W
9/93

RESOURCES IN AMERICA'S FUTURE

RESOURCES
IN
AMERICA'S
FUTURE

PATTERNS OF
REQUIREMENTS AND AVAILABILITIES
1960–2000

BY

Hans H. Landsberg, Leonard L. Fischman,
and Joseph L. Fisher

published for
RESOURCES FOR THE FUTURE, INC.
by
THE JOHNS HOPKINS PRESS

Resources for the Future is a non-profit corporation for research and education in the development, conservation, and use of natural resources. It was established in 1952 with the co-operation of The Ford Foundation and its activities since then have been financed by grants from that Foundation. Part of the work of Resources for the Future is carried out by its resident staff, part supported by grants to universities and other non-profit organizations. Unless otherwise stated, interpretations and conclusions in RFF publications are those of the authors; the organization takes responsibility for the selection of significant subjects for study, the competence of the researchers, and their freedom of inquiry.

Of the three authors, Joseph L. Fisher is president of Resources for the Future, Inc., Hans H. Landsberg is director of RFF's resource appraisal program, and Leonard L. Fischman is a consulting economist in Washington, D.C.

Staff Editors, Henry Jarrett and Vera W. Dodds

PREFACE

ONE OF THE GREAT QUESTIONS before any nation concerns the adequacy of natural resources to provide the kind of living its people want, or in some countries, merely to keep the population alive. The question is not new or transient. Even in the United States, with large resources of land, water, energy, and minerals, and the world's highest average level of living, one finds concern regarding the over-all adequacy of resources to support the rate of growth of the economy that is within the nation's reach. And if sheer quantities of raw materials and of resource services will suffice, then what will happen to the quality of the resource base itself and its capacity to sustain further economic growth? How may resource conservation and development reflect proven social values and at the same time promote such changes as society at its best would like to make? More specifically, can the flow of useful materials be increased without higher costs? Can necessary imports of raw materials be obtained effectively in ways that at the same time contribute to the economic development of the supplying countries? What reliance can be placed on discovery of new sources, and on technological advances in extraction, processing, and use? Can shifts in demand from one material to another be foreseen and accomplished with minimum disturbance to the existing work force and pattern of industrial location? What are the prospects for surplus production as well as for shortage of particular items?

These are some of the questions that gave rise to this book, which essentially is an effort to build a framework within which answers may be worked out.

The core of the book is the projections of demand and supply of natural resources —their products and services as well as the basic land, water, and minerals—to the year 2000 for the United States. The projections make a comprehensive, interrelated system consistent with more general projections of population, labor force, production, and income. The picture that emerges, we believe, will be helpful to anyone who bears a responsibility for, or is interested in, the resources future of the country.

We have made the estimates as carefully and soundly as we could within the limits of available data and practicable methods, but we are under no illusion that time will not prove us wrong, or at least wide of the mark, in many instances. The entire set of projections ideally should be made, say, once every five years in the light of new demographic, technological, and economic knowledge, improvements in projection methodology, changes in the outlook for war and peace, economic changes in other countries, discoveries of new sources and substitutes, and so on. Since so many of the basic resource decisions have to be made by government and a number of federal agencies already make their own projections for resources within their particular fields, there would be merit in having an agency of government assume the continuing responsibility for making and improving such a set of comprehensive projections.

Firms and individuals in the private sectors of the economy may also find some guide lines for decision in the projections as presented here or as modified for their own purposes. Many business firms, particularly larger ones, already make their own projections of future economic trends, at least for those parts of the economy immediately relevant to their products and markets.

Any future reworking of the projections presented here may be possible on a procedural basis which for this study was not feasible—one involving the establishment of a series of models of the economy, rapidly solved by electronic computer for any new data and variation of assumptions that might be entered into them.

In addition to presenting and interpreting the projections, we have indicated at many points in the book the problems which loom in the future as a result of lack of correspondence between estimated demand and supply. These are the visible gaps, the closing of which is the business of public policy and private management to accomplish to the extent the job is not to be done more automatically by the operation of the price system. We have not gone extensively into the kinds of policies and actions that may be employed in helping to close the demand-supply gaps at chosen levels although the general directions that policy might take are often mentioned. Mainly, however, the book serves as a background for considering policies, not as a treatise on policies themselves.

In focussing on the United States for the next forty years we have resisted temptations to look further ahead into the twenty-first century, or to examine world trends in any detailed or comprehensive way, although we did find it necessary to consider foreign trends in a very general way in estimating United States imports and exports. Even with these circumscriptions our book is an ambitious and complex one, and has involved rather deeply a number of persons, in addition to the three principal authors, on one or more specific parts or aspects of the study. Credit is given these persons in the Acknowledgments following this Preface.

Hans H. Landsberg, Leonard L. Fischman, and I have shared responsibility for the whole study; it is not easy, or particularly meaningful, to say who did what. In general, Mr. Landsberg took the lead in preparing the chapters on supply, and Mr. Fischman those on demand and the statistical appendices on demand projection. Mr. Landsberg, however, wrote the chapters on demand for heat and power and for mineral fuels and took charge of drawing the various chapters together. My part was principally in conceiving the study and how to go about it, and in supervision of the work.

In a work of this length and diversity the editing function was more important than usual; Henry Jarrett and Vera W. Dodds, of the Resources for the Future staff, contributed greatly to the final arrangement and presentation of material.

This study is one of several done in Resources for the Future, each of which has been drawn upon to some extent for the present volume. Two books which provide a comprehensive look ahead in particular resource fields have already been published: *Energy in the American Economy, 1850–1975,* by Sam H. Schurr, Bruce C. Netschert, and others; and *Land for the Future* by Marion Clawson, R. Burnell Held, and Charles H. Stoddard. A shorter study, *The Future Supply of the Major Metals* (Netschert, Landsberg), has also appeared. There is a particularly close relation between this book, which emphasizes the future, and *Trends in Natural Resource Commodities: Statistics of Prices, Output, Consumption, Foreign Trade, and Employment in the United States, 1870–1957,* by Neal Potter and Francis T. Christy, Jr., which traces the record of the past. The underlying meaning of the past record, and its implications for the future, are analyzed in a recently published study, *Scarcity and Growth: The Economics of Natural Resource Availability,* by Harold J. Barnett and Chandler Morse. Another study, *Regions, Resources, and Economic Growth,* by Harvey S. Perloff, Edgar S. Dunn, Jr., Eric E. Lampard, and Richard F. Muth, traces the connections between resources and economic growth in the United States by regions. These several studies, for which the present one provides a kind of capping, represent a broad and deep effort to see the place of natural resources and related products and services in American economic development, past and future. Other Resources for the Future studies examine particular problems and lines of solution; still others now being started deal more directly with resources on a world scale.

It is hoped that the findings of this study will prove stimulating to all concerned with natural resources and with the future economic growth of the United States.

September 28, 1962   JOSEPH L. FISHER, President
                                                RESOURCES FOR THE FUTURE, INC.

ACKNOWLEDGMENTS

THIS BOOK could not have been produced without the co-operation and assistance of many persons whose contributions included both intensive research on particular phases of the study and research and statistical analysis of a more general nature. The list of senior contributors includes a few persons who actually drafted smaller or larger portions of the text, but more generally comprises those whose contribution consisted of background papers, original analysis, and advice and consultation. Among the research assistants are several who contributed original statistical analysis and background papers.

Senior contributors

Edward Boorstein
David B. Brooks*
Francis T. Christy, Jr.*
Vera F. Eliasberg*
Irving K. Fox*
A. J. Goldenthal
R. Burnell Held*
Allen V. Kneese*
George O. G. Löf*
Frank Papp
Donald J. Patton
George Perazich
Bernard Sobin

Charles H. Stoddard*
Robert M. Weidenhammer

Research assistants

Lila Lee Abramson
Sylvia W. Bernstein
Bette K. Fishbein
C. L. Mastrantonis
Thomas H. Pendleton
Erna Peters*
Sedley Pyne
Selma Rein

Asterisks denote persons who were RFF staff members at the time the work was done. The others were consultants or temporary appointees.

We are indebted also to others of our colleagues on the RFF staff, in addition to those listed, for review, advice, and assistance throughout the long period of research and writing.

More than fifty persons outside the RFF staff, either as members of organizations or as individual consultants, reviewed relevant sections of the manuscript from the viewpoints of government agencies, industry, and university scholarship. Because it is impossible to identify all of the persons who participated in the institutional reviews, we shall not attempt a listing here. We do, however, want to express our deep gratitude to all of them; their assistance in catching errors and contributing new information and viewpoints was invaluable. Many of these same people also contributed technical advice in early stages of the work. The authors, of course, are fully responsible for the data presented and the conclusions drawn.

Pauline Manning prepared the index and assisted the RFF staff editors in editing the manuscript.

Clare O'Gorman Ford designed the charts.

H. H. L.
L. L. F.
J. L. F.

Contents

PART II. DEMAND FOR KEY MATERIALS

PART III. ADEQUACY OF THE RESOURCE BASE

(For Contents to Statistical Appendix see following page.)

STATISTICAL APPENDIX

TEXT TABLES

FIGURES

RESOURCES IN AMERICA'S FUTURE

*the study
in brief:*

RESOURCES IN THE NEXT 40 YEARS

AT THE BEGINNING OF THE 1960's the 180 million people of the United States enjoyed a level of living high beyond precedent for either their own country or any other. At the same time they were supporting an enormous peacetime defense establishment, conducting an impressive program for the exploration of outer space, and providing assistance to less developed countries in the interests of world stability, peace, and prosperity. By the year 2000 the United States probably will have well over 300 million people who will want and expect even higher levels of living than those of today—better diets, better housing, more consumer goods of all kinds, better education and cultural opportunities, more facilities for recreation and so on. There is little in the world outlook to suggest the probability (though there is always a possibility) of any large reduction in defense requirements. The need for economic aid overseas will continue; so will efforts to conquer outer space.

National aspirations call for accomplishing all of these things. Can the United States over the balance of the twentieth century count on enough natural resource supplies to sustain a rate of economic growth sufficient for their attainment? That is the central question behind this inquiry into future demand for natural resources and the goods and services derived from them, and into the prospects for meeting such requirements.

The question is not academic. Despite great and continuing gains in knowledge of how to locate and utilize natural resources, and the diminishing share of resource extraction in total economic activity, modern man, no less than his cave-dwelling ancestor, must work within the limits of the earth's natural environment. True, he has far greater scope as he broadens his understanding of physical, biological, and social processes; it is dangerous to predict just how far modern man can go through inventiveness, determination, and capacity for social organization and discipline. But natural resources—land and its products like crops and timber, water, fuels and other minerals—remain the indispensable physical stuff of which any kind of civilization must be built.

The fact that less than a century ago half of the working population of the United States was engaged in farming, mining, or other direct production of resource materials, and that now this work is done by only one-tenth of the working force (which turns out about five times as much), does not mean that natural resources have become less necessary. It suggests rather the growing extent and range of the other activities—manufacturing, transportation, education, national defense, the arts and sciences, and the many other aspects of modern society—that now rest upon the base of natural resources.

We have made our detailed study of future resource availability along the lines of economics, principally in terms of prospective demand-supply relationships. This approach was chosen as the best way of shedding light on a complicated and elusive set of problems. The broad implications of the resources outlook have been kept constantly in mind. Furthermore, although many of our findings are in terms of quantities, our aim is neither to predict what will happen nor to produce comparisons of numbers for their own sake. The objective, rather, is to uncover any serious situations of scarcity or surplus* that seem likely to occur if present trends continue and, through the analysis, to offer a useful guide to public or private actions that, if taken in time, might forestall such difficulties. One fundamental assumption underlies all of our projections: that there will be no large-scale, devastating war during the balance of the century. Such a catastrophe would change everything.

Our main conclusions can be summed up briefly: Natural resources are of basic and continuing importance to national economic growth and individual well-being, and vastly greater quantities of them will be required in the future. Figure 1 shows our projections. Neither a long view of the past, nor current trends, nor our most careful estimates of future possibilities suggest any general running out of resources in this country during the remainder of this century (or, if a broad impression may serve in the absence of detailed analysis, for a long time thereafter). The possibilities of using lower grades of raw material, of substituting plentiful materials for scarce ones, of getting more use out of given amounts, of importing some things from other

---

*NOTE: Terms like "scarcity" and "surplus," "demand," "requirements," and "supply" are not used in this study in their technical economic sense. Instead, such terms as "scarcity" and "surplus," for example, are used here simply to describe possible situations in which future consumption, as projected under our basic assumptions, appears to be significantly larger, or smaller, than the supplies that appear likely to be available. "Demand," "requirements," and "consumption" are used more or less interchangeably to indicate amounts that would be consumed under the same assumptions. The assumptions do not allow for changes in relative price, which as actual events unfold will tend to reduce demand and increase supply of a commodity for which "under-supply" is projected. A projected "deficit" (or "surplus") does not in itself necessarily imply desirability of special action to supplement the effects of market forces. (These considerations are discussed in detail later in this study, particularly pp. 41–53 and 60–61.)

countries, and of making multiple use of land and water resources seem to be sufficient guarantee against across-the-board shortage.

There is, however, great likelihood of severe problems of shortage (or, as in the case of agriculture during the next decade or two, of surplus) from time to time in particular regions or segments of the economy, for particular raw materials. Deficiencies either of quantity or quality in the environmental resources of land and water undoubtedly will also occur in some instances. Well-designed policies and timely actions can frequently prevent or reduce these difficulties. There is no policy panacea for all resource difficulties, but a few broad lines of action are clearly indicated:

maintaining the flow of new and improved resource technology in discovery, production, transportation, and use of natural resources;

maintaining and expanding a world trading and investing system that can enlarge the opportunities of the United States and other countries for importing raw materials at low cost;

conserving and using resources in accordance with sound ecological and economic principles.

These lines of action, in turn, are closely tied to further advances in science and education, wise investment in capital improvements, and enlightened foreign policy.

By looking ahead systematically at demand for natural resources and at their supply, impending difficulties can be foreseen and, to an extent, measured. An understanding of the prospects should encourage more intelligent and far-sighted responses, primarily better public policies and better private management of the nation's resources.

Resources AT A COST

The fact that there are limits to particular natural resources in particular places does not mean that through history resources have in any general sense grown increasingly scarce. The degree of scarcity in economic terms will vary not only with the size of the demand that is placed upon the resources but also with the technology of exploiting them. The early frontier farmer, hemmed in by forests and trying to work a field full of stones with a crude plow, was probably not impressed by superabundance of cropland.

Scarcity is not necessarily a function of growing economic maturity and has not necessarily increased with the inroads that man has made into the stocks of materials. Physical existence of resource materials cannot be equated with economic availability. The limits of economic scarcity have been pushed back in step with the growth in demand—and sometimes even faster. The long-continued rise in per capita consumption of nearly all raw materials, and the consequent general rise in levels of

Figure 1. Requirements for farm products, timber, water, outdoor recreation, metals, and energy
—1960 and projections to 2000.

*The projected increases in demand shown here and opposite for categories of natural re-
sources are those that would occur under the Medium assumptions for population, gross
national product, and other key factors that will govern future demand. High and Low
projections, based on alternative sets of assumptions, are not shown. The projections cannot be construed as predictions because there can be no certainty that the underlying assumptions will be borne out. They do, however, indicate the way in which things will
be heading if most major trends continue. Units for measuring projected requirements for
outdoor recreation are visits to the principal kinds of public areas—national parks, monuments, and recreation areas; state parks; and national forests. The withdrawal depletions
by which growth in water requirements is measured are the actual losses during use and
thus do not include withdrawn water that is later returned to lakes and streams (see page
260). "Steel equivalent" represents iron and steel, manganese, copper, lead, and zinc, aggregated by converting each metal to its steel equivalent in terms of specific gravity. For the
definition of roundwood as a timber measure, see page 252.*

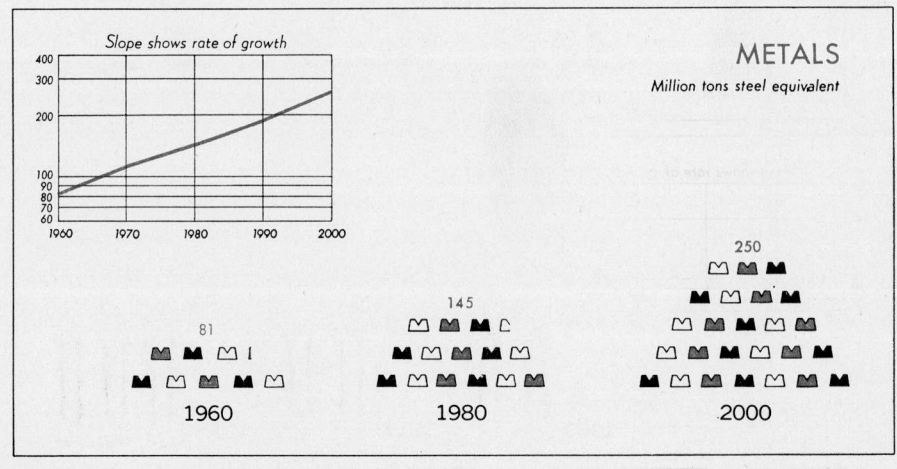

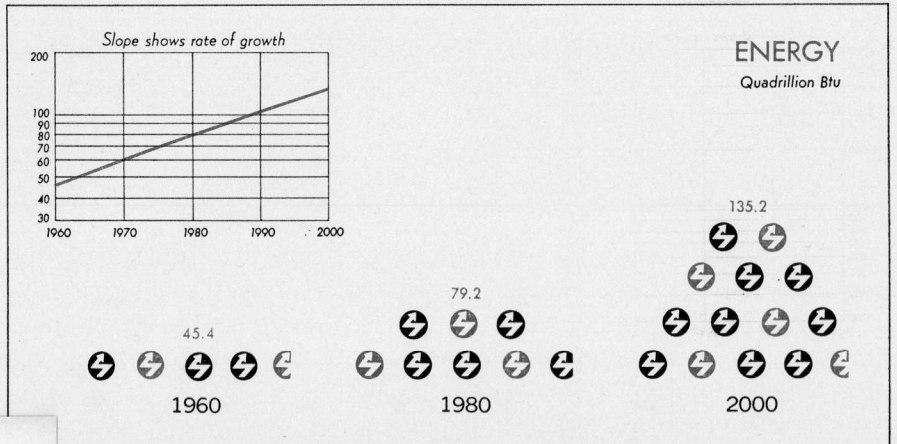

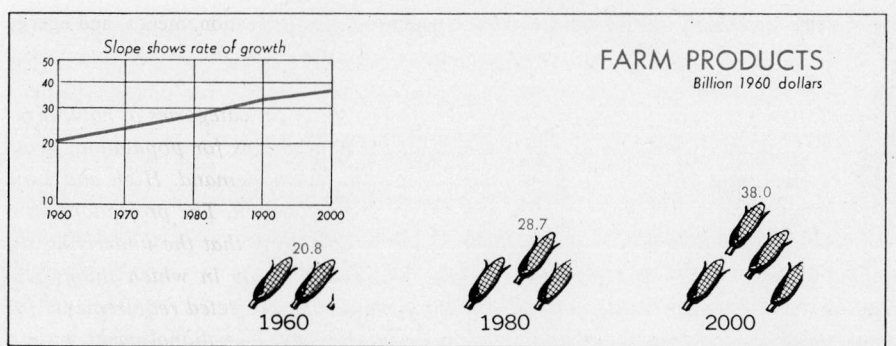

FARM PRODUCTS
Billion 1960 dollars

Slope shows rate of growth

20.8 1960
28.7 1980
38.0 2000

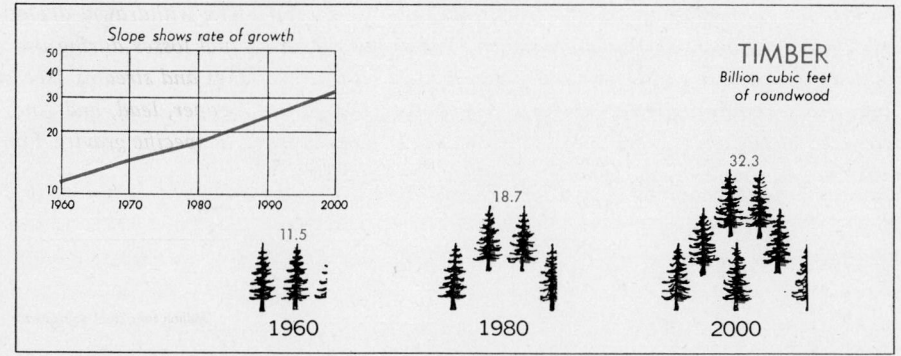

TIMBER
Billion cubic feet of roundwood

Slope shows rate of growth

11.5 1960
18.7 1980
32.3 2000

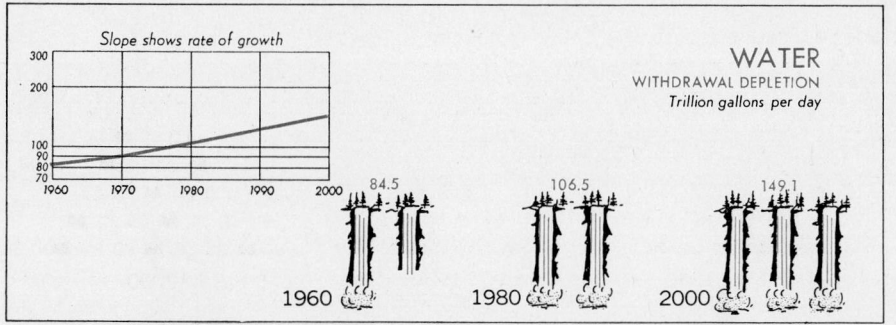

WATER
WITHDRAWAL DEPLETION
Trillion gallons per day

Slope shows rate of growth

84.5 1960
106.5 1980
149.1 2000

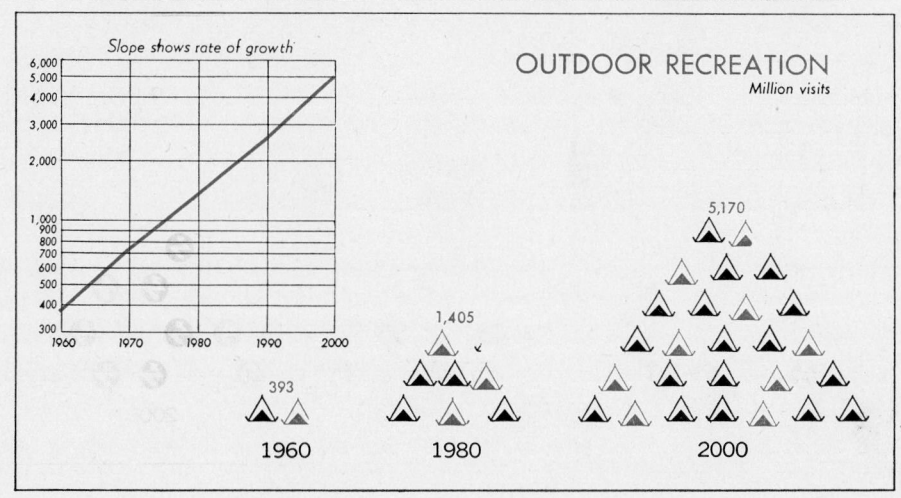

OUTDOOR RECREATION
Million visits

Slope shows rate of growth

393 1960
1,405 1980
5,170 2000

living, do not indicate scarcity, at least for some time to come. Malthus' pronouncement that population will eventually outstrip production is understandable in the light of the observable situation of his time, but it has not been borne out over the past century and a half, at least in western countries. The threat of scarcity has been held in check, largely by technological progress.

Since Malthus' day popular concern for resource adequacy has been cast largely in terms of physical limitations rather than of economic scarcity. Only in comparatively recent times has it been generally recognized that the limiting factor usually is not the physical volume that exists within the confines of the earth, but the cost of separating the desired materials from their environment and making them useful.

The oil content of the shales and tar sands on the North American continent or the sum total of aluminum contained in the earth's crust or the manganese known to exist with other metals in the millions of nodules that cover much of the ocean floor, or the virtually untapped tropical forests and the possibilities for fast-growing hybrid trees, these and similar resources are of such magnitude that concern with the adequacy of their physical occurrence has a very low priority in the ranking of contemporary problems.

The crucial question, then, is not simply how much there is, but what it will cost to produce needed resource materials and services most efficiently. As exploration and laboratory experiments enlarge the mass from which consumable materials can be economically extracted, the physical limitations recede into the background. The discovery of ready substitutes, either found in nature or produced in the laboratory by manipulation of familiar substances, further widens the potential supply.

Resource quality, however, is another question. Simply having enough oil, metals, land, and water would not spell a satisfactory life for most people. For example, there is surely enough land for urban expansion for many years to come and probably for outdoor recreation also, but the quality of it could be allowed to deteriorate to the point where it would yield unsatisfactory services. Similarly, burned-over forest land and abandoned strip mines lie ugly and useless for many years unless treated and restored. Pollution of water does not usually prevent its use, but it does make use less pleasant and more costly. The relationship of people to resources, which usually has been expressed in terms of quantity, needs to be restated for modern times to emphasize what is happening to the quality of resources.

Earlier Resource Appraisals and Reasons for a New One

Nonetheless, the specter of a globe robbed of the material riches with which it once was amply blessed has never ceased to prey upon people's minds; concern has been fed by suddenly emerging scarcities of one or another resource, and by the long-range prospect of greatly rising demand as declining mortality, high birth rates, and rising appetites for the paraphernalia of twentieth century living have reinforced one another. Sudden spurts in demand, coupled with stringency in labor supply, transportation, and international trade also have sharpened doubts about the future. The most recent of these was, of course, World War II, followed by the concentrated demand for the materials needed to rebuild the industries of Europe and to keep its population alive during the period of reconstruction. It was under the impact of these shortages and the associated drastic price increases of critical materials that the Administration of President Truman undertook to appraise broadly the country's natural resources position to the year 1975 and to formulate policies appropriate for achieving the satisfaction of prospective demand for resource materials at the lowest possible cost.

The President's Materials Policy Commission, which came to be known as the Paley Commission, after its chairman, William S. Paley, was created for this purpose. While its emphasis was on the formation of policy, it based its recommendations upon an analysis of prospective demand and supply of a range of resources; it is in no small part due to publication in 1952 of its report, *Resources for Freedom,* that the concept of resource availability *at a cost,* rather than the absolute depletion or "running-out" concept, was more fully developed and successfully brought to public attention.

While *Resources for Freedom* is more nearly a direct antecedent of this study, other broadly based investigations have had similar aims. Notable among them is the Twentieth Century Fund study by J. Frederic Dewhurst and associates, *America's Needs and Resources,* published first in 1947 and revised in 1955. Its coverage extended to human as well as inanimate resources. Its forward look was limited to a fifteen-year period, and its analysis of natural resource availability was largely in the nature of summary findings. Nonetheless, it stands as a milestone in the estimation of future needs and the likely means of satisfying them.

The Mid-century Conference on Resources for the Future was held in late 1953 under the sponsorship of Resources for the Future, Inc. Although this conference did not make recommendations for policy and action, nor provide a comprehensive framework of historical statistics and projections, it did provide a forum for the presentation of data, technical analysis, and opinions by leaders from government, industry, labor, agriculture, universities, and the professions. The summary record of the conference, *The Nation Looks at Its Resources,* was published in 1954.

The U.S. Forest Service report of 1958 on future timber resources did in more detail for this segment of the resource field what the broader-based studies have done for the economy as a whole, and other agencies of the U.S. Department of Agriculture have for many years been engaged in determining the future demand for food and fiber and, deriving from it, for land and other farm inputs. The President's Water Resources Policy Commission in 1950 examined the nation's prospects in regard to its water resources. A decade later, under the aegis of the United States Senate Select Committee on Water Resources, a number of federal government agencies estimated the demand for water to the end of the century. Earlier (1933–43) the library of resource studies of the National Resources Planning Board and its predecessor agencies had provided many useful ideas and benchmarks.

Resources for the Future, Inc. also has looked ahead in particular fields, with broad studies of land and of energy resources, and a reconnaissance survey, actually a forerunner of a portion of this book, on the future supply of the major metals. Private industry, too, in such fields as public utilities, transportation, energy industries, lumbering, and electronics, has explored the future as it seems to relate to particular goods and services and in so doing has contributed notably, in both techniques of projection and data made available, to the common pool of knowledge about resources and their adequacy.

In the past decade popular concern over future resource adequacy for this country seems on the whole to have lessened, if not in all then surely in most fields. Both in depth—through technological progress—and in breadth—through opening to investigation large geographical areas previously neglected—the resource horizon has widened in response to the actual and potential shortages that emerged during and soon after World War II. Indeed, it has widened to such an extent that many industries see the problems of the immediate future as those of glut rather than of scarcity.

This study looks forty years ahead and seeks to report objectively and in some depth on future adequacy of land—for cropping, grazing, forestry, recreation, and city-building—of energy sources, of major metal ores, and of fresh water. While it draws upon the investigations carried on in the organization since its inception ten years ago, it differs from them in that it covers all of the major resources and is set within a unified framework of major assumptions that underlie all projections of resource demand and supply with which it deals. We do not attempt to present a list of specific proposals for action, but content ourselves for the most part with presenting the evidence, making the projections, and indicating the problems.

Demand and Supply Prospects for Resources

This study is focused on the outlook in the United States for the four decades between our 1960 starting point and the year 2000. Had we looked ahead for a longer period, certain tentative conclusions about demand for some raw materials and the likely adequacy of their supply, which are imbedded in the projections, might have been altered. Had we looked only five or ten years ahead, certain other possibilities might never have come into view at all, for example the use of atomic energy on more than a very minor scale. Forty years seems to be about as far as it is profitable to look ahead. It is long enough to encompass most of the resource investments that have to be decided in the next few years. And it provides an ample time for the testing and working out of most policies. Beyond the year 2000 uncertainties multiply. The reasonable range in size of possible demands for raw materials would become far greater and make analysis that much more questionable.

Although our viewpoint is primarily domestic, it fully recognizes U.S. interests and responsibilities abroad, especially in regard to trade in resource-derived raw materials. While our study is cast in domestic terms, we do take account of world demand and supply trends because U.S. import and export possibilities cannot be projected without some eye to what is happening in the rest of the world. We do not think this procedure has materially altered statistical projections or the conclusions they imply in regard to demand-supply problems for this country. It should be pointed out clearly, however, that our conclusion that there is no general resource shortage problem for the balance of the century applies specifically to the United States; it cannot be extended automatically to other countries. In many less developed countries, especially in Asia, Africa, and Latin America, population presses hard on available natural resources; for them a sustained increase in living levels can by no means be guaranteed with the assurance that it can for the United States and other more advanced industrial countries. This does not mean that the developing countries will not continue the slow gains they have recently been making; it means rather that such gains will be harder to win. In the next few decades there is little leeway between the incessant demands of rapidly growing populations and the realistic possibilities for supplying food and other necessary raw materials.

Within the United States, our detailed coverage is limited to the forty-eight contiguous continental states. Because the projections grow so directly out of historical statistics it was not possible to include Alaska and Hawaii, although some data for Alaska have been included in the discussion of forest products. It may well be that on the supply side, mineral deposits and hydropower in Alaska and conceivably bauxite in Hawaii can significantly enlarge the U.S. resource base. For food products as a group, the two new states will continue to exert a net demand on the mainland, although they will no doubt continue to produce more than they use of a few products—notably sugar and pineapples in Hawaii and salmon in Alaska.

The Past as Prologue

New developments in production and use of resources undoubtedly will take place over the next forty years. Nevertheless the present situation and the record of the past are our most reliable guides to what is likely to happen in the future. A web of events, policies, institutional arrangements, and attitudes determines the resources situation at any given time. The strands of the web are long and tough. Thus in looking ahead we start with current trends in consumption and supply of resources and their products and assume no drastic changes in this country's essentially free-enterprise mixture of private and government economic activity or in its political and social framework.

The long-term record is one of greatly increased production of resource materials —a fivefold rise between 1870 and 1960—and of comparable gains in consumption.[1]

1. Neal Potter and Francis T. Christy, Jr., *Trends in Natural Resource Commodities* (Baltimore: Johns Hopkins Press and Resources for the Future, Inc., 1962). The historical statistics in this book stop with 1957. Those cited here have been extended to 1960 by Mr. Potter for the purposes of this study.

Growth rates of consumption are compared with population in Figure 2. As time went on, vastly greater amounts were produced with far less manpower per unit (see Figure 3); in fact the number of workers engaged in resource industries in 1960 was about the same as in 1870—nearly 7 million in both instances. Productivity in the resource industries (agriculture, forestry, mining)—that is, output per man-hour of labor involved—has increased persistently; since the Second World War it has clearly exceeded the productivity gain in manufacturing.

The "real cost" of resource products, which over the long run can be measured by the behavior of their prices in comparison with the general price level, has shown no marked change. This is the classic economic test of increasing scarcity. Deflated prices, as adjusted to allow for the influence of the general price level upon each resource commodity, have moved erratically since 1870, with many ups and downs and possibly some slight tendency upward. (See Figure 4.) By far the most notice-able increase has been in forest products, for which relative prices recently have been nearly three times what they were in 1870 and nearly twice those in 1930 although they have risen little since the late 1940's. But the over-all picture does not indicate that resource materials have become scarcer on any general or alarming scale over a good many decades in the past. Increases in efficiency in technology and management have largely offset tendencies toward greater difficulties and costs of extraction. For example, ore containing only 0.7 per cent copper can now be mined profitably whereas at the beginning of the century the minimum economic grade was around 3 per cent. Meanwhile the relative price of refined copper has not gone up.

For some resource products consumption has outrun domestic production. Around 1930 the historical position of the United States as a net exporter of resource prod-ucts shifted to that of net importer. This country continues to export basic agricul-tural commodities such as wheat and cotton, and to import non-competing products such as coffee, cocoa, and natural rubber. But especially since the Second World War, the United States has become a fairly large net importer of such basic items as crude oil and iron ore, and has increased its imports of copper, lead, zinc, and cer-tain other metals, which were already considerable. The trends of U.S. foreign trade are shown in Figures 5, 6, and 7.

Without increased imports of some of these commodities, costs and prices of cer-tain items would have risen, at least temporarily. In some cases new sources or tech-niques undoubtedly set ceilings; for example, oil can be produced from ample re-serves of oil shale at only a little above existing oil prices; and at least for a time much additional production could be secured from present underground sources. Nevertheless, access to foreign supplies has increased in importance. From a national self-sufficiency viewpoint certain basic resources have become scarcer, although from a world viewpoint this has not been true on any general scale.

The increasing diversity of the country's technology, industry, and enterprise re-sulted in much substitution of more plentiful and cheaper materials for those that were rising in cost and price. The most notable example is the massive substitutions during the past century among the energy commodities: wood, coal, oil, and natural

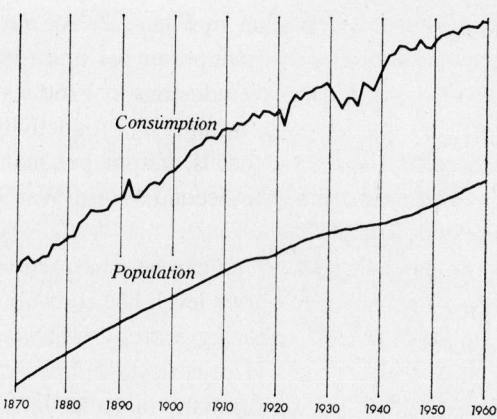

Figure 2. Rates of growth in consumption of all extractive materials compared with population growth, 1870–1960.

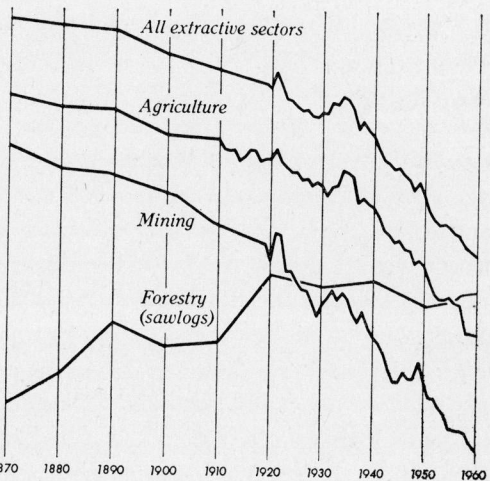

Figure 3. Relative trends in ratio of employment to output in resource sectors, 1870–1960.

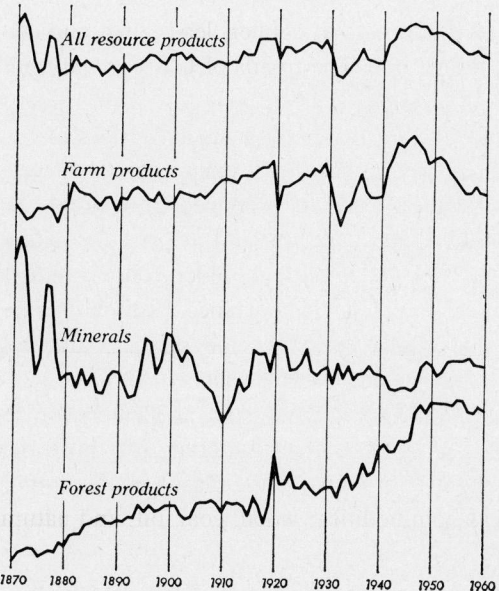

Figure 4. Relative fluctuations in deflated prices of resource products, 1870–1960.

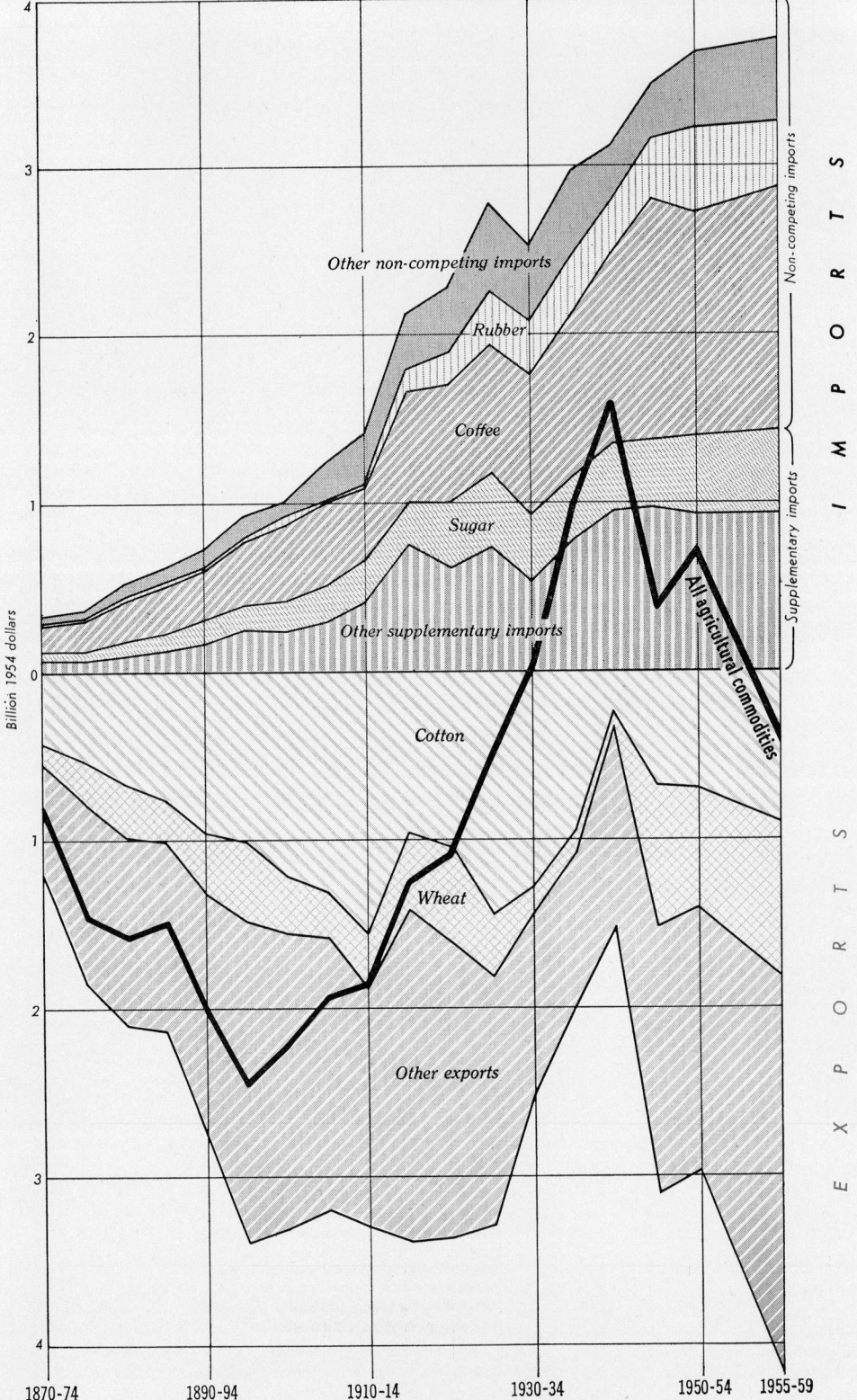

Figure 5 (opposite). Imports and exports of agricultural products, 1870–74 to 1955–59 (five-year averages).

Figure 6. Net foreign trade in petroleum and in all mineral fuels, 1870–1959 (five-year averages).

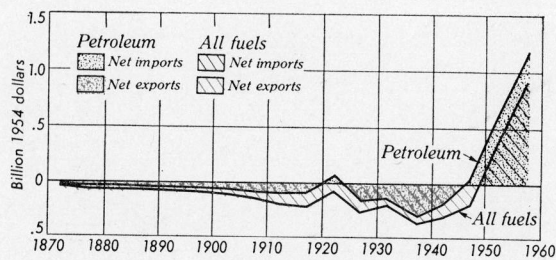

Figure 7. Net imports and exports of extractive commodities as per cent of U.S. consumption (1956–60 averages).

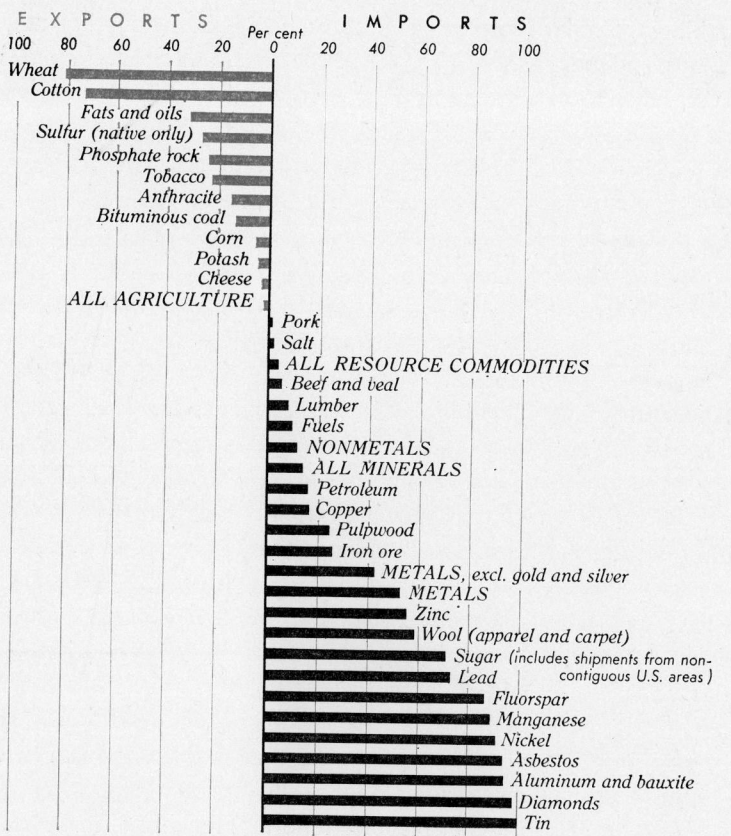

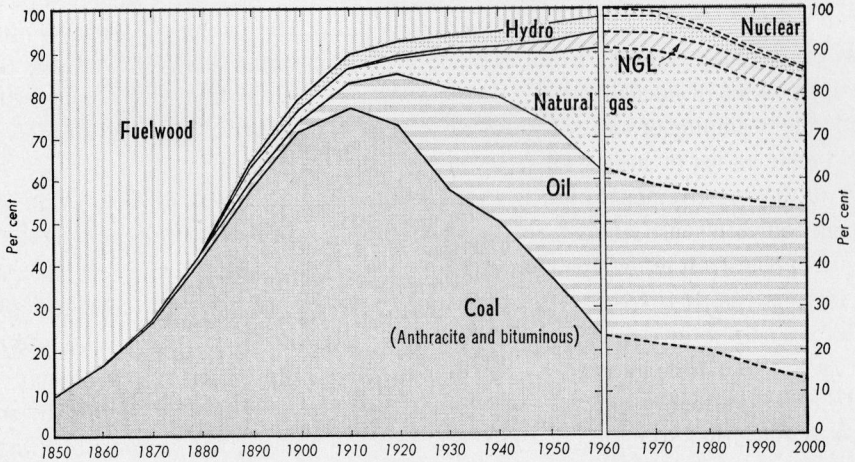

Figure 8. Changing proportions of energy sources, 1850–1960 and projections to 2000.

gas. In the future, it appears that nuclear energy will become significant. These shifts, past and prospective, are shown in Figure 8 (with rough data for fuelwood—not found in the later chapter on energy—inserted in the projections to assure historical comparability). Similar substitutions have occurred among building materials, metal alloys, foods, and many other categories of consumer and producer goods.

Since the early 1900's, programs of conservation have affected patterns of production and consumption. By conservation, we mean the deliberate shifting of the rate of use of a resource from the present to the future. Largely a matter of motivation and education, if not outlook on life itself, conservation in this sense can take place at any stage of economic activity, from the basic resources in place all the way through various forms of extraction and processing and to the later stages of industrial, household, and individual use. Public policies as well as business management can materially affect the time distribution of rates of use of resources. As the pressure of shortage mounts for a particular material or group of materials, conservation inducements and activities can restrain present use. Such activities frequently have pointed toward increased yields in the future, for example certain soil conservation practices which result in a reduction of crop output in the immediate future and an increase later on. Other efforts include postponing the cutting of timber or the catching of fish and killing of game until stock levels and growth rates are more favorable.

The past forty years and the next forty. In the four decades ending in 1960 the population of the United States increased by some 75 million—a rise of 70 per cent. Over the same period real per capita income doubled. Thus, by 1960 not only did the average U.S. citizen enjoy twice the income of his 1920 counterpart, but the country provided this scale of living for more than two-thirds again as many people. During those years came mass acceptance of the automobile, the emergence of radio and television, the rise of the airplane as a normal means of transportation, the application of chemical reactions—some long known, some newly discovered—to almost every phase of living from food and clothing to automobiles and missile fuels, the appearance of nuclear fission as a new means of producing energy, and most recently the beginning of man's breakout from the gravitational field of the earth.

No detailed list of such achievements could have been drawn up in advance. Nor, with all the improvements in projection making, is such a thing possible today, even though common sense suggests that many of the recent discoveries and inventions are bound to bear fruit in the coming decades and open the path to even more far-reaching innovations. It is hard to grasp what this may mean, but the backward look to 1920 can help to give some idea of the vast and fundamental changes that the next forty years may bring about.

To be aware that electricity output grew from less than 60 billion kilowatt-hours in 1920 to nearly 850 billion in 1960 helps one comprehend the prospect of a further growth to over 4,500 billion kilowatt-hours by the end of the century. Just as in 1920 it would have been hard to foresee that within forty years the state of California would produce more electricity than the entire nation was then producing, so today it is not easy to contemplate the probability that forty years from now one or two states will generate the equivalent of the nation's present 850 billion kilowatt-hours. Nor in 1920 would many informed persons have credited predictions that natural gas consumption, then little more than 800 billion cubic feet, would by 1960 climb close to 13,000 billion cubic feet. The effects of such growth upon the consumption of basic resources—farm products, minerals including mineral fuels, and forest products —in the past and the projected future impacts are shown on a per capita basis in Figure 9.

But along with the gains in technology and in total production and consumption, the past forty years have brought difficulties, some of which, it seems in retrospect, could have been avoided. There has been much misuse of resources, especially when judged by standards other than those of the market. The remarkable running up of gross national product and per capita income has had its price, and the ingredients of GNP and the side effects of its increase sometimes seem less impressive than its total size. Much good topsoil has been lost that could, at small cost, have been retained on the fields. Water pollution has increased rapidly and in some places has become a blight. The pattern of land uses in metropolitan areas leaves much to be desired, and the need for more parks, nature areas, and open spaces has become acute. In making this study we have been aware that the next forty years may see an intensification of quality deterioration of American resources and their use. In many of our demand and supply projections we have tried to allow for trends in conservation and related considerations.

To predict what will happen in the next forty years is a feat beyond the powers of social science. Our object here is to evaluate the consequences of the most realistic assumptions we can make on the basis of past history, current trends, and reasonable expectations of new discoveries, substitutions, more intensive use of existing materials, imports, new patterns of multiple use, and other such developments. Projec-

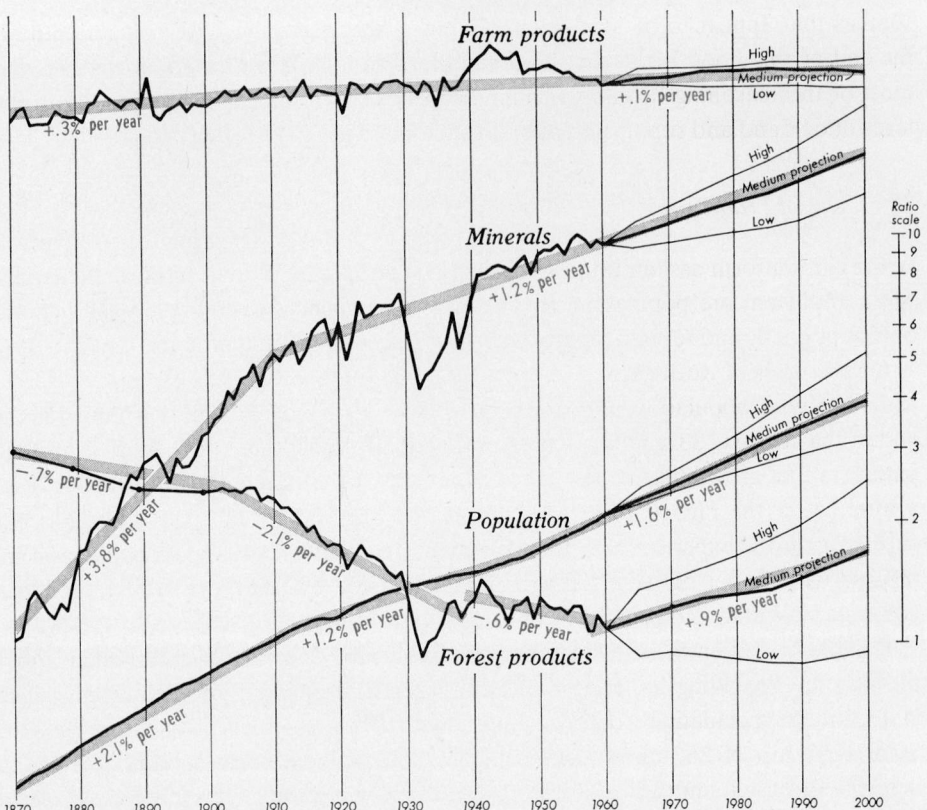

Figure 9. Rates of change in per capita consumption of all extractive materials, 1870–1960 and projections to 2000, compared with growth rate in population.

tions from such assumptions will show the supply problems either of scarcity or of surplus that would be likely to emerge in the absence of changes in relative price trends or corrective policy action. We have deliberately not allowed for further substitutions or other adjustments that would occur if a resource product became scarce. To do so would obscure the very situations we are trying to uncover. Throughout the study, therefore, we have assumed that there will be no significant changes in present price relationships.

Even so, the number of possible combinations of demand factors that could arise under the basic assumptions is so great that we have made our projections in terms of ranges—High and Low as well as Medium. Because of the wide opportunities for substitution, we begin with projections of major human needs and wants, such as food, clothing, housing, and transportation. Only then do we move to the resultant demands that each of these will make upon resources—how much metal or plastic rather than wood and brick might go into new housing, for example. In a second operation we estimate the sum of these possible demands for key materials, and in the third round we compare the various aggregate demand projections with the resources that appear to be available. In a sense, therefore, the statistical appendix at the end of this book is the core of the study, although it is in the text that we give most of the reasoning behind the numerical projections and discuss alternative patterns of demand and supply and some of their implications.[2]

The General Framework[3]

Certain uniform assumptions lie behind our projections for all resource materials. Most important are population growth and the associated increases in the nation's output of goods and services, represented by the gross national product.

On the basis of work carried out by the U.S. Bureau of the Census, this study uses as its Medium population projection for 1980 a figure of 245 million[4] and for the end of the century, 331 million, compared with 180 million in 1960. As a compound annual rate of growth this works out to about a 1.55 per cent net increase per year, or a little below the rate that prevailed between 1940 and 1960. Such a rate exceeds substantially the experience of the two decades ending in 1940, when population increased by only 1.1 per cent per year; but it is lower than any twenty-year or forty-year rate preceding 1920.

Population forecasts are not exempt from the rapid obsolescence that afflicts other projections. Providing for High and Low variants is one way of widening the field of legitimate speculation. The two additional marks set in this study for the year 2000 are a low of 268 million and a high of 433 million, corresponding to rates of net growth of 1.0 and 2.2 per cent respectively, the first 50 per cent below recent experience, the second nearly as much above it.

Principally because of changes in the age composition of the projected population, the nation's labor force is going to increase somewhat more rapidly than suggested by absolute population growth: by 2000 it is likely to be 142 million strong—almost double its 1960 size. And even based on what many might regard as a moderate assumption as to growth in productivity—roughly 2 per cent in terms of GNP per member of the labor force—the projected average annual growth in the national product of about 3.8 per cent per year (flanked by a High of about 4.8 per cent and a Low of about 3 per cent) represents slightly more than a *doubling* of GNP between 1960 and 1980 and approximately the same again between 1980 and 2000. (See Figure 10.)

Recent experience carefully interpreted does not suggest any radical reductions in hours worked per week and weeks worked per year for the labor force as a whole. Outside of agriculture, the projection envisages a drop from the current actual workweek of forty hours to just below thirty-seven hours in 2000. Productivity of non-

---

2. For further details on how the projections were made, see pp. 53–66.
3. For details see Chapter 1.
4. The Census Bureau expresses no preference for any of its series of projections to 1980, except for considering the highest less likely. The series chosen as the Medium estimate here is No. III of the Census Bureau.

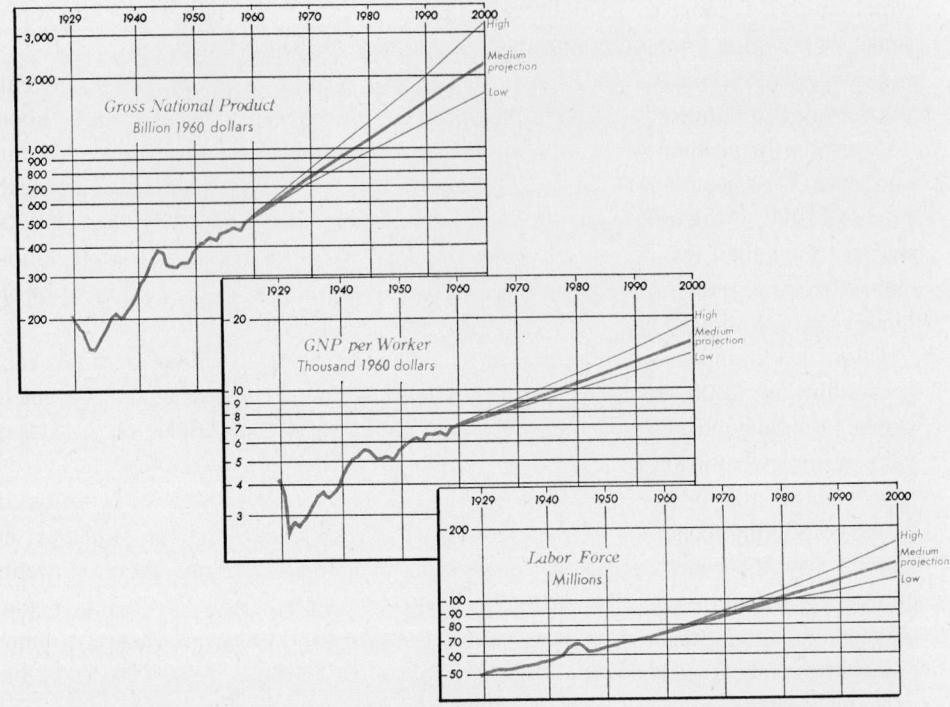

Figure 10. Growth of gross national product, labor force, and output (GNP) per worker, 1929–1960 and projections to 2000.

agricultural privately employed workers increased 53 per cent between 1940 and 1960, and is projected to rise 62 per cent from 1960 to 1980 and 69 per cent from 1980 to 2000.

It is this projection that the gross national product will somewhat more than quadruple between 1960 and 2000 that makes plausible the size of many of the increases in demand for resource materials that emerge from a combination of these basic factors and the projected changes in use of specific materials that are superimposed on them. For example, if electricity generation were to increase in step with GNP, this would yield a figure of not quite 3,700 billion kilowatt-hours in the year 2000. The actual projection of 4,700 billion kilowatt-hours, which is larger by nearly one-third, represents principally the results of continuing shifts in energy use toward electricity.

The assumptions underlying the development of the different major segments of the economy suggest relatively little change in its growth pattern. A moderate decline in the private as compared with the government sector (federal, state, and local) still leaves personal consumption expenditures accounting for 60 per cent of GNP by the end of the century (as against 65 per cent in 1960); government purchases correspondingly will have climbed from the present 20 to 25 per cent. Non-defense expenditures slowly increase their lead over defense outlays: from the present 55 per cent, non-defense expenditures are projected in the Medium projection to reach 60 per cent of total government outlay by the end of the century. In the High projection, which in itself is more than double the Medium, defense expenditures would represent 53 per cent of total government outlay, instead of 40 per cent.

Gross private domestic investment, which had risen 110 per cent in the twenty years ending in 1960, is projected to increase by 130 per cent to 1980, and by about 115 per cent from then to 2000. Within this category, investment in new plant and equipment is projected to advance considerably less rapidly than residential construction. By 2000, residential construction reaches a level of nearly 120 billion (1960) dollars, more than five-and-a-half times the 1960 value of residential construction. This is because of the rather high rates of family formation and of replacement of old houses that are allowed for.

Construction and services are projected to climb faster than output of goods, each quintupling by 2000, compared with a little less than a quadrupling in output of goods. Of total goods, durables quintuple and non-durables only triple. These rates of gain are somewhat lower than those prevailing during the past twenty years.

It is within this broad framework that use of the nation's resources is analyzed. Given continuing technological progress and access to foreign sources of supply, no major across-the-board crisis, slow or sudden, is in prospect during the next twenty or more years, although shortages may well occur for particular materials at particular times and places. In the closing two decades of the twentieth century the United States might face a substantial changeover to new sources in some of the fields, but probably with only minor increases in real cost.

Beyond this general observation, no single conclusion can legitimately be drawn for the resource outlook as a whole. We must turn instead to a separate consideration of each of the major resource categories—land, for agriculture, grazing, forestry, outdoor recreation, and urban living; water; the energy fuels; and nonfuel minerals.

Land[5]

Adequacy of land will vary with its many uses. There should be least concern over the supply of cropland to feed the growing population. Indeed, our calculations show cropland acreage surpluses for the greater part of the period. However, this position will obtain only if increasing demand is accompanied by continuing and substantial improvements in crop yields—such as a rise by the year 2000 to 100 bushels per acre for corn and 35 bushels for wheat, from recent average levels that were one-half lower for corn, about one-third lower for wheat. Rising yields would also be required for grazing land: some 50 per cent for open permanent pasture, the largest single constituent of non-crop grazing land. It is assumed that improvements in livestock feeding efficiency will continue, but at a moderate rate. Indeed, for cattle and calves, the largest feed consumers, no improvement is assumed over the checkered experience of the postwar years. For other branches of livestock raising, assumed improvements rarely exceed 20 per cent over forty years.

5. For details see Chapters 2, 3, 4, 8, 11, 12, 13, and 18.

These conclusions for the Medium projections also hold, with some qualifications, for the Low and High demand situations, which are conceived in this study as those that minimize or maximize the need for land. (See Figure 11.) Thus, the High demand projection is based not only on the High population figure but also assumes patterns of consumption that require relatively more land per calorie (that is, meat and milk rather than bread and noodles). Nonetheless, when high demand is combined with high efficiency in both livestock feeding and crop yields—a reasonable combination of conditions—not only is there no cropland shortage in sight through the rest of the century, but the calculated surplus exceeds that for the Medium projection. Even with somewhat lower efficiency in feeding and crop yields, no deficit in cropland acreage would be in sight. At the other end of the spectrum, the Low demand projection combined with low efficiency and low yields works out to a cropland shortage: low demand is more than balanced by poor productivity of soil and animals. The importance of yields is shown even more clearly by calculations that eliminate differences in level of demand. When the cropland acreages needed to satisfy Medium food and fiber demand under conditions of Medium yields in the year 2000 are compared with the acreages needed to meet the same demand at Low and High yields, it appears that 80 million more acres would be required with the low yields, and 50 million acres less with the high yields.

There is nothing very scientific about these yield projections, but it is a curious fact that projections made in recent years along more scientific lines have consistently proved to be conservative. Although the rate at which American farmers have dipped into the pool of available technology has greatly exceeded expectations, the gap be-

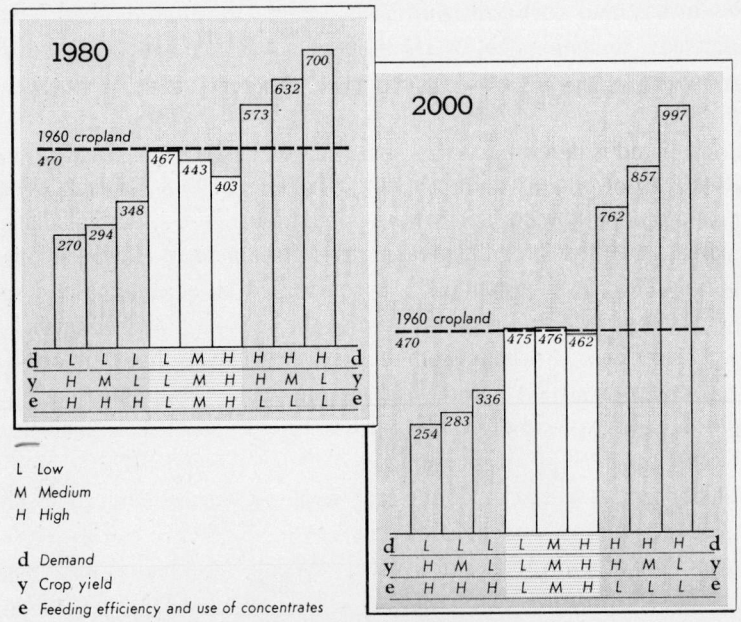

Figure 11. Cropland requirements projected under varying assumptions for 1980 and 2000.

tween top performance and the national average indicates that a wide margin for improvement remains. Meanwhile, technology will not stand still; the margin will continue to re-establish itself.

To complete the picture one may consider the consequences of calculations based upon the less likely combinations of assumptions: high demand combined with low feeding efficiency and low demand combined with high feeding efficiency, each of these then in turn combined with different assumptions as to yield. In all instances the result is what one would expect: large shortages of cropland in the High demand, and large surpluses in the Low demand projections, both of them emerging not in the dim distant future, but within the next twenty years.

These "outside" projections are less likely because High demand, arising from rapid population growth and a diet that stresses the more expensive and land-demanding kind of agriculture, would tend to provide the drive and the opportunity for reaching high efficiency in both crop yields and feed conversion. The converse is true for the Low projections. Thus, these projections serve mainly as warning signs of possible danger.

The generally reassuring picture for cropland is subject to qualifications. An implicit assumption is that the projected improvements in yield can occur even if the quality of the land should suffer through regional shifts, i.e., through inroads of more lucrative, non-agricultural land uses into areas of good cropping soil. With urban land projected to absorb some 25 million additional acres by 2000, there is ample room for encroachment upon good soils now in agricultural use. It is further assumed that idle land will be concentrated in areas of low land productivity. And, a very important qualification, it is assumed that the substantial changes in crop pattern, such as increases in hay and soybeans and decreases in pasture, can be made by substitutions that leave unchanged the total land area required. But despite these qualifications the prospect for not only adequacy, but continuing surplus acreage, for more than half the forty-year period seems reasonably clear.

Need for cropland is determined to some extent not only by demand for crops but by the productivity of grazing lands. In the Medium projection it has been assumed that throughout the period some 60 per cent of roughage feed will come from off-farm grazing. The yield increases assumed for range and woodland grazing still leave productivity of non-farm grazing soils vastly below that on farms. These increases may turn out to be modest, but progress to date in improving such lands has not been such as to counsel more optimistic assumptions. If the situation for cropland should become tight toward the end of the century, increasing attention might well have to be given to substitution of range for cropland and to increasing the productivity of the range.

Meanwhile demands upon land for other uses will mount—outdoor recreation, space for growing cities, for highways and airfields, reservoirs and watershed management, and wildlife refuges. Even when we assume that the rate of increase in recreation demand will fall off considerably from its present pace, our Medium projection calls for some 130 million acres for recreation in the year 2000, three times the 1960 figure. (See Figure 12.) In view of the expected increases in popula-

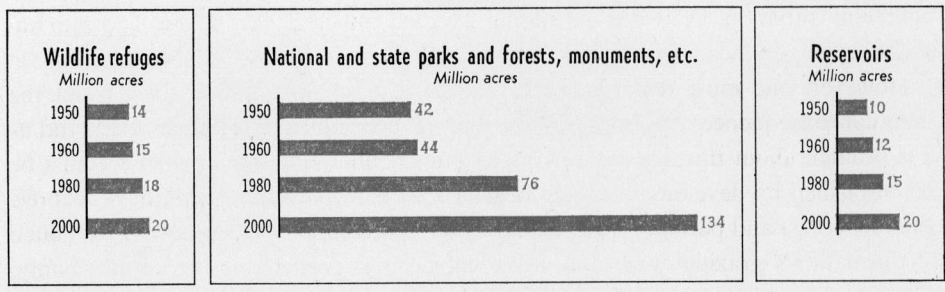

Figure 12. Acreage of publicly owned recreation land, 1950, 1960, and Medium projections for 1980 and 2000.

tion, leisure time, family incomes, and desire to get away at intervals from city living, this may be a conservative estimate. Urban land requirements are projected to total 45 million acres by 2000, more than double the 1960 acreage. And, for reasons we shall note a few paragraphs farther on, no increase has been projected for acreage of commercial forest despite the projected rise in demand for timber.

Given their full play, all of the identified demands for land by the year 2000 add up to more than the 1,900 million-acre total area of the forty-eight contiguous states. Our calculations show a land "deficit" of 50 million acres in the Medium projection for 2000, even assuming that every last square foot of mountain, desert, and swampland has found a use in one of the categories of demand. Eliminating even as little as 60 million acres as not suitable for any of the projected uses, the indicated deficit rises to 110 million acres. These calculations, shown in detail below, suggest a severely

			Medium projections	
	1950	*1960*	*1980*	*2000*
	(Million acres)			
Cropland, including pasture[1]	478	447	443	476
Grazing land[1]	700	700	700	700
Farmland, non-producing	45	45	45	45
Commercial forest land[2]	484	484	484	484
Recreation (excluding reservoir areas and city parks)	42	44	76	134
Urban (including city parks)	17	21	32	45
Transportation	25	26	28	30
Wildlife refuge	14	15	18	20
Reservoirs	10	12	15	20
Total specified[2]	1,815	1,794	1,841	1,954
Other land (residential)	89	110	63	−50
Total land area	1,904	1,904	1,904	1,904

1. All adjustments for feeding requirements are made in cropland, with grazing land held constant.

2. Does not provide for increased acreage to meet projected commercial forest demand. Requirements to close the projected gap in 2000 might run as high as 300 million acres to be put into forest use at this time.

tightening situation, even without taking the case for increasing forest land into account.

However, one must remember the nature of these projections: they depict the eventual consequences of trends, not the final reconciliation of supply and demand as it is brought about through market forces and public policy. Reconciliation must be accomplished by developing a great deal of land for more than one purpose, above all more forest and perhaps grazing land to serve recreation. The feed value of much of the nation's grazing land makes a small eventual contribution to food supply, yet something like one out of every three acres of land falls into one or the other category of grazing land. Intensified range management, substantially beyond the assumptions made in this study, could free some cropland for non-agricultural uses. Since cropland is far more evenly distributed than is range land, this would be a more useful source of land for recreation than if range land were freed directly for non-agricultural uses. In any event, pressures upon land as a whole are likely to increase in the second half of the period under review.

One additional potential source of pressure upon land demand has been barely touched upon: forests. The estimated demand for forest products by the end of the century is so much larger than the foreseeable domestic supply that something like 300 million acres would have to be added to the existing 484 million of commercial forest land in order to meet the Medium projection in the year 2000. It is not reasonable even to discuss such a development. In all likelihood forestry will have a hard time holding the land it now has; some curtailment, in fact, is generally expected. The situation can be improved by raising growth rates through regional shifts in cutting, from east to west; better fire, disease, and pest control; and improved management generally; better waste utilization; and continuing efforts to use hardwood in place of softwood. As in the case of cropland, higher demand would probably be accompanied by higher yield of timber per acre and of derived products, but even then it is doubtful that projected demand could be met without a substantial rise in cost or depletion of the country's forest cover. Obviously the future will see continued and intensified efforts to find substitutes and perhaps larger imports, as well as more intensive management of existing commercial forest land.

For these reasons our formal projections hold commercial forest acreage at its present size throughout the forty-year period. Modifications of demand are clearly in prospect. Combined with better growth they will result in a demand and supply balance that differs substantially from the trends pictured in Chapter 18. But these trends and their implications must stand as indications of an impending problem in land use.

Water[6]

The nation's total demand for fresh water has been growing even faster than population, and is expected during the balance of the century to keep growing at a rate at least equal to that of population. Irrigation, by far the greatest single withdrawal

6. For details see Chapters 14 and 19.

use, may increase by half by the year 2000; municipal use may double and manufacturing use quadruple.

Some local and even regional stringencies of water supply have already appeared. There will be more in the future, and efforts to mitigate them or head them off will probably justify large investments in water and sewage treatment facilities and in dams and reservoirs, greater economies in use of water to make a given amount go farther, and considerable political and social ingenuity in devising better institutional arrangements for planning and carrying out water development. There is no prospect, however, of water shortage on a nationwide scale and little evidence to suggest that, given sufficient thought and effort, localized water shortages will be a serious impediment to continued national growth during the next four decades.

Until very recently numerical estimates were made only for the withdrawal uses of water—the measurable amounts actually taken out of surface streams and lakes and underground supplies for use in households, factories, thermal electric plants, and irrigation. But also important are the flow and on-site uses for which water does not have to be withdrawn but is used as it moves for hydroelectric generation or, whether it moves or not, for a variety of purposes, including waste-carrying, navigation, recreational activities like swimming and boating, and maintenance of wetlands for wildlife.

For a number of reasons the uniform statistical structure upon which most of this study rests is of limited value in forming a useful idea of water requirements and supplies over the next four decades: (1) The historical statistics that would indicate past trends are meager. Water has been taken so much for granted in most parts of the country that few data on its use in manufacturing were collected before 1954. Attempts to estimate the quantities of water required for flow and on-site uses are so recent that as yet there are no data firm enough to be incorporated into our formal system of projections. The pioneering estimates made in 1960 for the Senate Select Committee on National Water Resources are highly tentative and preliminary. (2) Available estimates of supply tell little about quality of water, a key factor in its usefulness for many purposes. (3) Nationwide figures on water demand and supply mean little in appraising the regional and local water problems that currently are causing concern.[7] The cost of moving large quantities over long distances is so great that there is no national market for water. The fact that the total flow of all U.S. river basins is far greater than any conceivable aggregate of requirements for the year 2000 does not help areas that already are in trouble in the 1960's.

In looking ahead, therefore, it is necessary to give separate attention to three large regions—the East, the Pacific Northwest, and the West—within each of which common characteristics appear to outweigh diversity. Even so, many details are blurred

---

7. In the very long view, probably well beyond the forty-year span we are considering, the national totals also are significant. The generous national annual average of thirty inches of precipitation, eight of which are runoff and thus potentially available for use, means that national economic growth need not be impeded even if water should become scarce and costly in a whole region. Increases in population and water-using activity in agriculture or manufacturing could take place in areas where water still was plentiful.

because of the variety of situations inside of each region—often also within the river basins of which each region is composed.

In estimating the fresh water supply of each region we begin with the average annual flow of its watercourses and then indicate (see Chapter 19) the quantity that can be depended on throughout a full year, the quantity that can be depended on half of the time, and the largest dependable flow that could be developed with a complete storage and control program. (See Figure 13.) We have not assumed any changes in basic supply between now and the end of the century. Progress in weather modification conceivably could bring some increases in total precipitation within the next forty years, and desalting of seawater or brackish water will probably come into commercial operation for specialized purposes in at least a few localities of especially high water cost. But because of the lack of basic knowledge of rain-making and the present difficulties of reducing costs of desalinization, there is little basis for expecting either method of augmenting total supplies to affect materially the outlook of any large area during the rest of the century.

Our demand estimates, shown in Figure 14, have been based largely on projected increases in population, irrigated acreage, electric power generation, and manufacturing production in industries that use water in large amounts. These projections are in terms of withdrawal depletion—the amounts of water actually lost by evaporation or otherwise—rather than of total withdrawals. Total withdrawals include large percentages returned to water courses for further use, and thus in many circumstances can exceed average flow. The quality of the water returned is another matter, however—one that lies at the heart of the pollution problem. While we have not made comparable estimates of flow and on-site demands, they undoubtedly will be large;

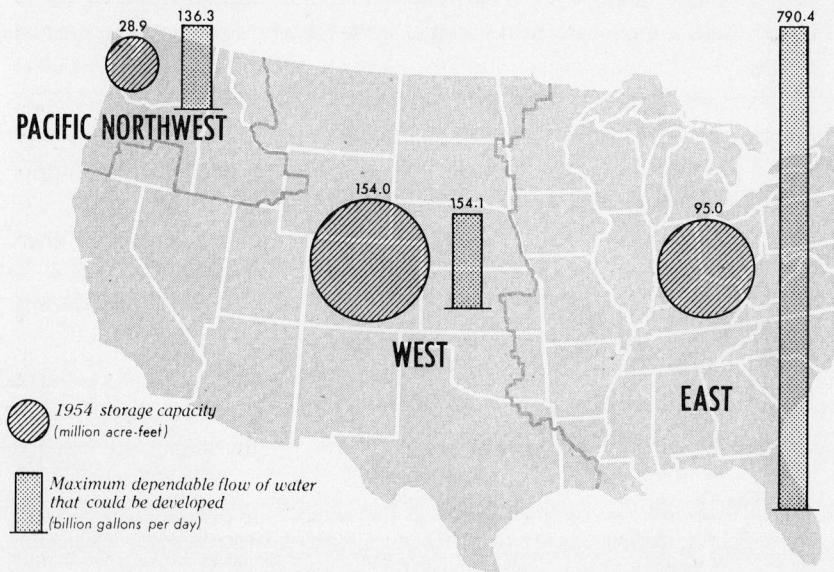

Figure 13. Maximum dependable flow of water that could be developed regardless of cost, and 1954 storage capacity, by region.

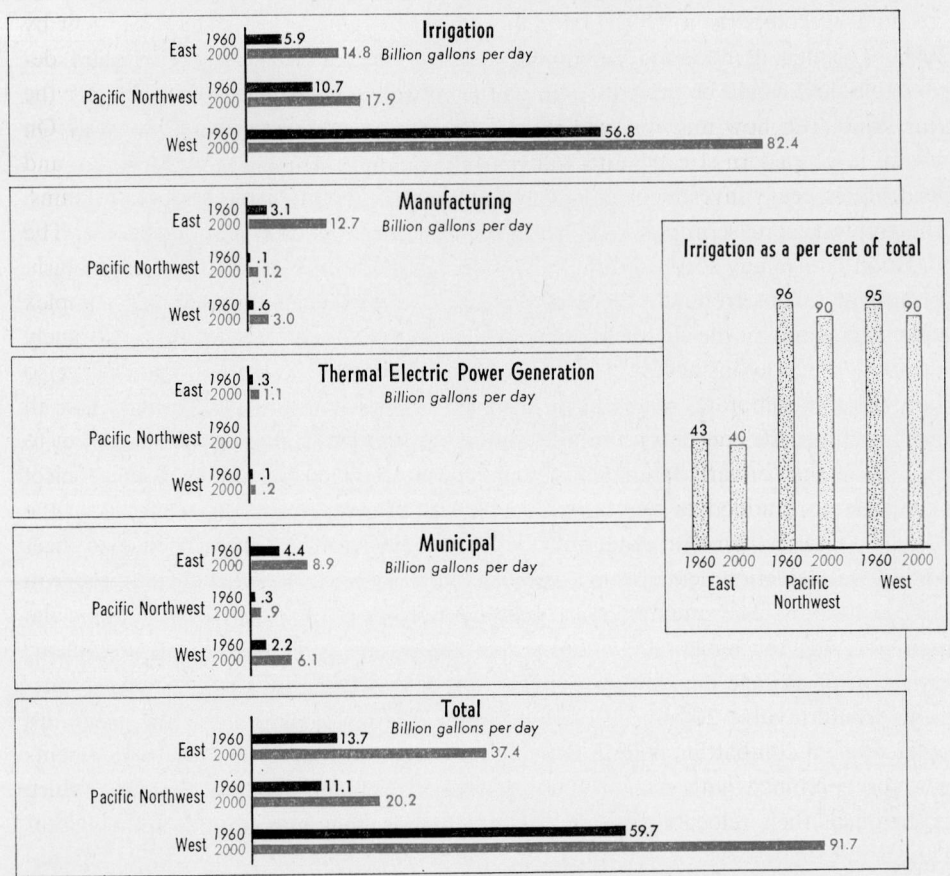

Figure 14. Withdrawal depletions of water, by region and use, 1960 and projections to 2000.

the two combined might be close to the projected withdrawal depletion in the West and Pacific Northwest and several times its size in the East.[8]

Although other withdrawal uses, manufacturing in particular, are expected to grow faster, irrigation will remain by far the largest contributor to withdrawal depletions.

The overwhelming importance of irrigation in the use pattern of both the West and the Pacific Northwest is evident; the projected declines in relative position through 2000 are slight. Figure 14 also shows why pollution is predominantly an Eastern problem: municipal and industrial use, the two main causes of pollution, between them account for more than half the withdrawal depletions (and a far higher share of total withdrawals because they return so much more of the used water than does irrigation).

In the *East,* with plentiful rainfall and a heavy concentration of people and industry, quality of water will be the main problem. Projected withdrawal depletions

8. The Senate Select Committee on National Water Resources estimates, cited in Chapter 19, show flow and on-site uses as even larger in relation to withdrawal depletions. See Committee Print No. 32 (Washington: U.S. Government Printing Office, 1960).

are small in comparison with maximum available supplies: less than 5 per cent by 2000. Through a moderate amount of new storage capacity, the year-round dependable flow would be twice as large as the withdrawal depletions projected for the year 2000. But how much of this statistically ample supply will be fit for use? On several large eastern streams and many smaller ones pollution is already severe and necessitates heavy investment in treatment plants and pollution abatement programs. The greatest increase in pollution has come within the lifetime of older people. The pollution is of many sorts—biological, chemical, soil particles, and general rubbish. Treatment ranges from the relatively simple and inexpensive to the very complex and costly; some of the chemical pollutants cannot be eliminated except at extremely high cost. In many instances one way out is the development of additional storage so that with less elaborate treatment there will be a sufficient flow of fresh water at all times to dilute the concentration of pollution and to flush contaminated water out to sea. When the forward estimates of such dilution flow made for the Senate Select Committee are added to our present depletion projections, it appears that by the year 2000 more than half of the maximum available flow would be needed to meet withdrawal depletion demands and at the same time insure reasonably clean water in eastern streams. The preliminary estimates made for the Committee may be on the high side, but the magnitude of the East's pollution problem is nonetheless clear. Provision of storage capacity to preserve enough of the total runoff for these purposes would involve 200 to 300 million acre-feet beyond the 1954 level. There are other ways of combatting pollution, including more thorough purification of effluents perhaps combined with recirculation, alteration of industrial processes to reduce pollution or their relocation to places more distant from other users, and substitution of salt or brackish water for certain purposes. Characteristically these alternatives are costly, but so are dams and reservoirs.

In the *West,* the great problem remains the actual using up of the available annual supplies. The region has only a fifth as much water as the East, but its withdrawal depletions are four times as large. With the expected growth in population and industry, the West's projected withdrawal depletions in the year 2000 would equal about 60 per cent of maximum available water supply and far exceed the present dependable flow—that is, the minimum daily flow that can be counted on throughout the year with present storage facilities. In some parts of the West supplies allocated to various uses already exceed the highest dependable flows that could be developed even with maximum storage. And all this without taking account of flow or on-site uses. If one adds the Senate Select Committee estimates for those uses, the combined demand even by 1980 would exceed maximum supply.

The West needs far more than development of new supply through construction of dams and reservoirs, long-distance transport of water, desalinization, and water conservation; the region's problem, above all, is one of working toward better allocation of water, at least of new supplies.

As settlers established themselves in the West, it became necessary to invest in water development, and the doctrine of prior appropriation—first in use, first in right—grew up naturally. Agriculture was the predominant economic activity and was possible only if water could be made available for irrigation. Irrigators have established claims, or ownership rights, for most of the water that so far has been available. Only during the more recent decades have population growth and industrial development entered the picture with sufficient force to contest with irrigators for remaining supplies of water. It is clear, however, that in areas where the demand exists water used for domestic, industrial, and even recreational purposes will yield much more in terms of employment and income than additional water used for irrigation. Indeed, it is hard to see how the anticipated large growth of population in the West can be supported without shifts toward those uses which will yield higher returns.

On the whole the *Pacific Northwest* is, like the East, a high-runoff region with large supplies of water in comparison with present and projected demands. Much of the region east of the Cascades, however, has an arid or semi-arid climate. Concentration of cities and industries is not nearly so great in the Pacific Northwest as in the East, so that neither its present nor projected pollution problem is so intense. Although parts of the region will have difficulties in abating pollution as well as in maintaining total water supplies, the distinctive water problem of the region as a whole is fuller realization, in co-operation with Canada, of the great hydroelectric potential of the Columbia River.

Energy[9]

The total demand for energy to supply the many forms of heat and power that modern America requires is expected to triple by the end of the century. At least through the seventies it appears that such needs can be met at no significant increase in real cost and with no sweeping changes in the relative contributions of the three great energy sources of the present: oil, natural gas, and coal. Toward the end of the century the patterns may change, notably through the rising importance of nuclear energy in generation of electricity and perhaps a decline in the relative importance of oil and gas. There is little indication, however, of major difficulties in meeting the nation's energy requirements over the next forty years.

Figure 15 shows projected Medium demand for energy in the principal economic sectors for 1960, 1980, and 2000, all in terms of the common unit of measurement, British thermal units or Btu's. The current total of 45 quadrillion Btu can be thought of as the energy contained in some 8 billion barrels of oil, not quite 2 billion tons of coal, or nearly 45 trillion cubic feet of natural gas. The tripling of energy requirements projected for the end of the century compares with not quite a doubling in population and a quadrupling in GNP. Thus, per capita use would continue to rise, but, as has been true since World War I, energy use per constant dollar of GNP would decline, as shown in Figure 16.

9. For details see Chapters 10, 15, and 20.

SECTOR	1960 C	O	G	E·HN	AS	E·AS	1980 C	O	G	E·HN	AS	E·AS	2000 C	O	G	E·HN	AS	E·AS
Residential	1.8	2.8	3.7	0.4	9.0	2.4	3.2	2.3	6.8	1.9	14.5	6.1	3.0	2.0	6.9	6.0	18.2	10.2
Commercial	1.4	0.9	1.2	0.2	3.8	1.4	1.6	1.6	2.2	1.0	6.6	3.2	1.6	2.6	2.1	2.8	9.3	4.8
Transport	0.1	7.7	0.4	—	9.2	—	—	15.9	0.7	—	18.5	—	—	33.3	1.0	—	37.2	—
Industry	6.3	2.4	6.0	0.8	16.0	4.4	9.2	3.7	11.5	3.1	29.1	10.1	11.8	6.6	19.9	12.0	55.6	20.4
Total (incl. sectors not shown)	11.1	17.4	13.2	1.6	45.3	9.3	15.8	28.8	24.2	6.4	79.2	20.8	18.0	53.0	33.8	21.7	135.2	37.0

Quadrillion Btu

C	O	G	E·HN	AS	E·AS
Coal	Oil	Natural gas	Electricity based on hydro and nuclear sources	All sources (incl. NGL not shown separately)	Electricity from all sources
(Including amounts consumed in electricity generation)					

Figure 15. Energy demand by source and economic sector (including allocable losses), 1960 and Medium projections for 1980 and 2000.

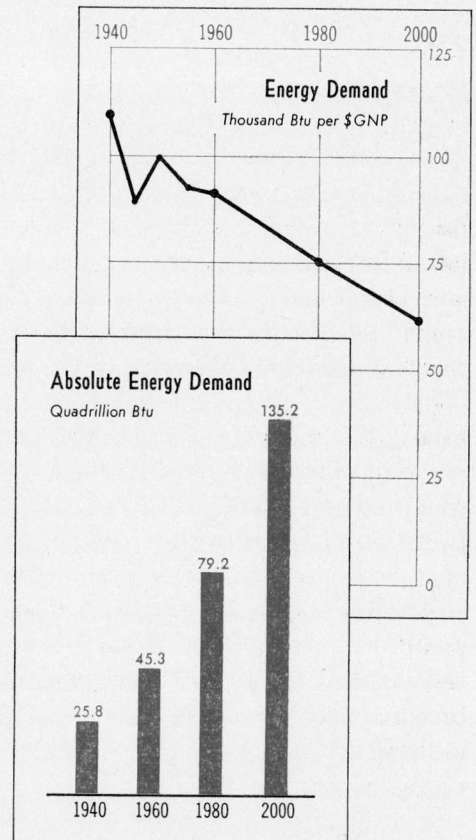

Figure 16. Energy demand per dollar of gross national product, 1940–1960 and projections for 1980 and 2000, shown together with absolute energy demand.

Changes in the projected pattern of requirements are significant but not radical for a forty-year span. They result from different assumptions of efficiency of energy use within the different sectors as well as from the relative growth or decline projected for the sectors themselves. Thus the projected decline in the share of residential use is chiefly the result of large assumed gains in efficiency.

The assumptions behind the demand projections do not specifically include any major uses that differ greatly from those around us today, although within these uses provision is made for changing technology, including some entirely new devices. Thus energy is presented as being used in the future home in conventional ways, such as heating, cooking, lighting, and the like, but it is also assumed that an increasing amount of energy will be used for applications that we cannot today identify. Among other possible developments that have not been specifically considered are electrification of railways, large-scale use of electric highway tracks, and the spread of pipeline transportation to material other than oil and gas. None is impossible, and for some of them significant data should appear in the next few years; but even taken together they are unlikely to make a substantial dent in the over-all requirement for energy, although they might change somewhat the proportions coming from the different energy sources. Also, some leeway for such changes is inherent in our projections, which are in large part extensions of past trends that themselves were in no small way shaped by technological progress.

The projected changes in amounts contributed by the different fuel sources rest largely on assumptions of consumer preference and technological development that affect both methods of use and relative price. Figure 15 shows the projections in absolute amounts. In relative terms, coal requirements continue the declining trend that between 1940 and 1960 halved the share of coal in national energy use. However, the rate of decline is much slower: it is projected that not until 2000 will it be halved again. Oil maintains its position with only minor fluctuations, and natural gas does the same with a gradual decline setting in by 1980. The gainer is nuclear energy which rises from 0.6 per cent of total energy use in 1970 to 14 per cent in 2000. Hydropower, only 3½ per cent of the national total in 1960, declines to 2 per cent in the projection for 2000, although it will remain much more significant in certain regions, notably the Pacific Northwest. The proportion of all energy, regardless of source, used in the form of electricity is expected to keep on increasing, but not so rapidly as in the recent past. Between 1940 and 1960 the share of electricity rose from less than 12 to more than 20 per cent. By 1980 projected electricity use is equivalent to over 26 per cent of national energy consumption; thereafter the share levels off to just over 27 per cent.

When the cumulative call on each source of energy is compared with the estimated magnitude of each of the resources involved, this study confirms the conclusion reached in an earlier Resources for the Future study[10] that required energy should be available in the pattern projected at substantially constant real cost through 1975 or thereabouts.

10. Sam H. Schurr, Bruce C. Netschert, *et al.*, *Energy in the American Economy, 1850–1975* (Baltimore: Johns Hopkins Press and Resources for the Future, Inc., 1960).

In the last two decades of the century, energy supply problems may arise for oil and gas. Reserves of coal appear ample for a much longer period than this century. In expressing concern for oil and gas supply we are acutely aware of the constantly changing scene and of the long list of similar statements that have been proven wrong in the past. Each of these fuels can be located only through costly efforts, and therefore search has been slow to move beyond geological areas that conform to traditional ideas of oil and gas location. Thus even the most optimistic estimates of oil yet to be found and recovered cannot quite shake off a conservative bias; an aura of doubt must always surround predictions of depletion. On the other hand, whatever the volume of oil and gas that can be proved to exist in the ground, there is no certainty that it will be produced. Exploration and exploitation, measured against competing investment opportunities, may become unrewarding well before resource stringency becomes an operating factor; various alternative energy sources and conversion methods are ready for use if rising cost of crude oil or gas production should create the opportunity. It seems possible that before the end of the century the country's petroleum and natural gas resources will be sufficiently depleted to bring into play an expanding flow of alternative energy sources. The Medium projections seem to point that way, and the High projections even more so; only the Low requirements projections would not raise the adequacy issue within this century, though they would soon thereafter.

Assuming a level of future imports at 20 per cent of demand, cumulative requirements for domestic petroleum in the Medium projection are calculated as about 185 billion barrels between 1960 and 2000, with total demand at 10 billion barrels in the year 2000 itself. Adding a minimum reasonable level of reserves to support such production leads to a figure in the neighborhood of 260 billion barrels. Would such an amount perhaps exceed the aggregate oil supplies that may be recovered in the future? On certain reasonable assumptions the answer would be yes. On more optimistic assumptions, involving principally higher rates of recovery from reservoirs, such a demand-plus-reserve figure would not equal future recoverable supplies, though it would come close. In either event, however, one would expect production to start levelling off a good many years before a situation is reached in which estimated remaining deposits are the equivalent of only a few years' output.

Similar considerations govern the outlook for natural gas. The projected cumulative demand plus a minimum provision for reserves would bring the nation close to —if not take it beyond—what can be estimated as the quantity of natural gas awaiting recovery. Annual demand by 2000 would have risen to 33 trillion cubic feet, not quite three times the current level, but well above the 22 trillion cubic feet that many have assumed as the peak of future gas production in this country. Unless the old story repeats itself and supplies now believed recoverable without major cost increases are grossly underestimated, production must be expected to level off many years before the end of the century, though apparently not before 1980.

The impact upon the economy of an incipient resources problem for oil and gas will be greatly mitigated, if not offset, by several factors. Outstanding among these is the expectation that electric energy derived from nuclear fission will make an increasing contribution, beginning slowly in the late sixties and gaining momentum in the seventies. By the end of the century the projections provide for roughly half of all electricity to be generated in nuclear reactors. This will reduce the relative demand for all hydrocarbon fuels.

Second, there are the shales of the Colorado plateau and tar sands of northern Canada, each with an enormous content of extractable liquid petroleum. While afflicted with a location problem they nonetheless give promise of commercial exploitation at prices not substantially above those of domestic crude oil.

A third possibility is the gasification of coal into a high-Btu fuel. The problem is to produce at a competitive cost a coal-derived gas that is sufficiently high in heat content to make it economical for long-distance transmission by pipeline and thus competitive with long-distance transmission of natural gas or electricity or of coal to central power stations. Much research has gone into this effort, and the goal may well be reached within the next forty years.

Finally the world outlook for oil and gas suggests that demand outside the United States is unlikely to grow at a sufficiently rapid rate to pre-empt the vast supplies available in the Middle East, North Africa, the Soviet Union, and probably in other parts of the world not yet thoroughly explored. However, this judgment must remain tentative, given the insufficient data on future demand, which, especially in the developing countries, might upset current speculations. The growing possibility of economic long-range shipment of natural gas in liquid form, combined with the virtually untapped reserves of natural gas in most of the oil-rich parts of the world, should make available new sources of supply the magnitude of which has not yet been established. Any such development would ease the pressure on world oil resources and thus benefit the United States at least indirectly.

A currently minor, though fast-growing, demand is the use of oil and gas as raw materials in the petrochemical industry. Projections in this area are particularly hazardous, for the chemical industry's growth is characterized by rapid changes not merely in magnitude but in materials, processes, applications, and relative prices. It appears, however, that even at the very rapid rates of growth assumed in our projections, total demand for gas and oil in the petrochemical industry could not materially alter the total supply position of either of the two resources. On the other hand, it is not unlikely that if raw material costs for the chemical industry should rise there might be a shift to substitute raw materials. Should this happen, coal, from which many of the current processes originated, would be a likely candidate.

Nuclear energy has already been mentioned briefly for its possible impact upon oil, gas, and coal. The outlook for nuclear energy as such has had many ups and downs since its commercial utilization first came into view almost twenty years ago. At the present time progress seems to be slow. Few reactors are in operation, and among them they amount to only a tiny fraction of the country's generating capacity. On the other hand, technology has been moving rapidly to bring costs nearer the levels that are attained by conventional generating methods.

Our projections here have been made largely by combining an appraisal of competing fuel costs on a regional basis with expectations of rapid progress in technology as experience yields new data and design benefits from operations. These give a modest place to nuclear energy by 1980: less than 5 per cent of all energy use and less than 20 per cent of all electricity generation. By the end of the century, about half of all electricity and 15 per cent of all energy is projected to come from nuclear reactors. A workable way of exploiting fusion rather than fission might change the timetable, but no account has been taken of this possibility.

No estimates are advanced for such sources as solar, wind, geothermal energy, or far-off devices like the biological fuel cell, which converts bacterial growth into electric energy. These would add directly to the resources upon which man can draw for his energy requirements, but there are too many open questions of technology and economics to permit quantitative speculation now on their place in the American energy pattern. Of the four, solar energy might before the end of the century create a niche for itself in some parts of the country, in residential and perhaps commercial use. At present, cost of equipment for any industrial use like power generation is far out of reach of commercial application.

Some fifty companies are currently doing research work on the fuel cell, a device that utilizes the electric current arising when two different gases react upon one another in the presence of a catalyst. It is difficult to believe that the fuel cell will not eventually become a commercial product. But while it has already proved itself in several applications, and has the advantage of very high conversion efficiency, it is not yet sufficiently developed to permit calculation of its impact upon the conventional fuel sources.

Several other departures in the energy field are based upon new conversion techniques. Thermionic and thermoelectric energy, both associated with the heating of metallic substances by a conventional fuel, as well as magneto-hydrodynamic generation, achieved through the flow of a very hot gas through a magnetic field, may give either higher efficiencies of conversion into electricity or such advantages as lower maintenance cost, silent operation, and lower weight; their effect upon energy resources will be principally through making reserves of conventional sources last longer rather than through adding to the substances from which energy is drawn.

Nonfuel Minerals[11]

There is no one way in which to sum up the outlook for all of the nonfuel minerals, each of which must be examined in the light of its own situation. Generally speaking, however, it is the metals that present problems of future adequacy. For most of them the supply prospects, as they appear in the light of information on mineral reserves and resources publicly available today, are such that the United States could not expect to meet its demands from domestic sources beyond a relatively brief time, if at

11. For details see Chapters 4, 5, 6, 7, 9, 16, 17, and 21.

all, without encountering higher costs, sometimes for only a brief transition period, sometimes permanently. In some instances the costs might be moderate, in others much higher. As a consequence there is need in the case of all but a few metals for (1) continued access to deposits beyond the U.S. borders and frequently outside the Western Hemisphere, and (2) advances in technology that would permit commercial exploitation of deposits now classified as potential ores with less costly methods than those in use today.

Domestic requirements for the major metals are expected to grow much faster than population during the remainder of the century, although generally not so fast as GNP. According to our Medium projections, the smallest rise—for lead—would be slightly over 100 per cent by the year 2000. Aluminum requirements are projected to rise by 800 per cent. An increase of 200 per cent is projected for steel, which now provides over 90 per cent of the tonnage of all major metals used and will continue to dominate the field.

As Figure 17 suggests, there are likely to be some significant changes over the next forty years in the pattern of metals use. Projected substitution of aluminum for steel in motor vehicles, construction, and containers is the reason for the most striking of these shifts. The extent of the change is brought out most sharply when one compares the major metals in terms of volume rather than tonnage. On this basis steel and aluminum together account for over 95 per cent of major metals use, both in 1960 and over the forty-year period of our projections. In 1960 iron and steel accounted for 90 per cent of metal volume and aluminum for 5.6. By 1980 these shares are projected to have shifted to 84.5 and 11.2 per cent respectively, and by the year 2000 to 79 and 17 per cent.

Our Medium projection for each metal is based on only one of the many patterns of demand that could result from over-all economic growth, substitutions among metals, and changing importance of the different end-uses during the next forty years.

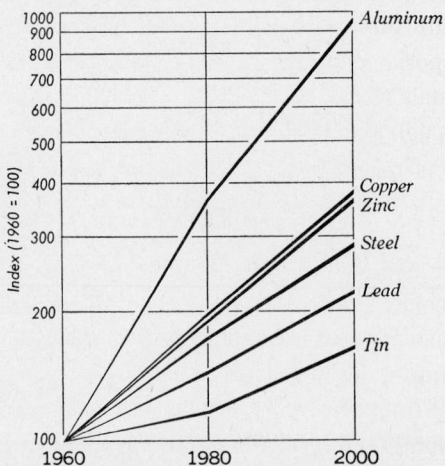

Figure 17. Comparative growth in the consumption of principal metals, 1960–2000.

For example, different but still plausible combinations of circumstances might result in a rise in aluminum consumption from 1.5 million tons in 1960 to as high a figure as 31 million tons or as low a one as 6.6 million in the year 2000 instead of to the 14.7 million tons of the Medium projection. Or iron and steel consumption, in terms of end-uses, might go from its 1960 level of 72 million tons to as high as 383 million or as low as 90 million instead of 196 million.

What are the prospects of meeting even the Medium projected U.S. demand for metals? The first step toward an answer is to compare the estimated cumulative demand for new metal over the balance of the century with domestic reserves. (The term "reserves" is used here in its strict definition as the mineral deposits currently estimated to be available that can be mined profitably at current prices with current technology.) Cumulative demand for iron and steel through the end of the century exceeds currently identified domestic reserves of iron ore in this country by some 40 per cent.

Domestic reserves of manganese, a metal that is indispensable to steel production, are just about equivalent to one year's consumption at present rates of steel production. Domestic reserves of bauxite are somewhat larger—equivalent to some five years of production at present rate—but basically the country is in a have-not status. The sum total of identified domestic reserves of copper equals not quite one-half projected cumulative requirements in the Medium projection. Lead and zinc occupy an intermediate position. Domestic reserves of lead are equivalent to not much more than one-tenth of projected demand; zinc reserves to more nearly one-third. Among the ferroalloys (other than manganese) that are essential in specialized kinds of steelmaking, domestic reserves appear to be sufficient only for molybdenum.

In addition to the identified reserves, however, there are other domestic deposits of a number of metals that can be mined at higher costs. In some instances, notably iron ore, these quantities of potential ore are very large. Better methods of extracting and using such materials would convert some of them into reserves, and a number of such gains in technology are sure to occur within the next forty years. Also, exploration will turn up new deposits that can be mined profitably by current methods. One cannot tell which metals would be affected, when, and how much, by these various possibilities. It seems unlikely, however, that creation of new reserves will come anywhere near keeping pace with increases in demand. Imports, which have grown rapidly since the 1930's, will become even more important in the future. (See Figures 18 and 19.)

Iron ore. Domestic deposits of potential ore are extremely large, since they embrace most of the taconite occurrences in the Lake states. Mining of this low-grade ore, much of it non-magnetic and therefore hard to separate and concentrate, would assure supplies well into the next century, but at present the high cost of production qualifies only a small fraction for inclusion in the reserve column. The remainder awaits further developments that would reduce the cost of winning the iron content from the hard and fine-grained rock.

As for import possibilities, world reserves appear adequate to U.S. needs through

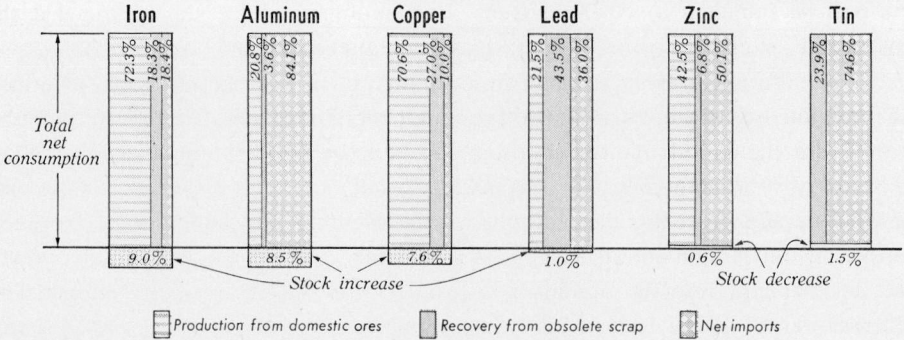

Figure 18. Sources of supply of principal metals consumed in the United States, as per cent of total net consumption, 1960.

the remainder of the century unless the demands of other countries should simultaneously grow at quite extraordinary rates. The twin avenues of advancing technology to enlarge use of domestic resources and recourse to foreign deposits—many of them in the Western Hemisphere—should relieve Americans of much of their concern over future supplies. If for any reason the United States should be restricted to its own iron resources, it seems unlikely that exploitation of the lower-grade, higher cost domestic sources, combined with advancing technology in steel production, would, after an initial period of adjustment, cause a major increase in steel prices.

Aluminum. World-wide reserves of bauxite, now practically the sole source of aluminum, are only just equivalent to world-wide cumulative demand as projected under an assumption of a moderate rate of growth. While the reserves are probably understated and new deposits of high quality are likely to be found, it is still reasonably certain that if the growth in demand outside the United States should be faster than we have assumed, lower-grade bauxite and high-alumina clays would be drawn upon. If this were done a truly spectacular rate of growth in world demand—above 10 per cent per year compounded—could be supported. Such a rapid development has been known, but never over a long period across the entire globe. Given continued access to them, foreign sources of good-grade bauxite should as in

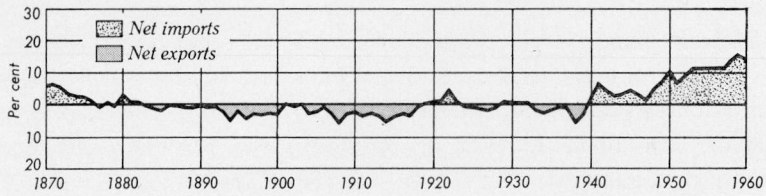

Figure 19. Net imports and exports of all minerals except gold and silver, as per cent of consumption, 1870–1960.

the past be sufficient to meet demands. Furthermore, it does not appear that the cost penalty of changing over to what is now potential ore would be unduly large.

Copper. There can be little doubt that reserves of copper, not only those identified in the United States but throughout the non-communist world, are insufficient to provide for the cumulative demand that can be expected in the next four decades. U.S. reserves, which even a generous interpretation cannot lift above 50 million tons of copper content, are less than half the projected cumulative demand of 110 million tons. And for the non-communist world as a whole, even at as low a yearly growth rate as 4 per cent, reserves amount to little more than half of the needed supply. The reserves, however, are backed up by an ample reservoir of potential ore of lower copper content. Considering that copper now mined abroad usually has a content of three, four, or five times (and in some places even more) that of copper mined in the United States, the transition from reserves to potential ore as a basis for production probably can be accomplished without real cost increases, as has been the case in this country.

Cost increases, if any, should be very gradual and small through the end of the century, for the projected magnitude of demand is such that by the year 2000 it would not be necessary to use ore with an average copper content of less than 1 per cent, which is a substantially better grade than the average ore now being worked in the United States.

Up to now exploration has been sporadic, even in areas that are outstanding producers of copper. Application of the modern tools of exploration will in all likelihood lead to the discovery of additional reserves and thus postpone the time when mining of lower-grade deposits will have to be tackled. Thus, improved and extended exploration is expected to be an important factor in future adequacy of copper.

Lead and zinc. Future adequacy is uncertain for the United States as well as for the rest of the world. The available data do not permit even an approximate conclusion, for in contrast to the other major metals reserve data are deficient in that they do not include inferred reserves, i.e., those that are estimated to be mineable but whose extent has not been ascertained through ample drilling.

Even with allowance for understatement, domestic reserves amount to barely one-eighth of projected cumulative requirements of lead, and about one-third for zinc. For the non-communist part of the world a mere continuation for the next forty years of the current level of lead consumption would require more than twice the amount that can now be regarded as reserves of the metal in these countries; in the case of zinc cumulative demand exceeds reserves by nearly 50 per cent.

Large discovery of lead and zinc reserves would have to take place to satisfy demand, but the history of government-subsidized exploration in this country suggests that either the costs of finding new deposits are far higher than even the recent government program indicated them to be—judging from the relatively poor results —or that indeed there is little additional ore to be found.

Manganese. The United States is poorly provided with manganese and heavily dependent on foreign supply. The domestic potential ore is limited in quantity and low in grade, the bulk of it containing less than 10 per cent of manganese as compared with foreign material containing 45 per cent and more. Even if continued effort by government and industry should enable the steel industry to utilize this potential ore, domestic supplies might be gone before the close of the century. Demand, now running at about 1 million tons a year, is projected to triple by the year 2000. However, recent research raises the distinct possibility that unit manganese requirements in steel production might be substantially reduced.

Because the United States now imports nearly all of the manganese it consumes, the situation abroad is especially important. Identified reserves in the non-communist world barely exceed projected demand. However, there seems to be a large potential for increased production. New reserves will undoubtedly be found (total world reserves were increased by 10 per cent recently by discoveries in the new African nation of Gabon); slagheaps near steel mills contain large amounts of recoverable used manganese; and there are large deposits of the metallic nodules containing manganese on the ocean floor. The technology for utilizing steel mill slag would receive an important impetus from indications that depletion of world reserves was in sight. So would the technology for exploiting the ocean-floor nodules.

The metals noted above account for nearly all of the total U.S. consumption of metals in both tonnage and value but only a small portion of the entire list of metals in commercial use. Many of the latter are of critical importance in certain functions. One group consists of the ferroalloys used principally in making certain types and grades of steel—chromium, nickel, molybdenum, tungsten, cobalt, and vanadium. Also there are some significant nonferrous metals—notably tin, magnesium, and titanium. Finally a large number of minor metals have come into prominence in recent years, often in connection with defense programs, atomic reactors, and space exploration—lithium, beryllium, columbium, and many others, used singly or in combination with major metals or with one another.

The ferroalloys occupy positions in the scale of adequacy all the way from a good prospect for self-sufficiency plus a large export trade for most of the period, as in the case of molybdenum, to nearly complete dependence upon foreign resources, as for tungsten, reserves of which in the non-communist countries appear insufficient to meet demand in those countries for more than perhaps two decades. Judgment of adequacy of chromium and nickel resources depends largely upon the ease and cost at which ore now classified as potential will lend itself to commercial exploitation, and the constellation of political forces in some of the areas of actual and potential production, such as Cuba.

The uncertainty of demand for other minor metals, and the wide range over which they can be substituted for one another, make judgment even more hazardous. However, for only a few of them are the reserves that can be estimated at this time anywhere nearly in line with projected requirements through the end of the century.

The non-metallic nonfuel minerals present few serious problems of adequacy over the next forty years. Lime and the various types of rock and sand required for cement, road-building, and other purposes are abundant on a nationwide basis, though some local problems of supply may arise as growing cities and suburbs or the expanding highway construction program put pressure on quarries of this or that material.

The reserves of potash and phosphate, so vital for helping to attain the high crop yields stipulated in our agricultural projections, seem equally adequate, with additional deposits in Canada promising to backstop U.S. supplies if necessary. And ocean-bed occurrences of phosphates might before long contribute to the needs of the West Coast.

Only sulfur is a candidate for a moderate measure of concern. The bulk of current sulfur production comes from subterranean sulfur domes the sum total of which is smaller than foreseeable demand. It is possible, but by no means certain, that new domes will be found. Discoveries in the past have been quite discontinuous—one might almost say fortuitous.

On the other hand, a relatively new source—sour oil and gas—has been contributing an increasing share of the world's sulfur supply. The recoverable sulfur content of the world's oil and gas reserves is apparently large, but it seems unlikely that enough of it will be tapped between now and the end of the century to fill the gap between the known dome reserves and cumulative requirements. It has also been estimated that Canada's bituminous tar sands contain two billion tons of sulfur. Even assuming that U.S. exports of sulfur will gradually decline and all domestic sulfur will be used domestically and that this country would also absorb some Mexican production, there would still remain a gap, even in our Medium projection. For the time being one must therefore assume that sources of supply not now visible would have to come into play toward the middle of the period under consideration. Though the long-run outlook is hopeful, it is possible that between now and the end of the century some tightness may develop.

Some Major Problems and Directions for Policy

This is not a book on resource policy; its aim is to present systematically and comprehensively a view of the future demand for resource materials along with a broad consideration of supply possibilities. Notwithstanding, our demand and supply projections in agriculture, forestry, water, minerals, and the rest have inevitably led to conclusions as to problems of resource shortage or surplus, some of which have been indicated already. In this section we shall consider briefly a number—but by no means all—of major resource problems cast into view by the projections, and what they seem to imply for future policy directions. It is recognized, of course, that many resource policy issues do not arise primarily from problems of demand and supply;

instead they are related more directly to matters of ownership, to conflicts in use, and to the incidence of benefits and costs among individuals, groups, and regions.

Future resource policies evolve from past policies just as future demand trends grow out of those of the past. The history of resources development and policy in the United States is the story of interaction between events, policies, and policy objectives. The so-called "first conservation movement" culminating in the administration of Theodore Roosevelt and the activities of his chief forester, Gifford Pinchot, grew out of recognition that the geographic frontier period was about over, that tendencies toward monopolistic control of certain basic resources needed curbing, and that large advantages could be secured through development of resources for multiple purposes. Policy objectives conceived during this period, however vague, did guide and shape the unfolding of specific policies which followed in regard to forests, water, oil, and other resources.

The great depression of the 1930's gave rise to new policies and policy objectives in the resource field. The raising of incomes in agriculture and the stimulation of the economy through programs of public works, many of them resource projects, became of central importance. The Tennessee Valley Authority was created at this time. The dust storms on the Great Plains plus the growing awareness of water erosion led to the launching of soil conservation activities across the country.

The Second World War and the re-establishment of the economies of the western European countries after the war placed heavy demands on raw materials which continued during the cold war and Korean War that followed. Population growth spurted during the latter half of the 1940's. This country became more dependent on imports of oil, iron ore, and many other metals. A huge stockpiling program, mainly for metals, was undertaken against the possibility of a protracted war. Economic growth was given increasing emphasis as an objective of national policy. In the resource field, for the most part, policies were confined to modifications and extensions of the policy innovations of the 1930's.

These major events in the resource field called for major shifts in objectives of resource development and for major policy responses consistent with a new role in world affairs, enlarged responsibility for aiding underdeveloped areas, an increasing net import position for important raw materials, new and uncertain defense requirements, and an urgent need to maintain a stable and growing domestic economy. A number of notable studies of the impact of these changes, such as that of the President's Materials Policy Commission, were made in the postwar period, each in its field attempting to state the problems and recommend more comprehensive and consistent public policies. These recommendations, however, have not thus far called forth great response from policy makers. Agricultural policies continue to be characterized by price supports and surplus stocks, acreage controls and fertilizer payments, and soil banks and subsidized irrigation—all underscoring stubborn inconsistencies. Water resource policies and administration continue in a tangled condition with rival claimants, purposes, and agencies competing for position. In the face of some real difficulties mineral industries seek tariff protection and favored tax treatment while comparative cost trends and the need of less developed countries to export raw materials inexorably lead this country to import more and more.

These inadequacies and dilemmas point to the need for recasting resource policies in a new mold of greater internal consistency and of greater harmony with the broader policies of foreign relations and defense. In any such new mold resource policies to achieve these objectives should find a place: multiple purpose management frequently on a regional basis; efficient production and use of land, water, and mineral resources; wide diffusion of benefits from resource development projects with equitable sharing of costs; adequate consideration for the qualitative, more or less nonmonetary aspects of resources such as clean air and unspoiled scenery; strong national defense, progress toward world peace, and sustained contribution to economic growth and stability in this country and elsewhere.

With this as background we turn to a brief characterization of several major problems for policy to deal with.

Research, development, and investment. At many points in this study the need for continued gains in technology stand out clearly—advances without which ever-present tendencies for demand to outrun supply cannot be held in check. Yields will have to continue to increase in agriculture. Reuse of water within industries, improvements in pollution treatment, and many other adaptations of new technology—perhaps even the beginning of desalinization—will be called on. Continued advance in techniques of exploration for ores and in their extraction and processing, plus increased efficiency in getting heat and power from fuels, will most certainly be necessary if demands for mineral materials and energy are to be satisfied. By the last two decades of the century nuclear power and liquid oil from shales and tar sands will probably have to make significant contributions. The main escape hatch from scarcity is technological advance across a broad front, and behind this have to be large, varied, effective programs of research and development in science, engineering, economics, and management. And backing this up has to be a strong system of general education at all levels.

Total research and development (R & D) expenditures in 1960, governmental and private, apparently were on the order of $12 to $15 billion, of which perhaps 10 per cent, or upwards of a billion and a quarter dollars, was probably in the resources field. A doubling of expenditures for resources research and development in each of the next two decades—a slower rate of increase than during the past decade for all R & D—would lift the total to $5 or $6 billion by 1980, which would come to about one-half of 1 per cent of gross national product. Quite probably the more basic research portion will increase compared with all R & D—it is now about 10 per cent of the total—and this will be true also of the resources component.

Policies can have decisive influence on the amount and emphasis in research and development activities. Tax treatment and other measures designed to affect R & D expenditures of private firms as well as government R & D budgets for agricultural research, atomic energy, geological investigations, and other resource programs can set the tone and direction for all resources R & D; private policies within industry can have a similarly important influence. Without attempting to be more specific here, we may conclude that R & D expenditures on resources will most certainly have to increase greatly in the future if an ample flow of low cost materials is to be continuously available and if the resource base is to be maintained and utilized effectively; it is evident, also, that a variety of public and private policies will have to be employed for this purpose.

In addition, expanded programs of investment in resource conservation and development will be needed along many lines if projected demands are to be met. Here again statistics are none too good in indicating historical trends. Total government expenditures for resources in 1960 were probably around $7 or $8 billion, somewhat less than half of which was by the federal government, and the larger portion of the remainder was for local water and sewage works. Some of this was for operating and maintenance, rather than for investment proper. Perhaps $3 or $4 billion was invested privately, mostly by the oil and gas industry. Total annual investments for resources were in the neighborhood of $9 billion in 1960, nearly 1.8 per cent of gross national product in that year.

If 2 per cent of GNP were invested in resources by 1980, the total would come to about $22 billion, an increase of two and one-half times over 1960. The cumulative amount for the twenty-year period would exceed a quarter trillion dollars. If the concept of resource investments were broadened to include investments in partially processed raw materials, such as steel and aluminum, and those devoted to production of substitutes, such as plastics, then total resource investment figures would be much higher.

Various estimates have been made of the amount of investment "needed" to conserve and develop the resources of the nation to meet anticipated demands and leave the resource base in a productive state at all times. For the most part these estimates lead in the direction of demonstrating the inadequacy of investment in terms of the standards laid down. We do not examine this question in this study, but we do venture the opinion that if our Medium levels of demand are to be satisfied, while at the same time allowing for improvements in the condition of the resource base of land and water, a considerable over-all increase in capital outlays for resources will be necessary during the coming years over and above what would result from a continuation of the modest increases of the past decade. For example, if, as our projections show, hydroelectric capacity were to expand by some 33 million kilowatts by 1980, the total investment at an average cost of $500 per kilowatt would be more than $16 billion over the period, which implies annual outlays well above those for new hydro capacity in recent years. A similar story can be told for forestry, outdoor recreation, minerals mapping and exploration, oil and gas development, and other resource fields. Steadily increasing capital outlays for resources are the means for translating research and development findings into practical applications; any serious diminution or delay of investment in these lines will undercut one of the foundations of the economy.

A reasonably free world trading system. The United States already leans heavily on imports for numerous mineral commodities which are vital to its economic growth and national defense; for about three decades it has been a net importer of extractive materials. By 1948 the United States for the first time became a net importer of oil, and shortly afterwards of iron ore. It is clear that in the future even larger amounts of certain items will have to be drawn from foreign sources if demand is to be satisfied without marked increases in cost. On the other hand the United States remains a large net exporter of a number of basic agricultural crops, notably wheat and cotton. To whatever extent the world trading system should deteriorate so that less goods were traded internationally, U.S. supply problems in minerals and market problems in agriculture would be intensified.

American energy and minerals policy has never been clear as to whether it should move in the direction of encouraging substitution to take full advantage of cheaper and more plentiful sources wherever located, or whether it should favor perpetuation of existing patterns whatever they may be. The objective of obtaining an adequate and dependable flow of raw materials at least cost, which has large general appeal, has had to be reconciled with the requirements of national defense, the position of affected industries and regions, and the interests of friendly nations. The lowest cost dictum would mean, for example, a considerable increase in imports of oil, as well as other raw materials, and this might not square with the national security objective. On the other hand, the case has been made that larger imports would enhance national security by making it possible to retain more domestic oil, for example, in the ground, available in time of need. A counter to this argument, however, is that a modern all-out war most likely would be a short one so that underground stocks of oil would be of no benefit; all that would count, so this argument runs, would be stocks of aviation gasoline and jet fuel already refined and stored close to airfields. Further problems arise when the interests of friendly nations are considered. Larger U.S. imports from the Middle East and Venezuela would promote economic development of those areas; on the other hand, a large domestic U.S. capability in oil production and refining is important to western Europe in case countries there should be denied access to oil from their principal sources of supply in the Middle East.

Despite difficulties in reconciling general objectives to be served by foreign trade policy regarding raw materials, and added difficulties in translating objectives to specific policies, the inescapable fact remains that for many items, especially among the minerals, the United States now draws heavily on sources in other countries and will have to continue to do so unless costs in many instances are to increase considerably. U.S. policy regarding imports and treatment of foreign investments, therefore, should strike its compromises with this clearly in view.

Multiple use of the nation's fixed area of land space. Increasing demands on land space for outdoor recreation, urban growth, highways, airports, and perhaps forests by the year 2000 will far exceed whatever saving may be made in land needed for crops and whatever amount of unused land that may be pressed into service. According to our Medium estimates for 2000, counting each use separately, land requirements would add up to 50 million more acres than the country has. Two escape routes from this untenable situation are possible: more intensive single purpose use of land, and multiple purpose use of land. Our projections already make allowance for the first, while the second offers new and expanded opportunities for ingenuity of policy and management.

Much of the demand for outdoor recreation land can be met by stepping up the use of national, state, and private forests for this purpose through investment in access roads, parking and camping areas, trails, and other facilities. Locations can be chosen which will be accessible to urban dwellers and at the same time minimize the sacrifice of timber production. Outdoor recreation use of forests usually complements other purposes such as watershed protection. With proper safeguards some range land and even farm land near cities may also be used for recreation. The economics of these newer patterns of multiple land use have not yet been proved out for private owners, although in isolated cases fees, rentals, and lease arrangements have succeeded.

Urban land uses will expand outward from presently built-up centers; many of the country's metropolitan areas will tend to become joined in continuous urban and suburban bands. To the extent that small parcels of vacant land now by-passed or surrounded can be filled in with urban development, the demand on nearby farm land will be reduced. With the necessary public support, the techniques of urban land use planning can help bring about a more efficient and an aesthetically pleasing pattern, with increased emphasis on reservation of parks, nature areas, farm land, and open spaces separating built up portions. Great, wide strips of megalopolis—Boston to Washington, Buffalo to Milwaukee, perhaps San Francisco to Los Angeles—can be planned for multiple purposes including urban living, industry and commerce, outdoor recreation, transportation facilities, and even some agriculture and forestry.

Prospective shortage of forest products. Supply limitations are more likely to be a barrier to meeting projected demand for forest products and services than for any other major category of resource materials. Because it is not easy to see how very many additional acres can be shifted into forest production even for the long pull, the solution here, so far as it involves the increase of supply, will have to be sought chiefly through improvements on existing forest land. A greater concentration of cutting on the mature stands in the West will be helpful over the coming twenty years or so, combined with strenuous efforts to improve and upgrade the more rapidly growing stands in the East. A large potential remains if only losses to insects, disease, fire, and other causes can be reduced. Direct annual losses from such damage amount to about a quarter of the total cut, and the further losses of growth that otherwise would have taken place are more than twice as large as the actual timber mortality.

Much of the commercial and potentially commercial forest land of the nation is in small farms and other holdings in the South and East, on much of which lack of incentive prevents the practice of good forestry. Improvements await the design and implementation of new forms of consolidated management, more suitable types of credit, possibly insurance against losses, tax arrangements which will further discourage premature cutting, aid in reforestation, along with other measures.

For the very long pull, a vigorous program of research and experimentation through genetics and physiology may lead to hybrids which will be more productive in terms of annual growth than present trees. Work along this line has already shown spectacular results on a small experimental scale. Further efforts to make use of species, sizes, and wood material now left behind in the forests can also make a contribution. In particular, technological improvements which will make economic the use of eastern hardwoods for pulp on a much larger scale than at present should return handsome dividends over time. The opportunities for increased imports, except possibly from Canada, do not seem particularly favorable, though eventually it is possible that tropical hardwoods from Central and South America, or their products, may find larger markets in this country.

Efficient and comprehensive development of water resources. The broad task of water policies over the coming years will be to promote the integrated development and efficient use of water for a wide range of purposes deemed important to the nation. The chief water problems of this country are impending shortage of supply in the West and serious deterioration of quality in the East. In the West, in addition to reservoir construction, watershed management, measures to control water-using but useless plants, and reduction of losses from reservoirs and canals, there remain the social, economic, and legal problems of facilitating a shift toward higher value industrial and municipal uses and away from the low-value use in irrigation agriculture. It is recognized that water law and practices have solidified in most parts of the West under the prior appropriation doctrine so that 90 per cent or more of the water is used for irrigation, and that this situation cannot be changed drastically without hardship to certain users and certain geographic areas. However, the preferred direction of policy seems to be clear, at least as regards new supplies of water that might be developed. To the extent that market forces can be utilized more fully in guiding the water into its most productive uses, this particular situation might over time be further ameliorated. For example, a movement toward pricing water more in accord with the full cost of developing supplies, preparing them for use, and distributing them could result in much greater conservation of water all along the line, from the irrigated field and the factory to the family sink and shower.

The problem for the East is primarily one of improving the management and use of water rather than one of shortage, and most importantly the prevention and abatement of water pollution. The economics of pollution control is far from simple; an optimal system of waste disposal ordinarily involves selection from a wide range of techniques, including water storage for maintenance of flow in dry periods, recycling in use, and treatment. Water flow requirements, especially in the heavily populated industrial areas, inevitably will increase greatly in the future, although extension of sewage treatment and other techniques can mitigate this tendency somewhat. Pollution prevention and abatement programs will have to be intensified and carried out over wide geographical areas, frequently on an interstate scale, as in the case of the Ohio River Valley and a number of other basins. Water quality standards need further definition for various uses and various locations.

Ample supplies of good quality fresh water will be wanted for outdoor recreation. Management of water for this purpose will require compromise and reconciliation with other major uses. For example, the largest number of water recreation facilities should be in or near metropolitan centers for convenience of users. Yet it is in these areas that both competition for water supplies and pollution tend to be concentrated. Planning to restrict water polluting activities to certain areas would be helpful as would the strict designation of certain areas for outdoor recreation.

At the other end of the scale from water shortage is the problem of floods, which continue to occur and cause as much or more damage than they did before flood prevention and control work was installed. This is in part the inevitable consequence of the increase in population and industrial and agricultural activities, exacerbated by a lack of proper incentives to locate structures and transportation facilities in more protected areas out of the flood plains. Dealing with the flood problem will involve choices among a variety of possible measures—flood forecasting, the construction of flood retention facilities, flood plain zoning for suitable uses, the requirement that structures be flood resistant, flood damage insurance, evacuation and other safety measures, and a number of others.

The efficient management of water for the various purposes is a complicated task. Engineering and economic analysis which will present the alternative strategies for development and control in such a way that they can be compared will help to guide public and private policy makers in making good choices. Not all the benefits to be received as the result of water development lend themselves to economic estimation in dollars, and the same is true on the cost side. On the other hand, dollar estimates of benefits and costs almost always can give clues as to the magnitude and incidence of benefits and costs on various groups; at a minimum such estimates can rule out extreme solutions as being too costly. Then there is the immensely difficult problem of comparing benefits and costs in the more distant future with those of the near future.

Those policy and administrative processes will serve best which make possible the more efficient and integrated patterns of water use. This, of course, does not necessarily mean a highly centralized structure since regional differences are of the essence in understanding the country's water resources and their potentialities.

Impact on particular industries and areas. New technology, product substitutions, new resource discoveries, depletion of older sources, changes in foreign trade policy and other shifts in the world scene frequently adversely affect particular resource industries, or segments of industries, and geographic areas. The coal industry and producing areas are hurt by substitution of other fuels. Mining areas in the West are abandoned when the richer mineral veins are worked out. Cut-over forest areas become depressed. Most widely prevalent of all, greatly increased productivity in agriculture during the past thirty years, notwithstanding a drop in farm employment from 12.5 to 7.1 million, has left more people in agriculture, particularly in certain regional and other segments of agriculture, than can find a reasonably good level of living.

In a relatively free and flexible economy, such as that of the United States, such problems inevitably accompany growth and change. To a large extent they can be handled by maintaining a growing, prosperous economy generally over the country so that displaced workers, managers, and enterprisers can find satisfactory opportunities elsewhere. Beyond this, special efforts are usually desirable to ease and promote necessary transitions, to minimize individual and social damage, and to direct aid especially to those most seriously hurt.

Unfortunately, programs ostensibly designed to serve these purposes sometimes are really installed and maintained for other reasons—for example, to perpetuate a special position or privilege long after the need for it has disappeared. Policy solicitude for disadvantaged industrial, agricultural, and labor groups is sensible for obvious reasons of social welfare and fairness to individuals, but only if it can be progressively diminished over the period of a few years. Usually this will require positive efforts to retrain and relocate displaced workers, to assist adversely affected industries, to diversify their activities, and to promote the establishment of new enterprises which can prosper in the areas undergoing these transitions. An economic system which aims to be competitive within its own national boundaries, and on a world scale as well, must not allow particular segments to receive protection permanently from the changes that competition insists be made. The net gains from technological innovation, the opening up of new low-cost sources of raw materials, and reduction of trade barriers are substantial; a legitimate concern for those disadvantaged as a consequence of such changes can be translated into effective policies without thwarting the changes themselves. But success along this line is sometimes too long delayed.

International price stability for minerals. Looking at minerals and certain agricultural products on a world scale, one of the most severe and intractable problems has been the sharp fluctuations of price, output, and prosperity in those industries. In large, wealthy, and diversified economies, this problem is troublesome enough, but in smaller, less developed countries and regions, which frequently depend heavily on one or a few mineral commodities, the effects of instability can be devastating. For example, in recent years about three-fourths of the total value of exports from Chile have been made up of copper and nitrates; somewhat less than half the exports of Mexico have been made up of coffee, cotton, and nonferrous metals and ores; in the Congo some 60 per cent of total exports have been copper, cobalt, coffee, and cotton. Basic causes of instability in minerals markets are to be found partly in the sharp fluctuations in the demand for metals in the major industrial countries due principally to business cycle ups and downs, which tend to be especially severe in the metal-using industries; partly in the ease with which metals and their products can be stockpiled in consuming countries, thereby throwing the burden of supply adjustments back on the mining sector; partly in the slow response of supply in the producing countries to price changes—that is, output can be neither expanded nor contracted rapidly except at considerable cost and difficulty, as price in the world markets goes up or down.

Various stabilizing schemes have been tried for minerals, some of them organized privately or semi-privately under cartels, and some more officially through treaties or under international auspices. Most of these arrangements have had a short and not conspicuously successful life. Occasionally reasonably successful efforts to stabilize the domestic mining industries of a country have impeded international stability and, typically, international schemes as well as domestic have operated to the disadvantage of ultimate consumers of metal products. There appears to be need for the creation and testing of new policies and arrangements. Care will have to be taken such arrangements do not result simply in the perpetuation of uneconomic locations and privileged positions.

Short-term vs. long-term resource policies. By approximately dating the onset of a shortage or surplus problem, or the changeover from one to the other, our statistical projections of demand and supply tell a good deal about the degree of emphasis that should be given to policies aimed toward a long-term as against a short-term effect. For example, with an outlook for surplus production of most basic crops for the next decade or two, a shift in the relative emphasis in soil conservation would appear to be in order, from practices whose main effects would be to increase output in the next few years, toward practices from which the gains in output could be deferred. Soil conservation activities thus become a kind of long-term insurance against the possibility that yields will not increase as much as expected or that domestic and overseas demand increases beyond expectations. Similarly, emphasis on basic research in agriculture the returns from which would not come until well into the future would be appropriate.

Another example comes out of our projections for nuclear energy which, we anticipate, will become increasingly significant during the last two decades of this century. In the next two decades conventional sources should suffice to meet demand without cost increases. In this circumstance research and development efforts need not bear down on immediate commercial feasibility, but can continue to stress a number of promising alternative types of fission reactors and can pursue more basic research on nuclear fusion possibilities.

In forestry, where the response to present actions tends to be slow and long deferred, more emphasis on development programs will be in order. Planting and stand improvement, disease, insect, and fire control programs, and efforts to improve management of small holdings would have to be enlarged now if appreciable effects are to be seen in the more distant future.

Non-economic considerations. The natural resources of a country, or of the world viewed as a whole, are so basic to the maintenance of life and civilization that no one special approach or set of considerations can be allowed to dominate the selection of broad policies. A rising level of living is assumed to be a primary objective, particularly as this may be promoted by vigorous development and wise use of natural resources. Sustaining a rising level over an indefinitely long period, however, requires a respect for the basic processes of nature. Economic calculation and technological ingenuity, as these are expressed in practice, do not always take sufficient account of the injunctions of ecology. In a number of ancient civilizations the misuse of water, soil, and grass led to, or was accompanied by, disintegration. In the exploitation of land and water resources, there are ecological "points of no return" beyond which the resource cannot be rebuilt except at exorbitant cost, if at all. These points should be respected as a matter of social insurance for the distant future, if not as a matter of "right conduct."

The maintenance of resource quality standards, and their improvement, will become of increasing concern as the material level of living rises and the elemental needs for food, clothing, and shelter are adequately met. Broadly speaking, this is the aesthetic part, although health and welfare of both individuals and society are also involved. The preservation of scenic beauty and the enhancement of recreational amenities beyond what might result from good business practices are parts of the story. Care and discrimination in the use of pesticides which may exterminate wildlife is another part. Polluted water and air may be burdens on whole cities and may limit severely future growth and improvement. The balancing of private and social responsibilities in these matters is difficult, not only because of the lack of a coincidence between those who cause the pollution or disfigurement and those who are harmed by it, but also because of the scale and cost of prevention and abatement programs. For the future the quality of growth, the aesthetics of resource use, will be as much a part of the standard of living as the sheer amounts of things to be consumed —probably more so as people's appetite for material goods becomes more nearly satiated.

Thus policy makers must weigh ecological and aesthetic considerations in the balance along with economic and technological factors, as a matter of promoting the public welfare in a broad sense. Further efforts to bring these considerations sensibly within the ambit of economic analysis, perhaps under the heading of welfare economics, are worth making.

Resource policies and national policies. From the viewpoint of this study, the overriding aim in natural resource policies is that the flow of resource materials and services be adequate for a vigorously growing economy and that the quality of the resource base be maintained and, where possible, improved.

Although resources are of basic importance in the American economy, labor and capital to produce needed goods are basic too. Nor are economic goals the only ones. Resource policies are not sufficient unto themselves; they operate in conjunction with other policies across the whole range of national concerns. Thus, resource policies at many points ought to be integrated with public works policy, tax and subsidy policy, transportation policy, foreign trade policy, military policy, and so on. Making resource policies pull together with policies in these other fields is a difficult undertaking, analytically and administratively, and calls for improved processes of policy formulation, operation, and evaluation.

Many examples of the importance of policy consistency can readily be found. Oil has already been mentioned, for which national security, relations with particular other countries, solicitude for the domestic industry, concern for short-run business stability, and development of sub-national regions, are among the considerations that constrain the working out of the principles of least cost. The constructive resolution of these conflicting aspects requires the highest order of statecraft. Policy objectives have to be cast in a broader frame than resources, or anything else, alone; techniques and processes of reconciliation become a necessity. Another example would be inland waterway transportation policy, which is a part of national transportation policy involving rail, highway, air, and pipeline transport as well as water. Government regulations are of considerable scope and significance in the oil and water transportation examples just mentioned as well as in other resource situations. The kind and degree of regulation depends considerably on prevailing views regarding government regulation of private business activities.

There are various levels of policy depending on the range of resources under view, the broader categories of national policy being considered, and the extent of the geographic area in mind. An all-embracing standard of consistency and performance is difficult to conceive, much less state explicitly and apply. Whatever specific resource policy may be under consideration, it should be tested and evaluated not only against broad objectives for resource policy but also against objectives in surrounding fields of policy. Across the board, economic standards of efficiency related to least-cost production, equating of marginal returns to resource users, and the ordering of development projects according to benefit-cost or return-on-investment measurements will be helpful if used with caution and with due regard for non-economic aspects. Administrative feasibility provides another series of tests for resource policies. Ecological constraints must be understood and obeyed, by common consent where possible, by government enforcement where necessary. In both government and industry the processes by which policies are made—political, consultative, budgeting, competitive, and bargaining processes—require most careful attention if good results are to be secured.

We do not envision any single, monolithic Resource Policy, through the application of which all resource problems will be solved. Nor would we expect ever to find a single water policy or energy policy unless these are stated in such general terms as to be rather useless. Policies, like actions, tend to come in bits and pieces, never thoroughly consistent in their direction. The real task is to make them more consistent, to fit them more to a well-conceived pattern. Clearly established general objectives and well-designed processes of policy debate and formulation, plus systematic review and evaluation, offer the best guarantee of policy improvements.

In our long look ahead at demand and supply of resources we do not see any general running out; instead we see the prospect of sustained economic growth supported by an adequacy of resource materials, *provided* technologic advances and economic adaptation of them continue, *provided* foreign sources of raw materials remain open through maintenance of a viable world trading and investing system, and *provided* government resource policies and private management of resource enterprises improve in farsightedness, flexibility, and consistency. Each of these provisos presents difficulties and opportunities which are well within the capacity of research, policy, and action to deal with successfully.

How the Estimates Were Made: A Note on Method, Scope, and Uses

The study starts with projections of U.S. population, labor force, gross national product, and other aggregates that indicate what the general size and shape of the American economy would be between 1960 and the year 2000, if current consumption trends as modified in the light of already discernible patterns of change should continue. Another key variable, the progress of technology, also is considered. Then future consumption levels, consistent with the over-all productive performance of the economy, are calculated for the important human needs such as food, clothing, shelter, heat and power, producer and consumer hard goods of all sorts, transportation, the military, and other identifiable and separable aspects of industrialized society. From these are derived the demand for numerous intermediate items: agricultural raw materials, steel, lumber, textile fibers, basic chemicals, and the like, with allowances for substitutions among materials and for future economies of use through better technology. Finally, the projected demands thus arrived at are considered in relation to availability of supply as determined by the underlying resources of land, water, and minerals.

Out of this approach, there emerges a comprehensive view of the likely future pressure on basic natural resources. Wherever requirements appear to come up against inadequate resources, there is a problem to be dealt with. The problems are not framed in the fear of running out, or of not having enough to support a rising level of living. The idea is, rather, that through long-range demand and supply projections future resource problems can be anticipated and dealt with through policy and management in an orderly way rather than through emergency action later on.

The study is held together by a common framework of assumptions as to economic development, set forth in Chapter 1, which underlies all parts of the projections. When claims upon each resource from all relevant end-uses and for all relevant resources from each end-use are aggregated, the chance that an undue share of the market will be assigned to any one of the resources is minimized. The advantage of this approach has been shown in earlier RFF work, most notably in its study of energy. The producers of competing sources of energy are, not unnaturally, tempted to claim unrealistically large portions of future demand for their particular product. Comprehensiveness of treatment minimizes this particular aberration.

Comprehensiveness means approaching the final level of each projection in successive stages. Frequently, a magnitude has to be put down as a first rough guess in order to estimate others depending on it. Since each item feeds into one or more other items, the entire structure is not completed and consistent until all the feedbacks have been accommodated and the quantities originally roughed in have been adjusted. In the present study this process sometimes has been cut off when only minor adjustments were left to be made; the resultant flaws that remain are the price of convenient short-cuts.

Requirements for each product and, deriving from it, for each resource, are affected by requirements for competing products and resources. All consumer goods compete for the consumer's dollar; only an over-all constraint in terms of total disposable income or consumer expenditures can keep the parts from exceeding the total. Metals, lumber, cement compete as structural materials; what is projected to happen to the use of one affects the projected use of the other. Thus, one cannot be "more or less" comprehensive, except for omission of those parts of the picture that can be clearly demonstrated to be of small significance in their impact upon resources. Figure 20 illustrates the kinds of cross-relationship that were involved in arriving at our projections of resource adequacy.

In numerous instances projections were carried out not so much because the item involved would in itself play a significant role in determining resource adequacy but because its consumption pattern would affect that of another item that might pose a resource problem within the period under review. Thus, there will undoubtedly be enough limestone to furnish the basic material for concrete, but the growth in use of concrete is intimately intertwined with requirements for steel. Or, certain statistical series needed as guides or reference series for resource-oriented projections had to be projected even though this involved the preparation of estimates for portions of the series not of direct interest in themselves. The projection of some of the details of the Federal Reserve Board index of industrial production is the most striking example of projecting unimportant parts of an important aggregate.

Comprehensiveness also facilitates double-checking. The product of labor force and productivity must equal the gross national product built up from its demand components, and the sum of the demand components must in turn equal the sum of the "type of output" components. Other than moderate residual differences call for adjustment of the projections.

Because none of these magnitudes in the future can be known, even these checks and constraints are speculative and are based upon judgment. In general, however, the larger the aggregates at which one guesses, the smaller the relative magnitude of the misjudgment. Projections of growth of population, gross national product, total industrial production, and similar large aggregates are likely to vary within a narrower range than, say, the consumption of tin, cotton, or natural gas liquids. Thus an independent projection of the major parameters hems in the vast number of projections in the various subdivisions and branches of the economy. Comprehensiveness thus serves to provide both consistency and discipline—at the cost, it is true, of a complex and time-consuming operation that is open to criticism at many more points than a simpler structure would be.

What is a projection? In economic parlance the term "projection" generally refers to the process of determining what a given set of starting assumptions means for the future course of some economic or social statistical measure. Sometimes, as in straight extrapolation, the starting assumption is no more than that the future will unfold exactly as did the past. Whether this or a complex set of parameters is the starting point, a projection is not a forecast, for the latter is an avowed attempt to foretell the future. While people who make projections usually try to start with assumptions which are as realistic as possible, the logic of the assumptions normally determines the end results regardless of their apparent plausibility or margin for error.

In this study we are working in terms of projections. We have, however, sought to make our projections both individually plausible and consistent with each other, as well as consistent with such general notions of the future as we could gather from specialists in one phase or another of the U.S. economy. An important exception is that the projected requirements do not reflect the impact of relative price changes that might result from any future supply stringency or surplus upon levels of demand. Implications of this lack of "price feedback" are noted on pages 60 and 61 of this section, where the characteristics of the projections are discussed.

A range of possibilities. Recognizing that the future is uncertain, we have rarely made a unique projection for a given item. Instead, we have projected a range of magnitudes. For some items this range is very large; for others, quite narrow. For many magnitudes—especially the larger aggregates—the possible limits are circumscribed either by physical limitations, or by institutional factors, or by already existing elements which determine the future for some time to come. For example, physiology places fairly narrow limits on the amount of food which might be consumed per capita. Or again, the number of young people already born largely determines the number of new households to be formed in the United States for the next two decades or so. The range grows wider, however, as we get into the details and subdivisions or move farther into the future. For example, while the total amount of food which can be consumed per capita cannot vary much, its particular composition can change considerably with tastes, habits, and prices.

Figure 20. Resources and Economic Growth:
Some examples of resource/output relationships,
1960, 1980, and 2000.

The selected items in the chart illustrate how
(1) the estimated future demand for various
consumption items on the basis of population
and general economic growth, (2) the demand
for key materials, and (3) the demand for basic
resources were derived in this study. The chart
also indicates the numerous cross-relationships
that must be investigated in a study of this sort,
and how very different elements in the economy
combine to create the level of demand for particular resources. It does not attempt to show all
of the interrelationships investigated even for the
items selected, nor the exact lines of derivation,
which ordinarily involve many steps intermediate to those shown.

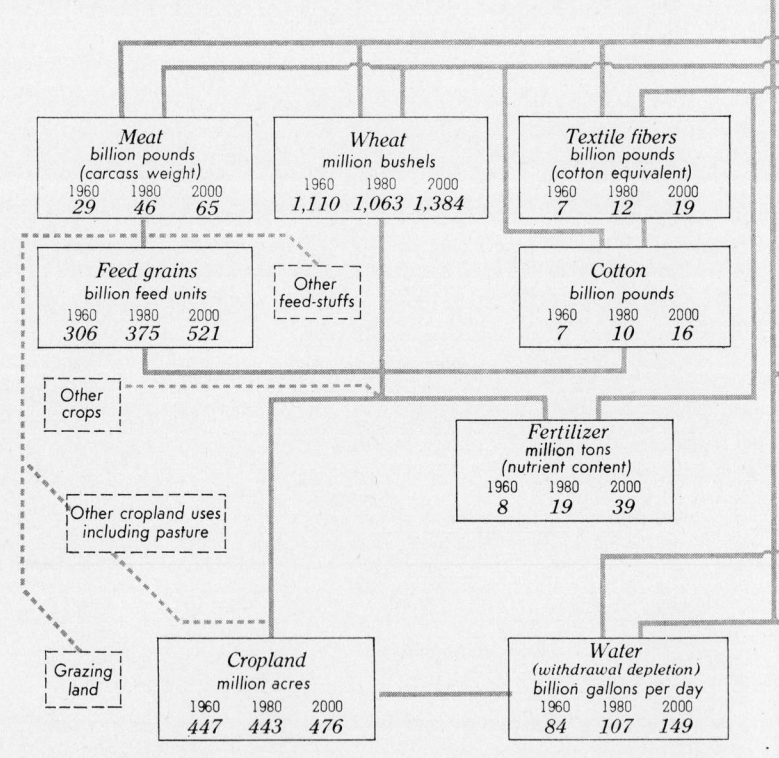

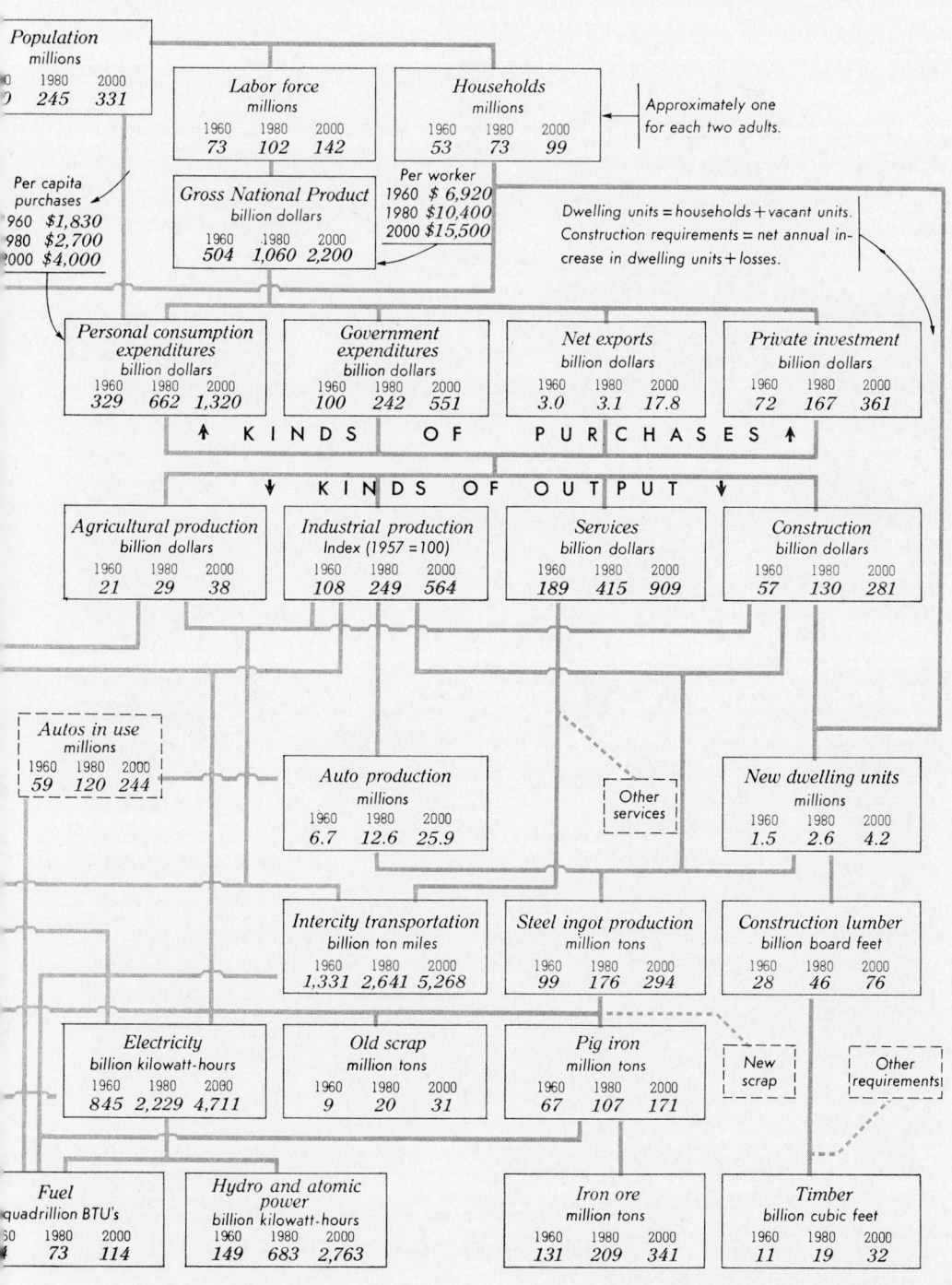

Population
millions
	1980	2000
245	331

Labor force
millions
1960	1980	2000
73	102	142

Households
millions
1960	1980	2000
53	73	99

Approximately one for each two adults.

Per capita purchases
1960	$1,830
1980	$2,700
2000	$4,000

Gross National Product
billion dollars
1960	1980	2000
504	1,060	2,200

Per worker
1960 $ 6,920
1980 $10,400
2000 $15,500

Dwelling units = households + vacant units.
Construction requirements = net annual increase in dwelling units + losses.

Personal consumption expenditures
billion dollars
1960	1980	2000
329	662	1,320

Government expenditures
billion dollars
1960	1980	2000
100	242	551

Net exports
billion dollars
1960	1980	2000
3.0	3.1	17.8

Private investment
billion dollars
1960	1980	2000
72	167	361

↑ K I N D S O F P U R C H A S E S ↑

↓ K I N D S O F O U T P U T ↓

Agricultural production
billion dollars
1960	1980	2000
21	29	38

Industrial production
Index (1957 = 100)
1960	1980	2000
108	249	564

Services
billion dollars
1960	1980	2000
189	415	909

Construction
billion dollars
1960	1980	2000
57	130	281

Autos in use
millions
1960	1980	2000
59	120	244

Auto production
millions
1960	1980	2000
6.7	12.6	25.9

Other services

New dwelling units
millions
1960	1980	2000
1.5	2.6	4.2

Intercity transportation
billion ton miles
1960	1980	2000
1,331	2,641	5,268

Steel ingot production
million tons
1960	1980	2000
99	176	294

Construction lumber
billion board feet
1960	1980	2000
28	46	76

Electricity
billion kilowatt-hours
1960	1980	2000
845	2,229	4,711

Old scrap
million tons
1960	1980	2000
9	20	31

Pig iron
million tons
1960	1980	2000
67	107	171

New scrap

Other requirements

Fuel
quadrillion BTU's
60	1980	2000
	73	114

Hydro and atomic power
billion kilowatt-hours
1960	1980	2000
149	683	2,763

Iron ore
million tons
1960	1980	2000
131	209	341

Timber
billion cubic feet
1960	1980	2000
11	19	32

Yet as we work back through the production system toward the natural resources, we find that the range once again narrows. Variations in the types of foods consumed can alter land requirements only to the extent that land productivity differs for these different types of food; and this range is moderate, compared with the variety of combinations in which food may supply calories. Or as another example, the future demand for lumber, plywood, shingles, and other wood products used in housing construction may vary much more widely than the demand for housing itself in accordance with relative prices of these and other construction materials. The derived demand for the basic resource, timber, however, may exhibit a narrower band because of the converging effect of the various wood products that go into houses—they all have to come from trees.

Besides including a range between High and Low projections for each item, we have also indicated in a Medium projection the magnitude resulting from assumptions that in our judgment are most likely to conform to what actually happens, except for relative price adjustments. Why would not just the middle estimate be enough for the purposes of this study? The answer lies in the nature of the High and Low projections. These are not maximum and minimum estimates, but rather reasonably conceivable outer limits of demand, where only future supply as influenced by resource conditions is absent in determining reasonableness. (Or, more precisely, is present only insofar as supply has affected *past* trends that have been extended into the future.) The Highs and Lows are the outcome of calculations based upon sets of assumptions different from those which give rise to the Medium projections. These assumptions also are reasonable extensions of past history, neither extravagant nor set up merely to satisfy the niceties of an outside chance estimate. They are, nonetheless, clearly meant to reflect avenues of development that must be considered less likely.

The area between the middle and the outside projections does not measure a margin of error. It represents, instead, an infinitely large number of paths that demand for a commodity might travel between 1960 and 2000 depending upon the particular combination of circumstances that actual events will weave together. Each such path within the area of projections, which widens as it moves farther into the future, has its corresponding underlying set of assumptions. Each projection—even the outside ones—theoretically has its own margin of error, but we are not concerned here with this statistical phenomenon.

Different assumptions underlying the growth of population alone will cause divergence. A substantial portion of the population of forty years hence is alive today, but there is less certainty of the number of people under forty in the year 2000—an age group that in the present population accounts for roughly two-thirds. Fertility in the years to come is the chief unknown factor, though there is also some uncertainty as to mortality rates and as to gains and losses by immigration. The population projection to the end of the century must thus allow for reasonable differences in assumptions.

The outcome is a Low population projection 20 per cent below, and a High projection 30 per cent above the Medium, or a spread of 50 percentage points between the High and Low. Neither of the two are in any sense extremes, nor do they measure error. They are simply different possibilities. The same holds true for other basic parameters. Different growth rates of national product that seem to make little difference in short-term comparisons will force the resulting totals far apart when compounded for forty years. At an annual growth rate of 4.8 per cent (the High rate implicit in our study) GNP would have more than sextupled by the end of the period, but at a rate of 3.1 per cent (our implied Low rate) it would have not much more than tripled. Yet neither of the two rates is at all unreasonable.

This approach can result in very wide ranges of estimates. To the extent that assumptions tending to raise demand for any particular item are independent of one another, i.e., can occur together, the grafting of high assumption upon high assumption leads to a final compounded projection that can amount to a multiple of the Medium projection. For example, the quantity of aluminum used in automobiles is determined basically by the size of the population of driving age, the number of cars per driver, and the amount of aluminum in the vehicle body and engine. There is no reason why high population growth, high vehicle ownership, and high use of aluminum in the vehicle should not occur together. While each of the High assumptions is less likely to occur than its Medium counterpart and a combination of the three is even less likely, the possibility remains, and would result in a vastly larger quantity of aluminum than the compounding of the Medium estimates. The fact that it might be two, three, or five times as high does not disqualify it.

The High and Low ranges are useful principally because the infinitely large number of variables acting and reacting upon one another cannot be dealt with adequately over a long period by any system of single-valued projections. But despite the ever-widening range of uncertainty that results from compounding over time, there still are limits in each case beyond which the deviations from the line of development judged most probable are not likely to go; to state the "reasonably possible" range of such deviations should enhance rather than detract from the value of a "most probable" projection.

The advantages of a range of estimates can perhaps be grasped best by the simple exercise of retreating forty years into history to 1920 and, with the knowledge then available, looking forty years ahead to 1960. What would have been projected regarding the automobile, the airplane, or synthetic rubber and plastics? Or the light metals? Or commercial fertilizer? Or, for that matter, population, hours of work, imports of raw materials, petroleum, and many other things? The trends and possibilities of new technology are susceptible to some degree of prediction as are the economic forces and interactions which will guide new technology into use, but a single exact measure obviously is not possible. Rather than being a refuge for timid statisticians, the presentation of a range of demands is called for in the name of common sense.

Also, a range will frequently serve to illuminate the likelihood and degree of a future problem. With only Medium projections, one could not be entirely sure that an indication of tight supply was not simply the result of the inevitable margin of error in the single projection. But if one then finds that even at the minimum requirements there will be a shortage, there is little doubt that the problem is a real one. Conversely, if a particular set of projections shows no shortage at the maximum, it is quite clear (as it would not be when using only one central line of projection) that there is no problem of resource availability.

The very width of the range of uncertainty can be useful in determining the appropriate lines of policy action. If there is a wide range of uncertainty as to the future, policy cannot be designed to be consistent only with the most likely figure, or only with the High, or only with the Low, but must allow for any eventual outcome within those ranges.

For these reasons, we talk in terms of High, Low, and Medium projections, although with major emphasis on the Medium figures. One thing must be borne in mind, however, for all three levels: of necessity we are discussing the possibilities for the future only as these can be foreseen from the vantage point of the present. What today appears improbable may be a reasonable possibility tomorrow, depending on how far the trend that actually develops diverges from the middle course that has been projected for it. These, like any other set of projections intended as guides to policy, must be reviewed from time to time and adjusted to changed horizons. In fact, to the extent that they may come to influence policy they would contribute to their own obsolescence.

Characteristics of the projections. The magnitudes that emerge as the result of projecting past consumption, whatever the assumptions, are not forecasts of sales volume, not predictions of the quantities that will in fact be disposed of in the market place. To acquire that quality they would have to reflect the influence of supply conditions, whereas those conditions, as they emerge in Part III of this book, have been kept from affecting the requirement projections.

Instead of identifying the effect of resource depletion, if any, through projecting a smaller volume of consumption at a higher real price, we find it more instructive to show the physical quantities "demanded" prior to adjustment to supply conditions and then to discuss what adjustments the economy might make in response to the supply situation, of which price change surely is one. We want to open up the problem to clear view by allowing an initial divergence of demand and supply to be carried forward for the full length of our forty-year projection period. Only at the end of the line do we consider the kinds of supply adjustment that may have ensued as a result of intermediate demand-supply divergence.

Our assumptions as to price relationship are implicit in the projection technique. As past consumption trends have been shaped by a variety of influences, including, naturally, supply conditions and relative prices of competing products, so does extrapolation imply continued operation of these factors. While, therefore, in our calculations of projected consumption future supply conditions—via price—are not an explicit variable, we are implicitly allowing for the continuing, but unspecified, operation of supply conditions by virtue of extrapolating past trends. By the same token, past changes in tastes, technology, etc., affect our projected trends of the future. There appears to be no escape from this particular dilemma: any trend-extrapolation technique carries with it the effects of whatever has happened in the past—the general sweep and drift of earlier influences, technologic, economic, demographic, or whatever. Our method merely highlights the effects of these influences on future demand, as modified by foreseeable changes in them, far into the future.

Modifications are introduced where informed judgment suggests a change in course for this or that past trend for such reasons as changes in technology or consumer preferences. To illustrate, the historical increase in the percentage of food consumed as meat can be extrapolated for a certain length of time; sooner or later it can be expected to flatten out, perhaps even reverse itself. Or, the trend to space-heating by natural gas can be expected to continue for some time, but eventually to slow down or be reversed when gas has captured from other energy sources those areas in which it can prevail and when developing new sources of house-heating, notably electricity, in turn begin to encroach upon the gas market.

As to the specific choice of coefficients—technical and otherwise—one is largely swayed by past performance, by the fact that changes are apt to work their way through the economy slowly and that the large stock of things in existence favors gradual changes in trend.

Even the Medium projection is not designed as a model in which all supply-demand conflicts are reconciled, that is, a forecast. It can only suggest to any individual industry the extent to which the projected demand for the resource or resources upon which it is based is likely to encounter a supply, or cost, problem, and if so, how imminent such an event might be. The economy may—and usually does—find ways and means of combatting the emergence of resource stringency, and thus the picture is bound to change from the way it appears in the projections to the way it will finally work itself out. The projections thus remain tools for identifying some of the potential trouble spots of the nation's resource situation, not a means for constructing a model of the future economy.

This does not preclude the use of the data for the additional purpose of approximating the level of both price and volume at which, at any given time, the material in question might enter into consumption. In the case of some minerals, for example, there is scattered material from which one can draw conclusions as to prices at which additional quantities of supply might be had. But again, one cannot foresee whether in fact this will be the response of the economy or whether, threatened by a developing scarcity, the substitution of competing materials or of imports will not obviate a rise in price. In the context of this study we are satisfied to uncover the likely trouble spots and indicate the rough timing, as guides to public and private policy making.

The treatment of technological progress. Rather than ignore technological change, or take into account only such change as was clearly already in the making, we have elected to deal with all such change as appeared to be reasonably possible. Where the implications of such change could be translated into quantitative magnitudes, we have incorporated them with the projections. Where only qualitative magnitudes were assignable or where the timing or the very possibility of developments was so uncertain that they could not be dealt with statistically, we have contented ourselves with description and speculation. But we have rarely refrained from quantitative expression merely because no material was at hand to serve in establishing a formula deemed beyond controversy.

In doing so we have trod a difficult path between (1) uncritically developing all of the future implications of information now available and (2) overlooking all but the sure things. There is evidence to go on—more than might at first glance be supposed. Few of today's amazing triumphs of science and technology were not discernible, at least in outline or principle, in the research and experiments of forty years ago. But it also is true that many of the laboratory possibilities of 1920 have not yet come into general use and that the speed, or lack of it, with which the others have been adopted would have been most difficult to anticipate. Furthermore, it may well be that the modern world is on the threshold of an unprecedented flowering of technology to which the past record is a poor guide. In any event, we believe that in striving for the closest possible appreciation of the future, it is better to guess, even on slender evidence, than to ignore. A footloose speculation four decades ago about dieselization of the railroads would have yielded a better projection of future coal and oil demand than one based on the assumption that locomotives would forever carry boilers. Similarly, a guess made today on what the bill for materials for the family vehicle of the future will be, or how much atomic energy will be generated forty years hence, is likely to give us a more useful focus on the future than the assumption that what we cannot clearly see will not be or should not be translated into figures.

Our efforts to allow for changing technology are reflected in continuing changes in a vast number of coefficients, many of them technical, but others hard to classify; all of them represent the kinds of quantitative relationships between two time series that enter almost all projections: steel to automobiles, sulfur to industrial production, or cubic feet of lumber per dwelling. Just as the direction of population growth is assumed as beyond doubt, so is the direction of technological progress in terms of output per unit of input, its speed being determined by what is theoretically possible and what is already known to be practical, by past rates of advance, and by current instances of individual achievements above the average.

To give an example on which there is wide agreement, it seems clear that ten years from now thermally generated electricity will be produced, on the average, at a rate better than the present fourteen ounces of coal per net kilowatt-hour. Even now the best stations need only twelve ounces; perhaps by the end of the century electricity will be generated at an average of, say, no more than ten ounces. It is quite possible, of course, that this could be an underestimate; the rate of improvement might rise in response to technological innovations now not even dreamed of. But whatever the assumption finally chosen, it seems preferable to be specific and err than not to provide for change at all. This is especially important when one is considering a period as long as four decades.

The quite widespread resistance to introducing provision for technological change into projections is perhaps rooted in inability to demonstrate systematically and methodically the means by which this will be achieved; and one who fails to do so is in danger of being put down as a "blind believer in technology." That danger has been courted throughout this study. There are numerous instances in which relationships have been assumed to change in the direction of increased efficiency without an accompanying technical justification. At times we have gone even further. For example, in the projection of residential electric energy consumption, an increasing amount has been set aside for unspecified uses. These might be currently developed applications in their infancy, such as snow removal, or dust precipitation, or luminous walls, or uses that have yet to be developed and can thus not even be named. We believe it would be less realistic to restrict projections of consumption to applications now in existence than to make room for the appliances of the future.

Time dimensions. In this study we have chosen to look all the way forward to the year 2000, with stopping points along the way. Not all of the points in time should be regarded with equal seriousness for all projections. Where, for example, there are potential problems of resource shortage or surplus and only a few years of "lead time" is necessary to take appropriate action, a twenty-year look forward, or often a shorter one, is sufficient. Such is the case where new processing facilities are required, as in thermal electric power generation. For some materials and resources, on the other hand, a much longer look is essential. Should we discover an impending shortage of some types of lumber, for example, the lead time necessary to take action might run into the decades, not only if the indicated solution consisted in the planting of more trees but also if it were the planning of research and development to provide substitutes for the wood product.

When no problem looms for the next decade or two, it often is helpful to have some general notion of what might take place in the last part of the century. For instance, looking forward only to the year 1980 might conceivably induce a belief that there are no problems with respect to the future supply of the conventional fuels. Even a vague notion of what might transpire in the two decades beyond 1980, however, makes it clear that we cannot wait until that time to push forward in developing substitute sources of liquid and gaseous fuels, not to mention nuclear power, against the time when other dependable sources of petroleum or natural gas may become inadequate. The long look offers a further advantage of perspective. For a number of resources, at least in this country, recent years have been marked by exceptional abundance. Public policy has had to concern itself more with mitigating the consequences of glut than of scarcity—for example, wheat, cotton, corn, crude oil. It is easy in such a climate to lose sight of long-term trends; this could be unfortunate because physical changes in resource management are not typically short-term matters. On the other hand, one must take care that some of the problems that appear to emerge in the more distant future are not more apparent than real. In many fields—especially minerals—long-run concern is uncommon and present estimates of statistically defined reserves may afford a poor comparison with long-term demand projections.

The data are for the most part presented in ten-year intervals. This should provide checking points for the degree of realism of the projections. However, the values given for any particular year are trend values; the actual magnitudes that will one day replace them will be determined by the factors immediately at work, such as the phase of the business cycle, the particular shape of our national defense, and other short-term elements. And where the demand projections are clearly incompatible with prospective supply considerations, relative price changes and substitutions will take place and affect the actual requirements.

Within these limitations, looking ahead is more satisfactory for some segments of the economy than for others. The chemical industry comes to mind as one in which developments are so rapid that it is hazardous to focus even at a ten-year range. At the other extreme, forestry and water are two resource fields in which a short time perspective neither reveals the problems ahead nor gives adequate time for policy formation. For basic agricultural crops a five- or ten-year perspective of overproduction with no look beyond would lead to a land-use outlook quite different from one based upon prospects for the next thirty years or more.

It is possible, of course, to extend projections farther into the future than forty years, but this would call for even more heroic assumptions regarding population, labor force productivity, new technology, and sources of raw materials than we have ventured. Over longer time spans, the problem of ever-widening ranges of possibilities in population, technology, institutions, and world affairs becomes more and more troublesome. We believe that in looking ahead to the year 2000 we are pushing about as far into the future as is useful for economic and planning purposes. This is not to say, however, that longer range attempts are not stimulating and, for a few general purposes, instructive.

Extent of coverage. Time perspective is one of the factors that determine the depth of analysis in the various segments into which the economy has been divided in this study. There is not much profit in engaging in painstaking analysis of demand trends in any field where the past record or the nature of the industry strongly suggests that the picture is bound to be altered by currently unknown and unpredictable elements that will appear early within the period under review.

Depth of treatment is also governed by the economic importance of the various resource products, and also by the outlook for each commodity. Especially in the minerals field, only cursory treatment is accorded to those resources that appear to be in such easy supply for such long periods ahead that little is to be gained by comparing them with detailed demand projections. Thus we have little to say about sand and gravel. Another consideration is the feasibility of arriving at even a rough kind of demand projection. Many of the minor minerals fall into this category. Some of them may have highly strategic importance in a few specific applications. As far as continued growth of the economy as a whole is concerned, however, their cost is not a pertinent factor, and little is gained from the adequacy analysis used elsewhere. Policy for these metals is firmly dictated by national goals, be these military security, morale, or prestige, and most considerations that normally enter into resource economics are presently irrelevant.

Other such materials, including numerous minor metals and plastic materials, though not so strategically important, have so ill-defined a future market that even projections as short as five years ahead are extremely uncertain. Many of them are substitutable for one another, and wholesale substitution will occur with price changes. Prices have tended to fluctuate violently for most of these materials, and the history of demand is thus confused and of little help in looking ahead. Such materials are dealt with in a summary fashion. Still other products, for example fish, are but a small part of a total category, in this case food, and have been furnishing an approximately constant portion of the total. These have usually not been considered in any depth, and sometimes not at all.

By and large, regional considerations have not entered directly into the projected demand pattern for the major resources. While greater effort in that direction would have improved the quality of the study, proliferation into geographical detail would have added excessively to the size of an already inevitably big task. There are exceptions, however. Projections of nuclear energy generation can hardly proceed without regional analysis, nor can discussion of relative fuel use, or implications of forest product demand for the future of the nation's forests, or the adequacy of fresh water supplies. Indeed, the last field is pre-eminently region-oriented.

The geographical scope of analysis is equally limited where issues transcend the borders of the United States. Unable to expand the study into an appraisal of world demand and resource adequacy, we had to limit sharply the amount of effort that went into projecting foreign trends. There are implicit assumptions that where the United States will continue to be dependent upon foreign resources, and where such resources are known to exist on a scale commensurate with some reasonable extrapolation of world demand, the United States will be in a position to attract them. This is perhaps less of an obstacle to meaningful analysis than the definition of what constitutes a "reasonable extrapolation" of consumption outside the United States. Criteria will be found to be rough, and reasoning is often circumstantial and indirect. Much work remains to be done here to fill numerous, large gaps in knowledge and analysis.

There are, we believe, no major, and few minor gaps in resource coverage. The significant resources have been identified and analyzed; if not in particular then as elements of larger categories, such as land for minor crops. There exists sufficient detail, moreover, to enable anyone who wishes to elaborate any estimate or who disagrees with any particular assumption to substitute his own more precise figures. Working out the consequences of any such new figures through the whole projection system would be tedious, but working them through the relevant portion will usually be fairly simple. Therefore, the expert on one or the other material or resource who disagrees with our projections may want to adopt the general framework of population, national product, and the like, and also the general methodology, but substitute his own estimates in the field of his specialty.

REQUIREMENTS FOR FUTURE LIVING

I N THESE ELEVEN CHAPTERS we shall first consider across-the-board factors that will help determine the level and direction of the U.S. economy through the next four decades and then study, one by one, the large categories of consumer needs and wants that have an important bearing upon resource problems, their magnitudes and possible ways of being satisfied. We shall also look to the construction and investment goods required and their principal kinds and quantities. We shall examine, finally, the kinds and quantities of some of the demands upon the economy —like transportation and energy—which are neither wholly items of "final demand" nor wholly "intermediate" requirements, but whose role is sufficiently universal as to warrant unified treatment. In each case, as we look at these end-use sectors, we shall try to determine the quantities of key agricultural and industrial materials which each implies.

Later in this study we shall (in Part II) attempt to gauge the demand that the sum of the various consumption requirements will make upon each of the principal categories of resource products and (in Part III) to appraise the adequacy of the nation's natural resources to meet the projected needs.

Carrying out these two steps is by no means a simple matter of adding and comparing. Possibilities of substitution, already large and still growing, will widen the alternatives for meeting consumers' material needs during the rest of the century. Perhaps the key conclusion one might derive from Part I of our study is that of more and more variety in the things that America consumes, the ways in which it gets things done, and the materials it uses.

Moreover, we are moving rapidly from dependence on "natural" resources to ability to utilize "synthetic." This flexibility, which has increased over the years as man has learned to manipulate matter in its smallest dimensions—the molecule, the atom, and now subatomic particles—enables us to build our technology upon what is plentiful or practicably renewable.

The great range of possible substitution is one of our chief forms of insurance against resource scarcity. This does not mean, however, that there are no resource problems worth revealing. Even with kaleidoscopic change, there are main currents that change but slowly. For example, some houses may be built before long solely of plastics; but most houses will be composed for some time to come of familiar materials. One part after another of automobiles may come to be made of aluminum, or plastics, rather than steel, but not all the parts of all makes of automobiles at once. A preponderant portion of our future resource requirements can be approximated under reasonable assumptions as to rate and character of national growth. Also, the variety of forms in which materials enter into final output of goods and services does not connote an equal variety of starting materials. By one route or another, we must depend in the final analysis on our basic natural resource endowment, and there can still be—no matter how devious the route—pressure upon one part or another of this endowment.

To the extent that resource problems are soluble only by substitution, there are both adjustment costs and ultimate costs. Moreover, the substitutions and readjustments may be more or less painful depending upon the extent to which we are forewarned and prepared. And despite all of our flexibility, we may find at times that our only adjustment to a comparative resource scarcity is a restraint upon consumption which we have a choice of making—in distribution and timing—according to the dictates of the market place or according to the choices of advance planning.

chapter
1
Basic Economic Patterns

BEFORE SEPARATELY EXAMINING possible future requirements for food, clothing, construction, and other human needs and wants whose satisfaction will entail demands upon natural resources, it is necessary to have some idea of the common economic and social climate that will condition events in each of the specific areas. Size of population and general level of economic activity are controlling factors but by no means the only ones: What changes may there be in the kinds of goods and services people will most prize, in their technology, in their ways of organizing business and governmental enterprises? Since this study concerns not the next year or even the next ten years, but the four decades of the remainder of this century, differences in consumers' tastes, or methods of organization, or any relaxation in technological limits, could over the years have marked effects upon demand for natural resources of all kinds.

Except for assuming some further gains in technology along general lines that already can be perceived, we have made no specific allowance for new scientific discoveries or for striking changes in the social and political rules of the game. This choice results not from any conviction that no such developments are likely in the next forty years but simply from our inability to hazard even a plausible guess as to exactly what might happen when.

Consequently, we have restricted ourselves to a few purely economic indicators in supplying the common background for projections of the principal categories of consumer requirements. Use of these more manageable criteria, however, does not entirely exclude broader considerations, which are built in to the extent that they have influenced trends in consumption and production in the past and thus will automatically make themselves felt in projections of the future.

While a study of past trends can help us develop a feel for which aspects of the economy change slowly, which rapidly, and which remain relatively fixed, it must be admitted that, looking back over the last forty years, the progression of events has been rendered largely discontinuous by two major wars and one major depression, with the result that much of useful economic history begins, so to speak, less than two decades ago. One faces the further hazard that the pace of man's social and economic evolution—even when it seems to falter—has come to resemble the compound interest curve, so that twenty years into the future—the halfway point in our forward outlook—is comparable in absolute amount of change with forty, fifty, or even a hundred years or more back into the past. We need go back only fifteen years to lose most of the detail in one of our principal statistical guides to the shape of the economy, the Federal Reserve Board Industrial Production Index; thirty-odd years exhausts nearly all of our continuous National Income Accounting history.

Two underlying assumptions. We live in a period of world tension and conflict and of matching military expenditure. The fact that almost one-tenth of our national productive effort is directly accounted for by defense expenditures means that the sum total of that effort will be profoundly influenced in its magnitude and character by the circumstance of how much longer the cold war may last and how much hotter or colder it may get.

In a study like this the only practicable way to deal with the cold war problem is by assumption. To each of our three levels of projection of various phases of the future economy, we append the reservation, "provided there is no general war." In our specific projections for defense outlay, our Medium projection rests on the assumption that the cold war will continue at about the same tempo as at present, with continuation of the current relationship of defense expenditures to gross national product. The High projection assumes that because of continued high tension and the increasing military power of potential adversaries, we shall be constrained to increase the proportion of our output devoted to defense. The Low projection assumes that in the not-too-distant future there will be a general international political settlement and that our military expenditures will at that time taper off. In and of itself, no one of these three defense assumptions determines the size of our future productive effort. Like any other principal demand component, however, each has a significant bearing upon the output engendered.

The prospects of prosperity and depression also must be a matter of assumption. Faith in our ability to take appropriate action leads us to exclude the possibility of any very deep or protracted depression. On the other hand, we admit the possibility of minor cyclical swings: in fact, since all of our past data are affected by business cycles, it is virtually impossible to eliminate their influence altogether in projecting the future. What we do have to assume, however, is that the particular target years toward which we are looking are reasonably "normal"—that is, that they will be years of full employment and not of labor shortage, that they will be neither at the top of a cycle nor at the bottom, but somewhere along the trend line. These are far from precise concepts. As a practical matter, we have defined "full employment" as employment ranging from 95 to 97 per cent of the labor force, depending upon the projection level (Low, High, or Medium). Higher relative employment levels have occurred only during war periods, and lower levels only during periods generally conceded to be abnormally depressed. There has been talk of higher relative unemployment being chronically with us, but the record has not yet established anything more than 5 per cent as the upper limit for a valid "normal-year" value.

Beyond these two necessarily arbitrary across-the-board assumptions are several other general economic determinants which, though also pervasive, can be arrived at more through analysis than adopted as articles of faith. Table 1–1 summarizes most of the data described hereafter.

People as Producers and Consumers

Population

The importance of population in the nation's future growth can hardly be overemphasized. On the size of the population depends the future consumption of the many things whose level of demand is determined primarily by the number of consumers. The size and composition of the population by sex and age help to determine the number of households, which in turn largely determines the required numbers of new houses, automobiles, items of home furnishing, etc. The age and sex composition of the population also bear heavily upon the size of the labor force, which is, in turn, a principal determinant of total output. The total output of the economy, or gross national product, is in turn the fundamental referral point to which most other projections of the components of national production and consumption must be directly or indirectly related.

The past history of population projections,

TABLE 1–1. Principal Elements in Future GNP and Its Disposition

Item	1940	1960		1980	2000
Population (millions)	132	180	L	226	268
			M	245	331
			H	279	433
Population 14 years and over (millions)	102	127	L	172	212
			M	176	242
			H	188	292
× Participation rate (per cent)	55.3	57.6	L	56.8	57.4
			M	57.8	58.7
			H	58.1	59.9
= Labor force (millions)	56	73	L	98	122
			M	102	142
			H	109	175
× Annual output per worker (1960 $—thous.)	4.2	6.9	L	9.8	13.8
			M	10.4	15.5
			H	11.5	18.8
= Gross national product (1960 $—billion)	234	504	L	965	1,680
			M	1,060	2,200
			H	1,250	3,290
of which:					
Purchased by consumers	159	329	L	610	1,070
			M	660	1,320
			H	750	1,730
Purchased by government	39	100	L	150	320
			M	240	550
			H	340	930
Invested	34	72	L	110	170
			M	170	360
			H	240	670
Net exports[1]	2	3	L	–10	—
			M	—	20
			H	—	–10
Errors, omissions, and not accounted for[2]	—	—	L	105	120
			M	–10	–50
			H	–80	–30
or produced as:					
Durable goods	37	96	L	151	261
			M	229	514
			H	322	918
Non-durable goods	89	162	L	246	349
			M	293	518
			H	354	760
Construction	24	57	L	80	119
			M	130	281
			H	200	590
Services	84	189	L	375	746
			M	415	909
			H	483	1,234
Errors, omissions, and not accounted for[2]	—	—	L	+108	+205
			M	–7	–22
			H	–109	–212

L = Low projection   M = Medium   H = High.
1. Negative number denotes net imports.
2. Negative numbers mean that the total GNP has been over-accounted for.

Source: Appendix to Chapter 1. There may be minor discrepancies in the data, owing to rounding.

... course of events, ... grounds for confidence. For ... , an estimate of 1975 population made in 1947 by a leading demographic authority had already been exceeded in 1955. The "high" projection for 1970 made in 1947 by another authority was reached in 1959. The "medium" Bureau of the Census projection which was made in 1950 for the year 1959 was actually surpassed in that year by nearly 10 million. On the other hand, the "high" projections made at the same time are running about neck and neck with the recorded totals since.

The best that one can hope for, under the circumstances, is to work out a set of population projections whose range encompasses the reasonable eventualities. To do so, it is necessary to consider the determinants of population growth and within what limits they are likely to affect future totals.

For the period through 1980 the projections used in this study are essentially those made by the U.S. Bureau of the Census in 1958 and published in their *Current Population Reports,* as well as in the 1958 *Statistical Abstract.* For the subsequent period we have been guided by some unpublished, tentative calculations, also made by the Census Bureau. For both periods we have modified the Census Bureau assumptions in order to provide for the additional variation which it seemed to us was "reasonably possible." These modifications were minor, however, since we felt that these new Census Bureau projections did, in the main, cover most of the range of population variation that could reasonably be foreseen at this date.

Of the three factors which account for rates of population change—fertility, mortality, and net immigration—fertility is the least predictable and can cause the greatest amount of variation. Many respected demographers have misjudged it in the past. Nor has the analysis yet been done which will give a definitive answer to the question of which way the birth rate is now trending. The consensus among the experts, however, is that if it goes up, it cannot be much more; it is more likely already to have reached a peak; and it is most likely going to trend downward, but how fast and to what point are questions on which consensus ends.

The kinds of birth rates assumed in this study may perhaps best be understood in terms of reproduction rates. In our Low projection we arrive ultimately at a reproduction rate of "1," which means that by the turn of the century, the population would just about be reproducing itself. At the Medium level, it would be reproducing itself, during the course of a generation, about 1¼ times over and at the assumed High level, about 1½ times over. On the other hand, if present birth rates were to continue, the population of the United States would be reproducing itself 1¾ times over.

That birth rates do not vary as much over the very long run as might be expected from their variability over the shorter run is because the short-run changes are the result of several influences that eventually tend to cancel out in the long run. These include speed-ups or slow-downs in the rate of marriages, the ages at which families are started, and the rapidity with which the desired sizes of families are achieved. In the long run, fashions in family size play the dominating role.

In terms of total number of births, however, as contrasted with birth *rates,* the long run adds a new factor of uncertainty—the effects of geometric progression. Virtually all of the women who will give birth between now and 1980 are already born; around two-thirds of the population of the year 2000, on the other hand, and perhaps one-quarter of the women who will have produced it, are not. One needn't be very far wrong about the number of births in the next decade or so to be much further off about the ones occurring two decades later.

The second most important factor in population change is the death rate. This is also the most predictable factor, since the death rate in the United States is very low and further changes (much of the year-to-year variation results from differences in the age composition of the population) can occur only very slowly. Consequently, very little of the spread in the projected population levels is attributable to

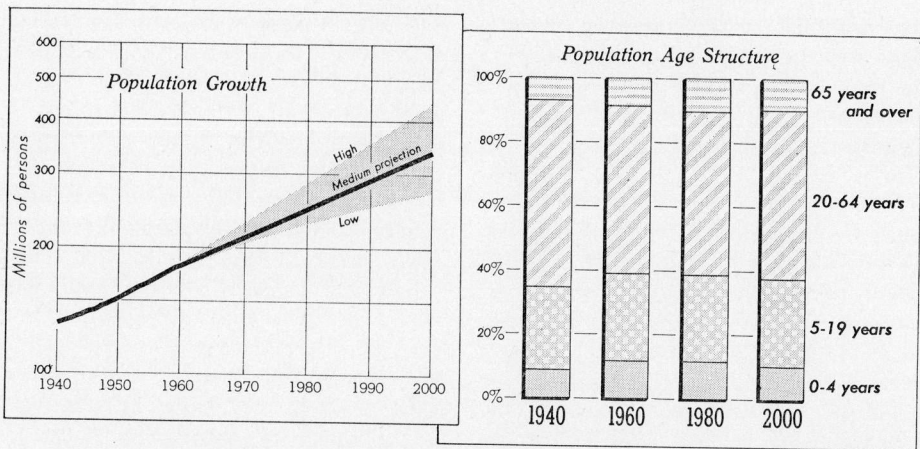

Figure 1–1. Population growth in the United States, 1940, 1960, and projections to 2000.

variations in mortality. Since the Census Bureau used only a single set of mortality assumptions, a crude adjustment was made in the projections to allow for slightly higher and slightly lower rates, but this adjustment in itself did not significantly affect the results.

The least important element in U.S. population change (at least in recent decades) has been net immigration; this will, in terms of *absolute change,* probably continue to be so. However, the annual rate of immigration that will occur in the years to come is difficult to foresee. It could conceivably increase greatly over present levels if the United States should liberalize its immigration laws and regulations, or it could decrease substantially if relative gains in levels of living abroad or other factors should decrease the motivation for emigration to the United States. Moreover, variations in levels of immigration not only have a direct effect on U.S. population levels, but a substantial secondary effect resulting from the fact that immigrants usually include a high proportion of women who are, or will soon be, within the principal child-bearing age span. Thus, the range that may open up between the high and low population possibilities could be significantly affected by this factor. Consequently, the single Census assumption of 300,000 immigrants per year was varied for the High and the Low to allow for the further population variation that might result from this influence.

The way in which population might grow over the next forty years, in comparison with the way it has grown in the past, is shown in Fig. 1–1. Summed up, it may be stated that a likely line of development will be the expansion of the U.S. population from the 180 million of mid-1960 to 245 million by 1980 and 330 million by the end of the century— equivalent to a compound rate of increase of around 1½ per cent a year. (This is slightly lower than the post-World War II average, but much higher than the depression and wartime growth rates.) It is possible, however, that the growth rate will rise to 2 per cent and higher, to yield a population of 280 million in 1980 and 430 million in 2000, or that it will gradually decline below 1½ per cent to yield a population of only 225 million in 1980 and 270 million in 2000.[1] Looked at another way, the population level which we regard as likely for 1980 may actually be reached as early as 1974 or may not be reached until 1988.

Urbanization. Several characteristics of population other than total size have an important bearing upon the future shape of the economy.

1. It is idle to speculate on which of these three is the most likely projection. The Bureau of the Census makes things especially difficult by presenting four levels of projection so that there is no middle estimate to be chosen as the candidate. Nonetheless, by the mere fact that the Bureau qualified its top estimate as more unlikely than the other three to come true, the Medium projection here presented, equal to the Census Bureau's Series III, may for our purposes be regarded as the most likely.

One is the extent of urbanization. Relating demand factors quantitatively to this characteristic is hazardous, however, and the rate of increase in urbanization is difficult to project. We do know that the population of the United States has developed from one which was only about 50 per cent urban in 1920 to one which is more than two-thirds urban today and that this trend will continue. However, what was once a clear distinction between "urban" and "rural," with rather well-defined differences in way of life, has increasingly lost meaning. The rapidly advancing homogenization of the American people and the radical growth in suburbanization have been erasing many of the differences of consumption habits between country and city. The chief significance of country/city distribution of residence today is with respect to its meaning for municipal services (such as water supply) and for means of transportation. The demand for the former, however, is spreading out well beyond formal municipal boundaries, and the demand for mass transportation, once a well-defined characteristic of cities, is becoming a most difficult item to quantify as people move farther out from city cores, depend more upon private automobiles, and find it harder to get to the center of town with them.

What seems fairly clear is that the distinction between urban and rural, between town and country, between city and suburb, will become hazier and may well necessitate such further periodic revisions of concept as those which the Census Bureau has had to make from time to time in the past. Some authorities look forward to the development, in the more thickly populated sections of the United States, of continuous urban belts completely linking the largest cities with one another and necessitating substantial revision of our arrangements for municipal services and mass transportation, not to mention the redistribution of our commercial and cultural centers and places of work. Some of these trends are obviously well advanced. Large masses of people now shun city centers in favor of neighborhood shopping centers; factories that once depended upon bus, street car, and subway to deliver their daily work forces now dot the country-

side. Increasing mobility of persons and penetration of modern distribution may be expected to erase the notion of rural isolation completely by the end of the century.

These trends are already in progress and are reflected in consumption and other demand statistics. While we cannot neglect to keep a weather eye on the particular modifications that may be called forth by the changing pace and character of urbanization in the United States, for the most part we can rely for our quantitative answers upon the extension of national trends without regard to the rural/urban factor.

Households

An important element in future demand for a large variety of items is the way the population groups itself into households. As a technical term used by the Bureau of the Census, it is equivalent to the number of occupied "dwelling units" or "housing units"—private homes, apartments, and other distinct and separate quarters. It is thus of obvious significance in anticipating the demand for new residential construction and for all of the things that go to equip a household—ranges, refrigerators, radios, TV sets, living room furniture and the like.

Though households are closely related to families, the two are not quite the same. For example, an individual living alone in a separate apartment constitutes a household and will be purchasing many of the same things as would a family. On the other hand, a family —a married couple, or parents and children, etc.—may be living with relatives or otherwise be doubled up or be living in a hotel or rooming house. In none of these cases would they constitute a separate household, nor would they require their own set of the principal items of household equipment.

In 1960, there were over 52 million households in the United States. Of these, 85 per cent consisted of what the Census calls "primary families"—that is, married couples with or without children, or individual parents with children, or any other person who had relatives living with him, provided that each of these groupings included a "head of household." Because of the "undoubling" that has steadily been taking place since the end of the war, only about 3 per cent of all families (2 per cent of married couples) were not maintaining their own household, so that there is now a very close relationship between the marriage rate and the rate of increase in household numbers.

What complicates the relationship is the growing trend toward single-individual households. In 1960, around 15 per cent of all households were constituted by such single individuals living either alone or accompanied by one or two roomers or boarders. In 1940, the figure was only 10 per cent. Of the total growth in households between 1940 and 1960, such individuals accounted for one-fourth.

The growth in the number of households can be estimated rather closely between now and 1980 because household heads are almost exclusively of age groups which as of this time have already been born. Thus the highly unpredictable factor of fertility is eliminated. Moreover, another uncertain factor in household formation—the rate of marriages—is partially self-compensating. A higher number of marriages than expected would increase the number of households by pulling individuals out of existing families, but it would also tend to decrease the number of households by bringing together individuals previously living alone.

Census Bureau estimates of the number of households in 1980 range from 69 million to 76 million. Applying the aggregate rates of household formation implied by the Census estimates to our own somewhat wider estimates of the adult population suggests a range of 69 million to 79 million and a most likely Medium level of 73 million.

Should the higher level eventuate, it would mean that the households-based demands we have arrived at for 1980 will be upon us about four years earlier than expected; should the lower level eventuate, these demands will not generally develop until as late as 1985.

Because so many persons yet to be born will be part of the adult population in the year 2000 and will be the heads of households at that time, the range of error for that year is

necessarily much greater. We are assuming that the number of households in 2000 will approximate 100 million, but that it could be as high as 125 million or as low as 85 million. This means that the associated magnitudes we are assuming for the year 2000 might actually occur as early as 1990, or not until twenty years later.

Particularly with respect to the year 1980, these ranges do not at first glance seem to offer any serious problems for forward planning, especially when one considers that they can progressively be narrowed down as one approaches the actual date. As will be seen later on in this study, however, many of the demands associated with households depend, not on the number of households as such, but on the rate at which new ones are being formed. This aspect, mathematically the first derivative, is much more volatile than the relatively predictable series which it determines, and relatively small differences among the projection levels for total households may mean relatively large percentage differences among the net annual additions that each implies. When it comes to the homes for households to live in and the major items of equipment, it is the annual additions, not the total stock, that loom up as the chief determining factor.

Labor Force

One common way, and the one here used, of estimating future national output is to multiply the number of workers by their average productivity to get the gross output of the particular segment or of the whole economy. We must, therefore, take into account the size of the labor force. In this study we have worked with the total labor force (including military personnel and a small percentage of normal unemployment) and a composite average annual output per worker.

The implication of this approach to projecting the gross national product (GNP) is that the labor force is an independent variable —that is, that it helps to determine the size of the GNP without being influenced in its own size by what the GNP, for other reasons, may turn out to be. This, of course, is not entirely true. In one sense, the labor force is in fact independent of the GNP, in that its size is determined by the number of persons of working age and their propensity to engage in gainful employment. But the degree of pressure upon the economy to turn out goods and services also has some bearing upon what the "labor force participation rate" will actually be; in that sense the size of the labor force is not independent.

Our method of covering this situation is typical of an approach used often in this work. With the aid of analyses carried out by the Census Bureau and the U.S. Bureau of Labor Statistics, we have made projections of the labor force and of the GNP based upon it. But since the GNP is not only a measure of output, but of what consumers, business, and government jointly spend, we have also estimated what the GNP ought to be on a spending basis, i.e., independently of labor force and productivity; by balancing one approach against the other and by verifying that the projected labor force could produce the independently projected GNP with plausible rates of increase in output per man-year, we have in effect confirmed that the labor force estimates are at levels that make two-way sense.

Over the next two decades there is comparatively little room for error with regard to the size of the labor force. Nearly every person likely to be working in 1980 is already born, and the desire of people in each age-sex group to hold a job changes but slowly. Our 1980 projections have a narrow range—from a Low of 98 million workers to a High of 109 million. In terms of time, our Medium projection of 102 million for 1980 is unlikely to be more than four or five years off the mark.

Because of the substantial importance of future births, the year 2000 is not as easily foreseen. Probably the labor force, like the population, will come close to doubling by that time, reaching a total of about 140 million. Our year-2000 labor force could be as much as 15 per cent lower than that, however, or 25 per cent higher.

About 58 per cent of the population 14 years of age and over are now members of the labor force—only a few percentage points

more than at the beginning of World War II. An even smaller increase seems likely between now and the year 2000, but this relatively unchanging average participation conceals a number of conflicting trends. For example, nearly all males between the ages of 25 and 55 are gainfully employed, but only about two out of every five women. Total male participation (14 years of age and over) is around 80 per cent and declining; total female participation, around 36 per cent and rising. The reason is that younger people of both sexes are tending to stay more years in school, while more and more adult women are taking on jobs and, just as important, going back to jobs as their children grow up. At the same time, older people have increasingly been leaving the labor force and taking advantage of retirement benefits. Also, younger women have recently been showing an increasing preference for babies as against employment; this not only decreases labor force participation directly, but later on indirectly by raising the relative number of potential workers in the age groups still largely at school. Thus, the exact course of future labor force participation rates will depend heavily upon trends in the babies/jobs choice, as well as on the economy's need for, and ability to hold, older workers. According to our projections, participation could go from the present 58 per cent to 59 or 60, or drop back to 57.

Productivity

The average American worker, aided by the nation's plant, equipment, and resources, turns out about $7,000 worth of goods or services every year. This is one-quarter more than he turned out ten years ago, three-quarters more than in 1929 and two and one-half times as much as he produced in the depths of the Great Depression. By 1940, this productivity had barely returned to pre-depression levels, but since then has been increasing at an average annual rate of 2.6 per cent, if you look at the whole period; at a rate of 2.1 per cent, if you look at the period since 1950; and at a rate of only 1.2 per cent, if you look at the last few years. All of these comparisons are made on the basis of dollars having a constant (1960) purchasing power.

With limited possibilities for variation in the labor force between now and 1980, it is productivity that makes most of the difference in what the nation's output might be; after 1980, it is at least of comparable importance with the size of the working force. A difference in rate of growth between 2 and 2½ per cent, for example, means a difference in annual output per worker of over $1,000 in twenty years, and this, in turn, means a difference in gross national output of over $100 billion, or about 10 per cent of the general magnitude of the GNP two decades from now.

In view of this uncertainty and of historical evidence that the productivity of the U.S. economy responds at least in part to the demands made upon it, we have sought to confirm our productivity choices by comparing the resultant GNP with the total product which is likely to be demanded by the various consuming sectors of the economy. The choices can also be confirmed by examining whether there are reasonable patterns of change in the general composition of the labor force, in hourly productivity, and in weekly and annual hours which will produce the predetermined aggregate result. This, too, we have done.

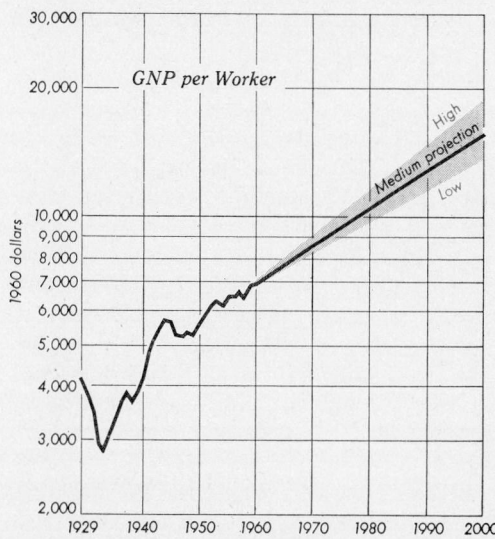

Figure 1–2. Gross national product per worker, 1929–1960 and projections to 2000.

The picture that emerges is one of an output per worker which will most likely continue to increase at the average rate of the last decade (2 per cent per year), but might also increase by as much as 2½ per cent per year or as little as 1¾ per cent (see Figure 1–2). One uncertainty is the relative level of government expenditures, particularly for the national defense. There is also the factor that a relatively faster-growing population makes greater demand on the labor force by increasing the relative numbers of people in the younger, nonproductive age groups and conversely for a relatively slower-growing population. Should our high-population-growth assumption prevail, the increase in population will outpace the growth of the labor force for most of the next three decades. Should the low-population-growth assumption prevail, the growth in labor force will outpace that in population for the rest of the century; the average worker will be able to provide better for himself and others and have longer vacations to boot (which is equivalent to having relatively lower annual productivity).

Our whole range of projected rates of increase in productivity is below the average increase that has taken place over the last two decades. However, those two decades saw, first, an all-out war mobilization, and then a period when the population was growing twice as fast, on the average, as the number of those of its members who were producing. Nothing comparable to this is either assumed or implicit in the calculations for the balance of the century. Moreover, much of the productivity gain in recent decades has resulted from a relative shift in employment from agriculture, with substantially lower (although rapidly rising) annual productivity, to non-agricultural pursuits, with higher productivity; with agricultural employment down to 8 per cent of the labor force and still declining, the potential effect of this shift is small and it may even be replaced in importance by a relative shift into the service industries and government, which have lower levels of productivity than the rest of the non-agricultural economy. Productivity will rise in all sectors of the economy, but the fastest gainers in output per person may be the less significant (and there is some relationship here) in numbers of persons employed.

Although it is clear that there is a relationship between rates of investment—the relative amount of current production devoted to capital goods—and the advance in the economy's productivity, the lessons that may be drawn from history about the quantitative effects on output per worker of different kinds and rates of investment are insufficiently precise to be applied confidently to projections.[2] What history does seem to show is that the American economy, under pressure, generates both higher levels of investment and higher rates of productivity gain. Our projections show this joint response, and we have tested it to verify that the relationship between the two elements falls within the limits of what the historical record suggests is plausible.

Gross National Product

The most informative single measure of the size of the American economy is the gross national product, or the sum total of all the expenditures in a single year for all of the end products of the economy—consumer goods and services; goods and services purchased by federal, state, and local governments; new construction; business purchases of capital equipment; and net purchases by foreigners. To this measure and the components thereof, as well as to the closely allied measures of national and personal income, may be related, directly or indirectly, most of the important productive series of the economy.

Yet because it is such a comprehensive measure of the multifarious activities that go to make up an economy, GNP is at the same time one of the least precise in meaning. For one thing, the dollar is the only available common denominator for all of these varied kinds of production—from automobiles to haircuts, from electric power to the current rental value of houses, from bread to ministerial services.

Not only does the value of the dollar change from year to year, but at thousands of different rates, depending upon the particular kind of purchase. Many such conceptual problems are inherent in the notion of real GNP, or GNP in constant dollars. No one solution will satisfy all theoretical objectives. In this study we have adopted a notion of "constant dollars" which will give us series for GNP and its major components roughly consistent in meaning with the official constant-dollar series produced by the U.S. Department of Commerce.[3]

Despite conceptual and statistical shortcomings, the relationships between real GNP and a great many other economic series are remarkably consistent. If alert to possible developments that may upset these relationships and aware of the degrees of precision within which projections may reasonably be used, one may utilize GNP and its principal components as the framework of a broad picture of the consumption of the various kinds of goods and services that make up the economy and eventually of the broad magnitudes of future material and resource requirements.

In 1960 the U.S. gross national product was slightly over $500 billion. On the assumption here used, it should by 1980, measured in 1960 prices, approximately have doubled, and by the year 2000, doubled again. Although the influences bearing upon it have been quite different, GNP has also more or less doubled over the last twenty years. During the preceding two decades, which include the Great Depression, on the other hand, the growth was somewhat slower, and it was also somewhat slower during the first two decades of this century.

Because the GNP level for 1980 is dependent largely upon the rate of growth of a fairly

2. For the most recent attempt to determine the relative roles of the different factors in productivity growth, see Edward F. Denison, *The Sources of Economic Growth in the United States and the Alternatives Before Us,* Supplementary Paper No. 13 (New York: Committee on Economic Development, January 1962).

3. The Department of Commerce real GNP figures, it should be noted, are sensitive to increases in output which result not only from growth within categories, but from shifts between lower- and higher-value categories. They do this, however, in terms of the comparative values which existed in the base year. The fact that in actuality these comparative values change is of small consequence so long as one deals in data close to the base year; but the continuing emergence of additional types of production, changes in their relative importance, the complete disappearance of some types and the emergence of new, and the substantial importance in the whole of that elusive type of production we call "services," all combine to make a constant-dollar GNP increasingly vague in meaning as we look farther and farther into either the past or the future.

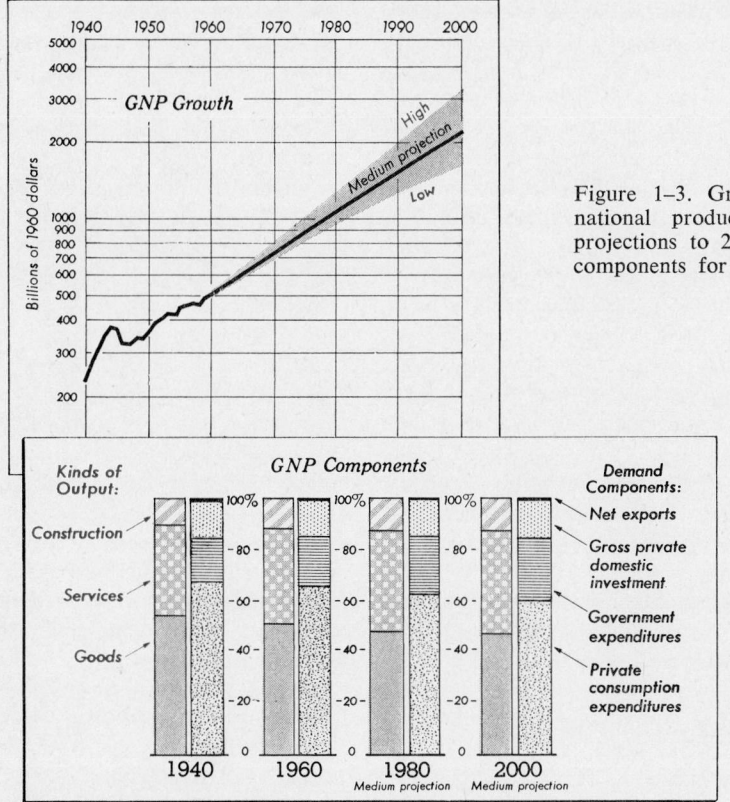

Figure 1–3. Growth of gross national product, 1940–1960, projections to 2000, and GNP components for selected years.

predictable labor force, the possibilities for variation are at least somewhat restricted. Specifically, as against a likely level of $1,060 billion, measured in 1960 dollars, one might expect a Low level falling short by no more than 10 per cent, or a High projection of no more than 20 per cent above the Medium. Looked at in terms of time, it means that the 1980 GNP might be upon us as soon as 1976, or not until 1984. Business cycle variations might, of course, magnify these comparatively small differences.

For the year 2000, we cannot project with anything like the same precision. Depending upon population growth and other circumstances, it is quite possible for our projected Medium GNP of $2,200 billion to be exceeded by 50 per cent or fallen short of by nearly 25 per cent. It could be upon us some ten years sooner or later.

A summary of these trends is shown in Table 1–1 and in Figure 1–3. Since the latter is a ratio chart, the degrees of slant of the different lines reflect the relative rates of growth. Our projected rates—any one of which, it is apparent from the chart, may be considered a plausible extension of past trends—vary from an average, over the next four decades, of about 4¾ per cent per year for the High down to 3 per cent for the Low, with a Medium level of a little over 3¾ per cent. The record of the past ten years tells little about whether the projected rates are reasonable. That decade saw a growth rate of over 4¼ per cent in its first half and less than 2½ per cent in its second half. Nor can we lean too heavily on the record of the decade immediately preceding, which spanned a war and a postwar boom, or on the decade before that, when the course of the GNP followed the deep "V" of the Great Depression. The long-term historical rate, which most economists expect the future to better, has been around 3 per cent.

In Figure 1–3 we show also how the GNP for 1940 and 1960, and the projected levels for 1980 and 2000 break down into expenditures by consumers, by government, and for private investment, and into different kinds of output.

Although other combinations are entirely conceivable, the Low projection of GNP levels for 1980 and 2000 is based largely on assumptions of low defense expenditures and low population growth. These, in turn, are likely to be accompanied by relatively high non-defense expenditures per capita, relatively low investment, and relatively high personal consumption expenditures per capita. Opposite tendencies would accompany a high-population/high-defense combination. Both of these combinations, plus the Medium combination and alternate Low- and High-population models, are shown in Table 1–2.

Measures of Expenditure

Personal and Family Income

Disposable personal income—the income consumers have left after taxes—is somewhat more predictable than GNP. The range in GNP, as we have seen, is due in large measure to government expenditures; but government expenditures will be offset, more or less, by taxes, so that as far as consumers are concerned, this element of GNP by and large cancels out. Eliminate the range in size of population, which is the other principal determinant, by reducing disposable personal income to a per capita basis, and the predictability becomes quite great. This is used as the take-off for projections.

The average U.S. citizen, young or old, now has at his disposal a personal income per year of a little less than $2,000, roughly 50 per cent higher, in real terms, than at the start of World War II. The prospects are for another 50 per cent rise over the next twenty years and a similar one in the twenty years after that. This Medium projection comes out, in money terms, to about 3,000 of today's dollars in 1980 and 4,300 in 2000. Our Low projection is $2,600 in 1980 and $3,500 in 2000; and our High, $3,200 for 1980 and $5,300 for 2000.

How the average family will fare may be approximated by a calculation of disposable personal income per household. From about $6,500 now, this should rise to nearly $10,-000 by 1980 and be somewhere between $13,-000 and $15,000 by the end of the century. This average figure is significantly inflated by the incomes of a relatively few households with very high incomes; it is a less revealing measure than a ranking of families by income. Federal Reserve Board data, arranged in this way, suggest that the middle-income family is now close to the $5,000-a-year mark. Using the rate of increase indicated by our household averages would raise this figure to about $7,500 by 1980 and $10,000–$12,000 by 2000. This

TABLE 1–2.   Variations in Principal GNP Demand Components in 1980

(Billion 1960 dollars)

Demand component	Low-population models		Medium	High-population models	
	Used herein[1]	Alternate[2]		Alternate[1]	Used herein[2]
Personal consumption expenditures	651	610	662	753	684
Government purchases	154	306	242	184	336
Private investment	113	221	167	121	236
Net exports and statistical error	47	33	−11	−28	−6
GNP	965	1,170	1,060	1,030	1,250

1. Assumes low defense.
2. Assumes high defense.

Source: Appendix Tables A1–10 and 11.

means that the typical household will be able to afford a standard of living, by 1980, enjoyed now by only the highest 20 per cent and, by the end of the century, will be at levels now considered quite well-to-do. This continued liberation of the mass of the American people from preoccupation with meeting basic needs for food, clothing, and shelter cannot help but bring about important changes in the pattern of total personal consumption expenditures.

Personal Consumption Expenditures

While modern economic systems are not quite as hand-to-mouth as those of an earlier day, they are still essentially concerned with providing for day-to-day living, with only a minor portion of human effort devoted to building up the capital and the inventories to provide for a more abundant future. Personal consumption expenditures remain the principal component of GNP in the United States.

Personal consumption expenditures have drifted downward from about 80 per cent of GNP at the beginning of the twentieth century, to 75 per cent in the twenties, to somewhere around 65 per cent in the last decade, with aberrations in time of war and depression. The decline has been due to the increasing role of government as a provider of defense and other services not obtainable in the marketplace; the portion of GNP devoted to private investment has basically remained unchanged. In our Medium projection, the proportion of personal consumption expenditures is projected to decline only slightly from now on, yielding a few more percentage points to increased expenditures by government. The picture would be different, however, for a high-defense economy, where personal consumption expenditures are likely to be little more than half of the GNP, or in a low-defense economy, where personal consumption expenditures could easily return to 70 per cent.

The uncertainties of world politics and population growth thus leave us with a broad range of uncertainty in the share of consumers in the GNP in the years to come. This is mostly due to the possible eventualities for the other claimants on GNP. Personal consumption ex-

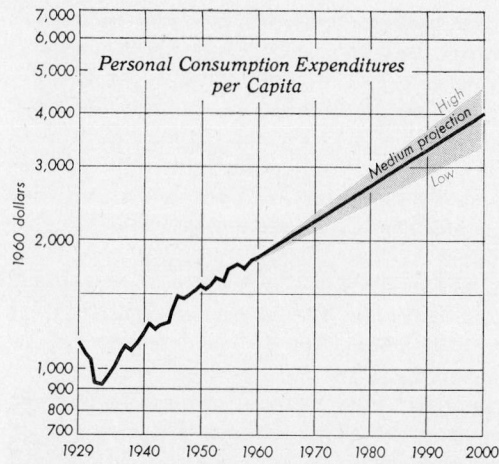

Figure 1–4. Personal consumption expenditures per capita, 1929–1960 and projections to 2000.

penditures have grown at a steady 1½ per cent per capita (disregarding wars and depressions) over the last several decades. The productivity of the American economy that one can reasonably project is such that per capita expenditure seems likely to grow during the balance of the century at an average rate of about 2 per cent per year. If both population and defense expenditures expand rapidly, this may bring it back to the historical 1½ per cent; under opposite circumstances (low population, low defense), it might go as high as 2¼ per cent. (See Figure 1–4.)

The lowest aggregates of personal consumption will occur when high defense expenditures coincide with low population growth; the highest aggregates will occur when low defense accompanies high population. The net result of these influences is illustrated by the various models in Table 1–2. In this table, the second, third, and fourth models are all calculated at the same per capita rate of increase in personal consumption expenditures (2 per cent). This is assumed to represent not only the Medium, but as low a rate of growth as could accompany low population growth and as high a rate of growth as is consistent with high population.

What this 2 per cent growth rate means for the average consumer is an increase in standard of living of almost 50 per cent in the next twenty years, a more than doubling by the end of the century. What it means in aggregate consumption is a doubling in twenty years (from the 1960 consumption level of about $330 billion) and a quadrupling by the end of the century. Whatever the population growth, the Medium projection of $660 billion in consumption expenditures for 1980 is not likely to be missed by more than $50 billion, on the down side, or $90 billion, on the high side. We shall most likely be passing the $500 billion mark in personal consumption expenditures in the early seventies and the trillion-dollar mark in the early nineties. Should there be continued rapid population growth under conditions of real world peace, the U.S. consumer market would probably exceed $1½ trillion before the end of the century. Under the opposite circumstances, we should barely have hit one trillion by the end of the century. These and other variations are set out in detail in Appendix Table A1–11.

We can be surer of that trillion than how the American consumer is going to spend even the next hundred billion. The way in which the consumer distributes his income between saving and spending and among such general classes of expenditures as food and clothing, housing, automobiles, furniture and appliances, recreation, etc., varies (disregarding the year-to-year fluctuations, with which we are not here concerned) only slowly. Relatively small variations in the proportions of these major components, however, can conceal very large variations in the proportionate expenditure on individual items; moreover, even very small percentage variations can mean very large absolute differences, after a time, in the demand outlook for important categories of goods with important raw material content. Most important of all, the stability of trend which some of these categories have shown in the past appears to depend in large degree upon certain institutional and relative-price influences which are apart from the simple matter of consumer preferences. There is no assurance that these institutional factors (living and working arrangements, sales ingenuity of individual industries, etc.) and relative-price trends will remain unchanged. While it is not so difficult,

therefore, to point to the most probable lines of development, it would be ill-advised not to allow, in most consumption categories, for very substantial possibilities of variation.

The most likely outlook is for consumption in all categories to rise, but there may be some rather wide variations among the contributions of the various categories to the over-all doubling per capita by 2000. There is also wide variation, as shown by the projected Lows and Highs for 1980 and 2000, in the degree of confidence which we may attach to our individual projections. The largest consumer expenditures today are for food, shelter, and clothing. Except for clothing, these are likely to retain top priority in the year 2000, but as a proportion of the consumer budget both food and clothing expenditures have been in a long-term slide, and it is logical to expect these trends to continue. This is what would be expected in a relatively high-income society, where the demand for such necessities becomes inelastic (increasing more slowly than income) as one-time luxuries take over. In addition, as will be discussed further in Chapter 3, the revolution in apparel fiber use and durability has been making it relatively cheaper for consumers to maintain an adequate wardrobe.

Surprising, perhaps, is the expectation that expenditures on housing will grow at about the same rate as total expenditures and that the share of expenditures on other necessities like food and clothing does not decline more sharply. Discretionary spending for items that are not absolutely necessary does increase, but the area of discretion has a way of developing ahead of demand, not confined to nonessentials but affecting virtually the whole range of consumer expenditures. As such spending ability grows, it may be exercised just as well on food as on automobiles, on housing as on recreation. The average consumer cannot get much more food down his gullet, but he can buy meat instead of bread, can get more of his food in restaurants and more of it in frozen or prepared forms, and so on. He may need only one house to live in, but he can easily be attracted to larger and more comfortable houses, and more land and landscaping; moreover, he might also want to maintain a summer cottage. As the mass of the population moves within reach of these embellishments upon necessities, the economy has a way of providing them to an extent it could not when the market was limited to a relative few.

Nonetheless there are a few areas of consumer spending in which discretionary spending is more significant than in others; these will most likely grow at a somewhat higher rate than total expenditures.

One of these areas is household appliances. As is shown in Chapter 6, a mere saturation of potential markets by presently-developed appliances could easily raise consumer expenditures on furniture and appliances to the levels shown in Figure 6–2, and it goes without saying that there are numerous new kinds of appliances on the way. Recreation is still another area likely to experience a faster than average growth, and this may include everything from golfing to foreign travel. Also likely to grow at a greater than average rate are the kinds of expenditures which the U.S. Department of Commerce groups under "personal business." The discretion here is slightly elusive, however; mostly the expenditure increase will be the inevitable result of higher automobile payments, bigger insurance policies, and the manipulation of more financial assets.

Government Expenditures

Second largest consumer of the national product (or contributor to it if one looks at the output side of the ledger) is government —federal, state, and local. Since we are following Department of Commerce concepts, this does not include the relatively self-supporting commercial type activities (including even the Post Office) which are designated as "government business enterprises."

Were it not for the uncertainties of the cold war the prospective expenditures of government might be somewhat more predictable. As it is, we must stay with our three rather different government-expenditure projections. These vary from a decline in the share of government to about 19 per cent of GNP in a completely peaceful world, to an increase to some 28 per cent in a world of highest tension. For our Medium projection, we have assumed

a non-defense component (defense is assumed as a constant percentage) which causes a gradual rise in the government share to 25 per cent from today's level of about 20. Government expenditures have fluctuated around this latter level for all of the past decade. They were only 10 per cent of GNP in the twenties, went as high as 45 per cent at the height of World War II, and fell below 15 per cent during the post World War II demobilization. There is little reason to doubt that government participation, at all levels, in social services, education, and the like, will increase.

The relation between the defense and non-defense components of our government expenditure projections is, of course, different for each of our three assumptions. At present, non-defense exceeds defense by about 20 per cent. Given an end to the cold war, we might be spending five times as much on government non-defense services as on defense. Given its intensification, defense could once again, as it did until very recently, come to dominate.

Private Investment

While investment may sound like a purely financial term, and the measurements are almost necessarily expressed in monetary units, what is under scrutiny is actually the additions to the physical stock of plant, equipment, and goods in process, from which current production, or income, is derived.

It is clear that there is a relationship between investment, so defined, and rate of economic growth: the less developed countries, with generally lower investment relative to GNP, generally grow at lower rates than the more developed countries and, in any one country, periods of more rapid growth are also usually periods of more rapid investment. It is clear, too, that there is a relationship between investment and worker productivity; the more and the better the machinery the individual worker has at his disposal, the more he can turn out. It is clear, finally, that there is a relationship between investment and savings: consumers and government must refrain from appropriating all of current output for current purposes if there is to be something to invest.

The study of all of these relationships is complicated, however, by the difficulties of defining savings and investment, the difficulties of distinguishing long-term phenomena from cyclical, and the difficulties of ascertaining which side of any of these relationships is cause and which effect.

In this study, therefore, we have not based our investment projections upon any hypothetical relationships between investment and any other of the factors named. Instead, we have built them up from their principal components—new construction, purchases of producer durable goods, and expansion of inventories. At the same time, we have tried to make sure that the resultant total—the gross private domestic investment—was not implausible either as a proportion of GNP or in relation to the growth rates in our Low, Medium, and High projections. Specifically, in our Medium projection, investment fluctuates around 15–16 per cent of GNP—precisely the level at which it has been for the last decade (ignoring cyclical fluctuations). In our Low-GNP projection it declines gradually to around 10 per cent, and in our High projection it jumps quickly to 19 per cent and rises gradually thereafter to 20.

Of the three prime components of gross private domestic investment, construction is the most important, accounting for better than half. This should be five times as large by 2000, most of the gain, in absolute terms, being in residential construction, simply because this element is, and will continue to be, about half of all private construction. It follows that at least one-quarter of investment has no direct connection with worker productivity (that is, by way of providing industrial plant and equipment) and is related to GNP only in the sense that current rental income arises out of the occupancy of residential properties.

Most of the rest of private investment—about 40 per cent—consists of purchases of "producers' durable equipment"; the 5 per cent remainder is accounted for by the net accumulations of inventory that must gradually occur in order to fill up the pipelines of a growing economy. Neither of these elements is likely to grow quite as fast as private con-struction (something like a quadrupling may be looked for), so that their relative importance in the investment picture will slightly diminish as the years go on. Partly, however, this is merely a matter of definition. Large pieces of equipment, such as go into chemical plants, refineries, and power plants, as well as the air-conditioning and other equipment that "come with" industrial and commercial buildings, are usually classified in the Department of Commerce accounts as "construction" rather than "equipment."

Not all of the non-residential construction or durable goods investment is, of course, strictly "industrial." A significant portion is devoted to office buildings, warehouses, stores, restaurants, garages, and other "commercial" facilities, not to mention such activities as mining and public utilities, all of which, combined, far surpass industrial plants as such in importance. Further consideration is given to the various categories of construction and of producer durables in Chapters 4 and 6.

Should investment follow the Low or the High trend, rather than the Medium trend we have been implicitly discussing, there would be large differences in the investment required. This is largely because of the relationship of population growth to residential housing and the fact that housing demand depends less on the level of population than on the more unpredictable factor of how fast it is changing. There is something like a 2½ to 1 ratio between the High and the Low projections of residential construction in 1980 and a 4¾ to 1 ratio in 2000. This is reflected in similar ratios for the range in possible levels of gross private domestic investment.

Exports and Imports

From the standpoint of the economy in general rather than from that of resources, we are interested in only the aggregate of foreign trade, on a net basis, and on such basis it has rarely exceeded 1 or 2 per cent of the gross national product, either as net imports or as net exports. It is unlikely that this situation will change much in the future, since the balance of trade (which, in the national accounts, includes some purely financial flows) cannot for very long remain far out of balance.

2

We have a greater interest in some of the particular kinds of U.S. exports and imports. These will be discussed, as we come to them, later in the study.

Goods, Services, and Construction

So far, we have drawn a picture of the future economy in terms of principal spending sectors—consumers, business (on capital account), government, and the rest of the world (net exports). It is also useful for many purposes to divide up the GNP according to the kinds of things produced, regardless of purchaser. Such a breakdown was instituted a few years ago by the Department of Commerce, and we have projected these categories in much the same manner as those already discussed. Since there are subcomponents common to each of the two breakdowns, for the most part all that is involved is a reshuffling of these subcomponents into the new classification.

The general distribution of the productive effort along these lines, past, present, and future, is shown in Figure 1–3. In interpreting these, it should be remembered that "goods" represents all things which, when finally consumed or added to capital by consumers, business, or government, are in the form of goods, regardless of how much in the way of services went into their making. "Services" includes not only consumer services, but the comparable things, like personal services and transportation, purchased by government. "Construction" includes not only private construction, but that carried on by government.

At present, construction accounts for about 11 per cent of the gross national product, services for about 38 per cent, and goods for about 51 per cent. This division has been relatively stable in the past. In the future there will probably be a slight increase in the share of construction and of services at the expense of goods. Should our High-GNP projection come to pass, however, its high investment content would mean a definitely higher share for construction, and conversely for the Low-GNP projection; in both cases, output of services, rather than of goods, would undergo most of the relative adjustment. Put in another way, the output of goods, like the gross national product, will, by 2000, probably have quadrupled; services and construction will more nearly have quintupled. The low line of development would entail a tripling of goods, nearly a quadrupling of services, but only a doubling in level of construction. The high line of development would bring goods output to about six times its present level, services to about six and one-half times, and construction to over ten times. Thus, the uncertainties of the future have greatest relevance, in a way, to the sector which, as we shall see later, presents some of the more difficult resources problems: construction.

Hard goods and soft. A further distinction that is useful for a number of purposes is between "durable" goods and "non-durable" goods, or between "hard" goods and "soft." We have already discussed producer durables —machinery and equipment—which, as "capital" or "investment" goods are the only goods purchased by business that are counted (as such) as part of the GNP. We have also mentioned some of the consumer durables, such as automobiles, furniture, and appliances, and non-durables, such as food and clothing; all consumer expenditures other than services may be similarly divided. Government expenditures on goods may similarly be divided between durables like automobiles and office equipment and non-durables like fuel and paper.

This distinction between durables and non-durables, it should be realized, is largely a matter of convention and does not completely coincide with the actual durability of particular goods. Shoes and apparel, for example, are classified as non-durable; yet, much clothing lasts as long or longer in use than some of the books, kitchenware, rubber tires, and other items classified as durable. By and large, however, the distinction does indicate what has to be repurchased day after day, month after month, or year after year, as against what generally lasts over longer periods, and the relative expenditures (nearly two dollars on non-durables for every dollar on durables) reflect this use characteristic. Moreover, there is a general relationship—although a declining one

—between these two classes of goods and the kinds of resources involved. The durables, or hard goods, are heavy consumers of the metals, glass, clay, and rubber; the non-durables exert their draft mostly on agricultural land and on the fuel minerals. Both groups call upon the forests, but the former demands larger trees (for lumber and furniture wood), while the latter can get by (if need be) with younger ones (for pulp). Both groups call upon chemicals and plastics, and it is the inroads of these more universal materials, more than anything else, that is erasing the importance of the old distinction between hard goods and soft goods.

The distinction between durable and non-durable goods also lies behind the standard industrial classification system to which a great many economic statistics are tied. In particular, there is a close correspondence between the output of these two classes of goods and the corresponding categories in the Federal Reserve Board's Industrial Production Index, which, with its further subdivisions, forms an important guide to the levels of demand of many individual materials and resources. This index is further discussed below.

There is a steady increase in the importance of durable, as against non-durable, goods. Before World War II, non-durables were nearly two and one-half times as important as durables; they are, as mentioned, something less than twice as important now; and by the end of the century the two categories should be about equal. This last, however, is true only for our Medium and High projections and is closely tied up with continuation of the cold war. The reason is that military equipment is an important part of durables expenditures; the higher durable goods requirement of higher investment levels is also a factor. If our Low GNP projection materializes, the relation between durables and non-durables will probably not change very much from what it is today.

Looked at in terms of prospective increases, the most likely prospect is for a tripling in non-durable output by 2000 and a quintupling in durables. Given the Low-GNP eventuality, both would somewhat more than double. Given the High-GNP outcome, durables output would be almost ten times as high in 2000 as it is today and non-durables over four times as high.

Farm and non-farm. Another "goods" breakdown, significant both in relation to projections of industrial production and for its implications as to comparative productivity, is that between "farm" and "non-farm." In this breakdown, also instituted a few years ago by the Department of Commerce, "farm" refers to the value of goods when they emerge from the agricultural sector; everything else, including the further value added to foodstuffs and fibers by industrial processing, is designated as "non-farm." This latter is roughly equivalent in scope to that of the Industrial Production Index, which covers all "value added" in manufacturing, utilities, and mining, while "non-farm goods" also includes all the value added in wholesale and retail distribution.

The relative importance of farm goods is steadily decreasing. Representing about 13 per cent of total goods before World War II, they are now down to less than 10 per cent, and are expected to decline to 6 per cent by 1980 and to 4 per cent by the end of the century. Roughly this relationship should hold no matter what the level of GNP. Even with the low increase in total GNP, however, this allows for a 50 per cent increase in agricultural output by the year 2000; with the Medium GNP this becomes a doubling, and with the High GNP a tripling. Given the prospective decrease in number of farmers, this also allows for a rate of increase in farm output per capita (and presumably farm incomes) substantially outpacing that in the rest of the economy.

Non-farm goods output seems likely to triple by the end of the century under the Low-GNP projection, to more than quadruple under the Medium projection, and to approach eight times present levels under the highest projection. This does not mean corresponding increases in demand for non-agricultural resources. Aside from the fact that it includes the processing of farm goods, a larger and larger proportion of this increased output will consist of value added subsequent to the raw materials stage.

Industrial Production Index

Up to this point, we have been talking mostly about the end-items of the economy, the "final" goods and services and construction that go to make up the GNP. Because nearly all of these end-items have gone through many and varied stages, involving a host of intermediate products and services, before they reach their final form, it is impracticable to try to relate the requirements for many material and energy inputs directly to them, especially for the purpose of projections well into the future. Instead, it is possible to sum up a substantial portion of the "intermediate productive economy" in terms of the Industrial Production Index and its principal components and subcomponents. The total index refers to the whole manufacturing, utilities, and mining sector of the economy, and may be derived from the projections of non-farm goods. The various components and subcomponents may be derived from some of the other sectors, such as durable goods, as well as from many of the projections of individual end-items which will be discussed in the chapters that follow. The particular industrial activ-

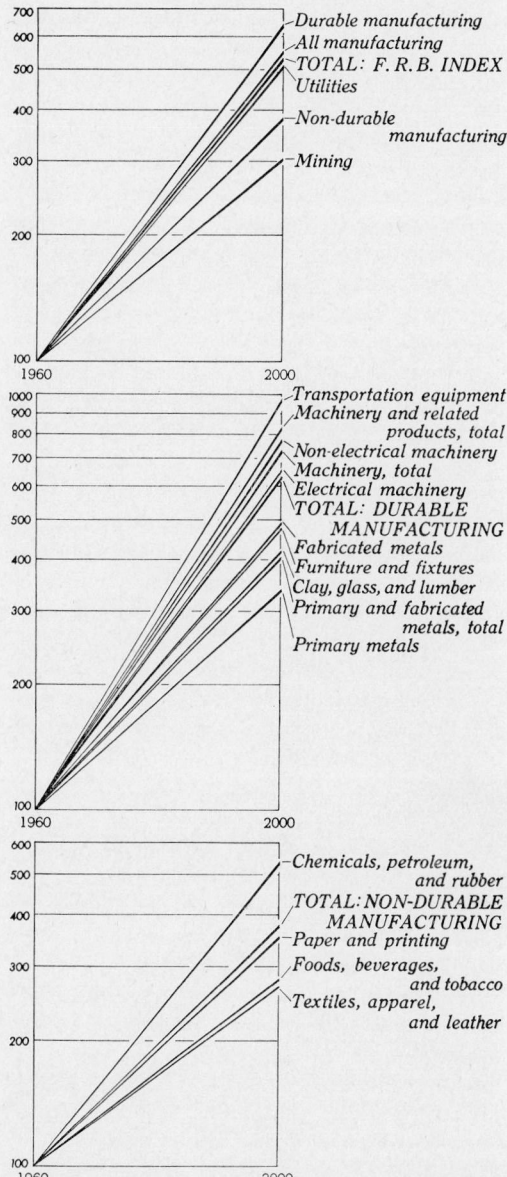

Figure 1–6. Growth of industrial production and various components, 1960–2000 (Medium projections).

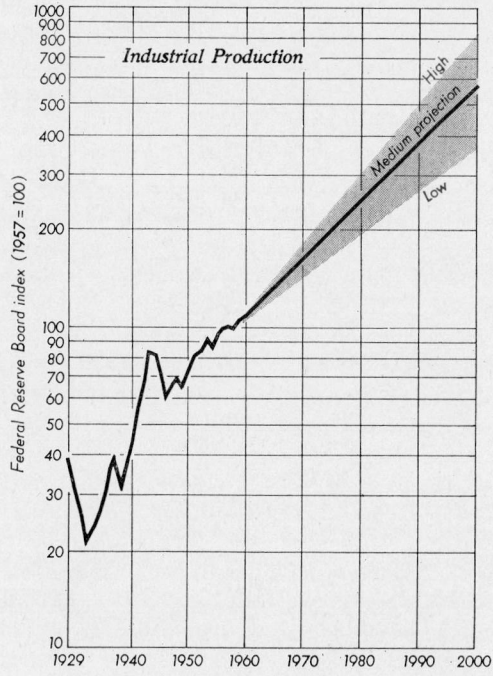

Figure 1–5 (opposite). Industrial production, 1929–1960 (Federal Reserve Board index), and projections to 2000.

ity involved does not in each case necessarily bear a constant relationship to the output of the relevant end-item, but frequently changes over the years according to the relative contribution to that end-item which the particular manufacturing sector makes.

The over-all industrial production index something more than quintuples by the end of the century—or, in other words, closely follows the course of the GNP. In the Low projection, it somewhat more than triples, again following the course of the GNP. In the High projection, it ends up at seven and one-half times present levels, compared with six and one-half times for the GNP; the difference is due to the relatively greater growth rate of goods and construction, compared with services, in the High projection.

The course of industrial production since 1929 and the range of projected possibilities to the end of the century are shown in Figure 1–5. Growth from 1960 to 2000, in the Medium projection, for some of its principal components is shown in Figure 1–6.

FOOD

FOOD IS BY FAR THE LARGEST single item in the American family budget, taking somewhat over a fifth of all consumer expenditures, after taxes. In 1960 the nation's retail food bill came to around $70 billion. In one way or another, the task of keeping people fed involves about 15 per cent of the productive activity of the whole economy.

In comparison with other large categories of personal wants and needs, food demand per capita is quite stable. Because everybody has to eat and nobody—no matter how rich—can eat more than so much food at one sitting, there are bottom and top limits on food consumption per person. In most of the years between 1929 and 1958, from 23 to 25 per cent of the average family budget was spent for food. Even during the war years and those immediately following, when other goods were harder to come by and families spent relatively more for food, the percentage did not go higher than 28.

All the same, there are many uncertainties in looking ahead. Stability in percentage shares does not necessarily mean stability in dollars spent. Some of the current trends in food demand are conflicting. Some are hard to understand, so that it is difficult to say how strong they will be in the future or how long they will

last. Even more important in a study like this one, where the basic interest is in future natural resource requirements and the adequacy of the nation's resource base, are the complex and shifting relationships between what people actually eat, their food purchases at the retail level, and agricultural acreage. The average productivity of crop and pasture land has about doubled since 1900. No doubt this trend will continue, but at what rate? Variations in the acreage requirements for different kinds of food are still wider. To provide a person with 3,200 calories a day for a year would at present take just a little over half an acre if the food were all in the form of bread, around two acres if it were milk, and more than ten acres if it were all beef. Clearly, we cannot get very far in calculating possible future patterns of food resource requirements without close inquiry into today's and tomorrow's menus.

That is our main purpose in this chapter, in which we shall analyze some of the general trends and then inquire into the prospects for the more important groups of foods. Later, in Chapter 12, we shall bring together these findings (along with others affecting agricultural production, notably those on textiles from Chapter 3) for an analysis of aggregate future de-

RELATED MATERIAL: Appendix to this chapter, pp. 586–95. Demand for crops, Chapter 12, pp. 233–51, and appendix, pp. 778–803. Land for agriculture, Chapter 18, pp. 335–55, 373–77, and appendix, pp. 969–84.

mand for key crops and pasture. Still later, in Chapter 18, we shall compare these projections, in terms of acreage, with the nation's land resources.

Problems of Measurement

In terms of farm value, meat and milk account for nearly three-quarters of the American diet; in terms of retail value, about half; and in both calories and pounds, less than half. Food grains, in contrast, account for about 10 per cent of farm value, 15 per cent of retail value, 10 per cent of weight, and 20 per cent of calories. Except for farm value, which is more pertinent to the discussion in later chapters, we are concerned here, in our inquiry into food requirements, with all three of the other measures. Simply for convenience, we shall base our projections for the individual food items on quantities for which available historical statistics are most abundant and dependable. In most cases this stage is at or near the farm level. The necessary conversions can be made from that starting point.

Statistical estimates of retail sales of food are precarious at best, but they can be made. The extent to which food is wasted between that point and the point of ingestion is an even greater unknown. Presumably, higher processing, better preservation, better home refrigeration, family-sized packages, and the like should cut down the waste that occurs in the household. At the same time, however, more lavish consumption standards, more "eating out," and other factors may be working in the other direction. It is not impossible that the 3,100-odd calories per person that Americans are purchasing at retail—considerably more than are physiologically necessary to sustain life and health—may reduce to around 2,600 calories actually consumed. Considering the build, age distribution, and work habits of the American people, this quantity is still more than is necessary, but it is, of course, only an average figure.

Some Over-all Trends

As the table below indicates, the average American is eating somewhat less, in terms of pounds and calorie values, than he did fifty years ago, but somewhat more in terms of retail value. One reason clearly is that people are buying more of the expensive and less of the cheaper foods. In addition, families today must

	Calories	Pounds (retail)	Price-weighted index (1947–49 =100)
1909–13	3,520	1,593	88
1926–30	3,500	1,556	91
1936–40	3,328	1,531	92
1946–50	3,280	1,560	101
1956–60	3,182	1,476	103

spend relatively more on the transportation, processing, and distribution steps that move food from farm to table. For example, in 1929 the farm value of food was about 43 per cent of what it cost the final consumer; in 1960 it was only about 34 per cent. Food is being transported farther, processed further, stored longer, and served up more luxuriously and more often in hotels and restaurants.

Some of the increased handling costs are the simple result of farmers themselves growing less of their own food. Between 1947 and 1960, for example, they increased their sales volume by 26 per cent, but decreased their production for home use by 45 per cent. Thus, in recent years a greater percentage of food produced than in the past has required marketing services.

More obvious evidence of expanded marketing services may be found among the several thousand items on supermarket shelves. Increasingly our food comes to us in highly processed and specially packaged forms. This does not always increase costs; savings in transportation and handling sometimes more than compensate for pre-consumer processing. There is less bulk to transport: a 6-ounce can of frozen concentrated orange juice, for example, replaces over 2 pounds of fresh oranges, and a medium-sized jar of instant coffee replaces a pound of coffee beans. Standardization and consumer-sized packaging have also spurred the growth of the supermarket chain, resulting in wholesaling and retailing economies of scale.

Aside from cost, the value of some of these changes to the consumer has been substantial in terms of the year-round availability of reasonably priced products which once, in unprocessed form, were considered luxuries.

Production of "convenience" items such as baby foods and partially prepared packaged dinners, pastries, and cake and cookie mixes will undoubtedly continue to grow at a rapid rate. Measured in today's prices, they had a farm value in 1939 of little more than $2 million. By 1947, their farm value had passed $10 million; by 1954, nearly $200 million; and by 1958 it was closer to $300 million. Still, however, they account for only a small percentage of total food production.

In general, the contradictory factors governing differences between retail food purchases and human consumption may cancel each other out, so that the downward trend in calorie consumption at retail is probably also reflected in a downward trend in calories actually consumed. The decreased amount of physical labor, improvements in house heating, migration toward warmer climates, growing public distaste for obesity and, importantly, population shifts toward a higher proportion of women, young children, and old people—all of whom are usually smaller eaters—these factors have been operating to reduce the requirements for food energy, and most of the trends will continue. Average requirements per person for calories at retail level, therefore, should continue to decline. But because some of the trends are nearing their limits, and because there are also countervailing trends (like that toward greater average heights), the rate of decline should slow down. Americans cut their per capita calorie consumption by around 10 per cent during the last forty years; for the next forty, this study assumes the cut will be more like 3½ per cent.

Competition among Food Groups

Among the several factors involved in the competition among food commodities and groups are changes in price relationships, income levels, consumer tastes and preferences, and relative availability.

The effect of price changes often eludes analysis. For example, two of the food groups that have shown absolute decreases in consumption

per capita—flour and potatoes—have also shown decreases in price relative to the prices for all foods. Consumption of meat per capita has been rising in the face of an increase in relative meat price. On the other hand, the price of sugar per calorie has fallen to where it is now less than the price of flour and cereal products per calorie, and this change has been accompanied by an increase in sugar consumption per capita and a decrease in flour and cereal products per capita. In the competition between meat versus cereals and potatoes, price has not been decisive, although it has undoubtedly moderated the outcome. In the case of sugar, which comes to us largely in candies, pastries, and canned fruits, the effect of price may be more apparent than real.

The influence of price changes upon closely related food commodities is more readily detected, but even here prices may not seriously alter long-term trends. Up to the end of World War II, for example, there was a close inverse relationship between changes in the price of beef relative to pork and the relative consumption of each. But since 1947, a preference for beef has been shown regardless of the relative price.

Changes in income do strongly affect the consumers' choice of foods. Higher personal incomes, for example, have been largely responsible for increasing the per capita consumption of meat and decreasing that of potatoes and cereal products, the cheap calorie sources.

As incomes continue to grow, indifference to price also grows, so that consumer preference—given ever-widening scope by improvements in transportation, packaging, and preservation—is rapidly becoming the principal arbiter of food consumption. Such preferences change. In an increasingly cosmopolitanized United States succeeding generations have abandoned old family customs. Changes in home and workplace environment have decreased the appeal of meals that "stick to the ribs," while broader popular education and scientific advance have fostered an interest in newer nutritional standards. So responsive has the public become to the latest variations in scientific finding as publicized through the mass media, that uncertainties as to future findings have become a serious hazard of forward estimating in the food field. Such a fac-

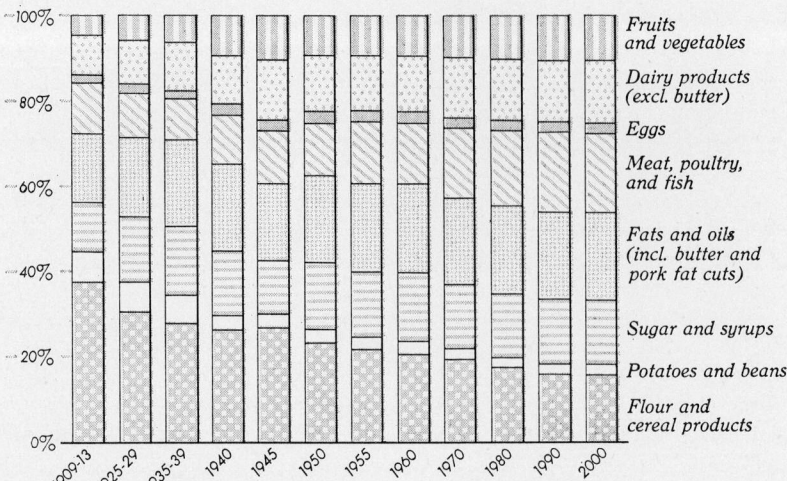

Figure 2–1. Percentage contribution of principal food groups to total food consumption, in terms of calories, 1909–13—1960 and Medium projections to 2000.

tor as the outcome of cholesterol research is likely to have far greater bearing on future patterns of American food consumption than variations in the price of butter.

About the only guides through this maze are past trends and the knowledge that, for something so central a part of daily life as food consumption, change in the habits of the whole population does not occur abruptly. The relative shares of the large food groups are particularly slow to change. While there can be considerable question as to how much of, say, pork or beef we shall consume, the basic roles of meat, wheat, dairy products, etc., are less difficult to predict. Moreover, we can be reasonably sure of at least one constant—a continued desire for variety—so that whatever the trends for particular foods, they must have limitations.

As measured in calories, the percentage contributions of the principal food groups to total consumption, past and future, are shown in Figure 2–1. The trends are those applicable to the Medium projections for each of the foods and for total caloric intake. The specific projections for individual food groups and food items, and the range of variation possible, are discussed below. Because of the differing ultimate land requirements of the different foods, especially meats, the specific trends have major relevance

to our agricultural resource discussion in Chapter 18.

Meat. Meat currently accounts for about 25 per cent of the total food budget. The responsiveness of meat consumption to changes in personal income is closer than for almost all other food commodities, and, as incomes increase, people will increase their expenditures for meat more than they will for other foods.

In a study of meat consumption patterns, based on a 1955 Household Food Consumption Survey conducted by the U.S. Department of Agriculture,[1] it was found that for every 10 per cent difference in level of income per household, there was an accompanying difference of 2.6 per cent in the *value* of meat consumed per capita. More of this response came from changes in prices paid than from changes in quantities bought. For each 10 per cent increment in income, there was only 1 per cent difference in quantity, compared with a 1.6 per cent difference in price paid. The higher level income classes were using their greater buying power to buy better grade meat, more highly processed meat, more expensive cuts, and only to a lesser extent to buy more meat.

1. Harold F. Breimyer and Charlotte A. Kause, *Consumption Patterns of Meat* (Washington: U.S. Department of Agriculture, Agricultural Marketing Board, May 1958).

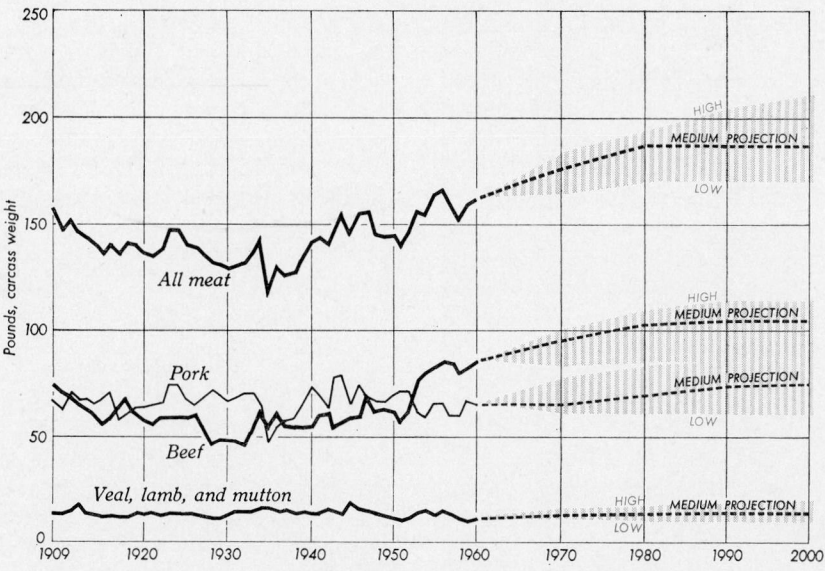

Figure 2–2. Meats—per capita consumption, 1909–1960 and projections to 2000.

This phenomenon is reflected in recent consumption trends. Meat consumption was fairly stable in the first part of this century, although it swung downwards to a depression low of 117 pounds in 1935. It then gradually rose to a peak of 167 pounds in 1956, since when it has—temporarily, it is assumed—declined slightly. These and future trends are shown in Figure 2–2. Here the unit used, "carcass weight equivalent," refers to weight in terms of large wholesale cuts; about 15 per cent of this is lost or trimmed before meat reaches the ultimate customer.

Consumption of meat per capita is likely to be higher in the future than it is now. For 1980 our projections indicate a range of 170 to 195 pounds, and for 2000, between 170 and 210 pounds. The Low estimate of 170 pounds is based upon the Low estimate of income per capita and allows for the development of storage and processing techniques that may reduce waste and lead to lower requirements for meat at the farm level. The upper limits are based upon estimates of high income per capita, which will permit fullest gratification of taste preferences for meat. It is also assumed that there will be a development of "factory-type" beef pro-

duction, similar to that of poultry, which will exert a downward influence on price.

A level of 210 pounds per person probably represents the maximum consumption of meat that could be expected under any conditions. It is true that certain other nations (New Zealand, Australia, Argentina, Uruguay) have a higher rate of meat consumption, but in these countries other foods have been relatively scarce and there is evidence that meat consumption tends to drop when alternative foods are more readily available to supplement a heavy meat diet.

Beef and pork are by far the most important components of the meat group, accounting for about 90 per cent of total consumption in terms of pounds. As a rule, the United States has consumed more pork than beef. Although people have a preference for beef, its consumption has been restrained by higher unit cost and, in the past, by the fact that beef has been more difficult to store in popular types of product than pork, much of which can be easily cured in the form of hams, bacon, and the like. The Breimyer-Kause study, cited above, indicates that families moving to the higher income levels are likely to consume relatively more beef and less pork. Taste preferences, however, vary among the regions according to differences in the historical and present availability of beef and pork in the region, historical differences in general income levels, and differences in family backgrounds. The South, which consumes more pork than beef, has a higher marginal preference for beef and less liking for pork than the United States as a whole. The opposite is true of the West, where the marginal preference for pork is greater than for beef, while actual consumption is the reverse. The example of the West is a significant indicator of the demand for variety in meat consumption.

In recent years beef consumption for the nation as a whole has shown a sharp increase over pork consumption and is now more than 30 per cent higher, a level never before attained. This has happened during a period in which beef prices have been rising relative to pork prices. There may be several reasons for this. Over the long run, more beef has become available, both geographically and seasonally. The curing process today can be matched by refrigeration and, particularly, freezing. Larger incomes have permitted greater gratification of the taste preference for beef. Lower-priced poultry may have cut into the pork market. And finally, there seems to be a growing distaste for fat pork, which may be partially attributed to popular opinion connecting high fat consumption with ill health.

It is quite likely that the spread between beef and pork consumption will continue and possibly increase. Support for this may be found in the Breimyer-Kause study, which shows that households with incomes below $8,000 consume between 25 and 30 per cent more beef than pork per person, while those above $8,000 consume about 50 per cent more. On the other hand, a further spread may be inhibited by the desire for food variety.

A range of 85 to 110 pounds of beef per person is expected for 1980, with a possible increase to 115 pounds by 2000. The lower limit, similar to the current level, may be maintained under conditions of small increases in income and a high preference for variety in consumption. The upper limits assume high income levels, a continuation of the preference for beef over pork, and the development of factory-type beef production.

For pork, the range is relatively wider. At the upper limit (83 pounds in 1980 and 85 pounds in 2000) we assume substantial production of a lean hog, plus the consumer demand arising from a desire for variety. The lower limit of 60 pounds represents a persistence of today's apparently widespread disinclination to eat fat pork.

The other "red" meats in the diet—veal, lamb, and mutton—make up about 10 per cent of per capita consumption, a little more than they did a few years ago. (Game also comes within this classification, but the amount of venison, bear, etc., consumed per capita is statistically insignificant.) Annual consumption of veal per person, which runs between 5 and 10 pounds, has decreased in recent years, and that of lamb and mutton, which together is about 5 pounds, also has shown some decrease. Consumption of these meats is largely related to the supply, which depends in turn on the demand for dairy products and wool. Demand for these primary commodities is unlikely to result in significantly larger supplies of veal and lamb, but there is a possibility that a meat-type lamb, already raised in certain areas, might show marked output increases.

On the basis of recent trends, veal consumption is expected to range between 7 and 9½ pounds per person in 1980 and perhaps as high as 11 pounds by 2000. Consumption of mutton and lamb may go down to about 3½ pounds, but it seems more likely that it will rise with higher incomes and the greater production of meat-type lambs. By 1980 consumption may reach 6½ pounds, slightly less than the thirties' average of 7 pounds; by 2000 it may be as much as 7½ pounds.

Not only total meat consumption, but the particular combination of beef, pork, and other meats, will have a significant bearing on the eventual resource requirement. Several of the possible patterns of consumption in 1980 and 2000 are summarized in the table which follows. Here, High and Low totals are based upon estimates of High and Low income levels per capita. Within the totals there is assumed, under "High beef," a marked taste preference for beef coupled with a gradual development of factory-type beef production, resulting in a lowering of price; and, under "Variety," fuller development of a lean hog and substantial demand for variety in meat consumption. Figures are in pounds, carcass weight equivalent, per capita. Historical data and projections for ten-year intervals may be found in Appendix Table A2–5.

	1980				
	High total			Low total	
	High beef	Variety	Medium	High beef	Variety
Lamb & veal	10	16	14	10	15
Beef	110	96	103	100	85
Pork	75	83	70	60	70
Total	195	195	187	170	170

	2000				
	High total			Low total	
	High beef	Variety	Medium	High beef	Variety
Lamb & veal	15	18	15	10	15
Beef	115	107	105	100	85
Pork	80	85	75	60	70
Total	210	210	195	170	170

Poultry. Past trends in the per capita consumption of poultry are a striking example of how management practices and technological development can affect patterns of food use. (See Appendix Table A2–1.) For thirty years, between 1909 and 1940, the level of poultry consumption did not change significantly. Then suddenly consumption started to rise; within the next eighteen years it had doubled.

Impetus was given by the relatively greater availability of poultry over other meats during the early stages of the Second World War, but the foundation for the change had been laid several years before. Over the years 1934–60, commercial broiler production increased at a rate of over 18 per cent per year, or from less than 5 per cent of total chicken production to almost 85 per cent. At the same time, the relative price of commercial broilers fell by more than half.

This marked increase in production in the face of falling prices has been made possible by the high degree of efficiency in modern broiler production. Growers are closely integrated with the suppliers of feed. In some cases, the integration is represented by a simple contract between the farmer and the feed supplier, in which the latter extends credit to the former to help ensure an adequate market for his feed. At the other extreme, the feed supplier owns the farm and employs hired labor to operate it.

In a typical arrangement, the feed dealer provides feed and medicine, pays for the chicks, provides technical advice on management practices, and frequently provides credit for the broiler house and equipment; moreover, he usually absorbs any deficit between costs of production and value of output. The large investment of the dealer and the large numbers of birds in which he shares responsibility facilitate rapid and full application of good management practices and of the results of scientific research.

The increase in commercial broiler production has been accompanied by a decrease in production of the farm chicken (the chicken produced as a by-product of the egg industry). This has occurred for two reasons besides the competition of the commercial broiler. First, the sex of chickens can now be determined at the age of one day; as a consequence, the males of a batch which has been bred for egg-laying qualities rather than for meat can be disposed of without waste of feed. Second, egg-laying hen flocks have decreased, since increases in yield of eggs per hen have been greater than the slight increases in total egg consumption.

Chickens account for about 80 per cent of the poultry industry. The balance is almost entirely turkeys, although there are some ducks, geese, and other fowl. About half the turkey production is integrated to some degree, and the pattern follows that of the commercial broiler industry.

By and large, the increase in per capita consumption of poultry since 1940 has been due to the falling price, the development of a standardized product, and the improvement of marketing channels. Continuation of the rate of increase since 1940 would result in a per capita consumption level of about 80 pounds (ready-to-cook basis) by 1980, or double the recent amount. However, it is not likely that the factors affecting the present rate will continue to exert the same degree of influence. Integration of poultry grower and feed supplier, which is accompanied by reduced costs, already covers about two-thirds of production. It will continue to spread, but at a slower rate, and price reductions gained through increased efficiency will also tend to slacken off. Furthermore, increases in the consumption of red meat will tend to hold down increases in poultry consumption. Consequently, we assume that the rate of increase will diminish rapidly. In 1980, depending upon intake of red meat, poultry consumption per capita should be somewhere between the current 35 pounds (ready-to-cook basis) and 45 pounds.

It is assumed that the level of consumption per capita established by 1980 will continue unchanged to the year 2000.

Eggs. In 1909, about 300 eggs were consumed each year per person. Consumption reached a peak of 400 in 1945 and has fallen to slightly below 350 in recent years. This measure of consumption, however, contains inaccuracies that may obscure the present trend. First, there has been an increase in the size of eggs—from 1.45 to 1.52 pounds per dozen. This means that the decline in pounds consumed since 1945 has been about 13 per cent, rather than 17 per cent (based on 1960 consumption). And second, there are no satisfactory methods for measuring the number of eggs produced in non-farm households and consumed at home. Such consumption was probably higher during World War II than it is today.

Statistical difficulties aside, the future consumption of eggs is unlikely to be very different from what it is today. Over 10 per cent of eggs produced are consumed in bakery goods and other processed foods. Because of their higher unit cost, the use of eggs for this purpose may decrease in proportion to that of other raw materials, but there will be an increase in the amount of processed foods consumed per person. In home baking, housewives will probably use fewer eggs as they turn to prepared mixes. On the other hand, the 1955 Household Food Consumption Survey indicates that higher income groups in all urban areas tend to consume more eggs per person than the lower income groups.

In view of these factors, we assume that egg consumption will range from 330 to 400 eggs per person in 1980 and 2000.

Dairy products. Milk is the most versatile of foods. The wide range of its products (bever-ages, desserts, additives, spreads, etc.) makes it difficult to find a common denominator by which milk consumption can be measured and projected into the future. The two chief nutrients —milk-fat solids and non-fat solids—have been consumed in varying proportions over the past twenty years. (See Figure 2–3.)

In terms of production, the ratio of these nutrients is relatively fixed: that is, 100 pounds of fluid milk contains about 4 pounds of fat, 9 pounds of non-fat solids, and 87 pounds of water. However, in recent years the relationship between the solids has been changing slightly (Figure 2–4). Following a tendency to decrease until 1950, there has been a definite steady increase in non-fat solids relative to fat. This has been accomplished by a shift in breeding to lower fat producers. Milk of high fat content is no longer a premium commodity. Within a few years a major trend has been reversed. From 1924 to the late 1940's, the butterfat content of fluid milk rose gradually from 3.92 per cent to 3.98 per cent; then it dropped sharply to 3.79 per cent in the late 1950's. The three states producing the largest quantities of milk—Wisconsin, New York, and Minnesota—have led the way, producing in 1959 milk averaging 3.65, 3.60, and 3.50 per cent butterfat, respectively. As the other states follow this trend the U.S. average will tend to reach the level of the three big states. Projections to the year 2000, culminating in an average butterfat content of 3.6 per cent, have been made on this basis.

Fat solids have always been used for human food more or less in their entirety. On the other hand, food use took only 50 per cent of the non-fat solids produced in the twenties, and now takes about 75 per cent.

The different trends in consumption suggest that milk fat and non-fat solids need to be treated as partially independent commodities. Per capita consumption of milk fat (or butterfat, to use the older, perhaps more familiar term) has declined about 20 per cent since 1924–28, primarily because of its high price relative to the price of substitute fats. In addition, there has been an outright reduction in the fat content of dairy products.

The outstanding example of milk-fat replacement is the shift from butter to margarine, given

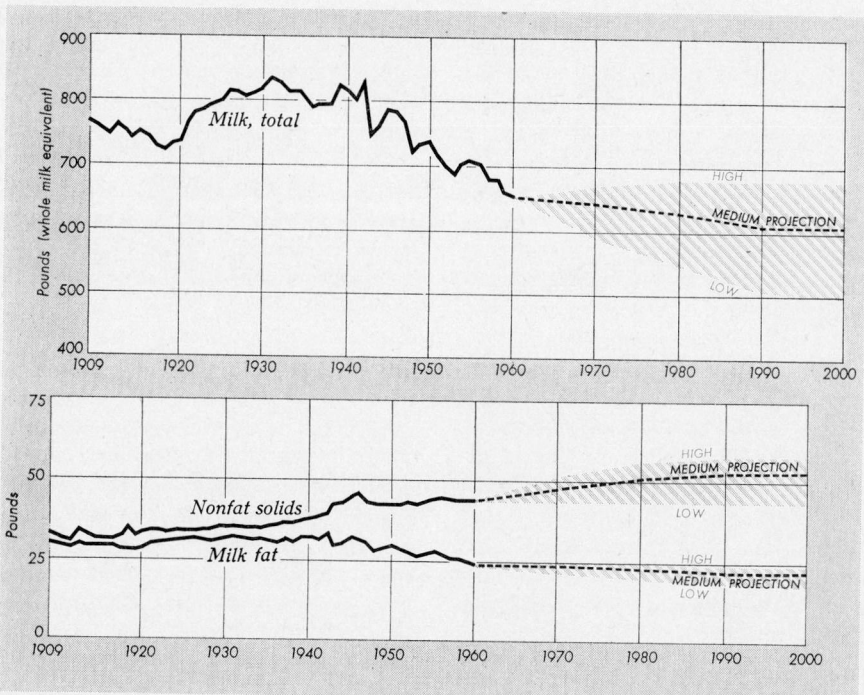

Figure 2–3. Milk—per capita consumption in terms of fat and non-fat solids, 1909–1960 and projections to 2000.

impetus by short supplies of butter during the Second World War and aided by the elimination of legal restraints on the coloring, packaging, and selling of margarine. The end of rationing did not result in a shift back to butter, indicating that there had been a lasting change in consumer tastes and preferences. At twice the price, butter was no longer preferred. Between 1935–39 and 1954–57, butter consumption per capita dropped almost 50 per cent. This was mostly due to the substitution of margarine, although a 15 per cent decline in total consumption of spreads (butter plus margarine) also played a part.

Milk fat is also giving way to substitutes in the form of so-called "filled dairy products," from which the milk fat has been removed and fats from other sources added. Substitutes of this nature have been developed for the butterfat in ice cream, whipped cream, and, recently, even fluid milk. On top of this, there has been an over-all drop in the fat content of fluid milk, ice cream, and cream.

While milk-fat consumption per capita has been decreasing, consumption of non-fat milk solids per capita has been rising and is currently about 28 per cent higher than it was in 1924–28. This has largely been brought about by relative increases in the consumption of those dairy products with relatively low fat content. Fresh whole milk, the most important of these, has increased about 10 per cent per capita since 1924–28; evaporated whole milk, 30 per cent; and cheese, which typically contains no more than one-third butterfat, 75 per cent. There have been even greater increases in the consumption of cottage cheese, cultured buttermilk, skim milk in chocolate drinks, non-fat dry milk solids (as part of other foods), and evaporated and condensed skim milk. On the other hand, consumption of both skim milk as such and natural buttermilk has decreased about 35 per cent.

Because of the wide variety of dairy products, we have chosen to estimate future demand on the basis of the two chief nutrients of milk—fat solids and non-fat solids. This assumes that these constituents can be estimated independently, which is true only to a certain point. Past experience indicates that consumption of the non-fat solids will continue to increase and consumption of the fat solids will continue to decrease. However, such independence of behavior on the part of the two kinds of solids will be decreasingly possible.

Until recently, the divergence in trend has been made possible by using more and more of the non-fat solids for human food and less and less for livestock and other purposes. But a point will be reached at which no more shifts from non-food use can be expected. At this point, the ratio of non-fat solids *consumed* per pound of fat solids consumed will be the same as the ratio of non-fat solids *produced* per pound of fat solids, assuming that both foreign trade in milk fat and its non-food use will be negligible. (See Figure 2–4.)

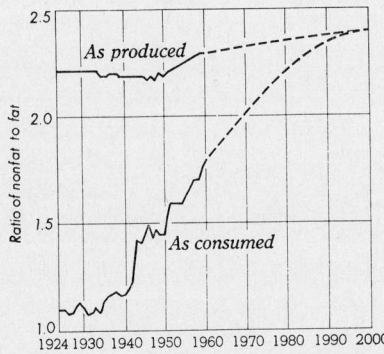

Figure 2–4. Ratio of milk non-fat solids to fat solids, 1924–1960 and projections to 2000.

With a reduction in butterfat content and only slight or insignificant decreases in percentage of non-fat solids, the ratio of all non-fat to fat in dairy products should increase to about 2.4 from the current one of about 2.3. As shown in Figure 2–4, this is also likely to be a ceiling for the consumption ratio between the two. Based on this ceiling and on the recent trend, consumption of non-fat solids per capita is not likely to exceed 58 pounds in 2000, nor, given contrary circumstances, is it likely to be less than today's level of approximately 44 pounds. Similarly, the decline in fat solids may be arrested either at today's level of 24 pounds,

or not until it reaches 18 pounds. The table below summarizes the consumption trends per capita for dairy products.

	1960 (pounds)	1980 Projections (pounds)			2000		
		Low	Me-dium	High	Low	Me-dium	High
Fat solids	24.6	20	23	25	18	22	24
Non-fat solids	44.2	44	51	56	44	53	58
Total milk solids	68.8	64	74	81	62	75	82

Estimates of future consumption per capita could be significantly affected by sharp and unexpected changes in relative price or consumer preference. The relative price of dairy products is dependent upon government price support programs as well as upon supply-demand relationships. We assume that the former will not be abolished in the near future. As to the latter, we conjecture that increases in total demand can be met by increases in efficiency and yield. In any case, the low price elasticity of dairy products means that demand is affected only by large changes in price.

A considerable part of the demand for dairy products is related to their nutritional value. In 1947–49 dairy products, excluding butter, contributed 13 per cent of the food energy (calories) consumed per person, 24 per cent of the protein, 14 per cent of the vitamin A value, 76 per cent of the calcium, and high percentages of other essential items of diet. The taste preference for milk is influenced by its high nutritive value and its traditional role in child feeding.

Grains. The cultivation of food grains has been the foundation of all agricultural societies. Food grains are still of considerable importance. The United States, with one of the lowest rates of food grain consumption in the world, currently consumes more than 20 per cent of its calories in this form. But the relative importance of the food grains is diminishing rapidly in the face of advanced technology and growing incomes.

Wheat has long accounted for some three-fourths of food-grain consumption in the United States, with corn, rye, rice, and oats making up most of the balance. With total grain consumption declining, per capita consumption of wheat has also declined—from over 300 pounds (measured at the farm level) to around 165 pounds a year. In addition to the factors making for the total decline in calories and the proportion of calories consumed in the form of grain products, there have been some influences peculiar to wheat. Among them is the fact that commercial bakers, over the years, have quadrupled the amount of non-flour ingredients in their products. In addition, there is less waste in the use of flour and less spoilage of baked goods as a result of better packaging and use of preservatives.

The 1955 Household Food Consumption Survey showed that the higher income groups and more urbanized households consume wheat in more highly processed forms (commercially baked goods and prepared flour mixes) than do the low income groups and farm households. While home baking of bread had declined, home baking of cakes, pies, and biscuits had increased—evidence of the growing popularity of prepared mixes. The Survey also found indications that bread consumption had decreased while consumption of other baked goods had gone up.

Wheat's basic advantage over other foods is that it provides a cheap source of food energy. Both the anticipated increases in income and decreases in requirements for calories therefore buttress the conclusion that consumption of

wheat will continue its downward trend (Figure 2–5). There is undoubtedly a bottom limit, but there are no clear indications as to what this is and when it will be reached.

The long-term decline in the consumption of wheat per capita has proceeded at varying rates. Following World War II and until 1953, the rate was gradual (about 0.8 per cent per year). A continuation of this rate to 1980 would lead to a level of 145 pounds per person, probably the upper limit that might then be expected. The decline since 1953 has been much sharper and, if extended to 1980, would result in a figure that seems unreasonably low. A more satisfactory bottom range to wheat consumption is obtained by extending the trend since 1935, which produces a consumption per capita in 1980 of about 120 pounds. Between 1980 and 2000 we have assumed that the rates of decrease will be retarded and that consumption at the century's end will range between 100 and 140 pounds per person.

Corn flour and meal and the products made from them once accounted for nearly 90 per cent of human consumption of this grain; now it is under one-third. On the other hand, once minor uses such as corn sugar and syrup, starch, and breakfast cereals have increased in volume or held their own, with the result that the overall trend of corn food consumption has been not unlike that of wheat (save for the two war pe-

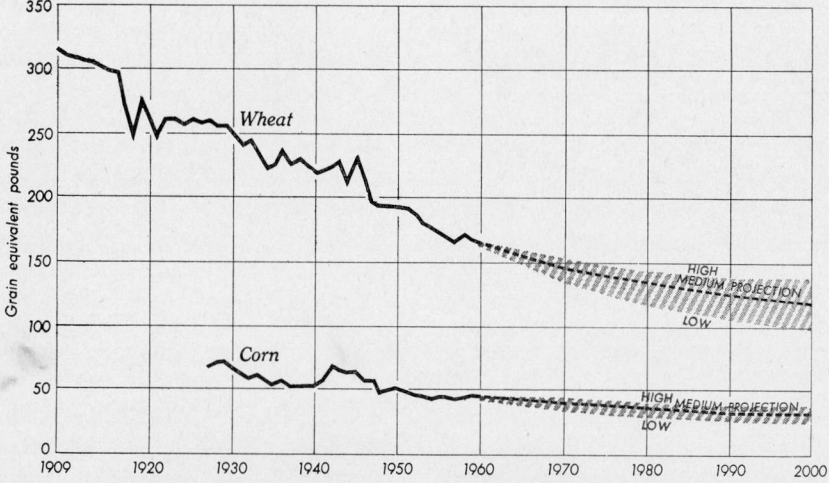

Figure 2–5. Wheat and corn for food—per capita consumption in equivalent grain, 1909–1960 and projections to 2000.

riods, when use of corn syrup boomed). Future corn consumption, therefore, is projected roughly parallel to the expected trends in wheat.

Projected per capita consumption of wheat and corn for food purposes, in terms of equivalent grain, is summarized in the table below.

	1960 (pounds)	1980 Projections (pounds)			2000 Projections (pounds)		
		Low	Medium	High	Low	Medium	High
Wheat	165	120	135	145	100	120	140
Corn	46	31	35	40	26	31	38

Vegetables. Unlike grains and meat, the growing of vegetables and fruits has relatively small impact upon land use; but in terms of the processing these foods undergo, their consumption involves the use of such items as metals, paper, and plastics, and therefore must be taken into account as part of the future resource-use pattern.

Between the First and Second World Wars, per capita consumption of vegetables remained quite steady. During World War II vegetable consumption reflected the tendency toward increases in general food consumption, and later reflected decline in general calorie intake. However, these over-all trends conceal widely divergent movements among the principal types of vegetables. (See Appendix Table A2–1.) It is to these that we must look for a reasonable appreciation of what may happen to vegetable consumption. The large and steady decline in the consumption of potatoes has been a clearly defined change in the pattern of food consumption. Between 1909–13 and the 1950's, per capita consumption of potatoes and sweet potatoes dropped 46 per cent. As a proportion of total vegetable consumption, the drop since the end of World War I has been from nearly one-half to less than one-third.

Many factors were operating to effect this change. Increased availability of other vegetables and rising incomes have permitted people to enjoy a greater variety of foods. Immigrants from potato-eating countries have become fewer and have become assimilated, which also has had its effect. Farmers, heavier consumers than city dwellers, have become fewer. Contributing to the decline has been the widespread belief that potatoes are fattening.

In looking to the future it is clear that certain of these factors are of diminishing importance. The "unassimilated" balance of immigrants is not great, and future off-farm movements will be relatively small. New kinds of demand have arisen: potato chips, dehydrated potatoes, and "french fries" are growing in popularity and may help to mitigate the downward trend. On balance, the decline in consumption per capita over the past decade has been minimal, and although this is too short a period to provide a reliable basis for projection, it does indicate that future decreases may not be as great as they have been in the past.

Among vegetables other than potatoes, three principal changes have been taking place. The first is typical of all foods, namely, a shift towards consumption in more highly processed forms. The development of canning processes has made vegetables available on a year-round basis and has permitted increases in per capita consumption even while consumption of fresh vegetables (purchased and home-grown) has remained level. Consumption of frozen vegetables, although still a small part of total consumption, has increased greatly in recent years. These tendencies are likely to continue with the expected increases in per capita income.

Increases in the processing of vegetables have been accompanied by increases in contract farm operations and decreases in production for auction markets and production in home gardens. Currently, about 90 per cent of the vegetables produced for canning and freezing are grown by processors, or under contract to them, and about half of the fresh-market vegetables are supplied by integrated operations. In some cases, even retail chain stores have established packing operations in shipping areas.

Use of home-grown vegetables decreased from 50 to 22 per cent of the consumption of all fresh vegetables (other than potatoes) between 1919 and 1960.

The third change in vegetable consumption relates to shifts in the relative importance of the commodities. There are more than twenty-five kinds of vegetables consumed in the United States, but only one, besides potatoes, is of sufficient importance to make up more than 10 per cent of total consumption. Tomatoes, which now account for a fifth of the total, have increased 40 per cent in consumption since the early 1920's—an increase apparently due to the development and wide use of such processed products as catsup, paste, sauce, and juice. Among the vegetables accounting for 5–10 per cent of the total, lettuce consumption per person has increased threefold, sweet corn has doubled, celery has increased 50 per cent, onions have remained the same, and cabbage has fallen by half.

The sum total of changes for vegetables other than potatoes and tomatoes has resulted in three periods of distinct trends. Prior to the Second World War, consumption per capita rose gradually. During and immediately following the war, consumption first increased and then fell sharply. In the last decade there has been a gradual and steady decline. It is possible that the trend will continue downward, but one may assume that it will not fall below 175 pounds (farm weight) per person, which is 11 pounds less than the previously recorded low in 1919. On the other hand, the recent downward trend could be reversed, primarily because of the growth in frozen vegetables. Since high-income families consume about four times as much frozen vegetables per capita as low-income families, it may be inferred that consumption will respond markedly to rising incomes. The importance of fresh (or frozen) vegetables to the diet is expected to gain wider public acceptance in the future and this, together with technological development in processing techniques, may lead to increases instead of decreases in vegetable consumption per capita. Continued increases, still essentially due to gains in processed products, may be expected for tomatoes. This means that by 1980 and 2000 the following patterns of vegetable consumption (in terms of farm weight) might prevail:

	1960 (pounds)	1980 Projections (pounds)			2000 Projections (pounds)		
		Low	Me-dium	High	Low	Me-dium	High
Potatoes (incl. sweet potatoes)	120	85	95	115	85	95	115
Tomatoes	77	70	80	88	70	80	90
All other	192	175	190	210	175	195	220
Total	389	330	365	413	330	370	425

Fruits and melons. Since the early part of the century the pattern of fruit consumption per capita has been marked by little change in the total and widely varying trends among the components. Prior to the mid-1930's there was significant competition between citrus fruits and apples. More of the latter were available, because they were easily stored and widely grown. This advantage, however, disappeared with the development of canning and freezing techniques (especially important for citrus products) and better transportation facilities. Together, increased availability and growth in incomes per capita have permitted consumers to enjoy larger quantities of citrus, the nutritional values of which are by now widely recognized. From the mid-1930's to the end of World War II, apple consumption remained steady while citrus fruit consumption continued to increase at a rapid pace, along with total fruit consumption. Since World War II, total fruit consumption has been rather steady. It is quite possible that the pattern has become fixed and that the consumption in 1980 will be closer to today's than today's is to that of fifteen to twenty years ago. Our estimates for 1980, however, allow for continued increases in citrus consumption and slight decreases in consumption of other fruits. The table below shows our projections of per capita consumption in terms of farm weight.

	1960 (pounds)	1980 Projections (pounds)			2000 Projections (pounds)		
		Low	Me-dium	High	Low	Me-dium	High
Citrus fruit	86	100	115	125	100	115	130
Apples	28	20	23	25	20	23	25
Other fruits and melons	120	101	115	125	100	115	125
Total	234	221	253	275	220	253	280

Fats and oils. For nearly four decades, except for brief periods during the Depression and wartime food rationing, consumption of food fats and oils has ranged between 65 to 70 pounds (retail weight) per person. As is the case with other food groups, however, the components have shown considerably different trends. Consumption of butter and lard has decreased; that of pork fat cuts (bacon, etc.) and shortening has fluctuated but maintained a level trend;

TABLE 2–1.   Aggregate Demand for Principal Food Items, 1920, 1940, 1960, and Projections for 1980, 2000

(Billion pounds, except for eggs)

Food	1920	1940	1960		1980	2000
Meat (carcass weight)	14.5	18.8	29.0	L M H	38 46 54	46 65 91
Poultry (ready-to-cook basis)	1.5	2.3	6.2	L M H	8 10 13	9 13 19
Dairy products (whole milk equivalent)	78.4	108.2	117.7	L M H	124 154 190	134 202 294
Eggs (billions)	31.8	42.1	60.1	L M H	75 88 112	88 119 173
Wheat (grain equivalent)	28.0	29.1	29.7	L M H	27 33 40	27 40 61
Potatoes & sweet potatoes (farm weight)	19.2	19.4	21.6	L M H	19 23 32	23 31 50
Tomatoes and other vegetables (farm weight)	26.9	38.4	48.4	L M H	55 66 83	66 91 134
Fruits and melons (farm weight)	24.9	32.2	42.0	L M H	50 62 77	59 84 121
Sugar and syrups (refined equivalent)	11.1	14.8	20.8	L M H	23 26 32	27 35 50
Fats and oils (retail weight including pork fat cuts and butter)	6.9	9.4	12.1	L M H	14 16 20	16 22 30
Coffee, tea, and cocoa (retail weight)	1.4	2.3	3.1	L M H	3.4 4.2 5.6	4.0 5.6 8.7

L—Low projection   M—Medium projection   H—High projection.
Source: Appendix Tables A2–1 and 2, except for 1920, which is similarly approximated.

and that of margarine and other edible oils has risen.

Stability over so long a period is a strong indication that future consumption per person of all fats and oils will continue to be within the 65–70 pound range, but there is also reason to believe that if the consumption level does change it will fall rather than rise. Despite the rise in margarine consumption, the consumption per capita of all table fats has lessened, a trend which is likely to continue with decreased consumption of wheat products. Salad oils and dressings of low-fat content may be expected to take an increasingly large share of the market. The only indication of contrary movement is the strong increase in per capita consumption of potato chips and processed french-fried potatoes.

With these factors in mind, the projections of consumption of food fats and oils have been adjusted to a range of from 60 to 70 pounds (retail weight) per person. This includes, it should be noted, the pork fat cuts and butter. These items, which represent about 40 per cent of the total, have also been considered in the meat and milk projections.

Other foods. Except for the Depression and war periods and the most recent years, consumption of fish per capita has not changed significantly since the early part of the century. A slight decrease may occur in the future in view of the expected high levels of red meat and poultry consumption. On the other hand, increased ease in home preparation, made possible by frozen fish and fish sticks, may help to maintain present levels. It appears reasonable to expect consumption in 1980 and 2000 to range between 9 and 11 pounds (edible weight) per person.

Since the mid-1930's, the combined per capita consumption of sugars, syrups, and honey has fluctuated between 110 and 115 pounds per person, with the exception of the war period and a few other years. It is unlikely to go above this level in the future, and 115 pounds may be considered an upper limit. The lower limit is more difficult to see, primarily because of the advent of artificial sweeteners and the growing popularity of the so-called dietetic foods. There is no way to measure the impact that these may have upon sugar consumption, but if it is on the order of 10 per cent the Low estimate of sugar consumption would be about 100 pounds per person in 1980 and 2000. This includes sugar used in processed products, such as candy, baked goods, and canned and frozen fruits, juices, and vegetables.

Of the three beverage commodities, coffee, tea, and cocoa, coffee is by far the most important in the U.S. dietary pattern, accounting for about 80 per cent of the total consumed. By 1980 this total may range from 15 to 20 pounds per person, measuring coffee and tea as sold at retail and cocoa in terms of the "chocolate liquor" equivalent of cocoa and chocolate products.

Total Demand

In all of the foregoing, we have been discussing demand on a per capita basis, and in many cases it has appeared that demand is declining. True though this may be, the relentless increase in population converts nearly all per capita food demands into a continuingly larger call upon the nation's natural resources. From the standpoint of knowing how great this call will be, the uncertainty as to which foods consumers will prefer, and in what measure, is multiplied by the uncertainties as to rate of population growth discussed in Chapter 1. For there is no a priori reason to believe that either a high or a low demand for meat, or milk, or any other of the various food commodities is not equally possible with a high or low population. At a later stage we shall examine, in the light of the resource base, whether the full range for each item does or does not engender any supply problems. For the moment, we may sum up our analysis of prospective food demand in terms of the data shown in Table 2–1.

chapter

3

CLOTHING
AND TEXTILES

APPROXIMATELY ONE-TENTH of the productive effort of the American economy is devoted to the provision of clothing and footwear, textile items for the household, and textile products for trade and industry. Clothing and textiles are thus important determinants of resource requirements. Moreover, they bear heavily upon a single key material—cotton.

A little more than half of textile consumption in recent years has gone into clothing. The remainder has been almost equally divided between household and industrial uses, with the former slightly in the lead. Leather is used predominantly for wearing apparel, with shoes accounting for four-fifths of the leather market. The outlook for leather demand will be appraised briefly at the end of this chapter, after discussion of all types of demand for textiles.

Textiles

The already complex problem of projecting future demand for textiles is further complicated by the rise of synthetic fibers, which in recent years have been replacing natural fibers

like cotton and wool in many uses. There are important differences in weight, durability, and other properties, not only between the natural and synthetic fibers, but also within each of these classifications.

Kinds of Fibers

In analyzing fiber consumption data for purposes of projection, it is convenient to take some of the differences between fibers into account by converting the original data into what are known as "cotton equivalent pounds." As worked out by Lowenstein and Simon of the U.S. Department of Agriculture,[1] these are based on (1) differences in average processing waste between the various fibers, and (2) differences in the average weight of generally comparable end-products produced from the different fibers.

In 1937, man-made fibers had only 12 per

1. Frank Lowenstein and Martin S. Simon, "Textile Fiber Consumption in Cotton Equivalent Pounds," *The Cotton Situation* (Washington: U.S. Department of Agriculture, November, 1960).

RELATED MATERIAL: *Appendix to this chapter, pp. 596–602. Demand for crops as key materials, Chapter 12, pp. 233–34, 248–51, and appendix, pp. 795–97. Plastics derived from petrochemicals, Chapter 17, pp. 317–25, and appendix, pp. 961–62. Land for agriculture, Chapter 18, pp. 335–55, 373–77, and appendix, pp. 969–84.*

cent of the market (speaking in cotton equivalent terms); cotton, 79 per cent; wool, 7 per cent; and other fibers, 2 per cent. By 1949 the synthetics' share[2] had gone up to 28 per cent and cotton's down to 65; now it is something like 40 and 55 per cent. These new fibers are finding increasing use not only as exclusive content of fabrics, but in combination with each other and with natural fibers.

There are many man-made fibers, some no longer new. Names like rayon and acetate have been with us for a long time. Nylon has been a familiar word since the war, and Dacron and Orlon also have a few years behind them. But this is only the beginning: the full roster reads almost literally from A (for Acrilan) to Z (for Zefran), and more are being added yearly. We also have the so-called metallic fibers, most of which are really metallized plastics, and a non-metallic mineral fiber—glass—which is finding an increasing variety of both textile and non-textile uses.

The steady gain of man-made over natural fibers for all uses has some important resource consequences. The great variety of trade names covers alternative forms of a limited number of basic products. These basic products, in turn, fall into two principal groups—cellulosics and non-cellulosics. The former, which comprise various forms of rayon (including the viscose type, which is what is usually meant by "rayon," and acetate type, which is usually referred to as "acetate"), are derived overwhelmingly from woodpulp, although they also come in part from the short fibers (linters) adhering to ginned cotton seed and later separated in the seed processing. The non-cellulosic, resin-based fibers break down into several subgroups, like the acrylic (e.g., Acrilan), polyamides (like nylon), polyesters (Dacron), polyvinylidene chloride (Saran), and other basic compositions whose number is constantly being added to. Directly or indirectly, most of these non-cellulosics are derivatives of petroleum or natural gas, or combinations of such derivatives with other materials.

2. "Synthetic" is used herein as synonymous with "man-made," rather than in its narrower technical sense of fibers (essentially the non-cellulosics) which are derived from synthesized materials like petrochemicals. In this narrower sense, rayon and acetate are not considered synthetic.

Clothing

To project future requirements for clothing, one must gauge the effects of two strong and conflicting current trends. On the one hand, there are more people in the country every year with more money to spend per person. On the other hand, outlays for clothing have been taking a progressively smaller share of the family budget—so much smaller, in fact, that absolute per capita expenditures for clothing (in constant dollars) have decreased in recent years. The net result has been a moderate increase in aggregate spending for clothing that has, however, lagged well behind the rise in population and total buying power.

A constant-dollar increase of more than one-fifth in per capita personal consumption expenditures since World War II has been accompanied by a net decrease of nearly one-third in expenditures on clothing. Clothing and footwear combined made up 12 per cent of total consumer expenditures in 1929, were down almost to 10 per cent at the onset of World War II, rallied in importance to reach 13½ per cent by the war's end and have since declined to a new low of 8½ per cent. Consumer demand for clothing has clearly been inelastic.

More important to the resources picture than dollar expenditures—which reflect not only the costs of fiber but the very much larger costs of processing it into yarn, cloth, and finished garments—are apparel trends in terms of fiber consumed. Here the inelasticity of consumption is even more marked. Judging by fiber trends for all uses (data distinguished by end-use are available only for recent years), not since World War I has consumption kept up with income. This has been particularly apparent since the end of World War II. Ever since 1949, fiber consumption for apparel has been on a plateau of 19 to 20 pounds per year per person.

This much fiber, of course, implies no small wardrobe. By this measurement, the average American is consuming twice as much as the average western European and four times as much as the resident of a country like India. Twenty pounds is enough for a man to outfit himself annually with something like a half-dozen shirts, six sets of underwear, a suit, a pair of slacks, a dozen pairs of socks, and two sets of pajamas, and still have enough left over for ties and handkerchiefs. A woman could outfit herself with several skirts and blouses, several dresses, a half-dozen pairs of hose, two nightgowns, a sweater, coat, bathing suit, and plenty of underwear. These are examples and not average buying habits, which are hard to determine.

In any case, it is clear that the clothing consumption level in the United States is at a point where clothing is clearly not a top priority as an expenditure item. This has helped to hold down per capita fiber consumption in recent years, but it does not entirely account for its stagnation. Additional explanation must be found in the changes occurring in the weight of clothing used and in the materials of which it is made.

Both by choice and by virtue of lessened physical requirements, the American taste has been running to increasingly lighter clothes. Better heating in homes, work places, and means of transportation has played a part, as has the tendency of many families to move to milder climates. So has the tendency for an increasing proportion of the labor force to spend its working day indoors.

Forty years ago the average man's suit appears to have been made of fabric weighing as much as 20 ounces per linear yard. By 1952, the clothing trade regarded "regular-weight worsteds" as meaning material weighing 12 to 13 ounces per linear yard; by 1958 the term was taken to mean 11 to 12 ounces. Men's summer suitings now run as low as 6 ounces. An index of the trend can also be found in the Census-compiled statistics on fabric production. For example, of the various weights of wool fabrics used for men's and boys' apparel, those falling between 13 and 16 ounces per yard constituted 45 per cent of the total yardage as recently as 1948, while fabrics of 9 to 13 ounces were only 38 per cent. By 1960, the lighter weight fabrics were more than 66 per cent of the total, and the heavier were down to less than 10 per cent —or hardly any more than the proportion of fabrics *under* 9 ounces. Similar trends hold for topcoats and overcoats.

Not only are fabrics lighter, but style changes over a long period have moved in the direction of less fabric per garment. Gone now is the vest as a regular component of a man's business suit. Even earlier, the American woman had been released from the yards and yards of fabric which fashion once required.

The big change in kinds of materials—to judge from the limited available data—came with World War II. From roughly 13 per cent of total apparel fiber poundage in 1937, man-made fibers jumped to 22 per cent by 1949 and to a peak of 24 per cent by 1951. Since then, their share has oscillated around 21 to 22 per cent, with the rayon fibers (including acetate) giving way to a steady growth in the newer synthetics. Cotton and silk took the initial brunt of the rise in man-made fibers, but in more recent years most of the impact has shifted to wool. Cotton in 1960 was once again about two-thirds of all apparel fiber consumption (not far from the prewar level), while wool had declined to less than 11 per cent (compared with 15 per cent in 1937 and 16 per cent in 1949), and silk and linen had become negligible factors.

The significance of synthetic fibers goes beyond their mere share of weight in the market. Pound for pound, they usually provide more fabric than their natural counterparts. Yard for yard, they last longer, and thus enable consumers to maintain larger wardrobes without correspondingly larger current purchases. Allowance for the former factor alone makes per capita apparel consumption look about 22 per cent higher than before the war, instead of only 17 per cent. Add the latter factor, and it is clear that wardrobes have improved to an extent which is not evident from the crude fiber consumption data.

Translated into the cotton equivalent pounds of Lowenstein and Simon, synthetic fibers come to about 30 per cent of total apparel fiber consumption in recent years, rather than 22 per cent based on actual weight. This is about 3 percentage points below the 1951 peak; and on a per capita basis as well, apparel use of man-made fibers has not shown any tendency to increase in the last decade.

Still another adjustment may be made in order to put the data on a basis more suitable to project. Some of the past variation in consumption per capita is explainable by differences in the composition of population by sex and age.

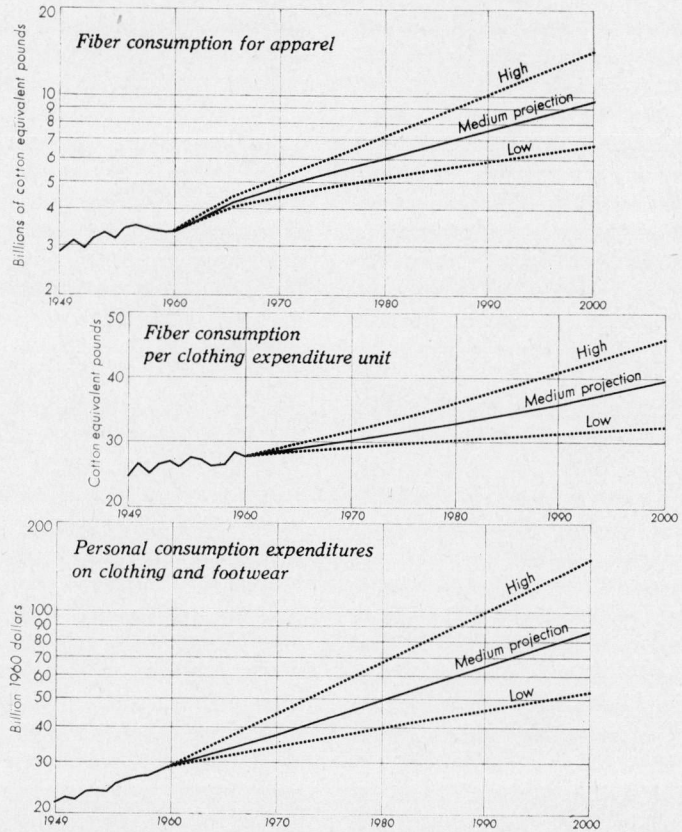

Figure 3–1. Trends in the consumption of clothing and footwear, 1949–1960 and projections to 2000

Over the last two decades, the U.S. population has become increasingly weighted with young children and older adults, who require less fiber than young adults. Sooner or later, depending upon the rate of population increase, this trend is due to change. By reducing consumption per capita to consumption per "clothing expenditure unit," both past and future changes in age-sex distribution may be conveniently taken into account. Simon has worked out factors which may be used for this purpose.[3] Although based upon statistical data on value of clothing expenditures, rather than on physical consumption, they afford a rough index to age-sex variations in the latter and explain some of the apparent consumption weakness in recent years.

3. Martin S. Simon, "Clothing Expenditure Units: A New Time Series," *Agricultural Economics Research*, Vol. F., No. 2, April, 1958.

After all of these adjustments, we find that apparel consumption—as measured by cotton equivalent pounds of fiber consumption per clothing expenditure unit—has exhibited some upward trend since the war, but only a slight one: less than 10 per cent in the past decade. What, then, of the future? The projections used in this study are shown in Figure 3–1. Our conclusion is that consumption per clothing expenditure unit probably will continue to trend upward, and at an accelerating rate. The increases will, however, still fall short of increases in per capita income.

Two factors that exerted downward pressure in the recent past may be expected to relax. Because clothing is a semi-durable item, the acceleration of per capita purchases at the end of World War II, and to some extent again at the start of the Korean War, most likely built up clothing inventories to the point of significantly lessening the priority on new clothing purchases. Inversely, in the 1954 and 1958 recessions, clothing purchases (at least for adults) became postponable. The experience of 1951–58, therefore, would represent a lower level of purchases than might have occurred had events followed a more normal course and, in fact, the increasing need for clothing replacement seems already to be contributing to accelerated purchases. Another factor, discussed above, has been the decreasing amount of fabric per garment and of weight of fiber per yard of fabric. While these trends can, and probably will, continue, the rates of decline and their relative effect on fiber consumption must inevitably be slowed.

A third factor at work, which may continue to exert a depressant effect for a while longer, is the high rate of family formation. This has caused many adult consumers to concentrate on the purchase of essentials other than clothing. Reinforcing the effect is the suburban living which a large proportion of these young households have adopted: much of their time is spent in casual clothing. While the suburban trend, as such, may go on for some time, its differential effect upon per capita clothing purchases may be expected to lessen.

One may conclude, therefore, that despite relative surfeit and temporary depressants, and barring emergence of additional retarding influences, the push of rising income will over the longer period cause a distinct upward movement in per capita money expenditures on clothing. If this movement turns out to be fairly rapid, it will probably mean that relatively more of the increase is going into style and workmanship than into fiber; if very slow, the materials content will be correspondingly higher. In other words, fiber consumption as such may be somewhat more narrowly projected than clothing expenditures in dollars.

Household Uses

Of the total fiber consumption in cotton equivalent pounds, the apparel segment accounts for half, and this proportion will probably continue. In the other half, household and industrial use are currently of nearly equal importance,

although, depending upon circumstances, their future growth rates could be substantially different. (See Figure 3–2.)

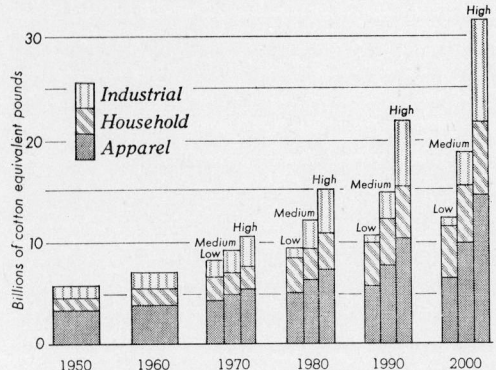

Figure 3–2. Trends in total fiber consumption, 1950, 1960, and projections to 2000.

In value terms, the most important item of household textile consumption is carpets and rugs, followed roughly by sheets, towels, and pillowcases; blankets and other bedcoverings; upholstery materials; and curtains and drapes. In terms of fiber requirements, however, "linens" are far and away the most important item. This lends a basic stability to household textile requirements, since per capita demand for linens can be expected to change even less than for clothing, and there is little, if any, prospect of displacement of cotton by lighter-weight fibers.

The slight upward trend in household textile consumption per household over the last decade is explained mostly by the growth in floor coverings and other decorative requirements. Unlike apparel, this sector of demand definitely responds to rising incomes and has been given further impetus by the high rate of establishment of new and larger homes. In terms of materials, the natural fibers (cotton and wool) have managed to maintain a substantial importance, but the significant gains have been made by rayon and other synthetics. Thus, the upward trend in household textiles shows up more clearly in cotton equivalent weights than in crude weight of fibers. For the future, we have assumed a continuation of this trend at a slightly increasing rate.

Industrial Uses

Although sanctioned by long tradition, the industrial category of fiber use is a misnomer if one thinks in terms of the eventual user, because perhaps one-fourth goes into automobile tires, which are a direct-consumption item; another large amount goes into other parts of automobiles; and an additional (though declining) amount finds its way into packaging. While industrial use of fibers has increased, in relation to total industrial output it has fallen steadily behind. Much of the explanation lies in the rapid substitution of synthetic fibers, which go farther because of their greater strength and durability per pound. In addition, textile fibers have, in some uses, given way to entirely different materials. For example, the automobile industry has found increasing numbers of ways to substitute plastics (and foam rubber) for fibers of all kinds. Paper has driven cotton out of the packaging field for consumer items like salt, sugar, and flour, as well as in the bagging of such industrial materials as cement and feed; the latter, in fact, are more and more being taken out of bags entirely and transported in bulk.

In the industrial arena, inroads of synthetics upon natural fibers are particularly dramatic. Man-made fibers used for industrial purposes in 1937 were only 1 per cent of the total. By 1949 the percentage had become 25 and by 1960, 48. An even sharper picture is drawn when these figures are adjusted to reflect the savings in processing waste and the greater utility per pound of the synthetics. In cotton equivalent terms, synthetics went from 3 per cent of industrial use in 1937, to 34 per cent in 1949, and 64 per cent in 1960.

The downward drift in the relation of industrial fiber consumption to industrial production is assumed to continue. However, as shown in Figure 3–2, industrial production will be increasing fast enough for this sector of fiber use to maintain its relative importance.

Shifts among Fibers

Shifts among fibers thus far appear to have resulted in relative conservation of resources. It takes, for example, about 3 acres of forest land to yield enough woodpulp in a year for a ton of rayon; it takes about 4 acres of cotton land to produce as much cotton, and cotton goes only seven-tenths as far. Thus, even though the average productivity of cotton acreage is likely to rise more rapidly than that of woodpulp acreage, the shift from cotton to rayon is likely to involve some net saving of land for some time to come. However, cotton is of relatively small importance in relation to cropland acreage (currently around 4 per cent), and woodpulp for rayon is even less significant (2 or 3 per cent) in relation to the total demand for woodpulp.

Further and greater conservation is involved in the shift from cellulosic synthetic fibers to non-cellulosic. Any imaginable expansion of the latter would hardly ripple the total demand for petroleum and gas. The continued availability of by-product sources, sufficient not only for non-cellulosic fibers but for all other non-cellulosic plastics, is almost without question (cf. Chapter 17), and this would continue to be true even if new sources of petroleum, such as oil shale, have to be brought into play.

So far, the cellulosics have had the bulk of the synthetic market. They were first on the scene, and they have one important use, high-tenacity tire cord, which alone accounts for about 15 per cent of synthetic fiber consumption. But just as rayon cord has displaced cotton, so rayon in turn now has a competitor in nylon. The battle is still being waged and rayon still has an advantage in price, but the trend indicates a growing preference for nylon.

The trends are the same for the uses of synthetic fibers in general. Before the war, non-cellulosic fiber consumption was confined to minor quantities of nylon. By 1950, one pound of non-cellulosic fiber was being consumed for every eight pounds of cellulosic (actual weight); by 1955 the ratio was one to three and before 1965 it seems likely to be one to one.

Increasingly, we shall be witnessing a situation where newly discovered synthetics come to displace, not so much natural fibers, as earlier types of synthetics. In few cases, if any, are these displacements likely to be complete. More and more, mixes of fibers are coming into vogue as manufacturers try to achieve the best cost-utility combinations for specific fabric uses. Nor are the natural fiber producers simply bowing to events; rather, research is finding ways of adding to and conditioning the natural fibers to give them some of the characteristics—such as crease resistance and wash-and-wear-ability—that have made the synthetic fibers popular. Some of the additives used are themselves plastics, so that the difference between natural and synthetic fabrics is beginning to blur.

One development, still in its infancy, may bring about a resurgence of woodpulp as a source of clothing and household textiles, even though not of rayon itself. This is the production of cheap, felted fabrics, made on something akin to paper-making machines instead of in weaving or knitting mills. Already, garments made of these fabrics are in widespread use in industrial plants and laboratories, and some observers look forward to the day when we shall all be clothing ourselves in disposable "paper" clothing. Undoubtedly, the cheapness of such fabrics will make them increasingly important contenders (in some cases in competition with non-woven plastics) for such articles as napkins, towels, diapers, tablecloths, drapes, and ultimately both inner and outer wear. However, it is hard to imagine felted fabrics taking over the clothing field completely. Moreover, there is reason to believe that woodpulp will no more retain an exclusive role here than it has in the synthetic yarns. It is the felting process that provides much of the economy, and it is likely that a whole range of natural and synthetic fibers may, for one purpose or another, be so processed. Statistically, therefore, we have not taken specific account of "disposable clothing" as a future phenomenon. Until the prospects become clearer, we shall have to assume that the relative contribution of natural fibers, woodpulp, and oil and gas to U.S. requirements for apparel and related products will be distributed much as it would have been had felted fabrics not come into the picture.

Summing up future demands for clothing and other textile products as they reflect themselves in the demand for fibers, we may project the call upon cotton, wool, and synthetic fibers as shown in Table 3–1. Since the resource consequences of all of these fiber sources are quite

TABLE 3–1. Principal Trends in Demand for Clothing and Related Products and Its Impact upon Key Materials, 1950, 1960, and Projections for 1980, 2000

Item	1950	1960		1980	2000
Total fiber consump-			L	9.47	12.36
tion (cotton-equiv-	5.94	7.08	M	12.01	18.97
alent billion lb.)			H	15.10	31.64
			L	5.12	6.73
Apparel use	3.10	3.68	M	6.10	9.92
			H	7.20	14.57
			L	3.04	4.74
Household use	1.23	1.67	M	3.23	5.59
			H	3.51	6.97
			L	1.31	.89
Industrial use	1.61	1.73	M	2.68	3.46
			H	4.39	10.10
Shares of the market					
(per cent)	100	100		100	100
			L	42.0	38.0
Cotton	64.0	55.9	M	46.0	44.0
			H	49.0	48.0
Wool	6.7	4.4		2.5	1.9
			L	48.3	50.0
Man-made (synthetic)	29.1	39.4	M	51.3	54.0
			H	55.3	60.0
Other	.2	.3		.2	.1
Shares of the synthetic					
market (per cent):					
Cellulosic (rayon			L	15	5
and acetate)	86.8	50.5	M	21	10
			H	32	20
			L	68	80
Non-cellulosic	13.2	49.5	M	79	90
			H	85	95
Consumption in actual					
weight (billion lb.):					
			L	4.0	4.7
Cotton	3.8	4.0	M	5.5	8.4
			H	7.4	15.2
			L	.5	.2
Rayon and acetate	1.1	1.0	M	.9	.7
			H	1.9	2.7
			L	1.7	2.7
Other man-made fibers	.1	.8	M	2.7	5.1
			H	3.9	10.0
			L	.44	.42
Wool (clean)	.71	.57	M	.55	.65
			H	.69	1.09
Shoe consumption (mil-			L	678	807
lion pairs)	465	528	M	784	1,120
			H	952	1,640
Demand for leather for all			L	18	10
uses (million cattle-	36	30	M	24	19
hide equivalents)			H	34	38

L—Low projection   M—Medium   H—High.
Source: Appendix Tables A3–2, 3, and 4.

limited, we shall, except for cotton, be giving them only incidental attention in the remainder of this study.

Footwear and Other Leather Products

Shoes were once almost as synonymous with leather as clothing was with cotton and wool. So were luggage, handbags, belts, and a number of other products. In every one of these uses leather has felt the effects of plastics competition —even more so than have natural fibers in the textile field. It has also had important competition from rubber and textiles.

As a result of such substitutions, the modest prospective increases in shoe consumption per capita (shoes are about four-fifths of leather's market) are unlikely to arrest leather's decline, except at the highest rates of population growth, while cattle slaughter, the chief determinant of leather availability, may be expected to continue steadily upward. (See Chapter 2.) Thus, the matter of having sufficient leather to keep Americans shod and supplied with handbags, wallets, etc., merits only summary attention, since it presents no problem of resource scarcity. Rather, there may be an important surplus problem in the making, which will be touched on in Chapter 12.

Summary data on shoe consumption and leather demand are included in Table 3–1.

chapter
4

CONSTRUCTION

ALTHOUGH CONSTRUCTION IS USUALLY VISU-ALIZED as primarily the activity of men and machines in digging, moving, shaping, erecting, etc., the relative use of materials by the construction industry far exceeds its share in the gross national product. Particularly is construction important for that special class of materials —sometimes referred to as the "physical-structure" materials—out of which the more or less durable, and durably shaped, things of our civilization are made. Its impact upon certain of these materials—notably wood, steel, and cement—is basic.

Principal Types of Construction

In value, about one-third of all construction consists of housing. The other components that make up the construction category of the gross national product consist of a large variety of activities both public and private, the most important of which are the construction of highways, public utilities, and stores and offices. Not included in the GNP as a "final product," but of substantial importance in terms of its impact upon resources and virtually on a par with housing in terms of dollar cost, is the

general category of maintenance and repair. (See Figure 4–1.) Conversely, included in the GNP and important for materials, but not always categorized as construction, is oil and gas drilling—about 4 per cent of new construction expenditures.

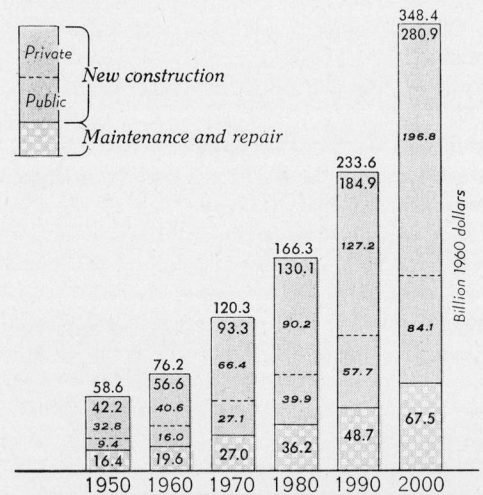

Figure 4–1. New construction, maintenance and repair, and the private and public components of new construction, 1950, 1960, and Medium projections to 2000.

RELATED MATERIAL: Appendix to this chapter, pp. 603–34. Lumber and woodpulp, Chapter 13, pp. 252–57, and appendix, pp. 804–15. Metals, Chapter 16, pp. 293–316, and appendix, pp. 859–939. Chemicals, Chapter 17, pp. 320–24, and appendix, pp. 940–56.

TABLE 4–1. Principal Categories of Construction, 1950, 1960
and Medium Projections for 1980 and 2000

(Billion 1960 dollars)

Category	1950	1960	Medium projection 1980	2000
Total construction	58.6	76.2	166.3	348.4
New construction	42.2	56.6	130.1	280.9
Maintenance and repair	16.4	19.6	36.2	67.5
of which for residential construction	6.2	7.2	10.8	14.7
Residential new construction incl.				
additions and alterations	19.6	22.6	54.7	126.4
Non-residential new construction	22.7	34.1	75.4	154.5
Private new construction	32.8	40.6	90.2	196.8
Public new construction	9.4	16.0	39.9	84.1
Components of public new non-				
residential construction:	9.1	15.3	37.2	77.8
Schools and hospitals	2.3	3.2	5.0	7.4
Highways	2.6	5.5	16.1	34.6
Military & industrial	.6	1.8	5.1	12.3
All other (water, sewerage, etc.)	3.6	4.8	11.0	23.5

Source: Appendix Table A4–3.

Table 4–1 shows the principal categories, past, present, and projected, all in billions of 1960 dollars.

Housing

Shelter, along with food and clothing, is among man's basic material needs. Housing, however, as we use the term in this study, includes not only shelter as such but also the additional values attributable to the gap between "shelter" and what modern Americans now expect of their homes.

The value attributed to housing in the National Income Accounts is largely a theoretical one, consisting of the imputed rental values arising out of home ownership. Looked at as a capital expenditure, however, its importance in the economy is without question: more than one dollar out of every three expended upon new construction; about one out of every four going into investment and about one out of every twenty-five in the gross national product.

Without regard to the very volatile short-term influences upon housing demand, we may distinguish two basic components in the long-term trend of annual demand for new dwelling units: (1) net additions to "stock," or what is needed to provide for the increasing number of households; and (2) net disap-

pearance of existing units, or what is needed in the way of replacement. Projections of both of these factors are very sensitive to small variations in assumption.

The number of households which we shall have in the year 1980 is fairly predictable. Compared with 53 million now, we may expect about 73 million in 1980, and the figure is unlikely to be off by as much as 10 per cent one way or the other. The outside estimates for the end of the century are projected to be at most 20 to 25 per cent below or above the "most likely" figure of 99 million.

The range of possibilities opens up considerably, however, when instead of considering differences in total stock of dwellings, we look at the net additions. In the Low projection an increase of 16 million occupied dwelling units (from 53 to 69 million between 1960 and 1980) compares with one of 20 million in the Medium and 26 million in the High projection (cf. Appendix Table A4–5). Here, the Medium would be some 25 per cent larger than the Low and be about the same percentage smaller than the High. On a net basis we might have to add 800,000, 1 million, or 1.3 million units per year, on the average, to take care of the increase in households, and the highest likely increase thus would top the lowest by over 60 per cent. At each projection level, of course, the annual additions towards the end of the period would be higher than those in the early years.

The range of possibilities is not radically widened when we consider the period ending in 2000 rather than 1980. Talking again in averages, the Low projection would require additions between 1960 and 2000 of 32 million units (or again 800,000 per year on the average), 47 million (or 1.2 million per year) in the Medium, and 71 million (or 1.8 million per year) in the High projection. Here the Medium number of additions would be 50 per cent above the Low and one-third below the High projection. The highest likely increase would top the lowest by more than 100 per cent.

Under our Medium estimate, the average levels are not much different from what we have already been experiencing. We can then take care of our growing number of households with an average annual addition of only 1.2 million units between now and the end of the century—similar to the rate at which we have added them over the past decade, though the actual numbers would be lower at the start and higher towards the end of the period.

This estimate needs to be raised somewhat for the reason that there is not exactly one dwelling unit in existence for each household. Instead, at all times a certain number of units are unoccupied, or vacant—and the vacancy rate is going up. In recent years, this has been partly because we have had an easier housing supply, the cumulative effect of the large volume of residential construction in recent years, which has not only provided for the growing number of new households, but dealt with much of the Depression-born and War-aggravated housing shortage. More important for the long run, however, is the fact that Americans have started along the road toward not only the two-car, but the two-house family. Not many families as yet have a country home and a town house, or even a winter home and a summer cottage, but the trend is there and it means that the vacancy rate—which includes unavailable as well as available units—is rising. In the earlier part of the century, something

like 3 or 4 per cent of all dwelling units were normally vacant, and nearly all of these were available for rent or sale. At the time of the Census Bureau's *1956 National Housing Inventory,* almost 10 per cent of all dwelling units were vacant, but less than one-third of them (about 3 per cent of all dwelling units) were on the market.

According to our Medium projection, about 5 million more dwelling units will be required in the year 2000 than would be needed if the vacancy rate remained what it is today. This would increase the annual construction need between now and then by about 10 per cent.

Much more important than vacancy rates in projections of future construction is what one assumes with regard to replacement demand—the rate of disappearance both of existing houses and of those yet to be built. The statistics of the last decade offer little guidance, and the statistics of the last several decades, if we take them at face value, can be downright misleading.

The concept of "net disappearance" of dwelling units does not cover a simple matter of houses becoming old and being demolished. Many dwelling units are demolished prematurely, in terms of serviceability, to make room for highways, office buildings, apartment houses, and other structures. Many others, like trailers and shacks, are temporary to begin with and often (but not always) are quickly scrapped or abandoned. Disappearance also occurs as the result of migration, which frequently means abandoned units, deteriorating to the point where they are lost to the housing supply.

Even demolition and abandonment do not tell the whole story. Dwelling units are lost through disaster—an estimated 40,000 a year from fire, flood, and windstorm.[1] Some are converted into rooming houses (not counted as dwelling units), stores, and offices. They are lost by merger with other units—as when two apartments are turned into one, or when basement apartments are turned into recreation rooms, and so on.

1. See Forest Service, *Timber Resources for America's Future,* Forest Resource Report No. 14 (Washington: U.S. Department of Agriculture, 1958), p. 377.

Obviously, these losses are to some degree balanced by gains. Units are not only merged, they are subdivided. Stores, garages, barns, and other buildings, or parts of them, are converted to residential use. Rooming houses have individual cooking facilities added and become tenements.

The *1956 National Housing Inventory* for the first time gave us a rough picture of the details of such change. The net disappearance of over 1½ million units between April 1950 and the end of 1956 was the result, on the one hand, of some 1 million demolitions, 700,000 mergers, and 1½ million losses through abandonment, disaster, and conversion, and, on the other hand, of 700,000 additions through subdivision and 900,000 from conversion of non-dwelling unit structures or quarters to individual dwelling use. On the supposition that all of the various conversions and mergers approximately canceled each other out, the 1½ million net loss is probably a fair approximation of the numbers disappearing either because of old age or because of prior demolition or abandonment.

About the only reasonably reliable set of statistics for earlier years is that on the total stock of dwelling units which, with a deduction for vacancies, has to approximate the total number of households. Attempts have been made in the past to approximate net disappearance for non-farm dwelling units, using as a guide the series on housing starts long maintained by the U.S. Bureau of Labor Statistics. Not only does this omit farm units but, judg-

ing from the evidence of the *1956 National Housing Inventory* as well as a revised survey of housing starts inaugurated by the Census Bureau in 1960, it seriously understates non-farm construction as well. It does not even attempt to include trailers and other non-permanent units which, even in normal times, account for some 2 or 3 per cent of new construction and in the Depression years may have surpassed 25 per cent.

We do have some clues, however, from which we have reconstructed an approximate picture, shown in Figure 4–2.

There is little apparent consistency in the figures shown in Figure 4–2, other than that at all times within the period (except 1956–60) the number of additions to stock has exceeded the number of replacements. Beyond that, it is clear that the levels of housing construction are profoundly affected by the vicissitudes of wars and business cycles, and that when the need for net additions runs high, replacement demand tends to be postponed. From an analysis of the age distribution of dwelling units as given in the 1940 and 1950 Censuses and in the *1956 National Housing Inventory*, and from a comparison with the numbers of occupied dwelling units which earlier censuses tell us existed in the past, we can, however, piece together some crude "life tables" for dwelling units and deduce some of the elements of past events.[2]

During the Depression decade, construction

2. For detailed calculations and derivations see Appendix Tables A4–5 and A4–6.

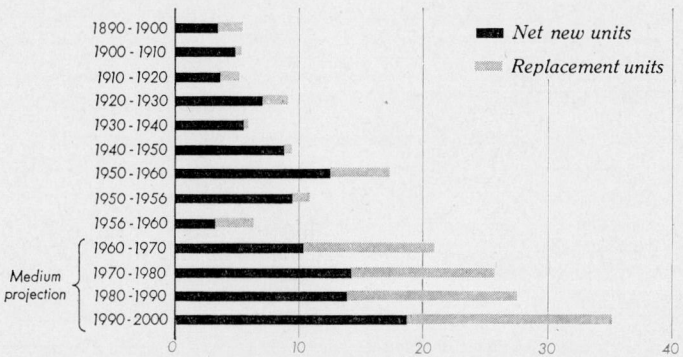

Figure 4–2. A record of new residential construction, 1890–1900 to 1956–1960, with Medium projections to 1990–2000.

was low and attention to replacement demands was minimal. A great many makeshift units were constructed to take care of the needed expansion for new households, but this did not keep the housing stock from aging significantly. By 1940, the average house was about 30 years old. In the War years, attention to replacement needs was again minimal, so that even the first flush of postwar building was insufficient to keep the average age of houses from rising further, to about 35 years in 1950. (This is partly because first priority appears to have been given to the replacement of makeshift War and Depression housing, rather than of older structures.) Since 1950, new construction has kept up with current aging, so that the stock has remained around the 35-year level.

It is assumed in our Medium projection that future rates of replacement will be such as to start to bring down the average age of the housing stock: to about 30 years by 1970 and 25 years by the end of the century, at which level a kind of equilibrium appears to be in prospect. This projection has as its necessary hypothesis the supposition that there will not be much change over the next several decades in the typical kinds of houses we live in, at least not in their durability; it also supposes that mortgage credit and other background conditions will permit the continued elimination of older units at rates characteristic of the past few years. Of the two conditions, the former is the more dependable, for most of the units which will be in use even as late as 1980 are already on the scene today. Close to half of the units in use at the end of the century will have been built before 1980, and it would take a much more rapid introduction of change into residential building methods and materials than has ever occurred before for the characteristics of new housing construction to change very much within the next two decades.

It is, of course, possible that the foregoing conditions will not hold. If, for example, despite the aging of the housing stock, it proves impossible for the construction industry and its credit facilities to keep up both with the heavy need for net additions and that for replacement, mature stock may disappear at a net annual rate of as low as 1½ per cent, instead of the 3 per cent which we have estimated to be the current (and long-run) norm. This might also occur if there is continued substantial subdivision of units and if the units are widely repaired and restored, instead of being totally eliminated. At the other end of the scale is the possibility that a high rate of income growth might accelerate the rate of abandonment and demolition of the near-million units which were classified by the 1956 Housing Inventory as "dilapidated" and the 8½ million more which lacked either a private toilet or bath or hot running water. The heightened new construction might then mean the more rapid introduction of new methods and materials (see the discussion later in this chapter) and eventually the advent of "annual model" houses. It is clear that housing is one area not in the past given over to revolutions, but it is conceivable that its pace could be quickened, assisted perhaps by a far-reaching urban renewal program, to the point where the replacement of mature stock would take place at a rate as high as 5 per cent per annum and where, by the end of the century, fully two dwelling units out of three would be no more than two decades old.

The importance of the three different assumptions for replacement demand is clear. Compared with the 10½ million replacement units required over the next decade under the Medium assumption, 16 million would be required under the High assumption and only 5 million under the Low. By the final decade of the century, when the Medium replacement demand had risen to 16½ million, the High would have reached 25½ million, but the Low would be less than 9 million. More of this range is due to the rate of replacement demand than to the size of housing stock. For example, applying the High disappearance rate to the Low 1990 stock, would still produce a replacement need of as much as 19 million in 1990–2000, compared with 25½, when applied to the High stock; but applying the Low disappearance rate to the High 1990 stock would reduce the need, even at those high population levels, by nearly half, to some 12 million.

Non-residential Construction

Non-residential new construction accounts for nearly two-thirds of total construction, but no single sector is of outstanding importance. Highway construction, amounting to about $5½ billion in 1960 (compared with housing's $22½ billion), is among the larger categories along with public utility construction ($5¼ billion), commercial facilities ($4¼ billion), schools and hospitals ($3¼ billion), and private institutional construction ($3¼ billion). General industrial construction, at less than $3 billion, is a scant 5 per cent of new building activity.

In general, non-residential construction shows a slightly slower rate of growth than does housing. Whereas the latter is projected to increase by roughly 140 per cent between now and 1980 and by nearly as much again between 1980 and 2000, non-residential construction may be expected to increase by only 20 per cent in the former period and little more than double in the latter. Fastest growing—at least between now and 1980—is highway construction, whose tempo may be expected to respond to the heavy appropriations of the new Federal Interstate Highway Program. Especially rapid growth may also be expected—for as long as the cold war persists—in the construction of military facilities and related governmental industrial enterprises.

A little more than half of all non-residential construction is financed privately and a little less than half, publicly. Because of rapid expansion in highways and military installations (launching sites, etc.) this relationship will probably be gradually reversed. (See Figure 4–3.)

In projecting these various sectors of the economy, the general rule followed has been to tie the dollar amounts to time series to which they seem to bear both a logical and statistical relationship and to estimate their future course in some proportion to that series. For example, private industrial construction, i.e., building of factories and other processing facilities, is linked to a series on investment in manufacturing, projected elsewhere in this study and, on the basis of the historical record, is assumed to rise slightly better than in proportion. Or, construction of institutional and miscellaneous buildings is tied to population growth, at a rate rising significantly faster than population; utility construction is based on utility gas and power sales, and so forth. One of the largest single items, highway construction, is projected on the basis of highway miles travelled by automobiles and trucks, with highway construction rising faster than miles travelled. While this reflects merely a statistical ratio, the underlying reason would be large-scale renewals of existing highways and additions of new ones, most of them wider and generally more costly than in the initial era of highway building.

This procedure carries many hazards. The relationship between the construction series and the reference series to which it is tied may be tenuous to begin with, or it may become so in the future. In addition, the projected changes in the relationship between the two, the coefficient, may not behave as the past, aided by reasoning, suggests. Nonetheless, there are at present no more reliable ways of estimating the future values of the various construction activities.

Maintenance and Repair

"Maintenance and repair" amounts to one-fourth of all construction activities in value, and at the end of the century it will still constitute, according to our Medium projection, around one-fifth (see Table 4–1). Distinguished from "alterations and additions" only by a shadowy margin, it is not part of the construction activities included under this label in the investment accounts of the gross national product, but its resources significance is nonetheless real.

The relative decline in maintenance and repair is largely a function of the relative increase in new housing. With the high rate of new residential construction gradually reducing the age of housing stock, it is to be expected that the proportionate amounts devoted to maintenance and repair will tend to decrease. About 40 per cent of all maintenance and repair activity is currently applied to residential structures; according to our Medium pro-

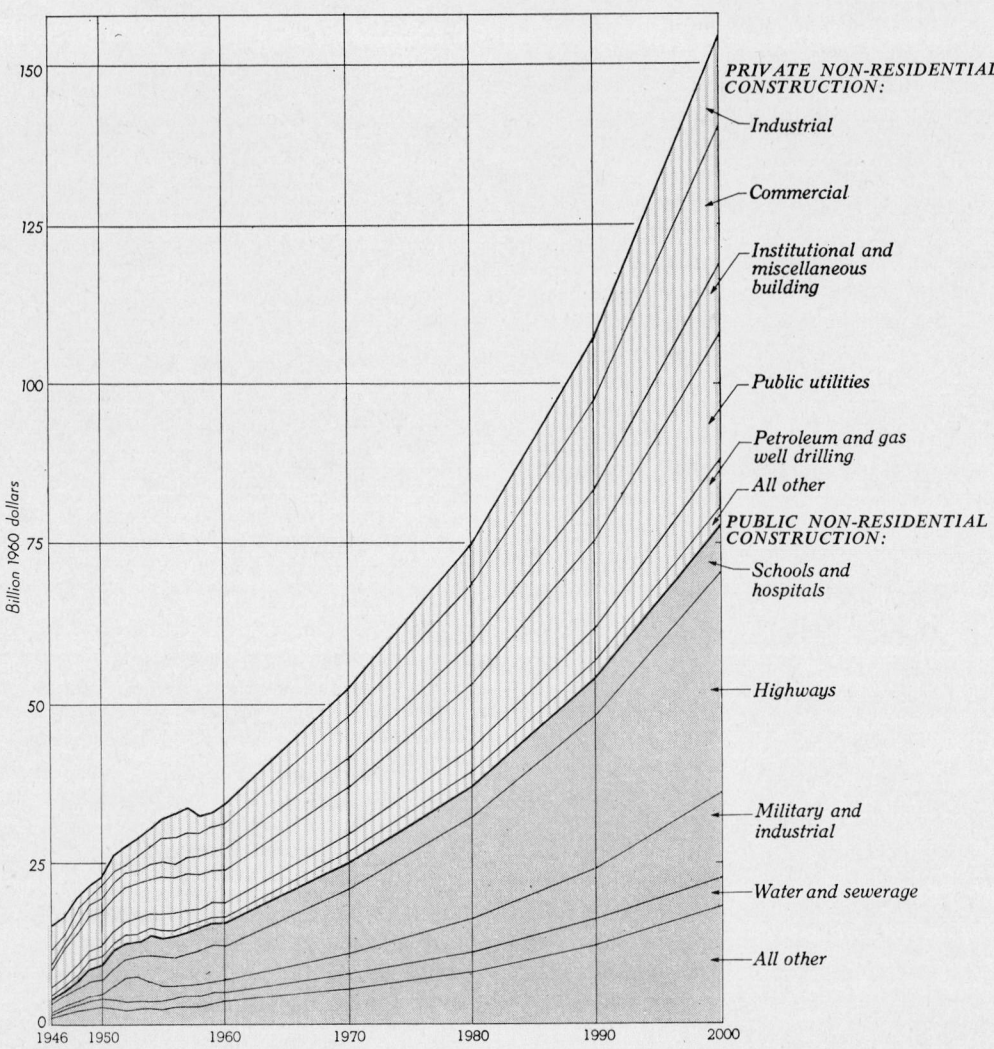

Figure 4–3. Principal categories of non-residential construction, private and public, 1946–1960 and Medium projections to 2000.

jection, the century-end percentage will be more likely half that much. In terms of residential construction, this means that for every three dollars now spent on new residential construction, at least one is spent on keeping existing houses in good repair. Forty years from now, it should be more nearly one against eight.

Materials and Methods

The historical record of construction in terms of dollar values or numbers of new buildings, and the likely trends in population and consumer income, are the chief elements in projection of future demands upon natural resources. But they are not the only ones. Methods of construction and choice of building materials also are important, and here simple projections of past performance can often be an untrustworthy guide to the future. Although construction technology, especially in home building, is relatively slow to change, some significant departures from tradition are under way in both methods and materials and must be taken into account in projecting requirements for particular resource materials. Some of the important trends and possibilities that are already clear are discussed below.

Materials for Construction

In weight and in volume (although not in value), more materials have to be mined, quarried, harvested, and moved to build our homes, roads, schools, bridges, pipelines, dams, etc., to outfit them with plumbing, electricity, heating, and fixtures, and to keep them maintained and in good repair, than are required for any other type of activity. Construction, directly or indirectly, uses up the overwhelming bulk of our lumber, virtually all of our cement, clay, stone, asphalt, and gypsum, half of our steel, and about a third of our copper and aluminum. It is above all because of their importance in the national economy that we shall direct our attention mostly to the "big three"— steel, lumber, and cement. We shall not ignore, however, the materials for which, if they are not so important in construction, construction is an important end-use. The ways in which construction materials are used in general also merit review, to illuminate trends and possibilities for substitution.

Building construction of all kinds uses materials for roughly the same purposes and according to the same general requisites. If we divide buildings, regardless of purpose, into large and small, each of the two groups becomes even more homogeneous in the uses to which construction materials are put. The other important construction categories— like electric power, highways, oil and gas lines, railways, etc.—have requirements which are more special for each, although some of the functions which construction materials must fulfill in each of these cases are the same as they fulfill in buildings.

The use of construction materials falls into five general classes: (1) structural, (2) architectural, (3) ancillary, (4) specialized, and (5) indirect. The first two have to do with the structures as such. The third comprises the materials utilized in structures, but which are not integral parts of them, such as the heating, plumbing, electrical wiring, and elevators in buildings, and the railings, lampposts, etc., that might be installed on bridges and highways. The fourth group includes such restricted applications as the firebrick used for the lining of blast furnaces and the lead or concrete shielding in atomic reactors. The last comprises materials used in construction—like scaffolding and concrete formwork, but which do not become even auxiliary parts of the final structure. In terms of volume, the first two categories are the important ones, and it is these which we therefore primarily consider.

Since structures are designed to support not only people, furniture, machinery, moving vehicles, etc. (live load), but also their own weight (dead load), it is important not only that structural materials be strong, but that they have a favorable strength-to-weight ratio. This is also important from the materials-handling standpoint. Because there are usually wide differences among the individual specimens of any material, the allowable working stresses of structural members are smaller, sometimes much smaller, than their average ultimate breaking strength. The more uniform the different specimens of any material, however, the more this safety factor can be reduced. Another important characteristic is thermal expansion, or volume changes relative to changes in temperature. This is particularly important when different materials are to be used in conjunction with one another.

At the opposite end of the scale from these structural characteristics is appearance—a purely architectural characteristic. Color and texture and sometimes ease of cleaning may have no significance at all from the standpoint of structural soundness, but they still condition the choice of materials in particular circumstances.

Of mingled structural and architectural significance are such characteristics as durability (resistance to dampness, frost, corrosion, and wear), fire resistance, and electrical, thermal, or acoustical conductivity.

Next to the consideration of how well particular materials fulfill the physical and aesthetic roles intended for them, the most important factor determining their relative use is cost. Three different kinds of cost-saving technological development have a bearing upon the selection and relative use of different kinds of construction materials: the technology of their manufacture, which may reduce their original cost; the technology of their transportation, which may reduce their delivered cost; and the technology of on-site handling and erection, which may reduce their in-place cost. For example, one of the reasons for the continued use of steel frames in tall buildings despite the technical feasibility of using a much cheaper material, reinforced concrete, is the expenditure involved in the erection of forms and shorings for concrete construction.

In addition, a conglomeration of factors—which includes such elements as design, tradition, custom, and institutional restrictions—has a very considerable bearing upon the relative use of different structural materials. Its effects are most felt in areas like residential construction, where tradition and style are strongest, and are of least consequence in fields like heavy construction (e.g., highways, dams, and railways), where aesthetic considerations are given less play. Particularly restrictive are the various municipal building codes, designed to protect the public against shoddy and unsafe structures, but which are so slow in being adapted to developing new technology that they seriously retard its application. A factor which may change this situation somewhat in the future is the increasing adoption of so-called performance codes, which specify not the materials to be used, but the performance requirements they have to meet.

Trends in Construction Methods

Especially with respect to large building construction, more and more architects and builders have begun to exploit the endless possibilities of design opened up by new types of concrete construction, new alloys, composition, synthetic, and other new or improved materials. Buildings without corners; increased utilization of arches, domes, and shells; new colors and color combinations; new kinds of exterior coatings; pre-colored panels; cable-suspended roofs—these are only a few manifestations of the revolution in style.

If this trend away from the conventional, combined with increased stress on off-site fabrication of components, were to make substantial inroads into home building, there could be radical changes in the consumption of construction materials, but so far, there is no evidence of any rapid movement in this direction.

More than four out of five new residential units in the United States are built in the form of small, one-to-four-family structures, of which the great bulk, in turn, are one-family. From the technological viewpoint, such building (representing 35 to 40 per cent of the value of new construction, if one includes the structurally similar motels, small garages, stores, etc.) may be distinguished from large-building and long-span construction by the fact that the engineering problems encountered in erecting the frame are insignificant relative to the architectural considerations.

The major structural developments in home building since the war are (1) the beginning of a shift away from the wooden frame house (still four out of five houses) to masonry structures and to an even more limited extent to metallic frames and structural panels; (2) the increased sheathing of frame houses with insulation board, gypsum board, and plywood, instead of wood boards; and (3) a trend, in some areas, toward brick veneer and brick-wood combination facing. All-plastic and all-aluminum homes are still essentially in the experimental stage. The prefabricated home industry—a pioneer in new types of panel construction—ships only around 70,000 units a year, far less than the output of mobile homes and trailers.

Large buildings, like apartment and office buildings, industrial plants, warehouses, oil pumping stations, railroad terminals, etc., account for about 25 per cent of the value of new construction. The major structural materials used in this field are steel and concrete. Wood walls and loadbearing-masonry walls of bricks or blocks hardly ever appear in modern large-building frames, although non-loadbearing, so-called curtain walls of masonry have gained in popularity. Some of the late developments in design and method include (1) frequent use of enameled steel, aluminum, or plastic panels for curtain walls and spandrels (the space between the windows on successive stories); (2) thin-shell roof construction utilizing not only metal and concrete, but also plywood; (3) the reduction of concrete construction costs largely by on-site precasting operations; (4) the growing utilization of prestressed concrete, heretofore confined in the United States mostly to tanks, large-diameter pipes, runways, and highway bridges; (5) the development of the plastic design theory of working stresses, which reduces the amount of steel needed for framing; and (6) most recently, the accelerated development of many kinds of prefabricated sandwich panels, consisting of facings and a core, and intended mostly for use as curtain walls, but also usable in many cases as loadbearing walls in residential and other light structures, thus eliminating the need for most of the framing. The facings, ready to serve the purposes of an exterior wall on one side and an interior wall on the other, may be of metal, plastic, asbestos board, wood composition board, asbestos cement, plywood, or light-weight concrete. For the core material in these sandwiches, which is selected for its insulating properties, plastic foam (polystyrene or polyurethane) seems to be the leading contender.

Flooring generally involves both the visible flooring and a subflooring. Most frame houses utilize boards for subflooring, but plywood is gaining ground. In buildings which use concrete beams, concrete flooring slabs are generally poured right along with the beams. Steel structures may be floored with poured concrete or with precast concrete or gypsum slabs.

Wood still is used for finish flooring in the living areas of about four out of five homes, although plastic tiles and other materials are gaining ground. In other lines of building there is a pronounced tendency toward the use of cement, ceramic, and plastic tiles, poured cement, terrazzo, and composition flooring like asphalt and magnesite (poured in a plastic state). The more successful resilient floor materials are asphalt, vinyl, cork, rubber tiles, and linoleum.

The outstanding single development in ceiling and interior wall construction is the gradual abandonment of plaster in favor of "dry-wall" (mostly gypsum board) construction in all types of building.

The current trend in home building toward flat, or low-pitched, roofs has led to a partial shift from tile, wood, and asbestos shingles to tar, asphalt rolls, and sheet metal as exterior roofing materials. The flat roofs of larger buildings are associated with concrete slabs, poured concrete, or sheet steel for their subsurface sheathing. Roofs of frame houses are likely to be underlain with wooden board, plywood, or composition decking.

Gutters and downspouts, once mostly galvanized steel, are increasingly being made of aluminum. Copper is used, too, and is still the standard material for flashings.

Trends in Individual Materials

In the subsequent sections of this chapter we analyze the likely effect of the various trends discussed above on future material requirements.

Iron and steel. Iron and steel find their way into construction in a large variety of shapes and forms, including pipe, galvanized sheet, rails, concrete reinforcing bars, nails and staples, plumbing fixtures, and decorative wrought iron. By far the largest single portion, however, enters as structural shapes and piling. (See Figure 4–4 and Appendix Table A4–9.)

As the toughest and stiffest of commonly used structural materials, steel's continued importance in construction would seem to be assured. Yet this may cease to be primarily in the form of structural shapes. In the construction of large buildings steel has the advantage of being relatively easily transported to the site and assembled. On the other hand, it corrodes rapidly and fails at high temperatures. These qualities imply additional costs of painting, maintenance, and fireproofing not present in steel's nearest competitor, reinforced concrete.

Technological advance, at the moment, seems to be favoring reinforced concrete. But steel research has made progress. The plastic design theory of continuous framing was fi-

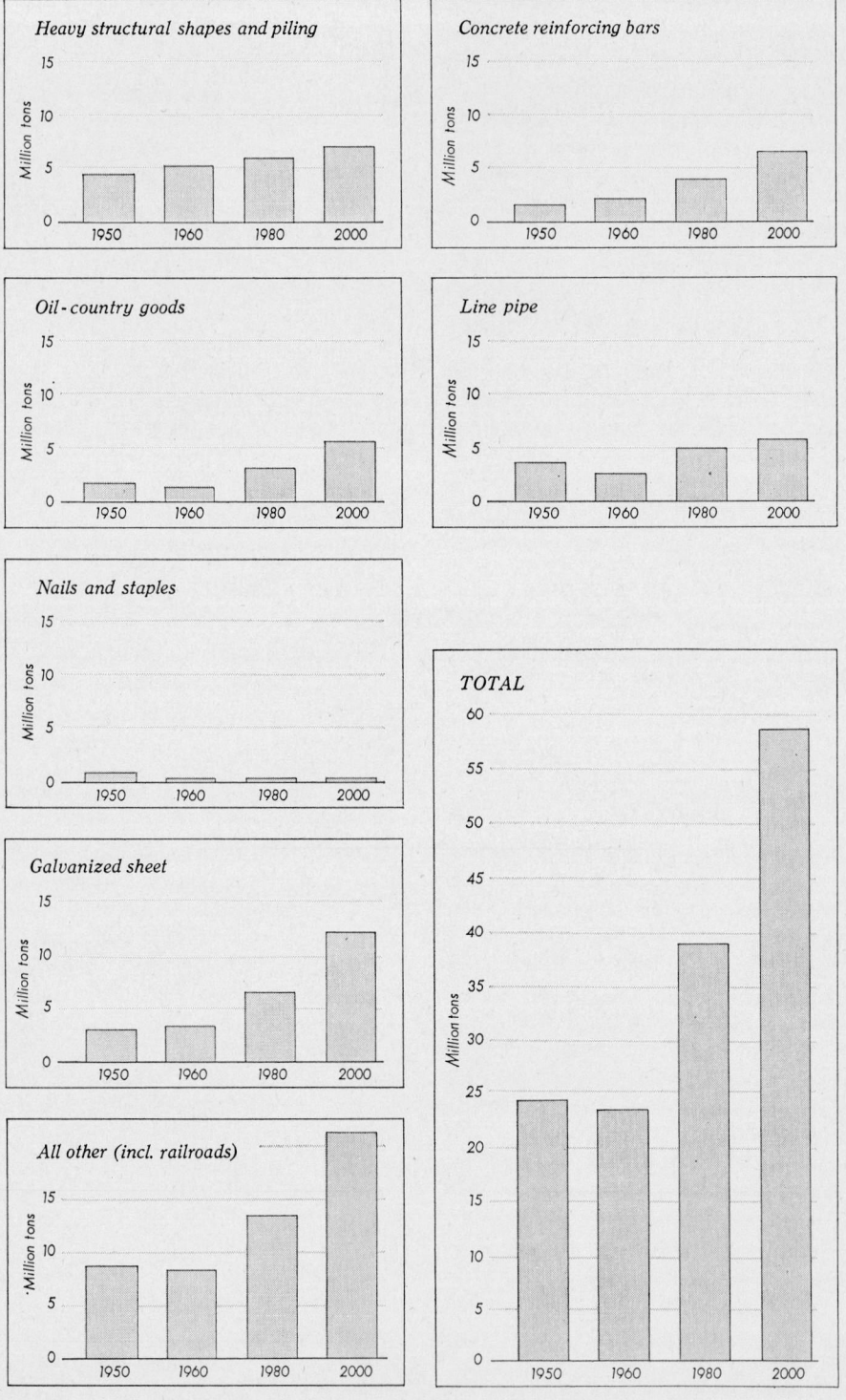

Figure 4–4. Principal uses of steel in construction, 1950, 1960, and Medium projections for 1980 and 2000.

nally perfected only a few years ago. Replacing the conventional elastic theory, it allows designers to take advantage of the reserve strength of steel beams and columns at portions not too heavily loaded. By permitting much higher working stresses, it would reduce the necessary amount and consequently cost of steel for a given structure. Such developments could very well retard, although they are not likely to reverse, the ascending role of concrete.

In smaller buildings, steel seems to be advancing its position only as light steel framing—a comparatively recent development, so far confined almost exclusively to prefabs. This means building the entire house frame out of light, copper-bearing steel members. The strength, durability, and speed of erection of such steel homes appear to counterbalance steel's greater original cost. Most of the steel going into residential construction, however, takes such forms as nails, staples, anchorage, windows and window frames, and heating, plumbing, and electrical equipment. Owing to the competition of aluminum, plastics, and ceramics, the relative importance of steel in a number of these applications seems likely to diminish.

On balance, the most likely course of events is for the relative use of steel structural shapes to decline, while that of concrete reinforcing bars rises. The growth of large building construction, however, may still be enough to sustain and even increase the aggregate use of steel structurals. Of the other large categories of construction steel, pipe for oil and natural gas production and distribution should be increasingly needed (though aluminum and plastics can be expected to make an impact), and galvanized sheet should also continue to increase in aggregate volume because of its role in heating, air conditioning, and guttering and roofing. Construction's use of steel in general should increase by more than half between now and 1980. At the upper range of possibilities, its use might nearly triple, and at a minimum it will more or less maintain its present level.

Wood. Because of its key role in residential construction, wood may be expected to do only slightly less well than steel. Although its relative cost has risen over the decades, it is still the most popular building material in the United States. Softwood enters the American home as framing, sheathing, siding, shingles, finishing panels, sash, and millwork; hardwood principally as flooring, panelling, and trim. In non-residential construction, wood serves as the most widely used material for concrete formwork, railroad ties, telephone poles, railings, fences, and many other uses. (See Figure 4–5 and Appendix Table A4–7.)

The principal advantages of lumber in construction are its ease of fabrication and of handling, its appearance, its low thermal conductivity, and its strength-to-weight ratio (which exceeds that of cast iron and equals that of the stronger concretes). Yet owing to its inherent weaknesses as an organic material, such as vulnerability to fungi and termites, its comparative lack of versatility from the standpoint of design, and its long-term rise in price relative to substitutes, the *relative* role of lumber as a building material has been steadily decreasing, and further substitution may be expected.

As a structural material in large building construction, wood has already been largely replaced by steel and concrete framing, brick or concrete walls, and concrete floors. This trend is likely to continue. On the other hand, wood framing is likely to retain its dominant position in the residential market, although yielding somewhat to steel, concrete, possibly aluminum, and sandwich panel type of construction.

The use of metal roof trusses is slowly reducing the amount of lumber required for roof structures, and for exterior surfacing wood is being increasingly replaced by brick veneer and by panels of such materials as asbestos, metal, and plastic. Dry wall construction and the use of gypsum plasterboard and of metal lath are also reducing the need for wood. A principal role for wood will probably continue in finished flooring, but there are recent trends toward substitution of composition and various types of synthetic materials even in living areas. Wood, as steel, is giving way to alumi-

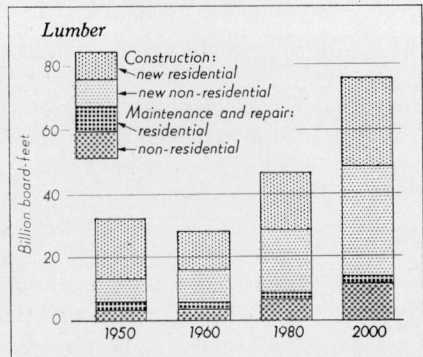

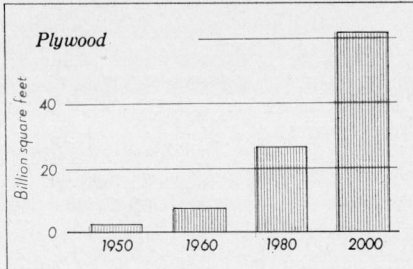

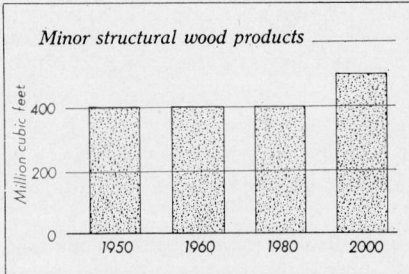

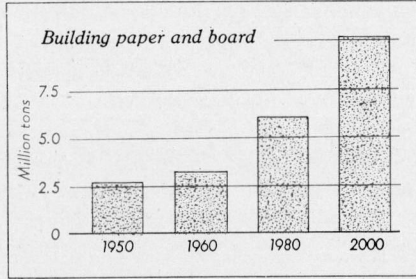

Figure 4–5. Principal uses of wood in construction, 1950, 1960, and Medium projections for 1980 and 2000.

num as the principal material for window frames, door frames, thresholds, trim, and other such applications.

In concrete construction the formwork will very likely shift from lumber to steel and plywood and eventually to plastics.

One element in the picture that may retard the trend away from wood is the apparently increasing popularity of plywood and of laminated structural members. Laminated wood arches, trusses, and roof systems have proved suitable for spanning distances up to 120 feet, and, because of their pleasing appearance, are currently in frequent use in the construction of churches, auditoriums, shopping centers, and the like.

Plywood, which in certain grades is stronger than lumber, may be substituted for lumber in almost any of its applications; it is already widely used in subflooring, sheathing, interior paneling, concrete forms, etc., and may be expected to grow in total utilization at almost twice the rate projected for lumber. The implications for total timber requirements are examined in Chapter 13.

Concrete. Use of cement in construction is overwhelmingly in the form of concrete (see Appendix Table A4–10), which is a variable mixture of portland cement, fine aggregates (almost always sand), and coarse aggregates (crushed stone, gravel, cinder, slag, or whatever else is locally available). The proportions of these ingredients are determined by the particular use to which the concrete is to be put, but they are usually 1:2:4, cement thus being the minor component.

The fact that concrete is the most widely used building material is explained by its versatility, its high crushing strength relative to bricks and other types of masonry materials, its cheapness relative to structural steel, and the essentially ubiquitous character of its ingredients.

The principal uses of concrete in the United States are in dams, water tanks, pipes and sewers, heavy walls, piers, caissons, columns, and road and sidewalk pavements. It is also used in the form of precast masonry units, such as concrete blocks and cast stone, whose principal advantage over brick and structural tile is their cheapness.

Because of the low flexural strength of concrete, it is combined with steel in most of its structural applications—a combination made possible by the coincidence of their coefficients of thermal expansion. The amount of reinforcing steel—rods, wire, wire-mesh, etc.—needed for a concrete structure is only one-third to one-half the amount needed for a similar all-steel structure. In the United States, the potentialities of this type of construction are just beginning to widen its use beyond massive structures.

The principal drawbacks of reinforced concrete in its competition with structural steel are the time and costs of erection, even if one takes account of the painting and encasing of steel members. It is expensive to build and remove forms, shores, and scaffolds. Most of the recent developments in methods of concrete construction are somehow related to economizing on forms: (1) Instead of the conventional lumber and plywood, steel—and more recently, reinforced plastic—forms have been tried. Plastics are especially promising, inasmuch as they are smooth and easily handled, retain water, may be given unusual shapes, and may be reused fifteen to twenty times. (2) "Slip-form" pavers have been successfully employed in laying road pavements. (3) Precasting of concrete members has been used as a mass production device and to provide stronger and more uniform concrete, but introduces transportation problems. (4) So-called tilt-up and lift-slab construction has permitted walls, floors, and columns to be poured on a horizontal surface and then either tilted or lifted into place. (5) Reusable, adjustable-length steel trusses have eliminated the need for the multiple shoring that otherwise has to be placed under the usual built-up forms. The faster such form-saving processes are perfected and adopted by builders, the faster reinforced concrete is likely to spread as a structural material.

Another limitation of ordinary concrete is its low insulation value. For this reason concrete walls are sometimes of a non-loadbearing, sandwich type, consisting of a layer of insulating material cast between two concrete slabs. In this application, concrete is seriously threatened by other types of curtain walls, including other types of sandwiches. Another way to give concrete insulating properties is to make it with light-weight aggregates—vermiculite, expanded clay, and the like. In this form, it no longer has sufficient strength to be used for loadbearing purposes, although it has been successfully employed in long-span roof construction.

Prestressed concrete has gained importance as a construction material. The principle of prestressing is that, by compressing concrete and keeping it under compression, the tensile stresses caused by loads are neutralized. The compression is achieved by casting the concrete around stretched rods or cables, the tension on which is released as the concrete sets. A prestressed beam needs only one-fourth the weight of the steel and one-half the weight of concrete required to support the same load by an ordinary reinforced concrete member.

Although it had been intensively used in Europe, prestressing for structural purposes was introduced into the United States only about a decade ago. So far, its applications have been limited mostly to pipes, tanks, runways, and sometimes highway bridges. As manufacturers gain experience and manage to reduce the manufacturing cost, prestressing may become competitive with steel and with reinforced concrete construction.

On balance, the trend is more toward a substitution of concrete for other building materials than of other building materials for concrete. The use of portland cement should more than double in the next two decades, may conceivably triple, and at its lowest is expected to increase by at least one-third.

Nonferrous metals. Most of the nonferrous metals are related to construction only indirectly—as builder's hardware, gutters and downspouts, flashing material, electrical and plumbing fixtures, etc. The principal exception is aluminum, which shows signs of continuing increase in various architectural applications. While virtually every nonferrous metal is used in construction in some capacity, only for aluminum and copper is construction a major outlet.

Aluminum has the highest strength-to-weight ratio of commonly used construction materials, resists corrosion, has low installation and maintenance costs, and is pleasing in appearance. These properties explain its widespread and ever-increasing application (see Appendix Table A4–12). Owing to its relatively high conductivity, a large-scale use has been in electric power installations. Its recent gains in such applications as doors and windows, gutters and downspouts, thresholds and other interior finish, roofing, and curtain walls are well known. There is little doubt of aluminum's maintenance advantage.

Nonetheless, as a structural material aluminum is unlikely to replace steel to any significant extent in the near future. Although the duralumin type aluminum alloys have the same strength as structural steel with only one-third the weight, their rigidity is considerably less. Also, they are susceptible to electrolytic corrosion when in contact with other metals or with alkalies like concrete and plaster, and their resistance to fire is only half that of steel. Since, in addition, its cost is relatively high compared with that of steel, aluminum is confined to a limited range of structural uses—particularly those where low weight or high resistance to normal types of corrosion are of great importance. Instances of this are fire escapes, easy-to-handle aluminum trusses that make it possible to replace factory roofs without interrupting work, and bridges on soils of low weight-bearing capacity. In small home construction, light-steel framing seems to be a more promising substitute for wood framing or for loadbearing masonry than does structural aluminum, although aluminum—particularly for roof systems—is definitely within the range of possibilities.

Taken together, the inroads of aluminum into the construction field make it the fastest growing major building material. It also has the widest range of possibilities as we project it further into the future. Between a doubling and a tripling of its use over the next two decades is within reason, but a quintupling cannot be excluded. Nearly seven times the 1960 use is the most likely projection for 2000, but a use three times as high is an outside possibility.

Copper—much of it in the form of brass and bronze—enters construction as electrical conductors; door knobs, locks, and other hardware; window screens; flashing, cornices, and guttering; pipe and tubing; and as an ornamental material. In many of these applications it is competitive with aluminum, in others with lead and galvanized iron. Owing largely to its use in wire and cable, however, aggregate copper consumption for construction should about double over the next twenty years, and again by the end of the century. (See Appendix Table A4–12.)

Other materials. Most of the other construction materials not yet mentioned fall into the general category of *stone, clay, and glass products*. Although stone is one of the most ancient materials of all, its use today is confined mostly to facing applications and to such incidental applications as sills, lintels, and steps. The ultimate compressive strengths of granite, limestone, and marble are rather high, but so are their necessary safety factors. They have little resistance to frost, dampness, and abrasion. Even as facing material, they are being partly replaced by concrete.

The two familiar burned-clay products are brick and structural tile. Brick is still used in independent loadbearing walls, but its main applications are as a facing material (brick veneer), in curtain walls for larger concrete or steel-frame buildings, and for cavity walls, chimneys, fireplaces, etc. The structural strength of both brick and clay-tile walls depends more upon the composition of the mortar and the skill of the masons than on the inherent crushing strength of the materials. The popularity of structural clay tile has increased recently, owing to its strength-weight ratio, its insulating properties, and its fire resistance. Because of their shape, clay tiles are generally more easily handled than bricks. They are used as surfacing material for roofs, walls, and floors, to build light walls and partitions, and in the fireproofing of structural steel. Terra-cotta-type tiles are used for decorative purposes.

Glass, as a construction material, appears in such form as window panes, glass blocks, and fiber reinforcing for plastics. Since glass blocks share most of the advantages of structural clay in addition to being translucent, they may find increased application in the buildings of tomorrow, though their heat-transmission property creates a problem.

Other non-metallic structural materials of significance are *gypsum, asphalt, and asbestos,* frequently used in mixtures with one another or with cement. The most important (aside from the special use of asphalt in road paving) is gypsum, marketed in such forms as plaster, plasterboard (gypsum lath), tile, and wallboard. It is valuable as a light-weight material, with good insulating qualities and sufficiently strong for partitions and sheathing. Its present commanding position as an interior walling material does not seem to be seriously threatened.

Plastics, discussed in detail in Chapter 17, are of potential importance in construction. Already they are much used in floor and wall tiles. Another important application takes the form of glass fiber-reinforced paneling used for some kinds of roofing and in many other applications where the color potentialities and translucent qualities may be valued. In addition to this use, plastics will probably increase as the principal core material and an important surface material for the sandwich panels mentioned above, as a substitute for wood in concrete forms, as floor surfacing, and as surfacing material for blocks and tiles of other substances. Plastic glues, some of which have proven stronger in joining metal sheets to each other than have rivets, are used in cabinet work and in the making of plywood.

Finally, both copper and steel used in pipes and fittings are likely to find their plastic counterparts an acceptable and even preferable substitute, once building codes permit and building contractors adopt their use.

The large-scale adoption of plastics as an architectural material depends ultimately on the nature of the new varieties to be produced, the relative prices, and such unpredictable, but crucial, factors as building codes and architectural styles. Even as a structural material, their future is not as dim as it once appeared. Future technical breakthroughs such as the imparting of strength through irradiation might alter this prospect radically, but presumably not soon enough to make any significant impact in the next two decades.

chapter

5

TRANSPORTATION

TRANSPORTATION IS NOT WHOLLY AN END-PRODUCT. Nearly all freight transportation, for example, is an intermediate product that becomes a component of various end-products like food or durable goods. At the other extreme is the kind of transportation bought by those who, for their own personal purposes, board railways, buses, or airplanes, or drop their tokens into a rapid transit turnstile, or hail a taxi. This kind of transportation is a definite end-product, as is also, by convention, the service embodied in an automobile purchased by the household consumer. But personal transportation may also be a matter of business, just as freight transportation may become an end-product if it involves, say, the transport of personal baggage. For our purposes, however, it is less important to make such distinctions than to divide up the transportation field by kinds of transport, each of which has its own particular set of consequences for use of materials. Regardless of the way it is used, therefore, we examine each type of transportation as if it were an end-product, project it as such, and then proceed to evaluate its materials requirements.

Transportation makes up a significant portion of consumer purchases. Between purchased local, intercity, and foreign transportation and the current costs of operating automobiles, it takes about 8 per cent of the consumer's income. Purchase of his car (or cars) costs him, on the average, about 5 per cent more. Its real impact, however, is hidden in the final cost of food, clothing, housing, durable goods, and all the other end-products of current consumption and of investment which contain a transportation component. It has been estimated (by the Transportation Association of America, June 1962) that one-fifth of the final value of all the end-products and services of the U.S. economy is accounted for by transportation expenditures.

Nor is transportation any less important as a user of materials. As we shall see, it accounts for a large proportion of the consumption of nearly all our metals. Indirectly, through construction of transportation facilities, it accounts for a substantial proportion of the building materials that were discussed in Chapter 4. And finally, it accounts for one-fifth of the nation's consumption of energy.

RELATED MATERIAL: Appendix to this chapter, 635–68. Construction, Chapter 4, pp. 117–18, 124–25, and appendix, p. 632. Durable goods, Chapter 6, pp. 153–55, and appendix, pp. 672–79. Demand for fuel, Chapter 15, pp. 277, 288–92, and appendix, pp. 848–52; for metals, Chapter 16, pp. 293–316, and appendix, pp. 859–939; and for rubber, Chapter 17, pp. 320–25, and appendix, pp. 957–60.

In the appendix to this chapter the relationships between the different segments of transportation and other aspects of the economy—size of population, volume of production, etc.—are presented and carried forward as a means of projecting transportation volume. The projections in turn provide the starting point for estimating bills for materials needed to build vehicles and fuel needed to power them.

Much of what follows here is in the nature of illustration of situations and trends that were taken into account in making projections presented in the statistical appendix. There is no way to link all the future features of transportation to the numerical projections, but among them they provide the rationale which underlies the numerical part of the study.

Because motor vehicles represent the biggest single claimant upon structural materials and fuels, we begin with a discussion of the largest segment of road traffic, passenger transportation. Then we analyze freight transportation, land, water, air, and underground, and finally, material and energy requirements.

Passenger Transportation

There are three principal elements in the passenger transportation picture, all worthy of separate consideration: domestic intercity travel, intra-urban or metropolitan transportation, and the use of school buses. Each involves an appreciable amount of equipment and the fuel to run it. Foreign travel, while growing rapidly in importance, is a negligible factor in its call upon domestic resource commodities.

Automobiles. The most important mode of passenger transportation, the personal or family automobile, accounts for about 90 per cent of intercity passenger movement and about two-thirds of all commuting to work and other local movement. Much more satisfactory than analyzing it in terms of its share in intercity and intra-urban passenger traffic, however, is evaluating it in terms of trends in automobile ownership.

Less than fifty years have passed since the beginnings of the mass-produced automobile, and, indeed, it is only sixty to seventy years

since the very first vehicles powered by internal combustion engines gave a rather feeble hint of the potentialities ahead. It is useful to recall how drastically the "horseless carriage" has transformed this country's way of living, within a span of years not much longer than the four decades to which we look ahead in this study. Even Henry Ford, who very early foresaw the automobile's appeal to the masses, is not on record as having predicted our present automobile population of more than one per household. Since 1914, when 1.6 million cars were registered in the United States and annual production first exceeded 500,000, the number of automobiles has risen rapidly to almost 60 million. Registrations have doubled in the brief period since World War II.

It does not follow that a similar rate of growth is to be expected in the four decades to come. Obviously, while the U.S. economy has not yet reached the saturation which more than one prophet has predicted in the past, it is substantially closer to such saturation than it was even ten years ago. We can look forward, perhaps, to more and more two car and even three car families, but by the time there is an automobile for every adult (there is already one for every two), we can reasonably assume that a point of strong resistance—if not actual saturation—will have been reached.

Saturation, of course, would not mean an end to the production of automobiles. Even if the percentage of automobile ownership did not grow, the number of households would. More importantly, the automobile is not a very long-lived object. Out of an annual output now fluctuating around 6 or 7 million cars, it takes 4 or 5 million just to replace those that are scrapped. The used car scrapper may be several ownerships away from the new car buyer, but his replacement needs inevitably travel through the chain of marketings back to the assembly line.

To project realistically the total stock of automobiles in use is an exceedingly difficult problem, for it is governed by many influences. Income plays a major role. Even if—thanks to installment credit and the almost universal tendency to regard the automobile as a necessity—ownership is spread throughout all income classes, it still progresses from 33 per cent among families at the lowest levels (under $1,000 a year) to 95 per cent among those with incomes of $10,000 and above. Second car ownership increases from 1 per cent in families at the lowest levels to fully 39 per cent among those in the $10,000-plus bracket. Thus, as time goes on and families move up the income scale, ownership—particularly of second cars—is bound to increase.

But income is not the only influence. Westerners own more cars per family than Easterners, and the population is moving west. Only one out of eight suburban families is without a car; one out of five such families owns two cars. One may say that suburban living and rising incomes go together, but what would be the result if there should develop a substantial "back to the city" movement of high income groups in years to come? Or what if new kinds of commuter transit systems, such as we describe below, in the section on common carriers, are developed? Another question is raised by the prospect of the increased use of rental automobiles—on call, perhaps, at each suburban apartment project. Fuller utilization of each vehicle under such circumstances would cut down the total stock required as well as space needed for parking and storage.

Likely to be of increasing importance in the future is the development of new types of automotive vehicles. While the trend has for some time been toward standardization of the automobile, with the apparent heterogeneity really consisting of surface variations upon relatively few basic types, a reversal of trend, spurred by the success of European cars and confirmed by the advent of the American compact car, seems to have set in. Will it last, and does it indicate the development of separate types of vehicles for long distance and for local travel? Such a distinction already is common in the vehicles owned by two and three car families, in terms of relative condition, if not size. Diversification may spread further: small, economical vehicles may appear on the streets in increasing variety and numbers; the appeal of sports cars has been more than demonstrated.

Looking further ahead, some foresee "land cruisers" equipped with magnetic or other controls which permit driving at speeds normally exceeding 80 or 90 miles per hour. Patents have already been applied for and prototypes of such cars have already been built. Another prospect is for the advent of the "auto-plane," a combination land-air vehicle safe to use in congested areas and taking little more skill to operate than that now possessed by the average driver. Again, some of the prototypes have been built.

Thus, what we are talking about when we refer to future ownership of automobiles is really the ownership of "user-operated vehicles." We can do little more than guess what these vehicles will look like beyond a decade or so—whether they will be confined to the ground or roam above it, ride on air bubbles (again, the prototype is in existence) or rubber tires, loom large and low or small and compact. In the materials evaluation that is the purpose of this book, this lack of knowledge is a serious drawback, but in projecting vehicle ownership, it does not make too much difference. Rising incomes, increased distances between home and place of work, more leisure, and the prospects for differentiation in types of vehicles are all objects of trends which may be relied upon with a high degree of confidence, and, considered in the light of the past, they promise increased numbers of vehicles, whatever shape they may take. Even if the firmly established pattern of family ownership should yield to rental or other arrangements, more and more vehicles will still be around in relation to the number of adults, for the "drive yourself" habit is too firmly ingrained in American life for even four decades to work much of a change.

Our projections, therefore, suppose that, in extension of a trend that carried the number of adults per car from 2.8 in 1950 to 1.9 in 1960, by 1980 there will be one owner-operated vehicle for every 1.3 adults and perhaps as many as one for every 1.1. By the end of the century, more than one vehicle for every adult is a definite probability, and we may have as many as three vehicles for every two. As a minimum, on the other hand, given a local transit revolution of the kind we refer to below, plus the interest in using air and improved rail transportation for the longer distances, there could quite conceivably be a marked slowing of the increase in automobile ownership, so that a car for every .94 adults may be as far as we go.

Coupling the different assumptions on possible rates of population growth with these ownership rates creates a substantial degree of uncertainty as to our future automobile stock, especially at the end of the century, for an adult population half of which is not yet born. The projected numbers, compared with today's level and that of twenty years ago, are as follows (with adults per car in parentheses):

	1940	1960		1980	2000
			L	114	199
				(1.3)	(.94)
Total stock of user-operated vehicles (in millions)	36 (3.3)	59 (1.9)	M	120 (1.3)	243 (.85)
			H	144	372
				(1.1)	(.65)

This is only half the story, however. The stock of automobiles gives us some clue as to current fuel requirements, but to determine what this future stock means for the steel, copper, aluminum, zinc, etc. that go into automobiles—and, next to construction, automobile manufacture is the largest single metallics consumer (see Chapter 16)—we also have to know how many will be built each year. Since, as noted above, more are built each year to replace those scrapped than to provide additions to stock, we are concerned with the extra uncertainty of not knowing how long today's and tomorrow's automobile will last. These are problems akin in many respects to those which we encountered in the projection of construction, another durable service item.

The average life of an automobile, according to scrappage figures for 1956, is about eleven years. (It used to be less.) Not all automobiles leave active service exactly at the end of eleven years, however; half a million cars of prewar vintage are still around, not a few of which date back to the twenties. Automobiles, like human beings, have different life spans; the number of "deaths" in any one year depends not only on the mortality that is specific to each age but on the current age distribution of the automobile population. As we did with

houses, we have used a kind of mortality, or attrition, table for automobiles, applying this not to automobiles manufactured in single years but to groups manufactured in each succeeding five-year period, and then summing for each age group the deaths for successive periods to obtain aggregate replacement need. The method has utilized for each projection level a single attrition rate, which we assume sets in after the car gets to be five years old (cf. Appendix Tables A5–4 and A5–5). Additional refinement seemed neither feasible nor indicated.

For our Medium projection, we have assumed an attrition rate which is equivalent to keeping the average lifetime of automobiles at about eleven years. For the Low projection— i.e., the projection that minimizes new car production—we assume that automobiles are replaced, on the average, after twelve years, and for the High projection, after nine years. All of these periods refer to the total lifetime of the automobile, which may involve several owners. While "antique" automobiles will still have their appeal (and our Medium projection provides for as many as 300,000 pre-1960 curiosities still on the streets in the year 2000), it is unlikely, in view of the hard life of most automobiles and of their rapid obsolescence, that average lifetimes of more than twelve years are much of a possibility. Conversely, while technological change and the modern tendency toward more and more "throwaway" articles may shorten the lives of user-operated vehicles, their purchase will still constitute an important enough expenditure that abandonment of half of all automobiles in less than 7½ years (equivalent, roughly, to the nine-year average age of the High projection) seems unlikely.

The wide range in replacement demand which even this limited range of assumptions gives us is shown in Table 5–1.

Clearly, the size of the future American automobile industry is hard to pin down. It could double its present size by 2000, or be ten times as large. If our Medium projection expresses the path of highest probability, the most likely rate of growth is one which is roughly commensurate with the over-all growth of the U.S. economy: an increase of 300 per cent by 2000.

TABLE 5–1. Purchases of Automobiles, 1950, 1955, 1960, and Projections to 2000

(Million vehicles)

Year and projection	Replacement demand (= abandon-ment and scrappage)	Net addi-tions	Total domestic purchases
1950	2.7	3.8	6.5
1955	4.0	3.7	7.7
1960	5.0	2.0	7.0
Low			
1970	5.9	2.8	8.7
1980	7.5	3.6	11.1
1990	9.4	4.2	13.7
2000	11.5	5.4	16.9
Medium			
1970	6.7	3.1	9.8
1980	9.6	4.4	14.0
1990	13.6	6.1	19.7
2000	19.5	9.3	28.8
High			
1970	8.3	4.2	12.6
1980	14.9	6.7	21.6
1990	27.8	11.1	38.9
2000	54.7	19.0	73.7

Sources: Historical data from Appendix Table A5–1. Projections are based on five-year averages from Table A5–3, although only the ten-year intervals have been reproduced; discrepancies in addition are due to rounding.

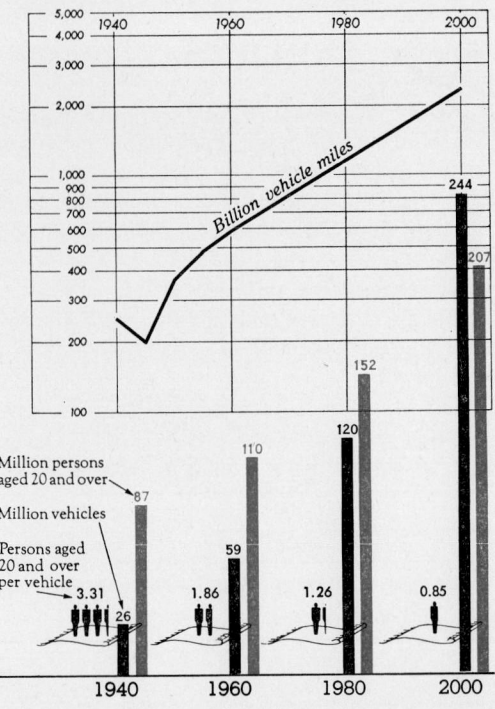

Figure 5–1. Stocks of owner-operated vehicles, vehicle ownership, and vehicle miles traveled, 1940, 1960, and Medium projections for 1980 and 2000.

Figure 5–1 portrays the Medium projection of vehicle miles, stock, and spread of ownership.

To some extent, the uncertainty is mitigated by the narrower ranges possible in value of production (and correspondingly, use of materials). A comparison of projected personal consumption expenditures on automobiles with the projected number of vehicles purchased shows (see Chapter 1 and Appendix Table A5–2) the low level of purchases associated with more expensive vehicles, representing, one might suggest, increasing average size and/or more complex equipment. In contrast, the high level of purchases is associated with a slight decrease in the average value of cars, an assumption consistent with the notion that such high purchases could come about only through heavy ownership of second and third cars, of relatively small size and shorter life. In the Medium projection, expenditure and number bought move together, implying an unchanged

value for automobiles. These relationships are utilized below in estimating use of materials.

Intercity transportation. Of the common carrier means of transportation, the airways already provide the largest share, measured in terms of passenger-miles, slightly edging out both railways and buses, which are now approximately on a par. The airlines actually carry far fewer passengers per year than do either railroads or buses, but they carry them on the average five or six times farther.

In the light of the potential ahead, air travel may be characterized as being in the stage of transition to the status of a mass transport industry. The two big questions regarding the future of air passenger transport are: (1) Will the airlines have only a major or an overwhelming proportion of the long-distance travel market? (2) Will they also make significant inroads into the short-haul market? Both questions reduce themselves to a matter of fares, equipment, and the influence of competitive forms of transport.

As for equipment, the industry has been in a state of flux for some time, and judgments as to the future are hard to reach. Large turbojets, originally thought of in terms only of long-distance hauls, are being introduced on medium hauls no longer reserved to the slower turbo-props. More and more powerful engines, including such new variations as the turbo-fan, which is rapidly being introduced, are being developed.

The airline industry can draw upon a huge past and prospective investment in military aircraft research and development. The large jets now in use are powered with engines directly evolved from those powering supersonic military aircraft. Such engines propel a four-engine, 120 to 180 passenger aircraft at high subsonic speeds, with operating costs per seat-mile, as the result of higher seating capacity and greater speed, comparable with those of large piston-engine planes.

If costs were the only consideration, the next line of development would probably be application of the same type of engine, perhaps in turbo-prop form, to an aircraft with three times the passenger-carrying capacity but somewhat lesser speed. Instead, the airlines are already looking ahead to supersonic planes. These may be powered by turbo-jets with afterburners, supplemented perhaps by ramjets ("pure" jets) for use at high altitudes. Speeds could vary from twice that of sound to four or five times. Aircraft producers have expressed confidence in their ability to build transports operating at three times the speed of sound by the mid-seventies or earlier, with no increase in seat-mile costs. Such planes could literally "beat the clock" from New York to California.

Given the time consumed in airport stops, none of these developments is significant for flight legs of less than 200 miles, and given the time consumed in ground transportation, check-ins, and schedule irregularities, none offers much for trips of less than 400 miles. If the airlines are to expand in this short-haul market, entirely different types of equipment need to be developed, such as the short-take-off and vertical-take-off-and-landing planes. The latter type includes the helicopter (which is also getting to be jet-powered), but is not limited to it. One research design, for example, utilizes jet engines which pull straight up for take-off and then swivel on their mountings to drive the plane forward. As in the long-haul market, airline gains in the intermediate and perhaps even the short-haul market would seem to depend upon the development of larger and larger planes, and equally of ground facilities that can cope with the increasing volume and technical requirements, and do so under conditions of more frequent scheduling.

Our projections for the future take for granted that the airlines will more and more displace surface transportation means from the long-haul market. The principal question concerns the shorter hauls, where a revitalized rail passenger transport could prosper if the airline industry's efforts go predominantly into long-distance flying.

At a minimum, we may expect the average citizen to be traveling twice as much by air in 1980 as the 192 miles yearly he does now and three times as much by the century's end. More likely is an increase of 130 per cent in the next two decades, to 440 miles per capita, followed by a 55 per cent increase in the two decades thereafter, to 680 miles. Coupled with population growth, this increase means expansion from the present 35 billion passenger miles to a likely 108 billion by 1980 and 225 billion by 2000. The rate of gain could be as much as 50 per cent greater, but not much smaller. Table 5–2 shows the assumptions that we have made regarding travel by air and other media, and Figure 5–2 charts the Medium results of our assumptions.

The basis for these projections is laid out in detail in the Appendix to Chapter 5; in a few words, most of the increase in airline traffic will come about simply because people will have the income and the desire (partly because it is increasingly convenient) to travel more. Some of it, however, is bound to be at the expense of surface transportation. Here the past is a good guide. Despite the considerable rise in incomes and the improvements in intercity travel since 1910, the travel rate per capita on

TABLE 5–2.   Revenue Passenger Miles per Capita, 1950, 1960, and Projections for 1980, 2000

Transport medium	1950	1960		1980	2000
Rail	181	96	L	44	30
			M	55	55
			H	73	70
Bus	174	113	L	60	40
			M	79	55
			H	90	85
Air	66	192	L	400	600
			M	440	680
			H	480	760
Inland waterways	8	11	L	11	11
			M	11	11
			H	11	11
Total	429	412	L	545	721
			M	585	801
			H	625	881

L = Low projection   M = Medium   H = High.
Lows and Highs are not additive.

Source: Appendix Table A5–7.

rail and bus combined is well below the rail level of fifty years ago.

The short-haul market accounts for most of today's intercity surface passenger transport. The average ride is about 70 miles for bus (including some commuter traffic) and 125 miles for rail (excluding commuter traffic). Excluding both first class and commutation traffic, the average rail journey has been about 100 miles since 1950. Many U.S. towns have only rail or bus service, not both. An increasing number of areas are being served by bus alone; this is true of both older towns on discontinued rail passenger lines and new towns which have grown up in the motor vehicle age without rail connections.

Given this increasing confinement of surface common carrier transportation to the short-haul market, it is likely that in this field surface travel per capita between cities will fall, by the century's end, to one-half or less of what it is now. At best it will still decrease moderately. Only with the High assumption in per capita use, coupled with the High assumption of population growth, can there be any expectation of increased aggregate traffic of surface common carriers, amounting to a possible 78 per cent increase in the next forty years. More likely, as assumed in the Medium projection, there will be a slight decrease; or a drop to little more than half of today's aggregate level is possible.

The division of this probably declining traffic between rail and bus is much more problematical, depending largely upon whether rail passenger transport develops, as it well could, into a series of medium distance networks providing, say, 100-mile-an-hour transportation within the large urban regions which are de-

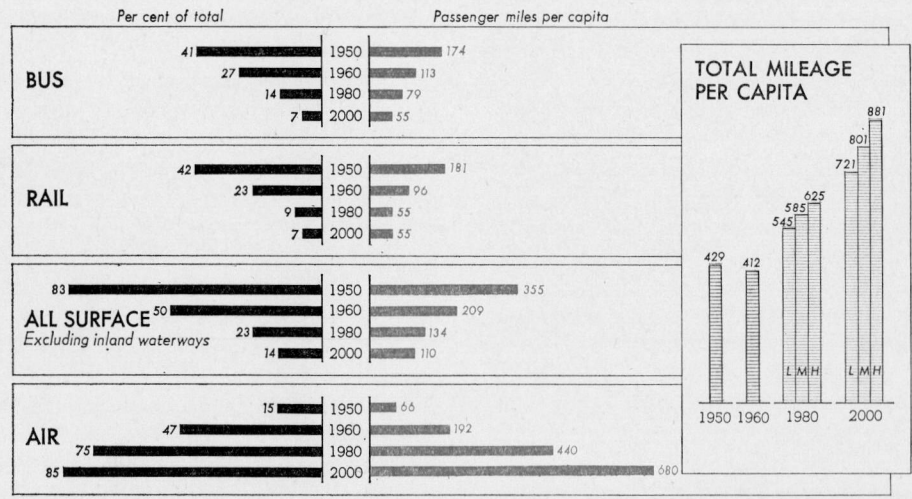

Figure 5–2. Passenger intercity mileage by common carrier, 1950, 1960, and projections for 1980 and 2000.

veloping in various parts of the country. The forms of this newer rail transport might or might not resemble the present binary-rail, locomotive-and-train system as we know it. Lightweight, high-speed, self-propelled cars or trains are a probable line of development, already under way. Also possible is some form of monorail. Super-high-speed railcars riding on air, instead of wheels, are being developed by the Ford Motor Company. Curtiss-Wright has designed a propeller-driven train which can accelerate and decelerate by reversing pitch and can negotiate hitherto impossible grades.

The exact division of traffic between rail and bus has only a limited bearing upon ultimate resource requirements. The kinds of materials used to construct new railway cars and buses are quite similar, as are the amounts needed per passenger. Diesel oil is, today at least, the common fuel of both trains and buses. Rubber, of course, plays a larger role in road than in rail transport, and highway maintenance needs differ from those of railroad tracks, but these are minor differences in terms of total raw material demand.

Because it is valuable, nonetheless, to have at least a rough notion of the breakdown between bus and rail, we have projected their individual shares, as shown in Table 5–3. On the assumption that rail transport will at least in part develop along the lines suggested above, we arrive at a Medium projection for rail which declines slightly over the next two decades from today's aggregate level of 17 billion passenger miles, then recovers to that level by the end of the century. For bus, under such circumstances, we foresee as most likely a slow, continuing decline from today's 20 billion passenger miles to 18 billion by the century's end.

Other trends are possible for both surface and air passenger traffic, depending upon assumptions made regarding population and regarding the sharing of the market between surface and air and, on the surface, between rail and bus traffic. Table 5–3 shows the variations for key years.

Intra-urban transportation is likely to become a far different thing, as the years go by, from what it is today, at least as far as moving

TABLE 5–3. Passenger Transportation, 1950, 1960, and Projections for 1980, 2000

(Billion revenue passenger miles)

Transport medium	1950	1960		1980	2000
Rail	27.5	17.2	L	9.9	8.0
			M	13.5	18.2
			H	20.4	30.3
Bus	26.4	20.4	L	13.6	10.7
			M	19.4	18.2
			H	25.1	36.8
Air	10.1	34.6	L	90.4	160.8
			M	107.8	225.0
			H	133.9	329.1
Inland waterways	1.2	2.0	L	2.5	2.9
			M	2.7	3.6
			H	3.1	4.8
Total	65.2	74.2	L	123.2	193.2
			M	143.3	265.1
			H	174.4	381.5

L = Low projection   M = Medium   H = High.
Detail may not add to total because of rounding. Lows and Highs are not additive.
Source: Appendix Table A5–7.

between home and place of work is concerned. The spread of suburban living and the constant increase of commuting distances, the growth of satellite cities around major metropolises, and the agglomeration of some metropolises into super-metropolises—these are all trends either well in progress or visible on the horizon.

Within supercities, some form of short-haul air transport is not to be excluded as a commonplace of the future, for it is already a reality, albeit on a small scale (in the form of helicopter service and suburb-to-city air commuter service); but its economics are such that, while it might grow from its present level of insignificance, it is unlikely, at least in this century, to become a principal means of local transportation. Similarly, taxi service—air or ground—is unlikely ever to provide any large proportion of intra-urban transportation. What we are really concerned with, in essence, is local mass transportation, or the moving of very large numbers of the residents of a given area daily between their homes and work and, to a lesser extent, between one point and another on other missions within the urban area by means of local trains, street cars, and buses rather than by private automobile.

Despite their continuing loss of business to the private automobile, local transit systems still are the most important single element in the public passenger transportation picture— measured either in number of passengers carried or in total revenues. Together, transit system and railway commutation revenues are larger than those of the domestic airlines or than the combined revenues of intercity buses and railways. If taxicab fares are included, outlays for local travel on public vehicles are about as large as those for all intercity common carrier travel combined.

Slow, crowded public transportation systems and the clogged automobile traffic on urban streets are among the increasingly less pleasant aspects of contemporary American life. Widespread dissatisfaction has lead to a plethora of plans and programs and some action. Fundamental decisions are in process of being made in a number of metropolises, and an increasing pace of action to solve local transportation problems is a reasonable expectation. Many billions are destined to be spent—some of it federal money—either on highways and expressways or on mass transportation arrangements. The way this money is spent, particularly as it is divided between facilities for common carrier and for private automobile travel, will have a considerable bearing upon the shape of local transportation in the next few decades and the nature and magnitude of its call upon resources.

New York City represents one extreme in local transportation arrangements. Without its highly developed system of rapid transit, the city as we know it could not exist. Fewer than one out of five riders enter the New York business district by automobile. At the other extreme is a city like Los Angeles, with its network of multi-lane expressways, where more than three out of every four people get downtown in their private cars.

The trend, so far, is in the direction of the Los Angeles pattern. Over the last several decades, even New York has been gradually expanding its system of elevated roadways, belt highways, tunnels, bridges, and expressways, and the proportion of automobile traffic into Manhattan—especially since World War II

—has also been expanding. It is difficult to say which is cause and which effect, but it is clear that the new roads fill up with traffic almost as fast as they are built. The rapid postwar growth of suburban living, beyond the reach of rapid transit facilities and frequently far from commuter railways as well, has had a large part in these developments. But the chief influence is plainly the consumer interest in, and ability to afford, the convenience of the private automobile.

Whether this trend continues will depend a great deal upon the competitive convenience of public transportation systems. For most cities, public transportation which will start attracting, rather than losing, customers will not be possible short of a revolution in public planning and public and private investment, including particularly a willingness to finance transportation systems based upon new technology and perhaps, as some suggest, to levy direct charges for urban highway use commensurate with cost, as is the practice on turnpikes. At the same time, much will depend upon the negative influence of the increasing costs of motor vehicle roads and expressways and parking facilities.

While it seems hardly realistic to assign the bus to the fate of the street car, new types of vehicles are likely to become increasingly important as the period of 1980 and beyond is reached. Private automobile traffic may come to be completely banned in many downtown areas, to be supplanted by "moving sidewalks" and other forms of short-distance haulage. New types of subway transport will appear in various areas, and existing subways will become increasingly automated. New types of automotive vehicles are likely to be developed, including, probably, a bus-type vehicle capable of maneuvering around suburban streets and then shifting to high speeds, under its own or some centrally provided power, on reserved streets, rails, or monorail, or in tunnels. Combination rail-street vehicles have already had limited application (partly for freight transport), and an advantage of the monorail is its adaptability to this type of operation.

For the nearer future, trends in the use of public transportation are likely to be determined less by the introduction of new technology than by the initiation of some kind of reserved-right-of-way rapid transit in cities which do not now have it. In a number of cities it will take drastic action to arrest the decline in local public transit use, which, measured in number of passengers, has dropped, for the country as a whole, by almost half in the last decade.

The range of future possibilities is indeed wide. If the decline is reversed, passenger volume might recover to the 1950 level of nearly 18 billion passengers by the late eighties and might end the century at nearly three times the level of less than 10 billion to which it has fallen today. If, instead, the trend is toward bigger and better expressways, urban public transport will probably end the century at half of today's level. A best guess between these extremes is that there will be continuing decline for the next few years, followed by a gradual recovery to something like the 1955 level of 12 billion passengers, mostly because of urban population growth.

School buses. The last, but not insignificant, element in the passenger transportation picture is the special problem of getting children to and from school. Suburban spread, increased school attendance, rural school consolidation, and simple decline in the habit of walking have all contributed to multiplying the number of children needing to be transported. In the last decade alone the proportion of pupils using school buses has increased from one-quarter to one-third; the total number of children attending primary and secondary schools has simultaneously increased by half.

School buses accounted for more than two-thirds of the 265,000 buses in the nation's stock at the end of 1959. Numerically, they also dominate annual production, nine out of ten of the 32,000 buses sold in 1960 having been destined for this use.

The foregoing figures, however, tend to overstate the importance of these vehicles. Most school buses are of the light-truck-chassis type, costing a fraction of the approximately $40,000 outlay required for an intercity bus. Fuel consumption per vehicle is less than one-

seventh that of other types of buses, partly because annual mileage is less than that of the average passenger car. Nonetheless, by virtue of sheer numbers, these vehicles are more important consumers of steel and fuel than other buses.

Over 12 million pupils now ride to school daily at public expense, and several million more are transported to private schools. Many other students, particularly in urban areas, rely on transit buses and other local transit facilities to get to school. These facilities are not considered in the school bus category, but their availability does have a bearing upon the future growth of school bus needs, since an increase in public transit systems that would to a degree "urbanize" suburban areas should before too long serve to slow down the rate of increase in the proportion of school children for whom special transportation is provided. For our projections, we have assumed that this proportion will increase from about 35 per cent now to 45 per cent in 1980 and 50 per cent by the end of the century. This is equivalent to assuming that the number of pupils transported will rise from today's 15 million to anywhere from 21 to 32 million twenty years from now and 26 to 58 million by the year 2000, depending largely upon the future birth rate that one assumes.

Freight Transportation

There has been a very close relationship, over the years, between intercity freight movement, the most comprehensive measure of the transportation of goods, and the gross national product. The relationship is even closer between intercity freight movement and the commodity components of GNP (total GNP less services). A U.S. Department of Commerce analysis in 1959[1] showed not only that both items had increased at the same annual rate of about 3 per cent between 1929 and 1958 but that, except during the war years, there has been almost perfect correlation between the two series even on a year-to-year basis.

For this reason our projections of this cen-

1. *Survey of Current Business,* June 1959.

tral element in the transportation picture are tied to the growth in output of goods and construction—which is another way of saying GNP less services. About two-thirds of the GNP falls within this combination, and for every dollar of it there are about four ton-miles of intercity freight movement. If goods and construction output doubles by 1980 (our Medium projection), we may expect intercity freight traffic also to double. By the same token, the longer range prospect is for quadrupling between now and the end of the century.

Much of the movement of goods in the process of production is, of course, within city boundaries or within local rural areas. At the extreme, it is hard to distinguish such movement from "materials handling." But if we eliminate conveyor belts, local pipelines, plant railroads, tractor-trains, and the like, we may just about identify local goods transportation with local trucking. A ton-mile figure for this type of movement is not very meaningful, and we have not tried to project it, but it may be estimated that well over half of all the miles driven by trucks in the United States is in such local drayage, or pickup and delivery service. Something close to half of this, in turn, represents rural mileage. In general, vehicles for local use are not as large as the 14- and 18-wheel behemoths that ply between cities, so that per trip they do not move very many tons, but they make many more trips per year and they each require not very much less in the way of materials and consume not much less fuel than their long-distance counterparts.

For intercity movement, the crucial and largely unanswerable questions have to do with the distribution of traffic among the different types of carriers, for while each uses largely the same kinds of materials and fuels, the amounts can be very different. And it does not take much acquaintance with the competitive history of railroads, trucking, pipelines, air transport, and inland waterways to realize that trends alone give only limited clues to the nature of the future transportation network.

In the thirty years covered by the Commerce Department analysis just cited, the rail share in intercity freight movement declined from about 75 per cent to 45 per cent. Some,

but not all of that share was taken up by trucking, which carried only 3 per cent of the traffic as late as 1929 but now accounts for 20 per cent. Only a slightly less spectacular increase has been shown by pipelines, whose share has increased from 5 per cent to just short of 20 per cent. The share of waterway traffic, at a little over 15 per cent of the total, has averaged roughly the same proportion of the whole over the entire period. Air freight, in percentage of total tonnage, is still negligible.

These changes reflect, to some extent, the competitive economics of the different forms of transport, as affected by the nature of the commodities being carried.

In the early years of this century, coal accounted for perhaps one out of every three tons of materials transported between cities. Both then and now, it has been the number one commodity—in terms of both weight and revenue—carried by the railroads, and it has been responsible for a relatively constant proportion of rail traffic over the entire period. In absolute tonnage, the amount of coal consumed in the United States now is not too different from what it was before our entry into World War I, and neither is the tonnage moved by rail. In relative terms, however, coal has declined from the position of supplying about two-thirds of U.S. energy needs at the end of World War I to supplying about one-fourth now, and with it has declined the relative fuel-carrying importance of the railways. Gas moves by pipeline, and petroleum and its products chiefly by pipeline, tank ship, and barge.

In the second largest segment of intercity carriage—that of manufactured products—rail has also maintained its absolute tonnage position, with very little change from the end of World War II, but this has meant a steadily declining position in relation to the total output of manufactured goods. Trucking has captured most of the increase. Except for grains, railroads have also lost out to trucking in the carriage of most agricultural commodities.

We can foresee that movements of bulk commodities over long distances will continue to be shared by the low-cost bulk carriage agencies—rail, waterway, and pipeline—and we have a notion of the quantities of the commodities which are particularly suitable for each. Two things fog the picture: the relatively growing proportion of manufactured goods, and a blurring of the distinction between different modes of transport.

It is reasonable to believe that trucks and railways will both participate in the growing volume of carload shipments, but trucks will probably take the greater share. For the smaller shipments, trucks have a preponderant advantage, although air shipments promise to become increasingly important. Regionally, trucks are the means by which increasingly large urban agglomerations can be kept welded into economic units. Long-distance trucking may also be expected to continue its expansion, and nationwide trucking has only just begun.

But is it still trucking when truck trailers travel their longer distances by being carried on the rails? This "piggy-backing" practice promises to increase; and it is not confined to the railroads. Truck trailers and truck bodies also move by coastwise ship and before long may regularly be carried aloft. The development of "container" transport, in general, is well under way and promises to erase much of the difference between the different modes of transport. It is already widespread practice for goods to move, by rail, truck, barge, and/or ship, in an unopened container (which is essentially a very large, reusable, standardized metal lock box) all the way from shipper to receiver; and standardized systems in the making hold promise of a speed of container transfer, onloading, and offloading that will make present transshipment procedures look antiquated.

These are not the only revolutionary changes under way. Pipelines, for example, are linking widely separated chemical plants into integrated complexes; and their use for carrying coal, in a coal-water slurry, has also begun. Conveyor belts are covering greater and greater distances. Increasing use of bulk carriage is converting general cargo, most appropriately carried by boxcar, truck, and plane, into bulk cargo, most suitable for ship and barge; even wine and fruit juices now fall into this category. Barges, extending their reach beyond inland waters, are affecting coastal and intercoastal tonnage move-

ments. Railroad cars are becoming more and more specialized; new, speedy loading and delivery systems have been initiated. And while tankers are getting larger, other ships, by virtue of being smaller, can traverse the St. Lawrence Seaway and carry freight directly between midwestern centers and foreign lands.

Even if we were able to predict the course and timing of all these technological trends, it would help us only in limited degree in defining the relative future roles of the different freight transport means. We must also give attention to such elusive or unpredictable elements as the probable course of governmental transportation policy, regulation, expenditures, and taxation; the geographical and industrial structure of the U.S. economy; management effectiveness, labor efficiency, and other elements affecting the relative competitiveness of systems.

In view of all these unknowns, the distributions we are able to project for future freight traffic cannot be expected to have a high order of dependability. The basic assumptions regarding the growth of each mode of transportation in relation to production of goods and construction are shown in Table 5–4, and the percentages that result from relating the aggregate ton-miles to the GNP in Figure 5–3. The chart, representing our Medium projection, illustrates one possible outcome—to us the most probable—based on a gradual halting of rail's relative decline, a matching increase and stabilization of trucking's share, unchanged relative participation of inland waterways, and a slight rise in the relative share of pipelines. The share of air transport in the projection of aggregate ton-miles, while increasing, would at the century's end still be negligible.

A slowing of the rate of decline in the relative position of the railways is to be expected, partly because of the exhaustion of some of the influences making for decline up to this time and partly because of the likely introduction of both new railroad technology and administrative improvements. One of the self-exhausting influences is the relative shift in the energy economy from coal to other fuels; this shift, as will be seen in Chapter 15, is projected to proceed at a decelerating rate; barring very speedy progress in the construction of coal pipelines, the railways will tend to maintain their relative role as fuel-carriers better than in the recent past. Another trend necessarily reaching its limit is trucking's capture of less-than-carload freight; there is already little left to the railroads. Of the technological factors slowing rail's decline, most important, perhaps, is the growth in piggy-backing and in container transport. This could mean keeping the railroads in the picture for small unit shipments. Further in the future, but a distinct possibility, is very full automation of railway operations and a consequent deep cut in rail freight costs. Management improvements, more favorable government regulation and taxation, heavier assignment of user charges to other modes of transport such as those via waterway and highway—these are among possible administrative developments that might favor the rails.

If our evaluation is correct, enough of these developments will occur to slow rail's relative decline; this, coupled with the increase in the total amount of goods to be carried, will produce an increase of better than 55 per cent in railroad ton-miles by 1980 and a near-tripling

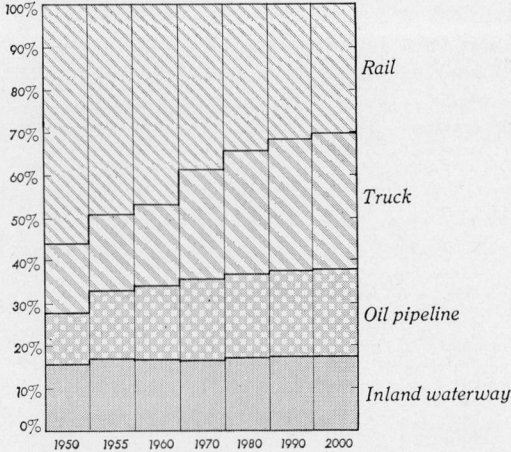

Figure 5–3. Domestic intercity freight transportation, by type of carrier, 1950, 1960, and Medium projections for 1970–2000.

TABLE 5–4. Ton-miles of Intercity Freight Transportation per Dollar of Goods and Construction, 1950, 1960, and Projections for 1980, 2000

Transport medium	1950	1960		1980	2000
			L	1.22	.93
Rail	2.52	1.84	M	1.43	1.24
			H	1.67	1.50
			L	1.05	1.20
Truck	.73	.95	M	1.18	1.30
			H	1.35	1.50
Inland			L	.61	.60
waterways	.69	.71	M	.70	.70
			H	.80	.80
			L	.66	.65
Oil pipelines	.54	.73	M	.82	.85
			H	.90	1.00
			L	3.70	3.50
Total	4.48	4.22	M	4.14	4.10
			H	4.60	4.60

L = Low projection   M = Medium   H = High.
Does not include air. Detail may not add to total because of rounding. Highs and Lows are not additive.
Source: Appendix Table A5–9.

by the end of the century. But when substitution effects are combined with differing assumptions as to the rate of economic growth, there can be substantially different patterns of development. A slower rate of increase in the national product, coupled with a more distant arresting of rail's decline (resulting in a lower rate of ton-miles per dollar of goods, as shown in the "low" line of Table 5–4), would mean a much slimmer increase in ton-miles over the next two decades and an increase by 2000 to about 30 per cent more than the present figure. The most favorable combination of GNP growth and rail participation would more than double rail volume by 1980 and quintuple it by 2000.

Under our Medium assumptions, trucking volume would catch up with total railroad volume by 1990; under the assumptions most favorable to truck transport, this would happen by 1980. The century's end could see trucking volume of anywhere from 3¼ to 11 times the present level, depending upon the growth of GNP and of truck participation.[2] Table 5–5 shows the aggregates under varying assumptions.

In one sense, trucking already surpasses the

2. As is explained in "The Study in Brief," pp. 55–60, neither the Highs, in competing enterprises such as railroads and trucking, nor the Lows could occur simultaneously. Each is considered in isolation as a possible result.

TABLE 5-5. Intercity Freight Transportation, 1950, 1960, and Projections for 1980, 2000

(Billion ton-miles)

Transport medium	1950	1960		1980	2000
			L	611	755
Rail	597	579	M	912	1,593
			H	1,384	3,192
			L	526	974
Truck	173	299	M	753	1,671
			H	1,119	3,192
Inland			L	306	487
waterways	163	223	M	447	900
			H	663	1,702
			L	331	528
Oil pipelines	129	229	M	523	1,092
			H	746	2,128
			L	1.70	2.30
Air	.33	.69	M	2.70	6.30
			H	4.20	25.30
			L	1,854	2,842
Total	1,063	1,331	M	2,641	5,268
			H	3,813	9,789

L = Low projection   M = Medium   H = High.
Totals for 1980 and 2000 are not sum of details, but have been independently projected.

Source: Appendix Table A5-9.

railroads in freight volume. It is estimated that the total tonnage handled by trucks, local as well as intercity, exceeds that moved on the railways. Since railway tonnage moves farther on the average, however, the output of railroads as measured in ton-miles still is much higher. From the resource point of view ton-mileage, in terms of material wear and tear, is a most important factor, though for other purposes revenue might better measure relative importance.

Achievement of high rates of increase in trucking's share of freight traffic depends not only on the competitive position of railroads (and air freight) but on factors within and affecting the industry itself. Although trucking's growth is closely related to its integrating role in regional economies, about half of its ton-mileage is in shipments moving over 400 miles. Continuation of a rapid rate of growth in this long-distance traffic would depend not only on slow development in the competitive piggy-back movement of goods but on generally favorable regulatory and taxation poli-

cies—in particular as they affect the carrying of larger cross-country loads. Some analysts foresee as much as a 50 per cent increase in such loads over the next twenty years as a consequence of use of multiple trailers. Specific consideration is already being given to permitting the operation of two- and three-trailer vehicles on toll roads in various states.

The use of trailer-on-flatcar and of container-on-flatbed service is certain to grow in the future, but the rate of growth is difficult to foresee. Only one or two per cent of railway car loadings are accounted for at present by these techniques, and there are many unresolved problems relating to standardization and ownership of equipment, policies of trucking and railway companies, and rates. The service is particularly suited to long-distance movement between major terminals, but since much trucking is between points not served at all by railways, the potential of rail-truck combination movements is limited to only a fraction of total truck traffic.

Inability to foresee these trends clearly does not necessarily imply a corresponding error in materials projections. Whether carried over the highway or on flatcar, the truck body or truck-sized container is likely to be materially the same. The principal differences would be in the numbers of truck tractors and in the volume of fuel consumption.

With respect to inland waterway traffic, whose tonnage we project as increasing more or less apace with that of total freight traffic, there is an omission, for lack of data, of that portion which is strictly coastal or intercoastal.[3] However, the volume of materials and fuels required for this part of the traffic is negligible.

Not the least interesting facet of waterway traffic is its potential role in the truck-rail piggy-back network. Already an important part of coastal and intercoastal traffic is in the form of roll-on/roll-off and lift-on/lift-off trailers, which have made it possible to effect savings in turn-around time.

In the past, the stability of water transport was to a large extent explained by the Great

3. Data on coastwise and intercoastal traffic for 1955–58 have recently been released by the Interstate Commerce Commission; these suggest a fairly constant relative position for this mode of intercity freight movement.

Lakes movement, which as recently as 1955 accounted for about half of the total. Its drop in the fifties has been offset by traffic on other inland waterways, which has taken a considerable spurt, aided by the improvement in channels, increased efficiency and size of towboats (which have become capable of propelling a so-called integrated tow with as many as thirty barges), increased capacity of tankers and barges, etc.

Bulk shipments of such commodities as coal, oil, sand and rock, sea shells, and lumber account for about four-fifths of all waterway movement. It is assumed here that this very dependence upon such bulk commodities will limit the relative amount of waterway traffic and that the steep rate of increase of recent years is therefore unlikely to be sustained.

Of the other now major forms of inland freight transport, oil pipelines are necessarily closely related to the growth of petroleum production and distribution and have been projected on that basis. (Gas pipelines are not statistically accounted for as transportation media.) Another form of inland freight transport, air freight, is still in its infancy, and widely different growth patterns are within the realm of possibility. Only in the High projection, however, have we assigned it a significant role, measured in tonnage, and even in this projection it would account for less than 1 per cent of the total. If there were a development of large, economical air freighters, air transport could become of considerable importance for certain types of traffic, such as the transport of food, apparel, machine parts, etc. But significant replacement of other inland transport means does not seem to be a likely prospect for the twentieth century.

Transportation Equipment and Materials

Steel, copper, aluminum, lead, zinc, glass, and rubber are the principal stuff (other than fuels) out of which transportation is made. The annual output of transportation equipment currently accounts for about one-fourth of steel consumption, 10 per cent of copper, one-fifth of aluminum and zinc, and 5 per cent of glass. Use of rubber for tires is about two-thirds of all rubber use, and of lead for batteries, about one-fourth of all lead.

Of the various sectors of transportation, motor vehicles (including trucks and buses) are the largest consumers of materials, taking in 1960 around 10 million tons of steel, nearly 2½ million tons of cast iron, 230,000 of aluminum, 310,000 of lead, 190,000 of zinc, and 160,000 of copper; and 1¼ million tons of rubber, 500,000 tons of glass, 70,000 tons of plastics, and 200,000 bales of cotton. These are the quantities actually contained in finished motor vehicles. Especially for most of the metals, the quantities which are initially put into production are substantially larger, but the extra amounts, except for some small loss, are returned as scrap for reprocessing and reuse and are therefore not part of the new materials requirement.

With such large amounts at stake, even moderate changes in the design of motor vehicles can make substantial differences in the future demand for different materials. The average compact car, for example, weighs about half a ton less than the average low priced standard automobile and contains correspondingly less cast iron and steel and half as much zinc. Less rubber is required for the tires, less glass for the windshield, less cloth for the upholstery. At present the market trend is toward the compacts, and even some of the standard cars are being trimmed in size. Yet the choices of materials for particular uses may be even more important than the over-all weight: the new aluminum-engine Buick contains less cast iron than did the Rambler of several years ago.

The displacement of iron and steel by aluminum began in earnest with the 1961 models. Several more General Motors cars have joined the pioneering Corvair among the ranks of those with aluminum engines. And the Rambler now boasts the first die-cast aluminum "six." Aside from its use in engine blocks, aluminum has made inroads upon cast iron's domain in terms of transmission housings and upon steel's domain in terms of piston heads, connecting rods, and other engine parts, as well as items of body trim. While aluminum is also giving zinc competitive troubles, its displacement of iron and steel is one of the most significant materials trends now under way. Yet it still accounts for less than 2 per cent of average car weight.

The exact materials content of automobiles is—strangely perhaps—not a matter of public record, but as an approximation, the average car produced in 1960 may be viewed as weighing about 3,500 pounds, of which 2,400 was steel, 600 cast iron, 60 aluminum (both cast and wrought), and the remainder other materials. While the rapid introduction of compact cars may for a few years overbalance the trend of big cars toward getting bigger, it would not be a bad guess to suppose that the apparently inevitable tendency of all cars (including compacts) to add dimensions and equipment would over the long run neutralize the continuing introduction of successive waves of new, smaller vehicles, with a resultant stabilizing effect upon average size. What will happen to average weight, however, is quite another question, for the introduction of aluminum definitely makes things lighter, and once vehicles are lighter they can be propelled by smaller power plants; this in turn means they need less strength of structure, and so they can become lighter still. Estimating these successive effects clearly gets one into the realm of speculation, but not nearly so much as estimating the rate of substitution for iron and steel in the first place. About all one can do under the circumstances is to assume the initial substitutions which seem reasonably possible and follow through to their logical consequences. We can also conjecture a plausible range of outcomes and reason through to a High and Low.

The average 600 pounds of cast iron per vehicle, for example, will probably dwindle over the years as more and more aluminum engine blocks and power-train housings are introduced. We are guessing that about half as much will be the average for 1980, and one-sixth by the end of the century. As an outside chance, cast iron use might disappear altogether by 1980, but, at the other extreme, as aluminum costs more than iron, its processing and weight advantages might still not give it even half the field by the century's end. In the case of steel, it is harder to imagine complete substitution even as an extreme case. Our best

guess is a disappearance of about one-sixth the unit use of steel by 1980 and about one-third before the century is done.

Although most of the gain will go to aluminum, it will obviously not be pound for pound. We assume it will take one pound of cast aluminum to substitute for three pounds of cast iron; this is a little less than equivalent volume, but aluminum engines can be a little smaller than cast iron ones, for not only do they have less of their own weight to push around but they can partially or wholly dispense with the iron engine's heavy water jacket. In the case of steel, one pound of aluminum might do for 2½ pounds of the heavier metal; this is a little more than equivalent volume, but it may take somewhat larger aluminum members to provide equivalent structural strength. Having thus cut down the total weight, we can turn around and further trim some of both the aluminum and the steel structure, with the end-results in the Medium projection shown in Figure 5–4.

When we multiply average material content by the number of new automobiles, and make some adjustment for the fact discussed above, in the section on automobiles, that the more cars the relatively smaller each and the fewer cars the relatively larger each, we come up with the total steel, iron, and aluminum picture tabulated below. Only in the case of cast iron

	1960		1980	2000
Number of vehicles produced		L	10.5	16.1
(millions)	6.7	M	12.6	25.9
		H	18.4	62.6
Steel used (mil. tons)		L	9.6	13.6
	8.0	M	12.8	21.2
		H	15.9	32.8
Cast iron used (mil. tons)		L	nil	nil
	2.0	M	1.9	1.3
		H	3.4	5.8
Aluminum used (mil. tons)		L	1.0	2.4
	.2	M	1.6	4.9
		H	3.3	8.1

Note: Net imports account for the differences between these production estimates and those for purchases on p. 132.

does it appear that a decreasing total consumption is likely, but the almost 25-fold increase in aluminum consumption will serve to hold down the rate of steel's gains.

This is not, of course, all the iron, steel, and

aluminum going into the automotive industry. Trucks and trailers are also important materials consumers, and here, too, heavy inroads of aluminum upon steel and cast iron are likely to take place. In the construction of trailer van bodies, in particular, aluminum is already the prime material, and an increasing proportion of all trailers are vans. Even if the bodies begin to be made detachable, the use of aluminum will be the same. All told, truck and trailer requirements (bus requirements are negligible)

ago of 12-volt instead of 6-volt batteries and more recently by the beginnings of a significant replacement demand for them. The larger batteries, however, use only 10 per cent more lead: something like 21 pounds as against 19 pounds. For the immediate future, the trend toward 12-volt batteries seems clear. Beyond that we do not know whether they will get still bigger (or more numerous) in order to service the new gadgets which automobiles will add, nor do we know for sure that they will

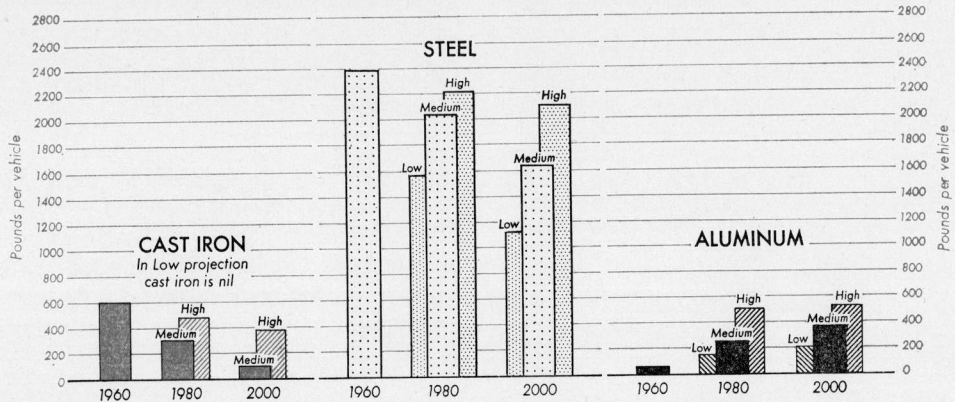

Figure 5–4. Principal metals in user-operated passenger vehicles, 1960 and projections for 1980 and 2000.

will add anywhere from 2.1 to 4.7 million tons to steel consumption in 1980, up to 1.1 million tons to cast iron consumption, and 80,000 to 390,000 tons to aluminum consumption, depending upon the assumptions as to growth in general and rate of substitution in particular. By 2000, trucks and trailers will be requiring 2.5 to 8.6 million tons of steel, up to 2 million tons of cast iron, and 170,000 to 1.1 million tons of aluminum. Except in the case of cast iron, these quantities are small compared with those used in automobiles.

Lead, zinc, and copper are the other principal metals in motor vehicles. Lead is almost wholly an ingredient of automotive batteries, and since batteries do not last nearly so long as automobiles its use is dependent more upon the replacement battery market than upon the production of new vehicles. Currently, the amount of lead per battery is tending to be pushed upward by the advent a few years

continue to be made of lead, rather than of some of the unconventional, more expensive materials (like nickel and cadmium) which contribute to smaller batteries with longer lives. Both an increase and a decrease in amount of lead per battery are thus conceivable, and when these alternatives are compounded with unknown developments in average life, plus the range in automobile stocks and production, a wide range of future lead use becomes possible. This range, together with projections of other metal use for motor vehicles, is shown in Table 5–6.

The use of zinc in automobiles is primarily in the form of die-cast parts, like door and window handles and elements of body trim. In some of these functions, it faces competition from aluminum, and this is likely to be intensified as auto makers develop captive aluminum casting facilities in order to produce some of the new aluminum engines. (Both zinc and

TABLE 5–6.   Consumption of Metals by Motor Vehicles, 1960, and Projections for 1980, 2000

Metal	1960		1980	2000
Steel (mil. tons)	10.1	L	11.7	16.1
		M	15.9	25.7
		H	20.6	41.4
Cast iron (mil. tons)	2.5	L	–	–
		M	2.3	1.6
		H	4.5	7.8
Aluminum (mil. tons)	.2	L	1.1	2.5
		M	1.8	5.3
		H	3.7	9.2
Lead[1] (thous. tons)	313	L	233	193
		M	459	721
		H	744	2,076
Copper (thous. tons)	159	L	192	242
		M	237	395
		H	347	926
Zinc (thous. tons)	190	L	300	465
		M	370	760
		H	542	1,780

L = Low projection   M = Medium   H = High.
1. Lead content of automotive batteries only. Excludes lead in radiator solder.

Sources: Steel, cast iron, and aluminum from Appendix Tables A5–11 and 12; lead, copper, and zinc from Table A5–13.

aluminum die castings also face competition from plastics.) But, judging from the rate at which new die-cast parts keep being introduced, it seems likely that the decline of the past few years in automotive unit use of zinc will be arrested. The potential use of zinc for undercoatings could equally help to halt the decline.

Copper, on the other hand, is likely to follow a declining unit trend. It has found its main automotive use in electrical wiring and in radiators, and the latter application, with the gradual introduction of aluminum engines, seems certain to decline. Increased production of motor vehicles, however, should still result in increasing automotive use of copper in the aggregate.

Automotive use of rubber, like that of lead, depends more upon the replacement market than upon the original-equipment market. Recently there has been some upward trend in the apparent rate of tire replacement, but this is probably due more to the increasing sale of snow tires than to any other factor and will presumably eventually expend itself. Over the long run, increasing tire life brought about by both more resistant cord and newer types of synthetic rubber, and the advent of some number of "tireless" vehicles, will probably depress the rate of tire replacement in relation to the number of motor vehicles, although it is not certain that the continued introduction of special purpose tires may not continue to push the trend upward. The average amount of rubber per tire (or tire-tube combination) will probably not change very much, if we are correct in assuming that the continued adoption of tubeless tires and the use of smaller sized tires by compact cars will be counterbalanced by trends toward lower-pressure and hence wider tires, as well as toward larger tires for trucks and buses and perhaps toward higher speed. Considering all these factors, and both the original-equipment and the replacement market, including the market for tubes and the small amount of rubber needed for recaps, we arrive at a probable total rubber consumption for motor vehicle tires which doubles by 1980 and more than triples by 2000. Ranges are wide, however: it is also possible that doubling may take place as early as 1970 or, at the other extreme, that it may not occur even by the end of the century.

Compared with that by motor vehicles, materials consumption by the other modes of transportation is distinctly minor. Railroads are most important, taking something like one out of every 20 to 30 tons of steel and one out of every 20 board-feet of lumber. Even these uses are declining in relative importance, however, so that, more and more, transportation use of materials is becoming synonymous with the materials content of automobiles, trucks, and buses. Add the highways, bridges, etc., upon which these vehicles ride (discussed in Chapter 4) and it is clear that this segment of demand has become and will continue to be the end-object of a large portion of our resource-exploitation activity.

Fuels for Transportation

Transportation takes about one-fifth of all energy currently consumed in the United States and nearly every other barrel of petroleum; and about 10 per cent of all energy goes into road transportation. As for liquid fuels—the energy source par excellence (at the time of writing) for transportation—the proportion used by motor vehicles is more than one-third.

Whether, for the next forty years, petroleum will continue to be the prime energy source for locomotion is open to question. A new kind of battery-powered automobile, rechargeable from house current, has already appeared in commercial models. As discussed in Chapter 20, fuel cell propulsion is regarded as a serious possibility. Nor is atomic power to be discounted, particularly for such large units as ships and railroad locomotives.

Even more uncertain is the particular form of petroleum which will be utilized. We have all seen how rapidly railroads have made the shift from coal to diesel oil. Why not as rapid a shift from, say, gasoline to kerosene, if by chance the turbine engine should come to surpass the reciprocating engine as the source of power for motor vehicles? There are some that foresee just such a development, and various manufacturers have installed turbine engines in experimental cars; others look forward to radical improvements in gasoline powered engines, of a kind that will not only maintain, but enhance, their present superiority. Or perhaps the diesel engine, already widely used by trucks and buses, could become important enough to switch a large portion of demand to diesel fuel; or the steam engine might conceivably be revived to the point where low grade fuel oil would become a significant propulsive source for motor vehicles.

From the standpoint of total petroleum requirements it makes little difference which of its forms it is used in. In fact, even if internal combustion engines go by the board altogether, it may not in all cases make as much difference in petroleum demand as might be thought at first. For example, should the fuel cell become important, there is a good chance that the usual fuel would be a derivative of petroleum (in addition to natural gas). On the other hand, should the battery operated car become important the loss of direct use of petroleum

would be offset to only a small degree by the need for fuel to generate the electricity; and the rather unlikely possibility of a successful automobile-sized atomic power plant would affect petroleum use even more. Therefore, our projections can be regarded as reasonably close in their magnitudes only if the kinds of power plants used—particularly in automobiles—remain on the whole fairly similar, in the sense just discussed, to what they are today. Any quantitative evaluation of the rates of introduction and the changed fuel efficiencies of radically different kinds of engines seems beyond the bounds of possibility at the present time.

There are also other situations in which we have assumed a relative lack of change, but in these cases on the basis of statistical evidence of customary behavior from which there is no great reason to expect much future deviation. For example, in no more than five out of the last twenty-five years has the annual mileage traveled by the automobile averaged less than 9,000: it averaged 9,300 in the late thirties and has fluctuated around 9,800 in the last ten years. We assume, therefore, that 9,800 miles per year is also a most likely figure for the future. Since average mileage would be inversely affected by the various possible rates of increase in car ownership, we have taken this 9,800 figure as being about as high an average as could accompany high levels of ownership and as low an average as could accompany low levels of ownership.

Although the number of miles squeezed out of a gallon would seem to be mostly a matter of engine and transmission efficiency, it actually depends as much or more on kinds of use made of cars, driving habits, traffic conditions (whose trend hardly needs statistical verification), and average condition of vehicles. Despite engineering improvements in automobiles, therefore, miles per gallon have shown a slight, but persistent, tendency to decline over the last three decades. For the last few years, however, the level has been maintained at between 14.3 and 14.4 miles per gallon, and we have consequently assumed that the decline has been halted—as the result, perhaps, of a decline in the average age of cars on the road. For the future we have assumed 14½ miles per gallon as not only the most likely efficiency level but the highest which is likely to accompany high annual mileage and the lowest likely to accompany low.

On the basis of the foregoing assumptions, the average automobile will use about 695 gallons of fuel a year, and the aggregate use of fuel by automobiles, like the automobile population, will double every twenty years. For trucks we have also assumed a constant average annual mileage, but in this case we consider it likely that miles per gallon, as the result of increasing size of trucks, will for a while continue to decline. The net result (Medium projection) is a little better than doubling every twenty years. Buses are a negligible factor in the fuels picture. Table 5–7 carries the pertinent figures.

TABLE 5–7. Use of Motor Fuels, 1940, 1960, and Projections for 1980, 2000

(Billion gallons)

Fuel user	1940	1960		1980	2000
Automobiles	16	41	L	77	135
			M	81	165
			H	97	252
Trucks	5	16	L	28	48
			M	36	77
			H	48	128
Buses	*	1	L	1	1
			M	1	1
			H	1	2
Total	22	58	L	106	184
			M	118	243
			H	146	382

L = Low projection M = Medium H = High.
* Less than half a billion.
Source: Appendix Table A5–15.

Much of the liquid fuel now used in transportation, aside from that used in motor vehicles, is the diesel oil consumed by railroads. This currently amounts to about 4 billion gallons per year and should grow, by 1980, to around 5 billion (3.4 billion Low, 8 billion High) and, by 2000, to around 8.5 billion (3.6 billion Low, 18 billion High). The rail-

roads also may be expected to use about half a billion barrels a year of diesel and fuel oil for non-motive purposes and negligible quantities of coal.

The fuel requirements of civilian airlines, despite their rapid growth, are of small consequence in the total transportation picture. They now account for about 3 per cent of all transportation consumption, and that proportion should remain approximately the same in the years to come. The anticipated switch from aviation gasoline to kerosene does not involve sufficiently large quantities to have an appreciable effect even on the tetraethyl lead picture. Military aviation is now of considerably more importance than civilian (about four times as much fuel consumed) but cannot be expected to grow very much, if at all, with missiles, space craft, and whatever else may be in the offing rapidly taking over the airplane's functions (see Chapter 9).

In the absence of exact figures, shipping—particularly the bunkering of vessels engaged in foreign trade—can be estimated to account for perhaps 5 per cent of total fuel for transportation. The continued maintenance of this

TABLE 5–8. Liquid Fuel Requirements for Transportation, 1950, 1960, and Projections for 1980, 2000

(Billion barrels)

Transport medium	1950	1960		1980	2000
Motor vehicles	.85	1.38	L	2.52	4.38
			M	2.82	5.77
			H	3.47	9.09
Railroads	.11	.09	L	.08	.09
			M	.13	.20
			H	.20	.42
Marine (foreign trade)	.06	.08	L	.19	.36
			M	.21	.45
			H	.27	.76
All other	.07	.10	L	.18	.32
			M	.21	.42
			H	.26	.67
Total	1.09	1.65	L	2.97	5.15
			M	3.37	6.84
			H	4.20	10.94

L = Low projection M = Medium H = High.
Source: Appendix Table A5–20.

relative position is a likely course for the future, assuming that atomic power does not take over an appreciable portion of large-vessel power plants. Movement of oil itself accounts for the overwhelming bulk of domestic shipping; even if there should be a relative shift in this movement in favor of oil pipelines or vice versa, the amounts of propulsive fuel required, in relation to transportation as a whole, would not be seriously altered.

Taking all transportation uses combined (see Table 5–8), the outlook is for a doubling of liquid fuel use between now and 1980 and a little more than a doubling in the subsequent twenty years. By the century's end we shall be using over 280 billion gallons per year to get us and our goods about, four times the quantity now needed and about twice current petroleum consumption for all uses. The quantity may be 25 per cent less, or 60 per cent more, but either way it will constitute a major claimant upon oil resources.

chapter
6

DURABLE GOODS

Much has been said about the importance of services in the mature U.S. economy. Yet half of the national output, even after inclusion of such purely statistical additions as "imputed rent," "financial services," etc., still consists of those tangible items called goods. As pointed out in Chapter 1, services may become a little more important between now and the end of the century; but the chances are that goods will at that time still constitute close to half of all production.

Within the goods category, roughly 40 per cent may be characterized as durable. The definition of "durable goods" is traditional and largely arbitrary. Along with excluding such quickly consumed items as foods, it also excludes a number of longer-lasting things, such as draperies and clothing. At the same time it includes some items, such as tires and tubes, whose lives are on the short side, as well as most military goods, whose durability in some cases is measured by one puff of smoke. Most durables (there are exceptions, notably tires and tubes) are known also as hard goods—all of the things that are rigid or semirigid in form but do not qualify as construction because they are not integral or original parts of

structures. The materials used for such goods include especially the metals, wood, and, more recently, plastics.

Consumption

Total consumption of durable goods came to nearly $100 billion in 1960. In the preceding chapter we have already considered the 30 per cent that qualifies as transportation equipment, including automobiles bought by private consumers as well as purchases by industry and government. In Chapter 9, we shall discuss another 15 per cent—the military hardware that constitutes almost four-fifths of all government durable purchases. In this section we consider the remaining 55 per cent, a miscellany that includes industrial machinery, furniture and fixtures, household appliances, electrical equipment, tools, instruments, tableware and utensils, and the like. The fact that this is such a mixed bag does not altogether interfere with its analysis and projection. Consumer purchases of durables, for example, may greatly change in character, but are not subject to wide quantitative ranges, even category by category.

RELATED MATERIAL: Appendix to this chapter, pp. 669–84. Durables in transportation, Chapter 5, pp. 128–45, and appendix, pp. 635–68; in military goods, Chapter 9, pp. 174–83, and appendix, pp. 709–21. Household appliances, Chapter 10, pp. 185–98, and appendix, pp. 722–50. Demand for metals, pp. 293–316, and appendix, pp. 859–939.

Consumer purchases. Leaving out automobiles, other transportation equipment and military equipment, consumer purchases represent just over one-half of the remaining consumption of durable goods. In other words, in the affluent U.S. society, the machinery, equipment, and furniture which consumers buy to keep around the house exceeds that purchased for use in factories, farms, and stores to produce the annual marketed output.[1] This situation is likely to change but little over the coming decades: the projections for both 1980 and 2000 indicate that consumer purchases of non-transportation durables will relate to producer purchases by approximately one and one-quarter to one.

In making the projections we have recognized that the market for any number of items appears to be saturated—that 98 per cent of all households already have refrigerators, 94 per cent radios, 95 per cent washing machines, and that many other devices are widely owned. However, these appliances do every so often have to be replaced. They frequently are replaced long before they wear out, because something new and better has come upon the market. Refrigerators of 11 cubic-foot capacity with shelving in the door and automatic defrost, are today considered a necessity to any number of families that would have been happy some years ago to do their own defrosting on a 7 cubic-foot model. The 90 per cent of households now content with black and white television may some day find they cannot get along without color.

For another thing, quite a few highly useful appliances are nowhere near market saturation. Only 7 per cent of all households, for example, own dishwashers, only 10 per cent have food waste disposers, and only 20 per cent clothes dryers. More importantly still, for many of these items there is really no point that can be called saturation.[2] It used to be that one radio per home was considered a limit; there are now relatively few that do not

have two or more, not counting sets for carrying around. Even for television, 100 per cent has ceased to be the saturation point. Two kinds of vacuum cleaners, plus a specialized scrubber or polisher, are no longer a rarity. Nor is it too uncommon for households to maintain an extra refrigerator in the recreation room.

There is no visible end to the stream of appliances which will in the future be invented, perfected, desired, and purchased. Some of today's dreams of the science fiction writers may be popular items of consumption a decade or two from now. For example, it is not inconceivable that the "automatic kitchen," already in the experimental stage, will achieve a substantial degree of reality before the century is out, with precooked dishes transferred to an automatic warming oven by pushing one button, and carted to the family dining table by pushing another.

Meanwhile, steadily increasing incomes are expanding both the range of felt needs and the practical limits of what can be acquired. Better-to-do families occupy larger living quarters and need more furniture; they acquire suburban homes with lawns, and need gardening equipment and lawn mowers. Do-it-yourself enthusiasts buy power tools and special-purpose equipment. Home libraries expand, and educational toys and home science kits multiply. Skates, skis, bowling balls, outboard motors, cameras, canoes, portable cooking equipment, and numerous other kinds of leisure-time paraphernalia become part of the family arsenal. The sewing machine gains new status as the means for pursuing a hobby, and begins to be supplemented by such more esoteric equipment as handlooms and portable kilns. Things that were once unknown, or known only to the rich, take but a generation to come within popular availability. Not all of these things fall within the traditional category of durables, but most of them do.

Projections of individual categories, such as shown below, were made as part of projecting the basic economic patterns in Chapter 1. Much of the relevant data will be found in Appendix Tables A1–22 to 27. The projections are based on historical trends in the share

---

1. Because we are interested in raw materials consumption as it develops in the future, the question as to what *stocks* of durables are larger is not here raised.

2. The statistics report only on households having the appliance, regardless of number, so that statistically this type of saturation cannot go above 100 per cent. See also Chapter 10.

of each in total consumer expenditures. On a judgment basis, affected by what information and guesses are available as to future patterns, these trends are extended into the future and applied to independently projected total consumer expenditures to arrive at aggregate dollar amounts spent in each category. These independently projected total expenditures act as constraints on the sum of the segments, though there is, of course, much room left for variation in the percentage shares. The sum total of these operations, put on a per capita basis, results in the projections for consumer durable outlays shown in Figure 6–1.

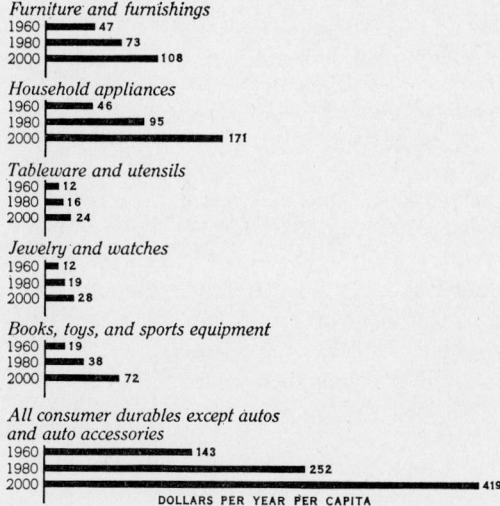

Figure 6–1. Per capita expenditures for principal types of consumer durable goods, 1960 and Medium projections for 1980 and 2000.

These increases imply no great rearrangement in the pattern of consumer expenditures. Household durables now occupy about 6 per cent of the family budget and are as likely as not to remain close to that level, with a little more emphasis, perhaps, on appliances, and relative stability in furniture. Books, toys, and sports equipment may double their relative importance, but even this would only make the difference between 1 per cent of the total budget and 2 per cent. Taking all durable

goods, including even automobiles and automotive accessories, the average consumer now commits less than 14 per cent of all his expenditures to this class of goods, and the probabilities are that even by the century's end, the share will not rise beyond 16½ per cent. The degree of uncertainty is measured by the High projection, in which this proportion would be as much as 20 per cent at the expense primarily of food and clothing, and the Low projection, in which it would remain just about at present levels.

Given the prospective increase in population, we may expect total consumer expenditures on durables other than automobiles and accessories to somewhat more than double by 1980 and again between 1980 and 2000. That is our Medium projection. In the High projection something like a tripling in each of the two periods is also possible; under the Low projection, on the other hand, the rate of gain might be as low as 1½ times for each twenty years. Which trend will eventuate depends largely upon whether the automobile remains a kingpin of family expenditure or preference shifts towards equipping the house. It is in connection with appliances, rather than furniture or the various other durables, that most of the uncertainty arises. A quadrupling of expenditures on household appliances over the next two decades is not beyond the realm of reasonable possibility, and this could be followed by something more than a tripling in the twenty years thereafter. Alternatively, it might take to the century's end for purchases of appliances to reach only three times what they are now.

The key figures, representing the application of per capita purchases to population, or, which is the same thing, percentage shares to total consumer expenditures, are shown in Table 6–1.

Producer purchases. The relationship between producer durable purchases and the output of the nation's economy is not well understood. There is no agreement on what is happening to the ratios between current purchases and the total stock of capital goods, between purchases of plant and purchases of

TABLE 6–1. Purchases of Consumer Durables, 1960 and Projections for 1980, 2000

(Billion 1960 dollars)

Consumer durables	1960	1980 Low	1980 Medium	1980 High	2000 Low	2000 Medium	2000 High
Furniture and furnishings	8	10	18	23	12	36	61
Household appliances	8	13	23	34	24	57	112
Tableware and utensils	2	4	4	5	6	8	12
Jewelry and watches	2	3	5	5	5	9	14
Books, toys, and sports equip.	3	6	9	14	11	24	45
All consumer durables except autos and accessories	26	39	62	85	62	138	253

Source: Appendix Table A1–27.
Total includes items not shown separately.

equipment, between stock of plant and equipment and the output of goods (capital/output ratio), between plant and equipment and labor force (capital per worker).

About two things there is no doubt: (1) output is impossible without some amount of capital, and (2) capital does not last forever. But it is also true, as was seen during World War II, that there is a wide range in the levels of output which any given stock of capital can support and that there is very broad leeway in the length of time that capital equipment may be retained in use. In view of these causes for uncertainty, we have chosen to make our projections by determining past trends, seeking to explain why they have been as they have been, and judging what variations, if any, may be expected in the future.

The analysis in this study has been concentrated chiefly on the period since World War II. If we look at the total plant and equipment expenditures—or investment—of all private businessmen, farmers, professional men, etc., we find that they rose quickly from only 6 per cent of the gross national product at the war's end to a peak of 12 per cent in 1948 and thence gradually, but steadily, declined to the 9 per cent level at which they now stand. The principal reason for these fluctuations is obvious: the need to make up for postponed wartime expansion and replacement. A look further back would tell us that we have also been making up for the low investment levels of the Depression years, but

that we seem to have ended up at a lower average investment level than during the twenties.

This new norm has at least three possible explanations: (1) that the capital/output ratio is decreasing, or in other words, that we are able to produce more goods with any given amount of capital; (2) that the life-span of capital plant and equipment has lengthened; or (3) that we are using them to a greater proportion of capacity. Most people think that the average life of capital equipment is, if anything, getting shorter because of more rapid obsolescence, and so far as utilization of capacity is concerned we are certainly not now operating at high levels. The remaining explanation—that the capital/output ratio has in fact been declining—is also the finding of a substantial body of analysis in recent years.

Some other factors must also be considered, though they do not upset this conclusion. There is, first of all, the changing mix of our national output. The difference between the role of government now and in the twenties is well known and substantial. It is almost inevitable, therefore, that a comparison of *private* investment with *total* output will yield a lower normal ratio now than thirty-odd years ago. But even a comparison of private investment with private GNP—eliminating all of the direct "output" of government as measured by what it pays out in wages and salaries—still shows a permanently lower ratio of capital to output. Second, there is a statistical inconsistency: the

TABLE 6–2. Plant and Equipment Expenditures, by Type of Industry, 1960 and Medium Projections for 1980, 2000

(Billion 1960 dollars)

Industry	1960	1980	2000
Durables manufacturing	7	15	32
Nondurables manufacturing	7	14	25
Total manufacturing	14	30	57
Transportation	3	7	13
Public utilities	6	10	18
Communications	3	6	13
Commercial, construction, services	8	15	32
Agriculture and mining	5	7	10
Professional and other	7	30	79
All plant and equipment expenditures	47	106	223

Source: Appendix Table A6–3.
Totals do not always equal sum of items, owing to rounding.

production of housing is measured on the output side, while the corresponding capital input —residential construction—is not included within the "plant and equipment expenditures" aggregate. We have not attempted to isolate the effect of this element. A third factor sometimes believed to distort the relationship is the inclusion of services in the gross national product, but since these have not varied significantly as a share, this factor offers little in the way of explanation.

Even if the statistics were made more precise, we would still have difficulty evaluating the over-all trends. Since the start of reasonably continuous national income data in 1929, "normal" years have been scarce. Whatever the basic relationships between capital and output, it is clear that trends in equipment purchases are pretty much lost in year-to-year fluctuations. The stock of capital equipment in use is much more stable over the years, but the amount of estimation required to get a notion of the size of this stock is such that only the most general conclusions can be drawn.

For our purposes, the best procedure has seemed to be to rely as little as possible on these over-all relationships and instead to evaluate separately each of the major industry investment components. On an industry-by-

industry basis, the relationships between capital input and industry output seem to be more reliable. They are still quite volatile and do not easily permit the identification of a trend, but the ranges of relationship are on the whole relatively narrow and thus limit the ostensible possibilities for the future. For most of the individual categories, it is the projected levels of output that serve as a basis for projecting plant and equipment expenditures: investment in durable goods manufacturing is projected as a fraction of durables output, investment in non-durables is similarly derived, and so forth. The resultant findings are summarized in Table 6–2.

It remains to narrow down expenditures for plant and equipment to purchases of equipment only, and to determine types of equipment. These are further used in the derivation of materials, but also provide useful insights into changing patterns of capital equipment. (See Table 6–3.) The conversion process involves assumptions as to the kinds of applications or industries in which particular kinds of equipment find their principal uses. Mostly, our projections have been made on the basis of trends in the relationship between each type of equipment and the predominant use. For example, industrial non-electrical machinery is projected with the historical relationship

TABLE 6–3. Producer Durable Purchases, by Type of Equipment, 1960 and Medium Projections for 1980, 2000

(Billion 1960 dollars)

Equipment	1960	1980	2000
Transportation equipment, including passenger cars	7	17	35
Electrical machinery	3	7	15
Furniture and fixtures	2	4	9
Industrial machinery, except electrical	5	12	22
Service-industry machinery	2	3	8
Other non-agricultural equipment (including office equipment)	6	14	30
Agricultural machinery, including tractors	1	3	4
All producer durables (estimated independently)	27	67	145

Source: Appendix Table A6–4.

between manufacturing investment and purchases of industrial machinery as a guide, and electrical machinery in the light of the historical relationship between investment in public utilities and communications and purchases of electrical machinery.

The differences between the sum of the detail and the amounts shown in Table 6–3 for all producer durables (the latter being derived from the difference between total plant and equipment expenditures and private nonresidential construction) are the result of two different ways of arriving at the same estimate.

The table once more illustrates the prime and growing importance of transportation which was brought out in Chapter 5. Not only is transportation equipment already the single largest component of annual business equipment acquisitions, but its relative importance grows. In fact, in our Medium projection, transportation equipment accounts for nearly 25 per cent of the total growth in annual equipment expenditures in the years to come.

Table 6–3 also indicates the relatively small annual cost of producer durables. In 1960 they were about 6 per cent of GNP; they might inch up to 7 per cent by the century's end. They amount only to about two-thirds of what consumers spend on hard goods and are likely to remain at that proportion.

Finally, the table helps put into perspective at least two widely noted current trends. One of these—automation—is presumed to be changing the character of America's industrial face, but since it is mostly upon industrial and office machinery that automation has its impact, it cannot materially alter the character of more than about one-third of equipment acquisitions. Another trend—the apparent relative shift from plant to equipment which may be appraised by comparing the two tables—reflects at least in part an increased relative expenditure on vehicles. There is also the rise in the relative importance in the total equipment picture of office and other non-industrial equipment, whose cost and number keep increasing without a corresponding increase in the buildings that contain them. Finally, the relative importance of electrical machinery plays a role, since the bulk of this is electrical

generating and transmission equipment, increasingly being installed out-of-doors or, because of growing size, housed more economically.

Materials Requirements[3]

Metals, wood, and plastics are the prime materials used in both producer and consumer durables. Neither weight nor volume provides an adequate basis for assessing their respective shares in the market. The proportions in which particular materials substitute for one another vary widely from application to application and may be based upon such diverse characteristics as strength, weight, thermal conductivity, hardness, or workability. In addition, data for lumber and plastics are hard to find. One gets the impression, however, principally on the basis of the tonnage involved, that metals are still, as they have been for many decades, the chief ingredient of durable goods, that wood is declining, and that plastics are growing.

Plastics. What little we know of plastics' use in durables may be illustrated by the growth in output of so-called moldings and extrusions. These are the "shapes and forms" of the plastics world, although a fuller accounting would also include reinforced plastics, which substitute for wooden planks and metallic sheet. As shown in Chapter 17, and especially in Appendix Table A17–1, the output of moldings and extrusions has nearly tripled in the last decade and, per dollar of durables output, roughly doubled. For the end of the century we have projected an output of fourteen times the present level. Such growth would make of plastics a prime durables raw material by the century's end, but in a field as dynamic as plastics such a projection must be considered with caution. For some kinds of durables— such as housewares and household appliances —plastics may have gone far ahead of metals even now, but the difficulty of finding a common denominator of comparison is especially

3. Materials requirements for transportation equipment were projected in Chapter 5 and are not, therefore, included in this discussion.

troublesome when one deals with the generally light-weight plastics.

The deficiencies of the projections we have made for plastics are explained in Chapter 17. So are the reasons why we have not delved more deeply. The developments are so recent and the variety of processing channels so numerous that adequate statistics are hard to come by, and since, fortunately, there is virtually no possibility that the growth of plastics, rapid though it is, will run into any problems of materials adequacy, we have only sketched in the rough outline.

Wood. Wood is still used in a great variety of durables but the only use that adds up to significant volume is in furniture and fixtures.

Here, as elsewhere, wood has lost ground to both metals and plastics, and its input per dollar of furniture and fixtures output has therefore been declining. The unit decline has not been enough, however, to keep total use of wood in furniture and fixtures from doubling over the last twenty years; on the assumption of a further gradual decline in unit use, a 75 per cent rate of gain seems probable for the twenty years to come and one of about 60 per cent for the twenty years after that. Greater rates of gain are quite possible: if wood merely holds its own against competing materials—i.e., if unit use remains stable from now on—there would be a tripling of its use in furniture and fixtures by

1980 and a growth to eight times present levels by the century's end. As a minimum, no more than a 20 per cent drop in aggregate use is to be expected from the 1960 level.

Metals. When it comes to metals use, we need to consider three different kinds of questions: (1) How much of the total value of durable goods is represented by their materials content and how is this proportion changing? (2) How does that ratio vary among different kinds of durables and what is the consequent effect of changes in "product mix"? (3) What substitutions are taking place among the specific metals? The research has not yet been done which will give adequate answers to these questions for the past, let alone the future, so our projections must approach the answers through crude statistics and general impressions.

We need not concern ourselves with considerations other than quantity, for although we have projected durable goods in terms of dollars, they are constant dollars that aim to measure physical volume of output. If we next refer to the quantities of metal input (of all kinds) per unit of dollar output, the absolute figures have little meaning, but the changes in the relationship from year to year are significant. Such figures for the past decade—shown in Figure 6–2 along with rough projections—confirm the general impression that the value

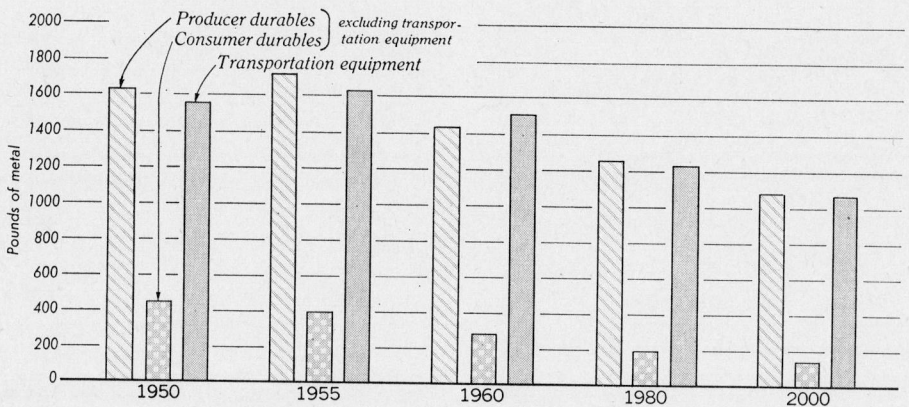

Figure 6–2. Contained pounds of metal per thousand 1960 dollars of expenditure on consumer and producer durables other than transportation, and on transportation equipment.

of the machinery and equipment used both by business and households in the United States is more and more a matter of fabrication, elaboration, and other value added, and less and less of materials content. This is true whether the metals are summed in terms of weight or in terms of volume. The figures also show that the materials content of consumer equipment is far less, proportionately, than the materials content of producer equipment. Partly, this contrast between producer and consumer durables is due to the relatively greater use in the latter of the lighter,[4] nonferrous metals, but even if all the metals were reduced to a volumetric equivalent in terms of steel, the story would be the same.

In our projections, it is assumed that the decreasing materials content for both producer and consumer durables will continue—and there is ample reason to believe that it will. All kinds of equipment are becoming more and more complicated, thus requiring more and more labor input; also the more complicated categories of equipment are becoming increasingly more important parts of the total. Data compiled by the Electronic Industries Association, for example, suggest that the output of industrial electronic equipment increased from less than a billion dollars in 1956 to 1.6 billion in 1959. Even after correction for price changes, this necessarily made electronics a more important component of total industrial equipment, whose output in constant dollars over the same period actually declined. On top of these shifts, miniaturization (for electrical equipment) and more economical engineering (for equipment in general) are constantly cutting down relative materials use. And weight-saving in one place results in secondary weight-saving in some other place: printed circuits, for example, not only save on copper wiring, but decrease the size of the finished unit which houses the equipment; lighter-weight working parts for machinery mean lighter-weight structural members; and so on.

We have not tried, in this study, to arrive at specific figures on how these metal inputs

will vary from item to item among the different kinds of producer and consumer durables, but have assumed that the change in the over-all relationship will be at least in part a result of changes in product mix to more complicated kinds of equipment. The effect is more noticeable in the case of consumer household durables, where, among the major items of equipment, the appliances, compared with furniture and fixtures, are projected to become progressively more important. In the case of producer durables, the relative position of electrical machinery as a whole is projected merely to hold its own and that of office machinery to increase only moderately; the decreasing ratio of materials to value added would be attributable mostly to detailed shifts within major product groups and to increasing complexity of function and simplification of design all along the line.

What then of the shifts among the individual metals? Again, the picture is quite different as between producer durables and consumer equipment. In terms of volume, more than nine-tenths of the metallic content of producer durables is steel or ferrous castings; and this is likely to continue with perhaps the slightest of declines. In consumer durables, by contrast, nonferrous metals already supply nearly 20 per cent of the volume requirement; by 1980 the proportion should reach 30 per cent and by 2000 be in excess of 40 per cent.

Despite these differing proportions, producer durables, because of their greater metal content per dollar, will account for the increasing demand for nonferrous metals in the future no less than will household goods. And so far as the ferrous metals are concerned, it is industrial demand that is by far the determining factor. Table 6–4 shows in summary form how prospective metals requirements for durables other than transportation equipment are likely to line up.

This table accounts for the overwhelming bulk of metals consumption for the durables (non-transportation) sector. But projections of individual metals present some problems. For example, there are the rather significant quantities of zinc which enter durable goods under the guise of "steel mill products" because they

---

4. The nonferrous metals are also more costly by both weight and volume; and steel is more costly than cast iron which is rarely used in consumer durables; this would account for part of the difference.

TABLE 6–4. Metals Requirements for Durable Goods Other than Transportation Equipment, 1960 and Projections for 1980, 2000

(Million tons)

	1960	1980 Low	1980 Me-dium	1980 High	2000 Low	2000 Me-dium	2000 High
Consumer durables:							
Steel mill products	3.2	4.0	4.8	5.4	5.4	7.8	9.9
Aluminum	.2	.4	.5	.6	1.0	1.4	1.8
Copper and zinc[1]	.2	.4	.4	.5	.6	.8	1.1
Total, in steel equiv.	3.9	–	6.6	–	–	12.7	–
Producer durables:							
Steel mill products	9.6	13.5	21.6	28.9	16.1	42.4	74.5
Ferrous castings	3.7	4.6	7.3	9.8	4.8	12.6	22.1
Aluminum	.2	.3	.6	.7	.5	1.3	2.3
Copper	.7	.8	1.3	1.8	.9	2.4	4.3
Lead and zinc[1]	.2	.2	.4	.5	.2	.6	1.1
Total, in steel equiv.	14.9	–	32.6	–	–	62.5	–

1. Zinc in die castings only.
Source: Appendix Table A6–7.

represent the coating applied in galvanizing. Because of the statistical problems involved, a separate estimate of these quantities has not been attempted. Nor has any allowance been made for the fact that the figures represent not quite the metal as such, but the metal in the form in which it is actually used, which may include all manner of alloys. These problems are further dealt with in Chapter 16.

That the table omits totals for the 1980 and 2000 Highs and Lows is a reflection of the intersubstitutability of the various metals. For the Medium, we have projected what seems as probable as any among possible future combinations. In the High and Low, we have calculated only the High or the Low each metal might assume individually, without attempting to work out the concurrent effect upon the others and thereby a High or Low for use of all metals combined.

chapter
7
CONTAINERS AND PACKAGING

THE TERM "CONTAINERS AND PACKAGING" applies to a combination of end-products which are used in transporting, preserving, and marketing many of the other end-products. The category is a diverse one, ranging from paper grocery bags to huge plastic pouches, from glass bottles for containing green olives to steel cylinders for storing gases under pressure, from portion-size food cans to 40-foot transport containers. These last—the "piggy-back" containers mentioned in Chapter 5—we have already accounted for as means of transport; this also seems the most suitable classification for the large plastic pouches which, at the end of a marine tow-line, are equivalent to deflatable barges.

Statistics relating to this group of products are widely scattered among the industries of which the particular product is a part: glass bottles of the glass industry, paper bags of the paper industry, etc. In addition, some 25 to 30 per cent of the products are not identifiable in the statistics of the Census of Manufactures, and are supplied only as dollar estimates by experts in the U.S. Department of Commerce. Table 7–1 presents for the last four census years data on the value of containers shipped, including the estimated "all other" category.

TABLE 7–1. Composition and Growth of the Container and Packaging Industry, 1939–1958

(Value of shipments in million current dollars)

Category	1939	1947	1954	1958
Paper and paperboard	737	2,508	4,065	5,053
Metal	490	1,013	1,808	2,318
Wood	222	550	493	411
Glass	156	423	629	842
Textile bags	113	340	214	175
Other containers and packaging materials	230	540	1,421	1,850
Total	1,949	5,375	8,631	10,648

Source: U.S. Department of Commerce, Business and Defense Services Administration, Industry Report, *Containers and Packaging,* Vol. XIV, No. 3, Autumn 1961.

RELATED MATERIAL: Appendix to this chapter, pp. 685–701. Transport of goods, Chapter 5, pp. 137–42, and appendix, pp. 650–51. Requirements for paper products, Chapter 8, pp. 170–73, and appendix, pp. 704–7. Demand for lumber and woodpulp, Chapter 13, pp. 252–57, and appendix, pp. 804–15; for metals, Chapter 16, pp. 293–315, and appendix, pp. 859–939; and for chemicals, Chapter 17, pp. 317–25, and appendix, pp. 940–56.

As may be readily seen, the container and packaging element in our national output is, in its hidden way, one of the largest sectors of the economy. The value of shipments of containers is currently around $11 billion, not counting other services performed, such as sealing, filling, labelling, etc. In terms of value added in the industry, a better standard of comparison, automobiles and steel are the only two individual industries that topped packaging in 1960.

The growth, which is shown in Table 7–1 in terms of dollars of the year cited, has been rapid in some lines and slow in others. Paper packaging still accounts for about half of the value of shipments, metals for one quarter. Coming up fast have been the "other" materials, among which the synthetics and aluminum foil are prominent. Wooden containers and textile bags have been losing ground and glass containers have been rising more moderately. When one allows for price changes, using the wholesale price index as a rough measure of adjustment, the annual growth rate for the industry as a whole works out to 4.7 per cent, and that of the paper segment alone to nearly 6 per cent.

The container and packaging industries are also significant end-users of a variety of basic products. For example, they account for nearly half of the U.S. consumption of paper (dealt with in Chapter 8), and about 10 per cent of steel (see Chapter 16).

General Trends

Per capita consumption of all major categories of containers except wooden boxes, crating, and the minor category of textile bags has been trending upward for many years—for some items slowly, for others quite rapidly. Use of tin cans, for example, has grown with the national tendency to consume more processed food. Consumption of food, coffee, and malt beverages in cans or jars has grown over the past two decades from 115 pounds per person per year to over 180 pounds. Aluminum foil has opened up new packaging markets, its per capita use more than tripling in less than a decade. Other packaging items have

benefited or suffered from the constant competition among different containers and container materials for particular markets. Although no meaningful quantitative additions can be made and comparisons must remain in terms of values, it is evident that total use of containers has been increasing more rapidly in recent years than has population.

This is a natural corollary to some of the other developing patterns of American life. As discussed in Chapter 2, our food needs are being met in more and more highly processed form, in wrappings and containers designed to fit individual or family convenience in food preparation. This means greater variety in size and form of container, which in turn increases the over-all requirement. Increased packaging use is a concomitant, too, of a declining retail sales force in relation to goods sold, the spread of self-service and vending machines, and attempts to improve the life and quality of perishable items. Added impetus is given by the still-growing emphasis on containers as a marketing device. With all or most of these trends destined to continue, it follows that relative growth in consumer goods packaging requirements will also continue.

Consumption of containers by business, while also trending upward, has in general tended to increase at a slower rate than has personal consumption. Several factors are responsible. First, recirculation of containers is more common for producer than for consumer goods. Second, in contrast with the increasing fractionalization of consumer goods into individually packaged purchase units, the trend in producer goods has been toward bulk handling. For example, in the case of certain industrial liquids, the old 13-gallon glass carboy has been all but replaced by great plastic drums containing from 200 to 500 gallons. Wherever possible, containers are being dispensed with entirely in favor of bulk handling in tank barges, tank trucks, hopper vehicles, and other forms of both liquid and dry bulk conveyance.

Some trends apply equally to consumer and to producer goods. One such trend, an extremely significant one, is toward the replacement of heavier containers by lighter ones. There is a slow but persistent reduction in the ratio of weight of container to product contained. This trend may also be viewed as an increasing value/weight ratio, a basic development under way for many years and applicable not only to the role of containers but to the other physical components of manufactured goods. With respect to containers, weight reductions have been taking such forms as thinner walls, thinner covers, thinner films, lower densities. Sometimes it is the same material which has been so adapted—glass is a notable example; sometimes the process involves the substitution of intrinsically lighter materials, such as aluminum for steel. It is, in fact, the latter threat of outright substitution that has in large measure spurred research toward improving the strength/weight ratios of traditional materials. There is every reason to suppose that trends such as these will continue, with the result that quantities of raw materials required for containers will not increase as fast as the quantities of containers themselves.

A related trend is the increasing versatility of individual types of containers and their consequent increasing substitutability for one another. This arises both out of improvement in the qualities of different container materials and out of advances in the design and engineering of the containers themselves. As an illustration, corrugated paperboard boxing has been so improved in strength and versatility in recent years that it has largely displaced heavier and costlier wooden crates. Each year brings new examples: aluminum cans in place of tin plate, rigid aluminum foil in place of container board, blown plastic bottles as a substitute for glass, polyethylene film instead of cellophane. It follows that relative price and weight, rather than a unique capacity to do a particular job, will increasingly become the arbiter of container markets.

However, another trend is tending to preserve a role for at least certain container materials. Attempts to improve the specific qualities of containers are leading to the use of two, or even three, materials in a single kind of packaging. Both rigid and flexible containers exhibit this trend: for example, paper sheeting is frequently laminated with plastic films,

aluminum foil bags are lined with paper, and rigid aluminum food containers sometimes are equipped with paperboard tops and plastic windows. It is likely that this trend will continue.

Thus, while per capita consumption of containers in general will grow at a fairly predictable rate, the prospective consumption of different kinds of containers is obscured by conflicting trends. As a consequence, our projections include Highs and Lows which are conditioned not only by divergent population growth possibilities, but by uncertainties as to which types of containers are most likely to prevail. (See Figure 7–1.)

Prospects for each of the principal container types are summed up in the sections that follow. Except where there is reason for supposing otherwise, our projections assume that the direction of historical trends will not be reversed. They are modified, however, by assumptions as

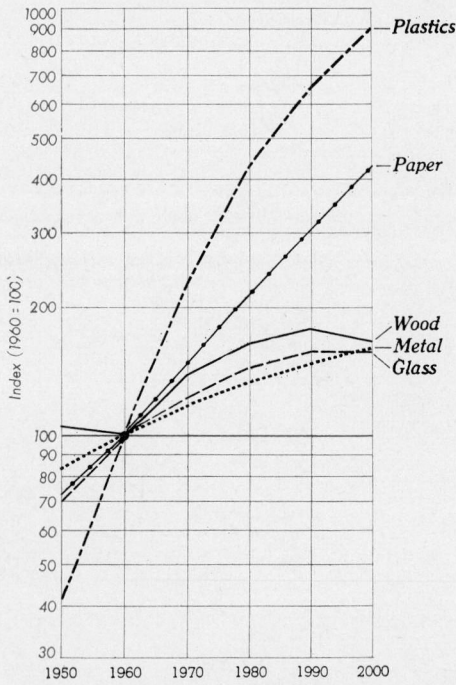

Figure 7–1. Relative growth of container materials consumption, 1950, 1960, and Medium projections to 2000.

to some potential technological developments whose effects already may be discernible.

Metal Containers

Metal containers fall into three separate classes: the "tin can" used primarily for food and beverages (and no longer exclusively made of tin plate); other rigid metal cans and containers, such as drums, barrels, etc.; and the group consisting of less rigid or non-rigid

products, such as foil and collapsible tubes. Each of these groups is projected separately, by reference to some broader development trend: cans to food consumption, other containers to national output of goods, and the non-rigid containers to population growth. The highlights of the projections are brought together in Table 7–2 for the key years and in such detail as to illuminate the connection between the discussion of general trends and the quantitative consequences.

TABLE 7–2. Past Use and Derivation of Future Use of Metals in Containers and Packaging, 1950, 1960, and Medium Projections for 1980, 2000

Item	1950	1960	Medium projection 1980	2000
Cans				
Consumption of canned food and beverages (mil. tons)	12.2	16.7	24.3	33.7
Pounds of tinplate per pound of food, etc., consumed	.249	.226	.240	.240
Metal used for canned food and beverages (mil. tons of tinplate equivalent)	3.0	3.8	5.8	8.1
Ratio of metal for all purposes to metal for food, etc.	128	128	132	134
Metal used for all purposes (mil. tons)	3.9	4.8	7.7	10.8
Per cent substitution of non-metal containers	—	—	2	10
Metal used for all purposes, allowing for substitution (mil. tons)	3.9	4.8	7.6	9.8
Per cent of cans made of aluminum	—	0.9	11.0	15.0
Aluminum use (mil. tons of tinplate equivalent)	—	0.04	0.83	1.46
Aluminum use (mil. tons of aluminum)	—	0.02	0.37	0.66
Steel use in conventional plate (mil. tons)	3.9	4.78	6.72	8.30
Adjustment for transition to thinner plate (per cent)	100	100	88.1	73.2
Steel use, adjusted (mil. tons)	3.9	4.78	5.92	6.08
Ratio of tin to tinplate	0.77	0.60	0.40	0.26
Tin use (thous. tons)	30	29	27	22
All other steel containers				
Output of goods ($ bil. 1960)	195	258	512	1,019
Tons of misc. containers per $ mil. (1960) output	16.7	13.9	8.8	5.9
Steel in misc. containers (mil. tons)	3.3	3.6	4.5	6.0
Total use of steel, gross (mil. tons)	7.2	8.4	10.4	12.1
Total use of steel, net of scrap generated in processing (mil. tons)	6.3	7.4	9.2	10.6
Aluminum in foil and collapsible tubes (mil. tons)	n.a.	0.13	0.40	0.68
Pounds per capita	n.a.	1.41	3.3	4.1
Population (mil.)	—	180	245	331

n.a. = not available.
Source: Appendix Table A7–4.

Tin cans. Preservation of food has always been the principal use of the tin can. In 1960, some 55 per cent of all tin plate consumed in container manufacture went into a variety of food cans, 4 per cent more into coffee cans, 18 per cent into beer cans, 5 per cent into oil cans, and the remaining 18 per cent into containers for a wide array of miscellaneous products. While further gains in the canning of beer and soft drinks will affect markets to some extent, the volume of consumption will continue to be bound up principally with the degree to which cans serve as food containers.

The typical tin can is composed of .01-inch steel plate coated both inside and out by films of tin only .000015 to .000080-inch thick. These thin coatings are relatively effective in protecting the steel from the corrosive action of the atmosphere without and from food acids and other reactants within. Since the sealed tin can is leak-proof, it is an excellent container of liquids and can also, by excluding air keep dry products fresh. It can be subjected to temperatures which will sterilize the contents, and be sealed before sterility is impaired. Another asset of cans is often overlooked: at present they have the highest filling speeds of any containers on the assembly line. On the other hand, even with the further protection of vegetable enamels, the protective coatings of tin are never completely corrosion resistant either inside or out; therefore, such corrosive substances as pickles and green olives must be packed in glass. Moreover, tin plate—or indeed any metal—has unfavorable taste effects on certain liquids, such as wine and whiskey.

Changes have been under way in the method of manufacturing cans, and even more important changes appear to be imminent. One such change relates to the amount of tin required. The shift from the so-called hot-dip process to electrolytic tin plating, begun in 1942 and all but complete at present, has already reduced the amount per can by more than 50 per cent. Further reductions are likely to come about, through the replacement of steel by aluminum (see below) which requires no coating, the increasing use of tinless steel cans, and the development of other coatings as tin substitutes. The comparatively high cost of tin per unit weight, as well as the dependence of the United States upon uncertain external sources of supply, provide incentives to discover such alternatives. Wherever possible, the preferred alternative is dispensing with tin entirely, as in many oil, coffee, and beer cans, and in other uses for which so-called black plate—ordinary cold-rolled steel plate of a certain thickness—is perfectly serviceable. The alternative of replacing tin with another metal or alloy or other coating is also an important one, however, and figures in our Low projection of future tin use (see Appendix Table A7–4).

The second major change that may be imminent is a large expansion in the proportion of the market served by aluminum. Aluminum cans have already begun to be used for such items as beer and frozen fruit juice concentrates. European canners have been using them for fish. If the present cost differential favoring tin plate can be overcome, canning in aluminum may increase rapidly. The fact that aluminum is already being used for this purpose despite the cost differential, reflects compensating advantages of lightness, ease of opening, high heat radiation reflectivity (which permits the contents to remain cold for a longer period of time than would be the case with tin plate), and superior corrosion resistance. Aluminum does not react with most liquids, nor does it corrode in the presence of air. The cold retentivity of aluminum cans favors their use for items refrigerated before consumption, such as soft drinks and beer. The external corrosion resistance was not significant so long as cans were stored under ordinary room conditions. With increasing consumption of frozen foods, however, many items now go through periods of storage in freezers, both in distribution channels and in the home. Under such subfreezing, humid conditions, aluminum containers are proving particularly serviceable.

The threat of aluminum to existing tin plate markets has provoked countermoves on the part of the steel industry. Tin plate will become lighter in the future, not only to contest the weight advantage of aluminum but also to reduce material input per can. This will be accomplished through new, thinner-gauge steels, providing strength and rigidity comparable to that of present tin plate, yet with thicknesses of as little as one-third. Commercial production of reduced gauge plate had begun by 1962. The degree to which it will compete with aluminum is as yet uncertain.

There is also the possibility, though a remote one, that metal cans may disappear from the market altogether. Glass is one possible substitution, although an unlikely one in view of the sturdy qualities of metal and the present price relationship between glass and metal. But plastics offer a large potential. Plastic containers start with the initial advantages of lower weight per unit of material packaged and the possibility of cubical rather than round shape, permitting more compact storage. It is significant that the Quartermaster Corps of the U.S. Army has been interested in the development of plastic substitutes for metal cans for precisely these reasons. However, if plastic containers are to prove a feasible substitution for metal, all of the positive attributes of metal cans must be preserved: rigidity and durability, leakproof containment of liquids, and the capacity to accept and maintain sterilization of contents.

Solution of the latter problem will probably not be through heat sterilization prior to sealing in the container, but rather through irradiation after the food has already been sealed. Thus, the technology of food irradiation, as yet in its infancy, may eventually provide the means for solving the food preservation problem and open the way to a large-scale use of plastic cans or pouches. At present, formidable problems remain to be solved, chief among them being the reactions of the plastic materials to the irradiation process. Radiation dosages sufficient to sterilize food also induce chemical reactions and deterioration in the plastics so far developed. It is thus not unlikely that the first substitutions of plastic for metal containers will occur where sterilization of the contents is not involved.

Balancing out all of the foregoing trends, we arrive at projections of materials used in cans, which flow from projected per capita consumption of food and beverages in cans to total metal use. As shown in Table 7–2, we assume a certain metal poundage per pound of food consumed, thence to cans for all purposes and,

by making use of the relationships discussed, to different types of metal. The final Low, Medium, and High projections, based upon Appendix Table A7–4, are as follows:

	1960		1980	2000
Aluminum used in cans		L	.16	.26
(million short tons)	.02	M	.37	.66
		H	.60	1.44
Steel used in cans		L	3.43	2.28
(million short tons)	4.78	M	5.92	6.08
		H	8.67	13.44
Tin used in cans		L	12	4
(thousand short tons)	29	M	27	22
		H	50	74

Other metal containers. Rigid metal containers other than cans include such items as pails, barrels, drums, and the steel cylinders used for compressed gases. While the use of some of these types has risen in recent years at rates roughly comparable to or slightly in excess of the rate of growth in the output of goods, over-all consumption has not kept pace with rising goods output. Output of certain categories has, in fact, not grown at all in the past decade. Most rigid metal containers other than cans are used for producers' goods, and both the increased handling of goods in bulk and the search for lighter containers, such as plastic pouches and fiberboard drums, have resulted in declining use of the older-type metal containers relative to output of commodities associated with their use. These trends, which first became marked in the 1950's, will probably continue to the extent that an absolute decline in steel requirements for such containers may take place.

Our projections, therefore, combine a declining ratio of metal tonnage use to future output of goods, with a resulting moderate aggregate increase in container tonnage: about 70 per cent by 2000. Coincident with this primary shift away from metal containers, a subsidiary trend toward the substitution of aluminum for steel is also likely to occur. In addition, the one important area of growth—transport containers (see Chapter 5)—is being served predominantly by aluminum.

Another group of metal containers, the nonrigid types, is experiencing exactly opposite trends—in fact, some of the most rapid rates of growth in the whole containers and packaging field. This group, essentially, comprises foils and collapsible tubes. Aluminum foil in particular has entered into both food and nonfood handling in numerous ways since 1945. Perhaps in no aspect of packaging have changing patterns of retailing and changing food preparation and consumption habits had greater impact. In particular, the rapid growth in importance of aluminum foil trays and other shapes which serve successively as retail packaging, home preparation dish, and even serving dish are responsible for an important part of the soaring consumption. The flexible foils are also contributing to the consumption increase, extending to use as an aid in cooking.

Present per capita consumption of aluminum foil in containers and packaging now exceeds one pound, which, compared with poundages of packaging elsewhere suggests a far from saturated market condition. Extension of both rigid and flexible foils to many other purposes not now so served would appear to be a reasonable assumption.

In sharp contrast to the foils, per capita consumption of metallic collapsible tubes ("squeeze-tubes") has been comparatively stable over the past fifteen years. The range of application for such tubes has been rather restricted in the past to a few conventional uses, and signs of recent upturn in per capita consumption appear to be confined to increased use in packaging medications. Collapsible tubes have in the past been made of pure tin, tin-coated lead, tin-lead alloys, and aluminum. Although lead-tin tubes are still the most important type, the percentage of the total tube market met from aluminum has been increasing steadily, particularly since the late forties. Our aggregate projection of aluminum in foil and collapsible tubes assumes that displacement of lead and tin tubes by aluminum will continue— slowly in the case of the Low projection, most rapidly in the High projection.

Combining the use of aluminum in foil and in collapsible tubes, we have assumed a per capita use of 3.3 pounds for the Medium projection in 1980, and 3.6 pounds for the High projection. The corresponding figures for 2000 are 4.1 pounds and 5.1 pounds, compared with 1.4

pounds in 1960. This reflects the belief that we are still in the initial stages of a growth curve for a new material so that per capita use in 2000 of about three times current consumption does not seem unlikely. When these per capita levels are multiplied by the projected population increase, total demand emerges as almost three times the current level in the 1980 Medium projection and over five times by the year 2000.

A further possible area of metals requirements in the containers and packaging field is in the developing sphere of foil/plastic and foil/paper laminates. Combinations of resin films and flexible aluminum foils may impart added properties to the package, combining such properties as imperviousness to liquids and gases, strength, tear resistance, and others. Uses parallel those served by the foils, films, and papers separately. The outlook at present, however, is that compared with foil used as such, only minor amounts of metal will be involved.

Glass Containers

When we move from metal laminates to glass, we move from one of the most recent to one of the oldest container materials. Glass is cheap—in fact, about the cheapest of all container materials. While it is breakable, it still affords a rigid container of relatively high strength. Perhaps most important is its almost complete chemical inertness—a characteristic not possessed by tin plate or aluminum. Glass accordingly continues to be used for those foods which would react corrosively with metals, as well as for those liquids the taste of which is impaired by contact with metal. Medicinals also are often packaged in glass for similar reasons. In many cases its transparency is the principal reason for its use.

The percentage distribution of the glass container market in 1960 was as follows:

	Per cent
Foodstuffs	41
Wine, beer, and liquors	20
Medicinal and health supplies	14
Toiletries and cosmetics	9
Household and industrial supplies	8
Non-alcoholic beverages	8

The importance of food and beverages for the glass container industry is thus almost as great as their importance for metal cans. In the beverage part of the market, however, glass has been losing ground to other materials. Much of milk retailing has shifted toward paperboard cartons, while beer distribution has partly shifted to cans. Where glass containers can be recirculated, as in the case of home delivery of milk, costs tend to favor glass over paperboard.

The use of industrial glass containers has also declined. With such losses of traditional markets, uncompensated by expansion into new ones, recent growth in consumption of glass containers has been unimpressive. In fact, the postwar growth rate has not been much greater than that of the national population.

In the light of the past and current trends, and in view of the advantages of other types of container materials, any quickening in the rate of growth of glass containers seems improbable. Instead, it seems likely that the position of glass in some of its traditional markets will be further eroded by shifts to competitive materials, including displacement by blown plastic bottles. Some counteracting effect may be felt from current research efforts looking toward technical improvements to enhance the competitiveness of glass vis-à-vis plastics and paper. One past accomplishment of such research is that unit weights of glass containers have been declining for many years, and further steps in the direction of thinner-walled glass containers are probable. Assuming further research successes, it is probable that the loss by glass containers of shares in certain markets will be at least counterbalanced by gains in the remaining markets. The demand for glass itself will increase more slowly than that for containers, because of the lighter weights. The decline that underlies our projections in Appendix Table A7–6 amounts to a loss of more than 50 per cent in weight per unit. This largely offsets the boost that glass container volume receives from the assumption that it will rise at a slightly faster rate than output of non-durables. The net outcome of the combination is an increase of 100 per cent in consumption of glass containers by 1980 compared with 1960, and an increase of 270 per cent by 2000, but at the same time the weight of glass consumed would increase by only 43 per cent and 58 per cent, respectively.[1]

Wood Containers

Wood for boxing and crating, after reaching an all-time peak during World War II, when it was used for shipping military supplies overseas, has neither grown nor decreased appreciably in amount since 1947. Since the total container field expanded rapidly over this period, the relative position of wood has declined even more than that of glass.

Wooden boxes and crates have been used principally for two general purposes: as containers for comparatively heavy durable goods and as containers for fresh fruits and vegetables. A large part of the former market has been lost, particularly for domestic shipments, to reinforced paperboard containers, which are of lower weight and less cost. But, because of the hazards of trans-oceanic transit, handling at the dockside, and the need for protection against pilferage, use of wooden containers has persisted for export goods. A further consideration in favor of wood for overseas consignments is its use in the form of slotted crates which can be handled by fork lifts without the need for separate pallets. Demand for pallets themselves also serves as a supporting element for lumber use. Nevertheless, a few large exporters have begun to dispatch goods in paperboard containers, and metal containers also are making inroads on those made of wood.

For shipping fresh fruit and vegetables, wooden crates continue to provide significant advantages, particularly in ventilating fresh produce under the high humidities associated with refrigeration. But paperboard boxes for this use too are partially displacing those made of wood.

1. While the raw material demands of glass have not been further pursued in this study, the projections of containers were nonetheless carried out in order to give a rounded picture of the container industry and to enable those especially interested to follow through to the materials implications.

In making our projections, we have related consumption of boxes and crating to durable goods output on the assumption of a continuing decline in the former per unit of the latter: to less than one-third the 1960 level by 2000. (See Appendix Table A7–6.) Aggregate consumption, however, would rise somewhat even in the Medium projection, reflecting the projected rise in durable goods output.

Paper and Paperboard Containers

Many different kinds of material are bracketed within the term "paper" when it is applied to its use for containers and packaging. Containers made of paperboard serve quite different uses from the group of flexible paper packaging materials. Each group has its special properties serving special uses, and each has its own relationship vis-à-vis competitive packaging materials. Trends among the flexible papers would not correspond to trends in the rigid and semi-rigid paperboards, and within these two general groups further differences in current growth rates are discernible among specific products.

When looked at as a whole, paper and paperboard have been both gaining and losing markets. Where rigidity is important, paperboards, particularly the category known as "container board," are invading many of the markets formerly supplied by wood. Where rigidity is not needed, paper has been losing ground to plastic films, and to some extent also to aluminum foils. Actually, the use of paper in flexible packaging has continued to grow in the aggregate, but the growth has been slower than would have been the case had these substitutions not occurred. Essentially, then, paper is being displaced from a part of the flexible packaging market, while it is at the same time enlarging its share of the rigid container market.

We have found no evidence to suggest that this latter trend will not continue. Further advances in the engineering of crush-resistant container board, upon which research is currently under way, should increase its serviceability and will probably enlarge its use for containers in overseas shipments. Similarly, the use of drums and cylinders made of what is popularly called "fiberboard" has mounted rapidly during the past decade, partly through displacement of both metal and wood. With further substitutions for metal and wood possible, paperboard use is likely to grow at a faster rate than that of the container and packaging market for paper as a whole, and slightly ahead of the output of goods in the economy. Other segments of the industry will probably have slower growth rates. Thus the "folding boxboards" (used in such products as cigarette cartons and for shipments of many foods from wholesaler to retailer and for many kinds of soft goods shipments) and the set-up box boards, such as those used in shoe boxes, have been growing at fairly stable rates related to the growth of non-durables output. There is little evidence of future major market gains or losses that will upset this relationship. Consequently, projections for container board were based on total goods output, assuming a slightly faster rate of increase; for folding boxboard on consumer purchases of non-durables, at the same rate of growth; and other components of this industry, on similar relevant series, as shown in Table 7–3.

In the flexible packaging field, papers will continue to prevail in some of their traditional markets (including the bagging market, from which they have by now largely displaced textile materials), while they will find themselves both competitive with and complementary to plastic films and metal foils in other market segments. For example, the kraft papers will undoubtedly have to share a growing fraction of their markets with various flexible plastic materials, but at the same time the use of plastic-coated paper packaging materials, and combination foil and paper containers for food, tobacco, and other items should also become increasingly widespread. The aggregate growth rate in the consumption of paper in flexible packaging during the past decade has been distinctly lower than that of the plastic films as a group—although the absolute increase has been large—and there is nothing to suggest that these trend relationships will not hold for at least two more decades, or quite possibly to the end of the century.

TABLE 7–3. Past Use and Derivation of Future Use of Paper and Paperboard in Containers and Packaging, 1950, 1960, and Medium Projections for 1980, 2000

Item	1950	1960	Medium projection 1980	2000
Use of *container board* (mil. tons)	5.8	8.2	19.2	41.3
Use of container board per $ bil. (1960) goods output (thous. tons)	29.6	31.6	37.6	40.5
Goods output ($ bil. 1960)	195.1	258.5	512	1,019
Use of *folding boxboard* (mil. tons)	2.5	2.9	5.3	9.2
Use of folding boxboard per $ bil. (1960) consumer purchases of non-durables (thous. tons)	21.0	19.2	19.5	19.5
Consumer purchases of non-durables ($ bil. 1960)	117.4	152.4	271	469
Use of *special food board* (mil. tons)	.65	1.5	3.2	5.4
Use of special food board per $ bil. (1960) Consumer expenditures on food and soft beverages (thous. tons)	11.7	21.2	27.0	27.0
Personal consumer expenditures on food and soft beverages ($ bil. 1960)	55.4	70.2	117.8	198.0
Use of *set-up boxboard* and *special paperboard* for containers (mil. tons)	1.2	1.4	2.6	4.5
Use of set-up boxboard and special paperboard for containers per $ bil. (1960) consumer purchases of non-durables (thous. tons)	10.0	9.3	9.5	9.5
Consumer purchases of non-durables ($ bil. 1960)	117.4	152.4	271	469
Use of *coarse and industrial paper* for packaging (mil. tons)	3.0	3.8	7.4	14.8
Use of coarse and industrial paper for packaging per $ bil. (1960) goods output (thous. tons)	15.3	14.7	14.5	14.5
Goods output ($ bil. 1960)	195.1	258.5	512	1,019
Use of *tissue paper* for packaging (mil. tons)	.13	.20	.46	.80
Use of tissue paper for packaging per $ bil. (1960) consumer purchases of non-durables (thous. tons)	1.11	1.31	1.70	1.70
Consumer purchases of non-durables ($ bil. 1960)	117.4	152.4	271	469
Total consumption of paper and paperboard in packaging (mil. tons)	13.2	18.0	38.2	75.8

Source: Appendix Table A7–8.

In total, the future use of paper and board in containers and packaging may be summarized as follows:

1960		1980	2000
	(Millions of short tons)		
	L	32	52
18	M	38	76
	H	47	114

Plastic Containers

Except for cellophane, plastics until recently have been comparatively little used for packaging and containers. But they have now quite suddenly appeared in quantity, and there are further large increments of growth in prospect. This dynamic surge is characteristic of recent plastics use in a number of end-use categories.

Two broad groups among a considerable variety may be distinguished: the transparent flexible films and the rigid and semi-rigid molded and blown plastics. A number of individual kinds of plastic materials are used in each of these two major groups, and some individual types, such as polyethylene, are represented in both. As in the case of paper and board, aspects of materials competition differ markedly between the two general categories.

Most transparent flexible plastic films are derived from petroleum and natural gas, though coal derivatives play a role in the manufacture of some of them; vinyl, polyethylene, and polypropylene are in this hydrocarbon group (see Chapter 17). Cellophane, however, introduced in 1924 and the first type of transparent flexible film to gain wide acceptance, is based on wood pulp. In 1960, it was still the most important single type in packaging use, although polyethylene was gaining on it rapidly.

The transparent films offer a number of advantages in the packaging field. Transparency has been most important, as it has helped to support the recent expansion in self-service retailing, particularly of meats and fresh fruits and vegetables. They have other advantages, however. They are permeable to gases but not to liquids, permitting fresh meats to maintain prime quality longer. They are odorless, tasteless, and colorless; they have considerable strength and tear resistance; and they conform well to the shape of the article being packaged. Some types can be made airtight and thus be used for vacuum packaging. In addition, the newer plastic films are strong enough to be used as pouches for loose fruit and vegetables, substituting for kraft paper sacks and facilitating self-service retailing through pre-packaging.

Cellophane had already partly displaced paper in its early period of growth, at the same time that it was being introduced as a packaging material for items previously unpackaged. More recently, cellophane has had to share the market with an increasing number of new films derived from the chemical industry, so that by 1960 its share of the market had dwindled to about 60 per cent. The position of cellophane to date has rested on its strength and tear-resistance, and particularly on its adaptability to high-speed packaging and printing. As petrochemical plastic films edge into the packaging market, however, we find them beginning to displace cellophane in much the same way as, earlier, cellophane displaced paper. And, similarly, the newer films are being applied in new markets, where packaging has not previously been used. They are also being used in conjunction with other new container materials—for example to provide transparent tops to aluminum foil trays. In general, the competitive strength of the newer plastics rests on cost advantages relative to cellophane, on their comparative strength, and, for certain uses, their gas permeability.

So rapid have been the changes in transparent flexible film applications to packaging in the past fifteen years that we must necessarily assume further major changes in the coming forty years. We must also assume that new plastic films, not yet synthesized even in the laboratory, will have an established market position long before 2000. In view of these uncertainties, we have restricted ourselves to an aggregate projection of the amount of plastic film for packaging as a whole, and then separated this into a cellulose-based segment and a petrochemical-based segment. In doing this we have assumed that the latter, regardless of the specific type, will rise from its present 38 per cent share to command 70 per cent of the total market by the end of the century. Since this percentage has risen from 12 to 38 in the short span of the period 1950–1960, it is entirely possible that the 2000 share may be even higher than 70. Thus, the ranges shown in the tabulation below reflect not only differences in the volume to be packaged, represented by consumer expenditures on food and tobacco, but also different allocations of the plastic container and packaging market:

	1960		1980	2000
			(Billions of pounds)	
Plastic transparent films		L	.92	1.46
(petrochemical-based)	.27	M	1.41	3.36
		H	3.31	11.99
Cellophane		L	.37	.29
	.44	M	.94	1.44
		H	2.07	6.66

Plastics in more rigid form are also making rapid inroads into the container and packaging field. Both molded plastics and plastics blown much as glass is blown are appearing in a variety of forms to serve the container needs of both consumer and producer goods. The versatility and substitution potential of some of the new plastics appear to be quite high. Already, blown plastic bottles have provided a limited amount of substitution for glass, particularly in uses where breakage is a critical factor. Based upon a rapidly rising poundage per dollar of food and tobacco, the aggregate consumption of this segment is projected to increase from less than 200 million pounds in 1960 to 3.2 billion pounds in 2000. (See Appendix Table A7–10.)

Offering equal displacement potential are the new expanded and foamed plastics, production of which can be integrated into the assembly lines of other goods' production to provide final envelopment prior to shipment. The factory product simply travels to its destination in a protective plastic cocoon. If this type of container production should become widespread in American manufacturing, plastic resins would gradually substitute for a portion of the paperboard market. Preformed sponge and rigid foam plastics are also coming into widespread use.

All of these inroads of plastics into the container and packaging market, rapid as they promise to be, represent only a small part of future plastics growth. But in terms of reduced requirements for other materials, notably paper, their significance is substantial.

chapter

8

PAPER PRODUCTS

IN THE PRECEDING CHAPTER, ON PACKAGING, we have already discussed the largest single end-use for paper. Kraft papers, bending board, bleached chemical pulp board, non-bending and special paperboards, and container board are all consumed largely or entirely for this purpose. Use of another important group of paper products—building board and paper—has been dealt with in Chapter 4 as an integral part of construction activities. In order to know the shape of future demand for paper and board, however, we must also appraise likely trends in the major classes of paper, not used in building or extensively for packaging. Among these, newsprint is of special significance. Other commercial grades consist of printing papers, fine papers, and tissue papers.

Like transportation and heat and power, paper products are both items of end-consumption and intermediate items which facilitate the production of many other end-products.

In all its uses combined, paper is more important to the United States economy than might be generally realized. Americans use paper on a lavish scale. The weight of American newspapers—especially the Sunday editions—has frequently been commented on by foreign visitors, conditioned to newspapers of usually under sixteen pages. Most of the other classes of commercial paper, including all those going into packaging, are used with similar lavishness. One American may consume more paper in one trip to a supermarket than an inhabitant of East or South Asia may consume in several months. Gross annual consumption of paper and paperboard has now reached about 40 million tons a year, about six times the paper consumption of any other industrial country, approaching one ton per family. In 1950 it had just reached 30 million tons, and in 1929 not even 15 million.

For every million dollars of gross national product, Americans consume fully 78 tons of paper in one form or another. Most important is the consumption of about 18 million tons annually for containers and packaging. Over 7 million more tons are consumed as newsprint and almost 5 million tons for printing paper. (See Figure 8–1.)

Considering these high consumption levels,

RELATED MATERIAL: Appendix to this chapter, pp. 702–8. Paper used in construction, Appendix to Chapter 4, p. 627. Paper and paperboard used in containers and packaging, Chapter 7, pp. 166–67, and appendix, pp. 698–99. Implications for lumber and woodpulp, Chapter 13, pp. 252–57, and appendix, pp. 804–15.

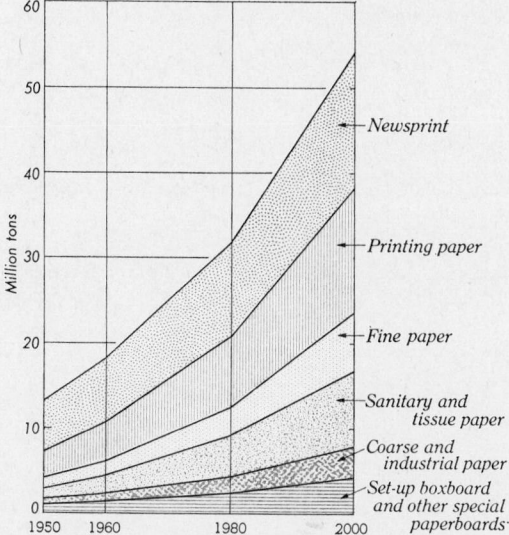

Figure 8–1. Consumption of paper (excluding paper for containers and packaging and construction), 1950, 1960, and Medium projections for 1980 and 2000.

one might well question the further scope for market expansion of paper above that implied by population increase itself. Yet per capita consumption of paper and board has been rising for a long time, checked only temporarily by the Depression and by the war years.

The general situation is illustrated by newsprint consumption. This has had a long-term growth rate which is appreciably higher than that of the population and equal to about 80 per cent of the rate of growth in disposable personal income. Daily circulation has been increasing and so, at the same time, has average number of pages per newspaper. Advertising lineage per paper has mounted, despite the growth of television advertising and the expansion of other media. As advertising lineage has grown, lineage of editorial and news copy also has expanded, since until recently newspaper policy did not depart too widely from a ratio of about 6 to 4 of advertising to non-advertising space. Countervailing trends in newspapers, such as closer spacing of columns, smaller print, and narrower margins have apparently about reached their limit. Unless all of these trends should cease—an unlikely de-

velopment—one may expect some further increase in per capita consumption of newsprint in the future.

Similar growth trends, different only in detail, exist in the other classes of commercial paper. Consumption of industrial papers has been rising fairly steadily for the past fifteen years. The consumption of printing papers is increasing, partly at least because of the stimulus which the paperback has been giving to the purchase of books. Rising income also boosts per capita consumption of fine papers. Finally, the consumption of building board and paper has risen in fairly close conformity with the expansion in construction activity, and should continue to do so unless widespread substitution, not now on the horizon, should occur, sufficient not only to dampen but offset the effect of such new uses as the application of building paper to highway construction.

The continuing rise in per capita paper consumption is probably nowhere better illustrated than in the increasing use of paper in the home. Indeed, our present material civilization in the United States can as truly be designated a "paper age," as a "steel age" or a "chemical age." The typical American household uses a wide and an increasing array of paper products—napkins, plates, cups, egg cartons, towels and many others. Several of the major commercial grades of paper are used in the manufacture of paper products for home use, but the boxboards and other special paperboards are of special importance in filling these requirements. Consumption of this general grade of paperboards for non-container uses alone, for example, doubled between 1946 and 1960.

The detailed procedures and assumptions by which consumption of each of the types of paper was projected are shown in Appendix Table A8–2. As in many other instances, a reference series was chosen that seemed to have a logical connection with the volume of consumption of the specific type of paper. Historical relationships were determined and analyzed, and then projected into the future on the basis of considerations as given above. The detailed work of the U.S. Department of Commerce, specifically its Forest Products Division, in establishing such relationships has been most

TABLE 8–1.   Past Consumption and Derivation of Projected Consumption of Paper, Other than for Containers and Packaging and Construction[1]

Item	1950	1960	Projected 1980	2000
Consumption of *newsprint* (mil. tons)	5.86	7.33	11.2	15.9
Population (mil.)	152	180	245	331
Consumption per capita (thous. tons)	38.6	40.7	45.9	48.0
Percentage imported (%)	82.9	73.9	57	45
Imports (mil. tons)	4.86	5.42	6.4	7.2
U.S. production (mil. tons)	1.01	2.01	4.8	8.7
Consumption of *printing paper* (mil. tons)	3.31	4.71	8.2	14.6
Disposable personal income ($ bil. 1960)	254	352	715	1,426
Consumption per $ bil. (1960) of disposable personal income (thous. tons)	13.0	13.4	11.4	10.2
Consumption of *fine paper* (mil. tons)	1.16	1.74	3.4	6.7
Consumption per $ bil. (1960) of disposable personal income (thous. tons)	4.57	4.95	4.7	4.7
Consumption of *sanitary and tissue paper* for other than packaging (mil. tons)	1.2	2.0	4.9	9.0
Personal consumption expenditures for paper products and other supplies ($ bil. 1960)	5.9	7.4	13.2	22.4
Consumption per $ bil. (1960) personal consumption expenditures for paper products and other supplies (thous. tons)	208.1	272.6	370	400
Consumption of *coarse and industrial paper* for other than packaging (mil. tons)	.7	1.0	1.8	3.7
Goods output ($ bil. 1960)	195	258	512	1,019
Consumption per $ bil. (1960) of goods output (thous. tons)	3.74	3.69	3.6	3.6
Consumption of *set-up boxboards and other special paperboards* for other than containers and packaging (mil. tons)	1.0	1.4	2.4	4.2
Consumer non-durables ($ bil. 1960)	117.4	152.4	271	469
Consumption per $ bil. (1960) of consumer non-durables (thous. tons)	8.41	9.08	9.0	9.0

1. For data on paper used for containers and packaging, see Chapter 7, Table 7–3; for paper used in construction, see Appendix Table A4–7.

Source: Appendix Table A8–2.

helpful in this respect.[1] A summary of these efforts is given in Table 8–1.

In the newsprint projections we have assumed that the United States will continue to meet a substantial portion of its newsprint needs through imports from Canada. This adjustment is important since we are ultimately interested in establishing the demand for wood (or pulp) by U.S. paper mills. With this allowance, total paper and paperboard consumption to be produced domestically and therefore representing a domestic demand for pulp

1. See especially *Pulp, Paper, and Board: Supply-Demand,* available as U.S. Congress, House Report No. 573, June 1957; and *Summary and Supplementary Correlation Charts* (Washington: U.S. Department of Commerce, June 1957).

and, ultimately, wood, may be summarized as follows:

	1960		1980	2000
		(Million short tons)		
Required U.S. production		L	59	93
of paper and board	34	M	70	134
		H	80	204

Large though these figures (which include paper products developed in this chapter as well as in Chapters 4 and 7) may seem at first glance, the approximate quadrupling which characterizes the Medium projection is quite comparable both with the growth rate of the economy as a whole and with the long-term trends of the past four decades.

As a step toward determining timber requirements to supply these amounts of paper it is necessary to convert paper tonnages into the equivalent of wood pulp needed to produce them. With minor exceptions it has been assumed that recent relationships between pulp and the different types of paper and board derived therefrom will remain valid throughout the period.

While our projections have been geared to the requirements to meet domestic paper needs, we should not lose sight of the fact that the prospects for expanding export markets for a number of commercial grades of paper appear quite favorable. Total international flows of paper are likely to expand sharply in the near future as overseas and particularly European paper requirements outstrip the productive capacity of Scandinavian mills. United States paper output, and concomitant pulp consumption, are therefore likely to rise somewhat above the levels projected in terms of domestic requirements, but data at hand have not permitted us to translate this anticipation into numbers.

chapter
9

MILITARY GOODS

THE SIZE OF THE DEFENSE EFFORT has great bearing upon future resource requirements in the United States. Its effect is largely indirect. In direct consumption of raw materials, national defense takes, with very few exceptions, only a negligible share. Higher defense levels would draw some resources away from other kinds of output, so the reconciliation of high (and low) defense expenditure possibilities with their compensatory adjustments elsewhere in the economy could theoretically be difficult. But because of the relatively low materials content of modern-day defense expenditures, and the apparent capability of the prospective labor force to meet high defense demands at the same time it meets high demand levels in other sectors, the reconciliation, as a practical matter, is unnecessary.

However, as suggested in Chapter 1, the levels of defense expenditure have in the past had major consequences for output and income throughout the economy and can be assumed to do so in the future, without, however, any implications as to desirability of the particular mix of goods and services that high defense expenditures bring about.

Any assumption of a major military conflict would make this entire study of little or no practical value. However, granted the absence of a major war, it may be shown that the three assumed future levels of defense expenditure assumed in Chapter 1 are quite consistent with the foreseeable range of prospects regarding the state of world tension, as well as with developing military technology.

The three assumptions have been made in terms of percentages of gross national product. The Low level, an eventual 3 per cent, is timed to be gradually attained by 1980. As one looks to the many points of friction around the globe, it seems most unlikely that a permanently low defense level can be achieved any sooner. That the Low level still is about twice as large a share of GNP as defense took during the twenties is ascribable to the now continuing prospect of an inescapable minimum international obligation, in contrast with the isolationism and relative unconcern about military threats which characterized the earlier period. It is also a consequence of the fact that in conformity with current national income accounting practice, space exploration forms part of defense expenditures.

RELATED MATERIAL: Appendix to this chapter, pp. 709–21. Basic economic patterns, Chapter 1, especially pp. 78–80, 83, and appendix, pp. 530–36. Demand for fuels, appendix Chapter 15, pp. 848, 852. Demand for metals, Chapter 16, pp. 293–316, and appendix, pp. 859–939.

The Medium assumption—that defense expenditures will remain at the recent average of 10 per cent of GNP (somewhat higher than the 1960–61 level)—is based upon the premise that nothing is likely to change the picture materially for the balance of the century. While it may be hard to imagine another forty years of unrelaxed tension without the advent of open and major conflict, the world has already lived through a dozen or more years of such tension after World War II.

The Medium assumption presupposes, too, that the gradual increase in absolute expenditure levels, which a continuing 10 per cent of GNP implies, is sufficient to meet the two most compelling cold war objectives: (1) the maintenance of a deterrent capacity sufficient to ward off full-scale conflict and (2) the maintenance of enough of a more conventional military capacity to handle limited wars. The Medium assumption is also presumed sufficient to comprehend whatever nonmilitary space expenditures are likely to be made by government, be it for scientific gains, for prestige maintenance, or for more immediate practical civilian use.

While we believe that the Medium projection—which amounts to a doubling of the present expenditure level within the next fifteen years—is consistent with the compromise between goals and costs which politics will produce, it is also quite possible that pressures will mount for a quickening of the pace. In a forty-year perspective, the contingency that the U.S.S.R. will choose to maintain constant its own proportion of defense expenditures to GNP while the Russian GNP still continues to increase more rapidly than ours, and that the military potential of Communist China will increase substantially, cannot be discounted. Nor can one write off a more rapid build-up in our space effort, or a much larger passive defense (including civil defense) effort. There are undoubtedly other contingencies, not now foreseeable, which could result in heightened defense outlay. Even our High projections, however—amounting to a tripling of absolute expenditures in fifteen years—are not in a range that would impose a substantial strain on the U.S. economy.

Kinds of Expenditure

Military technology has been changing so rapidly that any detailed specification of the nature of defense expenditures over the next four decades would be undependable, even if it were to come from more expert military analysts. About all one can say with reasonable certainty is that, barring general disarmament, men will become less and less important in the defense picture and materiel more and more. Missiles and space craft will take proportionately larger shares of increasing expenditures. These things are true regardless of the expenditure level, but the higher levels will be associated with the relatively larger role for the newer kinds of weapons. If general disarmament occurs, and defense expenditures consequently follow the Low projection, it is likely that the human element—more akin to police forces—will retain the greatest relative importance in relation to weapons, but even in this circumstance, developing technology and the inevitable pursuit of costly space-exploration programs will still combine to produce a continuing shift in emphasis to procurement and research costs.

The following specific judgments on growth in various kinds of military equipment are important not so much for their own sake as for the extent to which material requirements vary from one kind to another. In general, even assuming a relatively constant size of military establishment, dollar value of procurement can be expected to grow fairly rapidly. The rate of technological advance in military equipment and the penalty for not always keeping equipped with the latest are such that there are very rapid rates of obsolescence, calling in turn for a very rapid turnover in an increasingly more expensive capital stock. Among the factors contributing to the cost of the stock itself are (1) the increasing requirement for expensive electronic equipment and (2) the fact that increasingly higher-performance equipment calls for higher-quality materials and greater precision in metalworking and other manufacturing.

Very high rates of expenditure increase must be expected in the area of electronics and communications—especially in view of the new electronic equipment installed in ground, air, and space vehicles. Electronics each year takes over more and more of the functions of human senses, computing ability, and operation of equipment controls in air defense, bombing operations, navigation, and anti-submarine warfare. In outer space operations, it does virtually the whole control job. For purposes of defense against attack, increasingly more expensive radar is needed, to allow operation at the longer ranges implied by use of faster and higher-flying missiles and aircraft and to counter enemy jamming and counter-jamming devices. New, infra-red sensing devices being sent aloft in "early warning" satellites are the forerunners of a whole new family of devices.

Aside from increased electronic equipment, the amounts spent per man on ground vehicles, ships, weapons, and ammunition should not change materially. A possible exception is ships, for which proportionate costs may rise because of the increasing number of atomic submarines, but not enough to have a significant effect upon the general expenditure pattern.

Together, aircraft, space craft, and missiles can be assumed to grow at about the same relative pace as procurement as a whole (largely because they are about two-thirds of the total). Among them, however, missiles and space craft will have the lion's share of the growth, for the next several decades at least. Missile expenditures have already been climbing rapidly, and it is generally believed that missiles or rockets will largely replace manned bombers, manned interceptors, and fighter plane support of ground troops. In addition, there is the current resolve to catch up in the race for space. Ultimately, however, the comparative growth rates of missiles and of aircraft are likely to become quite similar. Manned combat vehicles will continue to have an important role, transport aircraft will continue to be needed and will also grow in size and expense, manned aircraft will find significant use as launching platforms for missiles, and operations on the fringes of space will be increasingly carried out by manned vehicles which are more the lineal descendants of airplanes than they are of ballistic or guided missiles.

Aside from procurement, a modest rate of increase may be expected in relative expenditures on military construction and on operation and maintenance. Much of the military construction step-up will be for protection of both personnel and missile-launching sites against nuclear attack, as well as for the continued dispersal of facilities; the Defense Department may also be involved in civilian shelter construction. Operation and maintenance consists largely of civilian salaries, fuels, power, supplies and spare parts. As a general overhead item, it necessarily must continue expanding in order to support over-all increased military budgets.

Finally, the area of research and development should experience the most rapid growth of all, for the evidence mounts that in this field lies much of the military rivalry between the United States and the Soviet Union.

To these tenuous qualitative judgments we have assigned arbitrary magnitudes. Taking the present size of the armed forces as our reference point, we have assumed that missile (and space) expenditures will grow by 5 per cent per year until—near the end of the century—they are twice as large as the expenditures on aircraft. Electronic equipment (including that made specially for missile and space craft systems) was assumed to grow at the same rate. Ships and ground vehicles and weapons were, in relation to manpower, assumed not to grow at all, while miscellaneous procurement was assumed to grow at 3 per cent. Research and development was assumed to grow at the most rapid rate—6 per cent— until at some time between 1980 and 1990 it became 20 per cent of all Defense Department expenditures. Expenditures on operation and maintenance, on military construction, and on atomic energy were assumed to grow at the relatively low rate of 1 per cent.

Under the three assumptions of defense expenditures and their attendant consequences for the size of the armed forces, the foregoing assumptions become the aggregates shown in Table 9–1.

TABLE 9–1. Defense Expenditures, by Major Categories, 1960 and
Projections for 1980, 2000

		1980			2000		
Category	1960	Low	Med.	High	Low	Med.	High
		(Billions of 1960 dollars)					
Military personnel	11	6	16	26	7	22	47
Operation and maintenance	10	5	20	34	8	34	77
Aircraft	6	3	13	23	5	25	57
Missiles and space craft	4	4	17	30	11	51	114
Other procurement	4	3	10	17	6	27	60
Research and development	4	5	18	32	9	42	95
Construction, atomic energy, and other	6	3	11	19	4	19	44
Total	45	29	106	181	50	220	494
		(Percentage distribution)					
Military personnel	25	21	16	15	14	10	9
Operation and maintenance	23	17	19	19	15	16	16
Aircraft	13	12	13	13	11	11	12
Missiles and space craft	9	15	16	16	22	23	23
Other procurement	9	9	9	9	12	12	12
Research and development	8	16	17	17	18	19	19
Construction, atomic energy, and other	13	10	10	11	8	9	9
Total	100	100	100	100	100	100	100

Source: Appendix Table A9–2.

Whatever the level of defense expenditures, outlays on missiles and space exploration may gradually be expected to take on top importance, reaching in the Medium projection a level that exceeds total defense cost in 1960.

Materials Requirements

Despite all innovations, weaponry still is mostly a matter of metals, primarily of steel. Chemicals are also important, as are some other non-metallics. The specific applications, however, are far from static; and many minor materials, for which defense applications are frequently the proving ground, ebb and flow rapidly in relative importance.

Arms still means metal, but metal no longer means arms. Only about 2 per cent of steel now finds direct defense applications; if there is a change, it will be toward a relative decline. About 2½ per cent of copper is now used for defense, and a figure more like 1½ per cent is likely by the century's end. Nor will alumi-

num, of which one pound in twelve now goes into a defense application, find much of its future growth in this area. Similarly, lead, chromium, molybdenum, and tungsten all have only small parts of their market in direct defense uses, and the situation is not likely to change.

On the other hand, about one-third of all nickel today ultimately finds a defense application, and the proportion, for the next couple of decades at least, is likely to be rising. Just about all of titanium metals goes into defense —though this has abated very recently. Fairly sizeable proportions of cadmium and cobalt, to take other examples, depend upon defense markets.

Of the non-metallics, building materials may become of increasing relative importance to defense. Plastics, ceramics, chemicals for fuel and destruction—all may be important, in rapidly changing ways, to the defense picture, but defense will be of little relative importance to the demand for these materials themselves.

A number of uncertainties are compounded

in any projections of defense materials requirements. To begin with, there is much we do not know of the present materials content of defense expenditures. The allocation among the various expenditure categories is in itself conjectural. And when we translate these expenditures into materials, we add at least two more kinds of uncertainty—(1) how much of the increasing dollar expenditure goes to materials as against labor and other inputs, and (2) what kinds of changes may be expected in the materials mix.

Thus, the defense materials projections must be regarded as essentially illustrative; they may be very wide of the mark. However, there is considerable similarity of materials use among the various kinds of defense expenditures. Because defense needs are small in comparison with the total use of the major materials, even the establishment of a crude order of magnitude for defense is sufficient for defining total resource demand. The finding that direct defense impact upon most materials is not significant is in itself worth making.

Estimates of the present consumption of materials in relation to defense expenditures must rest largely upon the special reporting systems that were set up to support the allocation systems of World War II and the Korean War. Of these systems, only the Defense Materials System (DMS), successor to the wartime Controlled Materials Plan (CMP), remains, and it is in limited use. Covered under this system are the requirements of the Department of Defense, the Atomic Energy Commission, and the contractors and subcontractors of these agencies for carbon steel, alloy steel, nickel-bearing stainless steel, copper, and several forms of copper and nickel alloy. Not included are the materials content of the many standard components and parts which eventually find their way into defense equipment. Moreover, because of security considerations, available information on current Defense Department requirements is limited and that on AEC usage is virtually nil. (However, it is known that the AEC demand is small enough to be of little significance.)

Piecing the available statistics together and adding some qualitative indications yields the following kinds of conclusions as to current materials usage and trends:

a) Only a very small part of defense expenditure pays for raw materials. For the more complicated pieces of equipment, like aircraft and missiles, materials (metals) account for only a few cents out of every dollar. The proportion is much more significant for ships and for ground vehicles; for ammunition, it is a sizeable fraction of total cost.

b) In almost all categories of defense expenditure, the relative importance of materials has been declining rapidly. For the most important categories, the drop has been on the order of one-third in the last five years.

c) The most important defense consumer of metals is now military construction, which takes more than a quarter of the metal tonnage, but accounts for little more than 10 per cent of all procurement expenditures. Only a few years ago, the principal metal consumer was ammunition, but this has by now dropped to little more than 10 per cent of the total and is no more important than several other categories.

d) Changes in the materials mix have been rapid. Only a few years ago military aircraft were more than 40 per cent aluminum; now the aluminum proportion is down to one-fourth, compensated by an increase in steel. On the other hand, aluminum use has gained slightly in missiles (and related ground equipment) at the expense of steel (still the major component).

e) Steel still accounts for two-thirds of the materials that go into the aircraft program, nine-tenths of ships, seven-tenths of missiles, and all but 5 per cent of ground vehicles. And while alloy and stainless steels are an important part of these proportions, ordinary carbon steel is still the bulk of the requirement.

The tendency for labor and other inputs to grow faster than materials use per dollar of military equipment will continue but the extent is difficult to estimate. For older, well-developed types of equipment, such as ammunition, artillery, ground vehicles, and ships, the change can be expected to be negligible. This does not, however, apply to the electronic equipment, if any, installed in these items; for electronic equipment in general, one may expect the relative materials content to dwindle at very rapid rates. Intermediate in the relative decline of material as against other costs will probably be such categories as aircraft and missiles. (See Figure 9–1.)

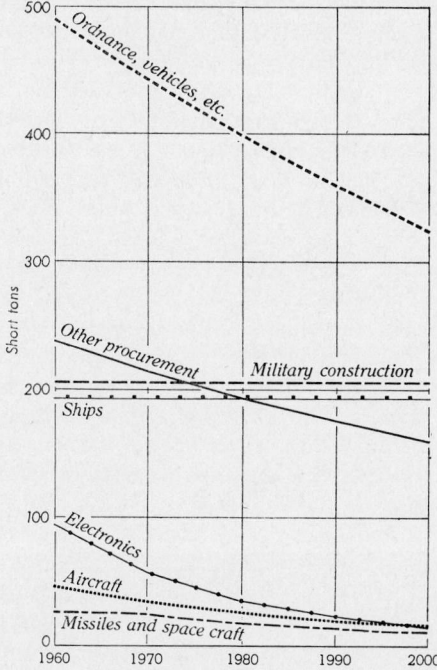

Figure 9–1. Metal used per million dollars of specified expenditure, 1960 and Medium projections to 2000.

In the case of electronics, we have assumed that the weight of materials per dollar of equipment would decline at the rate of 5 per cent a year, with the result that by the century's end such equipment would have only 14 per cent of its present weight per dollar. The 5 per cent rate is arbitrary; the assumption of a rapid decline is not. Computer operating speeds in weapon systems keep increasing, and the sensitivity and precision of radar, infra-red, and sonar equipment is constantly being stepped up. This in turn involves increasingly complex circuits. At the same time, advances are being made in the miniaturization of circuits: transistors and printed circuits are replacing heav-

ier electronic tubes and wiring and further advances in miniaturization keep occurring with amazing rapidity. For ground radar and computation equipment, size is not nearly so crucial, but reliability and capability are, and their achievement requires increases in total, but not materials, cost.

The rate of decrease in per-dollar weight of materials for aircraft was set at 3 per cent— less than that for electronics, but still substantial. As an illustration of how important the materials loss can be, the B-52 bomber, which came into production only a few years after the B-47, had a gross weight twice as high as the latter, but a cost more than three times as high. Even after allowance for price increases and more electronics equipment, this implies a substantial weight-per-dollar decline.

Missiles and space craft should eventually follow the same path as aircraft, but for the next decade at least counterbalancing forces are at work. One of these is the gradually increasing maturity of the industry. As manufacturers gain experience in the general field of missile production, and as a smaller proportion of missiles comes to consist of experimental and prototype models, costs may be expected to go down considerably, without corresponding changes in materials quantities. At the same time, the sizes of missiles and space craft are gradually increasing. Research and development will eventually counterbalance the latter factor, however, with the development of more efficient fuels; in particular, the introduction of solid fuels may be expected to eliminate the need for expensive fuel storage and handling equipment both in the missile and in the ground-support equipment. Since much of a missile (or space rocket) is simply a structure for storing fuel, increases in fuel power, whether the fuels are liquid or solid, will reduce the over-all weight.

Even harder to guess than the ratio of materials weight to constant-dollar cost in the defense categories is the kind of materials that may be used. Within the major procurement categories, the relative importances of subclasses will change, and new subclasses will appear with performance characteristics (and perhaps materials) now hardly dreamed of.

In addition, present metals will have new alloys, new methods of fabrication and heat treatment, and perhaps new protective coatings that will drastically change their relative attractiveness for particular kinds of uses. Or they may be replaced by non-metallics. Some of the assumptions we have made for important metals or metal alloys are shown in Table 9–2.

The metals most likely to be important in the aircraft of the future are alloys of aluminum, magnesium, and titanium; alloy steel; and alloys of nickel, principally with cobalt, chromium.

Aluminum is now the principal metal for

both aircraft and missile airframes. It is light; and at room temperatures it has high strength and corrosion resistance. It is also very easy to fabricate into aircraft parts. Unfortunately, available aluminum alloys lose their strength very rapidly as temperatures rise to a few hundred degrees Fahrenheit.

Magnesium is lighter still than aluminum, but lower in strength, and therefore does not account for a large proportion of present airframe weight. At temperatures under 400°F., however, the application of magnesium alloys has made it possible to use a lesser weight of aluminum in parts where strength is important.

TABLE 9–2. Consumption of Selected Metals per Million Dollars of Specified Expenditure, 1960 and Projections for 1980, 2000

(Short tons)

	1960	1980	2000
Carbon steel			
in aircraft	17.1	9.02	4.98
in missiles and space craft	12.3	8.97	4.95
in ships	122.0	122.0	122.0
in ordnance and vehicles	327.0	267.0	217.0
in electronics	53.3	20.1	7.58
in other procurement	219.0	180.0	147.0
in military construction	198.0	198.0	198.0
Alloy steels (including nickel stainless)			
in aircraft	12.84	10.89	6.04
in missiles and space craft	4.32	4.63	2.56
in ships	52.07	52.07	52.07
in ordnance and vehicles	123.98	100.80	82.65
in electronics	7.94	2.99	1.12
in other procurement	6.36	5.22	4.28
in military construction	1.91	1.91	1.91
Aluminum			
in aircraft	9.88	1.30	.72
in missiles and space craft	5.38	1.96	1.08
in ships	5.43	5.43	5.43
in ordnance and vehicles	13.2	10.8	8.8
in electronics	10.6	3.97	1.51
in other procurement	5.77	4.72	3.88
in military construction	.91	.91	.91
Nickel alloys			
in aircraft	.74	.77	.43
in missiles and space craft	.16	.24	.14
in ships	.78	.78	.78
in electronics	.50	.19	.07
in other procurement	.32	.27	.22
in military construction	.02	.02	.02
Magnesium			
in aircraft	.39	.28	.16
in missiles and space craft	.21	.20	.11

Source: Appendix Table A9–3.

At higher temperatures magnesium alloys lose strength less rapidly than aluminum; moreover, their temperatures rise less rapidly with friction (a consideration important for airframes having high speeds in the atmosphere for only short times). Thus in this range magnesium alloys begin to be superior to available aluminum alloys in applications where strength-to-weight ratios are important. Although strength declines substantially as still higher temperatures are reached, magnesium alloys now available have uses up to 800 or 900° F.

Titanium is newer as a structural metal. Although slightly denser than aluminum, titanium alloys are far stronger and retain much of their strength at temperatures up to about 1,100° F. Moreover, they have excellent corrosion resistance. The actual growth of demand, however, has been slower than many expected, applications having been limited largely to a few engine parts and to airframe parts heated by engine exhausts. This may be laid to problems in reducing its cost, difficulties of fabrication, and a technology that has moved fast enough to by-pass titanium in many uses and to relegate to a subordinate position the type of manned aircraft in which it was predominantly to be used.

Modern stainless steel alloys, although considerably heavier than aluminum, retain a great deal of strength to about 1,200 degrees F. They are cheaper than titanium and present far fewer problems in handling and processing. They have already largely replaced aluminum in the supersonic aircraft now in production and under development.

Nickel alloys have so far been used primarily in turbo-jet engines. The rapid revolution of a jet engine turbine sets up great stresses, and the temperatures are very high. As aircraft speeds create airframe temperatures exceeding the 1,200 degrees F. or so at which stainless steel can be useful, nickel alloys are likely also to be required in large quantities for airframes. Their strength-to-weight ratios would justify consideration of these alloys even at somewhat lower temperatures, but their cost makes aircraft designers avoid them whenever possible.

So-called tool steels were developed long ago to maintain hardness and strength at the high temperatures associated with fast operation of dies and cutting tools in the metalworking industries. Their high strength at elevated temperatures has led to their consideration as future structural materials for aircraft. But although they exceed stainless steel in strength-to-density ratios at the same temperature levels where stainless steel is the preferred material for airframes, they lack stainless steel's corrosion resistance. Suitable protective coatings will have to be developed before they can be used.

From present indications it seems likely that the great bulk of the aluminum applications for aircraft frames will be inherited by stainless steels, with titanium getting most of the remaining applications. Magnesium may be expected to get some of the surrendered alumi-

TABLE 9–3. Shares of Different Metals in Specified Defense Sectors, 1960 and Projections for 1980, 2000

(Per cent, by weight)

	1960	1980	2000
Aircraft:	*100*	*100*	*100*
Carbon steel	38	36	36
Alloy steel	21	20	20
Nickel stainless steel	7	23	23
Copper and alloys	4	4	4
Aluminum	22	5	5
Other metals	7	12	12
Missiles and space craft:	*100*	*100*	*100*
Carbon steel	52	53	52
Alloy steel	12	12	12
Nickel stainless steel	6	14	15
Aluminum	23	11	11
Other metals	7	10	10
Ships, ordnance, vehicles:	*100*	*100*	*100*
Carbon steel	66	66	65
Alloy steel	25	25	25
Copper and alloys	5	5	5
Other metals	4	4	5
Electronics:	*100*	*100*	*100*
Carbon steel	57	57	57
Copper and alloys	18	18	18
Aluminum	11	11	11
Other metals	14	14	14
Military construction:	*100*	*100*	*100*
Carbon steel	96	96	96
Other metals	4	4	4

Source: Appendix Table A9–3.

num applications, but later to give up some of its share in favor of titanium and stainless steel. The latter two metals are in turn likely to surrender some applications to nickel alloys and, perhaps, tool steels. These assumed developments are reflected in Tables 9–2 and 9–3, the latter showing the changing shares in aggregate use.

For missiles and space craft the principal difference is the somewhat lesser decline for aluminum and magnesium. We assume that for two reasons aluminum applications will continue to be relatively large. (See Figure 9–2.) First, a large part of the missile-system aluminum consumption is for ground equipment. Second, long-range ballistic missiles, which are likely to be important in future programs, spend very little time at low enough altitudes for aerodynamic heating and the entire rocket is at lowest altitude at the time that its speed is rising from zero, immediately after the launching. Speed is very high at re-entry into the atmosphere at the end of the flight, but only the nose cone and payload of the rocket have to survive this part of the flight, and these account for only a small part of the rocket metal.

Magnesium can play an important role as a substitute for displaced aluminum. The aerodynamic heating problems for many missiles are not so serious as for aircraft, and magnesium's low rate of heating will frequently be enough to keep the rocket structure together long enough for the rocket to accomplish its mission.

Nuclear reactors are almost the only users of zirconium. More would be used if it were cheaper in relation to stainless steel, for which it is a desirable substitute as a fuel cladding material. Other reactor materials consumed in significant amounts include hafnium, beryllium, cadmium, and non-metallic materials. Reactors and associated heat exchanger equipment also use high proportions of stainless steel and other high temperature alloys, but the absolute amounts of such materials for reactor use are relatively small at present levels of production. Ultimately, the production of military reactors or replacement of worn reactor parts may become large enough for use of high-temperature materials to become important. The use of reactors in military propulsion systems also requires lead or other shielding materials. Should reactors go into aircraft, there will be offsets in reduced needs for high-temperature materials in jet engines. There are no offsets for reactor requirements in naval shipping.

Based on considerations such as the foregoing, the prospective metals composition of the principal items of defense expenditure may be said to look somewhat as shown in Table 9–4.

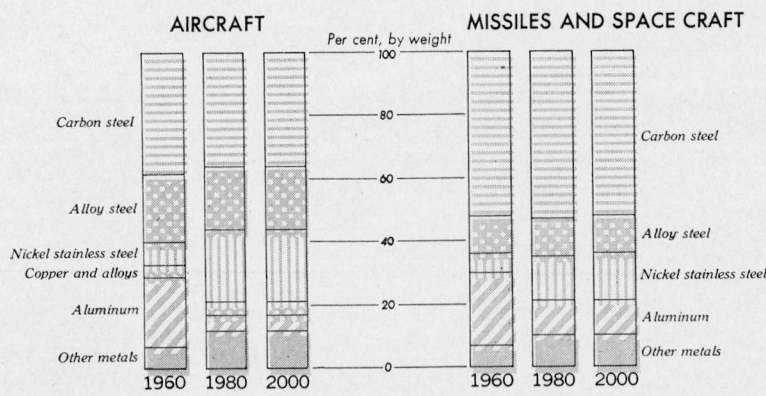

Figure 9–2. Shares of different metals in aircraft, missiles, and space craft, 1960 and projections for 1980 and 2000.

TABLE 9–4. Use of Major Metals in Defense, 1960 and Projections for 1980, 2000

(Thousand tons)

	1960	1980 Low	1980 Med.	1980 High	2000 Low	2000 Med.	2000 High
Carbon steel	994	478	1,824	3,172	631	2,956	6,658
of which:							
Aircraft and missiles	153	70	273	472	82	375	849
Ships	207	85	329	573	98	464	1,049
Ordnance, vehicles, etc.	131	53	160	294	43	195	434
Other procurement	153	90	378	648	162	764	1,720
Military construction	297	158	594	1,030	218	1,030	2,317
Alloy (including nickel stainless) steel	249	123	455	793	131	607	1,364
of which:							
Aircraft and missiles	96	57	224	386	62	283	637
Ships, ordnance, vehicles	137	57	211	390	58	272	612
Copper and copper alloys	67	29	108	188	34	157	352
Aluminum	111	25	103	179	33	153	343

Source: Appendix Table A9–4.

Few of the quantities are large, either in absolute terms or in relation to total demand for the metal in question.

Fuel Requirements

As with metals, fuel consumption for defense is a very small part of total fuel consumption—less than 5 per cent. Almost two-thirds of the current defense requirement is for aviation fuel, and of this, nearly three-quarters is jet fuel. As time goes on, jet fuel is likely to become by far the major portion of the total petroleum requirement (except in the event of the Low, end-of-cold-war, defense assumption, when it still would be the larger share). This is explained by the decline of naval needs, as atomic-powered ships take over, and by the gradual decline of piston-engine aircraft. The consumption of jet fuel itself will grow less than proportionately to expenditures on aircraft, partly for the same reason that materials use does not grow proportionately to such expenditures and partly because new types of fuels, such as solid chemical fuels, are likely to become significant in the total picture. The growth of petroleum consumption, in millions of barrels annually, has been projected as follows:

		Total defense consumption	Aviation fuel
1955		143	93
1960		262	168
1980:	Low	100	60
	Medium	270	230
	High	430	390
2000:	Low	100	65
	Medium	330	300
	High	720	685

In the Medium projection fuel use rises hardly at all by 1980, and only moderately through the end of the century. Even if nuclear-powered vessels should make a much-delayed appearance, the picture would not be greatly altered, for naval fuel consumption in 1960 accounted for only 20 per cent of the total.

HEAT AND POWER

REQUIREMENTS FOR heat and power in homes, in industry, and in commercial establishments together account for about two-thirds of the demand for energy in the U.S. economy. Industry alone—here defined as manufacturing and mining—now takes almost 35.5 per cent of the total; residential uses, 20 per cent; and commercial, about 8.5 per cent. The remaining 36 per cent of total energy demand is divided between transportation, 20.3 per cent, and a group of other activities which account for about 16 per cent, including agriculture, military requirements, petroleum products in highway building, public activities which are governmental or quasi-governmental in character, and certain losses.

Growth of population and economic activity during the remainder of the twentieth century is expected automatically to increase the energy needs of all categories (except perhaps those of the military, which may rise for other reasons). But a number of other factors, notably changes in technology and in consumers' tastes and preferences, may have marked effects on how the total increase in energy requirements is shared among the different types of use.

Residential Consumption

As man's standard of living has risen from finding shelter in a cave and feeding on unprocessed plants and animals, so have his needs for sources of heat, light, and, much more slowly, power. In the United States it is the variety of new ways in which energy sources have been utilized and their spread to the bulk of the population that have accounted for the great and sustained rise in domestic energy consumption.

In 1960, use of heat and energy in the country's homes, for purposes from warming the living room to operating the vacuum cleaner, was equivalent to roughly 350 million tons of coal. The growth in such residential uses has been rapid; U.S. consumption of *all* energy material for *all* purposes at the beginning of the twentieth century barely exceeded current energy consumption in just the American home.

Space heating—the technical term for keeping buildings warm—is by far the largest domestic use of energy. Other important requirements are for water heating, cooking, and lighting, and new applications are added to the list almost every year. Let a hurricane, flood, or industrial dispute interrupt the regular delivery of oil or electricity (which will also paralyze the thermostats on the gas appliances), and the modern household ceases to function. The significantly large domestic needs for energy are intimately tied to the requirements of the human body and therefore are not subject to wide ranges of uncertainty. To maintain an indoors temperature proper for assuring bodily comfort

---

RELATED MATERIAL: Appendix to this chapter, pp. 722–77. Requirements for petroleum products in highway building, Chapter 4, p. 127, and appendix, p. 632. Energy needs of transportation, Chapter 5, pp. 145–47, and appendix, pp. 660–62, 666; of the military, Chapter 9, p. 183, and appendix, p. 721. Demand for the mineral fuels, Chapter 15, pp. 277–92, and appendix, pp. 834–58. Adequacy of energy sources, Chapter 20, pp. 388–421.

is simply an exercise in arithmetic, given the outside temperature, exposure to sun and wind, and the characteristics of the shelter. Energy consumption for cooking is a function of eating habits—including preferences for degree of prior preparation of foods and for volume; both move within fairly narrow limits.

The obvious approach to calculating current domestic energy requirements would be to construct the "typical" home and, on the basis of reasonable assumptions, estimate its consumption of energy in each of the ways in which it is utilized: space heating, water heating, cooking, lighting, refrigerating, clothes washing and drying, television, etc.

This procedure serves up to a point and is used here wherever possible. Where it tends to founder is in the construction of the typical home. As a rule, no source of energy enters the home earmarked for one use only. Electricity fulfills a multitude of functions, and gas may or may not be used for half a dozen of them. But statistics are compiled at the point of wholesale or at best retail distribution, without distinction of use. Where a source comes nearest to meeting a single use, as is the case for oil in space heating, the quantities used in homes and those used in commerce or industry are not separately accounted for. They must be guessed at on the basis of types of oil sold. Thus we have

no adequate means for checking against actual consumption the theoretical or typical requirements we might construct. Nevertheless, our approaches to domestic energy use, while to a degree makeshift, can tell us a great deal about present situations and future possibilities.

Many of the technical details that bear upon our projections in this chapter have been relegated to the Appendix. But some remain, because our inquiry is directed less toward *what* will be done in the future—that is fairly clear given basic human needs—than toward *how* it will be done. Such an approach involves technological assumptions that cannot reasonably be divorced from our exposition.

Space Heating

The purpose of space heating is to provide, at least cost to the consumer, an environment of temperature and humidity in the home that the human body will find comfortable. To achieve this a range of familiar devices is used. There are individual space heaters or central systems. Some use hot water or steam and some use air; some use the traditional radiators, some baseboard devices, and some ducts and forced air; there are oil, gas, and coal burning furnaces; there are electric heaters, some of which are furnaces while others utilize resistance or the

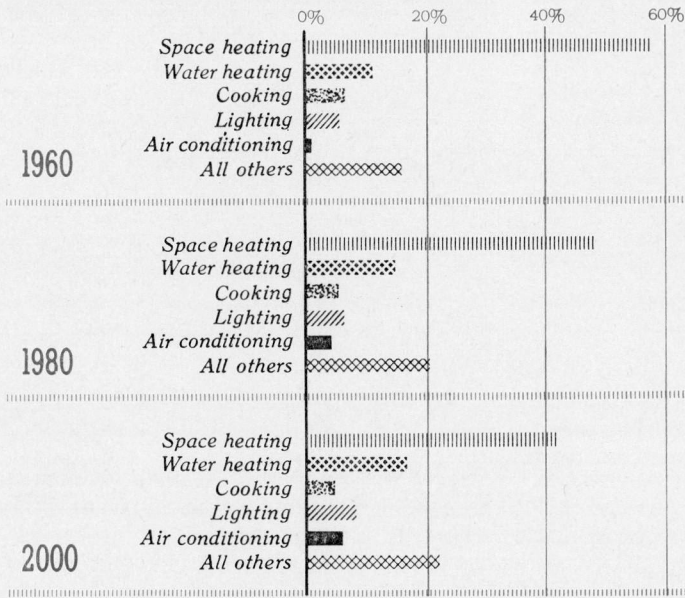

Figure 10–1. Relative importance of different domestic energy uses, 1960 and Medium projections for 1980 and 2000.

principle of heat exchange. And there are, of course, the open wood or coal burning fire, the kerosene stove, and the solar-heated house.

To find out how much heat American homes will require twenty to forty years from now is basically a matter of multiplying pertinent average heating requirements per household by a given number of potential households. A number of modifying factors relating to changing standards of housing space and efficiency need to be considered, however. And when the resulting estimates are looked at in terms of the kinds of fuels that will be involved in supplying domestic heat, it is necessary to consider what changes in consumer preferences and in heating equipment are likely to modify past trends. The thermal output values thus obtained for each source of heat can then be converted to fuel input data by use of efficiency factors which again are based on current experience and expectations of improvement.

Because specific end-uses are not covered by the recorded statistics, many of our projections must be based upon circumstantial evidence. Barring completely new modes of shelter or radical climatic changes, however, future consumption is bound to move within a fairly narrow range and errors of judgment are not likely to be large in terms of total heating needs. The distance between the High and Low projections, therefore, is not a wide one.

The search for a heating standard. The heating needs of a household depend upon such factors as climatic environment, size of dwelling, construction characteristics (especially age and the extent and nature of insulation), and certain features of the heating device itself (whether it supplies temperature regulation by individual room or by zone, or the degree of humidification it provides, for example).

Because these characteristics differ widely in individual dwellings and cannot be generalized, the future heating needs of the "average U.S. household" must be derived from historical statistical data, modified by the probabilities of changes in technology which may change patterns of consumption. The records of gas sales come closest to measuring what we are after. Whether the heat output of a gas furnace does or does not supply the precise caloric needs of bodily comfort is not here being argued; but

the facts that the fuel is reasonably consistent in quality, both in time and in space, that precise records are available, and that the user can adjust the amount of heat he draws from the gas furnace provide us with a close approximation of a standard with which to measure space-heating requirements, especially in view of the widespread use of gas for this purpose. Gas sales statistics have, therefore, been taken as our starting point, and these have been checked against a variety of other sources of information. Most of the statistical uncertainties involved in the data and their use are described and evaluated in the Appendix to Chapter 10.

The most remarkable fact about this information is the stability of consumption per customer. During the thirteen years in which data have been collected by the American Gas Association the difference between the highest and lowest consumption year per customer is of the order of 15 per cent; the slight increase on record is likely to have resulted from the spread of gas heating to colder areas. Here then emerges an indication of the "heat diet" of the average U.S. household—or almost so, for some qualifications must be made.

First, a customer is not always just one household. Inspection of data on multi-family dwellings (except those centrally metered, which fall into the commercial category) and central gas burners suggests that for every ten customers there are eleven households. This leads to an overstatement of use per customer. Second, customers for gas heating tend to be found disproportionately in the South and West, areas of the country which require least heating. This causes an understatement of about 10 per cent use per customer. Third, perhaps nearly half of the gas customers use non-central devices, the efficiency of which cannot be statistically verified. The first two factors work in opposite directions with similar force while the effect of the third is doubtful. The gas sales figure per customer which we use as our starting point is, therefore, pinned at 90 million Btu per household for the country as a whole, based upon the 82 to 97 million Btu per customer found in the gas heating territory. (See Appendix Table A10–1 for details of derivation.)

No fuel burning heater is 100 per cent efficient, for part of the fuel's inherent heat is lost, mostly up the stack. And so, to derive the effective output of heat, consumption data must be appropriately corrected. As is only natural, each branch of the energy industry tends to set its own efficiency at the maximum. In making inter-fuel cost comparisons, the American Gas Association uses 80 per cent efficiency for gas, 57 per cent for oil, 48 per cent for bituminous coal. Studies that may be biased toward electricity suggest efficiency factors of 60 to 65 per cent for oil and gas. And so it goes. In this study average efficiency of all installed gas equipment has been taken as 75 per cent, based on a normal design efficiency of 80 per cent and the relatively simple combustion process, which would cause only a moderate lowering of efficiency with age. Such a factor translates the input of 90 million Btu to an effective heat output of 67 million Btu per household. To be on the safe side in our requirement calculations we have rounded this upward to 70 million Btu. This then might be called the average annual heat requirement of the adequately heated American household as it exists today, i.e., with only a minimum of insulation.

It is apparent, however, that today's level of residential space heating does not, on the average, meet this "normal" standard. A lower actual level of not quite 60 million Btu for all households was calculated for the year 1955 in Resources for the Future's *Energy in the American Economy*.[1] In the projections, we have assumed that the 70-million-Btu level would be reached by 1980, through reduction in substandard-heating households (heated by means other than gas, oil, or electricity, or not heated at all) and the continuing trend towards central heating. We have further assumed that after 1980 the projected westward shift of the population combined with the effect of better insulation in the fast growing proportion of new dwellings—also promoted by the rising importance of air conditioning—would tend to lower the average national heating requirement and overshadow the effect of any possible growth in the average size of dwelling.

The scattered available statistics on insulation indicate that it is in its infancy, especially in non-custom-built housing. Its effects upon heat loss are substantial. Going from zero to 4-inch insulation can reduce heat loss in the wall by two-thirds, and increasing ceiling insulation from the customary 2 inches to 6 inches can cut down heat loss through that avenue by nearly one-half. This leaves windows and infiltration as the biggest sources of heat loss. It has been estimated that so-called 6–4–2 insulation (6–inch ceiling, 4–inch wall, and 2–inch floor) will reduce total heating requirements by no less than one-third and perhaps by as much as one-half.[2] On a conservative basis, this means that the "normal" 70 million Btu per household could be reduced to less than 50 million Btu by the adoption of better insulation practices. Naturally, such a reduction can become effective only gradually, above all through replacement of older houses and the engineering of relatively inexpensive ways for insulating walls and floors in existing houses. At present, the practice of ceiling insulation is widespread in all but the cheapest houses, but wall insulation occurs in no more than 50 per cent of newly built houses even in the highest cost bracket, ranging down to a mere 10 per cent at the lowest cost level.

In view of the wide scope for home improvement, our projection for the year 2000 calls for an average heat output requirement of around 60 million Btu per household, a 15 per cent drop from the estimated 1980 peak. This should leave the field open for incorporation of heat-conserving insulation or other efficiency-promoting devices in houses to be built in the next four decades.

The above considerations reflect a conservative approach to the future of heating which rules out any radical innovations such as solar heating or long-distance transmission of centrally generated heat. Efficiencies in the use of energy sources will change, and so will the relative importance of sources of energy, but the essential dependence upon a heating device pushing heat into an enclosed space and fed by energy sources now in use is not assumed to change materially during the rest of this century.

1. Sam H. Schurr, Bruce C. Netschert, *et al., Energy in the American Economy, 1850–1975* (Baltimore: Johns Hopkins Press and Resources for the Future, 1960).

2. See, for example, Southeastern Electric Exchange, *Economic Study of Electric, Gas and Oil Usage for Capehart and Other Public Housing Projects,* June 1958, pp. 32–33; *Load* (General Electric Co., Schenectady, New York), June 1957.

All other changes that reasonably can be expected are changes in the efficiency of the current types of heating device. Examples of more novel departures are the heat pump (discussed on pages 190–191), oil or gas furnaces burning at high temperatures without flame, electric heating produced by small oil or gas fired turbines driving generators (these are now beginning to make an appearance in commercial-type buildings), and perhaps the fuel cell or a related device. Just as the number of automatic furnaces has increased fivefold since the end of World War II, so there could be an equally rapid change to one or all such infant devices within the next twenty years or so. But it is hard to foresee a trend away from the traditional sources of heat: solid, liquid, and gaseous hydrocarbons, or electricity. These, we can be reasonably sure, will continue to form the energy mix in domestic heating.

Energy competition in space heating. Gas and oil between them now heat over 80 per cent of all households. The customers for gas heating have nearly tripled, from 7½ million in 1949, the first year for which data are available, to over 21 million at the end of 1960, and the prospects are that growth will continue, though at a more moderate rate, as more of the heating market is captured. In terms of energy input, oil and gas are running a close race, but in terms of heat output utilized in homes, gas has probably outdistanced oil owing to the higher average efficiency of existing gas-heating equipment. Of the remaining heat output, more than half is supplied by coal and the balance by such means as liquid petroleum gas (LPG), wood, and electricity.

There is much controversy over the factors that determine the choice of heating systems, and fierce competition among the suppliers for the consumer's dollar. More recently, the electric utilities have entered the fray, so that the struggle has now turned three-cornered: gas versus oil versus electricity. Coal supports electricity, with only slim hopes of re-entering the residential market on its own merit.

Since most people buy their homes ready made, the key to the choice lies more with the builder than with the eventual resident; this tends to make the cost of the original equipment, not the cost of operation, the important criterion. Gas-heating equipment, principally because of the simplicity of the burner, the absence of storage requirements, and the reduced requirements of piping and wiring, has had a clear cost advantage over oil. In addition, the gas industry has successfully merchandised gas as the more convenient, cleaner, more trouble-free heating mode, banishing all fear of fuelless days because the fuel is piped into the home as it is consumed. The price of fuel seems to have played only a secondary role. Gas prices have risen more than oil or coal since 1947–49, when gas heating began to expand rapidly. But in a recent poll fuel oil dealers themselves were inclined to consider the price of fuel as "immaterial" and believed that "gas prices would have to go up another 30%" to change the builders' preference for gas.[3] The matter of equipment cost, which affects the all-important "monthly payment," versus operating cost, about which the average home buyer knows little when he signs the sales contract, is a fruitful field for future investigation. There is apparently a large area of consumer indifference towards operating cost until prices rise considerably, though eventually higher prices can be presumed to have their effect upon demand.

The advance of gas heating has been held back only by the measure in which gas pipelines have failed to reach all parts of the nation. The Bureau of Labor Statistics surveys, taken in 1940, 1950, and 1956, show a rise of the share of gas-heating equipment installed by builders from 47 per cent in 1940 to 64 per cent in 1950 and to 72 per cent in 1956. Installations of oil-burning equipment, still on the upswing from 13 to 33 per cent in the forties, had receded to 21 per cent by 1956. Coal heating has practically vanished from new housing; the only real question is how rapidly it will be replaced in older dwellings. Figure 10–2 shows these trends very clearly.

The oil-heating industry is deeply concerned. The industry's newly merged top association, the National Oil Fuel Institute, made up of the National Fuel Oil Council and the Oil Heat Institute, is attempting to halt the decline by seeking new ways of making oil heating attractive. One of the problems it faces is that the

3. *Fueloil and Oil Heat* (Heating Publishers, Inc., New York, N.Y.), January 1961, p. 12.

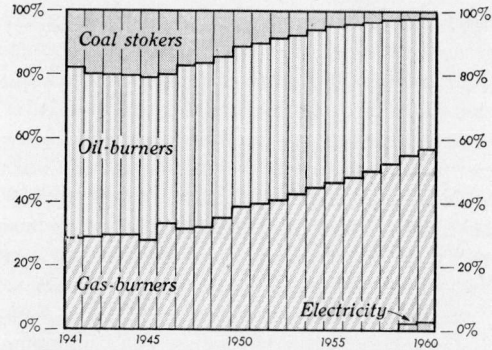

Figure 10–2. Changing shares of automatic heating devices in residential use, 1941–1960.

equipment is usually made by manufacturers that also produce gas-heating equipment, so that there is no independent push from the equipment side. At this time, emphasis within the industry seems to be shifting from conquering new territory to preventing old customers from converting oil to gas or electricity. The biggest wave of oil heat installations came right after the end of World War II, before natural gas expansion got under way. As the average life of an oil heater is customarily figured at sixteen to eighteen years, the industry expects a huge wave of replacement demand in the sixties. It is conducting much research into improved, and cheaper, oil-heating equipment to retain that market.

Recent experience, however, suggests a difficult task ahead. Oil has lost steadily and substantially, with around 80,000 to 120,000 conversions from oil to gas a year, plus a rising number of changes to electric heating—exceeding 10,000 for the first time in 1958; at the same time replacement of oil burners by new oil burners has been running between 100,000 and 200,000 units. On the whole, oil heating seems to have lost, year after year, at least one-third of the replacement market. This trend, coinciding with a declining share in heating equipment for new homes, a drying up of the coal-to-oil replacement demand, and projected below-average population growth in those areas where oil has had its strongest foothold, does not suggest a reversal in the decline of oil heating.

While increased gas use appears inevitable, electricity shows distinct signs of becoming a sizable competitor. In the new non-farm housing

market it may have captured close to 10 per cent of the heating installations in 1960, and the total number of electrically heated homes climbed from some 200,000 in 1955 (these early figures are not too reliable) to nearly one million by the end of 1960. The rate of growth, rather than the absolute numbers involved, is impressive, especially as some of the fastest growth rates are found not in the customary bailiwicks of cheap and aggressive electricity, like the TVA and Northwest Pacific areas, but in the colder North Central states where electrical heating poses some serious problems.

There are some advantages to electrical heating that give it an edge over oil and gas; for example, complete absence of any kind of piping, unquestionable cleanliness, individual room control, and, except for heat pumps, absence of noise and furnace space requirements. Lack of open flame may also have appeal. The anticipated continuing spread of air conditioning, in which electricity so far has dominated, and the urge of power companies to balance their summer peaks with heavy winter consumption have spurred utilities into increasingly active promotion; the consumer may be strongly attracted by the prospect of summer cooling and winter heating from the same energy source, especially in terms of operating cost.

The fact that storms can paralyze power transmission is a disadvantage that electric heating shares with other heating media, for thermostats and blowers rely on electricity, whatever the heat source. Only a self-contained gas furnace that produces its own electricity would alter the picture. Rising real incomes will bring homes with electrical heating, or heating and cooling, within the range of an increasing share of the population. The higher cost of electricity could to some extent be offset by better insulation—a possibility reflected in the insulation standards recommended, sometimes stipulated, by the utilities. While one may discount as a forecast the industry's picture of 29 million electrically heated homes by 1980, it must be taken quite seriously as a symbol of the role that heating plays in the plans of the utilities.

In our projections, the relative slowdown of gas is well discernible between 1970 and 1980, when the share of gas-heated dwellings is projected to rise by only 10 per cent, compared with a projected 22 per cent rise in the sixties. Between 1980 and 1990 no further rise is indicated. Just as oil heating can be anticipated to be kept in check by gas heating, so it seems safe to conjecture that the progress of gas will be slowed down, and perhaps eventually reversed, by electricity. How soon and how fast? This is more difficult to answer. Except for electrical heating, our projected pattern for all residences approaches the distribution of heating sources as it prevails in housing now being built. It may, therefore, be somewhat conservative regarding the further growth of gas heating, since it is possible that the decline in the percentage of new houses equipped with oil heating has not yet come to an end. The findings of the 1960 Housing Census, not yet available at the time of writing, and future sample studies should throw light on this question.

The data shown in Table 10–1 are the end-result of the projected trends in each type of heating. Perhaps most interesting is the fact that only in the High projection does gas heating account for substantially more than half the country's households.

Of the estimated 920,000 homes in the

TABLE 10–1. Distribution of Dwellings by Source of Heat, 1960 and Projections for 1980, 2000

(Per cent of total)

Fuel	1960		1980	2000
Natural gas	41	L	48	42
		M	54	50
		H	63	66
Oil	30	L	20	14
		M	21	15
		H	22	16
Coal	12	L	2	–
		M	3	–
		H	7	–
Liquid petroleum gas	9	L	6	3
		M	7	5
		H	10	10
Electricity	2	L	6	13
		M	12	31
		H	20	47
Other	5		3	–

L—Low projection   M—Medium   H—High.
Source: Appendix Table A10–8.

United States with complete electric space heating at the end of 1960, about 200,000 had been added during 1960.[4] The major part of the total were still located in the South, especially in the TVA area, and along the Pacific Coast; but the rest of the nation was beginning to catch on. For example, in 1960 nearly 10 per cent of electrically heated houses were located in the cold East North Central region; this was twice as many as in 1958.

Rather than project mechanically from the low present number and consequently fast annual growth rate of electric heating, we have made specific assumptions regarding the rate at which it might be introduced into new construction in each of the four decades to come. The rates we have stipulated are highly speculative, but one cannot but be impressed by the rapid rise in the rate of installation in the recent past— from a little over 2 per cent of all new construction in 1957, according to the trade reports, to nearly 10 per cent in 1960. In addition, one old house was converted to electric heating for every four new houses so equipped. Trade sources hope that by 1965 over 2 million homes, or over 3 per cent of all households, will be electrically heated; predictions range from 5 to 6 million for 1970, with a rise to 12 million by 1975 and to 29 million by 1980.[5]

Electric heating can be accomplished by methods that differ radically in efficiency. Resistance heating in various forms (radiant, convection, etc.) relies on the heating of wires or coils. The heat output equals the heat content of the energy input, i.e., the devices are for all practical purposes 100 per cent efficient. The so-called heat pump, on the other hand, has a much higher efficiency; its heat output is a multiple of the heat equivalent of the energy consumed. This multiple, referred to as the "coefficient of performance," varies with the conditions under which the heat pump, which is essentially a device transferring heat between environments of different temperatures, operates. The higher the outside temperature the higher the coefficient. Under most favorable

4. *Electrical World*'s Fifth Electrical World Heating Conference, Washington, September 25–26, 1961, Proceedings (New York: McGraw-Hill Publishing Co.).
5. *Ibid.*

conditions, the heat output may be as high as four or five times the energy input, but under most actual conditions, a coefficient not above three and often closer to two is likely.

There are as yet few pumps in operation, but growth is rapid—from just over 100,000 at the end of 1960 to over 150,000 estimated at the end of 1961. Most have been installed in the warmer parts of the country, where air conditioning is sought at least as much as heating. They are now beginning to make a bid for acceptance in colder climates. First cost is still high, though less so for the builder who is contemplating central heating *and* cooling and, correctly, compares the cost of the heat pump with the alternative of the combined costs of separate heating and cooling systems. Because the heat pump has the potential of a complete "climate control" tool, it seems to have a brighter future than might be indicated by its present sparse distribution. To the electric utility industry, it represents an ideal way of building seasonally balanced consumption and achieving the "all-electric house." To the consumer, it promises the elimination of any fuel storage, piping from and to the outside, and open flame. Its attraction is thus undoubted. Fulfillment, on the other hand, may have to await lower cost and technical improvements, especially such as will make the device more flexible: in different areas either heating or cooling may be the predominant need; therefore some way might be found to adjust the respective capacities of the pump so that as a heater it will not be significantly long or short on cooling capacity and vice versa. The utility industry looks forward to increased acceptance of the heat pump. One estimate is that at the end of the sixties one-quarter of all residential electric heating will be by heat pump, as against 11 per cent in 1960 and 14 per cent in 1961.[6]

Where does this leave us as far as projections of future electric power consumption are concerned? From what has been said about efficiency, it is clear that energy requirements will be lower for heat pumps than for resistance heating. Some assumption about the equipment pattern is therefore essential, but the attempt is more a bow in the right direction than the re-

6. *Ibid.*

sult of a closely reasoned analysis. The guess that by the end of the century over half the electric heating installations will be represented by heat pumps, or some descendants thereof, is lent substance by another projection: that by that time roughly half of all households should have central air conditioning and an additional third, room air conditioning. Given the expectations of the industry for the sixties, this may be a conservative outlook.

Efficiencies and physical energy requirements. The final step in the projection carries the estimates from heat output to physical demand for individual fuels, by way of estimated efficiencies.

The efficiency factors used reflect technically unspecified future improvements in heating devices. For gas and LPG only minor improvement has been assumed, in view of the high factors now presumed to prevail. (Even rather radical departures such as the porous ceramic tube, glowing at 2,000° with essentially flameless combustion, claim an improvement in efficiency of only 10 to 12 per cent.) Oil furnaces, on the other hand, have been assumed to become increasingly efficient between 1960 and 1980 under the spur of competition from gas now and from electricity later. Whatever coal-fired equipment survives is expected to become more efficient as older heating units disappear.

Average efficiency of currently operating heating devices is unknown. It is generally agreed that electric resistance heating is for all practical purposes 100 per cent efficient, i.e., involves no significant heat loss, and that gas, oil, and coal form a descending scale of efficiency. Beyond lies controversy.

The efficiencies that are assumed in this report represent the impression of observers as they review the claims made by rival industries and attempt to evaluate them in terms of likely bias as well as in terms of average age of equipment across the country. Overstated efficiencies would depress projected fuel requirements and understated efficiencies would exaggerate them. The efficiencies assumed here are intended merely as statistical bridges between heat output on the one hand and fuel input on the other. In no case are they to be interpreted as expert judgments reflecting on the quality of one type of equipment as compared with another, nor can they serve as clues to costs of heating.

Summary. The quantitative results of the projections are presented in Table 10–2. It should be noted that the electricity figures represent the energy input not in the home but at central power stations, i.e., the Btu content of coal, oil, or gas needed to generate the amount of electricity called for.

According to our projections total energy input will rise by less than 50 per cent between 1960 and 2000, compared with an increase of 84 per cent in population and 89 per cent in households in the Medium assumption. This does not seem unreasonable in the light of improved construction methods and higher efficiencies, increasing use of the heat pump, and the growing importance of single-occupant households requiring less heat. A swing to apartment dwelling, with the higher ratio of inside space to outside walls, would further accentuate this tendency, but it is too early to judge whether such a movement is indeed on the way. The increase in input between 1980 and 2000 is re-

TABLE 10–2. Energy Input for Residential Space Heating, by Source of Energy, 1960 and Projections for 1980, 2000

(Trillion Btu)

Fuel	1960		1980	2000
Gas	2,170	L	2,910	2,750
		M	3,585	3,715
		H	4,320	6,030
Oil	2,110	L	1,130	710
		M	1,670	1,430
		H	1,870	2,090
Coal	530	L	270	–
		M	285	–
		H	320	–
LPG	145	L	210	90
		M	225	105
		H	250	150
Electricity (Btu content of fuel input, excl. transmission losses)	129	L	621	920
		M	1,007	2,028
		H	1,547	3,427
All sources	5,084		6,772	7,278

L—Low projection   M—Medium   H—High.

Sources: Appendix Tables A10–9 and 11, the former converted to Btu's by use of Table A15–17.

markable for its small size. Declining requirements, due to better insulation and population shifts west and southward, as well as increase in electric heating, involving higher efficiency in both application and generation, are at the root of this projection. Lows and Highs in heat *input* have been computed only for individual fuels. The range in the High and Low estimates in total residential heat *output* is modest, even though it maximizes Highs and Lows by combining High household projections with High heat output per household, and similarly for Lows (cf. Appendix Table A10–11). Most of the amplitude depends on the range in the household projections rather than on differing assumptions regarding heat consumption rates. There is little reason for anticipating radical changes in the latter.

For the individual energy shares the range naturally widens. The projected continuing expansion in gas heating would by 1980 increase its use by 65 per cent above the 1960 volume. Thereafter it would expand very little, mainly because of the inroads of electric heating but also, to a small extent, because of the decline in per capita heating consumption. Under the Low assumption, expansion would be limited to 34 per cent above the 1960 level; the High projection would carry gas consumption to twice its 1960 level by 1980 and nearly three times by the year 2000. Should electric heating not come of age, then the High for gas might turn out to be more realistic than we would now believe likely.

The projected paths of oil heating point downward, even in the High model. The industry is so fully alive to this trend that one may expect major efforts to reverse it.

The recent sharp rise in electric heating appears to be only the beginning of a trend that will be strong throughout the rest of the century.

The growth through 1980 of LPG, as shown in the summary table, is due solely to the expansion in number of households, and so is its range. Main use is in more or less isolated areas or by two-home families, and since population growth is expected to be concentrated in urban areas it is difficult to foresee an increase in the relative share of LPG as a household fuel or a maintenance of position later in the century.

As for coal, the disappearance of automatic stokers seems to be merely a question of time: out of nearly 24 million automatic central burners in use at the end of 1960, fewer than half a million were coal burners. It is to be assumed that the non-automatic types will persist with somewhat greater success; under that aspect the Low estimate, showing half of 1960 consumption by 1980, is as far as pessimism can be allowed to proceed. Nonetheless, the halving in retail deliveries of coal between 1955 and 1960 raises the possibility that the decline in coal heating may accelerate rather than slow down. Continuation of this relative rate of decline would make coal retail deliveries negligible by 1975. While this is not impossible, it is improbable. On the other hand, only a major revolution in coal-heating techniques could prove the projection wrong after 1980. One idea, the firing of micro-sized coal, assuming most of the characteristics of a liquid, in a new type of burner, is in the experimental stage, but it raises institutional questions of such intricacy—apart from technical questions—that no quantitative account has been taken of this potential.

Other Household Uses

All other household uses, combined, require about the same amount of energy as does space heating alone, when electricity is measured in terms of fuel required in its generation. Water heating and cooking are the largest consumers of energy in this category; others examined individually below are lighting and air conditioning and, somewhat more briefly, television, refrigeration, food freezing, and clothes drying. Remaining uses are combined under an "all other" label which not only includes present appliances but also leaves room for some devices now in the design stage and some that are not yet known.

This last consideration makes long-term projections particularly vulnerable. Few of today's appliance array were on the drawing board forty years ago, fewer still were candidates for mass production. We are in a similar position today. The best we can do to guard against this source of error is to provide for a growing amount of unspecified energy use to be filled in by the inventiveness of tomorrow's engineer and designer. These "phantom appliances," as the trade calls them, and the likelihood of their success, cannot by their nature be discussed in substance; they are merely a statistical device to plug a source of underestimation. Most of what follows is devoted, therefore, to projecting the future of the principal appliances that are in use today.

Residential use of energy for purposes other than space heating is estimated to have consumed in 1960 some 3,900 trillion Btu—equivalent to some 150 million tons of coal, or close to 10 per cent of all energy consumed in the economy. Roughly half of this was by way of

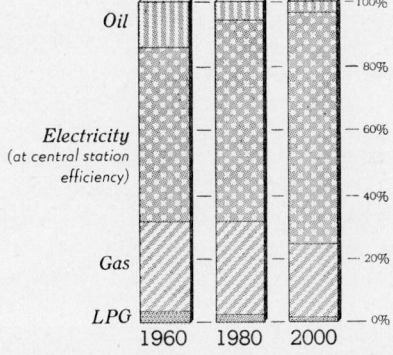

Figure 10–3. Shares of energy sources in domestic uses, excluding space heating, 1960 and Medium projections for 1980 and 2000.

direct home consumption of a fuel; the other half represented the consumption of fuel (or its equivalent in hydro power) in central power stations that send electricity into the home. In the direct consumption category, gas accounted for about two-thirds, oil and natural gas liquids for the balance. Use of coal outside the space-heating field is now rare and impossible to measure statistically.

Water heaters and ranges. In 1960 there were, on the average, more than one gas (including LPG) or electric range to each household, while two out of every three households claimed a gas or electric water heater. Undoubtedly, one-third of the nation was not without a source of hot water; it is rather that non-automatic water heaters are not included in the statistics and that coal was still a significant means of water heating, though, in all likelihood, most water heating by coal was done in furnaces, as an adjunct to space heating.

Medium projections summarized below assume continued growth in the percentage of households having one or the other appliance. Past rates of increase have been decelerated, however, especially for kitchen ranges, where better than 100 per cent saturation had statistically been reached in 1955. A significant slowdown in the growth rate of water heaters also has been assumed, especially after 1970, by which time it is projected that three out of four homes will be so equipped.

	1950	1960	1980	2000
Millions of households	43.8	52.6	73.0	99.4
Millions of ranges in use	[1]37.5	55.2	84.7	119.3
of which:				
Gas	[1]28.7	37.4	41.5	45.3
Electric	[1] 8.8	17.8	43.2	74.0
Millions of water heaters in use	18.5	32.0	62.1	99.4
of which:				
Gas	14.4	22.5	36.6	43.7
Electric	4.1	9.6	25.5	55.7

1. 1951.

How will the estimated total stock of these two appliances be shared between gas and electricity? Historical trends show a growing preference for the electric range. The same used to be true for water heaters, but in recent years the gas water heater—perhaps because of the growth of gas space heating—has grown in favor. As a result, growth in the share of electric water heaters has been kept moderate in our projections through 1970, but thereafter the effect of projected growth in electric space heating—accompanied by absence of gas connections—may be assumed to spur faster growth. The projected share of electric ranges reflects the probability of a gradual slowing down of the recent rapid rate of expansion.

There is little factual information on which to estimate future efficiency for these two appliances, whether they are fueled by gas or electricity. No doubt, innovations are in store which may result in larger sales of precooked, packaged foods. This will certainly reduce the heat needed in the home (and add it in the processing and distribution industry), but at least as much energy will be required to store it in its frozen condition.

In looking to the future, it has been assumed that greater use of prepared foods would cause a gradual decline in annual energy consumption for cooking, and that any improvements in the efficiency of water heaters would be offset by a more generous use of hot water in larger numbers of washing machines, dishwashers, and similar appliances.

Residential lighting. The level of consumption in electricity's original domestic use is less firmly known than one might imagine. All home use of electricity is centrally metered; consumption for any particular use can be estimated only indirectly or by special surveys. The base figure of 825 kwh here chosen for lighting consumption in 1960 is thus subject to controversy, though it is probably within 10 or 15 per cent of the "true" level. Very roughly, 825 kwh is the annual volume of electricity consumed by ten 60-watt bulbs turned on for an average of four hours a day. Available data suggest that ten to fifteen years ago each customer used only half as much light. Higher income and better understanding of lighting principles have undoubtedly made Americans less conscious of economy in lighting, but even so, the electric utility industry tells us that our lighting habits are still far from satisfactory.

In contrast to heating, where increasing space per person is offset by increasing efficiency of devices and housing construction, there is room for per capita growth in lighting. Among the reasons are: (1) the concept that a room should be illuminated evenly at all points; (2) the use of lighting for decorative as well as utilitarian purposes, which would include outdoor illumination; (3) relaxation of the economical room-by-room approach to lighting; and (4) increasing use of safety lighting indoors and outdoors. On the other hand, some technical innovations, such as fluorescent fixtures, would tend to reduce rather than increase consumption.

Considerations such as these have prompted the industry to set ambitious targets. Attainment of 1,725 kwh per customer by 1965, better than twice the 1960 consumption, is held to be possible provided there is aggressive promotion. Barring a complete revolution in living habits, this seems an extravagant goal; its attainment even in the latter part of the century is doubtful. The residential consumer has added only some 600 kwh to his annual lighting consumption in the nearly half century since World War I, most of it in the past two decades.

Some targets are even higher. The desirable end-result of special "lighting campaigns" planned by the industry, put by experts at 2,093 kwh per customer for 1965, has been adopted in our projections, summarized below, as the High for 1970. The Medium projection for 1970, 1,075 kwh, was arrived at by assuming a 25-kwh per year increase per customer; the result agrees closely with the trend estimated by a utility that has been a major factor in the lighting estimating field, the Middle West Service Company. Our projections for consumption of electricity per capita for residential lighting are tabulated below.

	Low projection (kwh)	Medium projection (kwh)	High projection (kwh)
1940	–	352	–
1950	–	602	–
1960	–	825	–
1970	975	1,075	2,100
1980	1,125	1,325	2,500
1990	1,275	1,575	2,900
2000	1,425	1,825	3,300

The decennial increase of 250 kwh per customer, based upon the trend of the past twenty years, was retained throughout the period for the Medium estimate; it was reduced to 150 for the Low and increased to 400 for the High. The past history of lighting use gives little reason to believe that changes will differ much from the 25- to 50-kwh increase per year that has prevailed in the recent past, but there is a good deal of unpredictability in the American consumer, especially as incomes continue their steady growth. Nor can the targets of the industry be ignored altogether, as they are bound to function as stimulants.

Although efforts to use gas as a source of lighting have never ceased and have recently been revived by some enterprising gas utilities

for special effects, no account has been taken of this development here. If at all susceptible to large-scale growth, this would seem to lie in the commercial rather than the residential field. Nor have we considered any other fuel, such as kerosene, as significant enough to be considered in this broad-brush portrait.

Air conditioning. Home air conditioning, which has only recently stepped over the threshold of acceptance, will result in a major new outlet for energy producers. It may also lead to serious seasonal load problems (it has already done so in some localities that now have summer rather than winter load peaks) unless supplemented by commensurate expansion of winter consumption of energy through heating. This circumstance partly explains the electric utility industry's drive for the acceptance of electric heating.

So far, gas has dominated in heating, electricity in air conditioning. Gas has not so far made significant inroads on air conditioning, or indeed any type of cooling or freezing device. By the end of 1960 an estimated 30,000 central gas-fired air-conditioning units were in operation in residential structures, and this figure was probably around 50,000 by the end of 1961. When energy requirements per unit of activity are compared, gas is at a disadvantage with electricity. While in water heating and cooking gas devices consume fewer Btu's than electric devices, when electricity is measured in terms of primary fuel input the ratio rises to two times in air conditioning and up to four and five times in refrigerators.[7]

It is possible that the efforts of the gas appliance industry to reduce the initial cost of gas-using air conditioners to that of electric units may reverse the situation. The industry is in fact quite optimistic, but the development is too recent and the head-start of the electric utilities too great to warrant quantitative consideration of gas air conditioning in this study. The situation, nonetheless, will bear close watching.

Forced air heating through a duct system was installed in 73 per cent of all new homes in 1956. Each of these homes, and their predeces-

7. Schurr, Netschert, *et al., op. cit.,* pp. 619–20, Table C-32.

sors back to 1940, is a potential customer for central air conditioning, even though the conventional location of the register at floor level reduces the efficiency of a later added cooling system. The step from using two different energy sources feeding into a single duct system to perfecting a single heating-cooling device seems logical, once efficiencies in cooling and heating can be equalized. But this development lies almost wholly in the future.

The starting point for the projection is provided by a 1958 Bureau of Labor Statistics survey,[8] which reported 6 per cent of new homes as having built-in complete cooling systems. This percentage might rise to some 15 per cent during the sixties, with further increases thereafter. To these basic figures of original installations must be added the estimated number of homes built between 1940 and 1960 (when forced air heating installations were general) which would add air conditioning as an afterthought. That a forced air duct heating system has favored the installation of a central system is suggested by a 1956 marketing survey of central residential air conditioning sponsored by the Du Pont Company, though the geographical distribution may have somewhat biased the results: 91 per cent of the respondents who owned such systems had forced air installations. This may not be as true in the future, should units installed in the attic become more popular.

Room air conditioners have been a fast-growing innovation. By 1960 one out of eight households had at least one unit. Rapid growth can be assumed to continue for some time, but should then slow down and eventually reverse itself as central systems expand. In our projections an upper limit of some 80 per cent of all households has been assumed for 2000, based on regional climatic differences. The outlook for use of electricity in various forms of residential air conditioning over the next four decades is tabulated below (Medium projections). As yet, there are insufficient data to provide the basis for making similar projections for the use of gas.

8. U.S. Department of Labor, Bureau of Labor Statistics, *New Housing and its Materials, 1940–56* (Washington, 1958).

	1960	1980	2000
Millions of households	52.6	73.0	99.4
with central air conditioning	0.5	12.7	43.7
with room air conditioning	7.4	29.2	34.8
Consumption of electricity:			
per central unit (kwh)	3,500	3,200	2,500
per household with room unit (kwh)	800	700	600
Aggregate annual (bil. kwh)	7.7	61.0	130.0

For room air conditioners, annual rates of power consumption per unit are projected to decline moderately from current estimated levels. There are different factors at work here. On the one hand, the increasing number of households equipped with room air conditioners will be accompanied by a rising number of units per home (estimated at 1.2 in 1960 and rising to perhaps 1.5 by 2000). Higher efficiency of the equipment itself and availability of two or more units should help lower unit consumption. On the other hand, the combined effect of two or more units may convey the impression of the "fully air-conditioned home" and actually lead to it and thus to higher unit consumption. On balance, however, the former influence should prevail.

For central systems, substantial improvement has been stipulated, based partially on better insulation, which may drop the cooling load by 30 per cent and more, on higher efficiency of equipment, and on gradual spread of central air conditioning to areas requiring less cooling. High power requirements were based on the assumption of no decrease in consumption per unit; Lows were based on a faster schedule.

Miscellaneous appliances. There remain the numerous appliances that consume relatively small amounts of energy. Only a few are enumerated individually; the remainder—steam irons, radios, dishwashers, etc.—are combined in an "all other" category which also includes the so-called "phantom" appliances discussed earlier, both those which exist on drawing boards or as prototypes (e.g., dust precipitators, luminescent walls) and, more importantly, the unknown ones.

For purposes of practicality all miscellaneous appliances but one are assumed to be in the electrical field. The exception is clothes dryers, about one-third of which today are estimated to be gas fired.

The problems of projecting electricity consumption vary from appliance to appliance. In some instances there is doubt about the per customer annual level of use, in others about the growth in the saturation rate. In the case of appliances such as refrigerators and television sets, where saturation is now close to 100 per cent and limits to expansion are therefore more rigid (though for TV by no means fixed), a single-valued projection has been considered satisfactory. Any excess beyond 100 per cent in terms of refrigerators per home could well be balanced by technical improvements, the influence of air conditioning upon room temperatures, and other factors. The continuous decline in energy consumption per unit by now apparently has run its course and can be assumed to remain at current levels throughout the period under review. For TV, the potential saturation rate will undoubtedly climb beyond 100 per cent, or an average of one set per home, but there are practical limits to the prospects of additional power consumption in terms of hours of viewing, and there also are possibilities of changing trends involving reduced power use—the adoption of transistor sets is an example.

In the case of freezers and dryers, both high power users but both carrying only a brief historical record, trends in annual consumption per household have been introduced into our projections. It appears likely that increased use of precooked and frozen food will lead to greater per customer use of freezers in terms of both size and load. But it has been assumed that the freezer, benefiting from the refrigerator experience, has reached a level of efficiency similar to that of the refrigerator, so that bigger loads will not be offset by increasing efficiency. Continuous decline in unit power consumption for clothes dryers has been assumed; this assumption is based upon the greater use of light and synthetic fabrics, requiring shorter drying time or merely exposure to room temperature.

The factors underlying our projections of energy use in miscellaneous appliances are summarized in the tabulation below (Medium projections).

	1950	1960	1980	2000
Saturation factors (per cent of households):				
Refrigerators	72.1	95.2	100	100
Television sets	16.4	87.1	100	100
Home freezers	5.5	22.1	53.0	70.0
Clothes dryers	0.9	18.3	60.0	75.0
of which electric (per cent)	90	70	50	50
Energy consumption per unit per year:				
Refrigerators (kwh)		350	350	350
Television sets (kwh)		250	250	250
Home freezers (kwh)		800	900	900
Clothes dryers:				
electric (kwh)		1,300	1,100	1,000
gas (mil. Btu)		4.5	4.0	3.5
All other electric appliances[1] (kwh)		330	850	1,600

1. Other than ranges, water heaters, and those listed above.

To accommodate the miscellaneous appliances too numerous to identify separately, we have made an allowance of 330 kwh per household in an "all other" category for 1960. This compares with survey data which show a range in consumption estimates for such appliances of from 150 to 400 kwh per customer in 1956.[9] Since we are dealing with averages and since, except in the field of TV, most appliances show relatively slow growth, this allowance is increased by only 200 kwh in the first decade and by somewhat more in the later stretches. Cumulatively, this category rises to 1,600 kwh in 2000; at that level it is equivalent to twice present per customer use for lighting, but only 13 per cent of projected 2000 average domestic electricity consumption. The "all other" category even now accounts for 9 per cent of power use per customer; its rise during the next four decades therefore appears not unreasonable, providing for either a proportionate expansion of the large variety of small uses and little innovation, or—which seems more realistic—a continuing small spread of uses not now looming large combined with some new significant application. The latter is all the more likely in view of the ubiquitous nature of electricity in the household, not only producing heat, light, and motive power, but performing auxiliary func-

9. Middle West Service Co. survey mentioned in Schurr, Netschert, *et al., op. cit.,* p. 624, Table C–35.

tions where other fuels are used for primary purposes.

Because this "all other" category is a rather speculative item, we have assumed, in addition to the Medium projection, a Low of 100-kwh addition every ten years and a rapidly rising High commencing with a 300-kwh addition between 1960 and 1970.

Our estimates for all the separately enumerated appliances and the "all other" total 193 billion kwh—equal to the total residential sales reported by utilities in 1960[10] plus a share of rural sales which is taken to be of the order of 4 billion kwh.

Miscellaneous gas consumption is covered through a statistical adjustment. For purposes of reconciling 1960 utility sales to residential customers with the aggregate of the individual uses separately estimated here for 1960, we have added to the latter what amounts to an "all other" gas consumption category. This includes uses of gas not computed separately and also corrects for errors in assumptions underlying those applications that are the subject of individual projections.

An estimate is also made for uses of petroleum products not separately considered, principally kerosene and range oil used for cooking and water heating and, in rare instances, lighting (see Appendix Table A10–18). These adjustments are rough and serve (1) to establish a 1960 base that is comparable with historical data and (2) as a reminder that detailed coverage is incomplete. The amount is roughly 25 per cent of the quantity consumed in space heating—and this proportion is assumed to continue. The impact on all petroleum consumption is insignificant: some 1½ per cent even by 1980.

Summary

We are now in a position to take an across-the-board look at energy use in the American home; for this purpose all forms of energy, including electricity, which is translated into the heat required to generate it, are expressed in terms of the actual or hypothetical heat content of the generating energy source materials. (The

10. Edison Electric Institute, *Statistical Year Book of the Electric Utility Industry for 1960* (New York, 1961).

principles underlying this operation are discussed in Chapter 15.)

The findings show (1) a substantially stable share of natural gas, (2) a continuously decreasing role for oil, until in 2000 it supplies a not much larger share of energy to the home than coal does today, and (3) rapidly increasing participation of electricity, which by the end of the century is projected to furnish over half the energy. LPG remains of peripheral significance, and coal as a direct source of domestic energy is projected to fade out of the picture after 1980.

It must be remembered, however, that all fuels will continue to furnish domestic energy by way of electricity, especially coal. At the same time, the projected emergence of nuclear-generated energy limits the contribution that the conventional fuels can be expected to make via electricity. For example, with roughly half of all electricity in 2000 projected to be supplied by atomic reactors, even exclusive use of coal in the remaining power stations could not bring the domestic use of coal to the level of gas use. Actually, substantially less than half of all electric power generation is projected to derive from coal.

Figure 10–4 and Table 10–3 show the leading role that electricity is projected to gain after 1980, and the large role of gas demand in direct fuel use (i.e., fuel burned in the home).

The second striking feature of this summary compilation is the slowdown in the growth

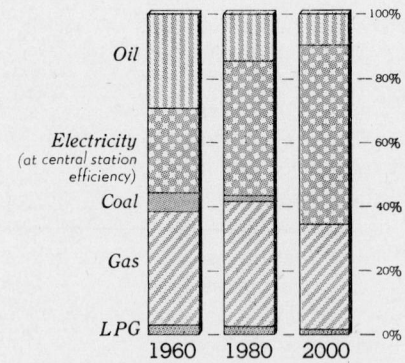

Figure 10–4. Shares of energy sources in all domestic uses, 1960 and Medium projections for 1980 and 2000.

TABLE 10–3. Consumption of Fuels for All Residential Uses, 1960 and Medium Projections for 1980, 2000

Fuel	1960	1980	2000	1960	1980	2000
	(quadrillion Btu)			*(per cent of total)*		
Natural gas	3.19	5.66	5.98	35.4	38.9	32.7
Oil	2.63	2.09	1.79	29.2	14.4	9.8
Coal	.53	.29	–	5.9	2.0	–
LPG	.28	.39	.28	3.1	2.7	1.5
Electricity (at central station efficiency and including transmission and distribution losses)	2.38	6.11	10.23	26.4	42.0	56.0
Total	9.01	14.54	18.28	100.0	100.0	100.0

Sources: Appendix Tables A10–19 and A15–18.

rate of total energy consumption after 1980. The reason lies above all in the lessened consumption for heating and the expansion of electric heating. Better insulation and shifts to warmer regions are contributing factors. Continuing technological advance in power generation is another, aided somewhat by the replacement of direct fuel burning—at best 80 per cent efficient—with electric heating, the efficiency of which may reach 200 to 300 per cent in the case of the heat pump. The effect of more efficient power generation, discussed fully in Chapter 15, cannot be overemphasized. While total residential electricity use is projected to rise from 594 to 1,188 billion kwh between 1980 and 2000, i.e., to double in volume, the heat required to generate this power (allowing for losses) is projected to rise only from 6.11 to 10.23 quadrillion Btu, i.e., by two-thirds. This exerts a powerful downward pull on total energy requirements. Table 10–4 summarizes the use of gas and electricity—the principal house-

TABLE 10–4. Domestic Electricity and Natural Gas Consumption by Main Uses, 1960 and Medium Projections for 1980, 2000

Energy source and use	Total			Per household[1]		
	1960	1980	2000	1960	1980	2000
Electricity	*(billion kwh)*			*(kwh)*		
All uses[2]	193	594	1,188	3,669	8,137	11,952
Lighting	43	97	181	817	1,329	1,821
Ranges	21	43	59	399	589	594
Water heaters	45	120	240	855	1,644	2,414
Air conditioning	7.7	61	130	146	836	1,318
Space heating	11.7	108	258	222	1,480	2,595
All other	63.7	165	319	1,211	2,260	3,209
Natural Gas	*(quadrillion Btu)*					
All uses	3.19	5.66	5.98	–	–	–
Space heating	2.17	3.58	3.72	–	–	–
Other	1.02	2.08	2.26	–	–	–

Sources: Appendix Tables A10–9, 12, 13, 14, 16, 18, 19.

1. Basis for projecting number of gas-using households is very uncertain; therefore figures per household are computed only for electricity, where number of users is assumed to equal number of households.

2. Sum of uses does not always add to all uses because of rounding.

hold energy sources—for the main domestic tasks.

Commercial Consumption

Commercial use of energy accounts for around 9 per cent of the nation's total consumption. Most of the commercial category is made up of well-defined types of customer—stores, warehouses, and other distributors of goods; offices, hotels, and clubs. The available statistics, however, include a miscellany of other users that are less easily identifiable. For example, the American Gas Association regards residential service in apartment houses as commercial provided the resident is not individually metered, presumably because the magnitude of demand and the commercial character of the tenant-landlord relationship outweigh the residential end-use.

In the case of electricity, the dividing line is no more precise, but it has long been assumed to coincide with that between "large" and "small" consumers, as they are tagged in the utility statistics. *Energy in the American Economy,* previously cited, contains statistical material confirming that by and large the division may indeed run along the line of the so-called "small" versus "large" consumers, though on a net basis, in that each of the two categories includes similar amounts of power that, by market criteria, would more properly belong to the other. The dividing line between commercial and residential service is as loose as in the case of gas supply, in that multiple dwellings not individually metered fall into the commercial class.

No attempt has been made here to account for the utilities' more than 6 million commercial customers in terms of economic characteristics. Retail plus wholesale outlets constitute the largest element, but would seem to add to at most one-third of the total. Service establishments of various kinds might account for another sixth, leaving some 3 million commercial customers in the heterogeneous group of "offices" (trade, professional, religious, educational, etc.), churches, private schools, clubs, societies; obviously, small industrial plants and above all apartment houses must represent a sizeable portion of the category.

To construct power consumption character-

istics that can form the basis of projection for so varied a collection of customers presents a problem. Yet, on the purely empirical level, commercial gas as well as electricity consumption has shown a remarkably stable relationship to one measure or the other of residential consumption, as is shown in Appendix Table A10–21. This is most fortunate; for the statistics of commercial consumption not only are vague in customer characteristics but are undifferentiated as to type of use. Space heating, cooking, water heating, air conditioning, and lighting are responsible for unspecified shares of consumption. The retail store, the hospital, the bowling alley, the apartment house, and the small manufacturing establishment undoubtedly have radically different consumption patterns. As was said by the authors of a recent Westinghouse study: "When we assay the history of the number of customers and the total kilowatt-hour sales, we have all but exhausted the real, quantitative knowledge available on the subject."[11]

Electricity. Over the past three decades, with almost uncanny regularity, there has been one commercial electricity customer for every eight residential ones. True, this relationship might change. A major reversal of the flow from the city core to the suburbs could affect the relationship, as might an accompanying, or even independent, shift from single-unit to apartment dwellings, although radical changes of this kind in the past two or three decades have not had this effect. For this reason, and in the absence of more than vague moves in that direction, we have estimated the number of commercial customers as a linear function of the number of households, in line with past experience.

There exists a similar consistent relationship in average electric power consumption between commercial and residential customer. This has not held constant, however, but has decreased for the past fifteen years, from a high in 1943, when the average commercial customer consumed 6.3 times the amount used by the average residential customer, to just below 5 in the last six years.

One may rationalize this evolution in several

11. Westinghouse Electric Corp., Headquarters Market Planning, *Twenty-Year Predictions of Electric Power Requirements, 1958–1978* (Pittsburgh, September 1958), p. 23.

ways, but it is difficult to test any hypothesis statistically. Possibly the big domestic appliance wave after World War II, not paralleled by anything comparable in the commercial field, boosted residential consumption in relation to commercial. Possibly the fact that commercial lighting has increasingly switched from incandescent to more efficient fluorescent and mercury lamps—though lighting experts contend that such developments have hardly scratched the surface of opportunities to establish satisfactory levels of illumination—has depressed commercial power consumption in relation to residential use. More recently, the rapid adoption of air conditioning in commercial premises as contrasted with slower acceptance in private residences, the adoption of higher lighting standards, and late hours for stores, especially in suburban areas, could be responsible for the comparative stability in the relationship in the last ten years. And there may be other explanations.

Without knowing cause and effect in the past, it is difficult to be rational about the future; but in view of the past trend, and the projected rather substantial growth in residential power consumption—especially in climate control—commercial consumption per customer is likely to continue its moderate relative decline. Appliance growth will affect only certain groups of commercial customers, and electric heating will boost commercial use less than residential. Our projections, therefore, are based upon maintenance of the current relationship as the maximum to be expected and on moderate but continuing declines of varying magnitude for the Medium and Low models. The pertinent data for 1960, 1980, and 2000 are summarized below (Medium projections):

	1960	1980	2000
Number of commercial customers (millions)	6.5	9.0	12.2
Electric power consumption per customer (thous. kwh)	17.1	34.2	45.4
Aggregate commercial power consumption (bil. kwh)	113	308	554

In the absence of differentiated end-use data and because of reliance on a few empirical statistical relationships, it is worth while to check the results here obtained with projections made by others. A recent thoughtful projection is the twenty-year forecast made in late 1958 by the Market Planning Group of Westinghouse.[12] It puts commercial sales for the years 1968 and 1978 at 217 and 328 billion kwh respectively. This compares with 190 and 308 kwh projected for the most comparable years in this study—1970 and 1980. Considering that the Westinghouse prediction is based upon departmentalized methods, such as separate projections of lighting, air conditioning, heating, and "all other" uses, and even considers the likely effect of fluorescent lamps, the similarity of the results, obtained by very different approaches, is reassuring.

Our projections for 1980 are also close to the future requirements estimated by the Federal Power Commission in 1959:[13] its 1980 figure of 306 billion kwh was a rise by 25 per cent from the 244-billion-kwh estimate it had made in 1955. For the year 2000, the FPC, which extended its 1960–80 trend graphically, projected sales of 670 billion kwh, some 20 per cent above our projection. Our assumption of a decline in commercial versus residential consumption probably accounts for the difference.

A third source worth commenting on is *Electrical World*. The last available projection, published in September 1961, forecasts for 1970 and 1980, respectively, 254 and 548 billion kwh. These projections are substantially higher than ours (or those of any other source, for that matter). Previously published projections suggest that the differences are due to the publication's more dynamic expectations of growth in both number of commercial customers and consumption per customer, but especially the latter. It is our feeling that these projections are based on maximum rather than average growth conditions and represent more nearly industry targets than expectations.

Unfortunately, similar projections for gas and other energy source requirements are not available for comparison with our own.

12. Westinghouse Electric Corp., *op. cit*.

13. U.S. Senate Select Committee on National Water Resources, *Water Resource Activities in the United States*, Committee Print No. 10, *Electric Power in Relation to the Nation's Water Resources* (Washington, 1960). Our projections are greatly below FPC's most recent (January 30, 1962) revision (Release No. 11,829), in which commercial requirements have climbed to 435 billion kwh, almost double FPC's projection made in 1955.

Gas. In the case of gas, there has been a remarkably stable relationship between total commercial and total residential consumption: in the past twenty-five years, commercial has never been more than 32 or less than 25.5 per cent of residential consumption. A peak was reached in the second half of the forties. Since then the percentage has returned to the level it held in the thirties.

The preference of the gas companies for the profitable residential outlets and the expansion of gas service to new areas further removed from the sources of gas, which renders it too costly for any but residential use, may be important reasons for the lag in commercial consumption in the fifties; but if this was indeed a factor, it seems to have been overcome more recently. Greater staying power of coal and oil heating in the commercial space-heating market may be another element. And there are undoubtedly others. But only detailed case studies could lead to persuasive explanations.

Various developments are possible in the future. Gas may penetrate the commercial space-heating and space-cooling market further and catch up with the rapid past and projected growth in residential consumption; it may fail to do so and in addition be displaced by electricity in other uses (in cooking ranges, for example); or it may remain stable at or near present levels. But, as with electricity, no violent departures are likely from the basic tie between residential and commercial consumption. The calculations shown in Appendix Table A10–23 trace out these assumptions.

Other energy sources. Most difficult to deal with, for reasons explained in the discussion of residential demand, is the commercial call on energy sources other than gas and electricity. The quantities involved are by no means negligible. Oil, for example, is a prominent commercial space-heating fuel. Yet there is no alternative to deriving it as a balancing item, after use of other fuels has been determined, and thus subjecting it to wide margins of uncertainty. In doing so, we have assumed that the number of commercial customers of electric utilities is the most reasonable measure of the number of commercial establishments in the country and that

its projection can therefore serve as an estimate of the number of commercial enterprises (as defined for utility purposes). We speculate that consumption of energy other than electricity will grow with the number of customers, but not as fast, because the bulk of it goes to space heating, which is likely to decrease per customer with rising efficiency, better insulation, inroads by electricity, and population shifts to warmer areas of the country.

This assumption permits us, starting from RFF estimates for 1955, to project total commercial energy requirements except for electricity and, deducting the amounts of gas already projected independently, to calculate coal, oil, and natural gas liquids as the balance. Coal consumption is expected to continue its rapid decline—evident in the statistics on retail deliveries—leaving the remainder to be supplied by oil and natural gas liquids.

The resulting changes in the role played by the various energy sources run in the same direction as in residential consumption except that between 1980 and 2000 oil is projected to raise its share significantly. (See Figure 10–5 and Table 10–5.)

Reasoning that is based upon projected residential use must remain quite speculative. For example, increased leisure time may lead to reduction in the hours that stores are open after dark, and even in the number of days that stores and offices are open. Chores now performed in commercial establishments may increasingly be undertaken at home with the aid of new appli-

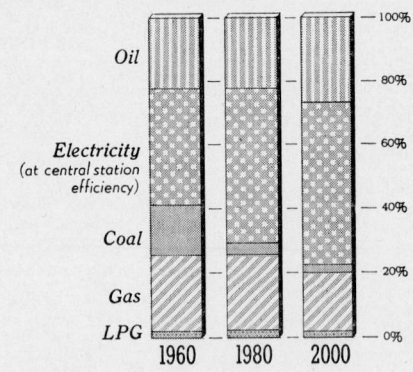

Figure 10–5. Shares of energy sources in commercial uses, 1960 and Medium projections for 1980 and 2000.

TABLE 10–5. Consumption of Fuels in Commercial Uses, 1960 and Medium Projections for 1980, 2000

Fuel	1960	1980	2000	1960	1980	2000
	(quadrillion Btu)			*(per cent of total)*		
Electricity (at central station efficiency and including transmission and distribution losses)	1.40	3.17	4.77	36.4	48.2	51.2
Gas	.92	1.58	1.67	24.0	24.1	17.9
Oil	.84	1.44	2.50	21.9	21.9	26.8
LPG	.08	.15	.18	2.1	2.3	1.9
Coal	.60	.23	.20	15.6	3.5	2.2
All sources	3.84	6.57	9.32	100.0	100.0	100.0

Sources: Appendix Tables A10–23 and 24 and A15–18.

ances. In that event, we would have overstated commercial energy consumption at the expense of household consumption, but total consumption would be affected only to the extent that centrally performed services are likely to enjoy an efficiency different from that prevailing in the home.

Industrial Consumption

Industry—that is, manufacturing and mining —is the largest single user of heat and power. It currently absorbs about one-third of total energy consumed in the country, either in the form of fuels burned in factories or mines or as electricity purchased from central power stations (in terms of fuel energy used in generation). For every unit of energy consumed in the home, nearly two are used up in mining and manufacturing. In the past, about one-fourth of energy use in manufacturing has taken the form of electricity, the remainder that of furnace and steam heat (sometimes called process heat):

	Energy used in industry as—	
Census year	*Furnace and steam heat (per cent)*	*Electric power (per cent)*
1939	78.3	21.7
1947	76.6	23.4
1954	74.6	25.4

Our projections indicate that the tendency toward increased participation of electric energy will continue:

	Energy used in industry as—	
	Furnace and steam heat (per cent)	*Electric power (per cent)*
1960	72.5	27.5
1980	65.4	34.6
2000	63.3	36.7

The persistent pre-eminence of non-electric heat and power is noteworthy, however, especially in view of the importance of electricity in automation. The large amounts of heat consumed in the processing of metals and crude oil account primarily for this relationship. Without the fuel burned in these industries the energy market in industry would be more nearly evenly divided between electric power and process heat. And even in the heavy industries, i.e., those that are engaged primarily in basic raw material transformation, electricity has made inroads. The electric furnace and electrometallurgy in general are specific examples. In particular, the relatively faster expansion projected for aluminum, the primary electricity user, than for steel, the primary fossil fuel user, will be an important factor in further strengthening the role of electricity.

Another tendency that the projections suggest will continue is the declining use of energy per unit of industrial output. In the past thirty years this has been the relationship, in terms of index numbers (1929 = 100):

	Census year			
	1929	1939	1947	1954
Industrial production	100	99	170	236
Energy consumption	100	84	134	169
Energy consumption per unit of industrial production	100	84	79	71

Between 1960 and 1980 our projections indicate a drop in energy consumption per unit of industrial output of 21 per cent, i.e., at a rate quite comparable to that prevailing in the 1929–55 period. Between 1980 and 2000 the rate of decline will decelerate somewhat, to 17 per cent. For the entire period unit energy consumption thus will drop 34 per cent, equivalent to an attrition rate of about one per cent per year. The relevant figures are as follows (1960 = 100):

	1960	1980	2000
Industrial production	100	231	522
Energy consumption	100	182	347
Energy consumption per unit of industrial production	100	79	66

Only in a superficial sense may this factor be called increased thermal efficiency. Industrial output is a complex composite; some of its constituents use much, some little energy. Shifts in the output mix thus influence the relationship between energy consumption and output, without necessarily any change in the technical efficiency of energy use. Output may increase at a rate faster than energy consumption for a variety of other reasons unconnected with energy use. And finally, there may be real improvements in the use of energy, such as, for example, reduced waste in the production process —less energy "going up the stack." Out of all of these changes there arises the concept as well as the measure of "energy efficiency," yet all one can legitimately say is that a unit of energy input has as its counterpart a larger amount, in value terms, of aggregate output. Projected changes in aggregate consumption in the next four decades result as much from changes in the industrial product mix as from changes in the application of energy to industrial processes.

One significant additional technical change is clearly in prospect: the full unfolding of the application of nuclear energy. The prospects of nuclear generation of electric power are dealt with in Chapter 15, where projections are made as to different types of generation of electric energy. In addition, nuclear process heat, generated in industrial plants or for groups of plants, is a definite likelihood in many industries. So is the use of nuclear energy for purposes other than heat generation, viz., the transformation of materials and the imparting to them of desirable qualities through exposure to radiation. Here again nuclear energy would take the place of conventional energy sources, but presumably at very different factors of efficiency not now feasible to estimate. Also, some processes and perhaps some industries will be entirely new.

At present, however, we are at the very beginning of this branch of application, and quantitative relationships cannot be foreseen. The projections do not, therefore, allow for the brave new world of what some atomic scientists believe will be the really exciting field of nuclear growth—industrial irradiation. All one can say is that there is every reason to believe that the future role of conventional fuels and energy sources employed in industry in uses other than the generation of electricity is likely to be diminished—no one can yet say by how much— through the utilization of nuclear energy.

We are thus left with the task of developing estimates of unit energy consumption for each industry or group of industries and, by applying these to projections of industrial production, of estimating the size of the future energy market in industry. The major source of energy consumption data for most of industry is the Bureau of the Census. From its annual reports on the use of electric power in industry and from its Census of Manufactures, one can derive tolerably accurate information on power input per unit of product output, the latter, as a rule, represented by the Federal Reserve Board index of production. This calls for care in interpretation, because the index is a composite weighted by value, and value does not necessarily reflect differences in intensity of power use; an index may remain constant while its constituent parts follow sharply differing growth rates.

Past trends have been used to establish these

relationships for the future, but some effort has been made to ascertain whether their future course accords with common sense. To illustrate, in the food, beverage, and tobacco industry group, electric power consumption per unit of output has been rising over the past decade. We have assumed that this rise is related to the continuing introduction of processing and handling phases in the industry that are electrically controlled, and that the rise will therefore continue.

Past changes typically have been in the direction of lower unit consumption for direct (non-electric) fuel use, and higher unit consumption for electric power. Though year-to-year change may seem negligible—not ordinarily exceeding one or two per cent—over a span of forty years such changes are most significant.

Wherever the past record seems to speak clearly, we have not hesitated to use it for projecting the future. The available data distinguish between electric and other energy use in industry, and the analysis follows this pattern. In both instances, some manufacturing processes are dealt with in greater detail than others, on the basis of their paramount importance as energy consumers and the far greater availability of data. One of them is the primary metals industry, within which the specific growth of aluminum and the future of electric-furnace steel (and ferroalloys) are important determinants of electric power consumption and steel making bulks large in coal requirements; both would otherwise get lost in the over-all index. Similarly, petroleum refining deserves separate treatment for its role as a large-scale consumer of natural gas.

Electric Power Consumption

Manufacturing in general. Broadly speaking, rising electric power consumption has been the result of three entirely separate movements: (1) better-than-average growth of some of the more power-intensive industries and industry branches; (2) a shift toward more power-intensive processes within industries (e.g., in chemicals); and (3) the intrusion of the "electric way of doing things" into existing non-electric processes or the complete replacement of

non-electric by electrical methods of fabrication. All three are intertwined in the aggregate picture, but to the extent that one or the other can be isolated in a given industry, it can assist in projecting future growth with a little more confidence. (See Figure 10–6.)

The primary metals industry, to give a practical example, is not only the largest electric-power-consuming industry; it also has been characterized by a rapid rate of growth in power consumption per unit, as shown below for a recent ten-year period:

	1947	1957
Elec. power consumed (mil. kwh)	40,645	77,766
Do., index (1957=100)	57	100
FRB index of prod. (1957=100)	81	100
Elec. per point of index (mil. kwh)	502	778
Do., index (1957=100)	65	100

Because the major products of the industry can be satisfactorily identified in physical form, one can determine why power consumption, instead of rising by 23 per cent, as did production, in fact increased by nearly 100 per cent, to 77.8 billion kwh. What caused the extra growth of 28 billion kwh?

Of first importance is the growth in aluminum production: primary aluminum accounted for 10.3 billion kwh in 1947 and for about 30 billion kwh in 1957. A second growth element has been the expansion in power-intensive electric-furnace steel: from 4.5 per cent of all ingot steel in 1947 to 7.1 per cent in 1957; estimated power consumption had simultaneously risen from 3.8 to 8.0 billion kwh. Third, production of electric-furnace ferroalloys rose 80 per cent between 1947 and 1957, with an estimated increase of 3.9 billion kwh in power consumption.

Had the three elements enumerated each expanded by no more than the 23 per cent growth rate of the primary metals industry as a whole, then 1957 power consumption would have been smaller by some 23 billion kwh. Only 5 billion kwh remain to be accounted for, compared with the 28 billion kwh that we started out with. These might be explained by a variety of de-

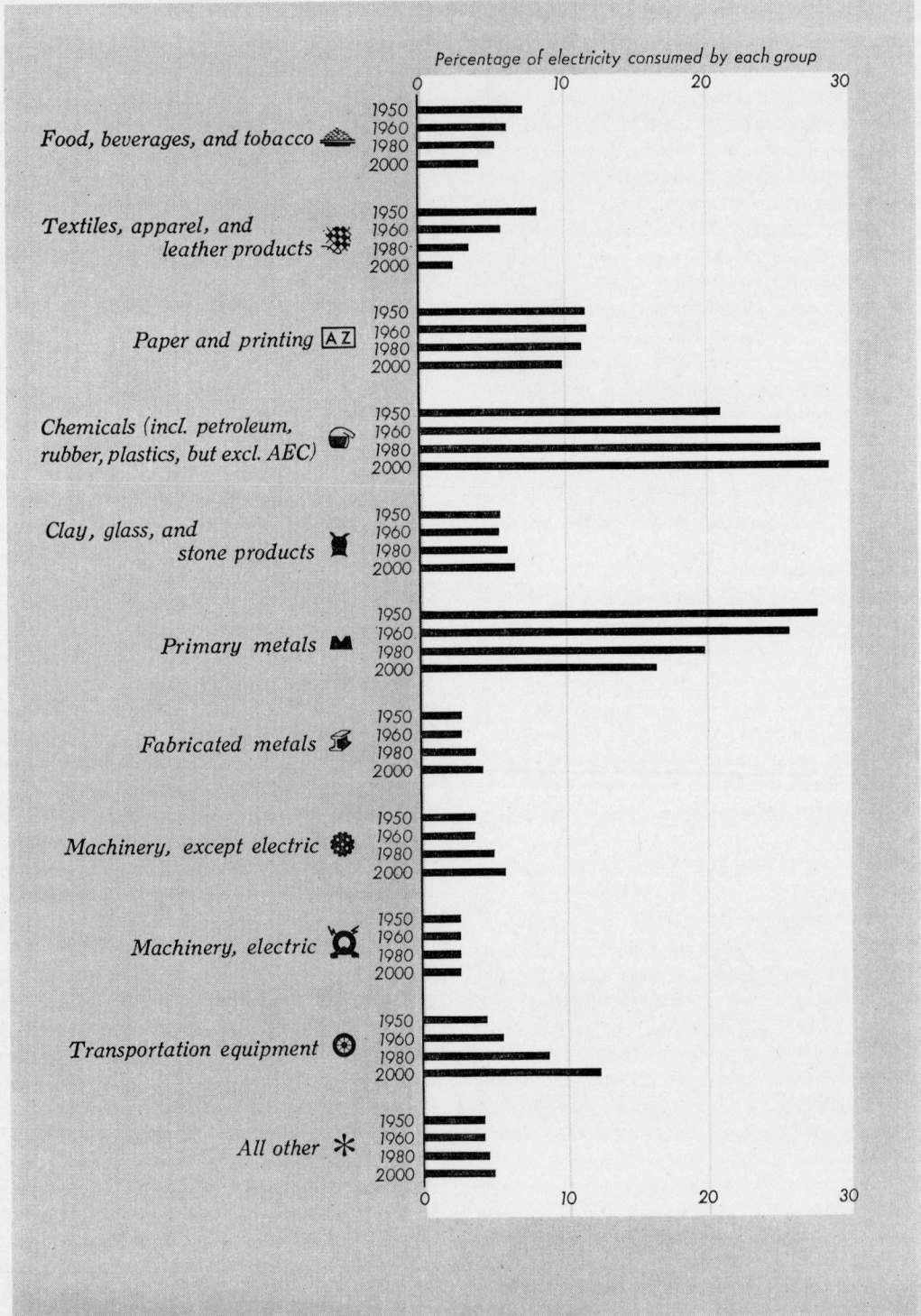

Figure 10–6. How electric power consumption is shared among manufactures, 1950, 1960, and Medium projections for 1980 and 2000.

velopments in processes that are more intensive users of power than those they have been replacing. Undoubtedly, a residual fraction is due to replacement of non-electric mechanical processes by electrical ones and to such auxiliary services as dust control, better lighting, etc.

The significance of the analysis lies in the fact that a shift in the importance of only a handful of the "subsectors" of an industry has produced a significant change in power consumption per unit for the industry as a whole. Unless one finds a way of allowing for such shifts in the projection, one may go seriously astray.

Similar conditions exist in other industries. For instance, in pulp and paper manufacture the growing importance of newsprint, requiring the power-intensive mechanical pulp, the expansion in lightweight products (tissues) requiring additional processing, and the preference for bleached items all have contributed to an increase in power consumption per unit. The transportation equipment industry offers a similar picture. According to Census data, power consumption in the industry's principal component—manufacture of motor vehicles and parts—rose by some 70 per cent between 1947 and 1954, while the FRB production index rose by only 29 per cent. The second largest segment, aircraft, showed power consumption rising almost precisely in step with the production index. Thus the impressive rise in electric power consumption per point of the index is due principally if not exclusively to developments in the motor vehicle industry. Unfortunately, the low production level of 1954 is likely to exaggerate power consumption, much of which is only loosely a function of production. To the extent that one were to expect future growth rates in these two subsectors to move in substantial contrast to past performance, as exemplified by the 1947–54 period, one would distort the projection if one dealt with aggregate electric power consumption for the entire transportation equipment industry.

In the absence of detailed studies of the components of each major industry group, there is little one can say in comment or explanation of the changes shown by the large aggregates, most of which exhibit an upward trend—of different

intensity—in power per unit of output. As a minimum, however, we can utilize this knowledge to the extent of identifying the most power-intensive elements and projecting them separately whenever we feel sufficiently sure about future growth trends of these subgroupings. Unless we can develop reasonably persuasive answers to questions regarding future technology, our projection will not improve merely by our knowledge of the past, of the technical coefficients, and of the degree to which specific segments of the industry have caused power consumption to rise faster than physical output. However, since a ton of aluminum requires some sixty times the electric power that goes into the making of an average ton of steel, even vague ideas as to future divergent trends in production are bound to be an improvement over the treatment of heterogeneous aggregates.

But for two reasons this cannot be carried very far. One is the increasing difficulty of constructing the required statistical data, and the second is the far greater hazard of projecting the parts than projecting the whole.

There is a great deal of basic research to be done in this field, both in the development and refinement of historical data and in speculating about future trends stemming from developing new technology. Perhaps the chemical industry causes most concern in this respect. It is here that new technology springs up with great rapidity (and sometimes becomes obsolete almost as quickly) and that electric power consumption can play a large part. Electrolytic processes even now are widespread and may become even more important.

Primary metals, dealt with in detail below, and chemicals have in the past accounted for half or more of industrial power consumption. Our analysis indicates no broad change in that aspect of future consumption, but brings to light a number of substantial shifts, as indicated in Figure 10–6.

The typical consumer goods industries, food processing and textile manufacture and related activities, are projected to lose in significance, from consuming 15 per cent of electric power in 1950 to consuming less than 7 per cent in 2000. One of the gainers would be the chemical

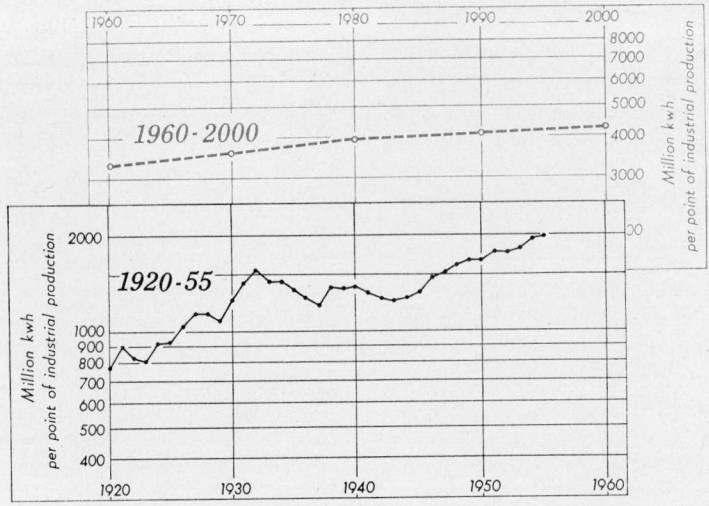

Figure 10–7. Rate of growth in electric power consumed by manufacturing, per unit of industrial output, 1920–1955 (production index: 1947–49 = 100) and Medium projection for 1960–2000 (production index: 1957 = 100).

industry, in 1950 ranking second, behind the metals, but indicated to have pulled even in 1960. By 2000 it is projected as absorbing nearly one out of every three kilowatt-hours consumed in industry. Most of the remaining industries are scheduled to retain their relative share of the power market, except for the transportation equipment industry, which is projected to triple its share, largely because of the steep rise in output that is projected for it.

It is owing above all to the joint predominance of the primary metals and chemicals that the pattern for the remaining groups does not change substantially in the projection.

The end-result, a generally rising trend of power consumption per unit of output, shown in Figure 10–7, continues the historical pattern. The rate of growth, however, is greatly reduced in our projection for the future: 40 per cent in the years 1960–2000 as against over 100 per cent from 1920 to 1955.

The unit power consumption coefficients combined with projected production indexes, as developed in Appendix Table A1–29, and augmented by consumption in mining, yield Low, Medium, and High estimates of industrial power consumption as follows:

1960		1980	2000
	(billion kwh)		
	L	745	1,466
355	M	977	2,391
	H	1,343	4,188

Such growth would, in the Medium projection, represent not quite a tripling in twenty years. The rate of growth would be 5.2 per cent per year in the first half of the period and more nearly 4½ per cent in the second half. This compares with a rate of nearly 7½ per cent in the twenty years ending in 1956, according to the data developed in *Energy in the American Economy* (these, as here, exclude AEC installations). Disregarding the insignificant effect of any lack of comparability, due to differences in projection methods or coverage, the data indicate a gradual slowdown in the rate of growth of industrial power consumption. As we are here dealing with compound growth, this is a reasonable expectation. The above-cited RFF study also projected a decrease in the rate of growth in consumption, but only down to 6½ per cent for the period 1955–75. This is only slightly lower than the utility industry's own estimate of 6.9 per cent derived from forecasts for 1960–80.[14] The Federal Power Commis-

14. *Electrical World,* September 18, 1961.

sion's estimate, made in October 1959,[15] implies a growth rate, between 1958 and 1980, of not quite 5 per cent for utility and non-utility industrial consumption, including that of the Atomic Energy Commission. Since nobody expects any significant rise in AEC consumption, the FPC data excluding the latter would probably show a slightly higher rate of growth.[16]

The primary metals. In the steel industry, the growing share of electric-furnace steel and the more than proportionate growth in electric power consumed in the manufacture of electric-furnace ferroalloys have been primarily responsible for past growth in power per ton of ingot produced. Feeling in the industry is that the rise of the electric furnace has gone about as far as power costs will allow it to go and that the improvement in vacuum smelting as an alternative way of producing high-grade metals will be a further factor in confining future expansion of electric-furnace production. Recent data on electric-furnace capacity and production seem to bear out this opinion. Ferroalloy production in electric furnaces, on the other hand, is more likely to remain a factor in the future growth of electric power consumption in the industry. On balance, consumption in these two sectors is projected as rising much less rapidly than in the past, owing also to the expectation that unit requirements will decline as efficiency improves.

This is reflected in Appendix Table A10–29, as also is the projected growth of power consumption relative to output in the balance of the steel industry. The evidence of the past supports the latter projection even though it is by no means unequivocal—largely because of the effect upon power consumption of the degree of plant utilization as determined by business conditions, strikes, etc. Increased emphasis on high-grade steel involving increased resistance to rolling, on cold-rolled products, on electric-welded pipe, and on the power-hungrier lighter products, both in flat-rolled and structural products,

contributes to this trend. Other past influences—such as the shift from dipped to electrolytic tin plate—have reached the point where they have practically pre-empted the field and thus will no longer exert much upward pressure on power consumption. An opposing influence will be the energy-saving effects of higher vertical integration and continuity, which, by maximum preservation of heat between successive processing steps, would lower resistance to rolling and other operations and thus reduce power requirements. The main effect of this would be felt, however, by non-electric energy sources. If steel were given the highest possible finishing temperature, faster rolling speeds would equally work in the direction of reduced power requirements.

A detailed comparison of 1958 and 1959 throws some additional light on the effect of operating rates upon the statistical evidence. The differences are radical: 1958 was a year of low-capacity year-round operation with high power consumption per ton of steel, while 1959 was a strike year of top-capacity production for over eight months and tightly shut mills during the remaining months, resulting in extremely low unit power consumption. Such distortions notwithstanding, we have on balance assumed a moderately rising power consumption per unit of output, partly on the basis of past developments and partly on the strength of the enumerated factors that point in the direction of higher power requirements. The resulting projections for electricity consumption by the principal metal industries are summarized in Table 10–6.

The role of aluminum as a large-scale consumer of power is bound to grow as its significance in the metal field increases. (See Figure 10–8.) The only damper consists of continuing improvements in ampere efficiency. Radical changes, such as direct reduction of bauxite (i.e., skipping the alumina stage), are in the offing, but they are surrounded by so much secrecy that it is impossible to say whether they involve a greater or lesser rate of power consumption. Perhaps the main effect would be a further impetus to aluminum production near bauxite locations, which are overwhelmingly outside the United States. A more immediate de-

15. U.S. Senate Select Committee on National Water Resources, *op. cit.*, Committee Print No. 10, pp. 1–8.

16. In the FPC's January 30, 1962 revision (Release No. 11,829), the implied growth rate has risen to 5.8 per cent between 1960 and 1980.

TABLE 10–6.   Electricity Consumption by Principal Metal Industries, 1950, 1960 and Medium Projections for 1980, 2000

Industry	1950	1960	1980	2000
Electric furnace steel:				
Output (mil. tons)	6.0	8.4	21	41
Power coefficient (kwh/ton)	700	700	600	500
Electricity consumption (bil. kwh)	4.2	5.9	12.6	20.5
All other steel:				
Output (mil. tons)	90.8	90.9	155	253
Power coefficient (kwh/ton)	154	169	265	350
Electricity consumption (bil. kwh)	14.9	16.9	41.1	88.6
Electric furnace ferroalloys:				
Output (mil. tons)	.93	1.25	2.8	4.6
Power coefficient (kwh/ton)	6,000	6,000	5,000	4,250
Electricity consumption (bil. kwh)	5.6	7.5	14.0	19.6
Aluminum (primary):				
Output (mil. tons)	.719	2.01	4.66	10.57
Power coefficient (thous. kwh/ton)	18.4	18.1	16.4	15.5
Electricity consumption (bil. kwh)	13.2	38.2	80.2	172.0
All other nonferrous metals:				
Electricity consumption (bil. kwh)	n.a.	7.8	12.3	22.8

Sources: Appendix Tables A10–29, 30, 31, 33.

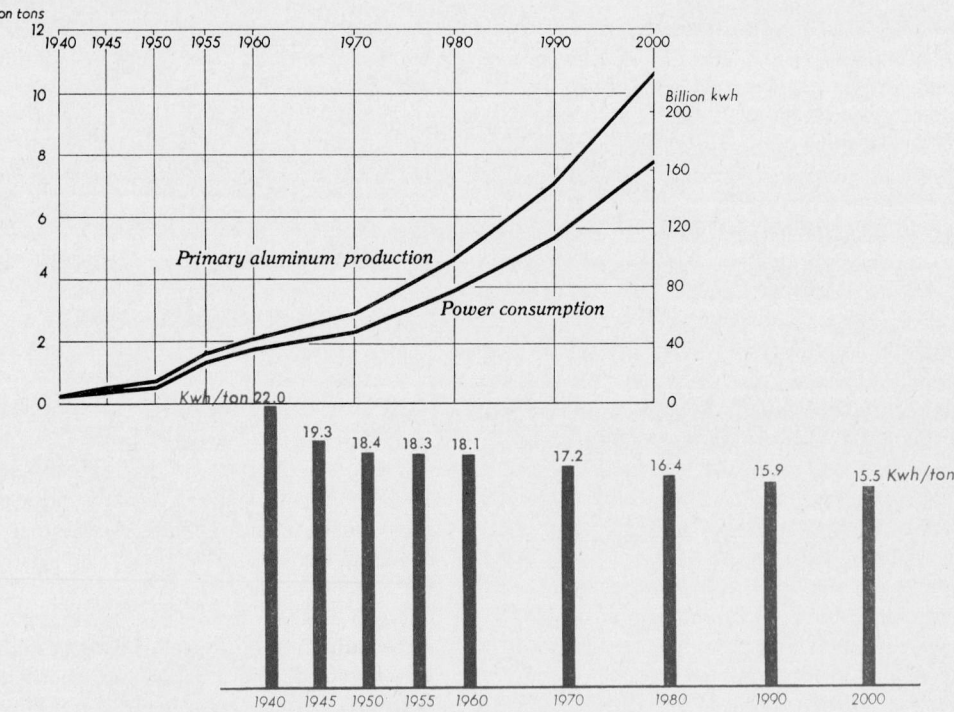

Figure 10–8. Aluminum production and power consumption in the manufacture of aluminum, 1940–1960 and Medium projection to 2000.

velopment is foreshadowed by recent announcements of electrode efficiency that is said to reduce power consumption by up to 15 per cent.

Improved efficiency in power utilization was assumed also for magnesium.

Electric power consumption for the remaining nonferrous metals is not large in comparison with that for either steel or aluminum. Moderate increases in power coefficients over those derived from Census data were allowed for copper, to reflect the increased processing of the metal imported in refined form, and for zinc, to reflect the growing share of electrolytic reduction, which requires roughly twice as much power per ton as does non-electrolytic processing.

This leaves us with "all other" nonferrous activities, a category which includes the primary production of lead, gold, silver, titanium, etc., the secondary production and casting of *all* nonferrous metals, and the rolling and drawing of nonferrous metals other than aluminum and copper. The inclusion of titanium and of all new metals now in their infancy makes this a highly volatile group, and one that cannot be matched with a satisfactory measure of the volume of physical output.

The statistical approach, given the negligible significance of the group, which is estimated to have consumed less than one-fourth of one per cent of all electricity in 1960, is described in the Appendix to Chapter 10. In appraising it, it is well to remember that titanium, here included, requires some 40,000 kwh per ton of sponge and considerably more per ton of end-product. Had the hopes held only a few years ago been fulfilled, titanium alone would by now consume well over one billion kwh per year. As it is, there is little reason now to allow for a great surge, but in a forty-year perspective titanium remains a fused statistical time bomb among the metals.

Mining. Mining is a relatively small user of electricity: in 1954 it consumed some 7 kwh for every 100 kwh consumed in manufacturing. This was a decline from 1939, when it had consumed more nearly 10 per cent of manufacturing power consumption. The drop in relative

importance took place despite a doubling in total power consumed in the mining industry.

In recent years, the four principal branches of mining—coal, oil and gas, metal, and non-fuel non-metal mining—have absorbed about equal amounts of electric power, in 1960 estimated at some 4 billion kwh each. From a prewar position in which it consumed only one-fourth as much electricity as did coal, oil and gas extraction has rapidly forged ahead of the other branches. Presumably, this tendency will continue into the future, in line with the projected slower growth rate of coal mining and the trend towards electric pumping in oil and gas recovery—a trend that is evident in primary production and, increasingly, in secondary recovery of oil.

Matched against an over-all mining index, power consumption per point of the index has been remarkably steady during the past two decades, showing only a very modest tendency towards increasing power use. The projection assumes that this will continue, though the scale is too moderate to justify an assumption of ranges in this coefficient. The following consumption pattern results:

		Index of minerals prod. (1957= 100)	Mil. kwh per point of index	Power cons. (bil. kwh)
1960		97	170	16.5
1980	L	130	–	26
	M	167	200	33
	H	222	–	44
2000	L	188	–	39
	M	292	210	61
	H	514	–	108

Thus, electric power consumption in mining is projected to decline to less than 4 per cent of total industrial consumption by the end of the century.

Industrial Fuel Consumption

Manufacturing in general. Energy consumed in industry in a form other than electricity performs a variety of tasks, most of which fall into one of two broad categories: those using furnace heat—such as metal processing, cement manufacture, or glass making—and those using steam heat. Steam's principal function used to be to drive mechanical devices, but in this it has been superseded by electricity and stationary direct drives, which as a rule burn diesel oil. Today, steam is employed mainly as a direct element in processing—to cook, bake, dry, sterilize, evaporate, distill, vulcanize, serve as a source of hydrogen, and generally facilitate or speed desirable reactions. In addition, it provides space heat.

As in the case of electricity, the primary metals industry (above all the steel industry) and the chemical industry (especially petroleum refining) are large consumers of fuel-generated heat. In recent years these two segments have accounted for about two-thirds of the consumption of coal, oil, and gas in manufacturing. The only other substantial consumers are the cement industry and—largely because of steam and heat requirements in beet sugar, canning, and meat packing plants—the food industry. Replacement of some of the heat processes by irradiation, in both the chemical and the food-processing industry, could appreciably alter the energy consumption pattern in the future; but it is too early to take quantitative account of this contingency. Our Medium projections of fuel consumption in manufacturing other than ferrous metals and petroleum refining are summarized below.

	1947	1954	1958	1960	1980	2000
Mfg. index (1957=100)	65	86	94	110	264	622
Fuel cons. per index pt. (tril. Btu)	54	49	44	45	33	26
Fuels consumed (quadr. Btu)	3.49	4.26	4.10	4.95	8.79	16.42

The projections are based primarily upon the work done in recent years by Perry D. Teitelbaum[17] and are keyed to material gathered in Census years, from 1939 to 1958. Unfortunately, these data are discontinuous and influenced by the events of the year in which the

Census of Manufactures is taken. For example, 1939 was a buoyant year, 1947 was still beset by postwar problems, and both 1954 and 1958 were years of partially depressed business conditions; fuel requirements, being to some extent overhead elements, are unduly affected thereby.

Because primary metals and petroleum refining account for nearly half the fuel consumption in manufacturing, and because year-to-year comparability of data becomes more disturbing as one slices the manufacturing pie finer, the treatment has been simplified despite the knowledge that projection of large aggregates is not the ideal way of allowing trends to work their influence.

Thus, while the fuel needs of the primary metals and petroleum products have been projected in much detail, all other manufacturing has been lumped together. A fuel requirement figure for 1960 has been estimated for this aggregate and related to an appropriately constructed index of manufacturing output. This relationship has been extrapolated on the basis of historical background, and the resulting fuel requirements per unit of manufacturing output applied to the projected index of production.

The reduction in relative fuel requirements has been put at 1.5 per cent per year to begin with, declining gradually to 1 per cent. Resting only on interpretation of the Census data (see Appendix Table A10–37), it has been checked against the better documented fuel efficiency improvements in the electric utility industry, which have been of the order of 2 per cent per year and better during the past decade. Power generation cannot perhaps benefit as much from radical changes in organization of production, with attending fuel economies, nor engage in a radical switch as manufacturing has done in changing from non-electric to electric power. Nevertheless, over the broad range of industry one would not expect the rate of improvement to be larger, as in electricity generation efficient fuel use is the focus of effort.

The primary metals. Some branches of industry are sufficiently crucial in the projection to call for separate consideration. First among them are the primary metals and especially the steel industry, from the coke oven to the basic intermediate steel product—the bar, sheet, wire,

17. Perry D. Teitelbaum, *Energy Production and Consumption in the United States: An Analytical Study Based on 1954 Data*, Bureau of Mines Report of Investigations 5821 (Washington: U.S. Bureau of Mines and Resources for the Future, 1961); and Teitelbaum, *Nuclear Energy and the U.S. Fuel Economy, 1955–1980* (Washington: National Planning Association, 1958).

or plate—but not extending to truly fabricated products.

The steel industry consumes close to one-third of all industrial energy other than electricity. From the moment the coal is put in the coke oven until the sheet or bar emerges from the rolling mill or the seam is welded on the pipe, heat is a factor of production. The historically declining trend in fuel consumed per ton of ingot has been projected into the future, but at a slightly less rapid rate, a projection based above all upon the reasoning that improving technology leads fuel consumption ever closer to the theoretical minimum.

The resulting figures might be compared with an industry generalization that an efficient, integrated steel mill should eventually consume no more energy than a ton of coal (including consumption for generation of electric power) per ton of ingot.[18] In the year 2000 electric power consumption (except in electric furnaces) would be 350 kwh per ton, equivalent at an assumed heat rate of 7,500 Btu per kwh generated to one-eleventh of a ton of coal, which, added to projected direct fuel consumption of 0.66 tons, would total roughly three-quarters of a ton. Thus, by 2000, the 1:1 ratio would have been left behind. Statistics in the Appendix to this Chapter suggest that it would have been reached sometime in the seventies. Assuming a theoretical limit of 15 million Btu per ton of ingot, chemically necessary for reduction, the above projection would be equivalent to 20 per cent above the minimum. This represents a great improvement over current practices but at a reduced rate. Our Medium projections for fuel consumption in the iron and steel industry for purposes other than electricity generation are summarized below.

	1950	1960	1980	2000
Tons of coal equiv. per ton of ingot, other than elec. furnace	1.2	1.1	.8	.7
Steel production, other than elec. furnace (mil. tons)	90.8	90.9	155	253
Fuel consumed (mil. tons coal equiv.)	114.9	103.5	124	177
of which:				
% coal	81	76	70	66
% oil	12	10	12	14
% gas	7	14	18	20

18. See, for instance, U.S. Steel, *The Making, Shaping and Treating of Steel,* Seventh Edition (Pittsburgh, 1957), p. 82.

The iron and steel industry is probably on the threshold of major changes in technology, all tending toward lower fuel, and especially coal, consumption. Once proved to be worth the investment, their acceptance will tend to be rapid. Among the most recent has been the widespread installation of oxygen injection equipment to speed the output of steel furnaces (and thus greatly increase their capacity). On the horizon are oxygen enrichment of the blast furnace, and the introduction of gas, oil, and powdered coal streams into the blast furnace in order to economize on coke and increase furnace capacity by shortening the duration of the blast. Since coke acts as a contributor of carbon as well as a source of heat, part of its function can be taken over by other fuels that are cheaper or more efficient.

Greater attention paid to the physical characteristics of ore has equally led to higher output per ton of fuel. Sintered ore and high-grade pellets are rapidly becoming the preferred ore feed; they add capacity to the furnace without the addition of a single cubic inch of space.

Of quite a different order of importance are radically new departures in steel making, above all those known as direct reduction processes. It is too early to try to assess their impact upon the industry and especially the industry's energy demand, but fuel savings undoubtedly will be one of the features accompanying the development. On the other hand, much will depend on the cost of electric power and of the gas used in reducing the iron ore—normally hydrogen (and indirectly, therefore, on the energy requirements of hydrogen production). A situation might develop, for example, where the reduction of energy requirements at one stage is offset by an increase elsewhere. Moreover, in an integrated plant the loss of the by-product fuels generated in the blast furnace would further complicate the energy balance.

Much more imminent is the widespread adoption of the so-called oxygen converter in lieu of the open-hearth furnace, in which the substitution of oxygen for air, aided by novel design features, is responsible for a substantial reduction in fuel needs (but possibly narrower limits to the use of scrap).

These are the factors behind the projected further drop in the ratio of energy use to steel production, but they are cited only to substantiate the direction, not the measure, of change. The latter must remain a matter of judgment.

In a recent study of the European steel industry,[19] the United Nations Economic Committee for Europe attempted to estimate the fuel savings that might result from the various technological changes. In general, these are substantially larger than are projected here. However, they are cast in terms of the individual production unit that uses the new process, not the industry as a whole with its spread from the most to the least efficient. Furthermore, some of the innovations will cause increases in energy consumption elsewhere, such as in sintering or pelletizing plants not included in the primary metals industry. For both these reasons, and in order not to minimize the fuel demands of the industry, we have preferred to keep assumptions as to rising efficiency on the conservative side. Especially in the next decade, these new developments will bear close watching, provided, of course, that the effects of technological progress will not be overshadowed or washed out by the diseconomies attending erratic or persistently low rates of capacity utilization.

The nonferrous metals are not a large enough consumer of fuels—as opposed to electricity—to warrant detailed attention. Because in the industry's most significant growth segment, the light metals industry, direct consumption of fuels plays only a small part (the bulk of fuel is converted to electric energy), we have assumed that the 1954 Btu input coefficient, as evolved from Census data, can be considered valid for 1960 and have then assumed that it will decrease at a modest constant rate.

Petroleum refining. The second large fuel consumer is petroleum refining; it absorbs nearly 20 per cent of the industry total. In its beginning petroleum refining was nothing but a distillation (i.e., boiling) process, and to this day most refining operations, which consist essentially in rearranging the hydrocarbons, occur in the presence of great heat. Notwithstanding enormous advances in processing the crude oil

and the continuing addition of new, presumably more efficient units to keep pace with rapid growth in capacity, statistics stretching over many years fail to disclose any discernible trend in energy requirements per barrel of crude.[20] One of the reasons why energy consumption has not declined has probably been the continuing addition of more highly refined products that require more elaborate and more energy-intensive processes. Thus the output mix of the typical refinery has been changing in such a way as to require more and more energy to crack the top fractions of the hydrocarbon family and give the refinery an increasing number of chemical-industry appendages. There could, of course, be a reversal. The switch from aviation gasoline to kerosene, called forth by the change-over from propeller to jet planes, has been a change to a less highly refined fuel. Air transport consumption of fuel is relatively too small, however, for this shift to have affected energy requirements significantly. Of course, similar developments on a larger scale, such as the possible emergence of internal combustion engines burning low-grade motor fuels, could drastically lower energy requirements. At the same time, the separation of the portions needed in petrochemical production—the butanes, propanes, ethanes, etc.—is a highly energy-intensive process and will undoubtedly increase in importance.

On balance then, the future of energy requirements per barrel of crude is uncertain; the wisest course is to make no assumption of future change. It may be noted, incidentally, that the refining requirements are roughly equivalent to one-tenth of the fuel value of a barrel of crude; almost two-thirds are supplied by petroleum products, the remainder by natural gas. (See Appendix Table A10–45.)

Mining. Consumption of fuel in mining has quantitative significance only in the case of oil and gas extraction. Census data indicate that in 1954 fuel burned for that purpose, most of it natural gas, amounted to about 10 per cent of the quantities of fuel burned in all manufacturing, and 4 per cent of the oil and gas pro-

19. Economic Committee for Europe, *Long-Term Trends and Problems of the European Steel Industry* (Geneva: United Nations, 1959), especially Chapter IV.

20. Cf. Schurr, Netschert, *et al., op. cit.,* p. 569.

duced. In the coal industry fuel burned represented at most one-half of one per cent of the amount of coal produced. Finally, the amount of fuel burned in non-fuel mineral extraction is quite small: about the equivalent of 6 million tons of coal, or less than 2 per cent of the fuel burned in all of manufacturing.

Accordingly, the effort devoted to projecting these magnitudes has been kept at a minimum, but, given the differences in projected growth of the various branches of mining, care has been taken to proceed separately in at least two main divisions: oil and gas, and all other minerals.

The available statistics record the use of gas in the oil and gas fields (the amount of oil and coal used there is so small as to be entirely unimportant for our purposes) in a category termed "field use." This accounts for gas used in the field for all "useful purposes" (as defined by the Federal Power Commission) prior to its arrival in a pipeline distribution system, a refinery, or any of the various end-use points. It thus goes beyond the needs of oil and gas field operations. One of the "useful purposes" is the burning of fuel in gas liquid plants; another is separation of certain amounts of gas from it in the form of gas liquids. Mining, in this instance, thus embraces not merely extraction but also partial processing, and the fuel consumed includes the product itself as well as the quantities burned in processing it. This explains why this use is equivalent to more than 15 per cent of fuel use in manufacturing. A rough technique is developed in the Appendix to Chapter 15 for isolating the amounts stripped from the gas and projecting separately the field use proper; the latter has shown a decisive relative decline in the past. It has been assumed that this trend will continue to operate (though on a more moderate scale), as it appears to have been due largely to the rising price of gas in uses outside the oil and gas fields and, more recently, to the increased use of electricity, which has released gas for sale or for re-injection into the wells.

Fuel use in the remaining branches of the mining industry, stretching from copper and lead to potash and clay mining, is the least satisfactory element to project or even to speculate about in non-quantitative terms. However, the relegation of this segment to the role of a cover-age adjustment, in Chapter 15, is fully justified by its minor role in the total energy picture: the 1.2 million tons of coal, the 9.2 million barrels of oil, and the 89 billion cubic feet of natural gas that the 1954 Census records as having been burned in the mining of materials other than oil, gas, and coal are of negligible weight in the total reckoning. And even the amount of coal used in coal mining does little to give weight to this group.

Fuel shares. Since World War II natural gas has become the preferred source of energy of industrial producers other than the coke-using iron and steel industry. When the basic research was done for *Energy in the American Economy* it was calculated that in 1955 natural gas contributed 39.3 per cent of all energy used in the so-called "general industrial group" (which represented all manufacturing except primary metals, petroleum refining, and cement); coal, 37.4 per cent; and oil and NGL jointly, 23.3 per cent.

Parallel though rough calculations for the same industry grouping for 1960 suggest that gas contributed no less than 48 and perhaps as much as 53 per cent of the non-electric energy consumption; coal, possibly as little as 25 per cent, but certainly no more than 30 per cent; and oil and NGL, somewhere between 22 and 25 per cent.

It is difficult to project this pattern into the future. We see no slowdown in the replacement of coal by gas, but one must recognize that, disregarding electricity, in and near coal-producing regions coal will continue to be the principal energy source. Such reasoning does not lead easily to quantitative expression. The available data are not nearly so well adapted to projection-making as are those for electric power generation. As elsewhere, one must note that here is a field for future study: how much further will the share of coal fall in general manufacturing below its approximate present level of 25–30 per cent, equivalent to 35–40 million tons?

On the mere basis of continuing expansion of the natural gas pipeline system in the North Central states, the Northwest, and Florida, and the possibility, within the time span of this projection, of pipeline delivery or tanker shipments of gas in liquid form to the northernmost portions of New England, one must project further growth in natural gas consumption. But the actual pattern will be determined, among other factors, by the relative growth, region by region, of the industries affected. Impressed by the sharp rise in the share of gas, the sharp fall in the share of coal, and the relative stability in the share of oil and NGL, we have projected a further substantial development in that direction, modifying it only in two respects: (1) by moderation in magnitude to symbolize the "rock-bottom" idea of certain regional linkages to coal, and (2) by a slight decline in the oil share on the assumption that the advance of gas will take place in some regions that are now largely oil consumers (though here the picture is blurred by the ever-present possibility of cheap foreign residual oil's competing successfully not only with coal but also with pipeline gas). In addition, we have allowed for a slight increase in the use of NGL, given its rapid strides in recent years.

For industry as a whole—i.e., including the primary metals industry and petroleum refining but omitting the field use of natural gas—the distribution of fuels resulting from the assumptions is shown in Table 10–7 and Figure 10–9.

If its field use were added, the share of natural gas would of course be even larger: 44 per cent in 1960, rising to more than half of total industrial fuel consumption in 1980 and 2000.

It is easier to feel reasonably certain about the direction than about the speed of change in these figures. An important consideration is that

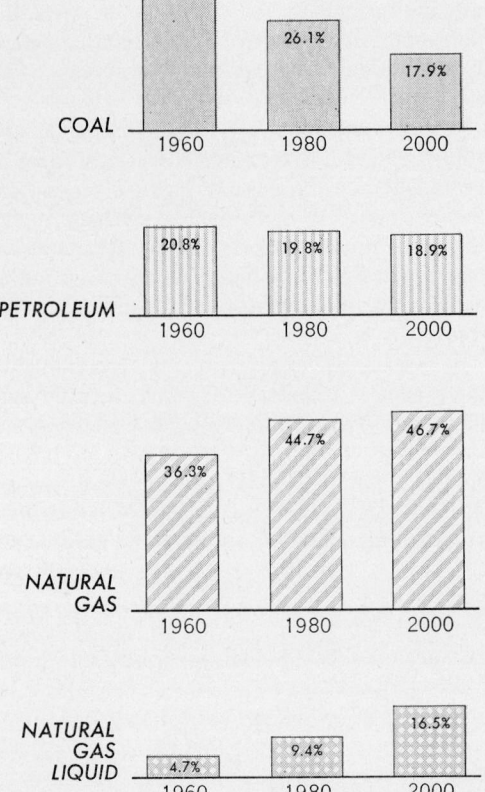

Figure 10–9. Distribution of fuels in industrial use, 1960 and Medium projections for 1980 and 2000.

underplaying the share of coal would represent an attitude of conservatism, since in the use of coal we are least concerned with resource deple-

TABLE 10–7.   Consumption of Fuels in Industrial Uses, 1960 and Medium Projections for 1980, 2000

Fuel	1960	1980	2000	1960	1980	2000
	(quadrillion Btu)			*(per cent of total)*		
Coal	3.90	4.43	5.76	38.2	26.1	17.9
Petroleum	2.13	3.36	6.12	20.8	19.8	18.9
Natural gas[1]	3.71	7.58	15.13	36.3	44.7	46.7
Natural gas liquids[2]	.48	1.59	5.33	4.7	9.4	16.5
Total	10.22	16.96	32.34	100.0	100.0	100.0

Source: Appendix Table A15–18.
1. Excluding field use of natural gas.   2. Including liquid refinery gas.

tion. Thus by stressing gas first and oil second we are turning in the direction of assuming maximum demand for those resources most likely to come under depletion pressure.

Unconventional sources. In considering the future role of unconventional energy sources in providing industrial process heat we are only at the threshold: estimates become too highly speculative to discuss in terms of quantitative, tabular projections; they must be discussed rather as possible forces that might bend foreseeable trends.

It is true that in terms of the future market the gradual replacement of conventionally produced heat by nuclear-origin heat offers an incomparably more impressive chance for radical change in industrial processes and structure than does electric power generation. Uses for other purposes than heat offer even more revolutionary change. However, as George Perazich has pointed out,[21] the growth of nuclear process heat will depend on a combination of factors that need practically plant-by-plant analysis before a diagnosis can be made.

First of all, while the cost of fuel is a major consideration in the generation of electric power, the cost of heat is usually only a very small fraction of manufacturing cost. Thus the incentive for installing a nuclear reactor cannot be expected to be strong, even if cost of heat produced by it were to be competitive or better. Second, cost is not likely to compare favorably with that of conventional fuels unless heat is used continuously throughout the year, at a high load factor, and in large blocks, even apart from the fact that for some time to come conventional fuel costs would have to be high in any event to justify nuclear process heat. (This situation is mitigated by the fact that industry usually pays more for its fuel than do utilities, so that the competitive threshold will usually be at a higher cost level.) Third, until further technical developments make it possible to develop high temperatures, the industries requiring principally high temperature heat will not be in a position to install nuclear reactors.

These limitations still leave a wide field of possible application, and it is altogether likely that the field will become still wider in the coming decades, at one end of the scale through the development of materials that will permit the construction of reactors capable of withstanding higher temperatures, and at the other end through design and construction of low-pressure, small reactors that serve the specific needs of the manufacturer. The chemical industry especially comes to mind as a likely pioneer in this field. However, as Karl M. Mayer has pointed out,[22] the contemporary concentration on the development of the power reactor with high-pressure and high-temperature characteristics could succeed in further deferring the day when nuclear process heat becomes a feasible factor in industry; for the bulk of industrial steam is required at a pressure so far below that of power-generating plants that the equipment constitutes quite a different animal.

In 1958 Mayer estimated that at a cost level of 70 cents or more per million Btu there was a heat market in the United States (counting only *new* equipment to be installed) for the equivalent of some 6 million tons of coal; at 60 cents or more that market would be more nearly the equivalent of 50 to 60 million tons, provided that nuclear process heat could take the place of all newly installed conventional process heat in all manufacturing processes. These estimates therefore represent maximum guesses. And since, according to Mayer, design is only approaching the 70–80 cent level, the immediate outlook is not promising. However, this is a field in which major revisions in the direction of reducing the demand for conventional fuels are sure to be needed in the future.

Miscellaneous Uses

Other well-defined activities whose energy requirements, though relatively small, are worth separate consideration in this chapter are in the fields of agriculture and of public use, such as street lighting or the uses of public agencies, including the special case of the Atomic Energy

21. George Perazich, *Nuclear Process Heat in Industry* (Washington: National Planning Association, 1958).

22. In "The Economic Setting for Nuclear Power and Heat Development," Second International Conference on the Peaceful Uses of Atomic Energy, Geneva, June 1958, printed in *Progress in Nuclear Energy, Series VIII: The Economics of Nuclear Power* (Pergamon Press, 1959).

Commission. Among them they account for less than 5 per cent of total energy consumption in the United States.

Of the remaining uses of fuels, several, such as use of gas and oil as ingredients in manufacturing chemical products or carbon black and in venting gas at the wellhead, are not related to heat and power requirements. These miscellaneous uses, amounting to another 8 per cent of total energy consumption, are noted in Chapter 15, where total demand for the mineral fuels is estimated.

Agricultural Production

Once we eliminate those farm uses that are clearly domestic rather than productive, consumption of energy in agriculture is low in comparison with consumption in other branches of the economy. This is true despite the impressive surge of mechanization that since the thirties has replaced the energy derived from the carbohydrates consumed by man and beast with energy derived from the hydrocarbon contained in oil and gas.

Inclusive of the fuel needed to supply electricity for farm operations, total energy consumed in farming in 1960 probably absorbed about 3 per cent of all energy consumed in the economy as a whole. Since coverage is incomplete in various respects, this is undoubtedly a minimum estimate. All farm trucking, for example, has already been covered in estimates of petroleum used in transportation; so has the fraction of farm automobiles that should logically be allocated to productive purposes. No continuing statistics exist concerning natural gas consumption on farms, let alone consumption of that portion that is used in production. Teitelbaum, in his estimates for 1954,[23] puts natural gas use on farms at 40 billion cubic feet, split roughly 3:2 between household and production uses. This is only a fraction of 1 per cent of total natural gas consumption. Finally, even the data on electricity are deficient as a measure of productive use in that only such power as is estimated to have been consumed in pumping and irrigation is separately accounted for, while such modern uses as those applied in cooling,

milking, incubating, etc. are reported as part of total rural consumption, which includes all residential uses.

These omissions apparently are not serious. The available data suggest that, even if we included as productive all fuel consumed in trucking and half the fuel consumed by automobiles, the resulting increase in estimated petroleum consumption would still not raise the share of total energy consumption on farms to much above 3 per cent of the country's demand. Only when petroleum is taken by itself are farmers important consumers, purchasing nearly 10 per cent of all petroleum products sold and using about two-thirds of it in production and distribution. Expenditure data available from special surveys conducted in connection with the 1954 Census indicate that productive use of nonpetroleum fuels is quite limited, so that coverage deficiencies actually distort the picture but little.

Table 10–8 represents the estimated use pattern of petroleum and natural gas liquids in 1955, starting from the data used and developed in *Energy in the American Economy* and supplemented by guesses as to productive uses,

TABLE 10–8. Agricultural Uses of Petroleum and Natural Gas Liquids, 1955

(Million barrels)

Fuel		Total consumption	Estimated to be used in production
Gasoline		185.2	–
As motor fuel		184.7	–
Automobiles	58.8		29.4
Trucks	35.4		35.4
Tractors	86.1		86.1
Other engines	4.3		4.3
Other uses		0.5	0.5
Fuel oil		26.7	5.3
Diesel oil		7.7	7.7
Tractor fuel (principally kerosene)		5.4	5.4
Kerosene		10.7	5.0
LPG		39.2	12.0
All liquid fuels (rounded)		275.0	190.0
Same, excl. all truck and automobile use (rounded)		–	125.0

Source: See footnote 24.

23. Teitelbaum, *Energy Production and Consumption in the United States, op. cit.*

based principally on Department of Agriculture data.[24]

As the statistical coverage of farm energy consumption is limited, on the whole, to occasional surveys rather than to data emanating regularly in the form of shipment or sales statistics, it is difficult to judge how fuel consumption—or more accurately consumption of liquid fuel—has varied with changes in farm output.

It seems clear, however, that fuel consumption has had its direct bearing mainly on labor requirements and has been only an indirect factor in the expansion of farm output. More fuel does not "produce" more wheat, cotton, or poultry, in the way in which more steel is based upon more coke. Increased output has been achieved without increased acreage; thus there is no case here of larger acreage requiring more, or more intensively used, machinery. On the other hand, fuel has been an indirect factor in increased productivity, by way of implements, brought about by the growing size of the average farm, the timely execution of crucial chores, the better coverage, and more perfectly performed operations in cultivation. These productivity gains are discussed at some length in Chapter 18. But for indications of future fuel consumption we must look above all to the notable slowdown in the growth of mechanized equipment, the negligible amount of animal power still to be replaced, and the high incidence of machinery use that has already been achieved in much of the nation's farm economy. All of these factors suggest a retardation in the growth of liquid fuel consumption on farms.

It would be only a slight exaggeration to say that the replacement of horses and mules on farms is complete, as shown in Figure 10–10.

A survey made in 1956[25] established that, on the average, workstock remaining on farms was used only nine days a year, and fewer than three days on one-third of all farms. It follows that, given no increase in acreage, possibilities of substitution are even more limited than is indi-

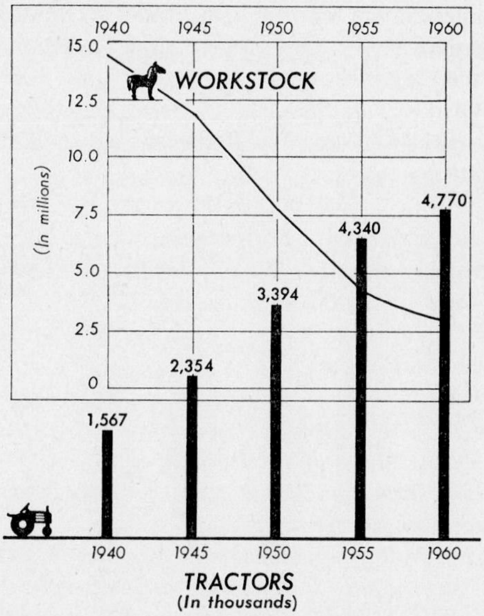

Figure 10–10. Trends in the use of animal and mechanical power on farms, 1940–1960.

cated by the drop in the number of animals. By now 40 per cent of all animals that remain are found on small farms in the Southern Atlantic and East South Central regions, where the drop has been gradual.

Not only the number of animals but also the use of animal-drawn implements has declined. Horse-drawn mowers still kept on farms were used on an average 54 acres per year in 1941, but on only 16 acres in 1956, as their use became restricted to smaller farms and often to supplementary harvesting. "Most of the nontractor farms," the U.S. Department of Agriculture judges, "contain less than 100 acres and many of them are part-time operations. . . ."[26]

As of the beginning of 1956, four out of five commercial farms had one or more tractors, and there were, on the average, 137 tractors for every hundred commercial farms and 175 tractors for every hundred commercial farms with tractors. In the principal branches of food raising—the raising of cash grain and of live-

24. U.S. Department of Agriculture, Agricultural Research Service and Agricultural Marketing Service, *Liquid Petroleum Fuel Consumption for Farm Purposes,* Statistical Bulletin No. 188 (Washington, July 1956).

25. Agricultural Research Service, *The Use of Horses and Mules on Farms,* ARS 43–84 (Washington: U.S. Department of Agriculture, March 1959).

26. These and subsequent data, except tabulation, from Department of Agriculture, *Farmers' Expenditures for Motor Vehicles and Machinery with Related Data, 1955,* Statistical Bulletin No. 243 (Washington, March 1959).

stock (other than poultry), and dairying—between 80 and 90 per cent of all farms had tractors, suggesting that growth may in the future be more pronounced on non-commercial farms and the less tractor-saturated branches of the farm economy.

Despite the marked slackening in tractor growth, shown below, it is reasonable to expect some further increase in the number of tractors on farms. This is unlikely to occur in the principal areas of tractor use—the Corn Belt from Ohio to Iowa and Missouri, the Lake states Michigan, Wisconsin, and Minnesota, and the six Plains states from North Dakota down to Texas—where growth in tractor stock has practically come to a halt. In these fourteen states, which account for half of all the tractors in the United States, the number of tractors now substantially exceeds the number of farms. Growth for the country as a whole is shown in Figure 10–10.[27]

The areas of potential expansion would thus seem to be the Atlantic-Appalachian states, the South and, to a more limited extent, the West (though substantial shifting of land from farm to urban use and concomitantly from virgin status to farm use gives a special potential to the West). Drawing again on type-of-farm data (limited to commercial farms), we find that only some 60–70 per cent of cotton, poultry, and fruit farms owned tractors on January 1, 1956. Because of the operating features of many of these farms, growth of tractors would be limited. Stipulating, however, at least one tractor for every commercial farm (of all types) that existed in 1956 would add some 700,000, or 15 per cent, to the current number of tractors. Assuming for every existing commercial farm the same number of tractors now found on those farms that have them would add some 1.3 million tractors to the current stock. This would certainly be a maximum assumption of what could be expected over the long term.

Relating the above considerations to the stock of tractors existing on January 1, 1960, we

27. Data from Department of Agriculture, *Number of Selected Machines and Equipment on Farms*, Statistical Bulletin No. 258, Agricultural Research Service and Agricultural Marketing Service (February 1960); and *Changes in Farm Production and Efficiency*, Statistical Bulletin No. 233 (1961).

might select an increase of 1 million to be reached by 1980 as a reasonable Medium projection, an increase of 1.3 million as a High, and an increase of 700,000 as a Low.

Beyond 1980, meaningful projections in this field are extremely hard to construct. It has therefore been assumed that only expansion in acreage will be a factor and that fuel consumption by tractors will grow at the rate assumed for acreage expansion.

There are, in addition to the limited prospect for gainful use, other reasons that might have a depressing effect on tractor use. More effective weed control through chemical agents would reduce the amount of tractoring for cultivation, and so would the possible integration of various crop operations in order to minimize compacting of the soil, root damage, and other side effects of tractor farming.

Little can be said about the final variable in this projection: the efficiency with which fuel is used by farm machinery. There have been divergent trends. On the one hand, horsepower ratings have risen, largely to enable tractors to perform the heaviest conceivable task they might meet. While tractors are used below their top-rated capacity, the increase in their horsepower has undoubtedly caused less economic average performance. On the other hand, a rapid switch to the more efficient diesel-engine tractors has recently occurred, accompanied by an increase in small tractors. Indeed, there has been substantial import of tractors smaller than those made customarily in the United States. So insistent has been the demand that domestic makers have decided to manufacture small models with which to recapture the part of the market that has been lost to imports. Though the impression one gains is that a reduction in unit consumption is the more likely of the two events, the evidence does not justify an adjustment on this score. On this basis, the projection of liquid fuel consumption works out at a slow pace of growth: a rise of 22 per cent from 1960 to 1980, and of 13 per cent from 1980 to 2000.

The only other energy source in farming that can be identified is the electric power consumed in irrigation and drainage. Here we accept the projections made by the Federal Power Commission late in 1959,[28] according to which this type of demand will total 19 billion kwh in 1980 and 29 billion in 2000, compared with 10 billion actually consumed in 1960.

Extension beyond 1980 is most speculative, but it can be safely assumed that in the West scarcity of water will become an increasingly notable factor and will raise the requirement for pumping from either surface or underground sources. Conversion of brackish or even sea water, if available at a cost comparable to that of sweet water, might put a major burden on pumping requirements in the last decade or two of the twentieth century. It is therefore probably conservative to extend the absolute rate of growth assumed by the Federal Power Commission beyond 1980, but the order of magnitude is not such as to warrant a more sophisticated approach. As it is, the year 2000 projection accounts for less than 1 per cent of total electric power demand projected for that time. Thus even a 50 per cent boost would not appreciably affect the aggregate electricity projection for the year 2000.

Public Consumption

The principal public users of energy are government (federal, state, and local) and a large variety of quasi-governmental public bodies. Of these, the Atomic Energy Commission is considered separately below, the defense establishment in Chapter 9, and transportation in Chapter 5. Energy consumption trends in the rest of the public sector presumably would not differ radically from those prevailing in residential and commercial use. For electricity and natural gas there are statistics to support this view. There is a good chance that growth trends will be similar in commercial establishments and in what are called "other public authorities" in the electric utility statistics and "other" in the natural gas statistics. Both types of customers have a public connotation and have, by and large, moved similarly in the past. For electricity, in fact, the relationship has been astonishingly constant. Appendix Tables A10–25 and A10–26

make use of historical relationships to establish projections.

In view of the relatively small importance of public energy use—less than 2 per cent of the total for the nation—and the probability that past relationships are reliable as at least a rough measure, no attempt is made here to derive refined estimates. Only if one could see radical changes ahead, in terms of altogether new uses or a significantly changed role of traditional uses, would it be important to devote much effort to the public sector.

One possibility, however, is worth noting. There is the prospect that street lighting and highway lighting, which have long fallen back as compared with the dynamic expansion of residential use of electricity, may be on the verge of a rebirth. In such an event, the much greater efficiency of fluorescent and mercury lighting will be more than offset by the raising to more satisfactory standards of those parts of cities and towns that hitherto have been neglected and by the continuous illumination of highways which may develop in the manner adopted along certain superhighways in the vicinity of large cities. In a 1960 survey of street and highway lighting,[29] it was found that only 15 per cent of all residential streets were illuminated at or above the level set by the lighting code, whereas over half the streets in commercial areas and highways were so lit. In the rural areas no more than 7 per cent of the roads met the standard.

This survey, regardless of one's judgment of the standard, at least suggests the existence of a large growth potential. Not considered in this projection is the significance of the recent limited resurgence of gas street lighting. Recent news articles report that more than half a million gas lights are now in use, some of them old but the majority of recent vintage. It is too soon to shrug the matter off as a passing fancy or to give it long-range significance. Certainly, it is difficult to picture a large-scale switch from electric to gas street lamps, if only in terms of replacement cost to municipalities. What is more likely is capture of a relatively small part of the

28. Senate Select Committee on National Water Resources, *op. cit.,* Committee Print No. 10, p. 4. The 1980 figure was raised to 26 billion in FPC's January 30, 1962 revision.

29. 2nd Annual Survey, *Electrical World,* November 14, 1960, p. 69.

total public lighting market by gas where special reasons other than economic exist. Resort towns and historic places might be among the more important customers.

Oil and coal statistics do not lend themselves to the establishment of relationships of the kind utilized for electricity and gas. Whatever public consumption occurs is subsumed in the adjustment of aggregate consumption in identified uses to total disappearance of oil and coal.

Atomic Energy Commission. Despite the fact that it currently accounts for some 7 per cent of total electric power consumption, assumptions of future power consumption in AEC installations have to be based principally upon "general impressions." This leads to the conclusion that an indefinite continuation of the current level of consumption, rounded to 60 billion kwh, is probably as good a guess as can be made, but one that will require revision at an early date. A more sanguine view is taken, for example, by the Westinghouse group cited in connection with commercial power consumption. Their projection foresees a power take in 1978 of 90 billion kwh. We have taken this magnitude to be the "maximum" in the year 2000.

chapter
11
OUTDOOR RECREATION

ONE OF THE FASTEST GROWING ACTIVITIES in the United States is outdoor recreation. More people, higher incomes, more leisure, and greater mobility are among the factors that have caused the rapid growth. This trend may be traced through many indicators: the increased construction in commercial recreation facilities, increased sales of fishing tackle, hunting equipment, and outboard motors, and above all, the increasing number of visits to parks and outdoor recreation areas of all sorts.

Looking at the publicly supplied part of outdoor recreation—which includes national parks, monuments and other areas, state parks and the larger metropolitan and regional parks, national and state forests, wildlife refuges, and the like—available statistics indicate that the use of such areas has been increasing rapidly for several decades. The principal factors lying behind this growth, while interrelated, may be sorted out as follows:

1) Population has nearly doubled during the last fifty years, which is as far back as we have any statistics at all regarding outdoor recreation on a national scale.

2) Incomes too have about doubled over this same period: on a per capita basis, the increase (in 1960 dollars) has been from $970 to $1,990.

3) Leisure time, a particularly tricky concept, undoubtedly has increased. The average work week in non-agricultural work has declined from fifty hours in 1910 to less than forty hours in 1960, a drop of about 20 per cent. Summer vacations on the average have lengthened, and more and more firms continue their employees' pay through the vacation period. The two-day week-end is now widely prevalent.

4) Mobility has increased tremendously over the past fifty years, mostly because of the family automobile. Cheap intercity bus routes, plus increased availability of airplane travel to most points in the country, have brought about a long-distance mobility which matches the shorter distance mobility of the automobile and local bus line.

5) The increase in the proportion of the population in the younger pre-work age brackets and in the older retired brackets, now widely accompanied by higher incomes, may well have exerted further pressure on outdoor recreation facilities. The shift from rural to urban living may have had a similar effect.

RELATED MATERIAL: Requirements for transportation, Chapter 5, pp. 129–37, and appendix, pp. 640–49. Demand for water, Chapter 14, pp. 258–60, 272. Adequacy of land, Chapter 18, pp. 373–77; and of water resources, Chapter 19, pp. 378–87.

The combination of these and other factors has resulted in a growth in the use of parks and related facilities of something approaching 10 per cent a year during the past several decades. The only interruption of any consequence in this trend took place during World War II, when the work week lengthened and gasoline rationing was enforced. The general growth in use was spread over all the major types of recreation areas, from city parks to national parks and forests, but with noticeable differences among them. The annual rate of growth in visits to national parks has been 9 per cent since the end of World War I, a little less since the end of World War II; in national forests, 8 per cent since the mid-twenties but over 12 per cent in the more recent past; in state parks, 9 per cent since the end of World War II; and in city and metropolitan parks, 4.5 per cent since 1929. These trends are shown in Figure 11–1.

The difficulties of projecting future demand for outdoor recreation are particularly vexing. The historical statistics are meager and the concepts underlying them not clearly worked out. National aggregates within which are submerged a 2-million-acre park in Alaska and a 1,000-acre park in Arkansas are difficult to deal with. Above all, past growth trends, if projected for the next forty years, seem to lead to a most unlikely situation. The uneven character of recreation land distribution is well exemplified in the finding by the Outdoor Recreation Resources Review Commission that recreation areas of over 100,000 acres in size constitute only 1 per cent of all areas but 88 per cent of the total recreation area.[1]

Projections are presented in Table 11–1, in the form of per capita visits, at different levels: High, Low, and Medium. The High level through 1980 simply projects past trends— specifically the period 1946–60. If extended to 2000, this approach would yield what appear to be astronomically high figures: nearly 1 bil-

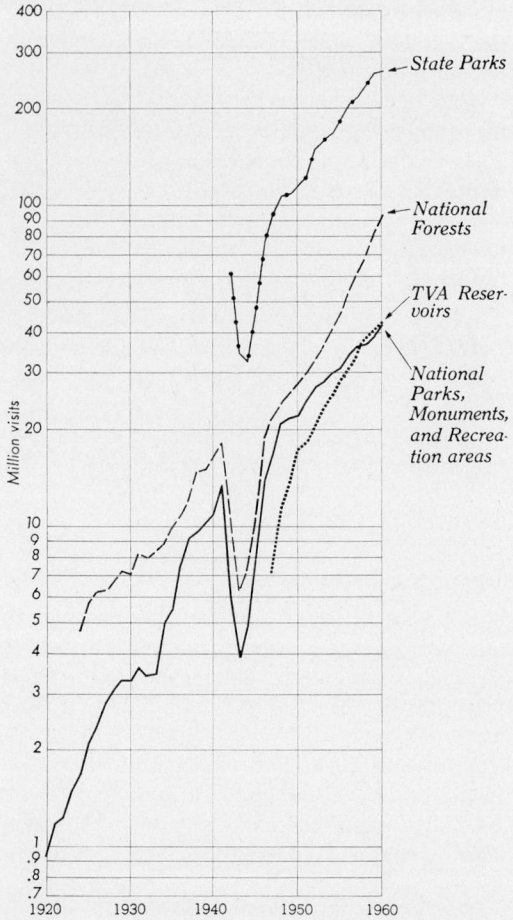

Figure 11–1. Annual visits to various types of recreation areas, 1920–1960.

1. Outdoor Recreation Resources Review Commission. *Outdoor Recreation for America*, A Report to the President (Washington: U.S. Government Printing Office, 1962), p. 52. For background data, see also Marion Clawson, *Statistics on Outdoor Recreation* (1958), *The Crisis in Outdoor Recreation* (1959), and *Methods of Measuring the Demand for and Value of Outdoor Recreation* (1959) (Washington: Resources for the Future, Inc.).

lion visits to the specified areas in the national park system by the year 2000 (over 3 visits each year by every man, woman, and child), and in the neighborhood of 9 billion visits each to the national forests and state parks (better than 2 visits per person each month). The additive effect, not counting visits to other areas, such as reservoirs, which score high on the visitor scale but are of less consequence in terms of space, carries into a quite implausible range, where the mere availability of time becomes a factor of constraint, no matter how fast and far we might travel. As a consequence, the projected High rate of gain after 1980 has been modified somewhat to yield a level of visits in the year 2000 which is about 27 per cent lower, but still a liberal high.

The Low estimates are made by relating the number of visits to the projected 1960–2000 increase of population and per capita disposable income, in each case using the middle-range estimate for these two items. On this basis, much smaller estimates of total visits result: 150 million to the national parks and

TABLE 11–1. Visits to Principal Recreation Areas, 1920–1960 and Projections for 1980, 2000[1]

(Per thousand population in year indicated)

Year		National parks, monuments, and recreation areas	National forests	State parks[2]
1920		9	n.a.	n.a.
1925		18	n.a.	n.a.
1930		26	[3]65	n.a.
1935		42	84	n.a.
1940		82	122	n.a.
1946[4]		97	129	534
1950		144	180	753
1955		186	277	1,108
1960		[5]229	516	1,439
1980[6]	L	330	750	2,100
	M	520	1,760	3,460
	H	820	3,840	5,820
2000[6]	L	490	1,110	3,100
	M	1,180	6,070	8,370
	H	2,340	19,820	18,290

L = Low projection   M = Medium   H = High
n.a. = not available.
1. Historical data by Marion Clawson, *Statistics on Outdoor Recreation* (Washington: Resources for the Future, Inc. 1958), and releases by Department of the Interior and U.S. Department of Agriculture.
2. Statistics of visits to state parks reflect not only growth but also changes in classification. Growth rates from 1960 on are based on number of visits adjusted to minimize these distortions.
3. 1931.
4. 1945 too heavily distorted by World War II factors.
5. Not strictly comparable to preceding years. On old basis of enumeration, figure would have been more nearly 210.
6. Per capita visits derived from projection of aggregate visits divided by Medium population projections (Appendix Table A1–2). Aggregate visits projected as follows: Low—3.5% growth per year, which is growth rate of per capita disposable income from 1960 to 2000 (Appendix Table A1–27), and thus reflects effect of population and income growth only; High—1960–80 extension of 1946–60 trend, 1980–2000, reduced by one-fourth the difference between that and the Low rate of growth; Medium—growth rate halfway between Low and 1946–60 trend.

related areas in 2000, not quite 350 million to the national forests, and some 950 million to state parks. The Low estimates, therefore, are presented as a kind of floor. Most likely, demand lies somewhere between this population-income-determined floor, and the extension of past trends.[2]

The Medium estimates are predicated upon a rate of gain midway between the projected Low rate of growth and the rate of postwar gain. This choice fully takes into account increases in population and income, but increases in other demand factors that have operated in the past are only partially allowed for.

This halfway estimate may be expressed as the result of projecting at annual compound growth rates varying between 6 and 8 per cent, according to type of area. Visits to national forests grow fastest; and those to national parks are slowest. By coincidence, we obtain a growth rate in the same range when we multiply the individual growth rates projected for the factors that appear to have most bearing upon demand for outdoor recreation: population, per capita income, leisure time, and per capita travel. This raises a good many questions for which as yet we have no answer. We do know that since the end of World War II recreation demand, in terms of visits to national and state parks and to national forests, has been increasing at a rate approaching 10 per cent a year. It can be shown that the four factors just named would be associated with a rise of only some 6 per cent, if conceived as acting in multiplicative fashion. Thus little less than half of the postwar rise remains to be "explained."

We can only guess at the functions here involved. On the one hand, it is rather audacious to assume these factors to be multiplicative. Equally likely, one or two of them might be mutually constraining, or might be thought of as the *sine qua non* without which the others might not be effective at all. On the other hand, one or more might have a mutually reinforcing effect on others and a dispropor-

2. In its report to the President, the Outdoor Recreation Resources Review Commission projects a tripling of demand for recreation facilities. This would place it below our Low projections, since even on a per capita basis these show about a doubling between 1960 and 2000.

tionately large effect on total demand: as per capita disposable income rises, changing tastes might boost outdoor recreation expenditures out of proportion; or, changing age, occupational, or regional distribution of the population (relative increase in urban population comes to mind as a potent factor) might give added impetus to the push that aggregate population growth imparts.

Thus, it is easy to see that there are many possible combinations of factors. What combination has spawned the past 10 per cent growth rate, we do not know; this makes it more difficult to estimate what the future holds. Thus, the fact that mere multiplication of the four factors yields a rate very much like the halfway mark between our High and Low growth rates is as interesting as it is unrevealing of the deeper relationships involved.[3]

Visits per Acre

If the Medium figures appear high—an average of 16 visits a year per capita compared with just above two in 1960—one must realize that the recreation-seeking portion of the population is composed of a great many multiple users (especially in beach and skiing areas) whose visits compensate for the non-users. As more people use the areas, so also will there be an increase in the number of people who visit them frequently. Looked at in this light, the per capita figures may appear less phenomenal. A great deal of planning would be required to meet this level of demand, probably involving the acquisition of many more tracts of land, and certainly entailing large investments in facilities to permit more intensive use. At this point it is helpful, therefore, to present our Medium projections of visits to areas in the national park system, the national forests, and state parks in terms of visits per acre. (See Figure 11–2.)

3. City parks have been omitted from our estimates because, in total, they require little land in comparison with national and state parks and forests. Since the ultimate object of our estimates is to translate recreational land use into acreage requirements, omission of city parks is of little consequence. The total land in city parks in 1960 was less than 1 million acres; this might increase in proportion to increases in the larger recreation areas through the remainder of the century. City park acreage is included in urban land as considered in Chapter 18, pp. 370–372.

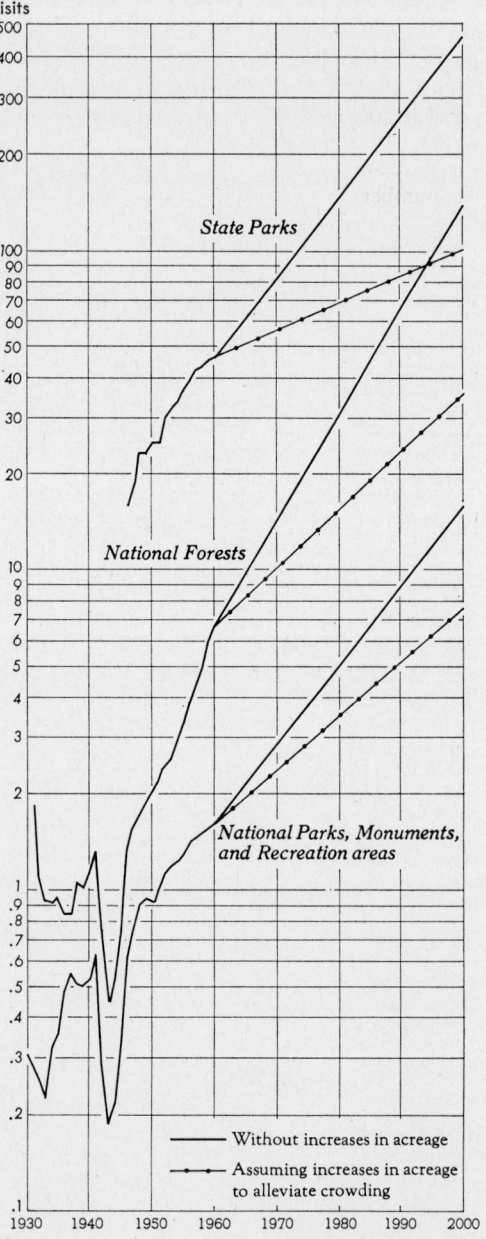

Figure 11–2. Annual visits per acre to principal recreation areas, 1930–1960 and Medium projections to 2000.

Disregarding World War II years, when use of the parks and forests dropped off, visits per acre to these three types of recreation areas have increased persistently with only a few brief interruptions. These interruptions occurred, not because fewer persons visited the parks or the forests, but because from time to time large pieces of new land were acquired.

Visits per acre vary greatly from one area to another. The degree to which they varied in 1960 is shown below for selected areas.

	Visits, 1960 (thousand)	Acres (thousand)	Visits per acre
National Parks			
Mt. McKinley	22	1,939	.011
Isle Royale	6	539	.011
Big Bend	76	692	.11
Everglades	579	1,259	.46
Yellowstone	1,443	2,213	.65
Glacier	725	1,000	.72
Olympic	1,160	889	1.3
Yosemite	1,150	758	1.5
Sequoia	611	385	1.6
Kings Canyon	760	454	1.7
Grand Canyon	1,187	673	1.8
Zion	576	129	4.5
Grand Teton	1,430	300	4.8
Great Smoky	4,529	508	8.9
Shenandoah	1,780	193	9.2
National Monuments			
Death Valley	356	1,866	.19
Joshua Tree	320	491	.65
Organ Pipe Cactus	262	328	.80
White Sands	379	140	2.7
Badlands	879	104	8.5
Petrified Forest	912	86	10.6
Muir Woods	509	[1]	[2]
State Parks			
Maine	691	205	3
New York	34,490	2,540	14
Maryland	4,913	18	27
Tennessee	3,860	131	29
Virginia	1,079	26	42
Washington	7,059	78	91
Oregon	10,918	60	181
Connecticut	4,497	22	204
New Jersey	6,399	29	221
Wisconsin	5,364	19	282
Rhode Island	2,597	8	325

1. Less than 500 acres.
2. Approximately 1,000.

Mt. McKinley National Park in Central Alaska experiences infinitesimal use per acre, but for the Shenandoah or Great Smoky national parks, both easily accessible to population centers on the Northeastern seaboard, there were 9 visits per acre in 1960. For state parks, which generally are more accessible, visits per acre tend to be larger, but they vary considerably from state to state and even more from park to park, especially in those states, such as New York and Maine, with very large wilderness parks.

While far from satisfactory, the use of "visits per acre" as a basis for estimating future use of recreation areas does offer a means for translating visits as a measure of demand and use into acres required. Perhaps the misleading characteristics of the measure for individual areas will be averaged out when numerous areas covering the whole country are taken together. It must be admitted, however, that more precise definition of use intensity standards for different types of recreation areas would simplify the estimating task.

It may be helpful to consider the upper limits of what might be called the carrying capacity of different types of recreation areas, in order to understand what is implied by our estimated number of visits per acre in the year 2000. Yosemite National Park, one of the more popular and accessible large recreation areas, now has about 1.5 visits per acre per year—that is, 1.2 million visits in a park measuring 760,000 acres. This, however, does not tell the whole story since nearly all the visitors spend most of their time in a 10,000-acre portion of the park, the floor of Yosemite Valley. Assuming that three out of four visitors stay in the Valley, this amounts to about 15,000 visits per acre of Valley land. Many would agree that Yosemite Valley is now developed and used very nearly to the maximum. While, conceivably, other areas in the park could be used almost as intensively, none offers such superlative natural scenery. However, by rationing the use of the Yosemite Valley floor through strict limitation on the time any visitor could spend there, the camping and overnight load might be shifted to other parts of the park. On this basis, visits per acre to the Valley floor might be increased considerably. The same would be true for the Old Faithful and other geyser areas in Yellowstone Park, and for the equally attractive spots in other national parks and monuments. It is difficult to say by how much visits per acre could be increased in this way, but it is within the realm of possibility that, for Yosemite Park as a whole, they might rise from 1.5 visits per acre per year to several times this number.

The Shenandoah National Park is a different type of park in many of its essential characteristics. It might be called a "drive-through" or touring park. The main feature, the Skyline Drive, is a beautifully engineered blacktop highway going along the Blue Ridge itself. There are a few camping and picnicking areas, but most visitors simply make the drive in one day. There were 9.2 visits per acre in 1960. This undoubtedly could be increased a good deal by rationing or curtailing use on certain week-ends of the year, notably in the summer and in the autumn when the foliage is at its most colorful. It seems within the realm of possibility that use could be increased considerably by judicious rationing on the few crowded week-ends of the year, and perhaps by providing additional access from the valley floors to the Skyline Drive. The Great Smoky National Park is similar to the Shenandoah National Park in these respects.

Another kind of area in the national park system might be called the "drive-to and walk-in" park. Muir Woods, across the Golden Gate Bridge from San Francisco, may be taken as an example. This area is visited by private cars or buses which are left in a large parking area while the visitors walk into the magnificent stand of redwoods. Recently there have been about 1,000 visits per acre a year. The limits here seem to be set by the damage pedestrians may do to the ground by upsetting balances in the plant and ground-cover ecology. To an extent, paved walks can be laid through the woods, although this seems to change the drainage characteristics of the area. Further study is needed before the maximum use, from the ecological and preservation point of view, can be determined. Here, as in the case of the Shenandoah and Great Smoky parks, more visitors could probably be accommodated if they could be spread out over the week and over the months of the year more than at present. It may be that the use of Muir Woods could be doubled or trebled, although this is a hazardous judgment. Mammoth Cave, in Kentucky and Carlsbad Caverns, along with many

historical sites, would fall within the same "drive-to and walk-in" category.

At the other end of the scale are the wilderness areas, those located within national parks or forests as well as those separately designated as such. Visits per acre here must remain few if the wilderness is to retain its characteristics. But it may be compatible with standards of wilderness to increase the intensity of use in some areas by spreading the use over winter or non-hunting months and by strict enforcement of use regulations which will preserve the desired characteristics.

Somewhere in between the parks and the wilderness areas are large portions of many of the national forests. At present, less than 10 per cent of national forest area is used primarily for recreation. Here, as in the case of Yosemite, large numbers of additional visitors could be accommodated if roads and trails to presently inaccessible areas were developed and if suitable facilities in these more remote places were provided. This kind of further development in forests as well as parks constitutes a reserve for expansion of great size.

Adjustments to Increased Use

A number of ways of adjusting to a large increase in demand for outdoor recreation come to mind. First, of course, is the adding of more acres. Even at the greatly increased carrying capacities assumed—and they may not perhaps be compatible with acceptable standards of nature enjoyment—we would have to add nearly 90 million acres to existing sites in the national park system, the national forests, and the state parks: 32 million additional acres by 1980, another 57 million by 2000. (See Table 11–2.) Many observers believe that the number of acres of national parks and national forests available for recreation may be expected to increase only slowly in the future as it has in the past; they see no likelihood of really large physical increases. The cost per acre is rising, and demands for other types of use may be expected to grow as population increases and the economy develops further. More likely than large physical expansion will be the conversion of land now used mainly for other purposes—such as growing trees—to recreation use, if not *in toto* then through multiple use of the land for recreation as well as forestry. Larger acquisitions may be expected for state parks, especially if strenuous efforts are made to acquire and develop more ordinary scenic areas.

A second way of meeting increased demand will be through the more intensive use of existing acres. This means more investment in access roads, in camping and picnicking facilities, in roads and trails of all sorts, in development of water supply and sewage handling facilities, and so on. As has been indicated, the limits here are difficult to foresee. Even in the few selected parks already discussed there appear to be wide ranges of possibilities. Much will depend on public policy and on the willingness of users to substitute for their first choice well-developed areas in less than superb natural surroundings. Such a substitution would be difficult in areas like Yosemite National Park or Grand Canyon National Park, whose attractions for most people are quite localized. In many of the national forests and state parks, however, it should be possible, with adequate investment, to add greatly to the intensity of use and therefore to the carrying capacity. Increases in intensity will involve sacrifices and compromises: large populations of wildlife have proved to be incompatible with large numbers of people; the same is true of fish, unless fishing regulations are very strict. A more elaborate grading of park and forest areas, ranging from wilderness to highly developed camping and picnicking areas, will be helpful.

Finally, growth in demand can be checked or redistributed in various ways. Strict limitation can be placed on length of stay. Higher fees can be charged for entrance and use. Vigorous efforts to spread the use over less used portions of the week, month, and year can be made. In addition to providing for more intensive use, these various schemes of rationing would have the effect of modifying the actual amount of use, depending upon the vigor and strictness of the rationing.

The quantitative precision of the calculations presented in Table 11–2 should not mislead one into thinking that they are based on agreed standards. As yet there is little agreement on what such standards might be. Nor is there much understanding of their implications. What has been done here is to scale down the steep increase in intensity of use that would result from failure to add acreage, even when visits are taken to grow at only their Medium rate, i.e., at a speed substantially below recent experience.

The adjustments made in Table 11–2 have employed a few rough benchmarks. Average

TABLE 11–2. Acres Required in 1980 and 2000, Principal Recreation Areas, Based on Medium Projection of Visits

	National parks, monuments, and recreation areas			National forests[1]			State parks		
	1960	*1980*	*2000*	*1960*	*1980*	*2000*	*1960*	*1980*	*2000*
Visits (millions)	41	125	390	93	430	2,010	259	850	2,770
Acreage (assuming no change from 1960, in millions)[2]	25	25	25	14	14	14	6	6	6
Visits per acre (rounded)	1.6	5.0	15.6	7	30	134	43	140	460
Visits per acre, adjusted[3]	1.6	3.5	8.0	7	15	35	43	70	100
Areas required (million acres)[4]	25	36	49	14	29	57	6	12	28

1. National forest area of 180 million acres is potentially available for recreation. Acreage figure shown here refers only to the 14 million acres of primitive, roadless, wilderness, and wild areas, which are *primarily* for recreation.
2. Acreage rounded to nearest million.
3. Adjustment is arbitrary to reduce intensity of use to more tolerable level; see text.
4. Based on adjusted visits per acre and projected visits.

use per acre in all national parks has been held just below the level of current use in the most heavily visited parks, and use per acre in national forests has been allowed to rise roughly in proportion to use per acre of national parks. Perhaps this approach produces too high an intensity by 2000, i.e., five times current use, but, again, standards are lacking.[4] As for state parks, which already show very high use per acre, we have allowed roughly for a doubling of average intensity by 2000. This yields a level even now greatly exceeded in some parts of the country (cf. the listing above), but without analyzing each of these situations it would be hazardous to adopt the current standard of, say, state parks in Rhode Island, as one acceptable for the country as a whole.

Certain growth factors will be at work in the next forty years, as in the past, along with certain growth-limiting or growth-retarding factors. The growth factors include more people, higher income per capita, more leisure time, greater ease of transportation, and more retired people. Among the growth-limiting factors are: the amount of time that will be available for using outdoor recreation areas, such as the fixed number of week-ends in the year; the number of recreation sites of high or desired quality; the amount of investment in the development, improvement, and maintenance of recreation sites; the degree to which other kinds of recreation may be substituted

4. In addition, there is a good deal of uncertainty as to the proper acreage figure in national forests that should be related to visits.

for the outdoor kind discussed here; and, of course, the kinds of policies that are pursued with regard to entrance fees, rationing, and so forth. We have found it impossible to tie our estimates of demand in this chapter tightly to identifiable growth and growth-limiting factors; rather, we have set what we believe to be the outer limits and then have arbitrarily chosen a middle estimate between the extremes. Evidence of both growth and growth limitations has been presented, but both the future demand in terms of visits and the future supply in terms of acres reflect a great deal of judgment, open to argument.

National parks and monuments, national forests, and state parks are the most space-devouring types of outdoor recreation facilities. Reservoirs, whether sponsored by TVA, Corps of Engineers, or Bureau of Reclamation, have had a spectacular growth in popularity and will undoubtedly provide increasing outlets for the more water-minded among vacationers and weekenders. Trends are far too short, however, for assessing future growth, even with the degree of uncertainty that attaches to the categories we have been discussing. Nor are the space implications of matching concern.

To an extent, the impending pressure on public recreation lands can be eased by increases in private facilities. But information on privately owned land, lakes, and beaches is far too meager to warrant speculation on this score. Publication of the ORRRC study reports will undoubtedly widen knowledge of this area of the recreation industry.

DEMAND FOR
KEY MATERIALS

MOST OF THE REQUIREMENTS for future living considered in Part I will draw upon more than one natural resource product for their fulfillment. Transportation, for instance, calls upon metals, textiles and plastics for the equipment itself and upon fuels for motive power; construction, upon wood, metals and several others; durable goods, upon an even wider range. Here in Part II we bring together these scattered items into projections of total future demand upon each of six groups of materials.

In so doing we start with the relatively homogeneous raw materials that go into the production of final products. But since many of these materials already have undergone transformations before they reach that point, we seek insofar as possible to follow them back to a stage at which they can be best compared (in Part III) with the resources from which they are derived.

Apart from this common purpose, no rigid pattern is followed in the next six chapters. Different approaches and different methods of measurement are needed to define patterns of future demand for such a wide diversity of materials of which chemicals and water are especially elusive.

One thread that runs through most of the chapters, however, concerns reuse—scrap—and "free" use—by-products. The first is particularly important for the metals and the second for food and for lumber, but both have wider application as means of holding down net demands for materials. Our interest here is on articles that have actually entered into end-use consumption. Other quantities of materials are reclaimed before that stage. We are not particularly concerned with them here except as they affect the total volume of particular materials needed to circulate in industrial pipelines at any given time. On the other hand, we must take into account the amounts of currently irreclaimable processing waste which never end up in final products but which are just as surely a drain on the materials supply.

chapter
12

CROPS

IF THE KEY MATERIALS OF THE AMERICAN ECONOMY were to be grouped by origin and ranked in order of value, at least equal contender for top rank would be agricultural crops. Roughly $20 billion worth of raw materials is accounted for under this heading, compared with a roughly equal amount for mineral materials and no more than $5 billion for all other materials combined. If the value of pasture were to be added in, agriculture would have a clear first place, and it would be several lengths ahead if the finished value of livestock were substituted for the value of their feed.

In this book, we have considered livestock as a semi-finished product and the various agriculturally produced feeds—including pasture —as the key materials entering into this product. Other agricultural materials are the food crops (wheat, rice, fruit, vegetables, etc.), the fiber crops (cotton, flax), and crops yielding food, feed, and industrial materials, such as soybeans. From the demands for food and clothing, plus some industrial materials, projected in Part I we could derive the demands for each one of these agricultural materials in turn. Yet if we look ahead to our goal of evaluating the call upon land resources, it is apparent that most such effort would be wasted. Of the total crop acreage harvested, fully 90 per cent is accounted for by only eight crops: corn, wheat, oats, barley, grain sorghums, hay, cotton, and soybeans. Of the five principal grain crops, all except wheat are primarily grown as feed for livestock, are to a large extent inter-substitutable, and may therefore be considered as a single crop—feed grains. The crops we shall specifically consider, therefore, are feed grains, hay, wheat, soybeans, and cotton. By adding pasture, we account for most agricultural acreage. We shall also give brief consideration to sugar and to two non-food animal products—leather and wool.

Even if we regard soybeans as a food crop, because they do supply edible vegetable oils, we find that only about one-fourth of harvested acreage, and perhaps 6 to 7 per cent of all agricultural land—that is, cropland and grazing land, is used for crops which are the immediate source of food for human consumption. Hardly 5 per cent of harvested cropland and just over 1 per cent of all agricultural land is devoted to raising fibers for clothing. Over 90 per cent of all agricultural land is devoted to the feeding of animals, and much of such land, being un-

RELATED MATERIAL: Appendix to this chapter, pp. 586–95. Food, Chapter 2, pp. 89–103, and appendix, pp. 778–803. Clothing and textiles, Chapter 3, pp. 104–11, and appendix, pp. 596–602. Use of land, Chapter 18, pp. 335–55, 373–77, and appendix, pp. 969–84.

suitable for crops other than grass, could not produce human food in any other way. Clearly, even though the low productivity of grazing land exaggerates its importance in terms of acres, the demand for animal products and the proficiency of animal husbandry are by far the principal determinants of agricultural, and through agricultural of total, land resource requirements in the United States.

The purpose of this chapter is to bring together, for all goods other than forest products, the requirements that ultimately constitute a demand for land as a producing agent. In Chapters 2 and 3 we projected the demand for food and fiber and looked into the various possible combinations in which these demands might be met: by different diets and by different fiber mixes. We did not, however, consider the impact of foreign trade: how large foreign demand for wheat, feed grains, or cotton is likely to be, to what degree domestic requirements for sugar may be supplied from abroad, etc. Above all, in evolving demand for food we did not proceed to demand for livestock feed; but it is only the latter that can be directly translated into demand for land, the ultimate resource in which we are interested.

Animal Feeding

Of all the problems that we must disentangle in this chapter in order to carry to Part III, and specifically Chapter 18, figures on size of crops to be harvested or grazed, the most complex is that of livestock feed. Livestock can be fed in a variety of ways, each of which has a different impact upon demand for land; feed grains, like corn or sorghum, yield more nutrients per acre than does hay, and hay more than pasture. Open range provides fewer nutrients than does pasture, and different types of grazing land differ in their productivity. High-protein feeds, such as oilcake or fishmeal, are even higher in feed content than grains, and, to the extent that they are by-products, the claim on land is already taken care of in connection with the main product. Thus, the proportion in which the various feed sources will be used makes all the difference in estimating land requirements.

It follows that an infinite variety of models can be constructed. We have limited the number to five: a Medium—or most likely—projection; a set of extremes in which all the factors that would tend to maximize land use (High) or minimize it (Low) are picked up; and a set of Modified Highs and Lows, in which at least one of the factors that tend to maximize or minimize land use is relaxed. We thus come out with two Highs, two Lows, and a Medium. In terms of occurrence, the modified projections are judged the more likely, while the extremes serve to highlight tendencies that can be identified and should be considered but represent outside probabilities.

Having made these observations on concept we shall now see how they work out in actual calculations. Many a factor besides consumer demand for meat, milk, eggs, and poultry enters into the demand for feed crops. The kinds of animals, how they are fed and what they are fed for, how their health is taken care of, what biochemical means are used to stimulate their growth—all of these have a bearing. The essential questions for this study are best understood if they are divided into two parts: (1) feeding efficiency, or the quantity of feed needed for a given output of meat, milk, or eggs, and (2) the sources of feed.

Feeding Efficiency

The list of feedstuffs is a lengthy and lengthening one. They range all the way from grass to corn to fishmeal. They may be fresh, dried, or fermented. And each feed has a different nutritive value per pound. Under the circumstances, analysis of feeding efficiency is dependent upon the use of some sort of common denominator, or "feed unit." As worked out by Ralph D. Jennings, of the U.S. Department of Agriculture,[1] a feed unit is taken as the feeding equivalent of one pound of corn. The relationship is not fixed, but varies with different animals and over time, depending upon the relative amounts of different kinds of feed that are used. While the conversion ratios are thus subject to error, particularly when used as an

1. See especially *Consumption of Feed by Livestock, 1909–56,* USDA Production Research Report No. 21 (Washington, November 1958).

all-animal average, they form as good a basis as is available for discussing total feed consumption. Without such a nutritive equivalent it would be impossible to aggregate different feedstuffs or analyze their relative roles in the feed picture.

Also useful is the division of feedstuffs into two principal categories—concentrates and roughage. The former includes grains and oilseed meals and other commercial by-products, while the latter includes hay, silage, pasture, and bulky feeds that have a relatively small amount of digestible nutrients. Concentrates are fed to all classes of livestock, but roughage is of particular importance in the ration of the ruminants—cattle, goats, and sheep. Ruminants can be maintained, if need be, on roughage alone, but swine and poultry, as a practical matter, depend overwhelmingly on the concentrates. By and large, there is a considerable range of substitution between concentrates and roughages, which has an important bearing both on the demand for various crops and on their dispensability in the event of supply tightness.

Besides the roughages and concentrates, livestock rations also include additives—minerals, urea, vitamins, antibiotics, etc. While of great importance in food production, these are at present and for the foreseeable future inconsequential from the standpoint of their own call upon resources, directly or indirectly. Urea (a synthetic nitrogen compound) is sometimes mixed with cattle feeds which contain large quantities of crushed corn cobs or other cellulosic material. The urea enables bacteria in the rumen of the cattle to convert this material into a digestible form. Increased use of urea thus might put a dent into the demand for feed crops. However, to the extent that trends like this are already implicit in the statistics of the past, they have at least partly been taken into account in the forward estimates. To assume much greater inroads would at this point be highly speculative. Waste materials are neither limitless nor costless and, depending upon the quantities demanded and readily available, will not necessarily come cheaper, after collection and processing, than the freshly produced items with which they may compete.

Since different animals—and even the same species of animal bred and raised for different purposes—have different feed requirements, it is of great consequence for projecting the range of demand in feed crops and pasture just how the demand for food in the United States is distributed among beef, veal, pork, poultry, eggs, and milk; between fat pork and lean pork; among the various grades of beef. In order to place a frame of reference around the multitudinous combinations of possibilities, we shall seek here, as elsewhere in this study, to establish a reasonably possible High and Low and a probable Medium. Whereas in Chapter 2, however, we were primarily concerned with Highs and Lows in terms of pounds consumed, here we are more interested in which combinations of meat and poultry consumption make the greatest and the least call upon feed units. We shall continue to assume that consumption of milk and eggs is relatively independent.

The efficacy of feed units in producing pounds of beef, veal, pork, poultry, etc., changes constantly as the technology of animal husbandry moves forward, as price relationships vary, and as, for one reason or another, different breeds of animals come to be preferred.

Take the milk cow for example. In 1910, it required, on the average, 120 pounds of corn equivalent to produce 100 pounds of milk; today, it takes about 109 pounds. The amount went as low as 95 pounds in 1929 and 1930, and one might conclude that feeding in those days was more efficient. This is true, in a sense, despite the fact that today's heavier milk producers are more efficient converters of feed. Today's efficiency arises largely from the fact that the input of feed required merely to raise and sustain the cow is spread over a greater number of units of output; but the principle of diminishing returns applies, and the last few units of output require more feed than those which precede. The cows of some thirty years ago had better marginal efficiency than today's cows because they were not being pushed quite so close to capacity and because the cost of feed was relatively high.

The statistics for beef cattle also show apparently greater feed efficiencies in 1929 and part of the thirties than obtain today. As with the milk cows, this is partly because the marginal pound of feed produces greater results in somewhat underfed cattle than in fully fed ones. But it is also because beef-raising economics places a premium not only on high added weight per pound of feed but on speed of growth. And the faster growing animals of today require more feed per pound to achieve this speed.

The ranges in types of livestock and their productivity are wide. For example, the average dairy cow produces about 6,000 pounds of milk a year; the average cow belonging to a herd-improvement-association farmer produces over 10,000. Many cows produce only 3,000 pounds; prize cows have exceeded 40,-000. Similar differences in productive capacity can be found in beef cattle, hogs, and poultry.

Feed efficiencies are also highly dependent upon progress in the development and use of mixed feeds, and of the already-mentioned additives, which can truly make the whole greater in nutritive value than the sum of its parts. Formula feeds, now widely used by the poultry industry and to a considerable extent by the dairy industry, enable the farmer to take advantage of precisely mixed combinations. The additives are highly important both in stimulating livestock growth and in permitting greater inter-substitution of usual feedstuffs by supplying the essential ingredients which some of them may lack. Antibiotics reduce susceptibility to disease and have by now become an essential in poultry rations. Hormones, which are relative newcomers among the additives and have had remarkable effects in speeding up growth, face an uncertain future because of unsettled questions as to their ultimate effect on the consumer of the animal or its products. Among other additives are such diverse items as vitamins, arsenicals, detergents, and even tranquilizers to quiet livestock during shipment to market.

Much of the improvement in feeding efficiency over the years has been associated with advances in veterinary knowledge and techniques. The most dramatic example is in the commercial broiler industry, which owes its existence to the development of methods that have permitted the close confinement of large flocks. These advances have reduced the need for sunshine by provision of vitamin D in the ration and have inhibited the spread of dangerous infections. Fatal and debilitating diseases still exist in all livestock enterprises and cause heavy losses of feed and labor, but the major scourges are under control.

Projections of feeding efficiency. Continued rapid advance in animal husbandry is in prospect. As with other aspects of agricultural technology, the continuation of change is guaranteed if only because it takes long periods of time, in most kinds of farming, for new technology to spread to all enterprises. In addition, however, research and development in animal husbandry may be expected to produce continued innovation and improvement, especially over the next few decades, of the following kinds: (1) further increases in the productive period of egg-laying hens and of milk cows; (2) increases in the rate of growth of meat animals and in the rate of output of milk per cow and eggs per chicken; (3) achievement of a technique, especially in cattle, for producing young of a predetermined sex; and (4) achievement of techniques for inducing multiple births.

The beneficial effect of all such potential developments on farm economics is clear; their effect on feed efficiencies may be quite mixed. By feeding hormones, for example, it may be possible to keep a milk cow in production over a greater proportion of her lifetime. As noted above, because of diminishing returns such a development may or may not be feed-saving. The saving, if any, would result from the fact that relatively fewer animals need be raised to the period of production. Similarly, the feeding of hormones to beef cattle has already resulted in increased rate of weight gain but no decrease in units of feed per pound of weight. On the other hand, speeding up the growth and productivity of laying hens produces significant feed savings, since most of a hen's feed is required for maintenance of the animal and only a small amount for the production of eggs.

The production of young of desired sex may in the future be achieved by electronic or centrifugal separation of male-producing and female-producing spermatozoa and the use of artificial insemination. With such a technique in beef cattle, the birth of females could be limited to the number required to replace breeding stock. Since steers make more economical weight gains than heifers, this would lead to a moderate saving in unit feed requirements.

Increasing the incidence of multiple births among beef cattle would have more substantial effects. If twins could be produced at every calving, the breeding stock could be cut virtually in two, and this might result in a 10 to 15 per cent saving in feed for beef cattle. The net effect for dairy cattle is difficult to foresee, because of limitations resulting from the need for freshening cows and the separate demand for veal. The development would have little application to hogs because large litters are normal.

Aside from technology, feeding patterns depend essentially on the supply of various feeds, their relative prices, and the prices of livestock products. As already noted, some of the most efficient feeding in the United States occurred during the early 1930's, when feed grains were in short supply and relatively expensive. The high cost of grains resulted in underfeeding, so that there was less output per animal but more per unit of feed. At the other extreme is the sort of price relationship where there are relatively low feed prices and high livestock-product prices. This makes it profitable to raise heavy hogs and beef, with a resultant lowering in efficiency.

While such differences in price relationships have important shorter term implications for feed/output ratios, one may assume that over the longer run, prices of livestock products and of feeds in general will move sufficiently in parallel that technical improvements, rather than relative prices, will be the principal determinant of total feed use. Relative prices will still have much to do with the specific feeds utilized, but in terms of broad groups future price trends are not likely to be so different from those of the past as seriously to alter the patterns of change already under way. In any event, it is the method of this study to base the various demand estimates on what it is reasonable to extrapolate on the basis of past trends and known or expected technical relationships and leave until the very last the

consideration of such decisive price changes as may be implied by our findings of prospective shortage or surplus.

The room for variation in prospective technical relationships is represented by our three levels of projection. The projected Low levels of feed efficiency (or, as we have calculated them, the high levels of feed input per unit of output) are in most cases assumed as remaining roughly what they are today. This does not mean that no change is to be expected in the component influences, but that the increased levels of efficiency in feeding which technology makes possible may be neutralized by the pursuit of faster growth or higher per-animal yields. The projected High levels of feed efficiency (low inputs per unit of output) are based upon optimistic projections of past trends, as modified by the judgment of various experts. The Medium, as usual, represents our judgment as to the in-between trend that seems most probable.

In the case of *cattle and calves,* it currently takes somewhat over 1,000 pounds of corn equivalent to produce 100 pounds of animal on the hoof, ready for slaughter (or about 55 pounds in terms of carcass weight). This requirement is somewhat higher than the one that prevailed earlier in the past decade; the higher level may be caused by relatively low prices of abundant feed supplies. The ratio relates feed for all cattle except milk cows to the slaughter of all cattle and calves, including cows which have passed their productive period. Our High projection (low feed efficiency) assumes some increase in the requirement, to 1,100 pounds in 2000; the Low projection, 25 per cent decrease by the end of the century; and the Medium, a steady 950 pounds, which has been the average over a considerable past period. Figure 12–1 illustrates these projections and those for the other animal products discussed in this section.

U.S. consumption of beef has been shifting more and more to the "good" and "choice" grades that require high degrees of finish. These grades come from the heavier animals, that usually have been fattened on grain. Being heavier than average, they require relatively more feed units per pound of product. A continuation of the shift to higher grade,

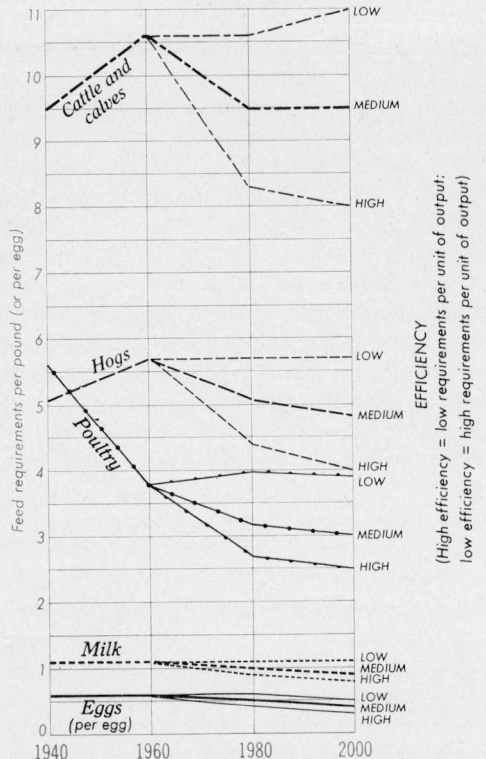

Figure 12–1. Feed efficiency for various animal products, 1940, 1960, and projections for 1980 and 2000. Except for eggs, this is calculated in relation to pounds (liveweight) of product.

grain-fattened beef consequently would tend to decrease feed efficiency. The High projection assumes such a condition, moderated by the application of some feed-saving practices.

The Low projection assumes that feed-saving techniques will more than compensate for the inefficiencies of overfeeding cattle, and that in addition there may be a tendency to revert, in part, to leaner beef. Grain fattening of beef in recent years has been associated with the development of commercial feedlots, each of which may carry up to 30,000 head of cattle at any given time and which feed beef continuously throughout the year. Such large-scale operations obtain benefits similar to those in the commercial broiler industry. By depending upon outside sources of feed, they gain greater flexibility in the kinds of rations used. The scale of operations permits more concentrated application of veterinary care and

facilitates the application of new techniques and research results.

Clearly more economical of feed on a liveweight basis than are cattle, *hogs* also yield more per pound of feed in terms of carcass weight. Moreover, gains in the efficiency of feeding hogs are more certain, as reflected in our projections, and can be assumed even in the Medium projection. Our upper trend, representing low efficiency, shows no change over the next forty years. The Medium projection, which improves in line with the trends of the past half-century, probably cannot be achieved without some shift—which is assumed—toward leaner hogs. To comply with the Low projection, the hog-raising industry would have to follow the road pioneered by commercial broiler production, and certain similarities in the raising of hogs and broilers suggest that such a development might occur. Both broilers and hogs depend almost entirely upon concentrates for their feed, and both can be raised in close confinement. In the case of hogs, however, there are problems to be overcome. Experiments thus far, for example, have been plagued by problems of disease and parasite control.

Aggregate feed requirements for *milk* production are second in importance only to those for beef and veal. Increases in requirements per unit of output are quite unlikely, but certain conditions could combine to keep feed efficiency from improving beyond present levels—for example, a low rate of gain in the relative numbers of higher yield dairy cattle, coupled with a high rate of feeding or with the extension of a practice, now current in some places, of prolonging the milking periods of cows well beyond the point of maximum feed efficiency. More likely, however, there will be continued gains in average feed efficiency, and this is reflected in our Medium estimate, which continues the over-all rate of improvement registered in the last forty years. The lowest curve on the chart represents a more rapid rate of change than has occurred over the long run. This decrease, to less than three-fourths of today's unit requirements by the end of the century, could be achieved if no more than the best management techniques already known were universally adopted. Although this is unlikely, widespread diffusion of presently known techniques, plus the perfection of new techniques still in the experimental stage, could still bring about the indicated high-efficiency trend.

Prospective feed requirements for *poultry* are not understandable without an examination of the trends in different types of poultry and the essentially by-product relationship of a portion of the supply. The takeover of chicken-meat production by the commercial broiler industry has been sweeping. Farm chickens furnish only 17 per cent of the total poultry supply; 20 years ago they furnished 72 per cent. Most such chickens now are Leghorns or crosses, bred for their egg-laying capabilities, and since they cannot compete on a meat basis, very few males are any longer raised. Because it is possible to determine the sex of chicks at the age of one day, farmers no longer need buy chicks of undetermined gender, but can confine themselves to pullets. The future importance of farm chickens is related to per capita consumption of eggs. Furthermore, the elimination of the roosters and introduction of other efficiencies means that less and less by-product meat will accompany each dozen eggs produced. The combined result is that while poultry consumption should double by the end of the century, the meat available from farm chickens will probably increase less than two-thirds.

Commercial broilers already require little more than half as much feed per pound of meat as do farm chickens and will continue to improve more rapidly than farm chickens in feed efficiency, because of their specialization. This shifting of the product mix should mean continuing large gains in feed efficiency for poultry as a whole—at least for the next decade or so. It took almost 5½ pounds of feed in 1940 to produce each pound of liveweight poultry. That included turkeys, which now provide about one-fifth of total poultry consumption and are slightly more economical of feed than farm chickens, but which then were only one-eighth of consumption and less economical to feed. By now, average requirements for poultry as a whole are down to less than 4 pounds; there should be a further gain to 3¼ pounds by 1980 and just below 3 pounds—or approxi-

mately the present level for broilers—by the end of the century. It is possible, though less likely, that average requirements could decrease more rapidly, to less than 3 pounds by 1980 and 2½ pounds by 2000. This speed-up could come about if declining egg consumption were to lower still further the proportion of meat from farm chickens and if one of the largest remaining problems in broiler production—the 10 to 20 per cent death loss among baby chicks—were more quickly and completely eliminated. On the other hand, an augmented per capita egg consumption, plus a trend to heavier, or roasting type, chickens, could nullify other influences and keep average feed inputs per pound of poultry more or less what they are today. The last contingency forms the basis of our Low feed efficiency projection.

Eggs themselves should be produced with rapidly increasing efficiency in the future. An average of about 9 ounces of corn equivalent feed units currently goes into the making of an egg—only a little less than twenty years ago. Twenty years from now, 8 ounces will be more probable, and by the end of the century, 6¼ ounces. Some of this prospective step-up in the rate of gain in efficiency is more apparent than real. Unaccounted for in the statistics of earlier years was the considerable amount of feed scavenged in the barnyard; although still unaccounted for, this supplement has by now been reduced to small proportions. Moreover, the size of the average egg has increased—another trend which has probably reached its culmination. On the technological side is the gradual conversion to production of eggs by caged hens. Should this trend be hastened and egg production follow more closely in the footsteps of the commercial broiler industry, it is possible that not 6¼, but 5 ounces of feed will be sufficient to produce an egg by the end of the century. On the other hand, factory methods may conceivably be sufficiently retarded in their spread that improvement in efficiency will take place at perhaps only half the rate assumed for the Medium projection.

Total feed requirements. There is no particular problem in deducing total feed requirements for a single Medium projection. But beef consumption is not independent of pork con-

sumption, nor pork of beef, and the two together are not independent of lamb and poultry consumption. These animals have different
feed requirements; thus the Highs and Lows
we may project are, quite apart from the levels
of population, dependent upon the particular
combinations of meat and poultry consumption
which we assume. Furthermore, while we may
suppose that higher consumption of any particular type of meat would result in higher
efficiency of production, this may not be taken
for granted, for there are other influences upon
the efficiency ratios which could easily be overriding. To determine the range of total feed
requirements we must evaluate the consequences both of treating feed efficiencies as an
independent factor and of adopting as test
models those combinations of meat and poultry
consumption which per se are most and least
feed-intensive.

The basis for doing this was laid in Chapter
2, where both low and high per capita meat
consumption were distributed as they might be
under the alternatives of emphasis on beef
and of a greater emphasis on variety in the
diet. We have already noted the smaller return in pounds of meat per unit fed of beef
compared with pork, and since these are the
two major elements in the meat diet, it must
follow that the highest feed requirements will
follow from an emphasis on beef and the lowest from an emphasis on variety. Poultry consumption may be assumed to respond inversely
to total red meat consumption, being lowest
when the latter is at a high and highest when
the latter is at a low.

If to our feed-intensive high consumption
pattern we add our low-feed-efficiency, and
therefore land-extensive, method of achieving
it, we may determine our high contingent lia-
bility for land, and if we reverse the procedure
for the low consumption pattern, we may determine how little land we may conceivably
require. We shall also determine what different
results would ensue if we were to meet our
high consumption pattern in the most rather
than the least efficient and least rather than
most land-extensive manner, and vice versa for
the low.

These calculations are summarized overleaf
in Table 12–1, which starts with low and high

demand levels (liveweight of animals), and
goes on to determine their possible meaning
for total feed requirements. The table also
shows the Medium projections for ease of
comparison.

As illustrated in Figure 12–2, there is a
considerable difference in total feed requirements for any particular food consumption
level under the alternate assumptions on feeding efficiency. Meeting the high demand levels
in the least efficient way (group 11) requires
a tripling of feed availability by the end of
the century; meeting them in the most efficient
way (group 10), little more than a doubling.
High efficiency in meeting the low demand
(group 7) would get us by with barely more
feed at the century's end than we use now;
low efficiency (group 8) would entail an increase of 50 per cent. Given medium population, medium demand, and medium rates of
increase in feeding efficiency (group 9), we
would need about 85 per cent more feed by
the year 2000.

The Sources of Feed

Feed grains. To what extent will demand for
feed grains follow the patterns for all feed?
The answer involves a number of complex interrelationships and several more assumptions.
Chief among the latter is one regarding the
basic subdivision of feed into concentrates and
roughage—a distinction set forth earlier in this
chapter. It will be noted, in Table 12–1, that
the greatest prospective increases in feed are
those for cattle and calves. Since these are primarily roughage-consuming animals, one would
expect a more than proportionate increase in
future requirements for roughage and a less
than proportionate increase in those for concentrates. Offsetting this, however, is the tendency toward more and more grain-fattening of
market-bound cattle, which raises the concentrate requirement. The net effect of the two
influences is likely to be close to compensating (see Appendix Table A12–3).

To ascertain the contingent liabilities, however, we must consider not only probabilities
but reasonable possibilities. Most of the concentrates (feed grains, oilseed meals, etc.) tend
to be more economical of land than the roughages (hay, pasture, etc.). When we compare

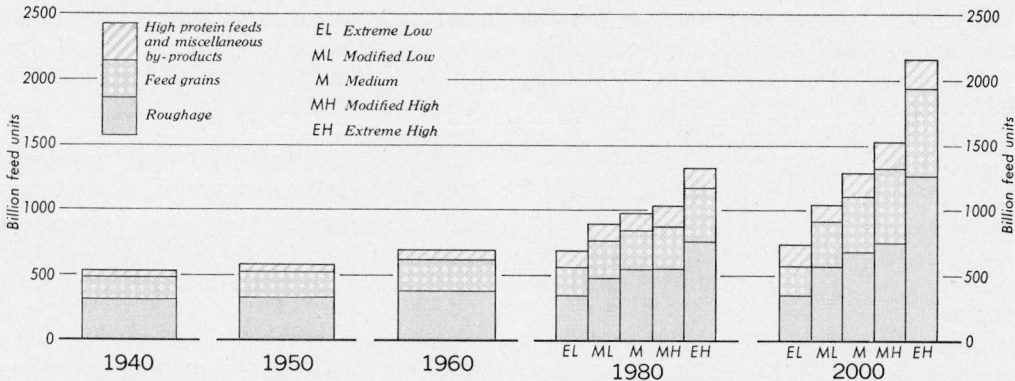

Figure 12–2. Combinations of feed supply, 1940, 1950, 1960, and projections for 1980 and 2000, under various assumptions as to consumption and efficiency.

projected patterns of demand with land requirements, in Chapter 18, we shall estimate the Extreme Low land need by associating low demand for feedstuffs with a liberal estimate of concentrate use and our Extreme High need by associating our high demand for feedstuffs with a conservative estimate of concentrate use. The various implications of meeting the low demand in a land-extensive sort of way (by keeping concentrates in the ration low) and the high demand in a land-economical sort of way (by keeping concentrates in the ration high), worked out animal by animal, may be found in Appendix Table A12–16. A summary, comparing them with the Medium projection, follows:

	1980	2000
Concentrates required, in billion feed units:		
Extreme Low (low demand, high efficiency, concentrates high in ration)	346	404
Modified Low (low demand, low efficiency, concentrates low in ration)	409	474
Medium	432	600
Modified High (high demand, high efficiency, concentrates high in ration)	480	780
Extreme High (high demand, low efficiency, concentrates low in ration)	559	893
Concentrates as percentage of total feed:		
Extreme Low	50	54
Modified Low	46	45
Medium	45	47
Modified High	47	51
Extreme High	42	41

Most of the range which shows up within each of the two demand levels may be traced to the assumptions on efficiency. In part, however, the high proportion of concentrates which the table shows as being reasonably possible with the Extreme Low demand may be explained by the higher emphasis in this demand level upon consumption of pork, product of an animal that eats almost exclusively concentrates.

Something like one-fourth of all concentrate consumption, measured in terms of feed units, is in the form of by-product feeds—chiefly oil cake and meal derived from soybeans and cottonseed, but also including other oilseed meals, tankage and meat scraps, fishmeal, brewers' and distillers' by-products, and various grain mill by-products. This is an increase from the period before World War II, when these by-product feeds accounted for about one-fifth of all feed units; and the prospects are that their relative importance will continue to grow. Most such feeds have such high nutritive content that they go much further, pound for pound, than feed grains. The protein content of many of the "high protein" feeds of this group ranges between 30 and 50 per cent, compared to a range of 6 to 11 per cent for feed grains.

The supply of oilseed meals—and hence in large measure the supply of by-product feeds in general—has historically been dependent upon the requirements for edible vegetable oils and for cotton. As for the future, it is

TABLE 12–1.   Variations in Total Feed Consumption under Different Patterns of Consumption and of Feeding Efficiency, 1940, 1960, 1980, and 2000

A. *Variations in Projections of Demand for Animal Products*

(Billion pounds liveweight, except eggs)

Item	1940	1960	1980	2000
1. Low total consumption with emphasis on variety in types of meat:				
Cattle and calves	15	29	40	47
Hogs	18	20	28	34
Milk	109	122	124	134
Poultry	4	9	14	17
Eggs (billions)	40	62	75	88
2. Medium consumption:				
Cattle and calves	15	29	51	70
Hogs	18	20	30	44
Milk	109	122	154	202
Poultry	4	9	13	18
Eggs (billions)	40	62	88	119
3. High total consumption, with emphasis on beef:				
Cattle and calves	15	29	60	99
Hogs	18	20	37	62
Milk	109	122	190	294
Poultry	4	9	13	21
Eggs (billions)	40	62	112	173

B. *Variations in Projections of Feed Requirements per Pound (or per Egg)*

(Corn equivalent pounds)

Item	1940	1960	1980	2000
4. High efficiency (low requirements per unit of output):				
Cattle and calves	9.5	10.6	8.3	8.0
Hogs	5.1	5.7	4.4	4.0
Milk	1.1	1.1	.9	.8
Poultry	5.6	3.8	2.7	2.5
Eggs	.6	.6	.4	.3
5. Medium efficiency:				
Cattle and calves	9.5	10.6	9.5	9.5
Hogs	5.1	5.7	5.1	4.8
Milk	1.1	1.1	1.0	.9
Poultry	5.6	3.8	3.2	3.0
Eggs	.6	.6	.5	.4
6. Low efficiency (high requirements per unit of output):				
Cattle and calves	9.5	10.6	10.5	10.5
Hogs	5.1	5.7	5.7	5.7
Milk	1.1	1.1	1.1	1.1
Poultry	5.6	3.8	4.0	3.9
Eggs	.6	.6	.5	.5

Table 12–1 (cont'd)

C. *Variations in Total Feed Units Required, Following from Combination of Above Two Sets of Assumptions*

(Billion corn equivalent pounds)

Item	1940	1960	1980	2000
7. Low consumption, high efficiency (Extreme Low):				
Cattle and calves	144	302	330	378
Hogs	89	115	124	134
Milk	117	134	108	100
Poultry	23	35	38	41
Eggs	23	35	28	27
Other livestock and pets	112	74	59	65
TOTAL	508	694	687	745
8. Low consumption, low efficiency (Modified Low):				
Cattle and calves	144	302	422	519
Hogs	89	115	161	192
Milk	117	134	136	147
Poultry	23	35	53	60
Eggs	23	35	41	41
Other livestock and pets	112	74	77	91
TOTAL	508	694	890	1,050
9. Medium consumption, medium efficiency:				
Cattle and calves	144	302	481	663
Hogs	89	115	156	213
Milk	117	134	146	182
Poultry	23	35	43	54
Eggs	23	35	42	46
Other livestock and pets	112	74	101	132
TOTAL	508	694	969	1,290
10. High consumption, high efficiency (Modified High):				
Cattle and calves	144	302	501	795
Hogs	89	115	164	248
Milk	117	134	165	220
Poultry	23	35	38	53
Eggs	23	35	43	54
Other livestock and pets	112	74	106	159
TOTAL	508	694	1,017	1,529
11. High consumption, low efficiency (Extreme High):				
Cattle and calves	144	302	640	1,093
Hogs	89	115	213	353
Milk	117	134	209	323
Poultry	23	35	53	80
Eggs	23	35	62	81
Other livestock and pets	112	74	138	228
TOTAL	508	694	1,315	2,158

Sources: Appendix Tables A12–1, 3, and 16. Data are from unrounded figures in appendix and will therefore not multiply out exactly.

unimaginable that cotton will ever be grown especially for the cottonseed. Soybean meal, however, has proved to be of great value in feeding poultry, dairy cattle, and hogs, and its inclusion in formula feeds is quite customary. There have been times when the meal from a bushel of soybeans has been worth as much as or more than the oil, and soybeans tend to be grown as much for the meal as for the oil. But it is only in the highest range of concentrate demand that the prospective by-product supply of meal would appear to be, in and of itself, insufficient.

Table 12–2 summarizes, for the Medium projections only, the way in which cotton and vegetable oils are related to feed grains. Not only is there a continuing trend for vegetable oils to take over more and more of the edible oil market, but the fact that cotton consump-

tion is increasing at a slower rate than oil consumption means that expansion in the role of soybeans is being additionally accelerated.

The potential saving in feed grain requirements resulting from the availability of by-products is significant. Already, high protein by-products alone account for about 17 per cent of the total concentrate supply, and we might have expected the proportion, from a straight extrapolation of the trend, to go up to about 18½ per cent by 2000 (see Appendix Table A12–7). More likely, however, the availability of by-product cake and meal and other by-products will permit nearly 23 per cent of the total concentrate requirement to be supplied from by-products in 2000. Thus, despite the little changed role of concentrates as a whole in the feed picture (in the Medium projection), feed grain supplies will have to be

TABLE 12–2.   Summary of By-product Concentrate Availability and Residual Demand for Feed Grains, 1960, 1980, and 2000

Item	1960	1980	2000 (Medium Projection)
Domestic food use of fats and oils (bil. lb.)	12.1	15.9	21.5
Production of soybean and cottonseed oil[1] (bil. lb.)	6.2	12.7	19.4
Soybean and cottonseed oil as per cent of total fats and oils food use	51	80	90
Cotton ginned (mil. bales)	15	22	33
Cottonseed oil produced (bil. lb.)	1.9	2.9	4.5
Oil per bale of cotton (lb.)	128	133	135
Soybean oil produced (bil. lb.)	4.3	9.8	14.9
Cake and meal produced:			
Cottonseed (bil. lb.)	5	8	13
Per pound of oil (lb.)	2.7	2.8	2.8
Soybean (bil. lb.)	18	41	60
Per pound of oil (lb.)	4.4	4.2	4.0
Cake and meal consumed[2] (soybean and cottonseed combined):			
Billion pounds	22	47	69
Billion feed units	34	75	110
Total high-protein feeds (bil. feed units)	54	99	137
Per cent soybean and cottonseed meal	64	76	80
Total concentrates (bil. feed units)	317	432	600
Per cent high protein	16.9	22.9	22.8
Concentrates other than high protein	264	333	463
Per cent feed grains	90.3	90	90
Feed grains (bil. feed units)	238	300	417

Source: Appendix Tables A12–7, A12–16.

1. Includes oil for export—currently about 1¼ billion pounds.
2. Balance assumed to go into export (and stocks).

increased between now and 1980 not 40 per cent, as is true for all feed, but less than 30 per cent; and by 2000, not 86 per cent but only 75 per cent.

The relative contribution of by-product feeds becomes even more pronounced in our Low demand projection. The lower the total requirements for animal feed, the more important, relatively, is likely to be the by-product contribution; thus, where the high-efficiency mode of meeting low requirements suggests a slight decrease in total feed requirements between now and 1980, the decrease for feed grains is on the order of 10 per cent. An effect of the opposite sort may be found in the High projection.

After an adjustment is made to cover the net effect of exports, non-feed uses of feed grains (in breakfast cereals, starch, alcoholic beverages, etc.), feeding of wheat and rye, and requirements for seed, the combined final picture for the four principal feed grains (corn, oats, barley, and sorghum) looks somewhat as follows:

	1960	1980	2000
		(billion feed units)	
Extreme Low projection	–	260	295
Modified Low projection	–	365	425
Medium projection	305	380	520
Modified High projection	–	430	725
Extreme High projection	–	520	830

The demand for feed grains, in other words, could dip from present levels and not recover even by the end of the century—or, at the other extreme, it could come close to tripling. More likely, however, something less than a doubling seems to be the prospect. Figure 12–3 shows these trends, along with those for other principal crops.

Hay. Currently about half as important as feed grains in terms of acreage, hay supplies only about one-third as many feed units. Pound for pound, it averages less than half the feeding value of grain, but the low figure is offset in part by the greater weight of hay harvested from an acre. Hay provides about one-fourth the roughage consumed by cattle and other livestock, and, whatever the pressures upon land, it is likely that this proportion will increase. It is the gradual disappearance of horses and mules over the past half-century that has kept the trend toward greater feeding of hay to meat and dairy animals from having very much effect so far on total hay consumption.

There is also the prospect, both because of shifts in the types of hay and because of better methods of cutting, curing, and preservation, that the average feed value of hay will have a tendency to rise. The shift is toward alfalfa, a

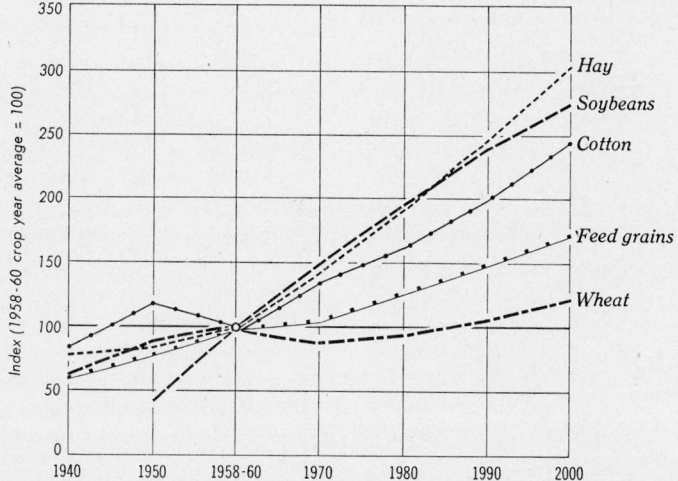

Figure 12–3. Comparative rates of growth in output of principal crops, 1940, 1950, 1958–60, and Medium projections to 2000.

protein-rich hay with high nutritional value. High quality alfalfa hay will supply more digestible nutrients per acre than corn and much more digestible protein, given recent national average yield relationships. The improved processing means a fuller utilization of the harvested tonnage. These two influences could conceivably combine to raise the feed unit value of hay to at least 55 per cent of that of corn. However, in line with the past trends as worked out by Jennings, we have assumed only a token increase above the present 41 per cent.

The combination of these factors, in terms of our five models, results in approximately the following prospects for hay consumption:

	1960	1980	2000
		(billion feed units)	
Extreme Low projection	–	135	170
Modified Low projection	–	135	175
Medium projection	100	185	300
Modified High projection	–	215	375
Extreme High projection	–	215	385
		(million tons)	
Extreme Low projection	–	165	205
Modified Low projection	–	165	210
Medium projection	119	225	355
Modified High projection	–	260	445
Extreme High projection	–	260	460

The most likely prospect is for a tripling in consumption by the end of the century. Under the most extreme circumstances, however, consumption might quadruple, or not quite double.

Pasture. Hay and pasture together make up about 90 per cent of all roughage. This percentage, we feel, is unlikely to vary by more than 5 percentage points within the period we are looking at. It follows, then, that the relatively rapid gains in prospect for hay mean relatively slower increases in the demand for pasture. In fact, meeting the low demand level in the most efficient manner means that the role of pasture may be cut by half. This matter of efficiency (including both feeding efficiency and relative emphasis on harvested crops) is all-important for the size of the residual call upon pasture, for even the high demand level may be met, under optimum conditions—i.e., the Modified High—with no increase from present output of pasture, and at medium

levels of efficiency the medium demand may be met with only a small increase. Meeting the low demand in the least efficient, most land-extensive manner, on the other hand, would entail a 50 per cent greater call upon pasture (the Extreme Low), and meeting the high demand in the same manner (the Extreme High) would mean something more than a tripling.

The five pasture projections work out as follows:

	1960	1980	2000
		(billion feed units)	
Extreme Low projection	–	160	120
Modified Low projection	–	300	365
Medium projection	240	290	315
Modified High projection	–	250	260
Extreme High projection	–	475	800

Wheat

The United States today consumes no more wheat than it did twenty years ago; yet production is half again as great. The reason for the unchanged domestic consumption is the drop in per capita consumption which was discussed in Chapter 2—just about enough to offset the growth in population. The United States has become one of the principal wheat suppliers to the world. Before World War II, the United States exported 5 to 10 per cent of its wheat crop; today, it exports about as much as it eats, supplying about one-third of all wheat moved in world trade. The uncertain future of world demand and the U.S. share in it have, therefore, a substantial bearing upon the future adequacy of our agricultural land resource. Recent export levels have been achieved only through a subsidy program.

In arriving at some idea of future exports, dietary needs in the rest of the world are only one of many factors. We must consider also the ability and willingness of other countries to pay for U.S. wheat; politically oriented exports from Communist countries; competitive damage to farmers in the areas supplied and the areas of other suppliers; and sources of financing. On a short-term basis, we might conceivably assess all these factors. Looking forward over a period of four decades, we simply extrapolate per capita trends, modifying them by some political-economic judgments.

A continental breakdown of population in non-communist countries, derived from United Nations projections, forms our basic factor. The total stands now at about 1¾ billion; by 1980 it should be somewhere around 2½ billion and by 2000, between 3 and nearly 4½ billion— most likely on the high side of 3¾. Latin American population, by the year 2000, will at least double, and perhaps more than triple; Asian and African populations should multiply at a slightly lesser rate; Western European, probably by only one-third (less than the most conservative expectations of U.S. growth). In absolute numbers, by far the biggest increase will take place in Asia, which already provides about half the non-communist world's population and over the next four decades will probably add another 1½ billion people.

The distribution of our wheat exports among the continents has so far been in accordance more with the relative emphasis in our foreign rehabilitation and aid programs than with the sizes of populations. Thus, for a time, the lion's share went to Western Europe (including Yugoslavia), financed mostly under the Marshall Plan and other special arrangements. With the recovery of Europe and the growing importance of exports paid for in local currencies under Public Law 480, the main flow has now shifted to Asia.

Our projections of wheat exports have been made on the assumption, for the High, that there will be, and, for the Low, that there will not be a long-run continuation of such noncommercial exports. Coupled with the United Nations' low, medium, and high population projections, these assumptions lead, in the Low, to a projected decline in wheat exports from the approximately 510 million bushels of 1960 (the all-time high) to about 372 million in 1980, followed by a recovery to 474 million by 2000. The Medium projections work out to 405 million bushels in 1980, followed by a gradual rise to 610 million bushels; the High follow the population trends to 685 million bushels.

Except for modest declines in the relative amounts retained for seed and used for other than human feeding, domestic consumption of wheat should follow the trends shown in Appendix Table A2–4. Our Medium expectation, on this basis, is an increase of something like 25 per cent in total requirements over the next four decades (see Figure 12–3), with a little more of our output going into domestic consumption than into exports. In the Low, total use would end up virtually unchanged, with some dip between now and 1970 and a subsequent recovery; exports would eventually account for about two-fifths of the total. In the export-dependent High, total demand for wheat would come to nearly 40 per cent above present levels, exceeding the 1.5-billion-bushel mark.

Soybeans

Soybeans were introduced commercially into the United States early in this century, but it was not until the twenties that soybean processing got a good start and not until the thirties that it attained a large scale. The plant is grown primarily for processing, but some is also grown for hay and pasture, to furnish direct feed in the form of beans, or for soil rebuilding. Of the many edible and inedible uses of processed soybeans by far the largest are in the form of oil for human consumption and cake and meal for animal feeding. The oil goes mostly into shortening and oleomargarine, and its principal competitor is cottonseed oil. The meal is used overwhelmingly for feedstuffs, and its principal competitor is cottonseed meal.

So far, soybean meal has been the by-product (or at best a joint product). What the future may hold in store has been dealt with above, in the discussion of feed grains, and summarized, for the Medium projection, in Table 12–2. We may now determine what the controlling product means for the total demand for soybean output in each of our five projection models. In doing so, we could conceivably rely upon the relationship of either product to the whole, since either will closely determine the bean demand. Since we have allowed for some trend, however, in both the individual and the joint extraction factors, we present the picture, in Table 12–3, in terms of the projected quantities of soybeans crushed, the quantities of each of the products, and the implicit extractive yields. It should be noted that the product

TABLE 12–3. Soybean Crushings and Soybean Products Projected under Different Consumption Patterns, 1960, 1980, and 2000

Model	1960	1980	2000
Extreme Low (oil the principal product, but emphasis on meal yield):			
Beans crushed:			
Million bushels	393	960	1,310
Billion pounds	23.6	57.6	78.6
Yield (bil. lb.):			
Oil	4.3	10.3	14.1
Meal	18.3	46.4	63.4
Per cent:			
Oil	18.2	18	18
Meal	77.5	81	81
Total recovery	95.7	99	99
Modified Low (oil the principal product,[1] with increased oil yield):			
Beans crushed:			
Million bushels	393	880	1,150
Billion pounds	23.6	52.8	69.0
Yield (bil. lb.):			
Oil	4.3	10.5	14.4
Meal	18.3	41.0	53.5
Per cent:			
Oil	18.2	20	21
Meal	77.5	78	78
Total recovery	95.7	98	99
Medium (oil the principal product, with moderately increased oil yield):			
Beans crushed:			
Million bushels	393	870	1,250
Billion pounds	23.6	52.2	75.0
Yield (bil. lb.):			
Oil	4.3	9.8	14.9
Meal	18.3	41.2	59.6
Per cent:			
Oil	18.2	19	20
Meal	77.5	79	79
Total recovery	95.7	98	99
Modified High (oil the principal product, but emphasis on meal yield):			
Beans crushed:			
Million bushels	393	700	880
Billion pounds	23.6	42.0	52.8
Yield (bil. lb.):			
Oil	4.3	7.5	9.5
Meal	18.3	33.8	42.8
Per cent:			
Oil	18.2	18	18
Meal	77.5	80	81
Total recovery	95.7	98	99
Extreme High (meal the principal product, with emphasis on meal yield):			
Beans crushed:			
Million bushels	393	870	1,510
Billion pounds	23.6	52.2	90.6

Table 12–3 (cont'd)

Model	1960	1980	2000
Yield (bil. lb.):			
Oil	4.3	8.1	11.0
Meal	18.3	42.1	73.4
Per cent:			
Oil	18.2	16	12
Meal	77.5	81	81
Total recovery	95.7	97	93

Source: Appendix Table A12–16.

1. For 1980. By 2000, meal is at least a joint product, so that low oil and high meal yield are used for that year.

mixes shown represent (except in the Medium) possible, rather than probable, combinations of circumstances and are intended only to establish the possible high and low contributions of soybean meal to future high or low feed supply.

If soybean demand continues to be determined—as we assume in all but the highest projection—by edible oil demand, its future is far less sure than if meal is the essential determinant. The higher levels of demand for cotton could provide enough cottonseed oil to more than counterbalance higher per capita oil consumption by a high population and thus limit the increase in oil-oriented demand for soybeans to little more than a doubling, instead of the possible tripling under circumstances where less cotton is produced. Where meal is the determinant, the demand might come closer to quadrupling.

Exports and direct feed uses of the beans could serve to even out the picture. If these are taken into account, as well as the amounts required as seed, the total demand for soybeans (as beans) might look somewhat as follows:

	1960	1980	2000
		(million bushels)	
Extreme Low	–	1,120	1,490
Modified Low	–	1,040	1,320
Medium	570	1,090	1,540
Modified High	–	1,020	1,360
Extreme High	–	1,200	2,020

Cotton

As we saw in Chapter 3, the outlook for domestic consumption of cotton is somewhat uncertain: from about 4 billion pounds now, it might increase to 8 billion pounds by the year 2000, under the Medium projection, or to as little as 5 billion or as much as 15 billion pounds. The prospects for cotton exports are even more uncertain. We have to contend not only with the same substitution factors and the same uncertainties as to population growth which are present in the United States, but with the added uncertainties of income growth in markets in which purchases of clothing are much more responsive to income gains than is the case here. On top of all this is the uncertain share of the United States in world markets.

The last is of no small importance. Over the length of time which we are surveying, both domestic production in large consuming countries like India and competitive supplies from large exporters like Egypt and potentially large exporters like the U.S.S.R. and China could change very markedly. It is difficult, in view of the wide year-to-year fluctuations, even to determine the "base" from which to make export projections. The last decade has seen exports of anywhere from 2¼ to 7½ million bales— or roughly 1 to 3½ billion pounds. From one season to the next, the United States has shifted from supplying one out of ten bales consumed in the non-communist countries to supplying one out of five. However, the 4½ million bales average of the past decade is as good a reference point as any, and we may reasonably expect exports to follow world population growth up to around 14 million bales before the century is over. Yet under different sets of circumstances, it would not be beyond reason for exports to settle down to only 3 million bales or, alternatively, rise to as high as 23 million.

On balance, we might most reasonably look forward to a total cotton demand rising from the recent average of 13½ million bales to something like 22 million in 1980 and 33 million in 2000 (see Figure 12–3). On the low side, demand may continue around present levels for the next four decades; or it may be up to 28 million by 1980 and 57 million by the century's end, under the assumptions underlying the High projection.

These ranges of possibilities raise questions

not only concerning cotton acreage but, as we have already pointed out, concerning the availability of oil and by-product feed. In the demand for cotton lies some part of the answer for corn and a good deal of the answer for soybeans.

Import Crops

Three of the principal crops consumed in the United States are produced either partly or wholly outside the United States—sugar, coffee, and cocoa. Little needs to be said here of coffee and cocoa, which are not produced at all in this country. Any effects that foreign trade in these products might have on U.S. crop production and ultimate land requirements would be both tenuous and small.

Sugar. About 30 per cent of the nation's sugar supply is produced from sugar beets and cane grown in the continental United States, and an additional 10 per cent from cane grown in the new state of Hawaii. Another 10 per cent comes from Puerto Rico, classed under the U.S. Sugar Act as a "domestic area." The rest is imported.

Of the total demand for sugar and syrups discussed in Chapter 2 (see especially Table 2–4), 85 to 90 per cent has been for cane or beet sugar, and there is no particular reason to expect a change in this proportion. Since almost all sugar is used for human consumption, it takes but a small additional adjustment for refining loss to estimate the future demand for raw cane and beet sugar approximately as follows:

	1960	1980	2000
	(million tons)		
Low	–	10	12
Medium	9	11	15
High	–	14	22

The 6½ million tons of sugar currently imported into the continental United States constitutes something over one-third of all the sugar moving in world trade. No serious problems of supply of offshore sugar have arisen, even after cessation of shipments from Cuba, which until recently accounted for about half of the U.S. overseas requirements. Over the longer future there is a possibility that political considerations might curtail shipments from some other producing areas, as they have from Cuba. However, there are a number of tropical areas with substantial room for bringing land into sugar cane production and for increasing present yields.

An important question is how fast the rest of the world will increase its consumption and thus compete with the United States for sources of supply. Were the United States standard of nearly 100 pounds per capita enjoyed by the world as a whole, global sugar consumption per year would be 150 million rather than the actual 45 million tons. The potential combined rate of increase resulting from world population growth and from greater per capita use could easily triple present world requirements by the end of the century. Fortunately, much of the increase will be taking place in countries which can themselves meet a good part of the increased requirements. Yet, to add the 100 million tons or so annual production that may be needed is a task of such magnitude that the developing of supply stringencies along the way is not at all to be discounted.

U.S. requirements are sufficiently small in relation to the potential world total that the very gearing up of world production to meet such a demand should reduce the size of any problems resulting from our dependence upon any one area. Moreover, substantial increases in yields in the United States and its outlying areas—particularly Puerto Rico—can, with time, be brought about in order to meet part of the future requirement.

Even if foreign supply should become notably tighter or more plentiful in the future, effects on land requirements in the continental United States would be negligible. Something under 1½ million acres—less than ½ of 1 per cent of crop acreage—is planted to sugar crops.

Animal By-products

Among domestic agricultural products must be included numerous animal by-products used in footwear, clothing, medicines, cosmetics, industrial chemicals, and other applications. Of these by-products, two—leather and wool—definitely belong among the key materials of the U.S. economy. It is of some interest, there-fore, to see whether or to what extent the demand for these items may be met in the future.

Leather. The demand for leather, as we saw in Chapter 3, is more likely to decline than to rise. Within the past decade the United States has passed from being a net importer of hides and skins to being a net exporter. The export surplus—result of a considerable trade in both directions—is still very slight, but sufficient to depress cattlehide prices in the United States and elsewhere. It takes only a superficial comparison of the demand for meat with the prospective decline in leather demand to see that this surplus will grow progressively. Even at the lowest levels of meat consumption, it may be expected to rise to about 25 million cattlehide equivalents by the century's end; the Medium projections suggest a surplus of about 40 million; and the High projections, mitigated by the modest rise assumed in leather demand, are of about the same magnitude as the Medium. What is more, these rising U.S. surpluses promise to occur against a backdrop of similar increase throughout the world, occurring for basically the same reasons: substitution of other materials for leather and hence a more rapid rise in per capita meat consumption than in leather consumption.

One may suppose, under the circumstances, that our original projections of leather demand should be subjected to some modification. Very likely, part of the adjustment to an increasing glut in hides and skins will be the development of new uses, made possible by the inevitable price declines. These same price adjustments should serve to cushion the weakening position of leather as a raw material and result in somewhat higher consumption than we have initially assumed. But these are some of the "escape hatches," this time for escape not from scarcity but from glut, that we have discussed in the beginning of this book and that are not used to revise the demand projections.

Wool. We saw in Chapter 3 (Appendix Table A3–3) that wool will experience somewhat the same demand softness as leather, although the drop should not be as severe. Whatever the course of domestic wool output, the impact of any softness in demand may be expected to fall in the first instance more harshly upon our foreign wool suppliers than upon U.S. sources, for a disproportionate share of wool displacement is occurring in carpet, rather than apparel, wools, and these have been primarily imported. The U.S. tariff, moreover, provides a considerable measure of protection to domestic growers.

Wool used to be the principal product of sheep raising on the Western range, but both there and in the Middle West feeder areas, lamb and mutton (mostly the former) are now the principal products, and the wool, which is either shorn from the sheep in flocks or on their way to slaughter, or pulled from the pelts of slaughtered animals, is the by-product (with some local exceptions). The average fleece per animal is something like 8 pounds, and the average meat yield is something like 96 pounds, liveweight. Because many animals are shorn more than once, however, the ratio of wool to lamb and mutton production is not 1:12 but more like 1:6. Thus, implicit in our lamb and mutton consumption estimates is a wool production most probably rising from about 300 million pounds now to 500 million in 1980 and 700 million in the year 2000. Depending upon population growth and the relative emphasis upon lamb and mutton as an alternative to beef, the range of uncertainty is wide—from a Low projection of some 340 million pounds even in 2000 (it has exceeded 400 million in times past) to a High projection of 650 million in 1980 and 1,200 million in 2000.

Before we can compare these production figures with consumption requirements we must make an allowance for the loss of weight from scouring, in which the lanolin and other products are removed from the crude wool. Since this so-called grease accounts for a little more than half the total weight, domestic production reduces to the following figures:

	1960	1980	2000
	(million pounds)		
Low	–	130	150
Medium	140	220	320
High	–	290	520

We must adjust our consumption figures as well—downward by about one-third to allow for the consumption demands satisfied by reprocessed and reused wool, by such non-sheep wools as mohair, alpaca, etc., and by the import of wool yarns and textiles. Roughly, then, our prospective consumption of scoured sheep's wool boils down to:

	1960	1980	2000
	(million pounds)		
Low	–	290	280
Medium	380	370	440
High	–	460	730

The comparison suggests that there is likely to be a decline—somewhat abrupt at first—in the gap between the total demand for wool and domestic output. (The slowing down in the supply increase is due mostly to the assumption of a tapering off in the increasing per capita demand for lamb and mutton.) The respective Lows and Highs need not occur simultaneously, since per capita consumption of wool and of lamb and mutton are essentially independent of each other, but the likelihood at any level is still for domestic supply to come closer to demand. It is to be noted that lamb and mutton consumption is the less predictable of the two consumption factors and will have the greater bearing on the ultimate import requirement.

Should a quite high demand for wool combine with a quite low demand for lamb and mutton, it is conceivable that the need for imports will not only continue but increase. The amounts which may possibly be involved, however, would not seem to offer any supply problems. Although the trend of world consumption is upward, the United States absorbs only about one-eighth of the total lamb and mutton and only a slightly larger proportion of the wool moving in international trade. If, as seems more likely, U.S. wool imports should decrease, it would, by the same token, appear to be in amounts that could before too long be absorbed by other markets.

chapter

13

LUMBER AND
WOODPULP

FOR AT LEAST THREE DECADES, the total volume of forest products consumed by the American people has been virtually unchanging, but within this total there have been some important shifts. Consumption of pulpwood has been rising rapidly, especially since World War II. Consumption of veneer logs, the source of plywood, has also been rising rapidly, while the use of wood for fuel (still nearly 15 per cent of the total) has continued a long downward trend from its late nineteenth century peak. Only the consumption of sawlogs has, except for the Depression years, exhibited relative stability and remains now, as in 1929, around half of all timber consumption.

In view of a population increase of about 50 per cent since 1929, it follows that per capita consumption of forest products is trending steadily downward. One reason for this, the continuing development of substitutes, is well known and has been dealt with in Chapters 4, 6, and 7. In addition, there has been a trend toward more economical use of wood, chiefly through the replacement of lumber by plywood, use of which is favored by lower construction labor costs.

The fact that consumption of both pulpwood and veneer logs has quadrupled over the past three decades does not imply that the two are equally important. In absolute terms, pulpwood consumption amounts to four times that of veneer logs and now accounts for more than one-fourth of all wood utilization—compared with one-sixth in 1950 and one-tenth a decade earlier. Since wood for pulping does not necessarily have to be of saw-timber size, this shift has important implications for the nature of the future resource base which can be drawn upon to meet U.S. timber demand (see Chapter 18).

The stability in total consumption has been reflected in a corresponding stability in forest production. Including fuelwood, about 11.2 billion cubic feet of "roundwood" (logs and other round sections as cut from trees) was removed from our forests and woodlands in 1929, about 10.8 billion cubic feet in 1960. (Ex-

---

RELATED MATERIAL: Appendix to this chapter, pp. 804–15. Uses in construction, Chapter 4, pp. 123–24, and appendix, pp. 626–28; in durable goods, Chapter 6, p. 155, and appendix, p. 684; in containers and packaging, Chapter 7, pp. 165–67, and appendix, p. 697; in paper products, Chapter 8, pp. 170–73, and appendix, pp. 702–8. Adequacy of forest land, Chapter 18, pp. 355–70, 373–77, and appendix, pp. 985–87.

cluding fuelwood, on the other hand, there was an increase from 8.1 billion to 9.3 billion cubic feet.)

This close correspondence between consumption and production exists because, for forest products as a whole, net imports contribute less than 10 per cent of domestic consumption. Since World War I, to be sure, the United States has changed from a net exporter to a net importer, but neither exports nor imports have been an appreciable percentage of total supply. Even in the case of woodpulp, which is one of our top-ranking imports, the combined importation of both pulp and pulpwood has constituted only a comparatively minor addition, about 15 to 20 per cent of supply.[1] Only for a few special products do imports have any greater significance. One of these products is hardwood plywood, which recently has been purchased in increasing quantity from Japan and the Philippines.

If one were to go merely by the experience of the last thirty years, estimates of future increase in forest products demand would be modest; a rise of not more than one-half between now and the end of the century would be within the realm of reason. More likely, however, is a two-thirds increase between now and 1980 and a tripling between now and the century's close. This higher expectation results from an examination of the three principal areas of timber use: (1) construction, (2) containers and packaging and other paper products, and (3) miscellaneous wood manufactures.

Except for the World War II period, roughly three-fourths of the consumption of lumber (i.e., sawn wood) and close to 40 per cent of all wood consumption has been in construction. The factors affecting lumber use for both residential and non-residential building have lead us, in Chapter 4, to the conclusion that despite a continued shift away from lumber in both applications, aggregate lumber consumption is likely to increase. Particularly in non-residential construction, much of the shift away from lumber may be expected to be into plywood. The requirements for construction lumber and plywood together may triple construction timber requirements between now and the century's end.

The one-fourth of lumber that does not go into construction is about equally divided between wooden containers and other wood manufactures. Add the timber going into paper and paperboard containers via pulp, however, and containers may be seen to account for about 20 per cent of all timber utilization. Other kinds of paper products would account for another 12 per cent.

As pointed out in Chapter 7, wooden containers have largely become obsolescent, but paper containers and paper for other uses promise to keep pace with the over-all growth of the U.S. economy. To some extent the over-all outlook for consumption of pulpwood depends upon a continued steady growth in newsprint consumption, plus the probability that an increasing percentage of this newsprint will be manufactured within the United States. But even should newsprint imports rise more than projected, this would have only a moderate effect on pulpwood requirements for total paper manufacture. Other varieties of printing, writing, and household papers are also presumed to rise, in the aggregate, at moderately rapid rates. It is through use in containers and packaging, however, that the rapid growth in paper consumption will primarily be sustained. Pulp for other than paper and paperboard is only a small part of total pulp consumption; through the remainder of the century its share should be relatively insignificant.

While there could be some surprises, the use of lumber for the "other manufactures" category listed in Table 13–1 would seem to have a limited future (but still some growth), and the use of plywood and veneer somewhat brighter prospects. To a large extent furniture is the key. It accounts for about half of the lumber comprised in "other manufactures," compared with about one-third thirty years ago. Other uses, like truck bodies and agricultural implements, have been declining rapidly. Better sustained have been such miscellaneous uses as caskets, handles, and small boats; since 1954, in fact, the construction of pleasure craft has been one of the most dynamic "growth industries" in the American economy, with the

---

1. As for the trade picture in newsprint, see Chapter 8.

TABLE 13–1.   Consumption of Wood Products, 1950, 1960 and Projections for 1980, 2000

Wood products	1950	1960		1980	2000
Lumber (billion board feet):					
			L	26	26
For construction	33	28	M	46	76
			H	68	157
			L	2	1
For containers	4	4	M	7	7
			H	11	17
			L	2	2
For furniture and fixtures	2	2	M	4	6
			H	6	17
			L	3	2
For other manufactures	3	3	M	5	9
			H	9	23
			L	33	31
Total consumption	42	37	M	62	98
			H	94	214
Plywood and veneer (billion square feet):					
			L	16	26
Softwood (⅜″ basis)	3	8	M	27	63
			H	44	137
			L	20	30
Hardwood (surface measure)	11	14	M	32	70
			H	50	147
			L	47	76
Pulp (million short tons)	17	27	M	56	110
			H	70	170

L = Low projection   M = Medium   H = High.
Source: Appendix Table A13–5.

result that boats are now approaching furniture as a wood consumer. Both boats and furniture, however, are prime targets for plastics and other substitutes, and these will undoubtedly limit their use of lumber.

The relative requirements for the principal kinds of wood products are summed up in Table 13–1. The ranges shown here for lumber and plywood, it should be noted, are independent of each other; that is, the actual occurrence of the Low shown for lumber, for example, is dependent upon and would imply a somewhat higher Low for plywood than the table indicates.

Translating these material requirements into cubic volume of timber is not an easy task and involves a number of assumptions. Conversion of logs into sawn products and veneer entails the "waste," on the average, of something like 40 to 50 per cent of the original volume of logs. While a considerable part of these "mill residues" are actually used for other purposes, such as fuel (about half), pulp, and particle board, their generation is an unavoidable concomitant of sawmill and veneer cutting operations and contributes to the drain on the stock of standing timber in the forest. Stated conversely, these residues are at present purely "by-products," and insofar as they substitute for roundwood their use supports a larger production of wood products per unit of timber output than would be possible if all of the raw material for each wood product had to come from timber cut for the specific purpose. To the extent, particularly, that pulp output grows faster than that of lumber, as we have projected, maintenance of even the present relative dependence upon residues would mean increasing inroads either upon the two-fifths of residues not now used or on the amounts burned for fuel. Since not all residues can be used for all purposes and since it is not always economical to substitute other fuels for mill waste, the limit upon by-product use is perhaps narrower than might at first appear. Nonetheless, it has been assumed that present trends toward increasing use of mill residues can continue for at least the rest of the century without running into a ceiling which would require a relative reversion to fresh timber cuttings.

Combined, construction and paper account for nearly all of the increase in roundwood consumption between now and the end of the century—about 7 billion cubic feet for paper and 12 billion for construction out of a total gain of 21 billion. For both of these sectors we have assumed important technological changes that would serve to reduce the relative requirement for wood. The accuracy of our projections hinges not only upon our estimates of the growth of construction activity and the use of containers, but also upon our estimates of the rate of shift into plastics and other new materials together with fuller utilization of the domestic forest output. The two sources of error tend to some extent to be compensatory: if activity is higher than we have estimated, the relative trend away from wood is likely to be faster, and the opposite is true if activity is less than estimated. In accordance with the method of this study, we have taken no account of any future price adjustments, aside from current long-term trends, that would condition these substitutions. It remains for the comparison of demand and supply, in Chapter 18, to suggest implications for the effect of these demand levels upon lumber prices in the light of the resulting size and composition of forests, and the consequent feed-back upon consumption.

Although in absolute terms the growth in construction requirements for wood is considerably greater than that for paper and paperboard, the projected rate of growth for paper and board is much faster—a gain of about two and one-half times in forty years compared with a gain of about one and one-half times for

construction. Roundwood pulp requirements (virtually all for paper and board) should increase from about one-fourth of timber volume in 1960 to nearly one-third in 2000. This is true at least for the Medium projection: should the Low projection eventuate, the proportion for pulp would be even higher, since it is in construction volume and materials use, rather than in the prospects for paper, that the greater uncertainties prevail.

From a resources standpoint, the future division of timber consumption between sawlogs and veneer logs is of particular interest. In recent decades, the softwood plywood industry has grown rapidly, largely at the expense of lumber. The greater strength of plywood compared with lumber means that thinner crosssections will do the same job. And the fact that by the century's end softwood plywood use is likely to be about eight times as high as it is today means a saving of perhaps 4 billion cubic feet of timber annually, at demand levels projected for that time, over what would be required were all of this increase to be met by lumber. Hardwood plywood and veneer consumption should also grow, but not as rapidly as softwood, since almost half of the hardwood veneers are used to surface ordinary lumber in furniture, cabinet work, panelling, and the like. By the end of the century consumption of hardwoods for veneer stocks should be only about one-fourth the cubic volume of softwood veneer logs consumed.

Future Timber Consumption

Table 13–2 sets forth the amounts of timber of each major type which we shall necessarily have to take out of our forests (or import) to support the key material requirements stated above. As indicated earlier, that part of the cubic volume of pulpwood requirements which comes out of mill residues is netted out here as being pure "gravy."

In this table, the figures shown for veneer logs are those consistent with the indicated sawtimber consumption. Veneer logs alone might be projected at a 2000 high, for example, of 13 billion cubic feet, but then the sawtimber requirement would be more than compensat-

TABLE 13–2. Consumption of Roundwood, 1950, 1960, and Projections for 1980, 2000

(Billion cubic feet)

Roundwood	1950	1960		1980	2000
Sawlogs for lumber	6.3	5.8	L M H	5.1 9.6 14.5	4.9 15.1 33.2
Softwood	5.2	4.9	L M H	4.2 8.0 12.1	4.1 12.6 27.6
Hardwood	1.1	.9	L M H	.9 1.6 2.4	.8 2.5 5.6
Veneer logs	.4	.8	L M H	1.6 2.5 3.7	2.6 5.8 11.2
Softwood	.2	.6	L M H	1.3 2.0 2.9	2.1 4.6 8.7
Hardwood	.2	.2	L M H	.3 .5 .8	.5 1.2 2.5
Pulpwood	1.9	2.7	L M H	4.3 5.1 6.3	6.9 9.9 15.3
Softwood	1.6	2.1	L M H	3.2 3.8 4.7	4.8 6.9 10.7
Hardwood	.3	.6	L M H	1.1 1.3 1.6	2.1 3.0 4.6
Miscellaneous timber	.8	.7	L M H	.4 .7 1.0	.4 .9 1.8
Softwood	.4	.3	L M H	.2 .3 .5	.2 .4 .8
Hardwood	.4	.4	L M H	.2 .4 .5	.2 .5 1.0
Fuelwood	2.3	1.4	L M H	.7 .8 1.0	.3 .6 .9
Softwood	.6	.3	L M H	.2 .2 .2	.1 .1 .2
Hardwood	1.7	1.1	L M H	.5 .6 .8	.2 .5 .7
Total timber consumption	11.6	11.5	L M H	12.1 18.7 26.5	15.0 32.3 62.4
Softwood	7.9	8.3	L M H	9.1 14.3 20.4	11.2 24.7 48.1
Hardwood	3.7	3.2	L M H	3.0 4.4 6.1	3.8 7.6 14.3

L = Low projection　　M = Medium　　H = High.
Source: Appendix Table A13–6.

ingly lower. The table illustrates further what has already been noted: that a simple extension of past trends defines almost the lowest of future timber consumption possibilities. Given the more probable course of paper consumption and of construction, a sharp step-up in the growth of demand is in the offing, starting in the relatively near future. Since, as is pointed out in Chapter 18, the potentials for forest product imports are relatively limited, this means eventual heavy pressures on the U.S. forest resource.

chapter
14

WATER

EVERY DAY SOMETHING LIKE 300 billion gallons of fresh water are used in homes, factories, steam generating plants, or on irrigated farm land. Other huge quantities are "used" without being withdrawn from natural water courses for such varied purposes as turning the generators of hydroelectric plants, carrying off wastes, supporting inland navigation, pleasure boating and swimming, and simply providing lovely and restful scenery.

Industry, already a heavy user of water, is increasing its demands each year. The effects of population growth upon demand for water will be intensified by the continuing rise in outdoor recreation and the growth of cities, where use per person is much higher than in rural households. From these and other indications it is clear that the nation's daily water needs by the end of the century will be much larger than they were in 1960.

In quantitative terms the demand for water as an end-product is substantially the same as for water as a key commodity or as a resource. Thus it is not necessary to translate end-use requirements into commodity demand, as was done in Part I of this study for food, clothing, heat and power, and other human needs. After consider-

ing, in this chapter, projected future levels of water use, we can turn directly to supply considerations in Chapter 19.

On the other hand, water demand has two distinctive characteristics that make future projections more complicated than for most other resource products. Both result chiefly from the supply side of the picture and consequently will be further examined in Chapter 19; but because both strongly affect the dimensions of demand we shall need to anticipate them here.

One of these characteristics concerns quality. Several kinds of use produce changes in quality that affect the acceptability of water for other uses. To cite the most extreme example, intense pollution can create an entirely new demand: a sufficient flow of clean water to dilute waste loads that make streams unfit for many purposes.

The second characteristic is the essentially regional character of water supply and—consequently—demand. The relatively high cost of transporting water long distances, in comparison with its value in productive activities, means there can be nothing like a national market for water. It is entirely possible for one area to have economic activities limited by water supply

RELATED MATERIAL: Appendix to this chapter, pp. 816–33. Adequacy of water resources, Chapter 19, pp. 378–87. Discussion of hydropower, Chapter 15, p. 282; and Chapter 20, pp. 416–17. Reference to navigation, Chapter 5, pp. 141–42.

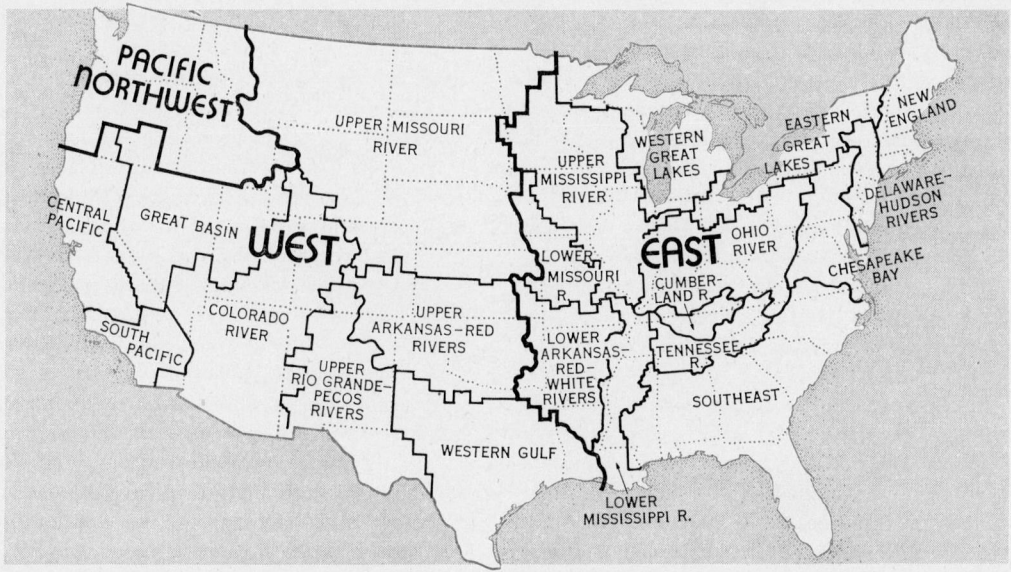

Figure 14–1. Major regions of water supply and demand in the United States.

stringencies, or to be faced with comparatively high costs for developing additional supplies while large amounts of good quality fresh water are flowing into the ocean elsewhere in the nation. Nationwide comparisons of demand and supply are of limited significance.

Some sort of *regional* comparison is in order. The river basin is sometimes used as the geographical unit for this purpose. This has much to commend it, but on the other hand, water often is used outside of the river basin in which it naturally flows. Other water services such as power may be marketed a considerable distance from the basin in which the power is generated. People may come from anywhere to enjoy a basin's recreation facilities, or industry not now located in a basin may move there. Moreover, it is extremely difficult to pinpoint the future impact of demands spread over a large area, some nationwide or international, upon the water supply of a particular basin. Accordingly, while the basin provides a convenient geographic unit for assessing supply, it is far from satisfactory as a unit for considering demand.

To provide a meaningful comparison of demand with supply in the absence of a national market for water, we have for purposes of this study divided the nation into three major re-

gions each of which has certain supply characteristics in common. Although this procedure requires an allocation of demand among the three regions, it reduces the allocation task to the minimum necessary to highlight the problem of providing adequate water supplies in the future.

The regions to be separately analyzed are: *The East*—a humid region of generally large continuously available supply, as indicated by stream runoff; this is roughly the part of the United States lying east of the 95th meridian (see Figure 14–1). *The West*—a region that is largely arid and semi-arid; it includes the Great Plains, all but extreme northeast Texas, the Rocky Mountain area and all of the Far West to the Pacific except the Pacific Northwest. *The Pacific Northwest*—a region that is partly humid and partly arid and semi-arid but which nevertheless has a large streamflow. The differing supply characteristics of these regions are described in greater detail in Chapter 19.

The great difference in the way the various uses of water affect the utility of the supply remaining, together with the flowing characteristic of water, has made difficult the devel... ment of concepts for describing differe... so that they are quantitatively comp...

irrigation, domestic, and industrial purposes water is withdrawn from surface or underground sources. Navigation, the production of hydroelectric power, and many forms of recreation use water in a stream or lake. To maintain vegetative cover in order to prevent soil erosion, runoff from rainfall is retarded so that more water becomes available to plants and less reaches stream channels and underground reservoirs. Each of these uses requires a supply of water; no one of them completely consumes the water used, but each has a different effect on the utility of supply remaining after use.

In our approach to the complex problem of making these varied uses comparable, we have generally followed the definitions and concepts of water use developed by Nathaniel Wollman while with Resources for the Future.[1] Working with the Senate Select Committee on National Water Resources and with the benefit of data and analyses by a number of federal economists and other specialists, Mr. Wollman embodied the preliminary findings of his research in one of the series of background papers published by the Committee.[2]

We shall in this chapter examine the water demand outlook for each of the regions defined. Following Mr. Wollman's system of classification, there are three classes of demand to be considered: (1) withdrawal uses, in which water is actually removed from sources of supply; (2) flow uses, like hydropower generation, recreation, and waste-carrying; and (3) on-site uses, like maintenance of wetlands as wildlife habitat and land treatment measures for soil conservation.

As Mr. Wollman has pointed out, the quantity of flow in the nation's various watersheds appears to be the one common measure of supply to which demand and use might be related in a practicable fashion. Most uses are concerned not with the total quantity of water available but with the flow that can be depended on. This is as true of hydropower generation and navigation

as for irrigation, industrial consumption, and other withdrawal uses.

The withdrawal uses are the only one of the three categories for which there are enough data to support numerical projections of future use patterns or, for that matter, dependable estimates of current use. And even for withdrawals there are great gaps in the historical statistics. Until quite recently, the supply of fresh water was simply taken for granted nearly everywhere but in the arid West. Not until 1954, for instance, did the Bureau of the Census first collect detailed statistics on industrial water use.

We do, however, feel that current estimates of water withdrawals give us enough to go on in making useful projections up to the year 2000. But the techniques of measuring use and projecting future demand for the flow and on-site uses of water are not yet good enough to yield figures that would justify an effort to project them in a study of this kind. Therefore we have attempted no numerical estimates in these two areas. We shall, instead, rely on the Senate Committee study to indicate broad trends and relationships and their significance.

The Outlook for Withdrawal Uses

The effect of a withdrawal use on water supplies may be conveniently thought of as consisting of five distinct elements: (1) withdrawal or intake, (2) use, (3) depletion or loss, (4) the location of effluent discharge, and (5) the quality of effluent discharged.

The customary way of measuring withdrawal uses of water has been simply to record the amounts taken out of streams, wells, and other sources of supply. Although this kind of information is valuable for planning of local water requirements, it does not tell much about the impact on regional or national supplies. Water withdrawn by an industrial or thermal power plant may be used once or recirculated several times. In 1954, for example, water use by industry and thermal-electric plants was, because of recirculation, some 45 per cent higher than the amount of water they withdrew from freshwater sources (see Figure 14–2). Water used by households and irrigation farmers is not recirculated, so use and intake are identical in

1. Mr. Wollman, professor of economics at the University of New Mexico, was a staff member of Resources for the Future during the academic year 1959–60, while on leave from his university post.

2. U.S. Senate, Select Committee on National Water Resources, *Water Resources Activities in the United States, Committee Print No. 32, Water Supply and Demand* (Washington, August 1960).

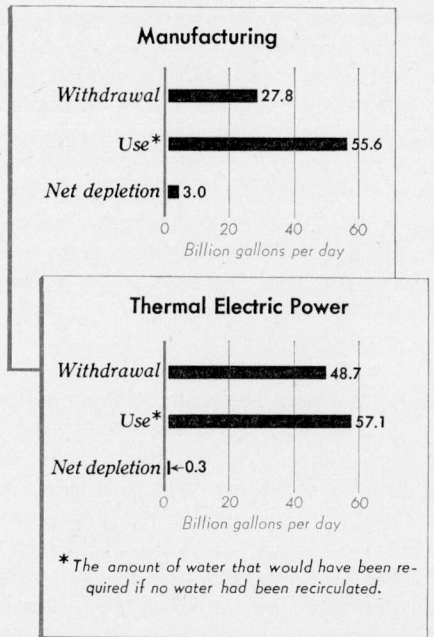

Figure 14–2. Fresh water withdrawals, use, and net depletion for manufacturing and thermal-electric power, 1954.

these cases. Since use of water is much more closely related than withdrawal to actual water losses and to water quality deterioration, the most important effects from the viewpoint of society, this concept underlies the projections and analysis of this chapter. Subsequent references to *use* or *withdrawal use* indicate the total amount of water put through industrial processes, cooling facilities, household water supply systems and irrigation facilities, not, as has ordinarily been the case in past studies, the amount withdrawn from water sources.

Most of the water used by both industry and municipalities is eventually returned to the watershed supply system so that, depending on how much it has been physically altered, it can be used downstream perhaps several times.

Some portion of the water used is, however, "used up." In general such depletion is almost entirely accounted for by evaporation and transpiration. For example, use of water for industrial cooling induces evaporation in the industrial plant or in the water body that receives the effluent. However, by far the largest (relatively and absolutely) depletion of water by a withdrawal use is in irrigation. Estimates indicate that currently about 60 per cent of the water withdrawn for irrigation purposes is lost through evaporation and transpiration. Most of the evaporation and transpiration loss resulting from household use is due to the irrigation of lawns and gardens and in some areas to the operation of evaporative air coolers. Almost all of the remaining water used in homes is for washing and waste disposal, neither of which leads to the depletion of supplies. Air conditioning is the greatest cause of evaporation of supplies used in commercial establishments. A more indirect but nevertheless significant way in which the withdrawal uses result in depletion is by evaporation from reservoirs in which water is stored to permit its release in accordance with the time patterns of withdrawal by users. Since there is presently very little basis for assigning reservoir losses to specific uses, further discussion is deferred to Chapter 19, where they will be treated as a reduction in the supply which can be made available by flow regulation reservoirs.

In most instances the effluent from "used" water is discharged into fresh water at locations that make it available for subsequent use. Thus total use often can be much larger than the recorded flow of a river basin without implying shortages, because by far the larger proportions of water used for industrial, steam electric, and municipal purposes are returned to water courses. It is necessary, however, always to make allowance for ultimate users—usually coastal cities or industries that discharge their effluent into the ocean or into saline estuaries. From the point of view of the amount of water "used up," the total amount of water they withdraw from the fresh-water source represents a net loss.

If there are *flow use* requirements in the stream from which water is withdrawn for municipal and industrial uses, the effects of discharging effluent into the ocean or saline estuary may be somewhat more complicated. Nevertheless, for reasons set forth in the appendix to Chapter 14, this study has counted discharges into saline water as net losses.

All withdrawal uses alter the quality of the

water used in some measure. This in turn affects the quality of the water supply into which effluent is discharged. As a result of leaching from the soil, the concentration of salts in the return flow from irrigation is greater than it was in the water originally diverted. The effluent from cooling processes is warmer than the water withdrawn. The effluent of municipalities and industries includes many organic and inorganic wastes. These quality-degrading consequences of withdrawal uses are treated in this study as a separate type of water use—namely, a flow use which is referred to as waste carriage and disposal. Accordingly, this type of demand is discussed under flow uses below.

In view of the foregoing considerations, this analysis of withdrawal uses is limited to measuring the effect of use upon the total supply of water available for possible use. This measure is referred to as the *withdrawal depletion*. It is quantitatively defined as (*a*) losses resulting from use as a consequence of evaporation, transpiration, or incorporation of water in a manufactured product, plus (*b*) total effluent discharges in circumstances under which the used water is unavailable for reuse. The sum of these quantities reflects with reasonable accuracy the flow required to meet a specified level of use, provided the quality is satisfactory.

Projections of Withdrawal Depletions

Separate projections are provided for municipal, industrial, thermal-electric power, and irrigation uses. These four categories include almost all depletions resulting from withdrawal use; the small residual consists primarily of rural household supplies, livestock watering, and mining operations.

In making these projections of withdrawal depletions, the projections of population and industrial growth have been allocated among the three water supply regions in accord with the distribution adopted in the Report of the Senate Select Committee on Water Resources.[3] Second, it has been assumed that technological and managerial advances would result in a moderate

increase in the efficiency of water use for thermal-electric power and agricultural purposes. However, major technological breakthroughs have not been anticipated. Third, no significant changes in public policy which would influence future use are assumed. Fourth, the projections assume in general the present level of water supply costs. No effort has been made to take into account possible price elasticities of demand for water supplies. These and other points of methodology are described in more detail in the appendix to Chapter 14.

Municipal use. The water supplied through municipal systems serves the uses with which people are generally most familiar (washing, drinking, lawn watering, fire fighting, etc.). Yet municipal water supply accounts for a relatively small proportion of all water used. In 1960 less than 5 per cent of all use was for municipal purposes. In recent years, however, use by municipalities has been growing rapidly —both because of the extension of public water supply systems to serve a growing population and increased per capita use.

Particularly in cities, a relatively lavish use of water for all domestic purposes has become characteristic of American life; in rural areas personal use is about half as much, but still very high compared with the standards for the rest of the world. Measured in terms of total withdrawals, each urban resident is supplied with about 60 gallons of water per day for domestic use, including lawn watering, air cooling and laundering. Another 26 gallons per person per day is supplied to commercial establishments connected to public supply systems, and 25 gallons goes for purely municipal functions like street cleaning, and fire fighting. These proportions, as well as total use, vary regionally; use for lawn sprinkling and irrigation is much heavier in the less humid areas.

While municipal use per capita has been increasing, it is difficult to foresee exactly how the factors affecting use per capita may be expected to balance out in the future. For example, recent analyses suggest that somewhat lower use per capita of water prevails in large urban areas (when industrial use is excluded) than in smaller cities and towns, owing to the

3. Committee Prints No. 5, *Population Projections and Economic Assumptions;* No. 8, *Future Water Requirements for Principal Water-using Industries;* No. 32, *Water Supply and Demand* (Washington, 1960).

prevalence of apartments and other multi-family dwellings. On the other hand, further increases in automatic appliances, air conditioning and swimming pools will tend to push use per capita upward unless water costs rise significantly. The projections made in this study are based on the assumption that factors affecting depletion per capita will about cancel out.

Net depletions per capita vary greatly among the three regions. For example, it appears that net depletions per capita for Salt Lake City are about four times as great as for Cincinnati because of the heavy use of water for lawn watering and evaporative air conditioning in an arid area. The projections assume that evapotranspiration losses will be approximately 10 per cent of total municipal use in the East and Pacific Northwest and 20 per cent of use in the West. Projected depletions due to effluent discharge into saline waters have been separately calculated for coastal areas.

The High, Low, and Medium projections are directly related to the High, Low, and Medium projections of population growth. The same coefficients of water use have been utilized for each of the three levels.

The application of these assumptions and procedures in the Medium projections indicates nearly a tripling of depletions for both the West and the Pacific Northwest and about a doubling for the East by the year 2000. (See Table 14–1.) The High level projections involve an increase of about three and three-quarter times for the western regions and a near tripling for the East. It is noteworthy that the year 2000 Medium projections of municipal depletions for the West are only about 7 per cent of the Medium projections for all depletions in withdrawal uses in the West. For the Pacific Northwest the percentage is about 4; for the East, on the other hand, municipal losses account for nearly a quarter of total depletions.

Thermal-electric power generation. Thermal-electric power plants withdraw more water—fresh and saline combined—than any other category of use except irrigation, and by the end of the twentieth century it is to be expected that power generation will lead all other withdrawal uses. The saline water used varies in concentration of salts from brackish to sea water; most of it is brackish except at coastal locations. Approximately 99 per cent of all water used for steam-electric generation is for condenser cooling. Consequently, it undergoes little change in use except temperature modification.

TABLE 14–1. National and Regional Fresh Water Depletion from Municipal Use, 1954, 1960, and Projections to 2000

(Billion gallons per day)

Region	1954	1960		1970	1980	1990	2000
U.S. Total	5.9	6.9	L	8.1	9.4	10.6	11.6
			M	8.6	10.8	13.3	15.9
			H	9.5	12.9	17.1	22.1
East	3.8	4.4	L	4.9	5.4	5.9	6.2
			M	5.3	6.4	7.6	8.9
			H	5.8	7.7	10.0	12.6
Pacific Northwest	.3	.3	L	.4	.5	.5	.6
			M	.4	.6	.7	.9
			H	.5	.7	.9	1.3
Total, high runoff regions	*4.1*	*4.7*	*L*	*5.3*	*5.9*	*6.4*	*6.8*
			M	*5.7*	*6.9*	*8.3*	*9.8*
			H	*6.3*	*8.3*	*10.9*	*13.9*
West, except Pacific Northwest	1.8	2.2	L	2.8	3.5	4.1	4.8
			M	2.9	3.9	5.0	6.1
			H	3.2	4.5	6.2	8.2

Source: Appendix Table A14–1.

Where cool water is readily available in large quantities, it is usually economical for generating plants to use the water on a once-through basis. However, under some circumstances it is more economical to run the water through cooling towers and reuse it. The central factor is the relative cost of water and of additional equipment. At the present time about 17 per cent of the water withdrawn for thermal-electric cooling is recirculated. The proportion recirculated may increase substantially in the future, depending upon water costs and possible public regulation designed to avoid excessive water temperatures in streams. While recirculation reduces both total withdrawals and heating of streams, it does not materially alter net depletion per kilowatt-hour of power generation. Accordingly, recirculation does not affect the losses from the total water supply of a region substantially unless effluent is discharged in such a manner that it is not available for reuse. Since at coastal locations saline water is generally used for cooling purposes, evaporation losses from fresh-water withdrawals are accepted as a satisfactory measure of thermal-electric power depletion. In projecting depletions the increased evaporation from the watercourse receiving the heated effluent, as well as evaporation losses within the plant, are taken into account. (See Appendix 14 for a detailed explanation.)

Saline water can be a substitute for fresh water for cooling purposes. In 1954 it represented about 20 per cent of total use. Non-corrosive equipment capable of utilizing saline water is somewhat more costly than equipment used for fresh water and, except at locations near saline water sources, a transportation cost is involved. These cost factors will determine the rate of substitution of saline water for fresh water. In this study it has been assumed that the percentage of saline water used in thermal-power generation will not change between 1960 and 2000. Since power generation is expected to increase several-fold in this period, a substantial increase in saline water use is anticipated.

The amount of cooling water depleted is dependent upon the amount of heat to be dissipated. With equipment now in use it is estimated that approximately ¾ gallon of water on the average is evaporated to dissipate the surplus heat produced in the generation of a kilowatt-hour of electricity. This estimate reflects a decline of 20 per cent since 1954 as a result of increases in the physical efficiency with which fuel is now utilized in power generation. The rate of increase in physical efficiency seems destined to decline in the future as the physical maximum in efficiency is approached. In this study it is assumed that by 2000, average efficiency will have increased to the point that only

TABLE 14–2. National and Regional Fresh Water Depletion from Thermal-electric Power Generation, 1954, 1960, and Projections to 2000

(Billion gallons per day)

Region	1954	1960		1970	1980	1990	2000
U.S. Total	.3	.4	L	.5	.6	.7	.8
			M	.6	.8	1.1	1.3
			H	.7	1.2	1.7	2.2
East	.23	.3	L	.4	.5	.6	.7
			M	.5	.7	.9	1.1
			H	.6	1.0	1.4	1.8
Pacific Northwest	–	–		–	–	–	–
Total, high runoff regions	.2	.3	L	.4	.5	.6	.7
			M	.5	.7	.9	1.1
			H	.6	1.0	1.4	1.8
West, except Pacific Northwest	.04	.1	L	.1	.1	.1	.1
			M	.1	.1	.2	.2
			H	.1	.2	.3	.4

Source: Appendix Table A14–2.

about 4/10 gallon of water will be required to dissipate the surplus heat produced in the generation of a kilowatt-hour of electricity. The same assumption is applied to both nuclear energy and to conventional fuels.

Revolutionary technological and scientific advances could drastically alter the future demand outlook. Conceivably a type of air cooling that uses no water whatsoever might be substituted for conventional cooling processes. Should it ever become economically feasible on a large scale to convert fuel—either fossil fuel or nuclear energy—directly into electricity without the intermediate step of producing steam, cooling water demands for electric power generation would be drastically reduced.

The High, Medium, and Low projections are directly related to the High, Medium, and Low projections for thermal-electric power generation. The coefficients of water use remain the same. (See Table 14–2.)

The projections suggest an increase of three and two-third times in depletion for thermal-power generation between 1960 and 2000. Although thermal-power generation is a heavy source of water withdrawal, actual depletion for this purpose does not appear large in comparison with water used for other purposes.

Manufacturing. Manufacturing establishments use large quantities of fresh water. In 1960, for example, it has been estimated that water use for manufacturing totaled around 78 billion gallons a day (bgd) as compared with about 89 bgd for thermal power generation, about 121 bgd for irrigation, and around 14 bgd for municipal purposes. Only a small fraction of the water used is actually used up. The 1960 net depletion of fresh water by manufacturing was less than 5 per cent of depletions attributable to all withdrawal uses. As in the case of municipal withdrawals, the primary effect of manufacturing use is the degradation of water quality through the discharge of effluents into water bodies. These effects are considered later as a waste carriage and disposal use, which imposes another type of demand upon water supplies.

While each of the major industrial groups uses substantial quantities of water, only seven

account for over 80 per cent of the total depletion. These are petroleum refining, pulp and paper, chemicals, iron and steel, nonferrous metals, food products, and coke. Since these industries are likely to continue to account for the predominant portion of industrial water use, the demand for water by manufacturing in the future will depend primarily upon the growth they experience.

Water is used by industry in a variety of ways. It is incorporated in some products; it is a cleansing agent; it is used to transport materials within a plant; it is utilized in chemical processes of various kinds. However, by far the largest proportion of the water withdrawn is for cooling purposes. According to data collected by the Bureau of the Census in 1954, the percentages of total withdrawals applied to cooling for the seven major water-using industries are as follows:

Petroleum refining 82
Pulp and paper 20
Chemicals and related products 82
Iron and steel 70
Food products 50
Nonferrous metals 82
Coke 74

Note: Data relate only to establishments with 1954 gross water intake of 20 million gallons or more for the year.

Evaporation resulting from cooling is also the major source of depletion from manufacturing water use. Losses attributable to other factors are comparatively small.

The detailed procedures followed in projecting future use for each of the major water-using industries are described in Appendix 14. Since very few data on manufacturing use were collected prior to 1954, it was not possible to examine past trends. By using Bureau of the Census data for 1954 and examining the way water is used by each major water-using industry, coefficients of water use per unit of product were developed. Inasmuch as cooling is the major cause of depletion, it was necessary to estimate the heat dissipation requirements per unit of product for each industry in much the same manner as this was done for thermal-electric power. Account was also taken of other types of losses.

It is not assumed that net depletions per unit

TABLE 14–3. National and Regional Fresh Water Depletion from Manufacturing, 1954, 1960, and Projections to 2000

(Billion gallons per day)

Region	1954	1960		1970	1980	1990	2000
U.S. Total	3.0	3.9	L	4.9	6.2	8.0	10.1
			M	5.7	8.2	11.7	16.8
			H	6.9	11.5	19.2	32.0
East	2.4	3.1	L	3.8	4.8	6.0	7.5
			M	4.5	6.4	9.0	12.7
			H	5.5	9.1	15.1	25.0
Pacific Northwest	.1	.1	L	.3	.5	.6	.8
			M	.3	.6	.8	1.2
			H	.3	.7	1.2	1.9
Total, high runoff regions	*2.5*	*3.3*	*L*	*4.1*	*5.2*	*6.6*	*8.2*
			M	*4.8*	*6.9*	*9.8*	*13.8*
			H	*5.9*	*9.8*	*16.3*	*26.8*
West, except Pacific Northwest	.5	.6	L	.8	1.0	1.4	1.9
			M	.9	1.2	1.9	3.0
			H	1.0	1.7	2.9	5.2

Source: Appendix Table A14–3.

of product will decline between now and 2000. It is likely, of course, that some industries will reduce use per unit of product very substantially in this period. For example, for some types of petroleum refining, air fin cooling is now used instead of water cooling. General extension of this practice would substantially reduce water demand by the petroleum industry. However, technological change has a varying effect on depletion per unit of product; it is reasonable to anticipate that decreases in some instances will be offset by increases in others.

Where water serves primarily as a coolant, saline water, where available, can to varying degrees be employed in place of fresh. On the other hand, in process uses opportunities for saline water use are much more limited. Saline water may be satisfactory where it does not come into contact with the actual product; waste removal frequently meets this criterion. The projections of manufacturing losses generally assume that there will be no increase in the proportion of water obtained from saline sources during the period under consideration. However, since projections of industrial growth are large, the implicit absolute increases in saline water use for manufacturing are also large.

The High, Medium, and Low projections are directly related to the High, Medium, and Low projections of manufacturing output. The same coefficients of water depletion are applied to each level. (See Table 14–3.)

The projections obtained indicate a large absolute increase in depletions. The East and the West would experience about a fourfold and fivefold increase (Medium projections) respectively and the Pacific Northwest would have almost an eightfold increase (when calculated from unrounded estimates). In addition there would be a substantial increase in the percentage of total depletions attributable to manufacturing. According to the Medium projections, depletions from manufacturing will increase from less than 5 per cent of total withdrawal depletions in 1960 to about 11 per cent in 2000.

Irrigation. Irrigation was already being practiced in certain parts of the West in the pre-Columbian period; Spanish colonists brought water to additional small areas; but these efforts have been dwarfed by the expansion in irrigated acreage that began with the diversions from the Wasatch Mountain streams in Utah in 1846. Since then the total irrigated acreage in the West (including the Pacific Northwest) has increased continually, though fitfully, through almost twelve decades.

By 1949, irrigated acreage (full or partial) was in excess of 25 million. By 1954 this had increased to over 27 million, and by 1957 to an estimated 32 million acres. The rate of growth between 1954 and 1957 was one of the highest in the entire history of western irrigation, and was due in part to the tapping of deep aquifers through the sinking of large numbers of wells by individual landowners.

Of the various categories of withdrawal use, irrigation accounts for by far the largest amount of fresh water depletion. Moreover, irrigation is heavily concentrated in the arid and semi-arid western half of the United States where it is essential to crop production. It is estimated that in 1960, about 80 per cent of the water withdrawn for irrigation use was in the West, about 15 per cent was in the Pacific Northwest, and about 5 per cent in the East.

Public policy has been an important determinant of the growth of irrigation in the United States. Specific state and federal policies have been designed to promote irrigation development in the arid and semi-arid West. In addition, public agricultural policies generally have encouraged intensive agricultural practices such as irrigation. If it is assumed that public policies are likely to continue to be an important factor influencing agricultural output, market forces will only be partially responsible for the extent of irrigation in the future.

Accordingly, our basic projections of future irrigation water use are based upon past trends in irrigated acreage and existing plans for irrigation development. It has been assumed that the upper limits on irrigation development would be imposed by such factors as topographic and soil conditions that determine the practicability of irrigation and by the unavailability of water except at very high costs. The projections, that is, are not based on the demand outlook for agricultural products, nor, except for extreme cases just mentioned, on the cost of water inputs in comparison with other possible inputs to achieve a given level of agricultural production. No major changes in public policy are contemplated.

Because both public policies and climatic conditions in the western states are quite different from those in the remainder of the country, the projections for the West and Pacific Northwest are based on somewhat different assumptions than the projections for the East. The first step for both regions has been to project irrigated acreage and then to apply coefficients of water use to the projected acreages to obtain projected amounts of water diverted. A percentage loss attributable to evapotranspiration was applied to the estimated diversions to obtain projected depletions. Projected acreages and associated depletions are set forth in Appendix Table A14–4.

For the two western regions, the High projections assume that all potentially irrigable land (as indicated by topography, soil conditions, and some prospects of a water supply) would be irrigated by the year 2000. The Medium projections assume that in addition to the 1957 acreage, private and public plans known to the Bureau of Reclamation and reported in a 1958 document (Report of the Commissioner of the Bureau of Reclamation) will be completed by 2000. The Low projections assume no net increase in irrigated acreage by 2000, i.e., new irrigation would be offset by land taken out of irrigation.

For the East, the High projection assumes that all land with suitable soils and topography for supplementary irrigation would be irrigated by 2000. The rate of increase in irrigated acreage is the same as the rate of increase in the High projections of cropland requirements set forth in Chapter 18. The Medium projection is a straight-line extension of the trend in eastern irrigated acreage from 1949 to 1957, whereas the Low projection is a straight-line extension of the trend in eastern irrigated acreage from 1939 to 1957.

The amount of water required per acre of irrigated land is much greater in the West and Northwest than in the East because of climatic differences and differences in techniques of applying water to crops. For the East it is assumed that 2.6 acre-feet of water per irrigated acre were diverted in 1960, but that this amount would decline to 1.9 acre-feet in 2000. This is based on the expectation that the efficiency of irrigation practices will increase. It is assumed that about 88 per cent of the water withdrawn for irrigation in 1960 was depleted, that by 1980 the percentage will have increased to 89 per cent and by 2000 it will have increased to 91 per cent. For the two western regions it is assumed that on the average about 4 acre-feet of water per acre irrigated was diverted in 1960, and that this average will continue to 2000. While diversion per acre is assumed to remain constant, depletion per acre will increase because of anticipated increases in the efficiency of irrigation practices; i.e., irrigation would use up more of the water diverted so there would be less returned to streams and aquifers. It is estimated that in 1960 about 60 per cent of withdrawals were depleted. It is assumed that by 1980 depletions would increase to 62 per cent and by 2000 they would be 65 per cent of withdrawals.

The projections which result suggest that irrigation will continue to dominate the depletion of water through withdrawal uses. According to the Medium projection for the nation as a whole for 2000, about three-fourths of withdrawal depletions would be attributable to irrigation. However, this is a decline from over 85 per cent in 1960. It is also noteworthy that

most of the depletion from irrigation (about 70 per cent for the 2000 Medium projection) occurs in the West. It is significant, however, that the Medium projections for this region indicate that irrigation would account for about 90 per cent of the depletion in 2000, compared with around 95 per cent in 1960. The Medium projections suggest that in the East irrigation will continue to account for around 40 per cent of total depletions. (See Table 14–4.)

Summary Outlook for Withdrawal Depletions

The Medium projections made in this study indicate that depletions attributable to withdrawal uses will increase by about three-fourths over the next four decades. (See Figure 14–3.) Irrigation will continue to be by far the largest source of depletion. However, its importance relative to other uses will have declined slightly. The percentage of total depletions accounted for by manufacturing in particular would rise substantially—from a little less than 5 per cent in 1960 to about 11 per cent in 2000. The broad regional pattern of use remains much the same, with depletions by far the greatest in the West because of irrigation. However, depletions in the East would grow in relative importance—

TABLE 14–4. National and Regional Fresh Water Depletion from Irrigation, 1954, 1960, and Projections to 2000

(Billion gallons per day)

Region	1954	1960		1970	1980	1990	2000
U.S. Total	61.3	73.3	L	75.7	79.4	82.8	85.3
			M	77.1	86.7	102.2	115.1
			H	77.1	86.9	123.8	165.1
East	4.2	5.9	L	7.2	8.6	9.7	11.0
			M	8.6	10.9	12.7	14.8
			H	8.5	10.7	28.4	48.2
Pacific Northwest	9.0	10.7	L	10.8	11.2	11.6	11.7
			M	10.8	12.4	15.5	17.9
			H	10.8	12.0	15.0	18.3
Total, high runoff regions	*13.3*	*16.5*	*L*	*18.0*	*19.8*	*21.2*	*22.7*
			M	*19.4*	*23.3*	*28.2*	*32.7*
			H	*19.3*	*22.7*	*43.4*	*66.5*
West, except Pacific Northwest	48.0	56.8	L	57.7	59.7	61.6	62.5
			M	57.7	63.4	74.1	82.4
			H	57.7	64.1	80.4	98.6

Source: Appendix Table A14–4.

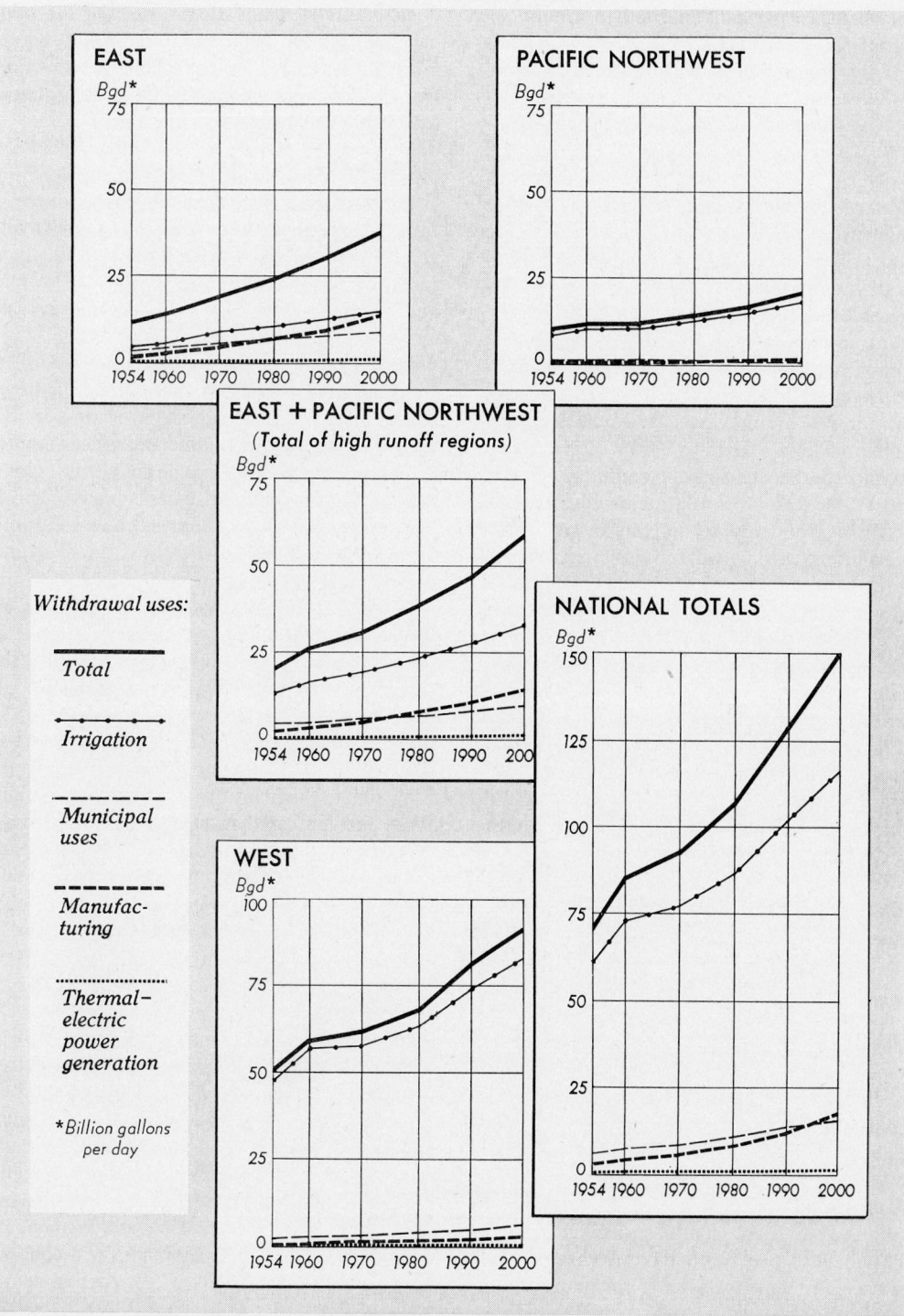

Figure 14–3. Net depletion, by region and type of withdrawal water use, 1954, 1960, and Medium projections to 2000.

from about 16 per cent in 1960 to around 25 per cent for the Medium projections in 2000—primarily because of rapidly increased irrigation.

The Future Outlook for Flow Uses

Water is used in a stream channel or lake for a number of purposes, including navigation, the production of hydroelectric power, the provision of habitat for aquatic life, and waste carriage and disposal. It is difficult, indeed, to arrive at a regionally or nationally significant common measure of use for these purposes that is at the same time comparable to the measures of withdrawal use previously utilized. Although the methodology devised by Mr. Wollman in his report to the Senate Select Committee on National Water Resources is a major advance, the problem is so complex and so many of its aspects have yet to be worked out satisfactorily, that the results can be viewed only as relatively crude indicators. Under the circumstances, no new projections for flow uses have been made especially for this study, even though the projections for the Senate Select Committee are based on slightly different projections of industrial output than ours. Accordingly, our appraisal of the future outlook for flow uses rests primarily on the work of Mr. Wollman, federal agency personnel, and other consultants who participated in the preparation of materials for the Senate Select Committee. The procedures used are described in detail in the reports to the Committee. It should be noted, however, that these flow-use projections are used as guides to the direction and scale of future trends. They are not put forward on the same footing as the great body of projections in this study; in some instances, as the reader will note below, we believe that certain estimates may turn out to be far out of line.

Table 14–5 summarizes the projections of flow uses for 1980 and 2000 and compares them with estimated use for 1954 for the three water supply regions. The quantities specified are not to be added to one another to arrive at a total flow use. The same water used for one purpose may also be used for all other flow uses. Thus the total required for flow uses is the largest flow required by any single use. On the other hand, the total flow requirement so derived must be added to on-site use and depletions from withdrawal uses to arrive at a measure of total use for all purposes.

Hydroelectric Power

Flowing water has been used as a source of energy for many centuries. In this century hydro power has been one of the major products of river basin development, although it supplies only a small percentage of all the energy used by the national economy.

Maintenance of hydro-power production levels requires the maintenance of certain flows. Depletion through withdrawals or on-site uses reduces energy output. Other flow uses tend to be compatible with hydro, although differences in timing of flow requirements can result in some incompatibilities. Thus in comparing total demand with supply, hydro must be taken into account.

Future potential hydro facilities will tend on the average to be more costly than those built in the past because generally the least costly facilities are built first. This factor presumably will tend to hold down construction of new hydro plants. On the other hand, with the advent of high-pressure, high-temperature steam-generating units which lose something in flexibility, hydro has increased in value per kilowatt-hour for peaking purposes—for use, that is, to supplement steam-generated power at certain hours of the day when use of electricity goes far above the average load on a system—because it can be turned off and on almost instantly without serious losses in efficiency. This characteristic is so useful that it has led to pump storage, whereby water is pumped into an elevated reservoir with off-peak energy from thermal plants and then used to produce hydro during periods of peak demand. Pump storage does not add appreciably to flow requirements because the same water may be reused almost endlessly. Because of its value for peaking purposes, and the fact that a few favorable new sites still remain, the outlook is that hydro development will continue in spite of the availability of alternative energy sources. (See Chapter 15, page 282.)

As indicated by the report to the Senate Se-

TABLE 14–5.   Regional On-site Depletions and Flow
Uses, 1954 and Projections for 1980, 2000

(Billion gallons per day)

Region and use	1954	1980	2000
East			
Total on-site uses[1]	(45.8)	35.3	48.0
Flows:			
Hydroelectric	253.6	405.4	423.1
Navigation	176.8	199.2	199.4
Sport fish habitat	60.0	125.4	170.5
Waste dilution[2]	413.3	251.5	342.3
West, except Pacific Northwest			
Total on-site uses[1]	(46.3)	34.5	47.5
Flows:			
Hydroelectric	27.7	77.7	79.5
Navigation	3.3	4.7	5.0
Sport fish habitat	14.9	40.0	62.2
Waste dilution[2]	101.9	51.9	76.2
Pacific Northwest			
Total on-site uses[1]	(1.2)	.9	1.3
Flows:			
Hydroelectric	93.7	133.0	133.9
Navigation	100.8	35.2	37.8
Sport fish habitat	3.1	5.6	8.7
Waste dilution[2]	4.7	28.9	28.0

1. On-site uses depletion for 1954 is estimated by backward extrapolation from 1980 and is not to be deducted from runoff. Losses for 1980 and 2000 are increases over 1954.
2. Total streamflow needed to maintain dissolved oxygen at an average of 4 mg. per liter, for level of treatment that minimizes total cost of treatment and storage. 1954 waste dilutions estimated on basis of 70% treatment for municipal and 50% treatment for industrial wastes, both higher than actually prevailed.

Source: U.S. Senate Select Committee on National Water Resources, Committee Print No. 32, *Water Supply and Demand* (Washington, August 1960), Part IV.

lect Committee, it is difficult to project future development in terms of water use. Energy output is determined by the "head"—that is, the fall of a stream in its course to the sea—as well as by the quantity of water. Existing operating arrangements assume considerable variation in flow; thus near average flows are not required during the low flow season. Further, when withdrawals are downstream of the hydro facilities, which is often the case, hydro is not incompatible with withdrawal depletions. Finally, because good substitute sources are available, hydro is a comparatively low value use, consequently it will probably be subordinated to other uses if conflict arises.

In short, although hydro is a significant use, it is difficult to express demand for hydro in comparative quantitative terms. This may not be too serious in assessing the supply-demand outlook because, as indicated, (1) hydro tends to be a residual that is only developed to the extent compatible with other uses, and (2) alternative energy sources are relatively abundant.

Navigation

The inland waterways have been major arteries of commerce and communication since this country was first settled. Early river development was primarily concerned with the improvement of navigation. With the advent of the railroads, navigation went into a decline that continued to World War II. Since then, inland waterway navigation has experienced a major comeback—in part as a result of improved equipment. Between 1940 and 1957 ton-miles per year increased about 500 per cent. The prospects are that for bulky low-value commodities in long-distance transit the inland waterways will continue to offer the lowest cost transportation between points served by the system. Some extensions of the system may be justified but how much of an increase this would be must await further analysis.

Successful navigation requires certain minimum water levels in navigation channels. Translation of such levels into generalized flow requirements is a difficult task for several reasons. First, navigation is only practiced at a limited number of locations—usually on the main stems of large rivers or major tributaries or in the lower reaches of smaller rivers. Thus such use tends to be localized. Second, flow requirements depend upon the kind of facilities provided. So-called slack-water navigation, in which locks and dams are provided at frequent intervals, requires relatively little water. Run-of-river navigation requires substantial flows. Third, navigation, like power and for similar reasons, is a low-value use and therefore is not competitive with withdrawal uses.

Fish Habitat

The demand outlook for outdoor recreation opportunities is appraised in Chapter 11. Associated with the large increase in demand for outdoor recreation will be a demand for sport fishing opportunities as one form of such recreation. The projections set forth in Table 14-5 for fish habitat are based upon assumed "relationships between population and fisherman, between fisherman and harvest of sport fish, between volume of water and fish harvest."[4]

It is doubtful that existing relationships among these factors are a very satisfactory guide to future flow use of water. No doubt some storage will be justifiable on the basis of increased demand for sport fishing opportunities provided by artificial lakes and regulated flows downstream. However, relatively large lake areas can be maintained with modest amounts of depletion or flow. We judge, however, that preservation of water quality to maintain fish life will be the primary need, rather than quantity of flow, if future demand for fishing opportunities is to be met.

4. U.S. Senate Select Committee on National Water Resources, Print No. 32, *op. cit.*, p. 19.

Waste Disposal

The Wollman report to the Senate Select Committee recognized that the projections for hydro power, navigation, and fish habitat were unsatisfactory guides to future flow use. Instead, the flows considered necessary to maintain water quality for a variety of uses were selected as setting the level of demand for all flow uses. This fact, together with the growing seriousness of water pollution, makes it desirable to consider in some detail the nature of the waste disposal problem as it influences water use.

Here it is necessary again to concentrate on the strategic elements in an extremely complicated situation, and again to anticipate some considerations of water supply in order to arrive at even an approximation of an increasingly important type of water demand.

Many kinds of pollutants get into water courses and affect the utility of supply—sediment from soil erosion, agricultural pesticides washed off fields and chlorides for ice control washed off highways, salts dissolved in a stream bed or leached from the soil by irrigation water, organic wastes from households and both organic and inorganic compounds from manufacturing.

Steam electric plants and many factories return water to streams much warmer than when it was withdrawn. Such heat pollution can have far-reaching effects on the quality of water. By stimulating the metabolism of microbes it hastens the breakdown of organic wastes and thus helps streams purify themselves. On the other hand, high temperatures lower the oxygen saturation level, harming fish and producing other ecological results that are mostly unfavorable. When stream temperatures are raised for only short stretches in relatively clean water, the effects are much less clear. Moreover, heat pollution loads can be mitigated by recirculation of cooling water.

Although the results of these diverse kinds of pollution are generally regarded as harmful, some, like salinity from irrigation, are serious but limited to certain river basins; some, like certain types of chemical pollution, still are little understood technologically; and few are promising subjects for systematic projection. The exception—a large one—is the problem of organic wastes from homes and industries.

Organic pollution. Dilution of organic wastes may well constitute one of the largest future demands for fresh water as urban populations continue to grow and industrial activity to expand. And, though many important areas still need fuller exploration, enough information is now available for reasonably systematic analysis of the situation and outlook.

A measure of the organic pollution load is Biochemical Oxygen Demand (BOD), which indicates the rate at which dissolved oxygen is drawn upon in a waste-receiving water. The rate at which a given quantity and type of organic waste exerts oxygen demand is a function of a variety of factors, among the most important of which are temperature and chemical characteristics of the receiving water.

The rate of BOD combined with the rate at which oxygen is restored determines the level of dissolved oxygen. In flowing water the combined effect of BOD and reaeration results in a fall and then a rise in dissolved oxygen as wastes are carried downstream. The degradation of wastes, together with the restoration of dissolved oxygen in receiving water, is often termed "self-purification." Through speeding up and controlling the processes which naturally occur in a stream, biological treatment plants can reduce BOD and take some of the burden off the streams, lakes, and estuaries into which wastes are discharged.

If the level of dissolved oxygen is carried very low in the waste-receiving water, fish are killed and other usually undesirable ecological changes occur. If dissolved oxygen in the receiving water is exhausted, septic conditions arise. Unassimilated organic wastes may also add to the difficulty and expense of treating withdrawals for municipal and industrial purposes.

While receiving waters are capable of recovering from the oxygen demand imposed by organic waste loads, and waste treatment plants are able to reduce waste loads, other effects may follow the biological degradation of organic wastes. The residual products of organic waste degradation are plant nutrients (nitrogen, phosphorus, carbon) which may foster algae growth. Since algae produce organic matter by means of photosynthesis, they at least periodically release oxygen, but when they die they become organic material which exerts an oxygen demand. Thus they are involved in the oxygen balance of the receiving water. Also, if algae occur in great quantities, they affect the appearance, taste, and odor of water.

There are several ways other than augmented flow of fresh water in which the organic waste disposal problem might be met so as to avoid degradation of water quality below levels necessary for the maintenance of aquatic life. Treated effluents can be held in lagoons, algae growth fostered, and the algae harvested which would, in effect, remove the plant nutrients. This process has only been operated experimentally. At some locations, effluent might be discharged into a separate channel that would empty into the ocean without polluting the natural stream. Wastes can be held in lagoons and discharged when flows are high, but for large cities and big plants this may not be practicable because of the space required. Conceivably, chemical and physical processes (distillation, for example) might be applied to waste water treatment to extend purification beyond that achieved through orthodox treatment, although known processes appear to be too costly for use on a large scale.

The practices envisaged by the report to the Senate Select Committee are a combination of treatment of wastes by orthodox methods with regulation of streamflows to increase the quantity of water in the effluent-receiving channel during low flows. The additional flow would provide more oxygen to complete the waste degradation process and prevent excessive algae growth. The oxygen standard adopted was 4 parts per million parts of water. This was assumed to be high enough to maintain fish life in most streams. The waste treatment levels assumed for the Wollman projections set forth in Table 14–5 are based on a combination of waste treatment and storage regulation measures designed to provide the desired oxygen content at a minimum cost.

Organic Pollution and Water Use

As the brief discussion above suggests, the relationships involved in estimating the demand upon a given water supply for organic waste disposal are extremely complex. The capacity of the receiving water to absorb wastes is determined by such factors as quantity of stream flow, rate of flow, temperature, and chemical content. Another significant variable is the degree of treatment, i.e., the extent to which organic wastes have been removed. Up to a point an increase in removal through treatment reduces oxygen demand on the stream. However, at higher levels of treatment the addition of plant nutrients fosters algae growth which has several undesirable effects. Among these is an increase in oxygen demand when algae die and decay. Under these circumstances, estimates of the effects of stream flow regulation upon the oxygen content of the stream when specified quantities of organic wastes are contributed can be no more than general approximations. The margin of error could easily increase when large areas with differing conditions are covered. In addition, there is great difficulty in assessing the demand for water quality maintenance because market forces cannot function effectively to establish the demand, and the political process is just becoming sensitive to the question. Consequently, demand expressed in terms of economic criteria can be no more than an informed judgment.

Nevertheless, it is abundantly clear that such demands will be great. The outlook for population and industrial growth indicates that organic waste loads will multiply in the decades ahead. Waste loads from municipalities and industries prior to any treatment will increase from 304 million population equivalents of BOD in 1954 to 894 million population equivalents in 2000, according to projections of the U.S. Public Health Service.[5] These projections are based on the Medium population projections set forth in this study and industrial growth projections not greatly different from the Medium projections in this report. As indicated in Chapter 11, outdoor recreation demand may experience an increase by a factor of 10 between 1960 and 2000, much of which will involve use of fresh

5. U.S. Senate Select Committee on National Water Resources, Print No. 9, *Pollution Abatement* (Washington, January 1960). One "population equivalent" is the amount of BOD exerted, on the average, by the domestic organic wastes generated by one individual.

water areas. Today regulation of streamflow to provide more water during low flow periods is looked upon as the least costly means of supplementing traditional treatment measures to maintain quality in most areas. Unless this prospect changes—which it could through technological advances—waste water dilution could be the determinant of flow use demand and require much larger quantities of water in the East than withdrawal depletions.

Summary of the Flow Use Outlook

With the methodology that has been developed so far, it is difficult to arrive at a clear quantitative picture of demand for flow uses. Yet, the projections for the Senate Select Committee indicate that flows for waste dilution in 2000 in the East might be eight times as great as our Medium projections for withdrawal depletions. There is little doubt that flow uses for navigation and hydro power will be large. However, since these are low-value uses for which there are low-cost substitution possibilities, such uses need not conflict with withdrawal depletions. Fish habitat demand will also be great, but it is our estimate that the major concern in meeting demand for fishing opportunities is the preservation of water quality.

The outlook for waste dilution is dependent in large part on future advances in techniques and development of economical alternative measures for dealing with the waste disposal problem. Doubtless, pressures to maintain water quality will be great and with mounting costs encountered in meeting the objective, opportunities and incentives will increase for searching out the most economical combinations of measures to deal effectively with the problem. Given an expectation of reasonable success, it seems likely that flow demand for waste dilution should fall somewhat below the levels indicated in the Report of the Senate Select Committee.

The Future Outlook for On-site Uses

The on-site uses are of two kinds: the provision of wetlands and swamps for wildlife habitat, and the provision of farm ponds and the use of other soil conservation measures. Swamps and wetlands deplete water supplies through evapotranspiration. Farm ponds influence evaporation losses and soil conservation measures, by retarding runoff, make more moisture available to plants and thus increase evapotranspiration.

As in the case of flow uses, the methodology for projecting demands for on-site use is still primitive. For one thing, the effect of changes in vegetative cover upon losses to the atmosphere cannot be estimated with precision. Market forces do not operate to indicate existing demand for these uses and there has been relatively little study of possibilities of systematically measuring these demands. Consequently, it is still impossible to make projections that are reasonably reliable. The best effort to date is in the work done for the Senate Select Committee on National Water Resources. Projected losses for on-site uses for 1980 and 2000 for the three water supply regions as reported to the Committee are set forth in Table 14–5.

Swamps and Wetlands

Land areas that are wet and marshy are essential to the maintenance of wildlife populations, particularly waterfowl. The extent to which such areas are provided will affect the availability of water for other purposes. If existing swamps and wetlands are maintained, past rates of flow will not be altered by such use. If they are drained, flows will be increased. If they are expanded, evapotranspiration losses will increase and historic flows will be reduced.

To project future water use for this purpose, it is necessary to estimate the demand for this type of wildlife habitat. One approach is to extend the trend in the hunting of game requiring swamp and wetland habitat—particularly waterfowl hunting. Since 1935 when the federal government began accumulating data on the number of waterfowl hunters, in connection with the sale of duck stamps, the number of hunters has increased rapidly. If it is assumed that this trend will continue and that each hunter will bag what is considered a reasonable quantity of game, an estimate can be made of the swamp and wetland area that will be required to support such a harvest. This essentially is the procedure followed by U.S. Fish and Wildlife Service in its report to the Senate Select Committee.[6]

6. Committee Print No. 18, *Fish and Wildlife and Water Resources* (Washington, April 1960).

The results obtained indicate a large depletion of water for this type of use. Moreover, much of this would occur in the West where water supplies are limited. Several problems are involved in these projections. First, maintenance of waterfowl populations—which are migratory—is dependent to a considerable extent on habitat conditions in Canada and Mexico. Accordingly, a specified population level cannot be assured through unilateral action. Second, it is difficult to appraise the various factors that will influence future demand. Will the number of hunters continue to increase, or will a more urbanized population turn to other forms of recreation? How will future demand respond to the costs of providing the land and water required to enlarge wildlife habitat? Too little is known about these matters now to subject them to reliable evaluation.

Farm Ponds and Land Treatment

The last several decades have seen soil conservation become a land program of major importance in the United States. All signs indicate the nation will proceed with efforts to conserve the soil mantle so as to assure the sustained productivity of its soil resources. In part as a result of federal assistance, the number of farm ponds has increased rapidly for watering stock, for domestic supplies, to retard runoff and thus reduce erosion, and for recreation purposes. No doubt many more of these will be constructed in the future.

The projections by the Department of Agriculture for the Senate Select Committee[7] suggest that continuation of these programs will deplete only modest quantities of water. Although estimates of this nature are subject to a large margin of error, they seem reasonable and, since they are small, substantial error can be tolerated.

The Water Demand Outlook in Summary

Demands upon the nation's resources of fresh water are expected to multiply between 1960 and the year 2000. Part of the increase will

7. Committee Print No. 12, *Land and Water Requirements for Irrigation* (Washington, December 1959).

come about simply from increases in population and in industrial activity. This general trend will be reinforced, however, by continued urbanization (people in large cities use much more water per capita for individual and community purposes than do country people), the mounting boom in outdoor recreation in which fresh clean water is so often an element, and by rising needs for stream flow to dilute organic wastes. The last of these requirements is for all practical purposes a large new use; because up to a certain level a flowing stream can usually clean itself up, the need for dilution flow did not appear in many areas until quite recently, when concentrations of people and industry pushed pollution beyond the point of tolerance.

Net losses of water resulting from the withdrawal uses—the only category of water demand for which numerical projections are made in this study—will, according to our Medium projection, nearly double by the year 2000. This forward estimate, it should be noted, is subject not only to the qualifications that hedge most of our projections in this study, but also to the circumstances that some types of water demand are not determined by market forces so that in looking ahead judgments must be made of the possible course of political decisions.

Although irrigation apparently will continue to be the largest single source of water depletion,

municipal and industrial withdrawal losses will represent steadily increasing shares of total withdrawal losses.

As noted earlier in this chapter, data are still so scanty and methods of analysis still so primitive that we have made no projections of flow and on-site uses. It is apparent, however, that future requirements in both these categories could be very large and that the flow uses almost beyond doubt *will* be. In fact, it seems likely that in the East, where the basic water problem is quality rather than quantity, needs for dilution flow could be much larger than all withdrawal losses. The most thorough study to date, though still preliminary—that of the Senate Select Committee—indicates dilution requirements at about three times our projections for all withdrawal losses for the country as a whole. However, these tentative estimations of dilution flow, even more than most resource-use projections, are subject to great uncertainties as to the future course of technology. New methods of treating organic wastes of cities and industries would in many instances be direct substitutes for dilution flow.

The significance of such relationships, and of the other indications on future water needs developed here, can be assessed in a meaningful way only by relating them to available regional supplies. This is done in Chapter 19.

chapter

15

MINERAL FUELS

THE PROJECTED U.S. REQUIREMENTS for heat and power developed in Part I constitute almost the entire basis of future demand for the mineral fuels. The few other elements in demand, consisting largely in non-fuel uses (such as oil and gas as building blocks of synthetics and other manufactured products) or transmission losses before final use, are noted later in this chapter (pages 288–89). Table 15–1 indicates how total heat and power requirements are projected to be shared among the main users over the forty-year period.

Here the several parts of the requirements picture are brought together and added up in terms of possible future demand for each of the mineral fuels. The results are summarized at the close of the chapter in Table 15–3. It is from this base that we can proceed in Chapter 20 to compare the demand pattern with the resource outlook.

But before such a summary of fuel demands can be constructed it is necessary to examine the total electricity requirements as developed in

Chapter 10 and elsewhere in Part I and state them in terms of the fuels and other sources of energy from which the electric power is likely to be derived. As illustrated in Figure 15–1, a substantial part of the raw fuel energy utilized must first be converted to electricity before it is available for end-use.

TABLE 15–1. Distribution of Heat and Power Requirements among Main Users, 1960 and Medium Projections to 2000

(Per cent)

Year	Residential	Commercial	Transportation	Industrial	Other
1960	19.9	8.5	20.2	35.2	16.2
(Medium projection)					
1970	19.0	8.3	21.5	36.2	15.0
1980	18.4	8.3	23.4	36.7	13.2
1990	16.0	7.6	25.6	39.0	11.8
2000	13.5	6.9	27.5	41.2	10.9

Source: Appendix Table A15–18.

RELATED MATERIAL: Appendix to this chapter, pp. 834–58. Requirements for construction, appendix Chapter 4, p. 632; for transportation, Chapter 5, pp. 145–47, and appendix, pp. 660–62, 666, 668; for containers, Chapter 7, pp. 167–69, and appendix, pp. 700–1; for military goods, Chapter 9, p. 183, and appendix, p. 721. Requirements for heat and power, Chapter 10, pp. 184–222, and appendix, pp. 722–77. Use of water in generating electricity, Chapter 14, pp. 270–71, and appendix pp. 825–26, and Chapter 19, pp. 378–87. Adequacy of energy sources, Chapter 20, pp. 388–417. Unconventional sources of energy and new technology, Chapter 20, pp. 417–21.

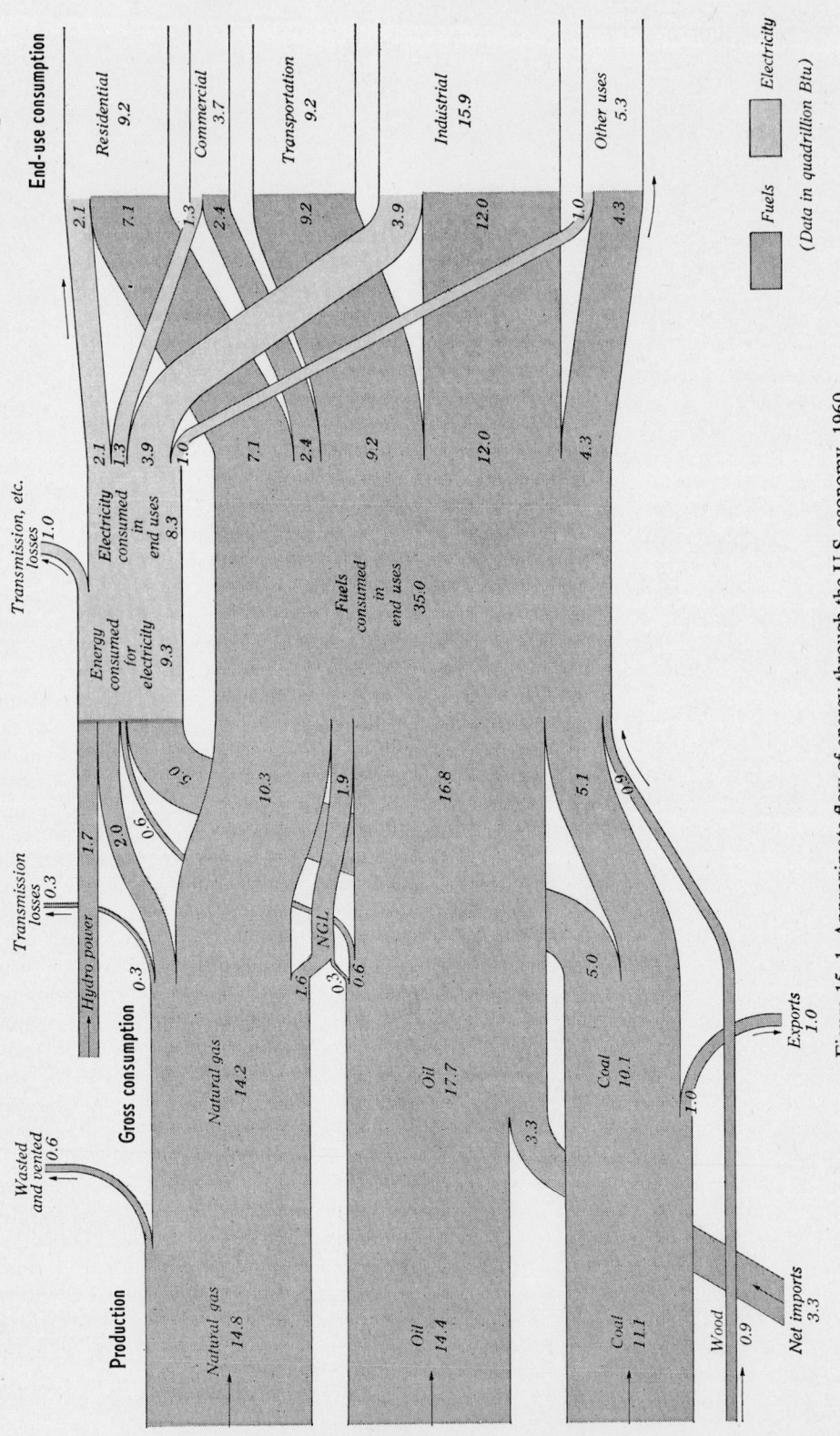

Figure 15–1. Approximate flow of energy through the U.S. economy, 1960.

Fuel Components of Electricity

Projection of the components of future electricity generation calls for analysis along three lines: After the most likely dimensions of future total demand have been indicated, (1) the role of nuclear energy as a nonconventional source of electric power has to be estimated; (2) the conventional sources—coal, oil, gas, and hydro —have to be allocated their share of the market; and (3) some assumption has to be made as to the future path of power generating efficiency.

Our projections indicate large and continuing increases in electricity generation throughout the rest of the century, but at a progressively slower rate. The quantities of electric power that would have to be generated to meet projected demand in the United States, as compared with output over the past twenty years, are as follows:

| | Past and projected | | | Decade rate of growth (Medium) |
| | Low | Medium | High | (per cent |
		(billion kwh)		per year)
1940	–	182	–	–
1950	–	390	–	7.9
1960	–	845	–	8.0
1970	1,200	1,400	1,780	5.2
1980	1,710	2,230	3,090	4.8
1990	2,260	3,240	4,880	3.8
2000	2,970	4,710	7,770	3.8

Growth from 1940 to 1960 was equivalent to doubling every nine years. The growth rate in the next two decades is equivalent to doubling in fourteen to fifteen years and doubling in nineteen years thereafter. On the other hand, projected absolute growth remains impressive. The increase in generation between 1960 and 1980 would be equal to nearly twice the total amount generated in 1960.

The estimates take no account of the very small quantity—less than 0.5 per cent of the nation's total supply—that is generated abroad and imported; supply is treated here as though all of it originated in the United States. Account is taken, however, of the gap between demand and generation caused by losses in transmission and distribution. Nearly all such losses—for our purposes we may say all—occur in the utility

field. Generating stations operated by consumers of electricity, concentrated mostly in industry, suffer only very limited losses. In utility practice, the average loss has never greatly exceeded 10 per cent of generation and has recently dropped below 9 per cent. Mainly on the expectation of greater load density (i.e., greater sales per capita for a gradually expanding number of customers, rather than constant sales per capita for a rapidly expanding number of customers), one may reasonably expect this slow downward trend to continue, declining to somewhere around 6 per cent by the century's end.

But as the rate of loss drops, the utility share of the market, where the losses are incurred, is expected to increase. Self-generated power constituted more than 40 per cent of the total industrial take in 1940; eleven years later it had dropped to less than 30 per cent, and by 1960 it represented only 21 per cent. We have assumed that it will decline to 14 per cent in 1980 and 10 per cent in 2000. Minor adjustments for these two opposing trends have been made in our projections (see Appendix Notes to Chapter 15).

The past—and projected—decline in industrial generation, noted above, is probably due to the economies that can be obtained in large-scale utility operations. Lower capacity cost and charges enjoyed in utility generation are another driving force. As utility efficiency approaches heat rates of 8,500 Btu per net kwh, the advantages of industrial generation, where by-product heat can generate electricity at 4,500 to 5,000 Btu per net kwh, become less and less significant. Nonetheless, the decline is likely to be less rapid in the future. A rock bottom of economical by-product utilization of steam or low-cost fuel (e.g., in chemicals, coke ovens, pulp and paper mills) will remain. Self-generation will persist also in industries that have a high load factor and for which, as in aluminum, electric power is an important cost element. And in small establishments or as stand-by equipment, diesel engines and gas turbines will continue to exist.

Growth in demand for electricity is expected to vary between different uses. Over the forty-year period consumption is projected to grow most rapidly in general ("other") manufactur-

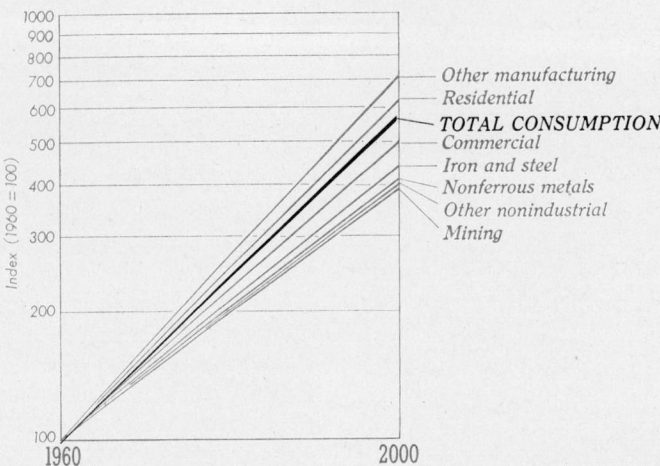

Figure 15–2. Growth in the consumption of electricity, by use, Medium projections for 1960–2000.

ing: by over 600 per cent, compared with less than 500 per cent for all uses. Growth of the different segments is depicted in Figure 15–2.

The High model points toward generation in 2000 about nine times its 1960 level, at a rate of growth not quite twice that projected at the Medium level, and the Low projection in turn reaches less than two-thirds the Medium level. Here again, different segments would share unevenly. Because of the greatly different paths that aluminum consumption might take, the spread is very wide in power consumption by the nonferrous metals industry. It is quite narrow in commercial use and in use by public authorities (including street lighting). One might summarize that the greatest chances for better than medium growth lie in industrial, followed by residential consumption.

If one were to assume for purposes of comparison that electricity consumption moves proportionately to gross national product, the High and Low GNP levels would by themselves call for a High electricity figure of about 7,100 billion kwh and a Low of about 3,600 billion kwh. This theoretical calculation indicates that more than half of the range occurs through assumed differences in the basic factor of economic activity, and less than half through technological changes and substitutions of energy sources.

Figure 15–3 indicates what the relative im-

portance of the various uses in the 1980 and 2000 economy might be compared with the present. Relative changes in position are unlikely to be violent. The growth in the role of industrial use—outside of the primary metals—is perhaps the single most noticeable feature.

Some comparative projections. How do our projections compare with some others, arrived at differently? A 1960 Edison Electric Institute study[1] forecasts 2,895 billion kwh of output for 1980, in contrast to our projection of 2,229 billion kwh. This significant difference is due principally to the utility industry's much more sanguine view of growth in residential and commercial consumption. On the other hand, the gap between the Federal Power Commission's projection for total power output and ours is quite small: for 1980 RFF's projection exceeds the FPC estimate of 1960[2] by less than 70 million kwh or 3 per cent. By 2000, our projection exceeds that of the FPC by 220 million kwh or some 5 per cent, again not an appreciable difference. We appear to be higher principally in estimated industrial consumption; the history of

1. U.S. Senate Select Committee on National Water Resources, *Water Resource Activities in the United States,* Committee Print No. 10, *Electric Power in Relation to the Nation's Water Resources* (Washington, 1960), pp. 9–34.
2. *Ibid.,* pp. 1–8.

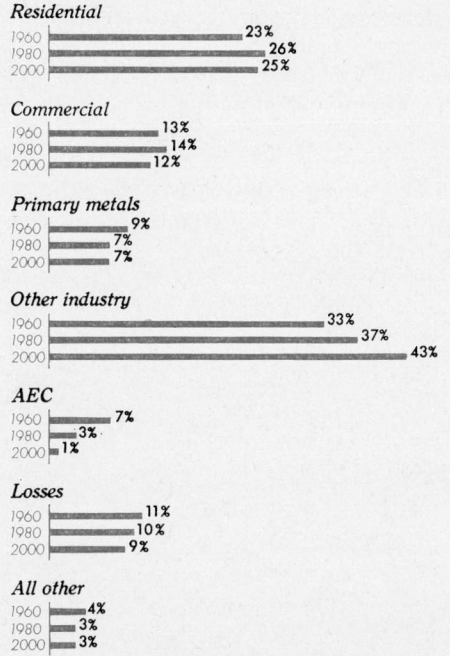

Residential
1960 ▬▬▬▬▬▬▬ 23%
1980 ▬▬▬▬▬▬▬ 26%
2000 ▬▬▬▬▬▬▬ 25%

Commercial
1960 ▬▬▬▬ 13%
1980 ▬▬▬▬ 14%
2000 ▬▬▬▬ 12%

Primary metals
1960 ▬▬▬ 9%
1980 ▬▬ 7%
2000 ▬▬ 7%

Other industry
1960 ▬▬▬▬▬▬▬▬▬▬ 33%
1980 ▬▬▬▬▬▬▬▬▬▬▬ 37%
2000 ▬▬▬▬▬▬▬▬▬▬▬▬ 43%

AEC
1960 ▬▬ 7%
1980 ▬ 3%
2000 ▪ 1%

Losses
1960 ▬▬▬ 11%
1980 ▬▬▬ 10%
2000 ▬▬▬ 9%

All other
1960 ▬ 4%
1980 ▬ 3%
2000 ▬ 3%

Figure 15–3. How electric power supply is shared among uses, 1960 and Medium projections for 1980 and 2000.

FPC projections, moreover, suggests that they are generally conservative.[3]

A Westinghouse estimate[4] of 2,532 billion kwh for 1978 compares with our 1980 figure of 2,229 billion; it exceeds ours by essentially similar percentages for residential, commercial, and industrial output and thus, on a somewhat higher aggregate level, has a similar consumer structure. Allowing for the difference in timing, our projection falls short of the Westinghouse estimate by between 20 and 25 per cent.

For the year 2000, the only other ready comparison is with the projection made by Philip Sporn,[5] that some 6,000 billion kwh might be required. This exceeds our projection of 4,700 billion by 25 per cent. As the American Electric Power Company, of which Mr. Sporn was presi-

dent at the time, has been substantially ahead of the national average in consumption per customer, his greater optimism is easily understandable and may turn out to be well justified.

Sources of Power Generation

Fuels not only compete vigorously with one another in the generation of electricity; they also jointly compete with falling water, and will before long compete with nuclear reactors. Today, even the most efficient power plants convert just over 40 per cent of the fuel energy into saleable electric energy. For the country as a whole the efficiency is much lower: not more than 32 per cent. While these efficiencies represent striking progress during the past two decades—in 1940 efficiency was barely above 20 per cent—the search for more direct ways of generation is stimulated by the magnitude of the remaining gap between the 24 million Btu contained in a typical ton of coal used by utilities and the almost 14.5 million or so Btu that are lost even in the most efficient plants in the process of burning coal in a boiler to produce steam to drive a turbine to generate electricity. New ways in the offing of generating electricity aim chiefly at converting more of the inherent energy of the fuels into electric energy.

Despite the fact that any energy source, including nuclear fission, may be utilized for producing steam as the driving force in a generator, coal has remained the predominant boiler fuel. Nearly 60 per cent of all electricity is today generated in coal-fired stations. Over the years coal has lost some of this market, but has recently shown a tendency to regain it.

The exceptions are oil on the Pacific Coast, in much of New England, in New York City, parts of western New Jersey, and in Florida; and to a much stronger degree, gas in the Southwest, the Mountain and Pacific states, and some of the West North Central states.

What the future pattern will be, no one can say, but one can narrow down the possibilities of substitution by observing regional patterns, effects of price, and past trends. First, however, it is convenient to identify the parts likely to be played by hydro and nuclear generation; the balance can then be considered to be available for sharing between coal, gas, and oil.

3. The FPC January 30, 1962, revision (Release No. 11,829) puts the Commission's 1980 estimate (including Alaska and Hawaii) at 2,994 billion kwh.

4. Westinghouse Electric Corp., Headquarters Market Planning, *Twenty-Year Predictions of Electric Power Requirements, 1958–1978* (Pittsburgh, September 1958).

5. See, for instance, U.S. Congress, Joint Economic Committee, Subcommittee on Automation and Energy Resources, *Energy Resources and Technology* (Washington, 1959), pp. 49–132.

Hydro power. Although every foot difference in height in the course of a river constitutes a potential source of power, actual exploitation remains far below this level and utilization of existing installations has been declining.

Hydro capacity almost doubled between 1950 and 1960. At the same time, fewer kilowatt-hours have been derived from each kilowatt of installed capacity, so that 1960 generation was only 50 per cent above that of 1950. It is unlikely that the next doubling of either capacity or generation will occur in less than the next two decades. In the final two decades of the century, growth in capacity and output is more likely to be around 35 per cent. At the same time, foreseeing a gradual reorientation of hydro stations from being base-load to becoming peaking facilities—permitting the most efficient thermal stations to serve as base-load—we have assumed that utilization will decline further to just over 45 per cent, or 4,000 kwh per year.

The estimated output series follows FPC thinking as expressed late in 1959 in connection with FPC's estimates prepared for the Senate Select Committee on National Water Resources. Its projections on this occasion represent a substantial upward revision of its earlier work. Our projections differ only in a minor respect: we are inclined to believe that installed capacity may turn out to be larger and utilization somewhat lower, in view of the growing tendency to consider hydro installations as peaking facilities and especially in anticipation of much wider use of pumped-storage installations, in which cheap off-peak thermal power will be used to refill reservoirs that will supply supplementary hydro energy during peak periods.

At the projected 2000 level of 90 million kw of installed capacity, some 75 per cent of what the FPC considers the country's hydro potential —others believe it to be larger—would be exploited. There is no reason why this should not occur, despite the inequalities in the geographic distribution of the potential. For example, if the entire Pacific Northwest potential were exploited and operated at 4,000 kwh per year per kilowatt installed, the amount generated would be about sufficient to fill demand in that area as projected by FPC in 1960 for 1980. Thus, even for this extreme case the level of exploitation

projected would not create any local imbalances, quite apart from the likelihood that by that time extra-high-frequency transmission will have given a vastly different meaning to the term "local." Our projections of future hydro generation, as compared with the record of the past two decades, are as follows:

	Installed capacity year-end (mil. kw)	Generation (bil. kwh)	Generation per year per kw installed (kwh)
1940	11.2	47.3	4,700
1950	17.7	95.9	5,600
1960	32.4	145.5	4,600
1970	55.0	245.0	4,450
1980	65.0	280.0	4,300
1990	78.0	320.0	4,100
2000	90.0	360.0	4,000

Even under these dynamic assumptions, the projected share of hydro power in total power output would decline continuously: from the present 18 per cent to 12.5 per cent in 1980, and to less than 8 per cent by the year 2000. Substantially more optimistic or pessimistic perspectives would not affect the significance of the competing sources of electric power sufficiently to make High and Low projections worth while, especially in a field in which exploitation of power potential is so greatly affected by considerations outside the field of economics, and certainly outside the field of power generation.

Nuclear power generation. The timetable of nuclear power development changes with the rate of progress in reactor technology, actual and anticipated; the experience accumulating in operating stations; and estimates of future costs of nuclear power relative to those of conventional generation. Despite the many uncertainties there are nevertheless some areas of substantial agreement. One is that nuclear power capacity will remain negligible for the first half of the sixties and begin to gather momentum, though only slowly, in the second half. A second is that the seventies will see substantial growth of nuclear power. And a third is that by 1980 upward of one-half—some go as far as two-thirds—of all new additions to generating capacity are likely to consist of nuclear power equipment.

Within this general framework there are substantial degrees of difference in timing. Thus, in their 1957 projection Davis and Roddis, then of the Atomic Energy Commission's Division of Reactor Development, anticipated gross additions to capacity (i.e., inclusive of replacement of retired plant) and nuclear generation's share of total power output as follows:[6]

	Additions (per cent)	Share of output (per cent)
1960	0.7	0.3
1965	8.2	1.9
1970	26.0	7.8
1975	53.0	21.9
1980	67.0	37.8

In a National Planning Association report, Karl Mayer, starting from a detailed analysis of comparative conventional power costs in the eight power supply regions into which the Federal Power Commission has divided the country, has developed a different timetable, far more conservative in terms of share of nuclear power in total electric power generation:[7]

	Per cent
1965	0.8
1970	3.5
1975	11.2
1980	21.3

Mayer's estimates are crucially dependent upon nuclear power costs. Subsequent studies suggest that he has been somewhat pessimistic. His assumption of 9 mills by 1970 now appears on the high side, though not by much. Cost estimates sponsored by the AEC caused the Commission to suggest estimates for plants yet to be built (often referred to as "potential") in a range of 8.3 to 11.8 mills per net kwh, all for sizes in excess of 200-mw capacity, and of 7 to 8 mills for 300-mw plants. Comparative power costs for coal-fired plants, estimated by the same engineering firms, range from 6.9 to 7.4 mills.

6. W. Kenneth Davis and Louis H. Roddis, "The Latest Prospects for Economic Nuclear Power," presented at Fifth Atomic Energy in Industry Conference of National Industrial Conference Board, Philadelphia, March 14, 1957.
7. Karl M. Mayer, "Regional Aspects of Nuclear Power," in *Nuclear Energy and the U.S. Fuel Economy, 1955–1980* (Washington: National Planning Association, July 1958), p. 153.

Construction of any one of the units involved would not be likely to see operation earlier than 1967. Should actual costs be confirmed by operating experience, one might expect similar units to be established after 1970; Mayer's cost assumption of 9 mills by 1970 would then turn out to be within reach for the smaller plants, but would probably be bettered for the larger ones, which are more likely to determine the course of nuclear power generation. Currently, nearly half of all new conventional generating units rate 300 mw and better. Given the much greater significance of capital versus fuel cost in nuclear plants it is reasonable to assume that builders will try to take advantage of economies of scale, to the extent that units are kept small enough to promise high-capacity utilization.

However, even 8 mills does not open up vistas of revolutionary change. According to engineering estimates made for the 1960 McKinney Report,[8] conventional steam plants could reach the nuclear plant unit cost of 8 mills at fuel costs as high as 46 cents per million Btu for coal, 53 cents per million Btu for gas, and 54 cents per million Btu for oil, in plants of similar size and operating characteristics. (The oil and gas prices can be higher because of the higher fixed cost of coal-burning plants.) The national average costs now paid by utilities are 26 cents for coal, 24 cents for gas, and 34 cents for oil, so that it is obvious that the competitive threshold at 8 mills for nuclear power would exist only in areas of exceedingly high fuel cost and locations where large plants are economical.

Utility fuel cost data for 1958 indicate that less than a dozen stations in the country would fall within that range, and the majority of those owe their high fuel costs to freakish situations, such as extremely low operation and consequently high prices. For example, the seven plants in Massachusetts that are involved purchased only 50,000 tons of coal between them in 1958, five of them less than 7,000 tons each. Published state averages of fuel cost are often apt to mislead, as they may include, in a region burning coal, one or two plants burning a mi-

8. Joint Committee on Atomic Energy, *Background Material for the Review of the International Atomic Policies and Programs of the United States*, Vol. 4, October 1960, pp. 1031–92.

nute quantity of oil at a very high price: hence a very high oil price for that state. In 1958 the statistics show sixteen states burning oil at a cost of 53 cents or more (up to 92.1 in West Virginia) per million Btu. Yet in the entire country only two plants burn oil in significant quantities at a price above 53 cents. Thus it is obvious that only at a level substantially below 8 mills would even high-fuel-cost areas become interested in nuclear reactors on a significant scale.

When newly constructed plants, rather than all, are considered, the competitive cost threshold that nuclear installations must attain drops even lower. In its steam station cost survey for 1960, *Electrical World* culled from the FPC data some fifty-odd new plants or old (but post-1950) plants with new units for which it computed energy cost.[9] Here the average was 6.9 mills per net kwh, with a sizeable number turning in performances below this level.

However, only three of these plants were in New England and two in the Pacific region, and all of these had energy costs above 7 mills per net kwh. Other plants, in areas scattered from the southern Atlantic states to the Canadian border, showed costs both below and above the 6.9 mill level. This suggests that there is no one cost level at which nuclear energy will become competitive; in this regard Mayer's projections are on the right track, even though beset by difficulties of predicting future conventional generating cost.

Actually, there is now in sight an installed nuclear capacity of close to 2 million kw by 1965. Even at the low rate of 5,000 hours of operation per year (most cost calculations are based upon an 80 per cent operating factor, equal to 7,000 hours), total generation in 1965 or 1966 would approach 10 billion kwh. This is similar to Mayer's projection of 7.8 billion kwh, but there is one difference: only a small portion of this generation is likely to be competitive in 1965. Even those now claimed to be competitive are so by the narrowest of margins and by assumption of a 90 per cent plant factor. The question of competitiveness is still quite open, and is likely to remain so for a few years. Nor are there any significant plans for nuclear instal-

9. *Electrical World,* October 2, 1961.

lations beyond the 2 million-kw capacity to be in operation by 1965. It is possible that much will be learned from the 300,000-kw reactor that the Pacific Gas and Electric Company is planning to build at Bodega Bay, California. By assuming a very high operating rate, power costs have been demonstrated to be less than 6 mills per kwh and just barely below those achievable with conventional fuels (in this instance, oil). One of the motivating factors in proceeding now is undoubtedly that such a plant, even if not now competitive, may be competitive over its life-time, since its performance can be continually improved as better efficiency in fuel elements is reached. Plants using conventional fuels can look forward to little or no improvement of this kind, once the generating unit has been installed.

Under these conditions, it seems reasonable to interpose an initial "hesitancy" factor that has little to do with the theoretical level of cost but much with a wait-and-see attitude. With experience in the first half of the sixties and further research and development, one can expect a new wave of construction that will bear fruit by 1970 but will lag behind the timetable computed by Mayer.

We have therefore adopted Mayer's approach and extended it in a rough-and-ready manner to the year 2000. However, except for the final decade, in calculating nuclear generation's share of all electricity generation the results of applying the percentage shares developed in Mayer's projections to projected total generation have been reduced, in view of current hesitations.

On the assumption that the principal element in differing estimates is timing, there is good reason for hazarding High and Low projections of nuclear generation. We have assumed half the Medium rate of additions as the Low and twice the Medium rate of additions as the High.

The three levels of projection take the following shape:

	Low	Medium	High
		(*billion kwh*)	
1960	–	–	–
1970	20	35	50
1980	220	400	580
1990	620	1,200	1,680
2000	1,230	2,400	3,480

Because of the slow development of nuclear power, which is the most nearly commercial new source of energy, we have made no quantitative projections of other unconventional energy, such as solar, tidal, wind, geothermal, and other sources. Nor have we new conversion devices, such as magneto-hydrodynamics, thermionic devices, and others, been taken into account statistically in our projections. Their nature is, however, discussed further in Chapter 20, and their positive effect on the heat rate on page 288.

Conventional thermal generation. Sharing of thermal generating equipment among the fossil fuels is determined principally by relative price movements as well as by relative growth rates in the economy of the different regions. As the Southwest burns gas, so New England burns oil and the East North Central states fire coal. With differences in growth come differences in fuel emphasis.

The regional growth pattern seems to favor gas. On the assumption that reported future additions to generating capacity constitute a reasonable preview of expansion, we note that the majority of the regions which show an above-average utility expansion program are regions in which gas is either the sole fuel (West South Central), or the predominant fuel with a consistently growing share of the total (Mountains and West North Central), or a region in

which gas has been gaining (South Atlantic and Pacific). East South Central is the only region with above-average expansion and domination of coal, indeed almost to the exclusion of any other fuel. Furthermore, imports of gas from Canada are likely to augment the future supply in many areas.

This becomes especially striking when a similar quick rundown is made for oil. It can then be seen that oil is strong only in New England and the Pacific states, though it has been rapidly losing ground to gas in the latter, holds a stable but weak position in the South Atlantic region, and has been especially weakening in the regions in which increases in capacity are likely to run above average. Future hydro capacity (with qualifications explained below), imported gas, and nuclear installations all represent potential competition to oil in the regions in which it is now of significance. (See Table 15–2.)

The favorable short-run prognosis for gas as boiler fuel developed up to this point is, however, dampened by considerations of price, and price in turn is strongly connected with regulation and with the future development of gas storage. A significant portion of the gas consumed by utilities is sold on an interruptible basis, as a means of providing a market when more lucrative uses are seasonally depressed; it carries a correspondingly low price tag. The creation of increased storage would enable gas

TABLE 15–2.   Regional Utility Expansion Plans and Pattern of Fuel Use

Region	Steam capacity at end of 1960[1] (mil. kw)	% of total	Planned post–1960 addition[1] (mil. kw)	% of total	Generation by coal as % of total[2] 1948	1952	1958	Generation by oil as % of total[2] 1948	1952	1958	Generation by gas as % of total[2] 1948	1952	1958
New England	5,397	4.3	1,618	4.1	82.2	51.6	65.0	17.8	48.4	30.2	–	–	4.8
Mid-Atlantic	21,400	16.9	4,308	11.0	94.5	85.2	79.7	5.5	9.9	11.3	–	4.9	9.0
E. N. Central	28,951	22.9	6,553	16.7	97.1	90.1	96.1	1.2	0.7	0.5	1.7	9.2	3.4
W. N. Central	8,981	7.1	3,670	9.4	53.6	42.0	42.0	12.3	6.9	2.2	34.0	50.8	55.8
S. Atlantic	19,601	15.5	6,748	17.2	80.5	74.6	75.0	14.5	16.1	16.9	5.0	9.3	8.1
E. S. Central	13,269	10.5	5,306	13.5	82.3	72.3	92.6	0.6	0.2	0.1	17.1	27.5	7.3
W. S. Central	15,335	12.1	5,725	14.6	1.5	0.6	–	3.5	1.1	0.2	95.0	98.3	99.8
Mountain	3,389	2.7	2,295	5.9	31.5	20.1	18.0	10.1	13.7	8.7	58.1	65.9	73.3
Pacific	10,167	8.0	2,961	7.6	0.2	0.1	–	53.4	49.6	32.5	41.9	47.1	67.5
United States	126,490	100.0	39,153	100.0	76.4	66.5	68.3	8.4	10.1	8.0	15.0	23.2	23.7

1. *Electrical World*, February 27, 1961, pp. 92–103.
2. 1948 and 1952: Computed from Reports by the Federal Power Commission; because of small amounts of other fuels burned, sum of items does not always add to 100. Data for 1958 from Edison Electric Institute, *Electric Utility Industry Statistics*, 1959.

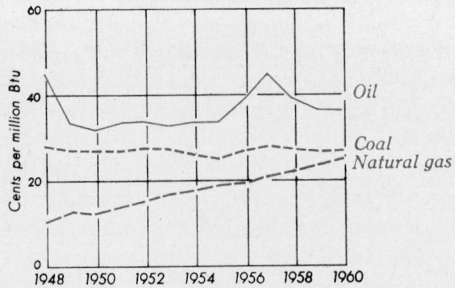

Figure 15–4. Prices paid by electric utilities for delivered fuel, 1948–1960.

distributing companies to accumulate stocks during periods of low residential, commercial, and other premium-price demand and thus benefit from year-round high-load pipeline operations without being forced to sell cheap off-season gas to utilities and other industrial users.

The development is not an unlikely one, though it would add just one more boosting factor to the gas price. The price of gas to utilities more than doubled between 1948 and 1960, while the cost of coal and oil to the utilities on the whole remained stable, or even declined. This by itself would not threaten the position of gas (indeed the share of gas in the utility market nearly doubled during the same twelve years) unless in any given area its price per unit of heat value were to exceed that of coal or oil.[10]

A comparison of cost per million Btu illustrates that, *on the national average,* this has not as yet happened. However, there has been a marked creeping up of the gas cost to the coal cost (as shown in Figure 15–4). Whereas in 1948 the cost of coal to utilities was 170 per cent above that of gas, in 1960, coal, on the national average, cost barely 7 per cent more than gas. Thus, as gas has penetrated from the areas of production in the West South Central states to the North and East, its price has risen by having to carry heavier transportation charges (apart from increases in the wellhead price and the effects of escalation). To the extent that the states more remote from sources of gas will increase their consumption, the rise in the na-

10. This is a crude yardstick and would need adjustment for economies or diseconomies attending the use of one or the other fuel.

tional average price is slowed only by the growth in supply from areas other than the Southwest and the emergence of the gas price from an era of underpricing in terms of heat value. On balance, further price increases appear likely, though at a more moderate pace.

The national average, however, is broadly indicative rather than helpful in quantitative analysis. The margin between the price of gas and that of coal is sufficiently large in the Southwest, the major portion of the Mountain states, and in parts of the Midwest to make these areas immune to significant inroads of coal for the foreseeable future. One cannot overlook the fact that in 1950 oil held as high a share as 14 per cent of the utility fuel market, at a time when its national average cost to the utilities was almost 20 per cent above that of coal; or that between 1955 and 1960 consumption of gas as utility boiler fuel in the Middle Atlantic states increased by some 110 per cent, of coal by less than 15 per cent, while the cost excess of gas over coal increased from 2.4 to 5.7 cents per million Btu.

One would not want to formulate new laws of price and demand relationship on the basis of such data, but look for meaningful relationships and magnitudes. For one thing, size of the "preempted" areas is very important. Counting the West South Central states as a gas preserve, we implicitly set a floor of 11 per cent of the utility fuel market for gas. With parts of the Mountain, Pacific, and the southern portion of the West North Central states (Kansas, Missouri) having similar characteristics, it is hard to foresee a rapid decline in the share of the market held by gas, and even after the emergence of nuclear energy as a competitive force in power generation it is likely that there will remain a solid core of power facilities that will enjoy sufficiently low gas prices to ward off competing fuels or modes of generation.

Even within smaller areas the effect of price is difficult to isolate and analyze. Sometimes emergence of a single new plant, located in a part of a state that has—or can create—economic access to a fuel not previously important, can completely obscure the situation. For example, the long-term contract of a Tampa utility company for coal created a large, low-cost coal market in that area, giving the price of coal in 1960 an advantage of over 10 per cent for Florida as a whole. This compares with a price penalty of almost 20 per cent in 1955. Yet, in the same five years, natural gas, the cost of which to utilities in the area rose from 22 to 34 cents per million Btu, managed to raise its share of the fuel market from 7 to 44 per cent, simply by replacing oil.

In six out of fifteen states in which coal in 1960 enjoyed a cost advantage over gas, coal's advantage had narrowed since 1955, in contrast to the national picture in which gas prices have been rapidly catching up with coal.

Out of such conflicting data one cannot fashion directly any projection of the share that gas is likely to hold of the future utility fuel market. On balance, the use of gas as utility fuel may well be approaching its peak, but its eventual decline, for the reasons cited, is likely to be slow. The development of the percentage shares shown below reflects this view.[11] (These percentages are established without regard to the long-run supply of each fuel or, consequently, to the long-run cost picture. Whatever modifications seem to be called for by such considerations are dealt with in Chapter 20.)

	1960	1980	2000
		(Per cent)	
Nuclear	–	17.9	51.1
Hydro	17.6	12.7	7.6
Coal	53.7	47.1	29.6
Oil	6.9	3.8	2.3
Gas	21.8	18.5	9.4

The same table also indicates our conclusions concerning the future role of oil as a utility fuel. It seems extremely unlikely that oil will be able to retain even its present small share of the market. It is subject to competitive threats by gas, and nuclear energy in many areas, also by

11. A somewhat different view has been advanced by Philip Sporn. In his projection of 6,000 billion kwh requirements by the year 2000 (noted on p. 000) he assigns shares of total generation as follows: nuclear, 53.4 per cent; hydro, 5.8; coal, 37.5; oil, 0.8; and gas, 2.5. Sporn calls his nuclear estimate a maximum. "It may—and most likely will—be quite a bit lower, and the share provided by fossil fuels correspondingly higher," he testified before the Senate Committee on Interior and Insular Affairs in 1961 (*National Fuels Study,* Hearings before the Committee, June 12, 1961, p. 79). In absolute terms, it amounts to 3,200 billion kwh, compared with the Medium estimate of 2,400 billion kwh projected in this study.

coal in Florida, and perhaps by hydro in California. Accordingly, we believe its relative share will decline slowly but continuously through 1980; for the balance of the period we have left it at the 5 per cent of the total thermal generation market it is assumed to reach in that year. It is in any event of little consequence in the total oil picture, and only a radical liberalization in import policy that would allow heavy landings at low prices would cause any change in this outlook.

Efficiency: The Heat Rate

There remain to be estimated the amounts of fossil fuels required to generate the calculated output of electricity. This is perhaps the least shaky of the many projection bridges we have to cross in this sequence. The amounts of coal, gas, and oil that have in the past gone into utility generation are known with precision. Second, the historical record of the heat rate, that is, the amount of Btu's required to generate one kilowatt-hour of electricity (net of power consumed in generating stations for auxiliary purposes), exhibits a trend of improved efficiency that is both consistent and logical. Third, the further technological improvement that is expected may be estimated by the current gap between the experience of the most advanced and that of the average plant, as well as by criteria in the engineering field.

The systematic improvement in generating efficiency is shown in Appendix Table A15–10. Heat rates do differ between the three fuels, but more because of the engineering characteristics of the array of central stations in which each fuel is used than because of intrinsic qualities of the fuels themselves. For example, in 1960 eleven of the twelve most efficient plants—generating at a heat rate of 9,250 Btu per net kwh or less—were coal-fired stations. Located in areas accessible to low-priced coal, the majority of these efficient coal-burning plants had large, newly built generating facilities and boasted the most progressive engineering features. On a broader basis (as shown in Appendix Table A15–8), coal-fired stations have the lowest heat rate (or highest efficiency); gas-fired plants are next and, in fact, show a slightly faster rate of improvement than coal plants. Relatively more gas-fired plants have been built in the past decade than oil-fired ones, so that they are on the whole the more efficient group.

The reduction in Btu requirements per net kwh between 1948 and 1960 has been 32 per cent for coal, 34 for gas, and 26 for oil. The over-all reduction has been about 32 per cent. This rate of improvement is unlikely to continue. Larger size of turbo-generators, as well as higher temperatures and steam pressures, will be increasingly more difficult to attain and bring less and less spectacular advantages, so that a leveling off in the heat rate improvement may be expected. Only sharp increases in fuel prices —not in prospect—would stimulate the kind of capital investment that would be required for an all-out effort at efficiency. On the other hand, the level of performance attained in today's most efficient plants clearly sets a target toward which one may expect the average to move—as has indeed happened in the past with a time lag varying from ten to twenty-five years. The 9,000-Btu/kwh threshold was successfully crossed in 1960 and has been improved since, and the number of plants doing better than 10,000 Btu per kwh grew from two in 1950 to eighty-three in 1960.

On this basis one might perhaps assume top performance in coal-fired utility plants of 7,500 Btu per net kwh by 1980, corresponding to a thermal efficiency of 45 per cent, as has been suggested in recent years.[12] Assuming that it takes twenty years for the top accomplishment to become the industry average, it is difficult to anticipate the 7,500-Btu/kwh rate to become general much before the year 2000. The rates for the intervening years can then be interpolated, with 1960 as a point of departure.

There is one important qualification here: to the extent that new means of conversion from heat to energy become commercially feasible, far better heat rates could be obtained. With magneto-hydrodynamic generation, efficiencies of 60 per cent and better might be reached

12. See, for example, James H. Harlow, "Steam Plant Improvements Projected to 1980," *Prospects for Economic Nuclear Power,* Studies in Business Policy, No. 83 (New York: National Industrial Conference Board, 1957); or C. W. Elston and J. E. Downs, in "Future of the Steam Heat Cycle," 19th Annual Meeting, American Power Conference, March 1957.

(equal to 5,700 Btu/kwh). Similar levels could be attained by combining steam generation based upon nuclear reaction with some direct, thermionic conversion of the extreme heat generated in the reactor. It is possible that either or both of these developments will bring down heat rates below those here assumed. But it is unlikely that the *average* rate for the industry as a whole will be much affected, except perhaps toward the very end of the century. Philip Sporn, in his projections, assumes an average heat rate of 7,000 by the end of the century.[13] His utility system's Breed plant was the most efficient operator in 1961—at less than 8,800 Btu per kwh—and thus optimism is well founded. But for the purposes of this study the somewhat more conservative assumption of an industry-wide rate of 7,500 has seemed more appropriate. This would represent a decline of roughly 3,000 Btu per kwh, or nearly 30 per cent from present levels.

Other Fuel Requirements

Now that we can add projections of fuel requirements for generation of electricity to the energy requirements already developed in Part I, it remains only to take account of the miscellaneous uses, many of which are not related to heat or power, that have not previously been covered. When these trends have been noted, we are in a position to consider the possible future course of total demand for mineral fuels.

Natural gas. The following four classes of gas use have not been previously examined:

a) Losses of gas in the shape of gas vented or wasted. These have experienced a steady decline since the end of World War II, as the value of gas has risen and steps have been taken to capture an increasing percentage for commercial use. In 1960 the total amount so lost was no more than it had been in the late thirties, although in the meantime total gas production had risen five- to sixfold. Theoretically, it is entirely possible for this ratio to decline to zero. It was halved between 1947 and 1953 and halved again between 1953 and 1959. Indeed, in some producing states it is nil even now, and in

13. U.S. Congress, Joint Economic Committee, *op. cit.*

the biggest producing state, Texas, it runs less than 4 per cent. In some other states, however, where distribution lines or other consumption channels are less accessible, waste reaches 10 per cent and more. For our purposes we have assumed a decline to 4 per cent by 1970, 3 per cent by 1980, and a stabilization at that level thereafter. While such losses of gas do not represent "demand" in the ordinary sense, they must be regarded as a mode of disappearance when resource adequacy is considered. There is probably a tendency to understate this category statistically because wasting gas is illegal, or at least frowned upon, in most states. Spectacular disagreement between Census data and Bureau of Mines data has been pointed out by Teitelbaum for 1954.[14]

b)Transmission losses. These include quantities unaccounted for, as otherwise the percentage that such losses form of marketed production would seem unreasonably high. They have in the last two decades constituted a rather unvarying percentage of marketed production, never exceeding 3.8 per cent or falling below 2.2 per cent.

c) Carbon black manufacture. At its peak, during the mid-forties, this specialized outlet for natural gas accounted for nearly 10 per cent of all net marketed production. By 1960 it had dropped to about 2 per cent. New processes and the substitution of oil for gas have led to the declining importance of carbon black manufacture as a gas consumer. We have assumed that this process will continue, but that a hard core of plants will remain as gas users.

d) Pipeline fuel. Here again, projection is aided by historical constancy. For the past ten years the relationship between marketed quantity—as defined in the Appendix—and fuel consumed to power the gas pipelines has stuck so close to 3½ per cent that one feels no compulsion to project anything different for the future.

Petroleum. A number of minor products derived in the refining process, and some secondary uses of principal products need to be

14. Perry D. Teitelbaum, *Energy Production and Consumption in the United States: An Analytical Study Based on 1954 Data,* Bureau of Mines Report of Investigations 5821 (Washington: U.S. Bureau of Mines and Resources for the Future, 1961).

dealt with briefly to complete the demand picture. Among the former are lubricants, wax, petroleum coke, and naphtha; the latter include the use of petroleum for carbon black manufacture and for chemical processes (not to be confused with the use of refinery *gas* for such processes), the quantity lost in handling, and finally "miscellaneous" uses. In the past, these uses have aggregated something of the order of 5 per cent of total petroleum demand. We have used this figure to raise the demand projections accordingly throughout the period. The slower demand for lubricants in evidence for some time now, based upon the emergence of permanent or less frequent lubrication of machinery and vehicles, can be assumed to be balanced by more rapidly growing demand for carbon black from petroleum and for crude oil as a basis for chemicals.

Natural gas liquids. The only significant demand for natural gas liquids not projected in Part I is their use in the manufacture of chemical products, a fast-growing segment of the economy. Indeed, growth has been so explosive that it is difficult to derive meaningful past relationships with other elements of the economy. An attempt to do so has been made in Chapter 17 (Chemicals) and the results have been taken account of in the comprehensive projections set down in Table 15–3.

Future Energy Demand Trends

The aggregate demand for the conventional fuels can now be established. There are a few technical difficulties that are dealt with in the Appendix to Chapter 15. One concerns the allocation of demand for natural gas liquids (natural gasoline and liquid petroleum gas) to crude oil and natural gas, respectively; demand exists only for finished gasoline as such, and for LPG as such, regardless of origin. Another is due to the fact that there are as a rule no statistics for specific end-uses of energy materials. These of necessity must be rough approximations, and only the sum of the end-uses can be checked against apparent consumption of the energy material. For 1960, aggregated end-uses, as here developed, have in all cases accounted for at

TABLE 15–3.   Demand for Energy, by Source, 1940, 1960, and Medium Projections for 1980, 2000

Source	1940	1960	1980	2000
	Physical quantities			
Petroleum (bil. bbl.)	1.41	3.19	5.34	10.03
Natural gas (tril. cu. ft.)	3.29	12.87	23.47	32.78
NGL (bil. bbl.)	.06	.34	.75	1.56
Coal (mil. tons)	499	436	630	718
Hydro (bil. kwh)	52	149	283	363
Nuclear (bil. kwh)	–	–	400	2,400
	Btu (quadrillion)[1]			
Petroleum	8.2	17.7	29.5	54.8
Natural gas	3.4	13.3	24.2	33.8
NGL	.2	1.6	3.4	6.8
Coal	13.0	11.1	15.8	18.0
Hydro	.9	1.6	2.6	2.8
Nuclear	–	–	3.7	19.0
Total	25.8	45.3	79.2	135.2
	Percentage distribution[1]			
Petroleum	31.8	39.1	37.2	40.5
Natural gas	13.3	29.2	30.5	25.0
NGL	0.9	3.6	4.3	5.1
Coal	50.4	24.5	19.9	13.3
Hydro	3.6	3.6	3.4	2.1
Nuclear	–	–	4.7	14.0
Total	100	100	100	100

Source: Appendix Table A15–19.
1. Totals may not add because of rounding.

least 95 per cent of statistical disappearance. End-use summations have been raised—or lowered—to conform to the statistical disappearance in 1960 and adjusted similarly throughout the projection period. The implicit assumption that the omissions (or errors) will be moving proportionately with the total of the identified end-uses is not disturbing in view of the magnitudes involved.

Table 15–3 incorporates the summary results of the Medium demand projections, both in terms of physical quantities and, for purposes of illuminating the relative magnitudes, in Btu's. For the latter comparison (see also Figure 15–5), both hydro and nuclear power generation have been converted to Btu's on the basis of the projected heat rate that has been assumed to prevail in conventional thermal generation for the particular year.

This tabulation does not represent a forecast or prediction. The quantities shown to be "demanded" are abstractions that have not been subjected to the test of cost involved in supply-

ing the requisite amounts. With that qualification, we may note several surprises. One is the relatively minor role that, even forty years hence, nuclear energy is projected to play. By the year 2000, its share in total energy consumption emerges as 14 per cent, or about the same as the share of coal at that time. The latter, of course, represents a greatly diminished share, though in absolute terms coal is slated to rise by nearly 65 per cent, fast in the sixties and seventies and more slowly thereafter. Indeed, our projections would strongly indicate that the early sixties might prove the turning point in the domestic demand for coal, bituminous and anthracite jointly. Nonetheless, the forces making for its emergence from a long decline do not seem powerful enough to prevent it from sliding back in its relative share of the energy market. The 700 million ton level projected by the end of the century is only 15 per cent above the level reached during the peak years of the forties. Given the vast advances in coal-mining technology since that time and, one must pre-

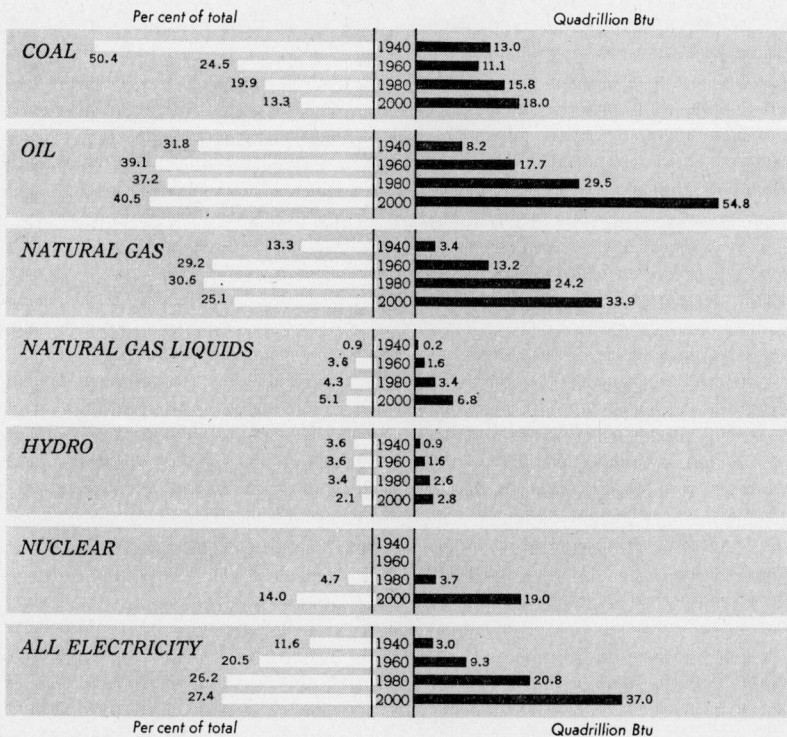

Figure 15–5. Changes in energy source patterns, 1940, 1960, and Medium projections for 1980 and 2000.

sume, further progress in the future, it seems likely that coal mining will continue to provide a livelihood for a steadily declining labor force.

Oil and natural gas, on the other hand, are projected to increase enough, or more than enough, to maintain their place in the demand pattern for fuel, provided supply conditions are such that the demand can be filled at stable relative prices, a question further explored in Chapter 20.

The emergence of nuclear energy affects gas in the latter part of the period, and the growth in demand for gas in other uses (principally households) is not strong enough to keep it from sliding. Oil shares so little in power generation and other industrial uses, and is so preponderantly the fuel for transportation uses, that only the development of nuclear-powered land vehicles could seriously threaten its position. Such a development is not at present in sight, but it might well come into view in the

course of the next decade or two. Similarly, a fuel cell based on energy sources other than liquid hydrocarbons could seriously jeopardize the role of oil in the energy picture.

The rate of growth of all but one of the different energy sources is projected to decline; the exception is coal, which appears to be in for a reversal of trend, from decline to increase. But there is not enough difference in the behavior of the various fuels to greatly affect the relative shares after 1960, other than coal, as shown by the percentage distributions in Table 15–3.

One other comparison is of interest. Energy use per unit of GNP has been declining ever since World War I.[15] This decline will apparently continue during the balance of the century, though not at the rapid rate at which it occurred prior to 1960. The projected drop in energy

15. Sam H. Schurr, Bruce C. Netschert, *et al., Energy in the American Economy, 1850–1975* (Baltimore: Johns Hopkins Press and Resources for the Future, 1960).

TABLE 15–4.   Energy Use per Unit of Gross National Product, 1940–1960 and Medium Projections to 2000

Item	1940	1950	1960	Medium projection			
				1970	1980	1990	2000
GNP (1960 $ bil.)	234	363	503	746	1,060	1,510	2,200
Energy use (quadr. Btu)	25.8	36.4	45.3	60.2	79.2	101.9	135.2
Energy use per $ GNP (thous. Btu)	110	100	90	80	75	67	61

Sources: Appendix Tables A1–12 and A15–19.

consumed per constant dollar of GNP is about 10 per cent every ten years. Over the entire period of forty years it would decline by 32 per cent, equal to an annual compound rate of decline of 1 per cent. This is roughly equal to the assumed rate of decline in the heat rate of electric power generation. It thus appears that the net effect in output changes and energy use will be to bring about the same improvement in the efficiency of total energy use as is in prospect for the electric power industry. This is not a bad prospect, and one that might even be improved by the development of new technologies that reap far greater economies in terms of efficiency than could be hoped for from the improvement of conventional methods.

chapter
16

METALS

GROWTH IN METALS CONSUMPTION is one of the best single measures of man's material progress. Since the start of the nineteenth century U.S. population and income growth have been accompanied by a growth in iron and steel production from less than 100,000 tons annually to about 100 million tons today—or from some 30 pounds per capita to around half a ton. This latter figure is roughly double the per capita consumption of most of the industrialized countries of western Europe. In general, the United States accounts for about one-third to one-half the non-communist world's total consumption of all of the principal metals.

In spite of recent increasing use of plastics and other synthetics, and the possible future use of relatively greater quantities of stone, gravel, and cement, it is improbable that the relative importance of metals will diminish much between now and the year 2000; certainly, absolute growth will continue to be large. If we use the primary metals portion of the projected industrial production index as the means of summing a large and heterogeneous group, we may foresee an average annual metals growth of 3.1 per cent in the next forty years (Medium projection), compared with 3.3 per cent during the last forty years. The 3.1 per cent rate compares with a projected average growth of 3.8 per cent per year in our Medium GNP series and 1.5 per cent in population. It seems clear, therefore, that metals use per capita in the United States will continue to rise while per dollar of gross national product, it will decline.

Not all of the future growth in metals consumption will be confined to present-day applications, even though the breadth of these applications is already vast. Passenger cars, machinery, and steel girders are among the obvious uses of materials characterized by strength, toughness, and endurance. But at the other extreme are such uses as that of nickel as a catalyst in vegetable oil hydrogenation, zinc oxide in rubber, or lead in gasoline. Metals can withstand the influences of time, weather, and large loads, and they can also fulfill the functions of a paper clip. Some can withstand strong corrosive chemicals, others are excellent conductors of electricity. Metals

---

RELATED MATERIAL: Appendix to this chapter, pp. 859–939. Requirements for construction, Chapter 4, pp. 121–23, 125, 126, and appendix, pp. 629–31, 633, 634; for transportation, Chapter 5, pp. 142–45, and appendix, pp. 654–59, 663, 665, 667; for durables, Chapter 6, pp. 155–57, and appendix, pp. 680–84; for containers, Chapter 7, pp. 161–64, and appendix, pp. 693–95; for military goods, Chapter 9, pp. 177–83, and appendix, pp. 715–21. Adequacy of the nonfuel minerals, including the minor metals, Chapter 21, pp. 422–83.

that can retain their characteristics under intense heat have been developed along with others that will not succumb to severe cold. Metals are being used for rocket fuel; indeed, in the field of outer space we may see more and more of a topsy-turvy situation in which metals are burned and petroleum, as plastic, makes up the structure of things.

This chapter does not attempt to deal with all of U.S. metals consumption. Iron and steel, aluminum, copper, lead, zinc, and tin are covered in more or less detail, as are the additives and alloying elements that go into steel production. Other metals are briefly dealt with in Chapter 21. The complete list of metals is a long one, and it does not detract from the importance of some of the more unfamiliar metals, whose quantities used commercially are very small, to point out that their range of intersubstitutability is quite large, so that scarcities in any one usually involve only inconveniences of redesign rather than stumbling blocks to end-item production. Shortages of these small-quantity metals, when they develop, are usually the result of new magnitudes of demand pressing upon exploration, mining, and extraction activity attuned to lower levels, and not of any basic scarcity of the resource itself.

General Trends and Concepts

There are great differences between the annual consumption of iron and steel and that of the nonferrous metals. The fact that the two groups are considered jointly at all is primarily due to the sharply increasing use of aluminum, which is replacing steel in so many ways as to have marked effect upon steel consumption. The extent of the substitution in regard to transportation equipment has already been indicated in Chapter 5. The more general picture of prospective substitution, including substitution of the nonferrous metals for one another, is shown in Table 16–1.

The percentages shown in the table are based on the assumption that the metals may be equated to one another in terms of their volume. This is far from an accurate equivalence for many kinds of applications, but as a general common denominator it is as good as

TABLE 16–1. Relative Consumption of tne Principal Metals, 1960 and Projections for 1980, 2000

(Per cent of total)

Metal	1960		1980	2000
Iron and steel	90.3	L	84.9	78.7
		M	84.5	78.5
		H	82.4	77.1
Aluminum	5.7	L	10.9	16.8
		M	11.2	17.0
		H	13.5	18.2
Copper	2.0	L	2.1	2.2
		M	2.2	2.4
		H	2.1	2.5
Zinc	1.1	L	1.3	1.6
		M	1.3	1.4
		H	1.3	1.5
Lead	.9	L	.8	.7
		M	.7	.7
		H	.7	.7

L = Low projection   M = Medium   H = High.
Source: See sources for Table 16–2. Original data converted to relative volumes on the basis of specific gravities.

any and better than weight. The importance of aluminum in the table comes about mostly as the result of its relative lightness and consequent high volume per pound. How small, for the most part, the tonnage of all of the non-ferrous metals continues in relation to steel is shown in Table 16–2.

Another caution must be added. Metals, in their pristine state, rarely find their way into any product. Rather, they are alloyed in countless combinations. To calculate consumption levels, therefore, we generally had to consider the metals as used—steel with its associated zinc, tin, tungsten, nickel, chromium, and the like; aluminum with its magnesium, copper, and zinc; copper with its lead and zinc; and so on. Then, wherever possible, estimates of the pure metal flows were abstracted.

In short, the capacity of the metallurgists to develop more and more alloys for more and more purposes has the consequence of progressively blurring the demand picture for the various metals. The demand for aluminum, for example, can really be worked out only in terms of "aluminum-base" alloys, and we must accept the uncertainty of not knowing how

TABLE 16–2. Consumption of the Principal Metals, 1960 and Projections for 1980, 2000

(Million tons)

Metal	1960		1980	2000
Iron and steel	72	L	76	89
		M	121	194
		H	176	378
Aluminum	1.6	L	3.4	6.6
		M	5.6	14.7
		H	10.1	31.1
Copper	1.8	L	2.2	2.8
		M	3.6	6.8
		H	5.2	14.0
Zinc	.9	L	1.2	1.7
		M	1.8	3.4
		H	2.7	7.2
Lead	1.0	L	1.0	1.1
		M	1.5	2.3
		H	2.2	4.9

L = Low projection   M = Medium   H = High.
Source: Appendix Tables A16–9, 32, 44, 52, and 61.

much of a deduction to allow for the fraction that is not aluminum. The proliferation of alloys has other consequences. By extending the range of capabilities of each it makes them increasingly substitutable for one another. On the one hand, this makes the future of each of the metals that much harder to project; on the other hand, it reduces the possibilities of shortage. Increasingly, it is not steel, or aluminum, or copper, etc., for which the economy of the future will be generating demands, but metals in the aggregate, and the specific form in which they appear will be as much a matter of competitive economics as of technical requirements.

Our High and Low projections for each of the metals reflect these uncertainties. For example, the trend of recent years has been toward a decreasing unit use of zinc in motor vehicles (employed primarily in the form of die castings). Our working judgment has been that this trend will probably continue, although at a gradually decreasing arithmetic rate, and this has been the basis for our Medium projection. One cannot ignore the possibility, however, of a more rapid decrease, resulting either from the faster substitution of aluminum for the hardware and decorative parts in which

most of the automotive zinc is used, or from a relative decline in the amount of decoration, or both. At the other end, one cannot ignore the first ventures into a completely new automotive use of zinc—as undercoating—and the possibility that this may become widespread, or the possibility that the substitution of aluminum for zinc has gone about as far as it can go. Our Low and High projections, therefore, indicate the substantial breadth of these possibilities. In doing so, we must continue to ignore the possible constraints or opportunities inherent in potential cost increases or decreases apart from current trends. For it is only after we have toted up the demand for each of the metals in its full potential breadth and compared this range with the supplies potentially available, as we do in Chapter 21, that one can reach any valid price inferences.

Concept of demand or consumption. In view of the foregoing assumption as to prices—continuation of past trends—our references to "demand," "requirements," or "consumption" have the common meaning: the actual or projected consumption for a metal given inertia (past trends) and prospective technological, sociological, and institutional changes to the extent that we can postulate them. This is only the beginning of definition, however, for there are few statistical measurements quite so ambiguous as the consumption of a metal. To understand the term, it is necessary to have an idea of the processes that metals go through from the time they leave the mine to the time they end up in a skyscraper, toaster, or automobile. These are not the same for all metals, but there are certain generalities that may be observed.

Most metals come out of the earth, in the form of ore. Ores are sometimes used almost in the form in which they are extracted: for example, bauxite, the ore of aluminum, may be subjected to a roasting process and then used directly (as alumina, or aluminum oxide) for the making of abrasive devices. The aluminum as such has never been extracted, but if we are eventually to compare demand with resources, we cannot ignore this as a form of consumption of aluminum. Similarly, some iron ore is used for the making of pigments rather than iron, much chromite for the making of firebrick rather than chromium, and most rutile (one of the ores of titanium) for the manufacture of paint. In each case, the metal has not been extracted, but there has been a drain on the primary metal supply.

More commonly, however, ore is mined for its metallic content, and the processes subsequent to mining are all designed to isolate the metal and to purify it. At or near the mine the ore is usually "concentrated," but it is still ore, i.e., a mineral or aggregate of minerals, not a metal. The next stage is usually "smelting," a furnace operation which chemically wrests the metal from the chemical compound in which it naturally occurs. The blast furnace is one of the instruments of this stage, wresting pig iron from iron ore. Other smelter products include blister copper and lead bullion. In some cases the smelter is not really a furnace—as in the case of aluminum and a large proportion of metallic zinc, which are electrolytically extracted from their chemical compounds.

Once the metal is extracted, it may be further refined, alloyed, or changed in its chemical or molecular structure for particular purposes. Steel is no more than iron with controlled amounts of carbon "impurities" chemically incorporated into it; thus treated, the iron is tougher and readier for the rolling mill or other processing into shapes and forms. Similarly, copper is electrolytically refined before being drawn into wire or processed for most other uses, aluminum is alloyed, lead is softened and "desilverized."

Whatever the processes, there is a stage at which the metal shows up in its most homogeneous form. Thereafter, it begins to be differentiated—mostly in shape and size, but sometimes chemically as well. The principal processes involve forming the metal into billets, rods, bars, wire, rails, beams, sheet, foil, extrusions, castings, and other basic forms, all of which are ordinarily referred to as the products of a mill or a foundry (the latter for castings). Each of these mill or foundry products is, in most cases, still potential raw material for a great variety of end-products and does not go into its final differentiation (or commitment to a specific end-use) until it gets into the succeeding stage—generally referred to as "fabrication."

If all of the metal ending up in products for consumption or investment flowed right on through this pipeline, there would be little problem in measurement: whatever the metering point, the amount would be the same. A glance at Figure 16–1, however, quickly shows that the facts of industrial life are not as simple as that. The output (or consumption) of steel ingots is not the same as pig iron; it includes also large quantities of metal refashioned from scrap. Nor is the volume of ingot production the same as the volume of rolling mill and foundry production; in between, something is lost and some part of this is channeled back. In addition, a substantial part of the metal shipped to fabricators is also lost—as borings, punchings, clippings, turnings, trimmings, shavings, and even processing dust, or simply faulty product—but any part of this so-called loss that can be scraped up in some quantity goes back again to an earlier part of the production process.

Statistically, this "runaround" scrap goes by various names. If it never leaves the plant in which it is generated (say, is dumped back into the furnace for remelting), it is called "home" scrap; but only for the steel industry are there data for this item and these data include not only the true runaround, but the scrap that comes about from tearing up obsolete parts of the mill itself. The stuff that is sold by fabricators back to smelters (or to special secondary smelters) or at least is transferred from plant to plant is usually recorded as "new scrap," or as "prompt industrial scrap." The outright losses usually do not get recorded at all.

Plainly, one can get a very different picture of the quantities of metal consumed in any one year if one makes the measurement at the ingot (refinery) stage, compared with the shapes and forms (mill and foundry) stage; the latter is always smaller by the amount of the intervening loss and runaround. Similarly, the amount of metal which actually leaves fabricators as end-products or destined to end-products is smaller still, yet more closely than

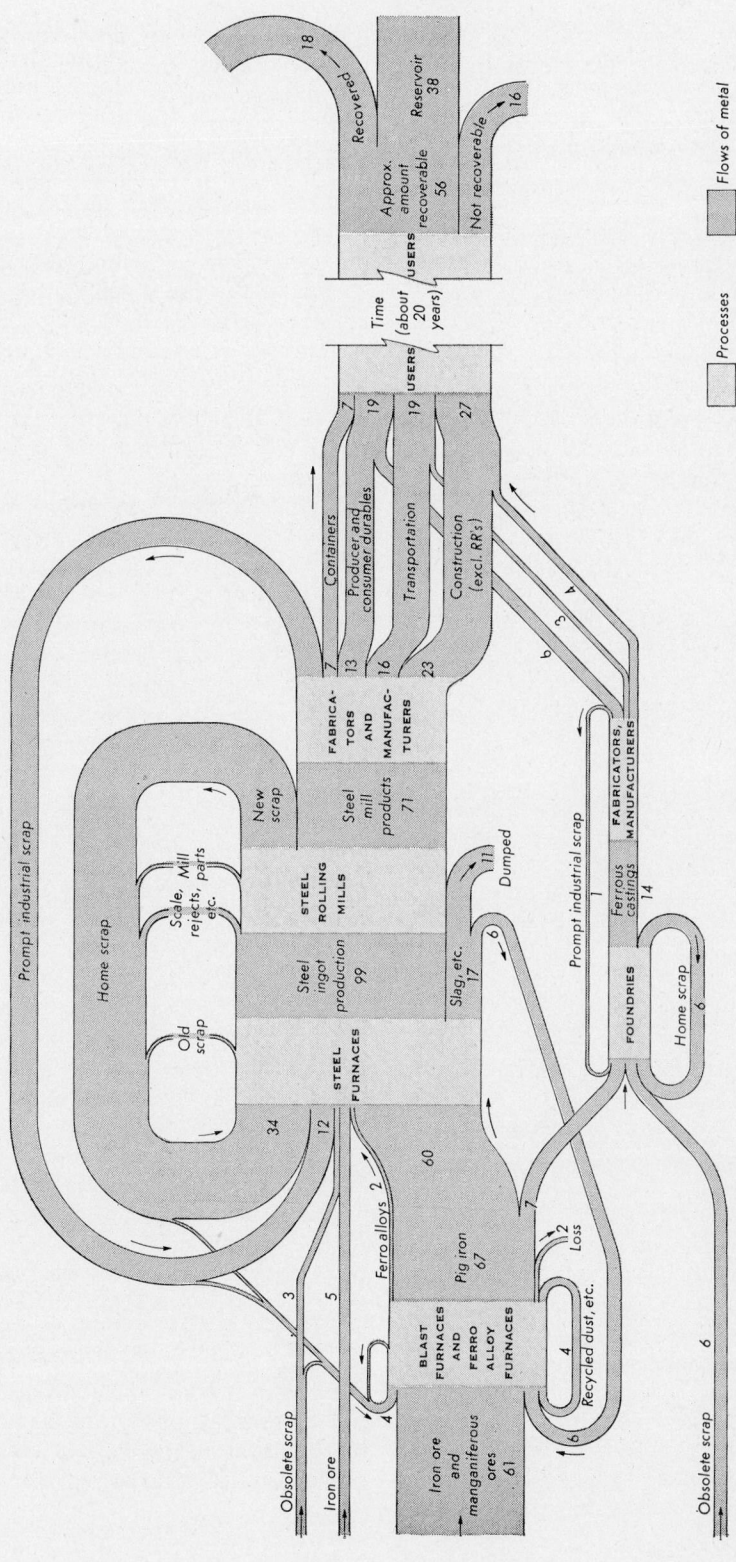

Figure 16–1. Approximate flow of ferrous metals through the U.S. economy (in millions of tons), 1960.

any others does this measurement approximate what in any one year actually is consumed. Moreover, it closely approximates what in the same year enters the input end of the pipeline—"new" metal, extracted from its ores, plus "old" scrap, or the metal consumed years back and now ready to lead a second life.

Most of the published statistical series that record consumption of metal measure gross consumption at one or more of the earlier processing stages. The fact that they do not go further toward the consuming end of things is a consequence of the virtual impossibility of gathering firm statistics at the latter point. Yet the "apparent consumption" series published by the same agencies generally do come close to end-use magnitudes (when not distorted by government stockpiling), for what they measure are the amounts of metal that need to be put into the front end of the pipeline to push the net end-use amounts out the back. Because the final objective of this study is to evaluate the prospective call upon basic resources, we have chosen to base our projections upon an estimation of the apparent-consumption/net-end-use equivalence, even though this has required the adaptation of reported end-use consumption to make it conform with the net end-use definition (i.e. by deducting prompt industrial scrap).

Even on this net consumption basis we come up with an input demand that need not be met wholly by extracting more metal from newly mined ore; more and more of our stock of material is already above ground and production can come from this as well. We could, in fact, treat this metal above ground as a reservoir from which some part of our future consumption demand could be met. However, because it is simpler to think of this source as an annual crop of metallic articles scrapped, we have chosen to regard old, or "obsolete," scrap as a diminution of the demand for new metal instead.

Iron and Steel

With invention of the Bessemer converter, in 1856, steel production in the United States started to grow rapidly. By the turn of the cen-

tury, annual output had reached 10 million tons. At the peak of World War I, it approached 50 million tons, then dropped back to a mere 15 million in the trough of the Great Depression. World War II saw production in excess of 80 million, and output has exceeded 110 million tons in several years since.

The foregoing figures refer to steel ingot production and as such exceed the levels of net end-use consumption, which we are attempting to estimate. However, because this single series is so central and well-known an indicator of the level of ferrous metals output, it is included here in order to provide easily understood comparisons with our net end-use projections. Moreover, the technology of iron and steel is such that the ingot production series provides a convenient way of relating a variety of iron and steel inputs (pig iron, scrap, manganese, and other additive metals) to the point in the production process at which most of these materials actually enter.

Table 16–3 indicates how, in retrospect and in prospect, steel ingot production and a number of other key measures of iron and steel demand shape up. The excess of ingot production over mill products and castings production holds despite the fact that most of the castings production is actually iron rather than steel. The similar excess of mill and foundry products over net domestic consumption (end-use consumption) reflects the further industrial scrap generation at the fabricating stage. The tendency for pig iron production to be still lower is a consequence of the extent to which requirements for metal are ultimately satisfied by the recovery of iron from old ferrous scrap.

Comparing projected ingot production with gross national product, it is apparent that, per dollar of GNP, future steel production declines. This is a continuation of the downward drift (with considerable fluctuations) that has been going on for some time. In 1929, about 300 tons of steel were produced per million dollars of GNP; in the thirties, the figure averaged around 200 tons; in the forties, 250 tons; in the fifties, 240 tons. For the last several years the amount has been a scant 200 tons, which is the level projected for the immediate future

TABLE 16–3. Measures of Iron and Steel Demand, 1926–30—1960, and Projections to 2000

(Million tons)

Year		Steel ingot prod.	Steel mill prod.'s	Ferrous castings	Net domestic iron and steel consumption	Domestic consumption of pig iron
1926–30 avg.		53	40	17	49	41
1931–35 avg.		27	19	7	23	17
1936–40 avg.		52	36	11	38	35
1950		96	73	16	74	65
1955		117	85	18	84	77
1960		99	71	14	72	67
1970	L	106	76	12	73	66
	M	141	101	17	99	88
	H	178	127	22	126	111
1980	L	115	82	10	76	67
	M	176	126	19	121	107
	H	253	181	30	176	157
1990	L	129	92	9	82	74
	M	225	161	21	151	134
	H	367	262	40	252	221
2000	L	140	100	9	89	79
	M	294	210	25	194	171
	H	554	396	57	378	330

L = Low projection M = Medium H = High.
Source: Appendix Tables A16–1, 2, and 9.

as well. It is possible that this level may be retained as late as 1980, but a more likely prospect is decline to around 170 tons per million dollars, or even as little as 120; by the century's end, 130 tons seems most likely, with a possible range of 80 to 170.

On a per capita basis the story is a little different. True, ingot consumption per person did drop from about 1,000 pounds annually in 1929 to as little as 250 pounds in the depths of the Depression, but it rose again to as much as 1,200 pounds in World War II and to 1,400 pounds at the peak of the fifties. Despite the recent drop back to less than 1,100 pounds, the most likely outlook is for 1,400 pounds in the eighties and 1,800 pounds by the century's end. It could go much higher (our High projection for 2000 implies 1¼ tons), but there is also the real possibility that the shift to other metals may be strong enough to keep even per

capita consumption of steel from rising above present levels.

To better understand these trends it is necessary to observe the development of steel consumption in each of steel's major categories of use. This is shown, in Figure 16–2, for the principal consumption categories. Table 16–4 shows the same trends in terms of percentage changes, and Table 16–5 shows the shifts in the relative contribution of the various categories to total steel demand.

By comparing the two tables, one may see where most of the growth in steel consumption will come from. Construction is the most important contributor: its growth rate is rather unspectacular, but because of its relative importance in the total market structure for steel, it accounts for most of the absolute increase in demand. By the same token, it is also the sector that introduces the greatest uncertainty

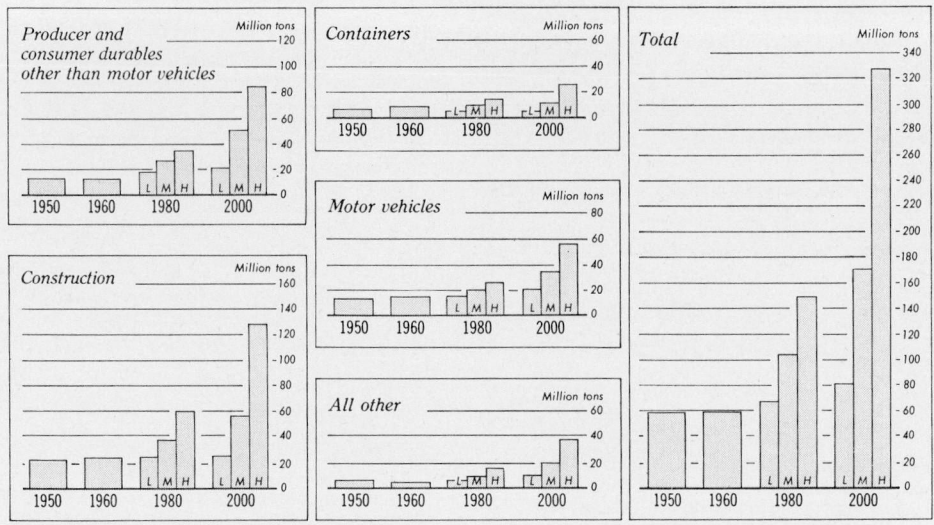

Figure 16–2. Net domestic consumption of steel mill products, by end-use category.

into the picture. If construction alone were to reach its High potential, and all else remain as in the Medium projection, the outlook for steel demand would be 40 per cent higher; should construction steel remain unchanged from what it is today, as is possible, the total steel prospect would be 20 per cent lower.

Next most important contributor to growing steel demand will be producers' durables and, farther down the line, railroads. These, too, are areas of uncertainty, though neither of them to the extent of the construction industry.

The most significant laggard among steel consumers, and a brake upon its increased consumption, is the container industry.

All of these conclusions must be somewhat qualified owing to a lack of knowledge concerning the precise market distribution of ferrous castings. This portion of iron and steel output has, however, been steadily declining in relative importance over the years and undoubtedly will continue to do so. Moreover, it is known that the primary consumers of castings are the construction and transportation

TABLE 16–4. Percentage Change in Steel Consumption by Category of Use, 1940–1960 and Projections for 1960–1980 and 1980–2000

Category of use	1940–1960	1960–1980			1980–2000		
		Low	Medium	High	Low	Medium	High
Construction (excl. railroad)	+104	+4	+69	+166	+3	+52	+115
Automotive	+96	+14	+56	+102	+38	+61	+101
Rail transportation	−36	+18	+150	+368	+100	+114	+138
Water and air transportation (incl. military aircraft)	−33	+167	+183	+233	+69	+106	+165
Producer durables	+112	+41	+125	+201	+19	+96	+158
Consumer durables	+72	+25	+50	+69	+35	+62	+83
Containers	+112	−22	+28	+86	−21	+15	+73
Ordnance	–	−50	–	+100	–	+50	+50
Ferrous castings	–	−29	+36	+108	−4	+35	+92
Total	+58	+6	+68	+144	+18	+60	+115

Source: Appendix Tables A16–4, 10, and 12.

TABLE 16–5. Percentage Distribution of Steel Consumption, by Category of Use, 1940, 1960, and Projections for 1980, 2000

Category of use	1940	1960	1980 Low	1980 Medium	1980 High	2000 Low	2000 Medium	2000 High
Construction (excl. railroad)	25	31	31	32	34	27	30	34
Automotive	16	18	20	17	15	24	17	14
Rail transportation	10	4	4	6	7	7	8	8
Water and air transportation (incl. military aircraft)	2	1	2	1	1	3	2	1
Producer durables	9	12	18	18	17	18	22	20
Consumer durables	6	6	5	4	3	6	4	3
Containers	8	10	7	8	8	5	5	6
Ordnance	–	–	.1	.2	.2	.1	.1	.2
Ferrous castings	24	18	12	14	15	10	12	13
Total	100	100	100	100	100	100	100	100

Source: Appendix Table A16–20.

equipment industries, so the course of castings consumption will largely follow the use of steel in general in these sectors, although most likely at a more moderate pace.

The particular influences upon steel consumption in these various sectors have been discussed in the appropriate chapters of Part I. In summary, however, it may be stated that the growth in use of aluminum and plastics is conspicuous among reasons for the failure of steel to keep pace with the growth of the economy. At the same time steel is making its own inroads—principally in residential construction and principally at the expense of wood. It is also making inroads upon itself—importantly, in the substitution of steel-reinforced concrete for steel framing—but this, of course, means a diminution in total requirements.

Perhaps the least predictable of iron and steel markets is the automotive industry. There is considerable reason to expect the substitution of cast aluminum for cast iron in automobile engine blocks, transmission housings, and other such parts, which add up to a substantial portion of the total weight of an automobile; yet the moves so far made by the automotive industry in this direction have been sporadic and uncertain. There is also reason to expect that in automobile bodies and framing steel will give way to aluminum or to reinforced plastics; yet at the moment the major automobile makers seem to be giving greater

consideration to the substitution of galvanized steel for non-galvanized.

There are other reasons why any forecast of total metal requirements per vehicle must be almost completely conjectural. Despite the move in the last few years toward smaller vehicles, enough large ones remain that there has been little change in the average size, and the suspicion must be that, while any chance of future major increase in this average is small, it will not decline much more either. It is because of this that our Medium projection assumes no change, over the next forty years, in the total volume of material required to produce each user-operated vehicle.

The container industry is another sector in which aluminum, in many ways, seems to be replacing steel. And here plastics also may make some inroads. But steel container research is not standing still and at present the kind and rate of long-term trend that will set in is wholly conjectural.

Steel's most dependable market is probably that of industrial and agricultural tools and machinery. While use of other metals may make some inroads in this sector, in most of the high bulk and volume uses there has been no real challenge to steel and there is little reason to doubt that, despite year-to-year fluctuations, the output of industrial equipment will undergo a substantial and steady growth.

In a number of markets the unit use of steel

is affected by materials/value relationships even more than by the use of other materials. Investment, consumers' purchases, military procurement are all measured in dollar value of final product, and, in a substantial sense, the limit of total output is the limit of funds with which to purchase this final value. Within this total value, technological change works to the disadvantage of steel and to the advantage of labor and of other metals. Steel is for structure; advancing technology serves to de-emphasize structure. The more complicated, more miniaturized, more electronified equipment—producer, consumer, and military—which is constantly being developed requires more assembly labor, more copper and aluminum, but rarely more steel. Yet, even with these influences working to diminish its relative position, steel is so large a part of the great bulk of our hard goods that its continued substantial growth is assured.

Pig iron and scrap. For all practical purposes, pig iron is new iron; and demand for new iron is what we need to know about to judge the adequacy of the resource base: iron ore. The link between pig iron and consumption of steel by end-products is a matter of iron and steel technology. The sort of question for which we need the answer has to do with scrap generation rates in rolling and in fabricating, the advent of direct casting and its effects on steelmaking and on scrap generation, the development of steelmaking technology as such and its effect on the future relative use of scrap and pig iron, and the extent of introduction of direct reduction, which also modifies the relative use of scrap.

Most of the answers on scrap generation, such as they are, come from a 1957 study by the Battelle Memorial Institute for the U.S. Department of Commerce and a follow-up study made by the Department of Commerce itself.[1] Of the quantities of shapes and forms shipped by mills and foundries to fabricators,

anywhere from 3 to 30 per cent become industrial scrap, available for reuse in earlier parts of the production process; the average is about 16 per cent. Of the total input of ferrous metallics into iron and steelmaking, not more than about 62 to 63 per cent is shipped out as shapes and forms. About 8 per cent is lost in melting and pouring operations and almost 30 per cent is fed back into the furnaces as home scrap. Although some of this home scrap is generated right at the blast and steel furnaces, the bulk of it results from the cropping of ingots, "losses" during hot and cold rolling, trimming and cutting, or from faulty castings. With the improvement of rolling mill and foundry techniques, one should expect a diminishing ratio of both permanent loss and home scrap production to iron and steel shipments.

That this has not occurred despite accumulating experience and perfection of methods is due to the ever more exacting demands of steel consumers for better quality and a larger variety of shapes. Since in this study steel consumption has been projected under the assumption that steelmakers will continue to improve their product and service in order to compete with other materials, it is expected that the number of stages in hot and cold rolling will grow, the milling operations lengthen, and the ratio of home scrap to finished output tend to increase. This tendency, it is assumed, would be roughly balanced by improvements in milling methods and by the spread of continuous casting.

The ratio of all metallics input to gross output of iron and steel (from furnaces) will probably remain close to its present 108 to 110 per cent, any gain in percentage recovery being sufficiently small to be counterbalanced by increased needs for inventory-in-process. Of the total metallics input (into both steel furnaces and foundries), that of pig iron has for years been running at 48 to 50 per cent and scrap at 45 to 48 per cent, with the balance being made up of ferroalloys and directly used iron ore. The immediate trend is toward a slight increase in the pig ratio and a corresponding decrease in scrap, but it is hard to say that this is the turn that the ratio will take over

1. Battelle Memorial Institute, *Final Report on a Survey and Analysis of the Supply and Availability of Obsolete Iron and Steel Scrap* (Columbus, Ohio: January 17, 1957); Business and Defense Services Administration, *Industrial Scrap Generation* (Washington: U.S. Government Printing Office, 1957).

the long run. Tending to depress the scrap proportion are the beginnings of direct reduction techniques and the introduction of an improved Bessemer-type technique—the basic oxygen process—which uses only up to about 30 per cent scrap. Operating in the opposite direction is the potential growth of electric steelmaking, which uses scrap in preference to all other sources and which could easily be stimulated by the combination of lower scrap prices and electric steel's inherent flexibility. Of lesser consequence, but also predisposing toward greater relative scrap use, are improvements in open-hearth steelmaking.

Of all factors, however, probably the most important is the huge present investment in integrated steel mills, with their blast-furnace "hot-metal" (pig iron) output geared to open-hearth output and so supplying a relatively stable pig iron quantity. Additions to steelmaking capacity come not only from the construction of completely new facilities—which gives greater opportunity for new processes to creep in—but from the continual modification of existing ones. Steel plants do not behave like the "wonderful one-horse shay." If whole plants were to become obsolete all at once, the pace of technological change could be rapid indeed; replacement of bits and pieces is so continual, however, that hardly any steel plant is really "old."

The iron and steel industry satisfies its scrap needs from three major sources: its own operations (home scrap); the operations of fabricators of finished products (prompt industrial scrap); and discarded articles flowing from railroads, auto wreckers, demolition of structures, etc. (obsolete scrap). Currently, only about 15 to 20 per cent of the total is obsolete scrap, whose availability is limited by the accumulated reservoir and annual crop of retirements and demolitions. Home and prompt industrial scrap generation necessarily fluctuate more or less with the pace of current production and are both the most readily available and the highest quality sources, so the call upon the old scrap supply is essentially residual. So far, at least in normal years, this residual has been small enough in relation to the annual retirement crop that there has been no question

of availability—in fact, large amounts of surplus scrap have been exported.

An increasing surplus of obsolete scrap seems to be in prospect. Of the present annual crop, so far as it can be estimated, only about one-third is being used in domestic iron and steel production; the balance is exported (recently about 10 to 20 per cent) or is simply accumulated in the reservoir. Around 35 per cent of the annual crop appears to be the long-term need, in our Medium steel projection, even to the end of the century; and to support High steel production the need is only about 45 per cent. That this should be so is because even old scrap has a runaround character and, even though the time taken for the runaround may be decades and scores of years, the ultimate consequence of relatively higher growth rates in steel production is relatively higher growth rates in obsolete scrap generation.

The implication of the foregoing is that the level of our requirements for pig iron (see Figure 16–3) is a consequence less of actual need

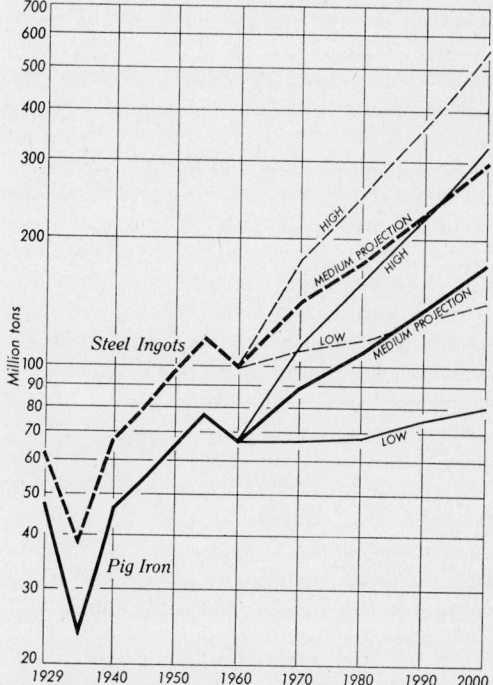

Figure 16–3. Production of pig iron and steel ingots, 1929–1960 (five-year intervals) and projections to 2000.

for new iron than of a steel technology which implies the use of new iron and scrap in certain proportions. It follows, however, that should resource stringency push up the relative cost of new iron, there are more than ample reserves of old iron to which a partial shift can be made. Should the circumstances require it, it may be assumed that production technology would adapt itself.

The Additive Metals

Manganese, molybdenum, nickel, chromium, vanadium, tin—these are a few of the many metals whose consumption in the United States is primarily or almost wholly associated with steel. Partly, their use is as alloying elements, partly as scavenger materials to remove impurities from the steel, partly as coating or plating materials. In this last category zinc also is important, but its other uses involve greater volumes. Similarly, while tungsten is an important steel alloying element, more of it is used directly in tungsten carbides.

Some of the additives serve more than one purpose: for example, manganese is both a purifying and an alloying element, nickel and chromium are used both for alloying and for plating. A number of these metals also serve as additives or alloying elements for metals other than iron and steel.

The two most important coating metals—tin and zinc—will be considered separately, later in this chapter. What we are concerned with here are the metals that are intimately involved in the process of steelmaking, of which manganese is the most important. Since far more manganese goes into the making of ordinary steel (carbon steel) than into alloy steels, our projections of steel ingot production as a whole have already established the principal reference for the future use of manganese.

Among the alloy steels, stainless steel is frequently distinguished from other types, as is high-speed, or heat-resistant, steel, but since at the fringes the compositions of these and other alloys fade into one another, we consider all alloys here as one group. The combinations of

composition are so numerous, and so constantly changing, that only the roughest of long-term conclusions can be drawn.

Of the total consumption of alloy steels, automotive and producer durable uses each currently account for nearly one-third. Both are assumed to use relatively more alloy steel, in contrast to carbon steel, as the years go on. The reason for this assumption, despite recent apparently declining trends, is the increasing need wherever steel is used—and in many applications where it is not now used, but where its superior strength sooner or later is likely to insure its use—for anti-corrosive and heat-resistant qualities, which only alloy steels can provide. Stainless steel, particularly, seems destined to be increasingly called upon in our modern technology, in applications ranging from tableware and construction trim to high-temperature uses on the fringes of space. About one-third of all steel currently used for transportation equipment (including military aircraft) is now alloy, and the proportion should continue to rise. A little over one-third of steel falling into other military categories is alloy, too, but the absolute quantities involved are relatively minor. Table 16–6 shows the varying prospects for end-use consumption of alloy (including stainless) steel.

Of the total quantities of additives used in steelmaking, an important proportion gets into the steel by virtue of its presence in the inputs of iron and steel scrap. The new amounts needed are added predominantly in the form of ferroalloys, which are metallic products combining iron with controlled amounts of one or more alloying elements.

Although they represent only a small proportion of all ferrous metallics input, ferroalloys (ferromanganese, ferrosilicon, ferrochromium, spiegeleisen, etc.) are actually the second largest category of metals produced in this country, exceeding the tonnage of aluminum or any of the other nonferrous metals. Because of their controlled composition, they facilitate the introduction of required amounts of the desired additives. Since they do not represent all of the amounts of the principal additives used in steel, however, it is simpler, for

TABLE 16–6. Alloy (including Stainless) Steel: Net Domestic Consumption, 1960 and Projections for 1980, 2000

(Million tons)

Market category	1960		1980	2000
Construction	.7	L	.8	.9
		M	1.3	2.2
		H	2.0	4.9
Automotive	1.2	L	1.5	2.3
		M	2.0	3.7
		H	2.6	5.9
Railroads	.3	L	.3	.7
		M	.6	1.5
		H	1.1	3.1
Water and air transport	.2	L	.6	1.1
		M	.6	1.4
		H	.7	2.1
Producer durables	1.1	L	1.9	2.6
		M	3.0	6.8
		H	4.0	11.9
Other	.2	L	.2	.3
		M	.3	.5
		H	.4	.8
Total	3.7	L	5.2	7.8
		M	7.8	16.1
		H	10.9	28.8

L = Low projection   M = Medium   H = High.
Source: Appendix Table A16–18.

our purposes, to consider the particular additives in terms of total content, whether they arrive by the ferroalloy route or not.

Manganese. Because of its hardening effects, manganese is important as an alloying element for both ferrous and nonferrous metals; as a reagent in the steelmaking process it is considered essential. Currently, over 90 per cent of U.S. consumption is taken up by the iron and steel industry; the remainder is used in nonferrous metallurgy, dry cells, and in various chemical applications.

The analysis of manganese requirements for iron and steel production is complicated by the multiplicity of channels through which the metal is consumed. To the extent that it derives from manganese ore (35 per cent or more manganese), it usually arrives at the steel furnace or ladle in the form of ferroalloys, but some of it is also introduced as ore and as manganese metal. A somewhat larger amount arrives in the form of pig iron, into which it is introduced mostly by way of manganiferous iron ore, but also, in part, through recycled steel-mill slag. Additional amounts arrive as content of iron and steel scrap. Excluding recycled material, an input of about 35 pounds per ton of steel is estimated to be required, of which only about 11 pounds shows up in the finished steel ingot. About 7 pounds of the difference ends up in blast furnace slag heaps, where it is considered to be totally irrecoverable, the rest in other slag dumps.

Current statistical series do not exist even on all of the manganese in ore, let alone in scrap, so historical knowledge of new metal consumption is severely limited. However, a liberal estimate of total manganese and manganiferous ore requirements per ton of steel is about 18 pounds, manganese content, and this figure is projected to persist as the result of a counterbalancing of increased additive use by more intensive steel slag recovery. Higher requirements seem unlikely, but lower requirements could result from technological advance towards less manganese use per ton of steel and from the development of direct extraction from steel-mill slag. (See also Chapter 21, pages 435–38.) Assuming that manganiferous iron ores maintain a constant contribution, the demand for manganese ores (including non-steel use) can be projected as detailed in Appendix Table A16–22 and summarized below.

(Million tons, manganese content)

1960		1.0
1980	Low	1.2
	Medium	1.8
	High	2.4
2000	Low	1.5
	Medium	2.9
	High	5.2

Nickel. While its principal application is in ferrous metallurgy, the uses of nickel are ubiquitous and growing. Over 3,000 alloys, ferrous and nonferrous, are at present estimated to contain nickel, in amounts varying from a mere fraction to 99 per cent. Strength, hardness, corrosion resistance, resistance to deformation at high temperatures, and pleasing appearance are among its qualities—and it often takes the addition of very little nickel to impart them. Altogether, about four-fifths of nickel goes into such alloys, the remainder into plating, chemical, and other uses.

Because nickel is relatively costly, future consumption trends are likely to be influenced in part by tendencies to minimize its ultilization. In general, the association of nickel with ferrous metals is likely to become relatively stronger and that with nonferrous metals to decline.

Our projections of alloy steel, above, provide the base for estimating the ferrous portion. Increased nickel use per ton of alloy (from about 25 pounds in recent years to 35 in 2000) should result from increasing emphasis on nickel-bearing stainless and from increased use of nickel in ferrous castings. The increasing demand for materials that are corrosion-resistant at high temperatures will be an important factor in this process.

The distinctive and common property of the multitude of nonferrous nickel alloys—many of them nickel-based—is resistance to heat, abrasion, and corrosive chemicals. Typical applications are as monel metal, in food-processing, paper, and textile machinery; nickel silver, in plated silverware and marine hardware; cupro-nickel condensor tubes and resistance wire; Inconel, in exhaust manifolds or combustion chambers of aircraft and in chemical industry and heat-treating equipment. Data on relative inputs into these various uses are unavailable; the constant input per dollar of producer durables output, which has been used in our projections, is equivalent to assuming a somewhat faster growth rate for nickel than for other materials.

Nickel consumption by electroplaters is highly irregular, since this industry has historically drawn down the nickel content of its electroplating baths in times of nickel shortage and built it up during periods of easier supply. Most of the consumption is for consumer durables, to which, in our projections, we have related the plating use. The assumed decline in unit input is to be explained primarily by the partial substitution of other metals (e.g.,

TABLE 16–7. Nickel: Net Domestic Consumption, 1960 and Projections for 1980, 2000

(Thousand tons)

Market category	1960		1980	2000
Alloy (incl. stain-		L	78	133
less) steel	51	M	117	273
		H	164	490
		L	4	5
Ferrous castings	5	M	8	12
		H	12	26
		L	54	72
Nonferrous metals	41	M	100	218
		H	172	535
		L	25	33
Electroplating	17	M	30	48
		H	38	76
		L	7	10
Other uses	5	M	8	12
		H	8	15
		L	169	253
Total	118	M	263	563
		H	394	1,142

L = Low projection   M = Medium   H = High.
Source: Appendix Table A16–24.

cadmium, with a nickel under-coating) and the use of thinner surfaces, sometimes on a stainless base. In addition, stainless steel as such is a partial competitor. (See Table 16–7.)

Chromium. The metallurgical industry accounts for over 60 per cent of U.S. chromite (chromium ore) consumption, measured in terms of contained chromium. Twenty-five per cent goes to refractories (firebrick, etc.), and the rest ends up in chemical uses such as in pigments, electroplating, leather tanning, and photographic supplies. As in the case of manganese, chromium is introduced into steel largely as a ferroalloy—ferrochromium, ferrochromium-silicon, etc.—although there is a growing practice of adding chromite directly. It is the essential ingredient of stainless steel and also imparts strength, better hardening characteristics, and other values. Chromium is expected to hold its own, both in stainless and in other alloy and plating applications, somewhat increasing in actual net unit use, but without additional input because of probable reduction in the rather high (some 20 per cent) processing-loss ratio.

Refractory use of chromite, closely related to pig iron output because of its application in blast furnaces, has been on an upward trend which is expected to taper off. Competition of magnesite may even cause declines. Chemical uses will probably remain stagnant.

In sum, an increase to about 3½ times the present consumption seems a likely prospect; but technological gains and competitive factors could combine to reduce this to less than twice, or opposite influences, added to high alloy steel production, could raise 2000 consumption to 6 times what it is today.

Molybdenum. In contrast to most other additives, which are largely imported, molybdenum produced in the United States supplies around 85 per cent of the needs of the noncommunist countries. As an alloying element, it imparts high strength and hardness to steel and to ferrous castings, especially at high temperatures. As such, it is in competition with several other additives, notably tungsten and nickel. It is likely that molybdenum will tend to gain in this competition and that extensive research will result in the discovery of new applications. Moreover, molybdenum metal itself and molybdenum-base alloys are becoming significant for nuclear applications and other advanced technology. Consequently, an increased domestic use of as much as ten times the present seems probable over the next forty years and has been assumed for our Medium projection. While exports are important, no basis for judging their future course was available (see also Chapter 21, pages 449–50).

Tungsten. Although it is consumed in quite small amounts compared with the other metals so far discussed, tungsten has a wide range of uses, often of critical significance. It is a long-used alloying element for steel, bestowing high-temperature strength and hardness. Its largest classes of ferrous applications are in high-speed steels for such products as drills, machine tools, and hacksaw blades. Tungsten metal itself and various tungsten alloys are used as electric or electronic components (elec-

trodes, heating elements, resistance wire, etc.) and in such high-temperature uses as jet engines. Tungsten carbides, use of which has risen spectacularly in recent years, are employed in tools for shaping and cutting metals and as small inserts at friction points. At present, the consumption of tungsten is about evenly divided between ferrous additive, tungsten metal and nonferrous alloy, and tungsten carbide.

For the future, relative tungsten use per ton of alloy steel is expected to remain unchanged; recurrent supply difficulties, together with the possibility of substituting molybdenum or other alloying elements, are among the factors tending to hold down consumption gains. Substitution of semi-conductors for vacuum tubes, miniaturization, and the advent of cheaper substitutes all suggest decreasing use of tungsten per dollar of electrical machinery. Carbides, the most likely form of growth, should remain about constant in relation to dollar output of industrial machinery.

As is the case with manganese and chromium, a substantial portion of tungsten production has been purchased by the government in recent years, resulting in a large discrepancy between apparent and actual end-use consumption. Although end-use consumption should quadruple by the end of the century, this will show up as only a small rise compared with the apparent consumption of the recent past.

Cobalt. Cobalt has a wide variety of applications, of which about three-fourths are metallic and about equally divided among three principal groups: permanent magnet alloys, high-temperature steels, and a miscellany composed mostly of tool steels. The non-metallic uses are as chemicals employed in the enameling of metals, in pigments, and in salts and driers.

Large increases may be expected in all but the chemical uses (where growth is likely to be fairly modest). Most rapid expansion will probably come in the permanent magnet use, as a direct result of the rapid growth in output of the electrical equipment in which such magnets find their principal application. The uses in tool steels and other industrial machinery, which have been tending toward greater unit consumption of cobalt, should be second in importance, followed closely by high-temperature alloys, which are an important constituent of spacecraft and missiles. Because of the small quantities used and the fluidity of the technology in many of its applications, projections for cobalt are particularly hazardous. Our Medium calculations sum to a consumption of 10,000 tons in 1980 and 19,000 in 2000, compared with 4,500 tons in 1960. The 1980 range is from a Low of 6,000 to a High of 15,000 tons, and that for the year 2000 from 9,000 to 38,000 tons.

Vanadium. The uranium boom of the fifties resulted in overproduction of vanadium pentoxide, which is a by-product of uranium output. Consequently, the search for new uses has been more intensive than in the case of most other metals. At the same time the United States has turned from being a net importer to supplying about 70 per cent of the non-communist countries' needs.

At present, around 75 per cent of domestic end-use consumption is absorbed by the steel industry. Although several other metals can substitute for vanadium in its ferrous applications (high-speed, heat-resistant, and other alloy steels), there are no signs that vanadium will be replaced. Thus, it is expected to increase at the same rate as alloy steels.

Prospective uses for vanadium metal as such and for vanadium compounds include: a weldable high-hot-strength sheet alloy for airframes, fuel-element cladding for atomic reactors, a part of automobile exhaust purifiers, and an element in a drug for discouraging heart attacks. The diversity suggested by this sampling suggests rather rapidly growing demand for vanadium in other than its steel-alloying uses. In addition, the United States should continue to supply large amounts to the rest of the world.

In total, vanadium consumption forty years hence may be estimated at about four times what it is today. This amount could be reduced if progress is made in reducing the present relatively large processing losses.

Aluminum

Since 1954, yearly production of primary aluminum in the United States has been larger than that of any other nonferrous metal—a new-found pre-eminence which is the result of spectacular growth in the past two decades. Between 1939 and 1960, primary ingot production increased by 1,100 per cent, net requirements for new metal by 900 per cent. Total end-use consumption—primary and secondary—increased by 800 per cent.

Aluminum's future looks almost as bright. If our Medium projection is correct, end-use consumption will be three and one-half times as high in 1980 as in 1960, and about two and one-half times as high in 2000 as in 1980. If all factors favor the demand for the metal, consumption by 1980 may rise to six times what it is today, and by 2000 to three times that of 1980. Even under the least favorable circumstances, an increase of about 120 per cent by 1980 seems to be in the cards, although the subsequent twenty years might see only a 90 per cent gain.

The properties responsible for the phenomenal rise of aluminum are its light weight, its high strength-to-weight ratio, and its versatility in forming, plus good electrical and heat conductivity, corrosion resistance and pleasing appearance. In addition, its cost per unit of volume is relatively low, although not in comparison with that of steel.

The applications of aluminum in modern industry and construction are innumerable. Its defense uses have been in a class with steel. It finds expression in plate, sheet, foil, extruded and drawn shapes; rod, bar, wire and cable; in sand, permanent-mold, and die castings; in forgings; in pigments, powders, and other "dissipative" uses.

Transportation, although second to construction at present, should become the most important single consuming category of the future, taking one-third to two-fifths of the total volume by 2000 (if military uses are included), compared with only one-sixth now. The underlying assumption is that aluminum will continue its substitution for steel in such items as bus and truck-trailer bodies; for cast iron in automotive engine blocks, transmission housings, etc.; for copper and zinc in other automotive parts. Although military transportation use is included, it will become a progressively smaller part of the total, owing to aluminum's disadvantages in supersonically travelling structures. Absolute growth in transportation uses should be on the order of twenty times, with the highest rates of increase taking place during the next twenty years.

The prospective drop in construction's share from over 40 per cent now to about 30 in 2000 is a reflection of the faster growth in some other categories, not of absolute loss. Construction uses should, in fact, nearly triple between now and 1980 and more than double in the twenty years following. Structural parts, contractors' products, power transmission facilities—these are a few of the applications where aluminum is being increasingly used, despite higher initial costs, because of its economy of maintenance. Contractors' products are at present the largest outlet—doors, windows, trim, awnings, screening, guttering, duct-work, and the like; however, aluminum use for framing and for panelling should come increasingly to the fore. Current use of aluminum for major structural uses is still limited, but roof trusses, bridges, and transmission-line towers are among the potentially large-bulk applications where a start has been made. Our Medium projection of 4½ million tons of construction aluminum in 2000, however, is still only about one-thirteenth that of steel.

The field of containers and packaging offers another large opportunity for aluminum's use. Although, through such products as aluminum foil and, just beginning, aluminum cans, it now accounts for less than 10 per cent of the aluminum market, use in this field will probably rise to 12 per cent before 1980. In view of countering moves by the steel industry and potential competition from plastics, the rate of growth is anything but certain, but a fivefold increase in the next two decades, followed by a more modest increase thereafter, seems likely.

Compared with the foregoing, other uses of aluminum will be relatively minor. What was

once aluminum's primary use—consumer durables—has declined from 26 to 12 per cent in the past decade and should drop below 10 per cent a decade hence. It is not that aluminum use in pots and pans, furniture, air conditioners, etc., will decline, but that it will not increase as rapidly as its later uses. Similarly, the assumption that producer durable uses, now at about 11 per cent of the total, will gradually decline to less than 9 per cent before the century's end means only that the growth in electrical machinery, heat exchangers, and other industrial uses will be dwarfed by the more dynamic sectors.

Prospective growth of net aluminum consumption (i.e., after deducting returned process scrap) in each of the principal market categories is shown in Table 16–8. Strictly speaking, the data shown in the table apply to aluminum and aluminum alloys. There are very few applications in which pure metal is

TABLE 16–8. Aluminum: Net Domestic Consumption, 1960 and Projections for 1980, 2000

(Million tons)

Market category	1960		1980	2000
Building and electric power construction	.7	L	1.0	1.6
		M	1.8	4.6
		H	3.4	13.8
Consumer durables	.2	L	.4	1.0
		M	.5	1.4
		H	.6	1.8
Producer durables	.2	L	.3	.5
		M	.6	1.3
		H	.7	2.3
Containers	.2	L	.4	.6
		M	.7	1.2
		H	1.0	2.3
Transportation	.3	L	1.2	2.9
		M	2.0	6.1
		H	4.2	10.6
Defense and misc. uses	.1	L	–	–
		M	.1	.1
		H	.2	.3
Total	1.6	L	3.4	6.6
		M	5.7	14.7
		H	10.1	31.1

L = Low projection   M = Medium   H = High.
Source: Appendix Table A16–32.

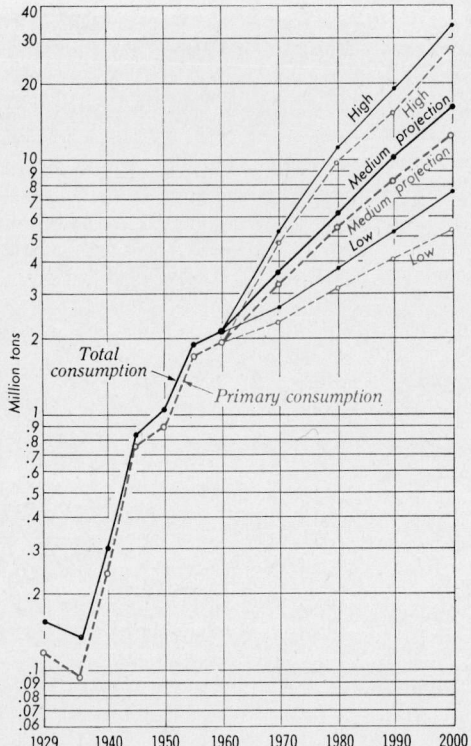

Figure 16–4. Total end-use consumption of aluminum (including exports) compared with primary aluminum consumption, 1929–1960 (five-year intervals) and projections to 2000.

used, but, on the other hand, most of the commercially used alloys contain only insignificant amounts of other elements. Thus, the average aluminum content of the aluminum shown in the table is something over 96 per cent—only a few percentage points under aluminum ingot —and further refinement of the projections is therefore not attempted.

Old scrap. More important than the alloying additives is the old scrap content of aluminum consumed; its importance, in absolute terms at least, will be growing. The two decades of useful life which may be estimated as characterizing the average aluminum product means that a large proportion of current scrap returns are coming from aluminum's infancy. Thus the reprocessing of obsolete scrap provides only about 5 per cent of current end-use requirements. The continued rapid growth of

aluminum demand will keep the percentage low; nonetheless it should rise to some 20 per cent of total requirements by the century's end.

Not all aluminum consumed returns as scrap, of course. A small portion (around 10 per cent) is dissipated through irrecoverable processing loss and through such uses as incorporation into paints and other chemicals and deoxidation of steel. A larger proportion, about 20 per cent, is rendered irrecoverable by the fact that its use is so widely distributed (as in consumer durables) that collection is difficult or (as with containers, foil, etc.) it becomes too thoroughly commingled with other "waste." Of the recoverable balance, not all is recovered immediately and some is exported. Thus, currently, only about half of the estimated annual crop of recoverable obsolete aluminum scrap is being used in domestic production. This is partly the result, however, of a current excess of primary capacity; as consumption mounts, return to a much higher rate of utilization of the scrap potential seems probable.

Given our projected volumes of old scrap recovery, and allowing for some exports, the resultant net demand for primary aluminum is projected as shown in Figure 16–4.

Copper

During the first half of the twentieth century copper was the most widely used nonferrous metal; for the rest of the century it will be second only to aluminum. Copper's use today is in no small part attributable to its ability to conduct electricity. More than half of the metal now consumed goes into uses related to electricity or electronics—even if many of such uses happen to be statistically classified as "electric power construction," "motor vehicles," "consumer durables," and the like.

Apparent total consumption of the "red metal" (including exports) rose to and stayed close to 1 million tons through the first three decades of the century. Following a big dip during the Depression, it gained momentum in the late thirties, exceeding the 2 million mark during the war and again in 1950, hovering around that level ever since. Some 20 to 25 per cent of that amount has been regularly recovered from old scrap, implying current new metal requirements of around 1.7 million tons per year.

Copper consumption is unlikely to keep pace with the growth in consumption of most other major metals, but substantial increases may be expected nevertheless—most likely on the order of 100 per cent between 1960 and 1980 and 90 per cent in the following two decades. Fastest absolute growth should come in building construction and in communications construction, primarily because of the underlying activity in these two fields. Electric-power construction might also have been important, were it not for the substantial displacement of copper by aluminum in transmission and distribution facilities.

Building construction makes use of copper —mostly as brass and bronze—in gutters, flashings, plumbing fixtures, fittings, and hardware. In piping particularly, copper is still displacing other metals, but shifts to aluminum, stainless steel, and plastics in other applications will at best leave copper with a proportionately unchanged role.

Producer durables, currently the largest user of copper, will probably drop behind construction over the next forty years. About one-third of the use in this field is for electrical machinery and equipment—as motor windings, wiring, and structural components. Pumps, compressors, valves, and fittings constitute another sizeable quantity. Resistance to the competition of aluminum is higher here than in construction, and the increasing emphasis on electronic equipment will also favor copper. But the relatively slower gain in producer durables output than in construction still makes this an area of slower copper growth.

Copper in automobiles may come to be replaced by aluminum, in the case of radiators, but the growth of air conditioning and electrical equipment in vehicles will work in the opposite direction. Use in other consumer durables will similarly feel the compensating effects of greater use of electrical equipment, offset by miniaturization and competition of other metals.

Railroad use of copper looks possibly even

TABLE 16–9. Copper and Copper Alloys: Net Domestic Consumption, 1960 and Projections for 1980, 2000

(Million tons)

Market category	1960		1980	2000
Motor vehicles	.2	L	.2	.2
		M	.2	.4
		H	.3	.9
Other durables (excl. railroad equip.)	.8	L	1.1	1.3
		M	1.6	2.9
		H	2.1	4.9
New building construction	.4	L	.5	.7
		M	.9	1.9
		H	1.5	4.7
Communications and electric power construction	.1	L	.1	.1
		M	.2	.5
		H	.3	1.1
Railroad equipment	.1	L	.1	.1
		M	.1	.2
		H	.2	.3
Defense	.03	L	.01	.01
		M	.05	.06
		H	.08	.15
Maintenance, repair, and operation	.1	L	.1	.2
		M	.2	.4
		H	.3	.9
Miscellaneous	.1	L	.1	.2
		M	.2	.4
		H	.3	.9
Total	1.8	L	2.3	2.8
		M	3.6	6.8
		H	5.2	14.0

L = Low projection   M = Medium   H = High.
Source: Appendix Table 16–44. Discrepancies due to rounding.

less promising, largely because of the tendency for a shift away from journal bearings. The outlook is quite uncertain, however, for development work is being done on at least one new type of bearing which would use ten times as much copper per unit as the present ones.

Despite these relative concessions to other metals, there is a general upward trend in nearly all uses, as is shown in Table 16–9.

It is to be emphasized that the foregoing figures include both copper and copper-base alloys. Unlike aluminum, copper contains substantial proportions of alloying elements in many of its uses. Wire mills turn out products which are predominantly pure copper; but

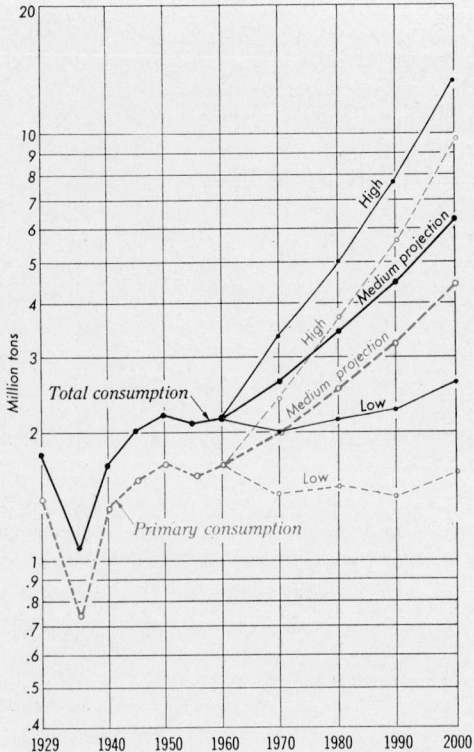

Figure 16–5. Total end-use consumption of copper (including exports) compared with primary copper consumption, 1929–1960 (five-year intervals) and projections to 2000.

products on which future emphasis was assumed, wire mill products—unalloyed copper—were likely to expand relative to brass and bronze. Moreover, if substitution by aluminum should occur, this trend would be accelerated. On the basis of similar considerations, a trend from bronze to brass may be foreseen in building construction, of brass to copper in military uses, and so forth. On the whole, there seems to be some tendency for increasing copper content in the "copper and copper alloys" consumed, but the increase is sufficiently mild that the future demand for copper, as such, has been estimated to persist at approximately 90 per cent of the aggregate end-use in both pure and alloyed form.

Because of its longer history and its slower growth rate, a larger proportion of copper than of aluminum requirements may be satisfied from old scrap. Currently, the proportion is about 20 per cent; by the century's end it should rise to nearly 30. Copper in end-products has a slightly lower life expectancy than aluminum—not because of an inherently lesser durability, but because of the different ways in which the two metals are used. In terms of pure copper, the prospective demand for this metal is summarized in Figure 16–5.

brass mills, which produce most of the shapes and forms of the copper world, lean heavily, as the name implies, to brass;[2] and foundries lean toward bronze. Brasses are primarily alloys of copper and zinc and bronzes of copper, lead, and tin. There are numerous variations and the two categories tend to fade into one another, but on the average, brass contains about 80 per cent copper and bronze closer to 90.

To ascertain how much of the consumption of copper alloys was actually copper, an analysis was made of the proportions in each of the market categories supplied by each of the principal types of mills, and of what changes were likely. For producer durables, for example, it was found that, given the kinds of

Lead

Lead, a heavy, soft metal, with excellent working and alloying properties, has long been valuable for its corrosion resistance and, more recently, for its impenetrability by radiation. Except for the Depression, consumption has been remarkably constant over the past thirty-five years. As traditional uses have disappeared and as more suitable or economical materials have assumed some of its roles, compensating new applications for lead have been found.

About half of lead's current use is associated with motor vehicles—about 35 per cent going into storage batteries and 16 per cent into tetraethyl lead (TEL) and tetramethyl lead. Despite the declining need for TEL in aviation fuel, these combined uses should continue to increase in importance, approaching three-fifths of the total (batteries, 35 per cent; TEL and tetramethyl lead, 24 per cent) before the

2. However, enough of relatively pure copper products are turned out that these mills have recently decided to refer to themselves as copper mills, instead of brass mills.

century is out. Of the two categories, however, it is the lead gasoline additives that really represent the important call upon resources, for they are literally "blown into thin air," while the battery lead recirculates in a runaround pattern so short (two to three years), with recovery so complete (virtually 100 per cent), that it is almost an inventory item. Less than one-third of the battery lead is really a drain on the new metal supply, although the proportion is increasing. By the same token, any misestimation in future battery-lead requirements entails compensating errors in scrap availabilities, so that the final estimate of new metal requirements is little affected.

The reason for expecting continuing large increases in consumption of lead additives to gasoline is the steadily increasing amounts of gasoline used, a consequence of the increasing automotive population projected in Part I. Containing 64 per cent lead, TEL (or its alternate) is the active ingredient imparting antiknock qualities. In addition to the aviation shift to jet fuels (i.e., commercial and military—private aviation still requires plenty of TEL), the advent of reforming (a way of producing antiknock gasoline without TEL) has slowed TEL's relative growth, but there are limitations on the quantities of gasoline that can be produced by the reforming process. Potentially more important as a possible cause of reversal in trend is the possible shift in automobile engines from the reciprocating, internal combustion type to some other type not requiring high-test gasoline as fuel. For the time being, however, we must regard this outcome as somewhat less likely than that of increasing numbers of gasoline engines demanding high-test.

Almost as important as tetraethyl lead, currently, are other dissipative uses—in paints and in other chemicals. Here, however, the relative trend, even the absolute consumption over the next twenty years, is downward so that the century will end with this as a relatively unimportant outlet.

Growth in the structural uses of lead is likely to be rather slow. One of the largest single uses—cable coverings—will probably yield to the pressures of aluminum above ground and polyethylene underground, but a certain basic

market, especially for underground use, should remain. A fair quantity of lead should continue to be used in a miscellany of metal products, mostly for industrial equipment. The calking use should rise in step with water and sewerage system installations, although there is some possibility of competition from plastic piping. The soldering use will tend to be depressed by the probable decline in copper automotive radiators, as well as by the spread of miniaturization and printed circuits in electronic devices, but the total complex of uses requiring soldering will nevertheless grow enough to produce an absolute increase in demand.

As already noted, the very substantial recovery of lead from scrap is largely a consequence of returned automotive batteries. There are other large sources, however—notably the solder in automobile radiators, type metal, and cable coverings. End-use demand is summed up in Table 16–10, and requirements for primary metal are shown in Figure 16–6.

TABLE 16–10. Lead: Net Domestic Consumption, 1960 and Projections for 1980, 2000

(Million tons)

Market category	1960		1980	2000
Storage batteries	.4	L	.3	.2
		M	.5	.8
		H	.8	2.2
Solder and calking	.1	L	.1	.2
		M	.2	.3
		H	.3	.6
Cable covering	.1	L	.1	.1
		M	.1	.1
		H	.1	.2
Other metal products	.2	L	.2	.2
		M	.3	.3
		H	.4	.6
Tetraethyl fluid	.2	L	.3	.4
		M	.3	.6
		H	.4	.9
Other dissipative uses	.1	L	.1	.1
		M	.1	.2
		H	.2	.4
Total	1.1	L	1.0	1.1
		M	1.5	2.3
		H	2.2	4.9

L = Low projection   M = Medium   H = High.
Source: Appendix Table A16–52.

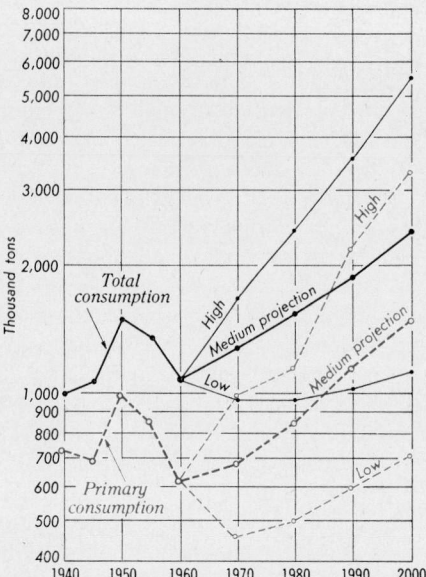

Figure 16–6. Total end-use consumption of lead (including exports) compared with primary lead consumption, 1940–1960 (five-year intervals) and projections to 2000.

Zinc

The statistical basis for tracing zinc to its end-use consumption is virtually nonexistent. Zinc usually finds its use in a number of intermediate products, each of which has an array of end-uses. Of these, galvanized steel, die-castings, brass, and zinc oxides account for nearly 90 per cent of total consumption, and the proportion should grow.

Galvanizing, which currently accounts for about one-third of zinc's use, is a way of protecting iron and steel from corrosion, by giving it a zinc coating. When exposed to the air, the zinc forms an impervious layer of zinc carbonate, which resists further attack. It is also electropositive in relation to iron, which means that when the iron is subjected to corrosion, the zinc is sacrificed in its stead. Zinc's use for galvanizing is thus closely associated with the use of steel in applications where such protection is important—currently, about 8 per cent of the steel used in construction, 12 per cent of that used in agricultural equipment, and 8 per cent of that in consumer durables. Since, of these categories, construction is the

largest tonnage user, it also accounts for the largest quantity of galvanized sheet—almost two-thirds of the total. The trend is toward even higher percentages of galvanized sheet in construction, raising this category by the year 2000 to more than half the total, and, in the process, total demand for galvanized sheet to five times (Medium projection) what it is to-day. Allowing for some thinning of the coatings, this means more than four times as much zinc. Other galvanized products (e.g., nails) are slower growing, leading to a tripling by 2000 as the over-all growth projection.

There is a "sleeper" in the galvanizing picture, however. Should galvanized sheet be adopted as the standard for automobile bodies, much larger quantities of galvanizing zinc would eventually be used.

Currently, just behind galvanizing as a zinc use is the making of die castings. This area, although aluminum is an active competitor, is potentially the most important for zinc's use and the one having the greatest rate of growth. In our Medium projection, output of zinc die castings should more than double between now and 1980 and again in the balance of the century, bringing it up to something like 40 per cent of zinc's total market.

The use of zinc in brass is dependent upon the outlook for copper already discussed. Its immediate future growth promises to be faster than that of die castings, and it should before long be accounting for 18 per cent of zinc consumption, compared with 14 per cent to-day.

Relatively, the use of zinc in oxide is declining, despite a wide range of uses for this chemical. Zinc oxide finds an outlet, among other places, in the vulcanization of rubber, in paints, ceramics, floor coverings, cosmetics, and pharmaceuticals. Probable declines in its relative vulcanizing and paint-pigment uses will help to depress this use from about 10 per cent of the total to 6 per cent by 2000. Other uses of zinc, which now sum to about 11 per cent of the total, should similarly experience relative decline.

Table 16–11 sums up the prospective end-use consumption of zinc, and Figure 16–7 indicates the total requirements for new metal.

TABLE 16–11. Zinc: Net Domestic Consumption, 1960 and Projections for 1980, 2000

(*Million tons*)

Market category	1960		1980	2000
Galvanizing	.3	L	.4	.4
		M	.6	1.0
		H	.9	2.2
Brass products	.1	L	.2	.2
		M	.3	.6
		H	.5	1.4
Die castings	.3	L	.5	.8
		M	.6	1.4
		H	.9	2.7
Oxide	.1	L	.1	.1
		M	.1	.2
		H	.2	.5
Other metallurgical and chemical uses	.1	L	.1	.1
		M	.2	.2
		H	.2	.4
Total	.9	L	1.2	1.7
		M	1.8	3.4
		H	2.7	7.2

L = Low projection   M = Medium   H = High.
Source: Appendix Table A16–61.

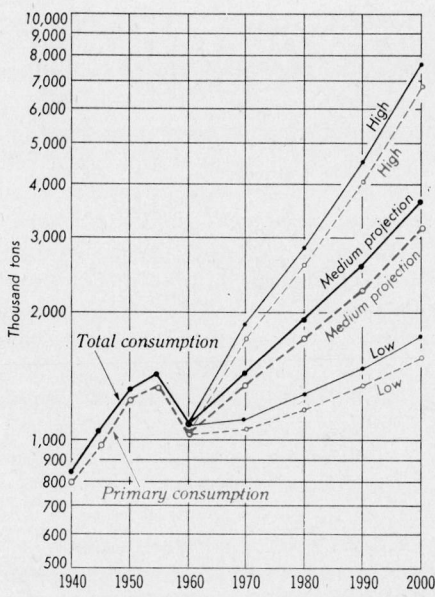

Figure 16–7. Total end-use consumption of zinc (including exports) compared with primary zinc consumption, 1940–1960 (five-year intervals) and projections to 2000.

Tin

Although it is important enough to rank with the principal nonferrous metals, the tonnage of tin consumed in the United States is currently less than one-tenth that of lead and zinc. At something like a dollar a pound, on the other hand, tin is quite comparable in value.

Aside from very small quantities intermittently obtained as by-product or mined in Alaska, there is no U.S. production of virgin tin. Consumption, therefore, is equivalent to secondary recovery plus imports. The latter arrive both as ore, for conversion at the lone U.S. smelter at Texas City, and as metal, which accounts for the greater proportion. Consumption of tin is about 40 per cent in tinplate and 25 per cent in the making of solder, with the balance about evenly divided between brass and bronze alloys and a miscellany of such items as bearings, chemicals, collapsible tubing, and type metal (see Table 16–12).

The consumption of tin for containers, already discussed in Chapter 7, accounts for about 95 per cent of the "tin and terne plate" category and thus has a major influence on whether the total consumption of tin quintuples by the end of the century, or declines. The

TABLE 16–12. Tin: Net Domestic Consumption, 1960 and Projections for 1980, 2000

(*Thousand tons*)

Market category	1960		1980	2000
Tin and terne plate	33	L	13	4
		M	28	23
		H	52	78
Solder	21	L	18	24
		M	30	51
		H	45	105
Brass and bronze	13	L	16	20
		M	28	55
		H	47	126
Miscellaneous	13	L	8	10
		M	28	55
		H	47	126
Total	80	L	55	58
		M	104	165
		H	179	401

L = Low projection   M = Medium   H = High.
Source: Appendix Table A16–71.

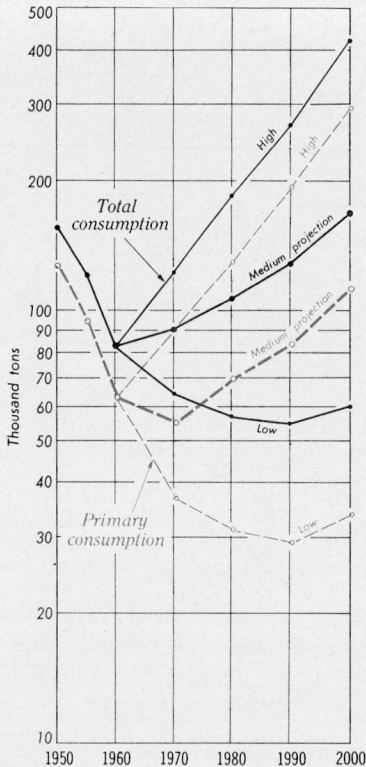

Figure 16–8. Total end-use consumption of tin (including exports) compared with primary tin consumption, 1950–1960 (five-year intervals) and projections to 2000.

wide range in the projections reflects the fact that in the contest between tinplate and aluminum the outcome is as yet undecided. The range in solder reflects in part the uncertain fate of automobile radiators, discussed in Chapter 5, but more importantly is a function of the rate of introduction of printed circuits and other technological changes in electronics and wiring, of the variety of piping used in future plumbing, and of numerous other technological cross-currents.

The proportion of tin requirements which is satisfied by recovery from old scrap (either as tin or as a constituent of alloys) has been slowly increasing and now stands at about one-fourth of net requirements. The outlook is for further increases, to a range of 28 to 43 per cent by the century's end. The percentage will be highest if the Low projection of requirements obtains and conversely lowest if the High develops. Given this modifying effect of old scrap availability, the requirements for imported tin (see Figure 16–8) may decline by the year 2000 almost to half of 1960 consumption, or they may almost quintuple. Our Medium projection is for an increase of 78 per cent.

Minor Metals

There are over fifty different metallic elements which find some sort of commercial application in the United States today. Including the alloying elements, we have discussed only thirteen of these. Some of the others are discussed in terms of both supply and demand in Chapter 21. For metals whose known availabilities are very small or whose difficulty of extraction is reflected in a very high price, demand trends independent of supply possibilities and problems become relatively meaningless. Many of these metals are substitutable one for the other, and the extent to which they are designed into products depends largely upon current technological developments which affect their costs of extraction and application. Many are connected with such frontier fields as electronic ultra miniaturization, space technology, and very high and very low temperature materials. Many are purely by-products of the extraction of other minerals, so that the extent of their utilization is highly conditioned by the demand for the principal products. Nearly all of them are utilized in quantities which, in comparison with most of the key materials dealt with in this study, are extremely small.

chapter

17

CHEMICALS

BOTH BY DEFINITION AND BY STATISTICS it is difficult to come to grips with the chemical industry. To be sure, there are traditional boundaries. The steel industry, even though it is replete with chemical reactions, from the production of pig iron by the combined impact of heat and hydrocarbons to the making of steel through the removal of excess carbon in the pig iron, the pickling, and the plating, is not a part of the chemical industry. Nor are the tanning of leather, or the conversion of wood into pulp and paper. Yet all of them rest on precise chemical reactions. What then are we to consider as the chemical industry for the purposes of this study?

The answer lies partly in tradition and partly in the inclusion here of a good many things simply because they are not included elsewhere. We can easily distinguish several major groups of products: the chemical fertilizers, the paints and varnishes, the soaps and detergents, the pharmaceuticals, the pesticides, and the vast and rapidly growing field of synthetics, within which fall, for instance, the rubbers, the fibers, the plastics in general.

Figure 17–1 sets out the scheme on which the statistics of the chemical industry are based by most federal agencies, but especially by the Federal Reserve Board in its production index.

Altogether, chemical products are counted in the tens of thousands, with the number growing apace. In place of just toilet and laundry soap, there are now dozens of different types of detergents: liquid, granular, flaky, foaming and non-foaming, green, blue, and pink, based on a variety of different chemical building blocks and processes. The same is true for fibers, to the bewilderment of the consumer, who can no longer remember, even if he can understand, the relative advantages of fibers based on acetylene, butadiene, ethylene, or xylene, and for most other chemical products. At the same time that they have led to increased variety, chemicals have greatly widened their competitive impact. Where they initially invaded mainly the field of household utensils, fibers, and rubbers, they now vie in efficiency with metals and concrete as construction materials, with glass, with leather, with fats and oils—one is almost tempted to say

---

RELATED MATERIAL: Appendix to this chapter, pp. 940–68. Requirements for clothing and textiles, Chapter 3, pp. 109–14, and appendix, pp. 598–601; for construction, Chapter 4, pp. 120–27; for durable goods, Chapter 6, pp. 154–55; and for containers, Chapter 7, pp. 167–69, and appendix, pp. 700–1. Use for fertilizers, Chapter 18, pp. 339–44.

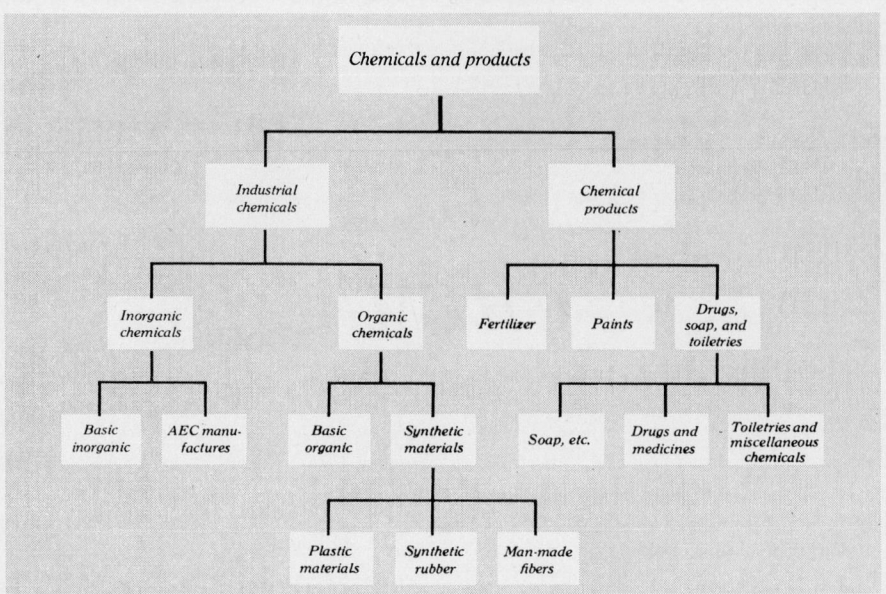

Figure 17–1. Chemicals and products, as defined by the Federal Reserve Board in its production index.

with anything but food, and even here there are portents of coming competition.[1]

The chemical product has this advantage over its natural counterpart: it can be synthesized so as to fit the intended use, whereas the natural substance which it displaces has, by and large, to be taken as found and the use adapted to its relatively inflexible characteristics. We can make a wood-like substance without appeal to termites and with other advantageous features wood does not possess, or a clothing material that moths won't eat and rain won't wet. We can manufacture a pipe that won't corrode in the ground and that will be less heavy than steel or aluminum, and a wrapping material that will be light, transparent, and waterproof and have a tensile strength many times that of paper.

If the world of chemicals is paradise for the designer it is purgatory for the statistician. Because of the numerous way-stations in the course of manufacture, the use of different units of measurement, the ease of sub-

stitutability in process and material, and the differences in degree of industrial integration, statistical duplication flourishes, and great difficulty besets the projecting of specific material requirements. In addition, the industry is characterized by fast development and equally fast obsolescence. High-pressure polyethylene is followed by low-pressure polyethylene, and both are followed by polypropylene. They all keep going for a while but it soon develops that each has advantages in given uses, so they must share the market, albeit an expanding one. Facilities are rapidly expanded and as rapidly become surplus because someone else has discovered a better process or product. Thus even a ten-year period is a very long stretch in which to project the development of the chemical industry, or at least some of the more dynamic parts of the industry. A forty-year span is for the chemical industry what a 200-year span might be for the metals or for energy. It is a time span in which anything might happen.

This is not as true for some of the industry's branches as it is for others. Traditional work horses, like sulfuric acid or the fertilizers, or

1. See Chapters 3, 4, 6, and 7.

the basic organics, such as chlorine and the alkalies, can probably count on a relatively stable rate of development. Their consumption can be projected with a good deal of confidence. But when it comes to the organics, the possibility of combining, under different conditions of pressure and heat and in the presence of different types of catalysts, different sets of hydrogen, carbon, nitrogen, and chlorine atoms (plus some others) opens up vast numbers of paths, charted and uncharted, to ever new end-products.

Most of the chemical industry is based upon raw materials that do not appear to face depletion in the time span of this review. To the extent that the basic sources are salt, lime, phosphate, or potash, the known deposits in the United States are of such magnitude as not to raise questions of even moderate cost increases due to their exhaustion (see Chapter 21). In addition, though this argument is apt to lose cogency when extended to more than a few areas of the economy, raw material costs in the chemical industry are a very small part of end-product costs. Processing equipment and energy, increasingly skilled manpower and research are characteristically far more important than the raw material. A pound of ethane, the forerunner of ethylene, costs less than half a cent; ethylene costs more nearly five cents; but by the time we have advanced to the resin, i.e. polyethylene, the price has gone to more than 30 cents a pound (this includes the cost of the various ingredients such as fillers, plasticizers, etc.). And to the consumer, the end-product, resin, appears as a raw material, from which the film, the molding, or the coating is fabricated. Thus the raw material from which the resin is derived could rise in price by a substantial margin before such an event came to be reflected in the cost of the finished consumer good.

These considerations and the principal aim of this study, to test the adequacy of natural resources for the U.S. economy, have kept us from developing detailed demand estimates for a great many parts of the chemical industry. In view of the speed with which raw material sources change, this is hardly a matter for regret. One shudders to think what a forty-year preview of the chemical industry made in 1920 might look like. And though any researcher believes himself to be more sophisticated than his predecessor, the chemical industry might shipwreck the best.

Soaps and paints. To illustrate, let us look at two ancient chemical arts: soap-making and paint manufacture. Both industries have recently experienced a revolution in their raw material base. For soap the upheaval did not get under way until after World War II. In 1940 production of soap and detergents was 25 pounds per year per capita, of which less than 1 per cent consisted of synthetic detergents. Five years later not much had happened to change the picture: total production had risen to 29 pounds per capita, of which less than 5 per cent fell into the synthetic group. Then the synthetics curve started a steep ascent. By 1950 one-third of all soap products consisted of detergents, and by 1960 the revolution was nearly complete; synthetics had conquered all but 24 per cent of the market. The relative increases have naturally been enormous. Between 1940 and 1950 production of detergents rose nearly 50-fold. Between 1950 and 1955 it nearly doubled, and between 1955 and 1960 it still grew some 47 per cent. At the same time, soap production based upon the traditional fats and oils dropped to less than one-third its 1940 level by 1960.

It is obvious that the great rise in synthetic detergents has now come to a halt. Until the next revolution in cleansing materials comes around, synthetic detergents will be one of the stable elements of the chemical industry (stable in the raw material base though undoubtedly unstable in terms of finished product competition). Within fifteen years the fats and oils producers have lost a market in which at the peak they were selling more than half a billion pounds of vegetable oils.

This was the second great revolution in the history of soap-making; the first one was the transition from wood ashes to caustic soda, soon after the middle of the last century. Certainly, the second revolution has proceeded at unprecedented speed. And even within this general upheaval there have been continual changes. The transition from soap bars to flakes to powders to liquids, attending the rise in the use of washing machines and the different theories of "cleansing power," has been a never-ending source of bewilderment to house-wives. However, it has had singularly little effect upon the total amount of soap and deter-gents consumed per person, so that it is rela-tively easy to project future aggregate require-ments.

In terms of raw materials, the detergents can be reduced principally to phosphoric acid and benzene derivatives. They thus rest upon two sources which are unlikely to raise supply problems. Processing bottlenecks rather than raw material depletion have been causes of past stringencies, and the outlook is the same for the future. Benzene, as we shall see later, has in the past been a coke oven derivative, but more recently it has been obtained in in-creasing amounts from petroleum and natural gas processing. In either event it constitutes so small a share of these raw materials that one need not enter into a discussion of its supply characteristics, except as part of the petro-chemical industry, which is dealt with below.

Changes in the production of paints, var-nishes, and lacquers have been in the same di-rection, but far less drastic. There has been a slow reduction in the oil-based paints in favor of water- and rubber-based paints, both using chemical building blocks derived from petro-leum and gas processing. By now, per gallon of paints and varnishes produced, more plastic materials than fats and oils are used. During the past two decades the use of plastics in paints has risen about tenfold, and new worlds to conquer have been correspondingly reduced.

The general point here is that, impressive as these growth developments are—and there are probably few fields where the rise can equal that of the synthetic detergents—the volume involved is merely a drop in the bucket as far as raw materials are concerned. For example, production of surface-active agents—which are the organic ingredients that provide the pri-mary properties of synthetic detergents—to-taled roughly 1½ billion pounds in 1960. Had the entire volume been derived from petroleum processing, which it was not, this would have

been equivalent to perhaps 5 million barrels of petroleum fractions, or less than two-tenths of 1 per cent of refinery throughput.

Petrochemicals

What has been said about two chemical in-dustry branches that turn out typical end-prod-ucts holds true for a much larger and rapidly growing field of which they form part, the field of petroleum-based products, generally re-ferred to as the petrochemicals. Synthetic rub-ber and fibers, agricultural chemicals such as pesticides, certain drugs and medicinals, pack-aging and coating materials, and even flavors used in the food-processing industry fall into this category. Because of the extreme versa-tility of the resin materials, which form the basic substance for the so-called synthetics, there is hardly a field in which they have not made an appearance. By proper manipulation of pressure and heat, and the admixture of different auxiliary materials, these hydrocar-bons, that are stripped from the refinery or natural gas stream or to a decreasing degree arise in the coke ovens of the steel industry, can be made into fibers; paints, indoor and most recently also outdoor; an infinite variety of utensils in daily use through molding proc-esses of various types; structural or insulating material in building; a substitute for metal in pipe; a protective coating for paper or fiber material; adhesive and bonding material; and so on in a list that is long and growing. The surprising thing is that even when all uses are taken together, they draw on only a small por-tion of the hydrocarbon streams that pass through refineries and natural gas processing facilities in the United States.

Our approach here is not basically through projection of demand for well-identified end-products. Rather, in a more complex fashion, it is through the projection of broad groups of products that are somewhat akin to the "semi-finished" category in the steel industry. This leads directly into estimates of demand for the key materials, which in this instance are oil and gas.

The statistics that relate to the industry are voluminous, but their usefulness is impaired both by duplication and by omission. On the one hand, each pound or gallon of material is counted as often as it turns up in measurable form according to the accounting method of the particular enterprise in which it is made. Thus there may be an entry for the crude material, say ethylene, as it is produced in a refinery and either sold to a processor or further treated in a branch of the plant. Next the material may turn up as polyethylene, a molecularly changed form of the ethylene, and some of it may show up in the ethylene glycol statistics, or in the plastics and resins statistics. On the other hand, it is also possible, though not common, that no record will be kept of the product stream as it changes from the crude through the so-called intermediate form into the final shape in which it leaves the chemical industry. Thus at none of the stages is it possible to say with certainty what portion of production is covered, nor is it possible to say how much duplication exists when the various stages are added. Figure 17–2[2] presents, in greatly simplified form, a picture of the flow of products out of petroleum and gas processing which gives some idea of the complexity of the industry. It illustrates the degree of duplication that might result if output is recorded at the primary, the intermediate, and the final level of production.

The nearest we can come to a measurement of the demand for oil and gas arising in the petrochemical industry is a figure carried in the official statistics (compiled, through historic accident, by the U.S. Tariff Commission) which purports to portray the "production and sales of crude products from petroleum and natural gas for chemical conversion." According to the Tariff Commission this series is relatively, though not entirely, free of the above-mentioned defects, i.e., it has only a moderate incidence of duplication and of omission. On that basis the estimated production of 26 billion pounds of chemical materials in 1960 can be compared with total oil and gas output. Total throughput of crude in the same year was approximately three billion barrels, and natural gas processed amounted to some nine trillion

cubic feet. Adding the amounts processed from the two sources yields a total volume of roughly 1.5 trillion pounds of hydrocarbons (assuming 300 pounds per barrel of crude and 50 pounds per thousand cubic feet of gas). It would then appear that chemicals based upon oil and gas consumed about 1.75 per cent of the amounts processed.

Though there are important limitations to such a calculation, for reasons that have been discussed above plus some others set out in the appendix to Chapter 17, the order of magnitude is the important thing here. Whether the percentage is 1, 1½, or 2 is of minor significance. What needs justification is the fact that, in view of this relative insignificance of the entire sector, we find it worthwhile to bother with it at all, as in other parts of the study we have relegated such magnitudes to the "all other" category and dealt with them as a minor technical adjustment to be taken care of through "blow-up" factors.

There are two reasons for concern. One is the fact that the use of hydrocarbons from oil and gas has been growing at a very fast rate indeed. Between 1950 and 1960 the Tariff Commission category cited above shows an increase of nearly 15 per cent per year compounded. While at one time the tempo was slowing down, the most recent experience permits no assumption of a continuing retardation, at least for the immediate future. A compound growth rate of 15 per cent annually is equivalent to a quadrupling every ten years. Such a rate of growth commands respect, and even a very small segment may quickly assume large proportions, especially when competing uses of oil and gas show no comparable growth rates.

Second, the comparison of total oil and gas flows with the portion that is channeled into the chemicals industry is somewhat misleading. Typically some 80 to 90 per cent of natural gas consists of methane, but until now, at least, very little of this lightest of all hydrocarbons represents a chemical feedstock. Nearly all of the hydrocarbon fractions that are being utilized as feedstock come almost entirely from the remaining 10 to 15 per cent of the natural gas processed. Similarly the petroleum refinery stream yields a limited amount of the gases

2. From Humble Oil and Refining Co., *An Introduction to Baytown Refinery* (1958).

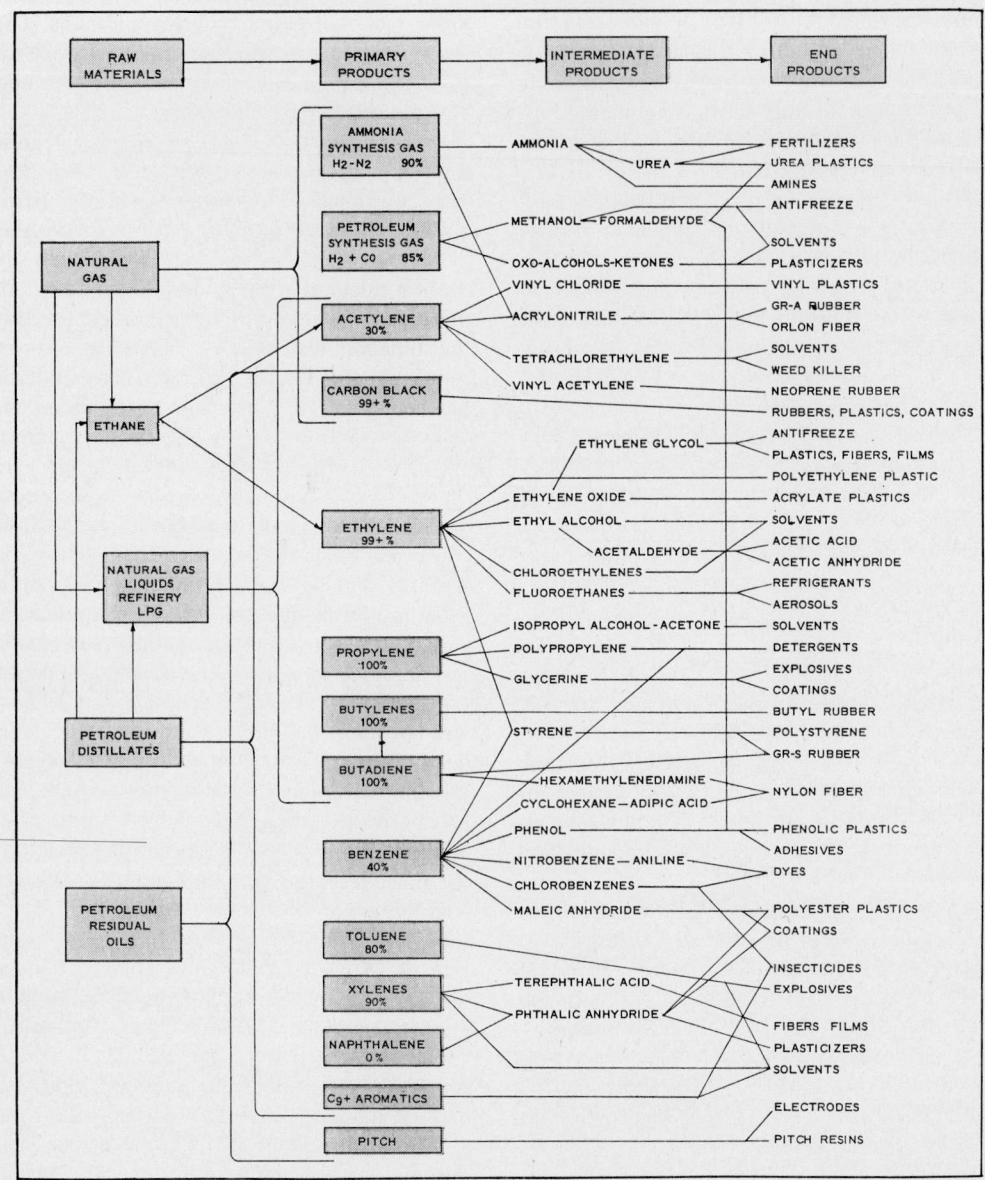

Figure 17–2. Chemicals derived from petroleum and gas.

that form the basis for the chemical industry. If demand for these were to rise, the production process would have to be reorganized so as to permit more of the crude to be transformed into the lighter hydrocarbons, less of it into middle distillates and gasoline. Not that these are unsolved technical problems—but they are matters of adjusting processing arrangements to demand. In the long run they would present little difficulty, but in the short run bottlenecks could certainly appear. (Such an instance arose some ten years ago in the production of benzene, demand for which is now far exceeded by the potential supply from refinery operations but cannot be met at will in the short run. The trend is clearly indicated by the fact that two-thirds of the country's benzene now comes from petroleum and that the last holdout—naphthalene—now is also being increasingly derived from oil.)

Given the high rates of growth in the last ten years, it is incumbent upon us to ask whether the prospects are for such rates to continue for long and whether this particular segment of the industry might not in the course of forty years become a claimant on oil and gas resources of such magnitude as to affect our analysis of gas and oil adequacy.

The diversity of the end-products makes this a difficult point to establish. Certain branches of the industry will expand slowly. Among these will be the manufacture of synthetic fibers, which has already captured large portions of the market previously occupied by other materials. As we have seen above, similar conditions are likely to prevail for the synthetic detergents and the paints. Growth in these fields will at best parallel the rate of oil and gas expansion needed to fuel the economy in general and thus will not contribute any special problem. Synthetic rubber is in a similar position, with emphasis shifting from replacement of natural material by man-made to replacement of one kind of synthetic rubber by another. The most dynamic group, and one for which we have gone to some pains in making projections, despite the general caution expressed earlier in this section, is the building blocks that form the basis for plastics and resins. "Organic crudes and intermediates" is as good a generic term for them as any other (even though the industry does not officially recognize the "intermediate" class anywhere except in the so-called aromatics: benzene, toluene, etc.). Actually, the crudes here are not especially "crude"; the term denotes more a processing stage than a physical quality.

The items covered are those that are at the base of plastic bondings, adhesives, moldings, extrusions, films, sheetings, reinforced plastics, floorings, coatings, fibers, and textile treating materials. Behind these general categories into which the industry divides its end-products are the thousands of familiar "plastics" products to

which each day seems to bring additions. They are by all odds the segment of the industry that could put the significant demand pressure upon future oil and gas production.

By projecting the end-uses, in the categories shown—relating each category in turn to a major economic classification, such as construction, or consumer durables, or fiber consumption; allocating the end-uses among the different types of resins; and calculating the amounts of primary material needed for their manufacture—we have attempted to approximate the requirements for each of the different materials. (Since allocation to different materials is based not on a range of such patterns but on a single percentage for each, and since the end-uses are on the whole not substitutes for one another, the Highs as well as the Lows are reasonably additive and have been so considered.) Not because of excessive faith in the precision of the procedure, but rather because we are not aware that this has been attempted elsewhere, we are reproducing in the appendix to this chapter the detailed routes by which we have arrived at these projections. We hope that any deficiency in procedure may act as a spur to better efforts by others in the field. The end-results are given in Tables 17–1 and 17–2, the first showing major market divisions for plastics only and the second showing the basic materials for plastics, fibers, and rubber.

The calculations are most revealing, above all in the very wide ranges that emerge, but also for the indicated steep growth. The Medium projection in Table 17–2 indicates a growth of 230 per cent between 1960 and 1980, and of nearly 150 per cent from 1980 to 2000. For the entire forty-year period the compound rate of growth works out at 5.3 per cent per year, dropping from 6 per cent for the first twenty years to 4.5 per cent for the second twenty years. This over-all growth rate is made up of a vast range of rates in the individual components. For example, one of the latest entrants, propylene, is projected to grow twentyfold in the first twenty years and not quite quadruple in the second. Use of ethylene (here confined exclusively to the portion used for the preparation of polyethylene) is projected to nearly quadruple, then more than double, in keeping

TABLE 17–1.   Requirements for Synthetic Resin Materials, by Major Markets, 1960 and Projections for 1980, 2000

(Billion pounds)

Major market	1960		1980	2000
Moldings and extrusions	1.8	L	5.2	10.9
		M	8.8	25.6
		H	15.5	64.2
Bondings and adhesives	0.6	L	1.0	1.6
		M	1.8	4.6
		H	3.7	16.1
Film for packaging	0.7	L	1.8	2.9
		M	2.4	4.8
		H	4.1	13.3
Sheeting and film (other)	0.4	L	0.8	1.3
		M	1.4	2.6
		H	2.2	5.7
Reinforced plastics	0.2	L	1.0	2.5
		M	1.4	5.2
		H	2.5	12.4
Flooring	0.4	L	1.0	1.5
		M	1.5	3.6
		H	2.5	8.0
Protective coatings	1.0	L	.9	1.2
		M	1.2	2.1
		H	1.8	4.5
Textile treating and coating	0.1	L	0.2	0.3
		M	0.3	0.5
		H	0.3	0.8
All above uses (about 85% of total market)	5.2	L	11.9	22.2
		M	18.8	49.0
		H	32.6	125.1

L = Low projection   M = Medium   H = High.
Source: Appendix Table A17–1.

with its status as an "old-timer." Another material, adipic acid, the basis for nylon and a veteran in the arsenal of synthetics, is projected to almost quintuple over the entire forty-year period.

What is important for this study is that, even at the high rates of growth assumed for some of the important building blocks, the group as a whole is not likely to affect significantly the total picture of demand for oil and gas in the next twenty or even forty years. The share that this group claims of petroleum and natural gas output is so small now that even large increments will leave it small in the future. One barrel of oil or a thousand cubic feet of gas goes a long way when converted to solid products.

Projected petroleum demand for the year 1980 is 5.3 billion barrels; for 2000 it rises to 10 billion barrels. Assuming for the moment that all petrochemical feedstock were to originate in the refinery, or rather to be derived from petroleum (it is conceivable that plants might be built at some future date that would process a *major* part of the crude barrel into chemical building blocks—as is done even now in some facilities abroad), then the 30 billion pounds of selected organic chemicals,

TABLE 17–2.   Requirements for Organic Crudes and Intermediates in Synthetic Manufacture, 1960 and Projections for 1980, 2000

(Billion pounds)

Material	1960		1980	2000
Acetylene	.64	L	1.31	1.88
		M	2.23	4.81
		H	4.16	15.66
Adipic acid	.29	L	.44	.60
		M	.82	1.38
		H	1.31	3.02
Butadiene	1.92	L	2.97	3.08
		M	4.55	7.50
		H	8.21	25.89
Ethylene (99% +)	1.31	L	2.95	4.94
		M	4.82	11.32
		H	9.15	30.70
Ethylene dichloride	.77	L	1.74	2.82
		M	2.83	6.67
		H	4.88	16.89
Formaldehyde (37% basis)	1.75	L	3.02	4.90
		M	5.68	14.81
		H	11.18	50.09
Phenol	.37	L	.54	.86
		M	.97	2.34
		H	1.87	7.39
Phthalic anhydride	.38	L	.50	.76
		M	.75	1.63
		H	1.26	3.90
Propylene (99% +)	.15	L	1.93	5.29
		M	3.08	11.88
		H	5.66	31.19
Styrene	1.73	L	3.12	4.98
		M	4.97	11.47
		H	8.83	30.24
All above	9.31	L	18.52	30.11
		M	30.70	73.81
		H	56.49	214.97

L = Low projection   M = Medium   H = High.
Source: Appendix Table A17–10.

largely resins and plastics, projected to be processed in 1980 (see Table 17–2), equivalent to perhaps 100 million barrels, would represent 2 per cent of total crude. In 2000 the projected production of petrochemical crudes, again limited to the field that we have defined here, would be equivalent to about 250 million barrels, or about 2½ per cent of total crude output. Since a sizeable fraction would, however, be derived from natural gas, the impact upon petroleum would be smaller than this figure suggests.

This does not measure the effect of *total* petrochemical production, for we have selected only one segment, namely the one that we believe is the most dynamic of those presently known. On the other hand, however, it is likely that other, presently unknown segments of the industry will in turn develop at even faster rates of growth and that the segment here measured will, therefore, represent a declining portion of the entire industry. Taking as our starting point the U.S. Tariff Commission's figure of some 26 billion pounds of materials representing the synthetic organics derived from oil and gas in 1960, and applying projected growth rates of roughly 6 per cent from 1960 to 1980 and roughly 4 per cent from 1980 to 2000 (in actual fact, there would not of course be any break of this kind in 1980; the division is here introduced only as a simplification to show orders of magnitude), we might expect demand to grow, at most, to 102 billion pounds by 1980, and not quite 370 billion pounds by 2000—the equivalent, in volume, of 340 and 1,230 million barrels respectively (see Appendix Table A10–11). Thus, petrochemical demand would exceed 6 per cent of total crude demand in 1980 and 12 per cent in 2000.

Since perhaps as much as half of the petrochemical demand would be met from natural gas processing and a small amount from coal-derived crudes, it is likely that demand for oil and gas will not exceed 5 to 6 per cent for each separately at any time in the next four decades. Thus, it can be said with a good deal of confidence that the issue of resource adequacy in the case of oil and natural gas is unlikely to be affected by the demands of the chemical industry, barring wholly unknown and unforeseeable new developments. What is indicated, however, is a continuing, growing need to strip increasing amounts of light hydrocarbon fractions from the basic material; this will have its impact primarily in the fields of research and capital investment and, to a lesser extent, energy demand, since the lighter the fraction the more energy it takes to isolate it and the more processes are involved in the isolation. Another likely answer to any developing feedstock problem would be greater use of natural gasoline, demand for which as an admixture to oil-derived gasoline is not going to rise nearly as fast as demand for it as a petrochemical base material.

These ramifications are not further pursued here. Suffice it to say that the flexibility which the industry has developed in converting one type of hydrocarbon molecule into another does not make one pessimistic as to its ability to strip five times or more the current relative fraction from gas and oil in the years to come.

A serious problem would be posed if the High petrochemical projection should develop along with the Medium or Low demand for gas and petroleum for other uses than petrochemicals. In that event petrochemicals would represent a major claimant upon total resources, and while there would be less question of adequacy of petroleum and gas as such, the relatively high demand for light fractions would call for a wholesale revamping of the industry in the image of the chemical industry. In that event the cost structure would in all likelihood undergo radical changes.

Inorganics

Chapter 21 deals briefly with the adequacy of supply of such diverse basic resources as salt, lime, phosphates, and potash, which are, with one exception, the heavy tonnage inorganic materials on which much of the chemical industry rests. The chlorine-soda industry, with its reliance on brine or other salt sources; the fertilizer industry, which is based largely upon the two natural nutrients phosphates and potash; and branches of the chemical industry (production of soda ash above all, calcium carbide, bleaches, insecticides, etc.) that rely on lime—all of these and more can be traced back to the four resources mentioned.

Save for the extent to which it is necessary for other purposes of this study to project demand for the basic chemical raw materials (above all, for the purpose of deriving a projection of the chemical production index as part of the projection of the manufacturing index; see Chapter 1), no attempt has been made to project the physical demand for chlorine, soda ash, etc. Various short-cut methods have instead been used to project the partial indexes that underlie the chemical manufacturing group index, as defined by the Federal Reserve Board. The pertinent estimates are summarized for the major groupings for 1960, 1980, and 2000 in Table 17–3.

The inorganic chemicals (chlorine, the alkalies, sulfuric acid, etc.) are projected in proportion to the index of all manufacturing. This relationship has been carried on historically, simply because the basic chemicals enter such a large variety of production processes throughout the economy. Similar relationships have been utilized to project other parts of the chemical index; for example, farmer outlays for

fertilizer have been used to estimate fertilizer demand, and personal consumption expenditures to project demand for toiletries.

Sulfur. The one resource which warrants a closer look among the inorganics is sulfur. It is not too long ago that most of the world was in the throes of an acute sulfur shortage. As so often happens, this very shortage was partly instrumental in opening the way toward a substantial widening of basic sulfur resources and a more optimistic outlook (see Chapter 21). The projection of demand is, therefore, of some interest.

Historical statistics show the remarkable harmony between the movement of sulfur consumption and that of industrial production. This is illustrated in Figure 17–3.[3]

The relationship in the last ten years between apparent consumption of sulfur and the revised FRB index of industrial production has been remarkably steady. Between 1951 and 1960 consumption of sulfur per point of the index was roughly 57,000 tons, and the remarkable fact is that in none of the nine years

3. Reproduced from *Chemical Week,* May 16, 1959, with permission of McGraw-Hill Publishing Company.

TABLE 17–3. Chemical, Petroleum, and Rubber Products Industry Production, 1960 and Medium Projections for 1980, 2000

Group	Index of production (1957 = 100)		
	1960	1980	2000
Chemical, petroleum, and rubber products	118	283	624
Chemicals and products	121	294	642
Chemical products	116	238	502
Drugs, soap, and toiletries	118	267	580
Paints	103	115	191
Fertilizers	115	209	333
Industrial chemicals	127	348	778
Inorganic	115	274	649
Organic	132	380	832
Basic organic	129	321	596
Synthetic materials (plastic materials, synthetic rubber, man-made fibers)	136	452	1,125
Petroleum products	108	185	342
Rubber and plastic products (tires and tubes, and misc. rubber and plastic products)	114	342	843

Source: Appendix Table A1–30.

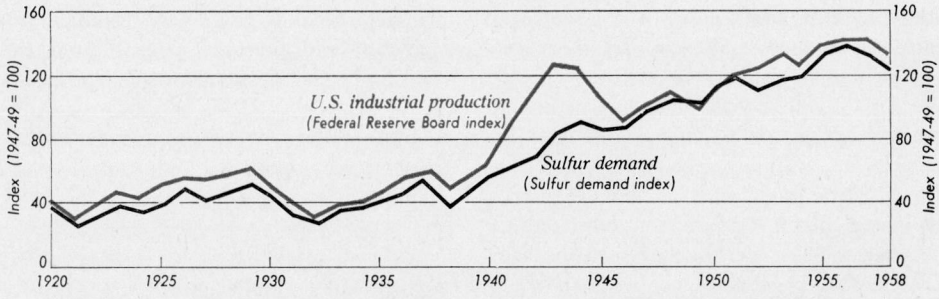

Figure 17–3. Rise of sulfur demand compared with industrial production, 1920–1958.

was it higher than 59,650 or lower than 54,300 tons. Indeed, if one were to omit 1951 and 1960, the absence of significant fluctuations would be even more marked. Prior to 1951 the level appears to have been somewhat higher, though again not substantially so. Altogether, considering the purposes of this study, one may legitimately speak of a constant relationship.

The question then arises whether one can confidently foresee the continuation of this relationship. In view of the enormous diversity in the use of sulfur, primarily in the form of sulfuric acid, such a continuation is extremely difficult to prove but less difficult to judge. Sulfur's most important single outlet, the production of fertilizers, is projected to grow at a rate substantially below that of manufacturing generally. The same is true, though less so, for another large-scale outlet, steel. And rayon production, which consumes substantial amounts of sulfuric acid, is not going to grow steeply. On the other hand, there will undoubtedly be increased use of sulfur in ore production and in metal processing in the nonferrous field. As lower grade ores are resorted to, more use will be made of leaching, a process in which sulfuric acid is likely to gain a steadily increasing market. The chemicals industry generally, with its above-average growth rate, will also remain a dynamic outlet for sulfuric acid, and so will the paper industry. Finally, it must be remembered that even now more than one-third of sulfuric acid is consumed in uses—numbering in the hundreds—each one of which takes only a small fraction of the total amount. These uses will most likely grow at the average rate of industrial production, as

will the manufacture of pigments, which is a large sulfuric acid customer. There is one final factor that might be of importance: to the extent that liquid fertilizer gains at the expense of solid material, the role of sulfuric acid will diminish. In the nitrogenous fertilizers this has already happened. It is not in sight for sulfur's principal market, the production of phosphatic fertilizer; yet it might happen.

Given the wide dispersion in consumption and the outlook for the factors that make for larger as well as for smaller than average increases in sulfur consumption, one does not feel especially uncomfortable assuming a rise in sulfur demand proportionate to the rise in industrial production. Such a rise would be from an estimated 6 million long tons in 1960 (this excludes export demand of roughly 1½ million tons) to 30 million tons in 2000, growing at an annual compound rate of 4.1 per cent. Over the forty years involved demand would cumulate to some 600 million long tons. Should sulfur demand grow at the rate of 6 instead of 4 per cent, not an inconceivable though a less likely rate, demand would cumulate to over 900 million tons. On the other hand, a lower rate is also possible, given the array of circumstances touched on above. At 3 per cent growth, total demand would reach only about 450 million tons. With sulfur production developing all over the world, largely on the basis of natural gas production and petroleum refining, it is unlikely that export demand will grow. No more than another 50 to 60 million tons might be added to cumulative domestic demand for the forty-year span. We shall see in Chapter 21 how these magnitudes relate to projected availability.

Fertilizers. While adequacy of basic raw materials for fertilizer production seems fully assured, the rough dimensions of the projected demand are still worth sketching in. The United States is so well provided with deposits that only the roughest approximations need be made. Total phosphate rock consumption, domestic and export, was at about 17 million tons in 1960, with a phosphoric pentoxide (P_2O_5) content of 5 million long tons. About 80 per cent of this went to domestic markets, and of domestic consumption roughly one-half was in the form of fertilizer. The remainder was absorbed largely by various branches of the chemical industry, especially soapmaking. We estimate that demand for phosphates will grow at a rate of 2.5 per cent per annum, on the basis of projected farm outlays for fertilizer and likely trends in growth rates for the different nutrients. At this rate cumulative demand for the forty years would amount to approximately 330 million long tons of P_2O_5 content. Should the rate of growth reach twice that assumed as most likely, i.e., 5 per cent, cumulative demand would instead total over 600 million tons.

The situation is not quite as clear-cut in the case of potash, but the net conclusion differs little. Because there has been a tendency for potash consumption to grow faster than that of phosphate in agricultural use, we start off with a somewhat higher growth rate for potash, 3.7 per cent per year. The cumulative demand at that rate would be not quite 200 million tons (measured in K_2O, or potassium oxide, content) for the forty-year period. This is equivalent to one-half of the recoverable reserves of the United States.

Since our initial growth rate is higher than that of phosphate demand, a more dynamic growth rate would not be as high as double the 3.7 per cent; but suppose the rate were 5 per cent over the entire period, what would be the implications? Cumulative demand would rise to more than 250 million tons, and again our judgment would have to be that such levels of demand would in no way cause a disconcerting rate of depletion. It has been estimated that currently our crop-raising activities remove some 5 million tons of K_2O from the soil. Starting from this estimate and projecting on the basis of rising crop production, one might establish a maximum demand case by assuming that all potash lost from the soil would be restored through fertilization. If this were to take place with immediate effect, the resulting demand for potash over the forty years might be in the neighborhood of 300 million tons (K_2O), on the basis of roughly a doubling of gross farm output and an initial consumption level of 5 million tons per year. Even such an extreme assumption reveals no alarming magnitude of demand.

In the case of the third of the plant nutrients, nitrogen, direct fixation of nitrogen from the air through vegetation, remains, of course, the principal source. But among additions made by the farmer, a radical raw material revolution has taken place in the last twenty-five years. Whereas through the mid-twenties the bulk of nitrogen (mostly in the form of ammonium sulfate) was a domestic coke oven by-product or imported, the balance began to shift toward what is called synthetic ammonia, produced from a hydrogen source, such as natural gas, and nitrogen in the air in the presence of a catalyst, around 1930. By 1935, the nitrogen contained in synthetic ammonia for the first time exceeded that contained in coke-oven ammonia. Not only has the situation never been reversed, but synthetic ammonia production has been steadily expanding, while that of coke-oven ammonia has been growing only slowly and has become stationary in the more recent past. The result has been that synthetic ammonia, based primarily on natural and refinery gas, now dominates the picture. Natural nitrogen sources, such as Chilean nitrate of soda, which began to fade after World War I, have for all practical purposes disappeared from the American scene.

To the extent that one can ignore all but synthetic ammonia, the resource situation here is similar to that of the synthetic materials already discussed: natural gas and oil demand for other purposes looms so large that the additional claim made upon them by the production of ammonia is negligible. At the rate of approximately 32,000 cubic feet of natural gas which is required to produce a quantity of ammonia containing one short ton of nitrogen, the roughly 3.5 million tons of nitrogen consumed in 1960 required somewhat over 100 billion cubic feet of natural (or refinery) gas, the equivalent of about 1 per cent of natural gas consumption for all purposes. Statistically it is included in total natural gas demand as presented in Chapter 15.

At a high rate of growth, say, 5 per cent per year, the present consumption of 3.5 million tons would rise to 25 million tons by 2000. Gas required would then be about 800 billion cubic feet, but because natural gas consumption would have risen substantially for other reasons, this quantity again would represent only a very small percentage, in the neighborhood of 2 per cent, of total gas withdrawal. The total demand for gas as shown in Chapter 15 includes this implicitly since it is projected from a 1960 withdrawal figure that comprises *all* uses. Especially in view of the fact that some refinery gas joins natural gas as a source of hydrogen for ammonia production, it is obvious that requirements will in no way be critical and can easily be met, or rather will not aggravate any shortage that might arise because of the demand for oil and gas in other uses.

Pharmaceuticals. If we omit other branches of chemical manufacturing, it is for the reason that, whatever resource problems the industry may have, they do not lend themselves to the gross quantitative approach that characterizes this study. The pharmaceutical industry may serve as an example. It has in recent years been the object of study, both in and out of government, but the focus has been not on its raw material supply situation but rather on its pricing practices and the competitive situation in the industry generally. What is of interest here is that discoveries of the past two decades have tended to broaden the raw material base of the industry. In a sense there has been a cycle that has now been closed, or is closing. From the early reliance on herbs, roots, and other botanical material, the drug industry moved on to an emphasis on aspirin, the sulfas, and a variety of vitamin and amino acid

products, all derived from coal tars and later from oil and gas. It is estimated that in the fifties three out of every four pounds of synthetic organic chemicals were coal- or oil-based. Recently there has been a return to the botanical base, but at quite a different level with different supply implications. The antibiotics have largely displaced the sulfas, for example, and grains are their base. Similarly, with the discovery of penicillin the supply base began to shift back to the ancient curative, botanicals.

But not only has the base shifted; it has also broadened, for many of the raw materials of the drug industry are not scarce herbs or roots (though some are) but waste products of the food industry. Thus the base has also cheapened. When it was found, for instance, that penicillin could be made from certain waste materials produced in the course of brewing, the industry gained an entirely new source of supply. As in many other cases science has created an important economic resource from waste products which previously had little or no value.

This changing pattern in raw material consumption relates primarily to the so-called "ethical drugs." By and large these are the types of products sold on doctors' prescription; their quality must meet rigid technical standards established by law. In the case of the so-called "proprietary drugs," which are patented and sold directly under various brands, the available statistical data do not permit a similar analysis. The proprietary drugs, however, represent a declining segment of the pharmaceutical industry. They accounted for nearly 50 per cent of all the industry's output in 1939 but the proportion has declined to less than one-quarter in recent years.

With so much research effort expended in discovering new drugs, it is difficult to say what raw materials may acquire new prominence in the future. But the availability of both the mineral and agricultural resources from which drugs will continue to be synthesized is more than adequate. Even allowing for large potential expansion of antibiotics as animal feed supplements, grain and sugar fermentation products will be plentiful enough for any future growth of the drug industry.

part

III

ADEQUACY OF THE RESOURCE BASE

I
T NOW remains to compare our projections of demand for resource products over the next four decades with the natural resources from which they must be met— that is, to test the adequacy of available resources to sustain continued economic growth in the United States. The resources we shall consider are largely domestic; they have been the traditional suppliers of most of the nation's needs and are likely to remain so. In a number of instances, however, especially for petroleum and a number of the metals, we shall also consider foreign sources in parts of the world that appear likely to be accessible to the United States during the balance of the century.

Here, as in earlier parts of this study, there is little that is clear cut in so long a look ahead. Just as the Medium, High, and Low projections of demand are no more than estimates of what seem to be future trends under varying sets of assumptions, our estimates of resource availability grow out of informed conjecture on the basis of imperfect present knowledge. Comparisons of demand and resources in the following chapters are in no sense predictions.

Inevitably there are great uncertainties in looking ahead over forty years that apparently will be marked by technological advance and political change; a further limitation has been built into our study from the start. The projections of demand have not been influenced by the supply considerations that will be discussed in the following chapters. No allowance has been made, that is, for market adjustments that normally would be expected in the form of lower demand for a given product (perhaps through a shift to cheaper substitutes) if its price rose. Such reactions obviously will continue to take place. But if we had taken account of them in our demand projections, most of the coming resource supply problems would have "solved" themselves, at least on paper: free-market adjustments would have brought supply and demand into balance at some level or other. Our purpose, instead, is to uncover possible supply difficulties of the future by inquiring into what would seem likely to happen without significant increases in the real cost of any resource product.

Limitations in concept and method are not confined to the demand side. Availability of a given resource in the amount required is not only a function of the physical environment, but also a function of the price that is offered.

With the necessary expenditure of effort (and therefore cost), cropland can be "created" where it does not exist today. Proper applications of fertilizer and water will—at a cost—allow crops to be harvested on once barren land. Similarly, the requisite price will bring forth reserves of metallic ores—or any other mineral—by raising the economic threshold at which a particular deposit can be considered worth exploiting.

Our judgments as to future adequacy must therefore be cautious and approximate. Timing cannot be firm, and the cost effect frequently cannot be spelled out in dollars and cents.

This would be true even if the United States were an economic island. Exposure to the uncertainties of international trade aggravates the problem. The reader must therefore be prepared to live with approximations, indications, and suggestions, with degrees of likelihood and with reasonable surmises, not with firm predictions. We cannot say that in such and such a year the country will be faced with an exhaustion or the beginnings of a severe curtailment in the supply of such and such a resource. We may, however, reasonably suggest that, given the demand projection, "sometime in the seventies," or "after 1980," supply is likely to be available only at a substantially higher price, or whatever the case might be.

Subject to such limitations we have in this part of the study brought together our best judgment (1) of the degree to which resources might be adequate to the task set for them by trends in demand and (2) of the period during which such problems as we foresee might begin to exert their influence.

Where it demands the analysis, estimates of resource availability are compared with the High and Low estimates of demand as well as with the Medium projection. Thus adequacy is tested not only for the "most likely" path of events but also for demand situations that are reasonably possible though less likely to occur.

chapter

18

LAND

LAND IS THE RESOURCE BASE not only of food, clothing, lumber, and other direct or indirect products of farms, grasslands, and forests, but also of the space required for towns and cities; highways, railroads, and airports; outdoor recreation, wildlife habitat, and reservoirs and other aspects of water management. Changes in the demands for land and for its products can often be quite different, in accordance with how intensively and efficiently land is used; the way in which the needs of 1980 and 2000 are met will depend to a large extent on how the nation's total land area can be made to serve a diversity of uses.

Except for fractional variations that result from land's being above water at some times and submerged at others, the land surface of the United States is a fixed quantity—1,904 million acres, not counting Alaska or Hawaii. By Census definition this total includes inland water courses less than one-eighth mile wide, lakes and reservoirs of less than 40 acres, and land partially or temporarily covered by wa-

ter, like marshland, swamps, and river flood plains.

Acreage, however, is by no means the only measure of the land's capacity to provide goods and services. To say that the United States has a land area of 1,904 million acres and is the fifth largest country in the world tells little about how such an area can support a population of 250 million, of 350 million, perhaps of 450 million people. No two pieces of land are exactly alike, even though many of the differences are too small to give cause to practical recognition or consequences. Climatic, topographic, and soil differences are among the most obvious; differences in location relative to population centers or transportation routes are others. Some are immutable, others man can change. Little can—so far—be done to change the basic temperature pattern or the hours of light and sunshine. But earth-moving machinery can alter the topography; chemicals can affect soil properties; reclamation, drainage, and irrigation works can modify the con-

---

RELATED MATERIAL: Appendix to this chapter, pp. 969–86. Urbanization section of Chapter 1, pp. 73–74. Food requirements, Chapter 2, pp. 89–103, and appendix, pp. 586–95. Clothing and textiles, Chapter 3, pp. 104–11, and appendix, pp. 596–602. Agricultural fuel requirements section of Chapter 10, pp. 218–21, and appendix, pp. 776–77. Outdoor recreation, Chapter 11, pp. 223–30. Crops, Chapter 12, pp. 233–51, and appendix, pp. 778–803. Lumber and woodpulp, Chapter 13, pp. 252–57, and appendix, pp. 804–15. Farm irrigation, Chapter 14, pp. 266–68, and appendix, pp. 832–33.

ditions of humidity; and river regulation or road construction can alter spatial relationships. Within limits, land characteristics can be altered to serve a particular economic and social purpose.

On the other hand, changes in the use of land, in response to population growth and changing demand, cannot be expected to be rapid. As Clawson and his co-authors have shown in their *Land for the Future* (cited in Table 18–1), changes in the United States since World War I have been relatively small.

Both in 1920 and in 1950 (the latest year for which nationwide census data were available at the time of writing) two-thirds of all land was devoted to agriculture and grazing; around one-quarter to forestry; and from 8 to 10 per cent to all other uses (see Table 18–1). For many years nine out of every ten acres have been used for growing crops to be consumed directly, to be fed to livestock, or to be turned into fiber and forest products.

Today's land use pattern is not the result of a systematic, planned allocation of sites to uses to which they are best adapted. Not all the best soil is in crops; some of the poorer soil is. Towns and cities may occupy good farming land, and crops are grown on millions of acres

that would better be grazed or support nonagricultural activities. Yet, on the whole, clashes between land capability and land use are gratifyingly small in the pattern that has evolved through trial and error.

We have no measure of change in the intrinsic quality of the average acre in cultivation. All we can say is that in 1960 the average cropland acre yielded about two-thirds again as much in crops as the average cropland acre in 1910, but this comparison rests on important factors other than land, including the state of scientific knowledge and technology and the extent of their application.

Will the combined pressure of rising numbers and higher incomes permit us to maintain the present pattern of land use? At what levels of population and income growth are strains likely to appear? And in what direction can we expect to find paths of adjustment, so that the same area that provides the highest standard of living in the world for some 180 million Americans now may enable perhaps as many as 430 million to enjoy a far higher standard in 2000? It is to these questions that this chapter addresses itself.

Although the uses of land for purposes other than farming, grazing, and forestry currently

TABLE 18–1.   Use of Land in the United States, Selected Years, 1900–1950

(Million acres)

Uses of land	1900	1910	1920	1930	1940	1950
Cities of 2,500 or more population (incl. city parks)	6	7	10	12	13	17
Public recreation areas (excl. city parks)	5	9	12	15	41	46
Agriculture	449	488	538	531	511	523
Crops	319	347	402	413	399	409
Pastured cropland	77	84	78	73	68	69
Non-producing (farmsteads, etc.)	53	57	58	45	44	45
Commercial forestry	525	512	500	495	488	484
Grazing	808	775	730	735	740	700
Transportation	17	19	23	24	24	25
Reservoirs and water management	*	1	2	3	7	10
Primarily for wildlife	*	*	1	1	12	14
Mineral production ⎫ Deserts, swamps, mountain tops, some non-commercial forest, etc. ⎬ Miscellaneous and unaccounted for ⎭	94	93	88	88	68	85
Total	1,904	1,904	1,904	1,904	1,904	1,904

* Negligible.

Source: Marion Clawson *et al., Land for the Future* (Baltimore: Johns Hopkins Press and Resources for the Future, 1960), p. 442.

account for only 10 per cent of all land, they include some of the most powerful in effective demand, such as urban and transportation use, and others that fall peculiarly within the sphere of public responsibility of one sort or another, above all recreation facilities. They cannot, therefore, be treated as the negligible tail end and be estimated by the "all other" method. For all we know, it might easily be the tail that wags the dog. Crop, grazing, and forest land might become scarce because of the effective inroads made by other uses.

In the rest of this chapter we shall consider the adequacy of agricultural and grazing land; then the demands of timber production upon the land base; and third, the projected impact of urban, recreation, and other uses. In conclusion, we shall bring together and, insofar as possible, reconcile these contrasting demands that all must be met from the nation's unexpandable total land area.

Agriculture and Grazing

In the production of food and natural fiber the need for space can be reduced but never eliminated. Somewhere along the line a green plant figures in the production process. Inquiry into the nation's capacity for growing the quantities of crops that will be needed between now and the year 2000 (as projected in Chapter 12) leads to land as the key resource. Not just any land will do. There is a wide range from the ideal acre to the barely marginal and the completely useless.

When certain land improvements become profitable, the process of substituting inputs of labor and capital for inputs of land begins, and useful acreage thus undergoes expansion without any physical addition. An acre of cropland, alternating between lying fallow and growing wheat in a system of dry farming, is hardly comparable to that same acre after water has been brought to it and it can be cropped every year. Drainage of land with many low spots where water might stand for long periods, preventing their use or even the most effective use of the entire area in a wet spring, may not show up in statistics as an increase in cropland acreage, yet it accounts for

as real an increase as a brand new acre of land added to the old supply. Similarly, the addition of fertilizer that has doubled the productivity of an acre for a given crop has effectively increased by one acre the total land base on which agriculture rests.

Agricultural Expansion

Whether or not it pays to make the required investment is determined by the economic and institutional conditions of the time. In that sense, the resource base is not fixed. Consumer demand and facilities for improving the land will determine the effective annual acreage.

The interplay of these factors in the United States in recent years has resulted in a farm output so large that it has more often been depicted as a national disaster than as a triumph of man over his environment. Yet, in a longer perspective, our present difficulties seem but a small blemish in the astounding accomplishments of technology and skill.

The physical acreage from which crops were harvested in 1960 was nearly identical with that of half a century ago, but the average acre in 1960 yielded some two-thirds more than did the average acre forty years earlier—adding the equivalent of nearly 250 million acres to our land supply. During the same forty years, moreover, the substitution of machines for work animals has freed some 80 million acres for non-feed uses. In 1920, 25 per cent of the cropland used for crops was used to produce feed for horses and mules and thus was not available to produce food or fiber crops; less than 2 per cent was so used in 1960. Furthermore, the production job was done with less than half the man-hours needed in 1920.

Figure 18–1 summarizes these developments by comparing input of all factors of production with farm output.[1] The changes are the net result of conflicting tendencies; the trend towards higher productivity is by no means a one-way street. Agricultural land of high quality in a particular location may be of much greater value for other uses than for farming;

1. From *Changes in Farm Production and Efficiency*, Statistical Bulletin No. 233 (Washington: U.S. Department of Agriculture, rev. July 1961), p. 47.

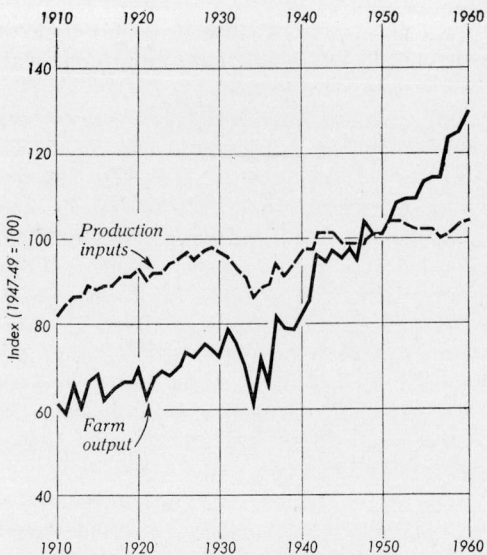

Figure 18–1. Farm output and production inputs, 1910–1960.

buyers can afford to bid it out of agricultural use. As land of high quality is lost, lower quality land will tend to replace it, requiring considerable investment of capital if it is to be equally productive. Some agricultural land today is no longer as productive as it was in 1910, for erosion has taken its toll over the years. Against these losses must be considered the gains from investments made to increase the productive capacity of other land. The extent of these changes and the nature of the balance between them is something that is not known, except as it is reflected in the size of the output of the nation's acreage. Over the past twenty years, there has been practically no increase in the sum total of input factors to support steady growth in output.

Until around 1920, the expansion of agricultural output in the United States came about in greatest measure as a result of the westward march of settlement and the resulting transfer of large areas of public domain land to private ownership. The productivity of the land changed very little. Yields per acre of cropland did fluctuate from year to year, but from the late 1860's, the earliest period for which national statistics are available, until the 1930's,

there was but the slightest over-all improvement in crop yields. The extension of farming into drier areas offset, partially or wholly, whatever gains in productivity per acre were being made elsewhere. Insect pests, plant diseases, and a decline in natural soil fertility brought about by cropping and by erosion losses were other factors.

As long as land was cheap and abundant and farm settlement outpaced the nation's needs for agricultural commodities, there was little reason for developing an intensive agriculture. With the limited technology and farming skills then available, it cost more to obtain an additional bushel or pound from an acre of land already cultivated than to raise it on new land. The financial resources of farmers on the frontier were often extremely limited, and labor, beyond that of the individual himself or his immediate family, was also scarce. It was only logical to spread these limited resources over as much of the more abundant land as possible.

In comparison with his European counterpart, the American farmer still makes extensive use of his cropland, but the additional requirements of a growing population can no longer be satisfied merely by increasing the acreage of land in cultivation. Changes in yield per acre make it clear that land is contributing less to the increases in output than it did in earlier times.

Figure 18–2 shows the percentage increase in the yield of selected crops over a quarter century.[2]

Factors in yield increases. There is no single cause for the great upsurge in yields. Some of the improvement can be attributed to a relocation of producing areas, which can bring differences in cropping practices and levels of managerial ability as well as differences in the quality of soil, topography, and climate. A striking instance of this is the shift of cotton production to California, with larger acreages per farm under irrigation. The average yield for the state in 1960 was 981 pounds of lint

2. Based on T. C. Byerly, "The Biological Sciences," *Journal of Farm Economics*, December 1958, Table 1, p. 1038.

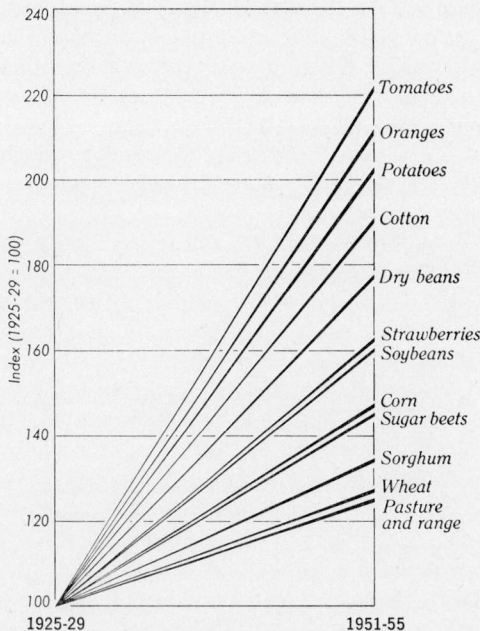

Figure 18–2. Increases in yields per acre, 1925–29 to 1951–55.

(graph labels, top to bottom on right side)
Tomatoes
Oranges
Potatoes
Cotton
Dry beans
Strawberries
Soybeans
Corn
Sugar beets
Sorghum
Wheat
Pasture
and range

(y-axis) Index (1925-29 = 100)
240 220 200 180 160 140 120 100

(x-axis) 1925-29   1951-55

value, with increased stress on high output of economically desirable factors, producible with the lowest input of feed.

But even the greatest potential may never reach fruition in a niggardly environment. To improve the environment, man has long resorted to soil additives, first of organic and more recently of inorganic origin. Nitrogen, phosphate, and potash are the mainstays of this group. Their influence has been vast. Ibach and Lindberg of the U.S. Department of Agriculture estimate that "average yields on the fertilized acreage of all crops and pasture in 1954 were 113 per cent above yields on the unfertilized acreage and 16 per cent above average yields per harvested acre."[3]

The use of fertilizer even in this country is still moderate: true, the use of chemical fertilizer in 1954 was five times greater than during the 1930's, but only half the acreage of inter-tilled crops, such as corn and cotton, and little more than a quarter that of the close-growing crops, such as small grains, was fertilized. At the 1954 rate of application, which was judged by Ibach and Lindberg to be "well below the rate of application that would have been most profitable for farmers whose capital resources would have permitted higher rates,"[4] one ton of plant nutrients produced the same results as 10.7 acres of land. The recent rate of consumption of 6 to 7 million tons of plant nutrients per year one might roughly conjecture to be the equivalent of 75 million acres of farmland, some 60 million acres more than in the mid-thirties, when the growth in fertilizer use really got under way. (These calculations make rough allowance for reduced use of organic manure.)

There has been some reduction in production losses through the ravages of insects, plant diseases, and weeds, which in the 1940's— the only period for which such estimates have been made—were equivalent to the output of about 60 million acres. Undoubtedly, the record has improved greatly since; the major wave of advance in pesticides and insecticides, the

per acre, in contrast to yields of 486 pounds in Mississippi and 329 pounds in Texas; her total production was second only to that of Texas. The weight of the California per acre yield certainly was a powerful influence in establishing the national average yield of 446 pounds, up 70 per cent from the level reached a decade earlier.

The plants themselves have undergone great change. Some crop varieties common today were unknown a generation ago. Crop improvement is not new in itself, but modern methods of deliberate and systematic crossing of plants, guided by a knowledge of genetics, have achieved striking results; increased yields, lessened vulnerability to natural hazards, greater ability to withstand drought, heightened resistance to insect, disease, and wind damage, adaptability of different varieties to different climatic conditions—all of these characteristics and more have been successfully bred into new strains. Parallel developments in the livestock field, notably artificial insemination, have produced animals of superior

3. D. B. Ibach and R. C. Lindberg, *The Economic Position of Fertilizer Use in the United States,* Agricultural Information Bulletin No. 202 (Washington: U.S. Department of Agriculture, 1958), p. 7.

4. *Op. cit.,* pp. 6, 9.

march of the alphabetical chemicals—from DDT to BHC and 2,4–D and its many successors and variants, did not really get under way until World War II, and it is still going. Improved machinery has helped in reducing damage from weather, especially through speed, allowing better timing of operations, and thus allowing full advantage to be taken of periods of favorable weather. But the acreage still claimed by losses gives an opportunity for substantial future gains, through improved chemicals and better methods of applying them and through improved cultural practices—timing of operations, choice of crop rotations, methods of seedbed preparations, etc.

Institutional factors have also been important in boosting crop yields. The various measures employed by the federal government to control production have been limited to the reduction of the quantity of land that may be planted to particular crops, without regard for differences in quality of land or the extent to which other factors may be substituted for land. These policies in turn have given farm operators an incentive to retire their less productive cropland and farm the remainder with greater use of fertilizer and increased application of other improved production practices. There was a net reduction of 20 million harvested acres between 1953 and 1958. Tobacco and cotton production fell during the period, but the output of feed grains, food grains, oil crops, and hay and forage crops actually increased.

Farmers are often said to prefer traditional methods to newer and more profitable techniques. The reputation may be deserved by many part-time, subsistence, and low-producing commercial farmers. But it is not among the 25 per cent of the nation's farmers who produce more than 75 per cent of all farm products sold in the market. Many of the low-producing farms are grossly inadequate in terms of soil resources, capital goods, or management skills and abilities. The farmers manage to survive as long as they are willing to accept a level of living much below the average for Americans today, and particularly if only part of the output is produced for the market. The human situations involved here are among the most

difficult of the country's farm problems, but they do not seem to constitute an obstacle to expanding total farm production in line with rising needs.

In the past, the fact that many farmers have been slow in picking up all the technological innovations has not caused any hardship for consumers. Existence of both a backlog of unused technology and large stocks of farm commodities in the early 1940's made possible the rapid expansion in farm output that was needed in the years immediately following.

It is difficult, if not impossible, to reverse technological advance in the face of a decline in the market, and even if it were easy, serious social and economic questions would arise. In the long run we do not look for reversal, or even a slowdown. Continuing advance in yields is needed if American agriculture is to meet the demands of the next forty years with little or no increase in agricultural land. This need does not necessarily point to great difficulties ahead. Average crop yields for the nation are a function of time, among other things. It takes time to discover the means for enlarging the productive capacity of agriculture within the relatively narrow confines of available cropland. It takes even more time for these changes to become established farming practices, although the period of adoption varies. Widespread acceptance of hybrid corn, for example, took place over a decade. While today's agriculture would be little match for the demands that can be anticipated for 1980 or 2000, the intervening years will provide an opportunity to exploit to the fullest the technology known today and, in addition, to permit initial application of technology as yet unknown. Agriculture's productive capacity may well be more than adequate for the job.

Projections of Yield

What yields could be reached before an effort to bring in large areas of marginal land would be needed to keep up with demand? The illustrative yield estimates which follow are an indication of reasonable capabilities. They cannot, of course, be supported with projections of all the factors that will bring them

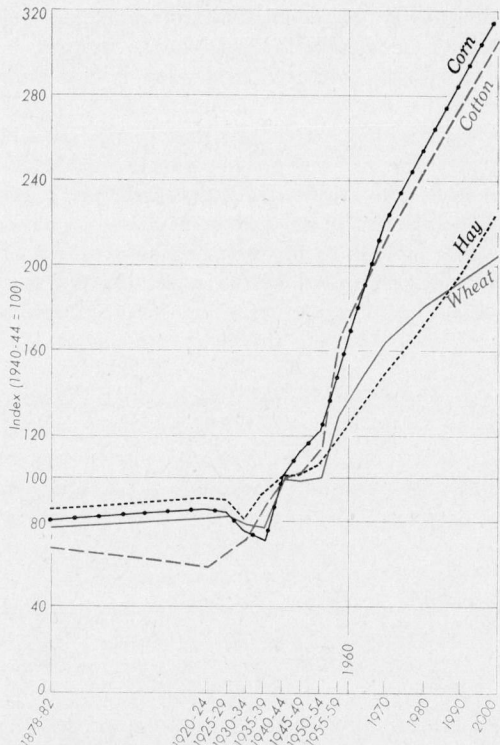

Figure 18–3. Yields of wheat, corn, cotton, and hay for five-year periods, 1878–82 to 1955–59, for 1960, and Medium projections to 2000.

about.[5] Like the other forward estimates in this study, they are a group's judgment of reasonable probability, derived from critical evaluation of available data and analyses but, in the last resort, a matter of judgment.

Some past developments. Food grains, feed grains, cotton, and forage production account for the bulk of the land devoted to crops in the United States. Figure 18–3 indicates the average yield per harvested acre of the major crops from these groups, wheat, corn, cotton, and tame hay, since 1920, as well as for a base period of some eighty years ago, 1878–82. These yields are contrasted with projections for the next forty years.

The first forty-year period produced no significant yield increases, bearing out our earlier

5. For example, irrigation development, as projected in Chapter 14, is not in any systematic way a condition of the projected yields.

observation that increases in the output of American agriculture were for many years achieved largely by the creation of new farm units on virgin soil. The late 1920's and the 1930's produced relatively undistinguished, and even declining, yields reflecting in part, in the latter period, the combined effects of drought and depression. Cotton yields, at a low point during the early 1920's, when the boll weevil infestation was at its peak, were beginning to climb above previous record yields by 1937. Corn and wheat yields began to show improvement with the return of more favorable weather and use of improved varieties. Most spectacular was the shift to hybrid varieties of corn which began, in a small way, in the early 1930's. Less than one per cent of the corn acreage in Iowa was planted to hybrids in 1933, but by 1939 over one-third of the Corn Belt's corn acreage and three-fourths of Iowa's corn acreage were in hybrids, and by 1942 the new hybrids accounted for 73 per cent of the acreage grown in the Corn Belt and 99 per cent of the Iowa acreage.

Most of the increase in hay yields has been through the rise of alfalfa rather than through improvements in the yield of any particular hay variety, including alfalfa. The traditional stand-by, a combination of red clover and timothy, yields only about two-thirds as much per acre as alfalfa. The rise in land planted to alfalfa from 16 per cent of all hay land in 1920 to 21 per cent in 1930, one-third in 1950, and about half in the late fifties has thus been of considerable influence on hay yields. At the same time, there has been only a beginning in raising the yield proper.

The effects of the use of commercial fertilizers were also beginning to be felt by the late 1930's. But increased farm production for the market during the inter-war years was made possible as much by the freeing of acreage from the growing of feed for horses and mules as by other factors, including rising crop yields.

The real boost in crop yields, across the board so to speak, did not set in until World War II. It is reflected in Figure 18–3 in the rise between 1935–39 and 1940–44. A second, even steeper, rise took place between 1950–54 and 1955–59; the middle and late forties presented a temporary lull, during which agriculture was for once kingpin in a seller's market. The most recent years, 1958–61, not here shown as such, have been marked by sustained high yields, first reached in 1958.

General trends. It is against this historical background that the forty-year projections must be seen. The crucial question is the extent to which the two great spurts in yield in the past can, with confidence, be projected into the future. Judgment will vary from crop to crop, but there can be little doubt that advances in yield represent a long-run trend.

For one thing, we have a fair idea of the range between the poorer performers and the high yield areas. Even on a state-by-state basis the leaders today operate at two or three times the yields obtained in low-yield states. Corn yields can illustrate: In the last few years the Corn Belt states, stretching from Ohio in the east to Iowa in the west and taking in Wisconsin in the north, have obtained from 60 to 70 bushels per acre and, most recently, even better. This is in sharp contrast with yields half that size and smaller elsewhere. However, yields in other areas have, on the whole, moved up even faster than those in the Corn Belt, as evidenced by the fact that the U.S. average yield has risen more rapidly than the yields in the leading corn states: by 70 per cent from 1938–47 to 1957–61, versus 30 to 40 per cent in Iowa, Illinois, Indiana, and Ohio; this spread of top performance to the laggards argues for a continuation of rising yields. And, yields in the leading states themselves have not stood still, despite the fact that the yield-increasing effects of hybrid corn cultivation no longer operate in these areas that have for some time embraced it on a 100 per cent basis. For example, in the top-ranking corn states the average yield has hardly ever dropped below 50 bushels per acre during the last ten years. Furthermore, there is ample evidence of the positive response of corn to fertilizer application and to irrigation. For instance, recent national average rates of nitrogen use—around 25 to 30 pounds per acre—are in a range where every additional pound will call forth a significant increase in yields and produce a

substantial dollar return above the additional cost of the fertilizer. (See Table 18–2).

In a whole series of trials held in the early 1950's it was calculated that the most profitable rate of nitrogen application was around 130 to 150 pounds in Nebraska, with corresponding yields of some 120 bushels per acre (about 2½ times current yield). In 1954, the most recent year for which, at the time of writing, there were adequate data, only 27 per cent of all Nebraska corn acreage was receiving nitrogen, and at the rate of only 42 pounds per acre. In a nationwide study on fertilizer use and crop yields, released in 1954, the unanimous agreement was that corn yields could be raised two to three times with increased utilization of fertilizer.

Both the percentage of the land fertilized and rates of application have been moving up, especially since 1950, as shown in Table 18–2; "acreage fertilized" refers to all types of fertilizers, "rate" only to nitrogen.

The figures bring out both the improvement in fertilizer use and its generally low level. Even in 1954, total fertilization for all acreage, including permanent pasture, averaged 27 pounds per acre on the 30 per cent of cropland fertilized, the equivalent of only 8 pounds per acre harvested in the United States.

We do not have this type of information on other matters such as the use of pesticides or selection of special breeds, but the uneven adoption of new practices, both in time and in space, is typical of the farm enterprise. It is this factor, together with the results achieved in practice, that is at the bottom of the yield projections. The wide range between the highest and lowest yield projected for each of the crops reflects the uncertainties not so much of the technical potential as of the farmer's decision to apply it. Nor is it easy to say under what conditions any one of the different levels may be expected to be found. On the whole, it is likely that high yields will tend to coincide with conditions of high demand, low yields with those of low demand, though one can by no means be dogmatic about it.

Principal crops. What about the prospects of yields for the crops shown in Table 18–3?

TABLE 18–2. Estimated Percentage of Harvested Acreage Fertilized and Rates per Acre Fertilized in the United States, 1947, 1950, 1954

Crop	Percentage fertilized			Rate of application (lb. nitrogen per acre fertilized)		
	1947	1950	1954	1947	1950	1954
Inter-tilled crops	43	45	50	19	20	34
Corn	44	48	60	10	15	27
Cotton	45	52	58	25	30	49
Tobacco	98	99	97	49	41	60
Sugar crops	70	69	91	32	23	58
Large seeded legumes	22	27	23	5	4	7
Fruits	60	51	58	55	44	78
Potatoes & sweet potatoes	75	73	78	60	45	71
Vegetables	76	68	63	40	34	59
Other	6	35	12	8	24	32
Close-growing crops	18	24	29	11	9	19
Wheat	18	22	28	5	8	18
Oats and barley	19	27	30	11	9	17
Other	12	32	30	14	14	27
Hay and pasture	7	7	12	4	5	14
Cropland	9	16	10	4	4	12
Permanent	5	5	27	4	5	16
Crops and pasture	23	21	30	15	15	27

Source: Fertilizer Used on Crops and Pasture in the United States, 1954 Estimates, Agricultural Research Service Statistical Bulletin No. 216 (Washington: U.S. Department of Agriculture, August 1957), pp. 54, 55.

For *wheat,* unless the downward trend in per capita consumption is halted or foreign markets take a much larger portion of the total output than they do now, only a gradual increase in yields may be expected, as continuing work in genetics makes possible varieties which combine high production potential with resistance to disease and insect damage. It is the kind of advance that is not peculiar to wheat but can be expected for the other major crops.

Fertilizer in this instance is unlikely to play a dominant role. The greatest potential increases in yield are in states in the humid areas; they produce less than half of the total crop but already have the highest yields and

TABLE 18–3. Crop Yields for Major Crops or Crop Groups, 1960 and Medium Projections to 2000

Year	Four feed grains (feed units per acre)	Corn (bu. per acre)	Wheat (bu. per acre)	Hay (tons per acre)	Cotton (lb. per acre)	Soy-beans (bu. per acre)
1960	2,352	53	26	1.8	446	23.5
1970	3,022	70	28	2.0	560	27.5
1980	3,416	80	31	2.3	640	30.0
1990	3,799	90	33	2.6	720	32.5
2000	4,179	100	35	3.0	800	35.0

Source: Appendix Tables A18–1, 2, and 3.

are the heaviest users of fertilizer. The original level of soil fertility has been depleted less in the drier states than in the rest of the nation largely because the low levels of moisture prevent plants from making the greatest possible use of the available plant nutrients. The response in yield from the use of additional quantities of fertilizer, except in connection with irrigation, is low in comparison to that in more humid areas. Wheat yields as high as, or higher than, the projection for 2000 have already been achieved in some states, among them Ohio, Indiana, Illinois, Michigan, and Wisconsin; Kansas in 1960 recorded 28 bushels per acre, compared with not quite 18 in the preceding ten years. The 1980 projection of 31 bushels per acre was equaled or exceeded by 14 states in 1960 or 1961. The yields achieved since 1958 suggest that substantially new levels of yield are being readied throughout the country.

Large increases in the production of *feed grains* could be achieved in the future with little trouble if the market for them develops; nor would increases in price be needed to stimulate their production. D. B. Ibach[6] has estimated that if fertilizers were to be used at the maximum economic rate now on all corn land, average yields could be increased to a possible 85 bushels per acre; this compares with a 1960 yield of 53 bushels. The estimate does not take into account the effect of increased supplemental irrigation or the spread of other cultural practices of demonstrated value now in only limited use. Additional increases can also be expected from genetic improvements and technological changes at present unknown. Thus, the 85-bushel yield, while estimated to be the extreme limit of what is economically feasible at the moment in terms of the increased use of fertilizer, provides a minimum yield estimate when the full yield potentialities of the years ahead are considered. The Medium projection exceeds this level in the last half of the projection period. The High projection reaches it sooner.

While corn has a decided advantage over

6. In *Substituting Fertilizer for Land in Growing Corn,* U.S. Department of Agriculture series ARS 43–63 (Washington: USDA, November 1957), Table 2.

other feed grains in both yield per acre and greater production of digestible nutrients per pound of grain, oats still occupy a considerable acreage in rotation with corn. Barley and grain sorghum would not occupy as great acreage as they do if it were possible to produce high yields of corn in the areas where they are grown. For the last several years, however, the acreages of these two grains have expanded for another reason: the necessity of finding crops that could take the place of wheat and corn, both limited by federal legislation. On the other hand, unless markets can be found for the wheat that the United States is now capable of producing, the feed grains will have competition from wheat itself as a livestock feed.

Because an acre of land in corn has greater productivity than one in other feed grains, the proportion of the total output of feed that corn is expected to provide is important in determining land requirements. There is a strong possibility that the increased use of fertilizers —especially nitrogen—may come to permit the continuous cropping of corn in areas of the Corn Belt where the erosion hazard is not great. It is more economical to apply large quantities of nitrogen fertilizer than to rely on oats and legumes in a rotation that keeps land out of corn one out of two or two out of three years. New chemical pesticides have eased the problems of weed and insect control. Even the maintenance of organic matter content of the soil is not too great a problem if the stalks are plowed under. In the feed grain projections, however, the proportion of corn has been kept constant at 60 per cent, owing to the uncertainties surrounding the future composition of the feed grain category.

Yield projections for the other feed grains appear in the appendix to this chapter. They form part of the "feed grains" projection in Table 18–3.

The pace at which *cotton* yields have increased since 1934 is remarkable, and there are prospects for its continuance. In our yield projections we have assumed acceleration of changes now under way in the organization of southern agriculture, particularly in the location of cotton production, the size of the farm on which it is produced, and the methods of

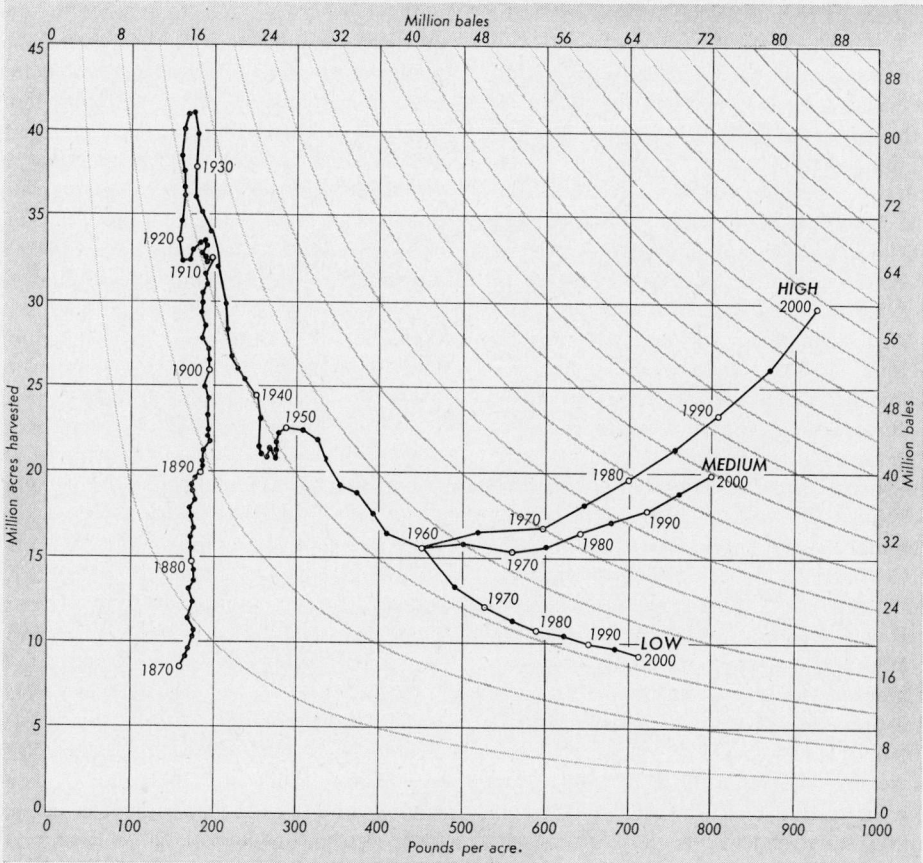

Figure 18–4. The shift from extensive to intensive cultivation of cotton, 1870–2000. Points on time line represent consecutive nine-year moving averages through 1957 and single years from 1960 on. Blue curves represent lines of constant production at different combinations of acreage and yields.

production used. The trend toward more intensive cultivation is illustrated in Figure 18–4.

The center of gravity of cotton production has shifted considerably in recent years. As recently as the 1939–48 period, 54 per cent of the land in cotton lay east of Texas. The proportion had dropped to 40 per cent by the late 1950's, giving the high-yield areas added weight. While cotton yields have already averaged more than two bales per acre in California and Arizona, Tennessee was the only state in the entire region from Texas east that averaged as much as a bale per acre prior to 1959. This national yield trend was further accentuated by government programs that begin-

ning in 1956 caused low-yielding land in the Southeast and Southwest to be taken out of production and, in addition, brought in extra-allotment land in the high-yielding Western and Delta regions under special legislative provisions in 1959 and 1960.

Higher yields have been favored by the westward shift in location to areas where cotton production takes place on level, irrigated land and large farms. In 1954—the most recent year of record—farms producing cotton had an average of nearly 90 acres in cotton in California in contrast to 11 acres in Alabama and 13 acres in Mississippi. More liberal use of fertilizer, especially nitrogen, also contributes to higher yields in the West and South-west.[7]

The cotton producer who has only a small acreage will be at an increasing disadvantage, while the producer who can acquire enough level land to justify machine picking will be in a position also to adopt the practices which will raise the general level of yields. Machine picking will be the only profitable method of harvesting cotton, especially if the price of cotton falls in relation to that of corn and soy-beans.[8] The trend to machine picking is already under way. With it will come greater use of high analysis chemical fertilizers, greater use of chemicals both to combat insects and weeds and to stimulate and control growth of cotton staple, development of cotton varieties that are adapted to mechanical picking, and increasing use of supplemental irrigation.

The yield of *hay crops,* as well as of *pasture,* has risen principally because of a change in types grown; except in irrigated areas it has lagged behind yield increases in other crops. There is good reason to expect large increases in yields once farmers come to appreciate the value of high quality forage, especially if there are improvements in harvesting methods that preserve the quality of the forage both during the curing state and while in storage. The wider use of the improved hay and forage crops now in existence would by itself do much to raise the average yield of hay and pasture. Alfalfa yields average about 50 per cent above those of clover, timothy, and winter grasses, and close to double those of other types. The Medium hay yield projected for 1980, for example, was reached or exceeded in 1960 and 1961 in alfalfa yield in 29 states, and of the 20 states producing over one million tons of alfalfa in 1960 only three produced less than two tons per acre.

Fertilizer is being used effectively on only a small acreage of hay and pasture. In 1950 it was calculated that hay crops in the North Central region, which produced only half the

nation's hay, were yielding only 39 per cent of their potential; and in the Northeast yields were 50 per cent of their potential.[9] In 1954 only 10 per cent of all hay land was fertilized. Estimates of the response to fertilizer use on hay in 1954 indicate that, at the very modest 1954 average level of use, the application of each ton of plant nutrients to hay crops yielded the equivalent of planting 13.5 acres. Comparisons for pasture land give similar results. Against these factors the increase of some 75 per cent in the Medium projection for hay yields appears almost conservative.

Of the *oil crops,* we have made explicit projections only for soybeans. Projections of cotton acreage, described elsewhere, naturally account for the oil yield as well as the fiber yield, and acreages in other oil crops, such as peanuts and flax, are too small to warrant separate projections. Soybeans, on the other hand, have in the past two decades attained a prominent place in American agriculture. The yield projection is shown in Table 18–3.

Some comparisons. In making long-range projections of yield, it is possible to be unduly influenced by the events of the more recent past. Comparison with projections made from time to time by the Department of Agriculture is, therefore, of interest. Table 18–4 brings together, for eight crops and cropland pasture, the projections made in this study and those recently made by the Department for the years 1975, 1980, and 2000. The Department estimates for 1975 are given in two categories: attainable and maximum. The attainable levels are in all instances but two lower than our Low projections for 1980; with exceptions, the maximum levels are reasonably close to our Medium projections. In a study for the Senate Select Committee on National Water Resources,[10] yields were developed for 1980 and 2000. What is of interest here is the Department's characterization of the estimates as "conservative."

7. *Fertilizer Used on Crops and Pasture in the United States, 1954 Estimates,* Agricultural Research Service Statistical Bulletin No. 216 (Washington: U.S. Department of Agriculture, August 1957).

8. Frank T. Bachmura, "Crop Alternatives to Cotton in the Arkansas-Mississippi Delta—a Prognosis," *Journal of Farm Economics,* November 1957, pp. 942–50.

9. *Fertilizer Use and Crop Yields in the United States,* Agriculture Handbook No. 68 (Washington: U.S. Department of Agriculture, December 1954).

10. U.S. Senate Select Committee on National Water Resources, *Water Resource Activities in the United States,* Committee Print No. 12, *Land and Water Potentials and Future Requirements for Water* (Washington: U.S. Government Printing Office, 1960), p. 8.

TABLE 18–4. Comparison of Yields per Acre Projected by RFF with U.S. Department of Agriculture Estimates

Crop	RFF[1] 1980			2000			USDA 1975[2]		1980[3]	2000[3]
	Low	Medium	High	Low	Medium	High	Attainable	Maximum		
Wheat (bu.)	28	31	33	30	35	37	24	27	25	31
Corn (bu.)	73	80	87	89	100	110	53	61	57	72
Oats (bu.)	49	54	62	55	61	80	42	52	44	52
Barley (bu.)	34	38	40	38	45	48	35	42	37	44
Sorghum (bu.)	54	55	59	56	59	65	35	42	37	46
Hay (tons)	1.8	2.3	2.7	2.2	3.0	3.7	1.8	2.1	1.9	2.2
Soybeans (bu.)	27	30	32	29	35	38	26	30	27	32
Cotton (lb.)	590	640	700	710	800	930	495	616	539	716
Cropland pasture (feed units)	–	1,620	–	–	2,120	–	1,725	2,450	1,874	2,470

1. Appendix Tables A18–1, 2, and 11.
2. *Our Farm Production Potential in 1975*, Agricultural Information Bulletin No. 233 (Washington: U.S. Department of Agriculture, September 1960).
3. Source: See footnote 10 above.

The report speculates that "increased future emphasis on production research plus programs to accelerate adoption of improved practices by farmers offer possibilities of attainment of yield levels much higher than those used in the present report." Apart from this general appraisal of its work, the Department had occasion to make upward revisions in the projection during the time—a number of years—the 1975 estimates were developed. Some of these revisions are substantial. For instance, the sorghum grain yield was raised from a preliminary maximum 1975 estimate of 32 bushels per acre to a final estimate of 42 bushels, and cropland pasture projected yield was raised from a preliminary maximum of 1,371 feed units per acre in 1975 to a final 2,450; at the latter level the figure substantially exceeds our 1980 projection of 1,620 feed units, which is close to the Department's attainable estimate.[11]

Other crops. The crops dealt with up to this point have in the past accounted for a maximum of 92 per cent, a minimum of 87 per cent of the crop acreage harvested. There has been a definite tendency for this percentage to increase. One of the reasons for the decline in the share of minor crops is that many of them are grown in a highly intensive type of agriculture and have benefited disproportionately from technological advances of all kinds. They probably will continue to do so. In addition, some crops, such as sugar, are not likely to encounter demand conditions that would call for expanded acreage, and they too are being grown under greater than usual scientific control because of their close tieup with the processing end of the industry. Finally, the starchy crops involved—potatoes, beans, and rice—appear destined for a decreasing role in the American diet. Unless stimulated by foreign demand, demand is likely to decline and incentives to yield improvement to decline with

it. On the other hand, rising incomes will raise demand for the more costly foods in this category. It has been assumed that the acreage in these minor crops will not again exceed 10 per cent of the acreage in those crops for which projections have been made. The average of 9 per cent which has prevailed during most of the past fifteen years has been assumed to continue throughout the period. This assumption is more a bow in the right direction than a calculated projection; the consequences of error are not significant.

Grazing. Because grazing is to a large extent a residual use, and because both cost-return relationships and tenure arrangements have often been unfavorable to investments that would increase the carrying capacity of grassland, much of the land is not as productive as it could be.

Grazing takes place on different kinds of land: farmland suitable for growing crops, open permanent pasture on farms or in public ownership, and woodland. Also, livestock are grazed on previously harvested fields, a practice usually referred to as aftermath grazing. Census data for 1950 and 1954 agree in putting the total area, exclusive of aftermath, at around one billion acres. Of this expanse, some 65 to 70 million acres are farm cropland, some 630 million consist of open permanent pasture, and some 300 to 320 million acres are wooded. The intensity of use of and availability of nutrients from the different types of pasture vary widely, so much so that, for example, Clawson, Held, and Stoddard, in their Resources for the Future study,[12] preferred to state the total acreage effectively used for grazing, exclusive of cropland, at only 700 million acres, on the grounds that grazing is of no real significance in some 250 million acres, mostly woodland. Figure 18–5 depicts the different estimates.[13] In

11. In January 1962, the Department of Agriculture released a preliminary study of land and water resource policy which assumed crop yield increases, across the board, of 56 per cent between 1959 and 1980. At this rate, the earlier Department projections for 1975 and 1980 would be exceeded by about one-third. Applying the rate individually would yield some 81 bushels for corn, 34 bushels for wheat, 60 for grain sorghum, etc. These yields would be extremely close to our Medium projections for 1980.

12. Marion Clawson et al., Land for the Future (Baltimore: Johns Hopkins Press and Resources for the Future, 1960).
13. Later estimates made by the U.S. Department of Agriculture on the basis of the Conservation Needs Inventory were not available at the time of analysis. Estimates for 1959 have since been published in Land and Water Resources (U.S. Department of Agriculture, May 1962), but do not appear to be wholly comparable with respect to woodland and forest grazing.

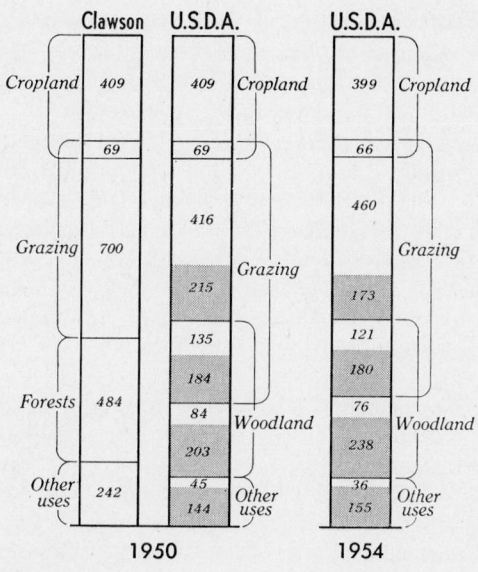

Clawson U.S.D.A. U.S.D.A.

Cropland	409		409	Cropland	399	Cropland
	69		69		66	
			416		460	
Grazing	700			Grazing		Grazing
			215		173	
			135		121	
			184		180	
Forests	484		84	Woodland	76	Woodland
			203		238	
Other uses	242		45	Other uses	36	Other uses
			144		155	

1950   1954

▨ Not in farms   Total area = 1,904 million acres

Figure 18–5. Distribution of land by use, 1950 and 1954.

Table 18–5 we follow the Census statistics for projection purposes so as to obtain a comparability that permits a calculation of feeding units derived from each of the different categories. In projection of total land use, in Table 18–15, the Clawson data are preferred.

With the aid of relative yield factors evolved by the U.S. Department of Agriculture, it is possible to express the diverse types of pasture in terms of cropland pasture equivalents. When that is done, the total grazing acreage is equivalent in yield to about 200 million cropland acres, to which we must add some 16 million acres as the equivalent of aftermath grazing.

Table 18–5 presents a summary of the projections of yields of the various types of pasture. Yields for cropland pasture are tied directly to hay yields, on the theory that, with a constant differential allowing for the fact that continuous grazing reduces the maximum quantity of feed that can be produced on a given area, growing conditions can be expected to parallel those assumed for hay: as the yield of hay rises, we assume, the yield of cropland pasture rises in proportion.

For other types of pasture a substantial lag

TABLE 18–5. Pasture Yields, 1950, 1960, and Medium projections for 1980, 2000

(Feed units per acre)

Year	Cropland (rounded)	Open permanent (on farms)	Woodland (on farms)	Grazing not on farms
1950	985	195	95	56
1960	1,230	220	100	60
1980	1,620	260	112	67
2000	2,120	310	125	74

Source: Appendix Table A18–6.

in the rate of yield increase must be assumed, and more so for woodland and pasture not on farms than for pasture that forms part of farm enterprises.

Unfortunately, we know little about past improvements on this score, except that they have been slow. Little significant research has been done until recently. Our assumptions are therefore rather arbitrary, based essentially on the thought that in a situation of ample cropland supply there will be little pressure for yield improvements in non-cropland pasture, but that tight cropland conditions will reverse this situation, up to the point where improvements in pasture will tend to keep in step with cropland pasture improvement. Actually, it is only in the case of farm permanent pasture that the assumptions are of special significance, for yields, in terms of feed units, are extremely low in woodland and non-farm grazing.

Idle land, fallow, and failure. Not all farmland is cropped or pastured every year. Some is left deliberately idle, while other land fails to produce a crop. These not inconsiderable losses form as much a part of the farm as does the surface that is cropped or grazed to yield a return to the farmer.

In the past twenty years between 2 and 4 per cent of the cropland used for crops each year has not been harvested because of damage from insects or disease or because of adverse weather conditions. In periods of drought the proportion has risen to as much as 7 per cent, and in the mid-thirties to over 10 per cent. While it can be expected that the insect and disease hazards will be considerably lessened in the years ahead and that some of the weather hazard, the greatest threat, can be reduced, allowance must still be made for crop failure, particularly in the drier parts of the country. Probably some 2 to 3 per cent of the land planted to crops each future year must be counted on to produce nothing.

In the nation's semiarid region some land is cultivated fallow each year in an effort to prevent the growth of weeds and rebuild soil moisture. In 1954, the practice was followed in the 17 states west of the Mississippi River on nearly 29 million acres, or 13 per cent of the land in those states. The extent of future summer fallowing is difficult to predict. Expansion of irrigation or measures to reduce runoff losses will reduce the need for summer fallowing, and both developments are decided possibilities. It is unlikely that the acreage left fallow will ever exceed 30 million acres, but it is quite possible that it will decline to as little as 15 million acres, especially if wheat growing—the principal cause of summer fallowing—were to be minimized in the drier western fringes of cropland. This reduction would come about through a more than anticipated rise in wheat yields in high-yielding regions and subsequent withdrawal from production of marginal land.

Finally, we must make allowance for cropland that each year is put under soil improvement or cover crops, or lies idle. The amount of land so treated has in the past been small, at least on the national level: in recent years it has averaged just below 20 million acres, the major portion of it idle.

Acreage Requirements

In the light of trends in yields and of the other technical and institutional considerations that we have just reviewed, how many acres are likely to be needed during the rest of the century to support the levels of crop production established earlier (in Chapter 12) as sufficient to meet the nation's requirements for food and fiber? There are so many possible combinations of circumstances that no single projection would give a worthwhile answer; it seems more useful to develop groups of projections that set upper and lower limits and, within such limits, to work out estimates for three of the more probable situations. We have done this first for crops alone, then for grazing, and finally for crops and grazing combined.

Crops. About 470 million acres within the 48 contiguous states, including some permanent pasture that would be suitable for crops, are classified as cropland. In 1960, 368 million of those acres were required for crop production, including crop failure, fallow, and other non-productive uses that must be allowed for each year.

The smallest conceivable future demands on cropland acreage—slightly over 250 million acres in the year 2000—would come about if high yields were coupled with the Low projections of population and demand developed in Part I, accompanied by low demand for livestock products (which require more land per calorie than direct food crops), high efficiency in converting feed into milk and meat, and maximum use of feed that requires the least land per unit of feeding value—that is, feed grains rather than roughage and hay rather than grazing. The highest conceivable acreage requirement—almost 700 million acres by 2000—would result from a reversal of all the assumed conditions: the highest of the population projections, high livestock demand, low feeding efficiency, and low yields. Although each of the separate circumstances in these two extreme cases is possible, the combination of all of them is most unlikely. Therefore we have worked out acreage estimates for three more probable sets of conditions—one based on Medium demand and yield assumptions, the other two on modified versions of the High and Low demand models that assume more likely combinations of conditions. In the Modified Low demand model, for instance, low population and general demand are accompanied by low feeding efficiency and land-extensive production of feed. Table 18–6 shows the calculations based on these assumptions.

To test the effect of yields, the Extreme High and Low demand models are also combined with Medium yields (lines 2 and 8) and finally with yields that tend to counterbalance the Extreme demand assumptions (lines 3 and

TABLE 18–6.   Cropland Requirements for Crops under Various Assumptions, 1960, 1980, 2000 (total cropland acreage in 1960: 470 million acres)

(Million acres)

Demand model	Yield assumption	Cropland required for crops			Excess of 470 million acres of cropland over crop needs		
		1960	1980	2000	1960	1980	2000
1. Extreme Low	H	–	270	254	–	200	216
2. Extreme Low	M	–	294	283	–	176	187
3. Extreme Low	L	–	333	336	–	137	134
4. Modified Low	L	–	364	368	–	106	102
5. Medium	M	368	368	418	102	102	52
6. Modified High	H	–	368	456	–	102	14
7. Extreme High	H	–	400	504	–	70	–34
8. Extreme High	M	–	440	572	–	30	–102
9. Extreme High	L	–	490	685	–	–20	–215

Source: Appendix Tables A18–11 and 12.

7). The conclusion is that such changes in the yield assumptions shrink but do not remove the acreage surplus in the Low demand projection, nor do they wipe out the shortage in the High demand projection, except in the greatly improved shortage position for 1980 (lines 8 and, above all, 7). At no level of yield can Extreme demand, on either the Low or the High side, be reconciled with persistence of the existing usage level of cropland acreage.

Indeed, it is only when we abandon the assumption of Low demand coupled with top efficiency in livestock feeding and intensive land use (and the reverse situation in the High model), and vary the feed efficiency factor, that the imbalances begin to dissolve. However, as soon as we add grazing requirements (see Table 18–8) the shortage reappears in aggravated form, so that this is only a temporary stage in the course of the calculation.

Pasture. Table 18–7 presents the pattern in which pasturing might be accomplished under varying assumptions of efficiency and yield and on the basis that Low demand coupled with the highest projected roughage availability from sources other than cropland will indicate the lowest demand for cropland pasture, and similarly for other levels. In the modified models these assumptions are reversed. It is our

working hypothesis that the acreage of the less efficient providers of roughage—i.e., all but cropland pasture—will remain available in their recent order of magnitude, but at rising rates of yield.

Quantitatively, as illustrated in Figure 18–6, this is least important for woodland pasture and for all off-farm grazing. Compared to what can be provided by cropland pasture, yields are so low that even substantial improvements would bring forth only relatively minor additions of feed supplies. For example, the 400 million acres of non-farm grazing land—largely the Western range—yield barely 60 feed units per acre per year, the equivalent of 60 pounds, or just about one bushel, of corn. This corresponds to one-sixtieth of a corn yield of 60 bushels per acre. Thus, it would take only seven million acres of corn land to yield the same amount in feed units now available from 400 million acres of range land. In terms of cropland pasture, an acre of off-farm grazing land is worth a little more: about one-twentieth of an acre. The 400 million acres thus are equivalent to 20 million cropland pasture acres.

It is principally in permanent farm pasture that the question of yields is of quantitative importance, for here an acre yields about one-fifth of the feed furnished by an acre of cropland pasture, or about one-fourteenth of what

TABLE 18–7.   Cropland Required for Pasturing, 1960 and Projections for 1980, 2000

Year	Demand model	Rough-age needed from grazing	Rough-age available from non-crop-land[1]	Apparent call on cropland pasture	Estimated yield of cropland pasture (feed units per acre, rounded)	Apparent call on cropland acreage (million acres)
		(billion feed units)				
1960		241	144	97	1,230	79
1980	Extreme Low	160	196	(36)		(22)
	Modified Low	303	136	167		103
	Medium	287	165	122	1,620	75
	Modified High	252	196	56		35
	Extreme High	476	136	340		210
2000	Extreme Low	119	249	(130)		(61)
	Modified Low	363	136	227		107
	Medium	317	193	124	2,120	58
	Modified High	262	249	13		6
	Extreme High	797	136	661		312

Note: Figures in parentheses denote excess of feed available from non-cropland grazing land over feed required from such land.

Source: Appendix Tables A18–11 and 12.

1. The lowest demand level is coupled with the highest projected non-cropland roughage supply to further minimize cropland requirements, and vice versa.

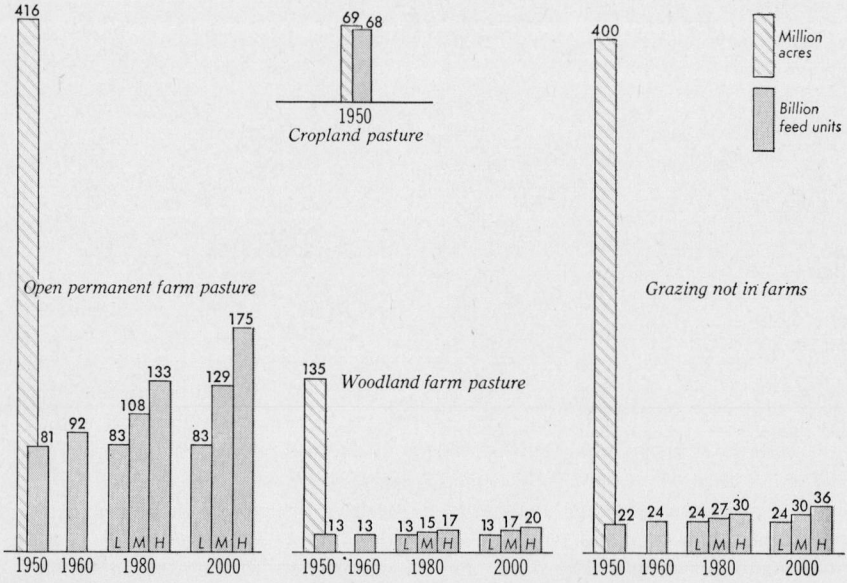

Figure 18–6. Grazing acreage and feed units available 1950, 1960, and projections for 1980 and 2000.

an acre would yield in corn. Thus the more than 400 million acres of open permanent farm pasture are even now the equivalent in feed value of over 80 million acres of cropland pasture. Anticipation of substantially rising yields makes the future of this type of land of exceptional significance. For example, a doubling of yields, not considered out of the question by some students of grazing problems, would add the equivalent of some 80 million acres of cropland pasture to the farm economy.

The over-all balance. Now, to bring together the two elements of our projections, let us assume that grazing will continue, at rising yields depicted in Figure 18–6, on currently used acreages and that cropland in excess of that required for raising crops will be available for pasturing. Under reasonable assumptions of efficiency and yields (which rule out both the Extreme High and Extreme Low demand models), a surplus position persists through more than half the period and a balance in agricultural land is indicated by the end of the century. This is shown in Table 18–8. The excess of 67 million acres in the Modified High projection (line 6) for 1980 is a sufficiently large percentage of cropland to indicate a real problem. It is due, however, largely to the fact that in this model we have assumed high yields not only in crops but also, to be consistent, in

grazing, so that requirements for cropland pasture drop to a minimum. Thus the effect of high demand is more than offset by greatly increased productivity of the range. The reverse is true for the Modified Low projection, which maximizes the demand for cropland pasture. By the end of the century, however, differences in demand about balance the yield effects. The shortages and surpluses of more than 100 million acres that arise in all but the middle three projections indicate that high and low demand cannot be reasonably reconciled with use of available cropland on any of the yield assumptions made.

How would the country fare if the Medium *demand* projection turned out to be more realistic than the *yield* projections? Suppose that the increase in yields that forms the Low projection were to represent the best effort in the next forty years, or that the Medium demand were to coexist with the High yield projection. The consequence has been calculated in Appendix Table A18–13. Disregarding pasture, we find that the attainment of only the Low yields would result in an increased cropland requirement of 50 million acres by 1980 and 80 million acres by 2000, while traveling along the High yield path would enable agriculture to dispense with 35 million acres in 1980 and 50 million in 2000.

It is instructive to examine the time inter-

TABLE 18–8. Cropland Requirements for Crops and Pasture under Various Assumptions, 1960 and Projections for 1980, 2000

(Million acres)

Demand model	Yield assumption	Cropland required for pasture			Cropland excess over crop needs[1]			Cropland excess over combined crop & pasture needs		
		1960	1980	2000	1960	1980	2000	1960	1980	2000
1. Extreme Low	H	–	–	–	–	200	216	–	200	216
2. Extreme Low	M	–	–	–	–	176	187	–	176	187
3. Extreme Low	L	–	15	–	–	137	134	–	122	134
4. Modified Low	L	–	103	107	–	106	102	–	3	—5
5. Medium	M	79	75	58	102	102	52	23	27	—6
6. Modified High	H	–	35	6	–	102	14	–	67	8
7. Extreme High	H	–	173	258	–	70	—34	–	—103	—292
8. Extreme High	M	–	192	285	–	30	—102	–	—162	—387
9. Extreme High	L	–	210	312	–	—20	—215	–	—230	—527

Source: Appendix Tables A18–11 and 12.
1. Cropland required for crops (as calculated) subtracted from 470 million acres estimated as total suitable for crop production.

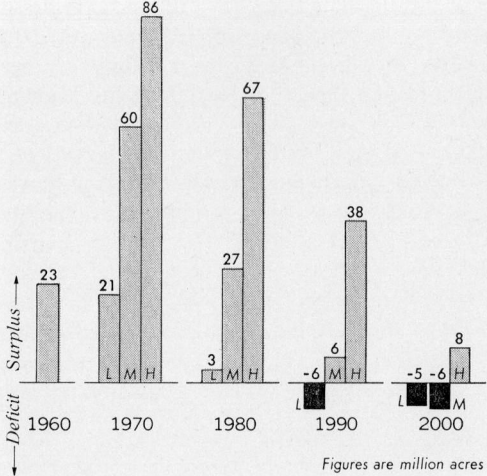

Figure 18–7. Cropland surpluses and deficits under varying combinations of demand and yield assumptions, 1960–2000. (See text below.)

vals indicated by the projections to see whether any striking breaks occur in the general picture. Figure 18–7, based on Appendix Table A18–11, shows the results.

Perhaps the most significant factor is the change in the Medium projection, from a position of 60 million surplus acres reached in 1970 to an acreage deficit in 2000. Between 1970 and 2000, there is a net shift of 66 million acres. The rapid decline in the surplus acreage and its eventual conversion to a deficit suggests that the pressure for better than the Medium yields and efficiency factors is not urgent in the next two decades but becomes increasingly so thereafter. In other words, failure to reach the Medium yields will not lead to acreage problems for the first half of the four decades but will result in a squeeze thereafter. In the Modified High projection, the surplus position remains impressive throughout most of the period, despite the steady decline in its size. This suggests not that higher demand leads to greater acreage surpluses, but rather that the high yields that we have assumed, in either crops or grazing, more than balance the effect of high demand, and that their attainment is not a crucial requirement for making acreage ends meet under this projection. In the Modified Low projection, the emergence of a deficit indicates that even a small improvement in

feed efficiency and yields over those assumed would lead to better balance.

The factor of feeding efficiency clearly needs emphasis, even though it is not directly connected with land use and yields. A substantial breakthrough in conversion of feed into livestock products, such as by admixture of certain chemical substances, would spell a reduction in feed grain, hay, and pasture needs. The efficiency factors used in Chapter 12 do not provide for such an occurrence, but over a forty-year period it can by no means be ruled out.

In evaluating the surplus acreage indicated in all but the Medium and Low projections for 2000, one must be aware that the estimate of required cropland comprises not only producing but non-producing acreage. Part of this is idle acreage. Acreage recorded as lying idle in the 1954 Census amounted to around 15 million acres, fairly evenly distributed over the eastern half of the United States (no separate data for idleness are recorded West of the Mississippi, see Table A18–5). In relation to cropland available, however, there was a marked concentration of idleness in the older portion of the Cotton Belt and in New England. These areas are perhaps involved in two separate fields of adjustment: a temporary unemployment of acreage in the South, triggered by the sharp drop in cotton acreage after the spurt of the early fifties, and a more permanent idleness of cropland in near-urban areas of New England. The extent to which the latter type of idle cropland can be properly thought of as surplus farm acreage is open to question. Some of it undoubtedly is cropland only in name, in transition to other uses.

Other parts of the catch-all category of non-producing land are equally debatable. These are, for example, the 25 to 30 million acres that are summer-fallowed, mostly in the semi-arid West and Midwest. To the extent that water becomes available to it, perhaps from desalinization in the second half of the forty-year span, or that better moisture-conserving measures are developed, much of this area might become continuously productive. In the projections it has been assumed that non-producing acreage will decline by 15 million acres. Should it be possible to reactivate a larger portion of this acreage, the surplus would rise correspondingly.

On the other side of the ledger, the developments portrayed in Table 18–8 would involve shifts of considerable magnitude between land uses and undoubtedly between regions. These shifts cannot be expected to work out on the land as neatly as they do on paper; this lack of perfection will tend to whittle down the statistically derived surpluses.

For example, in recent years some 65 to 70 million acres of cropland have been used for pasture. Both the Medium and the High projections for the year 2000 assume that some land so used would have to be taken up for raising crops (Table 18–8, lines 5 and 7–9). To the extent that these areas are among the poorer for growing crops, this development might conflict with any high yield assumptions underlying the High projections. On the other hand, in the Medium projection this encroachment on pasture land is not of significant proportions, and there is none whatever in any of the other projections except the unlikely low yield assumption in the Modified Low. The projected shifts between crops, as shown in Figure 18–8 and detailed in Appendix Table A18–8, do not appear to call for major changes that cannot be accomplished.

Hay provides the most extreme example, but even here the solution seems feasible, though it may be difficult. Decline in pasture would not suffice to make available for hay all the acreage projected. Additional acreage must come from a decline in the idle-fallow-failure category, and a drawing down of the earlier surplus acreage. This raises a question of substitution. Could the fallow acreage if planted to hay render the sort of hay yield we have stipulated? Would a decline in idle acres occur in the places where hay is needed to raise livestock?

The steep increase in soybean acreage equally raises a question of substitution. While the simultaneous decline in wheat and feed grain acreage would make land available, some of it would be in locations that are too northerly. In any case, wheat and feed grain acreage itself rises between 1980 and 2000. Thus, a residual acreage for soybeans would have to be found in land now idle.

These questions are not fully answerable in a broad survey. They do, however, serve to qualify the appraisal of the apparent acreage surpluses, in the sense that there are enough elements of incomplete substitutability to detract from the surplus character of this acreage.

In the calculations of feed availability we have chosen to assume continuing availability of grazing land at the levels that prevailed in the 1950's. This is believed to be a realistic assumption in that the statistics contain no indication that any of this land might be needed for raising crops. It is less realistic, however, to assume that grazing land might not be lost

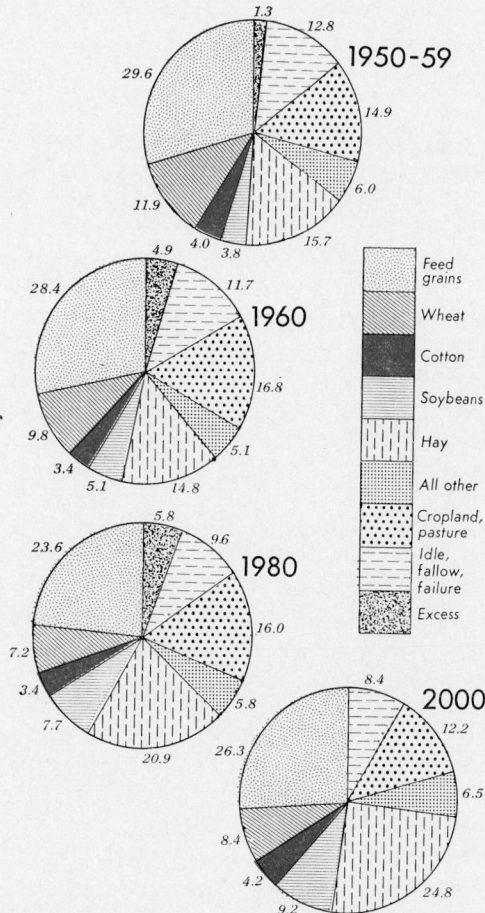

Figure 18–8. Shifts in percentage of cropland use, 1950–59, 1960, and Medium projections for 1980 and 2000.

to other than crop-raising activities and that cropland might not be equally lost. The surplus acreage arising in the projections must be thought of as a buffer to absorb such encroachment. Whether this buffer might be ample, we shall discuss in the succeeding sections.

At this point, however, it is important to point out yet another aspect of land use: soil suitability. We must ask ourselves whether the transfer which we assume of non-producing cropland to active use is feasible without major improvements. This is especially true for the latter part of the forty-year period, when excess acreage will be at its minimum (and eventually disappear) and substantial shifts between crops are indicated, even in the Medium projection.

According to the 1948–49 soil survey of the Department of Agriculture, some 50 million acres of cropland have severe limitations in cultivation and some 40 million acres are altogether unsuitable for crop production. (More recent data from the National Inventory of Soil and Water Conservation Needs estimate 55 million acres of cropland as having unfavorable soil in the root zone.) Some of this acreage undoubtedly overlaps with idle acreage, but some of it does not. Against this problem must be held the Department's finding that there are more than 200 million acres in grassland or woodland that are in varying degree suitable for cropping, given application of various improvement measures. About half of it is in grazing. Geographically, the bulk of this land is in the tier of states from North Dakota down to Texas, with some extension to the west and large woodland acreages in the Southeast. Conversion of such land to crop raising would have to be paralleled by improvement in the remaining grazing areas beyond the magnitude heretofore assumed, and, to the extent that portions of the soils to be transferred are situated in the more arid climate of the West, irrigation would have to be considerably extended. Because of the probably moderate amounts of land involved, the latter would be not so great a problem, but the raising of yields on the remaining pasture land might well turn out to become crucial in any situation of major encroachment of other uses upon cropland and the consequent plowing up of permanent pasture.

As for woodland, the definite possibility that we shall not be able to meet projected demand for forest products from current acreage, except under fairly stringent assumptions (see pages 359–69), makes it advisable not to count on transfers to agriculture of acreage now in commercial forests.

Possible new technology. The prospects of acreage needs through 1980 or thereabouts are not such that much attention has to be paid to revolutionary methods of supplying food and feed. Thereafter, on the other hand, excess acreage begins to thin out until it has turned into a small deficit by the year 2000. Any new method that can compete economically with traditional methods of production of nutrients therefore deserves serious attention. It has not been feasible in this broad treatment to work out the cost implications of such factors as yield increases or improvements in feeding efficiency.

Perhaps most revolutionary in concept are the efforts to produce protein in large quantities at low cost. Yeast culture is one of the methods sometimes mentioned. Even if the probability is slight that within the next forty years food for the American diet will be derived directly from yeast, one cannot ignore the much greater possibility that it could become an important source of protein in livestock rations. Already it is being used in animal feeds as a source of vitamins, particularly vitamin B, and other "unidentified growth factors." As a source of protein, its use is limited only by its cost in relation to that of other protein sources. Because the plant thrives on sugar solutions, it can make use of the sugary wastes and residues resulting from the processing of certain agricultural products. Yeast could become important enough as a source of protein that sugar solutions would be made specifically for its production.

Another food source, as yet largely untapped, is the ocean, where it is estimated that 85 per cent of all photosynthesis on earth takes place. Not only might a greater effort be made in the future to farm the seas for fish, but some say man ought to turn to the lowly alga, an extremely efficient organism, and develop it as a human food. In any case, as with yeast, the plant might well be used for livestock feed.

A development of recent years, not to be overlooked, could be of great importance in the future in making more efficient use of cheap roughage and such materials as corn cobs in the rations of cattle. It has been determined that cattle can obtain a third, and probably even more, of their total protein requirement from a ration high in cellulose if the ration includes nitrogen in the form of urea, ample quantities of phosphorus and sulfur, and certain trace elements. The necessary proteins are synthesized by micro-organisms in the rumen of the cattle. It is in this connection, incidentally, that the idea of feeding waste paper to livestock has recently received serious attention.

Forests

Projections of future demand for forest products—lumber, veneer and plywood, pulp, and miscellaneous products—were presented in Chapter 13. Whether and to what extent the projected demand for forest products can be met from domestic sources depends on how the productive capacity of the American forest grows or declines in the future.

Here, as in agriculture, the basic resource is the land. In many ways, forestry is agriculture in slow motion. Trees are just another crop, except for the difference in time between seed and harvest. This difference, however, is all-important. It is the time dimension that lies at the root of most of the forest problems that relate to demand, and that leads us in this study to give more attention to cutting rates and other forest practices than to forest acreage as such.

At any given point of time, it is the standing forest, not the land, that represents the resource; and it is the size of the cut removed from that resource in relation to its natural growth that determines the changing magnitude of the resource. Not only is there little chance of quick adjustments to changing demand, but every action today will affect the state of the forest tomorrow and for years to come. In taking our measurements for the next few decades, we must be thinking also of the legacy to be handed over to the next century, for while forests are renewable, it is only a growing forest of substantial age that will provide lumber, veneer, or pulpwood for our grandchildren.

Our main interest in this chapter is in the forest as a source of timber as a commodity. But in the course of our analysis we must bear in mind that our forest resource not only supplies lumber and wood but is basic for a host of other reasons, including its relations to the pattern of land use, the water balance, soil stability, the climate situation, recreation, and wildlife. Elementary wisdom and prudence indicate that our forest resource should be handled with great care and as rationally as possible.

Forests Past and Present

Faced with seemingly infinite expanses of woodland, our forebears cleared the land and planted crops—food, tobacco, and fiber. The wood was essential to the economy, for fuel, shipbuilding, log cabins and frame buildings, and, later on, railroad ties; but the land would have been cleared in any case. Originally, there were something like 830 million acres of what we now term commercial forest land; fewer than 500 million are left today. Of the timber volume estimated to have been standing when the white man arrived, only a little more than 10 per cent is left in the East, about two-thirds in the West. The most serious reduction, clearly, has been in the supply of standing timber rather than in loss of acreage through the clearing of land. Increased future supplies are more likely to arise out of a reversal of this trend than out of reforesting land now devoted to other purposes.

The rough measures of America's forest resources in 1952 are presented in Table 18–9, drawn from the U.S. Forest Service's comprehensive *Timber Resources for America's Future;* the data relate principally to the forty-eight contiguous states. In addition to the 484 million acres of commercial forest land shown for the forty-eight states—about one-fourth of the country's land area—there are another 4 million acres in the coastal lands of Alaska. There are also 175 million acres of non-commercial forest land, including 12 million in coastal Alaska; this is land with a forest cover but not contributing to production of forest products. Only 15 million acres in this class— most of it in the West—is productive forest land in the sense that it could yield a commercially useful forest, but it is reserved for special uses such as recreation in national parks, wilderness areas, etc.; the remainder is unproductive or economically inaccessible: swampiness, sparseness of tree cover, low site quality, composition of tree species, etc., render it of negligible value for timber production.

Definitions. Even within the category of commercial forest land, acreage figures in themselves tell little about capacity to meet projected demands. More significant than acreage are the age and species of tree and the complex relationships that determine net rate of growth; these vary widely from area to area and even from tract to tract.

Although this study does not need to go at all deeply into how forest trees grow and how they are cut and marketed, it will be useful to clarify a few technical terms that will recur in our analysis.[14]

Growing stock: The net volume in cubic feet of live trees of commercial species, on a given area, measuring at least 5 inches in diameter at breast height and at least 4 inches at the top of the central stem, not counting the bark. This is the most frequently used measure of timber supply.

Net annual growth: The annual change in cubic foot (or board-foot) volume of growing stock resulting from natural causes; that is, the increment from gross growth minus mortality. Occasional catastrophic losses from natural causes of extreme severity, such as great fires, hurricanes, etc., are not averaged into net growth figures.

Timber cut: The net volume in a given year, in cubic feet (or board-feet), cut or otherwise destroyed in logging.

Sawtimber: Trees of commercial species large

14. For fuller and other definitions see *Timber Resources for America's Future,* cited in Table 18–9, pp. 627 ff.

TABLE 18–9.   Basic Forest Data, 1952[1]

Category	Total	Soft-wood	Hard-wood
Commercial forests, including Alaska (mil. acres)	529	263	266
Commercial forests, including coastal Alaska only (mil. acres)	488	234	254
Commercial forests (mil. acres)	484	230	254
Growing stock, including Alaska (bil. cu. ft.)	548	377	171
Growing stock, including coastal Alaska only (bil. cu. ft.)	517	355	162
Growing stock (bil. cu. ft.)	498	336	162
Sawtimber (bil. cu. ft.)	362	274	88
Poletimber (bil. cu. ft.)	136	62	74
Net growth (bil. cu. ft.)	14.2	7.0	7.2
Timber cut (bil. cu. ft.)	10.8	7.5	3.3
Growing stock per acre (cu. ft.)	1,029	([2])	([2])
Annual growth per acre (cu. ft.)	29.3	([2])	([2])
Commercial forest land (per cent of total)	100	48	52
Growing stock (per cent of total)	100	67	33
Live sawtimber (per cent of total)	100	79	21

1. Alaska excluded, except where otherwise stated.
2. No figures given, since hardwood species grow in softwood-type forests and vice versa; establishing a direct relation would be misleading. However, size of growing stock per acre is substantially larger in softwood-type forests.

Source: Forest Service, *Timber Resources for America's Future* (Washington: U.S. Department of Agriculture, 1958).

enough and otherwise suitable to be sawn into lumber. Minimum specifications vary among species and regions, but no tree less than 9 inches in diameter at breast height is considered sawtimber. Growing stock of less than sawtimber size, but at least 5 inches in diameter at breast height, is *poletimber*.

Softwood and *hardwood:* These are commercial terms of long standing. Strictly speaking, the designations distinguish between conifers and non-conifers, rather than between lighter and denser woods. The leading softwoods are Douglas fir, Southern yellow pine, and ponderosa pine; oak is the principal commercial hardwood.

The nation's current timber inventory of 498 billion cubic feet of growing stock is supplemented by a non-growing stock—cull trees, salvageable dead trees, and usable tops and limbs—estimated at 88 billion. Over time, of course, the inventory is further supplemented by new growth that reaches the required 5-inch diameter. The growing stock clearly has a different and greater significance than the non-growing stock, which seldom meets merchantable specifications.

Regional differences. The geographic distribution of forest land is shown in Figure 18–9. The difference between the largely pri-mary growth in the West and the second-growth stands of most of the Eastern forests bears importantly on growth characteristics. Furthermore, practically all hardwood is found in the East, whereas the bulk of the softwood growing stock (but not forest land) is in the West. But while the West far outdistances the East in terms of softwood volume, with a growing stock inventory about three and a half times that of the East, its annual growth is only about 60 per cent as great. And the softwood cut in the West is roughly equal to that in the East. Thus there is great disparity between inventory, growth, and cut. (See Table 18–10.)

For the country as a whole, the 1952 softwood cut exceeded growth by about 0.5 billion cubic feet, or 6 per cent. But this is the net effect of two different experiences: a cut in the West which exceeded growth by about 1.2 billion cubic feet and a cut in the East about 0.7 billion cubic feet below growth. While softwood cut exceeded growth, softwood and hardwood growth combined exceeded cut by some 30 per cent, owing entirely to the fact that in hardwood the cut was less than half the annual growth.

Two factors above all others explain this relationship between inventory, growth, and cut. First, Western stands contain a larger propor-

TABLE 18–10. Growing Stock, Growth, and Cut, by Principal Areas, in 1952

(Billion cubic feet)

Item	West	East	Continental U.S. excl. Alaska	Coastal Alaska	Continental U.S. incl. coastal Alaska
Growing stock:					
Softwood	262	74	336	19	355
Hardwood	11	151	162	–	162
Total	273	225	498	19	517
Growth:					
Softwood	2.59	4.39	6.98	0.03	7.0
Hardwood	.15	7.08	7.23	–	7.2
Total	2.74	11.47	14.21	0.03	14.2
Cut:					
Softwood	3.73	3.75	7.48	.01	7.5
Hardwood	.02	3.25	3.27	–	3.3
Total	3.75	7.00	10.75	.01	10.8

Source: Forest Service, *Timber Resources for America's Future,* Tables 21, 29, and 32.

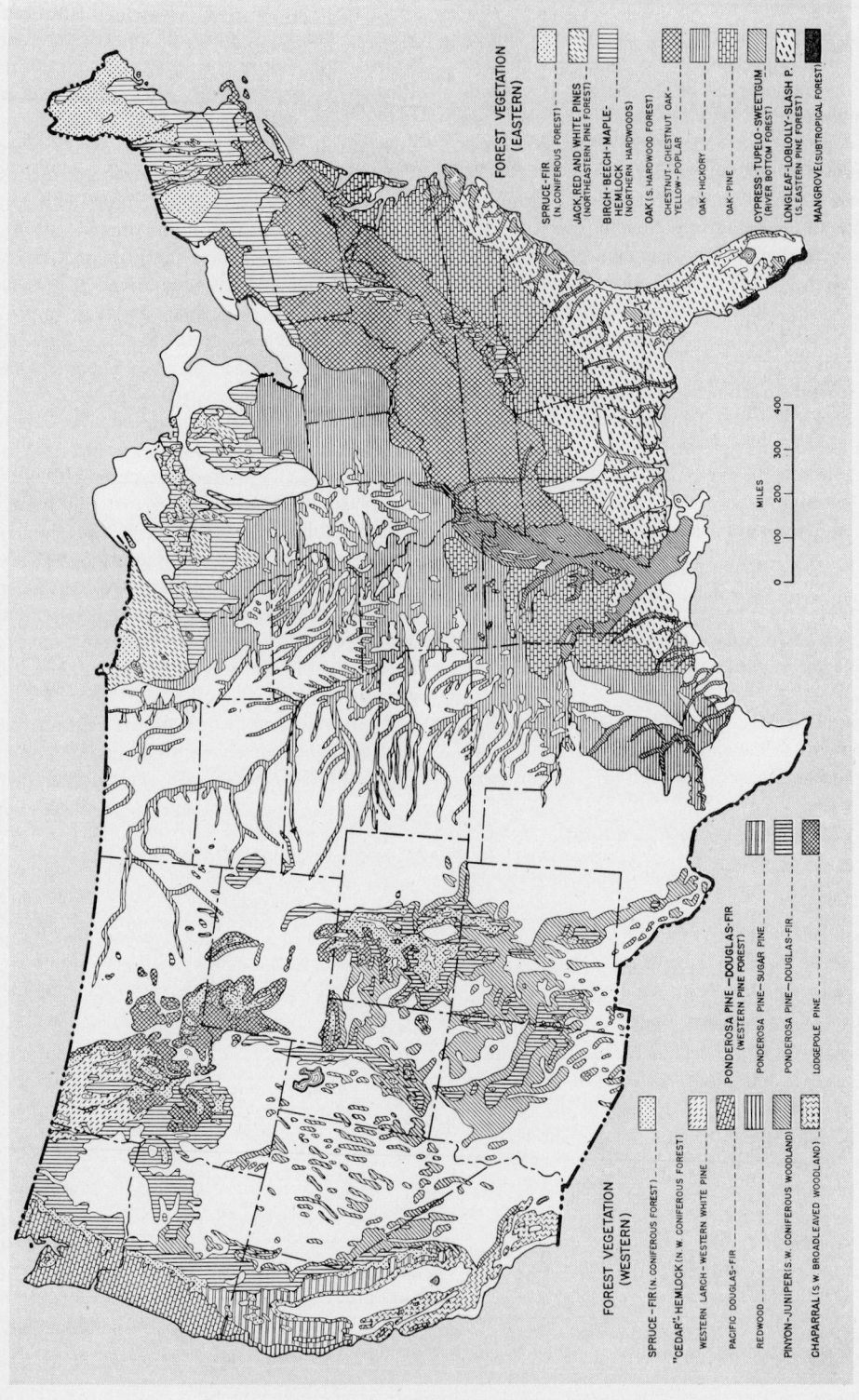

FOREST VEGETATION
(EASTERN)

SPRUCE-FIR
(N. CONIFEROUS FOREST)

JACK, RED AND WHITE PINES
(NORTHEASTERN PINE FOREST)

BIRCH-BEECH-MAPLE-
HEMLOCK
(NORTHERN HARDWOODS)

OAK (S. HARDWOOD FOREST)

CHESTNUT-CHESTNUT OAK-
YELLOW-POPLAR

OAK-HICKORY

OAK-PINE

CYPRESS-TUPELO-SWEETGUM
(RIVER BOTTOM FOREST)

LONGLEAF-LOBLOLLY-SLASH P.
(S. EASTERN PINE FOREST)

MANGROVE (SUBTROPICAL FOREST)

MILES
0   100   200   300   400

FOREST VEGETATION
(WESTERN)

SPRUCE-FIR (N. CONIFEROUS FOREST)

"CEDAR"-HEMLOCK (N. W. CONIFEROUS FOREST)

WESTERN LARCH-WESTERN WHITE PINE

PACIFIC DOUGLAS-FIR

REDWOOD

PINYON-JUNIPER (S.W. CONIFEROUS WOODLAND)

CHAPARRAL (S.W. BROADLEAVED WOODLAND)

PONDEROSA PINE-DOUGLAS-FIR
(WESTERN PINE FOREST)

PONDEROSA PINE-SUGAR PINE

PONDEROSA PINE-DOUGLAS-FIR

LODGEPOLE PINE

Figure 18–9. Forest vegetation of the United States. (Map from U.S. Forest Service.)

tion of sawtimber than do Eastern stands. Relative annual growth of a tree of sawtimber size tends to decline as the size of the tree increases. Thus, a stand of sawtimber will have a lower percentage growth rate than a stand of smaller trees. In addition, much of the Western commercial forest area supports original growth, as for example the giant redwoods and sequoias in California. Over a large area, such stands tend to achieve a balance of little if any net growth. Growth, mostly from the roots of old growth, is balanced by decay and death. The West including coastal Alaska is estimated to have close to 50 million acres of old growth sawtimber, a good deal of it unexploited virgin forest—over 40 per cent of its total commercial forest area. The East's old growth consists of a few remnant stands.

Finally, the stands that are below the sawtimber class contain large areas of cutover non-restocking land, young trees still too small to show measurable volume growth,[15] and a smaller acreage of old growth below sawtimber size, mainly at high elevations.

The East, on the other hand, contains most of the inadequately utilized commercial forest land. An estimated 73 million acres throughout the United States, or about 17 per cent of the combined East-West total of 438 million acres (leaving out the 46 million acres of old growth sawtimber stands) is poorly stocked (more than 10 per cent but less than 40 per cent of full stocking) and 42 million acres, about 10 per cent of the total, is non-stocked (less than 10 per cent of full stocking). Of the poorly stocked acreage, about 58 million acres are in the East and 15 million in the West; and of the non-stocked acreage, about 33 million are in the East and 9 million in the West.

As pointed out in *Timber Resources for America's Future,* "growth in the West still tends to be held down by the large residuum of virgin timber, which has little net growth." In the East the rate of growth in relation to inventory is much higher. But absolute amount and quality of growth in the East could also be much higher were it not for the under-

stocking. In effect, total growth volume is held down by a plethora of inventory in the West which depresses the growth rate, and by a shortage of inventory in the East, each in relation to the acreage devoted to forests.

With respect to the volume of cut, location of the forest areas is of importance. The West has the bulk of the softwood stands, but they are not only relatively remote from most of the consumers, but also predominantly publicly owned and managed. The Eastern stands are closer to the consumer, and since they are predominantly in private ownership and thus tend to follow market demand quickly, the pressure of demand tends to raise the ratio of cut to inventory in the East, and inventory is smaller.

These regional factors are of great importance in forest policy and management. Broadly speaking, well-planned cutting in the West promotes rather than inhibits future growth. The relatively small inventory in the East, on the other hand, has a high growth rate, but it minimizes the volume of growth. Heavy cutting here will reduce the growth volume; conversely, less cutting would permit inventory to accumulate (or be depleted less) and thus promote future growth. Such reduction of cutting would have to be accompanied, however, by thinnings, improvement cuttings, etc., and unless there is an incentive to perform such operations—preferably through a market for low-grade material—good management is hard to achieve.

It follows then, that one response to a tightening market would be to foster for some time the use of Western stands and to accumulate inventory for future needs in the East. The more the West is used, the less the pressure on the East. However, the fact that capital is tied up in the privately owned Eastern stands again means that such developments are not to be had for the asking.

How Demand Might Be Met

The demand for forest products may be met from net growth alone, or from net growth and growing stock. A cut that is smaller than net growth will increase inventory; this may increase the amount of future growth if, as is currently true in the East, the inventory is below the optimum level, or decrease it if the

---

15. No growth is recorded in the statistics until a tree reaches a minimum size of 5 inches diameter at breast height.

inventory is already excessive, as in the West. A cut which exceeds net growth will decrease inventory, and this will have the reverse effects on future growth. Only under conditions of "sustained yield" will, by definition, cut and growth balance and inventory remain constant. However, we are interested here in ascertaining the implications for the future of forests of projected demands upon them. Proceeding on the basis of sustained yields would reconcile the conflicting tendencies that we are anxious to identify.

Data developed in Chapter 13 indicate a sharp rise in the demand for forest products: the Medium projection shows a tripling between 1960 and 2000, from 11 to 32 billion cubic feet. In the High projection, demand in 2000 will be more than five times that of 1960. The relative increases in the demand are larger for softwood than for hardwood, despite an assumption of somewhat growing use of hardwood in pulp production. For both hardwoods and softwoods the demand for lumber increases much less than that for veneer and pulp.

Can prospective timber supplies meet the demand here projected, and if not, what types of adjustment to emerging shortages promise relief, singly or in combination? Because it takes decades rather than years for trees to reach useful dimensions, at least for most products other than pulp and fuelwood, most timber to be cut in the next four decades, certainly that of sawlog size, will come from trees now growing in the nation's forests. However, no judgment as to whether the size of the annual cut is excessive or insufficient can be made without reference to a long-term objective—above all, the inventory which one wishes to carry. For example, cutting into capital might be prudent if demand were declining, but would be self-defeating if demand were projected to rise.

As we shall see, under certain assumptions of cut and growth, our forests of trees of exploitable sizes would be entirely depleted by 2000, and even sooner. Disregarding factors other than timber supply, this would be unfortunate only if a continuing large timber demand is to be expected after 2000. Rising demand projections through 2000 make a decline or stagnation thereafter hardly a realistic

assumption. It follows that depletion of the kind depicted in the projections would work against satisfying demand past the period of projection. But depletion of existing stands could be alleviated if land either not now forested or poorly stocked were planted to trees which would reach maturity towards the end of our time span. Thus the fact that, for most purposes other than the production of pulp, several decades must elapse before commercial size has been attained does not in itself rule out acreage increases or stand improvement as paths of adjustment. Whether they are desirable, and if desirable, feasible, we shall discuss below.

Because of the different growing conditions, uses, and regional occurrence of the two principal categories, softwood and hardwood species, we discuss the two separately; and since the principal problems will arise in connection with the adequacy of the more desirable softwood group, we shall begin our analysis there.

But first a word of caution is called for. The data presented here are greatly simplified in comparison with those contained in their principal source, the Forest Service's *Timber Resources for America's Future,* which explores in detail the many aspects that cannot be accommodated in the present study. First, we discuss timber without differentiating between the more useful large trees (sawtimber) and the balance; second, we develop the growth vs. cut picture without reference to the use, in limited branches of consumption, of non-growing stock, such as cull trees, limbs, etc.[16] In general, the supply outlook for sawtimber is more critical than for timber of all kinds. Not only does the felling of trees of sawtimber size involve economies, but for many uses large trees are necessary. This explains why 84 per cent of the nation's timber cut in 1952 consisted of sawtimber, whereas the growing stock from which these trees were cut contained only 72 per cent sawtimber. Finally, the share of sawtimber in annual growth is even smaller than indicated by the inventory figure. It follows

16. Residues in the production of pulp are, however, allowed for in Chapter 13, and fuelwood, another important consumer of such products, is projected to become increasingly less important.

then that if the supply outlook for all timber is critical, the prospect of meeting sawtimber demand is still less promising. And since even in the Medium projection the year 2000 shows a large gap between demand and available growth, it follows that the sawtimber outlook is correspondingly dimmer.

A basic assumption to be born in mind is that the real price of timber and timber products is not, in these projections, responsive to the developing pressure on supply. As elsewhere in this study, this assumption is made so that our analysis can sharply bring out the possible effects of alternative courses.

Similarly, in the analysis that follows, cut and growth are juxtaposed and the consequences for the growing stock considered in order to pursue the implications, not to develop a realistic future supply and demand pattern. Indeed, we have here perhaps the best illustration of the general thrust of this study: to test future adequacy by comparing a reasonable extension of past consumption trends with resources availability, and to examine the implications of this confrontation.

Adequacy of softwood supplies. Table 18–11 summarizes the future movement of the softwood forest resource that would result from meeting each of the three levels of projected demand. It is assumed that part of the gross demand will be met through imports[17] and that these will increase moderately from the levels of recent years. It is further assumed that, as in 1952, East and West will each meet fifty per cent of net demand.

The assumed growth rates are of crucial importance. The key factors used in projecting these growth rates, starting from their known 1952 level, were the differences in age and structure between the Eastern and Western forests, and the consequent differences in relationship between inventory and growth rate. For the West, it was assumed that with increased cutting of old growth timber (some of it virgin forest) growth rates will tend to rise, and that, within broad limits, the faster the cutting the more rapid will be the rise in

17. The import assumptions are discussed below, pp. 367–69.

TABLE 18–11. Supply and Demand Relationships in Softwood, 1960 and Projections for 1980, 2000

(*Billion cubic feet unless otherwise indicated*)

Item	1960		1980	2000
Gross demand	8.3	L	9.1	11.2
		M	14.3	24.7
		H	20.4	48.1
Imports	0.8	L	1.6	2.4
		M	2.0	3.0
		H	2.4	4.0
Net demand	7.5	L	7.5	8.8
		M	12.3	21.7
		H	18.0	44.1
Cut from West	3.7	L	3.8	4.4
		M	6.1	10.8
		H	9.0	22.0
Cut from East	3.7	L	3.8	4.4
		M	6.1	10.8
		H	9.0	22.0
Net growth rate—West (per cent)	1.0	L	1.5	1.5
		M	1.7	2.1
		H	1.9	2.7
Net growth rate—East (per cent)	6.0	L	5.4	5.0
		M	6.0	6.0
		H	7.0	7.2
Net growth—West	2.5	L	3.6	3.5
		M	3.6	2.4
		H	3.6	nil
Net growth—East	4.6	L	5.5	7.2
		M	4.1	nil
		H	1.8	nil
Growing stock—West	253	L	244	234
		M	219	121
		H	193	nil
Growing stock—East	79	L	104	148
		M	72	nil
		H	36	nil

L = Low projection   M = Medium   H = High.

Source: Appendix Table A18–14.

growth rates. The doubling, in the Medium projection, goes about two-thirds of the way to the level that the Forest Service considers realizable (without any time reference or schedule). For the East, it was assumed that a substantial increase in inventory would bring a moderate decline in the rate of growth; that, with inventory at about the present level, growth rates would also remain at the present level; and that, with inventory declining, growth rates would rise. The effects of variations in mortality are allowed for, in line with the practice which is followed by the Forest Service.

Under the foregoing assumptions, the Low level of demand could be met, by the year 2000, with a decided improvement in the inventory position in the East and a modest reduction in growing stock in the West. Both are desirable targets. As a result of the cutting down of much old growth sawtimber, Western growth rates would increase and the volume of growth rise despite the decline in inventory.

The assumptions seem reasonable. The projected tripling in imports is substantial, but the resulting absolute magnitude of 2.4 billion cubic feet still modest. The assumption that 50 per cent of the demand will as hitherto be met from the West is not, at this level of demand, unrealistic. Changes in growth rate are modest and in the right direction both in the East (down) and in the West (up). Even if imports and growth rates were somewhat lower than those assumed, a small increase in the proportion of the demand met from the West could easily make up the difference; and similarly favorable results would be obtained. The margin by which projections are favorable in terms of terminal inventories is sufficient to warrant overlooking the problems of meeting demands for specific types of wood products such as sawtimber.

At the projected Medium level of demand the outlook would change sharply. Under that assumption the Eastern forests would remain substantially stable through 1980, but would undergo rapid depletion thereafter. Western inventory would hold up better, but by the end of the century it too would be rapidly moving towards depletion. This would not be serious through the 1980's, if we could assume that the Western cut would be substantially from old growth sawtimber. The shortfall thereafter would have to be met by cutting growth and thus depleting the capital stock.

The assumptions on which the projections rest clearly play a more crucial role in the significance of the results of the Medium projection than they do in that of the Low projections. Relatively small variations in the proportion of demand met from East and West and in the growth rates in the two areas can signifi-

cantly affect the results. At the same time, the question of meeting specific as opposed to over-all demand—for example, for sawtimber as opposed to wood in general, and for particular species—becomes much more important; even if there were indications that over-all demand could be met by net growth without significant stock depletion, this would not necessarily imply that specific demands could be met, as it is legitimate to infer in the Low projection.

Another factor that could clearly alter the outcome is the effect of losses through such menaces as fire, disease, and insects. In the projections, mortality rates have been allowed to decline, but not too radically. The theoretically possible increase in net growth through better forest practice can be gauged from the current level of losses from fire, disease, insects, etc. According to *Timber Resources for America's Future,* the total "growth impact" for both softwood and hardwood from these causes in 1952 was about 11 billion cubic feet, of which only about 770 million could be salvaged; the "impact" was made up of about 3.5 billion cubic feet in mortality and 7.7 billion in future loss of growth. The growth impact in 1952 was slightly greater than the cut in that year, and about 80 per cent of the growth (though the comparison is not fair in the sense that the "loss of growth" portion is distributed over the years of future growth). Eliminating these losses completely could thus raise growth rates spectacularly. In practice, complete elimination cannot of course be achieved. But gains beyond those assumed could significantly add to available supply.

Prevention of loss is only one aspect of more intensive management practices. The Forest Service estimates, for example, that "if forest land in each region were placed under the better forest management currently in effect in that region" the total volume of growth on present commercial forest land would ultimately be 27.5 billion cubic feet a year instead of the 14.2 billion attained in 1952. Even this is only little more than half the 50 billion cubic feet realizable under more extreme assumptions of optimum conditions all around, termed "biologically possible growth" by the Forest

Service. It is a sobering thought that the realizable growth would easily meet the Medium demand through 2000. This growth makes no assumptions other than the spread of good management. The Forest Service does not forecast that such a spread will in fact occur as a practical matter, and the continuance of rising cut and insufficient growth would of course make it less feasible, since inventory would decline, but it is well to keep the possibility in mind as a measure of the achievable.

It is obvious from the data that a shift from softwood to hardwood use, such as has been under way in pulp manufacture, would exert a strong influence on growth trends. If, from the approximately 30 per cent of total cut now met from hardwood species, the hardwood share would gradually increase to 40 per cent by the end of the century, the Western forests would decline to only 182 billion cubic feet by 2000, and the Eastern forests, instead of being rapidly depleted after 1980, would have an added lease on life, with depletion postponed though not eliminated. At the same time, the very large rise in hardwood inventory that is projected in the basic calculation (see Table 18–13) would be dampened. Such a shift towards hardwoods would mean a lessening of the pressure on softwoods, especially in the East, and at a later date also in the West, but it would be hard to achieve. Even now a large portion of hardwood utilization is for fuelwood. Excluding this, hardwood contributes only 20 per cent of domestic cut. Thus an increase to 40 per cent would be a doubling. Since the proportion of sawtimber is much lower in hardwood than in softwood, any such shift would aggravate the sawtimber problem. Indeed, one could say that relative hardwood utilization would have to far more than double in uses where trees of sawtimber size are not essential, especially pulpwood and miscellaneous uses. But since hardwood forests are largely in private ownership, such shifts depend on market forces and cannot be easily effected.

A second factor that exerts an influence on growth-cut relationships is the regional composition of the domestic cut. If instead of the 50/50 ratio between Eastern and Western

softwood cut we assume a gradual increase to 60 per cent in the West, the resulting inventory situation in the East is quite favorable through 1990, but again depletion is only postponed, not avoided. This increase would be accompanied by more rapid depletion in the West: by 2000 the Western forests would be only one-third of their 1960 size. This suggests a further variation. Heavier cutting in the West, especially of old growth, could be expected to increase the growth rate more than has been assumed in the basic pattern. Assuming a tripling, instead of a doubling, in the growth rate between 1960 and 1990–2000 (a rise that would be equivalent to that implicit in the Forest Service's realizable growth), depletion of the Western softwoods would be less rapid, amounting to some 100 billion cubic feet in forty years. While this seems a heavy load, one must recognize that the 50 million acres of old growth stands in the West carry probably no less—and possibly more—than 100 billion cubic feet of timber. To the extent that depletion were primarily to take place in those areas, a decline in growing stock of this magnitude would not be all bad. The problem is that by that time the required cut would be so large that depletion would accelerate.

To round out these speculations—all depicted in Figure 18–10 and detailed in Appendix Table A18–16—we have also calculated a combined pattern in which the shift to hardwood is linked to a shift to Western softwood and a rise in the Western softwood growth rate not of 200 but of only 150 per cent over the forty-year period. Such a model, based upon meeting Medium demand, indicates a moderate increase in the volume of Eastern forests, a rise of 50 per cent in hardwood forests, and a substantial, though greatly mitigated decline in Western growing stock.

Again, if it were feasible to concentrate cutting in old growth stands, then the inventory reached in 2000, under the favorable assumptions here made, would consist overwhelmingly of new growth. Under such conditions, the net annual growth rate might be substantially higher than the 2.5 per cent average assumed for the last decade of the century. If this were a possible development, then the declining

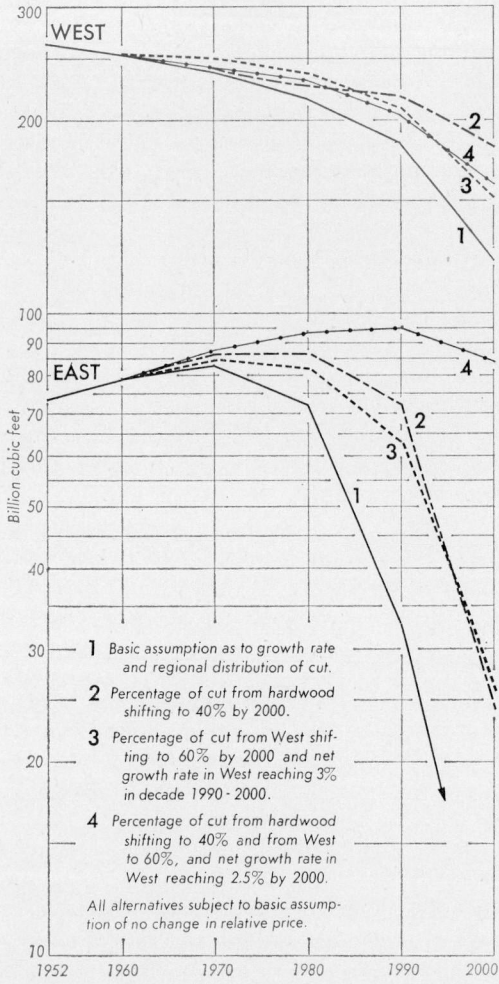

Figure 18–10. Changes in softwood growing stock under alternative assumptions of growth, 1952, 1960, and Medium projections to 2000.

trend in Western growing stock evident in Table 18–12 (col. 5) would not be nearly as disconcerting and ominous for the future, or, more realistically, the chances for meeting a demand not too far below the Medium projection would be greatly enhanced. Since old growth is predominantly in public ownership, such a development would depend above all on future timber sale policy.

The one variable not so far discussed is acreage. Obviously, our attitude towards depletion of forests now in existence would alter if we knew that new forests were being planted on acreage not now part of the commercial forest area. What acreage would have to be drafted into the forest category to yield enough wood by 2000 to plug the gap between domestic demand of over 29 billion cubic feet and net growth of only 12.4 billion? The answer must necessarily be a rough guess. On the basis of current growth of 30 cubic feet per acre as a minimum yield, we would have to shift some 600 million acres into commercial forest land to meet the shortage. Taking the Forest Service's figure for realizable growth on present acreage and translating it into a yield per acre figure of some 55 cubic feet, we might bring the total down to 300 million acres. New technology, such as faster breeding, higher rates of fertilization, etc., might further reduce this figure, but not substantially alter its order of magnitude. If the influence of shifts to hardwood and to Western softwood and of the higher growth rates achieved through improved management were brought to bear, this figure could again be reduced, but not greatly, for net growth in 2000, under the favorable assumptions of these shifts, would not rise beyond 16 billion cubic feet, compared with demand for 29 billion. An additional problem would be that much of the land would be in small lots, scattered all over the country, with little relationship to points of processing or consumption.

It seems clear from these considerations that the 2000 demand could be only partially met by expansion of the acreage basis even in the crudest physical terms, that is, completely disregarding the fact that, given the time element involved, all this acreage would have to be planted to trees in the next few years, with the first financial reward not in the offing for at least a couple of decades. But of course any expansion of forest acreage, and equally restocking of that portion of the commercial forest acreage that is now poorly stocked, would help to narrow the prospective gap. The first of these possibilities—acreage expansion—is, however, extremely problematical in view of the expected pressure of competing uses for land, some of much higher value. In fact, it is more likely that there will be some further shrinkage of commercial forest land.

TABLE 18–12. Effect upon Growing Stock of Meeting Medium Demand under Varying Assumptions of Source and Growth Rate, 1960–2000

(Billion cubic feet of growing stock)

Type, Location, and Year	Basic assumptions of source and growth rate	Cut shifting to 40% hardwood by 2000	Alternative assumptions		
			Softwood cut shifting to 60% in West by 2000		Combination of (2) and (4) but growth rate in West rising to 2.5% instead of 3% by 1990–2000
			Basic growth rate in West	Growth rate in West rising to 3% by 1990–2000	
	(1)	(2)	(3)	(4)	(5)
Softwood, West:					
1960	253	253	253	253	253
1980	219	227	212	236	228
2000	121	182	79	151	158
Softwood, East:					
1960	79	79	79	79	79
1980	72	86	82	82	94
2000	nil	24	25	25	84
Hardwood:					
1960	192	192	192	192	192
1980	299	280	280	280	280
2000	389	282	282	282	282

Source: Appendix Table A18–16.

Implications of the projections. The real question of how in the latter part of the century a balance might be achieved remains open. By price increases that will cut demand down, and by substitution of competing products? Or by stimulation of increased cuts? In either event projected demand cannot coexist with projected cuts without the shifts discussed and even then the 2000 position is not a tenable one.

It is highly probable that the Low demand can easily be met, and it is out of the question that the High demand can be met without the kind of inventory depletion that would very soon raise the most serious issues of conservation over a broad field far exceeding forestry matters.

We have already indicated that the odds on meeting demand for specific types, qualities, and species of wood would tend to be even longer than on meeting aggregate demand. A statistical demonstration of ability to meet the over-all demand carries no necessary implication, for example, that the specific demand for sawtimber can equally be met. While there is thus substantial possibility of over-all adequacy co-existing with specific shortage at least for the next two decades, there exists, on the other hand, a wide range of substitutability; and with improved technology, the margin of flexibility is growing. Specifically with respect to the division between sawtimber and other wood products, the margin of flexibility even now is substantial. In 1952 sawtimber constituted 85 per cent of the total cut, a much larger percentage than could be accounted for by end-products for which sawtimber is essential. Much sawtimber was used for end-products for which it was not essential. Fifty-six per cent of pulpwood, 34 per cent of fence posts, 30 per cent of mine timbers were made from sawtimber. The use of sawtimber for these products could be greatly reduced or even eliminated, but in all likelihood the switch to smaller trees would entail higher costs. This in turn would leave its mark upon the demand projections.

Another factor which would reduce the pressure on sawtimber is that the proportion of projected demand arising from pulpwood rises significantly between 1960 and 2000.

The extent to which various end-products can be made from waste residues of lumbering operations is increasing. The volume of residues is truly impressive. The amount occurring in logging and consisting of cut but unused or partly used trees and portions of trees totaled 1.4 billion cubic feet in 1952. This amount is part of the cut of growing stock and thus operates to reduce inventory. Better use here depends largely on improved and hence lower cost methods of collecting this material and delivering it to pulpmills, which would seem to be the most logical consumers. The amount available is 40 per cent of estimated pulpwood demand in 1960.

Even larger amounts are available as plant residues. These—totaling 3.4 billion cubic feet in 1952—occur mostly at sawmills and are of many different types, suitable for a long list of end-products, from brush handles to fiberboard. But only 60 per cent of plant residues were used at all in 1952 and, of this, 85 per cent was burned as fuel; only 15 per cent, or 9 per cent of total plant residues, remained to be used in wood products. It takes little imagination to foresee increasing use of the currently unused residues and declining use of residues as fuel, especially as demand pressure is likely to increase their value as wood rather than as fuel. (Indeed, the decline of fuelwood itself is built into the projections and so is the growing share of residues in pulpmaking.) This presumes, of course, that non-wood products manufactured either from plant fibers or from inorganic chemicals will not in the meantime provide an even cheaper substitute. At any rate, none of these potential sources of help are of such magnitude as to hold out hope that the projected demand for forest products may be met without inventory depletion for the rest of the century.

Adequacy of hardwood supplies. Table 18–13 presents essentially the same type of calculation for hardwood as was made above for softwood. The analysis of the data can be much more easily summarized, however. Since well over 90 per cent of the hardwood inventory is in the East, no regional differentiation has been

TABLE 18–13. Supply and Demand Relationships in Hardwoods, 1960 and Projections for 1980, 1990, 2000

(*Billion cubic feet unless otherwise indicated*)

	1960		1980	1990	2000
		L	3.0	3.2	3.8
Gross demand	3.2	M	4.4	5.7	7.6
		H	6.1	9.1	14.3
Imports	0.08		0.14	0.17	0.20
		L	2.9	3.0	3.6
Net demand	2.9	M	4.3	5.5	7.4
		H	6.0	8.9	14.1
Net growth rate		L	3.1	2.4	1.6
(per cent)	4.2	M	3.4	3.0	2.6
		H	3.6	3.2	3.2
		L	9.8	8.8	4.9
Net growth	8.0	M	10.0	10.4	10.0
		H	10.2	9.7	9.0
		L	308	372	416
Growing stock	192	M	299	352	389
		H	287	311	290

L = Low projection   M = Medium   H = High.

Source: Appendix Table A18–15.

introduced and the nature of the conclusions that emerge makes it unnecessary to determine the consequences of varying the assumptions.

The hardwood forests of the East are in various stages of regrowth following logging and fires. While the inventory may appear large, it is composed largely of pulpwood and small sawlog size trees, much of it of poor quality. There is very little old growth hardwood sawtimber. As a rule, hardwood forests in nature eventually evolve into uneven-aged, many-sized stands. Harvesting only the mature trees under selective logging makes room for younger trees to develop and at the same time accelerates the rate of growth. The current rapid growth rate is due to the youth of the stands; on a considerable area young stands are coming into merchantability by reaching the minimum pole size of 5-inch diameter.

At both its Low and Medium levels, the demand can be met in such a way as to permit the substantial growth of inventory which is essential for obtaining trees of the size needed for sawtimber. In each case this conclusion rests on an assumed decline in the growth rate, which in the Low projection is substantial.

Only in the High projection is it necessary to cut into inventory to meet demand late in the century. And the reduction starts from a level in 1990 which exceeds estimated 1960 growing stock by more than 50 per cent. These hardwood projections do not assume any increase in the net growth rate, but they do assume a reduction in mortality.

In concluding that the hardwood situation is clearly more favorable than the softwood, we must remember that this is true even though in our basic assumptions we have stipulated some replacement of softwood by hardwood (in pulp manufacture). Nonetheless, demands substantially higher than the Medium level could be met without inventory depletion. Only the upper reaches of demand signal a problem of resource adequacy, and then only after 1990. But even this problem could probably be held to tolerable limits by the spread of improved forestry practices, and it is not unlikely that by that time large areas of the world will have begun to exploit their hardwood forests more systematically and will constitute a larger source of supply of high quality woods for the U.S. market.

The role of imports. The assumed aggregate import levels have been stated in the basic projection tables. What are the potential sources of supply outside the U.S. borders? Compared with consumption of domestic softwood, softwood imports have not been large—less than 15 per cent. However, in relation to world timber trade they have been quite significant. In fact, the United States is a leading importer of softwood products.

About two-thirds of the softwood imported by the United States has been in the form of pulpwood and pulpwood products, almost all from Canada. The bulk of the remainder of softwood imports has been in the form of lumber, and over 90 per cent of this has come from Canada.

Canada undoubtedly remains the most promising source of supply in the future. The allowable cut for softwood alone in 1980 was estimated at 6.8 billion cubic feet in March 1957.[18] This is not to say that this amount of softwood *will* be cut in 1980 but that, barring cost considerations, 6.8 billion cubic feet of softwood *could* be cut if the demand for it existed. Part of the allowable cut may be lost to fire and disease, reducing the total to about 6.5 billion. Canadian domestic consumption may require about 1.5 billion cubic feet of softwood, leaving roughly 5 billion available for export. Allowance must be made for exports to areas other than the United States, primarily Western Europe. Although Western Europe is not a large importer of Canadian softwood at the present time, there are indications that the import requirements of this area may increase substantially in the next few decades.

Taking all these factors into account, it would seem that Canada may be able to supply to the United States between 2 and 4 billion cubic feet in 1980. Certainly, 2 billion would be a reasonable minimum, within the framework of a 6.8 billion cubic feet cut; whether Canadian shipments could bring relief beyond 4 billion cubic feet seems more doubtful. Allowing for imports of paper, principally newsprint, which has been dealt with in Chapter 8, the net import level of 2 billion cubic feet from all sources appears reasonable. The estimates of 1.7 and 1.8 billion cubic feet (for 1975 and 2000 respectively) advanced by the Forest Service's *Timber Resources* as deliberately "conservative" seem low even in the light of imports since 1952.

A look at the softwood problem for the year 2000 is even more speculative. The Low projection of imports again raises no problem, and towards the High of 4 billion cubic feet Canada may be able to make enough of a contribution to bring it within reach. Many improvements in Canadian forestry practices may occur in

18. Royal Commission on Canada's Economic Prospects, *The Outlook for the Canadian Forest Industries* (Hull, Que.: Queen's Printer and Controller of Stationery, 1957).

the intervening years, and perhaps the Canadian supply will increase enough to cover the imports required by the High and, by implication, the Medium projection. The U.S. Forest Service has suggested that the growth rate of timber in Canada may eventually increase by 50 per cent to 60 per cent; this growth may considerably augment the available supply.

Europe must be ruled out as a source of imports; indeed, as indicated, it is likely to compete with the United States for Canadian exports. In the long run no great increase in European softwood can be expected, since 96 per cent of the forests are now being utilized and forest management there is more intensive than in any other area in the world.

This leaves the U.S.S.R. as a potential supplier among the world's present large softwood producers. In sheer area and volume, the U.S.S.R. has a larger supply of softwood than any other country in the world. Its vast territory contains about one-fifth of the world's forested area; over 85 per cent of this is coniferous. However, accessibility greatly affects export possibilities. Over three-fourths of the U.S.S.R.'s forests are in the Asiatic portions of the country. Poor accessibility and lack of year-around navigable water routes minimize the chances of exploitation, barring revolutionary changes in methods of overland hauling in rugged terrain. Thus, the growth prospects that do exist are of only relative interest, as is the fact that at present annual growth is about twice annual cut. What counts economically is the situation west of the Urals. Here the forests have been heavily exploited, and the river system has been favorable to the timber industry, the rivers having by their northern flow in the past facilitated timber exports to Western Europe, primarily Great Britain.

The Soviet economy's rapid expansion, particularly in the field of construction, suggests that the demand for softwood will increase substantially. In the judgment of the U.S. Forest Service, no substantial volume of Soviet timber would be likely to reach United States markets even if trade between the Soviet bloc and non-communist countries were unrestricted.[19] If the softwood cut in the Soviet

19. Forest Service, *Timber Resources*, p. 351.

Union does increase faster than demand, an increase in shipments from Russia to Western Europe would decrease the latter's demand for Canadian softwood and thereby make more available to the United States. But these margins are not likely to be large. The Russian timber resources do not, even in the longer time perspective, hold out much promise for the American consumer.

We must conclude then that our basic import assumptions are probably stretched to the limit as far as supplies from traditional sources are concerned. Relief can be expected only from new sources, concentrated in tropical or semi-tropical areas and supplying hardwood rather than the softwood which has in the past constituted the bulk of U.S. imports. Both South America and Africa are in this category, but available information can lead to little more than speculation. Undoubtedly intensive economic development outside Europe and North America will in the coming decades lead to commercial exploitation of the forests in the now less developed countries of the world. Vast amounts of hardwood are physically available: they comprise two-thirds of the world's forests. But so far only valuable species, for specific uses, have been shipped to the United States: teak from Thailand and Burma, rosewood from Brazil, mahogany from equatorial Africa, and other species from the Philippines, Japan, and more than two dozen other countries. This is not the kind of trade here envisaged. To make a beginning towards supplementing U.S. lumber supplies would call for large-scale opening up of forests in hardwood areas and greatly reduced costs of long-haul transportation to make such supplies attractive to lower-grade uses—except in one area: The Canadian allowable cut of hardwood in 1980 has been estimated at 2.7 billion cubic feet and domestic demand is expected to be less than .6 billion cubic feet.[20] A large portion of Canada's hardwoods are in areas adjacent to the Great Lakes and the St. Lawrence Seaway, so that transporting this wood to the United States would not be a problem. If Canada has some 2 billion cubic feet of hardwood availa-

20. Royal Commission on Canada's Economic Prospects, *op. cit.*

ble for export in 1980 a significant part of any U.S. deficit may be supplied from this source.

As in the case of domestic supply, so in the import picture, the substitution of hardwood for softwood appears an almost inevitable means of meeting growing demand. Undoubtedly, this will raise major problems in technology. Only relative costs of hardwood supplies, the degree of inconvenience in substituting these for softwood, and cost and quality of competitive non-wood materials will eventually determine the balance.

Competing materials. The price of lumber and other forest products is quite sensitive to such factors as labor costs, location of supply in relation to demand, shifts in utilization, and other influences beside the simple supply-demand relationship here developed. Even in the lower reaches of demand for lumber and wood, prices may rise in relation to the general price level as they have been doing, except recently, for the last fifty or sixty years. Such increases may occur for various reasons: because the proportion of labor cost to total cost is high and wages rise; or because an increase in the proportion of cut coming from the West, while filling aggregate demand, entails higher transportation costs and thus an increased average price at the point of consumption. But whereas the net balance of these factors in the price situation is uncertain at lower demand levels, it seems probable that from a Medium demand level on up the price of wood and lumber would increase—probably substantially.

What might happen to forest products output at the somewhat higher levels of demand? Demand might for some time be met despite the depletion of the forests. But for how long? After a certain point, the community is likely to take measures to insure better management of the forests. But when would such measures be taken and what would be their nature and effects? The only thing it seems safe to say is that, over significant periods of time, particularly toward the latter part of the forty-year period, a substantial part of the demand for timber could not physically be met, and that, in any case, such wood as becomes available would command rising prices.

As this type of situation developed, it would call forth a variety of responses, some of which, like increased timber growth, shift in geographic source, and general improvements in management, already have been mentioned. In addition, it might promote further investment in and development of forestry and lumbering in Canada, further exploration of tropical forests, investigation of the qualities of tropical trees, and research into the uses to which they might be put. And it would tend to promote further economies in the use of wood, first by waste utilization and then by the further substitution of other materials: brick and concrete, aluminum, plastics, and fiber glass in construction; sugar cane bagasse and perhaps other non-wood vegetable fibers in making paper; aluminum foil and plastics instead of paper in packaging; materials other than wood in boxing and crating, or perhaps a basic change in shipping methods, for example in the transportation of vegetables, which would eliminate the use of boxing in its present form.

The tendency toward increasing use of substitutes depends as much on technological developments with respect to other materials as on developments in the price of forest products, for the use of competing materials is not merely a matter of the price relationship between these materials and wood. For example, in construction, aluminum or plastics may as materials cost more than lumber or wood, but it may be possible to do things with them which cannot be done with wood or even veneer. The use of these new materials may permit changes in the construction process; for example, a switch to prefabrication, which greatly reduces total construction costs despite the higher cost of the materials; or it may permit certain basic changes in the design of dwelling units and other buildings which could not be effected with wood. Aluminum in window frames, storm windows and doors, etc., possesses certain quality advantages over wood. Plastics and aluminum foil have properties clearly superior to those of paper for certain purposes, for example, in much of the wrapping of perishable foodstuffs. While technology is not likely to make wood and its products obsolete —indeed, wood is a preferable material in many aspects—the inroads of competitors must be reckoned with.

While substitution can be expected to continue at a certain pace independent of price, relative price is clearly of great importance, especially in end-products in which wood and lumber are a significant cost component. For example, price is very important in housing, which takes a large proportion of the country's lumber output. Even with a likely continuing reduction in the average use of lumber per dwelling unit, price increases would be significant.

The ultimate possibilities of new materials are still in the distant future. With further research and with development of their ability to take colors, resist heat, withstand weather, etc., and with reductions in their price, their range and volume of uses will increase greatly. As it is we are moving towards increasing liberation from traditional raw materials with their simple properties, towards a situation in which the raw materials are atoms and molecules. Increasingly, scientists and engineers are moving towards analysis of the properties and qualities desired for certain products, with a view to the creation of materials that will have these properties and qualities.

A tightening lumber and wood situation, as projected by rising demand during the latter half of the forty-year period, could greatly accelerate this movement by stimulating research and development, encouraging plunges into the new materials in otherwise doubtful situations by holding out the promise of a reliable mass market. Construction alone could eventually absorb vastly increased amounts of aluminum, plastics, fiber glass, etc. The pattern of material use is constantly changing and will change still further, and the interrelations between wood and the new materials are part of this process.

Other Uses of Land

Although about nine-tenths of the nation's area is devoted to crops, grazing, or timber, some of the varied uses of the remaining tenth are the most dynamic in terms of rapid growth, or the pre-emptive power of high pricing, or both. Prospective demand for outdoor recrea-

tion has been examined in Chapter 11. Other significant minor uses of land are for urban space, transportation, wildlife refuges, and reservoirs and water management. In our brief discussion of these we lean heavily on the data and analysis presented in Resources for the Future's recent full-length study in this field, *Land for the Future*.[21]

In addition, there are a number of miscellaneous types of land in this category, such as non-producing farmland (devoted mainly to homesteads), land used in minerals production, and true wasteland like deserts and inaccessible mountain tops. All told, this mixed bag of uses or non-uses occupied about 135 million acres in 1950. They are not separately considered here, but will be taken account of in the final section of this chapter, where the sum of projected demands upon acreage will be compared with the country's total land resources.

Urban Land[22]

In 1910, when the total U.S. population was around 92 million, less than half of the people lived in cities or towns large enough to be called urban places. By 1950, total population had risen to 150 million persons, of whom nearly two-thirds were town and city dwellers. All signs point to a continued growth of cities: larger urban proportions of a larger total population. By 1980, urban population may represent three-fourths of the total; by 2000, four-fifths.

Unmistakable as these trends appear to be in terms of people, their effect on future land requirements is less clear. Anyone driving from the downtown center of his home town through successive suburban and rural layers until he emerges into the open country will readily understand the difficulty of finding the statistical counterpart to the concept of urban land. Where does the city end, the country begin? What about the vacant lots? The wooded or grassy tracts surrounded by built-up sections?

21. Marion Clawson *et al., op. cit.*
22. For a full exposition of the estimates, the specialist is referred to *Land for the Future, op. cit.*, especially Chapters II, III, and VII. We have adopted the criteria of that study, with some modification to fit the general pattern of our projections. All that is attempted here is a summary of the argument of Clawson and his co-authors.

The as yet undeveloped subdivisions that border the open country, yet are no longer part of it?

The proper criterion, as Clawson points out, is not actual urban *use,* but *withdrawal* from alternative uses. Such a definition would include whatever land has been made idle by its urban context. The distinction between use and withdrawal is far from academic. Sample studies suggest that between one-third and one-half of all urban land is not in use. In his estimate for 1950 Clawson puts urban land used at 11 million acres, land withdrawn for urban uses at 17 million acres. The difference between the two figures represents land not now or, in all likelihood, in the future available for any use other than urban. Some of it may forever remain idle, but none is likely ever again to revert to cropping, grazing, or forestry.

Projection of urban land requirements, as shown in Table 18–14, incorporates the results obtained by Clawson but follows a greatly simplified projection procedure. As in his approach, population growth is assumed to accrue exclusively to urban centers, based on extrapolation of the 1940–50 experience. Growth in numbers of cities and urban places, in different size classes, based on past trends, and maintenance of density at the 1950 level for each size class (i.e., a city of 50,000 population is assumed to occupy the same amount of space in 1980 and 2000 as it did in 1950 and does now) is not separately worked out but rather implicitly accepted by our using his results. The density assumption, perhaps the crucial one in this type of projection, rests on the lack of evidence regarding changes in density for equal-sized cities over the past decade. Even a large margin of error here has relatively minor effect on the total land picture. Suppose that by 1980 the area picture were to change in such a way as to increase space requirements by 25 per cent for each size class; in that event the claim on land for urban purposes would rise by only 7.5 million acres, the equivalent of 0.4 per cent of all land, or of less than 2 per cent of all cropland. There is little reason, therefore, to quarrel with Clawson's assumption of a static size–density

ratio. The figures shown in Table 18–14 represent the estimated demand at the three population levels that might be expected in 1980 and 2000.

Two rough conclusions emerge from the study: urban population density has been increasing; but the increase has been gradual. The entire growth has been about 20 per cent in a century, while, as Table 18–14 shows, urban population, over the same span, has grown 25-fold. As the decline in acres per capita has only occasionally been interrupted and has in this century exhibited a definite tendency to flatten out (a behavior perhaps not entirely unconnected with more comprehensive definitions of "urban population"), we have not hesitated to extend this trend. For the Medium population model, we have used Clawson's fac-

TABLE 18–14. Urban Population and Land, 1850–1960, and Projections to 1980 and 2000

Year		Urban population (thousands)	Area (thous. acres)	Acres per capita
1850		3,544	720	.203
1860		6,217	1,200	.193
1870		9,902	1,958	.198
1880		14,130	2,785	.197
1890		22,106	4,190	.190
1900		30,160	5,545	.184
1910		41,400	7,450	.180
1920		54,158	9,535	.176
1930		68,955	11,780	.171
1940		74,424	12,800	.172
1950 (old def.)		88,927	15,040	.169
1950 (new def.)		96,468	16,750	.174
1960		125,000	21,400	.171
1980	L	171,000	28,000	.165
	M	193,000	32,000	.164
	H	225,000	36,000	.162
2000	L	213,000	36,000	.170
	M	279,000	45,000	.160
	H	378,000	59,000	.155

L = Low projection M = Medium H = High.

Source: Adapted from Marion Clawson *et al., Land for the Future* (Baltimore; Johns Hopkins Press and Resources for the Future, 1960), Table 16. Projection of urban population agrees with that used in Table A14–1 in the Medium projection but differs in High and Low, since regional estimates there used are possible Highs and Lows for each region and not additive.

tors, but have dropped the 2000 factor one notch—from 161 to 160—to take account of our slightly higher population projection.

The change in density ratio is conceived as related to population level rather than to time. Therefore, three different levels are assumed for each year of the projection. In each instance, the high population is coupled with the low acreage per capita, and vice versa, on the assumption that greater population pressure would make for more careful budgeting of urban land. The range in density ratios has been kept moderate. Even in 2000 the High falls only 10 per cent above the Low.

Transportation, Wildlife, and Reservoirs

Transportation. Chapter 5, although concerned primarily with the effect of future developments in transportation upon demand for materials, provides the general background for projecting space requirements. Quite small in terms of total land, these are of interest chiefly as specialized, high-value demands that through price or condemnation can pre-empt desirable acreage from other uses.

About 8 million acres now are in railroad rights of way. Even though the volume of freight traffic is increasing, gains in operating efficiency should make it possible to handle the greater load without additions to trackage. Any small net change that occurs is more likely to be a decrease in acreage as some rail lines are abandoned in the face of truck competition.

Highways and adjacent rights of way now occupy about 16 million acres. The current federal superhighway program calls for more than 40,000 miles in the interstate system and large mileage additions to other roads. With rights of way averaging 200 feet wide, this would add slightly more than 1 million acres; with 400-foot rights of way, a little over 2 million. (Each 8¼ feet of right of way requires an acre per mile.) Because of the efficiency of the new roads, construction will by no means have to keep pace with volume of traffic. Nevertheless, highway building clearly will continue throughout the century. A net increase of 3 million acres, resulting from extension of the primary road system, with allowance made for abandonment of superseded

roads and perhaps some rural roads, seems a reasonable assumption.

Airports and landing strips now occupy about 1¾ million acres. Here, even more than in the case of highways, heavier traffic does not require corresponding increases in acreage. Since 1927 total miles flown per year have risen 50-fold and passenger miles 200-fold, and airfield area has risen 7-fold. Our assumption is that present acreage in airfields and air strips will double by the year 2000.

With area in railroads holding steady or dropping slightly, total land requirements for transportation may be in the neighborhood of 30 million acres by 2000.

Wildlife refuges. Here we are concerned with land devoted formally and primarily to wildlife: as Clawson has pointed out, man shares nearly all of the nation's area with birds and other animals, even in cities and suburbs. About 15 million acres of public land, about two-thirds of which is federally owned and the other third state-owned, are now given over to wildlife. The additions that seem likely in the next four decades—perhaps on the order of 5 million acres—will probably be almost entirely wetlands set aside for the benefit of waterfowl.

Reservoirs and water regulation. About 12 million acres of land in the United States have been inundated by dam-created storage reservoirs or artificial lakes. This area does not include ponds of 40 acres or less, which in long-standing statistical practice are considered as land. (Consequently some acreage classified as farming or grazing land is actually under water. It appears, however, that little usable cropland has been flooded; most of the ponds are on gullied land.)

Growth of population and economic activity will greatly increase demand for dependable water supplies for industrial and municipal use, for recreation, and for adequate dilution flow to reduce concentration of stream pollution. More dams will be built. As pointed out in Chapter 14, most of them probably will be in the East, not only because most of the towns and factories are there but also because in much of the arid West fewer potential reservoir sites are left. It seems likely that on the order of 8 million additional acres will be covered by new reservoirs by the year 2000.

Other water regulation devices, such as levees, though often of great local importance, do not occupy enough acreage to create a nationally significant land requirement.

The Broad Outlook for Land

Having reviewed the outlook for the major uses of land in the United States (and the significant minor uses as well) we can now add up the various projected requirements and compare the sum with the total resource—the 1,904 million acres of the forty-eight contiguous states. The results are presented in Table 18–15. Miscellaneous land uses or non-uses not considered separately are lumped together in one item of the table.

On the face of it, the table appears to be a neat, clear-cut summation. In reality it is considerably less than that; several reservations and qualifications are in order.

First, the basic official classification of land uses, as we have noted earlier (and explain further in the appendix to Chapter 18), is by no means satisfactory. There are probably tens of millions of acres that can be considered woodland, grazing land, or "other" land, according to the enumerator's or owner's judgment at the time. Clawson, for one, has split the "non-commercial" forest category into grazing land, recreation land, wildlife land, and a residual that is relegated to the "all other" category. His procedure, however, makes it difficult to use the feed value data that the Department of Agriculture has evolved for the various grazing land categories contained in the official land use statistics. All our grazing projections (pages 349–51) have therefore been cast in terms of the official rather than Clawson's classification, but the latter is adopted in the summary land use projection in Table 18–15.

Another difficulty is that a substantial part of commercial forest land is used for grazing, while part is exclusively forest land; we cannot add grazing and commercial forest land as they appear in Census statistics without large-scale duplication of acreage (see Figure 18–5). On the other hand, the Census classification of

TABLE 18–15. Land Requirements (excl. Alaska and Hawaii), 1950, 1960, and Medium Projections for 1980, 2000

(Million acres)

Category	1950	1960	1980	2000
Cropland, including pasture[1]	478	447	443	476
Grazing land[1]	700	700	700	700
Farmland, non-producing	45	45	45	45
Commercial forest land[2]	484	484	484	484
Recreation (excl. reservoir areas and city parks)[3]	42	44	76	134
Urban land (including city parks)	17	21	32	45
Transportation	25	26	28	30
Wildlife refuges	14	15	18	20
Reservoirs	10	12	15	20
Total specified[2]	1,815	1,794	1,841	1,954
Other land (residual)	89	110	63	—50
Total land area	1,904	1,904	1,904	1,904

1. All adjustments for feeding requirements are made in cropland, with grazing land held constant.
2. Does not provide for increased acreage to meet projected commercial forest demand. Requirements to close the projected gap in 2000 might run as high as 300 million acres (see p. 364 above), to be put into forest use at this time.
3. Totaled from unrounded figures in Chapter 11.

"woodland" includes non-commercial forests that have little bearing on present or projected timber production.

Moreover, our discussion of the adequacy of the forest resource earlier in this chapter did not include formal estimates of acreage required to meet projected levels of demand. Attention was focused, instead, on growth rate and other variables beside land. The forest land acreage figures in Table 18–15 simply express our arbitrary assumption of no change during the next four decades. Obviously, diminution of commercial forest land would further aggravate a tightening supply situation and any expansion in forest acreage would ease it. Present trends suggest some loss of forest land to fast-growing other uses, particularly recreation.

Grazing acreage other than cropland pasture, like commercial forest acreage, has been assumed to remain available at the level estimated in the 1950 Census, with any adjustments for changes in feed requirements taking place—or rather showing up statistically—in cropland. Thus we do not possess true acreage requirement figures for grazing land in its various guises, but only for the sum total.

With all its shortcomings the table does bring out certain tendencies inherent in the data. The growing pressure of total demand upon the land resources, even allowing for substantial qualitative improvement, is clearly shown. Limiting ourselves to the Medium projection, we can see that by 1980 the "other land," which is the balancing item, will have shrunk considerably, and that by the end of the century it will become a minus quantity. This means that the projected requirements cannot be simultaneously met except by multiple use of substantial tracts of land.

Some of the specific implications in the tabulation are worth following up. Projected cropland requirements for 1980 are 35 million acres below the area so used in 1950. This difference would represent a net surplus situation if we could assume perfect mobility of land between changing uses, not merely between different crops but also between crop raising and pasturing. But clearly, substitutions are bound to entail some losses. In any case, let us look into the significance of a sizeable cropland surplus. Grazing acreage has been as-

sumed to remain available at the 1950 level, though with rising yields. To the extent that a cropland surplus emerges it may be feasible to use significant portions of it for pasturing. The grazing acreage that could in turn be released would be large. Let us assume that by 1980 some 15 million acres of cropland were truly surplus to crop raising and located in areas in which livestock feeding occurs on the appropriate scale; then, at the relative levels of feed values assumed for 1980, each acre of cropland pasture could take the place of 6 acres of permanent open farm pasture, or of 15 acres of farm woodland, or of 24 acres of non-farm range land. Pasture use of surplus cropland could thus release some 90 million acres of permanent farm pasture, or some 225 million acres of farm woodland, or some 360 million acres—more than exist now—of non-farm range land.

The simplifications in the above calculation are obvious: to be transferred easily, surplus cropland would have to be in zones which can switch directly from cropping to cropland pasturing or in which livestock raising either is practiced or is practical but dependent predominantly on provision of cropland pasturing; and the farm enterprises would have to be of such size and structure as to permit the switch from cropping to pasturing. Second, growth in such regions would have to be accompanied by decline in areas that rely on feeding land other than cropland pasture.

These severe limitations should qualify any impression that our projections do in fact intend to portray a constant acreage of grazing land. Instead, this has been merely a convenient first step in estimating the required acreage of cropland.

Even without any replacement of grazing land by cropland, agriculture as a whole is not likely to make increased net demands on land. On the contrary, it should be able on balance to release some land for other uses through 1980. Thereafter it appears that the surplus would decline sharply.

The basket category of land used by farms for purposes other than crop raising or pasturing remains constant in the forward projections. Since this classification includes rural roads, homesteads, etc., it might be argued that continuing shrinkage in the number of farms might gradually diminish this category, and release land for cultivation, but, in the absence of a better understanding of the many elements thrown together here, constancy has been projected.

All other uses trend upward, at various rates: transportation slowly, wildlife areas somewhat faster, reservoirs much faster, urban land very rapidly, and recreation land even more so. Aside from those for recreation, the projected increases in space requirements for uses other than agriculture and forestry is 41 million acres between 1960 and 2000. Where will this acreage come from? Will such magnitudes press hard against land availability?

Prospects for 1980. Looking ahead only to 1980 to begin with, we have seen that there is likely to be a surplus of cropland: perhaps as much as 25–30 million acres, more likely substantially less, depending upon the ease of adjustment to changing crop patterns. In addition, some 10 to 15 million acres might be squeezed out of the "other" category for purposes other than agricultural. Sufficient acreage is in sight to satisfy the growing needs of non-agricultural land demand. Again, however, regional qualifications are important. Since most of the rising demand—outside of that of recreation—will originate in urban growth, the land absorbed will be located near urban centers. Lush cropland may be lost to suburban sprawl, instead of land that it would be most desirable for agriculture to shed, such as areas now carried as "idle" or those of low-yield dry wheat farming. National average yields would be unfavorably affected by such a development and the loss of acreage would in effect be more serious than that portrayed by transfer of surplus acres in a statistical table. On the other hand, the loss of grazing land to non-agricultural uses and its replacement by smaller acreages of cropland elsewhere, or the loss of low fertility cropland in areas of reservoir and wildlife expansion, would be less disturbing. Whatever the path of adjustment, the surplus of cropland through 1980 is sufficiently large to permit expansion of other uses, even with a moderate amount of frictional loss in the process of substitution.

This picture begins to change when demand for recreation acreage, hitherto ignored, is included. This demand, on the assumptions explained in Chapter 11, rises by 34 million acres between 1950 and 1980. Table 18–15 suggests that such an amount can be made available for the exclusive purpose of recreation, but only by drawing on residual land, which encompasses wetlands, mountains, deserts, etc. We can presume that at this level we would not have broken into areas that are valueless even for recreation purposes, but we might be approaching such a situation, for the category of "other land" would by 1980 have shrunk by 26 million acres from its 1950 level, or nearly 50 million acres from the 1960 level which includes the cropland surplus. Thus, increased use of national forest and other land (including privately owned) that is not now used principally for recreation seems probable to help ease the stringency developing by 1980.

Prospects for 2000. For the year 2000 no such balance can be constructed. Satisfaction of all projected demand would presume use of *all* land, including deserts and marshes, and with a net deficit of 50 million acres at that. Assuming a rock bottom acreage of 60 million acres of true wasteland, unsatisfied demand for stated land uses would total some 110 million acres. This results from a rise between 1980 and 2000 of over 30 million acres in cropland needs, coupled with continuing expansion in non-agricultural demand, especially recreation. Even without growth in recreation demand beyond the level projected for 1980, demand would exceed usable acreage by the sizeable amount of some 50 million acres. The tightness is aggravated by the fact that, to the extent that cropland will have been permanently reduced to the 1980 requirement level by urban or other irreversible use, the renewed increase of cropland demand between 1980 and 2000 would call for inroads on permanent pasture and thus pose problems of capital investment for land improvement as well as possible regional shifts.

The shortfall in acreage emerging by the end of the century points to the need, on the one hand, for multiple use of land and, on the other, for intensification of range management.

And the above considerations apply solely to the Medium projections. Any of our projections that incorporate higher land demands are that much more unlikely to be met without multiple use and intensified range management.

What are these higher demands like? In the case of agriculture we can deduce from data presented in Appendix Table A18–12 that high demand coupled with low feeding efficiency and low yields would result in cropland demand for crops to be harvested that by the year 2000 would exceed the Medium projection by close to 300 million acres. It is useless to dwell on the prospect of a cropland demand that, without providing for cropland pasture, exceeds even the 600 million acres in the top three soil classes as defined by the U.S. Department of Agriculture, except as a reminder that continuing progress in technology and spread of skills and knowledge are the *sine qua non* of a continuing high standard of living based on an ample food supply available at a reasonable percentage of personal income.

When we abandon the implausible High demand model in favor of our "Modified High" model (which assumes the condition of high demand combined with high feed efficiency and high crop yields), the pressure on land becomes only marginally greater than in the Medium projection, because the high levels of feed efficiency and crop yields assumed largely compensate for the pressure of high demand. It would be prudent, however, to regard this increased elbowroom as a reserve against setbacks in expected feed efficiency and yield levels even though a surplus emerges statistically when demand for cropland pasture is added.

Outside of agriculture the effects of the High and Low models are likely to be more important. In urban growth, the High model adds some 12 million acres to land demand by the end of the century, further aggravating a tight situation. In recreation the limits of high demand are barely visible. In Chapter 11 only the Medium projection has been worked out in terms of acres, but, on the basis of visits to recreation areas in the High and the Medium projections, High demand can be projected to require, by the year 2000, three times as much

forest land, twice as much national park land, and more than twice as much state park land as under the Medium projection (unless carrying capacity is further increased), or some 200 million acres above and beyond the total assumed in the Medium projection.

Of course, long before such acreages were put at the service of recreation, sequences would be set in motion that would slow the upward trend. Certainly, nothing is gained from adding up these High model figures to arrive at a total high demand only to prove the country short by many hundreds of millions of acres toward the end of the century. What these figures, all pointing in the same direction, indicate is the pressures toward adjustment. In this context the pressure for additional recreation acreage is certainly formidable, but at the same time confined to public action channels and likely to call for investment in facilities far more than in land. Pressure from urban growth, moderate in magnitude, will be satisfied, while pressure from cropland is not likely to become a factor until some time during the second half of the time span here considered, when other uses will seriously encroach upon it, provided the efficiency and yield assumptions prove realistic.

There remains one major claimant hitherto discussed only in passing: forest land. We must recall that even assuming substantial increase in the growth rates of forests and shifts of supply from Eastern to Western areas and from softwood to hardwood, the Medium demand projected for 2000 is unlikely to be satisfied without serious depletion of forest stands. Any inroads of other uses upon forest land, and these are generally considered likely to occur, would further tighten the supply situation. A transfer of surplus acreage to forest use would of course ease the situation, but because of the nature of the forest resource projections no actual acreage requirements have been evolved. Furthermore, it seems likely that higher value uses will make claims on some acreage now in commercial forests. By showing the demand as constant, in Table 18–15, we are depicting a pattern that is inconsistent with meeting long range forest product demand. Thus, forestry represents in a way a latent force for expansion which seems more likely to follow the path of restocking and better management in general. So far, however, the easy supply outlook in the near and intermediate future seems to have discouraged private forest owners from planting even a fraction of the trees that the demand projections indicate might be required as a source of timber products, while the publicly owned forests are administered principally in the spirit of maintaining the growing stock.

Alternative possibilities. Assumptions of increased crop yields and improvement in efficiency in some of the livestock branches are crucial to the conclusion of adequate agricultural land supply at all three levels of projection. It is therefore important to inquire into the possibility of land shifts into agricultural use should the future prove these assumptions to be over-optimistic.

The estimates compiled in 1948–49 by the Soil Conservation Service[23] show that no less than 215 million acres of land in the first three capability classes—those most fitted for crop-raising—is in either grassland or woodland. Even of the top class almost 30 per cent is so used. Part of the explanation lies in the fact that the majority of farms are balanced producing units, active not only in crop raising but also in animal husbandry and sometimes forestry. It is therefore not surprising that the reverse also holds true; almost 50 million acres of land in classes IV to VII is in cropland use that should not be.[24]

While there are no regions that do not show some of these contrasts between use and capability, three regions in particular stand out in which good cropland is either grazed or wooded: the Southeast, which has about 25 per cent of such land, the Western Gulf region, principally Texas, which has 15 per cent, and the grazing lands from Montana and North Dakota down into Oklahoma, which account for yet another 15 per cent. In the Southeast it is principally woodland, in the other areas principally grazing land.

From the purely physical point of view, therefore, there appears ample room for extending the present crop acreage, should the need arise. The figures cited suggest also that deliberate shifts in acreage, based on soil capability, are an available means of yield improvement. Where grazing land is involved, the loss would be relatively small because of the low feed productivity of land in grazing. In fact, devoting a small acreage of the high-class land so shifted to pasture would normally compensate for the loss of grazing land.

As for conversion of forest land, the loss is far more serious, since much of the forest land most suitable for crop raising happens also to be land of high forest productivity. Since the forest situation is likely to be tight in any event, any inroads on the acreage, and especially on the more productive commercial acreage, would further aggravate the supply situation. On the other hand, conversion of non-commercial forest land, especially in the South, which now renders at best a low yield of animal feed, would appear a logical means of helping to satisfy expanding acreage demand.

It is our judgment that the land resource will be adequate to the demands upon it, but to sustain this judgment it will be very important that the yield and efficiency levels we project be reached. A path toward this goal is offered in the shifting of land from grazing to crop production—a shift which in all likelihood will entail investment in irrigation and soil-building practices.

23. Hugh H. Wooten and James R. Anderson, *Agricultural Resources in the United States,* Agricultural Information Bulletin No. 140 (Washington: U.S. Department of Agriculture, June 1955).

24. Preliminary data available at the time of writing from the National Inventory of Soil and Water Conservation Needs indicate that the "reserve" of regularly cultivable land now in forest land or pasture amounts to 240 million acres, and that 75 million acres now in cropland, classified in classes IV to VIII, are attended by serious problems.

chapter

19

WATER RESOURCES

IN CHAPTER 14 WE CONSIDERED the ways in which water resources are utilized and analyzed the water demand outlook for each of three water supply regions of the United States. Here we examine the concept of supply as applied to fresh water, describe existing and potential supplies for each of the three regions, and then compare them with projected demands. Finally, we analyze alternative solutions to some of the specific problems that may arise in view of supply-demand prospects.

The Nature of Fresh Water Supply

Over 99 per cent of the water in the earth's hydrosphere—i.e., the sum total of surface and ground waters and vapors above the ground—is either salty or is locked up as ice in the great caps of polar regions. The remaining small fraction of the earth's water supply may be separated into two parts. One part moves through the water cycle—from atmosphere to land and sea and back to the atmosphere—and is fresh water except at the stage when it is in the sea. In this cycle water is stored for intervals of varying length in lakes and rivers, as soil moisture, and

in underground aquifers. The other part for all practical purposes may be considered as unconnected to the water cycle. Most of this latter supply, accumulated over geologic time in various ways, lies at such great depths that it is not available to satisfy the demands with which we are concerned. Furthermore, since this supply is not replenished, except very slowly, withdrawal is akin to mining. For these two reasons—the costliness of exploitation in most areas and the non-renewable nature of water stored in deep aquifers—this study limits its consideration to those sources of supply involved in the water cycle.

Over the forty-eight contiguous states there is an average of approximately 30 inches of rainfall each year. About 70 per cent of this amount never becomes a concentrated supply but is evaporated or transpired by vegetation and does not reach a stream, lake, or aquifer. The remainder, totalling about 1,100 billion gallons per day and called runoff, is the gross potentially available water supply for the forty-eight states with which to meet the kinds of demands described in Chapter 14.

At any given location there are wide varia-

RELATED MATERIAL: Demand for fresh water, Chapter 14, pp. 258–76; appendix to Chapter 14, pp. 816–33. Discussion of hydro power, Chapter 15, p. 282; and Chapter 20, pp. 416–17.

tions in the average runoff. Within a year there will be fairly regular seasonal variations. In the mountains snow accumulates during the winter months and rivers rise when the snow melts. Most river basins have a higher percentage of runoff in the spring than in other seasons. On the other hand, southeastern basins experience a higher percentage of runoff in late winter and Florida has a higher percentage of runoff in the fall than in other seasons. In addition to these relatively regular seasonal variations, there are irregular variations from year to year. For example, the average runoff of the Colorado River at Lee's Ferry is 13.2 million acre-feet per year. However, annual flows as high as 24.0 million acre-feet and as low as 5.6 million acre-feet have been recorded. A third type of variation results from individual storms. Heavy rainfall may be concentrated over a few hours, causing a large amount of runoff to occur during a short period. As a result of these variations, runoff at a particular location at different times may vary widely. For example, at Lee's Ferry, where the average flow is 18,240 cubic feet per second (cfs), a peak flow of 220,000 cfs and a low flow of 750 cfs have been recorded.

During periods when runoff is too low to meet his needs, man relies upon storage in natural lakes, artificially constructed surface reservoirs, and underground aquifers. Artificial reservoirs regulate runoff and thereby reduce peak flows and increase low flows which otherwise would be experienced. Underground storage and natural lakes provide a source of supply during periods of natural low flow which is replenished when flow increases. Thus dependability of supplies is determined by the extent to which reservoirs (on the surface or underground) are capable of compensating for natural variations in runoff.

Generally it is considered that storage dams are the best means of compensating for natural variations in stream flow. At the same time, however, it is evident that there are opportunities for adjusting demand to variations in flow and for using underground storage that warrant greater consideration than they have received in the past.

If there were no losses from evaporation, sufficient storage could be provided to assure a dependable flow (the flow that is equalled or exceeded every day of every year) equal to average flow. However, evaporation increases with the surface areas of reservoirs. Such losses are particularly significant in arid regions. As a result, a dependable flow equivalent to average flow is not physically attainable. Moreover, successive increments of dependable flow require ever larger increments of storage and successive increments of storage are subject to rising costs. Accordingly, sufficient storage to provide dependable flows equivalent to average flows minus reservoir evaporation losses is seldom economically justified.

In considering the adequacy of the nation's water resources to meet prospective demands, we are concerned, therefore, not only with the total supply of water that is on the average available, but also with the flow that can be made available *at the time of demand*. Ideally, there should be provided a schedule of the cost of providing increments of dependable flow for comparison with the level of demand for a schedule of prices. Since data are not available for such a comparison, we must be content with the following supply data: (*a*) average annual runoff, (*b*) estimates of the largest dependable flow that can be made available, (*c*) the flows now available (with storage existing in 1954) 95 per cent of the time and 50 per cent of the time, and (*d*) an approximation of the additional storage that would be necessary to make available 100 per cent of the time flows equivalent to specified projected levels of use. All estimates of flow are totals available prior to any use whatsoever by man.

The Nation's Water Supply

Since the cost of transporting water great distances is high in comparison with its value, there is no national market for water. Thus supply-demand comparisons have relatively little meaning except on a regional basis. The country has been subdivided into three geographic areas for purposes of this analysis—the East, the arid West, and the Pacific Northwest.

(See Figure 14–1, page 259.) There would be advantages in having an even larger number of regions because the regions selected are still too large to represent a meaningfully localized demand. If a more elaborate regional breakdown were used, the margin of error in the demand projections would become very large because of the difficulty of estimating where economic activities might be located. The approach adopted is, therefore, a compromise in that it avoids projections of demand for numerous regions while requiring such projections for three relatively large geographic areas. The areas selected have comparatively homogeneous water supply characteristics. Also there is little prospect of major transfers of water between them.

The East. This region is humid and therefore it has a relatively high average annual runoff, generally about 14.7 inches per year. The region accounts for approximately 72 per cent of the runoff of the forty-eight contiguous states. For the most part, precipitation is reasonably well distributed throughout the year so that crops can be cultivated without irrigation. Nevertheless, there are periods of low runoff and at times there are droughts which have created demands for augmenting dependable supplies. The water supply of the region may be quantitatively summarized as follows:

	Billion gallons per day
Average total runoff	826.0
Maximum dependable flow that can be made available (total runoff minus evaporation)	790.4
Flow available 95% of time (with 1954 storage facilities)	76.0
Flow available 50% of time (with 1954 storage facilities)	436.6

The West. Most of this region is arid or semi-arid. Therefore, its average runoff is low—generally about 2.3 inches per year. Although the region covers more than half of the geographic area of the forty-eight contiguous states, it accounts for less than 16 per cent of the average runoff. Most of the runoff originates at high elevations from snow melt. Because of the deficiency of water, a relatively high degree of regulation through storage reservoirs is already

provided. The water supply of this region may be quantitatively summarized as follows:

	Billion gallons per day
Average total runoff	175.2
Maximum dependable flow	154.1
Flow available 95% of time (with 1954 storage facilities)	6.8
Flow available 50% of time (with 1954 storage facilities)	69.3

The Pacific Northwest. This area combines some of the features of both of the other regions. The coastal portion is humid, but east of the Cascades the climate is arid and semi-arid. Much of the runoff comes from snow melt in the mountains. However, runoff is high in comparison with the West, averaging about 11.7 inches per year. The water supply of the region may be quantitatively summarized as follows:

	Billion gallons per day
Average total runoff	143.0
Maximum dependable flow	136.3
Flow available 95% of time (with 1954 storage facilities)	9.7
Flow available 50% of time (with 1954 storage facilities)	76.0

Supply, Existing Use, and Prospective Demand

Table 19–1 compares the maximum supply of water that can be made available in each of the three regions with projected depletions as estimated in Chapter 14 and tentative estimates of flow requirements for on-site uses and waste dilution flows as estimated for the Senate Select Committee on National Water Resources.[1]

The East. Projected depletions even for the year 2000 are small in comparison with available supplies. They constitute only about 3 per cent of maximum available supplies in 1980 and less than 5 per cent in 2000. As of 1954, there were about 95 million acre-feet of storage capacity in the region. According to estimates for the Senate Select Committee, the provision of 18

1. *Water Resource Activities in the United States,* Committee Print No. 32: *Water Supply and Demand* (Washington, August 1960).

TABLE 19–1. Water Supply Compared with Projected Uses for 1980 and 2000

Supply and use	East	West	Pacific Northwest
Maximum dependable flow that can be made available (Bgd[1])	790.4	154.1	136.3
Present storage (1954) (mil. acre-feet)	95.0	154.0	28.9
Estimated depletions from withdrawal uses—Medium projections (Bgd)			
1960	13.7	59.7	11.1
1980	24.3	68.7	13.5
2000	37.4	91.7	20.0
On-site uses projected for Senate Select Committee (Bgd)			
1980	35.3	34.5	.9
2000	48.0	47.5	1.3
Waste dilution flows projected for Senate Select Committee (Bgd[2])			
1980	251.5	51.9	28.9
2000	342.3	76.2	28.0

1. Billion gallons per day.
2. Flow needed to maintain dissolved oxygen at an average of 4 milligrams per liter, for a level of treatment that minimizes total cost of treatment and storage.

Source: RFF projections of water depletion in withdrawal uses (see Chapter 14) and U.S. Senate Select Committee on National Water Resources, Committee Print No. 32: *Water Supply and Demand* (Washington, 1960).

million acre-feet of additional storage would make available all of the time a flow that now is available 95 per cent of the time. Such a dependable flow, of around 75 billion gallons per day, would be about twice as much as projected depletions for 2000. Considered in this fashion, it will be a relatively simple matter to fulfill prospective demands for municipal, industrial, and irrigation purposes, although possible alternative uses of prospective dam sites might raise serious local problems. Moreover, if the public were willing to cut back somewhat on water use for short periods of time (5 per cent), no increase in storage would be needed.

The on-site uses when added to estimated depletions would not alter this outlook materially, even though the projected on-site uses made for the Senate Select Committee somewhat exceed our projected depletions. The quantities involved remain small in comparison with available supplies.

The flow uses pose a more complex problem. The report to the Senate Select Committee assumed that the dissolved oxygen content of streams would remain at a relatively high level. For reasons set forth in Chapter 14, it was assumed that flows required for waste dilution would be the governing flows for all flow uses. If these assumptions and the projections based thereon are accepted, the demands upon the water supplies of the eastern region become large indeed. Thus by 1980 projected depletions plus the projections for the Senate Select Committee for on-site uses and waste dilution flows would total 311 billion gallons per day—almost 40 per cent of the maximum flow that could be made available and about four times the daily flow now available 95 per cent of the time.[2] This would mean that the indicated water quality standard would go unmet much of the time unless large additional storage were provided. Indeed, to assure fully dependable flows of this magnitude would require the addition of nearly 200 million acre-feet of storage to that available in 1954. A similar total for 2000 would

2. The waste dilution flows used in this estimate are those projected under a program of waste treatment and storage that would minimize total costs of meeting specified quality standards.

involve well over 50 per cent of the maximum available supplies, and probably around 300 million acre-feet of storage beyond the 1954 level would be needed to assure dependable flows.

Aside from the limitations of the projection techniques, especially with respect to on-site and flow uses discussed in Chapter 14, the prospects suggested by such a comparison pose several significant questions. First, it is not clear what water quality standards the nation will strive to maintain. Such a determination will not be made through market forces. Further, in terms of values measurable in dollars, it is probably cheaper to permit the dissolved oxygen content of many reaches of streams to fall periodically well below the dissolved oxygen content underlying the projections. This is already done in many areas and certainly is the practice over much of Europe. With proper precautions, this need not be a menace to public health. It is important to keep in mind that much of the time unregulated flows will be adequate for dilution purposes. It is only during periods of low flow that conditions might require release of stored water for dilution purposes. On the other hand, the explosive demand for outdoor recreation opportunities suggests there will be considerable pressure to maintain clean water supplies. It seems evident that the nation will make a considerable effort to assure the usability of water areas for recreation purposes. Nevertheless, any relaxation in the standards specified in the report to the Senate Select Committee—such as a decision to permit some streams to be heavily loaded with wastes while others would be kept comparatively clean—would greatly alter the demand outlook.

A second point is that new technology or new management techniques could also alter the demand outlook for waste dilution flows substantially. With existing technology, the extent to which treatment can economically substitute for dilution flows is limited. Plant nutrients contained in treatment plant effluent, even under the best present methods, foster the growth of algae, causing problems downstream. (See Chapter 14, page 274.) If these nutrients could be removed by processes involving less cost than presently known methods, the range over which

treatment could be economically substituted for dilution flows would be substantially increased. Similarly, if arrangements could be made to store some wastes during low flow periods and release them during high flows, less dilution water would be needed.

Third, should the demand for waste dilution flows be substantially reduced, there are still other flow uses that will make demands for water supplies, namely navigation, hydroelectric power, and recreation. Throughout the eastern region these uses are significant. Techniques for expressing these demands in meaningful quantitative terms have not been developed. However, it is pertinent that the value of water for hydroelectric power and navigation is generally considerably less than for agricultural, industrial, and municipal purposes. Accordingly, development for power and navigation would not, on economic grounds at least, interfere with municipal, industrial, and agricultural uses. Furthermore, since there are substitutable forms of energy and transportation available at moderate increases in cost, this should not pose a serious problem. It is conceivable that recreation use of water would be competitive with agricultural uses. However, supplies are so abundant in the East, there seems no possibility of serious conflict between these uses during the next several decades.

The West. The present water situation and future outlook in the West contrast sharply with the prospects for the East. Although considerably larger than the East in geographic area, it has only about a fifth of the water supply. A major proportion of this supply is currently used for irrigation, which results in estimated total depletions in 1960 which are nearly 60 per cent larger than projected total depletions for the East for the year 2000. (See Figure 19–1.)

By the year 2000, projected depletions for the West equal about 60 per cent of maximum available supplies. To provide a dependable flow of this amount would probably require in the neighborhood of 100 million acre-feet of storage to be added to the 154 million acre-feet of storage existing in 1954. This no doubt means that provision of the supplies to meet projected demands will involve sharply rising costs.

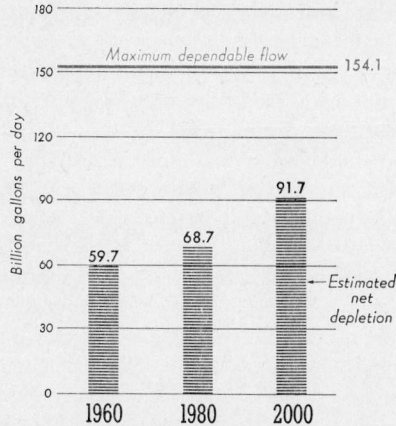

Figure 19–1. Net depletion from with-drawal uses, and maximum flow that can be sustained in the Western region, 1960 and projections for 1980 and 2000.

Region-wide comparisons, although sugges-tive of a relatively stringent water supply situa-tion, do not reveal some of the more serious situations within the region. The central part of the region—generally referred to as the Rocky Mountain West—is the most deficient in supply relative to existing and projected uses. About 60 per cent of the total supply of the region oc-curs in the Western Gulf Basin and the Cen-tral Pacific Basin (see Figure 14–1, page 259), leaving a relatively small amount for the re-mainder of the region. The stringency is most serious in the Upper Rio Grande and Pecos Basins, the Great Basin, the Colorado River Basin, and the South Pacific Basin. Available information indicates that generally over this area supplies allocated to various uses under state law already exceed maximum dependable flows. For example, the Arizona Water Program estimated in 1956 that annual depletions in that state alone exceeded long-term sustainable sup-plies by about 2,500,000 acre-feet (a situation made possible by overdrafts on ground water). Should the Supreme Court decide the current litigation over Colorado River water in favor of Arizona, that state would have available 1.2 million acre-feet more from the Colorado, but it would still be over a million acre-feet short of being able to maintain 1956 levels of use on a long-term basis.

The supplies available in the Western Gulf and the Central Pacific will permit depletions in the West, taken as a whole, to increase in the future. However, if the demands for flow uses projected for the Senate Select Committee are considered, regional demands will slightly ex-ceed total supplies by 1980 and by 2000 de-mand will be 140 per cent of estimated maxi-mum supply.

It is abundantly clear that the West, and particularly the Southwest, faces a difficult prob-lem in seeking to bring into reasonable balance its water demand with available supplies without causing serious economic complications.

In considering this problem, it is important to keep in mind the great differences that exist within the West as a whole. Some areas are actually depleting a larger quantity of water than they can anticipate having on a sustained yield basis; other areas have supplies yet to be developed. Some areas—mostly in the South-west—are experiencing a rapid rate of popula-tion and industrial growth. Other areas are growing very slowly or not at all; evidently they do not have intrinsic characteristics that attract population and industry. Therefore, there are exceptions to any generalizations that are made about the water situation in the West. Neverthe-less, substantial areas of the West face a situa-tion in which available supplies are being utilized fully and the cost of providing addi-tional supplies is so great as to raise serious questions about the economic merit of develop-ing them. In these areas consideration may be given to four kinds of ways of meeting future water demands:

1) *Diversion of supplies from water surplus to water deficient areas.* There are several pos-sibilities for such diversion. The most promising of these, and one now in the planning stage, is to divert water from the Central Pacific Basin to the Southern Pacific Basin (where Los Angeles is located). To go beyond the plans under discussion, this source might also be used to replace some of the water now taken from the Colorado River Basin for use in Southern California, thus making more water available for use within the Colorado River Basin. Aside from the engineering aspects, two kinds of problems are involved. First, studies indicate

that the diversion of water from the Central Pacific Basin to Southern California will cost several times more than water is ordinarily worth for irrigation purposes. Second, there is opposition from residents of Northern California to diverting supplies to Southern California, and California would be extremely reluctant to give up supplies it now secures from the Colorado River Basin.

From a purely engineering standpoint, water might be diverted from the Western Gulf Basin to other parts of the West. This does not appear to be remotely practicable because of the distances involved and the differences in elevation, which would require costly pumping. At one time a study was made of the feasibility of diverting water from the Columbia Basin to the Southwest. The costs of such a diversion appear to preclude such a possibility.

2) *Increasing supplies through weather modification, desalinization, reservoir evaporation suppression, and watershed management.* The possibility of these practices making significant additions to the total supply of the region depends upon advances in technology. It is impossible to predict what the results may be.

Weather modification promises appreciable increases in local supply, particularly in mountainous areas, at relatively low cost. However, increases in precipitation cannot be stimulated unless atmospheric conditions are just right and the location of the precipitation that results cannot be predicted with accuracy. Also, the extent to which weather modification efforts merely change the location at which precipitation occurs, rather than add to the total for a large region, remains an unsolved question. In view of these limitations, it is evident that considerable scientific advance will be necessary before weather modification can be relied upon for additional supplies.

Desalinization is still too costly to be economically justified at most locations. Pilot plants built or under construction by the federal government provide fresh water from the ocean at a cost of a dollar or more a thousand gallons. The outlook is that the refinement of existing technology may reduce costs to as little as forty or fifty cents a thousand gallons. A major technological breakthrough will be necessary to re-

duce costs sufficiently to permit widespread use of desalinized water for most purposes. Moreover, the areas of the West most hard pressed for water are relatively remote from the sea, so that desalinized sea water for this area could entail a high transportation cost. There are moderate amounts of saline and brackish water in underground aquifers; and in the lower reaches of the major rivers the return flows from irrigation are too brackish for most uses. Brackish conditions can be expected to become increasingly serious with the expansion of irrigation and industrial recirculation of water supplies. These brackish sources constitute the most likely supplies of water for desalinization to meet the more pressing demands of nearby areas. Also coastal areas that have been using inland sources of fresh water might reduce their demands by turning to desalinized sea water and thus increase available inland supplies of fresh water.

It has been estimated that western reservoir evaporation losses exceed withdrawals for municipal use in the United States. Some means of reducing evaporation losses at a reasonable cost would be a great boon to the Southwest where evaporation losses from reservoir surfaces may be as much as 100 inches a year, or on the average about 21 million acre-feet per year in seventeen western states. Greater use of underground storage could be a partial solution, but the science of ground-water management has not advanced far enough yet to make it a widely applicable alternative. Another possibility is that of applying hexadecanol to open water areas. This liquid, also known as cetyl alcohol, forms a monomolecular surface layer that will reduce evaporation as much as 90 per cent. However, to date this practice has not been successful in reservoirs because wind and wave action breaks up the film.

The replacement of deep-rooted plants and trees with shallow-rooted grasses results in an increase in runoff. Studies of the Salt River Basin in Arizona by the Arizona Water Program indicated that runoff might be increased about 20 per cent through such action. However, it is not clear whether the costs of instituting and maintaining such measures would be justified. Furthermore, it may be difficult to make such radical changes in vegetative cover without encountering serious erosion problems.

3) Reducing depletions per unit of product. In recent years considerable attention has been devoted to increasing the efficiency of water use. Domestic use could be reduced substantially by substituting refrigeration-type air-conditioning units for evaporative coolers. This, of course, would involve a substantial increase in energy costs. Also desert grasses and shrubbery in homes and yards might be substituted for conventional lawn and shrubbery landscaping. Industry may reduce depletions by substituting saline water for fresh water for cooling and other purposes. In some areas, air fin cooling can replace water cooling in petroleum refining. Widespread application of these and similar practices would reduce depletions significantly. In the West the major opportunity for reducing depletions per unit of product lies in agriculture because this is by far the heaviest user. The elimination of non-beneficial vegetation along canals, reduction of transportation losses, and selective application of proper quantities of water at the right time would minimize water requirements for irrigation. Beyond these is the use of available water supplies on the kinds of lands that are most productive instead of upon lands of relatively low productivity.

Although there are technological advances that would facilitate application of practices to reduce water consumption, there are also institutional obstacles. Many farmers do not know how to apply practicable water-saving techniques. Some students of the problem believe that farmers, manufacturers, and home owners lack financial incentives to conserve water because of features of western water law and public water pricing policies.

4) Adjusting the pattern of use to bring water supply and demand into balance. Barring the emergence of changes not now in prospect, it is evident that major adjustments in the *pattern* of water use—particularly in the Southwest —will be essential if this part of the arid West is to share in national economic growth to the extent envisaged by this report. Although the possibilities discussed above may help considerably, it seems doubtful that they alone will be sufficient. Attainment of a substantially higher level of economic development hinges upon the allocation of supplies among agriculture, municipalities, industries, recreation, and waste disposal.

In view of the priority accorded other demands, it seems doubtful that the West will ever allocate substantial flows for waste dilution purposes on the main stem reaches of its major rivers. The on-site uses projected for the Senate Select Committee are largely for sport fish and wildlife habitat. Although we have some question about the reliability of the projections (see Chapter 14), water devoted to recreation may merit a degree of priority in the allocation of western water supplies. Studies at the University of New Mexico indicate that water allocated to recreation may support considerably more economic activity than agriculture.

A significant shift from agriculture to higher valued municipal and industrial use appears essential in the parts of the region suffering the most serious water deficiencies if the economies of these areas are to grow. Municipal and industrial use supports a large amount of economic activity per unit of depletion in comparison with agriculture. Mr. Wollman[3] has estimated that in New Mexico an acre-foot of water used for municipal and industrial purposes engendered over $3,000 of total economic product (a combination of primary value-added and value-added by purchases). For recreation the range was from $200 to $300, and for agriculture the range was from $40 to $50. Thus a relatively modest shift from irrigation would have significant effects. For example, a transfer to municipal and industrial use of 10 per cent of the projected (Medium) depletions for 2000 for irrigation would support nearly double the projected 2000 level of depletions for municipal and industrial activity. If this were done, the nation would not suffer from the reduction in irrigated agriculture. In fact, the costliness of new irrigation indicates that alternative geographic sources of food and fiber supply would no doubt be less expensive in many instances. Plenty of water would remain for specialty crops such as citrus fruits that can only be

3. Nathaniel Wollman, *et al., The Value of Water in Alternative Uses* (Albuquerque: University of New Mexico Press, 1962).

grown in Florida and the Southwest. In short, a policy that fosters a shift in water use from agricultural to non-agricultural uses when economically justified would *permit* a manifold growth of the population and economy of the region otherwise precluded by inadequate supply of water. The extent and rate of growth would not be determined by water availability but by other factors that normally influence the location of population and industry. The agricultural sector of the economy might decline in this region but this should be no cause for concern either to the region or the nation during the foreseeable future.

The Pacific Northwest. This region, like the East, has a very large supply in comparison with existing and prospective depletion. Projected depletion for 2000 (Medium) is only about 15 per cent of maximum dependable supplies. If on-site uses and waste dilution flows projected for the Senate Select Committee are added to projected depletions for 2000, the total is still only about 36 per cent of maximum available flows. (See Figure 19–2.) Future storage planned primarily for hydroelectric power and for flood control promises dependable flows in much of the region that will be more than adequate to meet prospective demands.

The situation is not uniform, however, throughout the region. Since the area east of the

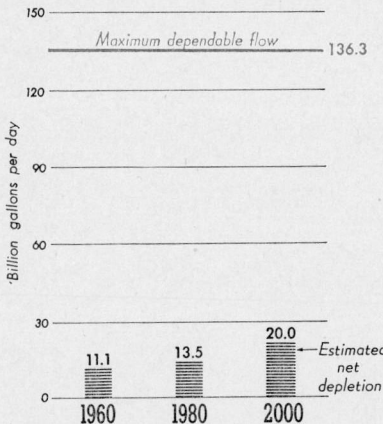

Figure 19–2. Net depletion from withdrawal uses, and maximum flow that can be sustained in the Pacific Northwest region, 1960 and projections for 1980 and 2000.

Cascades is arid, it is confronted with problems similar to those found in other parts of the West. On some tributaries available supplies are about all developed. In other instances the development of additional supplies for irrigation is of dubious merit because of costs. As in so much of the western part of the country, the problem is one of establishing a pattern and level of economic activity consistent with the availability and cost of water. Plenty of water is available to support a substantial growth of cities and industry, provided that other industry location factors are conducive to such growth.

Conclusion

The water supply-demand outlook in the United States should cause neither alarm nor complacency. The natural endowment of fresh water is more than adequate to support the levels of economic growth envisaged by this study. Yet, two problems of considerable significance are in prospect. One of these is the impact of prospective future use upon certain qualitative aspects of American life. The other might be characterized as a problem in regional economic and institutional readjustment.

The qualitative impact stems from waste disposal demands and possible increases in storage requirements. With a prospective quadrupling of gross national product and a near doubling of population, the potential demand for use of streams for waste disposal will be enormous. It also seems likely that a large, affluent, urbanized population will exert great pressure for preservation of the quality of the human environment. With regard to water, the issue is the extent to which water courses will be kept usable for recreation purposes and aesthetically pleasing. There is the further question of how quality standards are to be achieved. Are we to invest heavily in permanent reservoirs to dilute wastes, or are we to invest heavily in research with the hope of finding an alternative solution?

Prospective storage demands pose two kinds of problems. One involves the extent to which reservoirs will be permitted to encroach upon existing scenic areas. The other involves the question of whether artificial lake-type recreation, where justified, is to be provided by multiple-purpose reservoirs or facilities that are dominantly for recreation. Multiple-purpose facilities, while reducing costs, tend to be less suitable for recreation than single-purpose recreation lakes because of fluctuating water levels.

Problems of economic and institutional adjustment are most likely to arise in the West. In a large part of the West, particularly in the Central Pacific and Western Gulf Basins, water supplies appear more than adequate to meet projected needs. But in other areas, particularly in the Southwest, allocations already exceed sustainable supplies and the prospects are that conditions will become even more stringent. Should there be significant changes in the pattern of water use in these areas—from agricultural to non-agricultural uses—some of the people now on farms will be required to seek other occupations. In addition, it is conceivable that at some locations communities servicing irrigation projects will lose their economic base with the transfer of use. This occurred with painful consequences in the Owens Valley of California when Los Angeles bought the irrigation water rights in that valley. The basic question is not whether the readjustments will be made; the economic forces at work appear to be inexorable. Instead, it is a question of how efficiently the adjustment can be brought about. Will institutions—such as western water law and public investment policy—facilitate the change or will the change be forced? If the latter occurs, one can envisage farming areas and communities depressed but hanging on while their resource base gradually disappears from under them. One can also anticipate substantial public and private investments in irrigation that will have to be liquidated long before they can be amortized.

chapter

20

ENERGY

IN THIS CHAPTER we inquire separately into the adequacy of each energy source in the light of the demand that has been projected for it. It would be neater, of course, to devise aggregate figures for supply and requirements by using some common unit of measurement like the Btu. But although this is statistically possible, and satisfactory for some purposes, the results would mean little: there are too many important uses in which one fuel cannot be substituted for another. In transportation, for example, oil-based fuels provide nearly all the driving force and are likely to continue doing so throughout the remainder of the century. A plentiful total of energy resource base consisting mainly of coal would not help much, if the oil ran low, without advances in technology that would permit economic conversion of coal into oil.

However, where possible shortages are indicated in our fuel-by-fuel appraisals of adequacy we have investigated the directions in which a solution might be found in terms of substitute energy sources, first conventional and then the possible fruits of new technology.

Because this country's coal reserves can be

considered a resource of last resort in the foreseeable future, we shall discuss before coal those resources whose availability is least certain both in toto and at any point of time.

Demands are compared with resources for the conventional mineral fuels and hydro power that today account for practically all of the supply. Fuels for atomic fission are discussed only briefly, even though nuclear energy is expected to be an important source of electricity generation by the end of the century. The requirements for fissionable materials are so dependent upon the level of technology that is assumed, and the latter is so subject to change, that detailed discussion of the mineral resources supplying nuclear energy does not appear warranted.

Conventional Energy Sources

Oil

Along with most other mineral sources, oil shares the characteristics that it is not renewable, at least not in terms of the time span that one is normally interested in, and that its ex-

---

RELATED MATERIAL: *Principal sources of projected demand for heat and power, Chapter 10, pp. 184–222 and appendix, pp. 722–77. Other significant sources of demand: for transportation, Chapter 5, pp. 145–48, and appendix, pp. 660–62, 666, 668; for military goods, Chapter 9, p. 183, and appendix, p. 721. Aggregates of projected demand for mineral fuels, Chapter 15, pp. 277–92, and appendix, pp. 834–58; for petrochemicals, Chapter 17, pp. 320–25, and appendix, pp. 940–68.*

tent is only partially known. Inference, therefore, plays a large part in establishing the magnitude of the resource. There have been unceasing attempts to estimate its size. Unfortunately, disproportionate attention has been given to the so-called "proved reserves," data on which are compiled and published by the American Petroleum Institute.[1] This concept has very limited application and may prove positively harmful in long-range analysis. Despite frequent warnings this measure, which is quite independent of the technological outlook for either *discovery* or *recovery,* is frequently misunderstood and misinterpreted.

In essence, the proved reserves are but the current working stock or inventory of unrecovered petroleum carried by the producers for the accomplishment of rational commercial operations. Their size in the past has been equivalent to some twelve to thirteen times annual production (Table 20–1), a fact that has given rise to the image of oil reserves allowing only a dozen more years of continued consumption—or fewer at rising rates of demand. The seeming paradox of rising reserves accompanying rising consumption is simply the result of the oil industry's endeavor to drill far and fast enough ahead to keep the inventory immediately in sight, or "proved," at a suitable level. A related misconception is that all the oil could be in fact produced in as little as twelve years, though under certain conditions of annual flow this might not be far off the mark. Measurement of reserves in terms of annual consumption or production is merely a convenient index of magnitude that says nothing about producibility or adequacy of resources.

It is because there remains a substantial element of uncertainty as to whether oil will in fact be found where indications point to its possible occurrence, and because there are limits to the speed at which a given reservoir can be economically depleted, that exploratory drilling to the point of "proving" is required. Otherwise,

1. The official definition of the API is as follows:
"Proved reserves are both drilled and undrilled. The proved drilled reserves, in any pool, include oil estimated to be recoverable by the production systems now in operation, whether with or without fluid injection, and from the area actually drilled up on the spacing pattern in effect in that pool. The proved undrilled reserves, in any pool, include reserves under undrilled spacing units which are so close, and so related, to the drilled units that there is every reasonable probability that they will produce when drilled.

TABLE 20–1. U.S. Crude Oil Production and Proved Reserves, 1944–1960

(Million barrels)

Year	Production	End-year proved reserves	End-year proved reserves as multiple of production in preceding 12 months
1944	1,678	19,784	11.8
1945	1,737	19,942	11.5
1946	1,726	20,874	12.1
1947	1,850	21,488	11.6
1948	2,002	23,280	11.6
1949	1,819	24,649	13.6
1950	1,944	25,268	13.0
1951	2,214	27,468	12.4
1952	2,257	27,961	12.4
1953	2,312	28,945	12.5
1954	2,257	29,561	13.1
1955	2,419	30,012	12.4
1956	2,552	30,435	11.9
1957	2,559	30,300	11.8
1958	2,373	30,536	12.9
1959	2,483	31,719	12.8
1960	2,471	31,613	12.8

Source: Committee on Petroleum Reserves, 1961 Report to the American Petroleum Institute, March 10, 1961.

the producer could tackle just enough fields to meet current demand, exhaust them, and move on to the next. Proved reserves would then be a smaller multiple of current production. But in the face of the uncertainties, companies have no choice but to assure themselves a firm known supply sufficiently ahead of the time of exploitation. Therefore, as the tempo of production rises so does the size of the working inventory.

If there remains any mystery here, it is why the so-called life index has deviated so little from the 12:1 ratio and what pegged it to that figure to begin with. The oil man's spontaneous reply is that this is a "natural" level. By this he means that, assuming a range of life of five to twenty years per well, the average age of all wells taken together at any time might be in the neighborhood of ten to twelve years. In that situation the average well would be producing some 8 to 10 per cent per year of its lifetime production, or conversely reserves would equal ten to twelve times annual production. A tendency not to invest in excessive inventory nor to fall behind, combined with a certain institutional inertia, could then be expected to maintain the time-honored ratio. This does not, of course, preclude any one producer from carrying a smaller or larger inventory. Some major producers have in recent years carried thirty to forty times annual production, owing in some measure to production restrictions under prorating regulations.

For the reasons cited, the size and development of proved reserves cannot throw much light on the adequacy of the country's oil resources, except to serve as an example of how rising demand has continuously "created" the supply to meet it. Otherwise the level of proved reserves is a highly underexposed picture of our oil resources. It takes into account, broadly speaking, only those reserves believed to be producible at current cost and at current levels of technology from fields and facilities in operation; its size is closely determined by the amount of drilling done; and it fails to extend to all or to the bulk of known fields the experience gained in secondary recovery (by water flooding, gas injection, underground combustion and other thermal methods), allowing for it only where it has actually begun to be applied and has shown results in a given field.

Recoverable domestic supplies. The ultimate reserves form a more significant concept in appraising the adequacy of future supplies; the difficulty here lies in estimating their size even roughly.[2] Petroleum history is littered with the remains of obsolete guesses; some of them turned out to be spectacularly wrong in the light of subsequent developments. Yet none has tarnished the reputation of its author, for it is well understood that, short of systematically digging up the first 60,000 feet of the earth's crust from pole to pole, we can go only by inference, and that inference rests on a basis that experience continues to broaden.

The weakness of the ultimate reserve concept is that it does not allow for improved technology and, therefore, is affected by a conservative bias. One more step removed from the proved reserves concept is the concept of the resource base, the estimated total occurrence of the material in nature. By applying to this magnitude,

reduced by the amount produced in the past, a recovery factor, one may obtain an estimate of oil potentially available in the future. Such a figure would exceed that of ultimate reserves (equally reduced by the amount produced in the past) by the degree to which one assumes a rising ability to recover the resource.

In fixing upon a specific, contemporary appraisal of the resource base, reduced by past production, we see no reason to go beyond or modify the recent judgment of Resources for the Future,[3] that there are some 500 billion barrels in the ground "awaiting future recovery," or potentially available. This judgment was arrived at prior to Weeks's estimate of ultimate reserves of 460 billion barrels of liquid hydrocarbon (crude plus natural gas liquids),[4] of which perhaps some 400 billion barrels are crude alone. Excluding past production, of roughly 60 billion barrels, would leave some 340 billion available in the future. Considering that ultimate reserves do not provide for the effect of improving technology, as oil reserve estimates go these two can be said to be "in the same ball park." A doubling of historic recovery rates, principally on the basis of greatly expanded secondary activity, would, on the basis of the RFF resource-base judgment, yield some 300–350 billion barrels. A first calculation, therefore, starts with an assumption of two-thirds recovery, or recoverable supplies of 330 billion barrels. To obtain such an increase in recovery as an average over the entire forty years would require nearly 100 per cent recovery toward the final years, but it could also prevail by large initial increases in recovery, followed by stability at a high level short of 100 per cent.

We have, as an alternative, assumed a more limited future availability of 250 billion barrels, equivalent in the next forty years to the recovery of half the oil now estimated to be in place (in proved reserves, unrecovered oil fields, and fields yet to be found), even though we are aware that the estimate may turn out to be a minimum one.

3. Sam H. Schurr, Bruce C. Netschert, *et al., Energy in the American Economy, 1850–1975* (Baltimore: Johns Hopkins Press and Resources for the Future, 1960), especially pp. 356–59; also earlier RFF reports.

4. Lewis G. Weeks, "Where Will Energy Come From in 2059," *The Petroleum Engineer,* August 1959, pp. A–29–31.

2. Ultimate reserves have been defined as the sum of past production, current proved reserves, and reserves that will be discovered in the future (at current state of technology and cost).

These estimates have in common the fact that they do not assume a resource base broader than that assumed in *Energy in the American Economy*. It is quite conceivable, indeed probable, that estimates of the base itself will in the future undergo enlargement, as geologists become more confident as to the occurrence of oil (and gas) in non-traditional habitats. In this light, the two levels of recoverable oil could be interpreted to be the result of somewhat less increased recovery rates but a correspondingly higher resource base.[5] Thus, the 250 billion barrels here assumed (instead of the 167 billion barrels recoverable under static technological conditions from the remaining resource of 500 billion barrels)[6] might be drawn not at 50 per cent recovery from 500 billion barrels but, say, at 45 per cent from 550 billion barrels, or 40 per cent from 625 billion. It is obvious that in the last case, for example, the reserves still to be recovered at the recent rate of one-third would be 208.

The distinction here made between higher reserves due to higher recovery and those due to higher resource base is of particular importance when we deal with natural gas reserves.[7] Work proceeding in the U.S. Geological Survey will, we understand, result in reserve estimates for oil and gas that are substantially higher than those put forward by RFF in *Energy in the American Economy,* not because of higher recovery rates but because a larger resource base has been assumed. Zapp's work, quoted above, would lead one to conclude, indeed, that future recoverable oil in the United States might be put at 500 billion barrels or more, or twice the minimum figure put forward in this study (see especially pp. H-23 and 24 of Zapp's study).

It is worth drawing attention in this connection to the work of Paul D. Torrey and the Interstate Oil Compact Commission. In the latest of their biennial reports[8] it was estimated that of the original oil content of known U.S.

reservoirs (328 billion barrels), not quite 20 per cent (62.6 billion) had been recovered as of January 1, 1960, 10 per cent was in proved reserves, not quite 5 per cent was judged recoverable by conventional secondary methods—gas and water injection—and an additional 14 per cent was judged recoverable by improved secondary recovery methods. These figures add to a grand total of 50 per cent of original content. While this estimate throws light upon the limitations of the conventional reserve estimates (which equal about one-third of primary plus secondary reserves estimated by the IOCC) and the expectations for future recovery, a major point of interest is that the IOCC estimates represent an increase over their 1958 estimates of nearly 14 billion barrels of reserves—apart from 5 billion barrels produced in the two years elapsed. There can hardly be a better illustration of how technology alters the viewpoint under which future oil availability is considered, quite apart from the fact that the author of these estimates regards them as conservative.

The magnitude of recoverable supplies presented above does not rest on any level of costs or technology that we can specify. Yet the availability—as opposed to the physical occurrence—of oil today, tomorrow, and forty years hence will depend on the conditions under which the producers will find it profitable to exploit the known and explore the unknown.

Even if we were to assume that advancing technology will successfully overcome the physical obstacles to finding and lifting oil, we would have to determine the time schedule within which the exploitation of existing resources is likely to take place. Since the occurrence of oil, whatever its magnitude, is ultimately finite, exploitation should reach a peak—or perhaps several peaks or an extended plateau—then subside and terminate. Production probably would terminate before the resource was physically exhausted since economic forces would be likely to eliminate its use long before the last drop of underground oil had been brought to the surface. Indeed, it is almost impossible to imagine a situation in which "complete exploitation," in the physical sense, would occur; this is the reason the shape of the decline curve must be regarded as unpredictable.

There is no shortage of attempts to determine

5. While avoiding quantitative speculation, A. D. Zapp, in his recent bulletin, certainly points in that direction (*Future Petroleum Producing Capacity of the United States,* Geological Survey Bulletin 1142-H, Washington, 1962).

6. Schurr, Netschert, *et al., op. cit.,* p. 411.

7. See p. 407, below.

8. Paul D. Torrey, "Evaluation of United States Oil Resources as of January 1, 1960," paper presented to Mid-Year Meeting of Interstate Oil Compact Commission, Detroit, June 13–15, 1960.

the production peak in the United States, and those that place it any later than 1970 or any higher than 4 billion barrels per year are the exception. However, most of these estimates assume ultimate reserves far smaller than those described above. On the other hand, in Weeks's scheme, oil and gas reserves (the two, unfortunately, are inseparably joined in his presentation) would be produced over no less than a hundred years, and about 15 per cent of the reserves still would remain unproduced. A peak would be reached sometime during the last two decades of the century—if one were to hazard a guess, around 1990, the halfway mark.

This scheme, which is unaccompanied in its published form by the underlying reasoning, might contain a maximum crude oil production component of some 4 billion barrels at that peak point. This is substantially lower than the 6 billion barrels which, according to the RFF study, could be produced in 1975 at no appreciable increase in constant-dollar cost; and there is no implicit assumption in the study that 1975 will be the peak. Moreover, a 4-billion annual rate is barely more than the 10.6 million barrels per day which the industry was estimated on

January 1, 1960 as capable of producing (disregarding availability of transportation and other facilities). On this score, too, an annual rate of 4 billion barrels seems on the low side. Whether or not the 6-billion-barrel capacity figure errs on the side of generosity is hard to tell. The fragmentary data on particular fields or blocks of secondary oil production that are occasionally made available tend to show that additions to primary recovery that raise total recovery to 75 per cent are by no means exceptions. When it is recalled that secondary recovery involves no finding cost and no dry holes, its dampening effect upon average crude cost becomes obvious. The roughly 60 billion barrels that Torrey suggests can be recovered by secondary means is another factor that makes a 6-billion-barrel year by no means a remote possibility.

How do our demand projections stack up against the resource situation? Proceeding from the obvious to the doubtful, the meeting of the High demand projection from domestic resources is not likely.* This demand would amount to some 310 billion barrels for the forty years to 2000 (see Table 20–2, col. 2),

---

*NOTE

At this and other points in the discussion we have used the total of all High (or Low) demand projections for an individual energy source to illustrate the implications of the less likely but still possible demand trends. Elsewhere it has been pointed out that the extreme projections are not, as a rule, additive: High steel use and High aluminum use are unlikely to occur simultaneously; so are High natural gas use in electric energy generation and that in direct combustion for space heating. However, in the case of energy the consequent exaggerations are not likely to be severe, for most energy sources compete with one another in a given use but there is little competition between different uses of the same source. To illustrate, a High demand for petroleum in motor vehicle use does not exclude a High demand for petroleum in space heating, in steel production, or in the chemical industry. The same is true for other energy sources and their uses. The principal area of conflict is between use in electric power generation and what we have called direct use. In some applications

High use of electricity presupposes Low direct use. This is of little consequence for oil, given its insignificant role in electricity generation, and also for coal, given the preponderance of metal production and power generation, two uses in which coal competes with itself only to a very limited degree. It is principally in natural gas that there is significant competition between its use in electricity generation and as direct fuel. Consequently, the aggregation of all High demand figures for natural gas leads to substantial exaggeration of both the High and the Low. But even here the exaggeration is of little significance for the findings of this study, for the substantial doubts regarding future adequacy of natural gas resources in this country crop up sharply in the Medium projection. Obviously, any projection above the Medium level only accentuates the difficulties but injects no novel element into the situation. However, the Low projection is equally exaggerated on the low side. Therefore, a finding of adequacy at that projection level must be understood to be less certain than the statistics make it appear.

and it thus roughly equals the assumed upper recoverable quantity of 330 billion barrels, with all production concentrated in the next forty years.

The picture becomes only marginally more favorable when we introduce the realistic assumption that a minimum fraction, say 20 per cent, of domestic demand will throughout the period be met by imports. In that event, High demand for the projection span declines to 250 billion barrels, or 50 per cent recovery from 500 billion barrels. However, considering the reserves that would have to parallel the demand, it is doubtful that the High and for that matter even the Medium projection could be satisfied by domestic supply even when supplemented by a 20 per cent import allowance, a level not too far from the one now in existence for crude oil and its products.

Table 20–2 depicts these computations, but it has didactic significance only; it does not purport to show a likely course of development. A continuing increase in production, producing facilities, and proved reserves to a maximum, and attainment at that maximum point of an all-time high of reserves to which little if any future addition could be anticipated: all this does not add up to a reasonable pattern of growth, since the sum total of cumulative production from 1960 to 2000 and reserves in 2000 would amount to over 300 billion barrels in the Medium projection.

While the entire scheme is artificial, it drives home the point that, regardless of cost considerations, reserve additions would be far more likely to slow down and reverse direction long before 2000. So would production. It is impossible to state when this would occur.

Looking at the scheme depicted in Table 20–2 we see in Column 10 the rising ratio of gross additions to reserves to estimated reserves remaining to be proved. Exploration techniques have, of course, improved immeasurably in the past and must be assumed to continue doing so in coming decades; the difficulties of finding are related as much to what is available as a target area as to the state of technology. The first barrel ever proved was a very expensive one notwithstanding the fact that no oil had been discovered or taken from the ground. It stands to

reason, nonetheless, that it will be harder and more costly to add to proved reserves—though not necessarily to produce—one out of every three-and-a-half barrels remaining to be proved (1981–90) than one out of every eight barrels (1961–70), assuming future recoverability of as high as 330 billion barrels and the Medium demand projection. (See Figure 20–1.) But there is no basis for judging the point in this development at which costs could become prohibitive. In the High model it is more nearly in the seventies that one out of every three-and-a-half barrels left to be proved would have to become an addition to reserves.

It well may be that, as has been pointed out, assumption of an average recovery factor of two-thirds for the entire period represents too

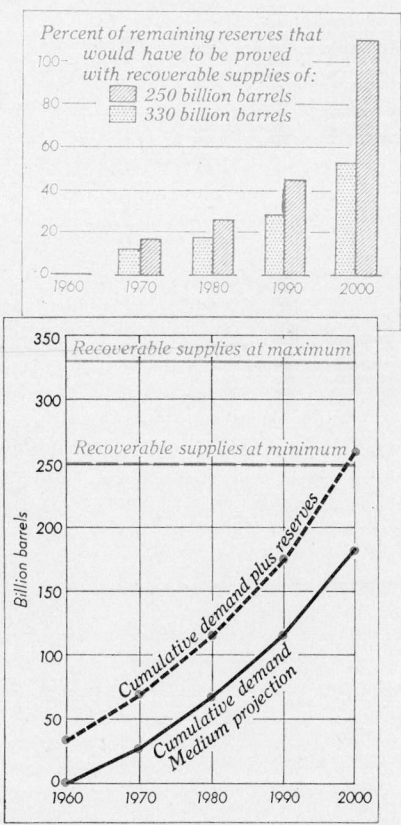

Figure 20–1. Implications of projected oil demand, excluding imports, for future adequacy.

TABLE 20–2. Implications of Projected Oil Demand for Resource Adequacy, 1960–2000

(Billion barrels)

Projection level and period	Demand Annual, in terminal year of period shown[1]	Demand In 10-year period	Demand for domestic oil only, assuming 20 per cent import level — In period shown	Cumulative	Proved reserves required at terminal year of period shown to continue domestic production (at ratio of reserves to output declining from 12 to 9 between 1970 and 2000)	Estimated reserves plus cumulative domestic demand	Implied gross additions to proved reserves — In 10-year period[2]	Annually	330 bil. bbl. — In bil. bbl.[3]	Gross 10-year additions as per cent of remaining reserves to be proved at beginning of period[4]	250 bil. bbl. — In bil. bbl.[3]	Gross 10-year additions as per cent of remaining reserves to be proved at beginning of period[4]
	(1)	(2)	(3)	(4)	(5)	(6)=(4)+(5)	(7)	(8)	(9)	(10)	(11)	(12)
Low												
Thru 1960	3.2	–	63	63	32	95	–	–	298	–	218	–
1961–70	3.6	34	27	90	35	125	30	3.0	268	10.1	188	13.8
1971–80	4.4	40	32	122	39	161	36	3.6	232	13.4	152	19.1
1981–90	5.6	50	40	162	45	207	46	4.6	186	19.8	106	30.3
1991–2000	7.1	63	50	212	51	263	56	5.6	130	30.1	50	52.8
Medium												
Thru 1960	3.2	–	63	63	32	95	–	–	298	–	218	–
1961–70	4.1	36	29	92	39	131	36	3.6	262	12.1	182	16.5
1971–80	5.3	47	38	130	47	177	46	4.6	216	17.6	136	25.3
1981–90	7.2	62	50	180	58	238	61	6.1	155	28.2	75	44.9
1991–2000	10.0	86	69	249	72	321	83	8.3	72	53.5	nil	110.7
High												
Thru 1960	3.2	–	63	63	32	95	–	–	298	–	218	–
1961–70	4.6	39	31	94	43	137	42	4.2	256	14.1	176	19.2
1971–80	6.8	57	46	140	60	200	63	6.3	193	24.6	113	35.8
1981–90	10.2	85	68	208	82	290	90	9.0	103	46.6	23	79.6
1991–2000	16.0	131	105	313	116	429	139	13.9	nil	135.0	nil	604.0

1. From Appendix Table A15–13.
2. Col. 3 plus net change from preceding period in Col. 5.
3. Starting recoverable supplies minus gross additions to proved reserves (Col. 7).
4. Col. 7 as per cent of Col. 9 in preceding period.

sharp a departure from current practices and that a factor of 50 per cent would be more reasonable. Columns 11 and 12 show the resulting picture. The combination of the High demand projection with a conservative supply assumption would be likely to lead to stringencies before the forty-year period has progressed even to the mid-point. In the first half of the seventies, or fifteen years sooner than on the assumption of the Medium projection and the less conservative availability, one out of six remaining barrels would have to be added to proved reserves. By the mid-eighties, practically no reserves would be left to be proved. Under this, the most unfavorable combination we could expect, the index of search intensity suggested by the last column would rise rapidly in the seventies, suggesting that real costs might be pulled up. A similar condition might not occur at more relaxed conditions of higher recoverability or lower demand until the early eighties, and might be delayed until the late eighties or early nineties when high recoverability and Medium demand are assumed.

Experience suggests, however, that what we now refer to as the "high" level of recoverability may ten or twenty years hence seem more moderate, with the result that a reappraisal would shift all the above time dimensions. For this reason, only moderate faith can be put in the calculations pertaining to the remote decades.

As for the more immediate future, as eminent an oil man as Morgan J. Davis, president of Humble Oil and Refining Company, has gone on record as confidently expecting availability of no less than 70 billion barrels in the next twenty years,[9] deriving his figure from extensions and revisions of fields discovered in the last ten years. His position has since been strengthened by the investigations of the National Petroleum Council published in 1961, which show that the estimate of recoverable oil in all fields discovered by 1939 had been put at 46.9 billion barrels in 1944, but now for the same fields must be raised to 64 billion barrels. His expectations are based on a moderate increase in recovery, of from

9. Morgan J. Davis, "The Dynamics of Domestic Petroleum Resources," paper presented at the 38th Annual Meeting of the American Petroleum Institute, Chicago, November 12, 1958.

one-third to one-half of oil in place, and new discoveries on undeveloped acreage (on the conservative basis of 2 per cent of the 350 million acres of land now leased yielding 5,000 barrels per acre). Such an increase, allowing 20 per cent imports, would take us safely into the mid-seventies on both the Medium and High demand projections, as is evident when 70 billion barrels are added to the 1960 figure of cumulative output and reserve in Column 6 of Table 20–2.

Ignoring the reasonable odds that the resource estimates will continue to shift upward, there is every chance that substitution for domestic crude would make increasing inroads as reserves are harder to prove, perhaps to the point that this country's oil resources may never be fully exploited or even explored. Indeed, were one free to leave aside considerations of national security, it is likely that one could afford altogether to table the guessing game of how extensive our domestic oil resources really are and take comfort in the certain knowledge that reasonably priced oil of foreign origin would flow to the United States for a term of years stretching beyond the normal focus of policy making. This point is dealt with below.

The conclusions reached above, however tentative, do not in substance differ essentially from those reached by others in the past, although the difference in timing is quite substantial. One of the most durable features of American petroleum history has been the prediction that within a specified time span, usually no more than a dozen years, the country's underground oil reserves will be exhausted. This recurrent motif in turn calls forth the contrapuntal theme: We are not running out of oil; it is all a statistical mirage.

What inspires this perennial duet? Basically it is the difficulty of exploring the habitat of oil in all of its ramifications, of estimating the extent to which oil may be technically subject to removal from the reservoirs in which it is found, and of defining the economic framework within which it might pay to lift the liquid to the surface.

"The fact is," an eminent petroleum geologist said in 1959, "that nobody knows the ultimate petroleum reserve of the United States or of any other country. . . . It has been estimated, for example, that not over one per cent of the sedimentary basins of the world has as yet been thoroughly explored."[10] New geological appraisals have led to successively higher estimates of reserves. The extension of petroleum production to offshore locations is only the most dramatic but by no means the most significant instance. The trend towards consideration of the so-called stratigraphic traps (i.e., those accumulations of oil that do not involve displacement or rock movement), as opposed to the more easily identifiable structural traps (abrupt shifts and irregularities in formations, such as faults, domes, etc.), may result in an even more far-reaching spread of areas considered potentially rich in oil, especially as even the most optimistic current reserve estimates that allow for stratigraphic traps are of necessity based upon only such limited samples as have come to the geologists' attention. "There is no imminent lack of potentially productive unexplored rock."[11]

Similarly, the degree to which oil reserves can be economically lifted is a constantly changing factor. New techniques have raised the industry's sights. Water, gas, heat, and chemicals, alone or in combination, have been harnessed to the job of dislodging the oil from the interstices of the bearing formation and pushing it to the surface. Nuclear explosions may some day join these techniques. As a result, it is no longer true that one must, on the average, write off as irrecoverable some two-thirds or more of the oil known to exist in identified deposits. Secondary recovery, that is, increasing the reservoir yield through lifting by means other than original or recirculated reservoir pressure, has become a potent production aid, now used extensively by both the major and minor producers. Already tertiary recovery, a second stage of sweeping out the reservoir, has become more than a vocabulary term. Yet in estimates of reserves and future availability little provision has so far been made for any but primary recovery. Whatever lack of allowance for new geological knowledge (both in depth and width of occurrence) holds down the under-

lying estimates also afflicts the resource base guess.

A few examples may serve to illustrate the persistence of the problem and thereby put in better perspective the conclusion reached in this study.

A report made in 1920 by the Chief Geologist of the U.S. Geological Survey estimated that there were some 7 billion barrels of petroleum left in the ground recoverable by contemporary methods (calling it "highly improbable" that the error was more than 50 per cent), that "the production of natural petroleum in the United States must pass its peak at an early date— probably within 5 years and possibly within 3 years," and that "a drain of over one-half billion barrels, even if the annual demand be not further increased would, if taken from the oil-fields of the United States, probably exhaust the oil resources remaining available in the ground in 14 years."[12] Forty years later, the ground has given up not 7 but 50 billion barrels, with an additional 30 billion barrels proved recoverable. For every barrel believed available in 1920, eight have since been lifted and five more have been proved. More recent instances abound. Indeed, the history of predicting ultimate oil reserves, be it of the United States or the world, has been and continues to be one of never-ending upward revisions at frequent intervals.

In a revision made in August 1959 by Weeks, ultimate oil and natural gas liquid reserves available through primary recovery climbed to an estimate of 270 billion barrels from an estimate of 240 barrels published in early 1958.[13] In addition, Weeks, for the first time in his published estimating practice, took quantitative account of secondary recovery potential, which he put at 190 billion barrels. Put differently, the revision, which represents an increase of nearly 100 per cent over the earlier, less inclusive estimate, allows for the effects of technological

10. A. I. Levorsen, paper presented to Fifth World Petroleum Congress, New York, 1959.

11. Zapp, *op. cit.*, p. H–24.

12. David White, U.S. Geological Survey, "The Petroleum Resources of the World," *Annals of the American Academy*, May 1920, reprinted in Part 8 of *Stockpile and Accessibility of Strategic and Critical Materials to the United States in Time of War*, Hearings before the Special Subcommittee on Minerals, Materiel, and Fuel Economics of the Committee on Interior and Insular Affairs, U.S. Senate, 83rd Cong., 2nd Sess., p. 213.

13. Weeks, *op. cit.*; and *Bulletin of the American Association of Petroleum Geologists*, February 1958, pp. 431–41.

progress upon recovery of oil in place as indicated by recent working experience in the field.

Perhaps the impression that we have entered an era of diminishing returns in the search for oil is created largely by the fact that the search has tended to concentrate in the same, gradually depleting oil habitat. It would then follow that until revised concepts had taken hold and new tools to indicate favorable locations had been developed, dry-hole drilling might substantially increase in a period of transition to new guides for exploration. Recent interest in Washington and Oregon, for example, and substantial discoveries in parts of Texas that had in the past been drilled up but abandoned as "dry," point in that direction. Results of one investigation[14] suggest the possibility of a 7.7 billion barrel petroleum occurrence in a wide onshore and offshore belt along the Atlantic Coast stretching from Maine to Georgia.

Hindsight makes it tempting to smile at the shambles of past estimates, but history may easily repeat itself, and looked at from the vantage point of 2000 a new estimate made in 1960 may give rise to just as much puzzled amusement as the 1920 estimate now tends to provide. If we have learned anything from past exercise, it is to cast estimates in the conditional rather than the declarative mood. That exploration of our environment is still most limited, and that a rising demand for oil has in the past created the incentive for investment to help widen this environment and is likely to do so in the future, these above all are the factors that render each estimate vulnerable and that reduce the sharpness of judgment.

Technology and costs. In assuming a remaining base of 500 billion barrels of which a substantial portion remains to be discovered, and recoverability factors greatly in excess of those that have prevailed so far, passing reference has been made to the effect of technology. For it is improvement in our ability to discover and recover that will afford access to and exploitation of the resource without significant cost penalties.

This is not the place to deal in detail either with technology and its effect upon cost in the past or with the likely future course of cost in the light of potential technological innovations. Both subjects have been treated in RFF's *Energy in the American Economy* and are receiving continuing attention in a number of RFF-sponsored research projects now under way. The arguments advanced in the *Energy* study, that technological progress in the past has prevented significant cost increases and is likely to do so in the future, stems from several considerations: (1) the unsuitability of many of the statistical series, above all the proved reserve data, frequently used in showing past cost increases; (2) failure of those predicting cost increases to widen sufficiently the area in which oil may occur in both orthodox and unorthodox geological formations, and to take account of occurrences at greater depths; (3) continuing progress in drilling technique, such as use of multiple wells; so-called "slim holes"; wells lined with cement rather than steel casings; and sonic, turbo, or percussion drilling and a host of improvements that speed the rate of penetration; and (4) various aids to recovery, most of which come under the general category of secondary recovery.

A few statistics illustrate recent progress.[15] Drilling time for wells drilled 15,000 feet or deeper has been cut from 222 days in 1949 to 105 days in 1960, and number of bits consumed per well has been cut from 199 to 66 during the same period, while average depth of well has just about remained stationary near 16,000 feet. (See Figure 20–2.)

In the span of only a few years the art of multiple completion has advanced rapidly from dual to septuple completion, with substantial attending cost reductions. An example of the immediate predecessor, a sextuple natural gas completion, illustrates the cost savings. Such a well, engineered in Texas in mid-1960 (tapping gas reservoirs at six levels between 4,700 and 6,600 feet), cost just above $75,000, whereas completion of six separate wells would have cost over $300,000 using conventional casing, or

14. John E. Johnston, James Trumbell, and Gordon P. Eaton, "The Petroleum Potential of the Emerged and Submerged Atlantic Coastal Plain of the United States," paper presented to Fifth World Petroleum Congress, New York, 1959.

15. These and subsequent deep well data from *The Petroleum Engineer*, March 1961, pp. B–19–23.

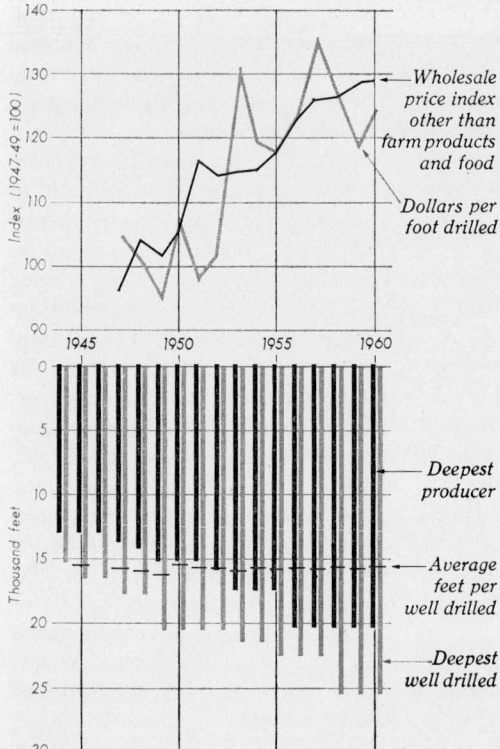

Figure 20–2. Trends in deep well drilling, production, and costs, 1945–1960.

$230,000 using the tubingless technique.[16] These are truly enormous cost differences. In the cited instance, even a less spectacular process of three dual completions, instead of one sextuple, would have cut the cost nearly in two.

In addition, development work stands to benefit along with exploration work from any advance in drilling. One cannot foretell what form such advance will take, but it is almost certain that during the next decade or two the time-honored rotary drill, now sixty years old, will be replaced by some radically different method of drilling in which above all (*a*) the power is applied only at the bottom and not dispersed in the effort of turning thousands of feet of steel pipe, and (*b*) the drilling or cutting device can be retracted and a new one lowered without having to pull up, disassemble, reassemble, and lower a long string of pipe. When one considers

that in some formations a rock bit may penetrate only half a dozen feet in ten or twelve hours before it is worn out and has to be lifted, and that a round trip for a bit at levels of 12,000 feet or so may take another eight hours, one understands the impatient wait for a radically new technology. Ventures such as the "Mohole" drilling operation may well make a significant contribution in that direction.

While it is true that wells have been drilled to greater depth and that the deeper the drilling, the greater the cost, technology has managed to offset these higher costs. Indeed, in the past fifteen years the cost per foot of deep wells drilled has risen barely as much as the wholesale price index, and this despite the fact that at the same time the maximum well depth has dropped from just over 15,000 to over 25,000 feet. This is impressive evidence of the impact of technology. While it "would be, perhaps, too much to expect that the average depth of new wells can continue to increase indefinitely at little or no increase in cost, . . . the achievement of technology to date is reasonable ground for assuming, at worst, only a modest cost increase in the period through 1975."[17] No single study has so far systematically disentangled and analyzed these elements: the prices of factors going into finding; the quantities of these factors used; the factors' relationship to changes in the depth pattern of wells; the results of exploration in terms of oil eventually found, including secondary recovery; the proper accounting for finding of gas, etc. The only published studies that have attempted to calculate costs per barrel of oil found are, to our knowledge, those conducted over a number of years by Robert E. Megill of Carter Oil Company, subsequently merged with Humble Oil and Refining Company. For the states covered in his studies, which unfortunately exclude Texas and Louisiana, the finding costs per barrel, even allowing for gas and secondary recovery, have been trending upward. However, in the last eight years or so, when allowance is made for gas finding, the trend in the largest of the areas studied by Megill—Kansas and Oklahoma—has not been steep. Indeed, if in spite of its erratic nature one can discern a trend since, say, 1950, costs may not

---

16. *Petroleum Week*, May 27, 1960, p. 24.

17. Schurr, Netschert, *et al., op. cit.*, p. 380.

have risen more than the general price level. None of these data, however, take one beyond the stage of suggestion.

In its May 1959 report, the Independent Petroleum Association's Cost Study Committee lamented the "lack of current information required to make a comprehensive study of the trends in the cost of finding, developing, and producing liquid hydrocarbons and natural gas." A year later, it noted that the "development of adequate factual information on the cost of finding, developing, and producing petroleum has proved to be a slow and difficult task" but also cited "growing awareness" of its value. Perhaps soon one may look forward to better data on finding costs and their relation to reserves as well as trends in depth and other features of drilling.

Secondary recovery by flooding oil reservoirs with water, liquid gas, petroleum, or carbon dioxide, by starting combustion in the reservoir and thus decreasing viscosity, and by other methods is being increasingly practiced. Continued progress and spread of this aid to production cannot but shift significantly the perspective of adequacy in both magnitude and timing, and of costs as related to findings. Estimates of the secondary recovery potential range at present from the conservative 60 billion barrels estimated by Torrey to another estimate of 85 billion barrels[18] and to Weeks's 190 billion barrels. These are far less closely connected than is primary recovery with drilling costs— and certainly not at all with any drilling costs related to finding, for these are amounts that have already been found! They cannot therefore be considered in the same framework as the primary recovery potential. Omission of most of this segment (for example, in proved reserve figures) is certain to lead not only to far too restricted a view of recoverable reserves but also to too pessimistic a view of costs. Even if finding costs rise and less oil is found per dollar spent in drilling, it is most important to recall that a declining share of oil produced participates in this particular expense item.

The record of technology is impressive, and the future seems to hold great promise for further advances in all phases of the industry: exploration, development, production, refining. Thus, from a resource point of view there is no reason why, through 1975 at any rate, the price of domestic crude should show any significant increase beyond that of the general price level. This judgment is obviously more difficult to maintain beyond the next fifteen or twenty years; with even optimistic estimates of total oil recoverability, the possibility cannot be excluded that in those more remote years stringent resource conditions might more than offset technological advance. Much will depend upon the ingenuity of the industry in finding and recovering domestic oil resources and upon its judgment of the sufficiency of the financial reward, the outlook for competing sources and for demand, and other factors. It is also true, however, that conditions outside the control of the industry circumscribe rather narrowly the level to which the price of crude might rise.

Indeed, the full or nearly full exploitation of domestic crude oil resources is unlikely for several reasons. For one thing, oil is closely hedged in by competing fuels as well as by foreign production. Should the more pessimistic forecasters be correct, and should increasing oil-finding costs push the price of domestic oil ahead of the general price level, it is difficult to see how such a price increase would be able to withstand the pressure from lower priced imported crude; from coal in most uses other than transportation, either directly or by way of electricity; from the application of new conversion methods in transportation, such as efficient batteries of one kind or another; and from shale or tar sands.

Import possibilities. Imports involve no foreseeable problem of supply, either in availability at the source or in transportation. Reserves abroad in most locations involve recovery cost at a level sufficiently lower than ours to absorb substantial additions to cost by taxation, transport, or other burdens before the question of competitive status in the U.S. market would arise. The cost of transportation is, furthermore, decreasing with the growth in size of the average tanker in service. Cost comparisons show that the relative cost of oil transport decreases by 50 per cent between the T-2 tanker (16,600

18. George Roberts, Jr., and Scott W. Walker, paper presented to Fifth World Petroleum Congress, New York, 1959.

deadweight tons) and a 45,000-tonner, and by another 10 per cent when we get into the super-tanker class of 85,000 tons.

Even the medium-sized 30,000-ton tanker can carry oil at less than two-thirds the cost of the war-born T-2. Construction figures, as presented in Table 20–3, show the increasing significance of the larger tankers. These will be especially prominent in crude, as opposed to product, carriage.

The tabulation shows the average size of tankers in construction to be 35,000 tons, compared with an average size of 19,000 tons for tankers in existence. Thus the outlook is for lower cost transportation to U.S. coastal locations.

While one may reasonably anticipate that rates of growth in demand for oil outside the United States will exceed the projected rate of demand at home, foreign oil reserves, however defined, are vast and continue to expand. Middle East oil reserves constitute roughly 60 per cent of the world's total oil reserves. They have increased four and one-half times during the 1950's, and recent extension of exploration to offshore locations in the Persian Gulf has further cemented the predominance of the area. In 1960 it was estimated that the Middle East had proved reserves of not less than 185 billion barrels. This compared with estimated proved

reserves of 32 billion in the United States, close to 20 billion in Venezuela, more than 30 billion in the U.S.S.R., and about 300 billion for the world as a whole. Sixty-two billion barrels of the Middle East oil reserves are in Kuwait; Saudi Arabia has 50 billion, Iran, 34 billion (or roughly the same as the United States), and Iraq, 27 billion.

The Middle East reserves are equivalent to roughly 60 times the total amount of petroleum and its products consumed in the United States in 1960, and about 125 times Western Europe's consumption in the same year. (See Figure 20–3.)

The foregoing estimates refer only to the proved reserves. Even though the magnitude of the reserves already discovered probably circumscribes the interest of established companies in further exploration and discovery, competition, especially from relative newcomers, provides a stimulus: annual gross additions averaged 16 billion barrels during the 1950's, an amount equal to one-half of total proved reserves in the United States. These vast resources have been located and are being produced with a minimum of drilling—with obvious implications for cost. In the Middle East, a total of fewer than 1,500 wells have been drilled, including both exploration and development wells. By comparison, close to 1.2 million wells have

TABLE 20–3.   Tanker Distribution by Size, October 1, 1958

Size (d.w. tons)	Tankers on order and under construction as of 10/1/58			Tanker tonnage existing as of 10/1/58		
	No.	Total d.w. tonnage (*thous. tons*)	Per cent of tonnage	No.	Total d.w. tonnage (*thous. tons*)	Per cent of tonnage
6,000–16,000	30	385	1.3	820	10,243	20.2
16,001–20,000	179	3,394	11.4	1,151	20,029	39.5
20,001–30,000	96	2,428	8.2	380	9,393	18.5
30,001–40,000	275	9,655	32.5	245	8,254	16.3
40,001–50,000	205	9,468	31.9	43	1,883	3.7
50,001–60,000	7	393	1.3	5	269	0.5
Over 60,000	57	3,987	13.4	7	599	1.2
All sizes	849	29,710	100.0	2,651	50,670	100.0

Source: Loren F. Kahle and A. J. Kelly, Jr., "The Role of Sea Transportation in the Petroleum Industry," paper presented to Fifth World Petroleum Congress, New York, 1959.

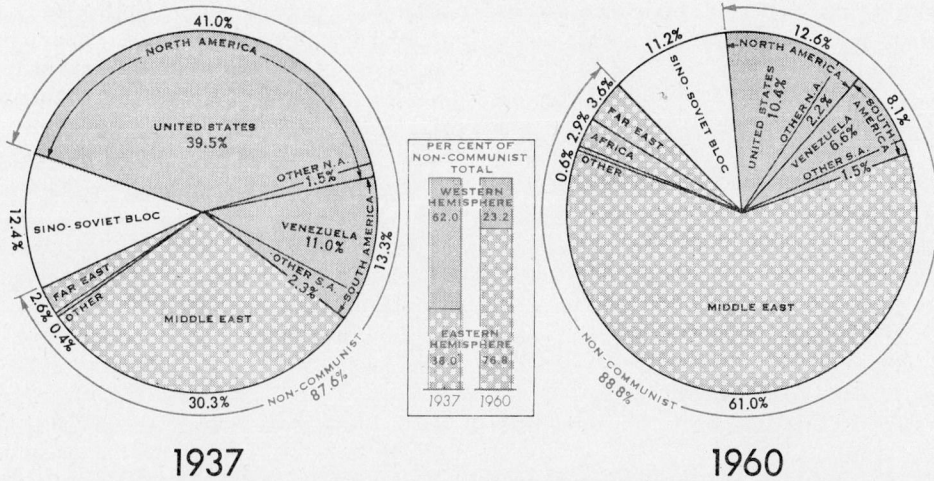

1937   1960

Figure 20–3. Proved crude oil reserves of the world, 1960 compared with 1937.

been drilled in the United States, of which those now producing total around 600,000. One must conclude that the amount of oil remaining to be discovered in the Middle East is probably substantial; it may be very large even in relation to the fabulous amounts already known to exist.

Middle East oil is extremely cheap to extract as compared with that of most other oil-producing areas of the world. Whereas the average U.S. well produces only 12 barrels a day, or about 4,500 a year, there are reports of wells in the Middle East producing over 600,000 a year. The U.N. Economic Commission for Europe, in its report, *The Price of Oil in Western Europe* (Geneva, 1955), has estimated the production cost of Arabian oil at about 35 cents a barrel. Others have put it at 20 cents or even less.

Although the Middle East is the most outstanding, it is not the sole example of the recent enormous increase in proved reserves, both in "traditional" oil countries and in places where oil had not previously been found. Put at not much above 30 billion barrels just prior to World War II, world petroleum reserves have multiplied by nearly ten in the short span of two decades.

Greatly increased demand has called forth this effort. Most important has been the rise of oil consumption in Western Europe, accompanied, as in an earlier era in this country, by less consumption of coal. By 1960 Western

Europe, defined for this purpose as the countries which were members of the Organization for European Economic Co-operation, consumed some 1.5 billion barrels, compared with not much above 400 million a decade earlier. In contrast to U.S. trends, industrial and heavy transportation uses, more than passenger cars, have been responsible for this rapid rate of growth. The ratio of persons to automobiles has declined from nearly fifty in 1950 to fifteen in 1960, but this is still five times as high as the U.S. ratio.

Absolute amounts consumed are small compared with U.S. levels. Even Western Europe consumed only about 7 barrels per capita, or far less than half of the U.S. level of nearly 20 barrels. Japan, which accounts for half the oil used in Asia, still uses only 230 million barrels a year, or about 2½ barrels per capita. In the rest of Asia, in much of Africa, and in some parts of Latin America use per capita is one barrel and less, but everywhere growth rates exceed sharply the 2½ to 3 per cent a year recently prevailing in the United States.

Listed overleaf are the relative average annual rates of increase in leading European countries and other parts of the world in petroleum product consumption between 1955 and 1960, according to United Nations statistics.

In a forty-year forward look, such rates of growth in oil consumption greatly overshadow

	Per cent
German Federal Republic	29
Italy	18
Netherlands	16
United Kingdom	13
Belgium-Luxembourg	9
France	8
Japan	23
Caribbean	6
Middle East	11
Africa	6
U.S.S.R. and Eastern Europe	11
Sino-Soviet bloc	12
World, excl. U.S.	11
World, excl. U.S. and	
Sino-Soviet bloc	11
World, incl. areas not listed	7

the fact that absolute levels are still far below U.S. experience. For example, an 11 per cent increase per year cumulated over four decades would mean attainment of more than sixty times 1960 consumption by 2000, and such a rate prevailed in the second half of the fifties throughout the world other than the United States. On the other hand, there is reason to assume that such rates will not prevail for a forty-year period, partly because, as in this country, competitive edging out of coal has its limits, partly because natural gas consumption has barely been tapped, and partly because the past five years have been especially dynamic ones in Western Europe.

Considerations such as these do not, however, help us in quantitatively appraising the energy growth outlook abroad. Only very rough orders of magnitude are feasible. For example, the Petroleum Department of the Chase Manhattan Bank has recently projected a ten-year 6.1 per cent annual growth rate in oil consumption in the non-communist countries of the world outside the United States.[19] If this high rate were to hold for forty years, consumption would rise from a level of about 3.4 billion barrels in 1960 to some 36 billion by the end of the century, for a roughly cumulated forty-year consumption of some 800 billion barrels. Adding a U.S. import demand equal to 20 per cent of U.S. consumption would raise this to approximately 850 billion barrels. This compares with 235 billion barrels of proved reserves outside the United States and the Soviet bloc. The apparent gap is in no

19. John G. Winger, et al., Future Growth of the World Petroleum Industry (New York: The Chase Manhattan Bank, Petroleum Department, September 1961).

way disconcerting. First, there is the history of the vast increase in reserves during the past decade—a near quintupling in the Middle East alone—accompanied by the opening up of entirely new areas of production. Second, total oil resources are usually a multiple of proved reserves. This has been discussed above for the United States. For the non-communist areas of the world no data are available, but if the situation in the United States carries any lesson, ultimately recoverable supplies abroad might be thought of as in the neighborhood of no less than seven times proved reserves. One may legitimately conclude, therefore, that even at high rates of growth in petroleum consumption it is difficult to anticipate any supply problems arising from the resource side during the balance of the century.

This is true even in the face of perhaps the greatest unknown variable—future consumption in the developing countries of Asia and Africa. It is well to keep one's perspective even over a period of forty years and not be carried away by the figures one can conjure up from prospective population growth and industrial expansion. Even in the Soviet Union after forty years of intensive centralized industrial development, consumption of oil is less than 4 barrels per capita—about one-fifth of what it is in the United States.

The resources aspect does not, however, encompass all the conditions that will determine supply. Much of the non-communist world's oil is located in politically unstable areas, unstable both domestically and as portions of the non-communist world (which for statistical purposes includes the so-called uncommitted parts of the globe). Most of the Middle East, the North African fields, and Indonesia must be put in this category. Thus, the question of continuing availability of supply—and more recently stable cost—which has long plagued this country is now of concern to Western Europe, which draws nearly 80 per cent of its supplies from the Middle East. Though matters have quieted down since the Suez crisis of 1956, the feeling of long-run stability is unlikely to return as a permanent feature of the international oil market.

How much oil can be supplied from abroad

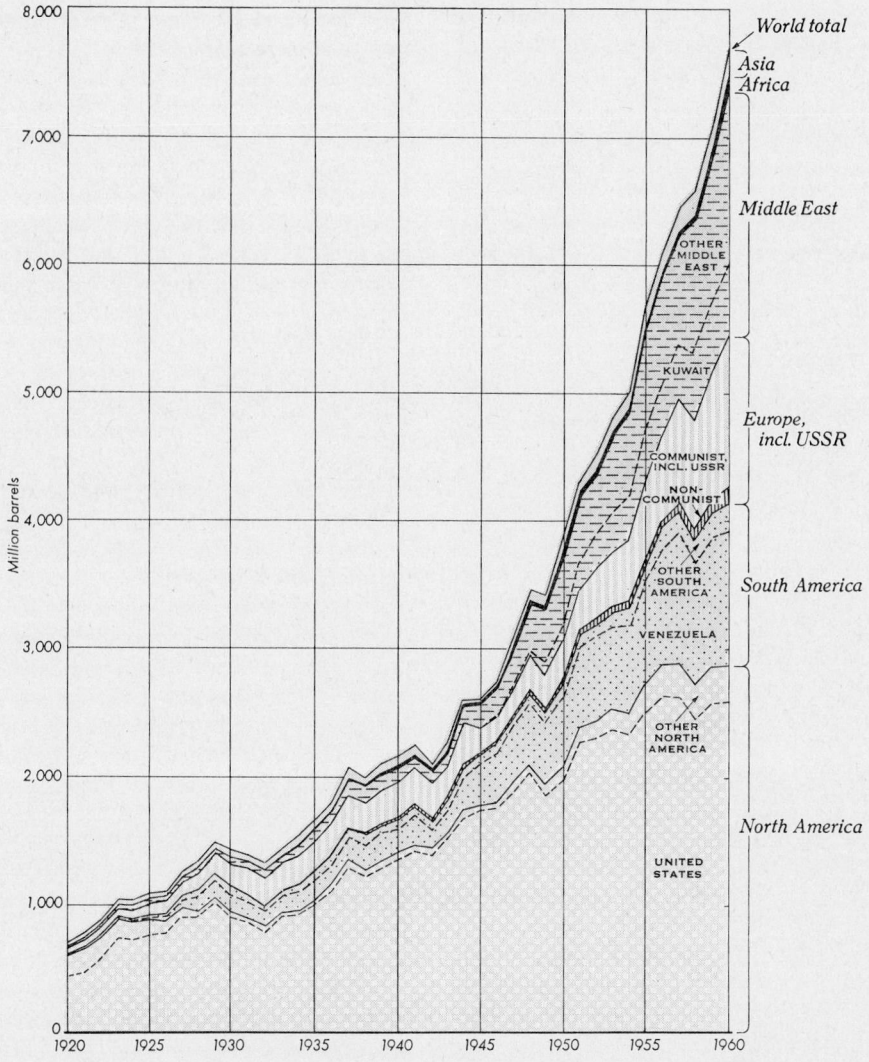

Figure 20–4. World oil production, 1920–1960.

to meet U.S. needs? Although this question cannot be answered in precise quantitative terms, the general lines of the answer are clear. For at least some time to come, the United States could obtain a very much larger proportion of the oil it requires from abroad—perhaps as much as a third, or half, or even more of its total requirements. Above all the Middle East, but also Venezuela, and in a few years Canada, could supply much larger amounts of oil to the

United States than is imported at present. (See Figure 20–4.) [20]

The effect of larger imports on the U.S. cost and price structure for oil and its products depends not only on institutional arrangements within the United States and among the oil companies, but also on the terms on which the

20. Data through 1959 from DeGolyer and MacNaughton, *Twentieth Century Petroleum Statistics, 1960* (Dallas, Texas). Data for 1960 compiled from various sources.

foreign countries are willing to make their oil available; these terms may be far above the basic cost of producing the oil and may vary with circumstances. But the low production cost of Middle Eastern, and to a lesser extent Venezuelan, oil suggests that with substantially larger imports a price structure in the United States could be supported that would be significantly lower than in the absence of imported oil. The magnitude of oil resources in the non-communist areas of the world thus suggests no problem in relieving any stringency in domestic supply that might develop. Cheaper imports are now supplementing domestic supplies and have been doing so for some years at an increasing rate, culminating in the present restrictions which in recent years have kept imports at the equivalent of 15–20 per cent of new supply. Thus imports cannot be viewed as a novel feature.

In the long perspective of this appraisal it is reasonable to assume that imports will not again decline below the current level except in a temporarily disrupted market and that, on the contrary, the percentage might increase. The rate of growth in imports will be determined largely by the spread between the domestic crude price and the landed cost of foreign crude, in the sense that a widening spread will put increasing strain upon import controls and the constellation of politico-administrative forces upholding them. Assuming that these might eventually give way to economic pressures, imports might then grow in continuation of the trend that prevailed until the imposition of controls. Such a development would relieve the strain on domestic petroleum resources and, by easing the pressure to discover every last drop of reserves, would equally ease any upward push of domestic prices.[21]

Alternative sources. Crude imports are only one of the substitutes for domestic crude. A second is coal, touched upon in the section dealing with future coal availability. Substitution here would, however, be confined to a narrower

field. Barring liquefaction of coal at prices competitive with those of other substitutes for crude petroleum, such as shale-oil or tar-sand derivatives—a step not now on the horizon—coal would compete principally as an industrial fuel. A return to coal is difficult to picture either in transportation or in residential use. New technology which—short of liquefying coal—is based upon giving it some of the handling advantages of oil has been attempted but has not sufficiently advanced to permit judgment. Substitution effects would be moderate, for industrial uses, as discussed in Chapters 10 and 15, account for only some 13 per cent of total petroleum consumption, and nearly half of that is in petroleum refineries. Locational considerations would also militate against substitution in many instances. Altogether, competition from coal cannot be anticipated to exert a very significant check should oil prices rise.

A third competitor, wholly potential so far but with a resource base that dwarfs that of crude oil, is shale oil. According to current experience here and abroad, there are no technical obstacles to producing shale oil (or gas) in commercial quantities. Commercial producers as well as small-scale pioneering organizations have successfully completed pilot operations in the heart of the Colorado shale oil country. The results suggest the probability that oil could be produced and transported to West Coast locations at prices competitive with that of California crude. A statement made forty years ago by the Chief Geologist of the U.S. Geological Survey is equally true today: "Our oil shales are an endowment of inestimable value on which we are certain, ultimately, to depend heavily, though the time and rate of that dependence will be largely controlled by the rate of development of foreign oil fields, the growth of world demand, and by consequent competitive prices of natural oil."[22] The question is: are we any closer to the point of entry of shale oil today than, it turned out, we were in 1920?

One can argue on both sides of this question. As yet, cost analysis has been based upon relatively small pilot plants and has not been sufficiently refined to establish beyond doubt the

21. The degree to which such a development would depress investment in domestic oil development depends upon the attractiveness of alternative channels of investment viewed in the light of new technology in oil discovery and production.

22. White, *loc. cit.*

potential competitiveness of shale oil. There is also the question of water supply. For example, although the known shale resource base (estimated at over one trillion recoverable barrels of oil just from rock yielding at least 15 gallons per ton) is a multiple of the estimated crude oil resources under even the most generous assumptions for the latter, problems of water supply alone might prevent production of more than 2 million barrels per day, though this would still total a respectable quantity over a year—three-quarters of a billion barrels or nearly 15 per cent of estimated oil demand in 1980—and perfection of a dry process cannot be excluded. A third drawback, however, is long-distance transportation cost. A Colorado-based shale oil industry would have to overcome substantial odds to compete in locations other than the West Coast, given the absence of low-cost water transportation of the kind enjoyed by Gulf Coast producers in supplying the East Coast.

Nonetheless, a small increase in the real price of crude could stimulate the construction of large-diameter pipelines and the acceptance of shale oil, provided sufficient capital could be channeled into such use. Investment might present a formidable barrier since, given the large and growing financial stake they have in foreign oil development, existing crude processors would probably prefer to turn to imports rather than to shale. At the same time, considering the magnitude of the task and the difficulty of breaking into the old or setting up a new marketing network, it might prove unfeasible for new and independent forces to undertake shale oil development on any significant scale. The sizeable acreages in Colorado that have been purchased or leased by a number of major oil companies bespeak their long-run interest in the potential, but for the moment they are more in the nature of an insurance policy.

Finally, at a time when Venezuela and the Middle East express rising concern over future market outlets, it is difficult to visualize the early emergence of shale oil as a crude oil substitute.

Nonetheless, one must not let the current mood of oversupply color the outlook for the next four decades. The general trend of our demand-resource comparisons points to tightness of crude oil in the latter part of the century. It is altogether conceivable that the reliance on imported oil may within the next decades suffer setbacks, and that development of an alternative domestic source of supply may appear prudent to the oil marketer, to the government, or to both. Shale oil would fill this role. It would also come into play if crude oil prices, owing to resource problems, should begin a steady upward movement. In either event, problems of location could probably be overcome with no more difficulty than has been experienced in bridging the distance between Texas and New York with pipelines and tankers. The fact that shale oil has been below the horizon for so long does not mean that it will not eventually appear above it. This is equally true, and perhaps more so, for the oil-rich tar sands of western Canada, which are easier to mine and have undergone substantial preliminary processing trials. While the locational problem is, if anything, even more serious, greater ease of production might offset this. The fact that several companies of substantial means are poised to go into action is certainly significant.

Natural Gas

As in the case of crude oil, the best-known measure of future gas supplies is the proved reserves (see Table 20–4). Their definition runs parallel to that of proved oil reserves (page 389), and their significance is similarly circumscribed. However, since between 75 and 80 per cent of gas deposits can be taken as economically recoverable—compared with nearly one-third in the case of crude oil—the proved reserve figure is not to a significant extent a function of the assumptions concerning recovery technology.

At the same time the concept of an ultimate gas reserve, comprising past production, proved reserves, and future discoveries (under the assumption of static technology) is not properly applicable to gas, because past production is only a partial measure of past gas withdrawals. Much gas has in the past been vented, flared, and wasted in other ways, as a concomitant of oil production.

The most practical concept is instead one of

TABLE 20–4. U.S. Natural Gas Production and Proved Reserves, 1945–1960

Year	With-drawals during year[1]	Estimated proved reserves as of end of year[2]	Proved reserves at end of year as multiple of withdrawals during preceding 12 months
	(trillion cu. ft.)	(trillion cu. ft.)	
1945	4.8	147.8	30.8
1946	5.3	160.6	30.3
1947	5.6	165.9	29.6
1948	6.0	173.9	29.0
1949	6.3	180.4	28.6
1950	7.1	185.6	26.1
1951	8.2	193.8	23.6
1952	8.9	199.7	22.4
1953	9.2	211.4	23.0
1954	9.5	211.7	22.3
1955	10.2	223.7	21.9
1956	10.9	237.8	21.8
1957	11.5	246.6	21.4
1958	11.7	254.1	21.7
1959	12.6	262.6	20.8
1960	13.3	263.8	19.8

1. From Appendix Table A15–12.
2. Report of the Committee on Natural Gas Reserves of the American Gas Association for year ending Dec. 31, 1961.

future recoverable gas resources, based upon (1) ultimate oil reserves exclusive of past production and (2) a gas/oil ratio. The latter may be derived from the quantitative relationship between the two forms of hydrocarbon as found in discovery, in past production, in proved reserves, or in other circumstances of nature, and it will differ accordingly.[23]

Available supplies. Given the two variables from which gas is estimated, it is understandable that past estimates have shown much divergence. In RFF's *Energy in the American Economy,* a ratio of gas to oil of 7,000 cubic feet per barrel—based essentially on proved reserves—was assumed and reasons were adduced for this selection.[24]

This ratio lies substantially above the ratio in

23. The various ratios are not measures of the true relationship of occurrence in nature. They are factors based upon different types of experience and are conditioned by the assumptions made in the commercial evaluation of the occurrences.
24. Schurr, Netschert, *et al., op. cit.,* pp. 403–410.

past oil and gas production, but gas wastage has been accounted for only since 1935 and therefore the recorded ratio is obviously too low. On the other hand, RFF's ratio is somewhat lower than the ratio in current proved reserves (which works out at 8,300 cubic feet per barrel), and again this is as it should be, for the high proved gas reserves are partially a result of low gas production in earlier years; in addition, we are confronted by the ever-present uncertainties arising from poor accounting of wastage.

Following the procedure in RFF's *Energy* study,[25] we have applied this ratio to an estimate of ultimate oil reserves, excluding past production, that represents a reasoned expert consensus. The estimate was actually derived as one-third of the total quantity of oil estimated to await exploitation—500 billion barrels—since current technology permits on the average about one-third of a reservoir to be recovered. Application of the ratio to that third, i.e., 167 billion barrels, resulted in an estimate of recoverable gas resources of roughly 1,200 trillion cubic feet. One could proceed from this quantity to the equivalent of a resource base concept on the basis that this quantity implies an 80 per cent recovery factor. However, little is gained by this additional step, given the high recovery level already reached in practice.

It follows from this summary description that assumptions of rising oil recoverability—such as we have made in the preceding section—will not affect the gas estimate. Given the high recovery of gas from any given deposit, increased recovery of oil would not, for all practical purposes, raise the amount of gas that can be recovered. In fact, an assumption of higher ultimate oil reserves that is predicated upon improved recovery ability would require a lowering of the gas/oil ratio, with no net increase in estimated gas recoverability.[26]

If, on the other hand, the oil estimate is raised because prospects of occurrence, rather than recovery, are judged to be more promising, and the resource base of oil is thus widened, then the gas estimate would also have to be raised. Indeed, on the grounds that the higher oil estimate

25. *Ibid.,* p. 411.
26. The only boost in the amount of gas recovered would lie in the relatively small portion of the gas associated with and dissolved in the additionally recovered oil.

is likely to be associated with deeper drilling and therefore higher gas occurrence, one could argue that in the latter circumstances, perhaps even the 7,000 cubic feet gas/oil ratio might be low. This is an important distinction, with immediate practical consequences.

It has been suggested above that the recoverable oil base on which estimates of gas recoverability must be predicated might not be the 167 billion barrels on which the estimate of 1,200 trillion cubic feet rests, but a higher though undetermined figure.

We are not here interested in putting forward yet another estimate of gas reserves; it is worth considering, however, that higher estimates of recoverable oil, based upon a higher assessment of the resource base—and these are bound to be made before long—set a different stage for estimates of natural gas reserves. Let us assume, for the sake of having a maximum supply with which to compare requirements, that at a one-third rate 210 billion barrels of oil can be recovered from 625 billion (see page 391). Then, figuring at a higher rate, say 8,000, suggested by deeper drilling which finds relatively more gas,[27] and on the basis of looking for gas alone rather than oil or oil and gas, we would obtain a reserve figure of 1,680 trillion cubic feet.

Disregarding the possibility that recovery might be boosted above 80 per cent, we shall in the following discussion compare the demand projections with 1,200 trillion cubic feet as a minimum and 1,700 trillion as a maximum estimate of recoverable gas resources in the light of present knowledge. The comments regarding the ephemeral, and essentially conservative, character of all such estimates, made earlier in this chapter in connection with oil, apply with equal force here.

Outlook for adequacy. How do these magnitudes, uncertain as they are, compare with projected demand from 1960 to 2000, both on a cumulative basis and at specific times? Table 20–5 presents the framework for analysis.

Ignoring supporting reserves, even the minimum estimate of 1,200 trillion cubic feet would be in excess of both the Low and Medium pro-

27. Zapp, *op. cit.,* p. H–32.

jections of cumulative demand by the year 2000 and would be exceeded by requirements implicit in the High projection only moderately. But the insertion of reserve requirements drastically alters the balance. Concentrating on the Medium projection, let us first assume that additional reserves would continue to be proved at the average rate of 20 trillion cubic feet per year which prevailed during much of the fifties. Then, in the forty years ahead we could anticipate proving of 800 trillion cubic feet, a figure which, when added to that of currently proved reserves of approximately 260 trillion, would come within 10 per cent of the lower range of anticipated recoverable resources, 1,200 trillion. Such a development would be paralleled by steadily increasing withdrawals, so that proved reserves would begin to decline, between 1970 and 1980, as shown in Table 20-5. The decline in reserves would accelerate. Each year the proved reserves would be a smaller multiple of production. Even before 1970, reserves would have dropped to less than twenty times output, the current minimum supply any company now has to prove to obtain Federal Power Commission certification for pipeline construction as a supplier to specified customers. By 2000, proved reserves would total less than three years' production.

Some 120 trillion cubic feet would remain to be proved—the difference between 1,200 trillion cubic feet estimated recoverable resources and the 986 trillion of cumulated demand plus 92 trillion of proved reserves. These remaining recoverable resources would suffice for barely another four years' consumption at then prevailing rates.

If the maximum recoverable resources of 1,700 trillion cubic feet were assumed, the picture would be substantially improved. Combining cumulative Medium demand and proved reserves would still leave some 620 trillion cubic feet to be added to proved reserves, but it is clear that the tempo of additions would have to be far greater than assumed in this example. (See Figure 20–5.)

Obviously, these are not realistic patterns. As in the case of oil, one cannot anticipate production's rising to a maximum, paralleled by falling reserves, only to be cut down to zero over-

TABLE 20–5.   Implications of Projected Natural Gas Demand for Resource Adequacy, 1960–2000

(Trillion cubic feet)

| Projection | | Demand | | | Fixed reserve additions[1] | | | Variable reserve additions | | | |
| | | | | | Gross additions to proved reserves, actual in 1960, and assumed at 20 tril. cu. ft. per year thereafter | Proved reserves | | Reserves required when ratio to prod. in year shown: | | Cumulative demand plus required reserves, end of period, when reserves: | |
Year	Period	Annual in year shown	10-year, in period shown	Cumulative		at beginning of year or period shown	at end of year or period shown	declines from 20 to 10 by 2000	remains at 20 throughout	decline from 20 to 10 times prod.	remain at 20 times prod.
(1)	(2)	(3)	(4)	(5)	(6)	(7)	(8)	(9)	(10)	(11)	(12)
Low											
1960	1960	13.3	—	—	14	263	264	266	266	279	279
1970	1961–70	16.4	148	161	200	264	316	287	328	448	489
1980	1971–80	19.6	180	340	200	316	336	294	392	634	732
1990	1981–90	21.7	206	546	200	336	330	271	434	817	980
2000	1991–2000	24.0	228	774	200	330	302	240	480	1,014	1,254
Medium											
1960	1960	13.3	—	—	14	263	264	266	266	279	279
1970	1961–70	19.3	163	176	200	264	301	338	386	514	562
1980	1971–80	24.5	219	395	200	301	283	368	490	763	885
1990	1981–90	28.9	272	667	200	283	211	361	578	1,028	1,245
2000	1991–2000	34.9	319	986	200	211	92	349	698	1,335	1,684
High											
1960	1960	13.3	—	—	14	263	264	266	266	279	279
1970	1961–70	22.3	178	191	200	264	286	390	446	581	637
1980	1971–80	31.0	266	457	200	286	220	465	620	922	1,077
1990	1981–90	41.4	362	819	200	220	58	518	828	1,337	1,647
2000	1991–2000	56.0	487	1,306	200	58	nil	560	1,120	1,866	2,426

Source: Appendix Table A15–14.
1. Without regard to maintenance of a given reserve/production ratio.

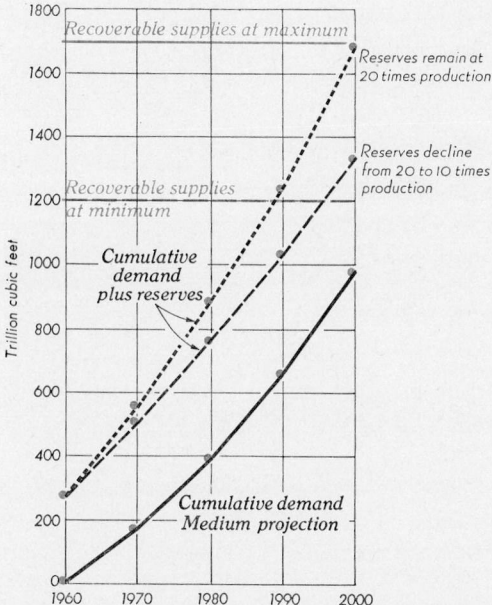

Figure 20–5. Implications of projected natural gas demand for future adequacy.

night. The question as to when production will reach a peak, or how fast the available gas can be withdrawn, then must be posed. On the assumption of 1,200 trillion cubic feet availability, the peak must come before 2000. The American Gas Association now sets it at 22.5 trillion cubic feet without specifying a date. In our scheme, this would place it between 1970 and 1980, to make it follow closely upon the peak in reserves, provided reserves continue to be proved at recent rates. Such would not be unreasonable timing, for, faced with declining reserves, the industry could be expected to slow down the rate of gas withdrawal. In that event a widening gap would open between projected demand and domestic supply, and the recoverable resources of natural gas would be stretched far beyond the year 2000; they would then supply a diminishing share of gaseous fuel consumption, assuming that there is an economic supply of natural gas from abroad, or a substitute source of gas from nongaseous sources. Otherwise, gaseous fuel will satisfy a smaller percentage of total energy consumption than has here been projected.

On the conservative assumption that proved reserves must be kept at twenty times consumption—given the long-term debt-financed investment in equipment, particularly pipelines—reserves would have to rise much faster. By 1980 they would have to reach some 490 trillion cubic feet. By 2000 they would reach 700 trillion. Such a figure, added to cumulative production between 1960 and 2000, would equal our maximum—a 1,700 trillion cubic-foot level of estimated recoverable resources. The turning point would surely come much sooner, with a gradual tapering off and exhaustion of reserves thereafter, for full production of a well cannot be maintained over its lifetime.

Looking at the situation in yet another way, by 1980 cumulative production plus required reserves at the twenty-year level would total 885 trillion cubic feet, or three-quarters of the minimum and over one-half of the maximum recoverable resources. Might not discovery of the balance stretch over a longer span of time?

In summary, these speculations suggest that somewhere around the midpoint of the forty-year period there may be a decline in gas withdrawal, provided cumulative knowledge does not in the meantime tend to support a figure well beyond 1,700 trillion cubic feet as more nearly realistic.

Suppose reserve requirements were permitted to decline gradually below twenty times, say to ten times annual production by 2000? This too is worked out in Table 20–5. The result is a stretching out of supplies. By 2000 demand plus reserves would reach nearly 1,350 trillion cubic feet, past the minimum estimate of recoverable gas resources and within 20 per cent of the maximum.

The principal effect of this variation would be lowered reserve needs after 1980, despite rising production. However, as of 1980 the relation of cumulative demand plus reserves to recoverable resources would be so similar to that in the previous assumption (cols. 11 and 12) that industry reaction would be unlikely to differ much. Probably the main result would be a stretching out of supplies at a lower rate of output. However, only a drastic change in financing methods, given the high share of funded financing customary in pipeline construction, would permit construction of new facilities under this assumption of declining reserve requirements.

Only a combination of high resource assumption and declining reserve requirements would permit one to view with relative equanimity the course of gas demand and supply through the end of the century. At that time, cumulative consumption would be just under 1,000 trillion cubic feet, required reserves 350 trillion cubic feet, and reserves yet to be proved thus another 350 trillion. But, given the high demand then reached, even these assumptions would not suffice to assure adequate supplies in the first decade of the new century.

The above conclusions pertain with added force to the High projection, since the 1980 Medium demand level will be reached as early as 1970 in the High projection. Even the Low demand would cause strain towards the latter part of the century under the minimum recoverability assumption, especially since, as we have pointed out, the simultaneous occurrence of the Low in all uses of gas is most unlikely and the Low is, therefore, somewhat exaggerated. On the other hand, given recoverable resources of 1,700 trillion cubic feet, stringency would be unlikely to appear in this century.

Imports and other alternative sources. Gas can be imported by two quite different means: by pipeline from Canada and Mexico, and by shipment in liquid form by special tanker. The first source of supply is a reality and its likely expansion may be expected to add to domestic supplies, especially in some of the northern fringe areas and areas along the Pacific Coast which have until recently been without gas or depended on meager supplies through long-distance pipelines from Gulf sources. But even in Texas, the country's principal supply area, imports from Mexico have been used to augment local supplies, which in turn are shipped out in interstate pipelines. A number of major projects for importing from Canada have recently come before the FPC and the Canadian regulatory authorities. They would among them bring over one billion cubic feet per day from British Columbia and Alberta mainly to the Pacific Northwest, California, and northern Lake States. These quantities, most of them now

flowing or about to flow, are equivalent to over 3 per cent of total current natural gas consumption in the United States. Thus Canadian supply is beginning to supplement domestic sources significantly, and may do so increasingly in the future, given the large reserves and the relatively limited home market.

The second potential source of supply is ocean-borne liquefied methane, the principal component of dry natural gas. In February 1959, 32,000 barrels of liquid methane (commonly referred to as LNG, for liquid natural gas) were shipped successfully to England from the U.S. Gulf Coast. Regular gas shipments from Algerian fields to England are planned to begin before 1965 on a significant scale. The price to the distributors has been estimated at 88 cents per thousand cubic feet, not too different from natural gas prices in some areas in this country.

Success of such export programs would give renewed impetus to earlier proposals to import liquid gas into some U.S. markets which are now near the end of long-distance pipelines, such as New England and places as far down the East Coast as Philadelphia. Under most active consideration are liquid gas storage plants in New England, designed to assist in meeting peak demand that cannot be filled by normal pipeline capacity. Whether such gas might be shipped in through pipelines at off-season periods and liquefied, or brought by ship from the Gulf, Venezuela, or even Middle East fields, will be determined by wellhead pricing and transportation costs. Even LNG shipments from Alaskan fields to the West Coast are now coming into competitive focus.

The supply base of natural gas is expected to expand greatly through perfection of this technology. If the larger ships that are now in an advanced stage of consideration can bring down costs of transportation sufficiently to make their importation economical, the gas resources of Venezuela alone would make a sizeable contribution to U.S. supplies. In 1958, 1.7 billion cubic feet of gas per day were flared in Venezuela, equal to about 7 per cent of 1960 net marketed production in the United States. Venezuelan gas reserves are estimated —quite conservatively, it appears—at 33 trillion cubic feet, or about one-eighth of proved U.S. reserves.

The Venezuelan example shows the magnitude of the unexploited potential. Economical transportation could influence the energy supply position throughout the world, directly by adding to natural gas supplies and indirectly by easing the supply situation of competing fuels. Thus, in a chain reaction, eventual shipment of Middle East natural gas may reduce Europe's need for liquid hydrocarbon and, by keeping the crude oil price lower than it would otherwise be, may in turn affect the U.S. petroleum supply position.

As in the case of oil, shale and tar sand are potential candidates for supplementing natural gas supplies, though most effort has been devoted to extracting oil rather than gas. The opposite is true for conversion of coal. Here the outlook is more promising for gasification than for liquefaction. The two principal obstacles are the cost of mined coal, which is high at the efficiencies that have been achieved in experimental operation, and the necessity for upgrading the low-energy gas which emerges. The latter need arises from the high cost per unit of energy sent through pipelines when the energy content per unit of volume shipped is low.

Efforts to overcome the coal cost obstacle have been primarily in the direction of eliminating mining and, instead, gasifying coal underground.[28] Costs of gas so produced have been estimated at a range of 62–77 cents per million Btu or, roughly, per thousand cubic feet. However, this gas has an extremely low Btu content, about one-tenth that of natural gas, and would thus have to undergo radical upgrading to make it suitable for pipeline transmission. *Energy in the American Economy* lists a large number of experiences in both underground gasification and conversion of mined coal, most of which show a similar cost range, but with more nearly commercially feasible Btu content per cubic foot in the case of mined coal gasification.[29]

Barring technical breakthroughs such as application of nuclear energy to coal in place, it is difficult to see synthetic gas competing with natural gas in the next two decades, for even continuing increases in the price of natural gas would not for a considerable time bring coal-based gas, delivered over substantial distances from coal fields to consuming centers, into a competitive situation. Later in the century, on the other hand, and in local situations especially favorable for premium uses, such as residential application, one cannot exclude the emergence of synthetic gas as an alternative to natural gas, should supplies of the latter begin to dwindle.

Natural Gas Liquids

Natural gas, like crude oil, contains a variety of hydrocarbons, the most plentiful of which is methane, followed in order of increasing heaviness by ethane, propane, butane, and others. All these compounds exist in gaseous form in reservoirs; but all, including methane, can be liquefied by precisely calculable changes in pressure and/or temperature. Broadly speaking, high pressure and low temperature conduce to liquefaction. The heavier the hydrocarbon, the higher the temperature or the greater the pressure at which the gas will liquefy. Thus, at constant pressure, methane, the lightest and simplest of the hydrocarbons, boils at $-161°$ C.; pentane, one of the heavier members, of substantial importance in gasoline, does not vaporize until the temperature reaches $36°$, and others, still heavier, remain in their liquid phase up to much higher temperatures. At constant temperature, the lighter the compound, the greater the pressure under which the gas must be kept to prevent it from vaporizing.

These relationships hold the key not only to petroleum refining but also to the processes commonly employed in the recovery of the so-called natural gas liquids (NGL). With the exception of condensates, described below, NGL production merely removes from the gas stream those components that liquefy at above normal but still relatively low pressures and at temperatures not too far above those encountered in the normal above-ground environment. Their removal is necessary in order to prevent spontaneous liquefaction—and conse-

28. See, for example, Bureau of Mines, Report of Investigations 5808, and Information Circular 8020, both 1961.
29. Schurr, Netschert, *et al., op. cit.;* see pp. 419–27 for a discussion of synthetic gas.

quent transmission problems—in high-pressure gas pipelines, and it is commonly profitable to utilize them separately.

Within the family of compounds ordinarily removed from natural gas by deliberate temperature and pressure manipulation, one conventionally distinguishes between natural gasoline and liquid petroleum gas (LPG). This classification has limited and decreasing usefulness, but is deeply embedded in tradition. Historically, the compounds that constitute the bulk of natural gasoline and which stay liquid under normal temperature and pressure were the first to be stripped from the gas stream and were found to be closely akin to crude-derived motor fuel, whence not only the name of the product but also the habit of referring to all natural gas liquids plants as "gasoline plants." Later on, with the application of higher pressures and lower temperatures, the less heavy compounds were recovered and only the lightest fractions—basically methane and ethane and varying proportions of propane and butane which are not ordinarily fully removed from the gas—remained in the gaseous phase. Because of ease in handling, these lighter compounds were kept in the liquid phase regardless of end-use and given the designation "liquid petroleum gas," in some ways an unfortunate name since the bulk originates in natural gas rather than in petroleum production. Terminology has not been improved by the addition of "liquid gas," by which is meant natural gas liquefied at low temperatures and high pressure to permit bulk transportation in an enclosed space, such as an ocean-going vessel (see page 410).

The one exception to the normal relationship between pressure, temperature, and the liquid gaseous scale is known as "retrograde condensation." The term applies to hydrocarbons of the heavier kind which are frequently recovered from high-pressure gas reservoirs. In the reservoir they exist in the gas phase, but upon pressure reduction at the surface they undergo spontaneous liquefaction and are so recovered. The reservoirs from which they are derived are separately classified as "condensate" reservoirs, short for "retrograde condensate."

Together with natural gasoline and liquefied petroleum gases, the condensates make up the natural gas liquids. To them must be added those liquid petroleum gases, often called liquid refinery gases, that arise in the course of refining crude oil. These are identical in nature and application with those derived from natural gas and are usually included in the NGL category.

In some of their uses NGL represent merely an alternative to refined crude, predominantly gasoline in transportation, or kerosene and diesel oil in agriculture, or, kerosene and light distillates in residential and commercial use.

Where natural gas liquids are relatively "on their own" is in their use as a feedstock for chemical transformation to plastics, fibers, fertilizers, drugs, rubber, and a host of other finished and intermediary products. It is in these uses, as we have seen in the demand projections, that the most rapid rise has taken place and can be expected to occur in the future.

Recoverable supplies. NGL availability is closely related to that of crude oil and gas. In general, the trend in the ratio of NGL to natural gas production has been upward, as increasing portions of the lighter hydrocarbons are extracted from the gas at or near the wellhead. If natural gas is stripped of all components other than methane, the yield of the heavier components might be as high as 20 per cent by volume and substantially higher by energy content. In actual practice, far from all the non-methane compounds are normally stripped, and most gases contain less than 20 per cent of them to start with. Thus the typical NGL yield is nearer 10 than 20 per cent on a volume basis.

NGL are not a truly additional fuel reserve, whether derived from natural gas or oil refining. However, since at least 1946 natural gas liquids recoverable from gas have been separately stated in the proved reserves estimates. The proved reserves of NGL are conservatively defined as those occurrences in proven fields that can be handled either by existing extraction facilities or by those under construction or planned for the immediate future. The reason for limiting NGL reserves by productive capacity is that, failing construction of such capacity, the potential NGL content of the reservoir may be produced as gas or oil and thus irrevocably lose its character as NGL.

Since natural gas reserves as published exclude NGL, no adjustment is needed when the reserves are expressed in heat values, for by convention wet gas, that is, gas inclusive of the NGL portion of gas, is taken to contain 1,075 Btu per cubic foot, but dry or stripped gas only 1,035 Btu. There is thus no double-counting involved when natural gas reserves are matched against natural gas demand, as long as the Btu factor of 1,035 is used, since demand also is conceived in terms of dry gas of 1,035 Btu/cubic foot heat content.[30]

In terms of volume rather than heat value, NGL in this country have been estimated to occur naturally at an average rate of 60 barrels per million cubic feet.[31] The currently feasible recovery factor is at least 51 barrels, or 85 per cent of the potential. Applied to an estimate of future gas recoverability of 1,200 trillion cubic feet, this would yield over 60 billion barrels of NGL yet to be recovered, equal to perhaps some 20 per cent of crude oil to be recovered; at 1,700 billion cubic feet, recoverability would be more nearly 85 billion barrels. In one respect, this would be a conservative estimate, as deeper drilling would be expected to raise the NGL content, through greater occurrence of condensates. In another respect, however, the acceptance of an 85 per cent recoverability factor presupposes installation of a type of equipment found today in only a few of the largest and most elaborate stripping facilities. In those, recovery appears to be about twice as high as the national average, based upon an informal check with in-

dustry sources. It is this gap between the large, efficient NGL producers and the mass of the "run-of-the-mill" installations that holds the key to increased NGL availability in the future.

Following the technique employed in the appraisal of oil and gas resources, we can now compare the NGL resources still to be recovered—60 to 85 billion barrels—with cumulative demand. The latter, as we have seen, does not in many instances constitute a demand for NGL. In the case of natural gasoline, for example, the demand is for motor fuel, whether derived from crude oil or gas. The NGL demand estimates derived as part of oil and gas demand projections are to that extent abstractions. They are useful only in terms of the separate availability projection and for the increasing range of products in the LPG family that have markets which overlap only partially or not at all with those of refined oil products.

Taking the NGL demand projections, then, at face value, we find that Medium demand totals some 30 billion barrels for the forty-year period, or 40 to 60 per cent of the estimated recoverable resources, and that at the High projection level demand would approach some 50 billion barrels, or 60 to 80 per cent of estimated recoverable resources.

The greater ease in supply here suggested, unless caused by the utilization of an extraction factor that is beyond economical reach, could help somewhat in easing any incipient supply tightness in oil, in that additional natural gasoline rather than a constant percentage, as assumed in the projections, could be channeled into use as motor fuel. However, the quantities involved, a maximum of 30 billion barrels in excess of demand for the forty-year period, are small in terms of projected oil demand of 10 billion barrels per year at the end of the century (see Table 20–2).

Finally, as discussed in Chapters 15 and 17, the availability of natural gas liquids is a rather elastic concept in that even current technology is capable of so breaking down the structure of crude oil that a major portion of it could be turned into the forms of hydrocarbon that comprise them. Thus, the comparisons here made have only limited significance and will, with

---

30. There is question, though, as to the correctness of the wet gas factor. Detailed calculations made by Teitelbaum for 1959 suggest that the wet gas may have a content of 1,100 Btu. (Perry D. Teitelbaum, *Energy Production and Consumption in the United States: An Analytical Study Based on 1954 Data,* Bureau of Mines Report of Investigations 5821 [Washington: U.S. Bureau of Mines and Resources for the Future, 1961].) But for our purposes in this broad study the conventional figure of 1,075 Btu per cubic foot of wet gas can be used.

31. B. R. Carney, "Natural Gas Liquids," *Progress in Petroleum Technology* (Washington: American Chemical Society, 1951), p. 255. Presumably because of the widely varying characteristics of gas fields, no other estimate appears to have been publicly ventured; at least none has come to our attention.

advancing technology, become less rather than more meaningful.

Coal

The coal resources of the United States—of the order of 1.7 trillion tons—are of a magnitude that dwarfs the requirements of even forty years of rising demand. Current recovery methods, according to recent Department of the Interior estimates,[32] would allow over 200 billion tons to be mined at current prices. Since the production required to meet the projected forty-year demand is of the order of 25 billion tons in the Medium projection, rising to 36 billion tons in the High, we need not concern ourselves here with the details of concept or derivation of these estimates.[33]

As far as cost is concerned, however, coal at the mine mouth is a far cry from coal at the place of consumption. Because of its bulk, coal suffers a heavy increase in cost in transportation, which currently amounts, on the average, to some 70 per cent of value at the mine.[34] To a large extent the price of delivered as against produced coal will of course depend on transportation policy, that is, on rates established for coal by its principal carriers, with government concurrence, compared with rates for competing fuels. Since the increase in annual coal demand developed in Chapters 10 and 15 is a moderate one (less than a doubling in forty years in the Medium assumption and a quadrupling in the High), it would seem that pressure on existing transportation facilities would be moderate. In addition, the anticipated concentration of coal demand in fewer uses—basically electricity generation and the metallurgical industries—would seem to favor the emergence of consumer-oriented types and policies of transportation that not only would prevent cost increases but might even bring

about cost reduction. One of these would be the linking of coal mines to utilities and possibly other consumers by pipelines that would carry a slurry of coal and water. The existing 108-mile line that brings coal to the Cleveland Electric Illuminating Company has by now successfully passed its test on the score of both technical feasibility and economic merit. More ambitious projects, such as the movement of West Virginia coal to several Atlantic seaboard utilities by way of a 24-inch pipeline, are in advanced stages of experimentation, with feasibility strongly suggested. However, no analysis of the impact of such a development is as yet possible. Certainly, it could assume major importance, especially to the extent that the slurry is directly fed to boilers. Finally, public transportation policy, shaped by competing interests of coal producers, railroads, coal consumers, and local, state, and federal authorities, would play an important part.

Another development that would save transportation costs is the expansion of long-distance high-voltage power lines. With decreasing need for closeness to power consumers, the generator could be located near the coal. Also, any increase in coal transportation cost might well be offset by developments in coal cleaning and preparation at the mine, which would represent a cost saving to the consumer. Thus, it is difficult to see why delivered coal should undergo any price changes other than those that reflect cost changes at the mine, and here the continuing advances in cost-saving mechanization, the consequent past record of increases in output per man-day, and the likelihood that coal wages will in the future increase with the same relative speed as wages generally, rather than faster as they did for a long period after the mid-thirties, all suggest relative stability of cost.

If the future were to bring a rising price of oil and gas, accompanied by a stable price of coal—delivered to identical classes of consumers—then a switch to coal, which is always a potential move in parts of industry and especially in power generation, could become an actuality and the substitution effects on which the High projection for coal is partly based would come into operation.

---

32. See for example, U.S. Geological Survey Bulletin 1136, and Department of Interior Report to Joint Committee on Atomic Energy, Vol. 4 of *Review of the International Atomic Policies and Programs of the United States* (2nd McKinney Report), Joint Committee Print, 86th Cong., 2nd Sess., October 1960.

33. For such details, see Schurr, Netschert, *et al., op. cit.,* Chapter 8.

34. It is important not to ignore the "average" qualifications, for there are significant areas—to mention only the recent seventeen-year agreement for coal delivery to a new TVA steam plant—where the mine-to-plant distance is but five miles and the transport cost correspondingly low.

There are, however, limits to such an eventuality. The geographic pattern of fuel occurrence tends to pre-empt given areas for given fuels; while a local situation may permit instances, it is hard to visualize, for some time at least, any substantial encroachment by coal on gas in the Gulf states or on oil in California. Similarly, aggressive development of Canadian natural gas resources could conceivably result in the pre-emption by gas of increasing territory in the hotly contested northern Midwest. Second, nuclear power generation, expected to gain momentum in the late seventies, is likely to make its impact with disproportionate strength in areas where fuel costs are high, principally areas not now predominantly served by coal. In that event, the area in which coal could widen its appeal by pricing oil and gas out of the market would be reduced; whereas one can visualize coal displacing oil and gas as alternative boiler fuels, it is difficult to imagine any one of the three as an alternative to a nuclear power plant once the latter has been found economical for the region. Finally, in most industries fuel is a minor expense item whose choice is affected by many considerations other than cost; therefore, relative price changes have less impact than in the very sensitive area of electric power production.

Even if coal were to make greater inroads on gas use in electricity generation than are assumed in our demand projection, the results would not affect the coal projection greatly. By 1980, gas-based generation is assumed to amount to only 18 per cent of all generation, and by 2000 this percentage is assumed to drop to less than 10 per cent. Thus, even the transfer of a substantial fraction of these market shares would not raise coal consumption significantly.

The effects on coal use in manufacturing might be somewhat greater, except for the iron and steel industry, for in our demand estimates we have proceeded on the assumption that in this sector coal would in any event lose little of its predominance. With the impressive showing made by natural gas in recent years and the corresponding loss in the position of coal, we have pictured coal as continuing to lose out vis-à-vis gas in the industrial fuel market. It is there that the tightening resource position of oil and gas, compared to the easy position of coal, could have a powerful effect on the competitive position. The results could be significant: if coal should make a stronger showing and retain for itself a share of the industrial fuel market more nearly equal to that held in 1960, when it supplied 25 per cent, the difference in annual coal consumption would amount to about 100 million tons in 1980 and some 300 million tons in 2000 in the Medium projection. Apart from the violence of the assumption,[35] even such levels would not lead us to question coal's availability at current prices, for the cumulative projected demand for coal under these conditions would not exceed 8 billion tons, still a small quantity in terms of the resource position.

Thus, the coal position may be viewed as providing a cushion capable of absorbing large chunks of industrial demand that gas and oil might find receding from their reach because of relative price increases. The rise from current levels would be moderate and spread over a sufficient period to provide time to overcome any obstacles that might develop at either the mining or the transportation end of the industry. Such problems, one may guess, might be largely of a regional nature, for example, as the Appalachian fields begin to show signs of exhaustion and the center of the coal mining industry shifts in a westward direction. While one would not have to assume anything comparable in impact to the southern migration of the New England textile industry, it would be reasonable to expect that those few industries for which fuel costs represent a crucial element would then locate plants nearer the source of coal, a tendency which even in the years since World War II has been a force in a good deal of industrial location, for instance in the choice of Ohio River valley sites.

While most of the above considerations are based upon the stipulation of a growing competitive advantage of coal due to oil and gas stringencies, the accompanying influx of imported oil and gas or entry of shale oil and tar

---

35. Since coal already supplies most of the fuel in steel making, its share in the remainder of industrial life would have to rise spectacularly.

sand oil and gas would act to limit the advantage of coal, depending upon the price at which these substitutes would appear and with regional differentiations that are difficult to specify. Coal gasification, on the other hand, would constitute one of the most powerful aids to coal production imaginable. This is discussed above in the section dealing with natural gas.

Hydroelectric Power

The absolute limits of the nation's potential hydroelectric capacity are those calculated from the average flow of all streams and the total vertical descent of each. This maximum potential for the United States (exclusive of Alaska and Hawaii) has been put at no less than 230 and no more than 390 million kw.[36] The concept is of use only in conveying some idea as to the likely order of magnitude of the resource. It is quite clear, however, that large portions of this purely theoretical capacity will never be developed. Absence of suitable dam sites eliminates a great deal of the stream flow from practical consideration, and competition with other economic and social objectives rules out much additional flow as a source of electricity generation. The Federal Power Commission, using a much more limited concept of the term, has recently set the potential hydro capacity of the forty-eight contiguous states at around 127 million kw, the component parts of which would operate for various fractions of the year.[37] Installed capacity, including non-utility, at the beginning of 1960 was 31.9 million kw.

As noted in Chapter 15 in the discussion of the share of the electricity supply that might be contributed by falling water, our projections for 1980 indicate a total installed capacity of 65 million kw, with a production of about 280 billion kwh. These figures, which are based largely on FPC estimates made in 1960, must be considered as relatively removed from controversy since they rest upon sites developed and licensed or planned to be developed.[38]

It is more difficult to look beyond 1980, since projected developments are far less certain for time spans of such length. Total capacity estimated to be developed by 1980 would represent over one-half of the U.S. potential (as estimated by FPC), excluding Alaska and Hawaii. As the technically and economically more reasonable sites are developed, increasing doubts arise as to the merits of remaining sites.

In the light of these findings, we hesitate in this study to project hydro capacity in the forty-eight states much beyond 90 million kw at any time in the future.[39] Potential hydro capacity differs, after all, from mineral reserves in that the latter are partly hidden, whereas all rivers are mapped and their flow and site characteristics known. Surprises can come only from altered circumstances that change the evaluation of a site previously considered unfeasible. It is doubtful that there are many quantitatively significant sites in that category today.

There is the additional fact that between 1980 and 2000 the rapid unfolding of nuclear power generation may reasonably be expected to occur. To the extent that nuclear power generation is less location-bound and more evenly available throughout the year than is hydro power, aggressive nuclear power development could have a dampening effect upon further hydro expansion, especially if nuclear power should become available at rates competitive with those now in prospect for the less cheaply exploited hydro sites. Finally, the uneven geographic distribution of technically promising but hitherto undeveloped hydro sites might act as a brake on hydro development.

On the other hand, the use of hydro installations, equipped perhaps with pumped storage facilities, to supplement nuclear stations run at a high plant-capacity factor is not an unlikely development. Such peaking facilities are well within the range of major future uses of hydro installations. Also, one can expect

---

36. Schurr, Netschert, *et al., op. cit.,* p. 476.
37. Federal Power Commission, *Hydroelectric Power Resources of the United States Developed and Undeveloped, 1960* (Washington, undated).
38. See, however, Appendix Table A15–4 for comment.
39. The Geological Survey Study of Potential and Developed Waterpower published in 1955 as Geological Survey Circular 367 raises questions of interpretation in terms of economic feasibility that are discussed in Schurr, Netschert, *et al., op. cit.,* pp. 445–62, and are not dealt with here, since, whatever the concepts or assumptions, hydro power is too small an element in future energy supply to warrant this degree of detail.

that new hydro generation plants will continue to be built as part of multiple purpose water development projects in which power production is only one of several objectives.

On balance, we can see no reason not to go along with the FPC estimate of generation of 360 billion kwh in 2000, to be derived from an installed capacity of 90 million kw, slightly above the 85 million kw proposed in the same document.[40] While this would represent a substantial decline in the rate of growth, as compared with current growth and even with the projected rate of growth between 1960 and 1980, the gradual approach to the potential, however defined, makes this reasonable. Such a schedule of production would fill 7½ per cent of our projected Medium demand for electricity in the year 2000.

Even if it were feasible to exploit by 2000 the entire 127 million-kw capacity potential estimated by FPC, which would produce some 530 billion kwh, only little over 10 per cent of projected electricity demand would be met by falling water. Thus, even under these extremely unlikely conditions, hydro electricity, though it may continue to play a dominating role in regions with unusually favorable sites, is bound to become a factor of decreasing significance in the nation's power economy.

Unconventional Sources

Apart from allowing for the gradual emergence of a large-scale nuclear energy sector in the electricity industry, and providing for improved efficiency in both production and consumption of energy, the approach taken throughout this study has been essentially conservative. Nor could it be different when the goal is a series of quantitative estimates. The future of the new uses, sources, and conversion methods of energy is far too uncertain to permit a numerical approach.

However, inability to quantify the consequences of new techniques does not bar one from considering the direction in which one or the other development would shift the pattern of energy demand and supply.

40. FPC release, dated December 17, 1959; cf. Appendix Table A15–4. In the same tabulation hydro potential was put at 122 million kw.

The New Technology

Some of the potential changes may be viewed merely as special cases of efficiency changes. For example, the demand projection for transportation rests essentially upon conventional means: automobiles, trucks, airplanes, ships, railroads, pipelines. Changes in design—multifuel engines, monorails, new types of short-distance air-borne vehicles—all would essentially be modifications of current modes; with exceptions such as exotic fuels for rocket propulsion or nuclear storage batteries, they would ultimately remain dependent upon conventional energy sources. This does not exclude inter-fuel shifts. Perfection of a rechargeable battery-operated automobile, for example, would ease the demand for oil and add to the demand for electricity, and—in the more remote future—for nuclear energy.

Likely consequences of other developments in engine design are less speculative. A switch from gasoline to diesel engines, on the way for some time now in trucks, but not yet in passenger cars, would reduce fuel requirements, eventually by as much as perhaps one-third to one-half—equivalent to some 10 to 15 per cent of all oil consumption. Development of the gas turbine, on the other hand, would work in the opposite direction: fuel requirements would rise, but not necessarily cost, since lower-type oil fuels could be utilized. The turbine cannot be excluded as a commercially successful passenger car engine and a possible booster of petroleum demand. Finally, there is the multi-fuel engine, with high efficiency and low-quality fuel demand. Though still beset by problems and not presently considered for mass transportation purposes, it could in a span of forty years easily come to fill that position. From all that is known, the multi-fuel engine would be similar in amount of fuel consumption to the diesel engine. Thus, except for high-consumption gas turbines (whose fuel hunger would no doubt decrease in time), all other potential design changes point to lower demand, and all, including the gas turbine, would be satisfied with a lower-cut type of refined product, somewhere in the light distillate class.

The one potential successor of the internal

combustion engine that would signify a more radical displacement of petroleum would be long-life batteries, specifically those versions that use materials other than hydrocarbon-based and whose electric recharge needs are small. Such batteries, which are principally a modification of the traditional storage battery, employing nickel, selenium, and other materials, have been tested, used in special applications, and may be expected to receive increasing prominence. At present their bulk, cost, and limited range seem to severely circumscribe their usefulness.

Fuel cells, which utilize the interaction of gases in the direct generation of electricity, have the advantage of high efficiency with which they can transform chemicals into electric energy. (See Figure 20–6.)[41] The effect of

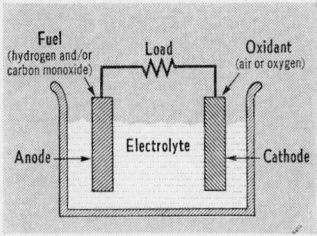

Figure 20–6. Fuel cell conversion method.

this promising development upon fuel demand is quite uncertain at this time, as is its range of applicability. In a manner somewhat analogous to the generation of electricity by the chemical reactions at the two electrodes of a storage battery, the fuel cell produces an electric current by reacting hydrogen gas supplied to one electrode with oxygen gas supplied to the other. A fused salt at a temperature of several hundred degrees separates the electrodes and forms a medium in which the reactions take place and through which the current passes. If the proper electrical connections are employed, power can be delivered from the cell to an external circuit and equipment. The efficiency of converting fuel energy to electricity in this unit is limited only by thermal

41. Figures 20–6, 7, 8, and 9 are reproduced with the permission of the General Electric Company, from slides accompanying a paper presented by J. J. William Brown at the Fifth Electrical World Heating Conference, 1961.

and electrical losses which in theory are very small.

It is too early to gauge either the probability of technical success in developing a commercially practical fuel cell or the approximate cost of electricity produced in this way. Even high efficiency could not make the process economically attractive without a drastic reduction in cost of hydrogen. But this is some way off. Even the necessary or desirable fuel gas components have not yet been determined. Some success along this line, however, has been achieved by use of a mixture of hydrogen and carbon monoxide known as water gas. This gas mixture is readily produced from coal or coke by reaction with steam. An over-all efficiency in energy conversion from coal to power of 50 per cent would be possible even in small units, substantially above current top efficiency in electricity generation.

Other research is directed toward the use of natural gas in a fuel cell. If the favorable preliminary experimental results of natural gas combustion in a fuel cell can be achieved on a practical scale, over-all conversion of chemical energy to electric energy could be doubled from its present rate in steam turbines of 35 to 40 per cent; and if the problems connected with the direct use of natural gas in the fuel cell should prove too great, this fuel might be converted to another form through one of several "cracking" processes producing hydrogen, carbon monoxide, and other compounds which might be more readily utilized in the cell. Here, too, research is at so early a stage that prediction of technical or economic success is impracticable, but the possibilities are good enough to have stimulated a great deal of research effort by fuel companies and independent laboratories. Planning cannot yet be based on assumptions of future fuel-to-electric efficiencies above 50 per cent, but conversions of 80 per cent, already achieved experimentally, should be regarded as attainable on a broader scale in the next two decades. There is no reason why the fuel cell might not eventually find employment in a range of uses from automobiles to power stations. Application in large stationary use might be the first to develop since no problem of gas storage would be involved, but even the developers envisage only a slow application to routine surface vehicles.

There is no reason to contemplate at this time the substitution of nuclear energy in motor vehicle propulsion. Size of engine, hazards, and waste disposal alone are formidable obstacles. Of more immediate interest, though of less quantitative consequence, is the likely use of non-conventional engines in marine—and perhaps air-borne—transportation. Our demand projections indicate that even a complete switch to nuclear-propelled ships by 2000 would reduce oil consumption by only 5 per cent. Aviation might raise this to 6½ per cent. From an over-all point of view, this would neither make nor break adequacy of hydrocarbon resources.

More readily calculable is the potential impact of nuclear energy, allowed for in our projections of electric energy generation but not in those pertaining to industrial process heating. Using the work done by George Perazich in his estimates for the National Planning Association,[42] we would judge that by 1980 the effect of this type of switchover would be minor, relieving the pressure on natural gas by perhaps 3 to 4 per cent, and similarly reducing the demand on coal. The substitution effect for oil would be negligible, because of its low use in industry, and since no significant relative increase is foreseen in the industrial use of oil, a similar pattern would hold true for the post-1980 years.

On the other hand, nuclear process heat could assist significantly in relieving any developing strain in the supply of gas for industrial purposes. To illustrate, a 50 per cent replacement of gas by nuclear-generated heat in 2000 would reduce total gas demand by approximately 25 per cent. This would reduce the 2000 level of demand, in the Medium projection, to approximately the size it would otherwise reach by 1985. In other words, a substitution of that order of magnitude would radically dampen further growth of gas demand after 1980. The big question, to which no answer is here attempted, is whether the generation of nuclear-generated heat can be made available on a sufficiently small scale to become a practical source of heat for even half of U.S. industrial demand.[43]

When we have dealt, even in summary fashion, with nuclear energy, we have gone as far as we can in quantitative consideration of unconventional sources. Beyond are nuclear fusion—the peaceful counterpart of the H-bomb, solar energy, wind, ocean tides, geothermal energy from hot springs or steam vents, and the temperature differences of ocean water at different heights. While most of these may have limited future usefulness in locations offering special advantages, fusion and solar energy have received more serious consideration—fusion because of the practically unlimited raw material and the absence of radioactive debris, and solar energy equally because of the universal availability of the source and the possibility of small-scale and low-cost equipment. Which of the two will attain significant commercial status first is impossible to tell, though it must be said that practical applications of solar energy do exist, whereas fusion is still deep in the laboratory stage. On the other hand, the payoff in perfecting commercially useful fusion is so high that we are likely to see much progress in the coming decades.

In contrast to other new forms of energy, solar energy is likely to find its application principally in residential use for space heating and warm water supply. Even now, solar water heaters are in use in Florida, and there are isolated instances of the experimental type of solar-heated houses. It is, however, a long way, in this country at any rate, from assuming commercial proportions. George Löf, a pioneer in the field, speculates that "400,000 solar (heated and cooled) homes might be in operation by 1984.[44] Even if one were to accept this outlook, it would not significantly affect the national energy demand picture, but it would help relieve any emerging strain on gas, both as a direct heating factor and by way of electricity.

42. George Perazich, *Nuclear Process Heat in Industry* (Washington: National Planning Association, 1958).

43. Cf. Chapter 10, p. 217.
44. George O. G. Löf, "Solar Energy," *The Petroleum Engineer,* January 1959, p. 201.

Direct generation of energy, that is, elimination of the steam boiler-turbine-generator detour, is a distinct possibility within the next forty years. Thermoelectricity, generated by the heating of two types of metals welded together, has been produced on a small scale and at low efficiencies.[45] (See Figures 20-7 and 8.) The simplicity of the operation would justify its application at efficiencies far below those achieved in modern conventional power plants and would be especially welcome in small-capacity installations. However, much improvement is required before even moderately high efficiencies are reached. At the same time, this method is theoretically useful

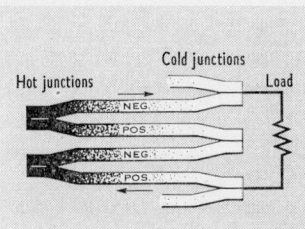

Figure 20-7. Thermoelectric conversion method.

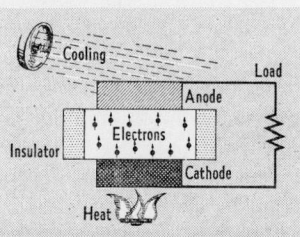

Figure 20-8. Thermionic conversion method.

as a source of power supply in vehicles. It would not only have the mechanical advantages of an electric drive but, as in the case of other substitutes for the gasoline motor, it would be able to operate on a lower-cut heat source (kerosene for instance) and thus counteract rising fuel prices that might be caused by a tightening in the petroleum supply picture.

45. A related method, referred to as thermionics (see Figure 20-8), currently is more promising as a cooling or heating device than as a means of generating electricity.

Another promising way of generating electricity without the steam cycle is magneto-hydrodynamics, consisting essentially in the passage of high-velocity gas through a strong magnetic field. (See Figure 20-9.) The attraction of this method lies in its mechanical simplicity, permitted by the absence of steam boiler, turbine, and generator, and in the high efficiencies that can be reached, perhaps up to 60 per cent. Fuel demand would be smaller

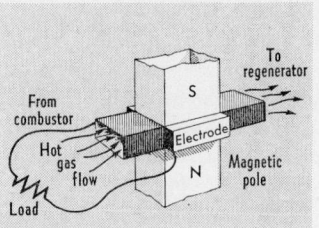

Figure 20-9. MHD conversion method.

than in conventional processes, even though far higher temperatures would have to be achieved than in the most modern steam electric plants. Even combinations of magneto-hydrodynamics and nuclear energy are possible. Estimates are that no less than ten and no more than twenty years will pass before MHD becomes a commercially feasible venture. For the time being, however, all that this prospect tells us is that the heat rates used in the conversion calculations of this study are not too daring, and might even be conservative.

The use of nuclear explosives underground is being investigated principally as a shortcut to recovering shale oil by *in situ* retorting. It could also be useful in recovering residual petroleum from formations not producible by conventional means. Finally, thought has been given to using an underground explosion for making available geothermal heat. Water would be allowed to percolate through the crushed rock down to the hot zone where steam at 400° F. would be generated and brought to the surface through drilled wells. The bulk of the energy thus produced would be not from the heat of the explosion but from the geothermal heat. No doubt, these new techniques will be greatly advanced during the next two decades. They could substantially ease any pressures on conventional sources of energy that might develop.

Uranium

Any attempt to measure the adequacy of the resources of fissionable material—uranium and thorium—requires knowledge about the "conversion factors" that specify the amount of fissionable material corresponding to a given level of power generation.

To illustrate, it is currently estimated that U.S. uranium reserves, in terms of U_3O_8, are of the order of magnitude of some 250,000 short tons. This quantity, at present levels of technology, may have an energy equivalent slightly above total U.S. energy consumption in 1960; or, at a more highly developed technology, of ten times 1960 consumption or at a highly advanced technology including so-called "breeding" (production of fissionable material during generation) a hundred times 1960 energy consumption. When a forty-year period is involved and sharp advances in technology must be anticipated, it becomes extremely difficult to strike some kind of balance among these greatly different developments.

To cite a realistic example, it can be estimated that a reactor of the Dresden type, now in operation in Illinois, requires 1.5 short tons of U_3O_8 per net electrical megawatt (1,000 kw); this includes both actual loading of the reactor and pipeline supplies to permit this loading level. Other reactors may need more, perhaps up to 2 short tons. In current-type reactors it may be very roughly assumed that about 50 kwh of electricity can be generated for every gram of uranium (measured in terms of U_3O_8) lost in the reactor. Thus in estimating uranium requirements that support a given amount of electric energy it is necessary to account for inventory and burnup requirements.

The Medium electricity projection for the year 2000 calls for, roughly, 2500 billion kwh to be produced in nuclear reactors. Assuming an 80 per cent plant factor, this would presuppose installed capacity of, say, 350,000 megawatts. At 1.5 short tons of U_3O_8 per megawatt, inventory requirements at that time (the total amount of uranium tied up inside reactors plus supporting amounts in various phases of the supply and distribution pipeline) would be 500,000 tons. Assuming that the pipeline requirement could be severely cut down, this amount might be reducible to perhaps 350,000 tons. In addition, uranium lost in burnup must be replaced. At the rate of 50 kwh per gram, and with projected cumulative power generation between 1960 and 2000 of roughly 30,000 billion kwh, uranium requirements (always in terms of U_3O_8 contained in uranium ore) would run to 660,000 short tons. Thus, the projected generation, at the low efficiency assumed would call for no less than 1 million short tons of U_3O_8, or four times currently estimated U.S. reserves.

Atomic technologists have no hesitancy in predicting that efficiency between now and the end of the century will increase greatly. There is no question in their mind that putting it even at twice the current level is a gross underestimation of future trends. When we recall that the energy potential of one gram of uranium equals that of three tons of coal and that, at efficiencies even now attainable in steam-electric plants, one gram of uranium is therefore a potential generator of 8,000–9,000 kwh of electricity, the range of possibilities is strikingly illustrated, for on those assumptions it would take only 4,000–5,000 tons of uranium to generate the 30,000 billion kwh of cumulative electricity projected for 1960–2000. In a sense, anything between these two extremes is open for exploration and exploitation by advancing technology.

Improvements in efficiency which would raise energy production per unit of uranium by three or four times above the current level would make current U.S. reserves adequate to see us through the end of the century. When reserves of thorium are added and when to this are added the potential reserves of both uranium and thorium, it becomes clear that the advance of reactor technology is a far more crucial development to watch than the varying estimates of ore reserves. Perhaps ten years from now it will become more rewarding to shift to an analysis of reserves.

chapter
21
NONFUEL MINERALS

IN THIS CHAPTER WE CONSIDER the outlook for adequacy of the metallic minerals and some of the important non-metallic minerals. Discussion of the latter is quite brief, mainly because there are few indications of critical supply problems between now and the end of the century.

Among the metals, most of our attention is given to steel and its alloys and to five major nonferrous metals: copper, aluminum, lead, zinc, and tin. For each of these we follow our usual pattern of comparing forty-year projections of requirements with estimates of resource availability. In the light of the nation's increasing imports that already are important for several minerals, considerable attention is paid to current production and estimates of future availability in other parts of the world. We have not attempted such projections for the minor metals, several of which have come into use only recently; their history is too short and their future too uncertain. Instead, we have sought to summarize the industrial structure of these metals, the circumstances of their oc-

currence and production, their principal uses, and the position of the United States for each of them.

We conclude the chapter with some general observations on future technology and possible new sources of minerals. Although quantitatively our supply-demand analyses for specific minerals are necessarily within the framework of current or clearly emerging technology, there is every reason to expect continued gains in methods of finding, extracting, and processing minerals. It is this broad advance that apparently can ease a number of otherwise stringent supply situations indicated by the formal projections.

Throughout the chapter principal attention is given to the Medium projections of requirements. Where these raise problems of adequacy nothing is gained by looking also at the High projection, but something may be learned by checking the position in the Low projection. On the other hand, where adequacy to meet Medium requirements seems assured, the High projection helps to test the degree of confi-

---

RELATED MATERIAL: Requirements for construction, Chapter 4, pp. 121–27, and appendix, pp. 629–32; for transportation, Chapter 5, pp. 142–45, and appendix, pp. 656–59, 663, 667; for durable goods, Chapter 6, pp. 155–57, and appendix, pp. 680–84; for containers, Chapter 7, pp. 161–64, and appendix, pp. 693–95; for military goods, Chapter 9, pp. 177–83, and appendix, pp. 715–21. Demand for metals, Chapter 16, pp. 293–316, and appendix, pp. 859–939; for chemicals, Chapter 17, pp. 325–29; for fertilizer, Chapter 18, pp. 337–43.

dence one may put into the conclusion of adequacy. All three levels are shown in Tables 21–3 and 21–12.

The effect of stockpiling has not been considered except insofar as it has biased the statistics of the past. For one thing, data on the amounts of material held in the different classes of stockpile have been released only gradually and too recently to be taken into account. Secondly, there is an important question of quality to be resolved. Undetermined portions of stockpiles may, upon analysis, turn out to be smaller in tonnage of equivalent standard specifications than is indicated by tonnage figures as they come to be released. Apart from these questions, it is clear that with few exceptions the amounts hitherto acquired are insignificant compared with requirements over a forty-year period. Cobalt stockpiles may be as large as a decade's requirements. Molybdenum stockpiles may also be larger than would be needed to meet the demand of two or three years, but in general the judgments given in this chapter will not be affected.

Concepts and Methods

The depletion or "wasting asset" concept— the idea that there is a finite stock in nature which is ineluctably reduced toward zero through the production process—has long been an important element of public policy concerning mineral resources. The validity of the depletion concept when applied to individual mines or deposits is undeniable, but it is only recently that the limited applicability in the social sense has been appreciated. Although "ore" has for many years been defined by the mining industry as material from which the contained raw metal or mineral can be extracted profitably at any given time, only with the report of the President's Materials Policy Commission in 1952 was the public made aware of the significance of this flexible definition over time in assessing the national mineral resource position. (The similar efforts of the U.S. Geological Survey and Bureau of Mines in 1947, and of certain mineral experts even earlier, did not attract public attention.) The Commission report emphasized that if the reserves of a particular

metal appeared inadequate for the long-term future, and if the prospects for future discovery of additional reserves were also poor, the nation would not "run out" of the metal, but would at worst be faced with rising costs.

Every metal occurs in nature under a wide variety of conditions which determine the cost of producing the metal. Given the circumstances of natural occurrence, the lower the cost criteria on which the material is to be classified as ore, the more rigorous are the conditions that must be met. Theoretically, an ore body that involved the absolute minimum costs of exploitation would be a large body of pure ore minerals, situated at the surface with no overburden so that the cheapest possible mining methods could be used, and located at the best possible site with respect to transportation and markets.

Such ore bodies exist only in theory. But with the progressive relaxation of the criteria— lower grade, higher percentage of deleterious impurities, greater depth, poorer location, and all the circumstances that increase the difficulties of winning the metal from its ore and delivering it to market in a usable state and thus make for higher cost—an increasing number of ore bodies, both known and unknown, with a larger cumulative metal content, are included within the criteria.

Thus, if the reserves of a particular metal within a country or in the world as a whole do approach exhaustion, the most that can happen in the absence of improved technology is higher cost for that metal, as sources with lower grade, greater depth, or other disadvantages are used. This does not mean that the rise in cost will necessarily be small, or that it will be economically insignificant. The spectrum of conditions of occurrence is not necessarily continuous, so that the cost change could be abrupt and even economically harmful. The general point is, however, that from the social viewpoint depletion is not absolute but is a matter of cost.

If this is true, one might expect to find instances of the cost effect of depletion in the historical record. But for the world as a whole an indisputable example of this effect has yet to be found. This is partly due to the fact that price, the only statistical measure of cost over the long term, is a very inaccurate measure and does not yield unequivocal results.[1] Of far greater importance, however, has been the countervailing influence of technological progress. Superior techniques for making a metal available to society, from methods of discovery through those of mining, extraction and refining, have conduced to lower cost. A technological innovation at a given time may result in lower costs of exploitation for current reserves and, in addition, may make possible the exploitation of previously potential ore at the same costs. By thus creating ore out of potential ore previously known to exist, it is even possible that over the short term technology may "create" more reserves than are discovered in the same period.

Against this wide-ranging benefit from technology must be placed the implications of the present level of world demand for many minerals and the prospects for future growth in that demand. Already, demand in many instances has reached such high absolute levels that past experience in maintaining an adequate current supply at no higher real cost may not be relevant in assessing the future. All indications of future economic growth point to truly enormous future demands, both annually and cumulatively. A large annual demand requires a large productive capacity, which in turn calls for a certain minimum reserve level to sustain such capacity. A large cumulative demand requires either the discovery of additional reserves to replace those used up in production or the conversion of potential ore into ore reserves through technology, or both, if real cost is not to rise. Estimated future demands are now attaining such magnitude that the adequacy of reserve discovery and of the effect of technology on potential ore usability cannot be taken for granted.

A note on terminology.[2] Mining technologists apply the term "reserves" to that portion of the known natural stock of a mineral raw material that can be worked commercially with the technology and economic conditions that currently exist and can be expected to exist in the short-term future. The material itself is termed "ore." They further distinguish categories of reserves by the certainty of knowledge of their existence. Such terms as "measured" and "indicated" describe reserves for which there is direct physical evidence on which to base quantitative measurement or estimation. "Inferred" reserves are those believed to exist on the basis of indirect, largely geological, evidence.

The distinction between measured and indicated reserves, on the one hand, and inferred, on the other, is important because of its relation to the concept of "discovery." The true total content of a mineral deposit is commonly known only after mining operations have exhausted the reserves in the deposit. A large mine usually has a lifetime of decades, so that it is uneconomic to "prove up" the total reserve content. Once the annual capacity of operations has been decided on, reserves are proved up only to the extent necessary to assure continuity of operations for several years ahead. Thus the bulk of the reserves in a working mine are normally in the inferred category and are transferred to the measured and indicated categories by current mining operations and by limited probing beyond those operations.

In a sense this transfer from the inferred to the other two categories may be considered "discovery," and it is sometimes referred to in this manner. In addition, there is true discovery, which consists in finding new deposits of ore bodies and extensions of known ore bodies, the existence of which was not even surmised.

The strict definition of reserves employs the criteria of current knowledge of their existence and current workability. The somewhat contradictory term "undiscovered reserves" is introduced here to emphasize the existence of

1. O. C. Herfindahl, *Copper Costs and Prices: 1870–1957* (Baltimore: Johns Hopkins Press and Resources for the Future, Inc., 1959), and "The Long-Run Cost of Minerals," *Three Studies in Minerals Economics* (Washington: Resources for the Future, 1961).

2. For a complete discussion of the concepts behind this terminology, see F. Blondel and S. G. Lasky, "Mineral Reserves and Mineral Resources," *Economic Geology*, Vol. LI, No. 7 (November, 1956), pp. 686–97; and Sam H. Schurr, Bruce C. Netschert, *et al.*, *Energy in the American Economy, 1850–1975* (Baltimore: Johns Hopkins Press and Resources for the Future, Inc., 1960), pp. 295–300.

material not yet discovered which if discovered would meet the criterion of current workability.

Material that cannot be worked under present economic and technological circumstances is termed "potential ore." This term covers both material that is known to exist and material that may be discovered in the future. Some of today's ore was known to exist in the past but was at that time potential ore; and much of today's ore, if it had been discovered in the past, would have been classified as potential ore at that time. Subsequent technological advances, and in some instances changed economic conditions, have converted that material into ore. The significance of today's potential ore is that it may become ore under the different technological and economic circumstances that will prevail in the future.

The distinction between reserves and known potential ore is rather hazy in an individual mining operation, and it is unfortunately even less determinable for a country or wider area. Many variables determine to what extent the material in a given deposit is or is not ore: the geological circumstances of the deposit, the mineralogy, the depth, the mining method that can be used, the processing techniques that can win the metal from the ore, the location of the deposit, and so forth. It is not possible to say which of these may be the major determinants; each occurrence of ore has its unique features. For this reason it is difficult to generalize the criteria that establish material as ore, especially between countries. In this study we have taken grade, or percentage metal content of the material, as the common denominator. One may generalize by saying that material above a certain grade is ore, all else is potential ore. Even within a given country this oversimplified definition is subject to many qualifications and is especially difficult to apply to larger areas or the world as a whole. Nevertheless, the distinction between reserves and potential ore is a highly useful one.

If the potential ore is defined as everything other than reserves, then, in concept at least, it includes all material in the environment with any metal content whatsoever. This may be meaningful for some purposes, but what is needed here is a more restricted conceptual level that bears some relationship to the technological progress that can be expected to occur in some definite period—say, by the end of the twentieth century. Such a level is termed the "resources," defined in this instance as the natural stock of the mineral raw material from which will come the supply of the metal within the period considered. Resources thus include both reserves and undiscovered material meeting the present reserve criteria, as well as both known and as yet unknown (undiscovered) potential ore.

If this definition is to be useful for present purposes it must be translatable into quantitative estimates. Unfortunately, there is no way of making a meaningful estimate of the quantity of "resources" so defined. There is no basis for estimating systematically what ores await discovery. There is, however, a useful approximation—the total of all reserves and of all potential ore for which there are quantitative estimates—the material that has been identified, so to speak. This approximation is termed "identified resources."

This chapter attempts to employ these concepts and associated terminology consistently, but complete consistency is impossible. The estimates that are cited and used all too frequently appear in the original with ambiguous terms. Difficulties thus arise from the use of precisely defined terms with ill-defined figures. We believe, nevertheless, that the definitions given above contribute to a better comprehension of future possibilities and probabilities in the materials discussed.

Method of analysis. In the future supply-demand position of the various minerals over the long term, there are three broad categories of possibilities:

(1) reserves are clearly ample to meet indicated needs through the end of the century;

(2) reserves are clearly inadequate to meet those needs;

(3) the situation is ambiguous.

If reserves are clearly adequate there is no reason to expect higher costs because of depletion during the period being considered. If reserves are inadequate or the situation is ambiguous, future needs can be met either through discoveries of additional reserves—which by definition would mean no higher costs—or by turning to what is now potential ore. The pertinent aspects of the latter alternative then become: (*a*) the degree of knowledge concerning resources (i.e., whether currently identified resources are sufficient for indicated needs), and (*b*) the nature of the resources and the effect their utilization would have on costs if the requisite technological advances were not forthcoming. Insofar as possible in the light of current knowledge, we attempt in the rest of this chapter to identify which of the three circumstances appears to exist for each of the minerals.

To answer these questions, the projected U.S. demand for each material from 1960 through 2000 is cumulated and compared with U.S. reserves and resources as currently estimated by the government or by other authoritative sources, to obtain an indication of the needed discoveries, and also is compared with identified resources. Where possible, the potential cost effects of turning to presently potential ore are indicated. In each instance where current domestic production is already insufficient to meet current demand at the prevailing price, a look at world reserves and resources as currently estimated and at world demand are called for. This procedure is extremely crude. Even though the projected U.S. demands rest on clearly spelled-out assumptions, they still contain a substantial share of subjective judgment. Future demand in the rest of the world is more nearly a straight guess, based upon recent growth experience.

On the opposite side of the ledger, the reserve-resource estimates make no allowance for the very wide range in quality that may be represented. The nature and degree of impurities are often passed over, as are the nature and proportion of co-products in some instances. The comparison of cumulated demand with estimated reserves and resources ignores many things. It assumes equal availability of all foreign sources to all countries in the world. It does not allow for locational factors at the processing level that would or could make certain sources uneconomic, or economic only at a higher cost level.

The matching of cumulated demand, as projected, against present reserves does not carry any assumption that a ton of reserves is the equivalent of a ton of output at any given time in the future. On the contrary, it is fully recognized here that reserve depletion is manifested in a decline in productive capacity well before exhaustion is approached. If cumulated demand is, for example, 100 million tons and reserves are 125 million tons, the demand could probably not be met without additions to reserves during the period. Such figures suggest that it would not require much in the way of new discoveries to assure an adequate annual rate of supply. Similarly, if demand totals 100 million tons and reserves are only 25 million tons, it is reasonable to state that discoveries of new reserves must be several times the total of current reserves to meet terminal annual demand levels, or else new reserves will have to be "created" from currently potential ore. Under these circumstances the nature of the lower quality resources becomes a matter of more than academic interest, and the possible effect on costs of resorting to such resources warrants attention even at this time.

The fundamental shortcoming of any attempt to assess the mineral future is the truly meager knowledge of the quantity and nature of mineral resources in general. Information is better in the United States and Europe than elsewhere, but throughout the world the knowledge is inadequate. Reserve data in this country tend to understate the true situation because of a tendency by companies to regard their own figures as confidential information, divulgence of which might harm their competitive position. Although this is possibly less true abroad, there is frequently no way of knowing the criteria by which the reserves are defined, so that data for different countries may not be on comparable bases. All reserve data, from whatever source, tend to reflect engineering caution and, as conservative estimates, are likely to understate the true extent of reserves to an unknown degree.

At the resource level the data situation is worse. Estimates of potential ore everywhere tend to be extrapolations from what few data are available. There is a common lack of definitions and limiting criteria accompanying estimates of what is here termed potential ore, so that it is impossible to judge comparability between countries. Estimates for underdeveloped countries, where direct observations may be entirely absent, depend on the conservatism or optimism of those responsible for the estimate and may be misleading in either direction.

Under the above circumstances it would be inappropriate to strive for detailed and precise conclusions or to use an elegant and sophisticated analytical procedure. Present knowledge can yield only broad indications as to future possibilities, and the analysis should match those limitations.

Metals[3]

As seen in Chapter 16, the demand for metallic minerals may be expected to increase sharply during the next forty years as the population increases and the economy expands. Such a rise in demand would continue a trend that has been in effect for a long time. Until fairly recently the growth in demand was primarily met by increased domestic output. Enough was produced of most metals not only to meet domestic needs, but to provide a significant amount of exports. Since the end of World War II, there has been rapidly increasing reliance on imports, so that today the United States has become a net importer of the basic metals and their ores.

Despite the large increase in demand and the general tendency for the more accessible deposits and richer ores to be used up with time, the real cost of minerals has not risen. Mineral prices have been subject to wide fluctuations, but for most of them the general long-run price trend has been sideways. Continuing discovery, improvements in extractive technology, and increasing supply from abroad have counteracted the factors making for higher costs.

It is probable that in the future the United States will become more dependent on foreign sources of supply. Whether the supply of a particular mineral will be adequate will thus depend not only on the domestic supply but increasingly on the supply that will be available from abroad. Rising economic development throughout the world will increase demand for minerals in other countries. This may tend to limit the amounts available to the United States, raise costs, or both. It also introduces greater uncertainty and injects yet less precise factors into a picture already full of uncertainties; but without consideration of at least the rest of the non-communist areas of the world no appraisal of adequacy in the field of iron ore, bauxite, copper, etc. could be complete.

How imports have assumed a progressively larger role in most of the principal tonnage materials is shown in Table 21–1. And, while imports have become more significant in the domestic supply picture, the pull that U.S. demand as a whole exerts on world supplies has diminished. This is brought out in Table 21–2 for consumption of copper, lead, zinc, aluminum, and steel, the latter as an indicator of iron ore consumption. Thus, despite the severe limitations of any projection of foreign requirements, it is better to guess poorly than to ignore altogether. Some idea of how U.S. metal ore requirements

TABLE 21–1. U.S. Imports as a Percentage of Apparent Consumption of Five Major Metals, 1930–1960

	Iron ore	Bauxite	Copper	Lead	Zinc
1930	5.00	64.46	64.55	9.11	3.89
1935	4.20	58.48	58.32	3.49	2.86
1940	3.09	65.22	48.69	35.42	22.91
1945	1.36	30.29	60.30	28.26	41.99
1950	7.72	76.33	47.71	43.46	40.20
1951	8.80	71.46	37.51	21.77	36.23
1952	9.70	81.88	45.51	55.53	45.75
1953	9.09	75.16	47.11	45.92	56.63
1954	16.77	77.60	48.16	40.46	56.51
1955	18.80	69.85	44.47	38.09	56.33
1956	24.28	73.15	43.58	39.67	57.63
1957	26.04	92.99	47.94	46.66	58.63
1958	29.92	110.52	42.87	58.52	60.00
1959	37.99	94.55	48.26	37.67	60.00
1960	32.01	98.44	45.68	35.26	59.98

3. A good deal of the material on the major tonnage metals (as in the preceding remarks) is drawn from: Bruce C. Netschert and Hans H. Landsberg, *The Future Supply of the Major Metals* (Washington: Resources for the Future, Inc., 1961).

Sources: Derived from data in U.S. Bureau of Mines, *Minerals Yearbook,* various editions; 1930–57, from Neal Potter and Francis T. Christy, Jr., *Trends in Natural Resource Commodities* (Baltimore: Johns Hopkins Press and Resources for the Future, Inc., 1962).

may change by the end of the century can be gained from Figure 21–1.

Iron and Ferroalloys

The category here used takes in, besides iron and manganese—both necessary ingredients of steel—the principal ferroalloys whose demand is related to steel production, though some are also used in nonferrous alloys. One large additive to the furnace charge, silicon, is not discussed because no resource problem seems to emerge. Tungsten only a decade ago found its main use as a ferroalloy, to give maximum resistance to steel under conditions of great heat. Today, its main use is in the manufacture of tungsten carbide, and filaments for electric lamps. Yet, by inertia it has remained as one of the "ferroalloy" group. Finally while all the alloying metals find a place in the tabular presentation of the "minor metals," some of them are dealt with only under that heading, principally because no demand projections have seemed feasible and the reserve-resource picture is even less subject to measurement than in other metals. The heading of this section is, therefore, only approximate. All pertinent cumulative requirements projections are shown in Table 21–3. These will be repeatedly referred to throughout the subsequent sections.

One other general observation must precede

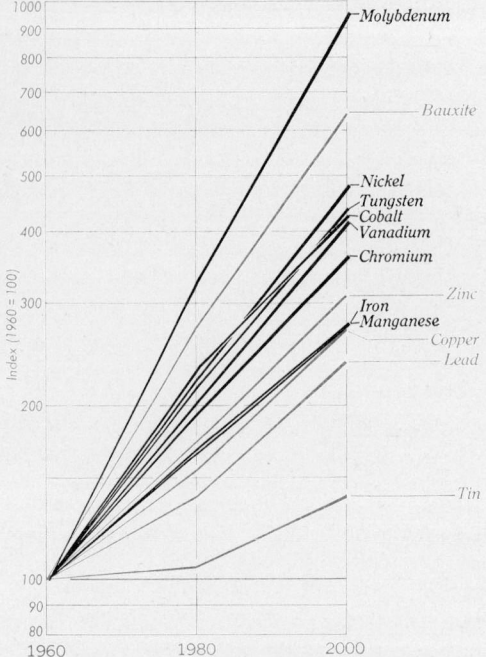

Figure 21–1. Projected changes in U.S. metal ore requirements between 1960, 1980, and 2000.

detailed discussion. As there is much room for substitution of one primary metal for the other, so there is, to an even greater extent a substitutability among the alloys. Criteria for substitution vary.

"In a peacetime economy the most desirable selection of ferroalloying elements . . . is the combination that meets service requirements at a minimum cost. From the standpoint of defense, however, the most desirable combination may be that which makes a minimum demand on alloying elements derived from foreign ores."[4] Whatever the determinants of substitution, it is important to have in mind that special steels represent a wide spectrum, and that in the past shortage of an alloying material has been successfully overcome by introduction of another, in more ample supply. Thus the judgment of resource inadequacy, where this should appear in the case of one or the other alloys, must be modified by these considerations.

TABLE 21–2. U.S. Shares of World Consumption of Some Major Metals, 1948–1960

	Copper	Lead	Zinc	Aluminum	Steel[1]
1948	48.6	47.2	43.1	n.a.	51.7
1949	41.7	39.2	38.8	50.3	44.2
1950	46.9	46.0	44.2	54.0	46.6
1951	43.7	37.2	41.2	50.4	45.6
1952	44.8	44.4	39.4	50.4	40.0
1953	45.8	39.9	41.4	60.4	43.2
1954	35.1	34.9	34.1	56.1	35.9
1955	37.2	34.9	37.9	51.1	39.3
1956	36.7	32.6	35.2	49.8	36.9
1957	32.1	30.0	32.0	49.6	34.9
1958	29.1	29.8	29.5	48.2	28.5
1959	31.3	27.4	29.8	47.9	27.8
1960	27.2	23.2	26.0	38.8	26.0

1. Production.

Sources: Nonferrous metals: *Yearbook of the American Bureau of Metal Statistics,* various editions; steel: U.S. Bureau of Mines, *Minerals Yearbook,* various editions.

4. U.S. Bureau of Mines, *Mineral Facts and Problems,* 1960 ed. (Bull. 585) p. 300.

TABLE 21–3. Ferrous Metals and Alloys: U.S. Consumption, 1960 and Projections to 2000

(Contained metal, unless otherwise specified)

Metal	1960	Low 1960–80	Low 1960–2000	Medium 1960–80	Medium 1960–2000	High 1960–80	High 1960–2000
Iron-in-ore (mil. long tons)	59.4	1,200	2,590	1,600	4,160	2,050	6,430
Manganese (mil. short tons)	1.05	22	48	28	73	35	107
Chromium[1] (mil. short tons)[2]	.52	12	29	15	43	19	63
Nickel (mil. short tons)[2]	.12	2.8	7.0	3.7	11.7	4.9	19.3
Tungsten (thous. short tons)[2]	4.6	110	250	150	460	210	800
Molybdenum (thous. short tons)[2]	15.9	460	1,390	650	2,560	860	4,180
Vanadium (thous. short tons)[2]	2.0	45	120	60	185	75	275
Cobalt (thous. short tons)[2]	4.5	110	260	140	430	190	690

1. In terms of Cr_2O_3.
2. Not adjusted for old scrap, judged to be only small part of supply.

Source: Appendix Tables A16–17, 22, 24, 25, 26, 27, 28, 29.

Iron ore. The outlook for iron ore reserves has changed sharply in the past ten to fifteen years. Greatly stepped-up wartime domestic mining and widely anticipated raw material shortages that appeared to threaten the domestic steel industry between the end of World War II and the Korean Conflict are at the bottom of this change.

United States companies took the lead in the search for new deposits, when consumption of previously unheard-of tonnages of steel during the war made drastic inroads upon the domestic reserves of high-grade ore. This was at a time when the technological breakthrough that permitted the use of low-grade iron-bearing material—the taconites, semi-taconites, jasperites, etc.—had not yet led to production on the large commercial scale which has since become practical.

Hundreds of millions of dollars were invested on the American continent, above all in Canada and Venezuela, and to a lesser degree in West Africa, to find and open up to exploitation new ore deposits. Roads were laid, railroads were built and ports constructed on such a scale that the entire concept of "accessibility" underwent radical revision. At the same time, care was taken to locate new steelmaking capacity within easy reach of ocean-going vessels. The opening of the St. Lawrence Seaway has further accentuated the role of foreign ores by widening the raw material area which can be economically tapped.

With only minor and brief interruptions iron ore imports have been on the rise since the end of the war. They first exceeded 5 million tons in 1948. Within the short span of eleven years they rose to 35 million tons, in 1959 and 1960. (See Figure 21–2 for summary trends and countries of origin.) U.S. imports were 4 per cent of the nation's iron ore consumption at the end of the war, and 30 per cent in the late fifties. By 1960, 4 tons were imported for every 10 tons mined domestically.[5] To appreciate the background for so striking a change in so short a period, it is necessary to take a brief look at the U.S. resource position.

U.S. reserves and resources. Basic to any appraisal of the domestic ore situation is the fact that foreign ore exports have in general superior qualities that enable them to overcome transportation disadvantages which might otherwise exclude them from locations distant from principal water routes. These qualities are high iron and low silica content, and sometimes physical structure, all tending to reduce processing cost in the blast furnace. Venezuelan ore shipments, for example, contain less than 1 per cent silica, compared with over 9 per cent in domestically mined ore. High silica content requires high limestone input and fuel consumption. The over-all effects of these requirements are a reduction in blast furnace capacity and an increase in the cost of producing iron.

5. U.S. Bureau of Mines, *Minerals Yearbook, 1960,* Vol. I, p. 562.

There is now little if any domestic ore that can compete on a quality basis with such foreign ore, unless it is first treated and upgraded into pellets or other types of concentrates, which will raise its iron content to 60 per cent or more, and give it desirable physical attributes. Taconite ore—a very hard, siliceous rock with a relatively low iron concentration found in the Mesabi range of Minnesota—must be finely ground to liberate the iron; sub-

supplies the balance, recently close to 10 per cent of domestically mined tonnage.

The resource position suggests that this picture will change but little in the future, for in regional composition reserve estimates differ unimportantly from the past production pattern. Measured, indicated, and inferred reserves (i.e., those deposits that can be reasonably assumed to exist and be producible at constant real cost given the current state of

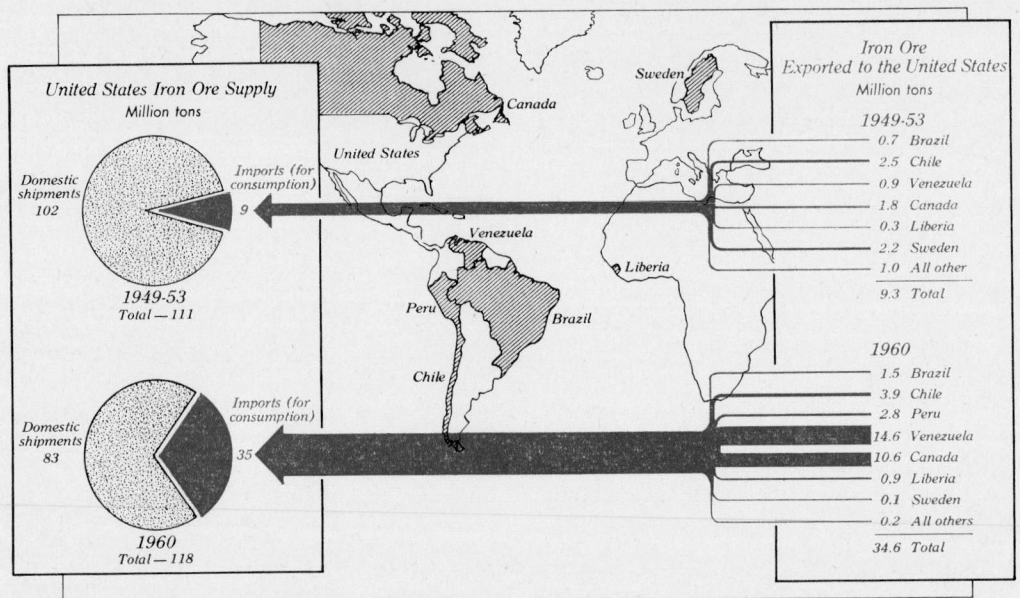

Figure 21–2. Sources of U.S. iron ore supply, 1949–53 and 1960.

sequent concentration is required to turn it into ore usable in furnaces. Since concentration is a necessary concomitant of taconite mining, the entire technology has from its inception been developed within this framework and magnetic taconites have thus found it easier to establish their competitive status in a market that increasingly demands partially processed ore.

With the exception of the western states, the pattern of domestic sources of supply has been remarkably steady. By and large, the Lake Superior ores have contributed some 80 per cent of the total, the southeastern states, some 6 to 8 per cent, and the Adirondack deposits some 4 to 5 per cent. The West (principally southern Utah), a relative newcomer,

technology) have most recently been estimated by the U.S. Geological Survey at 5.5 billion tons of ore (or 3 billion tons of iron) after concentration of low-grade material to commercial standards; not quite 75 per cent of reserves are located in the Lake Superior region, about 9 per cent in the West, some 10 per cent in the Southeast, and 5 to 6 per cent in the Northeast. In addition, however, there exist substantial deposits of potential ore, i.e., ore which at the present time it is not technically or economically feasible to produce but which might become usable in the future. Eighty per cent of this ore, aggregating some 65 billion tons and estimated conservatively by the Bureau of Mines to be equivalent to some 15 billion tons of iron when concentrated to commercial standards (but more likely to be larger as shown in Table 21–4), is found in the Lake Superior region and consists of the taconites, semi-taconites, jasperites, and related low-grade material of the Mesabi and neighboring ranges. The balance is located mostly in Alabama, but at such depths that, given the low grade and thin seams, it is presently not considered realistic to count these deposits as part of the reserves. Table 21–4 summarizes the information.

U.S. resources vs. requirements. How does this resource picture compare with estimated ore requirements, in terms of long tons of iron-in-ore? First of all, as indicated in Figure 21–3, domestic reserves slightly exceed the forty-year demand in the Low projection, but are only two-thirds as large as demand in the Medium projection. Whether domestic reserves would

last beyond the middle or end of the century depends upon the extent to which they are drawn upon. But when iron contained in potential ore is taken into account, demand at all three levels of projection could easily be met, even by using only the Lake Superior deposits of some 16 billion tons.

Use of the potential domestic ore is not blocked by unsolved technical difficulties but rather by relative cost; it is more economical at present to resort to foreign ores. Apart from having a low iron content, most of the domestic ore in question must either be separated by a complex flotation process or by roasting and conversion into the magnetic oxide. The fact that much of the domestic ore is very hard or very fine-grained poses further obstacles to low-cost processing. In any event, additional costs are incurred, though the magnitude of

TABLE 21–4.   Estimated Iron Ore Resources of the United States as of 1955

	Reserves			Potential ore		
Region and type of resource	Ore tonnage (mil. long tons)	Iron content (per cent)	Iron tonnage (mil. long tons)	Ore tonnage (mil. long tons)	Iron content (per cent)	Iron tonnage (mil. long tons)
Lake Superior						
Direct shipping and intermediate crude ore	2,000	50	1,000			
Magnetic concentrates (from magnetic taconite)	2,000	63	1,260			
Crude ore (taconite and other)				35,000	25–45	12,250
Crude ore, recoverable magnetically				15,000	22	3,300
Southeastern						
Direct shipping ore	550	36	200			
Concentrates	60	50	30			
Crude ore				11,220	31–50	3,535
Northeastern						
Concentrates	300	60	180			
Crude ore				2,850	27–43	1,000
Western						
Concentrates	490	50	250			
Crude ore				500	40–50	200
Central and Gulf						
Concentrates	50	48	25			
Crude ore				116	40–50	50
Alaska						
Crude ore	5	45–52	2–3	large		
Total	5,455	54	2,948	64,700		20,300

Source: M. S. Carr and C. E. Dutton, *Iron Ore Resources of the United States Including Alaska and Puerto Rico, 1955,* Geological Survey Bulletin 1082–C (Washington: U.S. Government Printing Office, 1959), p. 87.

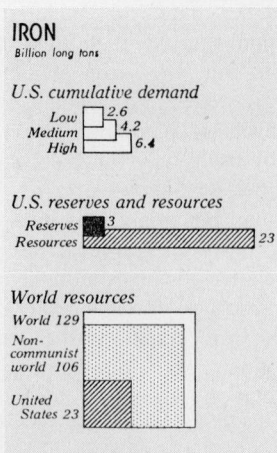

Figure 21–3. U.S. cumulative demand for iron-in-ore, 1960–2000, compared with approximate 1960 U.S. reserves and resources and world resources.

these costs appears to be moderate. Roasting, for example, appears to add between one and three dollars to the cost of ore per ton, or around 20 per cent to the cost of the ore delivered to a typical midwestern steel mill. With the cost of iron ore representing some 10 per cent of the cost of the finished ingot of steel, the added cost arising from additional processing would be of the order of 2 per cent per ton of steel. However, what, in the long perspective of steel price changes, can be called a minor cost factor in steel would be of sufficient magnitude in the cost of ore itself to give it a decided disadvantage vis-à-vis high-grade direct-shipping ore, domestic or foreign.

Since mining of most low-grade ore is of the open-pit variety, expansion, in a persistent emergency, would not present the kind of problem that faced the country at the end of World War II, when rapid growth in steel production had made such inroads on open-pit mining areas that the alternatives appeared to be either expansion of underground mining, necessarily slow and costly, or a search for new deposits abroad. However, expansion of taconite and similar mining would require much handling equipment (presently three tons of lower

grade ore are mined for each ton shipped), but present no real obstacles besides the necessity of handling very large tonnages. Drilling, blasting, and concentrating methods are undergoing continuing improvement and the chances of gradual cost reduction are thus good. It is legitimate, therefore, to conceive of domestic deposits as being available within the time dimensions of this study. As for the non-magnetic portion of the low-grade ores included in this class, it is reasonable to assume that a solution will be found for the commercial processing problems of these marginal materials.

Thus, all but the non-taconite low-grade ores may reasonably be expected to make the transition from potential ore to reserves within the balance of the century, and probably at an early date, with an iron content that might approach 16 billion long tons, depending upon the magnitude of the non-taconite resource included in Table 21–4. Only if these too could become reserves, a less likely prospect, could the entire tonnage of potential ore, totalling over 20 billion long tons of iron content, be reckoned as reserves at some future date.

Foreign resources and requirements. It is unlikely, however, that these ores will in fact be resorted to on a major scale during the next four decades. The last ten years have witnessed discoveries of high-grade foreign deposits in vast amounts, available at costs with which most domestic material cannot compete. As shown in Table 21–5, estimated reserves and identified resources in non-communist countries outside the United States approximate 83 billion tons of iron-in-ore, of which about half consists of direct-shipping ore.[6]

Significant U.S. suppliers are (1) Canada, with estimated reserves approaching 5 billion tons of iron-in-ore, and likely to be at the beginning of a phenomenal climb to the position of the world's top iron ore exporter; (2) Venezuela, with 1 billion tons of proven high-grade ore reserves, and another 3 billion in prospect as exploration continues; and (3) Brazil, with an estimated 16 billion tons of high-grade (60

6. There is room for doubt, but the most reasonable interpretation of the data leads to classifying them as largely reserves, although the ore needing beneficiation also includes potential ore. See Netschert and Landsberg, *op. cit.,* pp. 19–21.

TABLE 21–5. Iron Ore: Estimated World Reserves and Identified Resources, 1960

(Million long tons)

Region	Direct shipping ore	Ore needing beneficiation	Total iron content
North America	12,055	71,700	28,575
United States	5,455	64,700	23,248
Canada[1]	6,600	7,000	5,327
South America	23,708	36,600	24,991
Brazil	16,200	36,000	20,900
Venezuela	2,200	[2]	1,400
Europe	53,667	25,654	26,744
U.S.S.R.	33,757	23,984	18,928
Africa	9,459	[3]	5,288
Asia and Oceania	28,805	92,939	43,619
India	21,300	85,000	37,900
China	4,180	7,000	3,576
Total (rounded)	128,000	227,000	[4] 129,000
Non-communist countries (rounded)	90,000	196,000	[5] 106,000
Non-communist countries, excluding United States (rounded)	85,000	131,000	83,000

Note: Some regional totals include estimates for countries that are not listed.

1. The U.S. Bureau of Mines estimates 18,300 million tons of inferred ore. The Geological Survey of Canada (Gordon A. Gross) estimates 12 billion tons of low-grade reserves, in the Ungava Belt alone, to yield 4.8 billion tons of concentrate ("The Iron Ranges and Current Developments in New Quebec and Labrador, Canada," *Twenty-First Annual Mining Symposium, January 12 and 13, 1960.* Minneapolis: University of Minnesota, p. B–15).

2. No estimate available.

3. Over 50 billion tons, according to *Mine and Quarry Engineering*, September 1958.

4. Of which 62 billion tons likely to be in direct shipping ores at 48% iron content, the balance—67 billion tons—in other ore.

5. Of which 43 billion tons likely to be in direct shipping ores at 48% iron content, the balance—63 billion tons—in other ore.

Source: Adapted from F. G. Percival, *The World's Iron Ore Supplies* (London: British Iron and Steel Federation, rev. ed. 1959).

per cent) ore and another 6 billion tons of low-grade ore, both identified without the benefit of any profound search for material. A recent estimate of total South American reserves by two U.S. Bureau of Mines experts puts direct-shipping ore reserves at 20 billion tons and reserves of all types of iron ore at 60 billion tons.[7] Even disregarding the mounting West African deposits, one must conclude that demand at all three levels of projection, including the high figure of 6.4 billion tons of iron-in-

7. Horace T. Reno and Sumner M. Anderson, "Iron in Ore in South America," in *Twenty-first Annual Mining Symposium, January 12 and 13, 1960* (Minneapolis: University of Minnesota, School of Mines and Metallurgy).

ore estimated to be required in the United States for the period 1960–2000, should be readily available from sources identified today.

This would hold true irrespective of demand elsewhere. Cumulative demand for the entire world has been estimated at no less than 29 billion tons of iron-in-ore and no more than 62 billion tons. This includes both the United States and the Sino-Soviet bloc.[8] The latter figure, of course, equals the size of identified direct-shipping ore assuming an iron content of 48 per cent—the recent experience in world ore production. (See Table 21–5, footnote 4.) It

8. Netschert and Landsberg, *op. cit.*, p. 22.

would result from a growth rate in demand of 8 per cent sustained over the entire forty-year period, a most unlikely contingency, even though throughout the non-communist world iron ore consumption in the fifties grew much faster elsewhere than in the United States—at better than 8 per cent per year between 1950 and 1958.

Because of the industrial development to be anticipated in the now less-developed countries, it is reasonable to anticipate a higher rate of growth than the 2.5 per cent estimated for the United States, but less than 8 per cent. If growth in ore consumption were to be 5 per cent—twice as fast as assumed in the U.S. projection—cumulative consumption in the non-communist world, excluding the United States, in the four decades would be 16 to 18 billion tons of iron-in-ore. Added to the U.S. Medium projection of some 4 billion tons, this would result in total iron demand of 20 to 22 billion tons between now and 2000. Substituting the High for the Medium U.S. projection would raise this by another 2.5 billion tons to a total of roughly 25 billion tons of iron-in-ore.

In view of iron content in direct-shipping ore reserves of better than twice this level of demand, and considering the rate at which new deposits, miles from seaports and in areas previously considered inaccessible, have been opened up in the last decade, it should be feasible to mine supplies of that magnitude without even speculating on ore that needs beneficiation, the identified portions of which, in gross tonnage, are 1½ times the reserves. Certainly the immediate and perhaps even mid-term outlook might well be characterized as one of abundance. For the long run it must be pointed out that aerial mapping and systematic ground reconnaissance have barely begun to be applied on any substantial scale in Asia, Latin America and Africa, and even closer-home Canada undoubtedly will yield further surprises numbering in the billions of tons. New techniques described later in this chapter have already yielded substantial dividends.

Future U.S. supply pattern. Cost has been mentioned intermittently. By definition, as long as deposits now classified as reserves are the basis of supply, higher dollar cost cannot arise on the resource score. The implication for the United States is that between domestic taconite and similar material and other Western Hemisphere sources there seems to be no reason why costs should rise significantly any time in the indefinite future. This may eventually require commercial operation of the domestic non-magnetic taconites at current cost. In view of the already marginal position of the techniques and the long period of time over which it can be perfected before it must be drawn on, this is a reasonable speculation. But furthermore, additional costs arising in the preparation of the raw material may very well be partially offset by cost reductions in shipping charges and in the blast furnace, due to savings in fuel, especially in coke, and greater productivity of furnaces. Thus a mere increase in cost of iron ore without consideration of the characteristics of the ore would be quite misleading as an indicator of future steel cost, and it is the latter that in the final analysis interests the economy.

Because of the substantial corporate identity of ore producers and ore consumers in this country, the radical shift from domestic to foreign sources of supply has occurred with a minimum of public debate. The heavy investments made by the leading steel companies in foreign countries can be expected to lead to a preference for foreign ore, if for no other reason than to recoup the investment and to exploit the foreign sources as long as political conditions abroad permit. At the same time, a domestic industry will be kept in being, generally assumed at about the present capacity but with gradual replacement of direct-shipping ore by beneficiated low-grade material. The bulk of future growth in consumption is likely to be met from foreign sources.

One might speculate that the projected demand for roughly 100 million long tons of iron-in-ore in 1980 would be met from domestic sources to the extent of 50 million tons, of which in turn half might be beneficiated ore. By 2000, the proportions would have further shifted toward imports, which might fill 75 per cent or more of the over 160 million tons of iron-in-ore projected to be then in demand. At that time, it must be assumed that Lake Superior ore deposits, other than taconite and the like, would be exhausted or nearing exhaustion —forty years' production at the current rate of some 80 million tons of ore per year are greatly in excess of the estimated reserves of 2 billion tons of ore—and that substantial inroads would have been made into both the small deposits elsewhere and into the magnetic taconite reserves. Indeed, continued production of all types of ore through 2000 at recent levels of domestic production would total 2.5 billion tons, or close to currently estimated reserves of 2.9 billion long tons of iron-in-ore. At the same time, it must be presumed that much of the potential ore would by then have been shifted into the "reserves" column. In view of the size of this source—largely nonmagnetic taconite—this would assure a supply for many decades.

Manganese. Manganese is a relatively common metal in nature and occurs throughout the world in a variety of types of deposits. It is mined, like iron, with a wide range of methods at many different levels of concentration; this together with the complex mineralogy of its

ore bodies makes the distinction between reserves and potential ore difficult. Commercial manganese ore that can be shipped directly contains a minimum of 35 per cent manganese. A commercial concentrate, as well as so-called "synthetic ore," can be produced, however, from manganiferous ore of lower manganese content.

U.S. resources vs. requirements. In the United States the absence of high-grade deposits makes it easy to distinguish between reserve and potential ore. The only presently commercial reserves—including inferred ore—are in the Butte and Phillipsburg districts of Montana, and are estimated to contain almost 900,000 tons of manganese (see Table 21–6). None of the ore is of direct-shipping grade, but requires concentration.

At the resource level there are many districts, but over 90 per cent of the total is in four of them. In addition to the smaller districts listed in Table 21–6 there are many small deposits and districts representing a wide variety of manganese occurrences. The total manganese content of identified potential ore is estimated to be some 77 million tons.

TABLE 21–6. Manganese: Estimated U.S. Reserves and Resources, 1956

District	Ore (mil. short tons)	Average manganese content (per cent)	Contained manganese (mil. short tons)
Reserves:			
Butte, Montana	5.0	14	.70
Phillipsburg, Montana	0.8	22.5	.18
Total	5.8		.88
Potential ore:			
Cuyuna Range, Minnesota	504.0	5	25.20
Aroostook County, Maine	313.6	9	28.20
Chamerlain, South Dakota	77.3	15.5	12.00
Artillery Peak, Arizona	174.7	4	7.00
Three Kids, Nevada	5.0	10	0.50
Pioche, Nevada	4.0	10	0.40
Leadville, Colorado	4.0	15	0.60
Others	–	–	3.40
Total potential ore			77.30
Total identified resources			78.18

Source: L. Pavlides, "Manganese in the United States—Evaluation of Reserves," *Symposium Sobre Yacimientos de Manganeso* (Mexico: 20th International Geological Congress, 1956), Vol. 3, p. 214.

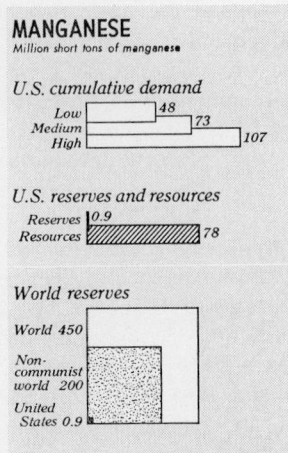

MANGANESE
Million short tons of manganese

U.S. cumulative demand
Low   48
Medium   73
High   107

U.S. reserves and resources
Reserves 0.9
Resources   78

World reserves
World 450
Non-communist world 200
United States 0.9

Figure 21–4. U.S. cumulative demand for manganese, 1960–2000, compared with approximate 1960 U.S. reserves and resources and world reserves.

Compared with the Medium cumulative demand projection of 73 million tons of manganese content, reserves are but a drop in the bucket and only total resources down to a 5 per cent grade material would meet demand. (See Figure 21–4.) Assuming no change in the present inability to utilize the potential ore, U.S. import needs through the remainder of the century can be taken to equal U.S. requirements, or 73 million tons of manganese. The fact that domestic production in recent years has been as high as 22 per cent of consumption is due only to the circumstance that most of it was produced under a special incentive program, at high prices, and ended up in the government stockpile.

Foreign resources vs. requirements. The foreign reserve situation is thus of utmost importance. The widespread occurrence of manganese ore, the variety of deposits, and the range in the grade which can be worked commercially, together with the incomplete knowledge common for all large-scale mineral deposits, make any tabulation of reserve-resource data little more than a minimum guess. Such a guess is given in Table 21–7 which lists a total of some 450 million tons of contained

manganese, of which perhaps 185 million tons are in non-communist countries.

In addition to the areas listed, dozens of countries throughout the world produce manganese ore or concentrates from all kinds of deposits. Total production from such sources, in fact, is greater than from the large-scale deposits. In 1958, for example, the countries listed in Table 21–7 produced 3.7 million tons of manganese ore; in addition, other non-communist countries produced 5.8 million tons. The reserve total shown in the table is both incomplete and subject to sudden change. Some new large-scale deposits (e.g. British Guiana) will soon be added. The large figure for Gabon would not have been included in any reserve estimate as little as five years ago. A figure of 200 million tons for the manganese content of total reserves in non-communist countries (carried in Figure 21–4) is certainly a minimum estimate.

Nothing can be said about potential ore. Low-grade manganese deposits, some of very large size, have been identified throughout the world, but with the current and prospective ample supply situation there has been no incentive to ascertain their size and content. By all indications, however, the total manganese content of potential ore elsewhere in the world is very large indeed.

There is in addition the potential afforded by the ocean floor, as discussed below (pages 495–96). The existence of manganese-bearing nodules on the ocean floor has been known for many decades, but only in the past few years has their extent and quantity become apparent. The tonnage involved in this type of occurrence cannot be estimated, but it is certainly equal to and more likely greater than known continental reserves.

How does demand in the non-communist world measure up to reserves? Since the metallurgical consumption of manganese is primarily a function of steel production, any projection of the former must be compatible with a projection of the latter. Steel production rose by 8 per cent between 1950 and 1960 in the non-communist countries of the world exclusive of the United States. Continuation of such a growth rate for a period of several decades is

TABLE 21–7. Manganese: World Reserves of the Larger Deposits[1]

Country	Ore (million tons)	Manganese content (per cent)	Contained manganese (million tons)
U.S.S.R.	625	20–50	213
Africa			
Ghana	10	52	[2]5
South Africa	60	37–52	27
Gabon	100	48–50	50
Morocco	50	25–45	18.5
Congo	10	45	4.5
Brazil	60	45–51	30
Asia			
India	100	47–52	50
China	50–100	40–50	22.5–45
Subtotal	1,065–1,115		420–443
All others	53		–
Total (rounded)	1,150		

1. Estimates have no common date, nor specification whether short, metric, or long tons.
2. Proved only.

Sources: Gabon—*The Mining Journal,* April 22, 1960, p. 456. China—U.S. Bureau of Mines, *Mineral Trade Notes,* Vol. 50, No. 3, Special Supplement No. 59, March 1960, p. 29. Others—U.S. Bureau of Mines, *Materials Survey: Manganese* (Washington: U.S. Government Printing Office, 1952), p. II–12; G. L. DeHuff, Jr., "Global Aspects of Manganese Ore Supply," *Symposium Sobre Yacimientos de Manganeso* (Mexico: 20th International Geological Congress, 1956), Vol. I, pp. 147–54.

highly unlikely. As a working assumption, a growth rate of 5 per cent is adopted to project foreign manganese production through the year 2000. This would mean a cumulative forty-year output of some 225 million tons of manganese. Together with projected U.S. import needs—which may be considered equal to total U.S. demand—the demand on foreign sources for the remainder of the century would be about 300 million tons. Confrontation with less than 200 million tons of identified reserves in non-communist countries suggests that "discoveries" of additional manganese reserves may be needed before 2000. But with allowance for the understatement in current reserve statistics and the possible overstatement of manganese requirements (see below), it would not seem to be a certainty. However, if we substitute the high U.S. projection, which by itself accumulates to some 110 million tons of manganese content, and allow for a certain loss in recovery, this magnitude of demand added to other demands of the non-communist world poses a real problem to be solved only by access to new, high-grade resources, or exploitation of known low-grade sources (which in the United States alone are enough almost to equal cumulative U.S. demand).

Given the large resources of the U.S.S.R., comparison of total world demand and resources yields a much more favorable picture. At the 3.2 per cent growth rate that prevailed between 1955 and 1960, world demand would cumulate to some 460 million tons.[9] This about equals reserves as now conservatively estimated.

Two other aspects of the future supply-demand situation in manganese warrant attention. The first concerns the ratio of manganese use to steel production. There is recent

9. Netschert and Landsberg, *op. cit.,* p. 29.

evidence that a satisfactory grade of steel can be produced with perhaps as little as 4 pounds of manganese per ton of ingot steel in comparison with the current average of 16 pounds. This creates a large field for technological advance. The pace of progress along this line may well depend upon the degree of availability at current prices of foreign manganese; but the high dependence of the major steel-producing countries on foreign manganese supplies may sooner or later call forth serious efforts to reduce a degree of reliance that is a source of potential commercial as well as strategic trouble. Any progress along this avenue would lessen total world requirements.

The second aspect is the loss of manganese in slag in the steelmaking process, and the consequent existence of a significant potential secondary source of supply. For every ingot ton of steel, some 12.4 pounds of manganese are wasted on the slag dump; this is only a little less than the manganese added in the steelmaking process.

The strategic weakness of the United States in manganese has been responsible for continued interest in methods of recovering and utilizing the manganese in slag, both in recovery of hot manganese from the slag as it is produced and in "mining" the accumulated slag dumps. Several processes are technically feasible, but the costs are so high that they cannot as yet be considered even potentially economic. Nevertheless, given the size of the source and the continuing strong impetus to exploit it, there would appear to be good probability of eventual economic use of secondary manganese. Steel mills are generally careful to segregate their slag and prevent its deterioration, not unmindful of its eventual exploitation.

The U.S. government has been active in attempting to lessen the national dependence on foreign manganese sources through the development of the large domestic deposits of potential ore. This activity has taken the form of direct governmental research on the exploitation of such ore and of purchase programs at incentive prices.

The problem of low grade would be solved by beneficiation of the ore or by extraction of the manganese in highly concentrated or even

metallic form. In addition, many of the ores are not amenable to treatment by heat and chemical reagents—which is the nub of the cost problem. The technical feasibility of some production methods has been demonstrated, but economic practicability is not yet in sight.

The recent government purchase program, which ended in 1959, included payments at prices up to twice or even more the commercial level. This, incidentally, is in line with the conclusion in the President's Materials Policy Commission report that utilization of the intermediate grade domestic ores (25 per cent or more manganese) would require prices from one and three-quarters to two and one-quarter times the commercial level, and the very low-grade resources (10 per cent or less manganese content) would need prices from two and three-quarters to three times that level.

Even on the assumption that future research and development efforts are no more successful than those in the past, there is little reason to expect that manganese costs for the United States will rise because of world resource depletion. The potential manganese ores of the world contain progressively larger tonnages at lower grades in what appears to be a continuous relationship. Thus a relatively slight decline in grade of ore mined could easily be accommodated by currently known and used beneficiation and concentration techniques.

But for the period through the year 2000 all this is probably academic. Between lower unit manganese requirements, "discoveries" of additional reserves in known deposits, true discoveries of new deposits, and the ocean floor opportunities, the manganese situation should take care of itself. It is predominantly U.S. dependence upon foreign sources which provides the stimulus for research, not the world resource situation.

Chromium and Nickel. The largest tonnage items among the additive metals other than manganese, which occupies a special role as a scavenger agent, are chromium and nickel. U.S. reserves of neither are sufficiently large, nor future discoveries sufficiently likely, to fill more than a small fraction of domestic requirements. Adequacy of resource is peculiarly dependent upon the situation abroad. This has recently been accentuated by the question of availability to the United States, or to the non-communist world as a whole for that matter, of Cuban deposits, among the most extensive low-grade orebodies in the world.

Apart from political considerations, there are wide ranges in estimates of reserves. Occurrences of low-grade resources are abundant. In addition, the various applications of chromium have in the past required different specifications of ore so that not all deposits can be considered available for all uses. Lack of sufficient knowledge to match type of orebody and type of application introduces an additional element of uncertainty. The summary impression one receives from studying the available data is one of qualified concern; not immediately, but, within the period under study.

Chromium. Nothing has happened in the last ten years to make one discard the judgment of the President's Materials Policy Commission that "domestic resources of chromite are meager." The description aptly characterizes both quantity and quality. The estimated 4 million short tons of measured and indicated domestic reserves, in terms of chromic oxide (Cr_2O_3), are low in chromium content, especially in the Montana field which contains the bulk of U.S. deposits, and difficult to concentrate, thus making the material undesirable for metallurgical use. However, the steel industry has in recent years been able to adjust its operations so as to use some of the domestic ores. Nonetheless, it is still true that only a few thousand tons a year are suitable for use in the steel industry. Large-scale government subsidization and stockpiling in most of the fifties has obscured the statistical picture, which shows a tenfold increase in domestic production between the early and the late fifties. When the government purchase program was terminated in 1958 all but one of the domestic mines shut down, and the remaining one, at Nye, Montana, delivers all its output to the government under a long-term contract. Under conditions prevailing in recent years the 4 million tons of domestic reserves material weigh but little in the balance, but possess rather the character-

istics of potential ore, available only under conditions of much higher chromium prices. On the other hand, when viewed as a potential orebody the Montana fields are likely to hold much more than 4 million tons, for it is known that the width of the chromite zone increases with increasing depth.

Domestic consumption of chromite ore has in recent years ranged between 1 and 1.8 million tons, or roughly 500,000 to 1,000,000 tons of chromic oxide fluctuating generally with the ups and downs of steel output. Chromium demand must thus be met predominantly from foreign sources. Of these the most important ones are located in Africa (South Africa and Southern Rhodesia), Turkey, and the Philippines. There are also sizeable reserves in New Caledonia, but quantity data on these are not available. Table 21–8 summarizes the estimates.

The fact that the data are tabulated by no means implies solid knowledge. The range of the estimated ore occurrence is very wide; in South Africa, for example, it is likely that the lower limit indicates the measured and indicated reserves and the upper limit includes inferred reserves to some assumed, but unspecified, depth. Second, the equivalence in terms of chromic oxide is approximate, especially where the ore material exhibits a wide range or is given without indication of content. Third, in no case is there an indication of cost implications that could lead one to rank the likely availability of the ore, at a scale of prices, nor is there, in most instances any hint of the degree to which inferred reserves are or are not included. The Cuban lateritic reserves, running into several billion tons of ore with a Cr_2O_3 content of only 1 to 4 per cent, are a special case. At present these reserves must clearly be labelled as potential ore, since they cannot be economically produced at the current stage of technology.

Imprecise as they are, the figures suggest that reserves are now larger than the 300 million tons of contained Cr_2O_3 that represented the best estimate of the President's Materials Policy Commission some ten years ago (though this would still be the estimate if one were to use the low point of the South African re-

TABLE 21–8.   Chromium: Estimated Principal World Resources[1]

Country	Chromite (mil. short tons)	Grade (per cent)	Cr_2O_3 (mil. short tons)
United States	n.a.	2–48	3.9
South Africa	200–2,000	40–45	80–800+
Southern Rhodesia	369–500	47.5	175–250
Turkey	10	40–48	4–5
Philippines	8–10	40–?	3–4
Canada	16+	4.6–25.2	1–2
Cuba (other than laterites)	1–2	40–50	.5–1.0
Cuban laterites	3,000	1–4	50

n.a. = not available.

1. The dating of the estimates is not feasible. All chromite and grade figures from U.S. Bureau of Mines, *Mineral Facts and Problems*, 1960 ed., pp. 190–1; also *Minerals Yearbook 1959*, Chromium chapter. Cr_2O_3 figures estimated on basis of ore and grade data. Extensive deposits are known to exist in the Soviet Union and in Albania which together accounted for 30% of world output in 1960. Another 10% of output came from countries not here listed. Recent reports of a 15 million-ton ore reserve discovery in Finland have not been reflected in the table.

serves). How much larger the reserves are is difficult to tell, but perhaps a figure of 500 million tons might not be far off. The estimates cover only areas for which estimates have been made at one time or other, and omit others that have not been sufficiently explored—for example, parts of Southern Rhodesia and Turkey—or for other reasons do not appear in the listing.

To form an idea of the demand-resource position, we must aggregate projected U.S. demand and guess at demand outside the United States, using as point of departure U.S. supply and world production. From these two components the Bureau of Mines estimates that from 1950 to 1958 chromite consumption in non-communist countries other than the United States rose from 750,000 to 1,600,000 short tons.[10] The estimate for 1950 appears somewhat to overstate consumption and thus may result in too conservative a rate of growth. Lack of reserve data in the Sino-Soviet bloc prevents any estimate of world consumption or supply.

These are very rough approximations. The

10. U.S. Bureau of Mines, *Mineral Facts and Problems*, cited above, p. 192.

President's Materials Policy Commission estimated 1950 consumption in the non-communist countries outside the United States at just under 600,000 short tons, but also did not claim great precision for its estimate, though it was based on somewhat more detailed data. However, assuming that foreign stock changes and shipments between the non-communist and communist countries did not significantly change between 1950 and 1958, we can deduce a growth in foreign consumption of 10 per cent compounded. Actually, net imports from communist countries appear to have increased of late so that the rate might be even higher. Apparent foreign non-communist consumption had as early as 1958 exceeded by 15 per cent the level of demand projected by the President's Materials Policy Commission for 1975. How much of this very rapid rate of growth is owed to the effects of postwar recovery and how much represents a long-run trend remains to be seen, but it is significant that the rise in the first four of the eight years under review is no steeper than in the second half. The chromium picture incidentally tallies well with the recent history of steel demand outside the Sino-Soviet bloc and the United

States which, as shown above, has risen by 8 per cent annually between 1950 and 1958, i.e., only slightly less than chromite consumption. Such a differential is thoroughly reasonable, as high-grade steels have undoubtedly experienced a boom superimposed upon that common to all grades.

In guessing at future foreign non-communist demand, it is probably safest to link chromium demand to steel demand. Starting from the previously set rise in steel consumption of 5 per cent per year as the outside limit (twice the U.S. rate of growth), and assuming a further relative increase of specialty steels within total steel output, we might select a 6 per cent growth rate. This would give us a consumption of 18 million short tons in 2000, or just about ten times that of 1960. Cumulative demand would amount to something like 380 million tons of chromite or, assuming an average grade of 43 per cent chromic oxide, 160 million tons of Cr_2O_3.[11]

U.S. Medium demand in all uses is estimated at 43 million tons of chromic oxide for the forty-year period, at less than 30 million in the Low and at not quite 65 million in the High model (cf. Table 21–3). As we have seen, there is at present no prospect that any of this demand can be economically met from domestic resources. Adding U.S. demand to that of the rest of the non-communist world results in cumulative demand in the Medium projection of about 200 million tons of Cr_2O_3.

Comparison with likely reserves leaves one in a twilight zone, for judgment of adequacy depends predominantly on three factors, all of them lacking precision: (a) just how large are African reserves; (b) what is the extent, nature, and workability of potential ores, other than those known to exist in Cuba; and (c) to what degree can grade specifications be expected to be progressively relaxed in the future? A fourth factor—efficiency of recovery—is ignored, as its quantitative importance pales before the uncertainties of the reserve data.

On the first point the size of the Rhodesian

reserves is of crucial importance; they are the best suited of the large deposits for metallurgical purposes. Eighty per cent of Rhodesian production is of metallurgical grade. The lower estimate of 175 million tons of chromic oxide reserves encompasses what is believed to be in place to a depth of 100 feet. If we assume that 60 per cent of the 200 million tons of demand estimated above—or 120 million tons—represents demand for metallurgical grade chromium (which is the relationship that has for some time prevailed in U.S. chromium consumption), this could be matched only if 75 per cent of Rhodesian deposits were of this grading, using the lower of the two reserve estimates. This is probably too optimistic an assumption. If we take the upper estimate, however, only one half of the reserves would have to be of metallurgical grade to match the above chromium demand for metallurgical purposes.[12] One cannot, of course, assume that all reserves could in fact be mined in the next forty years. Also, mining practice would call for discoveries of new or extensions of old reserves in order to guarantee continuity of output at the high level required toward the latter part of the century. Thus, the Rhodesian picture is encouraging but does not remove concern over resource adequacy.

The widely divergent guesses for South Africa represent general indications rather than precisely delimited and defined estimates, and it is not possible to bring any refinement to bear upon these. Nor can additional light be thrown on the matter of potential ore. However, here the magnitudes involved, in terms of Cr_2O_3, are not such as would tip the balance of the adequacy judgment one way or another.

Most of the South African material is not especially suitable for metallurgical use: much of it is low in chromium content, low in the ratio of chromium to iron, and crumbles easily. It is essentially chemical-grade material. Yet, the need for metallurgical-grade ore and its restricted occurrence make it important to find

11. There is no information on average grade of chromite consumed abroad. Given the fact that most consumption is in highly industrialized areas, predominantly for metallurgical use, the recent U.S. average experience has been used.

12. The Commonwealth Economic Committee estimates that about half of Rhodesia's reserves, put at 550 million tons, have metallurgical grade specifications; (see the Committee's *Iron and Steel and Alloying Metals* [London: Her Majesty's Stationery Office, 1962], p. 143). This would be nearly double the 120 million ton demand.

ways and means of processing the South African ore in such a manner as to render it acceptable to the steelmaker. Some progress has been made recently in that the metal industry can now use lower-grade material to a somewhat larger extent (though statistically this is not identifiable); this is due primarily to the fact that the makers of stainless steel have learned to use a lower-grade ferrochromium.

Reserves the world over are predominantly of the lower-grade variety, unsuitable for steel producers, while almost half the chromite demand in the world is for metallurgical use.[13] The outlook must, therefore, be termed uncertain in the Medium projection, with judgment suspended until more knowledge is available as to the nature of the African deposits. Should the African deposits turn out to be in the higher reaches of current guesses and if they can be made usable in steelmaking, then one could without hesitation cross off concern far into the next century.

The almost total dependence of the United States on foreign supplies that are available only via a long sea route and in areas that, in the perspective of forty years, may be subject to periods of political instability, makes the development of Western Hemisphere resources a matter of considerable interest. There is no indication, however, of large deposits, even of potential low-grade ore outside of Cuba. Thus, adequacy of chromium supplies is likely to rest on a shaky basis, and technological advance in improving the conditions under which low-grade ore becomes acceptable is of great importance, especially, as manganese and nickel as well are largely of foreign origin, leaving only silicon among the large-tonnage ferroalloys as a domestically produced material.

Nickel. Nickel in the short span of ten years has gone full cycle from extreme scarcity to relative abundance. Its value in defense equipment makes it appear critically short in times of emergency, and by the time expanded facilities furnish added supplies, civilian users have made adjustments to shortage that minimize nickel demand. The post-Korean shortage, together with stockpiling, left so strong an imprint that to convince the consuming public of its renewed and continued availability has been one of the main concerns of nickel producers. As far as resources are concerned, there is no doubt that the nickel-producing industry, assuming present trends in demand, will be amply able to cope with market demand for some time to come. It is in the longer future that a question of adequacy arises. And this may be due more to the insufficiency of the resource data than to any real resource inadequacy.

There is no lack of nickel deposits in nature. Its crustal abundance of 0.02 is twice as high as that of copper, lead, and zinc combined. But before a deposit can be considered the basis of a successful commercial venture, this natural abundance must be multiplied some eighty times and preferably more. In addition, it is necessary for the nickel to be combined with the other minerals with which it normally appears in the complex ore in a way that allows easy separation and utilization of each of them.

Deposits that satisfy these conditions are rare. Canada has been pre-eminent as the location of rich sulfide ores in which nickel together with copper, platinum, and other metals can be recovered economically. New Caledonia has been a second source, though of nickel only, extracted from silicate ores which are low in iron and chromite content. With few exceptions all other occurrences of nickel are in laterites, or nickel-bearing iron ores. The largest of these are found in Cuba, others are in the Philippines, Indonesia, and some probably occur in New Guinea. Appraisal of these deposits is critical for any judgment of adequacy, for they constitute the bulk of presently identified nickel resources: of some 50 million tons, in contained nickel, no less than two-thirds consist of the nickel contained in the laterites. Tables 21–9 and 21–10 portray the reserve-resource situation, with its proper qualifications, as it appears from a variety of sources, but principally the judgment of the U.S. Bureau of Mines.

No technical obstacle blocks the exploitation of the laterite-base nickel. The Cuban experience where large amounts of laterite have been successfully mined and have been sold

13. Only 15 to 20 per cent of reserves are of metallurgical grade, 5 per cent of refractory grade, the balance chemical grade (cf. Commonwealth Economic Committee, *op. cit.*).

TABLE 21–9.   Nickel: World Reserves[1]

Country and region	Company (where known)	Quantity (thous. short tons of nickel content)		Remarks
Canada				
Sudbury	International Nickel Co.	4,000		Proved
Sudbury	Falconbridge	636		Developed and indicated
Thompson	International Nickel Co.	1,200		Deduced from scope of operations
Lynn Lake	Sherritt-Gordon	131		Proved
	Total		5,967	
New Caledonia			4,600	Of which 2,200 laterites and balance silicates
Cuba				
Levisa Bay	Nicaro	930		Measured, indicated, inferred
Levisa Bay	Cuban Nickel (U.S. Govt.)	490		Indicated
Moa Bay & other	Nicaro	1,165		Indicated & inferred
Mayari, Moa Bay	Bethlehem Cuba Iron Mines	2,065		Measured, indicated, inferred
	Total		4,650	
United States				
Oregon	Hanna	257		
Other (incl. Alaska)		293		
	Total		550	
Total (rounded)			16,000	

1. Estimates have no common date and are minimum, since inferred, and sometimes indicated quantities not given.
   Principal Source: U.S. Bureau of Mines, *Mineral Facts and Problems*, 1960 ed. Most detailed previous listing in W. D. McMillan and H. W. Davis, *Nickel-Cobalt Resources of Cuba*, Bureau of Mines Report of Investigations 5099, Feb. 1955, and Bureau of Mines and Geological Survey, *Materials Survey—Nickel*, 1952. No data are available regarding nickel resources in the Sino-Soviet bloc.

profitably in the U.S. market without a price incentive or subsidy, and despite an ore royalty whose magnitude has long been embroiled in controversy, has marked a long step ahead in their utilization. There is reason to believe that, had it not been for the upheaval following in the wake of the Castro takeover, successful separation and disposition of the other constituents of the ore—cobalt and iron— would not have been far off.

Such a development would go a long way in putting the laterites on an equal footing with the more advantageous sulfide ores. Indeed when the Bethlehem Steel Company first acquired its Cuban claims, it considered them sources of iron ore, and it was only when it turned out that the iron ore was rendered unusable by the admixture of nickel and other

TABLE 21–10.   Nickel: World Potential Ore[1]

Country	Nickel content (thous. short tons)
Cuba	13,000–20,000
Philippines[2]	1,000– 4,400
Indonesia	5,000– 8,000
Venezuela	several 100
Brazil	several 100
Dominican Republic	700
Puerto Rico	1,000
Total	20,000–35,000

1. Based upon information in U.S. Bureau of Mines, *Minerals Facts and Problems*, 1956 and 1960 ed.; Report of Investigations 5099 (1955), 5532 (1959). Occasional articles in *American Metal Market* (e.g. 2/1/57, 8/2/56), Defense Production Act Progress Report No. 36, Joint Committee on Defense Production, 85th Congress, 1st Session.
2. Probably conservative estimate.

impurities that the deposits began to be thought of in terms of nickel rather than iron recovery. With the great abundance of high-grade iron ore, as described above, there is little incentive to work these deposits as sources of iron ore, but the recovery of iron ore as a by-product of nickel recovery would of course represent a different economic picture. A great deal depends, therefore, upon the cost of such an operation. Here, we are at sea: there is no indication at what price deposits containing 1 per cent or 0.9 per cent, etc., of nickel would represent workable reserves, nor what contribution the commercial exploitation of the iron and cobalt could make towards permitting the setting of a competitive nickel price.

Little is known about the connection between grade of ore and cost. Even if it were true—and there is no solid evidence—that, as has been suggested, costs tend to rise in proportion to the drop in grade, the question would then arise as to the upper limit of such a cost increase. This would eventually be set by the market price, but since the market price has in the past been that set by the International Nickel Company (INCO), the top producer, which rarely contributes less than two-thirds of the non-communist countries' consumption and which produces nickel as a joint product with copper, platinum, and other metals, this would not represent a very meaningful criterion.[14]

Because of these unknown factors, there is great looseness in the reserve data. Proven, indicated, inferred, and potential ore are thrown together in various combinations to arrive at varying totals. Nor are quick changes uncommon. In a Bureau of Mines publication of 1955 the newly found Mystery Lake deposits in Canada were called "not economic at present."[15] Yet exploration enabled INCO to announce in December 1956 a $125-million mining and refining project in the area which was to raise its capacity in 1961 by 25 per cent.

The uncertainties are aggravated by concentration of ownership. Even though there has been a widening of the circle of nickel producers, a single company, INCO, still is predominant to a degree known in only few lines of economic activity. In 1960 it owned about half the world's nickel-producing capacity. The current eclipse of Cuban production further strengthens its role. This situation has not been conducive to the appearance of meaningful reserve estimates.

The following will serve as an example. According to its annual reports, INCO's nickel reserves in its principal location, the Sudbury district northeast of Sault Ste. Marie, have steadily increased during the past three decades, briefly interrupted only during the war, when reserves were allowed to diminish. In 1929 ore reserves amounted to 203 million tons, all proved. By 1950 these had risen to 253 million tons and by the end of 1960 to 290 million tons. In terms of copper and nickel content combined—INCO does not report estimates of copper and nickel separately—reserves have increased over the same period from 6.9 to 8.7 million tons.[16] At the same time, several million tons have been mined. Over the period the company has done better than replacing each ton mined by a ton added to reserves.

The reserve estimates that INCO releases annually are for proven reserves only, i.e., they are strictly working inventories.[17] As for INCO's newest area of operation, in Manitoba, no reserve estimates have been released as yet, but the U.S. Bureau of Mines deduces from the company's scale of operations that they must be of the magnitude of some 1.2 million tons of nickel.[18] These are not very firm data on which to judge adequacy. In the case of Cuba, reserve estimates include proven, indicated, and inferred ores for the major locations, but, as mentioned above, there is uncertainty regard-

14. The fact that the quoted price of nickel dropped in the spring of 1962 was a major event in the industry. Apart from duty changes, the price had not declined in over thirty years, probably a record for a major resource material.

15. U.S. Bureau of Mines, Report of Investigations 5099, p. 8.

16. Figures cited in Table 21–9 suggest that about half of this quantity represents nickel.

17. "The proven ore reserves of the Company as reported are blocks of economic ore which have been explored by drilling or otherwise, in sufficient detail and in accordance with a standard practice, to enable accurate calculation of the number of short tons of ore and its nickel-copper content." *INCO Annual Report 1961.*

18. *Mineral Facts and Problems*, 1960 ed. See also Commonwealth Economic Committee, *op. cit.,* which puts them at "between one and two million tons."

ing exploitability of potential ore. Finally, in the case of New Caledonia, we have no indication regarding the criteria underlying the reserve estimates.

The individual estimates presented in Table 21–9 add to a total of under 16 million tons excluding the United States. One would be seriously misled to think that this estimate is anywhere near indicating the non-communist countries'—or for that matter this country's—possibilities of future nickel production. It is a minimum figure. First, the reserves controlled by principal producers are no doubt much greater than reflected in the reserve figures they publish. Second, the high degree of concentration in nickel production has until recently held back the drive behind finding and exploiting nickel deposits or new ways of dealing with unconventional ore sources. A good deal is vaguely known about the physical facts of occurrence of nickel but next to nothing about the size and cost of working of such deposits. It is estimated for example, that Indonesia has deposits totaling between 5 and 8 million tons of nickel content on the islands of Celebes and Borneo; that there may be as much as 4 to 5 million tons (others mention three or four times this quantity) of the metal in Philippine deposits—to name only the two most outstanding locations. The size of the Cuban nickel resource, whatever its destiny in terms of U.S. access to it, is still undetermined. In the early fifties it was estimated that the nickel content of the Cuban ores was close to 24 million tons,[19] and this figure was carried as recently as 1956 in a consultant's report to the Office of Defense Mobilization.[20] The Bureau of Mines commits itself to no more than 18 million tons at this time.[21]

These various guesses do not indicate whether the deposits could be profitably mined at current prices. But even if we did have some speculative cost studies, it would be hard to draw conclusions; first because the quality of these deposits has been estimated only roughly, not smoothly graded in tenths or hundredths

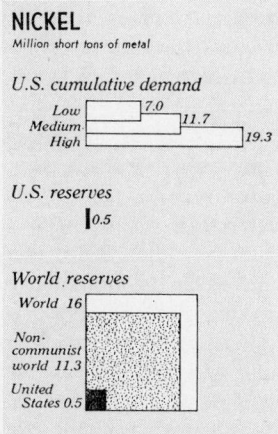

Figure 21–5. U.S. cumulative demand for nickel, 1960–2000, compared with approximate 1960 U.S. reserves and world reserves.

of percentage points of nickel content, and second because the price of nickel, in the largely non-competitive situation of the industry, is not a good guide to cost and therefore to the threshold at which additional productive capacity could profitably enter the industry. Yet cost differences between mining 1.3 per cent and 1.2 per cent nickel deposits may be sufficient to assign the first to the reserve, the second to the potential ore category.

U.S. nickel consumption, which is projected to rise from the current level of just over 100,000 tons of metal to more than 550,000 tons in 2000, would constitute a cumulative demand of nearly 12 million tons in the forty years. Demand in the rest of the non-communist areas of the world, if it were to grow at 6 per cent[22] as we have assumed for chromium, i.e., slightly faster than the 5 per cent growth for non-U.S. steel consumption, would cumulate to some 25 million tons, for a total of 37 million tons for the non-communist world as a whole.[23]

This magnitude is more than double the size

19. Bureau of Mines and Geological Survey, *Materials Survey—Nickel*, 1952.

20. The so-called Townsend Report (see Defense Production Act Progress Report No. 36).

21. *Mineral Facts and Problems*, 1960 ed., cited above.

22. This appears also the rate at which nickel consumption has been rising during the fifties. For data from 1951 to 1957 see *The Supply of Nickel 1958–61*, International Nickel Co., New York, May 1, 1958.

23. Because of lack of data no comparisons are made for the world as a whole.

of the minimum reserves listed in Table 21–9, and about equal to these reserves plus the low estimate of potential ore in Table 21–10. (See also Figure 21–5.) However, one-third of the reserves and two-thirds of the potential ores consist of the Cuban deposits. Not only are the potential ores very low grade, but availability of all material is questionable on political grounds. On the other hand, the reserves, as has been stressed, are minimum figures, often of the working-inventory type, and thus can be misleading. They are apt to grow, rather than dwindle, with production.

To satisfy demand on the scale projected, which would imply demand toward the end of the century of some 2 million tons per year, or six to seven times current capacity,[24] would be possible only if Canadian deposits of great extent consisting of the traditional sulfide ores were to be proved, or a transition made to the laterites in the semi-tropical or tropical latitudes. Since Cuba, the Philippines, and Indonesia between them can be assumed to hold at least some 30 to 35 million tons of nickel in such deposits, it would seem that between new Canadian discoveries and working of the laterites projected consumption could be satisfied.

It is instructive to appraise in this framework the striking expansion in nickel capacity, not quite concluded as yet, brought about partly through the financial encouragement offered by the U.S. government, a development paralleled by an expansion in INCO's own reserve basis. If nickel capacity in 1951–52 can be assumed to have equaled deliveries—a reasonable hypothesis—then 1960 capacity of just over 300,000 tons of metal, or 250,000 tons excluding Cuba, would just about be double that of 1951–52. Exploitation at capacity rate of the mining properties included in the 1960 capacity estimate soon falls short of projected demand for non-communist countries and would theoretically exhaust the minimum reserve estimate of roughly 16 million tons in some fifty years, or more nearly in forty years allowing for losses in recovery. Ample as current capacity appears to be in relation to demand, rates of growth in

demand are such that by the end of this decade new capacity would be called for.

Transition to poorer ore involves two distinct areas, both in Cuba. The first are the proved commercially successful deposits of ore testing between 1.3 and 1.4 per cent nickel content; but these are limited in extent and probably accounted for in the minimum reserve estimates (Table 21–9). Beyond, there are probably some 15 to 20 million tons of low-grade nickel, testing barely above 1 and less than 1 per cent nickel, enough—with the minimum reserves elsewhere—to match demand in non-communist countries to the end of the century and beyond. But at the time of writing we cannot assume that the Cuban ores will in fact be available to non-communist countries.

In the longer run it is probably prudent to assume that directly or indirectly the production of Cuban nickel would have its impact upon the world market, but availability to the Sino-Soviet bloc on easy terms would maximize consumption in that area and permanently reduce its availability to non-communist countries.[25] Nor can we be certain of future development of processes that will free the contained nickel at no significant increase in cost, though success in dealing with this type of ore during the past two decades gives good grounds for assuming success.

Then we must turn to the deposits in the Philippines, in the Celebes and Borneo (now beginning to be tapped by Japan), in Venezuela and generally throughout the Caribbean (Puerto Rico, the Dominican Republic, and perhaps others once the search intensifies), and, according to latest advice, New Guinea, where U.S. Steel is reported to be on the track of nickeliferous ores. These locations, between them, can be counted on holding 10 million, perhaps 20 million, tons of nickel. The problem of recovery is, however, more difficult. Closeness of Cuba to the United States has been an invaluable factor in the success of the Nicaro and Moa Bay ventures. New Caledonia has maintained its operations on the basis of exceedingly high-grade ore—up to 10 per cent

24. For example, see The International Nickel Co., *The Supply of Nickel, 1958–1961* (New York, 1958).

25. In addition, there are difficult technical problems that Cuba must solve to operate the plants in Moa Bay, formerly owned by Freeport Sulphur Company.

nickel content—and cheap hand-sorting operations that have made it feasible to ship semi-processed material to France for refining. It is unlikely that similar conditions could be anticipated in other locations. Thus, the entire process from mining to refining would probably have to be carried on in the country of origin, and thus problems of fuel, chemicals, etc., would have to be satisfactorily solved, for the shipping of the much larger amounts of raw ore for refining in the Western Hemisphere or Europe would probably render the metal non-competitive or result in a boost in price for all nickel.

In none of these speculations can one go very far. Three conclusions emerge: (1) identified minimum reserves, even if fully exploitable in the next forty years, appear insufficient to meet projected demand; (2) no one knows the real size of reserves, but past production and reserve history suggest that they are substantially larger than now recorded; (3) much rides on the significance of the potential nickel ores, but without systematic cost studies the status of the low-grade reserves cannot be assessed in a meaningful way.

Tungsten. The melting point of tungsten is higher than that of any other known metal; its desirability in the space and nuclear age is thus self-evident. But this country is ill equipped to match it from indigenous sources.

While there are substantial deposits of tungsten in the continental United States, they consist mostly of low-grade, high-cost material. Their commercial exploitation thus depends entirely upon the price level, except in those instances where tungsten is produced as a by- or co-product in some other mining operation, principally molybdenum. Thus between 1950 and 1956, when under a policy of incentive prices and stockpiling the U.S. government paid over $60.00 per short ton unit,[26] concentrates containing as much as 7,000 short tons of the metal were produced per year at domestic mines. By 1958 the price had dropped below $20.00 and production had declined to less

than 2,000 tons. While more than 700 domestic mines had produced tungsten in 1955 only two mines were left operating in late 1958. By 1960, price had recovered somewhat and production was up to half its peak level of the mid-fifties.

A 1957 reserve estimate of 71,000 tons of tungsten contained in 9 million tons of short-ton units of WO_3 in the United States, does not specify at what level of prices this estimate becomes operative, except that after the end of the domestic incentive program in 1956 only an undetermined but probable small part of these deposits could be termed reserves.

Nonetheless, it is useful to compare this estimate with projected demand as estimated in Chapter 16 and shown in Table 21–3. Even the submarginal domestic reserves are not of an order of magnitude that would supply requirements for many years. At the 1960 level of consumption—5,000 tons of metal—domestic reserves are equivalent to fourteen years. This calculation suffers, of course, from the fact that current consumption has reached its size at a price level far below that at which most domestic tungsten has in the past become available. Thus, if domestic material had to supply the bulk of consumption, presumably less of it would be used—possibilities of substitution being increasingly widened—and reserves would thus last longer. Even so, there can be little doubt that the United States, while attempting to improve the conditions under which domestic materials can be used, must look abroad for its tungsten supplies.

World reserves were last estimated as of 1954 and put at 174 million short-ton units of WO_3, or 1.74 million tons of WO_3, equivalent to approximately 1.4 million tons of metal. Less than one-fifth of this is located in the non-communist areas of the world. Actually, the source of many of these data go substantially further back than 1954: China to 1948, Burma 1938, Malaya 1940, Bolivia 1941, etc.[27]

How much of this quantity constitutes reserves depends to a large extent upon the

26. Defined as 1 per cent of a short ton, or 20 pounds of WO_3, in turn containing just below 16 pounds of tungsten metal (W).

27. *Materials Survey, Tungsten*, compiled for the Office of Defense Mobilization by the U.S. Department of Commerce, Business and Defense Services Administration, December 1956, Chapter II.

TABLE 21–11.   Tungsten: World Reserves[1]

(Thousand tons)

Country	WO$_3$	Contained metal
China	[2]1,345	1,067
United States	90	71
So. Korea[3]	70	56
Bolivia	55	44
Burma	48	38
Canada[4]	35	28
Brazil	25	20
Portugal	20	16
U.S.S.R.	17	14
Australia	16	13
Malaya	14	11
Total, incl. countries not listed	1,765	1,400
Non-communist countries only	405	321

1. 1954 except for Canada. Source: U.S. Bureau of Mines, *Mineral Facts and Problems*, 1960 ed., p. 913, unless otherwise noted.
2. This may be a conservative estimate. A recent Russian estimate puts it at 3,300; cf. U.S. Bureau of Mines, Special Supplement No. 59 to *Mineral Trade Notes*, March 1960, p. 29.
3. No data available for No. Korea which up to 1946 was responsible for about half of Korean tungsten output.
4. Includes recently discovered deposit. See U.S. Bureau of Mines, *Minerals Yearbook 1960*, Vol. I, p. 1146.

price at which tungsten is selling. *The Minerals Yearbook* of 1958 commented, ". . . relatively few tungsten deposits in the Free World properly could be classified as ore,"[28] meaning that at market prices exploitation was not a commercial proposition. At the same time, it suggested that figures very similar to those shown in the subsequent tables could be considered a "potential free-world reserve" provided prices ranged at the 1950–56 level. During that period the average price per unit of domestic WO$_3$ exceeded $60.00 compared to prices in the $20.00 range since 1958; imports at times fetched over $50.00, more typically $30.00, but now sell for around $20.00, prior to U.S. duty payment.

In the face of such severe price fluctuations, added to the age and questionable quality of the data to begin with, the determination of what does and does not constitute reserves be-

28. U.S. Bureau of Mines, *Minerals Yearbook, 1958* Vol. I, p. 1095.

comes a venture of doubtful value. Table 21–11 presents the available information.

Consumption in non-communist countries outside the United States has recently been at a rate of some 9,000 tons of metal per year. In addition, most if not all of U.S. demand must be met out of the above reserves. The reserves of the non-communist countries thus are the equivalent of twenty years' current consumption, or of substantially fewer years when faster growth of demand outside the United States is taken into account. (See Figure 21–6.)

Cumulative U.S. consumption alone, based upon Chapter 16 estimates, has been projected in Table 21–3 at 460,000 tons, equal to 140 per cent of reserves in non-communist areas. Were demand in the rest of these areas to rise at the same rate as projected for the United States, cumulative demand in non-communist countries in the next four decades might total 1 million tons, or about three times reserves. Reserves at face value do not look larger than the equivalent of fifteen to twenty years' consumption, at moderately rising rates.

There are, however, some important qualifications to be made. In the first place, while some of the deposits may be only potential ore, no comprehensive information is available on

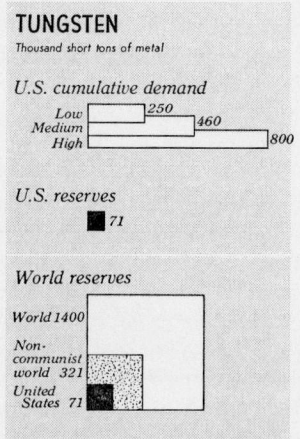

Figure 21–6. U.S. cumulative demand for tungsten, 1960–2000, compared with approximate 1960 U.S. reserves and world reserves.

potential ore as such; it is not feasible to speculate about the cost increases that would accompany gradual depletion. In the United States such occurrences are believed to amount to half again as much as reserves, but at what price they could be exploited is not known. The jump that might occur in a transition to domestic material is indicated by the experience of the fifties: a possible tripling in price; and it is likely that this would occur before recourse is had to material now labeled "submarginal," which refers to ore containing one-tenth of 1 per cent or less of WO_3, part of which can be recovered only as by-product.

Second, there has been a steady increase in estimated reserves. When the President's Materials Policy Commission report in 1952 suggested that "the future supply of tungsten in the free world may well be inadequate during the next 25 years,"[29] reserves of the non-communist countries were put at 270,000 tons, or some 20 per cent lower than they are now—roughly ten years later. In those ten years world production, in terms of contained metal, has totaled some 350,000 tons including China and the U.S.S.R., and 200,000 excluding both. The latter figure can be compared directly with the reserve estimate of 270,000 tons. It would then seem that of those reserves all but 70,000 tons were used up, but that an additional 250,000 tons of new reserves were found. This is not, presumably, how things happen. Rather, the nature of the reserve estimates is such that geologists have found no reason to change most of them during the past decade (or longer). And since production proceeds apace, the statistical outcome is one of unchanging or growing reserve estimates accompanying steady production. It is this kind of experience that makes one hesitate to speculate another twenty-five or forty years ahead, based upon reserve data that are poorly specified as to cost characteristics and seem to remain untouched by withdrawals for production.

Though of questionable practical effect for the time being, mention must be made of the truly enormous reserves estimated to be located in mainland China. The order of magnitude is four to five times that of the non-communist countries' reserves. If these deposits were to be exploited on any significant scale they would almost by necessity have to spill over into general international trade and would alleviate any impending tightness.

One cannot escape the judgment that major discoveries of orebodies or large-scale substitution of other metals, such as molybdenum, will have to take place long before the end of the century, indeed within the next ten to twenty years, if cost increases and reduced use of tungsten are to be avoided, provided the resource data are not as poor a guide now as they were ten years ago.

Molybdenum. The supply outlook for molybdenum has greatly improved over the recent past. When in 1957 the U.S. Geological Survey prepared the *Materials Survey* for molybdenum, recoverable molybdenum identified in the United States, Canada, and Chile, the world's principal sources, was estimated at 2.5 billion pounds. Since then the U.S. Department of the Interior has raised the estimate to more nearly 4 billion pounds[30] and even this appears to be a very conservative guess. The U.S. deposits alone have been estimated to contain 3 billion pounds. Of this, the principal molybdenum producer, Climax Molybdenum, controls some 2 billion pounds which the company claims could easily be doubled by indicated (but undefined) deposits. The remaining third, until 1960, was contained in western copper-bearing ores. Copper deposits in Chile may include a molybdenum reserve of 1 to 2 billion pounds, and those in Canada half a billion pounds.

In December 1960, the second largest U.S. molybdenum producer, Molybdenum Corporation of America, announced that explorations carried on during the past six years had resulted in identifying molybdenum ore in New Mexico estimated to contain nearly 800 million pounds of metal. Nor are these investigations concluded: apparently, subsequent to reporting

29. President's Materials Policy Commission, *Resources for Freedom*, Vol. II (Washington: U.S. Government Printing Office, 1952), p. 29.

30. U.S. Bureau of Mines, *Mineral Facts and Problems*, 1960 ed., cited above.

its findings to the Interior Department (which had aided in financing exploration) higher-grade deposits have been discovered. Thus one must suspend judgment of the size of U.S. reserves, but certainly 4 billion pounds even now appears conservative. Reserves of the non-communist countries would then total around 6 billion pounds.

Unlike most other metals, molybdenum happens to be practically a Western Hemisphere, and largely U.S., monopoly. Thus, comparison of domestic availability with domestic demand is meaningful. The latter has been running at around 30 million pounds (contained metal) a year in the second half of the fifties. In addition, exports have been approaching 15 million pounds. Based upon demand projections presented in Chapter 16, cumulative molybdenum consumption over the next forty years would exceed 5 billion pounds. (See Table 21–3.) If in addition the United States were merely to maintain its exports, another 600 million pounds or so would be required, and this figure, too, would rise with rising demand for steel, and especially alloy steel, abroad.

Thus one must with due prudence count on molybdenum demand to allow for both domestic consumption and exports of close to 6 billion pounds through the year 2000. Such a total, resting not only on the demand of the steel industry but also on the likelihood that the metal might gain importance in its own right in the field of space vehicles and similar uses, is so close to even a generous statement of reserves in non-communist areas that its satisfaction, on the basis of present knowledge, cannot be taken for granted. Only if one assumes the higher of the Chilean estimates, 2 billion pounds, and the doubling of Climax Molybdenum's reserves from 2 to 4 billion pounds, can one discount any resource problem in this field. Perhaps the only reasonable thing one can say is that molybdenum adequacy is not likely to become an issue until well into the latter part of the project period, at least in the Medium projection, and that recent discoveries give hope for a further boosting long before then.

The outlook is naturally far less reassuring for the High projection. The Low projection,

on the other hand, cumulating to less than 3 billion pounds, including foreign demand, is well within the realm of current reserves estimates.

Cobalt. A mineral with a wide spectrum of uses, from the pigment that produces blue-colored glass or ceramic ware to animal feeds and cancer-treatment application, cobalt has recently found increasing use as an alloy in both nonferrous and ferrous combinations. Resistance to wear and corrosion at high temperatures make it a desired element as an alloy in magnets, in missiles, jet engines, gas turbines, motors, generators, and other technical applications of the sixties. Its occurrence is widespread as a minor constituent in ores that bear copper, nickel, lead, iron, and other metals. Its recovery costs are high, and wherever feasible its use is avoided.

Given its markets, outlook for cobalt use is dynamic. Presently, the United States consumes some 4,000 to 5,000 tons of cobalt, valued at about $15 million. The course of the economy is unlikely to be bent one way or the other by resource problems that might arise in this particular metal. It has, however, been of strategic importance,[31] and its special properties in metallic and non-metallic peacetime uses are such that price considerations might be of secondary significance.

U.S. future use has been projected in Chapter 16 as rising from 4,500 tons in 1960 to 19,000 tons in 2000 in the Medium projection and twice as high in the High projection. Cumulative use in the forty years ending in 2000 would then be some 450,000 tons in the Medium, and 700,000 tons in the High projection.

Compared with estimates of reserves, these are not figures that conjure up the specter of tightness, provided far-away places remain accessible, for U.S. reserves are small: 43,000 tons with an additional 107,000 tons of potential ore.[32] Even jointly they amount to only a small part of projected use. Forty years of consumption at current levels would more than

31. See Chapter 9, especially pp. 177, 180.
32. U.S. Bureau of Mines, *Mineral Facts and Problems,* 1960 ed., cited above.

exhaust them. Reserves in the Congo, the area of principal production where cobalt emerges as a by-product of copper smelting and refining, have been put at 750,000 tons. These have for some time supplied the major portion of cobalt production in the non-communist world which in 1960 totaled 16,000 tons (metal content).

Ample cobalt resources exist in the lateritic ores of Cuba, together with nickel and chromium, but the program to exploit these ores has received a serious setback through the Castro revolution. Nonetheless, in the perspective of four decades the 370,000 tons of cobalt estimated to be contained in Cuban deposits of reasonably commercial quality, and another 700,000 tons in low-grade ore (between 0.07 and 0.1 percent cobalt content) are bound to have an effect upon availability. The Philippines, New Caledonia, Northern Rhodesia, and Canada are other areas known to have cobalt-bearing deposits; both Canada and Rhodesia have sizeable reserves from which they have recently been producing at the rate of 1,000 to 2,000 tons per year. However, lack of data on the cost implications of producing the cobalt contained in the mixed ores makes it impossible to classify these as either reserves or potential ore. Since there is much scope for substitution of cobalt, though usually with loss of efficiency, cost criteria take on especial importance in determining size of reserves.

Consumption data outside the United States are hard to find and, owing to stockpiling activities, world production is a misleading indicator. It is improbable, however, that U.S. consumption represents less than one-half of use in non-communist countries. More likely, it accounts for a larger share. Cumulative consumption in these countries through the year 2000 might then be of the order of 700,000 to 800,000 tons. While one cannot legitimately add the various estimates of reserves or resources enumerated above, the net conclusion is that cobalt consumption for most, if not all, of the remaining years of the century, is not likely to be held in check by depletion of reserves; but much more knowledge will have to be gained concerning the economic characteristics of deposits before one can be more certain of concomitant cost developments.

Vanadium. Both the reserves of and the resource base for vanadium are very large. Although it is only the twenty-second most abundant element in the upper portions of the earth's crust, it is the eighth most abundant metallic element. While it is widely dispersed in trace amounts so that much of the vanadium in the resource base is almost unavailable for use, vanadium is also found in large quanities, typically as a by-product, in a number of different types of ore deposits. In fact, much vanadium is extracted from the earth today but ends up in slag piles or mine dumps because it is not worth while to produce it as a separate product.

The best known source of vanadium is the Colorado Plateau of the United States, where it occurs with uranium in sandstones and limestones. Production from these deposits increased with the increase in uranium production and was encouraged by a purchase price guaranteed until recently by the Atomic Energy Commission. Production from these deposits has made the United States the world's largest vanadium producer. And U.S. consumption of vanadium in alloy steels has made it also the world's largest consumer of vanadium.

Uranium by-product production has in itself been more than enough for domestic needs and has provided a surplus of ore and of vanadium products for export. Indeed because of the purchase program, production for years was far in excess of consumption. An unfortunate result has been that interest in other sources of vanadium has been lagging. However, the content in some of these other deposits may far exceed that associated with uranium. These other modes of occurrence include vanadium associated with a number of types of iron deposits, with phosphate rock deposits, with shales surrounding phosphate rock, and with asphaltic material or other hydrocarbons.

A recent compilation[33] of calculated or estimated reserves of vanadium pentoxide—the form in which most statistics are cast—in

33. Materials Advisory Board, National Academy of Sciences–National Research Council, Report of the Committee on Refractory Metals (Washington, MAB-154-M[1] 1959), p. 231.

known domestic deposits indicates a total of just over 1,200,000 short tons, or more than 600,000 tons of contained vanadium metal. Deposits outside the United States contain about 375,000 short tons of metal. However, estimates for both known and undiscovered deposits suggest that very large tonnages exist beyond these figures. Titaniferous magnetites and vanadium associated with phosphate rock alone include probably as much again as the compiled reserves. Perhaps the most promising sources are vanadiferous phosphate deposits and the particular type of iron deposit known as titaniferous magnetite. Vanadium is already being extracted from the latter type of deposit in Finland and South Africa.

Projected use cumulated for the forty years through 2000 totals less than 200,000 tons in the Medium projection, and 275,000 tons in the High projection. The United States appears to be amply equipped with vanadium reserves to meet such demand.

Major Nonferrous Metals

The alloying materials, among the nonferrous metals, have just been discussed along with iron and steel to which they are principally tied. A few others are taken up briefly in a later section entitled "Minor Metals." The metals that we shall consider here are the five traditionally covered by the term "nonferrous metals," plus two relative newcomers, magnesium and titanium. The five traditional nonferrous metals were analyzed in Chapter 16 to the point of developing projections. These have

been cumulated and are presented, together with the 1960 level of consumption, in Table 21–12. All later comparisons of reserves and resources with projected demand refer to this table.

Copper. Although copper ore reserves have a history of steadily increasing deposits, both at home and abroad, it is hard to marshall statistical evidence that existing occurrences plus those to be added in the future will suffice to meet the demand of non-communist countries. (See Figure 21–7.) Much of the difficulty arises from the fact that half a dozen companies dominate the industry: three American, two British, and one Belgian. The small number of companies involved has tended to limit both quantity and quality of the available statistical information. Even now, government agencies often are loath to publicize information that might divulge operational details of individual companies. In addition, their knowledge frequently is limited to whatever a company is prepared to communicate.

This situation has its repercussions in the field of resource estimates. As in the case of petroleum, reserve estimates pertain almost exclusively to deposits that are either measured or indicated, but not inferred, for the reason that reserves fulfill primarily—almost exclusively—the function of a company's working inventory. Thus the known reserves have generally a low "life index" in comparison with the reserve/production ratio in iron and bauxite. As copper reserves in a particular area

TABLE 21–12. Major Nonferrous Metals: U.S. Consumption, 1960 and Projections to 2000

						(Million short tons of primary metal)	
		Low		Medium		High	
Metal	1960	1960–80	1960–2000	1960–80	1960–2000	1960–80	1960–2000
Aluminum	2.06	51	140	73	255	113	480
Copper	1.74	31	60	42	112	52	181
Lead	.64	10	23	15	38	21	68
Zinc	1.05	22	50	28	69	36	126
Tin	.07	.9	1.5	1.3	3.0	1.9	6.1

Source: Appendix Tables A16–35, 47, 56, 66, 72.

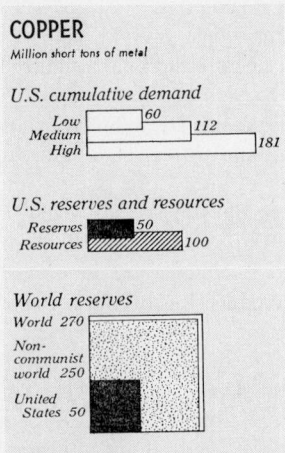

COPPER
Million short tons of metal

U.S. cumulative demand

Low | 60
Medium | 112
High | 181

U.S. reserves and resources

Reserves | 50
Resources | 100

World reserves

World 270
Non-communist world 250
United States 50

Figure 21–7. U.S. cumulative demand for copper, 1960–2000, compared with approximate 1960 U.S. reserves and resources and world reserves.

significance in copper because its occurrence in nature is low to begin with and highly localized. Copper is worked at a cut-off grade some fifty times below that of iron or bauxite, and at a level of concentration that is itself some fifty times the average copper content in the earth crust.

Copper reserves have increased in two ways: new deposits have been located and the specifications for suitable ore have been gradually reduced. Table 21–13 presents historical data on average tenor of copper ores mined in the United States during the past eight decades.

This tabulation is indicative of the progress of technology, especially when considered in conjunction with the long-run course of copper prices which shows no increase accompanying this decline in grade. While this is not proof that the lower-grade deposits are not more costly to mine, it does suggest that improved techniques have, in the past at least, successfully offset any cost-boosting effect that a decline of 70 per cent in copper grade might have exerted.

Whether or not higher costs necessarily accompany the transition to lower-grade material is a question that available information does not enable one to answer. As Herfindahl points out, lower-grade material may, for a variety of reasons, be less costly to mine; sufficiently so to offset the increased amount of raw material that must be handled. Among these reasons may be easier accessibility, attractiveness of mining ore which has low copper content but admixtures of other valuable minerals, decreased selectiveness, i.e., less sorting effort, and others. Whatever the reasons, the deterioration in quality of ore has certainly not boosted real costs in the past.

The average grade being mined today is 0.8 per cent ore. Will the phenomenon of constant

diminish, enough drilling or other exploratory activity is carried on to assure offsetting supplies (or alternatively the mine is closed down), but to judge from the information that is available, little if any effort is made to ascertain reserves that include those inferred from indirect geological evidence of one kind or another, accompanied by only a minimum of digging. Proving of reserves beyond the point which assures profitability of a given development for exploitation would seem to occur only as a by-product of this activity rather than as an aim in itself. In any event, reserve figures in copper are incomplete. Beyond the inferred reserves category there lie the unexplored and probably large amounts of potential ore whose extent is equally unknown, except for broadly based guesses. These elements have particular

TABLE 21–13. Grade of Copper Ore Mined in the United States, 1880–1956

1880 .... 3.0%	1906–10 .... 2.1%	1931–40 .... 1.6%
1889 .... 3.3%	1911–20 .... 1.7%	1941–50 .... 1.0%
1902 .... 2.7%	1921–30 .... 1.6%	1951–56 .... 0.8%

Source: Orris C. Herfindahl, *Copper Costs and Prices: 1870–1957* (Baltimore: Johns Hopkins Press and Resources for the Future, Inc., 1959).

cost hold good also for the next drop of one-tenth, two-tenths, or three-tenths of 1 per cent? The answer hinges to some extent on whether there is a minimum absolute loss entailed in processing the ore, no matter what the grade. The argument is often advanced that from 0.1 to 0.2 per cent of the copper-bearing material is lost under any circumstances; therefore this loss which can still be borne by 0.8 per cent average grade (probably having a cutoff point at or just below 0.6 per cent as the lowest type grade used at all) cannot be tolerated when the average drops to, say, 0.6, and the cutoff point to, say, 0.5 or 0.4 per cent. Clear proof of the proposition is lacking, however, and its nature is such that it seems among the problems likely to be successfully tackled by advancing technology. It does not run afoul of a law of physics such as exists, let us say, in conventional steam power generation, but is based upon a mechanical inefficiency. For example, leaching in place rather than refining after mining might lead to significantly higher recovery; the possible extent and cost implications of such a process, or others, cannot as yet be appraised. Nonetheless, one must provide for the likelihood that at one point or another there will arise that increase in cost that is no longer offset by improved technology.

These considerations provide a key to an understanding of the reserve estimates. Study of recent reserve history in the United States reveals that extension of reserves has in this century come about much more through progressive inroads upon the poorer portions of known copper fields than through the addition of entirely new copper-bearing provinces. Indeed, the latter event is somewhat of a rarity. Thus, when the joint efforts of the Bureau of Mines and the Geological Survey led to the discovery of the San Manuel deposit in Arizona, the occasion was characterized in the following terms: "Drilling at the San Manuel property near Tiger, Arizona, had developed enough ore by the end of 1946 to prove that a major copper ore body had been discovered. Thus, for the first time in a generation a substantial addition had been made to U.S. copper reserves from a recently discovered ore body."[34]

And even in this case, the general area—eastern Arizona—was one in which copper had previously been found in abundance.[35]

Such extension of existing deposits often calls for a changeover from underground to open-pit mining, and this again is a case of reduced cost as lower-grade ore comes into play. Indeed, it is the lower cost that permits the transition to lower grade. Perhaps the most striking such changeover in recent times has been the engineering of the so-called "Greater Butte" project in Montana, where in the heart of one of the oldest copper-producing areas in the country lower grades were tackled by a switch to open-pit mining. Though government sources, concerned about revealing company data, do not specify the composition of their reserve estimates, it is not hard to guess that it was this expansion, with a similar one in Michigan, that played a significant part in boosting copper reserve figures during the fifties.

In the absence of geological information, one of the most imaginative of mineral geologists, Sam G. Lasky, until recently of the U.S. Geological Survey, tried to fill the gap by formulating "laws" of mineral occurrence, in which a general relationship is established between the quantity of reserves and the grade of the ore, extrapolated beyond the grade down to which copper has in fact been worked. Developed in various articles[36] and used frequently in the President's Materials Policy Commission's report, the relationship—claimed by him to be generally valid because grounded in the history of deposits—postulates a steep increase in reserves as grade is allowed to decline, though this is not necessarily true for each of the great deposits now known. On this theoretical basis Lasky suggests the existence in the continental United States of some 100 million tons of copper in ore down to a tenor of —it seems from the chart in the PMPC report —just about 0.5 per cent,[37] or substantially be-

34. U.S. Bureau of Mines, *Minerals Yearbook 1946*, p. 458.

35. More recent Arizona discoveries (Mission, Pima, and Esperanza) may fall into the same category, but are in all likelihood not in the same size class.

36. See, for example, S. G. Lasky, "How Tonnage and Grade Relations Help Predict Ore Reserves," *Engineering and Mining Journal*, April 1950, pp. 81–85.

37. President's Materials Policy Commission, *op. cit.*, p. 144.

low current levels of profitability which keep the official estimate of reserves at only 32.5 million tons of copper.

In addition to the fact that it is net of inferred deposits, the current reserve estimate is probably conservative. In its 1956 edition of *Mineral Facts and Problems*—at a time when the official reserve estimate was only 25 million tons—the Bureau of Mines suggested, without further details, that there were some ten to fifteen years' worth of supply "around old mines and in new areas." One would not go wrong, therefore, in guessing at measured and indicated reserves of not less than 40 million and perhaps reaching towards 50 million tons. At projected Medium rates of domestic demand such amounts would be equivalent to less than one-half of cumulative demand and, if minable at will, would support domestic consumption through the late seventies. It is not, of course, suggested that the total deposits could in fact be worked up in this brief period. What is more likely is that domestic production will contribute each year no less than 1 million and perhaps as much as 1.5 million tons, with exhaustion of reserves postponed until the last decade of the century, always barring the development of lower-grade deposits.

Assuming that Lasky's curve reflects reality and that improved discovery techniques would permit location of all copper deposits, assumed by Lasky, the average grade mined would have to decline to less than 0.5 per cent in order to meet the estimated U.S. requirements of some 110 million tons of metal for the four decades; the Low projection, which cumulates to 60 million tons of copper demand, could be met from domestic resources by lowering the average grade worked—again reading from the Lasky curve—to some 0.7 per cent. Thus, not even at the Low projection level could domestic reserves, as now defined, be relied upon to meet domestic needs. And only the Low projection could perhaps be met by a further decline in grade of ore mined. One must look to the rest of the world, which even now supplies some 30 per cent of all copper ore refined in the United States. (See Figure 21–8.) Lasky's speculations are, of course, subject to two difficulties: (*a*) One would not of course, ever know whether all deposits had been discovered; and (*b*) discoveries of major high-grade deposits, though improbable, are still possible.

Foreign reserves. Complete estimates of foreign copper reserves are rare. The latest Bureau of Mines estimate was published in 1958, and at that time—as in the case of domestic

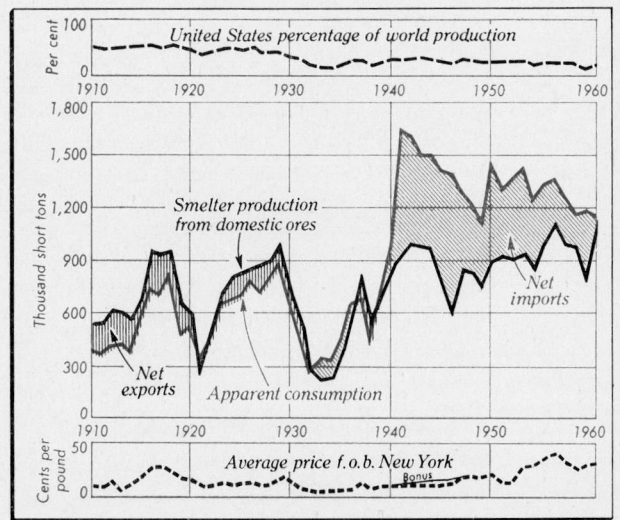
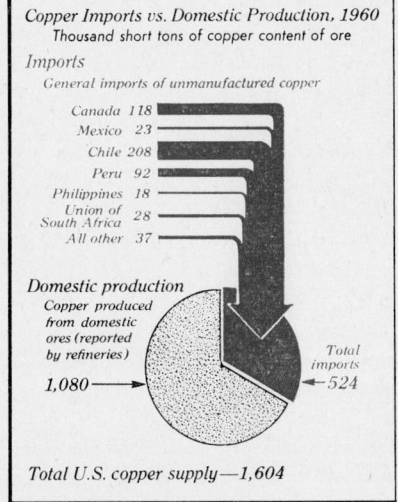

Figure 21–8. Sources of U.S. copper supply, 1910–1960.

reserves—only measured and indicated re-serves were accounted for. The total for non-communist countries other than the United States amounted to 122 million tons of con-tained metal (see Table 21–14). A substan-tially more generous estimate was put forward by the Geological Survey experts in their work for the President's Materials Policy Commis-sion, when they hazarded a guess at inferred reserves and suggested a total of 175 million tons. As new discoveries have since been made, it would not be unreasonable to put total for-eign reserves at a minimum of 200 million tons.

There are many uncertainties in this esti-mate. Measured and indicated reserves in Chile are put at 46 million tons, but inclusion of in-ferred deposits might raise this to as much as 75 million (which is the amount carried as "in-dicated" in the PMPC report). Similarly, the 25 million tons for Northern Rhodesia might be triple that quantity when inferred reserves are considered, and the Congo's reserves might go from 20 million to 40/50 million tons, depend-ing upon one's interpretation of past estimates.

As these deposits are worked by the same American companies that predominate in the U.S. industry, plus only three foreign ones, the uncertainty surrounding the size of the ulti-mate reserves, even those recoverable with

TABLE 21–14.   Copper: Foreign Reserves, 1958

(Million short tons)

Country	Measured and indi-cated	Possible inferred
Canada	7.0	?
Chile	46.0	30
No. Rhodesia	24.5	50
Congo (Katanga)	20.0	30
Peru	12.5	?
Yugoslavia	1.2	?
So. Africa	1.1	?
Philippines	1.0	?
Australia	1.0	?
Others	7.4	?
Sino-Soviet bloc	16.0	?
Total (rounded)	138.0	100+

Source: U.S. Bureau of Mines, *Mineral Facts and Prob-lems,* 1960 ed., p. 250; and President's Materials Policy Com-mission, *op. cit.,* Vol. II, p. 145.

present techniques and at present prices, again is rooted largely in this feature of the indus-try's structure. The matter is further com-plicated by the high-grade quality of most of these deposits: 6 per cent copper content in the Congo, up to almost 4 per cent in Rho-desia, and between 1 and 2 per cent in Chile. Reference to the generalized ore-tonnage curve mentioned above would lead one to assume that deposits down to an average of 1 per cent copper content—a better grade ore than is now being worked in the United States—might ag-gregate as much as 400 million to 500 million tons of copper metal, and this might be doubled if one were to lower the specification to 0.5 per cent average content.

There is always the possibility that new de-posits may be uncovered in areas that have not hitherto been known as copper bearing. This is particularly true for deep-lying deposits. Im-proved and expanded prospecting methods, briefly described in a later section, may bring surprises, less likely for the time being in the well-explored United States but more so in areas like Canada, Australia, and Africa.

The foreign reserves are large enough to meet U.S. demand for several decades, but can-not be considered as available without taking into account foreign demand. Even a rough guess at this demand is hazardous, as exempli-fied by the projection advanced for 1975 by the President's Materials Policy Commission, which so underestimated growth that, on any rough count, it was surpassed by the late fifties. Against the anticipated growth rate in demand of 1.7 per cent, the actual growth rate between 1950 and 1958 has been 9.4 per cent—some-thing of the order of the growth in aluminum. Assuming that this growth rate attained dur-ing the period of heavy European reconstruc-tion will not be maintained and that in the future even a rate of 5 per cent—which ap-pears to have prevailed since the big jump in consumption that took place between 1953 and 1954—might be on the generous side (U.S. experience as that of a developed country sug-gests a far lower rate, nearer 1 per cent and lower still if the recent recession years are in-cluded), cumulative demand in non-communist countries would total some 450 million tons,[38] excluding the United States, or 560 million tons including the Medium U.S. demand projection.

Short of the use of an indirect, generalized approach, such as the Lasky curve, we cannot point today to the resources to meet a cumulative demand of 500 to 600 million tons of copper. The most we see in terms of measured, indicated, and inferred reserves throughout the non-communist world are perhaps 250 million tons, or half the demand at the assumed rates of growth. It is only when foreign ores down to the 1 per cent grade level are taken into account and estimated according to the grade-quantity curve, that anything like 500 to 600 million tons come into view. Foreign demand would have to grow at a rate even lower than that projected for the United States for the copper reserves of 250 million tons to approach a level of adequacy. For example, if foreign demand should grow by only 2 per cent per annum, cumulative foreign demand for the four decades would aggregate some 160 million tons, and total demand for non-communist countries some 270 million tons. This begins to be more within the range of estimated reserves, though discoveries would still have to be sizeable to sustain such production. Moreover, these speculations contain the implicit assumption that all deposits would be exploitable within forty years, undoubtedly an unrealistic simplification. Thus even at very low rates of growth of foreign demand (and certainly at the High projection of U.S. demand), we possess no knowledge that permits us to foresee a supply-demand balance without the workings of deposits that presently lie outside the confines of economic mining. Additions to reserves amounting to four or five times present reserves are a task that even greatly expanded exploration activity might be unable to accomplish. Gradual lowering of grade has in the past been accomplished without cost increases. We will have to know more about these relationships at lower levels of concentration before we can feel more certain that this experience suggests a similar development in the next four decades, but the odds are in favor. Indeed, the economics often seem less disconcerting than the politics in the copper-rich parts of the world.

Nevertheless, the fact remains that the real price of copper has not increased in the past; if anything it has declined. Obviously, the producers of copper ore are not rushing to buy up promising sites and charging off their rising costs to their current sales. Perhaps there is no contradiction between this phenomenon and the uncertain long-run outlook, for the reason that forty years is not a span of time that businessmen ordinarily worry about. Or perhaps copper producers are confident from cost data in their possession that within such a period they can devise ways and means of economically exploiting the lower-grade deposits which they might have good reason to suspect exist in large amounts, not from any theoretical curve but from concrete geological evidence in areas where they have been mining successfully for many decades.

The high cutoff point in grade that now prevails in most foreign operations and the findings that the cutoff point in U.S. production has been drastically lowered over the years without cost increase strongly suggest that foreign production could be vastly expanded at constant cost. To the extent that local taxation practices cancel the cost advantage, such matters could be expected to undergo adjustment in the face of a declining copper market that would be the consequence of rigid tax policies and rising prices. However, neither knowledge of reserves and resources nor of future demand is such that any of these trends can be foreseen with much certainty.

Bauxite and other aluminum sources. Reserves of bauxite, the ore from which aluminum is obtained, more than doubled during the fifties. Indeed, it does not take much modification of official data to demonstrate that

---

38. The 1960 base of 2.8 million tons is much higher than the level of the immediately preceding years, but continued through 1961. Taking a 1956–59 average as a starting point, the figure would be more nearly 350 million tons. The hypothetical world demand figures used by Netschert and Landsberg (*op. cit.*, p. 47) for the world as a whole are indeed somewhat lower: 551 million tons at 5 per cent growth and 423 million tons at 3.9 per cent growth. These differences do not affect the judgment as to resource adequacy.

they may more nearly have tripled. And since systematic exploration and application of the fruits of technology in the use of ores have just begun, abundance seems the prospect. Aluminum is the metallic element that bulks largest in the crust of the earth—some 7.5 per cent of the total. However, for the contained aluminum to be of commercial significance it has to be present not only in concentrations that exceed its average occurrence, but also in such combinations with other elements as make its recovery technically and economically feasible.

Bauxites—which are hydrated aluminum oxides usually mechanically but not chemically mixed with silica and iron—are the primarily useful form from which aluminum has hitherto been recovered; the lower the silica and iron admixture, the better the ore. These ores are the end-result of a long weathering process during which other chemical components of the original clay or feldspar have slowly been leached out, leaving a relatively "clean" and high-grade ore for easy processing. By the same token, ores that are in a younger stage of development or that contain silicates as chemical rather than mechanical components, constitute potential raw material for the aluminum producer.

As the criteria are relaxed, the reserves expand—practically ad infinitum. This is precisely what has happened during the past two decades when improved processes have widened the tolerance for both silica and the iron content, and consequently lower alumina content has become acceptable. Today ores are mined and processed that only twenty years ago would not have been considered useful assets. From an average of 60 per cent in 1930, alumina content has declined to 50 per cent. Within the last two decades, the permissible silica content has rapidly risen from less than 8 to more than 15 per cent as new processes have been developed. High costs have been offset by higher rates of extraction of alumina and by the lower cost of less selective mining methods. Ability to use a 15 per cent silica material means in practice that material substantially higher (up to 25 per cent has been used) can be mined and then mixed with high-grade bauxite to raise its alumina content average. Elsewhere, in the

U.S.S.R. for example, much higher silica-content material is reported to have been used. In the United States the Bureau of Mines in 1947 reported alumina production costs from aluminum-bearing kaolin (reserves of which were put at over 100 million tons) as about 30 to 40 per cent above those prevailing in bauxite-derived alumina production. Kaolin, with an alumina content varying between 34 and 38 per cent—a silica content of over 40 per cent—is not qualified for inclusion in the reserve figures. Yet, the cost increase was such as to raise the price of aluminum ingot by no more than 10 per cent. Experiments with anorthosite, a plentiful non-bauxitic clay, have recently led the Bureau to similar conclusions.[39]

There is no reason to assume that the continuing research being carried on by the industry and, intermittently, by government will not bring results that will further broaden the specifications of useful aluminum-bearing ore. Reserve estimates are therefore of a transitory character, in need of frequent revision.

Apart from the broadening spectrum of the useful ore, the postwar years have also seen a vast expansion in the reserves of more narrowly defined bauxite ores, some of it accidental, most of it the result of systematic search. The most striking accidental discovery relates to the Jamaican deposits, until recently the largest single find. They owe their discovery to the concern of a landowner over the low productivity of his soil. A sample sent for analysis to London in 1942 was found to contain 50 per cent aluminum. Jamaican deposits now are estimated to contain some 600 million short tons of bauxite.

Intensified geological activity, especially in Africa but also in Australia, has since uncovered even larger deposits, and the end seems by no means in sight. It is only in relatively well-mapped areas like the United States that big surprises are unlikely. Here the principal expansion would seem to lie in the direction of lower-grade and silica-type ores of which hundreds of millions of tons may become available for exploitation.

39. See H. W. St. Clair, *et al., Operation of Experimental Plant for Producing Alumina from Anorthosite,* Bureau of Mines Bulletin No. 577 (Washington: U.S. Department of the Interior, 1959).

TABLE 21–15. Bauxite: World Reserves and Resources, 1950 and 1958

(Million long tons in place)

Region	Reserves 1950	Reserves 1958	Identified potential ore 1958
North America			
Caribbean			
Jamaica	320	550	450
Dominican Republic	n.a.	40	40
Haiti	23	23	7
United States	47	50	350
South America			
Surinam	50	200	200
British Guiana	65	80	70
Brazil	190	30	173
Europe			
Non-Soviet bloc	225	371	396
Soviet bloc	300	350	n.a.
Asia			
China	50	50	950
Other	61	98	273
Africa			
Guinea	n.a.	1,000	2,000
Ghana	229	229	n.a.
Oceania	21	603	403
Total (incl. areas not listed)	1,612	3,624	5,577
Estimated contained aluminum (mil. short tons)	400	900	1,100
Non-communist countries only in ground, wet	1,251	3,224	4,627
estimated contained aluminum (mil. short tons)	310	800	925

n.a. = not available.

Source: From U.S. Bureau of Mines, *Mineral Facts and Problems,* 1956 and 1960 ed., except for Guinea where latest reports suggest a different breakdown between reserves and potential ore (1:2 rather than 1:4). Also, 1950 figures for United States, given in source in dry tons, have been converted to equivalent wet tonnage.

As orders of magnitude the following estimates, going largely back to the President's Materials Policy Commission report, are offered: the equivalent of 25 million short tons of aluminum in potential, i.e., lower-grade bauxite ore, and more than 1 billion tons if ore specifications are further relaxed; finally, another billion tons in non-bauxitic minerals and rocks.[40] The conservative figure of 350 million tons of ore in place, shown in Table 21–15, is a more recent estimate made by the U.S. De-

40. Netschert and Landsberg, *op. cit.,* p. 35.

partment of the Interior. However, the far richer reserves elsewhere carried across oceans on low freight superbarges to tideland or river-based smelters, make it unlikely, except in a long-lasting emergency, that these potential resources will be drawn upon in our time.

While the rate and steadiness of annual growth in aluminum consumption and production is impressive, both here and abroad, the current level of output still is tiny when measured in terms of bauxite reserves. On the rough basis of 4 long tons of bauxite being required for each short ton of primary aluminum, the 1958 reserve estimate of 3¼ billion tons of bauxite reserves in the non-communist countries, shown in Table 21–15, represents the equivalent of 800 million short tons of aluminum. In 1960, aluminum production in non-communist countries was approximately 4 million tons: one-half of 1 per cent of reserves. Nonetheless these reserves, which at current rates of output would carry us into the middle of the twenty-second century, could be exhausted in a few decades at the steeply rising consumption levels that one must anticipate.

For the United States alone, Medium demand for aluminum has been projected to rise at a rate of 5.2 per cent in the first two decades from 1960 and a rate of 4.3 per cent in the period 1980–2000. At such rates of growth the cumulative demand would be just over 250 million short tons for the years 1960 through 2000. This equals not quite one-third of reserves for the non-communist countries, some-

TABLE 21–16. Aluminum: Per Capita Consumption in Selected Countries, 1950 and 1960

(Pounds)

Country	1950	1960
United States	11.9	[1]22.0
Belgium	1.6	14.5
France	2.4	10.3
Germany	2.3	12.5
Italy	2.3	5.0
United Kingdom	8.1	15.1

1. U.S. figure is for 1959–60 to average high 1959 and low 1960 consumption.

Source: Data from American Bureau of Metal Statistics, and U.N. Demographic Yearbooks.

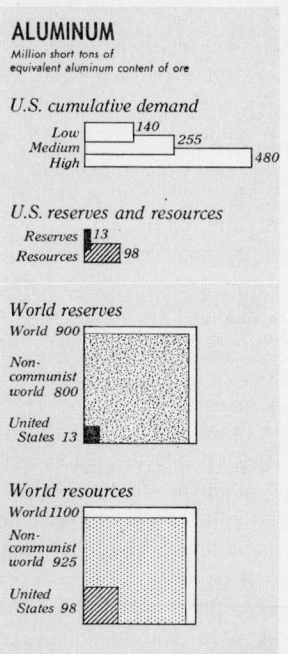

Figure 21–9. U.S. cumulative demand for aluminum, 1960–2000, compared with approximate 1960 U.S. reserves and resources and world reserves and resources.

what less than the present U.S. share in these countries' aluminum consumption, which is closer to one-half. (See Figure 21–9.)

It is hardly likely that demand outside the United States will grow less steeply, given the low per capita consumption for principal European consumers compared with the U.S. level. One might rather argue that growth rates outside the United States are likely to exceed projected U.S. rates, on the basis that rates of growth for the immediate future, commonly assumed at 8 to 10 per cent per annum at least in Europe, and probably at higher rates in the non-communist countries outside Europe, will stay at this level for some time.

On the assumption that foreign rates of growth would no more than match U.S. rates, aluminum consumption in non-communist countries, inclusive of the United States, would total 500 million tons from 1960 to 2000 and would thus claim two-thirds of the currently estimated reserves. Assuming consumption in these, outside the United States, to grow at rates one-half larger than the implied U.S. rate (i.e., at about 7 per cent per year), aluminum consumption for non-communist areas including the United States would cumulate to 900 million tons, or equal to reserves plus 10 per cent of potential ore. On a less conservative interpretation of reserves we might expect that even this demand will be more or less in balance with the reserve situation, as part of potential ore can be expected to be moving into the reserve category. It is important to add that this balance is in prospect at constant real prices, and perhaps even at a slight reduction in prices. The reasons are that the reserves today "on the books" are high-grade reserves of conventional composition, and that technological advance either in processing or in transportation can be expected to lead to savings. The likely shift of processing facilities toward the vicinity of bauxite deposits, as now planned in several major instances in West Africa, will sharply reduce the cost of transportation, as only half a short ton of alumina or one-quarter short ton of aluminum would have to be shipped for every long ton of bauxite now moving from mine to refinery, typically involving long sea journeys.

Mitigating factors. For several reasons, the above is a most conservative approach to the appraisal of adequacy. In the first place, the reserve data listed in Table 21–15 are minimum estimates. In one area alone, Australia, reserves three times as high as those shown are freely anticipated. The African reserves will certainly turn out to be much larger than now agreed. Only two areas—Guinea and Ghana—are shown in the table, and much more of the Guinea deposit than here shown may be in the reserve category, while no potential ore estimate exists for Ghana. Also, it is known even now that reserves exist in other parts of Africa: for example, in the Congo where erection of a half-million ton smelter has been talked about, in Liberia, and in Madagascar.

The mere fact that between 1950 and 1958 reserve estimates of bauxite deposits, as compiled by the U.S. Bureau of Mines, have been more than doubled to nearly 2 billion tons leads one to suspect that systematic exploration effort will raise these figures by several more billion tons in the next forty years, given the initial abundance of aluminum in the earth's crust.[41] Asian reserves are presently negligible, yet bauxite occurs predominantly in wet tropical or semi-tropical regions where weathering has sufficiently leached out the non-aluminum components of the basic rock. It is likely, therefore, that the warm regions of Asia

—as well as of South America and Africa— contain hitherto unrecorded bauxite deposits.

In the second place, aluminum-bearing material becomes a reserve as soon as quality criteria are lowered. In 1958, the Bureau of Mines put the potential resources of non-communist areas—largely bauxites and clays containing between 32 and 45 per cent of alumina only—at nearly 5 billion tons (of which 7 per cent were in the United States), or in terms of recoverable aluminum content a little more than the estimated reserves. But the potential tonnage of raw material that can technically be turned into aluminum runs into the tens of billions of tons. In the last resort, the pre-bauxite stages, i.e., the clay in our backyards, and ordinary feldspar, are potential aluminum reserves. One need not, however, be that radical. In the declining scale of values, there are first of all those bauxites that have a high silica or iron content and are therefore more wasteful to process. For example, removal of the 6 per cent maximum ferrous iron content limitation doubles U.S. reserves. Lowering the alumina content to 30 per cent—and such ores have been used elsewhere—would extend world resources indefinitely.

There are, third, the various non-bauxite aluminum-bearing minerals—anorthosite, nephelin, etc., some of which have in pilot operations here and abroad been processed into aluminum. In terms of the cost of refined aluminum the increased cost arising from the lowering of grade is of such a low order that the rise in price consequent upon the use of non-bauxite materials is not likely to be in excess of 10 per cent; this is the conclusion one must draw from the very careful investigations conducted by the Bureau of Mines. The latest report published in 1959,[42] estimates a cost increase of 2½ cents per pound of aluminum. Undoubtedly, within four decades this differential could be substantially reduced or might even disappear altogether with economies arising from processing on a large scale. There has been little urgency in estimating the size of potential resources of this nature. The PMPC guess that domestic sources of anor-

41. Between 1941 and 1953 reserve estimates grew by 50 million tons per year (on the average), as against 250 million per year between 1950 and 1958.

42. H. W. St. Clair *et al., op. cit.,* p. 26.

thosite are of the order of magnitude of 1 billion tons of aluminum content still stands. There is thus every reason to anticipate an abundance of aluminum-bearing material at substantially constant cost far beyond the end of the twentieth century.

In the narrower terms of domestically available material, the situation for the United States is less favorable. High-grade reserves aggregate only 50 million tons, equivalent to 42.5 million tons dry bauxite. These amounts would support production of some 10 million short tons of aluminum, no more than the equivalent of a five-year supply, at recent consumption levels (though they are, of course, likely to be mined over a longer period as a supplement to imported ores).

However, self-sufficiency in bauxites has not been a feature of U.S. aluminum production for many years. Since World War II when self-sufficiency was almost attained, aluminum producers have increasingly turned to foreign ores which they themselves have frequently helped to develop, a picture quite similar to that now emerging in iron ore.

By 1960, domestic bauxites contributed less than one-fifth to total bauxite consumption. In addition, the country had a net import balance of finished aluminum, further tipping the scales against self-supply. Since much of the aluminum industry has been located at the seaboard ready to receive bulk shipments of foreign bauxite, and since foreign reserves are infinitely larger than domestic reserves, this pattern is likely to continue, with the Arkansas mines producing between 1 and 2 million tons of bauxite per year for many years to come, while increased demand is met by increased imports.

At the same time, the larger reserves of lower-grade material provide a line of retreat in case of inaccessibility of foreign sources, which might, however, require substantial modifications of existing equipment. Perhaps the next stage, given peaceful conditions, will be a gradual change in emphasis from importing bauxite to importing alumina or even aluminum. For many of the new bauxite deposits are located in areas of potentially cheap hydropower generation, especially in West Africa, and the newly emerging countries are eager to exploit this resource. Even the most effective use of domestic low-grade ores, including tonnages in the hundreds of millions that appear to exist in the islands of Hawaii and about which more knowledge should soon be forthcoming, might not be enough to offset the combined advantages of low-cost electric power and 80,000- or 100,000-ton carriers that might in the not too distant future be available to the industry in its operations abroad.

While a reasonably open-minded interpretation of current reserve estimates of bauxites can easily be reconciled with meeting Medium projected demand for the balance of the century and beyond, the balance in prospect for the High projection is a little harder to establish, though still within reasonable limits of achievement. For the United States, it checks in at a level almost twice that of the Medium projection, or nearly 500 million tons of aluminum, and if demand in non-communist areas outside the United States should show a similar magnitude, total demand would be for about 1 billion tons, some 25 per cent in excess of reserves.

Whether or not this rate of demand is likely should become apparent in the next ten or fifteen years during which growth rates are likely to be at their maximum. For example, under the High projection, U.S. aluminum demand in 1970 would be 5.1 million short tons, requiring some 20 million long tons of dry bauxite. This is between two-and-a-half and three times the level of recent years. There is little doubt that such a development would greatly stimulate the perfection of methods for using clays and feldspars, and accelerate systematic exploration abroad. Times of stringency have always been times of technological advance. Indeed, one cannot read recent history of the search for more ore and better methods without being convinced of the probable fruitfulness of both approaches and the consequent likelihood that, even if future growth should be along the lines traced by the High projection requirements, these could be met for the balance of the century and beyond without a significant increase in cost.

A final note on direct reduction of aluminum-bearing ore which by-passes the intermediate alumina stage: It is possible that this development, which has now led to the establishment of at least one experimental plant, may have a technology in which neither the degree of impurities (silica, iron, etc.) nor the degree of concentration has significant cost complications. Such a path would radically shuffle the significance of domestic vs. imported aluminum. A basic advantage would be the elimination of a great deal of labor and facilities connected with the initial stage in which bauxites or clay are processed into alumina. The capital and labor savings—the former have been spoken of as perhaps one-third of present cost—would in turn make it feasible to utilize lower-grade ore without a corresponding increase in cost of the finished metal. Substantial resources have been channeled into research and more recently into construction of sizeable pilot plants, here and abroad (France, Japan, Canada). In the long run, this approach may be as successful in widening the industry's raw material base as continuing attempts to improve the recovery of alumina from clays. As for the latter, there are indications, though as yet no proof, that new processes can yield a production cost of alumina competitive with that of alumina from bauxites. From a security point of view this would be of first-rate significance, but in the long run it is likely to be overshadowed by the elimination of the alumina stage altogether.

Lead and zinc. A series of natural factors, aggravated by the reported difficulty of obtaining details of their operations from mining companies, makes the reserve situation for lead and zinc difficult to assess.

Among the natural obstacles to a quantitative assessment are: (1) the usual occurrence of lead and zinc deposits in combination, often not merely with one another but also with other metals such as gold, silver, and copper, and at other times with non-metals such as pyrites; (2) the characteristic smallness of deposits, compared to the massive nature found in iron, bauxite, or copper ore deposits; (3) their irregular shape and less continuity in degree of metal content; and (4) the fact that lead and zinc are generally mined by under-

ground methods. These factors make it difficult to draw conclusions as to ultimate size of reserves. There seems to be no systematic relationship between grade of deposit and cost; thus a principal indicator of what might or might not be reserves, in the accepted meaning of the term, is lost.

As for lack of data on the part of the mining companies, one gathers from comments in published accounts of the U.S. Bureau of Mines work, leading at times to a complete omission of data for the United States and Mexico, that the situation is far from satisfactory. Perhaps this is not to be wondered at in an industry that has suffered for years from foreign competition but whose largest members are at the same time active promoters of production abroad, financially, or as operators, or both.

Furthermore, as in the case of copper, foreign consumption of the primary material substantially exceeds U.S. consumption, so that judgment on future consumption abroad seriously affects the outlook for U.S. adequacy. In what follows, these cautions have to be kept in mind and the conclusions regarded as most tentative and subject to continuous revision.

Lead. The current official estimate of lead reserves in the United States, in terms of gross lead content—i.e., not allowing for losses in mining, milling, and smelting—is 2.9 million short tons of measured and indicated reserves and 2.7 million tons of inferred reserves. At a recovery factor of 80 per cent, total reserves of 5.6 million tons would thus be of the order of 4.5 million tons. This is equivalent to roughly seven times current demand for primary lead. However, timing also must be taken into consideration. Within the past ten to fifteen years mine production of domestic lead has ranged between 300,000 and 400,000 tons per year and, at that rate, has filled less than a third of domestic lead consumption. Assuming that production in any future year might not rise above the 300,000 ton level, and thus meet a share of demand dropping to less than one-third, domestic reserves, as given above, would still not last beyond the middle of the next decade, so that from any point of view domestic reserves, as defined so far, are deficient.

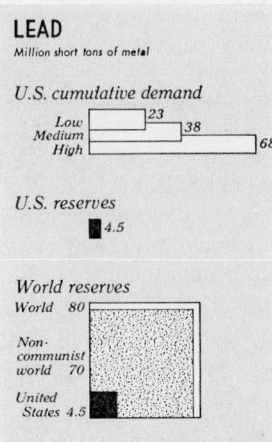

Figure 21–10. U.S. cumulative demand for lead, 1960–2000, compared with approximate 1960 U.S. reserves and world reserves.

Of added concern is the fact that the official estimate of reserves has been lowered substantially between the late forties and the late fifties. Inferred reserves, estimated at 5 million tons through 1955, have only recently been written down to 2.7 million tons, while at the same time measured and indicated reserves have been raised by a mere 400,000 tons. Since meanwhile lead has been continuously produced, there has not been a net loss: total reserves of 5.6 million tons still exceed the 7.5 million tons total reserves of ten years ago minus the roughly 3.5 million tons that have been mined in the intervening years. Nonetheless, it is obvious that under current conditions of costs and prices sizeable properties known to contain lead have reverted to the category of potential ore.

Beyond such vague indications there is no knowledge of potential ore reserves, either in terms of lower-grade ore now known but disregarded, or of ore yet to be discovered. Even such rough guesses at potential ore in the United States as have been ventured—the 8 million tons estimated by the President's Materials Policy Commission for example—might be on the low side, for it is uncommon that potential ore should be only just as large as reserves. Total identified domestic resources

then must be put at no less than 10 million and no more than 15 million tons gross, or 8 to 12 million tons recoverable metal. Compared with the Medium projection of U.S. demand of 38 million tons from 1960 to 2000, this is at best one-third. (See Figure 21–10.)

When foreign ores are taken into account, the picture becomes even less clear; data are lacking on both inferred and potential ore, and estimated demand for foreign mine production does not rest on the detailed analysis devoted to domestic demand. Measured and indicated orebodies, excluding the United States and eastern Europe, are put at 41 million tons, equivalent in terms of recoverable lead content to around 33 million tons (see Table 21–17). If we adopt the general supposition, advanced more recently by the Bureau of Mines, that inferred reserves must be put at no less than the amount of measured and indicated reserves combined, then total foreign reserves would, in round numbers, amount to 70 million tons of recoverable lead. Mine production has been growing and in recent years has tended to approach 2 million tons per year. At this rate of output reserves would be produced through most of this century, but output

TABLE 21–17. Lead: World Reserves, Measured and Indicated, 1957

(Thousand short tons metal content)

Region and country		Reserves
North America		14,600
United States	2,900	
Canada	8,000	
Mexico	3,500	
Other	150	
South America		2,500
West Europe		9,100
Africa		3,500
Asia		2,000
Australia		12,500
Total non-communist countries		44,200
Recoverable (at 80%)	35,400	
Eastern Europe		4,600
World total		48,800
Recoverable (at 80%)	39,000	

Source: Bureau of Mines, *Minerals Yearbook, 1957* (Washington: U.S. Department of the Interior, 1958), Vol. I, p. 725. For inferred reserves, see text discussion.

would not be sufficient to meet the projected requirements for U.S. imports and foreign demand. Besides the total content of domestic reserves, U.S. Medium demand of 38 million tons would over the period 1960–2000 require an additional 33 million tons of recoverable lead. If during the same time span foreign demand, excluding the Sino-Soviet area, were not to rise above current consumption levels, it would require some 45 million tons, for a grand total of some 80 million tons. This would exceed non-communist area reserves, including inferred, by one-fifth.

However, two corrections must be made. In the first place, the assumption of constant demand abroad is not realistic. Recent experience suggests a long-run rate of perhaps 2½ or 3 per cent per year, similar to the 2.9 per cent rate implied in the projection contained in the PMPC report in 1952. Over forty years, such rates would cumulate to an increase of 170 and 225 per cent respectively. Starting from a 1960 level of 1.1 million tons, we could expect cumulative demand over the forty years of 82 million tons at the 2½ per cent rate or 92 million tons at the 3 per cent rate. It follows that non-communist area demand would be large enough without U.S. import requirements added to it to absorb the estimated 70 million tons of foreign reserves and still remain unsatisfied to the extent of some 10 million to 20 million tons. Including the United States, it would total some 130 million tons.

Second, the assumption that inferred reserves only equal measured and indicated reserves might be conservative: only a few years ago a Bureau of Mines expert stated as accepted opinion that inferred reserves might be up to three times as large, and so he suggested a range of 100 million to 150 million tons as likely world lead reserves.[43] Here, too, the lower limit would not suffice to cover both U.S. and foreign demand, even if the latter were to grow only by 2½ per cent per year.

43. O. M. Bishop, *The Reserve Base for the World's Lead-Zinc Industries,* paper presented to American Zinc Institute and Lead Industry Association Meeting, Chicago, April 28, 1955. These figures may be compared with the world-wide cumulative demand hypothesis of 140 to 180 million tons, used by Netschert and Landsberg (*op. cit.,* p. 57). This includes the United States as well as Sino-Soviet bloc consumption.

The upper limit would just about be sufficient, allowing for the inclusion in the reserve estimate of communist areas of the world.

Only by supplementing our fairly definite knowledge of measured and indicated reserves —or working inventory—with crude guesses and analogies tending toward the optimistic, can we at this time see sufficient reserves to equal lead demand during the balance of this century. Also, meeting of the High U.S. demand of 68 million tons would presume that the United States could pre-empt upward of half of all foreign reserves even if these are put as high as 150 million tons; further, without a constant flow of discoveries supplies would begin to tighten long before the end of the century, as reserves now in sight and inferred could hardly be expected to be exploited in a steadily rising curve followed by sudden exhaustion; and finally, the Low demand projection for the United States—23 million tons— could probably be met by domestic production and foreign imports and still leave sufficient supplies to fully satisfy foreign demand even at a level of annual growth abroad up to 3 per cent.

These conclusions are based on reserves alone, without reference to potential ore. Some comments on these points follow the discussion of zinc. There is also the likelihood that lead reserves not as yet located at all will in time supplement the reserves now known. Past experience demonstrates that active search has normally resulted in the finding of new provinces—most recently, for example, eastern Tennessee and New Brunswick. The latter, unknown at the onset of the fifties, is estimated to hold close to 3 million tons of lead, or equal to total measured and indicated reserves of the entire United States. New discovery is a vital factor in the future adequacy of lead.

Zinc. The data are as unsatisfactory for zinc as they are for lead, and the conclusions are similar. Measured and indicated zinc deposits in the United States were last estimated (1957) at 13.5 million tons, equivalent to 11 million tons of recoverable zinc content. Inferred reserves, estimated in 1950, suggest a figure of 12.7 million tons, or 10.2 million tons in terms of recoverable metal content, but measured and indicated tonnage on that occasion was put at only 8.5 million tons, and 3.9 million tons were given as potential ore.

Considering the nature and timing of the data, it is reasonable to assume that reserves might at present amount to 25 million tons of metal content.[44] This compares with projected cumulative U.S. demand of 69 million tons for the next four decades. At current rates of domestic production, under which the major portion of demand is met from imports, these reserves would last through and beyond the end of the century.

Zinc reserves outside the United States and the Sino-Soviet area amount to 47 million tons of recoverable zinc (see Table 21–18). Assuming foreign inferred reserves at the minimum level suggested by the Bureau of Mines,

TABLE 21–18. Zinc: World Reserves, Measured and Indicated, 1957

(Thousand short tons metal content)

Region and country		Reserves
North America		37,000
United States	13,500	
Canada	16,700	
Mexico	6,600	
Other	200	
South America		6,000
West Europe		11,000
Africa		4,000
Asia		3,600
Australia		11,000
Total non-communist countries		72,500
Recoverable (at 80%)	58,000	
Eastern Europe and China		11,400
World total (rounded)		83,900
Recoverable (at 80%)	67,100	

Source: Bureau of Mines, *Mineral Facts and Problems,* 1960 ed. (Washington: U.S. Department of the Interior), p. 985. For inferred reserves, see text discussion.

i.e., as large as measured and indicated, reserves of non-communist areas outside the United States might total 94 million tons, or roughly 120 million tons including U.S. reserves.

While these tonnages are larger than those of lead, zinc demand not only is currently

larger than lead demand but is projected to rise somewhat more steeply in the future. Cumulative demand for the United States alone is projected at 69 million tons in the Medium projection, leaving at most some 51 million tons to satisfy demand in the remainder of the non-communist areas of the world. In the face of current consumption of slab zinc abroad of the order of 1.3 to 1.5 million tons per year— or 50 to 60 million tons in forty years at current consumption levels—a supply-demand balance based solely on measured, indicated and minimum inferred reserves is not in the cards.

But foreign consumption has not been stable. During the fifties it has on the average risen by 4 per cent per year, with relative increases especially striking in the newly developing nations. On the other hand, the second half of the decade has witnessed a decided slowdown so that a continuation of this rapid growth, reflecting to a considerable extent the emergence from postwar prostration, is unlikely. However, even a growth rate of only 2½ per cent for the next forty years would boost annual consumption from an approximate level of 1.5 million tons in 1960 to 4 million in 2000; cumulative consumption during the period would reach over 100 million tons. Including U.S. demand of 69 million tons, total demand of the non-communist countries would exceed 170 million tons, compared with reserves of 120 million tons.

Only on the basis of a more generous assumption of inferred reserves could reserves be made to even approximate cumulative demand. If it can be assumed that inferred reserves might be as much as three times the size of measured and indicated reserves,[45] then the 47 million tons of measured and indicated recoverable reserves in the non-communist areas (excluding the United States) might be matched by as much as 140 million tons of inferred reserves, for a grand total of some 190 million tons of recoverable zinc content. To this, U.S. reserves of 20 million tons of recoverable metal must be added, for a total for non-communist areas of 210 million tons. This calculation finds some support in a one-time esti-

44. See Netschert and Landsberg (*op. cit.,* p. 59).

45. See p. 465.

mate advanced by the Bureau of Mines in 1956, when it put forward a guess of "65 to 100 million tons" of inferred reserves for North America alone.[46] In recent publications, however, no mention has been made of this estimate.

The total of 210 million tons may be said to be a minimum position for meeting the projected consumption, provided foreign consumption is conservatively assumed to grow at a rate significantly below recent experience. (See Figure 21–11.)

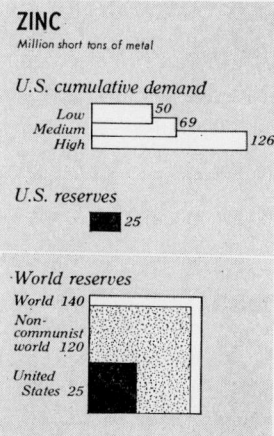

Figure 21–11. U.S. cumulative demand for zinc, 1960–2000, compared with approximate 1960 U.S. reserves and world reserves.

Barring the undertaking of careful geological surveys on an international scale, including estimates not merely of inferred but equally of potential ore, the judgment of adequacy of lead and zinc over the next forty years is bound to be inclined toward the negative and at the same time to remain a matter of highly speculative and unsatisfactory guesswork, based on the thinnest of assumptions and overshadowed by current ups and downs of the market as well as by the struggle of American lead and zinc producers to maintain the profitability of their domestic mines.

46. U.S. Bureau of Mines, *Mineral Facts and Problems,* 1956 ed., p. 993.

Potential ore of lead and zinc. Common to both lead and zinc resources data is the absence of information on and concern for potential ore. Why this marked gap? There are two possible explanations: (1) there is relatively little material below present cutoff grades; (2) such material exists, but for some reason there are no data.

There is evidence in support of both explanations. The lack of data may merely stem from differences between the geology of lead-zinc occurrence and that of the other metals. Since the lead-zinc deposits may be characterized by sharper boundaries, there is little point in pursuing exploration efforts beyond cutoff grade. In many iron and aluminum deposits, on the other hand, similar effort may indicate large tonnages of potential ore because of the lateral continuity of the deposits and the indefiniteness of the deposit boundaries. Moreover, if there is an anomaly in the grade distribution of lead and zinc, it would have been noted by the geological and mining professions, yet there is a notable absence of comment on such a circumstance.

Another reason for lack of data could be the prevalence of old districts as the sources of lead and zinc, at least in the United States, in which the continued development of existing mines does not require the delineation of ore and potential ore to the same extent as in new districts. For new districts more information may have to be acquired and made public in order to raise the capital for initial development. The problem of assessing coproducts and by-products may also contribute to the lack of data. Finally it can be argued, again for the United States at least, that depressed lead-zinc prices have discouraged exploration for additional reserves of these metals.

Yet there are disturbing arguments and evidence for the existence of relatively little potential ore.

Perhaps the strongest evidence is provided by the attempts during World War II and the Korean War to stimulate lead-zinc output in the United States. The government approved a high percentage of the proposals it received, but the resulting increase in production was only modest and insufficient for current needs (including stockpiling). The limited increase in production was all the more surprising since the subsidy was large in relation to the current market price.

It could be argued that the distribution of lead-zinc occurrence by grade is such that subsidies must be very high to bring large quantities of potential ore under consideration. But if this were so, the wartime subsidy programs should have yielded knowledge of a very large tonnage of potential ore as a by-product of the industry's efforts to find material that could be worked under the subsidy. Indeed, the exploration effort was directly subsidized and even carried on by the government itself during World War II. The fact that despite this effort the ratio of potential ore to reserves is still low for both lead and zinc suggests that there is comparatively little potential ore; or, what is the same thing, that the tonnage-grade relationship changes fairly abruptly not far below current cutoff grades.

If this *is* the anomaly that exists, and not merely a lack of data, then why has it not received attention heretofore? The situation remains puzzling, and adds an extra element of uncertainty to the long-run outlook for lead and zinc.

Tin. Analysis of adequacy of tin is handicapped by poor resource data. Only reserve data are available. Second, estimates of reserves have remained unchanged in the past ten years. Third, even the reserve figure that was then put forward by the President's Materials Policy Commission was "an exceedingly rough approximation, as it contains individual estimates made on varying assumptions and standards as to cost, grade, and other factors; nor can any distinction be made between measured, indicated, and inferred reserves."[47]

In the ten years since the last reserve estimate was put together, production has amounted to perhaps 40 per cent of these reserves. Yet, in its 1960 summary of the situation the Bureau of Mines reports the same reserve figure. The underlying assumption is that what has been absorbed in production has been filled in by gradual further development, and perhaps this is not a bad assumption. It has the crucial drawback, however, that the reserve figures become relatively meaningless, especially as they are not related to any upper resource limit (other than the judgment expressed in the 1953 Materials Survey compiled by the U.S. Department of Commerce that the non-prospected tin-bearing regions of Malaya, Burma, and Bolivia might have again as much tin content as the estimated reserves).

Actually, for the immediate years ahead, it would seem less crucial to know whether reserves are 5 million tons of tin content, carried since 1950 in the reserve column (see Table 21–19), or twice that amount, than to feel more reassured as to the practicality of producing the tin in some of the principal areas of tin mining.

Numerically, one can compare the 5 million tons of reserves with the 3 million-ton cumulative U.S. consumption under our Medium projection for the year 2000, or with the Low U.S. projection of 1.5 million tons; or one can say that the reserves are about equal to thirty years of consumption by non-communist countries at levels that have prevailed in the fifties. But such comparisons are of only relative significance. Considering supplies from Indonesia, the Congo, and Bolivia as subject to interrup-

TABLE 21–19. Tin: Reserves in Non-communist Countries, 1950

(Thousand long tons of metal content)

Country	Reserves
Malaya	1,500
Indonesia	1,000
Thailand	800
Burma	300
Congo	500
Nigeria	250
Bolivia	500
Other	150
	5,000

Source: President's Materials Policy Commission, *Resources for Freedom,* Vol. II (Washington: U.S. Government Printing Office, 1952), pp. 51–52.

47. President's Materials Policy Commission, *op. cit.,* p. 51.

tion, one can easily see that almost half of the non-communist countries' reserves are in a category of uncertainty, and that political problems loom large in any appraisal of future adequacy of tin. Moreover, the policy of the International Tin Agreement countries has, through production control, affected price and consumption, so that under this aspect as well the forward look has its limitations. All one can reasonably say is that there seems only moderate ground for concern over long-run adequacy of resources in the ground, while one must remain apprehensive regarding the nearer term. In either event, the poor knowledge of reserves and resources severely limits any judgment.

United States resources are negligible, and national interest is, therefore, focused on the situation in the producing countries.

One further element that must be kept in mind is the increased substitution potential. This is true especially in the canning field, where aluminum has been making significant inroads and where other, non-metallic forms of packaging and conserving may in the future further circumscribe the role of tin. In its indirect effect, too, the competition of the lighter metal has had a depressing effect upon tin consumption. In order to stay in the field, tinplate cans have had a decreasing tin content, first by the practical elimination of the dipping process (which takes more than twice the amount of tin per ton of steel than does plating), and most recently by a new process that promises further to reduce the share of tin. Thus, any cost increases due to depletion of tin reserves would merely add further impetus to existing moves aimed at reduced tin content and substitution, which have been taken into account in making projections of future use of the metal and explain why even in the Medium projection, net end-use of tin in 2000 exceeds the 1960 level by over 100 per cent, and tin ore requirements, given large-scale scrap recovery, in 2000 would be less than four-fifths larger than in 1960.

Magnesium and titanium. No consumption projections were derived in Chapter 16 for magnesium or titanium.

In the case of magnesium, the light metal par excellence, this decision was to a large degree based on the fact that the primary raw material today is sea water, and that, therefore, no resource problem is in sight. (Even in any sudden boost of demand processing capacity might not for long be a bottleneck.)[48] Secondly, the course of magnesium demand has been an erratic one, not solely in the United States, but worldwide, due partly but not exclusively to the importance of magnesium as a war material. Dating a mass market from the beginning of World War II, production at the height of the war reached 184,000 tons in 1943, dropped precipitously to 5,000 tons only three years later, was boosted to the 100,000 ton level once again during the Korean conflict (1952–53) and has since fluctuated between 80,000 and 30,000 tons per year. Consumption, more steady, has ranged between 30,000 and 50,000 tons in the last decade, without any indication of trend.

From what is known, the Soviet Union seems to have had a similar experience, suggesting that, given the cost of production, we are confronted here with continuing inability to handle some of the basic characteristics of the materials, such as poor corrosion resistance, high inflammability, and difficulty of producing alloys with improved properties.[49]

For these reasons we have abstained from projecting magnesium use into the future, with three exceptions: (1) in the projection of the Federal Reserve Board index of production an estimate was needed, and was made; (2) since magnesium is one of the intensive consumers of electricity, some provision had to be made to allow for it in the projection of electric energy consumption; and (3) an estimate emerged as one of the by-products of gauging materials consumption in military goods (Chapter 9). These instances are not, however, to be considered as carrying any well-

48. According to the executive secretary of the Magnesium Association (quoted in *New York Times*, October 15, 1961) "unlimited capacity could be built in less than two years' time, even under wartime conditions."
49. Perhaps the best publicized use is that made in the manufacture of the Volkswagen in West Germany. At similar magnesium poundage per automobile, magnesium consumption in this country would be 120,000 tons higher than it is now, but still not at the level of major tonnage metals.

supported implication for future use of the metal in all applications.

Similar considerations on the consumption side have been responsible for the absence of a titanium projection, although again some account was taken in military requirements and in the electric energy use projections, given the heavy use of electricity per pound of titanium. Like magnesium, titanium has had a checkered, though a shorter and even more erratic history.

With its high strength-to-weight ratio and great resistance to corrosion, titanium seems to combine some of the best characteristics of a high-grade steel and aluminum, but difficulties in workability, from ore reduction where its tendency for contamination by gases calls for special precautions, through machining and scrap recovery, have stood in the way of rapid acceptance. So has the simultaneous improvement in other materials, notably high-strength steel alloys. Titanium certainly seemed tailormade for the space age. It received large-scale and rapid financial encouragement by government as soon as it became obvious that the cold war would be of long duration. When, in mid-1952, the President's Materials Policy Commission published its report, titanium production was just climbing out of the less-than-thousand tons per year production class and seemed to be heading into the family of the major tonnage metals. Consumption levels of 100,000 tons were freely mentioned as not far off, and government efforts were bent toward bringing into existence annual production facilities of no less then 35,000, reduced later to 22,500 tons of metal (more correctly of so-called titanium sponge, which, named after its appearance, is the end-product of the ore reduction process, but still one step short of the ingot stage).

By 1957 the boom that had begun in 1948 was spent. Having risen from 500 tons in 1951 to over 17,000 tons in 1957, production dropped to less than 5,000 tons in 1958. Both production and consumption in 1960 remained near 5,000 tons (representing over half of world production) and only four U.S. producers had stayed on; at least two previous producers had closed down, and several potential manufacturers never began production. By 1960, sponge capacity had settled down at 21,000 to 22,000 tons.

These developments on the production side took place in the face of a continuing, sharp decline in the price of titanium metal. When it first made its commercial appearance in 1948, sponge was priced at nearly $5.00 per pound. At that time it was believed that, as the price declined due to increased capacity and improved technology, large new markets would open up. By 1960 the price had dropped beyond earlier expectations. Top-grade metal was quoted at— and sold for less than—$1.60 per pound, or two-thirds below the 1948 price. Much progress had been made in scrap utilization and in metal processing, both contributing to lower prices of products such as sheet, plate, wire, etc. Yet, large-scale commercial markets had failed to materialize,[50] and government interest had begun to shift from manned aircraft use— where much larger tonnage had been expected to take the place of aluminum and specialty steels than turned out to be the case—to missiles and space vehicles.

Thus, at the time of writing, the future of titanium remains in doubt. The judgment expressed by the authors of the President's Materials Policy Commission report, that 1975 demand could not be projected even within very wide limits, remains valid ten years later, but at one-third the price then prevailing the slow emergence of markets counsels a somewhat less sanguine view than was held in the early fifties.

No single development is likely to make titanium the tonnage metal anticipated ten years ago. A breakthrough in ore-reduction method resulting in a low-cost continuous production process, which so far has eluded the technologists, would help; so would progress in workability, welding, alloying, scrap utilization. In the meantime, production levels even at capacity, i.e., four times current rate of output, would not begin to strain the resource situation. Of the two raw materials ilmenite and rutile, the latter—more economical but

50. Even now the chemical industry consumes only 2 per cent of total titanium purchases, while the B-52 bomber program has at times absorbed as much as 50 per cent. (See *New York Times,* November 21, 1961.)

domestically less available—is the preferred. Ilmenite, on the other hand, is plentiful, both in the United States and in Canada, and whatever inconveniences might be connected with its use would have to be accepted if titanium were to become a large tonnage metal.

The Minor Metals

Besides the ferroalloys, already covered in connection with iron ore, there are at least two dozen minor metals now in common use, even taking all rare earths (sixteen metals including lanthanum and yttrium) as a single metal and considering the platinum group (six metals) as a single metal. These minor metals are discussed briefly here because of their relative economic significance—either present or potential—among minor metals.

These metals, grouped into three categories of origin, are:

Produced primarily as by-products of metallurgical processing of other metals

Antimony	Indium
Arsenic trioxide	Platinum group
Bismuth	Rhenium
Cadmium	Selenium
Gallium	Tellurium
Germanium	Thallium

Produced primarily as a by-product of mining other metals

Heavy sands group

Hafnium	Titanium[51]
Rare earths	Zirconium

Pegmatites

Beryllium	Lithium
Cesium	Rubidium
Columbium	Tantalum

Wholly or largely produced and processed independently

Mercury	Strontium
Silicon	

Table 21–20 gives 1960 production and consumption figures (insofar as they are available)

51. Dealt with primarily on p. 470, but because of the close geological relationship of rutile (the preferred ore of titanium metal) with other sand deposits, also shown here.

for these metals or groups of metals. Tables 21–21 and 21–22 list their major uses and the economically significant properties. These tables are selective rather than complete. Beyond this tabular information we shall not attempt to give details of the production, uses, and technology of individual metals; such information is readily available in a number of places.[52]

No projections of end-use consumption of the minor metals were made in Chapter 16. Many of them have only a short history; data have not been systematically collected; and most of the trends that might be established are based on such unusual and transitory circumstances that they would be poor guides to the future. The value of the minor metals was often first recognized for highly specialized military uses where cost was less central than performance; their long-run potential rests elsewhere. But commercial use must rest on demands (not heretofore made) for metals that can withstand very high temperatures, or are particularly corrosion resistant, or perform a special function in electronic components. The medical profession may find some useful. Others may be required as additives to plastics or ceramics, fields which may come to rival the ferroalloys in importance. All of these rest on new techniques for substitution, and on new ideas which are not subject to projection in the detail which would be necessary for estimation of consumption. Even less than other commodities can they be considered to have found a secure market for themselves. That they will be used seems certain, but not where and how much.

Finally, there is the old problem of percentage changes when dealing with small quantities. A new source can double or triple the available supply; a new use, quadruple consumption of one metal and eliminate that of another. Within a few years disinterest changes to a crash program and critically short supply, and then just as rapidly follow conditions of abundance and oversupply. This is the situation so vividly expressed by the sobriquet "Cinderella metals" given some of them. In these circumstances rates of growth, trends, and per-

52. Notably, U.S. Bureau of Mines, Bulletin 585, *Minerals Facts and Problems;* and *Minerals Yearbook,* various eds.

TABLE 21-20. (Part 1). Production and Consumption of Minor Metals, 1960 Data

Group (1)	Metal or metallic compound (2)	Basis of statistics (3)	Ore (thousand pounds)			Percentage	
			World mine production (4)	U.S. mine production (5)	U.S. consumption (if consumed as a mineral) (6)	Col. 5 as % of Col. 4[1] (7)	Col. 6 as % of Col. 4 (8)
1a........	Antimony	Content of ores and of by-products	122,000	(3,500)	–	(3)	–
1a........	Arsenic Trioxide (white arsenic)[2]	By-product	–	–	–	(6)	–
2b........	Beryllium	Beryl, beryllium content	(775)	(29)	(660)	(5)	(87)
1a........	Bismuth	By-product	–	–	–	(15–20)	–
1a........	Cadmium	By-product	–	–	–	(20–25)	–
2b........	Cesium	Content of ores	n.a.	0	–	0	–
2b........	Columbium	Columbium-tantalum concentrate, gross weight	6,350	0	(5,000)	0	(80)
1c........	Gallium	By-product	–	–	–	n.a.	–
1c........	Germanium	By-product	–	–	–	(25)	–
2a........	Hafnium (see Zirconium)						
1c........	Indium	By-product	–	–	–	(25)	–
2b........	Lithium[2]	Lithium minerals, gross weight	(235,000)	(50,000)	n.a.	(20)	–
3	Mercury (essentially identical with refinery production)						
1c........	Platinum group (totals)[3]	Metal content	82	2	–	(2)	–

2a........	Rare earths[4]	Rare earth oxides in monazite and bastnasite concentrate	n.a.	[5]1,250	--	(50)	
1c........	Rhenium	By-product	-	-	--	(60)	
2b........	Rubidium	Content of ores	n.a.	0	--	0	
1b........	Selenium	By-product	-	-	--	n.a.	
3........	Silicon (high purity) (not separable from silicon for other uses)						
3........	Strontium[5]	Largely celestite	22,370	100	13,400	(4)	(60)
2b........	Tantalum (see Columbium)						
1b........	Tellurium	By-product	-	-	--	n.a.	
1c........	Thallium	By-product	-	-	--	n.a.	
2b........	Titanium	Titanium dioxide content of ores and slags	(2,998,600)	852,534	1,145,302	(28)	(38)
		Rutile production, gross wt.	230,000	18,866	48,458	(8)	(21)
2a........	Yttrium (included with rare earths)						
2a........	Zirconium	Largely zircon, gross wt.	[2]385,754	(93,460)	178,000	(24)	(46)

Notes follow Part 2 of this table.

TABLE 21-20. (Part 2). Production and Consumption of Minor Metals, 1960 Data

Group (1)	Metal or metallic compound (2)	Basis of statistics (9)	Metal, alloy, and compound production (thousand pounds)			Percentage				U.S. secondary production (thous. lb.) (17)	Wholesale lots price in New York ($/lb. unless otherwise stated) (18)
			World smelter or refinery production (10)	U.S. smelter or refinery production (11)	U.S. consumption of new metal (12)	Col. 11 as % of col. 10 (13)	Col. 5 as % of col. 11 (14)[1]	Col. 12 as % of col. 10 (15)	Col. 5 as % of col. 12 (16)[1]		
1a	Antimony	*	(112,200)	19,908	26,534	(18)	(18)	(24)	(13)	80,208	0.31
1a	Arsenic trioxide (white arsenic)[2]	White arsenic*	94,000	10,378	53,250	(11)	(50)	(57)	(10)	–	[6]0.04
2b	Beryllium	*	n.a.	400	(500)	(70)	(7)	(80)	(6)	small	71.50
1a	Bismuth	*	5,200	(1,400)	1,527	(27)	(40)	(30)	(10)	nil	2.25
1a	Cadmium	Metal*	21,700	10,180	10,166	(47)	(40)	(47)	(40)	minor and incl. with primary	1.40
2b	Cesium	*	n.a.	[5]2	n.a.	(60)	0	n.a.	0	nil	540.00
2b	Columbium	Metal only	n.a.	(200)	200	n.a.	–	n.a.	–	n.a.	45.00
1c	Gallium	*	n.a.	<1	<1	n.a.	(100)	n.a.	(100)	nil	1,180.00
1c	Germanium	*	n.a.	54	75	(30)	(37)	(50)	(40)	n.a.	136.00
2a	Hafnium	Sponge	n.a.	70	n.a.	(60)	(60)	(60)	–	very small	[7]100.00
1c	Indium	*	n.a.	n.a.	[5]40	(33)	(60)	(60)	(33)	nil	18.25
2b	Lithium[2]	Lithium carbonate equivalent of chemicals*	n.a.	n.a.	7,700	(60)	(50)	(60)	(50)	nil	[6]0.67
3	Mercury	*	19,304	2,525	3,889	(13)	(100)	(20)	(65)	407	2.60
1c	Platinum Group (totals)[3]		80	4	53	(4)	(60)	(66)	(4)	5	1,200.00
2a	Rare earths[4]	Rare earth oxides*	n.a.	[5]7,600	3,200	(50)	(100)	(50)	(100)	n.a.	150.00–4,100.00
1c	Rhenium	*	n.a.	(1)	(1)	(60)	(100)	(60)	(100)	nil	580.00
2b	Rubidium	*	n.a.	[5]1	n.a.	(90)	0	0	0	nil	[6]390.00
1b	Selenium	*	1,777	620	810	(35)	n.a.	(46)	n.a.	41	6.50
3	Silicon (high purity)	Single crystal equivalent	(125)	105	72	(85)	(100)	(60)	(100)	n.a.	160.00
3	Strontium[5]	Strontium sulfate	n.a.	n.a.	n.a.	n.a.	–	(100)	–	nil	0.03
2b	Tantalum	Metal only	n.a.	300	400	n.a.	n.a.	n.a.	n.a.	n.a.	35.00
1b	Tellurium	*	390	260	340	(67)	n.a.	(87)	n.a.	nil	4.00
1c	Thallium	*	n.a.	[5]<4	<4	n.a.	–	n.a.	–	nil	7.50
2b	Titanium	Sponge	18,200	10,622	10,974	(58)	(60)	(60)	–	(4,400)	1.60
2a	Yttrium	*	n.a.	n.a.	[5]0.1	n.a.	–	n.a.	–	nil	245.00
2a	Zirconium	Sponge	n.a.	2,846	n.a.	n.a.	–	n.a.	–	400	[7]6.25

Data compiled from various sources of the U.S. Bureau of Mines, mainly *Minerals Yearbook*. Data approximate as numerous qualifications in the original have been omitted.

Groups:

1a—Metallurgical by-products, large tonnage
1b—Metallurgical by-products, medium tonnage
1c—Metallurgical by-products, small tonnage
2a—Mining by-products, heavy sands
2b—Mining by-products, pegmatites
3 —Individual products

nil = (Secondary production) means no production aside from intraplant recoveries.
n.a. = Data not available.
— = Column not applicable.

( ) = estimated by Resources for the Future, Inc.
* = Production and consumption figures include all or nearly all of the metal in question.

1. Estimates are made here even though columns 4 and 5 are not applicable as an attempt to estimate the content of minor metals in domestic major metal ores. The Bureau of Mines does not consider this as mine production because the ore is mined principally for its major metal content.
2. 1959 data (except price).
3. Ruthenium, rhodium, palladium, osmium, iridium and platinum.
4. Includes lanthanum and yttrium.
5. 1957 or 1958 data (except price). (Estimate in *Mineral Facts and Problems*.)
6. Price refers to a compound rather than to the metal.
7. Price refers to purity higher than usual commercial grade.

TABLE 21–21.   Principal Uses of the Minor Metals and of Their Alloys and Compounds

Metal	Ferrous alloys (steel making)	Electrical industry	Electronics industry	Chemical, rubber and petroleum industry	Food, textiles, other industries	Glass & ceramic industry (incl. refractories)	Paints, pigments and enamels	Structural metal: aircraft	Structural metal: other	Nuclear reactors	Storage batteries	Bearing metal	Soldering, welding and brazing	Machine tools	Control and measuring equipment	Decorative and uses giving special protection	Munitions and explosives	Insecticides and fungicides	Drugs and pharmaceuticals	Other
Antimony	(M)		C	C	(C)	(C)	C				(A)	(A)	A		A	A	AC		C	
Arsenic			C	C		(C)	C					(A)	(A)		M	A	M	(C)	C	
Beryllium			A			(C)		M						(A)	(A)					
Bismuth				M									A		(A)	(M)			(C)	
Cadmium		(M)	A				M			M	(M)		A		M					
Cesium																				Fuel
Columbium	(M)		M					M	A				A	A						
Gallium		A	A																	
Germanium			(M)	A		C							A							
Hafnium										(M)										
Indium			A(M)	M(C)								(A)								
Lithium		M		M(C)		(C)					M	C	M				(C)			
Mercury		MA		(M)		M	M							A	(MA)			M	M	Lamps
Platinum group	M	A		C		M		A	A				M	A		M				Catalyst
Rare earths	M	A		M		M			A											Carbon arcs
Rhenium		(M)	M	MC		(C)	(C)								(M)					Lubricants
Rubidium			M	MC		MC	C													
Selenium		(M)	(M)	A		(C)	(C)												C	
Silicon	(M)	M		C	C	A	(C)					C		C	(M)	M			M	
Strontium							C										(C)			
Tantalum	(M)	M	MA	MC		C	C	(M)	MA					C		M	(C)		C	High-speed alloys
Tellurium	(M)	M	C	MC		C	C								C			C	M	
Thallium			C			C									C			(C)	C	Lamps
Titanium	M		C	MA		(C)	(C)	(M)	MA					C		M				
Yttrium	M					A				M										
Zirconium	M	M	M		M	(C)			M	M			M		M	M				

M—used as a metal.
A—used as an alloy.
C—used as a compound.
Letters in ( ) indicate major uses of metal.

TABLE 21–22. Properties of the Minor Metals which are Most Important in Their Metallic Uses

Metal	Low weight	Melting point: high	Melting point: low	High thermal conductivity	Electrical conductivity: high	Electrical conductivity: low	Semi-conductive	Thermoelectric	Other special electrical properties	Good structural properties¹	Ductile and/or easily worked	Hard or hardener	Low friction coefficient	Reactive	Deoxidizer or reducing agent	Corrosion resistant	Coloring agent	Poisonous	Low neutron cross-section	Radioactive	Other
Antimony	M		A					A	A	X		A	A		A	A	C	C			Fire resistant (C)
Arsenic	X	MC	M					A	A	MA	X	A			A	A	C	C			Decolorizer (C)
Beryllium	M			MA	A				A	A		A				A		MC			Nonsparking (A)
Bismuth			A	X		C		A					M			M			M		
Cadmium			MA		A				A	A		A	M			M	C	MC	X		
Cesium			MA					M	MC					M			C	MC		M	
Columbium		MA							M	A		A			A	A			A	M	
Gallium			M		A	A			M	A		A			A	A	C		X		
Germanium		M	M			M	M		M				M	M		M					
Hafnium		M							MA	A		A	M	M	A	M	C				
Indium			AC								A		M	M	A	AC				M	Hygroscopic (C)
Lithium	MC													X	A					M	Luminescent vapor (M)
Mercury	X		M	X	MA	— VARIABLE —				A	MA	A		X	A	MA		MC	X	M	
Platinum Group	X	MA																			Sparking (A)
Rare earths	X	MA							M		MA	A		M	A	A				M	Incandescent (A)
Rhenium	X	MA							M		A				A						Absorbs light (M)
Rubidium						M	M		M		A			M							
Selenium							M		C			AC			AC	AC	C	C			Many variables (C)
Silicon	MC	C					M		M	A		AC			C	AC					
Strontium	C								M	A		C		X	A	MA	C		M		
Tantalum		MA					M		M	A	M	A			A	MA	C				
Tellurium							M	AC	M	A	X	C	X		C	MA	C	C			Luminescent vapor (M)
Thallium				X	M		M		C	C	X	C	X		A	MA	C	C			
Titanium	X	A								MA	MA	A			A	M			M	M	Transmits microwaves (C)
Yttrium	M	A													A						Magnetic (A)
Zirconium		C							C	M		A			A	M			M		

M—Property is that of metal itself.
A—Property is that of an alloy or intermetallic of the metal.
C—Property is that of a compound of the metal.
X—Indicates that metal has poor or opposite characteristic for the given property.

1. Strong and stiff relative to weight; creep resistance; fatigue strength; etc.

centages can all be less than poor indicators; they can be completely misleading.

Yet in a comprehensive look at the next four decades something must be said about the minors, even if we are unable to project consumption in terms of quantity. There is consolation in the fact that any problems arising from inadequate supply with attendant price increases could have only a minor effect on the economy. The issue is of a quite different order than a long-term cost increase in, say, iron ore, the effects of which would permeate the economy.

Available supply. The limitations on supply which make these metals minor are in large part a result of the geology. First, they may be sparsely found in the crustal portions of the earth. But this can be only a partial answer. Titanium is one of the nine most abundant elements; rubidium is six times as abundant as copper and more than twenty times as abundant as lead. Second, and more important, they may not be concentrated by as large a factor into deposits which can be easily worked. In its major source rubidium is concentrated barely five times whereas a 1 per cent copper deposit has been concentrated 180 times, and a 2 per cent lead deposit more than 1,300 times over their average abundances in the earth's crust. Third, the desired metal may be won only with great difficulty either from the rock masses which contain it or more commonly from sister metals of very similar chemical character. The necessity of separating by hand most beryl, the ore of beryllium, from associated minerals is an example of the former problem, and the pairs columbium-tantalum and zirconium-hafnium (so often referred to in just that way) is an example of the latter.

Another reason that some metals are minor is because they have not been looked for. The familiar case of uranium has proven that abundant supplies may exist largely unrecognized. Nevertheless, it is doubtful if any concentrations of these minor metals comparable to those of the major metals have been overlooked. At the same time there is something hopeful in the unusual nature and occurrence of the minor metals. It may merely mean that sources will not be found in the conventional locations or by using conventional techniques. The "ores" may turn out to be not rock but brines for instance. Even the United States and Europe, surely the best geologically explored areas, have by no means exhausted the possibilities of looking for these metals.

There is a large gap in quantity produced between iron and the nonferrous metals; there is an equally important gap between the major nonferrous metals and these minor ones. Annual domestic production of minor metals contained in ores is in a few cases less than one ton, more commonly amounts to a few hundred tons, and rarely is more than 10,000 short tons. Indeed, in most cases the gross weight of ores and concentrates (if they can be distinguished apart from ores and concentrates of major metals) is itself on the order of 10,000 short tons. For any one metal, the value of ore production may be several hundred thousand dollars, and only rarely up to ten million dollars. While complete data are by no means available, one may roughly estimate that the total value of primary forms of the metals (that is the unfabricated metals themselves, their alloys, and their compounds) cannot have exceeded $600 million, nor could the value of the ores and concentrates have exceeded $200 million.

For many of the minor metals, there is a fairly tenuous relationship between the price of the ore and the price of the final product. This is a result of the great difficulty encountered with many of these products in separating the metals from their ores, in separating the metals from one another, and in processing, fabricating, and sometimes just in handling the metals themselves. Where the price relationship is close, as with ferrocolumbium and its ore columbite, the reason is often that the ore is utilized directly (i.e., after only concentration to remove undesired *mineral* constituents) in the making of the product; in this case columbite is smelted directly into ferrocolumbium.

Not only are these commodities produced and consumed in minor total quantities, but commonly the amounts consumed per unit of final product are also very small. There are two aspects worth considering here. On the one hand, they are by no means as essential as often indicated by crash programs to find new sources of a particular one. All have substitutes, though in some cases not particularly good substitutes, which come into use when the economic conditions justify replacement of one by the other. Further, the use of alloys—and minor constituents can make the variations in alloying possibilities well nigh infinite—increases the range of useful substitution both in a technologic sense and also by narrowing the economic gap if one exists. On the other hand, where the consumption of some metal for some use is on the order of only a few hundred tons annually, it does not matter within a wide range what its price may be as long as it sufficiently outperforms other substitutes.

Clearly, then, there is no flat answer to the question of whether available supplies of the minor metals will be sufficient. However, it can be said that considering the world as the unit of supply as well as of demand, few of these metals seem to be in short supply.

This does not mean that there will not be price increases arising from abrupt increases in demand, such as often result from production for military requirements today. Nor does it mean that if new uses requiring large tonnages prove to be very efficient there will not be price increases. But it does mean that periods of substantially higher prices may well be short. Over the next ten to twenty years lower prices may be expected for many of these commodities as the focussing of interest on them induces the expenditure of man-hours and money on research involving their extraction and their properties.

The three main groups. Although we make no effort here to do more than comment, by way of example, on the prospects for individual metals, the three principal groups into which the minor metals fall have some common characteristics worth exploring. The groupings are (1) metallurgical by-products, (2) mining by-products and (3) independent products.

Metallurgical by-products. Quite a number of the minor metals are extracted from ores of the major metals at a stage in processing, usually the smelter, where the minerals are themselves broken down into their components. These metals, when classified on the basis of the quantities in which they are produced and consumed, break down into three subgroups: antimony, white arsenic, bismuth, and cadmium form the top group, each being consumed annually in the United States in quantities exceeding one million pounds; selenium and tellurium, which are annually consumed in quantities measured in several hundreds of thousands of pounds, form a poorly defined intermediate group; and finally there are those metals consumed in quantities of less than 100,000 pounds annually. (See Figure 21–12.) The last group is larger and more heterogenous than the others; it includes gallium, germanium, indium, rhenium, thallium, and the six platinum group metals—iridium, osmium, palladium, platinum, rhodium, and ruthenium. (The subgroups are based entirely on weight and not on value of domestic consumption; ordering on the latter basis would give quite a different classification.) There is no ambiguity about including any of these metals as metallurgical by-products. The few real antimony mines are entirely dominated by the by-product antimony. The same is true of placer platinum mines. And although most of the South African platinum is a main product rather than a by-product, the extractive process in a broad sense resembles the situation where it is a by-product, as in Canada.

By-products are not costless as is sometimes thought. They do of course occur as an extra product in the ore, and production is less costly than if each by-product metal had to be mined for its own sake and if its price had to cover all costs of production. Moreover, the recovery of one metal, say cadmium from flue dust, may place a firm in a favorable position to recover other products, such as germanium, from the same flue dust. However, their removal from the major metal, their recovery from flue dust, slimes or whatever, and their refining to a purified state are all additional costly processes. The first may have had to be performed in any case but the latter two are costs which must be assessed against that metal itself.

In the terms of economic theory these minor

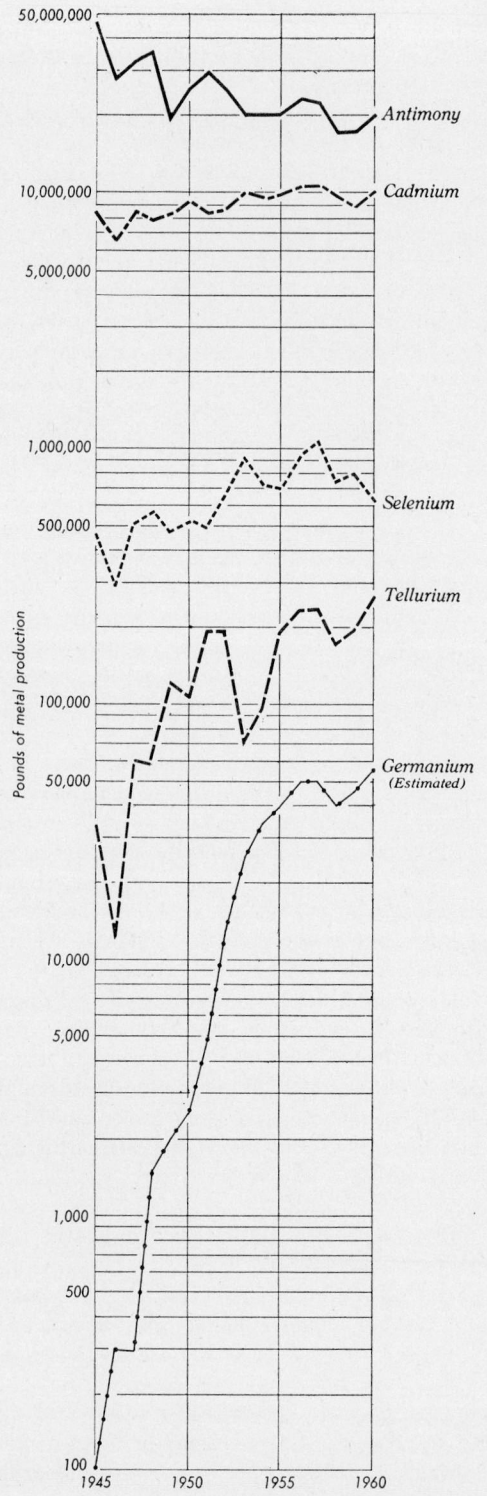

Figure 21–12. U.S. production of selected metallurgical by-products, 1945–1960.

metals are joint products. They are further characterized by economies of scale in their production, so that they tend to be produced by only a few companies: nine companies produce antimony in the United States; three, bismuth, two, indium; and only one produces thallium. But other firms stand ready to produce should the prices start to go up or even if the level of demand shifts upward; for example, with the increase in demand the number of germanium producers increased from one to three in a few years, and a fourth has recently begun production even though the price of germanium is now lower than it was when there was only one producer.

The recent price histories of most metallurgical by-product metals are quite similar. They exhibited a rising price between 1945 and the end of the Korean War. Since that time their prices have held steady or fallen somewhat as productive capacity has expanded to meet the higher level of demand. Selenium shows an identical pattern except that its peak was in 1956; and tellurium, although its price is still rising, will probably peak shortly. The six platinum metals also have a similar pattern but experience more fluctuations in price because they are subject to greater speculation. And the other metals of the small quantity subgroup are in general cheaper now than they were in 1945. All in all, there is little suggestion of a fundamental shortage of these metals, a conclusion which is reinforced by geological studies. However, there is a limit beyond which the available supply cannot be pushed without substantial price increases. This is that point at which practically all of the metal contained in mined ores of the major metals is being extracted (which in itself may require moderate price increases). When still more than this is demanded, the price must rise in order to eliminate the less productive uses of the metal or to induce further production. But the latter means that the price must rise high enough to make entirely new types of deposits economic or (still less likely) to induce higher production of the major metal from which it is extracted. In economic terms, the supply of the metallurgical by-product metals is inelastic after a point. If shortages do appear which force up prices in the next few years, it would be most likely among this group rather than among metals of the other groups, which do not have this limit on annual production. In particular could this occur with the top subgroup in terms of quantity, for it is with these that present possibilities for production have been most fully exploited.

Mining by-products. Metals that are separated from one another while still physically and chemically intact as a mineral are here designated as by-products of the mining stage. They then must pass through further stages of processing in order to extract the metal. (See Figure 21–13.) Just as with the metallurgical by-products this group can be further subdivided, here into a heavy sands subgroup and a pegmatite subgroup. There is also some pro-

duction of metals from saline lakes and brines which should probably be considered as falling within this group.

Because the mining by-products group is less cohesive than the metallurgical by-products group, fewer generalizations can be made about it. There is a mining stage through which all the co-products pass, not just as an inherent part of the major metal ore, but as recognized objects of value. Typically, they are produced in joint product fashion with other metals of the same subgroup and are all of approximately equal unit value. Thus rutile, zircon, and monazite concentrates may all be produced by the same operation. It is often not just feasible but necessary to sell all the co-products if the operation is to be profitable.

The heavy sands (or black sands) subgroup deposits are nothing more than extensive areas of beach sand, or less commonly river sand, from which the winnowing action of waves and currents has carried away the lighter minerals. A residual concentration of heavier metal-bearing minerals is left and if the concentrating action has been carried far enough, if the deposit is large enough and, most important, if it includes the desired minerals, the deposit may become an orebody.

Rare earth metals, thorium, titanium, and zirconium-hafnium, are the most important metallic products of heavy sands but a number of other metals and industrial minerals are recovered from some of the deposits as well. Characteristic metal-bearing minerals are monazite (rare earths and thorium), rutile (titanium), ilmenite (titanium), and zircon (zirconium-hafnium). Zirconium-hafnium and thorium sources are almost exclusively heavy sands but both titanium (in ilmenite) and rare earths (in bastnasite) are also mined from "hard rock" deposits.

There is hardly a geologic shortage of the metals of this group. Deposits of heavy sands are widespread throughout the world, though of course any country may be short of any one or two of the metals as the United States is short of thorium. Moreover, the production of any one of them increases the supplies of all the co-products. Thus shortage of thorium has induced accelerated production of monazite

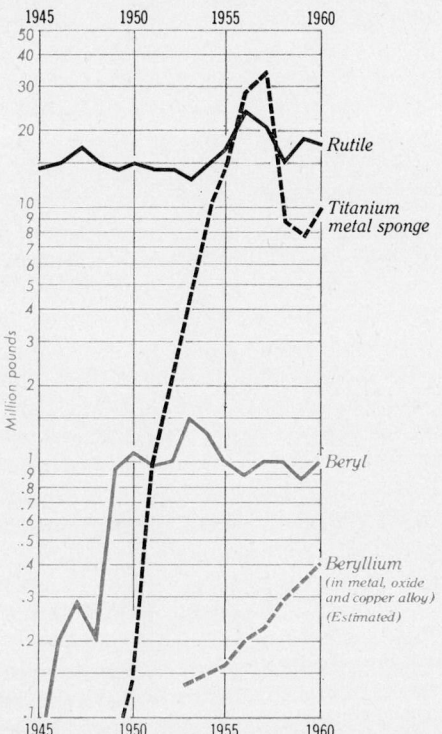

Figure 21–13. U.S. production of selected mining by-products and the metal extracted from them, 1945–1960.

which has in turn meant added production of rare earths. There is a fairly well-developed market for these minerals both because they are used directly in industry and because there is no major weight loss if they are processed further. Their prices tend to be rather variable compared to the prices of metals as they shift in response to differences in requirements and available supply. In general, heavy mineral mines have a flexible output up to the capacity of the processing plant. But as the capacities vary widely among the half dozen or so producers and, more important, as there apparently exist gradually increasing quantities of minerals in heavy sand deposits as the grade of ore gradually decreases, there is no reason to expect more than very mild price increases (if even that) under conditions of gradually increasing demand.

However, the very characteristics which make these residual minerals resistant enough to form sand deposits also make them resistant to reduction to the metal itself. Most of the cost of these metals comes from stages of production beyond the mining stage. But here technical advance has made cost reductions possible. The price pattern which titanium has set (see page 470) is likely to be repeated with other metals.

The pegmatite subgroup refers to those minerals which occur in vein or dike-like masses characterized by the large size of the crystals. The mines typically are fairly small, commonly involving only a few men on an operation which opens and closes with slight shifts in the economic situation. Yet pegmatite mining has been the mainstay of world supply for a great many of the minor metals, among them beryllium, columbium-tantalum, lithium, and cesium-rubidium. Today, however, only cesium and rubidium are exclusively the products of pegmatites. Columbium is now mined in part as an individual product from carbonatite rocks. Beryllium may also be derived from disseminated deposits in the future. Lithium is still an important pegmatite mineral but large amounts are also recovered from the brines of Searles Lake, California. And tantalum is mined from placer deposits as well as from pegmatites.

Domestic pegmatite mining for metals, with the partial exception of lithium, has in recent years been possible only because of government-supported prices which induced larger production than would otherwise have been the case. In part this is because many of the larger pegmatite deposits have been exhausted and in part because other areas, notably southern Africa, seem to have been better supplied with large metalliferous pegmatite deposits than the United States. In any event, and again with the partial exception of lithium, the mining of metalliferous pegmatites in the United States is not a promising source of supply. To a certain extent the same is true for many of the industrial minerals recovered from pegmatites. However, in every case except for cesium, rubidium, and tantalum, sizeable alternative sources are available in this country or in Canada. Moreover, in a world-wide sense there appear to be no particular shortages of these metals; in fact, in many cases joint production requires the stockpiling of unwanted minerals in hopes of future increases in demand. Nevertheless, there could well be short-term price increases for many of these metals. Not only is pegmatite mining an expensive and fairly limited type of operation in output, but the increase in production resulting from the reopening of old mines is small. And some of these metals are used in fairly substantial quantities.

Individual products. There is a miscellaneous group of minor metals which are mined with no by-products or with by-products of a decidedly lesser importance. The desired product is identifiable at every stage in the process of extraction so that costs can be fairly specifically assigned. Mercury is the example *par excellence* of this group as it has been mined extensively and practically without by-products for centuries. The other members of the group are strontium and silicon. Strontium is included because its deposits, resembling those of some industrial minerals, are formed by zones of strontium minerals contained in otherwise valueless sedimentary rocks. And the mining of silica is based on the location of almost monomineralic deposits.

Although domestic supplies of these minor metals (other than silicon) are inadequate at today's prices, in no case do world supplies appear to be so. This is particularly significant since their price must cover all mining and extraction costs if they are to be produced as individual products. Two trends appear to be working together. First, deposits of these metals seem to be available with a gradual decrease in grade so that deposits now just below economic grade can fill in any gap left by the exhaustion of richer deposits. The process of shifting to lower grades is going on slowly enough to allow technology to at least compensate for the lower grades without a long-term rise in price. This, of course, does not preclude the possibility of rapid price fluctuations, such as have been characteristic of mercury, or of the approaching exhaustion of individual deposits with attendant increases in costs, such as face the operators of some mercury and silicon mines.

Second, there seems to be a shift toward producing metals from this type of deposit, and away from pegmatite mining, based on lower costs and increased reserves. Pyrochlore (columbium ore) is the best example, but the cases of bastnasite deposits of rare earth metals and phenacite-bertrandite deposits of beryllium are similar. The minor metal-bearing minerals are typically disseminated through an uncommon rock type over a sizeable area. Such deposits offer the advantage that ore grade and reserves can be estimated fairly accurately so that planning of production is easier. They are of sufficient size to justify erection of mills and other treatment facilities which use modern separation techniques like flotation. Open-pit mining is feasible for many of them. In general the scope of the operation is such as to allow greater returns to technical advances than are available in pegmatite mining. This shift to disseminated deposits is on a small scale parallel to the shift in the early part of this century from mining vein copper deposits to disseminated copper. Like that early change, it awaits growth in the market but also induces it by providing sources that are dependable over long periods of time.

Nonmetallic Nonfuel Minerals

Between them the metals and fuels account for an overwhelming proportion, in terms of value, of the contribution of minerals to the modern economy. There are, however, many other useful minerals, only three of which are considered separately here: sulfur, phosphates, and potash. The others either are of small economic importance or, like stone and sand for construction, so plentiful and ubiquitous that supply estimates have never been compiled.

This does not exclude supply problems for specific grades (such as may occur in glass manufacture), or a given location, where a quarry may have to close down because of suburban encroachment, or new specifications eliminate the use of local deposits of sand and gravel for highway construction. These, in the face of nationwide abundance, are not dealt with here. For others, such as quartz and industrial diamonds, synthetic substitutes have come into wide use.

In fact, the prospect of ample supply over a long future applies to some minerals that are used in the chemicals industry as well as directly. For example, reserves of salt in the United States have been put at 60,000 billion tons. This compares with annual consumption of 20 to 25 million tons. The most likely supply problem in the years to come is one of salt abundance in connection with the desalting of brines or sea water in areas that suffer from fresh water shortage. The chemical industry takes some 70 per cent of total consumption, most of it going into chlorine and soda manufacture. Geographically, salt production is carried on in widely dispersed areas, from Louisiana and Texas to Michigan and California. No regional shortages are in sight, an important consideration as cost of transportation is a heavy charge upon salt consumers.

Most of the U.S. production of lime, to take another example, is consumed by the chemical industry, principally for the manufacture of alkalies and calcium carbide. The fact that 15 to 20 per cent of the surface of the United States is estimated to be underlain by limestone perhaps better than anything else explains why no one has bothered to compile reserve estimates. There are no indications of threatened resource depletion.

Sulfur. The nineteen fifties, beginning on a note of extreme scarcity, controlled distribution, and high prices of sulfur, ended in an atmosphere of not merely temporary abundance and low prices but stiff competition and probably long-term ease. As happens so often in the history of materials, the search for new sources of sulfur has been highly successful. At the same time the temporary stringency sent sulfur consumers hunting for alternate processes involving other less scarce materials and this too has been successful, at least to the point of stemming the rapid rise in sulfur consumption.

Several developments have contributed to the reversal. Perhaps the one of most permanent impact has been the tapping of the sulfur contained in many crude oil and natural gas deposits. Its presence had long been a source of annoyance and cost to the refiner or pipeliner, but it was not considered as worth recovering, or as seriously competitive with sulfur produced by the traditional Frasch process, in which underground native sulfur deposits are liquefied by the injection of superheated water and pumped to the surface. Even a decade ago when the President's Materials Policy Commission report was written, little was expected of this source in the near future; otherwise, total reserves from oil and gas refining would have been put at more than 6 million tons, with an additional 19 million tons believed to be forthcoming only at a 25 per cent increase in the price of sulfur. What in fact happened was that nearly 4 million tons of sulfur—two-thirds of then estimated reserves—were produced from 1950 to 1960, at a declining real price of sulfur. Production has topped 750,000 tons per year, and keeps rising. Between 1950 and 1960 production has grown nearly sixfold and now represents nearly 12 per cent of domestic sulfur production. In 1960 alone, newly installed capacity exceeded total production ten years earlier.

A thoroughgoing revision of reserve estimates would require an analysis, field by field, of recoverable sulfur content of known domestic oil and gas fields, with allowance for fields yet to be discovered and for quantities likely to be imported. Even without such an analysis, it would seem that the reserves must be counted not in the millions but in the tens of millions of tons. If 1960 refining of some 3 billion barrels of petroleum and processing of some 10 trillion cubic feet of natural gas yielded over 700,000 tons of sulfur, then surely future recoverable petroleum of not less than 250 billion barrels and 1,200 to 1,700 trillion cubic feet of recoverable gas should contain no less—and most likely much more—than 50 million tons of sulfur. For example, for every 1 per cent of H_2S in domestic natural gas reserves, there would, at a recovery factor of 40 tons of sulfur per million cubic feet of H_2S, result an estimated sulfur reserve in natural gas alone of 48 million tons. To this would have to be added the sulfur recoverable in oil refining, now contributing two-thirds of total sulfur recovered.

A second source that was equally known ten years ago but believed not to be available for commercial exploitation in the near future, are offshore sulfur deposits. The putting on stream in April of 1960, of the Grand Isle dome off the Louisiana Coast, eleven years after its discovery by the Humble Oil Company, has lengthened the time perspective, and this without the incentive of a price increase. Freeport Sulfur Company, which in 1960 acquired the sulfur rights, has never indicated the reserves believed to be contained in this dome, but there has been mention in the press of 30 to 40 million tons. In addition, Freeport holds two other offshore domes with undisclosed reserves.

Third, there has been great expansion in foreign sulfur production. This began a few years ago in Mexico, where sulfur-bearing salt domes, similar to those along the Gulf Coast, had previously been discovered. In a spectacular performance, Mexico shot up from a sulfur importer as recently as 1954 to being the producer of one-and-a-quarter million tons at the end of the fifties.

Another producer on the march is Canada, where past sulfur production has been principally from pyrites but for the future is based on the expansion of natural gas, some of it extremely rich in sulfur. Reserves of sulfur from Canadian gas fields that are now being tapped have been estimated at no less than 40 million tons, Canadian proved reserves from gas and oil, whether or not now producing, at 50 million tons, and those contained in estimated ultimate gas reserves at 260 million tons.[53] While recovered sulfur production is still relatively small—just over 400,000 tons in 1960— it is rising rapidly and estimated to reach 2½ to 3 million tons by 1965. By 1960 it exceeded for the first time sulfur production from either pyrites or metal smelters.

Perhaps the most spectacular recent sulfur development based on natural gas has been the Lacq field of southwestern France. Discovered in 1951, it has produced rapidly increasing amounts of sulfur. Production in 1956 was 2,300 tons; in 1960, 780,000 tons. By mid-1961 production was fast approaching operations at the annual design rate of 1.4 million tons. In the light of estimated gas reserves and current sulfur yield per unit of gas, total reserves are probably no less than 30 million tons.

What has happened in France and in Canada, and at a less rapid pace in the United States, is possible wherever gas and oil hold sufficient sulfur to make commercial recovery feasible. In 1959 alone, the Bureau of Mines reported the erection of refinery-connected sulfur-recovery units in Brazil, the United Kingdom, Egypt, the Union of South Africa, Australia, and Uruguay. One may expect this trend to continue and sulfur recovery to spread to those areas which have not as yet installed recovery equipment. These include the Middle East with vast reserves of sulfur-bearing crude.

It is clear that, barring discovery of a sizeable number of new salt domes with sulfur in their cap rock, the world production pattern will undergo a substantial transformation; in this country the first effects are likely to be felt in the export field, as foreign self-sufficiency is built up. It is worth noting that despite the fact that Frasch-process sulfur had always been the cheapest source of sulfur, recent years have seen a halt in the expansion of Frasch-type production and a steep rise in sulfur recovery from oil and gas to meet consumption. This

holds out the reasonable chance that the future expansion of demand can be met from recovered sulfur without a price increase.

U.S. salt domes were first estimated in 1944 to hold 60 million tons under then prevailing price conditions, with an added 22 million potentially available later, under unspecified conditions. In 1951 the U.S. Geological Survey put reserves at 50 million tons, but the President's Materials Policy Commission believed the true figure to be closer to 100 million tons.[54] No less than 50 million and no more than 100 million tons has remained the reserve estimate through this day, though in 1956 the Bureau of Mines called this "probably conservative," and industry sources have been suggesting a level closer to 200 million tons. To maintain the estimate unchanged, the Bureau of Mines presumed that unspecified additions to reserves have compensated for the production that has taken place in the meantime, at the rate of 5 to 6 million tons per year since 1950 and 3 to 5 million in the preceding decade. This would presuppose additions to reserves of the order of 50 million tons during the past ten years.

There is no evidence that this has or has not happened. Certainly, it would have involved the addition of a number of sizeable domes. The truth is that very little is known. The producing companies publish production figures, but are reticent when it comes to reserve figures. The Bureau of Mines candidly admits that the domestic reserve position of Frasch sulfur is "obscure."[55] As we have seen, Mexican reserves are estimated at 50 million tons, and Canadian ultimate reserves from gas fields at 260 million tons. Taking U.S. Frasch reserves at 150 million tons, and U.S. reserves recoverable from oil and gas at 75 million tons, total Western Hemisphere reserves add to some 500 million tons. Beyond this lie the immense reserves of pyrites, on which until recently most European production has been

53. See, for example, *Sulphur: The Magazine of World Sulphur* (London), December 1958.

54. When one realizes that the so-called Boling Dome of the Texas Gulf Sulphur Company has by now yielded over 50 million tons of sulfur since March 1929, when it went on stream, and is still a producer, the difficulties of reserve estimating become apparent.

55. *Minerals Facts and Problems, op. cit.,* p. 821.

based, and further off the supplies of gypsum and anhydrite which were first successfully used for sulfur (plus cement) production in Germany during World War I, and have more recently been of commercial significance in the United Kingdom. Omitted in this calculation is the sulfur to be derived from Middle Eastern and African oil and gas. Again, quantitative expression is not feasible, but given the size of the reserves—still mostly unutilized as far as gas is concerned—sulfur to be derived here may well run into the hundreds of millions of tons.

Finally, there are the potential hydrocarbon sources other than crude oil and natural gas. It has been estimated, for example, that the Athabaska sands in Canada contain more than 2 billion tons of sulfur. Some or all of this may be available for recovery, depending upon the production process, if and when these deposits will be drawn upon for petroleum supply.

A look at the past and the consideration that sulfur's principal use, sulfuric acid, apart from its role in fertilizer production, is an ingredient in a vast variety of industrial processes, point to the pace of industrial activity as an indicator of sulfur demand. The close relationship since the end of World War II has been discussed in Chapter 17. Projecting this relationship into the future, consumption in 1980 might rise to 15 million tons, from 6 million in 1960, and to 30 million by 2000.

It would seem that the cumulative domestic demand of over 600 million tons implicit in these figures, to which one would have to add at least some 75 million tons of exports,[56] could not be satisfied from U.S. reserves as presently identified; on the other hand, it would not take a great many new offshore sulfur domes to bring capacity up to this level. Moreover, by absorbing all or most of Mexico's and Canada's estimated reserves, U.S. requirements could be met, provided that Canada would tap and produce all its gas within that time. The latter assumption is hardly tenable, and thus our judgment must be that, barring new dis-

56. The degree to which rising foreign production will reduce U.S. exports is important but does not affect the magnitudes involved in the comparison of reserves and domestic demand.

coveries or substantial upward revisions of future production of known deposits, new sources will have to come into play: pyrites, anhydrite or bituminous sand. Some of these may come in at a somewhat higher price, but since they would be called upon to supplement gradually, rather than to suddenly replace customary sources, the price of sulfur might not in fact undergo a significant increase. As in some other resource situations, reserve estimates seem to point to inadequacy, but the steady pace of revision of such estimates puts a damper on concern.

Phosphates. Over 25 per cent of the world's phosphate reserves are located in the United States, where they are highly concentrated in a few areas: Florida in the East with minor amounts in Tennessee, and Idaho, Montana, Wyoming, and Utah in the West. In the past three out of every four tons of phosphate rock produced has come from Florida. Reserves are put at 2 billion tons (660 million tons P_2O_5) in Florida, 85 million tons (15 million tons P_2O_5) in Tennessee, and 3 billion tons of rock (870 million tons P_2O_5) in the western deposits. A great deal of this reserve is inferred and thus is subject to a considerable margin of error, but the magnitudes are such that no conceivable error could cast doubt on the adequacy of the reserves for future U.S. demand. Domestic use in 1960 for fertilizer alone was just above 3 million tons of contained P_2O_5. Using projected farmer expenditures as a reference series (see Appendix Table A1–16), this can be projected to rise to nearly 9 million tons in 2000, for a cumulative call on phosphate reserves approaching 250 million tons of P_2O_5. Adding requirements in other uses, and providing for continuing export at current rates would result in total use of less than 400 million tons, or perhaps 1,100 million tons of rock. None of these magnitudes raise questions of depletion. In terms of P_2O_5 content, Florida alone has about 50 per cent in excess of the reserves necessary to meet the demand, and western reserves are twice as large as demand. It is thus difficult to detect a resource problem.

Beyond the reserves it is estimated that

there are 12 billion tons of potential rock consisting of lower-grade material, awaiting economical methods of commercial exploitation. In the West the practice is to separate low-grade rock in processing the high-grade material, and in Florida phosphatic slimes are being accumulated, pending the discovery of ways to utilize them. Finally, there is the real promise of supplementing the continental reserves by mining phosphorite from the sea bottom. Encouraging news was reported on this outlook, in late 1960, by investigators from the Scripps Institution and the University of California.[57] It appears that phosphorite is found not far from both the Atlantic and the Pacific coasts in relatively shallow water (less than 300 feet) and that the characteristics of the material are similar to the rock now commercially exploited in Florida. Such a venture would be of great importance to the Pacific states, and especially to California, that import large amounts of phosphate by long overland routes. According to the investigators, there is every reason to assume that phosphate production from the sea is commercially feasible even now. If a commercial method can be developed, the inconvenience created by geographic concentration of supply would be eased.

Potash. Concentration of potash reserves is even more marked than in the case of phosphates. Ninety per cent of U.S. supplies come from the New Mexico deposits, the small remainder from California, Utah, Michigan, and Maryland. The discovery in 1925 of the New Mexico field was a direct consequence of the determined initiative by the federal government to locate domestic material and free itself of import dependence, that had hurt so badly in World War I when German sources were cut off. It was located largely by oil-drilling crews that became aware of the high potassium content and value of the lands on which they were operating. Actually, the area of active exploitation is extremely small: some 55 square miles east of Carlsbad, New Mexico. It is from this field that the United States satisfies most of its needs. Brine deposits in Searles Lake,

57. John L. Mero, "Minerals on the Ocean Floor," *Scientific American,* December 1960, p. 64ff.

California, and in the Bonneville salt flats are relatively unimportant; so are the Michigan brines.

The recoverable reserve in the United States is estimated at 400 million short tons K_2O equivalent, based upon material that has a K_2O content of not less than 14 per cent. If one were to lower the threshold to 10 per cent, the size of the reserves would double or better. If lowered to 5 per cent, the fields could be worked for a thousand years at the current rate, or be counted upon to supply the projected cumulative requirements through the end of the century at a rate of depletion not much more than 10 per cent—i.e., at the end of the century the fields would still retain 90 per cent of their present content.

The ranges mentioned are by no means academic. The German deposits are mined at 10 per cent, the former Polish potash fields were exploited at a 5 per cent grade level. We know of no investigations, however, that would show the cost implications of the lowering of grade in the New Mexico field. In view of the sizeable reserves at the 14 per cent cutoff level, it is perhaps not surprising that nobody has been much concerned with the effects of tackling lower-grade deposits. These reserves are not quite double the consumption that can be projected through the year 2000 on the basis of farmer expenditures for fertilizer and lime. Actually, potash use has been rising faster than phosphate, and thus a quadrupling of aggregate consumption has been assumed for this rough projection. In order to equal estimated reserves consumption would have to rise not fourfold but more than eightfold by the end of the century.

Given on the one hand the very comfortable margin of reserves over projected requirements and, on the other, the possibilities of gradually lowering the cutoff point and thereby greatly increasing the reserves, there is no reason to assume any supply problem in the time period we are considering. There is, in fact, an additional consideration that puts the time of concern into the indefinite future, and that is the vast occurrence of potash in Canada. Reserves in Canada are put at no less than the almost astronomical figure of 6,400 million short tons of K$_2$O content, taken at a minimum grade of no less than 25 per cent. Nor are these the largest known deposits. West and East Germany between them are estimated to have deposits four times as large as those reported in Canada.

Future Technology

Our analysis of the adequacy of mineral raw materials has been for the most part in terms of current technology. To be sure, allowance has been made for some developments that seem sure to come in the near future; and the whole history of the past few decades has a background of steadily advancing rather than static technology. On the whole, however, our approach has been conservative. In the many instances where increased discovery, or technological advance in the recovery of lower-grade and more complex deposits, or in the subsequent processing, appears a precondition for forestalling increased cost to society in the balance of the century, we have left the question open.

The fact that mineral prices have shown no clear tendency to rise over a period of more than half a century suggests strongly that one should not indulge in the easy generalization that they must rise as better deposits are depleted. But while they need not rise, they may. Increasing imports have altered the basic supply pattern, and uncertain factors have been injected into the determination of prices, such as the tax, price, and other economic policies of the countries from which the minerals are imported, competition from third countries for their purchase, and the political orientation of the exporting country. Beyond these factors, however, the possibilities of technology give long-range perspective: increased availability through exploration and discovery, higher rates of extraction from known deposits, and increasing ability to use low-grade materials—these are valid considerations that operate apart from the changing coloration of the world-wide market in which the United States must buy.

Here we bring together systematically the most significant technological factors in the development of minerals production—a good many touched on earlier in this chapter—that may help to counter rising trends in the cost of production. Some of these, as will be seen, are merely extensions and offshoots of operations that have been known and used here before. Others are radical innovations. While the latter hold more promise, at the same time their consideration is rendered less meaningful by the lack of cost data which will accumulate only gradually and sporadically.

New Techniques for Exploration and Discovery

Most of the word's deposits of commercially useful minerals have been discovered by locating a surface outcrop of the mineral itself and by following the vein or body of ore into the ground. In many cases, water and other agents have moved the minerals from their original sites, and prospecting has required the "trailing" of alluvial deposits back to their sources. But with all these methods, practically the only basis for discovery was surface indication of the mineral itself.

Geophysical methods. Although not as widely applied to the prospecting for solid minerals as in the search for petroleum, the geophysical methods are being used increasingly to supplement the more obvious surface indications. Underground discontinuities and anomalies located by these techniques can often be evaluated by the experienced geologist as possible indicators of mineralization and ore deposits, even where no outcrop exists. Several other methods for locating certain minerals involve the use of magnetic instruments for finding iron, nickel, and other metals associated with iron and nickel; gravity meters for showing indirectly, by means of underground rock density, the types of minerals which may be present; underground temperature recorders which indicate the presence of highly conductive minerals; and aerial photographs of the ground and its vegetation from which inferences can be drawn as in petroleum prospecting.

The airborne magnetometer has been particularly useful in exploring difficult terrain, where rapid aerial determination of electromagnetic anomalies is comparatively simple and cheap. Deposits of most metal sulfide ores, such as lead, copper, iron, nickel, are good conductors of electricity, and an electromagnetic wave from an airborne radio transmitter is reflected from these materials to an associated sensing device in a modified and identifiable manner. The magnetometer has been successfully used in locating ore deposits even as deep as 200 to 300 feet beneath the surface. Lead and zinc ores in New Brunswick and nickel in Manitoba are recent discoveries credited to this method. Since the instrument is not infallible and responds also to non-metallic conductors such as graphite, the principal value of the method is in eliminating large areas from expensive prospecting by ground parties.

A somewhat similar technique involves the use of a sensing device beneath the airplane to detect reflections of natural atmospheric electromagnetic currents. It is claimed to be more sensitive than the standard technique, and perhaps able to locate mineral deposits as deep as 2,500 feet. Evaluation of this development appears to require further data on its performance.

Geochemical methods. A relatively new technique which may become even more significant than geophysics is geochemistry. This technique, pioneered by scientists in the U.S.S.R., consists in the chemical analysis of rocks and soils to determine relative concentrations of small traces of the element being sought or of other elements which may be associated with the ones being sought.

The fundamental principle of geochemical prospecting is the determination of the "background," or normal trace amount of a given metal in the soil of a region, and the search for amounts of this metal which are significantly higher. By systematic sampling and analyzing, a pattern of such trace occurrences can be determined. Sometimes the anomaly will pinpoint the deposit, whereas, if much surface disturbance has taken place through erosion, volcanic action, or other means, further tracing and inferring will be required for final location. Occasionally, samples showing abnormally high metal contents may be far removed from the original site of the deposit. In addition to surface sampling, analysis of underground samples procured by drilling can be used to supplement surface data.

Experience to date is encouraging. Among the numerous recent examples of ore discoveries by application of geochemical prospecting was an extension of an antimony deposit in Alaska (1953), uranium in the Yellow Cat area of the Colorado plateau (1952), zinc and lead in an extension of the Chief mine in Utah (1950), a zinc and lead deposit in New Brunswick by testing stream sediment for copper traces (found in 1956 after negative geophysical results), a rich copper-iron deposit in British Columbia (1957), lead in France, copper in Angola, and cobalt in Morocco. About 6 million samples are being analyzed annually in the U.S.S.R., and deposits of lead, zinc, silver, nickel, bismuth, molybdenum, beryllium, tungsten, tin, vanadium, mercury, and antimony have been located. Large sampling programs by copper producers in the United States, Peru, and Africa are in progress.

Certain indirect techniques have also been successfully employed for the location of minerals. Some elements often occur in close association with others which may be easily determined analytically or which show wide anomalies. Arsenic, for example, is often thus used as a "pathfinder" for cobalt, because anomalies of arsenic may be many times greater than those of the cobalt metal being sought. Similarly, molybdenum can be used as a pathfinder for copper.

Another indirect indicator is the presence of specific plant life, the changed appearance of plants, and difference in the composition of plants. All three methods have only recently begun to flourish in this country. The location of uranium deposits in the Colorado plateau is a case in point: the western loco weed takes up large amounts of selenium—a pathfinder for uranium—from the soil, and since loco weed is toxic to animals the apparently unrelated death of sheep and horses pointed the way to uranium. Another notable example was the finding of exceptionally rich iron ore deposits in Venezuela through the use of aerial photographs of 11,800 square miles of jungle and mountain territory. The Copei tree, with its light-colored foliage and dogwood-like blossom grows most thickly where the richest iron ore deposits are located.

A more refined analytical technique has been used in the application of an anomaly involving the occurrence of two isotopes of oxygen in limestone near deposits of lead and zinc in Colorado. The distribution between these two naturally occurring forms of oxygen combined with calcium and carbon in calcium carbonate (limestone) was found to change systematically with distance from the mineral deposits. By use of a mass spectrometer, a laboratory instrument which measures the concentration of atoms of various atomic weights, orebodies have been outlined by determination of isotopic ratios of oxygen in numerous field samples.

Extension of basic geological knowledge. The steadily increasing knowledge of the earth's crust through geologic investigations, studies of deep formations pierced by oil wells, and basic studies of ore formation processes are of indirect benefit in prospecting for minerals. They facilitate interpretation of the findings of geophysics and geochemistry and increase the probability of discovering hidden commercial deposits of minerals.

A project which may have major significance of this sort is the proposed drilling of a deep well in the ocean floor to the so-called Mohorovicic "discontinuity." This is a deep rock stratum of high density from which seismic waves are reflected, but about which practically no other information is available. Depth of this layer under the land mass is about twenty miles, which is much beyond drilling limits, but it is only about three miles below the ocean bottom and at an attainable well depth. If the project can be successfully carried out, it is possible that very important information about the earth's crust will become available and a much better understanding of its formative processes can be obtained. Indirectly, this may lead to techniques for more systematic minerals exploring, particularly in deep formations.

New Techniques in Mining

Technology is continuing to yield new and improved methods for reaching minerals and moving them to the surface. Greater mechanization of mines, improved equipment of all types, better explosives, and so on, as well as greater knowledge of minerals occurrence and behavior are contributing to these gains. Improvement in such facilities may be expected to continue, but in the perspective of a forty-year outlook the further gradual evolution of mining and drilling techniques may be overshadowed by several radically new methods, the most promising of which are noted below.

Underground nuclear explosions. The mining method of perhaps the greatest potential importance, but which as yet has not been directly tested, involves the use of nuclear explosives underground.

Many pertinent technical data were obtained in a series of a half-dozen underground nuclear explosions in Nevada during 1957 and 1958. The first of these showed that the explosion could be confined completely underground, that a very large rock-shattering effect could be obtained (several hundred feet in diameter in this test), that extremely high temperatures could be developed in the underground formation which, if not reduced by the presence of water, could persist for months or years, and that the formation of an underground cavity could produce secondary fracture by caving so that many more tons of rock would ultimately be broken by the blast.

By varying the power of the device and the depth of burial, several important effects of large, deep explosions could be correlated. In the type of formation encountered, 420,000 tons of rock per kiloton TNT equivalent were crushed or broken by caving, and 600 tons melted. Radioactivity in the products of the explosion was confined almost completely to the layer of fused, compressed rock immediately surrounding the blast zone.

These test results indicate practical potentialities of underground atomic explosions for crushing very large quantities of underground mineralized rock for subsequent removal by tunneling, caving, dissolving, or other methods. It has also been suggested that subsequent to a nuclear blast in a deep deposit of low-grade ore, extraction of the metal by percolation of acidified water through the immense crushed ore bed could be affected. The mineral-bearing solution could be pumped to the surface for metal recovery, and the solution fortified and recycled to the mineral deposit through wells drilled into the fractured formation. Copper is a likely prospect for such a recovery procedure, since some copper is already being recovered by more elementary solvent extraction methods. If the ore does not lend itself to chemical extraction, mining of the shattered deposit might be effected by tunneling, block caving or other conventional method. If hydrated rocks are present or if another source of water is available to carry heat away from the blast vicinity, recovery of the crushed rock should not be unduly difficult.

Another probable future application of nuclear explosives is the stripping of thick overburdens from mineral deposits to permit open-pit mining methods. Although problems of radioactive contamination by the blast debris have not been solved, it is possible that methods may be developed so that millions of tons of earth may be cheaply and safely removed from the underlying deposits.

Mine drainage. Greater application of a technique for dewatering deep mines—gravity drainage through long tunnels constructed expressly for this purpose—may bring large new orebodies into commercial production in the decades ahead. Because the depth of commercial minerals production is often limited by the economics of pumping water from the workings, deep deposits of marginal grade ore usually have to be left in the ground. The new technical development which makes their recovery promising is equipment for more economical tunneling. New explosives, drilling equipment, and underground loading and haulage facilities have placed costs in a range justifying construction of long gravity drainage tunnels to dewater deep deposits of commercial ore.

Theoretically, any mine zone above sea level can be gravity-drained, but until recently drainage tunnels longer than a few miles have been rare. The new techniques are permitting economical construction of much longer drainage tunnels so that mines even in relatively low-lying or plains areas can be drained to distant valleys. A recent proposal for a drainage program in the eastern Pennsylvania coal mining region would involve construction of tunnels totaling more than 100 miles in length. Large deposits would be dewatered by this system.

New Techniques in Extractive Metallurgy

Some of the new processing methods are directly associated with the new mining techniques. Thus, if nuclear explosions are used to prepare metallic ores for percolation extraction, processing becomes part of the mining or recovery operation. The special methods of this type include solvent extraction of copper and other metal ores. Of more immediate importance are some of the new methods for treating raw minerals mined by conventional methods. These processes are of two types: (1) concentration and beneficiation techniques by which ores, especially of low grade or refractory nature, may be upgraded, broken down, and prepared for further processing; and (2) smelting, recovery, and refining techniques by which the final metallic and non-metallic products are made.

Concentration and beneficiation. The term "concentration" is generally applied to ore preparation processes by which all or part of the waste material in the raw ore is removed by a preliminary treatment, prior to smelting or some other final recovery process. "Beneficiation" includes not only concentration processes, but also methods, such as sintering or drying, which make ores more susceptible to subsequent treatment.

Flotation. One of the most important process metallurgy developments of all time was the discovery and introduction of ore flotation as a means of concentration: it permits otherwise worthless low-grade ores, usually of the sulphide type, to be concentrated to levels permitting economical smelting.

Among the more recent applications has been the utilization of the flotation process in recovering the iron content in non-magnetic taconites. Given the large domestic reserves of such ore, the significance of a successful recovery process is obvious, and it is reasonable to assume that a commercially useful process will not be long in coming. At a more general level of technology, the ion flotation process, where the metal ions in a liquid solution combine with soap bubbles to float to the surface to be skimmed off, offers possibilities of recovery from mine water and dilute lead liquors not hitherto economical. This or other processes developed in the laboratory will have to be proved on a plant level before they can be accepted as useful new tools. At the same time, a search for cheaper reagents can be expected to accelerate the time schedule for success.

Solvent extraction and other chemical processes. There have been numerous production metallurgy advances in recent years in the design and improvement of wet processes for ore treatment. The object here is to concentrate a low-grade ore or liberate the desired metal (or metals) from the compound, often with the aid of acids or alkalies or special treating agents. The ore or concentrate undergoes chemical treatments at moderate temperatures, usually in the presence of water. In uranium milling, for example, sulphuric acid is generally employed to leach uranium oxide or other uranium salt from the rock. Although the initial concentration of the mineral in the ore may be less than 1/10 of 1 per cent, this treatment nevertheless effects almost complete recovery of uranium and other heavy elements such as vanadium and tungsten. Further chemical treatment of the liquid extract results in precipitation and final recovery of a dry uranium salt. Improvements in the production of soluble salts such as potassium compounds, magnesium salts, borax, and various other products have been based on wet milling and dissolving processes.

Solvent extraction with organic compounds such as amines and organic phosphates is also beginning to enter the production metallurgy

field. The selective properties of solvents can be used to separate minerals from each other in solution, with resulting economies in processing. The fractions can then be treated to recover the solvent for reuse. In uranium ore treatment, this method has been used with such success that almost one-third of U.S. uranium ore is processed by solvent extraction. Use of low-grade nickel-cobalt ore is largely dependent upon a successful solvent extraction process.

In contrast with the widely used uranium recovery processes, chemical methods for obtaining aluminum oxide from clays have not yet been applied commercially. Availability of bauxite has postponed the day when it will be necessary to recover aluminum from ordinary clay, but the techniques are ready at probably only a minor cost increase, if any, in the aluminum ingot.

Another type of chemical process which might become important for recovery of certain minerals involves the use of ion-exchange resins. A number of natural and synthetic granular compounds will remove metallic and non-metallic ions from dilute solutions, substituting other ions for them. On subsequent contact with solutions containing suitable regenerating chemicals, the ion-exchange resin is converted back to its original composition and the valuable metallic or non-metallic fractions are released to the regenerating solution, usually in much higher concentration than in the original solution. Separation of the desired materials can then be effected by various chemical means. For compounds already dissolved in natural waters and brines, and for the selective separation of valuable small fractions in solid mixtures, ion-exchange processes will probably become increasingly important.

Some processes of extractive metallurgy can assume commercial significance only with recovery of valuable by-products present in the ore. Others become more profitable, or more stable in pricing, by this means. An example is the recovery of tungsten and tin from molybdenite ore produced in Colorado. Although not originally recovered when the mill was constructed, there is substantial recovery of tungsten and tin, which are present in the ore to the extent of only one part in 12,000 and one part in 600,000 respectively.

Thus, efforts are being made to find out what materials are in the ore, even in minute amounts; where in the refining process these trace elements concentrate; and how the valuable constituents can be recovered. Development along these lines should prove even more fruitful as the need for new materials and as demands for currently used materials increase. On a far larger scale, advanced efforts to recover nickel, cobalt, and iron separately from nickeliferous iron ore are crucial to the commercial exploitation of ore in Cuba and other locations.

Magnetic separation. Certain compounds of iron and nickel have magnetic properties. If such ores are finely pulverized, concentration of the metal can be carried out by use of magnetized belts or pulleys to attract the iron-bearing particles and allow most of the waste to pass on to disposal. This process, along with the pelletizing treatment described below, is now being used in a large new Minnesota plant to produce a good blast-furnace feed from domestic taconite ore. In addition, techniques are being developed for turning non-magnetic into magnetic taconites and thus making them subject to beneficiation.

Sintering and pelletizing. While not falling under the heading of extractive metallurgy, sintering and pelletizing are often necessary adjuncts. Finely powdered ores, particularly of iron, have been difficult to smelt, because they are carried out of the blast furnace in the gases. But if the powdered ore is first mixed with coal dust or some other carbonaceous material and heated nearly to the softening or fusion point of the ore, hard chunks of ore, or "sinter," suitable for the blast furnace result. The sintering process has rendered ores amenable to smelting that would otherwise remain in the ground.

If the sintering process is suitably conducted, small pellets rather than lumps will be obtained. These, too, can readily be smelted. Both are developments that can be expected to grow in importance.

Smelting and refining. As usually employed, the terms "smelting" and "recovery" apply to chemical processes used in converting a compound of a metal to the metal itself. Smelting involves high temperature reactions, whereas recovery may also include low-temperature chemical processes. Some ores may contain part or all of the metal in uncombined form, thereby making these processes merely the separation of the valuable components.

"Refining" is the term generally applied to the purification of a crude or impure metal or metal mixture. Both chemical and physical processes may be involved. Improvements at this stage of processing are important in that cost reductions here may offset cost increases at earlier stages.

Developments in smelting technology comprise principally the processing of metals of new importance, the application of new processes for decreasing the costs of smelting long-used metals, and the use of improved smelting equipment. In the processing of some of the "new" metals, such as titanium, zirconium, columbium, and germanium, several recently developed high-temperature reactions are employed. Titanium refining has been a particularly difficult and expensive process. The key to reduced costs lies largely in the replacement of batch processes by continuous processes. New developments, not yet applied on a substantial scale, appear promising.

An innovation in iron and steel smelting and refining, which has seen only minor process changes through many decades, is the use of oxygen. Its addition to the air-blast in the blast furnace increases productivity of the furnace and yields a better grade of pig iron. In the steelmaking operation, the rapidly expanding practice of direct oxidation and removal of carbon in pig iron by a stream of oxygen materially reduces the time required for finishing steel in the open-hearth furnace and thus raises the capacity of the furnace.

A whole new family of iron smelting processes which have been extensively tested and which under suitable circumstances appear to have commercial applicability, are those employing direct reduction of iron ore, usually by hydrogen from natural gas without the intermediate production of pig iron in the blast furnace. The process can also be used in the production of manganese and chromium.

The future adoption of any of these processes is likely to be influenced heavily by the price of the reducing agent, hydrogen. At present prices there is but limited interest, especially as current improvements in blast furnace efficiency through oxygen application make the traditional approach seem less in need of replacement. Another limiting factor is the greater value in integrated mills of hot molten iron as it comes from the blast furnace as compared to the cold iron produced by direct reduction. Nonetheless, in areas of cheap gas, high-cost coke, and suitable ore, where the economics of an integrated plant are not of importance, currently known direct reduction processes are likely to make headway in the next two decades.

New Sources of Minerals

The sea, the sea bottom, and deep underground strata, constitute unused or little-used sources of minerals. Also, as the space age begins, bodies in the solar system other than the earth are not entirely beyond the bounds of speculation.

The sea, and to some extent the sea bottom, are examples of known mineral "deposits" but, with a few exceptions, there is no known technology feasible for economic exploitation. Very deep deposits under the land and ocean and under the Antarctic ice are not only unknown but also not economically recoverable at the present time. For the remote Antarctic continent it seems unlikely that minerals production will commence during the present century.

Sea water. Sea water contains practically all of the chemical elements, the most plentiful of which are shown below.[58]

58. Adapted from Brian Mason, *Principles of Geochemistry*, 2nd ed. (New York: John Wiley and Sons, 1958), p. 186. The figures are based on a standard "chlorinity"—the total weight of the chlorine, bromine, and iodine—of 19 parts per thousand. Hydrogen and oxygen in ions and gas dissolved in sea water are neglected in the listing.

Element	Parts per thousand
Chlorine	18.980
Sodium	10.556
Magnesium	1.272
Sulfur	0.883
Calcium	0.400
Potassium	0.380
Bromine	0.065
Carbon	0.028
Strontium	0.008
Boron	0.005
Fluorine	0.001
All others	0.013
Total	32.591

Of these elements, only four—sodium, chlorine, magnesium, and bromine—are now recovered in substantial quantity, and a very few others are obtained in trace-amounts.

Several elements are recovered from the sea indirectly by use of marine life as concentrators of the substances. Iodine can be obtained from seaweed and kelp, which take up a considerable amount of iodide in the plant tissues. One source of lime (calcium oxide) is oyster shells which in turn are the result of biological processes utilizing calcium in sea water.

As yet, however, economical methods for recovering the dozens of other elements in sea water have not been devised. The volumes of water which would have to be processed for substantial production of some of these other elements would be tremendous, and practical processes would have to be based on the use of relatively small proportions of energy and chemicals. While all the dissolved elements *can* be recovered, cost will remain a deterrent, unless and until inadequacy of conventional sources should raise the price of the material sufficiently to push some of these substances dissolved in sea water into a competitive position. Since the total value of the dissolved materials in 1,000 gallons of sea water is only about $10.00, practically all of which is due to the sodium chloride content, processing costs obviously will have to be very small per unit of water treated. There seems no prospect of the required upward increase in mineral prices during the next four decades.

It has frequently been suggested that when substantial production of fresh water from sea water is achieved, recovery of minerals from the waste brine should become interesting. This may indeed come about, provided that overproduction of sodium chloride can be avoided. Advantages of such a combined minerals and water production system would be in avoidance of duplicate pumping costs and other treating expenses. It is not unreasonable to expect that within the next twenty to forty years, some by-product recovery will be carried out in sea water conversion plants built for meeting fresh water needs. But these plants will probably be of limited number in the United States, at least in this century; barring the achievement of extremely low-processing cost, application will probably not be of major significance except for the sea-water minerals already being recovered.

There may, however, be wider utilization of biological "convertors" or concentrators for recovering minerals from sea water. As iodine is concentrated in kelp, so also are other elements concentrated in certain plants and fish. It has been found, for example, that niobium and vanadium occur in considerable concentration in fish of the skate group. Further research may result in other discoveries of this type, leading possibly to commercial production of some of the more expensive elements by recovery from sea plants and animals.

The ocean bottom. It is probable that rock structures forming the continental shelf and parts of the ocean floor are mineralized much the same way as the land is. Some of these mineral deposits may be close to the "surface" of the ocean bottom, and others may lie deeply buried. Petroleum, gas, and sulfur are already being removed from deposits below the ocean floor, but no attempt has been made to look for other minerals.

A second type of deposit is the silt, slime, and solid debris covering the ocean bottom. These materials are derived from land erosion, ocean "fall-out," deterioration of submerged rock, and the products and remains of animal and plant life. Some of these deposits are comparatively recent, particularly those near the land masses, whereas others are millions of years old. Their degree of mineralization varies a great deal. Exploitation of these deposits depends first on the development of feasible systems for their removal from the ocean bottom and their delivery to the surface (and ultimately to the land), and secondly, on processes for concentration, extraction, and final refining.

A third source of minerals on the sea bottom is the nodular material distributed more or less generally over millions of square miles of ocean bottom, at considerable depth. These nodules, of unknown origin, commonly range in size from that of a pea to that of a billiard ball, but smaller and much larger sizes are also encountered. They are usually found on top of the sediments covering the ocean bottom, averaging several pounds per square foot in the major belts of occurrence. The nodules are primarily manganese, with a maximum content of 50 per cent and an average content of 20 per cent manganese. Usually between 1 and 2 per cent each of nickel, copper and cobalt accompany the manganese, the proportions varying as between different locations. The depth at which the nodules are found varies from 500 to 3,000 feet off the U.S. southeast coast to a range of 5,000 to 14,000 feet in the eastern half of the Pacific.

The magnitudes involved are startling: at 5 pounds of manganese per square foot (several such areas have been identified), one square mile would contain 70,000 tons of nodules or 20,000 to 35,000 tons of manganese. The value in merchantable form of the manganese alone on a square mile of ocean bottom is over $1 million. The locations of many of these deposits are known; nodules are often brought up in dredging operations. The only important deterrent to production is the technology of bringing the material to the surface of the ocean. The development of economical dredging or suction equipment for operation at such great depth may be successful enough in the next decade or two to bring these deposits into use, though the principal investigator, J. L. Mero, claims economic feasibility even now provided a very high capital investment is made. It appears that economical production will require a high volume, perhaps 5,000 tons a day. Hence, large investment and considerable risk would be involved in a development of this sort, especially as total U.S. consumption at this time amounts only to some 8,000 tons of manganese ore a day. Yet a breakthrough here would almost at once shake free the United States of growing dependence upon overseas sources. Recovery of phosphates from the ocean bottom, especially along the West Coast may precede that of manganese.

Outer space. It is possible, even probable, that rich deposits of minerals useful in our economy occur on the moon and neighboring planets of the solar system.

It has been estimated that the costs of transport from the earth to the moon, at such time when there is some "traffic" between the two, will be several million dollars per ton. This cost would include not only the expense of developing space ships but also their operating cost, including the energy to propel them. But assuming that other transport purposes could defray the costs of development, the energy requirements per ton of mineral shipped from the moon to the earth may be compared with the value of the mineral itself. Under the most optimistic conditions, the energy alone would probably cost many thousands of dollars per ton transported. There is no crude mineral having a value on earth sufficient to justify such a high transport cost let alone the cost of discovering it, producing it, and making it available for shipment. There is little prospect that total transportation costs could be decreased to a practical level. And, although there may ultimately be some minerals production on other solar system planets, this would appear to be only for use on those planets rather than for transport to the Earth. Hence, the prospects for augmenting the Earth's mineral supply by transport from space must be considered practically negligible.

APPENDICES

General
Notes

THE PURPOSE of these technical appendices is threefold:

(1) to make available, for the benefit of economists, businessmen, and others who wish to make further calculations and comparisons with other projections, the more important detailed derivations and analyses which were made during the course of this study;
(2) to present, for ease of reference, some of the comparable historical data;
(3) to present the salient elements in the methodology followed, some of the more important considerations involved in the methodological choices, and some of the corollary implications of the projections, to aid in their evaluation.

These data are presented essentially in the form of statistical tables, with explanatory footnotes and brief commentary.

It is to be noted that the data in the appendices are generally given in terms of two to four significant digits. However, the number of digits presented is not to be taken as an indication of the degree of precision attributed to the projections. Rather, it is determined primarily by considerations of convenience in showing the arithmetic and in providing a sufficiency of digits for further manipulation. It may be assumed that our ability to project into the future very seldom approaches the medium precision of ± 1 per cent which would be implied by two significant digits, let alone precision 10 or 100 times as great which would be implied by three or four; and that it must decrease as we peer further and further ahead. In fact, there are few *historical* series which may be considered "exact" to the extent of three significant digits, and it is only to avoid further error in computation that we work with these or larger numbers.

Although what we are attempting to delineate in these projections is a real, economic world, that world can be specified only in terms of the "language" which we have available for the purpose—namely, that of economic statistics. In a sense, therefore, what we are projecting is not really the nation's output, its use of automobiles, its construction of buildings and highways, etc., but a succession of statistical series which seek to represent, as well as possible, changing magnitudes of these various phenomena. Precision in the designation of exactly which series is being used to represent the change over time of some intrinsic phenomenon is therefore essential to exact communication. Even some of the most clear-cut economic and social phenomena (e.g., population changes) are represented in the public records by more than one statistical series, among which we must choose, and we frequently have the further choice (which, in the absence of due caution, is easy to exercise unawares) of varying the specifications and conditions upon which any one series is predicated. What we have tried to do in this appendix is to present the past statistical series of which each of our projections is the continuation and to designate the source and other distinguishing specifications of that series, so that the user can, if he wishes, go further into its exact meaning by consulting the reference publications. Where awareness of the special characteristics of a series was important to an understanding of the course of the projections, we have specified these characteristics in the footnotes and commentary. The few instances where we have deliberately varied the specifications of a projected series from those of its historical antecedent are also duly noted.

Two basic assumptions apply throughout: that there will be, during the period under study, no general war and no major depression. If either comes to pass, all of the projections must be considered invalid. If neither comes to pass, the projections are believed to encompass the probabilities and reasonably possible divergences as they can be foreseen *at this time,* since they allow for reasonable variations of assumption with regard to other pertinent social, political, and economic conditions.

It must be emphasized, however, that economic phenomena follow both trends and cycles. Even where a trend projection turns out to have been completely accurate both in its assumptions and the deductions derived therefrom, for few, if any, of the years shown could the actual, observed data be expected to fall on, or even very close to, the projected values. The continued existence of minor cyclical variations is assumed and is implicitly taken into account by the approach of using past trends as a starting point for judging the future, but each of the decennial points used in these appendix tables must be considered to be a "normal" year if the specific figures are to be closely approximated.

The fact that our Highs and Lows are net of cyclical variation is of little consequence for long-range resources policy. What is more important to remember is that the trend itself may be "right" today and "wrong" tomorrow. Our projected mean trends and broadening outer limits encompass only those possibilities that now seem reasonable.

The detailed derivations and the relevant historical series are contained in the tables. Most of the individual decisions and their rationale have been recorded in the footnotes. The few paragraphs of introductory notes on each subject record some of the more general aspects of the projection rationale as well as some of the general working hypotheses. It is not supposed that any of these hypotheses may be considered to have been demonstrated or that all of them will stand up under further investigation and scrutiny. This study is merely intended to provide a first approximation, in the form of a systematic framework more complete than has been available heretofore, of the future magnitudes upon which resources policy must be based. Sufficient care and analysis have been devoted to the establishment of the framework and the various projections to produce what is considered a plausible and internally consistent whole.

A particular word needs to be said about the use in this study of "High," "Low," and "Medium." The last really needs no explanation; it represents, in every case, our best judgment as to the probable course of a series. All the Mediums are intended to be consistent with one another; they add to the Medium totals whenever they form the component parts of a whole. In other words they constitute what is usually thought of as a complete and internally consistent "model."

Mutual consistency is also characteristic of the Highs and of the Lows, but not in the same way, and the attributes of an additive model do not obtain. Any given High, for example, is consistent with the Highs for any greater or lesser degree of aggregation, but it is, in nearly every case, as a matter of concept and definition, inconsistent with the other Highs at the same level of aggregation. Put in another way, the High and the Low models have internal vertical consistency, but not horizontal consistency. To illustrate with a concrete example, the Low personal consumption expenditures shown in appendix Table A1–10 are consistent with the Low gross national product shown in the same table; the Low GNP, similarly, is consistent with the Low labor force and that, in turn, with the Low population, as shown in appendix Table A1–11. The Low personal consumption expenditures in Table A1–10 are not, however, at the *only* level consistent with the Low GNP; they are at the *lowest* such level (in terms of what is regarded as reasonably possible). This level, as will be gleaned from Table A1–11, also is the *likely* (Medium) level accompanying the two conditions making for lowest aggregate personal consumption expenditures—namely, Low population and High defense expenditures. Should population (and labor force) be a little higher or defense expenditures a little lower, personal consumption expenditures would be a little higher—in the former case accompanied by a higher GNP; in the latter case, by a lower.

Similarly, the Low private investment, the Low government purchases, and the Low net exports given in Table A1–10 are all the lowest levels which seem reasonably possible, consistent with the Low GNP. Their total falls short of the Low GNP, but since they could not all be at a low simultaneously, such a total could never obtain. Thus, the "residual" shown in that table represents not only estimating "error" but the amount which, if we were to construct a "most probable" Low-GNP model, would have to be allocated to one or more of the subcomponents.

The question may be raised whether the Highs and Lows maintain a consistent degree of probability, particularly in instances where the values appear to be multiplicative. For example, if we arrive by successive derivations at the Low copper requirements for the Low automobile production for the Low population with Low per capita purchases of automobiles, will not the order of probability of these copper requirements be inordinately low—certainly of a much lesser probability than, say, the population Low?

It must be admitted that the methods used in the study for obtaining Highs and Lows do introduce a bias toward a lesser degree of probability at the end than at the beginning of any particular chain of derivations, although the decrease in probability, measured as it should be in terms of areas under a distribution curve, is not as rapid as might be suggested by a simple multiplication of probabilities of occurrence or non-occurrence of a particular value. However, there has been independent testing and reconciliation throughout the derivations. A great many of the projections have been arrived at from two or more different directions, and, where equal confidence seemed due to two different projections for the same series, that with the more restrictive range has generally been used. This has particularly been true with respect to aggregates and their components.

Since the aim of this study was to determine the reasonable range of contingencies with which resources policy must be prepared to deal, it seemed better to overestimate what was reasonably possible rather than underestimate it. The ranges of future possibilities will be capable of being narrowed both with more refined analysis and with the passage of time. Where we have unduly exaggerated our ranges, the error, because of the asymptotic effect of zero, is likely to be more with the High than with the Low. If in projecting requirements we must have error, this is where prudence would dictate we have it.

Cross-Reference
Index

EXCEPT FOR possible inadvertent errors and omissions, the source for each of the statistical series given in each of the appendix tables has been indicated in the table footnotes, either in terms of some outside source or in terms of some other table in the appendix. Thus, it is possible to trace any particular figure and determine the sources and methods by which it has been derived, or—stated differently—the various elements and assumptions which are implicit in it.

Since it is intended that the appendix material also serve as a tool and source of material for further analysis, it is equally important that the user be able to trace the consequences, in terms of derived and related figures, of any changes in assumption or magnitude with regard to any one figure whose implications he might wish more fully to explore or with respect to which he has later or better information. The cross-reference index which follows is intended to facilitate this type of use. Although it has not been possible, for want of space, to pinpoint each individual series in terms of each other individual series which it affects, the type of cross-referencing used—from table to table—will, in most cases, enable the user quickly to identify the particular series concerned. For example, if better information becomes available with respect to past "large building construction" (Table A4–1), it will be seen that corrections need to be made in the data on materials use in Table A4–8. Or again, if the projections on population growth are changed, this will necessitate revisions in numerous tables in the appendices to Part I. In each case, subsequent reference, in the left-hand column of the index, to the numbers of this "first order" of affected tables will reveal still further repercussions, and so on, so that by successive reference the effect of any one change may be traced through to its consequences in terms of the whole projections scheme.

Data in Table:	affect data in Tables:	Data in Table:	affect data in Tables:	Data in Table:	affect data in Tables:
A1–1	A1–2, 18, 24; A3–1; A5–6; A7–3; A8–1; A10–12, 13, 17, 20; A12–5, 11; A16–21.	A1–16	A1–13, 18, 30; A4–4.	A3–2	A1–30; A3–3; A17–1.
		A1–17	A1–12, 14; A5–20.		
		A1–18	A1–19, 20, 21; A6–3.	A3–3	A1–30; A12–14; A17–1, 8.
A1–2	A1–12, 13, 14, 15, 18, 19, 20, 21; A2–4, 6; A3–2, 3, 4; A4–3, 4, 5; A5–7; A7–4; A8–2; A10–12, 13, 14, 16, 18, 22; A12–14; A16–21; A17–11.				
				A3–4	A1–30.
		A1–19	A1–20, 21.	A4–1	A1–30; A4–3, 4, 8, 11; A17–12.
		A1–22	A1–23.		
		A1–23	A1–25, 27.	A4–2	A1–12; A4–1; A9–1.
A1–3	A1–2, 4, 5, 20; A3–2; A5–2, 7.	A1–24	A1–25.	A4–3	A1–13, 15, 30; A4–7, 9, 10, 12; A13–5, 6; A16–61; A17–1, 12.
A1–4	A1–5, 20.	A1–25	A5–7.		
A1–5	A1–2, 11, 12, 20.	A1–26	A1–24, 27, 30; A3–1; A6–6, 8; A7–7, 9; A8–1; A17–12.	A4–4	A1–12; A4–3, 7, 9, 10; A16–52.
A1–6	A1–7, 8, 11, 12, 13, 14, 15, 18, 26, 30; A4–1; A5–8, 10; A6–1, 3; A7–3, 5, 7; A8–1; A16–21.			A4–5	A4–4, 6, 8; A10–7, 9.
		A1–27	A1–14, 30; A3–2; A4–4; A5–2; A6–4, 5; A7–8, 10; A8–2; A17–12.	A4–6	A4–5; A10–7, 15.
				A4–7	A4–9; A8–2; A13–5.
A1–7	A1–26; A4–2; A8–1.	A1–28	A1–29, 30; A3–1; A6–1; A10–27; A14–3.	A4–8	A4–9.
A1–8	A1–6, 12, 13, 14, 15; A4–1; A6–1, 3; A7–7; A8–1; A9–1.			A4–9	A16–10, 12; A17–1.
		A1–29	A3–2; A4–4; A6–3; A10–28, 33, 34, 36, 38, 43; A14–3; A16–26, 52; A17–6.	A4–10	A4–9; A15–13.
A1–9	A1–8; A4–2.			A4–11	A4–12.
A1–10	A1–11, 15.			A4–12	A16–32, 44, 63.
A1–11	A1–12.	A1–30	A1–29; A4–4; A5–9.		
A1–12	A1–2, 10, 11, 13, 15, 17, 18, 20, 21, 25, 27; A4–3, 4.	A2–1	A2–2, 4; A7–1; A12–5, 11.	A5–1	A1–30; A5–2, 3, 4, 13, 14; A16–54.
		A2–2	A2–3, 4, 5; A7–2; A12–14.	A5–2	A5–11, 13, 15.
A1–13	A1–12, 14, 30; A5–9, 10; A6–3; A7–6, 8; A8–2; A16–10, 21, 52, 53, 71.	A2–4	A1–16; A12–1, 2, 7, 14.	A5–3	A5–2, 4; A16–54.
				A5–4	A5–3, 5.
		A2–5	A2–6.	A5–6	A5–7, 18.
A1–14	A1–13; A16–24; A17–1.	A2–6	A12–1.	A5–7	A5–15, 18.
		A3–1	A1–30; A3–2, 3, 4; A12–12.		
A1–15	A1–14, 18.			A5–8	A5–9, 10, 16, 18.

Statistical
Notes

IN THE following tables detail will not always add to totals, because of errors introduced by rounding. Some such minor discrepancies are due to roundings made after calculation of data on worksheets, and others to different degrees of rounding in different tables. These discrepancies should not be confused with those due to compensation among Highs and Lows (see discussion in General Notes, above).

The effects of "feedbacks" of derivative series upon antecedent series have been taken into account wherever they significantly modify the calculations. In some instances, where the effects are slight, footnotes indicate the omission of these further calculations. Such discrepancies as may remain unnoted, whether of the latter type or due to minor adjustments stemming from updating figures, are not considered to affect significantly the resulting calculations.

L = Low projection.
M = Medium projection.
H = High projection.
LL = Low Low (or Extreme Low) projection.
HL = High Low (or Modified Low) projection.
LH = Low High (or Modified High) projection.
HH = High High (or Extreme High) projection.
n.a. = not available.
A dash signifies "nil," "not applicable," or "negligible."
Tons refer to short tons, unless otherwise specified.

appendix

to

chapter

1

BASIC ECONOMIC PATTERNS

Notes

THE OBJECTIVE FOR this part of the study was to produce both a number of recognized indicators of the growth of the American economy and reference series to which the projections in Part I— dealing with end-products and generally used intermediates—could be related. The most important reference series are those for population, households, and gross national product. Also important are the components of GNP by consuming sectors (personal consumption, government, investment, export) and by types of output (goods, services, and construction), as well as the Federal Reserve Board industrial production index and its components. Most of the other projections shown in this part of the appendix (including even such important ones as labor force) have been worked out because they are necessary intermediates in the derivation of other basic aggregates or because they afford valuable checks for plausibility and internal consistency.

Population

What is presented in the historical data and the projections for population (Tables A1–1 and A1–2) is the well known series, "total population of the United States, including Armed Forces overseas." This is something more than the "resident" population and, for reasons of historical comparability and comparability with other series, is exclusive of Alaska and Hawaii. It relates to midyear and contains the same degree of "undercount" of children

under 5 that is estimated for the Censuses—an error that is corrected in certain of the calculations in order to arrive at valid age-sex breakdowns. As a general base for all population-oriented projections, this series is probably no more appropriate or inappropriate than others that might have been used, but in any event the differences among the series are in the neighborhood of only one or two per cent and have virtually no effect on the further derivations.

The population projections are based essentially on recent projections of the U.S. Bureau of the Census, published in *Statistical Abstract of the United States,* 1958, pp. 6–7, and in Current Population Reports, Series P-25, No. 187, Nov. 10, 1958.[1] The Census projections cover the years 1960–80, with detail by age-sex groups, and are in four series, with the following assumptions:

Fertility:
Series I: Averages 10% above 1955–57 level throughout the projection period.
Series II: 1955–57 level continues to 1975–80.
Series III: 1955–57 level declines to 1949–51 level by 1965–70, then remains at that level until 1975–80.
Series IV: 1955–57 level declines to 1942–44 level by 1965–70, then remains at that level until 1975–80.
Mortality: Based on mortality rate data developed

1. Minor partial revisions, not taken account of herein, were subsequently published in Series P-25, No. 241, Jan. 17, 1962.

by the Social Security Administration. These allow for a gradual decline in death rates throughout the projection period. The same mortality assumptions were used for all four series.

As shown in Chapter 1, Table 1–1, the fertility assumption has—especially for more distant years, where geometric rates of progression cause greater effect—primary bearing upon the population projections and for this reason is made the basis for the differences in the Census projections. For purposes of this study, the fertility assumption in Series I seemed to provide a reasonable "High." That in Series III seemed to provide the most reasonable "Medium," on the supposition that the very long term trend in fertility is downward and that the aberrations we have seen in recent decades are the result of depression, war, and certain variations in age of marriage and speed of family formation which have been having a more dramatic effect on recent birth rates than they are likely to have on long-term changes in sizes of completed families. Series IV of these "illustrative" projections, however, did not seem to provide, beyond the year 1970, a reasonable Low, since it in effect assumed a flattening out of the birth rate at a level higher than some of those which have already been experienced. While it is true that these lower levels were recorded mostly during the Great Depression, they have also been reached in some relatively prosperous years (1926–29, 1939–41, 1944–45). It is at least a reasonable possibility that birth rates will continue to decline after 1970, and for this reason our Low has been adapted from the Census Series IV projection by assuming such a continued decline. The method of calculation was crude, assuming a continued linear decline of Census's implied crude birth rate; considering that what was wanted was a Low, no greater precision was believed warranted.

Additional modifications, of lesser importance, were made in the same crude manner in order to provide a range in death rates and in immigration. Although the death rate has a greater absolute influence on the size of population than the immigration rate, room for variation in rate of decrease in mortality is small. Consequently the more important modification, affecting mostly the "High," was that in immigration, which was worked out as a rate relative to actual population rather than as an absolute amount. Both an increase in this rate, resulting from a relaxation of political objections to immigration, and a decrease in the rate, resulting from a diminution in motivation of foreigners (and

Puerto Ricans) to emigrate to the United States, were assumed to be reasonably possible.

For the years 1990–2000, guidance was taken from some tentative, unpublished work done by the Census Bureau. As with the series up to 1980, crude adjustments were made on the basis of diverging birth, death, and immigration rates.

Age distribution

The age-sex distribution (Table A1–3) calculated by the Census Bureau (and lying behind their total population projections) was adjusted for each age-sex-year bracket by correction factors. For the Low this included a cohort adjustment factor corresponding to the lower birth rate assumption from 1975; in addition, a minor, across-the-board adjustment was used to take into account the assumed lower immigration and higher mortality. For the High, the total adjustment by reason of higher immigration and births to immigrants (as well as the minor one resulting from the lower death rate) was arbitrarily distributed among the various age-sex brackets, since the numbers involved were too small to warrant more precise methods.

Labor force

Projections of labor force were obtained (Table A1–5) by applying age-sex participation rates (Table A1–4) to the corresponding projected age-sex population brackets. The rates were adapted from the rates and assumptions used in the sources given in the footnotes (projections by the Census Bureau and the Bureau of Labor Statistics), with adjustments to take account of actual levels recorded subsequent to the date of the BLS-Census projections and to conform the projections to a single estimated level for 1960.

The method of arriving at the labor force figures, it should be noted, was one of the exceptions to the method of multiplying extremes in obtaining derived Highs and Lows. The age-sex detail of the population figures is of necessity an additive model, since addition is the way the total High or Low population projection is arrived at. Conceivably, with a given High or Low population, there might be a higher or lower concentration, respectively, in the population of labor force age, but any substantial variation (except perhaps near the end of the projection period) would be unlikely. In the case of the labor force participation rates, on the other hand, lower or higher participations than are shown in Table A1–4 are quite conceivable. This is particularly true for the High, where the Census projection on which the rates are based was derived by projection of the average rates of change in participation rates between 1920 and 1954–56. For a few age-sex brackets, this means a decline rather than a rise in rates. Applying the highest reasonable rates independently to each age-sex bracket, rather than following the Census model, would, however, have increased the High by only about 2 per cent; and such complete independence of behavior cannot, in any event, be assumed.

Variations in the size of the labor force are shown in Table A1–5. It does not include all of the permutations possible with Low, Medium, and High population and Low, Medium, and High participation rates, but only those which are of future interest herein. Combinations of the two Lows, on the one hand, and the two Highs, on the other, yield the basic Low and High labor force projections used in most of the subsequent analysis. The Low-High combination and the High-Low combination, which would be brought about, respectively, under conditions of High demand with Low population and Low demand with High population, are relevant to the analogous variations in GNP models, which are given in Table A1–11.

The projections, in Table A1–2, of civilian labor force, civilian employment, private employment, and agricultural and non-agricultural employment are used in this study principally for "implication" checks—that is, to verify the plausibility of the implied rates of growth in productivity emerging from other projections. Hence, the methods used for derivation were designed only to achieve approximate results and are not always conceptually "pure." However, the principal conceptual requirement was taken cognizance of—namely, that respective components of any one level of projection should relate to the same basic GNP model.

Households

The definition and importance of households are discussed in Chapter 1 (pp. 74–75). The projections (Table A1–2) are based on those of the Bureau of the Census, which were derived from detailed consideration of the distribution of individuals by family and household status. Our projections were adjusted to our own population projections by application of the implicit Census ratios of households to population 20 years of age and over. These same ratios were extrapolated beyond 1980, the latest year projected by Census, in order to arrive at projections to 2000. Since there were four Census projections, an arbitrary choice was made, for our

Medium, of the higher (and more central) of the two medium Census household projections.

Especially for the less distant years, differences in participation rates among the several projections are not very great. Application of these rates to the different population levels still produces a relatively narrow range (+8% and —6% from the Medium in 1980 and +25% and —15% in 2000). For many purposes, however (e.g., residential construction), what is significant is not the absolute level of households but the magnitude of year to year change, which is much more volatile. Small errors in projection of household levels become large errors in annual increments. It is significant, therefore, that our method of applying High household ratios to High population, and vice versa for the Lows, tends to exaggerate the range in number of households and in their rate of formation, since there is actually some compensation likely between the two factors. However, the range in Census household projections is probably on the conservative side. Moreover, the wider ranges in households do not appear until the "second generation" and are caused more by the assumed range in birth rates over the next two decades than by the range in household ratios. It is felt, therefore, that the range both in number of households and in annual increments is within the limits of what is reasonably possible.

So far as the annual rates of change are concerned, it is easily possible that there may be substantially larger or smaller figures than indicated, as the result of speedups and slowdowns in the marriage rate, in family doubling or undoubling, and in the establishment of independent quarters for unmarried children and for older people. Such factors could cause annual increments in households (and demand for dwelling units) running as much as 20 per cent higher or lower than what we have projected. However, since the fluctuation for the most part would be causally connected with the business cycle, it may be regarded as part of the cyclical fluctuation which would be superimposed upon all the long term trends we are projecting.

Gross national product

The three projected levels of GNP stem from the basic hypothesis that the size of GNP results from an equilibrating of the productive potential of the economy with the demand forces pressing upon it. The Medium projection in Table A1–10 shows both the levels of consumer, investment, government, and external demand separately derived and the total output calculated from the Medium labor force and Medium rates of increase in man-year productivity. For High and Low models as such, it is necessary to refer to Table A1–11, in which the most likely combinations giving rise to the High and the Low GNP, as well as some variant models, are worked out. The High and Low demand components set forth in Table A1–10 do not constitute additive models. Each is consistent with the High or Low GNP, as the case may be, but not with the Highs and Lows for the other demand components. Each could easily reach the High or the Low shown, but only if one or more of the other categories is lower or higher than shown. The meaning of the "residual" in Table A1–10 is thus different for the High and the Low projections from what it is for the Medium. In the latter case it represents only "statistical error." For the High and the Low it contains the added element of the total overallocation (for the High) or underallocation (for the Low) among components which would have to be distributed negatively or positively, respectively, in order to produce an additive High or Low GNP model.

There is one qualification that needs to be made to the foregoing explanation. The Low personal consumption expenditures, it will be seen from Table A1–11, could not, by the logic of that table, accompany the Low GNP shown in Table A1–10, since that GNP would be a result of low defense expenditures, which would in return result in somewhat higher personal consumption. Similarly, the highest personal consumption could not occur with the highest GNP since the latter would be the result of high defense expenditures, which would in turn tend to depress personal consumption. Thus, what is shown in Table A1–10 for the Low personal consumption expenditures is the lowest level deemed consistent with Low defense, and for the High, the highest level deemed consistent with High defense. It was assumed that these combinations would produce a wider range, not only in GNP but in resources use, than that obtained by making personal consumption expenditures the principal determinant.

A similar qualification holds for net exports. In order to avoid a confusing residual, the independently possible extremes are not shown. Instead, what is shown for the Low is very strictly the Low net exports (actually negative, or net imports) consistent with the Low-GNP level and for the High, the High net exports consistent with the High-GNP level. That the latter is still low (compare the Medium net exports, for example) is due to the fact that even the highest levels of exports would be counterbalanced by the minimum import necessities of the high-GNP economy.

In the case of government expenditures and investment, the Highs and Lows shown may be interpreted as representing both the reasonably possible extremes and the levels consistent with the respective GNP's.

The derivation of GNP from labor force and productivity is shown in Table A1–12, which also contains the derivation of the several demand components. The selection of rates of growth was made on the basis of an examination of the graphed data. The Low rate is approximately the average rate of change from 1929 to 1960; the Medium rate, that from 1930 to 1960; and the High rate, that from 1931 to 1960. The Low also represents a continuation of what is suggested by the experience of recent years, while the Medium and High represent degrees of stepping up. It is felt that this increased rate of gain will be called forth by the increasing demand pressures described in Chapter 1. Some estimators in this field have assumed even faster rates of gain.

That the projected gains in annual productivity are consistent with plausible assumptions on the major sector breakdown of the labor force, annual hours worked, and hourly productivity is demonstrated in Tables A1–18 and 19.

Personal consumption expenditures are obtained, as indicated in the footnotes, by applying a single per capita rate of gain to the three population projections. Higher and lower rates of gain are reasonably possible, but would be inconsistent with the government expenditure assumptions at the particular GNP level. Gross private domestic investment is obtained by addition of the constituent elements, on the assumption that these are essentially independent of each other and cumulative in effect. The government expenditures projection is the sum of defense expenditures and a level of non-defense expenditures which is relatively higher with Low defense and lower with High (see Table A1–12, footnote 10). The derivation of net exports is described in footnote 11 to Table A1–12 and detailed in Table A1–17. The level of exports is taken as essentially independent of U.S. output, but the level of imports as closely associated therewith.

Table A1–13 shows the composition of the GNP by type of output. In the primary breakdown—by goods, services, and construction—there is a residual (in this table referred to as "non-allocable output") analogous to the residual in Table A1–10. In the second segment of the table, the total of goods, projected as an aggregate, is compared with the "built-up" total of durable goods and non-durable goods, with a corresponding residual. In both cases, the residual lies within the bounds that may be considered permissible for "statistical error" plus the non-allocable overage or shortfall described in footnote 6 of the table. The difference between total goods (in the Low and High) and the added total of farm and non-farm goods is of another kind, in that non-farm goods was actually obtained by subtraction of farm goods. However, to obtain, for example, the High non-farm, the element subtracted was neither the Low nor the High farm but the "Low farm associated with High population," since this and the High non-farm are complementary parts of the High goods total. This "Low farm associated with High population" was obtained by multiplying the High population by the Low per capita output of farm products.

The projection of changes in inventories was necessary both to derive the goods components and to derive private investment, since, with the long term growth in the economy, there must also be a growth in goods "in pipeline." Inasmuch, however, as it is a quite minor component of current output, the projection was made crudely (see footnote 11) on the basis of ratios to rates of growth in total sales of durables and non-durables, respectively.

Details of the derivation of durable goods, non-durable goods, and services are shown in Table A1–14. It will be noted that for each of the first two groups the Highs and Lows have been added to the total, as if the purchases by each of the demand sectors were "non-competitive." To the extent that this introduces error, the error becomes part of the "non-allocable" residuals shown in Table A1–13.

Table A1–15 presents a number of projections with respect to government employment, product, and purchases. It will be noted that, in keeping with the treatment of government product by the National Income Division of the U.S. Department of Commerce, "productivity" per government employee, measured in constant dollars, is maintained unchanged. There are small differences, in that the NID applies the constant factor to each of several principal classes of employees, while the series presented herein give effect only to the differences between military and civilian personnel.

Table A1–16, on farm output and product, is a link between the agricultural demand and output projections in the appendices to Chapters 2 and 12, on the one hand, and the national income magnitudes dealt with in this appendix. Since "gross farm product" and "farm goods" are identical by definition, the series affords a means of deriving, by subtraction from total goods, the non-farm goods

magnitudes which are given in Table A1–13 and also used, importantly, as a basis for the general industrial production index in Tables A1–29 and 30. It also permits, again by subtraction, the derivation of a "non-agricultural product" figure which can be used as part of an implications check for the plausibility and consistency of our various employment and output projections.

The implications checks are contained primarily in Tables A1–18 to 21, which examine growth rates in output and productivity for GNP and its principal components. There is a wide range of uncertainty concerning the fashion in which daily average hours and weeks of work per year may develop during the rest of the century, and for this reason both the man-hour projections and the hourly productivity rates shown in Table A1–19 should be considered as essentially illustrative. The annual output per worker figures appearing in Table A1–18 would appear to be somewhat more reliable in general magnitude. The non-agricultural trends, involving as they do smaller rates of change, would appear to be more dependable than the agricultural. In interpreting the data it should also be remembered that these are labor force concepts, which show total hours and output per individual and not per job. They therefore give effect to a probably increasing proportion of dual job holding, offset to some extent by a possibly increasing number of part-time workers.

The kinds of productivity gains projected are not out of line with those assumed by other analysts. Of particular interest are the implied relatively greater rates of gain in agricultural as compared with non-agricultural activity, bringing agriculture almost abreast of the rest of the economy by the end of the century. This is largely a function of the projected continued decline in agricultural employment. However, it is also to be noted that the comparison in real product assumes the same relative prices for agricultural and non-agricultural products as obtain in the base year.

Tables A1–20 and 21 compare past and projected growth rates, the former in the form of total change over successive 20-year periods and the latter as average annual rates of change over successive decades and scores of years. These may also be regarded as a form of "implications" check. In addition, Table A1–20 illustrates the relative contribution of each of the components of each aggregate to the over-all rate of change in the aggregate.

Personal consumption expenditures

Tables A1–22 and A1–23 present past and prospective breakdowns of consumer expenditures in percentage terms. Since the aim is to evaluate consumer behavior, which involves a relative disposition of available income based on actual prices, the historical percentages are calculated from data in current dollars. Extrapolation of trends so calculated implies a continuation of the same sorts of relative price changes as have occurred in the past. It is to be noted that calculation of past distribution of expenditures in constant, rather than current, dollars would not have removed the effect of such past relative price changes but would have distorted the proportions in which consumers made their expenditure distribution.

The projected expenditures are basically "judgment" extrapolations of past trends, modified by the kinds of considerations concerning changing habits and influences that are discussed in Part I. The Highs and the Lows give scope to the fact that in each instance a range of possible past trends and future influences may be perceived. As usual, the total of the Highs will exceed 100 per cent and the total of the Lows will fall short of it, for if the consumer goes "high" on some of these expenditure components, it follows that he will have to spend on the low side for some others. In evaluating Table A1–23, it should be noted that some of the components are too small, as a percentage of total expenditures, for the year-to-year changes or the High-Low range to be meaningful. Such items are carried in the table mostly to provide an order of magnitude and to account for the 100 per cent.

The place of disposable personal income in the picture is shown in Tables A1–22 and 23 in terms of its percentage relationship to personal consumption expenditures. The difference between the two is "saving," which it should be remembered is the concept of this term used in the U.S. National Income Accounts compiled by the Department of Commerce and whose proportion may be expected (despite considerable year-to-year variation) to change either slowly or not at all over the long term. While analysts frequently relate consumer expenditures to disposable personal income rather than to total expenditures, for the purposes of this book use of the latter relationship seemed both more practical and more dependable. The single per capita level of total personal consumption expenditures which it appeared logical to use could not so logically have been replaced with a single per capita level of disposable personal income. Moreover, to project disposable personal income independently, rather than "synthetically" as in Table A1–27, would have required an analysis of income flows which is not especially relevant to the purposes of this study and which would have required an additional array of assumptions. For certain parts of this study, however—primarily to take advantage of previous work in a particular field—the relation of categories of expenditures to disposable personal income as projected herein has been used.

Tables A1–24 and 25 deal with consumer expenditures on a per capita basis, in constant dollars. These series provide an added set of constraints for the judgments on the individual projected expenditures, which have to make reasonable sense not only as percentages of the total but in absolute levels per person, both in and of themselves and in terms of continuity with the historical base.

Tables A1–26 and 27, finally, show historical and projected consumer expenditures in the aggregate (i.e., for the aggregate of all consumers), in constant dollars. The historical table is derived from the published statistics in current dollars, using the specially devised deflators shown in the table footnote: the projections table results from applying the percentage distribution in Table A1–23 to the total personal consumption expenditure levels shown in Table A1–12. These are the series which form the bases for many of the end-use and materials-consumption derivations later in the book. They amount to a set of quantity indexes which, in their groupings, have the effect of aggregating quantities on the basis of their 1960 relative prices, but at the same time allowing for changes in consumption habits resulting from changing relative-price relationships. This is consistent with the general method of this study in allowing for the influence upon demand of a continuation of past trends in price relationships, on the grounds that abstraction from the influence of such changes is impracticable. Wherever prospective shortages based on these demands appear to be in prospect, Part III of this study considers the deviations from trends that might be entailed in the actual equating of demand and supply.

Not all the elements in Table A1–27 are direct take-off points for later evaluation of resource requirements. Some are included only for completing the array and thus establishing plausible relationships between the series of particular interest and the residuals which they imply for other expenditures. A number of others—e.g., food, clothing, housing, automobiles—are elsewhere evaluated, usually in detail, in quantity rather than value terms, on the basis of other determinants. In these cases, the value aggregates of Table A1–27 afford cross-checks for plausibility. Some of the components also afford cross-checks with each other. Automobile operating expenditures, for example, are not unrelated to passenger car purchases. Nor are they unrelated to purchased transportation. Much of the value of these various cross-checks would be lost, it should be noted, were not all consumer expenditure components considered, as they are in these tables, even if not of direct interest, to insure consistency with the consumer-expenditure total.

Industrial production index

Tables A1–28 to 30 give the historical data and projections on principal components of the Federal Reserve Board index of industrial production. As with the consumer expenditure tabulation, not all of these components find further use in derived projections, but it is necessary to have all the parts in order to confirm that any one of them is in plausible relationship with the others and with the whole. Some of the components are not precisely identical with those shown in the published FRB data but have been derived by the same method of averaging as is used in the FRB groupings.

Table A1–30 shows, in summary, the derivation of the indexes. The basic method was, for each of the components, to determine the coefficients which have historically obtained between the component and some related economic series for which, on the basis of other work in this study, an independent projection existed or was possible. As a rule, 1953–60 comparisons were emphasized, because of some discontinuity in the indexes at 1953, but whether this or the whole available period (1947–60) was used, the method was to fit a graphic trend line to the coefficients and extrapolate them —usually arithmetically but in some cases on the basis of free-hand curves. Judgment was applied, in the process, in terms of hypotheses as to the reasons for changing coefficients in the past and speculation as to whether these reasons would prevail in the future. Only a single level was projected for each of the coefficients, on the assumption that, since the reference series and the indexes were by and large only alternate means of presenting the selfsame quantity projections, a compounding of the ranges by the multiplication of Lows and Lows and of Highs and Highs would have extended them beyond the points of reasonable probability.

After application of the projected coefficients to the projected reference series, the individual index components were aggregated in the FRB manner. At particular points, these aggregates were checked against group series directly projected and systematic adjustments made until the differences appeared to fall within the confines of allowable statistical error. Thus construction of the industrial production index provided yet another means of

helping to insure that projections generated in various parts of the study are mutually consistent with one another.

LIST OF TABLES

*These tables also contain analogous data on disposable personal income.

TABLE A1–1.   Historical Data on Population, Households, Labor Force, Armed Forces, and Employment

(Millions)

						Labor force				
	Population[1]	Households[2]	Total[3]	Armed forces[3]	Civilian total[3]	Employed[3]	Civilian government employment[4]	Private employment[5]	Agricultural employment[3]	Private non-agricultural employment[5]
1929	121.9	29.6	49.4	0.3	49.2	47.6	2.8	44.8	10.4	34.4
1930	123.2	30.0	50.1	0.3	49.8	45.5	3.0	42.5	10.3	32.2
1931	124.1	30.3	50.7	0.3	50.4	42.4	3.0	39.4	10.3	29.1
1932	124.9	30.4	51.2	0.2	51.0	38.9	3.0	35.9	10.2	25.7
1933	125.7	30.8	51.8	0.2	51.6	38.8	2.8	36.0	10.1	25.9
1934	126.5	31.3	52.5	0.3	52.2	40.9	3.0	37.9	9.9	28.0
1935	127.4	31.9	53.1	0.3	52.9	42.3	3.2	39.1	10.1	29.0
1936	128.2	32.5	53.7	0.3	53.4	44.4	3.4	41.0	10.0	31.0
1937	129.0	33.1	54.3	0.3	54.0	46.3	3.5	42.8	9.8	33.0
1938	130.0	33.7	54.9	0.3	54.6	44.2	3.6	40.6	9.7	30.9
1939	131.0	34.4	55.6	0.4	55.2	45.7	3.7	42.0	9.6	32.4
1940	132.1	35.2	56.2	0.5	55.6	47.5	3.8	43.7	9.5	34.2
1941	133.4	35.9	57.5	1.6	55.9	50.3	4.1	46.2	9.1	37.1
1942	134.9	36.4	60.4	4.0	56.4	53.7	4.8	48.9	9.3	39.6
1943	136.7	36.8	64.6	9.0	55.5	54.5	5.5	49.0	9.1	39.9
1944	138.4	37.1	66.0	11.4	54.6	54.0	5.5	48.5	9.0	39.5
1945	139.9	37.5	65.3	11.4	53.9	52.8	5.5	47.3	8.6	38.7
1946	141.4	38.4	61.0	3.5	57.5	55.2	5.1	50.1	8.3	41.8
1947	144.1	39.4	61.8	1.6	60.2	57.8	5.0	52.8	8.3	44.5
1948	146.6	40.9	62.9	1.5	61.4	59.1	5.1	54.0	8.0	46.0
1949	149.2	42.5	63.7	1.6	62.1	58.4	5.3	53.1	8.0	45.1
1950	151.7	43.8	64.7	1.6	63.1	59.7	5.5	54.2	7.5	46.7
1951	154.4	44.8	66.0	3.1	62.9	60.8	5.8	55.0	7.0	48.0
1952	157.0	45.7	66.6	3.6	63.0	61.0	6.0	55.0	6.8	48.2
1953	159.6	46.5	67.4	3.5	63.8	61.9	6.1	55.8	6.6	49.2
1954	162.4	47.1	67.8	3.3	64.5	60.9	6.2	54.7	6.5	48.2
1955	165.3	48.0	68.9	3.0	65.8	62.9	6.4	56.5	6.7	49.8
1956	168.2	49.0	70.4	2.9	67.5	64.7	6.7	58.0	6.6	51.4
1957	171.2	49.8	70.7	2.8	67.9	65.0	6.9	58.1	6.2	51.9
1958	174.1	50.7	71.3	2.6	68.6	64.0	7.2	56.8	5.8	51.0
1959	177.1	51.6	71.9	2.6	69.4	65.6	7.4	58.2	5.8	52.4
1960	179.9	52.6	72.8	2.5	70.3	66.4	7.7	58.7	5.7	53.0

1. Total population, including Armed Forces overseas, as of midyear. Data contain no adjustment for under-enumeration, nor do they include figures for residents of Alaska or Hawaii (which, if included, would increase the July 1, 1960, total by 800,000). Sources: 1929–39, U.S. Bureau of the Census, *Statistical Abstract of the United States*, 1959, p. 5, Table 2 (1929 Armed Forces overseas assumed same as in 1930); 1940–60, Census Bureau, Current Population Reports, Series P–25, No. 223 (Jan. 26, 1961), data for "conterminous United States."

2. "Non-institutional" households, as of midyear, "1950" definition. Source: Current Population Reports, No. 92 (Mar. 5, 1959) and No. 109 (July 17, 1961), p. 20. For 1947–60, the original data relating to April or March are interpolated (or extrapolated) to July 1; 1960 also adjusted to 1950 definition and to exclude Alaska and Hawaii.

3. Yearly averages, including Armed Forces at home and overseas. "New definitions" from 1947 on, but these affect significantly only the allocation between employed and unemployed. Source: *Economic Report of the President* (Washington: Jan. 1961), p. 146. Data will not always add to totals because of rounding.

4. Excludes Armed Forces, employees of government enterprises, and work relief. Source: 1929–45, "Average Number of Full-Time and Part-Time Employees by Industry," U.S. Department of Commerce, *National Income* (supplement to *Survey of Current Business*), 1954, Table 26; 1946–60, Table VI–14 in *U.S. Income and Output* (1958 supplement to *Survey of Current Business*) and July 1961 National Income Number of *Survey of Current Business*.

5. Obtained as residual.

TABLE A1–2. Projected Population, Households, Labor Force, Armed Forces, and Employment [1]

(Millions, unless otherwise indicated)

	1940	1945	1950	1955	1960		1970	1980	1990	2000
Total population [2]	132.1	139.9	151.7	165.3	179.9	L	202	226	249	268
						M	208	245	287	331
						H	223	279	349	433
Households [3]	35.2	37.5	43.8	48.0	52.6	L	58.7	68.7	76.5	84.3
						M	61.2	73.0	84.3	99.4
						H	64.3	79.2	97.6	124.1
Labor force [4]	56.2	65.3	64.7	68.9	72.8	L	85.4	98	108	122
						M	87.1	102	119	142
						H	88.8	109	135	175
Armed Forces [5]	.5	11.4	1.6	3.0	2.5	L	2.3	1.4	1.4	1.5
						M	3.3	3.7	4.2	5.0
						H	4.5	5.9	7.8	10.6
Civilian labor force [6]	55.6	53.9	63.1	65.8	70.3	L	83.1	97	107	120
						M	83.8	98	115	137
						H	84.3	103	127	164
Civilian employment [7]	47.5	52.8	59.7	62.9	66.4	L	78.9	92	102	114
						M	80.4	94	110	132
						H	81.8	100	123	159
Civilian government employment [8]	3.8	5.5	5.5	6.4	7.7	L	10.7	14.3	18.0	22.3
						M	11.7	16.6	22.7	31.2
						H	12.8	19.6	29.0	43.9
Private employment [9]	43.7	47.3	54.2	56.5	58.7	L	66.6	74	78	82
						M	68.7	78	87	101
						H	70.7	84	101	128
Agricultural [10]	9.5	8.6	7.5	6.7	5.7	L	4.2	3.1	2.3	1.7
						M	4.7	3.8	3.1	2.5
						H	5.1	4.6	4.2	3.8
Non-agricultural [11]	34.2	38.7	46.7	49.8	53.0	L	61.5	69	74	79
						M	64.0	74	84	98
						H	66.5	81	99	126

1. Data are for "coterminous" United States, i.e., exclude Alaska and Hawaii. Historical data, unless otherwise indicated, are from Table A1–1.

2. From Table A1–3.

3. Household ratios applied to population 20 years and over (from Table A1–3). Household ratios for 1970 and 1980 based on Census projections of households (Current Population Reports, Series P–20, No. 90, Dec. 29, 1958, series D, B, and A for Low, Medium and High), and of population 20 years and over (series III for Low; series II for Medium and High). The ratios thus implied were extrapolated to the year 2000.

4. From Table A1–5. Low labor force equals Low population times Low participation rates; High labor force equals High population times High participation rates.

5. Related to defense expenditures (Table A1–12) by a formula by which relatively larger military expenditures have a relatively lower unit manpower content per dollar. Expenditures on Armed Forces (Table A9–2) are divided by average 1960 expenditure to obtain Armed Forces numbers, since expenditure projections follow National Income Accounts assumption of unchanging productivity.

6. Residuals, obtained by subtracting Low Armed Forces from Low labor force, etc. The Low and High thus represent the civilian labor force levels consistent with the Low and the High gross national product, respectively, rather than the possibly lower or higher levels that might accompany High defense activity in a Low labor force economy or Low defense activity in a High labor force economy.

7. Calculated at "full employment" levels of 95% of the civilian labor force for the Low, 96% for the Medium, and 97% for the High. These are thus, as in the preceding item, the levels consistent with Low, Medium, and High GNP, rather than those that might accompany a defense-oriented "Low" economy, on the one hand, or a non-defense "High" economy, on the other.

8. Projected as a percentage of civilian employment, increasing (arithmetically) from the 1960 level by 1% every five years in the Low, 1½% in the Medium, and 2% in the High. Historical percentages of civilian employment were around 6 in the thirties, 10 at the end of World War II, down to 8 in 1947, and back up to 11½ in 1960.

9. Residuals. The Lows are derived by subtracting the High percentage of government employment from the Low of civilian employment; conversely for the Highs.

10. Projected at an annual rate of decrease of 1% for the Low, 2 for the Medium, and 3 for the High. The long term average has been 2%.

11. Lows are derived by subtracting High agricultural from Low total private; vice versa for the Highs.

TABLE A1–3.   Distribution of Projected Population, by Sex and Age [1]

(Absolute figures in millions)

	1940	1945	1950	1955	1960 [2]	1970	1980	1990	2000
Low projection:									
Total population	132.1	139.9	151.7	165.3	179.9	202.2	226.0	248.6	268.5
Total population, adjusted [3]	133.0	140.8	152.5	166.1	180.8	203.0	226.8	249.4	269.3
Under 5 years	11.4	13.8	17.1	19.1	20.7	17.9	20.6	20.2	20.6
5–19 years	34.7	33.2	35.1	41.7	49.8	58.0	56.1	60.8	61.2
20 years +	86.8	93.7	100.3	105.3	110.3	127.1	150.1	168.4	187.4
14 years +	101.6	107.8	113.1	118.9	126.5	150.7	172.1	191.1	212.2
Male, 14 +	50.9	53.7	55.9	58.4	61.8	73.3	83.4	92.4	103.7
14–19	7.4	7.1	6.5	6.9	8.2	10.9	11.2	11.1	12.7
20–24	5.8	6.0	5.8	5.4	5.7	8.8	10.2	9.2	10.5
25–34	10.6	11.3	11.7	11.9	11.3	12.6	18.5	19.6	19.2
35–44	9.2	9.8	10.7	11.2	11.7	11.4	12.5	18.4	19.5
45–54	8.0	8.4	8.7	9.3	10.2	11.3	10.9	12.3	17.8
55–64	5.5	6.1	6.7	7.1	7.5	9.9	10.0	9.7	11.0
65 +	4.4	5.0	5.8	6.5	7.1	8.4	10.1	12.1	13.0
Female, 14 +	50.7	54.0	57.2	60.5	64.8	77.4	88.8	98.7	108.5
14–19	7.4	7.0	6.4	6.7	8.0	11.4	10.9	11.5	12.0
20–24	5.9	6.0	5.9	5.4	5.6	8.6	10.0	8.9	10.2
25–34	10.8	11.5	12.2	12.3	11.5	12.6	18.3	19.4	18.9
35–44	9.2	10.0	10.9	11.6	12.3	11.6	12.7	18.4	19.5
45–54	7.6	8.2	8.7	9.6	10.7	12.0	11.4	12.5	18.0
55–64	5.2	5.9	6.7	7.4	8.1	10.0	11.3	10.8	11.8
65 +	4.6	5.4	6.5	7.5	8.7	11.2	14.2	17.2	18.1
Percentage distribution: [4]									
0–4	8.6	9.8	11.2	11.5	11.5	8.8	9.1	8.1	7.7
5–19	26.1	23.6	23.0	25.1	27.5	28.6	24.7	24.4	22.7
20–64	58.5	59.2	57.7	55.0	52.3	53.0	55.5	55.8	58.0
65 +	6.8	7.4	8.1	8.4	8.7	9.7	10.7	11.7	11.5
Medium projection:									
Total population	132.1	139.9	151.7	165.3	179.9	208.2	245.4	286.9	331.1
Total population, adjusted [3]	133.0	140.8	152.5	166.1	180.8	209.0	246.2	287.7	331.9
Under 5 years	11.4	13.8	17.1	19.1	20.7	21.5	27.9	30.2	33.5
5–19 years	34.7	33.2	35.1	41.7	49.8	60.1	66.9	82.2	91.3
20 years +	86.8	93.7	100.3	105.3	110.3	127.4	151.5	175.3	207.0
14 years +	101.6	107.8	113.1	118.9	126.5	150.7	176.1	205.8	242.5
Male, 14 +	50.9	53.7	55.9	58.4	61.8	73.2	85.6	100.4	119.0
14–19	7.4	7.1	6.5	6.9	8.2	10.9	12.5	15.6	18.1
20–24	5.8	6.0	5.8	5.4	5.7	8.8	10.5	11.0	14.2
25–34	10.6	11.3	11.7	11.9	11.3	12.6	18.6	20.9	23.7
35–44	9.2	9.8	10.7	11.2	11.7	11.4	12.7	18.6	20.8
45–54	8.0	8.4	8.7	9.3	10.2	11.3	11.0	12.3	18.0
55–64	5.5	6.1	6.7	7.1	7.5	9.9	10.0	9.8	11.1
65 +	4.4	5.0	5.8	6.5	7.1	8.4	10.3	12.3	13.1

Table A1–3 (cont'd)

(Absolute figures in millions)

	1940	1945	1950	1955	1960 [2]	1970	1980	1990	2000
Female, 14 +	50.7	54.0	57.2	60.5	64.8	77.4	90.5	105.4	123.5
14–19	7.4	7.0	6.4	6.7	8.0	11.4	12.1	15.0	17.4
20–24	5.9	6.0	5.9	5.4	5.6	8.6	10.2	10.7	13.8
25–34	10.8	11.5	12.2	12.3	11.5	12.6	18.4	20.6	23.3
35–44	9.2	10.0	10.9	11.6	12.3	11.6	12.7	18.4	20.6
45–54	7.6	8.2	8.7	9.6	10.7	12.0	11.5	12.6	18.2
55–64	5.2	5.9	6.7	7.4	8.1	10.0	11.4	10.9	12.0
65 +	4.6	5.4	6.5	7.5	8.7	11.2	14.3	17.2	18.3
Percentage distribution:[4]									
0–4	8.6	9.8	11.2	11.5	11.5	10.3	11.3	10.5	10.1
5–19	26.1	23.6	23.0	25.1	27.5	28.8	27.2	28.6	27.5
20–64	58.5	59.2	57.7	55.0	52.3	51.6	51.5	50.7	52.9
65 +	6.8	7.4	8.1	8.4	8.7	9.4	10.0	10.3	9.5
High projection:									
Total population	132.1	139.9	151.7	165.3	179.9	222.6	279.3	349.4	433.1
Total population, adjusted [3]	133.0	140.8	152.5	166.1	180.8	223.4	280.1	350.2	433.9
Under 5 years	11.4	13.8	17.1	19.1	20.7	27.6	37.8	45.9	54.7
5–19 years	34.7	33.2	35.1	41.7	49.8	65.6	84.4	111.8	137.4
20 years +	86.8	93.7	100.3	105.3	110.3	130.1	158.0	192.6	241.9
14 years +	101.6	107.8	113.1	118.9	126.5	152.6	187.8	232.3	291.8
Male, 14 +	50.9	53.7	55.9	58.4	61.8	73.8	91.3	113.9	144.0
14–19	7.4	7.1	6.5	6.9	8.2	11.0	15.2	20.3	25.5
20–24	5.8	6.0	5.8	5.4	5.7	8.9	11.2	14.2	19.1
25–34	10.6	11.3	11.7	11.9	11.3	12.9	18.9	23.4	31.0
35–44	9.2	9.8	10.7	11.2	11.7	11.6	13.1	19.0	24.1
45–54	8.0	8.4	8.7	9.3	10.2	11.6	11.6	12.9	18.6
55–64	5.5	6.1	6.7	7.1	7.5	9.2	10.6	10.6	11.8
65 +	4.4	5.0	5.8	6.5	7.1	8.6	10.7	13.0	13.9
Female, 14 +	50.7	54.0	57.2	60.5	64.8	78.8	96.4	118.6	147.7
14–19	7.4	7.0	6.4	6.7	8.0	11.5	14.6	19.5	24.4
20–24	5.9	6.0	5.9	5.4	5.6	8.6	10.9	13.8	18.5
25–34	10.8	11.5	12.2	12.3	11.5	12.9	19.0	23.5	30.4
35–44	9.2	10.0	10.9	11.6	12.3	11.9	13.2	18.9	23.9
45–54	7.6	8.2	8.7	9.6	10.7	12.3	12.1	13.2	18.8
55–64	5.2	5.9	6.7	7.4	8.1	10.3	12.0	11.7	12.7
65 +	4.6	5.4	6.5	7.5	8.7	11.3	14.7	18.0	19.0
Percentage distribution:[4]									
0–4	8.6	9.8	11.2	11.5	11.5	12.4	13.5	13.1	12.6
5–19	26.1	23.6	23.0	25.1	27.5	29.4	30.1	32.0	31.6
20–64	58.5	59.2	57.7	55.0	52.3	49.3	47.3	46.1	48.1
65 +	6.8	7.4	8.1	8.4	8.7	8.9	9.1	8.9	7.6

1. Including Armed Forces overseas, as of July 1. Based on Census Projections IV, III, and I, for Low, Medium, and High, respectively. (For sources, see Notes.) The Low projections were adjusted for lower fertility and higher mortality; the High projections for higher immigration and births to immigrants. Historical data from Current Population Reports, Series P–25, Nos. 98 (Aug. 13, 1954), 146 (Nov. 12, 1956), and 170 (Dec. 18, 1957). Detail will not always add to totals, because of rounding.

2. 1960 as projected by U.S. Bureau of Census (Series III), except for "under 5 years" cohort, which was adjusted to 1955–60 births reported in Current Population Reports, Series P–25, No. 223 (Jan. 26, 1961).

3. Corrected for "net Census undercount" of children under 5 years of age.

4. Related to adjusted population as 100%.

TABLE A1–4.   Projected Labor Force Participation Rates, by Sex and Age [1]

(Per cent)

	1940	1945	1950	1955	1960	1970	1980	1990	2000
Low projection:									
Labor force, total	55.3	60.7	57.1	58.0	57.6	56.7	56.8	56.8	57.4
Male, total	82.5	85.7	82.2	82.3	79.8	80.1	80.9	81.5	81.7
14–19			52.3	49.0	46.4	48.6	49.6	50.5	51.1
20–24			89.7	89.4	89.0	89.4	89.4	89.4	89.4
25–34			94.0	96.4	96.2	96.4	96.4	96.4	96.4
35–44	[2]	[2]	92.5	96.8	96.2	96.8	96.8	96.8	96.8
45–54			93.1	95.0	94.3	94.8	95.0	95.0	95.0
55–64			86.6	86.3	85.1	86.0	86.2	86.3	86.3
65 +			43.1	38.7	32.1	37.6	38.3	38.5	38.7
Female, total	28.0	35.7	32.7	34.5	36.3	34.5	34.0	33.6	34.3
14–19			31.7	29.7	30.1	30.0	30.4	30.8	31.4
20–24			45.8	45.8	45.8	45.9	45.8	45.8	45.8
25–34			33.6	34.8	35.7	35.2	35.0	35.0	35.0
35–44	[2]	[2]	38.5	41.4	43.1	42.6	42.4	42.4	42.4
45–54			37.9	43.5	49.4	46.2	45.2	44.6	44.5
55–64			26.9	32.2	36.8	34.1	33.4	33.2	33.2
65 +			9.2	10.3	10.5	10.3	10.3	10.3	10.3
Medium projection:									
Labor force, total	55.3	60.7	57.1	58.0	57.6	57.8	57.8	57.7	58.7
Male, total	82.5	85.7	82.2	82.3	79.8	78.6	78.4	78.4	79.1
14–19			52.3	49.0	46.4	46.2	46.8	47.0	47.2
20–24			89.7	89.4	89.0	86.6	86.0	86.0	86.0
25–34			94.0	96.4	96.2	96.4	96.4	96.4	96.4
35–44	[2]	[2]	92.5	96.8	96.2	96.7	96.8	96.8	96.8
45–54			93.1	95.0	94.3	94.9	95.0	95.0	95.0
55–64			86.6	86.3	85.1	86.0	86.3	86.3	86.3
65 +			43.1	38.7	32.1	31.2	29.9	29.2	29.2
Female, total	28.0	35.7	32.7	34.5	36.3	38.2	38.3	38.0	39.0
14–19			31.7	29.7	30.1	28.2	28.0	27.8	27.6
20–24			45.8	45.8	45.8	45.3	45.2	45.2	45.2
25–34			33.6	34.8	35.7	38.3	39.1	39.1	39.1
35–44	[2]	[2]	38.5	41.4	43.1	47.0	48.4	48.9	49.0
45–54			37.9	43.5	49.4	54.8	56.3	56.4	56.4
55–64			26.9	32.2	36.8	42.8	44.4	44.4	44.4
65 +			9.2	10.3	10.5	12.0	12.9	13.0	13.0
High projection:									
Labor force, total	55.3	60.7	57.1	58.0	57.6	58.2	58.1	58.2	59.9
Male, total	82.5	85.7	82.2	82.3	79.8	78.0	76.1	74.6	76.1
14–19			52.3	49.0	46.4	42.0	38.8	37.6	37.3
20–24			89.7	89.4	89.0	86.0	83.3	81.0	78.8
25–34			94.0	96.4	96.2	97.2	97.7	98.1	98.5
35–44	[2]	[2]	92.5	96.8	96.2	97.8	98.3	98.5	98.7
45–54			93.1	95.0	94.3	96.3	97.3	97.7	98.1
55–64			86.6	86.3	85.1	88.7	90.5	91.6	92.4
65 +			43.1	38.7	32.1	24.8	18.9	14.7	12.0
Female, total	28.0	35.7	32.7	34.5	36.3	39.6	41.2	42.3	44.2
14–19			31.7	29.7	30.1	27.9	26.6	26.2	26.2
20–24			45.8	45.8	45.8	46.6	46.3	46.2	46.2
25–34			33.6	34.8	35.7	38.0	40.2	42.6	45.1
35–44	[2]	[2]	38.5	41.4	43.1	48.6	52.9	56.6	58.5
45–54			37.9	43.5	49.4	58.8	65.8	67.8	67.8
55–64			26.9	32.2	36.8	46.0	53.0	55.0	55.0
65 +			9.2	10.3	10.5	12.5	14.0	15.1	15.8

1. 1940–60 rates, and subtotals and totals for all years, are derived from absolute data on labor force and population (Tables A1–3 and 5, except that age-sex detail was calculated from unrounded data). The Medium age/sex bracket projection for 1970 is based on Bureau of Labor Statistics projections of participation rates (Bull. No. 1242, 1959), the Low and High on Census Projections IV and II, respectively (Current Population Reports, Series P–50, No. 69, Oct. 1956); these have been adjusted somewhat for better consistency with actual 1955–60 experience and extrapolated to 2000.

2. Yearly averages not available.

TABLE A1–5. Projected Labor Force under Various Assumptions as to Population and Participation Rates [1]

(Millions)

	1940	1945	1950	1955	1960	1970	1980	1990	2000
A. Low population, low participation:									
Labor force, total	56.2	65.3	64.7	68.9	72.8	85.4	97.7	108.5	121.9
Male, total	42.0	46.0	45.9	48.0	49.3	58.7	67.5	75.3	84.7
14–19			3.4	3.4	3.8	5.3	5.6	5.6	6.5
20–24			5.2	4.8	5.1	7.9	9.1	8.2	9.4
25–34			11.0	11.5	10.9	12.1	17.8	18.9	18.5
35–44	[2]	[2]	9.9	10.8	11.3	11.0	12.1	17.8	18.9
45–54			8.1	8.9	9.6	10.7	10.4	11.7	16.9
55–64			5.8	6.1	6.4	8.5	8.6	8.4	9.5
65 +			2.5	2.5	2.3	3.2	3.9	4.7	5.0
Female, total	14.2	19.3	18.7	20.9	23.5	26.7	30.2	33.2	37.2
14–19			2.0	2.0	2.4	3.4	3.3	3.5	3.8
20–24			2.7	2.5	2.6	3.9	4.6	4.1	4.7
25–34			4.1	4.3	4.1	4.4	6.4	6.8	6.6
35–44	[2]	[2]	4.2	4.8	5.3	4.9	5.4	7.8	8.3
45–54			3.3	4.2	5.3	5.5	5.2	5.6	8.0
55–64			1.8	2.4	3.0	3.4	3.8	3.6	3.9
65 +			.6	.8	.9	1.2	1.5	1.8	1.9
B. Low population, high participation:									
Labor force, total	56.2	65.3	64.7	68.9	72.8	88.2	101.9	114.4	129.7
Male, total	42.0	46.0	45.9	48.0	49.3	57.5	64.8	71.6	80.4
14–19			3.4	3.4	3.8	4.8	4.3	4.2	4.7
20–24			5.2	4.8	5.1	7.6	8.5	7.4	8.3
25–34			11.0	11.5	10.9	12.2	18.1	19.2	18.9
35–44	[2]	[2]	9.9	10.8	11.3	11.1	12.3	18.1	19.2
45–54			8.1	8.9	9.6	10.9	10.6	12.0	17.5
55–64			5.8	6.1	6.4	8.8	9.1	8.9	10.2
65 +			2.5	2.5	2.3	2.1	1.9	1.8	1.6
Female, total	14.2	19.3	18.7	20.9	23.5	30.7	37.1	42.8	49.3
14–19			2.0	2.0	2.4	3.2	2.9	3.0	3.1
20–24			2.7	2.5	2.6	4.0	4.6	4.1	4.7
25–34			4.1	4.3	4.1	4.8	7.4	8.3	8.5
35–44	[2]	[2]	4.2	4.8	5.3	5.6	6.7	10.4	11.4
45–54			3.3	4.2	5.3	7.1	7.5	8.5	12.2
55–64			1.8	2.4	3.0	4.6	6.0	5.9	6.5
65 +			.6	.8	.9	1.4	2.0	2.6	2.9
C. Medium population, medium participation:									
Labor force, total	56.2	65.3	64.7	68.9	72.8	87.1	101.8	118.8	142.3
Male, total	42.0	46.0	45.9	48.0	49.3	57.5	67.1	78.7	94.1
14–19			3.4	3.4	3.8	5.0	5.8	7.3	8.5
20–24			5.2	4.8	5.1	7.6	9.0	9.5	12.2
25–34			11.0	11.5	10.9	12.1	17.9	20.1	22.8
35–44	[2]	[2]	9.9	10.8	11.3	11.0	12.3	18.0	20.1
45–54			8.1	8.9	9.6	10.7	10.4	11.7	17.1
55–64			5.8	6.1	6.4	8.5	8.6	8.5	9.6
65 +			2.5	2.5	2.3	2.6	3.1	3.6	3.8
Female, total	14.2	19.3	18.7	20.9	23.5	29.6	34.7	40.1	48.2
14–19			2.0	2.0	2.4	3.2	3.4	4.2	4.8
20–24			2.7	2.5	2.6	3.9	4.6	4.8	6.2
25–34			4.1	4.3	4.1	4.8	7.2	8.0	9.1
35–44	[2]	[2]	4.2	4.8	5.3	5.5	6.1	9.0	10.1
45–54			3.3	4.2	5.3	6.6	6.5	7.1	10.3
55–64			1.8	2.4	3.0	4.3	5.1	4.8	5.3
65 +			.6	.8	.9	1.3	1.8	2.2	2.4

Table A1–5 (cont'd)

(Millions)

	1940	1945	1950	1955	1960	1970	1980	1990	2000
D. High population, low participation:									
Labor force, total	56.2	65.3	64.7	68.9	72.8	86.3	105.2	130.5	168.1
Male, total	42.0	46.0	45.9	48.0	49.3	59.0	72.6	90.3	116.6
14–19			3.4	3.4	3.8	5.3	7.5	10.2	13.0
20–24			5.2	4.8	5.1	8.0	10.0	12.7	17.1
25–34			11.0	11.5	10.9	12.4	18.2	22.6	29.9
35–44	2	2	9.9	10.8	11.3	11.2	12.7	18.4	23.3
45–54			8.1	8.9	9.6	11.0	11.0	12.3	17.7
55–64			5.8	6.1	6.4	7.9	9.1	9.1	10.2
65 +			2.5	2.5	2.3	3.2	4.1	5.0	5.4
Female, total	14.2	19.3	18.7	20.9	23.5	27.3	32.6	40.2	51.5
14–19			2.0	2.0	2.4	3.4	4.4	6.0	7.7
20–24			2.7	2.5	2.6	3.9	5.0	6.3	8.5
25–34			4.1	4.3	4.1	4.5	6.6	8.2	10.6
35–44	2	2	4.2	4.8	5.3	5.1	5.6	8.0	10.1
45–54			3.3	4.2	5.3	5.7	5.5	5.9	8.4
55–64			1.8	2.4	3.0	3.5	4.0	3.9	4.2
65 +			.6	.8	.9	1.2	1.5	1.9	2.0
E. High population, high participation:									
Labor force, total	56.2	65.3	64.7	68.9	72.8	88.8	109.2	135.2	174.9
Male, total	42.0	46.0	45.9	48.0	49.3	57.6	69.5	85.0	109.6
14–19			3.4	3.4	3.8	4.6	5.9	7.6	9.5
20–24			5.2	4.8	5.1	7.7	9.3	11.5	15.0
25–34			11.0	11.5	10.9	12.5	18.5	23.0	30.5
35–44	2	2	9.9	10.8	11.3	11.3	12.9	18.7	23.8
45–54			8.1	8.9	9.6	11.2	11.3	12.6	18.2
55–64			5.8	6.1	6.4	8.2	9.6	9.7	10.9
65 +			2.5	2.5	2.3	2.1	2.0	1.9	1.7
Female, total	14.2	19.3	18.7	20.9	23.5	31.2	39.7	50.2	65.3
14–19			2.0	2.0	2.4	3.2	3.9	5.1	6.4
20–24			2.7	2.5	2.6	4.0	5.0	6.4	8.5
25–34			4.1	4.3	4.1	4.9	7.6	10.0	13.7
35–44	2	2	4.2	4.8	5.3	5.8	7.0	10.7	14.0
45–54			3.3	4.2	5.3	7.2	8.0	8.9	12.7
55–64			1.8	2.4	3.0	4.7	6.2	6.4	7.0
65 +			.6	.8	.9	1.4	2.0	2.7	3.0

1. Includes Armed Forces overseas; new definitions beginning 1950. Source of historical data: 1940–50, Current Population Reports, Series P–50, Nos. 2, 69, 85; 1955, Bureau of Labor Statistics Bull. No. 1242 (1959); 1960, BLS, *Employment and Earnings*, Jan. 1961, Table 2. (The slight discrepancy between total labor force in this table and in Table A1–1 for 1950 is due to a later revision for which the age-sex breakdown is not available.)

The projections were obtained by applying projected participation rates (Table A1–4) to projected age-sex brackets of population (Table A1–3) in the manner described by each of the assumptions "A" through "E."

2. Yearly averages not available.

TABLE A1–6. Historical Data on Gross National Product and Its Principal Components

(Billion 1960 dollars)

| | | By type of purchaser[1] | | | | By major type of product | | | | | | | By economic sector | | | | |
	GNP	Pers. consump. expend.	Gross pvt. domestic invest.	Government purchases	Net exports	Goods Total[1]	Durables[1]	Nondurables[1]	Farm[2]	Nonfarm[3]	Services[1]	Construction[1]	Military product[4]	Civilian product[5]	Government product[6]	Private product[7]	Private nonagri. product[8]
1929	206.5	141.3	41.7	23.1	.4	104.5	34.8	69.7	15.8	88.7	70.9	31.1	1.2	205.3	14.1	192.4	176.6
1930	187.4	132.8	28.2	25.7	.7	91.6	23.4	68.2	14.5	77.1	70.0	25.9	1.2	186.2	14.7	172.7	158.2
1931	174.1	128.7	18.2	27.0	.2	84.9	17.0	67.9	16.9	68.0	68.3	20.9	1.2	172.9	15.0	159.1	142.2
1932	148.3	117.1	5.5	25.6	.1	70.2	8.8	61.4	15.9	54.3	64.1	14.0	.8	147.5	14.7	133.6	117.7
1933	144.4	114.3	5.7	24.9	-.5	69.6	12.0	57.6	15.7	53.9	64.8	10.0	.8	143.6	15.7	128.7	113.0
1934	158.1	120.3	9.4	28.6	-.2	78.9	17.6	61.3	13.0	65.9	68.3	10.9	1.2	156.9	18.2	139.9	126.9
1935	174.1	127.6	19.0	28.9	-1.4	90.1	22.4	67.7	15.8	74.3	71.1	12.9	1.2	172.9	19.4	154.7	138.9
1936	197.7	140.6	24.9	34.0	-1.7	103.2	29.7	73.5	13.5	89.7	76.5	18.0	1.2	196.5	22.8	174.9	161.4
1937	208.6	145.5	31.5	32.7	-1.0	111.8	32.4	79.4	16.9	94.9	77.3	19.5	1.2	207.4	21.4	187.2	170.3
1938	199.3	143.0	18.9	36.1	1.3	102.5	22.3	80.2	17.1	85.4	78.6	18.2	1.2	198.1	23.2	176.1	159.0
1939	215.6	151.1	25.8	37.2	1.5	112.2	28.7	83.5	17.0	95.2	80.8	22.6	1.7	213.9	23.5	192.1	175.1
1940	233.6	158.9	34.3	38.7	1.7	126.1	37.4	88.7	16.7	109.4	83.6	23.9	2.1	231.5	24.2	209.4	192.7
1941	272.1	169.4	43.0	59.7	.1	146.3	52.5	93.8	18.0	128.3	94.3	31.5	6.7	265.4	30.0	242.1	224.1
1942	309.1	165.9	22.1	124.7	-3.6	163.6	59.8	103.8	19.6	144.0	112.7	32.8	16.6	292.5	43.8	265.3	245.7
1943	348.6	170.4	13.1	171.4	-6.3	194.5	89.3	105.2	18.0	176.5	135.9	18.2	37.4	311.2	68.7	279.9	261.9
1944	374.3	176.4	15.1	189.2	-6.4	214.0	100.5	113.5	18.4	195.6	147.9	12.4	47.4	326.9	79.3	295.0	276.6
1945	368.8	188.8	20.9	164.3	-5.2	207.3	88.7	118.6	17.4	189.9	148.7	12.9	47.4	321.4	77.8	291.0	273.6
1946	322.3	211.5	50.1	55.9	4.8	180.6	60.7	119.9	17.6	163.0	116.9	24.8	14.6	307.7	40.8	281.5	263.9
1947	321.8	215.1	50.2	47.2	9.3	179.9	63.6	116.3	16.2	163.7	112.9	29.0	6.7	315.1	31.1	290.7	274.5
1948	334.1	219.3	59.3	52.7	2.8	184.5	63.4	121.1	18.5	166.0	116.0	33.7	6.2	327.9	31.1	303.0	284.5
1949	333.8	224.7	47.0	58.6	3.5	178.5	59.3	119.2	17.6	160.9	120.0	35.3	6.7	327.1	32.6	301.2	283.6
1950	362.6	238.4	66.2	56.8	1.2	195.1	73.9	121.2	18.5	176.5	125.2	42.2	6.8	355.8	33.9	328.7	310.2
1951	391.4	240.6	68.1	79.4	3.3	211.8	85.3	126.5	17.3	194.5	136.9	42.7	13.1	378.3	42.0	349.4	332.1
1952	406.5	246.9	60.4	96.9	2.3	218.5	87.2	131.3	18.0	200.5	144.0	43.9	15.3	391.2	45.3	361.2	343.2
1953	423.9	258.7	61.1	104.1	*	230.4	93.6	136.8	18.7	211.7	147.2	46.3	15.0	408.9	44.8	379.1	360.4
1954	416.8	262.1	59.1	93.7	1.9	218.5	82.7	135.8	19.5	199.0	148.7	49.6	14.1	412.7	44.1	372.7	353.2
1955	449.3	281.5	74.4	91.4	2.0	239.1	95.0	144.1	20.5	218.6	155.8	54.4	13.0	436.3	44.0	405.3	384.8
1956	459.0	290.9	73.7	90.6	3.8	244.5	97.2	147.5	20.1	224.4	162.2	52.3	12.7	446.3	44.6	414.4	394.3
1957	468.0	298.6	69.8	94.5	5.1	246.9	98.1	148.8	19.8	227.1	168.7	52.4	12.3	455.7	45.3	422.7	402.9
1958	460.1	301.2	59.1	98.9	.9	233.3	82.5	150.8	20.0	213.3	173.6	53.2	11.5	448.6	45.6	414.5	394.5
1959	490.7	319.0	72.8	99.9	-1.0	252.2	95.0	157.2	19.9	232.3	181.1	57.4	11.5	479.2	46.1	444.6	424.7
1960	504.4	328.9	72.4	100.1	3.0	258.5	96.7	161.8	20.8	237.7	189.3	56.6	11.0	493.4	47.3	457.1	436.3

Table A1–6 (cont'd)

* Negligible.

1. Aggregated from the detailed components given in Table A1–8. Owing to differences in the method of deflation, there are minor differences in the GNP and the major components as thus calculated from the values that would result from a simple transposition to 1960 dollars of the officially published constant-dollar data on a 1954 base. The implicit price deflators resulting from the values calculated herein are given in Table A1–7.

Because of the difficulties of adjusting the official data, the figures for 1960 include Alaska and Hawaii. Owing to some overlap between the GNP data as calculated for "coterminous" United States (48 States and D.C.) for earlier years and the gross product of Alaska and Hawaii, the comparability with earlier data is not affected by the full amount of Alaskan and Hawaiian product. The Department of Commerce estimates that the 1960 U.S. total comparable with those of earlier years would be only about $1 billion lower, of which about $.5 billion is in personal consumption, $.3 billion in state and local government purchases, and $.2 billion in construction. Source: *Survey of Current Business*, July 1961 National Income Number, p. 5.

2. From Table VII–10, *U.S. Income and Output* and July 1961 National Income Number of *Survey of Current Business*, transposed from 1954 to 1960 dollars on basis of deflators given in *U.S. Income and Output*, Table VII–11.

(For deflators transposed to a 1960 base, see Table A1–7, herein.) "Farm goods" is equivalent to "farm gross product"; for further explanation, see *U.S. Income and Output*, p. 53 and Table VII–9.

3. Total goods, less farm goods.

4. Compensation to both active and reserve forces, estimated as indicated in footnote 1 to Table A9–1. Average active forces pay: $4,160. Reserve components for 1953–60 from Department of Defense budget summaries (vary from $4 billion to $.6 billion); for 1950–52 estimated ($.1 to $.3 billion); prior to 1950 assumed negligible. Use of a constant multiplier for active forces is in line with the practice of the National Income Division, Office of Business Economics, Department of Commerce, in assuming unchanging productivity in government employment.

5. GNP, less military product.

6. From Table I–13, *U.S. Income and Output* and July 1961 National Income Number of *Survey of Current Business*, transposed from 1954 to 1960 dollars on basis of deflators given in *ibid.*, Table VII–8. (For deflators transposed to a 1960 base, see Table A1–7, herein.)

7. GNP, less government product.

8. Private product, less farm goods.

TABLE A1–7.   Implicit Price Deflators for Principal GNP Components[1]

(1960 = 100)

	GNP[2]	Pers. con- sump. ex- pend.[2]	Gross pvt. domes- tic in- vest.[2]	Govt. pur- chases of goods and serv- ices[2]	Goods Total[3]	Dura- bles[3]	Non- dura- bles[3]	Farm[4]	Non- farm[5]	Serv- ices[3]	Con- struc- tion[3]	Gov- ern- ment prod- uct[6]	Pri- vate prod- uct[7]	Pri- vate non- agri. prod- uct[8]
1929	50.6	55.9	38.8	36.8	53.8	52.0	54.7	62.2	52.4	52.2	36.0	30.8	52.0	51.1
1930	48.6	53.5	36.5	35.8	51.4	50.4	51.6	53.5	51.1	50.0	34.7	30.8	50.1	49.9
1931	43.8	47.6	30.2	34.1	44.1	47.1	43.4	36.6	45.9	47.1	31.6	31.1	45.0	46.0
1932	39.4	42.1	16.4	31.6	38.2	43.2	37.5	28.1	41.3	43.7	26.4	30.3	40.5	42.2
1933	38.8	40.6	24.6	32.1	38.9	42.5	38.2	29.3	41.7	40.3	28.0	29.8	39.9	41.3
1934	41.1	43.1	30.9	34.3	43.2	43.8	43.1	33.4	45.2	40.3	30.3	30.6	42.5	43.4
1935	41.6	44.1	33.2	34.6	44.3	42.9	44.6	43.9	44.4	40.4	30.2	30.5	43.1	43.0
1936	41.8	44.5	33.7	34.7	44.3	42.4	45.0	46.3	43.9	41.2	30.6	31.9	43.1	42.8
1937	43.5	46.3	37.1	35.8	46.0	44.8	46.3	47.9	45.6	42.6	33.8	32.2	44.8	44.5
1938	42.7	45.2	35.4	35.5	44.3	46.2	43.9	39.4	45.3	42.9	33.5	32.7	44.1	44.6
1939	42.3	44.7	36.0	35.8	43.8	45.6	43.1	38.2	44.9	42.7	32.7	32.4	43.5	44.0
1940	43.1	45.2	38.5	36.4	44.7	46.3	44.1	40.9	45.3	43.1	34.3	32.2	44.3	44.6
1941	46.2	48.3	42.1	41.5	50.0	53.0	48.5	51.9	49.7	43.4	36.8	31.3	48.1	47.7
1942	51.5	54.1	44.8	47.9	57.8	60.2	56.5	68.3	56.3	44.8	43.0	34.5	54.3	53.2
1943	55.2	59.0	42.7	51.7	62.4	61.1	63.4	85.0	60.1	46.1	47.3	37.3	59.6	57.9
1944	56.5	62.2	47.0	51.0	62.5	58.1	66.3	84.9	60.4	48.6	46.8	40.6	60.7	59.1
1945	57.9	64.5	49.8	50.5	63.0	55.8	68.5	93.3	60.3	51.6	48.4	45.2	61.3	59.3
1946	65.4	69.6	56.1	54.6	71.3	65.6	74.2	109.4	67.2	58.6	54.0	50.8	67.5	64.7
1947	72.8	76.9	62.7	60.2	79.9	74.5	82.9	128.1	75.2	63.6	64.5	53.6	74.9	71.7
1948	77.6	81.3	72.7	65.5	85.1	78.5	88.5	128.9	80.2	67.3	72.1	55.9	79.9	76.7
1949	77.3	80.6	70.2	68.6	83.6	80.8	85.2	109.7	80.8	69.6	71.4	59.4	79.2	77.4
1950	78.5	81.8	75.5	68.7	83.9	82.1	84.9	110.8	81.1	71.7	73.9	61.5	80.3	78.4
1951	84.1	87.2	82.7	76.2	90.6	87.2	92.8	136.0	86.5	75.2	80.1	64.9	86.3	83.7
1952	85.4	89.0	82.6	78.4	90.7	86.7	93.4	126.2	87.5	78.0	82.9	68.5	87.5	85.4
1953	86.2	89.9	82.3	79.5	89.8	85.3	92.8	112.0	87.9	81.2	84.2	70.8	88.0	86.8
1954	87.1	90.8	87.7	80.4	90.3	86.6	92.7	104.3	89.0	83.5	83.9	73.3	88.8	87.9
1955	88.5	91.3	85.8	82.7	90.8	88.7	92.2	95.5	90.4	85.6	86.2	77.2	89.7	89.4
1956	91.3	92.8	91.5	87.2	93.1	92.2	93.8	96.3	92.8	88.3	92.2	81.6	92.4	92.2
1957	94.6	95.5	94.7	91.5	96.5	96.3	96.6	98.0	96.3	91.6	95.6	85.9	95.6	95.4
1958	96.6	97.3	95.8	94.5	98.3	97.5	98.8	107.6	97.6	94.6	95.7	91.9	97.1	96.6
1959	98.4	98.4	99.4	97.2	99.2	99.9	98.9	100.0	99.2	97.3	97.9	95.7	98.7	98.6
1960	100.0	100.0	100.0	100.0	100.0	100.0	100.0	100.0	100.0	100.0	100.0	100.0	100.0	100.0

1. Derived by dividing reported data in current dollars by corresponding series given in Table A1–6. Current dollar data, unless otherwise indicated, are from the tables in *U.S. Income and Output* and July 1961 National Income Number of *Survey of Current Business* specified in the footnotes which follow.
2. *Income and Output* Table I–1 (see footnote 1).
3. *Income and Output* Table VII–5.

4. *Income and Output* Table VII–9. ("Farm goods" is equivalent to "farm gross product.")
5. Total goods, less farm goods.
6. *Income and Output* Table I–12 ("general government").
7. GNP, less government product.
8. Private product, less farm goods.

TABLE A1–8. Historical Data on Minor GNP Components[1]

(Billion 1960 dollars)

Year	Durable goods — Consumer[2]	Producer[2]	Government[3]	Net exports[3]	Change in inventories[4]	Non-durable goods — Consumer[2]	Government[3]	Net exports[3]	Change in inventories[4]	Services — Consumer[2]	Government[3]	Net exports[3]	Construction — Private[2]	Public[5]	Government expenditures — Defense[6]	Non-defense[7]
1929	15.8	13.5	.9	1.8	2.8	70.2	1.1	-2.0	.4	55.3	15.0	.6	25.0	6.1		
1930	12.6	10.7	.9	1.4	-2.2	66.7	1.4	-1.2	1.3	53.5	15.9	.6	18.4	7.5		
1931	10.9	7.2	.9	1.1	-3.1	66.4	1.7	-1.2	1.0	51.4	16.6	.3	13.1	7.8		
1932	8.2	4.3	.9	.6	-5.2	61.2	1.7	-.7	-.8	47.7	16.2	.2	7.2	6.8		[8]
1933	8.0	4.5	.7	.4	-1.6	59.3	2.2	-1.2	-2.7	47.0	17.4	.4	5.5	4.5	[8]	
1934	9.2	6.1	1.2	.9	.2	63.3	2.6	-1.6	-3.0	47.8	20.0	.5	6.1	4.8		
1935	11.3	8.2	1.2	.8	.9	66.8	1.8	-2.8	1.9	49.5	21.0	.6	8.0	4.9		
1936	14.0	11.1	1.4	1.0	2.2	74.5	1.8	-3.1	.3	52.1	24.1	.3	11.3	6.7		
1937	14.6	12.7	1.5	1.9	1.7	77.0	2.1	-3.3	3.6	53.9	23.1	.3	13.5	6.0		
1938	11.9	8.8	1.6	2.1	-2.1	78.3	3.2	-1.4	.1	52.8	25.2	.6	12.1	6.1		
1939	14.1	10.3	1.5	2.3	.5	82.5	2.0	-1.4	.4	54.5	25.7	.6	14.6	8.0	3.4	33.8
1940	16.3	13.3	1.6	3.6	2.6	86.1	3.0	-2.5	2.1	56.5	26.5	.6	16.3	7.6	5.9	32.8
1941	18.7	15.6	8.5	3.4	6.3	91.9	2.5	-3.4	2.8	58.8	35.5	-	18.3	13.2	31.4	28.3
1942	11.5	9.0	35.7	1.0	2.6	93.8	11.3	-2.5	1.2	60.6	54.2	-2.1	9.3	23.5	101.1	23.6
1943	10.0	8.4	69.3	1.2	.4	96.8	13.1	-3.7	-1.0	63.6	76.1	-3.8	5.3	12.9	153.0	18.4
1944	9.1	11.1	80.2	1.4	-1.3	101.0	16.7	-3.8	-.5	66.3	85.7	-4.1	5.8	6.6	171.2	18.0
1945	10.4	15.5	63.6	1.9	-2.7	109.0	11.0	-1.6	.2	69.4	84.8	-5.5	7.9	4.9	145.3	19.0
1946	20.6	19.6	8.4	3.6	8.5	115.7	1.4	1.5	1.3	75.2	42.0	-.3	20.7	4.1	27.8	28.1
1947	24.7	26.4	4.5	6.4	1.6	113.2	2.4	2.3	-1.6	77.2	35.1	.6	23.8	5.2	15.9	31.3
1948	26.1	27.7	5.4	3.3	.9	113.0	5.0	-.4	3.5	80.2	35.8	-	27.2	6.5	16.5	36.2
1949	27.9	24.1	6.6	3.3	-2.6	114.2	6.2	-	-1.2	82.6	37.2	.2	26.7	8.6	19.1	39.5
1950	34.0	25.8	6.9	2.5	4.7	117.4	2.5	-1.6	2.9	87.0	38.0	.2	32.8	9.4	19.9	36.9

Year																
1951	30.9	26.7	16.5	3.5	7.7	119.6	4.1	.2	2.6	90.1	47.2	-.4	31.1	11.6	42.8	36.6
1952	30.2	26.5	25.9	3.3	1.3	123.6	6.4	-.2	1.5	93.1	51.8	-.9	31.1	12.8	58.5	38.4
1953	35.1	27.4	27.0	3.0	1.1	127.2	11.2	-1.1	-.5	96.4	52.7	-1.9	33.1	13.2	62.5	41.6
1954	34.4	25.3	21.9	3.8	-2.7	128.3	6.9	-.3	.9	99.4	50.9	-1.6	35.6	14.0	51.4	42.3
1955	42.0	27.4	18.2	4.1	3.3	134.7	6.7	-.4	3.1	104.8	52.7	-1.7	40.6	13.8	46.8	44.6
1956	40.3	30.3	19.1	4.6	2.9	140.0	4.8	.7	1.8	110.6	53.1	-1.5	38.7	13.6	45.9	44.7
1957	40.9	29.9	21.0	5.2	1.1	142.4	4.5	1.2	.7	115.3	54.7	-1.3	38.1	14.3	48.1	46.4
1958	37.7	23.6	20.1	3.7	-2.6	143.2	7.4	-.6	.8	120.3	55.5	-2.2	37.3	15.9	47.2	51.7
1959	43.6	25.9	20.3	1.8	3.4	149.2	6.8	-1.2	2.4	126.2	56.5	-1.6	41.1	16.3	46.9	53.0
1960	44.3	27.5	18.5	3.9	2.5	152.4	7.2	.5	1.7	132.2	58.5	-1.4	40.6	16.0	45.5	54.6

1. Unless otherwise specified, data are derived by transposing to 1960 dollars the figures in 1954 dollars given in Table VII–6 of *U.S. Income and Output* and July 1961 National Income Number of *Survey of Current Business*. For 1954/60 price relationships, and implicit deflators, generally, see Table A1–9, herein.

2. Data for 1930–46 (not shown in *Income and Output* Table VII–6) are from *Income and Output* Table I–2.

3. Data for 1930–46 are from unpublished figures of the Office of Business Economics, U.S. Department of Commerce. Gross exports and imports separately deflated.

4. Data for 1930–46 are from *Income and Output* Table I–7.

5. Total construction, from *Income and Output* Table I–7, less private.

6. *Economic Report of the President*, 1961, Table C–2, except for 1960, which is from July 1961 National Income Number of *Survey of Current Business* (national defense less government sales).

7. Total government purchases, from Table A1–6, less defense.

8. 1929–38 not available separately.

TABLE A1–9.   Price Deflators for Minor GNP Components[1]

(1960 = 100)

	Durable goods			Non-durable goods		Services		Construction	
	Con-sum-ers	Pro-duc-ers	Gov-ern-ment	Con-sum-ers	Gov-ern-ment	Con-sum-ers	Gov-ern-ment	Pri-vate	Pub-lic
1929	58.4	43.2	43.5	53.7	54.3	58.0	33.4	34.8	40.5
1930	57.0	41.6	n.a.	51.0	n.a.	55.7	n.a.	33.4	n.a.
1931	50.4	39.4	"	43.6	"	52.3	"	30.5	"
1932	44.3	37.4	"	37.2	"	48.0	"	26.0	"
1933	43.4	35.5	"	37.5	"	44.0	"	26.0	"
1934	46.0	37.8	"	42.1	"	44.0	"	27.8	"
1935	45.1	37.5	"	43.9	"	44.2	"	28.5	"
1936	45.1	37.4	"	44.1	"	45.1	"	29.0	"
1937	47.4	40.1	"	45.7	"	46.7	"	32.6	"
1938	47.9	41.3	"	43.4	"	47.3	"	32.6	"
1939	47.3	40.7	"	42.6	"	47.3	"	32.6	"
1940	47.8	41.6	"	43.2	"	47.6	"	33.5	"
1941	51.6	44.4	"	47.0	"	49.3	"	36.2	"
1942	60.5	48.1	"	54.7	"	51.9	"	39.7	"
1943	66.3	48.1	"	61.2	"	54.5	"	44.2	"
1944	74.2	48.8	"	64.7	"	56.9	"	47.0	"
1945	78.0	49.4	"	67.2	"	58.2	"	48.2	"
1946	77.3	54.9	"	73.3	"	61.7	"	53.2	"
1947	83.3	63.2	69.8	82.5	92.7	66.7	55.9	63.9	66.7
1948	87.1	68.4	73.0	87.4	90.6	70.9	59.4	71.7	74.5
1949	88.1	71.6	76.9	84.6	86.7	72.6	62.5	70.4	74.1
1950	89.2	73.3	79.2	85.0	77.3	74.6	64.8	73.7	74.2
1951	95.3	79.7	83.3	92.1	119.0	78.0	68.7	79.5	80.8
1952	96.3	80.2	82.1	93.1	99.7	81.2	72.3	82.1	84.8
1953	93.7	81.5	78.3	92.7	98.1	84.8	74.5	83.6	86.1
1954	94.2	82.3	80.8	93.0	96.2	86.8	76.6	83.5	85.0
1955	94.3	84.4	83.0	92.6	96.9	88.3	79.8	86.1	87.0
1956	95.5	89.7	88.2	93.9	99.3	90.4	84.1	91.7	93.1
1957	98.7	95.2	93.2	96.7	103.6	92.9	88.2	94.7	97.3
1958	98.9	97.9	96.0	98.9	96.5	95.0	93.1	95.3	97.5
1959	100.2	100.0	98.1	98.7	98.2	97.7	96.3	98.0	98.8
1960	100.0	100.0	100.0	100.0	100.0	100.0	100.0	100.0	100.0

1. Computed by transposing from 1954 to 1960 dollars the implicit price deflators given in *U.S. Income and Output* and July 1961 National Income Number of the *Survey of Current Business:* Table VII–2, for consumer purchases, producer durables, and private construction; Table VII–7, for government purchases.

TABLE A1–10.   Projected GNP in Terms of Demand Sectors[1]

	1940	1945	1950	1955	1960	1970	1980	1990	2000
Billion 1960 dollars:									
Low projection:									
Personal consumption expenditures	159	189	238	282	329	448	610	819	1,070
Gross private domestic investment	34	21	66	74	72	92	113	134	168
Government purchases	39	164	57	91	100	129	154	223	318
Net exports	2	−5	1	2	3	−4	−8	−7	−3
Total	234	369	362	449	504	665	869	1,169	1,553
GNP	234	369	363	449	504	710	965	1,260	1,680
Residual[2]	–	–	+1	–	–	+45	+96	+91	+127

Table A1–10 (cont'd)

	1940	1945	1950	1955	1960	1970	1980	1990	2000
Medium projection:									
Personal consumption expenditures	159	189	238	282	329	462	662	944	1,320
Gross private domestic investment	34	21	66	74	72	119	167	238	361
Government purchases	39	164	57	91	100	160	242	365	551
Net exports	2	–5	1	2	3	1	3	9	18
Total	234	369	362	449	504	742	1,074	1,556	2,250
GNP	234	369	363	449	504	746	1,060	1,510	2,200
Residual [2]	–	–	+1	–	–	+4	–14	–46	–50
High projection:									
Personal consumption expenditures	159	189	238	282	329	495	753	1,150	1,730
Gross private domestic investment	34	21	66	74	72	148	236	377	666
Government purchases	39	164	57	91	100	197	336	555	927
Net exports	2	–5	1	2	3	1	2	2	–6
Total	234	369	362	449	504	841	1,327	2,084	3,317
GNP	234	369	363	449	504	798	1,250	1,980	3,290
Residual [2]	–	–	+1	–	–	–43	–77	–104	–27
Percentages of GNP:									
Low projection:									
Personal consumption expenditures	67.9	51.2	65.6	62.8	65.3	63.1	63.2	65.0	63.7
Gross private domestic investment	14.5	5.7	18.2	16.5	14.3	13.0	11.7	10.6	10.0
Government purchases	16.7	44.4	15.7	20.3	19.8	18.2	16.0	17.7	18.9
Net exports	.9	–1.4	.3	.4	.6	–.6	–.8	–.6	–.2
Total	100.0	100.0	99.7	100.0	100.0	93.7	90.1	92.8	92.4
GNP	100.0	100.0	100.0	100.0	100.0	100.0	100.0	100.0	100.0
Residual [2]	–	–	+.3	–	–	+6.3	+9.9	+7.2	+7.6
Medium projection:									
Personal consumption expenditures	67.9	51.2	65.6	62.8	65.3	61.9	62.5	62.5	60.0
Gross private domestic investment	14.5	5.7	18.2	16.5	14.3	16.0	15.8	15.8	16.4
Government purchases	16.7	44.4	15.7	20.3	19.8	21.4	22.8	24.2	25.0
Net exports	.9	–1.4	.3	.4	.6	.1	.3	.6	.8
Total	100.0	100.0	99.7	100.0	100.0	99.5	101.3	103.1	102.3
GNP	100.0	100.0	100.0	100.0	100.0	100.0	100.0	100.0	100.0
Residual [2]	–	–	+.3	–	–	+.5	–1.3	–3.0	–2.3
High projection:									
Personal consumption expenditures	67.9	51.2	65.6	62.8	65.3	62.0	60.2	58.1	52.6
Gross private domestic investment	14.5	5.7	18.2	16.5	14.3	18.5	18.9	19.0	20.2
Government purchases	16.7	44.4	15.7	20.3	19.8	24.7	26.9	28.0	28.2
Net exports	.9	–1.4	.3	.4	.6	.2	.2	.1	–.2
Total	100.0	100.0	99.7	100.0	100.0	105.4	106.2	105.3	100.8
GNP	100.0	100.0	100.0	100.0	100.0	100.0	100.0	100.0	100.0
Residual [2]	–	–	+.3	–	–	–5.4	–6.2	–5.3	–.8

1. Corresponding historical series are shown in Table A1–6. The derivations of the major projected components and of GNP itself are shown in Table A1–12.
2. The discrepancy for 1950 is due to rounding. For meaning of "residual" with regard to projections, see narrative Notes and footnote 6 to Table A1–13.

TABLE A1–11.   Principal Variations in Low and High Values for GNP and Its Demand Components under Alternate Assumptions

(Dollar amounts in $ 1960 billions)

	1960	1970	1980	1990	2000
Output levels:[1]					
Low population:					
Low labor force (mil.)	72.8	85.4	98	108	122
Low GNP ($ bil.)	504	710	965	1,260	1,680
High GNP ($ bil.)		768	1,127	1,588	2,290
High labor force (mil.)	72.8	88.2	102	114	130
Low GNP ($ bil.)	504	734	1,000	1,330	1,790
High GNP ($ bil.)		793	1,170	1,680	2,440
High population:					
Low labor force (mil.)	72.8	86.3	105	130	168
Low GNP ($ bil.)	504	718	1,030	1,520	2,320
High GNP ($ bil.)		776	1,210	1,910	3,160
High labor force (mil.)	72.8	88.8	109	135	175
Low GNP ($ bil.)	504	739	1,074	1,580	2,420
High GNP ($ bil.)		798	1,250	1,980	3,290
Demand models:					
Low population & high defense:[2]					
GNP	504	793	1,170	1,680	2,440
Personal consumption expenditures[3]	329	426	554	707	884
Gross private domestic investment[4]	72	147	221	319	493
Government purchases[5]	100	188	306	480	762
Added total	501	761	1,080	1,510	2,140
Residual ($ bil.)	+3	+32	+90	+170	+300
% of GNP	+.6	+4.0	+7.6	+10.1	+12.3
Alt. personal consumption expenditures[6]	329	448	610	819	1,070
Alt. residual ($ bil.)	+3	+10	+33	+60	+115
% of GNP	+.6	+1.3	+2.8	+3.6	+4.7
High population & low defense:					
GNP	504	718	1,030	1,520	2,320
Personal consumption expenditures[3]	329	511	804	1,260	1,970
Gross private domestic investment[4]	72	93	121	161	232
Government purchases[5]	100	137	184	298	483
Added total	501	741	1,110	1,720	2,685
Residual ($ bil.)	+3	−23	−80	−200	−365
% of GNP	+.6	−3.2	−7.8	−13.2	−15.7
Alt. personal consumption expenditures[6]	329	495	753	1,150	1,730
Alt. residual ($ bil.)	+3	−7	−28	−89	−125
% of GNP	+.6	−1.0	−2.7	−5.9	−5.4

Table A1–11 (cont'd)

(Dollar amounts in $ 1960 billions)

	1960	1970	1980	1990	2000
Low population & low defense:[2]					
GNP	504	710	965	1,260	1,680
Personal consumption expenditures[3]	329	463	651	901	1,220
Gross private domestic investment[7]	72	92	113	134	168
Government purchases[7]	100	129	154	223	318
Added total	501	684	918	1,260	1,710
Residual	+3	+26	+47	–	–30
High population & high defense:[2]					
GNP	504	798	1,250	1,980	3,290
Personal consumption expenditures[3]	329	471	684	991	1,430
Gross private domestic investment[7]	72	148	236	377	666
Government purchases[7]	100	197	336	555	927
Added total	501	816	1,310	1,923	3,023
Residual	+3	–18	–6	+57	+270

1. Labor force projections from Table A1–5. Low and High GNP for each labor force level calculated by applying the corresponding projections of output per man-year given in Table A1–12.

2. The initial assumption is that for any given population level, the High levels of defense (and hence government purchases) will be accompanied by High labor force participation and man-year productivity; conversely for the Low. Personal consumption expenditures are assumed to adjust inversely to the level of defense expenditures. (See introductory Notes to this part of the appendix.)

3. High defense models are initially assumed to imply Low per capita personal consumption (see Table A1–12); Low defense models, High per capita consumption. This assumption is later adjusted in two of the models (see footnote 6).

4. Approximated by using the ratios of investment to GNP in the appropriate one of the last two models shown, i.e., the one with the similar defense level. (See Table A1–10 for the calculated ratios.)

5. Sum of appropriate defense and non-defense expenditures. High defense is High ratio to GNP (Table A1–12), multiplied by appropriate GNP level; vice versa for Low. Non-defense expenditures calculated from single per capita rate (Table A1–12) and appropriate population level.

6. The size of the residual in the first approximation suggests that personal consumption expenditures need not be as fully compensating with defense expenditures as was initially assumed. For this alternate calculation the per capita level used in the Medium (Table A1–12) is taken as an approximation of what would more likely obtain in both the Low population/High defense economy and the High population/Low defense economy. It also enters into the final, non-additive Low and High models (Table A1–10) as the Low consistent with Low population and Low defense and the High consistent with High population and High defense.

7. From Table A1–12.

APPENDIX TO CHAPTER 1

TABLE A1–12. Derivation of GNP and Its Demand Components[1]

	1940	1945	1950	1955	1960		1970	1980	1990	2000
GNP ($ 1960 bil.)	234	369	363	449	504	L	710	965	1,260	1,680
						M	746	1,060	1,510	2,200
						H	798	1,250	1,980	3,290
Labor force[2] (millions)	56.2	65.3	64.6	6.89	72.8	L	85.4	98	108	122
						M	87.1	102	119	142
						H	88.8	109	135	175
GNP per worker[3] ($ 1960 thous.)	4.16	5.65	5.62	6.52	6.92	L	8.32	9.85	11.7	13.8
						M	8.57	10.4	12.7	15.5
						H	8.99	11.5	14.7	18.8
Personal consumption expenditures[4] ($ 1960 bil.)	159	189	238	282	329	L	448	610	819	1,070
						M	462	662	944	1,320
						H	495	753	1,150	1,730
Population[2] (millions)	132	140	152	165	180	L	202	226	249	268
						M	208	245	287	331
						H	223	279	349	433
Personal consumption expenditures per capita[5] ($ 1960 thous.)	1.20	1.35	1.57	1.71	1.83	L	2.11	2.45	2.84	3.30
						M	2.22	2.70	3.29	4.00
						H	2.29	2.88	3.62	4.55
Gross private domestic investment ($ 1960 bil.)	34.2	20.9	66.3	73.9	72.4	L	91.6	113	134	168
						M	119.3	167	238	361
						H	148.0	236	377	666
Private purchases of new plant and equipment[6] ($ 1960 bil.)	21.0	21.3	40.5	46.5	47.1	L	62.0	76.1	90.9	109.6
						M	74.4	106.2	152.2	223.4
						H	84.4	138.6	224.6	378.4
Private residential construction (non-farm)[7] ($ 1960 bil.)	8.5	2.1	18.2	21.0	21.1	L	26.0	32.7	37.4	51.1
						M	38.0	50.8	72.3	118.5
						H	52.6	79.6	124.8	243.0
Inventory change[8] ($ 1960 bil.)	4.7	−2.5	7.6	6.4	4.2	L	3.6	4.6	6.1	6.8
						M	6.9	9.8	13.8	19.3
						H	11.0	17.3	27.7	44.9
Government expenditures ($ 1960 bil.)	**39**	**164**	**57**	**91**	**100**	L	129	154	223	318
						M	160	242	365	551
						H	197	336	555	927
National defense expenditures ($ 1960 bil.)	5.9	145.3	19.9	46.8	45.5	L	45	29	38	50
						M	75	106	151	220
						H	105	181	295	494
Per $ of GNP[9] (¢ 1960)	2.5	39.5	5.6	10.4	8.8	L	6.4	3.0	3.0	3.0
						M	10.0	10.0	10.0	10.0
						H	13.2	14.5	14.9	15.0
Non-defense expenditures ($ 1960 bil.)	32.6	18.3	36.6	43.9	54.6	L	83.2	125	185	268
						M	85.7	136	214	331
						H	91.9	155	260	433
Per capita[10] ($ 1960)	247	131	241	266	304		412	554	744	1,000
Net exports[11] ($ 1960 bil.)	1.7	−5.2	1.2	2.0	3.0	L	−3.6	−7.5	−6.7	−2.7
						M	.9	3.1	8.7	17.8
						H	1.3	1.7	1.5	−5.6
Durables	3.6	1.9	2.5	4.1	3.9	L	2.0	.7	−.1	−1.8
						M	3.3	3.3	3.5	1.8
						H	3.3	2.9	.7	−7.4
Non-durables	−2.5	−1.6	−1.6	−.4	.5	L	−1.6	−3.8	−6.0	−10.2
						M	.2	1.2	2.8	4.6
						H	.4	1.2	2.3	2.8
Services	.6	−5.5	.2	−1.7	−1.4	L	−4.0	−4.4	−.6	9.3
						M	−2.6	−1.6	2.4	11.4
						H	−2.4	−2.4	−1.5	−1.0

Table A1–12 (cont'd)

1. Unless otherwise indicated historical data are from Tables A1–6 and A1–8. Projections are either the product or the sum, as appropriate, of detail under each major heading.
2. From Table A1–2.
3. Extrapolation of past trends, starting from assumed 1960 trend value of $7,030. Rate of increase is 1.7% per annum, 2%, and 2.5%, for Low, Medium, and High, respectively.
4. The Lows and the Highs shown are those established in Table A1–11 as being the Lows and Highs most consistent with the Low and High personal consumption models (Low population, High defense and High population, Low defense). See footnote 6 thereto.
5. Extrapolation of past trends, starting from assumed 1960 trend value of $1,820.
6. From Table A6–3, except for 1940, which is from *U.S. Income and Output,* Table I–2, transposed to a 1960 base per deflator in Table A6–1, herein.
7. From Table A4–4, except for 1940 and 1945, which are from *U.S. Income and Output,* Table I–2, transposed to a 1960 base per deflator in Table A4–2, herein.
8. From Table A1–13.
9. Arbitrary assumptions. See text.

10. Projected to increase at 3% per annum. This compares with 2.8% from 1955 to 1960 and 2.0% from 1950 to 1955 and is just slightly above the long-term (1929–60) trend rate. Use of a single rate does not imply improbability of a range. Rather, this rate is taken as both the lowest that might obtain for non-defense expenditures in a low-defense economy and the highest that might obtain in a high-defense economy.
11. From Table A1–17. Low and High to be interpreted as Low net exports associated with Low GNP and High net exports associated with High GNP, respectively, and to be read algebraically. The net import position associated with the Low is the result of using a High import propensity assumption. That for the High (in 2000) is the result, despite a Low import-propensity assumption, of the demands generated by a High GNP. A single level of exports, geometrically extrapolated, was used for all three GNP levels on the assumption that (a) these are largely externally determined and (b) the largest relative export capacity will occur at the lowest GNP levels, and vice versa, so that probable variations in export propensity will be compensated by inverse variations in export capacity. (Export propensity will probably be highest with a High GNP, owing to the indirect effect of U.S. GNP on world product and the need to pay for higher imports.)

TABLE A1–13.   Projected GNP in Terms of Kinds of Output[1]

(Billion 1960 dollars)

	1940	1945	1950	1955	1960		1970	1980	1990	2000
Gross national product[2]	234	369	363	449	504	L M H	710 746 798	965 1,060 1,250	1,260 1,510 1,980	1,680 2,200 3,290
Goods[3]	126	207	195	239	258	L M H	330 363 401	422 512 623	540 722 967	692 1,019 1,502
Services[4]	84	149	125	156	189	L M H	266 280 302	375 415 483	529 614 772	746 909 1,234
Construction[5]	24	13	42	54	57	L M H	67 93 124	80 130 200	93 185 326	119 281 590
(Non-allocable output)[6]	–	–	1	–	–	L M H	+47 +10 −29	+88 +3 −56	+98 −11 −85	+123 −9 −36
Output of goods: Durable[7]	37	89	74	95	96	L M H	122 154 188	151 229 322	200 343 540	261 514 918
Non-durable[7]	89	119	121	144	162	L M H	200 216 239	246 293 354	299 393 523	349 518 760
(Non-allocable goods)[6]	–	−1	–	–	+1	L M H	+8 −7 −22	+25 −10 −45	+41 −14 −85	+82 −13 −161

Table A1–13 (cont'd)

(Billion 1960 dollars)

	1940	1945	1950	1955	1960		1970	1980	1990	2000
Farm goods[8]	16.7	17.4	18.5	20.5	20.8	L	22.3	24.5	26.8	28.8
						M	24.1	28.7	33.6	38.0
						H	26.7	33.5	42.6	53.3
Farm goods per capita[9] ($ 1960 thousand)	.12	.12	.12	.12	.12	L	.11	.11	.11	.11
						M	.11	.12	.12	.12
						H	.12	.12	.12	.12
Non-farm goods[10]	109	190	176	219	238	L	306	395	510	660
						M	339	483	688	981
						H	376	592	929	1,454
Construction: Private[5]	16.3	7.9	32.8	40.6	40.6	L	47.7	57.3	65.4	83.8
						M	66.4	90.2	127.2	196.8
						H	88.3	138.1	219.7	403.0
Public[5]	7.6	4.9	9.4	13.8	16.0	L	19.3	22.8	28.0	35.6
						M	27.1	39.9	57.7	84.1
						H	35.4	61.6	106.0	186.6
Changes in inventories[11]	4.7	−2.5	7.6	6.4	4.2	L	3.6	4.6	6.1	6.8
						M	6.9	9.8	13.8	19.3
						H	11.0	17.3	27.7	44.9
Durable goods	2.6	−2.7	4.7	3.3	2.5	L	1.8	2.4	3.8	4.7
						M	4.3	6.0	9.1	13.4
						H	7.0	11.3	18.7	32.2
Non-durable goods	2.1	.2	2.9	3.1	1.7	L	1.8	2.2	2.3	2.1
						M	2.6	3.8	4.7	5.9
						H	4.0	6.0	9.0	12.7

1. Historical data from Tables A1–6 and A1–8.
2. From Table A1–12.
3. Projected at the growth rates of 2.5% per annum, 3.5%, and 4.5%. These are all reasonable extrapolations of past trends.
4. Projected at growth rates of 3.5%, 4.0%, and 4.8% for Low, Medium, and High, respectively.
5. From Tables A1–8 and A4–3.
6. The concept of "non-allocable," as used herein (referred to as "residual" in Table A1–10) is composed of two elements:

   a. *Statistical error,* or error arising from independent projection of components and total. In the Medium only this element appears. In cases where one component is calculated by subtracting another from the total, this element is absent by definition.

   b. *Cumulative error in the Highs and the Lows.* If the components stand in a substitutive (competitive) relationship to one another, a maximum value in one implies a less than maximum value in the other, i.e., the projected components cannot all simultaneously be at

maximum or minimum level. Totaling the Lows consequently results in a "non-allocable" shortfall compared with the reasonably possible Low for the directly projected aggregate. The "non-allocable" component in the High total is an overage, or negative quantity.

7. From Table A1–14.
8. From Table A1–16.
9. Derived as an implications check and as a basis for calculating non-farm goods.
10. For Medium, difference between total goods and farm goods. For Low, difference between Low total goods and farm goods calculated on basis of High per capita trend taken with Low population. Vice versa for High.
11. Sum of changes for durables and non-durables, which are calculated by applying to future sales (domestic consumption plus exports) the average postwar relationship of accretions in inventory to increments in sales (70% for durables and 45% for non-durables). The relevant historical data on sales are in Table A1–8, projections in Table A1–14.

TABLE A1–14.   Derivation of Aggregate Output Components of GNP[1]

(Billion 1960 dollars)

	1940	1945	1950	1955	1960		1970	1980	1990	2000
Output of durable goods[2]	37.4	88.7	73.9	95.0	96.7	L	122	151	200	261
						M	154	229	343	514
						H	188	322	540	918
Consumer purchases[3]	16.3	10.4	34.0	42.0	44.3	L	60.5	83.6	114	151
						M	65.1	98.6	148	218
						H	74.7	125.8	210	344
Producer purchases[4]	13.3	15.5	25.8	27.4	27.5	L	35.8	43.9	52.4	63.2
						M	46.1	66.9	97.4	145.2
						H	54.7	93.6	155.0	264.9
Government purchases[5]	1.6	63.6	6.9	18.2	18.5	L	22.1	20.2	30	44
						M	34.8	53.8	85	136
						H	48.3	88.1	156	284
Net exports[6]	3.6	1.9	2.5	4.1	3.9	L	2.0	.7	–.1	–1.8
						M	3.3	3.5	3.5	1.8
						H	3.3	2.9	.7	–7.4
Changes in inventories[7]	2.6	–2.7	4.7	3.3	2.5	L	1.8	2.4	3.8	4.7
						M	4.3	6.0	9.1	13.4
						H	7.0	11.3	18.7	32.2
Output of non-durable goods[2]	88.7	118.6	121.2	144.1	161.8	L	200	246	299	349
						M	216	293	393	518
						H	239	354	523	760
Consumer purchases[3]	86.1	109.0	117.4	134.7	152.4	L	191	237	287	335
						M	202	271	360	469
						H	221	323	473	680
Government purchases[5]	3.0	11.0	2.5	6.7	7.2	L	9.0	10.8	15.6	22.3
						M	11.2	16.9	25.6	38.6
						H	13.8	23.5	38.8	64.9
Net exports[6]	–2.5	–1.6	–1.6	–.4	.5	L	–1.6	–3.8	–6.0	–10.2
						M	.2	1.2	2.8	4.6
						H	.4	1.2	2.3	2.8
Changes in inventories[7]	2.1	.2	2.9	.9	1.7	L	1.8	2.2	2.3	2.1
						M	2.6	3.8	4.7	5.9
						H	4.0	6.0	9.0	12.7
Output of services[8]	83.6	148.7	125.2	155.8	189.3	L	266	375	529	746
						M	280	415	614	909
						H	302	483	772	1,234
Consumer purchases[3]	56.5	69.4	87.0	104.8	132.2	L	186	260	359	482
						M	195	293	436	634
						H	214	348	566	903
Government purchases[5]	26.5	84.8	38.0	52.7	58.5	L	76.9	99.2	133.3	180.2
						M	95.6	141.1	202.5	292.7
						H	111.3	181.6	286.1	459.6
Net exports[6]	.6	–5.5	.2	–1.7	–1.4	L	–4.0	–4.4	–.6	9.3
						M	–2.6	–1.6	2.4	11.4
						H	–2.4	–2.4	–1.5	–1.0
Non-allocable services[9]	–	–	–	–	–	L	7	20	37	72
						M	–8	–18	–27	–29
						H	–21	–44	–79	–128

1. Historical data are from Tables A1–6 and A1–8.
2. Sum of components. Output equals sales plus change in inventories; sales equals domestic purchases plus net exports.
3. Projections from Table A1–27.
4. Projections from Table A6–4.
5. From Table A1–15.
6. From Table A1–17.
7. See footnote 11, Table A1–13.
8. From Table A1–13.
9. Represents non-allocable purchases and statistical error. (See footnote 6, Table A1–13.)

TABLE A1–15.   Projected Government Product and Purchases[1]

(Billion 1960 dollars)

	1940	1945	1950	1955	1960		1970	1980	1990	2000
Gross government product[2]	24.2	77.8	33.9	44.0	47.3	L	60.1	73.5	91.3	111.9
						M	69.8	94.7	125.8	169.2
						H	80.1	118.7	171.3	253.9
Military product[3]	2.1	47.4	6.8	13.0	11.0	L	9.7	6.1	6.4	6.8
						M	14.6	16.4	18.8	22.1
						H	19.7	26.3	34.6	46.9
Civilian government product[4]	22.1	30.4	27.1	31.0	36.3	L	50.4	67.4	84.9	105.1
						M	55.2	78.3	107.0	147.1
						H	60.4	92.4	136.7	207.0
Civilian government employment[5] (millions)	3.8	5.5	5.5	6.4	7.7	L	10.7	14.3	18.0	22.3
						M	11.7	16.6	22.7	31.2
						H	12.8	19.6	29.0	43.9
Government purchases[6]	39	164	57	91	100	L	129	154	223	318
						M	160	242	365	551
						H	197	336	555	927
Durable goods[7]	1.6	63.6	6.9	18.2	18.5	L	22.1	20.2	30	44
						M	34.8	53.8	85	136
						H	48.3	88.1	156	284
Non-durable goods[8]	3.0	11.0	2.5	6.7	7.2	L	9.0	10.8	15.6	22.3
						M	11.2	16.9	25.6	38.6
						H	13.8	23.5	38.8	64.9
Services[9]	26.5	84.8	38.0	52.7	58.5	L	76.9	99.2	133.3	180.2
						M	95.6	141.1	202.5	292.7
						H	111.3	181.6	286.1	459.6
Ratio of services to government product	109.5	109.0	112.1	119.8	123.7	L	128	135	146	161
						M	137	149	161	173
						H	139	153	167	181
Construction[10]	7.6	4.9	9.4	13.8	16.0	L	19.3	22.8	28.0	35.6
						M	27.1	39.9	57.7	84.1
						H	35.4	61.6	106.0	186.6
Residual[11]	–	–	–	–	–	L	2	1	16	36
						M	–6	–10	–6	–
						H	–12	–19	–32	–68

1. Historical data, unless otherwise indicated, from Tables A1–6 and A1–8.

2. Represents total compensation of government employees. Projections by summing the components below.

3. From Table A9–2, total expenditures on military personnel.

4. Civilian government employment (below) multiplied by 1960 compensation per employee—$4,715.

5. From Table A1–2.

6. From Table A1–10.

7. Sum of expenditures on defense procurement (Table A9–2) and the following assumed percentages of government non-defense expenditures (Table A1–12): Low 8%, Medium 10%, and High 12%.

8. Assumed, on the basis of the historical record, to be 7% of total government expenditure.

9. Based on the ratios which follow, which are extrapolations of past trends.

10. From Table A4–3.

11. Represents non-allocable purchases and statistical error. (See footnote 6, Table A1–13.)

TABLE A1–16.   Projected Farm Production and Gross Product

(Billion 1960 dollars)

	1940	1945	1950	1955	1960		1970	1980	1990	2000
Value of production of principal items:[1]										
Principal livestock products	12.5	14.8	15.0	17.2	17.6	L	19.9	22.3	24.3	26.0
						M	21.9	26.6	31.7	36.6
						H	24.5	31.7	41.0	51.6
Principal crops	7.8	9.4	9.9	9.9	11.4	L	11.4	12.9	14.2	15.3
						M	12.9	15.6	18.5	20.6
						H	14.6	18.8	24.6	32.0
Total[2]	20.3	24.2	24.9	27.1	29.0	L	31.3	35.2	38.5	41.3
						M	34.8	42.2	50.2	57.2
						H	39.1	50.5	65.6	83.6
Current operating expenses:										
Per cent of output of principal items:[3]										
Fertilizer and lime	2.3	3.4	4.1	4.5	5.0	L	5.0	5.0	5.0	5.0
						M	5.7	6.3	6.9	7.5
						H	6.1	7.1	8.1	9.1
Repair and operation of capital items	8.7	10.2	13.8	13.5	13.8	L	14.4	14.2	14.0	13.8
						M	14.5	14.5	14.5	14.5
						H	15.1	15.3	15.5	15.7
Miscellaneous	6.3	5.2	7.5	8.1	9.4		10.5	11.2	11.5	11.5
Value:										
Fertilizer and lime	.47	.83	1.03	1.23	1.46	L	1.5	1.8	1.9	2.1
						M	2.0	2.7	3.5	4.3
						H	2.4	3.6	5.3	7.6
Repair and operation of capital items	1.76	2.46	3.43	3.65	3.99	L	4.4	5.0	5.4	5.7
						M	5.0	6.1	7.3	8.3
						H	5.9	7.7	10.2	13.1
Miscellaneous	1.27	1.25	1.86	2.16	2.73	L	3.2	3.9	4.4	4.7
						M	3.7	4.7	5.8	6.6
						H	4.1	5.7	7.5	9.6
Farm gross product[4]	16.7	17.4	18.5	20.5	20.8	L	22.2	24.5	26.8	28.8
						M	24.1	28.7	33.6	38.0
						H	26.7	33.5	42.6	53.3

1. Product of production or consumption of principal agricultural products and 1960 average prices. Former from Tables A2–4, A12–1, and A12–14; latter from, or estimated from, U.S. Department of Agriculture, *Agricultural Prices* (Washington: Jan. 1962).

2. This total of principal crops approximates gross farm income as estimated by the National Income Division, Department of Commerce, for historical years. It is therefore taken as a suitable measure of future gross farm income as well.

3. Historical data calculated from output value above and expenses (shown below) as reported in USDA, *Farm Income Situation,* July 1961, deflated by price index for production expenses reported in *Agricultural Prices,* Jan. 1962. Projections, which are basis for calculation of future expenses (below), are extrapolations made on a judgment basis.

4. Value of output, less expenses. Equivalent to "farm goods" production, in the National Income and Product sense.

TABLE A1–17.   Projected Imports and Exports, by Kind of Product

(1960 dollars)

	1940	1945	1950	1955	1960		1970	1980	1990	2000
U.S. imports per dollar of GNP (cents):[1]										
Total[2]	4.01	4.19	3.88	4.07	4.68	L	4.59	4.54	4.53	4.55
						M	4.97	5.21	5.47	5.74
						H	5.86	6.82	7.78	8.74
Durables[3]	.68	.57	.74	.87	1.18	L	1.35	1.45	1.55	1.65
						M	1.45	1.65	1.85	2.05
						H	1.70	2.10	2.50	2.90
Non-durables[4]	2.48	1.39	2.13	1.67	1.74	L	1.49	1.24	1.03	.85
						M	1.62	1.46	1.32	1.19
						H	1.96	2.12	2.28	2.44
Services[3]	.85	2.23	1.02	1.53	1.76	L	1.75	1.85	1.95	2.05
						M	1.90	2.10	2.30	2.50
						H	2.20	2.60	3.00	3.40
GNP[5] ($ billion)	234	368	363	450	504	L	710	965	1,260	1,680
						M	746	1,060	1,510	2,200
						H	798	1,250	1,980	3,290
Aggregate imports[6] ($ billion):										
Total[2]	9.3	15.5	14.2	18.3	23.6	LL	32.6	43.8	57.1	76.4
						HL	41.6	65.8	98.0	146.8
						M	37.1	55.2	82.6	126.3
						LH	36.6	56.8	89.7	149.7
						HH	46.8	85.2	154.0	287.5
Durables	1.6	2.1	2.7	3.8	6.0	LL	9.6	14.0	19.5	27.7
						HL	12.1	20.3	31.5	48.7
						M	10.8	117.5	27.9	45.1
						LH	10.8	18.1	30.7	54.3
						HH	13.6	26.2	49.5	95.4
Non-durables	5.7	5.1	7.7	7.5	8.8	LL	10.6	12.0	13.0	14.3
						HL	13.9	20.5	28.7	41.0
						M	12.1	15.5	19.9	26.2
						LH	11.9	15.5	20.4	28.0
						HH	15.6	26.5	45.1	80.3
Services	2.0	8.2	3.7	6.9	8.9	LL	12.4	17.9	24.6	34.4
						HL	15.6	25.1	37.8	57.1
						M	14.2	22.3	34.7	55.0
						LH	14.0	23.1	38.6	67.4
						HH	17.6	32.5	59.4	111.9
Exports:[7]										
Total	11.1	10.3	15.3	20.3	26.7		38.0	58.4	91.2	144.1
Durables	5.2	4.0	5.2	7.9	9.9		14.1	21.0	31.4	46.9
Non-durables	3.2	3.6	6.1	7.1	9.3		12.3	16.7	22.7	30.8
Services	2.6	2.8	4.0	5.3	7.5		11.6	20.7	37.1	66.4
Net exports[8] ($ billion):										
Total[2]	1.7	−5.2	1.2	2.0	3.0	L	−3.6	−7.5	−6.7	−2.7
						M	.9	3.1	8.7	17.8
						H	1.3	1.7	1.5	−5.6
Durables	3.6	1.9	2.5	4.1	3.9	L	2.0	.7	−.1	−1.8
						M	3.3	3.5	3.5	1.8
						H	3.3	2.9	.7	−7.4
Non-durables	−2.5	−1.6	−1.6	−.4	.5	L	−1.6	−3.8	−6.0	−10.2
						M	.2	1.2	2.8	4.6
						H	.4	1.2	2.3	2.8
Services	.6	−5.5	.2	−1.7	−1.4	L	−4.0	−4.4	−.6	9.3
						M	−2.6	−1.6	2.4	11.4
						H	−2.4	−2.4	−1.5	−1.0
Gross merchandise trade[9] ($ billion)	15.7	14.8	21.7	26.3	34.0	L	46.6	63.7	86.6	119.7
						M	49.3	70.7	101.9	149.0
						H	55.6	90.4	148.7	253.4

Table A1–17 (cont'd)

1. Refers to imports of goods and services as used in the National Income and Product Accounts. Historical figures are derived from unpublished data of the National Income Division, U.S. Department of Commerce.

2. Sum of the detail which follows.

3. Arithmetic extrapolations of alternate historical trends.

4. Low and Medium are geometric extrapolations of long term declining trends. (Geometric, rather than arithmetic, approach is used in order to take account of the asymptotic effect of zero.) High is an arithmetic extrapolation of a relatively recent (c. 1954–60) trend.

5. From Table A1–12.

6. Source of historical data as in footnote 1; projections by application of the coefficients above. "LL" (Low-Low) and "HL" (High-Low) projections represent, respectively, the Low and the High import levels consistent with the Low GNP; "LH" and "HH" those consistent with the High GNP.

7. Historical data as in footnote 1. Projections (except for the total, which is the sum of the detail) are geometric extrapolations of past trends. The single level for each category may be interpreted not only as the Medium, but as the Low consistent with the Low GNP and the High consistent with the High GNP. The Low GNP, with its underlying Low population and Low defense expenditures, implies a relatively higher export propensity than the Medium, and vice versa for the High. Moreover, the level of exports is to a certain extent independent of the U.S. GNP, being determined in large measure by foreign rates of economic and population growth.

8. Since what is desired is the Low *net exports* consistent with the Low GNP, they are calculated by using the High *import* levels consistent with the Low GNP (HL). Vice versa for the High.

9. Sum of imports and exports of goods only (used as a measure of ocean transportation volume). For this purpose, "LL" imports are used for the Low, "HH" for the High.

TABLE A1–18. Projected Output and Man-Year Productivity, by Economic Sector[1]

	1940	1945	1950	1955	1960		1970	1980	1990	2000
Gross national product[2]						L	710	965	1,260	1,680
($ 1960 bil.)	234	369	363	449	504	M	746	1,060	1,510	2,200
						H	798	1,250	1,980	3,290
						L	3.51	4.27	5.06	6.27
GNP per capita ($ 1960 thous.)	1.77	2.64	2.39	2.72	2.80	M	3.59	4.33	5.26	6.65
						H	3.58	4.48	5.67	7.60
						L	700	959	1,254	1,673
Civilian product[3] ($ 1960 bil.)	232	321	356	436	493	M	731	1,044	1,491	2,178
						H	778	1,224	1,945	3,243
Civilian product per capita						L	3.47	4.24	5.04	6.24
($ 1960 thous.)	1.76	2.29	2.34	2.70	2.74	M	3.51	4.26	5.20	6.58
						H	3.49	4.39	5.57	7.49
Civilian government product[4]						L	50.4	67.4	84.9	105.1
($ 1960 bil.)	22.1	30.4	27.1	31.0	36.3	M	55.2	78.3	107.0	147.1
						H	60.4	92.4	136.7	207.0
Civilian government product per						L	.25	.30	.34	.39
capita ($ 1960 thous.)	.17	.22	.18	.19	.20	M	.26	.32	.37	.44
						H	.27	.33	.39	.48
						L	646	887	1,166	1,566
Private product[5] ($ 1960 bil.)	209	291	329	405	457	M	676	966	1,384	2,031
						H	722	1,138	1,813	3,039
Private product per capita						L	3.20	3.92	4.68	5.84
($ 1960 thous.)	1.58	2.08	2.16	2.45	2.54	M	3.25	3.94	4.82	6.14
						H	3.24	4.08	5.19	7.02
						L	22.2	24.5	26.8	28.8
Agricultural product[6] ($ 1960 bil.)	16.7	17.4	18.5	20.5	20.8	M	24.1	28.7	33.6	38.0
						H	26.7	33.5	42.6	53.3
Agricultural product per capita						L	.11	.11	.11	.11
($ 1960 thous.)	.12	.12	.12	.12	.12	M	.11	.12	.12	.12
						H	.12	.12	.12	.12
Private non-agricultural product[7]						L	622	860	1,136	1,534
($ 1960 bil.)	193	274	310	385	436	M	652	937	1,350	1,993
						H	697	1,107	1,775	2,991
Private non-agricultural product						L	3.08	3.81	4.56	5.72
per capita ($ 1960 thous.)	1.46	1.96	2.04	2.33	2.42	M	3.13	3.82	4.70	6.02
						H	3.13	3.97	5.09	6.91

Table A1–18 (cont'd)

	1940	1945	1950	1955	1960		1970	1980	1990	2000
GNP per worker[8] ($ 1960 thous.)	4.16	5.64	5.62	6.53	6.92	L	8.32	9.85	11.7	13.8
						M	8.57	10.4	12.7	15.5
						H	8.99	11.5	14.7	18.8
Civilian product per employed civilian worker ($ 1960 thous.)	4.88	6.08	5.96	6.93	7.42	L	8.87	10.4	12.3	14.7
						M	9.09	11.1	13.6	16.5
						H	9.57	12.2	15.8	20.4
Private product per employed private worker ($ 1960 thous.)	4.78	6.15	6.07	7.17	7.79	L	9.70	12.0	14.9	19.1
						M	9.84	12.4	15.9	20.1
						H	10.21	13.5	18.0	23.7
Agricultural product per employed agric. worker[9] ($ 1960 thous.)	1.76	2.02	2.47	3.06	3.65	L	5.29	7.90	11.7	16.9
						M	5.13	7.55	10.8	15.2
						H	5.24	7.28	10.1	14.0
Private non-agricultural product per employed non-agricultural worker ($ 1960 thous.)	5.64	7.08	6.64	7.73	8.23	L	10.1	12.5	15.4	19.4
						M	10.2	12.7	16.1	20.3
						H	10.5	13.7	17.9	23.7

1. Historical data from, or calculated from, Tables A1–6 and A1–1. Population and labor force data used in calculating the projected ratios are from Table A1–2.

2. From Table A1–12.

3. GNP less military product (Table A1–15).

4. From Table A1–15.

5. For the Medium, civilian product less civilian government product. For the Low, there is subtracted from civilian product that civilian government product which would be obtained by applying the percentage which High civilian government product is of civilian product to the Low civilian product (equivalent also to multiplying the Low civilian product by the complement of the percentage which High civilian government product is of High civilian product). The Low is calculated inversely. This procedure is a way of approximating the less than "extreme" government proportions of civilian product which would be consistent with the "extreme" ranges of private product.

6. From Table A1–16.

7. For the Medium, private product less agricultural product. For the Low, the amount to be subtracted is determined by applying High per capita agricultural product to Low population, and vice versa for the High. The reasons are the same as those for the calculation described in footnote 5.

8. This is an assumed series (see Table A1–12), although it is balanced with the demand upon workers (Table A1–11).

9. In agriculture, the higher levels of productivity are associated with the lower levels of employment and output. This is probably due in part to the fuller employment per worker associated with a relatively smaller farm labor force, as illustrated in Table A1–19.

TABLE A1–19. Man-Hour and Hourly Productivity Possibilities Associated with GNP Projections

	1940	1945	1950	1955	1960		1970	1980	1990	2000
Agricultural:						L	4.2	3.1	2.3	1.7
Employment[1] (millions)	9.5	8.6	7.5	6.7	5.7	M	4.7	3.8	3.1	2.5
						H	5.1	4.6	4.2	3.8
Weeks worked per year[2]	50.5	50.6	50.4	50.5	50.3		50.3	50.3	50.3	50.3
Hours worked per week[2]	55.4	51.9	48.7	47.9	45.5		42.8	40.3	37.9	35.7
Annual hours (thousands)	2.80	2.63	2.45	2.42	2.29		2.15	2.03	1.91	1.80
Annual man-hours						L	9.0	6.3	4.4	3.1
(billions)	26.6	22.6	18.4	16.2	13.1	M	10.1	7.7	5.9	4.5
						H	11.0	9.3	8.0	6.8
Hourly productivity[3]						L	2.47	3.89	6.09	9.29
($ 1960)	.62	.75	.99	1.24	1.59	M	2.39	3.73	5.69	8.44
						H	2.43	3.60	5.33	7.84
Average rate of increase						L	4.5	4.6	4.6	4.3
over preceding decade	–	–	4.8	–	4.8	M	4.2	4.6	4.3	4.0
(% per annum)						H	4.3	4.0	4.0	3.9
Private non-agricultural:						L	61.5	69	74	79
Employment[1] (millions)	34.2	38.7	46.7	49.8	53.0	M	64.0	74	84	98
						H	66.5	81	99	126
						L	49.0	48.6	48.4	48.2
Weeks worked per year[2]	50.8	49.9	49.6	49.5	49.4	M	49.2	49.0	48.8	48.6
						H	49.4	49.4	49.4	49.4
						L	38.8	37.6	36.4	35.4
Hours worked per week[2]	40.9	45.0	40.7	40.9	40.0	M	39.2	38.4	37.6	36.8
						H	40.0	40.0	40.0	40.0
						L	1.90	1.83	1.76	1.71
Annual hours (thousands)	2.08	2.25	2.02	2.02	1.98	M	1.93	1.88	1.84	1.79
						H	1.98	1.98	1.98	1.98
Annual man-hours						L	119	130	136	141
(billions)	71.1	87.1	94.3	101	105	M	124	139	155	175
						H	128	152	182	226
Hourly productivity[3]						L	5.23	6.62	8.35	10.88
($ 1960)	2.71	3.15	3.29	3.81	4.15	M	5.26	6.74	8.71	11.39
						H	5.45	7.28	9.75	13.23
Average rate of increase						L	2.3	2.4	2.3	2.7
over preceding decade	–	–	2.0	–	2.3	M	2.4	2.5	2.6	2.7
(% per annum)						H	2.7	2.9	2.6	3.1

1. From Table A1–2.
2. Historical data from, or derived from, tabulations in U.S. Bureau of the Census, Current Population Reports, Series P–50 (1940–55) and U.S. Bureau of Labor Statistics, *Special Labor Force No. 14* (1960). Projections are extrapolations of recent trends: the single projection for agriculture is assumed to be as low a level as would be consistent with Low agricultural employment and as high a level as would be consistent with High employment. For non-agricultural employment, it is assumed that the forces making for lower employment will also tend to eventuate in relatively lower weeks worked and lower hours per week; and vice versa for the High.
3. Low productivity equals Low "product" (Table A1–18) divided by Low man-hours, and vice versa for the High.

TABLE A1–20.   Principal Components of Actual and Projected GNP Change, 1940–60, 1960–80, and 1980–2000[1]

						Relatives (%)			
	Amounts					1940–60		1960–80	1980–2000
	1940	1960		1980	2000				
GNP ($ 1960 bil.)	234	504	L	965	1,680	215	L	191	174
			M	1,060	2,200		M	210	208
			H	1,250	3,290		H	248	263
Labor force (millions)	56.2	72.8	L	98	122	130	L	135	124
			M	102	142		M	140	139
			H	109	175		H	150	161
GNP per worker ($ 1960 thous.)	4.16	6.92	L	9.85	13.8	166	L	142	140
			M	10.4	15.5		M	150	149
			H	11.5	18.8		H	166	163
Labor force:									
Population of labor force age (millions)	102	126	L	172	212	124	L	137	123
			M	176	242		M	140	138
			H	188	292		H	149	155
Average participation rate (%)	55.3	57.6	L	56.8	57.4	104	L	99	101
			M	57.8	58.7		M	100	102
			H	58.1	59.9		H	101	103
GNP components ($ 1960 bil.):									
Government product	24.2	47.3	L	73.5	111.9	195	L	155	152
			M	94.7	169.2		M	200	179
			H	118.7	253.9		H	251	214
Private agricultural product	16.7	20.8	L	24.5	28.8	125	L	118	118
			M	28.7	38.0		M	138	132
			H	33.5	53.3		H	161	159
Private non-agricultural product	193	436	L	860	1,534	226	L	197	178
			M	937	1,993		M	215	213
			H	1,107	2,991		H	254	270
Private non-agricultural employment (millions)	34.2	53.0	L	69	79	155	L	130	114
			M	74	98		M	140	132
			H	81	126		H	153	156
Output per employed non-agricultural worker ($ 1960 thous.)	5.64	8.23	L	12.5	19.4	146	L	152	155
			M	12.7	20.3		M	154	160
			H	13.7	23.7		H	166	173
Hourly productivity ($ 1960)	2.71	4.15	L	6.62	10.88	153	L	160	164
			M	6.74	11.39		M	162	169
			H	7.28	13.23		H	175	182
Hours worked per year (thousands)	2.08	1.98	L	1.83	1.71	95.2	L	92	93
			M	1.88	1.79		M	95	95
			H	1.98	1.98		H	100	100
Average non-agricultural hours per year:									
Hours worked per week	40.9	40.0	L	37.6	35.4	98	L	94	94
			M	38.4	36.8		M	96	95
			H	40.0	40.0		H	100	100
Weeks worked per year	50.8	49.4	L	48.6	48.2	97	L	98	99
			M	49.0	48.6		M	99	99
			H	49.4	49.4		H	100	100

Sources: Tables A1–2, 3, 4, 5, 12, 18, and 19.

1. Includes implied components, derived for checking and illustrative purposes.

TABLE A1–21. Growth Rate Implications of Principal Projections[1]

(Per cent per annum, compounded)

	1940–50	1950–60		1960–70	1970–80	1980–90	1990–2000	1940–60	1960–80	1980–2000
Population	1.4	1.7	L	1.2	1.1	1.0	.7	1.6	1.1	.9
			M	1.5	1.7	1.6	1.4		1.6	1.5
			H	2.2	2.3	2.3	2.2		2.2	2.2
Labor force	1.4	1.2	L	1.6	1.4	1.0	1.2	1.3	1.3	1.1
			M	1.8	1.6	1.6	1.8		1.7	1.7
			H	2.0	2.1	2.2	2.6		2.0	2.4
Private non-agricultural employment	3.1	1.3	L	1.5	1.1	.7	.7	2.2	1.3	.7
			M	1.9	1.5	1.3	1.6		1.7	1.4
			H	2.3	2.0	2.0	2.4		2.2	2.2
Agricultural employment	−2.3	−2.7	L	−3.0	−3.0	−2.9	−3.0	−2.5	−3.0	−3.0
			M	−1.9	−2.1	−2.0	−2.1		−2.0	−2.1
			H	−1.1	−1.0	−.9	−1.0		−1.1	−.9
Gross national product	4.5	3.3	L	3.5	3.1	2.7	2.9	3.9	3.3	2.8
			M	4.0	3.6	3.6	3.8		3.8	3.7
			H	4.7	4.6	4.7	5.2		4.7	5.0
Civilian product	4.4	3.3	L	3.6	3.2	2.7	2.9	3.8	3.4	2.8
			M	4.0	3.6	3.6	3.9		3.8	3.7
			H	4.6	4.6	4.7	5.2		4.6	5.0
Private product	4.6	3.3	L	3.5	3.2	2.8	3.0	4.0	3.4	2.9
			M	4.0	3.6	3.7	3.9		3.8	3.8
			H	4.7	4.6	4.8	5.3		4.7	5.0
Private non-agricultural product	4.8	3.5	L	3.6	3.3	2.8	3.0	4.1	3.5	2.9
			M	4.1	3.7	3.7	4.0		3.9	3.8
			H	4.8	4.7	4.8	5.4		4.8	5.1
GNP per capita	3.0	1.6	L	2.3	2.0	1.7	2.2	2.3	2.1	1.9
			M	2.5	1.9	2.0	2.4		2.2	2.2
			H	2.5	2.2	2.4	3.0		2.4	2.7
Civilian product per capita	2.9	1.6	L	2.4	2.0	1.7	2.2	2.2	2.2	2.0
			M	2.5	2.0	2.0	2.4		2.2	2.2
			H	2.4	2.3	2.4	3.0		2.4	2.7
Personal consumption expenditures	4.1	3.3	L	3.2	3.2	3.0	2.7	3.7	3.1	2.8
			M	3.4	3.7	3.6	3.4		3.6	3.5
			H	4.2	4.3	4.3	4.2		4.2	4.2
GNP per worker	3.1	2.1	L	1.9	1.7	1.7	1.7	2.6	1.8	1.7
			M	2.2	2.0	2.0	2.0		2.1	2.0
			H	2.7	2.4	2.5	2.4		2.6	2.5
Civilian product per employed civilian worker	2.0	2.2	L	1.8	1.6	1.7	1.8	2.1	1.7	1.7
			M	2.0	2.0	2.0	2.0		2.0	2.0
			H	2.6	2.4	2.6	2.6		2.5	2.6
Private product per privately employed worker	2.4	2.5	L	2.2	2.2	2.2	2.5	2.5	2.2	2.4
			M	2.4	2.3	2.5	2.4		2.4	2.5
			H	2.7	2.8	2.9	2.8		2.8	2.8
Agricultural product per employed agricultural worker	3.5	4.0	L	3.8	4.1	4.0	3.7	3.7	3.9	3.9
			M	3.5	4.0	3.7	3.5		3.7	3.6
			H	3.7	3.3	3.3	3.3		3.5	3.3
Private non-agricultural product per privately employed non-agricultural worker	1.6	2.2	L	2.0	2.2	2.1	2.3	1.9	2.1	2.2
			M	2.2	2.2	2.4	2.3		2.2	2.4
			H	2.4	2.7	2.7	2.8		2.6	2.8

1. Reference projections are contained in Tables A1–2 (population and employment), A1–12 (derivation of GNP and its demand components), and A1–18 & 19 (output and productivity by sector).

L, M, and H refer to the Low, Medium, and High GNP, etc., projections and not necessarily to the Low, Medium, and High growth rates for the particular items.

TABLE A1–22. Historical Data on Percentage Distribution of Personal Consumption Expenditures, by Type of Product[1]

	Type of pur- chase	1929	1930	1931	1932	1933	1934	1935	1936	1937	1938	1939	1940	1941
Disposable personal income[2]	–	105.3	104.8	104.1	98.7	98.6	100.2	103.6	105.8	105.6	101.6	104.2	105.8	113.6
Personal consumption expenditures	–	100	100	100	100	100	100	100	100	100	100	100	100	100
Food and tobacco	–	26.9	27.4	26.4	25.8	27.5	30.0	31.3	31.9	32.0	31.8	31.0	30.9	31.4
Food and soft beverages	ND	24.7	25.3	24.0	23.1	23.4	23.5	24.2	24.3	24.4	24.2	23.3	23.3	23.8
Alcohol and tobacco	ND	2.1	2.0	2.4	2.7	4.1	6.5	7.1	7.5	7.6	7.7	7.7	7.6	7.7
Clothing and accessories	–	14.2	13.7	13.4	12.3	11.7	12.6	12.5	12.2	12.0	12.4	12.4	12.3	12.8
Clothing and footwear	ND	11.9	11.3	11.3	10.2	10.0	10.9	10.7	10.5	10.2	10.5	10.6	10.3	10.7
Cleaning, storage, and repair	S	1.6	1.6	1.6	1.5	1.4	1.3	1.3	1.3	1.4	1.4	1.4	1.4	1.4
Jewelry and watches	D	.7	.7	.5	.5	.4	.4	.4	.4	.5	.5	.5	.6	.7
Housing	S	14.5	15.5	16.7	18.3	17.0	14.6	13.7	12.8	12.5	13.6	13.2	12.9	12.3
Household durables	–	6.0	5.6	5.0	4.2	4.1	4.3	4.5	5.1	5.3	4.9	5.2	5.5	6.0
Furniture and furnishings	D	3.0	2.6	2.6	2.2	2.0	2.1	2.3	2.7	2.7	2.5	2.7	2.9	3.1
Household appliances	D	2.3	2.2	1.7	1.2	1.3	1.4	1.5	1.7	1.8	1.6	1.8	1.9	2.2
Tableware and utensils	D	.8	.6	.7	.8	.8	.8	.7	.7	.7	.7	.7	.7	.8
Household supplies and operations	–	8.9	9.3	9.6	10.1	10.3	10.1	9.7	9.5	9.5	9.4	9.7	9.8	9.4
Paper products and other supplies	ND	1.7	1.7	1.7	1.6	1.7	1.8	1.7	1.8	1.9	1.8	2.0	2.0	2.1
Fuel and ice	ND	2.0	2.2	2.1	2.3	2.5	2.4	2.3	2.3	2.1	2.0	2.1	2.2	2.0
Gas, electricity, and water	S	1.8	2.1	2.5	3.0	3.0	2.8	2.7	2.5	2.4	2.6	2.6	2.6	2.3
Telephone and telegraph	S	.7	.8	.9	1.0	.9	.9	.8	.8	.8	.8	.9	.9	.8
Domestic service, maintenance, and repair	S	2.6	2.6	2.4	2.2	2.1	2.2	2.1	2.1	2.3	2.1	2.2	2.2	2.1
Passenger car purchases	D	3.3	2.3	1.9	1.3	1.7	2.0	2.7	3.1	3.0	1.9	2.5	3.1	3.3
Automobile operating expenses	–	4.3	4.3	4.2	4.7	4.9	4.9	4.8	4.8	4.9	5.0	5.1	5.1	5.3
Tires, tubes, and accessories	D	.8	.7	.7	.6	.6	.7	.7	.6	.6	.6	.7	.7	.8
Gas and oil	ND	2.3	2.5	2.5	3.0	3.2	3.2	3.1	3.1	3.2	3.3	3.2	3.2	3.2
Repair, insurance, and tolls	S	1.2	1.1	1.0	1.0	1.1	1.1	1.1	1.1	1.1	1.1	1.2	1.2	1.2
Purchased local transport and personal business	–	7.9	7.2	7.2	7.6	7.8	7.1	6.9	6.8	6.7	6.7	6.6	6.3	6.0
Purchased local transport	S	1.4	1.5	1.5	1.6	1.6	1.5	1.4	1.3	1.3	1.3	1.3	1.3	1.2
Interest, legal and financial services	S	6.4	5.7	5.7	6.1	6.3	5.6	5.5	5.4	5.4	5.4	5.3	5.0	4.8
Personal and medical care	–	5.9	6.2	6.5	6.8	6.5	6.4	6.3	6.1	6.2	6.4	6.4	6.4	6.1
Ophthalmic goods and appliances	D	.2	.2	.2	.2	.2	.2	.2	.2	.2	.2	.3	.3	.3
Toilet articles and drugs	ND	1.5	1.5	1.7	1.8	1.6	1.6	1.5	1.4	1.5	1.6	1.6	1.6	1.6
Medical and personal services	S	4.2	4.5	4.7	4.9	4.7	4.6	4.5	4.5	4.4	4.6	4.6	4.4	4.2
Recreation, travel, education, and religion	–	8.2	8.6	9.0	9.0	8.5	8.0	7.7	7.8	7.9	7.9	7.8	7.6	7.4
Books, toys, and sports equipment	D	.7	.6	.7	.5	.5	.5	.6	.6	.7	.7	.7	.7	.7
Newspapers, toys, and plants	ND	1.4	1.4	1.4	1.5	1.5	1.5	1.4	1.4	1.4	1.5	1.5	1.5	1.5
Amusements	S	2.1	2.3	2.5	2.4	2.3	2.2	2.2	2.2	2.3	2.3	2.2	2.5	2.2
Domestic intercity travel	S	.7	.6	.5	.5	.5	.5	.5	.5	.5	.5	.5	.5	.5
Foreign travel and remittances	[3]	1.0	1.0	1.0	.9	.8	.7	.6	.7	.7	.6	.5	.3	.3
Private education, religion, and welfare	S	2.4	2.7	2.9	3.1	2.9	2.6	2.4	2.3	2.2	2.4	2.3	2.3	2.2
Durable goods	D	11.7	10.1	8.9	7.4	7.5	8.1	9.1	10.0	10.3	8.8	9.9	10.8	11.9
Non-durable goods	ND	47.7	47.9	47.2	46.2	48.0	51.4	52.1	52.3	52.3	52.6	52.0	51.8	52.6
Services	S	40.6	41.9	43.9	46.4	44.6	40.5	38.8	37.5	37.4	38.6	38.1	37.4	35.5

ND = Non-durables.   D = Durables.   S = Services.

1. Calculated from data in current dollars. Sources: 1929–45, *National Income*, 1954, Table 30; 1946–55, Table II–4, *U.S. Income and Output* and July 1961 National Income Number, *Survey of Current Business*. For a cross-reference between the consumption categories shown here and those in the National Income Accounts as well as for definitions of certain of the items, see Table A1–26.

2. Calculated from data in current dollars in Table II–1 of *U.S. Income and Output* and subsequent sources as in footnote 1.

3. See Table A1–26, footnote 8.

1942	1943	1944	1945	1946	1947	1948	1949	1950	1951	1952	1953	1954	1955	1956	1957	1958	1959	1960
130.9	132.8	133.6	123.5	109.1	102.8	106.2	104.7	106.5	108.4	108.6	108.5	107.9	106.8	108.5	108.3	108.4	107.4	107.0
100	100	100	100	100	100	100	100	100	100	100	100	100	100	100	100	100	100	100
34.7	36.2	36.5	36.6	35.7	35.2	33.8	32.2	30.6	31.6	31.6	30.4	30.0	28.5	28.5	28.2	28.2	27.1	26.6
26.4	27.7	27.9	28.0	27.6	27.7	27.0	25.6	24.3	25.5	25.4	24.3	24.2	23.0	23.1	22.9	23.0	21.8	21.3
8.3	8.5	8.6	8.6	8.0	7.6	6.8	6.6	6.3	6.1	6.2	6.0	5.8	5.5	5.4	5.3	5.2	5.3	5.3
14.6	15.9	15.9	16.2	15.1	13.9	13.7	12.9	12.2	12.2	12.0	11.5	11.2	11.1	11.0	10.8	10.6	10.5	10.3
12.2	13.3	13.3	13.5	12.4	11.4	11.3	10.7	10.0	10.1	9.9	9.4	9.2	9.1	9.1	8.9	8.8	8.7	8.5
1.5	1.7	1.7	1.6	1.7	1.6	1.6	1.5	1.4	1.4	1.4	1.3	1.3	1.3	1.2	1.2	1.2	1.1	1.1
.8	1.0	1.0	1.0	1.0	.9	.8	.7	.7	.7	.7	.7	.7	.7	.7	.7	.6	.7	.6
12.1	11.3	10.8	10.2	9.4	9.4	9.9	10.7	10.9	11.1	11.5	11.8	12.2	12.0	12.1	12.4	12.8	12.7	12.8
5.2	3.9	3.5	3.8	5.9	6.6	6.7	6.4	7.2	6.8	6.4	6.3	6.2	6.4	6.5	6.1	5.9	6.0	5.7
2.8	2.6	2.5	2.5	3.0	3.0	3.1	2.9	3.1	3.1	2.9	2.8	2.6	2.8	2.9	2.8	2.7	2.7	2.6
1.6	.7	.4	.6	2.0	2.8	2.8	2.7	3.3	2.9	2.8	2.8	2.8	2.9	2.9	2.7	2.6	2.7	2.5
.7	.6	.6	.7	.9	.8	.8	.8	.8	.8	.7	.7	.7	.7	.7	.7	.7	.7	.6
9.8	9.6	9.6	9.4	8.6	8.8	8.9	8.8	9.1	9.1	8.9	8.8	8.9	9.0	9.2	9.2	9.4	9.4	9.6
2.3	2.4	2.4	2.2	2.3	2.5	2.5	2.4	2.5	2.5	2.3	2.3	2.2	2.2	2.2	2.2	2.2	2.2	2.2
2.1	2.0	1.9	1.8	1.7	1.8	1.9	1.7	1.7	1.6	1.5	1.4	1.4	1.4	1.3	1.3	1.2	1.2	1.1
2.3	2.1	2.0	1.9	1.7	1.7	1.7	1.8	1.9	2.0	2.1	2.2	2.3	2.4	2.5	2.5	2.7	2.7	2.8
.9	1.0	1.0	1.0	.9	.8	.9	1.0	1.0	1.0	1.1	1.1	1.1	1.2	1.2	1.2	1.3	1.3	1.3
2.2	2.2	2.4	2.5	2.0	2.0	1.9	1.8	1.9	1.8	1.8	1.7	1.6	1.7	2.0	2.0	2.1	2.0	2.1
.5	.4	.3	.3	1.7	2.8	3.2	4.5	5.5	4.5	4.0	5.1	4.8	6.2	5.0	5.1	3.9	4.9	4.8
3.5	2.4	2.5	3.0	4.5	4.7	5.0	5.4	5.6	5.7	5.9	6.2	6.2	6.4	6.4	6.5	6.4	6.5	6.5
.3	.4	.4	.5	1.0	1.0	.9	.9	1.1	1.0	1.0	.9	.9	.9	.9	.9	.8	.9	.9
2.3	1.3	1.3	1.5	2.1	2.2	2.5	2.8	2.8	2.9	3.0	3.2	3.4	3.4	3.5	3.6	3.6	3.5	3.5
.9	.7	.8	1.0	1.4	1.5	1.6	1.7	1.7	1.8	1.9	2.0	2.0	2.0	2.0	2.0	2.0	2.1	2.1
5.6	5.4	5.3	5.1	4.7	4.7	4.9	5.0	5.2	5.2	5.3	5.5	5.8	5.8	6.1	6.2	6.5	6.6	6.9
1.4	1.6	1.6	1.4	1.3	1.2	1.2	1.1	1.0	1.0	1.0	.9	.9	.8	.7	.7	.7	.6	.6
4.2	3.8	3.8	3.6	3.4	3.5	3.7	3.9	4.1	4.3	4.4	4.6	4.9	5.1	5.4	5.5	5.8	6.0	6.3
6.3	6.4	6.6	6.4	6.1	6.0	6.2	6.3	6.2	6.2	6.4	6.5	6.8	6.8	7.1	7.3	7.7	7.8	8.1
.3	.3	.3	.3	.3	.2	.2	.2	.3	.3	.3	.3	.3	.3	.3	.3	.3	.4	.4
1.8	1.9	1.9	1.8	1.6	1.5	1.5	1.6	1.6	1.6	1.7	1.7	1.6	1.6	1.7	1.8	1.8	2.0	2.0
4.3	4.2	4.4	4.2	4.2	4.2	4.4	4.4	4.4	4.3	4.5	4.6	4.9	4.8	4.9	5.1	5.4	5.4	5.6
7.8	8.4	8.9	9.2	8.4	7.9	7.9	7.9	7.6	7.6	7.8	7.8	7.9	7.8	8.1	8.1	8.4	8.5	8.7
.7	.6	.7	.8	1.0	.9	.9	.8	.8	.8	.8	.8	.8	.9	1.0	1.0	1.0	1.1	1.1
1.5	1.5	1.5	1.6	1.6	1.6	1.6	1.7	1.8	1.8	1.8	1.8	1.7	1.7	1.8	1.8	1.8	1.8	1.8
2.3	2.3	2.4	2.4	2.4	2.2	2.0	2.0	1.8	1.7	1.7	1.6	1.6	1.6	1.6	1.6	1.6	1.6	1.7
.7	1.0	1.0	.9	.8	.6	.6	.6	.5	.5	.5	.5	.4	.5	.5	.5	.4	.4	.5
.4	.6	.9	1.3	.5	.5	.6	.6	.6	.6	.7	.9	.9	.9	.9	.9	.9	.9	.9
2.2	2.4	2.4	2.2	2.1	2.1	2.1	2.2	2.1	2.1	2.2	2.2	2.3	2.2	2.4	2.4	2.6	2.7	2.8
7.7	6.6	6.2	6.7	10.8	12.4	12.7	13.6	15.6	14.1	13.2	14.1	13.6	15.4	14.3	14.2	12.7	13.8	13.5
56.9	58.6	58.8	60.1	57.6	56.5	55.4	53.3	51.1	52.5	52.4	50.7	50.1	48.6	48.7	48.3	48.4	47.0	46.3
35.4	34.9	35.2	33.2	31.5	31.1	31.9	33.1	33.3	33.5	34.4	35.2	36.3	36.0	37.1	37.5	38.9	39.1	40.2

TABLE A1–23.   Projected Percentage Distribution of Personal Consumption Expenditures, by Type of Product[1]

	Type of pur-chase	1950	1955	1960		1970	1980	1990	2000
Disposable personal income	–	106.5	106.8	107.0	L	107.0	106.0	106.0	106.0
					M	108.0	108.0	108.0	108.0
					H	109.5	111.5	113.5	115.5
Personal consumption expenditures	–	100	100	100		100	100	100	100
Food and tobacco	–	30.6	28.5	26.6	L	24.0	21.4	19.1	17.0
					M	24.4	22.2	20.2	18.2
					H	27.5	27.5	27.5	27.5
Food and soft beverages	ND	24.3	23.0	21.3	L	19.1	16.8	14.8	13.0
					M	19.6	17.8	16.4	15.0
					H	22.5	22.5	22.5	22.5
Alcohol and tobacco	ND	6.3	5.5	5.3	L	4.5	3.9	3.3	2.7
					M	4.8	4.4	3.8	3.2
					H	5.3	5.3	5.3	5.3
Clothing and accessories	–	12.2	11.1	10.3	L	8.9	7.7	6.6	5.7
					M	9.6	8.8	8.3	7.9
					H	10.6	10.6	10.6	10.6
Clothing and footwear	ND	10.0	9.1	8.5	L	7.4	6.4	5.6	4.9
					M	7.9	7.3	6.8	6.4
					H	8.8	8.8	8.8	8.8
Cleaning, storage, and repair	S	1.4	1.3	1.2	L	.8	.6	.4	.2
					M	1.0	.8	.8	.8
					H	1.2	1.2	1.2	1.2
Jewelry and watches	D	.7	.7	.6	L	.6	.55	.5	.5
					M	.7	.7	.7	.7
					H	.7	.7	.8	.8
Housing	S	10.9	12.0	12.8	L	12.2	11.7	11.5	11.5
					M	13.1	13.0	13.0	13.0
					H	14.8	16.6	18.2	19.8
Household durables	–	7.2	6.4	5.7	L	5.5	5.5	5.5	5.5
					M	6.2	6.8	7.2	7.6
					H	6.7	7.7	8.7	9.7
Furniture and furnishings	D	3.1	2.8	2.6	L	2.0	1.6	1.3	1.1
					M	2.7	2.7	2.7	2.7
					H	2.9	3.1	3.3	3.5
Household appliances	D	3.3	2.9	2.5	L	2.2	2.2	2.2	2.2
					M	2.9	3.5	3.9	4.3
					H	3.5	4.5	5.5	6.5
Tableware and utensils	D	.8	.7	.6	L	.6	.6	.6	.6
					M	.6	.6	.6	.6
					H	.7	.7	.7	.7

Table A1–23 (cont'd)

	Type of pur-chase	1950	1955	1960		1970	1980	1990	2000
Household supplies and operations	–	9.1	9.0	9.6	L M H	9.1 9.4 10.0	8.9 9.4 10.9	8.7 9.5 12.0	8.5 9.5 13.2
Paper products and other supplies	ND	2.5	2.2	2.2	L M H	2.0 2.1 2.3	1.8 2.0 2.3	1.6 1.9 2.3	1.4 1.7 2.3
Fuel and ice	ND	1.7	1.4	1.1	L M H	.7 .8 1.0	.4 .5 .8	.2 .3 .6	.1 .2 .4
Gas, electricity, and water	S	1.9	2.4	2.8	L M H	2.8 3.2 4.4	2.8 3.6 6.0	2.8 4.0 7.4	2.8 4.4 8.8
Telephone and telegraph	S	1.0	1.2	1.3	L M H	1.2 1.3 1.8	1.2 1.3 2.2	1.2 1.3 2.6	1.2 1.3 3.0
Domestic service, maintenance, and repair	S	1.9	1.7	2.1	L M H	1.7 2.0 2.7	1.5 2.0 3.3	1.5 2.0 4.0	1.5 2.0 4.6
Passenger car purchases	D	5.5	6.2	4.8	L M H	4.9 5.0 5.6	4.7 5.0 6.4	4.5 5.0 7.3	4.3 5.0 8.1
Automobile operating expenses	–	5.6	6.4	6.5	L M H	6.4 6.6 7.0	6.3 6.6 7.4	6.2 6.6 7.8	6.1 6.6 8.2
Tires, tubes, and accessories	D	1.1	.9	.9	L M H	.8 .9 1.2	.7 .9 1.4	.6 .8 1.4	.6 .8 1.4
Gas and oil	ND	2.8	3.4	3.5	L M H	3.4 3.6 4.2	3.2 3.6 4.8	3.0 3.6 5.4	2.8 3.6 6.0
Repair, insurance, and tolls	S	1.7	2.0	2.1	L M H	1.9 2.1 2.6	1.7 2.1 3.2	1.5 2.2 3.8	1.3 2.2 4.4
Purchased local transport and personal business	–	5.2	5.8	6.9	L M H	6.4 7.3 8.2	6.4 8.1 10.0	6.4 8.7 11.8	6.4 9.3 13.6
Purchased local transport	S	1.0	.8	.6	L M H	.4 .6 .6	.4 .6 .6	.4 .6 .6	.4 .6 .6
Interest, legal and financial services	S	4.1	5.1	6.3	L M H	5.8 6.7 7.7	5.8 7.5 9.5	5.8 8.1 11.3	5.8 8.7 13.1
Personal and medical care	–	6.2	6.8	8.1	L M H	8.0 8.9 9.9	8.0 9.6 11.7	8.0 10.2 13.5	8.0 10.8 15.3
Ophthalmic goods and appliances	D	.3	.3	.4	L M H	.4 .4 .5	.4 .4 .5	.4 .4 .5	.4 .4 .5
Toilet articles and drugs	ND	1.6	1.7	2.1	L M H	2.0 2.3 3.0	2.0 2.5 4.0	2.0 2.7 5.0	2.0 2.9 6.0
Medical and personal services	S	4.4	4.8	5.6	L M H	5.5 6.2 7.0	5.5 6.7 8.0	5.5 7.1 9.0	5.5 7.5 10.0

Table A1–23 (cont'd)

	Type of pur- chase	1950	1955	1960		1970	1980	1990	2000
Recreation, travel, education, and religion	–	7.6	7.8	8.7	L	8.5	8.5	8.5	8.5
					M	9.5	10.5	11.3	12.1
					H	10.5	11.5	12.5	13.5
Books, toys, and sports equipment	D	.8	.9	1.1	L	1.0	1.0	1.0	1.0
					M	1.2	1.4	1.6	1.8
					H	1.4	1.8	2.2	2.6
Newspapers, toys, and plants	ND	1.8	1.7	1.8	L	1.65	1.55	1.45	1.4
					M	1.8	1.8	1.8	1.8
					H	2.1	2.3	2.5	2.7
Amusements	S	1.8	1.6	1.7	L	1.5	1.4	1.3	1.2
					M	1.7	1.7	1.7	1.7
					H	1.8	1.8	1.8	1.8
Domestic intercity travel	S	.5	.4	.5	L	.4	.4	.4	.4
					M	.5	.5	.5	.5
					H	.6	.6	.6	.6
Foreign travel and remittances	[2]	.6	.9	.9	L	.9	.9	.9	.9
					M	1.2	1.6	1.8	2.0
					H	1.9	2.8	3.6	4.4
Private education, religion, and welfare	S	2.1	2.2	2.8	L	2.6	2.6	2.6	2.6
					M	3.1	3.5	3.9	4.3
					H	3.7	4.7	5.7	6.7

Totals:

Durable goods	D	15.6	15.4	13.5	L	12.5	11.8	11.1	10.7
					M	14.4	15.2	15.7	16.3
					H	16.5	19.1	21.7	24.1
Non-durable goods	ND	51.1	48.6	46.3	L	41.2	36.6	32.4	27.8
					M	43.5	40.7	38.2	35.8
					H	50.2	52.2	53.5	56.2
Services	S	33.3	36.0	40.2	L	37.2	36.0	35.4	34.8
					M	42.1	44.1	46.1	48.0
					H	49.8	59.1	68.0	76.8

Direct projections:[3]

Durable goods	D	15.6	15.4	13.5	L	13.5	13.7	13.9	14.1
					M	14.1	14.9	15.7	16.5
					H	15.1	16.7	18.3	19.9
Non-durable goods	ND	51.1	48.6	46.3	L	42.7	38.9	35.1	31.3
					M	43.7	40.9	38.1	35.5
					H	44.7	42.9	41.1	39.3
Services	S	33.3	36.0	40.2	L	41.4	42.6	43.8	45.0
					M	42.2	44.2	46.2	48.0
					H	43.2	46.2	49.2	52.2

1. Historical data from Table A1–22. Projections are on a judgment basis, having regard both to historical trends in percentage distribution and to per capita implications (Tables A1–24 and 25). For a discussion of expected expenditure patterns, see text.

2. See Table A1–26, footnote 8.

3. These totals, like the expenditure detail, are projected on a judgment basis (see footnote 1) and are used in lieu of the added totals when total consumer durables, non-durables, or services are required. In the Medium, where the direct projection method has the effect of "smoothing" the trend, the differences between the directly projected values and the added values may be regarded as statistical error. In the Low and High, the differences also include amounts "non-allocable." (See footnote 6, Table A1–13.)

(1960 dollars)

TABLE A1–24. Historical Data on Per Capita Personal Consumption Expenditures, by Type of Product[1]

	Type of purchase	1946	1947	1948	1949	1950	1951	1952	1953	1954	1955	1956	1957	1958	1959	1960
Disposable personal income	–	1,632	1,535	1,588	1,577	1,674	1,690	1,708	1,759	1,742	1,819	1,877	1,888	1,876	1,936	1,956
Personal savings	–	137	42	92	71	102	132	136	138	128	116	147	144	146	134	127
Personal consumption expenditures	–	1,496	1,493	1,496	1,506	1,572	1,558	1,573	1,621	1,614	1,703	1,729	1,744	1,730	1,801	1,828
Food and tobacco	–	513	490	471	465	463	462	469	473	469	478	488	485	476	485	487
Food and soft beverages	ND	390	377	371	367	365	368	369	375	375	384	394	393	385	390	390
Alcohol and tobacco	ND	123	113	100	99	98	95	99	98	94	94	94	93	90	95	97
Clothing and accessories	–	204	192	188	183	184	179	183	182	179	185	187	186	185	190	188
Clothing and footwear	ND	160	150	149	146	148	144	148	147	145	151	152	153	152	158	156
Cleaning, storage, and repair	S	31	30	29	27	26	25	25	24	23	23	23	22	21	20	21
Jewelry and watches	D	13	12	11	10	10	10	10	11	10	11	12	11	12	12	12
Housing	S	149	158	165	172	181	187	192	195	198	203	208	217	223	229	235
Household durables	–	74	86	89	84	99	92	91	96	92	104	107	103	100	107	105
Furniture and furnishings	D	38	40	41	39	43	42	41	42	39	45	48	47	45	48	47
Household appliances	D	25	36	37	36	45	40	40	43	42	47	48	45	43	47	46
Tableware and utensils	D	11	10	11	10	11	10	10	11	10	11	12	11	11	12	12
Household supplies and operations	–	122	130	132	129	139	141	139	140	140	150	160	162	164	169	175
Paper products and other supplies	ND	35	37	37	36	39	40	37	37	36	38	39	39	38	40	41
Fuel and ice	ND	25	27	28	25	26	25	24	23	23	23	23	22	21	21	20
Gas, electricity, and water	S	23	24	25	27	29	31	32	34	37	41	43	44	46	49	51
Telephone and telegraph	S	12	12	14	14	15	16	17	18	18	19	21	22	22	23	24
Domestic service, maintenance, and repair	S	27	28	29	27	30	29	28	28	26	29	34	35	36	37	38
Passenger car purchases	D	25	42	48	65	84	69	61	81	77	105	85	86	67	85	88
Automobile operating expenses	–	76	78	81	84	91	95	99	105	103	111	112	113	113	118	119
Tires, tubes, and accessories	D	16	18	14	13	17	15	15	15	14	16	15	15	14	16	16
Gas and oil	ND	34	35	38	42	44	47	50	54	55	59	61	62	62	64	64
Repair, insurance, and tolls	S	26	28	29	29	30	32	34	36	34	36	36	36	37	38	39
Purchased local transport and personal business	–	87	85	88	88	94	96	96	100	102	107	112	114	117	121	126
Purchased local transport	S	25	23	22	20	18	18	17	16	15	14	13	13	12	11	11
Interest, legal and financial services	S	62	62	66	68	75	78	79	84	87	93	99	102	105	110	115

Table A1–24 (cont'd)

	Type of purchase	1946	1947	1948	1949	1950	1951	1952	1953	1954	1955	1956	1957	1958	1959	1960
Personal and medical care	–	106	103	104	105	108	109	111	114	118	122	127	131	137	142	147
Ophthalmic goods and appliances	D	4	3	3	3	3	4	4	4	4	4	5	6	6	7	7
Toilet articles and drugs	ND	25	23	23	27	24	26	27	27	27	29	31	32	34	36	38
Medical and personal services	S	78	76	78	78	80	79	81	83	87	88	91	93	96	99	103
Recreation, travel, education, and religion	–	144	135	133	131	129	130	134	135	134	139	145	145	149	155	159
Books, toys, and sports equipment	D	12	12	12	11	11	11	11	13	12	15	16	17	18	19	19
Newspapers, toys, and plants	ND	25	24	25	25	27	28	29	29	28	30	30	30	31	33	33
Amusements	S	45	40	37	36	34	31	31	29	30	30	30	29	29	30	31
Domestic intercity travel	S	14	12	12	10	9	10	10	9	8	8	8	8	8	8	8
Foreign travel and remittances	S[2]	10	9	10	11	10	11	13	16	16	16	17	16	16	17	17
Private education, religion, and welfare	S	39	37	38	38	39	39	39	39	40	41	43	44	47	49	51
Durable goods	D	146	171	178	187	224	200	192	220	212	254	240	239	217	246	246
Non-durable goods	ND	818	786	771	765	774	775	787	797	790	815	832	832	823	842	847
Services	S	532	536	547	554	574	584	593	604	612	634	658	674	691	713	735

ND = Non-durables.　　D = Durables.　　S = Services.

1. Derived from series on personal consumption expenditures and population in Tables A1–26 and A1–1, respectively.　　2. See Table A1–26, footnote 8.

TABLE A1–25.   Projected Per Capita Personal Consumption Expenditures, by Type of Product[1]

(1960 dollars)

	Type of purchase	1950	1955	1960		1970	1980	1990	2000
Disposable personal income	–	1,674	1,819	1,956	L	2,260	2,600	3,010	3,500
					M	2,400	3,000	3,550	4,320
					H	2,510	3,210	4,110	5,255
Personal consumption expenditures	–	1,572	1,703	1,828	L	2,110	2,450	2,840	3,300
					M	2,220	2,700	3,290	4,000
					H	2,290	2,880	3,620	4,550
Food and tobacco	–	463	478	487	L	506	524	542	561
					M	542	600	664	726
					H	630	792	996	1,251
Food and soft beverages	ND	365	384	390	L	403	412	420	429
					M	435	481	539	598
					H	515	648	814	1,024
Alcohol and tobacco	ND	98	94	97	L	95	96	94	89
					M	107	119	125	128
					H	121	153	192	241
Clothing and accessories	–	184	185	188	L	188	189	187	188
					M	213	238	273	315
					H	243	305	384	482
Clothing and footwear	ND	148	151	156	L	156	157	159	162
					M	175	197	224	256
					H	202	253	319	400
Cleaning, storage, and repair	S	26	23	21	L	17	15	11	7
					M	22	22	26	32
					H	27	35	43	55
Jewelry and watches	D	10	11	12	L	13	13	14	16
					M	16	19	23	28
					H	16	20	29	36
Housing	S	181	203	235	L	257	287	327	380
					M	291	351	428	518
					H	339	478	659	901
Household durables	–	99	104	105	L	116	135	156	182
					M	138	184	237	303
					H	153	222	315	441
Furniture and furnishings	D	43	45	47	L	42	39	37	36
					M	60	73	89	108
					H	66	89	119	159
Household appliances	D	45	47	46	L	46	54	62	73
					M	64	95	128	171
					H	80	130	199	296
Tableware and utensils	D	11	11	12	L	13	15	17	20
					M	13	16	20	24
					H	16	20	25	32

Table A1–25 (cont'd)

(1960 dollars)

	Type of purchase	1950	1955	1960		1970	1980	1990	2000
Household supplies and operations	–	139	150	175	L M H	192 209 229	218 254 314	247 312 434	280 384 601
Paper products and other supplies	ND	39	38	41	L M H	42 47 53	44 54 66	45 63 83	46 68 105
Fuel and ice	ND	26	23	20	L M H	15 18 23	10 14 23	6 10 22	3 8 18
Gas, electricity, and water	S	29	41	51	L M H	59 71 101	69 97 1,173	80 132 268	92 176 400
Telephone and telegraph	S	15	19	24	L M H	25 29 41	29 35 63	34 43 94	40 52 136
Domestic service, maintenance, and repair	S	30	29	38	L M H	36 44 62	37 54 95	43 66 145	50 80 209
Passenger car purchases	D	84	105	88	L M H	103 111 128	115 135 184	128 164 264	142 199 369
Automobile operating expenses	–	91	111	119	L M H	135 147 160	154 178 213	176 217 282	201 263 373
Tires, tubes, and accessories	D	17	16	16	L M H	17 20 27	17 24 40	17 26 51	20 32 64
Gas and oil	ND	44	59	64	L M H	72 80 96	78 97 138	85 118 195	92 144 273
Repair, insurance, and tolls	S	30	36	39	L M H	40 47 60	42 57 82	43 72 138	43 88 200
Purchased local transport and personal business	–	94	107	126	L M H	135 162 188	157 219 288	182 286 427	211 371 619
Purchased local transport	S	18	14	11	L M H	8 13 14	10 16 17	11 20 22	13 24 27
Interest, legal and financial services	S	75	93	115	L M H	122 149 176	142 203 274	165 266 409	191 347 596
Personal and medical care	–	108	122	147	L M H	169 198 227	196 259 337	227 335 489	264 431 696
Ophthalmic goods and appliances	D	3	4	7	L M H	8 9 11	10 11 14	11 13 18	13 16 23
Toilet articles and drugs	ND	24	29	38	L M H	42 51 69	49 67 115	57 89 181	66 116 273
Medical and personal services	S	80	88	103	L M H	116 138 160	135 181 230	156 233 326	182 299 455

Table A1–25 (cont'd)

(1960 dollars)

	Type of pur-chase	1950	1955	1960		1970	1980	1990	2000
Recreation, travel, education, and religion	–	129	139	159	L M H	179 211 240	208 284 331	241 372 452	280 483 614
Books, toys, and sports equipment	D	11	15	19	L M H	21 27 32	24 38 52	28 53 80	33 72 118
Newspapers, toys, and plants	ND	27	30	33	L M H	35 40 48	38 49 66	42 59 90	46 72 123
Amusements	S	34	30	31	L M H	32 38 41	34 46 52	37 56 65	40 68 82
Domestic intercity travel	S	9	8	8	L M H	8 11 14	10 14 17	11 16 22	13 20 27
Foreign travel and remittances	2	10	16	17	L M H	19 27 44	22 43 80	26 59 130	30 80 200
Private education, religion, and welfare	S	39	41	51	L M H	55 69 85	64 95 135	74 128 206	86 171 305
Totals:[3] Durable goods	D	224	254	247	L M H	263 320 376	287 411 549	314 516 785	353 650 1,097
Non-durable goods	ND	776	816	847	L M H	869 966 1,149	895 1,100 1,502	921 1,257 1,961	948 1,430 2,557
Services	S	571	633	735	L M H	785 936 1,142	885 1,119 1,691	1,005 1,516 2,462	1,152 1,915 3,493
Direct projections:[3] Durable goods	D	220	250	250	L M H	280 310 350	340 400 480	390 520 660	470 660 910
Non-durable goods	ND	770	810	850	L M H	900 970 1,020	950 1,110 1,240	1,000 1,250 1,490	1,030 1,420 1,790
Services	S	580	640	730	L M H	870 940 990	1,040 1,190 1,330	1,240 1,520 1,780	1,480 1,920 2,380

ND = Non-durables.   D = Durables.   S = Services.
1. Historical data from Table A1–24. Projections derived by applying percentages in Table A1–23 to Low, Medium, and High per capita expenditures, Table A1–12.
2. See Table A1–26, footnote 8.

3. The differences between the added totals and the "direct" totals represent "statistical error," plus, in the Low and the High, "non-allocable" expenditures. See footnote 3, Table A1–23, and footnote 6, Table A1–13. For use in comparison, historical data in the "direct" series are rounded.

TABLE A1–26. Historical Data on Aggregate Personal Consumption Expenditures, by Type of Product[1]

(Billion 1960 dollars)

	Content in terms of NIA classes[2]	Type of purchase	De-flator[3]	1946	1947	1948	1949	1950	1951	1952	1953	1954	1955	1956	1957	1958	1959	1960
Disposable personal income	I	–		230.7	221.2	232.8	235.3	253.9	260.9	268.2	280.8	282.9	300.6	315.7	323.3	326.7	342.8	351.8
Personal savings				19.4	6.1	13.5	10.6	15.5	20.3	21.3	22.1	20.8	19.1	24.8	24.7	25.5	23.8	22.9
Personal consumption expenditures				211.5	215.1	219.3	224.7	238.4	240.6	246.9	258.7	262.1	281.5	290.9	298.6	301.2	319.0	328.9
Food and tobacco	I	–		72.6	70.6	69.0	69.4	70.3	71.4	73.6	75.5	76.2	79.0	82.0	83.1	82.8	85.9	87.6
Food and soft beverages	1–4	ND	3	55.2	54.3	54.4	54.7	55.4	56.8	58.0	59.9	60.9	63.5	66.2	67.2	67.1	69.0	70.2
Alcohol and tobacco[4]	5+[4]	ND	6	17.4	16.3	14.6	14.7	14.9	14.6	15.6	15.6	15.3	15.5	15.8	15.9	15.7	16.9	17.4
Clothing and accessories	II	–		28.8	27.6	27.6	27.3	27.9	27.6	28.8	29.1	29.0	30.6	31.4	31.9	32.2	33.6	33.9
Clothing and footwear	1, 3, 4	ND	4	22.6	21.6	21.8	21.8	22.4	22.2	23.3	23.5	23.5	24.9	25.6	26.2	26.4	27.9	28.1
Cleaning, storage, and repair	2, 5, 6, 8	S	10	4.4	4.3	4.2	4.0	4.0	3.9	3.9	3.9	3.8	3.8	3.8	3.8	3.7	3.6	3.7
Jewelry and watches	7	D	2	1.8	1.7	1.6	1.5	1.5	1.5	1.6	1.7	1.7	1.9	2.0	1.9	2.1	2.1	2.1
Housing[5]	IV	S	7	21.0	22.7	24.2	25.7	27.4	28.8	30.1	31.2	32.1	33.5	35.0	37.1	38.8	40.5	42.2
Household durables	V	–		10.5	12.4	13.0	12.6	15.0	14.2	14.3	15.3	15.0	17.2	18.0	17.6	17.4	19.0	18.8
Furniture and furnishings	1, 4	D	2	5.4	5.7	6.0	5.8	6.5	6.5	6.4	6.7	6.4	7.5	8.0	8.0	7.9	8.5	8.4
Household appliances[6]	2 & IX.5	D	2	3.6	5.2	5.4	5.3	6.9	6.1	6.3	6.9	6.9	7.8	8.0	7.7	7.5	8.4	8.3
Tableware and utensils	3	D	2	1.5	1.5	1.6	1.5	1.6	1.6	1.6	1.7	1.7	1.9	2.0	1.9	2.0	2.1	2.1
Household supplies and operations	V	–		17.3	18.7	19.4	19.3	21.1	21.8	21.8	22.4	22.8	24.8	26.9	27.8	28.6	30.0	31.5
Paper products and other supplies	5–7	ND	6	5.0	5.4	5.4	5.4	5.9	6.1	5.8	5.9	5.9	6.3	6.5	6.6	6.7	7.1	7.4
Fuel and ice	8d	ND	6	3.6	3.9	4.1	3.7	4.0	3.9	3.8	3.7	3.7	3.8	3.8	3.8	3.7	3.7	3.6
Gas, electricity, and water	8a–c	S	8	3.2	3.5	3.7	4.0	4.4	4.8	5.1	5.5	6.0	6.7	7.3	7.6	8.0	8.6	9.2
Telephone and telegraph	9	S	8	1.7	1.8	2.0	2.1	2.3	2.5	2.7	2.9	2.9	3.2	3.5	3.8	3.9	4.1	4.4
Domestic service, maintenance, and repair	10, 11, IX.6	S	8	3.8	4.1	4.2	4.1	4.5	4.5	4.4	4.4	4.3	4.8	5.8	6.0	6.3	6.5	6.9
Passenger car purchases[7]	VIII.1a	D	1	3.5	6.1	7.1	9.7	12.8	10.6	9.5	13.0	12.5	17.3	14.3	14.8	11.6	15.1	15.8
Automobile operating expenses	VIII.1	–		10.7	11.3	11.9	12.5	13.8	14.7	15.5	16.7	16.7	18.3	18.8	19.4	19.7	20.9	21.4
Tires, tubes, and accessories	b	D	1	2.2	2.2	2.1	2.0	2.6	2.4	2.3	2.4	2.3	2.7	2.5	2.6	2.5	2.8	2.8
Gas and oil	d	ND	5	4.8	5.1	5.6	6.2	6.6	7.3	7.9	8.6	8.9	9.7	10.2	10.6	10.8	11.3	11.6
Repair, insurance, and tolls	c, e, f	S	9	3.7	4.0	4.2	4.3	4.6	5.0	5.3	5.7	5.6	5.9	6.1	6.2	6.4	6.8	7.0
Purchased local transport and personal business	–	–		12.3	12.3	12.9	13.2	14.2	14.8	15.1	15.9	16.5	17.7	18.9	19.6	20.3	21.5	22.6
Purchased local transport	VIII.2	S	9	3.5	3.3	3.2	3.0	2.8	2.7	2.7	2.4	2.4	2.3	2.2	2.2	2.1	2.0	2.0
Interest, legal and financial services	VII	S	10	8.8	9.0	9.7	10.2	11.4	12.0	12.4	13.4	14.1	15.4	16.7	17.4	18.2	19.5	20.6

Item	Ref.	Type	Defl.	1946	1947	1948	1949	1950	1951	1952	1953	1954	1955	1956	1957	1958	1959	1960
Personal and medical care	—			15.0	14.8	15.3	15.7	16.4	16.8	17.5	18.2	19.2	20.1	21.4	22.5	23.8	25.2	26.5
Ophthalmic goods and appliances	VI.2	D	2	.5	.5	.5	.5	.5	.6	.6	.6	.6	.7	.8	1.0	1.0	1.2	1.2
Toilet articles and drugs	III.1, VI.1	ND	6	3.5	3.3	3.3	3.5	3.7	4.0	4.2	4.3	4.4	4.8	5.3	5.5	6.0	6.4	6.8
Medical and personal services	III.2, VI.3–8	S	10	11.0	11.0	11.5	11.7	12.2	12.2	12.7	13.3	14.2	14.6	15.3	16.0	16.8	17.6	18.5
Recreation, travel, education, and religion	—			20.4	19.4	19.5	19.5	19.6	20.1	21.0	21.5	21.8	22.9	24.4	24.9	26.0	27.4	28.6
Books, toys, and sports equipment	IX.1, 4	D	2	1.7	1.7	1.7	1.7	1.6	1.7	1.8	2.0	2.0	2.4	2.7	2.9	3.1	3.3	3.5
Newspapers, toys, and plants	IX.2, 3, 7	ND	6	3.5	3.5	3.6	3.4	3.8	4.1	4.4	4.6	4.6	4.9	5.1	5.2	5.4	5.8	5.9
Amusements	IX.8–12	S	10	6.3	5.8	5.4	5.3	5.3	5.1	4.8	4.8	4.8	4.9	5.1	5.1	5.1	5.3	5.9
Domestic intercity transport	VIII.3	S[8]	9	2.0	1.8	1.7	1.5	1.5	1.3	1.5	1.4	1.5	1.3	1.4	1.4	1.4	1.4	1.5
Foreign travel and remittances	XII	S	10	1.4	1.3	1.3	1.5	1.6	1.5	1.5	2.1	2.6	2.7	2.8	2.8	2.8	3.0	3.0
Private education, religion, and welfare	X, XI	S	10	5.5	5.4	5.6	5.7	5.9	6.0	6.2	6.2	6.5	6.7	7.3	7.6	8.2	8.6	9.2
Durable goods		D		20.6	24.7	26.1	27.9	34.0	30.9	30.2	35.1	34.4	42.0	40.3	40.9	37.7	43.6	44.3
Non-durable goods		ND		75.2	77.2	80.2	82.6	87.0	90.1	93.1	96.4	99.4	104.8	110.6	115.3	120.3	126.2	132.2
Services		S		115.7	113.2	113.0	114.2	117.4	119.6	123.6	127.2	128.3	134.7	140.0	142.4	143.2	149.2	152.4

ND = Non-durables. D = Durables. S = Services.

1. Sources of undeflated data: 1946–60, Table II-4, *U.S. Income and Output* and National Income Number of *Survey of Current Business*, July 1961. The current dollar data aggregated from these sources are converted to 1960 dollars by means of implicit price deflators (see footnote 3) for selected broad classes of consumer purchases (Table VII-13, *U.S. Income and Output* and July 1961 *Survey of Current Business*), shifted to a 1960 base. Consequently, the detail will not add to the totals of durables, non-durables, and services, which were differently deflated (see Note to Table A1–9), nor to total expenditures, which were deflated by the series for this item given in Table A1–7. Latter also used to deflate savings and disposable personal income.

2. NIA = National Income Accounts. Numerical references are to the items as numbered in *U.S. Income and Output*, Table II-4.

3. Reference numbers are to the following series of deflators:

	1946	1947	1948	1949	1950	1951	1952	1953	1954	1955	1956	1957	1958	1959	1960
Durables:															
1. Automotive	69.6	75.3	80.7	83.7	84.1	88.8	92.9	91.0	89.4	91.3	93.7	98.2	98.7	101.1	100.0
2. Other	81.6	88.3	91.4	91.2	92.8	99.9	98.8	95.5	97.8	96.2	96.9	98.9	99.5	99.6	100.0
Non-durables:															
3. Food	73.7	84.3	88.5	84.9	85.7	94.1	96.2	94.5	94.7	93.3	94.0	97.0	100.5	99.1	100.0
4. Clothing	80.6	87.1	92.4	88.5	87.6	95.3	93.6	93.4	93.6	93.8	95.6	96.9	97.3	98.4	100.0
5. Gasoline	63.0	70.6	79.2	81.0	81.1	82.7	84.4	88.0	89.8	90.8	93.5	97.6	96.6	97.5	100.0
6. Other	68.0	76.6	82.5	81.5	82.5	87.4	87.8	89.5	89.5	90.5	92.4	95.5	97.1	98.5	100.0
Services:															
7. Housing	65.8	68.6	72.8	75.0	77.5	80.7	84.2	88.1	90.7	91.8	93.4	95.1	97.0	98.5	100.0
8. Household	76.1	78.3	80.4	82.0	83.4	85.5	88.8	91.6	92.0	92.3	93.2	94.4	96.3	97.8	100.0
9. Transportation	55.8	60.9	66.1	69.6	72.4	75.1	78.6	83.8	85.8	87.1	89.5	90.8	92.5	97.4	100.0
10. Other	56.5	63.2	67.7	68.7	70.1	74.2	77.3	80.5	82.5	84.5	87.4	91.0	93.6	97.0	100.0

4. Alcohol transferred from food category to this category; see footnote to food item in *U.S. Income and Output*, Table II-4.

5. Includes rent, space-rental value of owner-occupied dwellings, and expenditures for hotel accommodations.

6. Mostly electric, including radio and TV.

7. Including home-type trailers and dealers' margins on used cars.

8. About half of this category is currently attributable to services and half to non-durable goods. The latter arises out of purchases by U.S. government personnel abroad. The former is net of expenditures of foreigners in the United States.

TABLE A1–27.   Projected Aggregate Personal Consumption Expenditures, by Type of Product[1]

(Billion 1960 dollars)

	Type of pur- chase	1950	1955	1960		1970	1980	1990	2000
Disposable personal income	–	253.9	300.6	351.8	L M H	479 499 542	647 715 840	868 1,020 1,305	1,134 1,426 1,998
Personal consumption expenditures	–	238.4	281.5	328.9	L M H	448 462 495	610 662 753	819 944 1,150	1,070 1,320 1,730
Food and tobacco	–	70.3	79.0	87.6	L M H	107.5 112.7 136.1	130.5 147.0 207.1	156.4 190.7 316.2	181.9 240.2 475.8
Food and soft beverages	ND	55.4	63.5	70.2	L M H	85.6 90.6 111.4	102.5 117.8 169.4	121.2 154.8 258.8	139.1 198.0 389.2
Alcohol and tobacco	ND	14.9	15.5	17.4	L M H	20.2 22.2 26.2	23.8 29.1 39.9	27.0 35.9 61.0	28.9 42.2 91.7
Clothing and accessories	–	27.9	30.6	33.9	L M H	39.9 44.4 52.5	47.0 58.3 79.8	54.1 78.4 121.9	61.0 104.3 183.4
Clothing and footwear	ND	22.4	24.9	28.1	L M H	33.2 36.5 43.6	39.0 48.3 66.3	45.9 64.2 101.2	52.4 84.5 152.2
Cleaning, storage, and repair	S	4.0	3.8	3.7	L M H	3.6 4.6 5.9	3.7 5.3 9.0	3.3 7.6 13.8	2.1 10.6 20.8
Jewelry and watches	D	1.5	1.9	2.1	L M H	2.7 3.2 3.5	3.4 4.6 5.3	4.1 6.6 9.2	5.4 9.2 13.8
Housing	S	27.4	33.5	42.2	L M H	54.7 60.5 73.3	71.4 86.1 125.0	94.2 122.7 209.3	123.1 171.6 342.5
Household durables	–	15.0	17.2	18.8	L M H	24.6 28.6 33.2	33.6 45.0 58.0	45.0 68.0 100.0	58.8 100.3 167.8
Furniture and furnishings	D	6.5	7.5	8.4	L M H	9.0 12.5 14.4	9.8 17.9 23.3	10.6 25.5 38.0	11.8 35.6 60.6
Household appliances	D	6.9	7.8	8.3	L M H	9.9 13.4 17.3	13.4 23.2 33.9	18.0 36.8 63.2	23.5 56.8 112.4
Tableware and utensils	D	1.6	1.9	2.1	L M H	2.7 2.8 3.5	3.7 4.0 5.3	4.9 5.7 8.0	6.4 7.9 12.1

Table A1–27 (cont'd)

(Billion 1960 dollars)

	Type of pur-chase	1950	1955	1960		1970	1980	1990	2000
Household supplies and operations	–	21.1	24.8	31.5	L	40.8	54.3	71.3	91.0
					M	43.4	62.2	89.7	125.4
					H	49.5	82.1	138.0	228.4
Paper products and other supplies	ND	5.9	6.3	7.4	L	9.0	11.0	13.1	15.0
					M	9.7	13.2	17.9	22.4
					H	11.4	17.3	26.4	39.8
Fuel and ice	ND	4.0	3.8	3.6	L	3.1	2.4	1.6	1.1
					M	3.7	3.3	2.8	2.6
					H	5.0	6.0	6.9	6.9
Gas, electricity, and water	S	4.4	6.7	9.2	L	12.5	17.1	22.9	30.0
					M	14.8	23.8	37.8	58.1
					H	21.8	45.2	85.1	152.2
Telephone and telegraph	S	2.3	3.2	4.4	L	5.4	7.3	9.8	12.8
					M	6.0	8.6	12.3	17.2
					H	8.9	16.6	29.9	51.9
Domestic service, maintenance, and repair	S	4.5	4.8	6.9	L	7.6	9.2	12.3	16.0
					M	9.2	13.2	18.9	26.4
					H	13.4	24.8	46.0	79.6
Passenger car purchases	D	12.8	17.3	15.8	L	22.0	28.7	36.9	46.0
					M	23.1	33.1	47.2	66.0
					H	27.7	48.2	84.0	140.1
Automobile operating expenses	–	13.8	18.3	21.4	L	28.7	38.4	50.8	65.3
					M	30.5	43.7	62.3	87.1
					H	34.6	55.7	89.7	141.9
Tires, tubes, and accessories	D	2.6	2.7	2.8	L	3.6	4.6	4.9	6.4
					M	4.2	6.0	7.6	10.6
					H	5.9	10.5	16.1	24.2
Gas and oil	ND	6.6	9.7	11.6	L	15.2	19.5	24.6	30.0
					M	16.6	23.8	34.0	47.5
					H	20.8	36.1	62.1	103.8
Repair, insurance, and tolls	S	4.6	5.9	7.0	L	8.5	10.4	12.3	13.9
					M	9.7	13.9	20.8	29.0
					H	12.9	24.1	43.7	76.1
Purchased local transport and personal business	–	14.2	17.7	22.6	L	28.7	39.0	52.4	68.5
					M	33.7	53.6	82.1	122.8
					H	40.6	75.3	135.7	235.3
Purchased local transport	S	2.8	2.3	2.0	L	1.8	2.4	3.3	4.3
					M	2.8	4.0	5.7	7.9
					H	3.0	4.5	6.9	10.4
Interest, legal and financial services	S	11.4	15.4	20.6	L	26.0	35.4	47.5	62.1
					M	31.0	49.7	76.5	114.8
					H	38.1	71.5	130.0	226.6
Personal and medical care	–	16.4	20.1	26.5	L	35.8	48.8	65.5	85.6
					M	41.1	63.6	96.3	142.6
					H	49.0	88.1	155.2	264.7
Ophthalmic goods and appliances	D	.5	.7	1.2	L	1.8	2.4	3.3	4.3
					M	1.8	2.6	3.8	5.3
					H	2.5	3.8	5.8	8.6
Toilet articles and drugs	ND	3.7	4.8	6.8	L	9.0	12.2	16.4	21.4
					M	10.6	16.6	25.5	38.3
					H	14.9	30.1	57.5	103.8
Medical and personal services	S	12.2	14.6	18.5	L	24.6	33.6	45.0	58.8
					M	28.6	44.4	67.0	99.0
					H	34.6	60.2	103.5	173.0

Table A1–27 (cont'd)

(Billion 1960 dollars)

	Type of pur-chase	1950	1955	1960		1970	1980	1990	2000
Recreation, travel, education, and religion	–	19.6	22.9	28.6	L	38.1	51.9	69.6	91.0
					M	43.9	69.5	106.7	159.7
					H	52.0	86.6	143.8	233.6
Books, toys, and sports equipment	D	1.7	2.4	3.5	L	4.5	6.1	8.2	10.7
					M	5.5	9.3	15.1	23.8
					H	6.9	13.6	25.3	45.0
Newspapers, toys, and plants	ND	4.1	4.9	5.9	L	7.4	9.5	11.9	15.0
					M	8.3	11.9	17.0	23.8
					H	10.4	17.3	28.8	46.7
Amusements	S	5.1	4.9	5.5	L	6.7	8.5	10.6	12.8
					M	7.9	11.3	16.0	22.4
					H	8.9	13.6	20.7	31.1
Domestic intercity travel	S	1.3	1.3	1.5	L	1.8	2.4	3.3	4.3
					M	2.3	3.3	4.7	6.6
					H	3.0	4.5	6.9	10.4
Foreign travel and remittances	[2]	1.5	2.7	3.0	L	4.0	5.5	7.4	9.6
					M	5.5	10.6	17.0	26.4
					H	9.4	21.1	41.4	76.1
Private education, religion, and welfare	S	5.9	6.7	9.2	L	11.6	15.9	21.3	27.8
					M	14.3	23.2	36.8	56.8
					H	18.3	35.4	71.3	115.9
Totals:[3] Durable goods	D	34.1	42.2	44.2	L	56.2	72.1	91	114
					M	66.5	101	148	215
					H	81.7	144	250	417
Non-durable goods	ND	117.8	134.7	153.5	L	185	223	241	308
					M	201	269	358	472
					H	248	396	623	972
Services	S	86.7	104.5	132.2	L	167	220	289	373
					M	194	292	432	624
					H	247	445	788	1,269
Direct projections: Durables	D	34.0	42.0	44.3	L	60.5	83.6	114	151
					M	65.1	98.6	148	218
					H	74.7	125.8	210	344
Non-durables	ND	117.4	134.7	152.4	L	191	237	287	335
					M	202	271	360	469
					H	221	323	473	680
Services	S	87.0	104.8	132.2	L	186	260	359	482
					M	195	293	436	634
					H	214	348	566	903

ND = Non-durables.   D = Durables.   S = Services.

1. Historical data from Table A1–26. The projections are computed by applying the percentages projected in Table A1–23 to projected total personal consumption expenditures, Table A1–12. They thus allow for the compensating effect of population size on range of per capita expenditures.

2. See Table A1–26, footnote 8.

3. The difference between the added totals and the "direct" totals represents "statistical error," plus, in the Low and the High, "non-allocable" expenditures. See footnote 3, Table A1–23, and footnote 6, Table A1–13.

TABLE A1–28. Historical Data on FRB Index of Industrial Production and Principal Components[1]

	1947	1948	1949	1950	1951	1952	1953	1954	1955	1956	1957	1958	1959	1960
INDUSTRIAL PRODUCTION, TOTAL	65.3	68.0	64.3	74.5	80.8	83.8	90.8	85.4	96.0	99.3	100.0	92.9	104.9	108.0
Manufacturing, total	66.1	68.6	64.8	75.5	81.5	84.8	92.1	85.8	96.7	99.5	100.0	92.4	105.3	108.2
Durable manufactures, total	61.8	64.4	58.5	71.3	80.3	85.1	96.0	85.0	97.9	100.0	100.0	86.8	101.5	104.3
Primary and fabricated metals	78.3	80.6	70.0	87.0	93.9	88.3	99.7	84.4	102.0	101.1	100.0	83.6	95.4	96.8
Primary metals	80.8	84.1	70.8	89.1	96.9	88.5	100.3	81.3	105.5	103.7	100.0	78.0	89.5	90.3
Iron and steel	81.7	85.5	73.0	89.9	100.5	88.5	102.0	80.0	105.7	103.2	100.0	75.4	85.9	87.9
Nonferrous metals and products	76.1	77.7	62.3	83.9	83.5	85.9	93.4	86.6	104.8	105.7	100.0	88.5	103.9	100.2
Primary aluminum	34.7	37.7	36.6	43.6	50.7	56.7	76.0	88.6	95.0	101.7	100.0	97.6	122.0	125.6
Other nonferrous metals	78.3	75.2	67.2	80.7	84.6	94.1	97.0	85.5	95.6	99.9	100.0	80.0	76.8	87.1
Primary copper (smelting and refining)	79.4	78.1	70.3	82.9	79.8	77.9	86.5	79.4	92.9	100.6	100.0	91.2	75.7	103.7
Primary lead	89.4	84.3	89.7	94.5	80.5	87.8	88.3	91.1	90.5	101.1	100.0	86.5	63.1	68.8
Primary magnesium	15.2	12.2	14.2	19.3	50.1	129.7	114.6	85.8	75.1	83.9	100.0	37.1	37.8	49.2
Primary zinc	81.0	79.8	82.0	85.3	87.9	90.3	91.5	81.4	96.8	99.6	100.0	78.8	81.3	81.9
Secondary nonferrous metals	102.6	96.5	71.5	100.2	107.8	103.2	103.0	94.3	110.9	106.7	100.0	84.1	100.1	93.5
Nonferrous shapes and castings	80.7	83.8	63.5	90.5	88.2	90.1	97.0	86.5	110.1	108.6	100.0	89.1	108.0	98.1
Fabricated metal products	74.9	76.2	68.8	84.2	90.0	87.8	98.8	88.8	96.9	97.4	100.0	91.6	103.9	106.0
Machinery and related products	51.4	53.7	49.9	60.6	72.5	82.6	94.9	83.7	95.0	98.4	100.0	85.8	101.7	105.8
Machinery	62.6	63.8	56.7	69.7	79.6	88.4	96.4	84.3	92.6	102.8	100.0	85.2	102.8	106.4
Non-electrical machinery	73.8	74.2	63.3	71.0	90.3	98.0	101.1	86.2	92.7	103.3	100.0	82.6	99.3	102.2
Electrical machinery	50.5	52.4	49.2	67.3	67.7	77.4	89.9	81.5	92.5	102.1	100.0	88.9	107.6	112.3
Transportation equipment	40.3	44.0	44.2	52.9	59.0	68.6	86.2	78.7	95.9	91.5	100.0	84.2	97.8	101.7
Motor vehicles and parts	64.2	69.6	71.4	91.8	84.1	72.1	91.5	82.5	117.9	94.7	100.0	76.5	100.3	114.7
Aircraft and other equipment	22.3	24.9	25.0	25.4	41.4	66.1	82.2	76.0	76.5	88.8	100.0	90.5	93.9	88.6
Instruments and related products	54.8	56.4	50.3	58.5	67.1	79.7	87.0	84.7	90.5	97.3	100.0	94.1	112.2	118.9
Clay, glass, and lumber	77.7	81.8	74.1	89.9	94.3	91.6	95.1	92.0	103.3	104.7	100.0	96.5	111.3	108.5
Clay, glass, and stone products	68.0	72.5	67.6	81.8	90.4	86.4	88.6	85.2	97.2	101.7	100.0	94.7	110.2	109.6
Lumber and products	91.8	95.6	84.3	102.5	102.2	100.9	106.7	103.9	114.2	109.9	100.0	99.7	113.1	106.5
Furniture and fixtures	70.1	72.7	67.1	81.9	77.4	79.6	83.2	86.8	98.6	101.8	100.0	96.1	114.9	119.7
Miscellaneous manufactures	80.4	85.8	79.5	89.6	86.8	89.2	100.6	91.1	102.0	105.1	100.0	95.2	108.6	112.6

Table A1–28 (cont'd)

	1947	1948	1949	1950	1951	1952	1953	1954	1955	1956	1957	1958	1959	1960
Non-durable manufactures, total	70.0	72.3	71.1	79.1	81.7	83.3	86.9	86.9	95.0	98.9	100.0	99.9	110.3	113.4
Textile, apparel, and leather products	83.5	87.1	83.1	91.9	90.1	92.2	93.6	89.6	98.4	101.1	100.0	99.2	115.2	114.8
Textile mill products	88.0	94.2	87.1	99.0	98.0	97.2	99.1	92.7	102.4	104.1	100.0	97.7	113.2	108.8
Apparel products	76.7	79.9	79.2	85.2	83.7	88.0	89.7	86.6	95.1	98.9	100.0	101.1	119.9	124.3
Leather products	93.4	89.0	84.7	91.6	85.9	91.4	91.8	90.9	98.8	100.6	100.0	96.8	105.5	100.4
Paper and printing	68.1	70.9	70.8	78.4	81.1	79.4	84.5	86.9	94.6	99.3	100.0	99.2	107.6	111.5
Paper and products	64.9	66.7	63.8	76.8	81.3	77.5	84.3	85.3	96.2	100.7	100.0	101.0	110.9	111.9
Pulp and paper	65.3	68.1	63.7	76.3	83.4	79.4	85.5	86.2	96.8	102.8	100.0	100.3	110.9	111.9
Converted paper products	64.4	65.1	63.8	77.3	79.2	75.5	83.1	84.2	95.4	99.1	100.0	101.7	111.0	111.9
Printing and publishing	70.4	74.0	75.9	79.5	81.0	80.8	84.6	88.0	93.4	98.3	100.0	97.9	105.3	111.4
Chemical, petroleum, and rubber products	50.6	54.1	52.7	64.7	71.8	74.5	80.2	79.3	91.8	96.3	100.0	98.8	112.7	117.7
Chemicals and products	45.4	49.1	48.4	60.5	68.6	71.7	77.5	76.8	89.2	95.5	100.0	99.7	114.3	121.2
Industrial chemicals	36.7	41.5	40.9	52.3	61.1	63.7	73.4	73.0	89.2	95.0	100.0	98.2	118.4	126.8
Chemical products	54.6	57.2	56.3	69.1	76.5	80.1	81.6	80.6	89.1	95.9	100.0	101.3	110.2	115.5
Drugs, soaps, and toiletries	47.8	51.0	52.2	64.3	74.2	77.7	79.1	78.2	85.4	94.8	100.0	102.3	111.3	118.4
Paints	83.0	82.6	71.7	89.3	85.5	88.5	90.1	87.1	103.5	100.3	100.0	97.3	104.6	102.5
Fertilizers	64.4	67.8	69.2	75.0	82.2	90.1	92.8	97.6	98.6	98.7	100.0	99.7	112.2	114.8
Petroleum products	63.8	69.1	66.9	73.8	82.5	84.4	89.5	88.8	95.4	100.1	100.0	98.8	105.4	108.1
Rubber and plastic products	57.8	58.7	55.4	71.7	73.3	75.2	80.7	79.2	98.1	95.7	100.0	95.0	114.0	114.3
Foods, beverages, and tobacco	83.4	82.7	83.6	86.5	88.3	90.2	91.2	92.8	96.2	99.8	100.0	102.1	106.5	109.4
Mining, total	76.4	80.3	71.2	79.5	87.3	86.5	88.8	86.2	94.8	100.1	100.0	91.4	95.3	97.1
Coal	137.3	131.1	96.8	111.3	114.2	100.4	94.8	81.7	96.6	103.4	100.0	82.5	82.3	82.6
Crude oil and natural gas	63.9	70.4	66.6	73.0	82.5	85.2	89.2	89.2	95.3	100.0	100.0	93.6	98.6	98.5
Metals	73.4	75.7	68.0	78.4	84.3	77.8	86.6	70.9	89.8	94.7	100.0	82.5	77.1	96.8
Stone and earth minerals	55.0	59.9	57.9	66.2	72.3	75.5	77.5	85.4	92.8	100.3	100.0	98.4	108.0	112.1
Utilities, total	38.9	43.4	46.3	52.7	60.1	65.2	71.1	76.5	85.4	93.6	100.0	104.5	115.0	123.1
Electricity	38.6	43.3	46.2	52.0	59.0	64.3	71.1	76.0	85.4	93.5	100.0	104.3	115.2	123.2
Gas	39.4	43.6	46.2	54.3	62.6	67.3	70.9	78.0	85.2	93.8	100.0	105.0	114.4	122.5

1. Source: Federal Reserve Board, *Industrial Production, 1959 Revision* (July 1960), and various current releases. In some instances, the data have been re-arranged or combined by means of arithmetic weighted averages (the method used by the FRB).

TABLE A1–29. Projected FRB Index of Industrial Production and Principal Components[1]

(1957 = 100)

	1950	1955	1960		1970	1980	1990	2000
INDUSTRIAL PRODUCTION, TOTAL	74.5	96.0	108.0	L	148	203	278	380
				M	164	249	375	564
				H	182	305	506	836
Manufacturing, total	75.5	96.7	108.2	L	150	208	287	395
				M	166	254	387	587
				H	184	311	522	870
Durable manufactures, total	71.3	97.9	104.3	L	139	181	248	334
				M	176	275	425	658
				H	214	386	670	1,175
Primary and fabricated metals	87.0	102.0	96.8	L	112	131	158	195
				M	143	195	270	388
				H	179	278	434	711
Primary metals	89.1	105.5	90.3	L	102	112	131	154
				M	129	168	222	303
				H	161	237	352	540
Iron and steel	89.9	105.7	87.9	L	92	95	105	112
				M	122	151	190	247
				H	156	220	317	474
Nonferrous metals and products	83.9	104.8	100.2	L	117	144	185	235
				M	157	237	351	532
				H	215	393	640	1,131
Primary aluminum	43.6	95.0	125.6	L	128	172	220	281
				M	178	292	439	661
				H	267	531	839	1,479
Other nonferrous metals	80.7	95.6	87.1	L	82	89	104	128
				M	109	138	194	279
				H	138	221	357	598
Primary copper (smelting and refining)	82.9	92.9	103.7	L	79	80	75	65
				M	107	136	170	231
				H	132	199	299	509
Primary lead	94.5	90.5	68.8	L	49	52	61	71
				M	72	88	115	148
				H	103	150	222	331
Primary magnesium	19.3	75.1	49.2	L	41	45	46	48
				M	57	76	92	113
				H	85	138	176	251
Primary zinc	85.3	96.8	81.9	L	77	86	96	110
				M	99	126	163	220
				H	128	188	290	469
Secondary nonferrous metals	100.2	110.1	93.5	L	126	157	218	302
				M	152	218	352	564
				H	181	315	583	1,030
Nonferrous shapes and castings	90.5	110.1	98.1	L	125	154	200	257
				M	168	254	378	576
				H	227	416	684	1,218
Fabricated metal products	84.2	96.9	106.0	L	128	157	198	255
				M	164	235	340	509
				H	204	335	550	955
Machinery and related products	60.6	95.0	105.8	L	143	180	253	351
				M	194	322	530	868
				H	255	505	975	1,882
Machinery	69.7	92.6	106.4	L	134	175	238	323
				M	182	300	478	753
				H	241	466	878	1,629
Non-electrical machinery	71.0	92.7	102.2	L	137	178	248	344
				M	186	303	490	781
				H	246	475	900	1,698
Electrical machinery	67.3	92.5	112.3	L	131	171	226	295
				M	177	296	462	713
				H	234	454	847	1,532

Table A1–29 (cont'd)　　　　　　　　　　　　　　　　　　　　　(1957 = 100)

		1950	1955	1960		1970	1980	1990	2000
Transportation equipment		52.9	95.9	101.7	L	148	176	255	366
					M	198	339	572	972
					H	263	541	1,087	2,200
Motor vehicles and parts		91.8	117.9	114.7	L	172	247	337	453
					M	188	304	470	741
					H	232	445	868	1,737
Aircraft and other equipment		25.4	76.5	88.6	L	124	108	176	282
					M	206	369	661	1,181
					H	290	628	1,287	2,634
Instruments and related products		58.5	90.5	118.9	L	218	347	508	716
					M	281	528	945	1,670
					H	334	739	1,504	3,046
Clay, glass, and lumber		89.9	103.3	108.5	L	122	141	160	198
					M	166	224	308	447
					H	213	330	524	911
Clay, glass, and stone products		81.8	97.2	109.6	L	130	159	189	241
					M	168	233	327	488
					H	213	338	543	962
Lumber and products		102.5	114.2	106.5	L	107	110	110	121
					M	162	209	275	376
					H	211	315	491	822
Furniture and fixtures		81.9	98.6	119.7	L	128	148	167	195
					M	178	266	394	570
					H	213	364	618	1,027
Miscellaneous manufactures		89.6	102.0	112.6	L	126	145	167	196
					M	141	182	238	312
					H	177	265	403	612
Non-durable manufactures, total		79.1	95.0	113.4	L	148	192	242	290
					M	160	228	318	430
					H	177	276	424	631
Textile, apparel, and leather products		91.9	98.4	114.8	L	134	151	175	198
					M	145	187	241	309
					H	168	246	363	533
Textile mill products		99.0	102.4	108.8	L	121	135	153	173
					M	136	172	211	266
					H	154	216	306	443
Apparel products		85.2	95.1	124.3	L	146	174	206	236
					M	161	215	288	380
					H	192	296	454	685
Leather products		91.6	98.8	100.4	L	110	121	131	141
					M	117	140	166	196
					H	129	170	222	287
Paper and printing		78.4	94.6	111.5	L	147	192	242	294
					M	156	217	295	392
					H	165	248	387	558
Paper and products		76.8	96.2	111.9	L	153	206	270	347
					M	167	245	352	498
					H	173	281	482	760
Pulp and paper		76.3	96.8	111.9	L	149	195	250	313
					M	162	232	326	450
					H	168	267	446	687
Converted paper products		77.3	95.4	111.9	L	157	217	291	380
					M	171	257	378	546
					H	177	296	517	833
Printing and publishing		79.5	93.4	111.4	L	144	182	222	257
					M	148	198	254	318
					H	159	225	312	416

Table A1–29 (cont'd)   (1957 = 100)

	1950	1955	1960		1970	1980	1990	2000
Chemical, petroleum, and rubber products	64.7	91.8	117.7	L M H	154 188 245	202 283 455	269 420 823	332 624 1,478
Chemicals and products	60.5	89.2	121.2	L M H	158 195 258	209 294 475	273 435 855	348 642 1,516
Industrial chemicals	52.3	89.2	126.8	L M H	174 224 296	237 348 547	315 520 980	404 778 1,745
Chemical products	69.1	89.1	115.5	L M H	141 164 218	179 238 402	229 348 727	289 502 1,279
Drugs, soaps, and toiletries	64.3	85.4	118.4	L M H	154 177 238	203 267 458	265 397 846	337 580 1,497
Paints	89.3	103.5	102.5	L M H	90 105 134	80 115 180	84 144 287	104 191 476
Fertilizers	75.0	98.6	114.8	L M H	116 155 186	139 209 279	147 271 333	162 333 588
Petroleum products	73.8	95.4	108.1	L M H	125 141 159	153 185 237	186 247 357	230 342 553
Rubber and plastic products	71.7	98.1	114.3	L M H	169 211 286	225 342 597	341 535 1,177	376 843 2,272
Foods, beverages, and tobacco	86.5	96.2	109.4	L M H	133 140 169	163 184 259	197 240 398	229 303 600
Mining, total	79.5	94.8	97.1	L M H	109 128 149	130 167 222	152 218 325	188 292 514
Coal	111.3	96.6	82.6	L M H	83 98 122	93 120 167	92 125 194	93 135 257
Crude oil and natural gas	73.0	95.3	98.5	L M H	114 132 147	139 173 223	171 232 335	215 321 534
Metals	78.4	89.8	96.8	L M H	92 116 145	90 134 190	92 155 246	92 182 342
Stone and earth minerals	66.2	92.8	112.1	L M H	127 165 209	156 228 331	185 320 532	236 478 943
Utilities, total	52.7	85.4	123.1	L M H	172 201 250	245 314 421	320 447 647	422 637 1,013
Electricity	52.0	85.4	123.2	L M H	180 209 265	265 342 462	358 504 732	486 739 1,172
Gas	54.3	85.2	122.5	L M H	148 175 204	181 227 291	199 267 382	220 318 514

1. Historical data from Table A1–28; projections from Table A1–30.

TABLE A1–30.   Derivation of FRB Index of Industrial Production and Principal Components[1]

	1957 prop. (wt.)	1947	1948	1949	1950	1951
INDUSTRIAL PRODUCTION INDEX—DIRECT	100.00	65.3	68.0	64.3	74.5	80.8
Non-farm goods output[2] ($ 1960 bil.)	–	164	166	161	176	194
Index points per $ billion[3]	–	.398	.410	.399	.423	.416
INDUSTRIAL PRODUCTION INDEX—ADDED	100.00	65.3	68.0	64.3	74.5	80.8
MANUFACTURING INDEX—DIRECT	86.49	66.1	68.6	64.8	75.5	81.5
Index points per $ 1960 bil. of non-farm goods[3]	–	.403	.413	.402	.429	.420
MANUFACTURING INDEX—ADDED	86.49	66.1	68.6	64.8	75.5	81.5
MINING INDEX	8.55	76.4	80.3	71.2	79.5	87.3
UTILITIES INDEX	4.96	38.9	43.4	46.3	52.7	60.1
DURABLE MANUFACTURES—DIRECT	49.66	61.8	64.4	58.5	71.3	80.3
Durable goods output[2] ($ 1960 bil.)	–	63.6	63.4	59.3	73.9	85.3
Index points per $ billion[4]	–	.972	1.02	.987	.965	.941
DURABLE MANUFACTURES—ADDED	49.66	61.8	64.4	58.5	71.3	80.3
Primary and fabricated metals	13.15	78.3	80.6	70.0	87.0	93.9
Primary metals	7.73	80.8	84.1	70.8	89.1	96.9
Iron and steel	6.21	81.7	85.5	73.0	89.9	100.5
Blast furnaces and steel works	3.31	76.7	80.0	69.8	85.7	94.0
Steel ingot production[5] (mil. tons)	–	84.6	88.4	77.7	96.5	104.8
Index points per mil. tons[6]	–	.907	.905	.898	.888	.897

1952	1953	1954	1955	1956	1957	1958	1959	1960		1970	1980	1990	2000
									L	148	203	278	380
83.8	90.8	85.4	96.0	99.3	100.0	92.9	104.9	108.0	M	164	249	375	564
									H	182	305	506	836
									L	306	395	510	660
200	212	199	219	224	227	213	232	238	M	339	483	688	981
									H	376	592	929	1,454
.419	.428	.429	.438	.443	.440	.436	.452	.454		.485	.515	.545	.575
									L	148	203	277	379
83.8	90.8	85.4	96.0	99.3	100.0	92.9	104.9	108.0	M	165	250	375	564
									H	184	309	511	847
									L	150	208	287	395
84.8	92.1	85.8	96.7	99.5	100.0	92.4	105.3	108.2	M	166	254	387	587
									H	184	311	522	870
.424	.434	.431	.442	.444	.441	.434	.454	.454		.490	.526	.562	.598
									L	143	186	245	315
84.8	92.1	85.8	96.7	99.5	100.0	92.4	105.3	108.2	M	169	255	379	561
									H	198	339	565	943
									L	109	130	152	188
86.5	88.8	86.2	94.8	100.1	100.0	91.4	95.3	97.1	M	128	167	218	292
									H	149	222	325	514
									L	172	245	320	422
65.2	71.1	76.5	85.4	93.6	100.0	104.5	115.0	123.1	M	201	314	447	637
									H	250	421	647	1,013
									L	139	181	248	334
85.1	96.0	85.0	97.9	100.0	100.0	86.8	101.5	104.3	M	176	275	425	658
									H	214	386	670	1,175
									L	122	151	200	261
87.2	93.6	82.7	95.0	97.2	98.1	82.5	95.0	96.7	M	154	229	343	514
									H	188	322	540	918
.976	1.03	1.03	1.03	1.03	1.02	1.05	1.07	1.08		1.14	1.20	1.24	1.28
									L	132	162	214	286
85.1	96.0	85.0	97.9	100.0	100.0	86.8	101.5	104.3	M	176	274	428	677
									H	227	418	763	1,420
									L	112	131	158	195
88.3	99.7	84.4	102.0	101.1	100.0	83.6	95.4	96.8	M	143	195	270	388
									H	179	278	434	711
									L	102	112	131	154
88.5	100.3	81.3	105.5	103.7	100.0	78.0	89.5	90.3	M	129	168	222	303
									H	161	237	352	540
									L	92	95	105	112
88.5	102.0	80.0	105.7	103.2	100.0	75.4	85.9	87.9	M	122	151	190	247
									H	156	220	317	474
									L	95	101	113	123
82.6	98.7	77.0	102.1	100.3	100.0	74.6	82.1	86.7	M	124	155	198	259
									H	157	223	323	488
									L	108	115	129	140
92.8	111.3	88.1	116.8	114.9	112.4	85.1	93.3	99.1	M	141	176	225	294
									H	178	253	367	554
.890	.887	.874	.874	.873	.890	.877	.880	.875		.88	.88	.88	.88

Table A1–30 (cont'd)

	1957 prop. (wt.)	1947	1948	1949	1950	1951
Steel mill products	1.68	78.8	82.4	72.6	90.2	98.6
Steel shipments[5] (mil. tons)	–	63.4	66.3	58.5	73.0	80.1
Index points per mil. tons[6]	–	1.24	1.24	1.24	1.24	1.23
Ferrous castings and forgings	1.22	96.9	101.9	81.5	100.3	118.2
Shipments of ferrous castings[5] (mil. tons)	–	15.3	15.9	13.0	16.2	18.1
Index points per mil. tons[6]	–	6.33	6.41	6.27	6.19	6.53
Nonferrous metals and products	1.52	76.1	77.7	62.3	83.9	83.5
Primary aluminum	.24	34.7	37.7	36.6	43.6	50.7
New metal requirements[7] (mil. tons)	–	.60	.78	.71	.96	1.01
Index points per mil. tons[8]	–	57.8	48.3	51.5	45.4	50.2
Other nonferrous metals	.31	78.3	75.2	67.2	80.7	84.6
Primary copper (smelting and refining)	.11	79.4	78.1	70.3	82.9	79.8
New metal requirements[9] (mil. tons)	–	1.33	1.41	1.26	1.69	1.47
Index points per mil. tons[8]	–	59.7	55.4	55.8	49.1	54.3
Primary lead	.03	89.4	84.3	89.7	94.5	80.5
New metal requirements[10] (mil. tons)	–	.68	.69	.76	1.00	.70
Index points per mil. tons[8]	–	131	122	118	94.5	115
Primary magnesium	.04	15.2	12.2	14.2	19.3	50.1
Primary aluminum index		34.7	37.7	36.6	43.6	50.7
Index points per alum. index pt.[11]		.44	.32	.39	.44	.99
Primary zinc	.05	81.0	79.8	82.0	85.3	87.9
New metal requirements[12] (mil. tons)		1.15	.99	.98	1.24	1.11
Index points per mil. tons[8]		70.4	80.6	83.7	68.8	79.2

1952	1953	1954	1955	1956	1957	1958	1959	1960		1970	1980	1990	2000
									L	96	102	115	125
85.0	100.2	78.9	106.0	104.1	100.0	74.8	86.8	89.2	M	126	158	201	262
									H	159	226	328	495
									L	77	82	92	100
69.0	80.2	63.2	84.7	83.2	79.9	59.9	69.4	71.1	M	101	126	161	210
									H	127	181	262	396
1.23	1.25	1.25	1.25	1.25	1.25	1.25	1.25	1.25		1.25	1.25	1.25	1.25
									L	79	66	66	66
106.3	112.8	89.3	114.9	109.8	100.0	77.9	95.2	89.3	M	112	132	152	185
									H	152	205	284	409
									L	12	10	10	10
15.7	16.5	13.5	17.5	16.7	15.3	12.2	14.6	13.8	M	17	20	23	28
									H	23	31	43	62
6.77	6.84	6.61	6.57	6.57	6.54	6.39	6.52	6.47		6.6	6.6	6.6	6.6
									L	117	144	185	235
85.9	93.4	86.6	104.8	105.7	100.0	88.5	103.9	100.2	M	157	237	351	532
									H	215	393	640	1,131
									L	128	172	220	281
56.7	76.0	88.6	95.0	101.7	100.0	97.6	122.0	125.6	M	178	292	439	661
									H	267	531	839	1,479
									L	2.44	3.33	4.35	5.66
1.08	1.57	1.72	1.80	1.84	1.84	1.88	2.28	2.06	M	3.38	5.66	8.67	13.33
									H	5.08	10.30	16.58	29.82
52.5	48.4	51.5	52.8	55.3	54.3	51.9	53.5	61.0		52.6	51.6	50.6	49.6
									L	82	89	104	128
94.1	97.0	85.5	95.6	99.9	100.0	80.0	76.8	87.1	M	109	138	194	279
									H	138	221	357	598
									L	79	80	75	65
77.9	86.5	79.4	92.9	100.6	100.0	91.2	75.7	103.7	M	107	136	170	231
									H	132	199	299	509
									L	1.45	1.49	1.43	1.26
1.52	1.55	1.57	1.59	1.63	1.71	1.63	1.48	1.69	M	1.97	2.55	3.25	4.50
									H	2.43	3.73	5.70	9.91
51.2	55.8	50.6	58.4	61.7	58.5	56.0	51.1	61.4		54.4	53.4	52.4	51.4
									L	49	52	61	71
87.8	88.3	91.1	90.5	101.1	100.0	86.5	63.1	68.8	M	72	88	115	148
									H	103	150	222	331
									L	.46	.50	.60	.71
.99	.87	.87	.85	.82	.86	.78	.71	.61	M	.68	.85	1.13	1.48
									H	.97	1.44	2.18	3.31
88.7	101	105	106	123	116	111	88.9	113		106	104	102	100
									L	41	45	46	48
129.7	114.6	85.8	75.1	83.9	100.0	37.1	37.8	49.2	M	57	76	92	113
									H	85	138	176	251
									L	128	172	220	281
56.7	76.0	88.6	95.0	101.7	100.0	97.6	122.0	125.6	M	178	292	439	665
									H	267	531	839	1,479
2.29	1.51	.97	.79	.82	1.00	.38	.31	.39		.32	.26	.21	.17
									L	77	86	96	110
90.3	91.5	81.4	96.8	99.6	100.0	78.8	81.3	81.9	M	99	126	163	220
									H	128	189	290	469
									L	1.04	1.18	1.34	1.57
1.03	1.19	1.09	1.34	1.34	1.30	1.04	1.08	1.02	M	1.34	1.73	2.28	3.15
									H	1.73	2.59	4.06	6.70
87.7	76.9	74.7	72.2	74.3	76.9	75.8	75.3	80.3		74.2	72.8	71.4	70.0

Table A1–30 (cont'd)

	1957 prop. (wt.)	1947	1948	1949	1950	1951
Secondary nonferrous metals	.08	102.6	96.5	71.5	100.2	107.8
Aggregate secondary recovery[13] (mil. tons)	–	1.27	1.19	.93	1.14	1.14
Index points per mil. tons[6]	–	80.8	81.1	76.9	87.9	94.6
Nonferrous shapes and castings	.97	80.7	83.8	63.5	90.5	88.2
End-use consumption of aluminum, copper, and zinc[14] (mil. tons)	–	n.a.	n.a.	n.a.	3.93	n.a.
Index points per mil. tons[6]	–	–	–	–	23.0	–
Fabricated metal products	5.42	74.9	76.2	68.8	84.2	90.0
Structural metal parts	2.91	64.8	70.0	65.6	76.0	81.4
Total construction (incl. maintenance & repair)[15] ($ 1960 bil.)	–	45.1	50.1	52.1	58.6	59.4
Index points per $ billion	–	1.44	1.40	1.26	1.30	1.37
Other fabricated metal products	2.51	86.6	83.4	72.5	93.7	100.0
Durable goods output[2] ($ 1960 bil.)	–	63.6	63.4	59.3	73.9	85.3
Index points per $ billion	–	1.36	1.32	1.22	1.27	1.17
Machinery and related products	28.98	51.4	53.7	49.9	60.6	72.5
Machinery	15.31	62.6	63.8	56.7	69.7	79.6
Non-electrical machinery	8.92	73.8	74.2	63.3	71.0	90.3
Priv. purch. of industrial mchy., tools, office, etc., and agric. mchy.[16] ($ 1960 bil.)	–	12.5	13.5	11.2	12.0	13.0
Index points per $ billion[17]	–	5.9	5.5	5.7	5.9	6.9
Electrical machinery	6.39	50.5	52.4	49.2	67.3	67.7
Priv. purch. of elec. mchy. & appl.[18] ($ 1960 bil.)	–	9.68	10.01	8.87	10.62	9.61
Index points per $ billion[19]	–	5.22	5.23	5.55	6.34	7.04

1952	1953	1954	1955	1956	1957	1958	1959	1960		1970	1980	1990	2000
									L	126	157	218	302
103.2	103.0	94.3	110.9	106.7	100.0	84.1	100.1	93.5	M	152	218	352	564
									H	181	315	583	1,030
									L	1.37	1.71	2.38	3.30
1.05	1.08	1.04	1.19	1.14	1.10	.96	1.09	1.04	M	1.66	2.38	3.84	6.16
									H	1.98	3.44	6.36	11.25
98.3	95.4	90.7	93.2	93.6	90.9	87.6	91.8	89.9		91.6	91.6	91.6	91.6
									L	125	154	200	257
90.1	97.0	86.5	110.1	108.6	100.0	89.1	108.0	98.1	M	168	254	378	576
									H	227	416	684	1,218
									L	5.42	6.90	8.71	11.19
3.88	4.31	n.a.	4.74	4.54	4.21	3.96	4.78	4.31	M	7.30	11.05	16.42	25.05
									H	9.85	18.08	29.76	52.95
23.2	22.5	–	23.2	23.9	23.8	22.5	22.6	22.8		23.0	23.0	23.0	23.0
									L	128	157	198	255
87.8	98.8	88.8	96.9	97.4	100.0	91.6	103.9	106.0	M	164	235	340	509
									H	204	335	550	955
									L	122	150	178	227
81.0	91.3	83.8	90.2	93.4	100.0	92.5	100.5	103.6	M	159	220	308	460
									H	201	319	512	907
									L	92.7	113.5	134.9	172.2
61.0	63.4	67.1	72.8	70.7	71.1	71.8	77.1	76.2	M	120.3	166.3	233.6	348.4
									H	152.4	241.4	387.6	687.0
1.33	1.44	1.25	1.24	1.32	1.41	1.29	1.30	1.36		1.32	1.32	1.32	1.32
									L	134	166	220	287
95.7	107.5	94.6	104.6	102.0	100.0	90.6	108.0	108.8	M	169	252	377	565
									H	207	354	594	1,010
									L	122	151	200	261
87.2	93.6	82.7	95.0	97.2	98.1	82.5	95.0	96.7	M	154	229	343	514
									H	188	322	540	918
1.10	1.15	1.14	1.10	1.05	1.02	1.10	1.14	1.13		1.10	1.10	1.10	1.10
									L	143	180	253	351
82.6	94.9	83.7	95.0	98.4	100.0	85.8	101.7	105.8	M	194	322	530	868
									H	255	505	975	1,882
									L	134	175	238	323
88.4	96.4	84.3	92.6	102.8	100.0	85.2	102.8	106.4	M	182	300	478	753
									H	241	466	878	1,629
									L	137	178	247	344
98.0	101.1	86.2	92.7	103.3	100.0	82.6	99.3	102.2	M	186	303	490	781
									H	246	475	900	1,698
									L	14.7	16.3	19.8	24.4
13.8	14.4	13.2	13.0	14.9	15.2	12.1	12.1	12.7	M	20.0	27.8	39.2	55.4
									H	26.4	43.6	72.0	120.4
7.1	7.0	6.5	7.1	6.9	6.6	6.8	8.2	8.1		9.3	10.9	12.5	14.1
									L	131	171	226	295
77.4	89.9	81.5	92.5	102.1	100.0	88.9	107.6	112.3	M	177	296	462	713
									H	234	454	847	1,532
									L	15.4	19.7	25.6	33.5
10.29	11.05	10.92	12.18	13.26	12.76	11.66	13.13	13.59	M	20.8	34.0	52.5	81.0
									H	27.5	52.2	96.2	174.1
7.52	8.14	7.46	7.59	7.70	7.84	7.62	8.19	8.26		8.5	8.7	8.8	8.8

Table A1–30 (cont'd)

	1957 prop. (wt.)	1947	1948	1949	1950	1951
Transportation equipment	10.76	40.3	44.0	44.2	52.9	59.0
Motor vehicles and parts	5.04	64.2	69.6	71.4	91.8	84.1
Automobiles	2.03	48.5	55.0	70.5	92.2	75.7
Annual production[20] (millions)	–	3.56	3.91	5.12	6.67	5.34
Index points per million[21]	–	13.6	14.0	13.8	13.8	14.2
Trucks and buses	.38	105.2	107.5	79.4	104.4	122.6
Annual output of trucks and trailers[22] (millions)	–	1.27	1.41	1.16	1.40	1.48
Index points per million[17]	–	82.8	76.2	68.4	74.6	82.8
Motor vehicle parts	2.63	68.8	74.2	71.7	90.6	84.4
Annual production of motor vehicles[23] (millions)	–	4.80	5.29	6.25	8.00	6.77
Index points per million	–	14.3	14.0	11.5	11.3	12.5
Trailers, boats, and cycles[24]	.22	–	–	–	–	–
Personal consumption expenditures on toys, sports equipment[25] ($ 1960 bil.)	–	1.7	1.7	1.6	1.7	1.7
Index points per $ billion	–	–	–	–	–	–
Aircraft and other equipment	5.50	22.3	24.9	25.0	25.4	41.4
Aircraft and parts	4.61	12.5	15.3	16.8	19.3	33.7
Defense exp. on mil. aircraft & missiles[26] ($ 1960 bil.)	–	n.a.	n.a.	n.a.	n.a.	n.a.
Index points per $ billion[27]	–	–	–	–	–	–
Private shipyards[24]	.55	–	–	–	–	–
Output of goods and construction[28] ($ 1960 bil.)	–	209	218	298	237	254
Index points per $ billion	–	–	–	–	–	–
Railroad equipment	.34	n.a.	n.a.	n.a.	n.a.	n.a.
Deliveries of rolling stock[29] (thousands)	–	99	118	100	48	100
Index points per unit	–	–	–	–	–	–

1952	1953	1954	1955	1956	1957	1958	1959	1960		1970	1980	1990	2000
									L	148	176	255	366
68.6	86.2	78.7	95.9	91.5	100.0	84.2	97.8	101.7	M	198	339	572	972
									H	263	541	1,087	2,200
									L	172	247	337	453
72.1	91.5	82.5	117.9	94.7	100.0	76.5	100.3	114.7	M	188	304	470	741
									H	232	445	868	1,737
									L	163	218	278	351
63.0	88.9	81.4	123.8	91.6	100.0	71.3	96.4	117.1	M	173	262	379	565
									H	211	383	708	1,365
									L	8.3	10.5	13.0	16.1
4.32	6.12	5.56	7.92	5.82	6.11	4.26	5.59	6.67	M	8.8	12.6	17.7	25.9
									H	10.7	18.4	33.1	62.6
14.6	14.5	14.6	15.6	15.7	16.4	16.7	17.2	17.6		19.7	20.8	21.4	21.8
									L	119	154	198	259
108.6	119.1	89.5	113.1	107.6	100.0	85.4	113.6	116.7	M	159	226	324	474
									H	212	349	553	909
									L	1.27	1.60	2.02	2.59
1.26	1.29	1.04	1.33	1.16	1.16	.92	1.20	1.25	M	1.69	2.35	3.31	4.74
									H	2.25	3.64	5.64	9.09
86.2	92.3	86.1	85.0	92.8	86.2	92.8	94.7	93.4		94	96	98	100
									L	186	282	402	560
73.0	89.4	82.4	114.0	95.1	100.0	79.3	101.7	112.6	M	204	348	562	915
									H	251	510	1,037	2,143
									L	9.5	12.0	14.9	18.6
5.54	7.32	6.60	9.17	6.92	7.22	5.14	6.73	7.87	M	10.4	14.8	20.8	30.4
									H	12.8	21.7	38.4	71.2
13.2	12.2	12.5	12.4	13.7	13.9	15.4	15.1	14.3		19.6	23.5	27.0	30.1
									L	189	262	361	471
50.9	64.8	59.1	76.9	85.7	100.0	103.1	138.0	131.4	M	231	400	664	1,047
									H	290	585	1,113	1,980
									L	4.5	6.1	8.2	10.7
1.8	2.0	2.0	2.4	2.7	2.9	3.1	3.3	3.5	M	5.5	9.3	15.1	23.8
									H	6.9	13.6	25.3	45.0
28.0	32.2	29.6	32.0	31.6	34.5	33.1	41.9	37.5		42	43	44	44
									L	124	108	176	282
66.1	82.2	76.0	76.5	88.8	100.0	90.5	93.9	88.6	M	206	369	661	1,181
									H	290	628	1,287	2,634
									L	125	101	174	290
60.8	79.7	77.7	78.3	90.1	100.0	91.7	95.2	87.7	M	215	398	730	1,326
									H	304	686	1,440	2,996
n.a.	11.6	10.7	10.4	10.4	11.9	11.8	11.1	10.1	L	11.5	7.7	11.4	16.6
									M	19.7	30.4	47.7	75.8
									H	27.9	52.4	94.1	171.2
−	6.87	7.26	7.53	8.66	8.40	7.77	8.58	8.68		10.9	13.1	15.3	17.5
									L	139	176	222	284
−	98.4	77.8	72.7	79.3	100.0	102.7	105.4	110.2	M	160	225	317	455
									H	184	288	453	732
									L	397	502	633	811
262	277	268	294	297	299	286	310	315	M	456	642	907	1,300
									H	525	823	1,293	2,092
−	.355	.290	.247	.267	.334	.359	.340	.350		.350	.350	.350	.350
									L	87	92	123	170
n.a.	90.0	50.1	58.2	86.4	100.0	54.8	57.3	65.9	M	162	202	285	386
									H	275	386	566	807
									L	71	73	95	130
83	86	40	44	68	102	45	40	58	M	133	160	221	295
									H	225	306	439	616
−	1.05	1.25	1.32	1.27	.98	1.21	1.43	1.14		1.22	1.26	1.29	1.31

Table A1–30 (cont'd)

	1957 prop. (wt.)	1947	1948	1949	1950	1951
Instruments and related products	1.66	54.8	56.4	50.3	58.5	67.1
Purchases of producers' durable equipment[16] ($ 1960 bil.)	–	26.4	27.7	24.1	25.8	26.7
Index points per $ billion[30]	–	2.08	2.04	2.09	2.27	2.51
Ordnance and accessories[24]	1.25	–	–	–	–	108.9
Defense expenditures on ships, vehicles, and ammunition[26] ($ 1960 bil.)	–	n.a.	n.a.	n.a.	n.a.	n.a.
Index points per $ billion	–	–	–	–	–	–
Clay, glass, and lumber	4.57	77.7	81.8	74.1	89.9	94.3
Clay, glass, and stone products	2.92	68.0	72.5	67.6	81.8	90.4
Total new & maint. constr.[15] ($ 1960 bil.)	–	45.1	50.1	52.1	58.6	59.4
Index points per $ billion	–	1.51	1.45	1.30	1.40	1.52
Lumber and products	1.65	91.8	95.6	84.3	102.5	102.2
Consumption of lumber for all purposes[31] (bil. bd. ft.)	–	33.3	35.9	33.7	41.6	37.6
Index points per bil. bd. ft.[32]	–	2.76	2.66	2.50	2.46	2.72
Furniture and fixtures	1.48	70.1	72.7	67.1	81.9	77.4
Consumer & producer purchases of furn. & fixtures[18] ($ 1960 bil.)	–	7.6	7.7	7.2	7.9	8.2
Index points per $ billion	–	9.2	9.4	9.3	10.4	9.4
Miscellaneous manufactures	1.48	80.4	85.8	79.5	89.6	86.8
Pers. cons. exp. on newspapers, toys, plants[33] ($ 1960 bil.)	–	3.4	3.6	3.8	4.1	4.4
Index points per $ billion[34]	–	23.6	23.8	20.9	21.9	19.7

1952	1953	1954	1955	1956	1957	1958	1959	1960		1970	1980	1990	2000
									L	218	347	508	716
79.7	87.0	84.7	90.5	97.3	100.0	94.1	112.2	118.9	M	281	528	945	1,670
									H	334	739	1,504	3,046
									L	35.8	43.9	52.4	62.3
26.5	27.4	25.3	27.4	30.3	29.9	23.6	25.9	27.5	M	46.1	66.9	97.4	145.2
									H	54.7	93.6	155.0	264.9
3.01	3.18	3.35	3.30	3.21	3.34	3.99	4.33	4.32		6.1	7.9	9.7	11.5
									L	104	57	65	67
135.9	161.9	118.1	122.6	105.4	100.0	95.9	107.9	116.3	M	183	208	254	315
									H	256	365	507	710
									L	1.7	.9	1.0	1.0
n.a.	6.4	3.7	2.4	2.0	1.7	1.8	2.0	2.1	M	3.0	3.3	3.9	4.7
									H	4.2	5.8	7.8	10.6
–	25.3	31.9	51.1	52.7	58.8	53.3	54.0	55.4		61	63	65	67
									L	122	141	160	198
91.6	95.1	92.0	103.3	104.7	100.0	96.5	111.3	108.5	M	166	224	308	447
									H	213	330	524	911
									L	130	159	189	241
86.4	88.6	85.2	97.2	101.7	100.0	94.7	110.2	109.6	M	168	233	327	488
									H	213	338	543	962
									L	92.7	113.5	134.9	172.2
61.0	63.4	67.1	72.8	70.7	71.1	71.8	77.1	76.2	M	120.3	166.3	233.6	348.4
									H	152.4	241.4	387.6	687.0
1.42	1.40	1.27	1.34	1.44	1.41	1.32	1.43	1.44		1.40	1.40	1.40	1.40
									L	107	110	110	121
100.9	106.7	103.9	114.2	109.9	100.0	99.7	113.1	106.5	M	162	209	275	376
									H	211	315	491	822
									L	34.2	32.8	30.5	31.5
39.4	38.1	38.5	41.1	40.5	35.5	36.4	39.9	36.8	M	51.6	61.9	76.1	97.6
									H	67.4	93.5	135.9	213.5
2.56	2.80	2.70	2.78	2.71	2.82	2.74	2.83	2.89		3.13	3.37	3.61	3.85
									L	128	148	167	195
79.6	83.2	86.8	98.6	101.8	100.0	96.1	114.9	119.7	M	178	266	394	570
									H	213	364	618	1,029
									L	11.2	12.3	13.4	15.1
8.0	8.3	8.2	9.5	10.4	10.1	9.7	10.5	10.5	M	15.6	22.2	31.5	44.2
									H	18.7	30.3	49.4	79.8
10.0	10.0	10.6	10.4	9.8	9.9	9.9	10.9	11.4		11.4	12.0	12.5	12.9
									L	126	145	167	196
89.2	100.6	91.1	102.0	105.1	100.0	95.2	108.6	112.6	M	141	182	238	312
									H	177	265	403	612
									L	7.4	9.5	11.9	15.0
4.6	4.6	4.6	4.9	5.1	5.2	5.4	5.8	5.9	M	8.3	11.9	17.0	23.8
									H	10.4	17.3	28.8	46.7
19.4	21.9	19.8	20.8	20.6	19.2	17.6	18.7	19.1		17.0	15.3	14.0	13.1

Table A1–30 (cont'd)

	1957 prop. (wt.)	1947	1948	1949	1950	1951
NON-DURABLE MANUFACTURES—DIRECT	36.83	70.0	72.3	71.1	79.1	81.7
Non-durable goods output[2] ($ 1960 bil.)	–	116.3	121.1	119.2	121.2	126.5
Index points per $ billion[4]	–	.602	.597	.596	.653	.646
NON-DURABLE MANUFACTURES—ADDED	36.83	70.0	72.3	71.1	79.1	81.7
Textile, apparel, and leather products	7.32	83.5	87.1	83.1	91.9	90.1
Textile mill products	2.78	88.0	94.2	87.1	99.0	98.0
Domestic consumption of textile fibers[35] (bil. lb. cotton equiv.)	–	n.a.	n.a.	5.21	5.94	5.88
Index points per bil. lb.[36]	–	–	–	16.7	16.7	16.7
Apparel products	3.44	76.7	79.9	79.2	85.2	83.7
Pers. cons. exp. on clothing & footwear[25] ($ 1960 bil.)	–	21.6	21.8	21.8	22.4	22.2
Index points per $ billion[37]	–	3.55	3.66	3.63	3.80	3.77
Leather and products	1.10	93.4	89.0	84.7	91.6	85.9
Shoe production[38] (million pairs)	–	437	437	419	465	422
Index points per million[39]	–	.214	.204	.202	.197	.204
Paper and printing	7.93	68.1	70.9	70.8	78.4	81.1
Paper and products	3.27	64.9	66.7	63.8	76.8	81.3
Pulp and paper	1.63	65.3	68.1	63.7	76.3	83.4
Paper & paperboard production[40] (mil. tons)	–	21.11	21.90	20.32	24.38	26.05
Index points per mil. tons[17]	–	3.09	3.11	3.13	3.15	3.20
Converted paper products	1.64	64.4	65.1	63.8	77.3	79.2
Paper & paperboard production[40] (mil. tons)	–	21.11	21.90	20.32	24.38	26.05
Index points per mil. tons[17]	–	3.05	2.97	3.14	3.17	3.04

1952	1953	1954	1955	1956	1957	1958	1959	1960		1970	1980	1990	2000
									L	148	192	242	290
83.3	86.9	86.9	95.0	98.9	100.0	99.9	110.3	113.4	M	160	228	318	430
									H	177	276	424	631
									L	200	246	299	349
131.3	136.8	135.8	144.1	147.5	148.8	150.8	157.2	161.8	M	216	293	393	518
									H	239	354	523	760
.634	.635	.640	.659	.670	.672	.662	.702	.701		.74	.78	.81	.83
									L	143	178	224	267
83.3	86.9	86.9	95.0	98.9	100.0	99.9	110.3	113.4	M	158	221	305	419
									H	190	312	514	838
									L	134	151	175	198
92.2	93.6	89.6	98.4	101.1	100.0	99.2	115.2	114.8	M	145	187	241	309
									H	168	246	363	533
									L	121	135	153	173
97.2	99.1	92.7	102.4	104.1	100.0	97.7	113.2	108.8	M	136	172	211	266
									H	154	216	306	443
									L	8.21	9.47	10.82	12.36
6.01	6.21	5.95	6.60	6.58	6.55	6.46	7.25	7.08	M	9.25	12.01	14.94	18.97
									H	10.49	15.10	21.85	31.64
16.2	16.0	15.6	15.5	15.8	15.3	15.1	15.6	15.4		14.7	14.3	14.1	14.0
									L	146	174	206	236
88.0	89.7	86.6	95.1	98.9	100.0	101.1	119.9	124.3	M	161	215	288	380
									H	192	296	454	685
									L	33.2	39.0	45.9	52.4
23.3	23.5	23.5	24.9	25.6	26.2	26.4	27.9	28.1	M	36.5	48.3	64.2	84.5
									H	43.6	66.3	101.2	152.2
3.78	3.82	3.68	3.82	3.86	3.82	3.83	4.30	4.42		4.40	4.46	4.49	4.50
									L	110	121	131	141
91.4	91.8	90.9	98.8	100.6	100.0	96.8	105.5	100.4	M	117	140	167	196
									H	129	170	222	287
									L	606	678	747	807
458	446	473	517	524	527	517	560	528	M	645	784	947	1,120
									H	714	952	1,260	1,640
.200	.206	.192	.191	.192	.190	.187	.188	.190		.181	.178	.176	.175
									L	147	192	242	294
79.4	84.5	86.9	94.6	99.3	100.0	99.2	107.6	111.5	M	156	217	295	392
									H	165	248	387	558
									L	153	206	270	347
77.5	84.3	85.3	96.2	100.7	100.0	101.0	110.9	111.9	M	167	245	352	498
									H	173	281	482	760
									L	149	195	250	313
79.4	85.5	86.2	96.8	102.8	100.0	100.3	110.9	111.9	M	162	232	326	450
									H	168	267	446	687
									L	44.9	58.7	74.7	92.9
24.42	26.53	26.72	30.14	31.34	30.70	30.82	34.05	34.46	M	49.0	69.7	97.2	133.5
									H	50.8	80.1	133.0	203.7
3.25	3.22	3.23	3.21	3.28	3.26	3.25	3.26	3.25		3.31	3.33	3.35	3.37
									L	157	217	291	380
75.5	83.1	84.2	95.4	99.1	100.0	101.7	111.0	111.9	M	171	257	378	546
									H	177	296	517	833
									L	44.9	58.7	74.7	92.9
24.42	26.53	26.72	30.14	31.34	30.70	30.82	34.05	34.46	M	49.0	69.7	97.2	133.5
									H	50.8	80.1	133.0	203.7
3.09	3.13	3.15	3.17	3.16	3.26	3.30	3.25	3.24		3.49	3.69	3.89	4.09

Table A1–30 (cont'd)

	1957 prop. (wt.)	1947	1948	1949	1950	1951
Printing and publishing	4.66	70.4	74.0	75.9	79.5	81.0
Newsprint consumption[41] (mil. tons)	–	4.66	5.14	5.53	5.86	5.87
Index points per mil. tons[17]	–	15.1	14.4	13.7	13.6	13.8
Chemical, petroleum, and rubber products	10.94	50.6	54.1	52.7	64.7	71.8
Chemicals and products	7.10	45.4	49.1	48.4	60.5	68.6
Industrial chemicals	3.61	36.7	41.5	40.9	52.3	61.1
Inorganic chemicals	1.08	33.3	35.5	36.7	42.7	50.5
General FRB industrial production index[42]	–	65.3	68.0	64.3	74.5	80.8
Points per point of general index[42]	–	.51	.52	.57	.57	.63
Organic chemicals	2.53	38.2	44.0	42.7	56.4	65.6
Basic organic chemicals	1.40	40.9	46.6	43.6	58.4	65.0
Synthetic materials index[43]	–	35.0	40.7	41.1	53.5	64.9
Points per synthetic index point[44]	–	1.17	1.14	1.06	1.09	1.00
Synthetic materials	1.13	35.0	40.7	41.1	53.5	64.9
Plastic materials	.49	22.0	26.1	31.7	41.9	52.9
Production of plastic materials[45] (bil. lb.)	–	n.a.	n.a.	n.a.	2.15	2.44
Index points per bil. lb.	–	–	–	–	19.5	21.7
Synthetic rubber	.14	n.a.	n.a.	n.a.	n.a.	n.a.
Production of synthetic rubber[46] (mil. long tons)	–	.509	.488	.394	.483	.845
Index points per mil. tons	–	–	–	–	–	–
Man-made fibers	.50	45.2	54.2	51.3	66.9	74.2
Domestic consumption of man-made fibers[47] (bil. lb. cotton equiv.)	–	n.a.	n.a.	1.45	1.73	1.84
Index points per bil. lb.	–	–	–	35.4	38.7	40.3

1952	1953	1954	1955	1956	1957	1958	1959	1960		1970	1980	1990	2000
									L	144	182	222	257
80.8	84.6	88.0	93.4	98.3	100.0	97.9	105.3	111.4	M	148	198	256	318
									H	159	225	312	416
									L	8.77	10.37	11.83	12.86
5.92	6.11	6.10	6.48	6.81	6.77	6.52	7.07	7.33	M	9.03	11.25	13.60	15.89
									H	9.68	12.81	16.58	20.78
13.6	13.8	14.4	14.4	14.4	14.8	15.0	14.9	15.2		16.4	17.6	18.8	20.0
									L	154	202	269	332
74.5	80.2	79.3	91.8	96.3	100.0	98.8	112.7	117.7	M	188	283	420	624
									H	245	455	823	1,478
									L	158	209	273	348
71.7	77.5	76.8	89.2	95.5	100.0	99.7	114.3	121.2	M	195	294	435	642
									H	258	475	855	1,516
									L	174	237	315	404
63.7	73.4	73.0	89.2	95.0	100.0	98.2	118.4	126.8	M	224	348	520	778
									H	296	547	980	1,745
									L	160	223	317	437
55.9	66.7	75.5	88.2	94.6	100.0	100.8	110.8	114.9	M	177	274	424	649
									H	196	336	572	961
									L	148	203	278	380
83.8	90.8	85.4	96.0	99.3	100.0	92.9	104.9	108.0	M	164	249	375	564
									H	182	305	506	836
.67	.74	.88	.92	.95	1.00	1.09	1.06	1.06	M	1.08	1.10	1.13	1.15
									L	180	251	315	391
67.0	76.3	71.9	89.5	95.1	100.0	97.1	121.6	131.9	M	245	380	562	832
									H	338	636	1,154	2,079
									L	175	212	245	280
71.2	81.1	76.4	92.4	98.3	100.0	95.0	114.1	129.0	M	223	321	437	596
									H	308	538	898	1,489
									L	214	299	402	528
61.8	70.3	66.3	85.9	91.1	100.0	99.5	130.9	135.5	M	271	452	717	1,125
									H	376	757	1,472	2,810
1.15	1.15	1.15	1.08	1.08	1.00	.95	.87	.95		.82	.71	.61	.53
									L	214	299	402	528
61.8	70.3	66.3	85.9	91.1	100.0	99.5	130.9	135.5	M	271	452	717	1,125
									H	376	757	1,472	2,810
									L	283	424	615	859
50.4	60.5	59.1	77.8	89.7	100.0	110.3	155.1	162.5	M	375	681	1,175	1,967
									H	562	1,222	2,539	5,105
									L	10.32	15.05	21.21	28.83
2.33	2.78	2.83	3.74	3.98	4.34	4.52	5.86	6.14	M	13.70	24.16	40.50	66.00
									H	20.50	43.33	87.56	171.30
21.6	21.8	20.9	20.8	22.6	23.0	24.4	26.4	26.5		27.4	28.2	29.0	29.8
									L	200	255	289	325
n.a.	75.9	55.7	86.8	96.3	100.0	94.1	123.4	128.2	M	242	359	494	660
									H	314	604	1,104	1,958
									L	2.27	2.89	3.29	3.71
.798	.848	.623	.988	1.080	1.118	1.055	1.380	1.469	M	2.74	4.07	5.62	7.52
									H	3.55	6.86	12.56	22.33
−	89.5	89.4	87.8	89.2	89.4	89.1	89.4	87.3		88.3	88.1	87.9	87.7
									L	150	189	226	260
70.8	78.5	76.3	93.6	91.1	100.0	90.4	112.4	110.7	M	178	254	330	431
									H	210	345	529	799
									L	3.69	4.57	5.40	6.18
1.99	2.10	1.95	2.32	2.29	2.41	2.42	2.84	2.79	M	4.38	6.16	7.90	10.24
									H	5.18	8.35	12.65	18.98
35.6	37.4	39.1	40.3	39.8	41.5	37.4	39.6	39.7		40.6	41.3	41.8	42.1

Table A1–30 (cont'd)

	1957 prop. (wt.)	1947	1948	1949	1950	1951
Chemical products	3.49	54.6	57.2	56.3	69.1	76.5
Drugs, soaps, and toiletries	2.73	47.8	51.0	52.2	64.3	74.2
Soap and related products	.61	62.9	65.9	66.2	78.6	75.1
Production of soap & syndets[48] (bil. lb.)	–	4.058	3.816	3.849	4.401	4.075
Index points per bil. lb.	–	15.5	17.3	17.2	17.9	18.4
Drugs, medicines, toiletries, & misc.[24]	2.12	43.5	46.7	48.2	60.2	73.9
Pers. cons. exp. on toilet articles & drugs[25] ($ 1960 bil.)	–	3.3	3.3	3.5	3.7	4.0
Index points per $ billion	–	13.2	14.2	13.8	16.3	18.5
Paints	.60	83.0	82.6	71.7	89.3	85.5
Production of paints, varnishes, & lacquers[49] (mil. gal.)	–	582	577	525	641	590
Index points per mil. gal.	–	.143	.143	.137	.139	.145
Fertilizer	.16	64.4	67.8	69.2	75.0	82.2
Farm outlays on fertilizer & lime[50] ($ 1960 bil.)	–	–	–	–	1.03	1.08
Index points per $ billion	–	–	–	–	72.8	76.1
Petroleum products	1.93	63.8	69.1	66.9	73.8	82.5
Total consumption of petroleum[51] (bil. bbl.)	–	1.86	2.05	1.97	2.18	2.40
Index points per bil. bbl.	–	34.3	33.7	34.0	33.9	34.4
Rubber and plastics products	1.91	57.8	58.7	55.4	71.7	73.3
Tires and tubes	.66	89.2	80.8	72.5	90.6	93.0
Cons. of rubber in tires and tubes[52] (mil. long tons)	–	.947	.857	.770	.961	.986
Index points per mil. tons	–	94.2	94.3	94.2	94.3	94.3

1952	1953	1954	1955	1956	1957	1958	1959	1960		1970	1980	1990	2000
									L	141	179	229	289
80.1	81.6	80.6	89.1	95.9	100.0	101.3	110.2	115.5	M	164	238	348	502
									H	218	402	727	1,279
									L	154	203	265	337
77.7	79.1	78.2	85.4	94.8	100.0	102.3	111.3	118.4	M	177	267	397	580
									H	238	458	846	1,497
									L	136	160	179	193
84.7	89.6	87.3	94.0	99.4	100.0	98.0	104.1	105.9	M	140	174	206	240
									H	150	198	251	312
									L	6.06	7.01	7.72	8.30
4.131	4.104	4.228	4.329	4.632	4.939	4.932	n.a.	5.220	M	6.24	7.60	8.90	10.30
									H	6.69	8.65	10.80	13.40
20.5	21.8	20.6	21.7	21.5	20.2	19.9	–	20.3		22.4	22.9	23.2	23.3
									L	159	216	290	379
75.7	76.1	75.6	82.9	93.5	100.0	103.5	113.4	122.0	M	188	294	451	678
									H	264	533	1,018	1,837
									L	9.0	12.2	16.4	21.4
4.2	4.3	4.4	4.8	5.3	5.5	6.0	6.4	6.8	M	10.6	16.6	25.5	38.3
									H	14.9	30.1	57.5	103.8
18.0	17.7	17.2	17.3	17.6	18.2	17.2	17.7	17.9		17.7	17.7	17.7	17.7
									L	90	80	84	104
88.5	90.1	87.1	103.5	100.3	100.0	97.3	104.6	102.5	M	105	115	144	191
									H	134	180	287	476
									L	537	460	472	578
583	665	635	719	693	669	663	650	663	M	629	659	809	1,063
									H	803	1,034	1,614	2,642
.152	.136	.137	.144	.145	.149	.147	.161	.155		.167	.174	.178	.180
									L	116	139	147	162
90.1	92.8	97.6	98.6	98.7	100.0	99.7	112.2	114.8	M	155	209	271	333
									H	186	279	333	588
									L	1.5	1.8	1.9	2.1
1.19	1.21	1.22	1.23	1.24	1.27	1.33	1.44	1.46	M	2.0	2.7	3.5	4.3
									H	2.4	3.6	4.3	7.6
75.7	76.7	79.9	80.1	79.6	78.7	75.0	77.9	78.6		77.4	77.4	77.4	77.4
									L	125	153	186	230
84.4	89.5	88.8	95.4	100.1	100.0	98.8	105.4	108.1	M	141	185	248	342
									H	159	237	357	553
									L	3.70	4.50	5.50	6.80
2.47	2.59	2.59	2.80	2.93	3.01	3.02	3.14	3.19	M	4.15	5.45	7.30	10.10
									H	4.70	7.00	10.52	16.30
34.2	34.6	34.3	34.1	34.2	33.2	32.7	33.6	33.9		33.9	33.9	33.9	33.9
									L	168	225	341	376
75.2	80.7	79.2	98.1	95.7	100.0	95.0	114.0	114.3	M	211	342	535	843
									H	286	597	1,177	2,272
									L	132	152	163	186
93.4	95.1	85.6	107.2	98.1	100.0	91.4	111.1	111.0	M	160	215	282	378
									H	204	344	593	1,048
									L	1.40	1.61	1.73	1.97
.990	1.000	.903	1.130	1.040	1.070	.996	1.180	1.140	M	1.70	2.28	2.99	4.01
									H	2.16	3.65	6.29	11.13
94.3	95.1	94.8	94.9	94.3	93.5	91.8	94.2	97.4		94.2	94.2	94.2	94.2

Table A1–30 (cont'd)

	1957 prop. (wt.)	1947	1948	1949	1950	1951
Rubber & plastic products (cont'd)						
Misc. rubber products	.78	59.3	61.3	56.8	65.6	72.2
Rubber consumption in non-tire products[52] (mil. long tons)	–	.463	.474	.441	.601	.574
Index points per mil. tons	–	128	129	129	109	126
Misc. plastic products[24]	.47	21.5	28.9	32.6	58.7	50.7
Consumption of moldings and extrusions[53] (bil. lb.)	–	n.a.	n.a.	n.a.	.677	.714
Index points per bil. lb.	–	–	–	–	86.7	71.0
Foods, beverages, and tobacco	10.64	83.4	82.7	83.6	86.5	88.3
Pers. cons. exp. on food, beverages, & tobacco[25] ($ 1960 bil.)	–	70.6	69.0	69.4	70.3	71.4
Index points per $ billion[54]	–	1.18	1.20	1.20	1.23	1.24
MINING	8.55	76.4	80.3	71.2	79.5	87.3
Coal	1.30	137.3	131.1	96.8	111.3	114.2
Coal production[55] (mil. tons)	–	688	657	481	560	576
Index points per mil. tons[56]	–	.200	.200	.201	.199	.198
Crude oil and natural gas	5.75	63.9	70.4	66.6	73.0	82.5
Crude oil	4.33	70.8	76.9	70.3	75.3	85.8
Crude oil production[57] (bil. bbl.)	–	1.86	2.02	1.84	1.97	2.25
Index points per bil. bbl.[6]	–	38.1	38.1	38.2	38.2	38.1
Natural gas	.32	42.8	48.0	50.7	58.7	69.3
Marketed production of nat. gas[58] (tril. cu. ft.)	–	4.58	5.15	5.42	6.28	7.46
Index points per tril. cu. ft.	–	9.34	9.32	9.35	9.35	9.29
Natural gas liquids	.33	49.9	54.8	58.4	66.6	73.9
Production of nat. gas liquids[59] (mil. bbl.)	–	132	147	157	182	205
Index points per mil. bbl.	–	.378	.373	.372	.366	.360

1952	1953	1954	1955	1956	1957	1958	1959	1960		1970	1980	1990	2000
									L	148	190	234	284
73.5	82.9	80.8	100.3	95.8	100.0	94.7	108.8	103.6	M	176	266	393	571
									H	235	482	952	1,845
									L	.866	1.054	1.267	1.519
.551	.624	.579	.715	.667	.664	.617	.742	.689	M	1.027	1.476	2.126	3.055
									H	1.375	2.677	5.145	9.867
133	133	140	140	144	151	154	147	150		171	180	185	187
									L	254	387	577	796
55.1	56.8	67.2	81.4	92.1	100.0	100.3	126.3	136.6	M	341	647	1,126	1,947
									H	485	1,144	2,369	4,699
									L	3.42	5.25	7.86	10.88
.647	.759	.858	1.166	1.237	1.221	1.311	1.813	1.809	M	4.59	8.78	15.34	26.60
									H	6.54	15.52	32.28	64.19
85.1	74.8	78.3	69.8	74.4	81.9	76.5	69.7	75.5		74.2	73.7	73.4	73.2
									L	133	163	197	229
90.2	91.2	92.8	96.2	99.8	100.0	102.1	106.5	109.4	M	140	184	240	303
									H	169	259	398	600
									L	107.5	130.5	156.4	181.9
73.6	75.5	76.2	79.0	82.0	83.1	82.8	85.9	87.6	M	112.7	147.0	190.7	240.2
									H	136.1	207.1	316.2	475.8
1.23	1.21	1.22	1.22	1.22	1.20	1.23	1.24	1.25		1.24	1.25	1.26	1.26
									L	109	130	152	188
86.5	88.8	86.2	94.8	100.1	100.0	91.4	95.3	97.1	M	128	167	218	292
									H	149	222	325	514
									L	83	93	92	93
100.4	94.8	81.7	96.6	103.4	100.1	82.5	82.3	82.6	M	98	120	125	135
									H	122	167	194	257
									L	438	490	484	489
507	488	421	491	530	518	432	433	436	M	514	630	658	711
									H	644	881	1,020	1,354
.198	.194	.194	.197	.195	.193	.191	.190	.189		.190	.190	.190	.190
									L	114	139	171	215
85.2	89.2	89.2	95.3	100.0	100.0	93.6	98.6	98.5	M	132	173	232	321
									H	147	223	335	534
									L	111	137	171	219
87.3	90.1	88.4	94.8	99.6	100.0	93.4	98.4	98.1	M	126	164	221	298
									H	138	209	312	495
									L	2.91	3.58	4.48	5.73
2.29	2.36	2.32	2.48	2.62	2.62	2.45	2.57	2.57	M	3.30	4.29	5.79	7.81
									H	3.62	5.47	8.18	12.95
38.1	38.2	38.1	38.2	38.0	38.2	38.1	38.3	38.2		38.2	38.2	38.2	38.2
									L	145	175	193	216
74.5	78.5	80.9	87.3	93.9	100.0	101.8	106.9	118.9	M	171	219	259	312
									H	200	281	370	504
									L	15.6	18.8	20.8	23.2
8.01	8.40	8.74	9.41	10.08	10.68	11.03	12.05	12.77	M	18.4	23.6	27.9	33.6
									H	21.5	30.2	39.8	54.2
9.30	9.35	9.26	9.28	9.32	9.36	9.23	8.87	9.31		93.0	93.0	93.0	93.0
									L	148	189	238	305
78.8	85.5	87.1	92.0	98.7	99.9	97.4	105.9	106.4	M	173	239	329	493
									H	199	309	469	753
									L	464	591	745	954
224	239	252	281	293	295	295	321	339	M	540	747	1,029	1,540
									H	622	966	1,467	2,352
.352	.358	.346	.327	.337	.339	.330	.330	.314		.32	.32	.32	.32

Table A1–30 (cont'd)

	1957 prop. (wt.)	1947	1948	1949	1950	1951
Oil and gas drilling	.77	52.0	61.8	62.3	72.4	78.4
Expenditures on oil and gas drilling[15] ($ 1960 bil.)	–	1.23	1.52	1.54	1.78	1.97
Index points per $ billion	–	42.3	40.7	40.4	40.7	39.8
Metal mining	.70	73.4	75.7	68.0	78.4	84.3
Primary metals index[60]	–	80.8	84.1	70.8	89.1	96.9
Index points per point of primary metals index[61]	–	.908	.900	.960	.880	.870
Stone and earth minerals	.80	55.0	59.9	57.9	66.2	72.3
Clay, glass, and stone products index[60]	–	68.0	72.5	67.6	81.8	90.4
Index points per point of clay, etc., index	–	.81	.83	.86	.81	.81
UTILITIES	4.96	38.9	43.4	46.3	52.7	60.1
Electricity	3.76	38.6	43.3	46.2	52.0	59.0
Utility sales of electricity[62] (bil. kwh)	–	218	241	248	280	318
Index points per bil. kwh[6]	–	.177	.180	.186	.186	.186
Gas	1.20	39.4	43.6	46.2	54.3	62.6
Net marketed production of natural gas[63] (tril. cu. ft.)	–	3.51	3.94	4.16	4.86	5.68
Index points per tril. cu. ft.[6]	–	11.2	11.1	11.1	11.2	11.0

1. This table shows the method of deriving the projections in Table A1–29. It includes not only the series shown there, but a number of subcomponent index series, which were not material to projections developed elsewhere in this study and which were projected only for purposes of deriving the principal series. These subcomponents are generally of a lesser order of reliability and in some cases are not even published by the Federal Reserve Board, although they can be deduced as residuals from the series that are published.

The elemental components in each case were derived by (1) calculating the historical coefficients between the desired index series and an appropriate reference series which is projected elsewhere in this study, (2) extrapolating the coefficients for future years, and (3) multiplying to get the desired index projections. The extrapolation in each case was based partly or wholly on graphic analysis, and in most cases it was on a straight-line basis. However, qualitative judgments were also applied in many instances; the more important of these are detailed in the footnotes below.

Series which do not show the foregoing kind of derivation have been derived by first multiplying the indexes in each subcomponent by the subcomponent weight in order to get a set of aggregates, then adding the aggregates and dividing by the combined weights. The aggregates have not been reproduced in the table, but they may easily be calculated using the indicated weights ("1957 proportion"). (Some minor discrepancies may appear in replication, owing to calculation of some of the original series before rounding.)

The series designated as "direct" were projected in the same manner as the elemental subcomponents. Where such directly projected series showed differences from their "added" counterparts which exceeded reasonable bounds for

1952	1953	1954	1955	1956	1957	1958	1959	1960		1970	1980	1990	2000
									L	106	114	131	151
83.7	90.5	98.0	102.7	105.4	100.0	89.2	93.3	85.4	M	131	180	241	339
									H	151	241	392	669
									L	2.6	2.8	3.2	3.7
2.10	2.21	2.36	2.55	2.63	2.46	2.06	2.24	2.19	M	3.2	4.4	5.9	8.3
									H	3.7	5.9	9.6	16.4
39.9	41.0	41.5	40.3	40.1	40.6	43.3	41.7	39.0		40.8	40.8	40.8	40.8
									L	92	90	92	92
77.8	86.6	70.9	89.8	94.7	100.0	82.5	77.1	96.8	M	116	134	155	182
									H	145	190	246	342
									L	102	112	131	154
88.5	100.3	81.3	105.5	103.7	100.0	78.0	89.5	90.3	M	129	168	222	303
									H	161	237	352	570
.879	.863	.872	.851	.913	100.0	1.06	.861	1.07		.90	.80	.70	.60
									L	127	156	185	236
75.5	77.5	85.4	92.8	100.3	100.0	98.4	108.0	112.1	M	165	228	320	478
									H	209	331	532	943
									L	130	159	189	241
86.4	88.6	85.2	97.2	101.7	100.0	94.7	110.2	109.6	M	168	233	327	488
									H	213	338	543	962
.87	.88	1.00	.96	.99	1.00	1.04	.98	1.02		.98	.98	.98	.98
									L	172	245	320	422
65.2	71.1	76.5	85.4	93.6	100.0	104.5	115.0	123.1	M	201	314	447	637
									H	250	421	647	1,013
									L	180	265	358	486
64.3	71.1	76.0	85.4	93.5	100.0	104.3	115.2	123.2	M	209	342	504	739
									H	265	462	732	1,172
									L	986	1,448	1,956	2,654
342	384	411	481	530	558	569	627	665	M	1,141	1,869	2,752	4,039
									H	1,448	2,525	3,998	6,404
.188	.185	.185	.178	.176	.179	.183	.184	.185		.183	.183	.183	.183
									L	148	181	199	220
67.3	70.9	78.0	85.2	93.8	100.0	105.0	114.4	122.5	M	175	227	267	318
									H	204	291	382	514
									L	13.13	16.04	17.65	19.50
6.15	6.26	6.97	7.58	8.31	8.80	9.06	9.97	10.58	M	15.51	20.13	23.63	28.15
									H	18.06	25.75	33.79	45.49
10.9	11.3	11.2	11.2	11.3	11.4	11.6	11.5	11.6		11.3	11.3	11.3	11.3

statistical error plus "non-allocable" (see footnote 6, Table A1–13), the two series (including the added subcomponents) were approximately adjusted to one another. The directly projected series, rather than the added ones, were used in further aggregation.

Source of the historical data is as in footnote 1, Table A1–28. In addition to its use as a statistical data source, *Industrial Production: 1959 Revision* was relied on for the details on sources and descriptions of the FRB series on the basis of which most of the judgments were made as to appropriate reference series and the changing nature of their relationship to the FRB indexes.

2. From Tables A1–6 and 13.

3. The long-run correlation between the industrial production index and non-farm goods output was pointed out by the Office of Business Economics, U.S. Department of Commerce, when the non-farm goods series was first published (*Survey of Current Business,* June 1957, p. 11). There is no obvious reason for the clear upward rise in the coefficients, other than the possibility of a declining role for goods transportation (which is not part of the industrial production index) in relation to manufacturing value added (cf. Table A5–9). This would affect both the manufacturing and the general industrial production index. The slightly slower rise of the latter than the former is presumably due to the drag imposed by mining—again a reflection of the declining role of physical mass in relation to total value added.

4. It was assumed that the apparent trend toward increase of the index in relation to the reference series would begin to taper as the industrial processing component accounted for an increasingly larger share of end-product value.

5. From Tables A16–1 and 9.*

Table A1–30 (cont'd)

6. The contents of the reference series used by the FRB and the reference series herein are so close that, in the absence of any clear trend, an average of the historical coefficients has been used (in some cases limited to less than the full 1947–60 period, owing to obvious discontinuities in the data).

7. From Tables A16–30 and 35.*

8. The declining coefficient reflects increasing relative satisfaction of domestic consumption requirements by net imports.

9. From Tables A16–38 and 47.*

10. From Tables A16–50 and 56.*

11. There is no very satisfactory reference series for magnesium, since magnesium metal requirements have not been projected in this study. The tie made here to aluminum is based on partial similarity of end-uses, as well as the joint application of magnesium and aluminum in many end-uses, including application in magnesium-aluminum alloys. The declining coefficient, on the other hand, reflects the fact that most of the projected growth in aluminum will be in applications in which magnesium does not play a significant role as well as in applications where the two metals are competitive.

12. From Tables A16–59 and 66.*

13. From Table A16–75, or aggregated from Tables A16–30, 38, 50, 59, and 69.*

14. From Tables A16–31, 32, 39, 44, 60, and 61.*

15. From Tables A4–1 and 3.*

16. From Tables A6–2 and 4.

17. The trend in the coefficients is presumably the result of changes in the product mix which, in the absence of evident reasons to the contrary, are assumed to continue.

18. From Tables A1–26 and 27 and A6–2 and 4.

19. The effects of changing product mix are assumed to taper off and the index eventually to rise proportionally to constant-dollar value of aggregate output. This outcome is suggested, in part, by the graphic analysis.

20. From Tables A5–1 and 11.

21. The sharp historical increase in the coefficients is presumed due to the faster rise in output of certain types of equipment (automatic transmissions, power brakes, etc.) which the FRB includes in the index, in relation to automobiles as such. This discrepancy in growth rates is assumed to taper off.

22. From *American Automobile Association, Motor Truck Facts,* 1961 ed.; U.S. Department of Commerce, Current Industrial Reports, Series M37L; and Table A5–10 herein ("total demand").

23. From Automobile Manufacturers Association, *Automobile Facts and Figures,* 1961 ed., and Table A5–13 herein.

24. Not published by Federal Reserve Board; inferred from the published data. In most cases not all years are calculable, owing to changes in index weighting and/or non-availability of related components.

25. From Tables A1–26 and 27.

26. From Tables A9–1 and 2.

27. Aside from past trend, two elements would seem to justify the rising coefficients in the future: (1) a presumably increasing role for non-military production in relation to the military production which is now the bulk of the output and on which the projection is based; (2) the assignment to a separate category, in our defense expenditures projections, of the increasing amounts of electronic equipment which will go into aircraft, missiles, and space vehicles and which will continue to influence the FRB index.

28. From Tables A1–6 and 13. With almost half of private shipbuilding being devoted to military output and the rest following a sporadic course, there is no really satisfactory reference series for this index. However, its relative weight is small and a very precise calculation was therefore not needed.

29. From Tables A5–16 and 17 (freight cars plus other rolling stock).

30. Aside from past trend, the rising coefficients would seem to be justified by the steadily increasing use of instrumentation in relation to producer durables as a whole.

31. From Tables A13–3 and 5.

32. Aside from historical trend, the increasing coefficient would seem to be justified by increasing relative amounts of processing (e.g., relatively more plywood, prefabrication).

33. From Tables A1–26 and 27. Although this index is part of the "durables" group, the most important of its three principal components is "misc. consumer non-durable goods." The other two components are "misc. consumer durable goods" and "misc. business supplies."

34. The downward trend in the coefficient, which has been extrapolated at a declining rate, may be due to the increasing relative contribution of imports. It does not seem to be particularly ascribable to items omitted from the reference series.

35. From Tables A3–1 and 2.

36. On the assumption that the declining historical trend is due to a lesser amount of mill processing for man-made fibers, the trend is continued, but permitted to taper off. A similar tapering has been projected (Table A3–2) in the declining relative participation of natural as against man-made fibers in total fiber consumption.

37. The historical upward trend is probably due to the declining relationship of raw material content (included in the reference series value) to value added in apparel manufacture. Based partly on the graphic record, the relationships between material content and value added are assumed eventually to stabilize, or to appear to stabilize because of counterbalancing factors, including (on the index-depressing side) advances in mechanization and automation and an increasing proportion of imports.

38. From Tables A3–1 and 4.

39. The declining historical trend is presumably due to the declining role for leather (included in the index) in relation to consumption of shoes. This relative decline should taper (see Table A3–4), largely because the substitution of other materials in non-shoe uses is approaching a hard-core limit.

40. From Tables A8–1 and 2.

41. Although job printing and periodicals have a greater weight in the index than do newspapers, no reference series has been projected herein which adequately represents the former group. It is assumed that there is a relatively uniformly changing relationship between the two segments, even though the first segment is increasing more rapidly.

42. This index has been related to the general industrial production index because of the varied and general use of inorganic chemicals (or items manufactured from inorganic chemicals) throughout industry. The ratio of inorganic chemical output to general industrial output has been projected at a lower rate of rise than in the recent past, however, on the grounds that much of the recent rise has been due to increases in "atomic energy manufacturing," which accounts for over one-third of the total weight; with the expected leveling off in atomic products output, the over-all relative growth in the inorganic chemicals index should be slowed.

43. Given below; the bulk of basic organic chemical output now goes into the production of synthetic materials.

44. Because of the decreasing proportion of basic organics going into substances other than synthetic materials, the coefficient is permitted to decline (geometrically, since the relative effect will be increasingly less).

45. From Table A17–4* and U.S. Tariff Commission, annual reports on *Synthetic Organic Chemicals: U.S. Production and Sales.*

46. From Table A17–7* and U.S. Department of Commerce, *Current Industrial Reports,* Series M30A.

47. From Tables A3–1 and 3.

48. From Table A17–11 and U.S. Department of Agriculture, *Fats and Oils Situation,* Mar. 1959, p. 24.

49. From Table A17–12* and *Fats and Oils Situation,* May 1961, p. 21.

50. From Table A1–16 or calculated as indicated in footnote 3 thereto. (1947–49 not calculated.)

51. Historical data from Sam H. Schurr, Bruce C. Netschert, *et al., Energy in the American Economy, 1850–1975*

Table A1–30 (cont'd)

(Johns Hopkins Press and Resources for the Future, 1960), Appendix Table VI, or similarly calculated from current Bureau of Mines data. Projections are from a preliminary version of Table A15–13. Later changes were not included in order to avoid extensive "feedback" corrections, but the petroleum index was not used as such and the effect of the corrections on the over-all chemicals, etc., index would be relatively insignificant.

52. From Table A17–6* and *Current Industrial Reports,* Series M30A.

53. From Table A17–1 and U.S. Tariff Commission, annual reports on *Synthetic Organic Chemicals: U.S. Production and Sales.*

54. The tapering represents the expectation that the rate of increase in the processed food components of the index will slow down and tend toward identity with the rate for physical consumption of food in general.

55. From Table A15–16* and from "Bituminous Coal" and "Pennsylvania Anthracite" chapters of *Minerals Yearbook.*

56. The historically declining relationship of the index to coal output in tons is presumably due to the decline in anthracite output (with a higher value per ton) relative to bituminous. (The FRB index is a composite of the two separate indexes.) So far as it may be significant enough to affect the future over-all coal index, it is assumed that this differential movement has about run its course.

57. Historical data from "Crude Petroleum and Petroleum Products" chapter of *Minerals Yearbook.* Projections by linking consumption, Table A15–13,* to production at 1960.

58. Historical data from "Natural Gas" chapter of *Minerals Yearbook.* Projections by linking "net withdrawals," Table A15–14,* to marketed production at 1960.

59. From Tables A15–12 and 15.*

60. From this table, above.*

61. The projected decline in the coefficient is based on the assumption of increasing relative utilization of foreign ores.

62. From Tables A15–3 and 1.*

63. Historical data from Table A15–12. Projections by linking "total identified uses plus pipeline fuel," Table A15–14,* to the historical series at 1960.

---

* A preliminary version was used, with the result that there are small discrepancies between the data now given in the reference table and the data (or derived) data given here. These discrepancies were insufficiently large to warrant revision of the FRB index.

appendix
to
chapter
2

FOOD

Notes

IN GENERAL, the projections of per capita demand for foods and food groups (Table A2–2) have been based upon the following: (a) past trends in per capita consumption; (b) indications from the Department of Agriculture's 1955 Household Food Consumption Survey (USDA, *Food Consumption of Households in the United States, 1956*); and (c) the judgment of persons who have been concerned with estimates of consumption of individual foods and food groups.

The extrapolation of trends into the future has been further modified by the assumption that the amounts of food consumed per person will tend to become relatively fixed some time before the year 2000. At present and over the past half century, changes in income have played an important role in the shift from one food to another. As incomes increase, however, their effect on the type of food consumed becomes less important. The high levels of income projected for the future will permit full gratification of *present* taste preferences. Although other factors affect patterns of consumption (medical knowledge, distaste for obesity, past experience, etc.), their effect cannot be clearly anticipated so far in the future.

With the exception of those of beef, we have made no specific allowances for changes in relative prices. However, the extrapolation of past trends implicitly assumes the continuation of all factors, including price changes, which have affected consumption rates in the past.

The basic per capita consumption data (Table A2–1) have been drawn from USDA, *Consumption of Food in the United States, 1909–52* (Agricultural Handbook No. 62), Supplements for 1956 and 1960 (Sept. 1957 and Aug. 1961).

In all but a few cases, the data refer to quantities as measured at farm or wholesale rather than retail level. The farm measure provides a convenient common denominator for most agricultural products, whether consumed in fresh or processed forms. The farm measure also facilitates making estimates of required farm output. It does not, however, directly provide a check estimate of the number of pounds which the consumer may be expected to eat or purchase in the future; this has had to be calculated (Table A2–2). And it presents problems in dealing with food groups whose components have had differences in trend between farm and retail levels.

The use of the term "consumption" is not absolutely precise. The historical data of the USDA actually refer to "domestic disappearance," which is a residual figure derived from estimates of output, stock changes, and foreign trade. We have added to this, wherever available, USDA estimates of consumption of foods which have been grown in home gardens and which do not appear in the regular output statistics. The USDA per capita estimates were derived by use of data that exclude military population and military consumption. For the sake of comparability herein, the historical aggregates in Table A2–4 have been reconstituted using the official "population, including Armed Forces overseas." This involves only slight differences from the USDA "domestic disappearance" totals for civilian food, except for the World War II years and where significant home garden production is involved.

In all cases we have used 1980 as the primary target for the projections of per capita consumption. With 1980 as a benchmark, we have then made rough estimates of demand for the year 2000. The intervening periods have been estimated by interpolation.

As in other sections of this study, the projections include ranges—the upper and lower limits within which consumption might reasonably be expected to fall—as well as a Medium figure which represents our judgment as to the most likely course of development. The ranges are intended to bracket the area of substantial uncertainty and thus reveal the contingent problems that may be faced. The meaning of the High and Low, however, differs somewhat from table to table in this chapter, depending upon the purpose to be served. In Tables A2–2 and A2–4, they represent the reasonably possible extremes for each different food item. In Tables A2–5 and A2–6, where models representing different patterns of meat and poultry consumption are shown, they represent the levels for individual items which, in combination, lead, respectively, to High and Low feed consumption.

It should be noted further that, as usual, the Highs and Lows are not additive, so that, for example, High and Low meat consumption (in Table A2–2) is not the sum of the High and Low components, but allows for compensation among them. Since it is not pertinent to the further derivations,

no attempt has been made to project the Highs and Lows of total consumption in either pounds or calories. These would not vary much from the projected Medium levels and would be well within the range which would be implied by the projected Highs and Lows of the individual food items were there no compensation among them.

This appendix deals with the principal food items in the physical form in which they are sold either at retail or at wholesale. In the appendix to Chapter 12 are shown the further conversions, where applicable, into farm crops and, for the items of animal origin, into feed implications.

LIST OF TABLES

TABLE A2–1.　Historical Data on Annual Per Capita Food Consumption[1]

(All quantities in pounds, unless otherwise specified)

	Total calories per day[2]	Total consumption in lb.[3] (retail wt. equiv.)	Meat[4] (carcass wt.) Total	Beef	Veal	Lamb and mutton	Pork (including pork fat cuts)	Fish[5] (edible wt. equiv.)	Poultry[6] (ready to cook basis)	Eggs[7] (no.)	Whole milk equiv.	Milk fat	Nonfat solids
1909	3,570	1,616	155.2	74.2	7.3	6.7	67.0	11.1	14.7	293	770	30.2	32.9
1910	3,530	1,589	146.4	70.4	7.2	6.5	62.3	11.3	15.5	306	759	29.7	31.1
1911	3,510	1,558	151.9	68.5	7.1	7.3	69.0	11.4	15.6	329	749	29.4	30.1
1912	3,500	1,619	145.9	64.6	6.9	7.7	66.7	11.4	14.9	312	763	29.9	34.1
1913	3,490	1,583	143.7	63.3	6.3	7.2	66.9	11.6	14.5	303	754	29.5	33.4
1914	3,480	1,552	140.0	62.0	5.8	7.1	65.1	11.8	14.5	295	747	29.2	32.0
1915	3,460	1,568	134.9	56.4	5.9	6.1	66.5	11.3	14.4	313	751	29.4	31.9
1916	3,410	1,508	140.1	58.9	6.4	5.8	69.0	11.1	13.8	299	747	29.3	31.6
1917	3,350	1,510	135.3	64.7	7.2	4.5	58.9	11.0	13.3	281	729	28.6	32.4
1918	3,400	1,560	141.6	68.5	7.3	4.8	61.0	11.0	13.3	284	725	28.4	35.2
1919	3,470	1,541	138.9	61.5	7.8	5.7	63.9	11.7	14.2	303	733	28.8	33.3
1920	3,320	1,542	136.0	59.1	8.0	5.4	63.5	11.9	13.7	299	736	28.9	33.9
1921	3,230	1,496	134.0	55.5	7.6	6.1	64.8	10.6	13.4	300	768	30.1	34.0
1922	3,460	1,561	137.7	59.1	7.8	5.1	65.7	11.4	14.2	316	783	30.7	34.0
1923	3,480	1,565	147.3	59.6	8.2	5.3	74.2	10.8	14.6	326	787	30.9	33.5
1924	3,500	1,572	147.3	59.5	8.6	5.2	74.0	11.1	13.7	324	796	31.1	34.3
1925	3,480	1,559	140.1	59.5	8.6	5.2	66.8	11.2	14.3	318	802	31.4	34.4
1926	3,500	1,567	138.0	60.3	8.2	5.4	64.1	11.5	14.2	339	818	32.0	34.6
1927	3,500	1,544	134.9	54.5	7.4	5.3	67.7	12.3	15.2	342	813	31.8	34.7
1928	3,520	1,561	131.6	48.7	6.5	5.5	70.9	12.2	14.6	338	804	31.5	34.9
1929	3,500	1,572	131.2	49.7	6.3	5.6	69.6	11.9	15.7	334	811	31.8	35.9
1930	3,480	1,537	129.0	48.9	6.4	6.7	67.0	10.3	17.2	331	819	32.1	35.7
1931	3,420	1,547	130.7	48.6	6.6	7.1	68.4	9.0	15.5	333	838	32.9	35.4
1932	3,360	1,509	131.1	46.7	6.6	7.1	70.7	8.5	16.1	313	832	32.7	35.6
1933	3,320	1,491	136.1	51.5	7.1	6.8	70.7	8.8	16.7	296	814	31.9	35.5
1934	3,280	1,492	143.9	63.8	9.4	6.3	64.4	9.3	15.3	289	814	32.0	35.0
1935	3,230	1,505	117.4	53.2	8.5	7.3	48.4	10.6	14.8	280	801	31.6	35.7
1936	3,320	1,511	130.6	60.5	8.4	6.6	55.1	11.8	15.9	289	792	31.3	36.3
1937	3,280	1,520	126.2	55.2	8.6	6.6	55.8	10.8	15.9	308	798	31.5	36.9
1938	3,290	1,519	127.1	54.4	7.6	6.9	58.2	11.0	15.0	310	796	31.4	37.1
1939	3,380	1,553	133.6	54.7	7.6	6.6	64.7	10.8	16.6	313	825	32.6	37.7
1940	3,370	1,551	142.4	54.9	7.4	6.6	73.5	10.6	17.0	319	819	32.5	38.1
1941	3,430	1,573	143.7	60.9	7.6	6.8	68.4	11.2	18.3	311	803	32.0	38.4
1942	3,370	1,568	140.3	61.2	8.2	7.2	63.7	8.8	20.7	318	833	33.2	41.0
1943	3,400	1,588	146.8	53.3	8.2	6.4	78.9	8.0	25.7	347	750	30.1	42.8
1944	3,390	1,640	154.2	55.6	12.4	6.7	79.5	8.8	23.1	354	763	30.6	43.0
1945	3,330	1,651	145.2	59.4	11.9	7.3	66.6	10.0	25.1	402	788	31.6	45.6
1946	3,350	1,647	154.1	61.6	10.0	6.7	75.8	10.6	23.1	379	786	31.4	46.9
1947	3,300	1,598	155.3	69.6	10.8	5.3	69.6	10.1	21.7	383	769	30.7	44.0
1948	3,240	1,528	145.5	63.1	9.5	5.1	67.8	10.6	21.4	389	724	28.8	42.4
1949	3,220	1,521	144.6	63.9	8.9	4.1	67.7	10.7	22.9	383	734	29.1	42.3
1950	3,290	1,505	144.6	63.4	8.0	4.0	69.2	11.6	24.7	389	741	29.4	42.7
1951	3,190	1,497	138.0	56.1	6.6	3.4	71.9	11.1	26.1	392	715	28.2	42.8
1952	3,230	1,494	146.0	62.2	7.2	4.2	72.4	11.0	26.8	390	700	27.3	43.6
1953	3,200	1,494	155.3	77.6	9.5	4.7	63.5	11.4	26.7	379	691	26.8	42.8
1954	3,180	1,486	154.7	80.1	10.0	4.6	60.0	11.3	28.1	376	700	27.1	43.3
1955	3,200	1,492	162.8	82.0	9.4	4.6	66.8	10.4	26.3	371	706	27.2	44.3
1956	3,200	1,499	166.7	85.4	9.5	4.5	67.3	10.3	29.6	369	703	26.9	44.9
1957	3,150	1,480	158.7	84.6	8.8	4.2	61.1	10.1	31.4	362	684	26.0	44.3
1958	3,160	1,465	151.6	80.5	6.8	4.2	60.2	10.6	34.1	354	680	25.7	44.0
1959	3,210	1,473	159.5	81.4	5.7	4.8	67.6	10.7	35.2	353	666	25.0	44.2
1960	3,190	1,465	161.5	85.2	6.2	4.8	65.3	10.5	34.6	334	654	24.6	44.2

| | | | | | Consumption of principal items | | | | | |

	Wheat[9] (grain equiv.)	Corn[10] (grain equiv.)	Potatoes & sweet potatoes[11]	Tomatoes[12]	Other vegetables[13]	Citrus fruit[14]	Apples[14]	Other fruits & melons[15]	Sugar & syrups[16] (refined)	Fats & oils[17] (retail wt.)	Coffee, tea, & cocoa[18]
1909	315	n.a.	229	n.a.	n.a.	–	–	n.a.	87.5	60	10
1910	310	"	238	"	"	17.8	62.2	"	89.9	59	10
1911	310	"	195	"	"	19.8	76.5	"	92.3	61	9
1912	306	"	217	"	"	18.5	78.0	"	90.8	58	11
1913	302	"	226	"	"	16.6	62.8	"	95.2	59	10
1914	301	"	192	"	"	24.1	74.2	"	94.6	62	10
1915	299	"	222	"	"	23.1	71.8	"	91.5	62	11
1916	298	"	180	"	"	22.0	68.6	"	91.5	62	12
1917	272	"	186	"	"	22.0	61.8	"	93.2	57	14
1918	247	"	212	"	"	16.5	62.6	"	94.2	60	12
1919	277	"	192	54	186	23.5	50.3	123.8	108.8	61	13
1920	263	"	180	52	201	26.0	67.6	138.0	104.3	58	13
1921	245	"	194	48	189	30.5	39.1	132.2	103.2	57	13
1922	259	"	181	50	195	24.6	60.6	146.7	122.1	62	13
1923	260	"	208	53	193	32.6	58.1	133.2	108.4	66	14
1924	256	"	180	52	206	34.1	56.8	141.6	118.4	66	13
1925	260	"	183	54	208	29.2	49.4	140.5	121.7	66	12
1926	259	"	157	55	210	31.7	65.0	154.0	123.1	65	14
1927	260	67.6	173	53	207	32.7	39.9	139.0	122.2	66	13
1928	255	70.5	175	52	207	30.0	51.3	150.9	124.0	67	13
1929	254	71.1	188	54	216	40.4	42.7	143.6	116.8	68	14
1930	247	65.9	157	58	219	32.2	45.3	139.3	128.7	67	13
1931	240	60.8	164	56	212	43.9	53.7	147.3	117.9	68	14
1932	242	58.9	170	57	209	37.5	41.1	123.7	112.4	67	14
1933	232	60.2	164	57	205	40.7	42.1	119.4	113.4	67	14
1934	222	56.3	167	57	216	41.2	27.7	126.4	112.8	67	14
1935	225	51.1	176	61	213	48.2	35.4	135.1	112.7	62	15
1936	235	54.2	158	61	217	49.4	30.4	134.8	114.8	65	16
1937	228	51.2	156	63	216	50.6	36.9	146.8	112.1	65	15
1938	229	51.2	158	65	220	55.7	31.3	138.9	111.2	65	16
1939	225	51.6	150	65	223	71.3	33.6	141.7	116.8	68	17
1940	220	51.6	147	66	225	67.1	33.8	143.3	112.1	71	17
1941	221	57.4	154	66	223	72.5	35.4	141.6	121.8	70	18
1942	223	65.7	154	72	234	72.1	31.7	119.0	106.4	66	15
1943	229	64.4	154	76	229	71.6	28.2	103.1	103.4	67	14
1944	211	62.3	165	80	234	89.3	28.8	116.1	111.9	66	16
1945	230	63.6	147	89	248	88.3	26.6	135.0	96.8	61	17
1946	214	58.8	147	86	241	95.3	27.9	147.3	98.3	64	21
1947	196	58.8	147	76	226	94.1	30.1	134.7	118.9	65	18
1948	194	49.0	122	71	221	93.1	31.3	127.9	110.7	65	19
1949	193	49.9	128	70	210	82.4	30.2	127.8	112.3	65	19
1950	192	50.5	124	71	213	73.3	29.3	119.8	118.0	68	18
1951	190	49.0	127	74	207	82.8	31.5	119.5	110.7	65	18
1952	188	47.5	115	71	206	84.4	28.2	121.8	114.2	68	18
1953	182	46.2	121	72	202	85.6	26.6	126.2	113.6	65	18
1954	178	44.9	121	70	200	86.0	26.2	122.4	111.5	66	16
1955	174	45.2	122	73	198	91.4	26.5	120.0	112.9	68	16
1956	170	45.2	115	73	200	88.0	26.3	120.7	113.4	67	17
1957	167	44.2	121	74	195	89.2	25.7	118.4	111.4	65	17
1958	169	45.5	114	74	194	75.6	29.8	119.4	113.9	66	17
1959	167	46.3	118	76	191	82.8	30.6	116.9	113.9	69	17
1960	165	46.0	120	77	192	86.3	27.7	119.7	115.4	67	17

Table A2–1 (cont'd)

1. Source citations under individual items are to tables in U.S. Department of Agriculture, Agricultural Marketing Service, 1956 and 1960 supplements to *Consumption of Food in the United States, 1909–52*. The figures from 1941 to date refer to civilian consumption, earlier data to all consumption.

2. Based on quantities of nutrients available for consumption per capita per day (retail basis), computed by the Institute of Home Economics and including estimates of produce of rural and urban home gardens, prepared by the Agricultural Marketing Service. Source: Table 44.

3. Source: Table 38.

4. Approximately at wholesale level of distribution. Source: Table 8.

5. Quantities for 1909–28 represent approximations, with fresh and frozen fish, canned fish, and cured fish consumption sub-components based on straight line projections. Source: Table 29.

6. Sum of chicken and turkey series, in equivalent eviscerated weight basis. Source: Table 8.

7. Measured approximately at wholesale level of distribution. Source: Table 8.

8. Total milk is whole milk equivalent of all dairy products on a milk-fat-solid basis. Sources: Tables 9 and 66 (1960 supplement).

9. Source: Table 88.

10. Includes quantities used for corn sugar and syrup. Source: Table 92.

11. Farm weight basis, including estimated home garden production. Sources: Tables 21, 22, and 36.

12. Farm weight basis, including estimated home garden production. Sources: Tables 21 and 36.

13. Farm weight basis, including estimated home garden production. Includes dry beans and peas and leafy green, yellow, and other vegetables. Sources: Tables 21, 22, and 36.

14. Farm weight basis. Beginning in 1934, apples are those grown only in commercial areas. Source: Table 16.

15. Farm weight basis, including estimated home garden production. Sources: Tables 16, 21, and 36.

16. Amounts include cane, beet, and corn sugar as well as honey and molasses. Data are on an approximate retail weight basis. Source: Table 37.

17. Series includes pork fat cuts, which is duplicated under pork, and butter, which is duplicated under milk fat, in retail weight equivalent. Source: Table 32.

18. Series is on basis of retail weight equivalent. It includes coffee on roasted basis (84% of green beans) and chocolate liquor equivalent of cocoa and chocolate products. Source: Table 38.

TABLE A2–2. Projected Per Capita Food Consumption[1]

(Pounds, except for eggs)

	1940	1945	1950	1955	1960		1970	1980	1990	2000
Total calories per day[2]	3,370	3,330	3,290	3,200	3,190		3,130	3,120	3,100	3,080
Total annual consumption[3] (retail weight equivalent)	1,550	1,650	1,510	1,500	1,460		1,470	1,490	1,490	1,490
Meat, total[4] (carcass wt.)	142	145	145	163	161	L	164	170	170	170
						M	175	187	190	195
						H	185	195	205	210
Beef (carcass wt.)	54.9	59.4	63.4	82.0	85.2	L	83	85	85	85
						M	95	103	105	105
						H	100	110	115	115
Veal (carcass wt.)	7.4	11.9	8.0	9.4	6.2	L	7.0	7.0	7.0	7.0
						M	7.8	8.5	9.0	9.0
						H	8.5	9.5	10.5	11.0
Lamb and mutton (carcass wt.)	6.6	7.3	4.0	4.5	4.8	L	3.7	3.5	3.5	3.5
						M	4.9	5.5	6.0	6.0
						H	6.0	6.5	7.0	7.5
Pork (carcass wt.)	73.5	66.6	69.2	66.8	65.3	L	60	60	60	60
						M	66	70	74	75
						H	78	83	85	85
Fish (edible wt. equiv.)	10.6	10.0	11.6	10.4	10.5	L	9	9	9	9
						M	10	10	10	10
						H	11	11	11	11
Poultry[5] (ready-to-cook basis)	17.0	25.1	24.7	26.3	34.6	L	35	35	35	35
						M	38	40	40	40
						H	43	45	45	45

Table A2–2 (cont'd)   (Pounds, except for eggs)

	1940	1945	1950	1955	1960		1970	1980	1990	2000
Eggs (number)	319	402	389	371	334	L	330	330	330	330
						M	360	360	360	360
						H	390	400	400	400
Dairy products (whole milk equiv.) [6]	819	788	741	706	654	L	590	550	510	500
						M	645	630	610	610
						H	675	680	680	680
Milk fat	32.5	31.6	29.4	27.2	24.6	L	22	20	18.5	18
						M	24	23	22	22
						H	25	25	24	24
Non-fat solids	38.1	45.6	42.7	44.3	44.2	L	44	44	44	44
						M	48	51	53	53
						H	51	56	58	58
Wheat (grain equiv.)	220	230	192	174	165	L	135	120	110	100
						M	145	135	125	120
						H	155	145	140	140
Corn (grain equiv.)	51.6	63.6	50.5	45.2	46.0	L	35	31	28	26
						M	39	35	32	31
						H	43	40	38	38
Potatoes and sweet potatoes (farm wt.)	147	147	124	122	120	L	95	85	85	85
						M	105	95	95	95
						H	120	115	115	115
Tomatoes (farm wt.)	66	89	71	73	77	L	70	70	70	70
						M	75	80	80	80
						H	83	88	90	90
Other vegetables (farm wt.)	225	248	213	198	192	L	175	175	175	175
						M	190	190	195	195
						H	205	210	220	220
Citrus fruit (farm wt.)	67.1	88.3	73.3	91.4	86.3	L	90	100	100	100
						M	105	115	115	115
						H	110	125	130	130
Apples (farm wt.)	33.8	26.6	29.3	26.5	27.7	L	22	20	20	20
						M	24	23	23	23
						H	26	25	25	25
Other fruits and melons (farm wt.)	143	135	120	120	120	L	105	101	100	100
						M	117	115	115	115
						H	125	125	125	125
Sugar and syrups (refined equiv.)	112	97	118	113	115	L	100	100	100	100
						M	105	105	105	105
						H	115	115	115	115
Fats and oils [7] (retail wt.)	71	61	68	68	67	L	60	60	60	60
						M	65	65	65	65
						H	70	70	70	70
Coffee, tea, and cocoa (retail wt.)	17	17	18	16	17	L	15	15	15	15
						M	17	17	17	17
						H	19	20	20	20

1. Historical data from Table A2–1. Projections on a judgment basis; see Chapter 2.

2. Based on detail shown in table and therefore slightly understated by reason of omission of edible offal and game. Also omitted from the calculation is the negligible per capita caloric contribution of cocoa. Conversions from retail weight are based on factors used in 1956 supplement to *Consumption of Food in the United States.*

3. Conversion from primary distribution weights, where necessary, based on factors used in 1956 supplement to *Consumption of Food in the United States.*

4. Total meat excludes estimates of edible offal and game.

High and Low detail will not add to total, since range in consumption of the individual items depends not only on range in total meat but on additional factor of possible substitutions among them.

5. Sum of chicken and turkey series in equivalent eviscerated weight basis.

6. Whole milk equivalent is based on projections of milk fat solids and of percentage of butterfat in milk (latter decreasing from 3.76% in 1960, to 3.65% in 1980, to 3.60% in 2000).

7. Includes pork fat cuts, which is duplicated under pork, and butter, which is duplicated under milk fat.

TABLE A2–3. Percentage of Food Energy Contributed by Major Food Groups[1] (medium projection)

	1940	1945	1950	1955	1960	1970	1980	1990	2000
Dairy products, excluding butter	11.3	14.1	13.2	13.6	13.2	14.0	14.4	14.7	14.8
Eggs	2.2	2.7	2.8	2.6	2.4	2.7	2.8	2.8	2.8
Meat, poultry, and fish	11.3	12.5	12.5	14.1	14.6	16.5	17.7	18.3	18.4
Fats and oils, including pork fat cuts and butter	20.4	17.5	20.2	20.5	20.5	20.2	20.3	20.4	20.6
Potatoes and sweet potatoes	3.6	3.6	3.1	3.2	3.1	2.7	2.5	2.5	2.5
Fruits, vegetables, and nuts	9.7	10.1	9.1	9.1	9.6	9.9	10.2	10.3	10.3
Flour and cereal products	26.5	26.9	23.2	21.4	20.7	19.2	17.4	16.0	15.6
Sugar and syrups	15.0	12.6	15.9	15.5	15.9	14.8	14.8	14.9	15.0
	100.0	100.0	100.0	100.0	100.0	100.0	100.0	100.0	100.0

1. Projections based on conversion of major food groups to retail weight equivalents multiplied by 1960 calorie factors per retail weight pound of food consumed, as derived from 1960 supplement to *Consumption of Food in the United States,* Tables 38, 44, and 47. The distribution shown is for the Medium projections only. Historical data are similarly calculated, except that the weight/calorie conversion factors used are those for the nearest year or period for which percentage distributions are published (*Consumption of Food,* Table 47) and apparent calorie factors may thus be calculated.

Fluid milk consumption data prior to 1960 have been revised, but effect on percentage distribution of calories not yet published.

TABLE A2–4. Aggregate Domestic Consumption of Principal Food Items, 1940–2000[1]

(Billion pounds, except for eggs)

	1940	1945	1950	1955	1960		1970	1980	1990	2000
Beef (carcass wt.)	7.26	8.31	9.62	13.55	15.33	L	16.8	19.2	21.2	22.8
						M	19.8	25.2	30.1	34.8
						H	22.3	30.6	40.1	49.8
Veal (carcass wt.)	.98	1.66	1.21	1.55	1.11	L	1.41	1.58	1.74	1.88
						M	1.62	2.08	2.58	2.98
						H	1.89	2.65	3.66	4.76
Lamb and mutton (carcass wt.)	.87	1.02	.96	.76	.86	L	.75	.79	.87	.94
						M	1.02	1.34	1.72	1.99
						H	1.22	1.81	2.62	3.25
Pork (carcass wt.)	9.70	9.32	10.50	11.04	11.74	L	12.1	13.6	14.9	16.1
						M	13.7	17.1	21.2	24.8
						H	17.3	23.1	29.7	36.8
Fish (edible wt.)	1.40	1.67	1.76	1.72	1.89	L	1.82	2.03	2.24	2.41
						M	2.08	2.45	2.87	3.31
						H	2.45	3.07	3.84	4.76
Poultry (ready-to-cook basis)	2.25	3.51	3.75	4.35	6.22	L	7.1	7.9	8.7	9.4
						M	7.9	9.8	11.5	13.2
						H	9.6	12.6	15.7	19.5
Eggs (billions)	42.1	56.2	59.0	61.3	60.1	L	66.7	75	82	88
						M	74.9	88	103	119
						H	87.0	112	140	173

Table A2–4 (cont'd)

(Billion pounds, except for eggs)

	1940	1945	1950	1955	1960		1970	1980	1990	2000
Dairy products (whole milk equiv.)	108.2	110.2	112.4	116.7	117.7	L	119	124	127	134
						M	134	154	175	202
						H	151	190	237	294
Milk fat	4.29	4.42	4.46	4.50	4.43	L	4.44	4.52	4.61	4.82
						M	4.99	5.64	6.31	7.28
						H	5.58	6.97	8.38	10.39
Non-fat solids	5.03	6.38	6.48	7.32	7.95	L	8.9	9.9	11.0	11.8
						M	10.0	12.5	15.2	17.5
						H	11.4	15.6	20.2	25.1
Wheat (grain equiv.)	29.1	32.2	29.1	28.8	29.7	L	27.3	27.1	27.4	27.0
						M	30.1	33.0	35.9	39.7
						H	34.5	40.4	48.9	60.6
Corn (grain equiv.)	6.82	8.90	7.66	7.47	8.28	L	7.07	7.01	6.97	6.97
						M	8.11	8.57	9.18	10.26
						H	9.59	11.16	13.26	16.45
Potatoes & sweet potatoes (farm wt.)	19.4	20.6	18.8	20.2	21.6	L	19.2	19.2	21.2	22.8
						M	21.8	23.3	27.3	31.4
						H	26.8	32.1	40.1	49.8
Tomatoes (farm wt.)	8.72	12.4	10.8	12.1	13.9	L	14.1	15.8	17.4	18.8
						M	15.6	19.6	23.0	26.5
						H	18.5	24.6	31.4	39.0
Other vegetables (farm wt.)	29.7	34.7	32.3	32.7	34.5	L	35.4	39.6	43.6	46.9
						M	39.5	46.6	56.0	64.5
						H	45.7	58.6	76.8	95.3
Citrus fruit (farm wt.)	8.86	12.4	11.1	15.1	15.5	L	18.2	22.6	24.9	26.8
						M	21.8	28.2	33.0	38.1
						H	24.5	34.9	45.4	56.3
Apples (farm wt.)	4.46	3.72	4.44	4.38	4.98	L	4.40	4.52	4.98	5.36
						M	4.99	5.64	6.60	7.61
						H	5.80	6.98	8.72	10.80
Other fruits and melons (farm wt.)	18.9	18.9	18.2	19.8	21.5	L	21.2	22.8	24.9	26.8
						M	24.3	28.2	33.0	38.1
						H	27.9	34.9	43.6	54.1
Sugar and syrups (refined equiv.)	14.8	13.5	17.9	18.7	20.8	L	20.2	22.6	24.9	26.8
						M	21.8	25.7	30.1	34.8
						H	25.6	32.1	40.1	49.8
Fats and oils [2] (retail wt.)	9.4	8.5	10.3	11.2	12.1	L	12.1	13.6	14.9	16.1
						M	13.5	15.9	18.7	21.5
						H	15.6	19.5	24.4	30.3
Coffee, tea, and cocoa (retail wt.)	2.25	2.38	2.73	2.64	3.06	L	3.03	3.39	3.74	4.02
						M	3.54	4.16	4.88	5.63
						H	4.24	5.58	6.98	8.66

1. Historical series are the product of July 1 population estimates including Armed Forces overseas and civilian per capita consumption. They thus differ from USDA's "domestic disappearance" (civilian and military). The actual military component for the war years appears to be inflated by sizable amounts of food probably destined for civilian use overseas, so that a theoretical inflation of civilian consumption to the "total population plus Armed Forces" base offers a better comparison for the projected quantities. Sources: Per capita consumption from Table A2–1; population from Table A1–1. Projections based on Tables A2–2 and A1–2.

2. This category includes butter and pork fat cuts and is thus duplicated to a considerable extent under milk fat and pork, respectively.

TABLE A2–5.   Projected Combinations of Per Capita Meat and Poultry Consumption under Alternate Assumptions[1]

(Pounds, carcass weight, for beef and veal, pork, lamb, mutton; ready-to-cook weight for poultry)

	1940	1945	1950	1955	1960	1970	1980	1990	2000
I. High total consumption, with emphasis on beef:									
Beef and veal	62.3	71.3	71.4	91.4	91.4	107	117	122	124
Pork	73.5	66.6	69.2	66.8	65.3	74	75	79	80
Lamb and mutton	6.6	7.3	4.0	4.5	4.8	4	3	4	6
Poultry	17	25.1	24.7	26.3	34.6	35	35	35	35
Total	159	170	169	189	196	220	230	240	245
II. High total consumption, with emphasis on variety:									
Beef and veal	62.3	71.3	71.4	91.4	91.4	101	105	113	118
Pork	73.5	66.6	69.2	66.8	65.3	78	83	85	85
Lamb and mutton	6.6	7.3	4.0	4.5	4.8	6	6.5	7	7.5
Poultry	17	25.1	24.7	26.3	34.6	35	35	35	35
Total	159	170	169	189	196	220	230	240	245
III. Medium consumption:									
Beef and veal	62.3	71.3	71.4	91.4	91.4	103	111	114	114
Pork	73.5	66.6	69.2	66.8	65.3	66	70	74	75
Lamb and mutton	6.6	7.3	4.0	4.5	4.8	4.9	5.5	6	6
Poultry	17	25.1	24.7	26.3	34.6	38	40	40	40
Total	159	170	169	189	196	212	227	234	235
IV. Low total consumption, with emphasis on beef:									
Beef and veal	62.3	71.3	71.4	91.4	91.4	100	107	107	107
Pork	73.5	66.6	69.2	66.8	65.3	60	60	60	60
Lamb and mutton	6.6	7.3	4.0	4.5	4.8	4	3	3	3
Poultry	17	25.1	24.7	26.3	34.6	43	45	45	45
Total	159	170	169	189	196	207	215	215	215
V. Low total consumption, with emphasis on variety:									
Beef and veal	62.3	71.3	71.4	91.4	91.4	91	95	95	95
Pork	73.5	66.6	69.2	66.8	65.3	68	70	70	70
Lamb and mutton	6.6	7.3	4.0	4.5	4.8	5	5	5	5
Poultry	17	25.1	24.7	26.3	34.6	43	45	45	45
Total	159	170	169	189	196	207	215	215	215

1. Historical data from Table A2–1. Projections from Table A2–2, with arbitrary adjustments to allow for models on various levels of feed intensity.

"Variety" refers to variety in consumption of "red meats" only (beef, pork, veal, lamb, and mutton); "emphasis on variety" allows for a relatively greater proportion of such meats being consumed in forms other than beef. Because poultry is, on the average, a more efficient channel for converting feed than is red meat in any form, the High (High feed) models both include Low per capita consumption of poultry and the Low models, High per capita consumption of poultry.

TABLE A2–6. Projected Combinations of Aggregate Meat and Poultry Consumption under Alternate Assumptions[1]

(Billion pounds carcass weight, for beef and veal, pork, lamb and mutton; ready-to-cook weight for poultry)

	1940	1945	1950	1955	1960	1970	1980	1990	2000
I. High total consumption, with emphasis on beef:									
Beef and veal	8.2	10.0	10.8	15.1	16.4	23.8	32.6	42.6	53.7
Pork	9.7	9.3	10.5	11.0	11.7	16.5	20.9	27.6	34.7
Lamb and mutton	.9	1.0	.6	.7	.9	.9	.8	1.4	2.6
Poultry	2.2	3.5	3.8	4.3	6.2	7.8	9.8	12.2	15.2
Total	21.0	23.8	25.7	31.1	35.2	49.0	64.1	83.8	106.2
II. High total consumption, with emphasis on variety:									
Beef and veal	8.2	10.0	10.8	15.1	16.4	22.5	29.3	39.4	51.0
Pork	9.7	9.3	10.5	11.0	11.7	17.4	23.2	29.7	36.8
Lamb and mutton	.9	1.0	.6	.7	.9	1.3	1.8	2.5	3.2
Poultry	2.2	3.5	3.8	4.3	6.2	7.8	9.8	12.2	15.2
Total	21.0	23.8	25.7	31.1	35.2	49.0	64.1	83.8	106.2
III. Medium consumption:									
Beef and veal	8.2	10.0	10.8	15.1	16.4	21.4	27.3	32.7	37.7
Pork	9.7	9.3	10.5	11.0	11.7	13.7	17.1	21.2	24.8
Lamb and mutton	.9	1.0	.6	.7	.9	1.0	1.3	1.7	2.0
Poultry	2.2	3.5	3.8	4.3	6.2	7.9	9.8	11.5	13.2
Total	21.0	23.8	25.7	31.1	35.2	44.0	55.5	67.1	77.7
IV. Low total consumption, with emphasis on beef:									
Beef and veal	8.2	10.0	10.8	15.1	16.4	20.2	24.2	26.6	28.7
Pork	9.7	9.3	10.5	11.0	11.7	12.1	13.5	14.9	16.1
Lamb and mutton	.9	1.0	.6	.7	.9	.8	.7	.8	.8
Poultry	2.2	3.5	3.8	4.3	6.2	8.7	10.2	11.2	12.1
Total	21.0	23.8	25.7	31.1	35.2	41.8	48.6	53.5	57.7
V. Low total consumption, with emphasis on variety:									
Beef and veal	8.2	10.0	10.8	15.1	16.4	18.4	21.5	23.7	25.5
Pork	9.7	9.3	10.5	11.0	11.7	13.7	15.8	17.4	18.8
Lamb and mutton	.9	1.0	.6	.7	.9	1.0	1.1	1.2	1.3
Poultry	2.2	3.5	3.8	4.3	6.2	8.7	10.2	11.2	12.1
Total	21.0	23.8	25.7	31.1	35.2	41.8	48.6	53.5	57.7

1. Historical data from Table A2–4. Projections based on data in Table A2–5, multiplied by High population for groups I and II, Medium population for group III, and Low population for groups IV and V. Population projections from Table A1–2.

appendix

to

chapter

3

CLOTHING AND TEXTILES

Notes

THE AIM OF this section, as of other sections of Part I and their appendices, is first to project the prospective growth in end-use consumption of particular items and then to evaluate their materials implications. The fact that in this particular case we plunge directly into a consideration of fibers and leather is due to the much greater convenience of measuring the future consumption of the large variety of items involved in terms of these common denominators, rather than in terms of the end-products themselves. This abbreviated treatment is also a reflection in part of the relatively limited resource significance of the raw materials concerned, which leads us to be satisfied with establishing only approximate orders of magnitude. *Silk and linen* have become a negligible factor in consumption. For *leather and wool,* it may easily be established that even liberally estimated increases are so modest as to be easily obtainable from present supply sources. The *non-cellulosic synthetics* are only a minor part of the whole petrochemical plastics complex, and even the very rapid expected growth of that complex as a whole is not enough to make much of a difference in total petroleum demand. *Rayon* presents less quickly answered questions, but here, too, it does not take very refined analysis to determine that its possible impact upon total wood pulp is of small importance. If for no other reason than its historical importance, *cotton* deserves some degree of elaboration, but it should be remembered that we are dealing with little more than 4 per cent of total cropland.

Despite the foregoing, the importance of clothing and textiles as end-products makes it desirable to establish their consumption pattern in a general way, the trends within each one of the principal consumption categories, and the relative participation of the different fibers in the total demand projections thus arrived at. This is done in Tables A3–1 to 3.

Although they are available as a consistent series only from 1949 on, the end-use statistics of the Textile Economics Bureau have been used as the basis for Table A3–1 and the projections in Table A3–2. Unlike data on mill consumption of fibers, which have been compiled for a longer period, the end-use series approximate quantities consumed at the "cutting level," as derived by the Textile Economics Bureau from various Census Bureau series. To the fiber content of garments cut, as deduced from the amounts and weights of cloth used, is added an allowance for fabric waste plus unspinnable fiber waste. While gross fiber requirements are thus approximated, the method eliminates any apparent consumption caused by changes in mill stocks and segregates exports of semifinished and finished textiles. The data still include in domestic consumption the finished garments which are exported, but a compensating bias arises from the exclusion of certain categories of consumption—like wallboard reinforcement, synthetic paper—for which data are not available.

Conversion to cotton-equivalents, as specified in footnote 1 to Table A3–1, was undertaken to arrive at a better common denominator than pounds. The equivalents are essentially fabric-weight ratios adjusted for differences in processing waste.

The clothing expenditure units used in reducing apparel consumers to a common denominator (see source cited in footnote 4 to Table A3–1) take the adult male in the 25–29 age bracket as unity. Females in the same bracket are taken as 1.21 units; children under 10 are less than half a unit, as are also adults over 60. Other examples are: males 15–19, .93 units, females 1.10; males 20–24, 1.02, females 1.29; males 30–34, .95, females 1.14. Although these equivalents are based on an analysis of expenditure patterns, they should also approximate relative physical consumption as well, particularly when the latter is measured in cotton-equivalents and thus happens to reflect to some extent the relative costs of fibers.

The extrapolations of coefficients, in Table A3–2, are made on a judgment basis, in the light of both past trends and the various considerations for the future which are described in Chapter 3. More refined methods of calculation were not deemed to be warranted, both because of the limited need for precision mentioned above and because no basis was found for a more convincing approach to the determination of fiber-consumption relationships this far into the future. In particular, the past record serves merely to demonstrate the relative inelasticity of fiber consumption and provides little basis for deducing future coefficients. It should be noted, however, that a check has been made to verify the plausibility of the relationship between quantities of fiber consumed, as projected here, and consumer expenditures on clothing and footwear, as projected in Table A1–27. The implicit relationship is that at the lower rates of growth of consumer expenditure on clothing, an increasing proportion of that expenditure will go for fiber as such, while at the higher rates, there will be a slight increase in the relative proportion expended for "confection."

While it may seem better (Table A3–3) to have analyzed separately the shares of the different fibers in each of the three principal consumption categories, the aggregation may be justified both on grounds of the degree of precision sought and because the joint treatment avoids the problem of augmentative error if we were to aggregate the individual Highs and Lows. Institutional and physical "frictions" may be expected to place somewhat greater constraints around possible variations in the total fiber-participation pattern than around the patterns in the individual sectors.

The summary calculations for leather in Table A3–4 are intended only to establish orders of magnitude. The declining role of leather in the American economy may be seen to be absolute as well as relative unless both high population growth and a slowing of substitution combine to alter the situation. It should be noted that the historical stability of shoe production (see Table A3–1) is in part due to the exclusion of rubber footwear, production of which has increased in recent years.

The impact of substitutes on the leather industry may be illustrated by the fact that the proportion of shoes with leather soles declined from 73 per cent in 1947 to 38 per cent in 1954, 31 per cent in 1958, and 28 per cent in 1960. Those with leather uppers declined from 90 per cent in 1947 to 83 per cent in 1954, 77 per cent in 1958, and 76 per cent in 1960. (U.S. Bureau of the Census, Current Industrial Reports, Series MC-31A and predecessor reports). In 1947, 20 per cent of the units of women's hand luggage were all-leather or chiefly leather; this had declined to 11 per cent by 1954 and less then 2½ per cent by 1958.

LIST OF TABLES

TABLE A3–1. Historical Data on Fiber and Leather Consumption

	1949	1950	1951	1952	1953	1954	1955	1956	1957	1958	1959	1960
Domestic consumption of fibers, by end-uses (billion lb., cotton equiv.):[1]												
Apparel uses:												
Total	2.84	3.10	2.99	3.14	3.23	3.15	3.36	3.42	3.39	3.38	3.70	3.68
Manmade fibers	.86	.97	.99	.97	.94	.90	.93	.95	.98	1.00	1.11	1.12
Cotton	1.75	1.89	1.80	1.95	2.07	2.04	2.20	2.24	2.19	2.17	2.36	2.34
Wool	.22	.23	.19	.21	.21	.20	.22	.22	.21	.20	.22	.21
Silk and linen	.01	.01	.01	.01	.01	.01	.01	.01	.01	.01	.01	.01
Household uses:												
Total	.97	1.23	1.14	1.20	1.32	1.31	1.46	1.51	1.51	1.52	1.70	1.67
Manmade fibers	.11	.18	.19	.21	.25	.27	.37	.40	.45	.47	.54	.56
Cotton	.76	.92	.87	.90	.97	.96	1.00	1.01	.97	.97	1.05	1.01
Wool	.10	.13	.07	.08	.09	.07	.08	.09	.08	.07	.10	.09
Silk and linen	*	*	.01	.01	.01	.01	.01	.01	.01	.01	.01	.01
Industrial uses:												
Total	1.40	1.61	1.75	1.67	1.66	1.49	1.78	1.65	1.65	1.56	1.85	1.73
Manmade fibers	.48	.58	.66	.81	.91	.78	1.02	.94	.98	.95	1.19	1.11
Cotton	.89	.99	1.07	.84	.74	.70	.75	.70	.66	.60	.65	.61
Wool	.03	.04	.02	.02	.01	.01	.01	.01	.01	.01	.01	.01
Silk and linen	*	*	*	*	*	*	*	*	*	*	*	*
All uses:												
Total	5.21	5.94	5.88	6.01	6.21	5.95	6.60	6.58	6.55	6.46	7.25	7.08
Manmade fibers	1.45	1.73	1.84	1.99	2.10	1.95	2.32	2.29	2.41	2.42	2.84	2.79
Cotton	3.40	3.80	3.74	3.69	3.78	3.70	3.95	3.95	3.82	3.74	4.06	3.96
Wool	.35	.40	.28	.31	.31	.28	.31	.32	.30	.28	.33	.31
Silk and linen	.01	.01	.02	.02	.02	.02	.02	.02	.02	.02	.02	.02
All uses: % distribution												
Total	100.0	100.0	100.0	100.0	100.0	100.0	100.0	100.0	100.0	100.0	100.0	100.0
Manmade fibers	27.8	29.1	31.3	33.1	33.8	32.8	35.2	34.8	36.8	37.5	39.2	39.4
Cotton	65.3	64.0	63.6	61.4	60.9	62.2	59.8	60.0	58.3	57.9	56.0	55.9
Wool	6.7	6.7	4.8	5.2	5.0	4.7	4.7	4.9	4.6	4.3	4.6	4.4
Silk and linen	.2	.2	.3	.3	.3	.3	.3	.3	.3	.3	.3	.3
Manmade fibers: % distribution[2]												
Rayon and acetate	89.4	86.8	84.2	81.6	78.7	72.6	70.3	65.6	61.2	57.0	54.2	50.5
Non-cellulosic and others	10.6	13.2	15.8	18.4	21.3	27.4	29.7	34.4	38.8	43.0	45.8	49.5
Coefficients of relationship:												
Total use: lb. per capita[3]	34.9	39.2	38.1	38.3	38.9	36.6	39.9	39.1	38.3	37.1	40.9	39.4

Apparel use:												
Lb. per clothing expenditure unit[4]	24.7	26.7	25.6	26.6	27.0	26.1	27.4	27.4	26.3	26.5	28.6	27.9
Clothing expenditure units (millions)	115.0	116.0	116.9	117.9	119.8	120.8	122.7	124.6	125.6	127.7	129.4	131.7
Household use:												
lb/household[3]	22.8	28.1	25.4	26.3	28.4	27.8	30.4	30.8	30.3	30.0	32.9	31.7
Industrial use: mil. lb/FRB manufacturing index point[5]	21.6	21.3	21.5	19.7	18.0	17.4	18.4	16.6	16.5	16.9	17.6	16.0
Apparel use: lb/$ 1960 of consumer expenditures on clothing and footwear[6]	.130	.138	.135	.135	.137	.134	.135	.134	.129	.128	.133	.131
Domestic consumption of fibers, by type of fiber (billion lb., actual wt.):[1]												
Cotton	3.40	3.80	3.74	3.69	3.78	3.70	3.95	3.95	3.82	3.74	4.06	3.96
Rayon and acetate	.99	1.07	1.10	1.15	1.17	1.00	1.14	1.06	1.04	.98	1.09	1.01
Other manmade	.09	.13	.16	.21	.26	.30	.39	.45	.52	.58	.73	.77
Wool	.63	.71	.51	.55	.58	.51	.56	.58	.54	.50	.58	.57
Domestic consumption of shoes and leather:												
Shoe production:												
Mil. pairs[7]	419	465	422	458	446	473	517	524	527	517	560	528
Pairs per capita[3]	2.81	3.06	2.74	2.92	2.79	2.92	3.13	3.12	3.08	2.97	3.16	2.93
Leather consumption:												
Mil. cattle-hide equiv.[8]	34.1	36.0	31.9	32.9	34.5	33.2	35.4	35.1	34.4	32.4	32.4	30.5
Per pair of shoes (cattle-hide equiv.)	.0814	.0774	.0756	.0718	.0774	.0702	.0685	.0670	.0653	.0627	.0579	.0578

* Less than 5 million lb.

1. Based on data, in actual pounds, from "Textile Fiber End Use Survey," in Textile Economics Bureau, New York City, *Textile Organon*, Nov. 1961.

"Apparel uses," as used herein, combines the *Organon*'s "men's and boys' wear," "women's, misses' and juniors' wear," "girls', children's and infants' wear," and "other consumer-type products" (principally retail piece goods and apparel linings). "Household uses" (sheets, towels, blankets, rugs, etc.) is the same as the *Organon*'s "home furnishings." "Industrial uses" includes tire fabric, auto upholstery, bags and bagging, etc. Data were added and converted to cotton equivalents before rounding.

"End-use consumption," as worked out by the Textile Economics Bureau, is measured at the "cutting" level or at other point as close to the consumer as possible, but with allowance for allocable processing waste up to that point. It excludes net exports of textile raw materials and semi-manufactures.

Cotton equivalent ratios are as follows: Rayon tire cord, 1936-53, 1.59; 1954, 1.64; 1955, 1.71; 1956, 1.74; 1957, 1.77; 1958-60, 1.80. Other rayon yarn, 1.51. Rayon staple, 1.10. Non-cellulosic synthetic tire cord, 2.73. Other non-cellulosic synthetic yarn, 1.74. Non-cellulosic synthetic staple, 1.37. Wool, .55. Silk and linen arbitrarily taken as 1.00. Assumed average ratios for 1960: Rayon, 1.4; non-cellulosic, 1.8. Source (except for silk and linen): Frank Lowenstein, and Martin S. Simon, "Textile Fiber Consumption in Cotton Equivalent Pounds," in USDA, *Cotton Situation* (Nov. 1957); also, *Cotton Situation* (Nov. 1960), p. 21, and unpublished data and corrections supplied by Mr. Lowenstein.

2. Sources and conversion factors as in footnote 1.
3. For population, households, see Table A1-1.
4. Unit allowing for age-sex variations in the population. Based on calculations by Martin S. Simon, in "Clothing expenditure units: a new time series," *Agricultural Economics Research*, Vol. X, No. 2 (April 1958).
5. For Federal Reserve Board (FRB) index, see Table A1-28.
6. For consumer expenditures in $ 1960, see Table A1-26.
7. Excludes slippers and rubber footwear. Source: U.S. Bureau of the Census, *Facts for Industry*, M68A-05 Sup. (March 8, 1957) and Series M31A. Data for 1947: 437 million pairs, or 3.03 per capita; for 1948: 437 million pairs, or 2.97 per capita.
8. Tanners' Council of America data on leather production (roughly equivalent to consumption since foreign trade in finished leather is negligible), converted to cattle-hide equivalents as follows: 1 cattle hide = 6 sheep or lamb skins, 4 calf or kip skins, 10 goat or kid skins. Crude data from U.S. Bureau of the Census, *Statistical Abstract of the United States*, 1961.

TABLE A3–2.   Projected Domestic Consumption of Fiber, by End-Use[1]

(Fiber quantities in cotton equivalents)

	1950	1955	1960		1970	1980	1990	2000
Total domestic consumption of				L	8.21	9.47	10.82	12.36
fibers[2] (bil. lb.)	5.94	6.60	7.08	M	9.25	12.01	14.94	18.97
				H	10.49	15.10	21.85	31.64
				L	4.42	5.12	5.90	6.73
Apparel use[3] (bil. lb.)	3.10	3.36	3.68	M	4.70	6.10	7.83	9.92
				H	5.18	7.20	10.25	14.57
Clothing expenditure units[4]				L	152	169	186	204
(millions)	116.0	122.7	131.7	M	154	182	214	248
				H	162	199	250	310
Apparel use per clothing expendi-				L	29.1	30.3	31.7	33.0
ture unit[5] (lb.)	26.7	27.4	27.9	M	30.5	33.5	36.6	40.0
				H	32.0	36.2	41.0	47.0
Check:								
Personal consumption expenditures				L	33.2	39.0	45.9	52.4
on clothing and footwear[6]	22.4	24.9	28.1	M	36.5	48.3	64.2	84.5
($ 1960 bil.)				H	43.6	66.3	101	152
Pounds of fiber consumed per				L	.13	.13	.13	.13
dollar of pers. cons. expend.	.14	.13	.13	M	.13	.13	.12	.12
				H	.12	.11	.10	.10
				L	2.25	3.04	3.84	4.74
Household use[3] (bil. lb.)	1.23	1.46	1.67	M	2.34	3.23	4.23	5.59
				H	2.46	3.51	4.90	6.97
				L	58.7	68.7	76.5	84.3
Households[7] (millions)	43.8	48.0	52.6	M	61.2	73.0	84.3	99.4
				H	64.3	79.2	97.6	124.1
Household use per household[5] (lb.)	28.1	30.4	31.7		38.3	44.3	50.2	56.2
				L	1.54	1.31	1.08	.89
Industrial use[3] (bil. lb.)	1.61	1.78	1.73	M	2.21	2.68	2.88	3.46
				H	2.85	4.39	6.70	10.10
FRB index of manufacturing				L	145	192	252	331
production (1957 = 100)[8]	75.5	96.7	108	M	165	246	365	540
				H	191	325	549	918
Industrial use per FRB index				L	10.6	6.8	4.3	2.7
point[5] (mil. lb.)	21.3	18.4	16.0	M	13.4	10.9	7.9	6.4
				H	14.9	13.5	12.2	11.0

1. Historical data from Table A3–1, except as otherwise indicated.

2. Sum of three principal end-uses, which follow.

3. Product of following two factors.

4. Calculated by applying the "clothing-expenditure" factors of Martin S. Simon (see Table A3–1, footnote 4) to the detailed projections of population by sex and age brackets underlying Table A1–3. It should be noted that these factors are not wholly appropriate in that they were derived on the basis of differences in *value* of apparel purchases by the different sex-age groups, rather than in *quantity* of fiber consumed. However, they do provide a better basis for projection than do the unadjusted population totals.

5. Extrapolations of past trends.

6. From Table A1–27.

7. From Table A1–2.

8. Based on preliminary calculations. The final manufacturing index projection (Table A1–29) does not differ from the preliminary sufficiently to make more than small differences in the final calculation of fiber consumption.

TABLE A3–3. Projected Domestic Consumption of Fiber, by Type of Fiber[1]

		1950	1955	1960		1970	1980	1990	2000
Cotton:									
Share of fiber market[2] (%)		64.0	59.8	55.9	L	47.0	42.0	40.0	38.0
					M	49.0	46.0	45.0	44.0
					H	51.5	49.0	48.0	48.0
Domestic consumption[3] (bil. lb.)		3.80	3.95	3.96	L	3.86	3.98	4.33	4.70
					M	4.53	5.52	6.72	8.35
					H	5.40	7.40	10.49	15.19
Manmade fibers:									
Share of fiber market[2] (%)		29.1	35.2	39.4	L	44.9	48.3	49.9	50.0
					M	47.4	51.3	52.9	54.0
					H	49.4	55.3	57.9	60.0
Domestic consumption[3] (bil. lb. cotton equiv.)		1.73	2.32	2.79	L	3.69	4.57	5.40	6.18
					M	4.38	6.16	7.90	10.24
					H	5.18	8.35	12.65	18.98
Rayon and acetate:									
Share of manmade fiber market[4] (%)		86.8	70.3	50.5	L	26	15	8	5
					M	32	21	14	10
					H	40	32	25	20
Domestic consumption (billion lb. cotton equiv.)		1.50	1.63	1.41	L	.95	.69	.43	.31
					M	1.40	1.29	1.11	1.02
					H	2.07	2.67	3.16	3.80
Domestic consumption, actual weight[5] (bil. lb.)		1.07	1.14	1.01	L	.68	.49	.31	.22
					M	1.00	.92	.79	.73
					H	1.48	1.91	2.26	2.71
Other manmade:									
Share of manmade fiber market[4] (%)		13.2	29.7	49.5	L	60	68	75	80
					M	68	79	86	90
					H	74	85	92	95
Domestic consumption (bil. lb. cotton equiv.)		.23	.69	1.38	L	2.21	3.11	4.05	4.94
					M	2.98	4.87	6.79	9.22
					H	3.83	7.08	11.64	18.03
Domestic consumption, actual wt.[6] (bil. lb.)		.13	.39	.77	L	1.23	1.73	2.25	2.74
					M	1.66	2.71	3.77	5.12
					H	2.13	3.93	6.47	10.02
Wool:									
Share of fiber market[2] (%)		6.7	4.7	4.4		3.4	2.5	2.0	1.9
Domestic consumption[3] (bil. lb. cotton equiv.)		.40	.31	.31	L	.28	.24	.22	.23
					M	.31	.30	.30	.36
					H	.36	.38	.44	.60
Domestic consumption, actual wt.[7] (bil. lb.)		.71	.56	.57	L	.51	.44	.40	.42
					M	.56	.55	.55	.65
					H	.65	.69	.80	1.09

1. Historical data from Table A3–1.

2. The share of wool, silk, and linen in total fiber consumption (in terms of cotton-equivalents) having first been projected (on a judgment basis), the remainder (i.e., the market for the principal fibers), was divided between cotton and manmade fibers under three assumptions regarding the future importance of cotton. The High market share for cotton is associated with the Low market share for manmade fibers. Since any one of these distributions might reasonably concur with the Low (or High) aggregate fiber consumption, Low (High) domestic consumption for each fiber was calculated by the application of its Low (High) market share to the Low (High) projection of total fiber requirements.

Silk and linen (flax) are not shown in the table but are assumed to decline from a current .3% of the market to .2% by 1970 and .1% by 1990.

3. Share of the fiber in the market, multiplied by total domestic consumption, Table A3–2.

4. Extrapolated by inspection, taking account of asymptotic effect of zero. Low share of "other manmade fibers" equals 100 minus High share of "rayon and acetate."

5. Converted at ratio of 1.4 lb. of cotton equivalent to 1 lb. of actual weight, which is the relationship around which historical ratios have gravitated. (See footnote 1, Table A3–1.)

6. Converted at ratio of 1.8 lb. of cotton equivalent to 1 lb. of actual weight.

7. Converted at ratio of .55 lb. of cotton equivalent to 1 lb. of actual weight.

TABLE A3–4.   Projected Leather Consumption[1]

	1950	1955	1960		1970	1980	1990	2000
Population (millions)[2]	152	165	180	L	202	226	249	268
				M	208	245	287	331
				H	223	279	349	433
Shoe production (million pairs)	465	517	528	L	606	678	747	807
				M	645	784	947	1,120
				H	714	952	1,260	1,640
Pairs per capita[3]	3.06	3.13	2.94	L	3.00	3.00	3.00	3.00
				M	3.10	3.20	3.30	3.40
				H	3.20	3.40	3.60	3.80
Leather consumption (million cattle-hide equiv.)	36	35	30	L	24	18	14	10
				M	27	24	22	19
				H	32	34	36	38
Consumption per pair of shoes[3] (cattle-hide equiv.)	.077	.068	.058	L	.039	.027	.018	.013
				M	.042	.031	.023	.017
				H	.045	.036	.029	.023

1. For sources of historical data and nature of series, see Table A3–1.

2. From Table A1–2.
3. Extrapolation of past trends.

appendix
to
chapter
4

CONSTRUCTION

Notes

THE PROJECTIONS of construction contained in this appendix serve a dual purpose: (1) they provide a basis for building up a value-of-construction series for "feeding back" into the projections of GNP; (2) they provide the reference series from which may be projected in turn the key material requirements for construction. The derivation of such requirements, grouped by principal kinds of materials (wood, steel, cement, nonferrous metals), is also included herein. In Part II, the requirements for each of these materials deriving from construction are aggregated, material by material, with the requirements deriving from other sectors of the economy.

The principal construction series for the United States is the one on "value of new construction put in place," until recently maintained jointly by the Bureau of Labor Statistics and the U.S. Department of Commerce and published in *Construction Review*. (Responsibility for the series was shifted in 1959 exclusively to the Department of Commerce; publication is still in *Construction Review*.) The data are broken down into private and public construction and, further, into as many as 30 subcategories. The "public construction" is equivalent in concept to public construction as it enters into the GNP. The "private construction" is equivalent to the private construction of the GNP, save for the omission of oil and gas well drilling, which is separately estimated and added into the GNP construction series by the National Income Division of the Office of Business Economics, U.S. Department of Commerce.

In addition to the oil and gas discrepancy, the *Construction Review* differs from the National Income Division data when presented in terms of constant dollars. Besides having a different base year, the *Construction Review* deflators usually take into account changes in materials and labor costs only; the National Income Division deflators include an allowance for contractors' profits.

Maintenance and repair expenditures are omitted from the monthly published series, which thus pertain only to "new" construction, and they are not, as such, accounted for as part of the GNP. (Included both in new construction and in the GNP, on the other hand, but not separately shown, are "major alterations and additions.") Annual estimates of maintenance and repair expenditures have been made on the basis of corollary data; the series are published in *Construction Review* and its supplement, *Construction Volume and Costs*. Since they account for about one-fourth the total value of all construction activity, maintenance and repair expenditures are of clear importance from a materials standpoint and have therefore been included among the historical and projected series given in this appendix.

Most of the construction data herein are based upon *Construction Review* rather than National Income Division estimates, in order to take advantage of the available detail. Adjustment of the original data to 1960 dollars and other estimation of our own are explained in the footnotes. The summary National Accounts data (transposed to 1960 dollars) are also shown, for purposes of comparison.

For the future, relative price movements are assumed to be identical for both series, so that the new construction totals in either terms will be the sum of the construction series detail.

With one exception, the projection for each of the categories of construction has been directly in terms of dollars. The exception is the important sector of residential building, which currently accounts for about 40 per cent of all new construction. Here the projection has been made in terms of dwelling units and the dollar series subsequently derived by applying unit values. The estimation, it should be noted, is for *all* residential construction, public and private combined. The data usually given in the statistical sources are for "private non-farm" and for "public" separately, farm dwelling unit construction being classified with other farm construction. To arrive at the projected totals herein, residential construction is included in its entirety in private construction and percentage adjustments are made to take account of the consequent small misallocation of public residential building. Treating residential construction in this manner has the double advantage of facilitating its derivation from the households projection and permitting a uniform evaluation of the totality of residential construction in terms of material requirements.

The full detail on value of new construction which is available in the *Construction Review* series has not been used. Instead, the historical data (Table A4–1) and the projections (Table A4–3) are in terms of those segments or combinations of segments which are either important because of their proportion of total construction value, or important for one or more kinds of materials, or else sufficiently different from other segments in characteristics and determinants as to warrant separate treatment. In aggregating the various projected segments, it will be noted that, except for the "private non-residential" total, Highs have been added to Highs and Lows to Lows. This, on the assumption that the segments shown are essentially independent of each other and that all could thus take on these extreme values concurrently. While this is not completely true, it would appear to be close enough to being true to justify the procedure.

Private and public construction

The projections of *residential building* (Tables A4–4 to 6) are based in part on parameters that are fairly secure, in part on ones that are quite insecure. Given the levels of the population projections and their implicit age distributions, there is little doubt that the numbers of households (and hence occupied dwelling units) will approximate those shown. The projected vacancy rate adds some uncertainty as to the total stock of dwelling units, but the trend toward "second" houses (summer dwellings, etc.) is at once apparent enough and slow enough that not too much error can be introduced on this account. The fact that almost a 5 to 1 range still results for the projected "net additions to stock" is a consequence not of additional uncertainty but of the fact that this series has the inherent volatility of a "first derivative."

Although not as important to the end result as the population assumptions, a significant source of possible error also lies in the projections of "net disappearance." This figure, representing replacement demand, is not simply equivalent to demolitions of obsolete structures, but is the net result of destruction of dwellings for many reasons; of mergers, conversions, and subdivisions of units; and of additions and subtractions of types of housing which are definable as dwelling units or not according to their occupancy.

This last is of some importance when considering the relationship of dwelling units to material requirements. A tent, trailer, temporary shelter, etc., is counted as a dwelling unit only if it happens to be somebody's principal residence. Such units may become increasingly important, especially in terms of vacation living. Since they are not part of the housing "stock" unless actually erected and occupied, there may be a growing understatement of materials use as the result of their partial exclusion. Balanced against this is the overstatement, or the erroneous statement, of materials use in the case of trailers, "mobile homes," prefabs, small cottages, etc., that do happen to be somebody's permanent dwelling. Since all occupied and other "permanent" units have been evaluated herein in terms of typical use of materials, the failure to account for these special types separately may have led to some overstatement of wood and cement, for example, together with some understatement of metals and plastics. The assumption, however, is that, net, the balance of such error is too small in relation to other unavoidable errors in the building materials projections to be worth taking account of.

The housing role played by hotels, rooming houses, and other "institutions" has not been specifically evaluated. In part such residences fall into the classification of "non-housekeeping" residential units and in part into the non-residential building category; in neither case are they of any great importance. Since their materials consumption has in effect been projected as part of the materials requirements for new dwelling units and for non-residential buildings, the principal conditions for avoidance of error are that the distinction between institutional and non-institutional dwelling quarters be maintained as consistent as possible over time and that there be no great shift in the proportion of the population "institutionally" housed. It is partly for reasons of such consistency that no use was made of the new "housing unit" concept adopted by the Census Bureau (see below). With regard to any shift in proportion of institutional and non-institutional quarters, while there has been some relative increase in non-housekeeping quarters in recent years they still constitute only about 3 per cent of the total value of residential construction and there is no reason to suppose that much further change in this proportion is likely.

Also not specifically evaluated is the effect of any potential shifts in proportion of single-dwelling-unit and multiple-dwelling-unit residential structures. In a general way, however, urbanization, suburbanization, and regional shifts in population have been considered in reaching judgments on prospective changes in the relative roles of the different types of building materials.

The figures on net disappearance of dwelling units (Tables A4–5 and 6) are discussed in a general way in the text, Chapter 4 (pp. 114–16). While long-term tabulations of disappearance have been made by other analysts (see, for example, U.S. Bureau of the Census, *Historical Statistics of the United States, 1789–1945*, Series H 84–88), both recent evidence and an evaluation of apparent long-run attrition, based on the age distribution of dwelling units in the 1940 and subsequent housing censuses, suggest that the past estimates of disappearance (and, correspondingly, new construction) have been too low. This is confirmed, in particular, by the data on components of change in the *1956 National Housing Inventory* (U.S. Bureau of the Census) and by the revised survey of new housing starts inaugurated by the Census Bureau in 1960. Components of change shown for 1956–60 in Table A4–5 herein were estimated on the basis of data on households, vacancy rates, and dwelling-unit starts as adjusted to the 1950–56 Housing Inventory benchmark, and may be somewhat overstated. However, the disappearance so obtained checks out closely with the theoretical attrition derived by using the Medium projection formula.

The new Census housing starts series, although better in coverage than the old *Construction Review* series and inclusive even of farm dwellings, was not used as such primarily because it was available only for 1959 and 1960. It still omits some

types of new units (notably trailers) and admittedly may still understate the number of units which it is supposed to include. Both the theoretical coverage of the new housing starts series and the coverage of the 1960 Housing Census (preliminary results of which began to be available as this study was being completed) are in terms of a new, broader "housing unit," in place of the "dwelling unit" which was previously the standard. The effect is to increase the count of dwelling units by several per cent, chiefly by including some of the units which were previously classified as non-dwelling-unit quarters. While the dwelling-unit and household series shown in this study will have no counterparts in future official statistics, it was nonetheless decided to maintain the projections on the old basis, since the new concept lacks enough of a history to provide a satisfactory basis for adjustments; it also has not as yet, like the old series, been made the subject of official Census Bureau projections. For illustrative purposes, we have shown an approximate conversion of our series onto an equivalent "residential non-farm" basis.

If we had had a number of housing inventories, like those of 1940, 1950, and 1956, which gave the age distribution of dwelling units and, better still, also came after some decades of "normality," we would have had some chance of building up "life tables" for houses and thus knowing the "deaths" that would occur by reason of old age and other casualty. The closest we can come to an indication of such normal attrition is on the basis of the 1940 Census, which contains data on age groups going back to before the Civil War. The further one goes back in time (i.e., in terms of age cohorts), the less reliable the data and the less comparable with current trends are the relationships they disclose. Yet only a relatively long period will indicate the attrition rate of "mature" houses and (this is especially true for the 1940 figures) erase the additional error introduced by the virtual halt in net disappearance during the decade 1930–40.

Comparing the stock of housing as it must have existed in 1890 (on the basis of number of households and estimated vacancies) with what was left in 1940, we find that 37 per cent of the original total was, at the later date, still on the scene—a loss at the average rate (compounded) of 2 per cent a year. The 1900 stock still around in 1940 was 54 per cent of the original, indicating a 1½ per cent per year disappearance, and the 1910 stock was 72 per cent of the original, indicating a 1 per cent per year disappearance. (These, of course, are net rates and would probably be higher if there were no subdivision and other conversion of units.) The declining annual rates (2, 1½, and 1) are not as inconsistent as they might seem, for what they involve mostly is the inclusion of an increasing proportion of "younger" dwellings, which do not disappear at as fast a rate as those which have already gone through three or four decades, and of increasing weight in the total for the period 1930–40, when there was very little attrition. In fact, if one should make the apparently arbitrary assumption that dwelling units disappear at the rate of 0.2 per cent a year for the first 10 years, 1 per cent for the next ten years, 2 per cent for the third decade, and 3 per cent a year thereafter, one would arrive at the following numbers reaching successive ages:

10 years—98%
20 years—89%
30 years—72%
40 years—53%
50 years—39%
etc.

The comparison with the apparent net disappearance deducible from the 1940 Census is rather close:

1930 stock still extant in 1940—99%
1920 "   "   "   "   " —89%
1910 "   "   "   "   " —72%
1900 "   "   "   "   " —54%
1890 "   "   "   "   " —37%

The "arbitrary" rates just cited constitute our Medium assumption as to future disappearance, which may be seen, by these standards, to be not as inconsistent with the historical record as the data in the last column of Table A4–5, relating disappearance to beginning stock, make it appear. The reason for the low level of this latter percentage in the thirties is self-evident. Its increase from 2 per cent in the forties to 10 per cent in the fifties is the difference between wartime restrictions and postwar boom but is still an understatement of "normal" replacement because of the emphasis, in those years, on providing for new households. The fifties themselves saw a rise from the 10-year equivalent replacement rate of 5 per cent in the 1950–56 portion to an approximate 16 per cent thereafter—only slightly less than our Medium projection for the rest of the century.

The Medium projection, therefore, is, despite first appearances, consistent with a good deal of past history and especially with the very recent past. The Low projection is roughly consistent with the record of the twenties and with the average experience for the fifties. The High projection, which is the most liberal in terms of the ultimate average lifetime of houses which it implies, could be brought about initially by a stepping up in the rate of replacement of the millions of substandard units still extant and be sustained later by new concepts of housing construction and obsolescence.

The average age of dwelling units actually disappearing between 1950 and 1956 may be estimated at as low as 30 years or as high as 45 years, depending upon whether one goes by the apparent evidence of the differences in age distribution between the 1950 and the 1956 counts or the age distribution of disappearing units according to the "Components of Change" survey (*National Housing Inventory*). Both sources contain large unknowns and it is likely that the true average age is somewhere in between—its lowness the result of a heavy amount of disappearance among "temporary" Depression and World War II units. The implicit age of units disappearing between 1956 and 1960, according to our construct, is about 55 years, slightly more than that of our Medium projection. These current average "ages at death" are only a crude reflection of life expectancy, however, since they are affected by the relative sizes of successive cohorts. Since we assume continuing growth in the future, the implicit average ages of disappearing units will sooner or later fall below the respective theoretical life expectancies under each of the attrition assumptions.

In moving from numbers of units constructed to value of residential construction (Table A4–4), we have multiplied the numbers by projected unit values and added an estimate for alterations and additions. The relatively small amount of "nonhousekeeping" residential construction has been implicitly included in the values attributed to ordinary residential units. On the assumption that the income elasticity (corrected by relative prices) of dwelling units will approximate unity, the average values have been assumed to rise proportionately to disposable personal income per household. Expenditures for alterations and additions have been assumed to maintain a constant relationship to new residential construction.

The remaining kinds of private construction have been in general projected in relation to the activity levels which they are to support or as proportions (similarly allowed to change) of total investment in the particular sector as developed in the appendix to Chapter 6 (the latter, in turn, being related to the appropriate current output levels). The relations or proportions have been allowed to change in accordance with possible interpretations of past trend. A few of the private sectors (e.g., institutional and miscellaneous buildings) and some of the public sectors have been related to population growth; other public sectors have been related to the activities supported (e.g., highway construction to vehicle-miles and military construction to total defense expenditures).

To avoid any compounding of errors in the Highs and Lows, total private non-residential construction has been derived "directly," as a percentage of total projected outlays for plant and equipment in all sectors (business, agriculture, and other), shown in Table A6–3. The differences between the totals so derived and the actual added sums are shown in Table A4–3 as "non-allocable." For the Medium projection, this "non-allocable" is equivalent to statistical error, whose size indicates the relatively close correspondence of the projections derived in the two different manners.

The Medium projections, as derived herein, may be compared with projections of construction activity to 1975 and 2000 which were published in September 1961 by the Construction Division of the U.S. Department of Commerce (*Construction Review,* Vol. 7, No. 9):

	1960	1975¹	2000
	(Billion 1960 dollars)		
Total new construction:			
Herein	54.4	108	274
Commerce	55.6	107	219
Total private:			
Herein	38.4	75	190
Commerce	39.6	75	147
Of which, residential nonfarm:			
Herein	21.1	45	118
Commerce	22.5	45	74
Total public:			
Herein	16.0	33	84
Commerce	16.0	32	71
Of which, highways:			
Herein	5.5	13	35
Commerce	5.5	12	27

1. RFF figures estimated for this purpose from 1970 and 1980 data.

The foregoing shows only the principal comparisons and involves some adaptations for comparability (such as the elimination from our data of oil and gas well drilling), but it points up the principal differences between the two sets of projections. Aside from rounding, the differences in 1960 arise from our use of residential value data from the National Income Accounts, which have not yet been adjusted to the new housing series. The differences in our projections are negligible for 1975, but are considerable for the year 2000 and may be seen to concern both private and public construction. On the private side, the difference is almost exactly ascribable to the different projections for residential construction; on the public side, a large part of it

is ascribable to our larger highway construction projections, but it also runs throughout the public sectors.

The lower Commerce residential projection for the year 2000 is in no wise attributable to a lower base population projection; in fact, their population assumption is about 15 per cent higher. Compensatory differences in our estimated rates of household formation and vacancies bring the two projections of annual net additions quite close (each at a little over 2 million). The differences are thus largely ascribable to the volume of replacement demand, in which we are about 50 per cent higher, but still at a reasonable level, in our judgment, for the reasons outlined earlier in these notes.

There may also be noted a significant conceptual difference between our projections and those of Commerce in that we have intended to include, while Commerce has not, the numbers of occupied mobile homes. This is probably partly responsible for our similar estimates of net additions in the face of differing population totals.

The reasons for the discrepancies with regard to public construction are more difficult to pinpoint. In general, we have projected a significantly higher role for government expenditures in 2000 than that postulated by the Department of Commerce. On the specific matter of highway construction, the differences seem to be related less to our respective projections of vehicle travel than to our appreciation of the unit cost in highway construction needed to support each vehicle-mile.

In addition to new construction, the Commerce Department also projected expenditures for repair and maintenance. The differences between these and our own Medium projections are so small as to be insignificant.

Materials used in construction

Projecting the materials content of construction is made extremely difficult by the almost complete absence of historical data from which it is possible systematically to link the inputs of construction materials to the volumes of different types of construction. For the purposes of the analysis herein, historical relationships were mostly deduced from the scattered estimates of earlier analysts or by the putative distribution of data on gross shipments of different types of materials into their end-use applications—again, on the basis of whatever scant evidence was available. The requirements for residential construction were calculated primarily on a per-dwelling-unit basis, those for other categories on the basis of unit value put in place.

Such historical data as are available on use of *wood* may mostly be found either originally estimated or reproduced in the U.S. Forest Service's *Timber Resources for America's Future* (Forest Resource Report No. 14, Jan. 1958). The historical estimates herein are largely based on those there given, although a choice of alternative estimates was sometimes necessary and further adjustments, interpolations, and extrapolations were also made. The construction use considered in this appendix has in recent years accounted for some 70–80 per cent of total use of lumber and plywood. Of this total, sawn products account for some 80 per cent and veneer and plywood for most of the rest. Maintenance and repair account for about one-fifth of the sawn lumber and the rest is divided between new residential and new non-residential uses in roughly comparable proportions.

While the projections of residential lumber have been made on the basis of over-all use per unit, judgments on prospective unit use have been based in turn upon a consideration of the separate trends in framing, flooring, and millwork. Decreasing unit use of lumber in the interval between 1940 and 1953 was partly the result of declines in floor space and in ceiling height (*Timber Resources,* p. 379) but more importantly was the result of certain changes in construction style and consumer preference, summarized in U.S. Bureau of Labor Statistics, *New Housing and its Materials, 1940–56,* notably: (1) a decrease in the relative number of frame houses (89% to 82%), reducing the need for studs and sheathing (about 20% of total lumber volume); (2) a trend toward flat or low-pitched roofs, reducing the need for rafters and sheathing (30% of volume); and (3) the use of concrete-slab (increasing from nearly nothing to 11%) in place of basement or crawl-space foundations, thus reducing the need for floor joists and subflooring (still 30% of total wood volume in 1950).

The unit-use estimates for 1950–60 in Table A4–7 take these trends, as well as the more recent reversal of trend in floor space, into account. They also allow for the important substitution, noted below, of plywood for wooden boards. The projection assumes that the principal downward trends will continue, but at a decreasing rate, partly compensated by increasing unit size. More specifically, it supposes that there will be a continued decrease in proportion of frame houses, an end to the relative decrease in basementless houses, and a continued shift to flat roofs.

About half of the lumber for new non-residential construction, in 1952, went into concrete formwork

and allied uses and about a third more into farm service buildings; most of the rest went into framing and other applications in small non-residential buildings. The mild 1950–60 decline in unit use which is shown in Table A4–7 may be ascribed to some substitution of plywood, metal, and plastics in formwork, coupled with relative stability in farm use of lumber. As a non-residential structural material, lumber no longer constitutes any threat to the use of steel and reinforced concrete, although some increased use may be expected for architectural effect. The principal difference among the three unit-use projection levels has to do with the relative role ascribed to reinforced concrete construction (see Table A4–10) and the relative contribution of sawn wood toward the formwork. The Low projection would suppose no relative growth in concrete construction coupled with a shift to plywood, plastics, etc., for formwork; the Medium projection, a counterbalancing of increased use of reinforced concrete by the substitution of new formwork materials; and the High projection, higher rates of gain in concrete construction plus (possibly) slower rates of substitution for wood. The High also presupposes some continued gain in the use of lumber for architectural effect; the Low, conversely, assumes that the net elimination of structural use of lumber in non-residential buildings will continue, but have decreasingly less effect on unit use as the zero point is approached.

As indicated in footnote 11 to Table A4–7, the total use (production) of softwood plywood has been taken as a rough measure of the combined use of softwood and hardwood plywood in construction. The increasing coefficients over the years have been projected into the future, the main element in the picture being a substitution of plywood for wooden boards (subflooring, sheathing, cabinet work) in residential construction, and some corresponding substitution for concrete formwork in non-residential construction. Since both of these substitutions have definite limits, the rate of increase in unit use, in all three projections, is assumed to slow down. The variations among the three projections may be assumed to reflect not only different rates of substitution of plywood for lumber but, as time goes on, different rates of displacement of plywood in turn—in sheathing, subflooring, panels, and formwork—by metals and plastics.

In addition to using it in the forms of lumber and plywood, construction also uses wood in the forms of building paper and board, which currently account for about 6 per cent of all wood pulp. The combined requirement is derived crudely, at the end of Table A4–7, in relation to projected total construction.

Because data are very limited on the distribution of *steel* by different types of construction, but a considerable amount of information is available on the different types (shapes) of construction steel, it was decided to analyze steel for construction on the latter basis, relating shipments of each type to the kind of end-use which most affected its consumption. The quantities thus obtained were then adjusted to the total level of steel use in construction, for which fairly reliable historical estimates can be made. The kinds of steel accounted for in Table A4–8 are utilized to the extent of close to 90 per cent in construction or in the manufacture of "contractors' products," such as furnaces, windows, etc. At the same time, the total tonnage of the types of steel analyzed is equivalent to about 80 per cent of all steel for construction, although about 10 per cent of this 80 is spuriously so allocated.

Trends in use of two of the largest steel items—heavy structural shapes and concrete reinforcing bars—are closely interrelated with each other and with the substitution of reinforced concrete for steel frame construction in large buildings. The projections of heavy structural shapes (Table A4–9) are based on rates of unit use which are the complement of expected increases in use of reinforced concrete construction, discussed below in connection with Table A4–10 on cement. Displacement is assumed to take place at the rate of 5 barrels of cement to one ton of structural steel, and in the Medium projection changes in the unit use of steel in Table A4–9 are based solely upon this relationship. In the case of the Low and the High, it is assumed that the extremes in possible unit use of cement for large buildings will be partly occasioned by influences not having to do with substitution for steel structurals, so that a somewhat lesser degree of complementarity is assumed. The Low also allows for the possible displacement of steel by other metals, as well as a possibly decreasing total use of framing materials in relation to value of building construction.

The use of concrete reinforcing bars follows directly, rather than inversely, from the use of cement, although allowance must be made for the relative amounts of cement devoted to "mass," rather than reinforced, concrete, as well as for the steel-saving spread of "prestressing." Failure of the High ratios to rise, and decline in the Medium, and part of the decline in the Low, result from an assumed increase in the role of prestressing, which may save as much as half of the steel per unit of cement. Steel used in prestressing is ordinarily in the form of cable, rather than bar, and the projections of concrete reinforcing bars are intended to include this substitute form, now a negligible part of the total.

The relationship of "oil-country goods" to oil and gas well drilling has shown considerable constancy, and all three projections are therefore based upon a continuance of the average ratio of the past decade. The relationship of line-pipe requirements to its predominant end-use, gas utility construction, seems less dependable, so that while the Medium projection is based upon a continuation of the postwar average relationship, the Low and the High allow for variations in either direction.

The use of nails and staples—a relatively minor component of construction steel—is assumed to decline in the future in relation to use of lumber as the result of displacement by glues and of the use of laminated, instead of nailed, panels.

What is now "galvanized sheet" has been treated as if it were equivalent to all of the miscellaneous steel used in residential construction, which it approximates. Some sheet steel goes directly into construction via such uses as wall panels and roofing sheet, but most reaches construction through contractors' products, such as heating and cooling equipment, doors, windows, and hardware. Both the direct and the indirect use of miscellaneous residential construction steel is expected to rise, as steel is substituted for other materials in contractors' products (e.g., for cast iron in plumbing fixtures) and for other types of paneling and framing in direct construction uses. The Low projection assumes that increased use in contractors' products will no more than cancel out a net loss in direct uses as some of the traditional galvanized sheet applications decline. The High projection, conversely, supposes a radical breakthrough in the use of light steel framing.

The summation in Table A4–9, adjusted to the level of total net shipments of steel for construction, is given both net of and inclusive of railroad construction. The latter is to complete the picture and to afford a comparison of the over-all input ratios over time. In deriving total use of steel in the appendix to Chapter 16, railroad construction steel is combined with other railroad steel.

Use of *portland cement* is fairly evenly divided among large-building construction, highway construction, other heavy construction, and maintenance and repair of all types, with new residential construction of only slightly lesser importance.

At the war's end, about two-fifths of the cement

consumed in residential building was employed in the form of concrete blocks, mostly for basement walls. The remainder was used in foundation slabs, subflooring, and concrete frames for multifamily units. A steady rise in unit use since then may be ascribed to (1) increasing average size, (2) an increasing proportion (in the last few years) of homes with basements, (3) a more rapidly increasing proportion built on flat slabs, and (4) a recent resurgence in multifamily construction.

Cement used in large buildings must be considered in conjunction with the competitive use of heavy steel structurals. Gradual substitution of reinforced concrete for steel structurals in large buildings is assumed to occur as the result of at least two kinds of developments: (1) improvements in technology which are decreasing both the cost and the erection time of reinforced concrete buildings and (2) a trend away from taller structures toward structures spread over a greater area for such purposes as industrial plants, schools, and hospitals.

Unit use of cement in highway construction has shown a slight tendency to rise in recent years—the net result of a relative yielding of concrete to asphalt in highway pavements, somewhat more than counterbalanced by the substitution of reinforced concrete for steel in bridges and other structures, similar to that occurring in large building construction. The combined unit use in any one year is also affected by the mix of highway construction as between paving and the building of bridges, etc., and it has been a relative shift toward the former that has dampened the recent rise in cement, despite a rapid increase in reinforced concrete structures. Also a factor has been a tendency toward heavier pavements utilizing both cement and asphalt.

In categories other than those already discussed, the use of cement is mostly in mass structures such as dams, piers, sewers, military airfield runways, etc. There has been some upward trend in unit use in this "other heavy construction" category, explainable primarily by changes in the relative importance of the subitems. For the future, it is assumed that a continued trend toward the higher cement using components will be most likely counterbalanced by lower unit consumption of cement in each, as the use of expanded aggregates and other materials gives equivalent bulk with less cement.

In the aggregate, an increasing unit use of cement per construction dollar, as shown in Table A4–10, is the probable outlook. At a minimum (Low projection), unit use might stabilize near present levels. Table A4–10 also includes a crude calculation of requirements for concrete aggregates and for bitumens, the former of interest only because of its large volume and the latter because it is a component of the demand for petroleum.

Of the presently more minor materials going into construction, *copper* and *aluminum* (and their alloys) are among the more important and are treated in Tables A4–11 and 12. Aluminum, at least, could one day become a major construction material. So also could plastics, but the statistical base for projecting the use of plastics in construction is virtually non-existent, and no such projection has therefore been attempted.

For both aluminum and copper, adjusted shipments data, as developed in the appendix to Chapter 16, have been used to derive the historical consumption coefficients. Projections of these coefficients (which are net of returned new industrial scrap) are based on recent trends, tempered by judgments as to the effect of technological developments under way or on the horizon. In the case of new building construction, the principal governing elements seem to be (1) relative gains for copper at the expense of steel in piping, (2) a longer term displacement of both copper and steel by plastic piping, (3) relative gains for both copper and aluminum at the expense of galvanized steel in such sheet metal applications as guttering and roofing, (4) some gain for aluminum in relation to copper in this same area, (5) gains for aluminum (along with plastics) at the expense of wood and masonry materials in outside walls, (6) the further spread of the use of aluminum door and window frames, thresholds, etc., and (7) a general decline in the use of materials per dollar of construction. In view of these factors, the Medium projection for copper assumes a continuation of the approximate present unit use, while the Medium projection for aluminum allows for the continuation—at a slower rate—of the rapidly rising trend of recent years. Even in the Low, the unit use of aluminum is assumed to undergo some increase, while the Low for copper allows for a possible modest decline. In the High, the assumed rise for copper is limited, while that for aluminum allows for possible revolutionary developments over the next two decades in the use of aluminum walls and framing.

In the electric light and power application, the principal trend seems to be a displacement of copper by aluminum, particularly for long-distance transmission lines, as well as in some local distribution equipment; but the continued significance of this trend is limited by the fact that most of the displacement has already occurred. Now entering into the picture is the substitution of aluminum for steel in transmission towers, which portends gains for aluminum without any effect upon copper. Again, there is the general expectation of decreasing total material use per dollar of total construction cost. On balance, there seems to be no other outlook for copper in this field except decline, and the three projections allow for this at various assumed rates. For aluminum, continued gains, although at a more modest rate than in the recent past, seem the most likely prospect, and this is the basis of the Medium projection; the High allows for a somewhat more rapid rate of gain and the Low for the possibility that the over-all decline in unit materials use may counterbalance aluminum's relative gains.

The remaining use of nonferrous metals in construction is predominantly copper's use in communications construction, and, despite a recently rising trend, this has been projected (Medium) as most likely to maintain the average level of recent years. The reason is a presumed growth in the unit value of other materials and of labor, resulting from the continued introduction of increasingly more sophisticated types of auxiliary equipment. The High and the Low allow for more or less arbitrary deviations in either direction.

LIST OF TABLES

A4–

TABLE A4–1. Historical Data on New and Maintenance Construction, by Type[1]

(Billion 1960 dollars)

	1946	1947	1948	1949	1950	1951	1952	1953	1954	1955	1956	1957	1958	1959	1960
Total construction	39.7	45.1	50.1	52.1	58.6	59.4	61.0	63.4	67.1	72.8	70.7	71.1	71.8	77.1	76.2
Total new construction[2]	24.8	29.0	33.7	35.3	42.2	42.7	43.9	46.3	49.6	54.4	52.3	52.4	53.2	57.4	56.6
Private	20.7	23.8	27.2	26.7	32.8	31.1	31.1	33.1	35.6	40.6	38.7	38.1	37.3	41.1	40.6
Public	4.1	5.2	6.5	8.6	9.4	11.6	12.8	13.2	14.0	13.8	13.6	14.3	15.9	16.3	16.0
Residential construction[3]	9.9	12.5	14.6	14.7	19.6	16.8	16.8	17.4	19.1	22.2	20.1	19.3	20.6	24.5	22.6
Additions and alterations[4]	2.4	2.9	3.3	3.0	3.1	3.0	3.3	3.4	3.5	3.8	4.0	4.1	4.1	4.5	4.9
Non-residential construction	15.08	16.38	19.23	21.18	22.68	26.27	27.36	28.85	30.16	31.67	32.43	33.50	32.32	32.60	34.05
Private non-residential construction[5]	11.60	11.58	12.88	12.79	13.58	15.14	15.12	16.12	16.54	18.28	19.02	19.52	17.43	17.36	18.80
Industrial	3.40	2.73	2.02	1.42	1.52	2.77	2.92	2.74	2.48	2.85	3.46	3.80	2.50	2.14	2.85
Commercial[6]	2.28	1.37	1.81	1.50	1.84	1.80	1.43	2.21	2.70	3.83	4.08	3.81	3.77	3.99	4.18
Institutional and miscellaneous buildings[7]	1.05	.94	1.40	1.80	2.04	2.18	1.96	2.04	2.45	2.37	2.36	2.60	2.84	2.87	3.14
Public utilities[8]	2.91	4.23	5.02	5.38	5.14	5.21	5.45	5.74	5.41	5.55	5.48	5.76	5.24	5.02	5.32
Electric light and power	.94	1.43	1.74	2.22	1.96	1.89	2.25	2.38	2.33	2.16	1.98	2.15	2.31	2.04	2.06
Gas utilities	.57	.98	1.13	1.41	1.70	1.78	1.47	1.60	1.40	1.52	1.50	1.69	1.54	1.67	1.76
Other utilities	1.40	1.82	2.15	1.75	1.48	1.54	1.73	1.76	1.68	1.87	2.00	1.92	1.39	1.31	1.50
Petroleum and gas well drilling[9]	1.11	1.23	1.52	1.54	1.78	1.97	2.10	2.21	2.36	2.55	2.63	2.46	2.06	2.24	2.19
All other private construction[9]	.85	1.08	1.11	1.15	1.26	1.21	1.26	1.18	1.14	1.13	1.01	1.09	1.02	1.10	1.12
Public non-residential construction	3.48	4.80	6.35	8.39	9.10	11.13	12.24	12.73	13.62	13.39	13.41	13.98	14.89	15.24	15.25
Schools and hospitals[10]	.39	.61	1.22	2.08	2.34	2.70	2.56	2.54	3.04	3.29	3.23	3.44	3.45	3.15	3.22
Highways	1.21	1.71	1.87	2.37	2.64	2.62	2.78	3.18	4.12	4.25	4.30	4.63	5.33	5.72	5.46
Military and industrial[11]	.58	.46	.49	.45	.56	2.40	3.81	3.72	3.07	2.39	2.00	1.85	1.87	1.84	1.80
Water and sewerage	.42	.66	.90	1.01	1.02	1.13	1.11	1.18	1.25	1.33	1.49	1.50	1.48	1.50	1.49
All other public[12]	.88	1.36	1.87	2.48	2.54	2.28	1.98	2.11	2.14	2.13	2.39	2.56	2.76	3.03	3.28
(Large-building construction)[13]	7.12	5.65	6.45	6.80	7.74	9.45	8.87	9.53	10.67	12.34	13.13	13.65	12.56	12.15	13.39
Maintenance and repair[14]															
Residential	5.38	6.50	6.65	6.85	6.20	6.31	6.50	6.36	6.85	7.54	7.76	8.05	7.34	7.84	7.23
Non-residential	9.55	9.58	9.72	9.91	10.15	10.40	10.57	10.72	10.63	10.84	10.65	10.69	11.31	11.82	12.33

1. Except where otherwise indicated, data are derived from series published in *Construction Volume and Costs, 1915–1956* (Washington: U.S. Departments of Labor and Commerce, 1958) and in Table V–3, *U.S. Income and Output* (1958 suppl. to *Survey of Current Business*) and 1961 National Income Number of the *Survey of Current Business*. Data for 1960 include Alaska and Hawaii, but are on an "old series" basis for residential construction; revision to "new series" basis has not yet been incorporated into the National Income Accounts series. For deflators, see Table A4–2.

2. From Tables A1–6 and A1–8. These summary series, which follow the definitions used in the National Income Accounts, differ from the detail that follows both in terms of classification and in terms of the deflators used. "Private," here, is less than the sum of "residential" and "private non-residential" by the very small amount of "public residential construction." The NIA deflators differ from the BDSA/BLS deflators used in the detail of this table in that they take into account not only materials and labor costs but the changing profit margins of construction firms.

3. Includes farm and public residential, as well as private non-farm.

4. Private non-farm only; public and farm residential presumed insignificant. Additions and alterations are part of the residential total on the preceding line.

5. Unlike the usual published series, this does *not* include farm residential, which has been included here with other residential construction, above.

6. Includes office and loft buildings, warehouses, stores, restaurants, garages, and other edifices.

7. Religious, educational, professional, social, recreational, and miscellaneous private buildings.

8. "Other" includes railroads, local transit, petroleum pipelines, and communications. Breakdown for 1946–56 from *Construction Volume and Costs* (see footnote 1). All items deflated by deflator for total public utilities. 1957–60 estimated on basis of distribution in *Construction Review* (Washington: Departments of Labor and Commerce), Dec. 1958, p. 6; Aug. 1960, p. 12; and July 1961, p. 7.

9. Sewer and water facilities, roads, bridges, and miscellaneous construction such as that in parks and playgrounds, plus non-residential farm construction. Deflated by deflator for "farm construction," which accounts for the bulk of this category.

10. The great bulk of this category is schools.

11. For most years, the bulk of this category is "military facilities." "Military" and "industrial" components separately deflated (see footnote 7, Table A4–2).

12. "Miscellaneous public service enterprises," "conservation and development," administrative, social, recreational, commercial, and miscellaneous.

13. Arbitrarily defined as total of private industrial, commercial, and institutional, plus school and hospital construction.

14. Basic data are from *Construction Volume and Costs, 1915–1956* and *Construction Review*, Dec. 1960 and 1961. Implicit deflator for total new construction used for the total; deflators for private non-farm residential construction for the residential portion (source: Income and Output Table VII–2, *U.S. Income and Output* (1958) and *Survey of Current Business* for July 1960 and Feb. 1961; transposed from 1954 to 1960 base). Non-residential maintenance and repair is obtained as a residual.

TABLE A4–2.   Price Deflators for Historical Data on Construction

Year	National Income Accounts deflators				Construction statistics deflators[1]									
	Total construction[2]	Private[3]	Public[3]	Private residential non-farm[4]	Total residential (incl. farm)[5]	Private non-residential[6]	Public utility	Petroleum and gas well drilling	Farm construction	Public non-residential[7]	Military	Highways	Sewer and water	Other public[8]
1946	54.0	53.2	n.a.	55.6	55.8	49.7	47.2	59.0	58.8	47.3	54.7	73.7	45.9	47.0
1947	64.5	63.9	66.7	67.4	67.5	62.3	55.3	62.6	72.3	60.9	67.0	84.9	53.5	56.0
1948	72.1	71.7	74.5	75.2	75.3	69.2	60.6	69.5	78.4	68.7	73.8	95.0	59.4	62.5
1949	71.4	70.4	74.1	72.8	72.9	68.4	61.8	68.3	76.0	67.9	72.9	89.8	61.0	63.4
1950	73.9	73.7	74.2	77.5	77.6	70.0	64.8	70.8	77.9	69.7	73.6	86.0	64.5	66.6
1951	80.1	79.5	80.8	83.0	83.1	76.3	71.5	75.6	86.2	75.5	80.1	96.1	68.4	71.4
1952	82.9	82.1	84.8	85.3	85.4	79.4	73.5	80.1	87.5	79.1	82.6	101.5	71.3	74.3
1953	84.2	83.6	86.1	86.7	86.9	81.2	76.9	84.2	88.0	81.6	84.2	99.3	74.9	77.5
1954	83.9	83.5	85.0	86.1	86.2	81.8	79.2	86.7	87.4	82.0	84.0	94.0	78.3	79.7
1955	86.2	86.1	87.0	88.8	88.9	84.1	81.8	91.1	89.4	84.1	86.0	95.2	81.4	82.6
1956	92.2	91.7	93.1	92.7	92.8	89.0	89.2	93.1	94.1	88.4	91.3	102.3	85.7	87.2
1957	95.6	94.7	97.3	94.4	94.5	93.6	94.0	92.9	96.1	92.3	95.9	105.7	89.7	91.2
1958	95.7	95.3	97.5	95.3	95.3	95.3	97.0	96.8	96.2	94.6	97.1	104.0	93.5	94.2
1959	97.9	98.0	98.8	98.4	98.4	98.0	99.4	99.7	99.0	97.6	98.8	102.2	97.3	97.7
1960	100.0	100.0	100.0	100.0	100.0	100.0	100.0	100.0	100.0	100.0	100.0	100.0	100.0	100.0

1. Unless otherwise indicated, transposed from series on 1954 base in Table VII–14 of *U.S. Income and Output* and 1961 National Income Number of *Survey of Current Business*.

2. From Table A1–7.

3. From Table A1–9.

4. Implicit deflator in National Income Accounts, transposed to a 1960 base. Used to deflate residential maintenance and repair.

5. Calculated by combining deflators for residential building (except farm), (93.3%), public residential construction (4.7%), and farm construction (2.0%).

6. Used for components of non-residential construction, but not for total, which is obtained by addition.

7. Used for schools and hospitals and industrial portion of "military and industrial" category. Total public non-residential construction obtained by addition.

8. Calculated by combining indexes for public non-residential buildings (37.3%), miscellaneous public service enterprises (11.1%), conservation and development (45.3%), and "all other public" (6.3%).

TABLE A4–3. Projected New and Maintenance Construction, by Type[1]

(Billion 1960 dollars)

	1950	1955	1960		1970	1980	1990	2000
Total construction, including maintenance and repair	58.6	72.8	76.2	L M H	92.7 120.3 152.4	113.5 166.3 241.4	134.9 233.6 387.6	172.2 348.4 687.0
Total new construction[2]	42.2	54.4	56.6	L M H	67.0 93.3 123.7	80.1 130.1 199.7	93.4 184.9 325.7	119.4 280.9 589.6
Private[3]	32.8	40.6	40.6	L M H	47.7 66.4 88.3	57.3 90.2 138.1	65.4 127.2 219.7	83.8 196.8 403.0
Public[3]	9.4	13.8	16.0	L M H	19.3 27.1 35.4	22.8 39.9 61.6	28.0 57.7 106.0	35.6 84.1 186.6
New residential construction[4]	19.6	22.2	22.6	L M H	28.2 41.1 56.4	35.4 54.7 85.0	40.3 77.6 133.0	54.7 126.4 257.9
Additions and alterations	3.1	3.8	4.9	L M H	5.1 7.4 10.2	6.4 9.9 15.3	7.3 14.0 24.0	9.9 22.8 46.5
New non-residential construction	22.7	31.7	34.1	L M H	38.8 52.4 67.3	44.7 75.4 114.7	53.1 107.3 192.7	64.7 154.5 331.7
Private non-residential construction[5]	13.58	18.28	18.8	L M H	20.9 27.4 34.7	23.7 38.2 57.3	27.1 53.5 93.3	31.8 76.7 158.0
Industrial	1.52	2.85	2.85	L M H	3.1 4.3 5.7	3.5 6.3 9.8	4.0 9.2 16.6	4.6 13.1 28.0
Commercial	1.84	3.83	4.18	L M H	4.5 6.4 8.9	5.3 8.9 15.0	7.0 13.3 25.3	9.3 20.2 44.5
Institutional and miscellaneous buildings	2.04	2.37	3.14	L M H	3.9 4.4 5.1	4.8 5.9 7.8	5.6 7.8 11.4	6.5 10.0 16.4
Public utilities	5.14	5.55	5.32	L M H	5.0 7.4 10.3	5.2 9.9 16.6	5.3 13.3 26.8	5.9 18.7 44.4
Electric light and power	1.96	2.16	2.06	L M H	1.4 2.4 4.5	.9 3.1 7.8	.5 4.2 12.4	.3 6.1 19.9
Gas utilities	1.70	1.52	1.76	L M H	1.8 2.4 3.1	1.8 2.8 4.4	1.9 2.9 5.7	2.1 3.2 7.7
Other utilities[6]	1.48	1.87	1.50	L M H	1.8 2.6 2.7	2.5 4.0 4.4	2.9 6.2 8.7	3.5 9.4 16.8
Petroleum and gas well drilling	1.78	2.55	2.19	L M H	2.1 2.8 3.3	2.4 3.7 5.4	2.8 5.1 8.7	3.4 6.9 14.8
All other private non residential construction	1.26	1.13	1.12	L M H	1.1 1.7 2.2	1.1 2.1 3.2	1.2 2.6 4.5	1.2 3.0 6.0
(Non-allocable private non-residential construction)[7]	—	—	—	L M H	1.2 .3 −.8	1.4 1.4 −.5	1.2 2.2 —	.8 4.8 +3.9

Table A4–3 (cont'd)

(Billion 1960 dollars)

	1950	1955	1960		1970	1980	1990	2000
Public non-residential construction[8]	9.10	13.39	15.3	L	17.9	21.0	26.0	32.9
				M	25.0	37.2	53.8	77.8
				H	32.6	57.4	99.4	173.7
Schools and hospitals	2.34	3.29	3.22	L	3.8	4.2	4.6	5.0
				M	4.1	5.0	6.2	7.4
				H	4.8	6.7	9.4	12.9
Highways	2.64	4.25	5.46	L	7.2	9.1	11.0	13.8
				M	10.1	16.1	23.8	34.6
				H	12.4	24.2	45.9	86.5
Military and industrial	.56	2.39	1.80	L	1.7	1.4	2.0	2.8
				M	3.3	5.1	7.8	12.3
				H	4.6	8.7	15.3	27.7
Water and sewerage	1.02	1.33	1.49	L	1.8	2.0	2.2	2.4
				M	2.2	3.0	4.0	5.3
				H	2.9	4.4	6.6	9.5
All other public	2.54	2.13	3.28	L	3.4	4.3	6.2	8.9
				M	5.3	8.0	12.0	18.2
				H	7.9	13.4	22.2	37.1
(Large-building construction)[9]	7.74	12.34	13.4	L	15.3	17.8	21.2	25.5
				M	19.3	26.1	36.5	50.7
				H	24.5	39.3	62.7	101.8
Maintenance and repair[10]	16.35	18.38	19.6	L	25.7	33.4	41.5	52.8
				M	27.0	36.2	48.7	67.5
				H	28.7	41.7	61.9	97.4
Residential	6.20	7.54	7.2	L	8.7	10.2	11.3	12.5
				M	9.1	10.8	12.5	14.7
				H	9.5	11.7	14.4	18.4
Non-residential	10.15	10.84	12.4	L	17.0	23.2	30.2	40.3
				M	17.9	25.4	36.2	52.8
				H	19.2	30.0	47.5	79.0

1. Historical data from Table A4–1. Projections of the individual categories of construction from Table A4–4.

2. Sum of private and public construction, and, except for historical data (see footnote 2 of Table A4–1), of residential and public and private non-residential construction.

3. Private construction is the sum of residential and private non-residential, less public residential, construction. For breakdown of residential construction, see Table A4–4. Public residential is added to other types of public construction to yield total public construction.

4. For breakdown into farm, non-farm, and public, see Table A4–4.

5. Independent projection, based on plant and equipment expenditures; see Table A4–4.

6. Computed as a residual.

7. Residual equivalent to "statistical error," plus unallowed-for compensation among Lows and Highs when these are directly added. (For the 2000 High, a positive statistical error may be assumed to outbalance the actual non-allocable, which should be negative.) For further explanation of "non-allocable," see footnote 6 to Table A1–13. See also Notes.

8. Sum of detail below.

9. Sum of private industrial, commercial, and institutional construction and public school and hospital construction.

10. Residential maintenance and repair is assumed to be $148 per household, the average for 1951–60, while non-residential maintenance and repair is assumed to be 2.4% of GNP. See Table A1–2 for household projections and Table A1–12 for projections of GNP.

TABLE A4–4.   Derivation of the Components of New Construction

(Billion 1960 dollars unless otherwise indicated)

	1950	1955	1960		1970	1980	1990	2000
Residential construction:								
New dwelling unit construction[1]				L	1.64	1.79	1.70	1.93
(million units)	1.88	1.79	1.54	M	2.39	2.65	3.06	4.21
				H	3.21	3.83	4.74	7.63
Equivalent residential non-farm				L	1.36	1.49	1.42	1.62
units (new series, millions)[2]	1.53	1.48	1.27	M	2.01	2.23	2.58	3.57
				H	2.70	3.23	4.02	6.50
Average value per unit[3]				L	14.1	16.2	19.4	23.2
($ 1960 thous.)	8.8	10.3	11.5	M	14.1	16.9	20.8	24.6
				H	14.4	18.2	23.0	27.7
Disposable income per household[4]				L	8.2	9.4	11.3	13.5
($ 1960 thous.)	5.80	6.26	6.69	M	8.2	9.8	12.1	14.3
				H	8.4	10.6	13.4	16.1
Value of new dwelling unit				L	23.1	29.0	33.0	44.8
construction[5]	16.5	18.4	17.7	M	33.7	44.8	63.6	103.6
				H	46.2	69.7	109.0	211.4
				L	5.1	6.4	7.3	9.9
Additions and alterations[6]	3.1	3.8	4.9	M	7.4	9.9	14.0	22.8
				H	10.2	15.3	24.0	46.5
				L	28.2	35.4	40.3	54.7
Total new residential construction[7]	19.6	22.2	22.6	M	41.1	54.7	77.6	126.4
				H	56.4	85.0	133.0	257.9
				L	26.0	32.7	37.4	51.1
Private non-farm	18.2	21.0	21.1	M	38.0	50.8	72.3	118.5
				H	52.6	79.6	124.8	243.0
				L	.8	.9	.9	.9
Farm	1.0	.9	.8	M	1.0	1.2	1.4	1.6
				H	1.0	1.2	1.6	2.0
				L	1.4	1.8	2.0	2.7
Public	.4	.3	.7	M	2.1	2.7	3.9	6.3
				H	2.8	4.2	6.6	12.9
Private non-residential construction:[8]								
				L	3.1	3.5	4.0	4.6
Industrial	1.52	2.85	2.85	M	4.4	6.3	9.2	13.0
				H	5.7	9.8	16.6	28.0
				L	16.4	18.7	22.4	26.8
Investment in manufacturing[9]	10.4	13.5	14.5	M	21.4	29.7	41.6	57.3
				H	27.2	43.7	69.3	110.6
Industrial construction as per cent				L	19.1	18.5	17.9	17.3
of investment in manufacturing	14.6	21.1	19.7	M	20.5	21.3	22.1	22.9
				H	21.1	22.5	23.9	25.3
				L	4.5	5.3	7.0	9.4
Commercial	1.84	3.83	4.18	M	6.4	8.9	13.3	20.2
				H	8.9	15.0	25.3	44.5
"Commercial and other"				L	9.0	10.6	14.0	18.8
investment[9]	7.90	8.85	8.44	M	11.5	15.4	22.1	32.5
				H	14.4	22.7	36.2	60.1
Commercial construction as per cent				L	50	50	50	50
of "commercial and other"	23.3	43.3	49.5	M	56	58	60	62
investment				H	62	66	70	74

Table A4–4 (cont'd)

(Billion 1960 dollars unless otherwise indicated)

	1950	1955	1960		1970	1980	1990	2000
Private non-residential construction (cont'd)								
Institutional and miscellaneous				L	3.9	4.8	5.6	6.5
buildings	2.04	2.37	3.14	M	4.4	5.9	7.8	10.0
				H	5.1	7.8	11.4	16.4
				L	202	226	249	268
Population [10] (millions)	152	165	180	M	208	245	287	331
				H	223	279	349	433
				L	19.4	21.0	22.6	24.2
$ 1960 per capita	13.4	14.4	17.4	M	21.0	24.2	27.2	30.2
				H	22.8	27.8	32.8	37.8
				L	5.0	5.2	5.3	5.9
Public utilities	5.14	5.55	5.32	M	7.4	9.9	13.3	18.7
				H	10.3	16.6	26.8	44.4
Investment in public utilities				L	9.7	10.6	11.3	13.5
and communications [9]	6.15	7.43	8.81	M	12.3	16.4	22.1	31.0
				H	16.1	25.6	40.6	66.2
Public utilities construction as per				L	52.0	49.0	47.0	44.0
cent of investment in public	83.6	74.7	60.4	M	60.4	60.4	60.4	60.4
utilities and communications				H	64.0	65.0	66.0	67.0
				L	1.37	.90	.54	.34
Electric light and power	1.96	2.16	2.06	M	2.36	3.01	4.18	6.13
				H	4.50	7.85	12.44	19.92
FRB index of electric power				L	180	265	358	486
production [11]	52.0	85.4	123.2	M	209	342	504	739
				H	265	462	732	1,172
$ 1960 million per point of				L	7.6	3.4	1.5	.7
FRB index	37.7	25.3	16.7	M	11.3	8.8	8.3	8.3
				H	17.0	17.0	17.0	17.0
				L	1.79	1.77	1.91	2.07
Gas utilities	1.70	1.52	1.76	M	2.36	2.77	2.94	3.15
				H	3.06	4.36	5.73	7.71
FRB index of gas utility				L	148	181	199	220
production [11]	54.3	85.2	122.5	M	175	227	267	318
				H	204	291	382	514
$ 1960 million per point of				L	12.1	9.8	9.6	9.4
FRB index	31.3	17.8	14.4	M	13.5	12.2	11.0	9.9
				H	15.0	15.0	15.0	15.0
				L	2.14	2.41	2.80	3.44
Petroleum and gas well drilling	1.78	2.55	2.19	M	2.84	3.72	5.06	6.88
				H	3.31	5.43	8.74	14.85
FRB index of crude oil				L	111	137	171	219
production [11]	75.3	94.8	98.1	M	126	164	221	298
				H	138	209	312	495
$ 1960 mil. per point of				L	19.3	17.6	16.4	15.7
FRB index	23.6	26.9	22.3	M	22.5	22.7	22.9	23.1
				H	24.0	26.0	28.0	30.0
All other private non-residential				L	1.13	1.08	1.18	1.25
construction	1.26	1.13	1.12	M	1.66	2.19	2.55	2.97
				H	2.18	3.22	4.51	5.97
				L	4.0	3.7	4.0	4.3
Farm investment [12]	6.1	4.8	4.1	M	5.4	6.4	7.5	8.5
				H	6.4	8.7	11.5	14.7
All other private construction as				L	28.2	29.3	29.4	29.1
per cent of farm investment	20.7	23.5	27.3	M	30.8	32.7	34.0	34.9
				H	34.0	37.0	39.2	40.6

Table A4–4 (cont'd)

(Billion 1960 dollars unless otherwise indicated)

	1950	1955	1960		1970	1980	1990	2000
Total private non-residential				L	20.9	23.7	27.1	31.8
construction[13]	3.58	18.28	18.80	M	27.4	38.2	53.5	76.7
				H	34.7	57.3	93.3	158.0
				L	21.8	24.7	28.2	32.9
Total, including farm dwellings[14]	4.60	19.33	19.60	M	28.3	39.3	54.8	78.2
				H	35.7	58.6	95.0	160.1
Public non-residential construction:[8]								
				L	3.8	4.2	4.6	5.0
Schools and hospitals	2.34	3.29	3.22	M	4.1	5.0	6.2	7.4
				H	4.8	6.7	9.4	12.9
				L	202	226	249	268
Population[10] (millions)	152	165	180	M	208	245	287	331
				H	223	279	349	433
				L	18.6	18.6	18.6	18.6
$ 1960 per capita	15.4	19.9	17.9	M	19.5	20.5	21.5	22.5
				H	21.3	24.1	26.9	29.7
				L	7.2	9.1	11.0	13.8
Highway construction	2.64	4.25	5.46	M	10.1	16.1	23.8	34.6
				H	12.4	24.2	45.9	86.5
				L	1,271	1,711	2,237	2,908
Auto-equivalent miles[15] (billions)	649	835	979	M	1,368	1,946	2,723	3,898
				H	1,531	2,412	3,825	6,177
				L	.57	.53	.49	.47
$ 1960 per 100 auto-equivalent miles	.41	.51	.56	M	.74	.83	.87	.89
				H	.81	1.00	1.20	1.40
				L	1.7	1.4	2.0	2.8
Military and industrial[16]	.56	2.39	1.80	M	3.3	5.1	7.8	12.3
				H	4.6	8.7	15.3	27.7
				L	45	29	38	50
Defense expenditures[17] ($ 1960 bil.)	19.9	46.8	45.5	M	75	106	151	220
				H	105	181	295	494
Military and industrial construction as per cent of defense expenditures	2.8	5.1	4.0		4.4	4.8	5.2	5.6
				L	1.8	2.0	2.2	2.4
Water and sewerage	1.02	1.33	1.49	M	2.2	3.0	4.0	5.3
				H	2.9	4.4	6.6	9.5
				L	202	226	249	268
Population[10] (millions)	152	165	180	M	208	245	287	331
				H	223	279	349	433
				L	9.0	9.0	9.0	9.0
$ 1960 per capita	6.7	8.1	8.3	M	10.5	12.3	14.1	15.9
				H	12.9	15.9	18.9	21.9
				L	3.4	4.3	6.2	8.9
All other public	2.54	2.13	3.28	M	5.3	8.0	12.0	18.2
				H	7.9	13.4	22.2	37.1
Total government expenditures				L	129	154	223	318
($ 1960 bil.)[16]	57	91	100	M	160	242	365	551
				H	197	336	555	927
Other public construction as per				L	2.8	2.8	2.8	2.8
cent of total government	4.5	2.3	3.3	M	3.3	3.3	3.3	3.3
expenditures				H	4.0	4.0	4.0	4.0

Table A4–4 (cont'd)

1. From Table A4–5. Data are the arithmetic averages of preceding and succeeding 5-year period, except for 1950, 1955, and 1960, which are calculated by adjusting BLS/Commerce housing-start data to the 1950–56 benchmark (see footnote 7 to Table A4–5). The average for 2000 requires an estimate for 2000–05, which has been constructed roughly, by extrapolating net additions and net replacements through that period.

2. Based on the 1950–56 relationship between BLS/Commerce series and Census Bureau *National Housing Inventory* data (see footnote 1), as well as the 1959 relationship between new and old BLS/Commerce series, adjusted for the relative amount of farm construction. The new series is not actually available for 1950 and 1955, but has been estimated back for comparison purposes. This series, which is presented for illustrative purposes because of its general familiarity, is believed to be an undercount of actual new housing units produced, omitting not only farm construction and mobile homes, but probably also some vacation cottages and other residential units built without permits.

3. Historical values obtained by dividing new residential construction, less alterations and additions, by number of units constructed. Projections are proportional to the change in disposable personal income per household (next item). While both higher and lower unit values are "reasonably possible," they could not reasonably be combined with the High and Low projections of number of units, which are partly dependent upon the relative price. The use of unit income elasticity is based on the apparent tendency of consumers to maintain a constant relative position of housing expenditure in their budgets in order to effect gradual improvements in housing standards in the face of more rapidly rising relative costs (cf. Tables A1–22 and 23).

4. Disposable personal income from Table A1–27; number of households from Table A1–2.

5. Historical data from Table A4–1—total new residential construction, less additions and alterations. Projections by multiplication of preceding factors.

6. Projected at 22% of new residential construction. This is on the low side of recent experience (see Table A4–1) and is selected as being consistent with the assumed relatively high levels of new residential construction activity (in turn consistent with the assumed full-employment economy). The single coefficient is used for all three projection levels, on the assumption that it represents not only a most probable value but as low a percentage as would be consistent with the Low new residential construction and as high a percentage as would be consistent with the High. While lower and higher levels of addition and alteration might also be reasonable, the interest here is in the amounts that may logically be added to new construction to obtain total residential.

7. Historical data for the total are from Table A4–1; for the breakdown, from the sources indicated in footnote 1 thereto. Projections of the total are the sum of the preceding two lines; the breakdown is on the assumption that "public" will constitute about 5% of the total and that farm residential construction will move proportionately to agricultural product (Table A1–16).

8. Historical data for each construction value series are from Table A4–1; the coefficients are calculated. Projections are the product of the extrapolated coefficients (graphically and/or on a judgment basis) and the reference series shown.

9. From Table A6–3.

10. From Table A1–2.

11. From Tables A1–29 and 30.

12. Farm purchases of new plant and equipment, from Table A6–3. Farm construction constitutes the bulk of the "other" category.

13. Historical data from Table A4–1. Projections derived by subtracting farm dwellings (this table, above) from total non-residential construction including farm dwellings (below). For explanation of the use of this method of derivation rather than addition, see Notes.

14. Historical data are sum of preceding line and farm dwellings (above). Projections from Table A6–3.

15. Arbitrary measure, reflecting rough space/weight equivalence. From Table A5–15—passenger car miles, plus 3 times truck and bus miles.

16. Cf. Table A9–2.

17. From Table A1–12.

TABLE A4–5. Housing Stock and Components of Change, 1890–2000

(Million dwelling units)

Period	Inventory, beginning of period[1] Occupied dwelling units[3]	Vacancy rate (%)[4]	Total housing stock[5]	Net change in stock	New construction Non-farm housing starts[6]	Est. total new dwelling units[7]	Net disappearance[2] Num-ber[8]	Per cent of be-ginning stock
1890–1900	12.69	3.0	13.08	3.27	3.94	5.4	2.1	16.1
1900–1910	15.96	2.4	16.35	4.75	3.95	5.3	.5	3.1
1910–20	20.26	4.0	21.10	3.72	3.89	5.2	1.5	7.1
1920–30	24.35	1.9	24.82	6.99	7.04	9.2	2.2	8.9
1930–40	29.90	6.0	31.81	5.52	3.69	5.9	.43	1.4
1940–50	34.85	6.64	37.33	8.66	5.95	9.5	.88	2.4
1950–56	42.83	6.87	45.99	9.35	8.11	10.9	1.57	[9]5.0
1956–60	49.87	9.88	55.34	3.2	4.76	6.4	3.2	[9]16.5
1950–60	42.83	6.87	45.99	12.5	12.87	17.3	4.8	10.4
1960–	52.6	10.1	58.5	—	—	—	—	—
Low projection:								
1960–65	52.6	10.1	58.5	2.2		4.7	2.5 ⎫	9.0
1965–70	54.4	10.4	60.7	5.0		7.8	2.8 ⎬	
1970–75	58.7	10.6	65.7	5.7		8.6	2.9 ⎫	9.9
1975–80	63.7	10.8	71.4	5.8		9.4	3.6 ⎬	
1980–85	68.7	11.0	77.2	4.9		8.5	3.6 ⎫	10.1
1985–90	72.9	11.2	82.1	4.2		8.4	4.2 ⎬	
1990–95	76.5	11.4	86.3	4.5		8.6	4.1 ⎫	10.3
1995–2000	80.3	11.6	90.8	4.8		9.6	4.8 ⎬	
2000–	84.3	11.8	95.6	—		—	—	—
Medium projection:								
1960–65	52.6	10.1	58.5	4.1		9.1	5.0 ⎫	18.3
1965–70	56.0	10.5	62.6	6.2		11.9	5.7 ⎬	
1970–75	61.2	11.0	68.8	6.9		12.0	5.1 ⎫	16.9
1975–80	67.0	11.5	75.7	7.3		13.8	6.5 ⎬	
1980–85	73.0	12.0	83.0	6.7		12.7	6.0 ⎫	16.6
1985–90	78.5	12.5	89.7	7.2		15.0	7.8 ⎬	
1990–95	84.3	13.0	96.9	8.5		15.6	7.1 ⎫	16.9
1995–2000	91.2	13.5	105.4	10.2		19.5	9.3 ⎬	
2000–	99.4	14.0	115.6	—		—	—	—
High projection:								
1960–65	52.6	10.1	58.5	6.9		14.8	7.9 ⎫	27.7
1965–70	58.2	11.0	65.4	7.7		16.0	8.3 ⎬	
1970–75	64.3	12.0	73.1	9.0		16.1	7.1 ⎫	22.4
1975–80	71.4	13.0	82.1	10.0		19.3	9.3 ⎬	
1980–85	79.2	14.0	92.1	11.0		19.0	8.0 ⎫	21.4
1985–90	87.6	15.0	103.1	13.1		24.8	11.7 ⎬	
1990–95	97.6	16.0	116.2	12.2		22.6	10.4 ⎫	21.9
1995–2000	106.6	17.0	128.4	22.8		37.9	15.1 ⎬	
2000–	124.0	18.0	151.2	—		—	—	—

Table A4–5 (cont'd)

1. Historical data are for the Census dates June 1, 1890 and 1900; Apr. 15, 1910; Jan. 1, 1920; and Apr. 1, 1930–50. 1956 data are from the *National Housing Inventory* and are as of Dec. 31. 1960 data are as of July 1. Projections are also as of mid-year.

2. Includes all changes other than new construction, namely: demolitions, conversions, mergers, units created from non-residential space or residential space changed to other uses, disaster losses, etc. For the period 1950–56 (benchmark period), net disappearance for reasons other than demolition exceeded demolitions by 434,000 units.

3. To maximize comparability of data, the figures for 1890–1950 are all from 1950 Census of Housing, Vol. 1, Pt. 1, and refer to "occupied dwelling units" (1940 and 1950) or "families" (earlier years). There are slight differences between these counts and the counts or estimates of households as determined by the Census Bureau Current Population Survey. 1956 data are from the *National Housing Inventory*, and the 1960 figure is the mid–1960 estimate of households from Table A1–1. Subsequent data are household projections, from Table A1–2.

4. For 1900–30, based on implied rates for non-farm housing units, as derived from ratio of families to available units, U.S. Bureau of the Census, *Historical Statistics of the United States, 1789–1945*, Series H 83. The rates have been arbitrarily adjusted (slightly) to allow for the differences in definition between "family" and "occupied dwelling unit" and also for the probably lower farm than non-farm vacancy rates. The 1890 rate is estimated on the basis of residential building activity trends (*Historical Statistics*, Series H 75). 1940–56 rates are implicit in the relation between total and occupied dwelling units. The 1960 rate is averaged from quarterly data in Bureau of the Census, Current Housing Reports: *Housing Vacancies*, Series H-111, No. 24 (May 1961). Projected rates are extrapolated by "inspection" and take into account increased stock of seasonal, or "second," dwelling units.

5. Occupied dwelling units, plus indicated vacancies.

6. 1900–40 from *Historical Statistics*, Series H 86. (Data for 1930–40—actually, 1930–39, inclusive—are BLS data, based on building permits, adjusted for esti-

mated number of makeshift units built. Earlier data are from studies by Twentieth Century Fund and National Bureau of Economics Research.) 1890–1900 estimated on basis of index of residential permits given in *Historical Statistics*, Series H 75. 1940 ff. are BLS data based on building permits, from *Construction Review* and other current sources, with an adjustment to include Jan.–Mar. 1950 in the 1940–50 period; 1956–60 includes an estimate for the first half of 1960, to bring the changes to the same date as the stock figure. (Estimate is on "old series" basis, but is derived in part from revised housing starts series, since old series is available only through Apr. 1960.)

7. 1950–56 from *1956 National Housing Inventory*, Vol. I, Pt. 1, Table C (p. 15). 1956–60 estimated from non-farm housing starts, applying proportional adjustment indicated by 1950–56 benchmark. 1930–50 are estimated from age distributions in 1940 and 1950 Housing Censuses, adjusted for non-reporting units; it was assumed that there was no net disappearance among dwellings built during the preceding decade (thus understating new construction by the small number of units both built and disappearing during the decade). Figure for 1920–30 is based on the assumption that there was virtually no net loss of stock built in 1920–30 in the following decade. Estimates for earlier years are based on rough guesses as to the probable understatement contained in the BLS housing start series. They are roughly consistent with the amount of understatement implied by the 1950–56 benchmark, with some additional allowance for less complete reporting as one goes back in time, plus a proportionately greater amount of farm dwelling construction. Projections are the sum of net change in stock and net disappearance.

8. 1950–56 from *1956 National Housing Inventory* (see footnote 7). The estimates of net disappearance for other periods in this table are considerably higher than those arrived at by other analysts (cf. for example, *Historical Statistics*, Series H 87–88) and are a reflection primarily of the higher estimates for new construction. Projections from Table A4–6.

9. 10 year equivalent.

TABLE A4–6. Derivation of Projected Net Disappearance of Dwelling Units and Age Distribution of Stock[1]

(Million units)

| | Total | Period built | | | | | | | |
		Pre–1930	1930–40	1940–50	1950–60	1960–70	1970–80	1980–90	1990–2000
1956 stock	55.3	30.0	5.0	9.4	10.9				
% distribution[2]	100	54	9	17	20				
1956–60: Net disappearance[3]	3.2	2.5	.3	.4	–				
New construction[4]	6.4	–	–	–	6.4				
1960 stock	58.5	27.5	4.7	9.0	17.3				
% distribution	100	47	8	15	30				
Low projection:									
1960–65: Net disappearance	2.5	2.0	.2	.2	.1				
New construction	4.7	–	–	–	–	4.7			
1965 stock	60.7	25.5	4.5	8.8	17.2	4.7			
% distribution	100	42	7	15	28	8			
1965–70: Net disappearance	2.8	1.9	.3	.2	.4				
New construction	7.8	–	–	–	–	7.8			
1970 stock	65.7	23.6	4.2	8.6	16.8	12.5			
% distribution	100	36	6	13	26	19			
1970–75: Net disappearance	2.9	1.7	.3	.4	.4	.1			
New construction	8.6	–	–	–	–	–	8.6		
1975 stock	71.4	21.9	3.9	8.2	16.4	12.4	8.6		
% distribution	100	31	5	12	23	17	12		
1975–80: Net disappearance	3.6	1.6	.3	.6	.8	.3	–		
New construction	9.4	–	–	–	–	–	9.4		
1980 stock	77.2	20.3	3.6	7.6	15.6	12.1	18.0		
% distribution	100	26	5	10	20	16	23		
1980–85: Net disappearance	3.6	1.5	.3	.6	.8	.3	.1		
New construction	8.5	–	–	–	–	–	–	8.5	
1985 stock	82.1	18.8	3.3	7.0	14.8	11.8	17.9	8.5	
% distribution	100	23	4	9	18	14	22	10	
1985–90: Net disappearance	4.2	1.4	.2	.5	1.1	.6	.4	–	
New construction	8.4	–	–	–	–	–	–	8.4	
1990 stock	86.3	17.4	3.1	6.5	13.7	11.2	17.5	16.9	
% distribution	100	20	4	7	16	13	20	20	
1990–95: Net disappearance	4.1	1.3	.2	.5	1.0	.6	.4	.1	
New construction	8.6	–	–	–	–	–	–	–	8.6
1995 stock	90.8	16.1	2.9	6.0	12.7	10.6	17.1	16.8	8.6
% distribution	100	18	3	7	14	12	19	18	9
1995–2000: Net disappearance	4.8	1.2	.2	.4	.9	.8	.9	.4	–
New construction	9.6	–	–	–	–	–	–	–	9.6
2000 stock	95.6	14.9	2.7	5.6	11.8	9.8	16.2	16.4	18.2
% distribution	100	16	3	6	12	10	17	17	19
Medium projection:									
1960–65: Net disappearance	5.0	3.9	.5	.4	.2				
New construction	9.1	–	–	–	–	9.1			
1965 stock	62.6	23.6	4.2	8.6	17.1	9.1			
% distribution	100	38	7	14	27	14			
1965–70: Net disappearance	5.7	3.3	.6	.8	.9	.1			
New construction	11.9	–	–	–	–	11.9			
1970 stock	68.8	20.3	3.6	7.8	16.2	20.9			
% distribution	100	30	5	11	24	30			
1970–75: Net disappearance	5.1	2.9	.5	.7	.8	.2			
New construction	12.0	–	–	–	–	–	12.0		
1975 stock	75.7	17.4	3.1	7.1	15.4	20.7	12.0		
% distribution	100	23	4	10	20	27	16		

Table A4–6 (cont'd)

(Million units)

	Total	Period built							
		Pre–1930	1930–40	1940–50	1950–60	1960–70	1970–80	1980–90	1990–2000
1975–80: Net disappearance	6.5	2.5	.4	1.0	1.5	1.0	.1		
New construction	13.8	–	–	–	–	–	13.8		
1980 stock	83.0	14.9	2.7	6.1	13.9	19.7	25.7		
% distribution	100	18	3	7	17	24	31		
1980–85: Net disappearance	6.0	2.1	.4	.9	1.3	1.0	.3		
New construction	12.7	–	–	–	–	–	–	12.7	
1985 stock	89.7	12.8	2.3	5.2	12.6	18.7	25.4	12.7	
% distribution	100	14	3	6	14	21	28	14	
1985–90: Net disappearance	7.8	1.8	.3	.7	1.8	1.8	1.3	.1	
New construction	15.0	–	–	–	–	–	–	15.0	
1990 stock	96.9	11.0	2.0	4.5	10.8	16.9	24.1	27.6	
% distribution	100	11	2	5	11	17	25	29	
1990–95: Net disappearance	7.1	1.6	.3	.6	1.5	1.6	1.2	.3	
New construction	15.6	–	–	–	–	–	–	–	15.6
1995 stock	105.4	9.4	1.7	3.9	9.3	15.3	22.9	27.3	15.6
% distribution	100	9	1	4	9	14	22	26	15
1995–2000: Net disappearance	9.3	1.3	.2	.5	1.3	2.2	2.2	1.4	.2
New construction	19.5	–	–	–	–	–	–	–	19.5
2000 stock	115.6	8.1	1.5	3.4	8.0	13.1	20.7	25.9	34.9
% distribution	100	7	1	3	7	11	18	23	30
High projection:									
1960–65: Net disappearance	7.9	6.2	.7	.7	.3				
New construction	14.8	–	–	–	–	14.8			
1965 stock	65.4	21.3	4.0	8.3	17.0	14.8			
% distribution	100	32	6	13	26	23			
1965–70: Net disappearance	8.3	4.8	.9	1.2	1.2	.2			
New construction	16.0	–	–	–	–	16.0			
1970 stock	73.1	16.5	3.1	7.1	15.8	30.6			
% distribution	100	22	4	10	22	42			
1970–75: Net disappearance	7.1	3.7	.7	1.0	1.2	.5			
New construction	16.1	–	–	–	–	–	16.1		
1975 stock	82.1	12.8	2.4	6.1	14.6	30.1	16.1		
% distribution	100	15	3	7	18	37	20		
1975–80: Net disappearance	9.3	2.9	.5	1.4	2.1	2.2	.2		
New construction	19.3	–	–	–	–	–	19.3		
1980 stock	92.1	9.9	1.9	4.7	12.5	27.9	35.2		
% distribution	100	11	2	5	14	30	38		
1980–85: Net disappearance	8.0	2.2	.4	1.1	1.8	2.0	.5		
New construction	19.0	–	–	–	–	–	–	19.0	
1985 stock	103.1	7.7	1.5	3.6	10.7	25.9	34.7	19.0	
% distribution	100	7	1	4	10	26	33	19	
1985–90: Net disappearance	11.7	1.7	.3	.8	2.4	3.7	2.5	.3	
New construction	24.8	–	–	–	–	–	–	24.8	
1990 stock	116.2	6.0	1.2	2.8	8.3	22.2	32.2	43.5	
% distribution	100	5	1	2	7	19	28	38	
1990–95: Net disappearance	10.4	1.4	.3	.6	1.9	3.1	2.4	.7	
New construction	22.6	–	–	–	–	–	–	–	22.6
1995 stock	128.4	4.6	.9	2.2	6.4	19.1	29.8	42.8	22.6
% distribution	100	3	1	2	5	15	23	33	18
1995–2000: Net disappearance	15.1	1.0	.2	.5	1.5	4.3	4.2	3.1	.3
New construction	37.9	–	–	–	–	–	–	–	37.9
2000 stock	151.2	3.6	.7	1.7	4.9	14.8	25.6	39.7	60.2
% distribution	100	2	1	1	3	10	17	26	40

Table A4–6 (cont'd)

1. The following attrition (net disappearance) rates have been assumed:

Portion of lifetime:	Annual attrition (per cent)		
	Low	Medium	High
First 10 years	.1	.2	.3
Second 10 years	.5	1.0	1.5
Third 10 years	1.0	2.0	3.0
Thereafter	1.5	3.0	5.0

As described in the Notes to this part of the appendix, the Medium rates are consistent with long-run experience, as derived from the 1940 Housing Census. They also check out quite closely, when applied to the 1956 stock, in explaining the apparent net disappearance between 1956 and 1960. The implied median and average life of units is approximately as follows:

	(years)		
	Low	Medium	High
Median life	65	43	35
Average life	74	50	38

Although the components of change between the 1950 and the 1956 housing stock were tabulated in the *1956 National Housing Inventory* by year built, the large "unreported" category and the unknown average age of the open ended pre-1930 category makes estimation of the average age of net disappearing units difficult. Moreover, the age distribution available for the components of change is not consistent with that provided by a comparison of age distributions of 1950 and 1956 stock (presumably because of differences in coverage and errors in response). One may estimate, however, that the average age of net disappearing units in this period was as low as 30 years—the result of rather heavy (and probably heavily underreported) disappearance of makeshift units and temporary sub-units added during the Depression and the war years. Between 1956 and 1960, the average age of net disappearing units may be estimated at a more normal 53 years. The Low projection of disappearance would thus represent a distinct slackening from the recent rate, although it would, judging from the meager evidence available, be roughly consistent with the rate obtaining in the twenties. It could occur because of a presumed elimination by now of relatively less well built structures, a slackening in conversions, and a concentration, in future construction, upon structures (including multiple dwelling unit structures) of relatively more permanent type. The High rate could come about through a stepping up in the rate of elimination of substandard structures and a greater concentration, in future construction, upon seasonal structures, trailers, prefabs, and other types of units designed for relatively short lives.

2. From *1956 National Housing Inventory*, Vol. III, Pt. 1, p. 15, proportionately adjusted to distribute "nonreporting" units and slightly readjusted so that post-1950 cohort does not exceed 1950–56 new construction.

3. Adjusted to apparent total net disappearance (Table A4–5). The implied attrition rate for pre-1930 stock is slightly under 3% per annum.

4. From Table A4–5.

TABLE A4–7.   Projected Use of Wood in Construction

	1950	1955	1960		1970	1980	1990	2000
Lumber:[1]								
Use in new residential construction[2]				L	11.5	12.0	11.4	12.9
(bil. board ft.)	19.0	16.1	12.2	M	16.7	17.8	20.5	28.2
				H	22.5	25.7	31.8	51.1
Number of new dwelling units				L	1.64	1.79	1.70	1.93
constructed[3] (millions)	1.88	1.79	1.54	M	2.39	2.65	3.06	4.21
				H	3.21	3.83	4.74	7.63
Lumber per new dwelling unit[4]								
(thous. bd. ft.)	10.1	9.0	7.9		7.0	6.7	6.7	6.7
Use in new non-residential construc-				L	8.9	8.0	7.4	7.1
tion[5] (bil. bd. ft.)	7.2	10.1	10.2	M	14.7	19.6	25.8	34.0
				H	19.5	31.0	50.1	82.9
New non-residential construction				L	38.8	44.7	53.1	64.7
($ 1960 bil.)[6]	22.7	31.7	34.1	M	52.4	75.4	107.3	154.5
				H	67.3	114.7	192.7	331.7
				L	.23	.18	.14	.11
Lumber use per $ 1960[7] (bd. ft.)	.32	.31	.30	M	.28	.26	.24	.22
				H	.29	.27	.26	.25
Use in residential maintenance and				L	2.2	2.0	1.9	1.8
repairs[8] (bil. bd. ft.)	3.0	2.7	2.3	M	2.4	2.4	2.4	2.5
				H	2.7	2.8	3.2	3.7
Residential maintenance and				L	8.7	10.2	11.3	12.5
repairs[6] ($ 1960 bil.)	6.2	7.5	7.2	M	9.1	10.8	12.5	14.7
				H	9.5	11.7	14.4	18.4
				L	.25	.20	.17	.14
Lumber use per $ 1960[9] (bd. ft.)	.48	.36	.32	M	.26	.22	.19	.17
				H	.28	.24	.22	.20
Use in non-residential maintenance				L	3.9	4.2	4.2	4.4
and repairs[8] (bil. bd. ft.)	3.3	3.4	3.6	M	5.0	6.6	8.7	11.6
				H	5.6	8.1	12.4	19.8
Non-residential maintenance and				L	17.0	23.2	30.2	40.3
repairs[6] ($ 1960 bil.)	10.2	10.8	12.4	M	17.9	25.4	36.2	52.8
				H	19.2	30.0	47.5	79.0
				L	.23	.18	.14	.11
Lumber use per $ 1960[10] (bd. ft.)	.32	.31	.29	M	.28	.26	.24	.22
				H	.29	.27	.26	.25
				L	26.5	26.2	24.9	26.2
Total use of lumber (bil. bd. ft.)	32.5	32.3	28.3	M	38.8	46.4	57.4	76.3
				H	50.3	67.6	97.5	157.5
Plywood:								
				L	11.1	15.9	20.2	25.8
Total consumption[11] (bil. sq. ft.)	2.7	5.3	7.7	M	16.8	26.6	42.0	62.7
				H	22.9	43.5	77.5	137.4
Total construction, including								
maintenance and repair[6]				L	92.7	113.5	134.9	172.2
($ 1960 bil.)	58.6	72.8	76.2	M	120.3	166.3	233.6	348.4
				H	152.4	241.4	387.6	687.0
Consumption per $ 1960 of total				L	.12	.14	.15	.15
construction, including mainte-	.046	.073	.101	M	.14	.16	.18	.18
nance and repair[12] (sq. ft.)				H	.15	.18	.20	.20

Table A4–7 (cont'd)

	1950	1955	1960		1970	1980	1990	2000
Use of lumber and plywood combined: Bd. or sq. ft./$ 1960 thous. of total construction, including main- tenance and repair:[13]								
Low								
Lumber (bd. ft.)	555	445	371		286	231	185	152
Plywood (sq. ft.)	46	73	101		128	154	169	172
High								
Lumber (bd. ft.)	555	445	371		330	280	252	229
Plywood (sq. ft.)	46	73	101		143	163	172	172
Bil. bd. or sq. ft.:								
Low								
Lumber (bd. ft.)	32.5	32.4	28.3		26.5	26.2	24.9	26.2
Plywood (sq. ft.)	2.7	5.3	7.7		11.6	17.0	22.3	29.1
Medium								
Lumber (bd. ft.)	32.5	32.4	28.3		38.8	46.4	57.4	76.3
Plywood (sq. ft.)	2.7	5.3	7.7		16.8	26.6	42.0	62.7
High								
Lumber (bd. ft.)	32.5	32.4	28.3		50.3	67.6	97.5	157.5
Plywood (sq. ft.)	2.7	5.3	7.7		21.8	39.3	66.7	118.2
Minor structural wood products:[14]								
				L	.31	.26	.24	.22
Total consumption[15] (bil. cu. ft.)	.37	.38	.36	M	.41	.42	.48	.54
				H	.52	.63	.84	1.11
				L	20.9	23.7	27.1	31.8
Private non-residential construction[6] ($ 1960 bil.)	13.58	18.28	18.8	M	27.4	38.2	53.5	76.7
				H	34.7	57.3	93.3	158.0
Use per $ 1960 of private non-resi- dential construction[16] (cu. ft.)	.027	.021	.019		.015	.011	.009	.007
Building paper and board:								
				L	3.6	4.1	4.5	5.3
Total consumption[17] (mil. tons)	2.6	3.2	3.2	M	4.7	6.0	7.8	10.6
				H	6.0	8.8	12.9	21.0
Use per $ 1960 mil. of total con- struction, including mainte- nance and repair[18] (tons)	45.2	43.8	42.1		39.2	36.3	33.4	30.5

1. Historical data for each category are estimated so as to add to the total shown, which is the sum of lumber consumption for construction plus railroads as reported in Lumber Manufacturers Association, *1960–61 Lumber Industry Facts*. Considerations in estimating each category are as shown in the respective footnotes. Except for such rough estimates, historical data on lumber use in the components of construction are lacking.

2. Except for the historical adjustment noted in footnote 1, both the historical series and the projections are derived by applying the unit use figures to the number of dwelling units (see footnote 4).

3. From Table A4–4.

Table A4–7 (cont'd)

4. 1950 from U.S. Forest Service, *Timber Resources for America's Future,* Forest Resource Report No. 14 (Washington: Jan. 1958), p. 383. 1955–60 estimated by assuming an annual rate of decrease of 3% for constant size units (see *ibid.,* p. 382) and adjusting for presumed increases in size and varying proportion of frame houses built. Projections of use per dwelling unit are based upon judgments as to the reasonably possible trends in sizes of units and in proportional use of lumber as against other materials. The single set of coefficients is taken as not only the Medium but as low a unit use as is consistent with Low dwelling unit construction and as high a unit as is consistent with High dwelling unit construction. For explanation of the considerations involved, see Chapter 4, pp. 120–24, and Notes, above.

5. 1950 and 1955 estimated on basis of use for 1949 and 1952 reported in *Timber Resources for America's Future,* Tables 222 and 223 (pp. 391–92), adjusted to include the additional lumber consumed in railroad and in farm non-residential construction (*ibid.,* pp. 399, 403, 405); the interpolation and extrapolation are based on the course of cement shipments and of farm non-residential building. (About 50% of new non-residential lumber consumption is for concrete forms and related uses and about 35% for farm service buildings). 1960–2000 derived by applying coefficients which follow.

6. From Table A4–3.

7. 1950 and 1955 derived from aggregate use, above. 1960–2000 projected on assumption, particularly, of declining use of lumber for concrete formwork. (See Chapter 4, pp. 120–24, and Notes, above.)

8. Both historical data and projections based on coefficients which follow.

9. Historical ratios assumed (see *Timber Resources for America's Future,* p. 396) to be half of the consumption per dollar of new residential construction. Projections, which are on a judgment basis decline, but in the High approach the ratios assumed to prevail in new residential construction.

10. Assumed, as in *Timber Resources for America's Future* (p. 396), to be the same as for new non-residential construction. (The inclusion by us of railroad and farm non-residential maintenance, which are separately considered by *Timber Resources,* would tend to give this assumption even greater justification because of the very similar nature of maintenance and repairs and new construction in both of these areas.)

11. Data on production of softwood plywood (⅜" basis) (source: U.S. Bureau of the Census, Current Industrial Reports, No. M24H(60)–1, July 27, 1961) are taken as approximations of the consumption of plywood in construction. Roughly one-fourth of softwood plywood has in recent years been consumed in non-construction uses, and an unknown, but probably similar, quantity of hardwood plywood has gone into construction, mostly in the form of cabinetwork, flush doors, and paneling.

12. The projections represent reasonably possible rates of increase, based on current trends. Reasons for the expected gains are given in Chapter 4, p. 124, and Notes, above.

13. The purpose of this calculation is to approximate the amount of compensation between the extreme projections for lumber on the one hand and plywood on the other. Since plywood substitutes for lumber, in use, on the basis of roughly 1 square foot for 1 board foot, but requires only half as much volume of wood, the adjustment is made in plywood, lumber being maintained at its originally calculated Low and High. For the Low, 10% of the cumulative decrease in lumber, in board feet per thousand dollars of construction, has been assumed to be possible only if the Low plywood use is higher by an equal number of square feet. For the High, an increasing percentage of the cumulative increase in High plywood consumption has been assumed to be possible only by "borrowing" from lumber consumption, and has been deducted from the High plywood coefficient. (The increasing percentages are to reflect the fact that the *gross* substitution of plywood for lumber becomes a greater and greater portion of the *net* increase in plywood use as plywood is in turn replaced by plastics and other materials.)

14. Includes posts, poles, piling, and mine timbers.

15. The 1950 estimate is from *Timber Resources for America's Future,* p. 372, Table 207, converted into cubic feet on the basis of the implicit 1952 conversions there shown. The 1955 and 1960 estimates are assumed to be identically proportionate as the 1950 estimate to "Other products, new supply" given in U.S. Forest Service, *The Demand and Price Situation for Forest Products,* Nov. 1960, p. 24 (48.2%). Projections by application of the coefficients which follow.

16. Projected on a judgment basis.

17. Historical data from House Committee on Interstate and Foreign Commerce, *Pulp, Paper, and Board—Supply-Demand* (H. Rep. No. 573, 85th Cong., First Sess.). Data for 1960 from U.S. Bureau of the Census, *Pulp, Paper and Board* (Current Industrial Reports, Series M26A). Projections by application of the coefficients which follow.

18. Extrapolation of 1952–60 trend. Trends prior to 1952 were erratic.

TABLE A4–8. Historical Data on Construction Steel[1]

(Million tons unless otherwise indicated)

	1948	1949	1950	1951	1952	1953	1954	1955	1956	1957	1958	1959	1960
Principal items:													
Heavy structural shapes and piling	4.55	3.97	4.54	5.32	4.37	5.36	4.88	5.13	5.78	7.39	4.40	4.43	5.26
Tons per $ 1960 thousand of large building construction[2]	.70	.58	.58	.56	.49	.56	.46	.41	.44	.54	.35	.37	.40
Concrete reinforcing bars	1.54	1.57	1.67	1.90	1.81	1.85	1.75	2.16	2.52	2.30	2.04	2.17	2.21
Tons per 100 bbl. of portland cement consumed in new and maintenance construction[3]	.78	.78	.75	.81	.74	.72	.65	.75	.83	.81	.68	.66	.71
Oil-country goods	1.54	1.37	1.69	1.88	1.61	2.02	2.29	2.54	2.56	2.82	1.16	2.07	1.20
Tons per $ 1960 thousand of oil and gas well drilling[4]	1.01	.89	.95	.95	.77	.91	.97	1.00	.97	1.15	.56	.92	.55
Line pipe	2.02	2.53	3.67	3.19	2.88	3.51	2.60	3.08	3.38	4.22	2.61	2.80	2.69
Tons per $ 1960 thousand of gas utility construction[5]	1.76	1.76	2.11	1.76	1.92	2.15	1.82	1.97	2.11	2.36	1.41	1.66	1.45
Nails and staples	.86	.73	.87	.86	.65	.53	.57	.65	.56	.45	.42	.39	.32
Tons per million bd. ft. of lumber used in construction[6]	31.3	28.3	26.8	30.3	21.7	18.5	19.1	20.1	18.1	16.5	15.2	12.7	11.3
Galvanized sheet, etc.[7]	2.30	2.33	2.98	2.64	2.53	2.70	2.80	3.29	3.30	2.66	3.04	2.96	3.21
Tons per new dwelling unit[8]	1.90	1.89	1.58	1.80	1.67	1.82	1.70	1.84	2.19	1.89	1.87	1.59	2.08
Total of principal items	12.8	12.5	15.4	15.8	13.9	16.0	14.9	16.9	18.1	19.8	13.7	14.8	14.9
Total steel for construction, except railroads[9]	19.0	17.2	21.9	24.4	20.6	24.2	20.3	25.0	26.7	26.6	19.9	23.0	22.5
All construction steel as per cent of total of principal items	148	138	142	154	148	151	136	148	148	134	145	155	151
Total steel for construction, including railroads[10]	21.0	19.0	24.2	26.8	22.4	26.6	21.8	26.7	28.3	28.1	20.5	23.8	23.3
Tons per $ 1960 thousand of new and maintenance construction[11]	.42	.36	.41	.45	.36	.42	.32	.37	.40	.39	.29	.31	.31

1. Data represent total shipments of each of the indicated types of steel, based on reports of the American Iron and Steel Institute (AISI). Some non-construction use is therefore included, as well as a small proportion of exports; however, construction is estimated to account for about 88% of the total shipments of these types.

2. "Large building construction" from Table A4–1.

3. Consumption of portland cement from U.S. Bureau of Mines, *Minerals Yearbook*, various issues.

4. Oil and gas well drilling from Table A4–1.

5. Gas utility construction from Table A4–1.

6. Consumption of lumber and wood products from *Lumber Industry Facts*, 1960–61. Includes lumber for "building and construction," plus "railroads."

7. Includes galvanized sheet, barbed and twisted wire, and woven wire fence.

8. New dwelling units estimated by adjusting BLS/Commerce housing starts (old series) to 1950–56 *National Housing Inventory* benchmark. (See Tables A4–4 and 5.)

9. Construction industry as defined by AISI, plus contractors' products; oil and gas drilling; mining, quarrying, and lumbering; and agricultural construction. Railroad steel omitted for later convenience in considering separately steel use for transportation. (See Table A16–4). Steel for military uses is also omitted, although some of this may be for construction. It is to be noted that the quantities shown include steel for maintenance as well as for new construction.

10. Coincides with construction industry as defined for the National Income Accounts, but includes maintenance. Railroad construction (predominantly trackage) from Table A5–16.

11. Value of construction from Table A4–9. Coefficients calculated as basis for implications check in Table A4–9.

TABLE A4–9.   Projected Use of Steel in Construction[1]

(Million tons unless otherwise indicated)

	1950	1955	1960		1970	1980	1990	2000
Principal items:								
Heavy structural shapes and piling	4.5	5.1	5.3	L	4.0	3.6	3.0	2.0
				M	5.8	6.0	6.6	7.1
				H	8.8	12.6	18.8	28.5
Large building construction[2] ($ 1960 bil.)	7.7	12.3	13.4	L	15.3	17.8	21.2	25.5
				M	19.3	26.1	36.5	50.7
				H	24.5	39.3	62.7	101.8
Tons per $ 1960 thousand	.58	.41	.40	L	.26	.20	.14	.08
				M	.30	.23	.18	.14
				H	.36	.32	.30	.28
Concrete reinforcing bars[3]	1.67	2.16	2.2	L	2.1	2.1	2.1	2.1
				M	3.3	4.1	5.0	6.6
				H	5.1	8.5	14.5	27.1
Use of portland cement[4] (mil. bbl.)	223	287	308	L	385	471	560	715
				M	520	742	1,072	1,644
				H	680	1,139	1,938	3,614
Tons per 100 barrels	.75	.75	.71	L	.54	.44	.38	.29
				M	.63	.55	.47	.40
				H	.75	.75	.75	.75
Oil-country goods	1.69	2.54	1.2	L	1.7	1.9	2.2	2.7
				M	2.2	3.0	4.1	5.5
				H	2.6	4.3	7.0	11.8
Oil and gas well drilling[2] ($ 1960 bil.)	1.78	2.55	2.19	L	2.1	2.4	2.8	3.4
				M	2.8	3.7	5.1	6.9
				H	3.3	5.4	8.7	14.8
Tons per $ 1960 thousand	.95	1.00	.6		.8	.8	.8	.8
Line pipe	3.67	3.08	2.7	L	2.3	2.0	1.7	1.5
				M	4.3	5.0	5.2	5.8
				H	6.2	9.2	12.5	17.7
Gas utility construction[2] ($ 1960 bil.)	1.70	1.52	1.8	L	1.8	1.8	1.9	2.1
				M	2.4	2.8	2.9	3.2
				H	3.1	4.4	5.7	7.7
Tons per $ 1960 thousand	2.2	2.0	1.5	L	1.3	1.1	.9	.7
				M	1.8	1.8	1.8	1.8
				H	2.0	2.1	2.2	2.3
Nails and staples	.87	.65	.32	L	.2	.2	.1	.1
				M	.3	.3	.3	.3
				H	.4	.4	.5	.6
Lumber for construction[5] (bil. bd. ft.)	32.5	32.4	28.3	L	26.5	26.2	24.9	26.2
				M	38.8	46.4	57.4	76.3
				H	50.3	67.6	97.5	157.5
Tons per million board feet	27	20	11		8	6	5	4
Galvanized sheet	2.98	3.29	3.2	L	3.4	3.8	3.6	4.1
				M	5.5	6.6	8.3	12.2
				H	8.0	11.1	15.6	28.2
New dwelling units constructed[6] (millions)	1.88	1.79	1.54	L	1.64	1.79	1.70	1.93
				M	2.39	2.65	3.06	4.21
				H	3.21	3.83	4.74	7.63
Tons per dwelling unit	1.6	1.8	2.1	L	2.1	2.1	2.1	2.1
				M	2.3	2.5	2.7	2.9
				H	2.5	2.9	3.3	3.7
Total of principal items	15.4	16.8	14.9	L	13.7	13.6	12.7	12.5
				M	21.4	25.0	29.5	37.5
				H	31.1	46.1	68.9	113.9

Table A4–9 (cont'd)

(Million tons unless otherwise indicated)

	1950	1955	1960		1970	1980	1990	2000
Total steel for construction, except				L	22.1	23.3	23.1	24.1
railroads[7]	21.9	25.0	22.5	M	32.4	38.0	45.2	57.6
				H	44.2	59.8	83.9	128.7
Ratio to principal				L	161	171	182	193
tons (%)	142	149	151	M	151	152	153	154
				H	142	130	121	113
Total steel for construction,				L	22.6	23.7	23.5	24.5
including railroads[8]	24.2	26.7	23.3	M	33.0	38.6	45.9	58.6
				H	44.9	60.7	85.2	130.6
Total new and maintenance				L	92.7	113.5	134.9	172.2
construction[2] ($ 1960 bil.)	58.6	72.8	76.2	M	120.3	166.3	233.6	348.4
				H	152.4	241.4	387.6	687.0
Tons per $ 1960 thousand				L	.24	.21	.17	.14
	.41	.37	.31	M	.27	.23	.20	.17
				H	.29	.25	.22	.19

1. Historical data from Table A4–8. Projections, except for last item, derived by applying the indicated coefficients, which have been projected on a judgment basis, taking into account the factors discussed in Chapter 4, pp. 120–23, and in the Notes, above.

2. From Table A4–3.

3. This category is to be interpreted as including cable used for prestressing, which may become a significant proportion of reinforcing steel in the future.

4. From Table A4–10.

5. From Table A4–7.

6. From Table A4–4.

7. Sum of items above multiplied by adjustment factor shown. The latter reflects in part the understatement involved in adding Lows which are partially interdependent (and similar overstatement in the Highs) as well as the likelihood that the lesser roles (Lows) for the items here specifically treated mean relatively larger importance for other construction steel (and vice versa for the Highs).

8. The relationship between this total and total new and maintenance construction is used as an implications check. Steel for railroad maintenance and construction from Table A5–17.

TABLE A4–10.   Projected Use of Cement, Aggregates, and Bitumens

	1950	1955	1960		1970	1980	1990	2000
Portland cement[1] (mil. bbl.)	223	287	308	L	385	471	560	715
				M	520	742	1,072	1,644
				H	680	1,139	1,938	3,614
Total new and maintenance construction[2] ($ 1960 bil.)	58.6	72.8	76.2	L	92.7	113.5	134.9	172.2
				M	120.3	166.3	233.6	348.4
				H	152.4	241.4	387.6	687.0
Barrels per $ 1960 thousand[3]	3.81	3.94	4.04	L	4.15	4.15	4.15	4.15
				M	4.32	4.46	4.59	4.72
				H	4.46	4.72	5.00	5.26
Aggregates[4] (bil. tons)	.55	.88	1.13	L	1.41	1.74	2.14	2.70
				M	2.26	3.83	5.97	9.00
				H	3.20	6.66	12.85	24.01
Heavy construction, including highways[5] ($ 1960 bil.)	11.90	15.65	17.35	L	19.1	22.0	26.7	33.8
				M	28.3	42.1	60.9	89.1
				H	38.1	67.3	116.8	205.2
Tons per $ 1960 thousand[3]	46	56	65	L	74	79	80	80
				M	80	91	98	101
				H	84	99	110	117
Bitumens[6] (mil. bbl.)	65.6	92.6	110.6	L	146	197	257	334
				M	157	224	313	448
				H	176	277	440	710
Vehicle travel in auto-equivalent miles[7] (bil.)	649	835	979	L	1,271	1,711	2,237	2,908
				M	1,368	1,946	2,723	3,898
				H	1,531	2,412	3,825	6,177
Bitumens per million miles[8] (bbl.)	101	111	113		115	115	115	115

1. From *Minerals Yearbook,* various issues. 1950–55 data are total shipments to destinations in continental United States; 1960 includes Alaska and Hawaii (see footnote 1, Table A4–1).

2. From Table A4–3.

3. Coefficients are projected on a judgment basis.

4. Sand, gravel, crushed stone, and slag.

5. Expenditures on public utilities, highway, military and public industrial, water and sewerage, and other public construction aggregated from Table A4–3. More than half of aggregate tonnage is estimated to be used in highway construction, about 30% in other types of concrete construction, and the remainder in such miscellaneous uses as railroad ballast, rip-rap, and filler.

6. From *Minerals Yearbook,* various issues—domestic demand for asphalt and road oil. Highway paving accounts for 80–90% of the total; the remainder is used principally for roofing.

7. From Table A4–4. This series reflects intensity of travel and is therefore preferable to the series on new highway construction for projecting paving demand, which comprises a substantial amount of repair and maintenance.

8. Historical figures calculated from series above. The approximate 1960 coefficient is assumed to continue through 2000 (rather than there being an extension of the apparent upward trend), because of the great strides which have been made in the paving of roads previously unpaved. In 1936, two-thirds of all roads were unpaved; in 1956, only one-third. Thus, the opportunities for new paving are shrinking, while at the same time the requirements for maintenance are rising. It is not unreasonable to expect these downward and upward changes in requirements, in the future, to balance each other out.

TABLE A4–11. Historical Data on Consumption of Copper and Aluminum in Construction

	1950	1952	1953	1954	1955	1956	1957	1958	1959	1960
Construction expenditures[1] ($ 1960 bil.):										
New buildings	27.3	25.7	26.9	29.8	34.5	33.2	33.0	33.2	36.7	36.0
Electric light and power	1.96	2.25	2.38	2.33	2.16	1.98	2.15	2.31	2.04	2.06
Public utilities other than electricity or gas	1.48	1.73	1.76	1.68	1.87	2.00	1.92	1.39	1.31	1.50
Use of metal[2] (thous. tons):										
New building construction:										
Copper	365	257	271	n.a.	411	376	366	380	437	401
Aluminum	225	180	n.a.	333	427	428	441	468	593	585
Electric light and power construction:										
Copper	83	82	76	n.a.	56	49	48	46	38	32
Aluminum[3]	70	89	n.a.	73	77	92	89	86	98	93
Public utility construction, except electricity and gas[4]:										
Copper	70	62	63	n.a.	69	89	96	81	82	89
Total:										
Copper	518	401	410	n.a.	536	514	510	507	557	522
Aluminum	295	269	n.a.	406	504	520	530	554	691	678
Unit use of metal (tons per $ 1960 mil.):										
New building construction:										
Copper	13.4	10.0	10.1	n.a.	11.9	11.3	11.1	11.4	11.9	11.1
Aluminum	8.2	7.0	n.a.	11.2	12.4	12.9	13.4	14.1	16.2	16.3
Electric light and power construction:										
Copper	42.3	36.4	31.9	n.a.	25.9	24.7	22.3	19.9	18.6	15.5
Aluminum	35.7	39.6	n.a.	31.3	35.6	46.5	41.4	37.2	48.0	45.1
Public utility construction, except electricity and gas:										
Copper	47.3	35.8	35.8	n.a.	36.9	44.5	50.0	58.3	62.6	59.3

1. From Table A4–1. "New buildings" is the total of residential, industrial, commercial, institutional and miscellaneous, and schools and hospitals.

2. Aggregate use of metal from Tables A16–39 and 31. Estimated on the basis of mill and foundry shipments, with allowances for returned industrial scrap.

3. Includes that part of "electrical" aluminum which appears to consist of ACSR cable and bare aluminum conductor wire used for power transmission.

4. Limited to copper for communications construction, which is the predominant use. Data on use in minor types of public utility construction not available.

TABLE A4–12.   Projected Consumption of Copper and Aluminum in Construction[1]

	1950	1955	1960		1970	1980	1990	2000
Expenditures[2] ($ 1960 bil.):								
				L	43.5	53.1	61.5	80.1
New buildings	27.3	34.5	36.0	M	60.3	80.8	114.0	177.0
				H	81.0	124.2	195.8	360.4
				L	1.4	.9	.5	.3
Electric light and power construction	1.96	2.16	2.06	M	2.4	3.1	4.2	6.1
				H	4.5	7.8	12.4	19.9
Public utility construction other				L	1.8	2.5	2.9	3.5
than electric or gas	1.48	1.87	1.50	M	2.6	4.0	6.2	9.4
				H	2.7	4.4	8.7	16.8
Unit use of metal[3] (tons per $ 1960 mil.): New building construction:								
				L	9.9	9.7	9.5	9.3
Copper	13.4	11.9	11.1	M	11.0	11.0	11.0	11.0
				H	11.5	12.0	12.5	13.0
				L	17.1	17.9	18.8	19.8
Aluminum	8.2	12.4	16.3	M	18.0	19.8	21.8	24.0
				H	19.7	23.9	28.9	35.0
Electric light and power construction:								
				L	6	2	5	2
Copper	42.3	25.9	15.5	M	10	6	4	2
				H	13	11	9	7
				L	45.0	45.0	45.0	45.0
Aluminum[4]	35.7	35.6	45.1	M	50.2	51.6	52.0	52.2
				H	52.9	56.4	58.0	58.8
Public utility construction, except electric and gas:								
				L	43.5	40.5	37.5	34.5
Copper	47.3	36.9	59.3	M	46.5	46.5	46.5	46.5
				H	49.5	52.5	55.5	58.5
Aggregate use of metal (thous. tons): New building construction:								
				L	431	515	584	745
Copper	365	411	401	M	663	889	1,254	1,947
				H	932	1,490	2,448	4,685
				L	744	950	1,156	1,586
Aluminum	225	427	585	M	1,085	1,600	2,485	4,248
				H	1,596	2,968	5,659	12,614
Electric light and power construction:								
				L	8	2	–	–
Copper	83	56	32	M	24	19	17	12
				H	58	86	112	139
				L	63	40	22	14
Aluminum[4]	70	77	93	M	120	160	218	318
				H	238	440	719	1,170
Public utility construction, except electric and gas:								
				L	78	101	109	121
Copper	70	69	89	M	121	186	288	437
				H	134	231	483	983
Total:								
				L	502	618	693	866
Copper	518	536	522	M	808	1,094	1,559	2,396
				H	1,124	1,807	3,043	5,807
				L	807	990	1,178	1,600
Aluminum	295	504	678	M	1,205	1,760	2,703	4,566
				H	1,834	3,408	6,378	13,784

1. Historical data from Table A4–11.
2. From Table A4–3. Building construction is the total of residential, industrial, commercial, institutional and miscellaneous, and schools and hospitals.

3. Projections are on a judgment basis, as described in the Notes.
4. Includes that part of "electrical" aluminum which is used for power transmission.

appendix
to
chapter
5

TRANSPORTATION

Notes

THE ANALYTICAL materials which follow with respect to transportation and the degree of analysis applied are selected with a view to their ultimate significance for resource requirements. Perhaps even more in the case of transportation than for most other "end-product" sectors, the selection is thus considerably different from what it would be if transportation trends and policy as such were the objects in mind. The tables also represent a distillation of a considerable amount of trial calculation which is not shown but which was performed in order to establish various of the orders of magnitude of materials and fuels use in areas which later proved to be of too small consequence to merit any more than summary treatment.

Since automobiles are by far the most important single element in transportation's call upon materials and fuels, the treatment of this particular category is the most extensive. Two elements in the analysis of future demand should, in particular, be borne in mind. One is the combined treatment of all automobiles, whether business-owned or privately owned, on the basis of criteria pertaining to private ownership and purchases. Data on business ownership of automobiles are virtually non-existent, and even the National Income Accounts utilize a more or less arbitrary allocation of purchases (currently 17% to business, 82% to consumers, and 1% to government) to separate "personal consumption" from "capital" expenditures. Aside from the fact that many of the automobiles charged to business accounts are actually for largely personal use, there appears to be no better basis on which to estimate fu-

ture business purchases of automobiles than to assume that their growth will parallel that of personal automobile purchases. Moreover, one of the uncertainties of the future is the extent to which consumers will continue to own their own vehicles rather than, as may be increasingly the case, rent them where and when needed. This will affect in a very uncertain fashion the division of automobiles and automobile purchases as between consumers and business, but it will not affect the total purchases and stock of automobiles except to the minor extent that such a trend would conserve vehicles.

The second element important to bear in mind is that while we frequently use the word "automobile" here and in the tables, what we really mean is "user-operated passenger vehicle." We cannot be sure of the future nature of this vehicle—whether it will consist mostly of the approximate equivalents of today's sedan and station wagon or devolve into a variety of shapes encompassing everything from motor scooters to personal helicopters. We can be quite sure that there will be considerable change and differentiation, however, so that it is well, for projection purposes, to assume that all of these different kinds of vehicles would fall into the future equivalent of today's automobile category. In so doing—and in particular in our inclusion of airborne vehicles—we are deviating from the present National Income Accounts classification, which places personal airplanes in the same basket as "wheel goods, durable toys, sport equipment, and boats."

As with dwelling units, additions to stock and replacements both serve to determine demand for automobiles, but in this case replacements, because of the shorter service life, loom much larger in importance. The future stock has been related to the adult population, defined, for convenience, as persons 20 years of age and over. It is not that persons under 20 do not drive automobiles, but only to a limited extent do they own them or have them reserved for their exclusive use. The 20-and-over population thus comes as close as any reference group can to being the car-owning population, and it is one for which we have Census Bureau projections. The degree of ownership among adults is projected essentially on the basis of past trends (shown in Table A5–1) with allowances for the factors that may speed these up or slow them down. The projected trends (Table A5–2) are, for convenience, tied to the points January 1, 1930, 1942, and 1960 but represent, in fact, judgments as to the increase in rate of ownership which will flow from the upward movement of the population through income brackets, the trend toward increased ownership within income brackets, and a presumed inverse relationship between average size of car and size of stock (a relationship suggested by consumer purchasing power, cost of highway construction, and sheer availability of space—particularly urban space). Jan. 1, 1930, represents the highest degree of ownership reached prior to the Great Depression, and Jan. 1, 1942, the peak at the start of World War II. The steepest rate of increase, between 1942 and 1960, is taken as the measure of the High and the 1930–60 rate as the measure of the Medium; the Low rate of increase in ownership has been set at a little less than the Medium. The expansion of the stock itself is then permitted to follow a somewhat broader path on the assumption that there will be no compensation between the rate of growth in adult population and the rate of growth in car ownership.

A technical point worth noting in connection with the relation of stock to population is that we have transposed the official Bureau of Public Roads registration figures by one year—this, on the assumption that cumulative registrations for any one year are a better measure of the stock in use during the following year than they are for the registration year itself. While the Bureau of Public Roads attempts to eliminate from its figures the duplications resulting from reregistration, it is probably unable to do so completely. Moreover, among the vehicles registered during the course of a year are a significant number later scrapped, abandoned, or simply not used. This overcount is assumed as being approximately equal to the actual net additions made in the following year between January 1 and our July 1 reference date for population. The transposed figure is also taken as being a more suitable measure of vehicle use during the ensuing year for purposes of computing unit mileage and fuel consumption.

It should also be noted that this overcount tends to exaggerate the historical statistics on "net additions" (which are shown in Table A5–1) and understate those on "apparent retirement." Were the overcount confined solely to vehicles later scrapped, and were the current year's scrappage fully included in the end-of-the-year registration total, the mathematical result would be to assign to net additions, rather than to retirement, the difference between the current year's and the preceding year's actual retirements (sometimes negative). More likely the case, in view of the fact that much of the current year's scrappage does not show up in the registration total, is that the true net additions and retirements are approximately the average of the figures shown in Table 1 for the current and the preceding year.

The cohort attrition method of projecting replacement demand, which is described in general in Chapter 5 (p. 131), is shown in Table A5–4, and the resultant replacement demand, as well as the net additions implied by stock changes, in Table A5–3. While the true attrition (or mortality) curve probably has more of a hump around the modal lifetime than the negative exponential curves which we have in effect used, the error introduced on this account is probably not nearly so great as that involved in lack of knowledge of changing average lives. As indicated in Chapter 5, it will take a fair number of additional years of statistical record before any kind of reasonable mortality table can be constructed on an actuarial basis and even this will face the added uncertainty, not applicable to human beings, of possible rapid change in "life expectancy." Both for the High and for the Low, in fact, such changes in life expectancy have been assumed, continuing to the end of the century. The Medium continues the apparent present expectancy.

Table A5–5 shows the net effect of additions and replacements on the average age of stock, for each of the projection levels, at successive points in the future. This has a bearing upon the possible average characteristics of automobiles at each of these points and hence upon how much change may be assumed in the use of fuel and other items needed for current operation.

In Table A5–6 are presented the salient historical data on the various forms of passenger travel other than private automobile, and in Table A5–7 the comparable projections. The projections in intercity travel and its distribution among types of carriers are based partly on past trends and partly on judgment. Despite the increased use of automobiles, per capita travel on public carriers is assumed to resume its long-term increase (there has been a declining tendency in very recent years). This is consistent with the projected trend in consumer expenditures on domestic travel and would occur less as the result of a larger number of trips than of longer ones. Consistent with the increasing length of journey and the steady tendency of air travel costs to fall within a broadening sphere of purchasing power capabilities, all of the increase, and indeed more, would fall to the airlines. Ground travel we have projected to continue its long-term decline, at least until the late seventies, but at a somewhat lessening rate. The projected trends for rail and bus are essentially based on the division of the surface transportation market between the two modes, although it is also assumed that rail, in its competition with air, will have the dominant role in determining the total size of the surface market. The range shown for rail is thus slightly wider than that for bus or for the total.

The Medium projection for per capita use of railroads envisions a decline of about 40 per cent by 2000, the Low a century-end usage of less than ⅓ of today's level, and the High a recovery to, and stabilization at about ¾ of today's level. In other words, while it is a distinct possibility that the decline of rail passenger traffic will follow its present trend (considerably slowed) to its ultimate conclusion, it seems more likely that the need for rail transport between the individual metropolises of some of the coming large urban regions will, among other factors, tend to preserve rail's share at a somewhat higher level. The High projection would serve only in the event of an early and thoroughgoing reorganization of railroad operations, with increased rates of investment and all-around better service.

While air travel has been projected essentially as a matter of alternate extrapolations of per capita trends, the High is believed possible only if air fares are reduced, by about 50 per cent, to a level comparable to those of surface transport. This would raise the proportionate amount of purely personal travel. In the Low projection, personal travel would remain, as now, a little less than half of total air travel. All three projections presuppose a rather high income elasticity for air travel.

Local transit is projected as being primarily related to urban employment and as continuing to decline as a means of getting people to work, except

in the High projection, which assumes a stabilization, at current levels, in transit's relative role. The Medium projection assumes a decline of roughly 40 per cent in its relative importance but, because of the numbers of urban workers to be transported, results in a slight recovery of aggregate traffic from the present trough. In the Low, the rise in non-farm employment is insufficient to arrest the transit industry's decline.

School buses are estimated roughly, on the basis of projected school attendance and a rising percentage of pupils to be transported by bus. Although these constitute the most numerous variety of bus, they are the least important of the three categories (school, local transit, and interurban) in terms of materials and fuels. Buses as a whole are, in fact, insignificant in the materials picture and of only small consequence in the fuels picture; hence relatively rough projections appear to suffice.

Tables A5–8 and 9 present, respectively, historical and projected data on intercity freight transport by type of carrier. Next to automobiles, this is the most significant sector of transportation in terms of materials and fuel requirements. The projection proceeds essentially by relating total freight transportation, and then each of the principal modes of goods transport in turn, to the "commodity" components of the gross national product (goods and construction). Past trends are extrapolated in each case and the Mediums, at least, slightly adjusted so that the parts sum up to the totals. (The High and Lows, which need not add, have been tested for consistency.) Omitted from the analysis was a relatively important segment of intercity transport—namely, coastwise and intercoastal shipping—for which data were not available at the time the work was done. While this form of transport appears to rank behind only railroads in importance, this reflects largely the fact that the ton-mile measurement for it is particularly inflated by virtue of the circuitousness of most of the routes. By more comparable measures, it probably ranks more nearly after trucking and somewhat ahead of inland waterways.

Table A5–10 lays the basis for the materials and fuels analysis of trucking by converting this type of freight transport successively into stock and into current production requirements of vehicles. While intercity freight carriage is predominantly by truck-trailer combination, by far the greatest number of trucks in use in general are single unit. These latter were related directly to the commodity components of GNP on the basis of recent average experience, since there is no apparent trend. For the intercity movement, an increasing percentage was assumed to be carried by "combos," since there is a clear trend in this direction. The output of ton-miles per combo was projected to increase—less on the basis of past trend than on the judgment that both average size and average highway speeds will move upward. On the basis of both slight trend indications and the judgment that utilization economies would push in that direction, the number of trailers per tractor was also projected to increase. Replacement demand for both trucks and trailers was roughly estimated as maintaining its past relationship to vehicle stocks; while the implied average life of vehicles would vary, on this basis, according to the rate of growth and hence average age of stock in use, it may be estimated as remaining somewhere in the vicinity of 10 years.

In Table A5–11 the cast iron, steel, and aluminum contents of automobiles have been projected on a "technical coefficient" basis, starting from an estimated 1960 content arrived at by first determining the approximate average weight of 1960 units (production year) and then distributing this according to scattered information as to relative steel, aluminum, and cast iron composition. This use of a bill of materials, rather than of statistical coefficients arrived at by comparing shipments of materials with output of automobiles, is justified by a number of factors, including the difficulty of segregating iron, steel, and aluminum for automobiles from other quantities of these materials shipped for the automotive industry; the avoidance of the necessity for estimating how much of such shipments was not actually consumed but returned as circulating industrial scrap; and the avoidance of error caused by inventory changes at various stages of shipment and processing. Moreover, the future coefficients have not been projected on a trend basis, but on the basis of judgments as to the possible rates of changeover to aluminum engines and other parts, the theoretical substitution factors in terms of specific gravities and changed volume requirements, and the secondary savings resulting from over-all weight reduction. The projections are admittedly crude, and the ranges reflect the wide degree of present uncertainty as to the turns that the future engineering of automobiles might take. Although the estimates have been checked with industry sources, it is not unlikely that closer study by those more thoroughly familiar with the research and development under way as well as with the limits of engineering practicability might result in more definitive projections for at least the nearer-future years.

In Table A5–12, iron, steel, and aluminum content of trucks and trailers has been treated in a similar manner to that of automobiles. The estimates of present content are even more precarious than those for automobiles and the difficulties besetting projection at least as great. The aggregate quantities involved are substantially smaller, however, and the consequences of error therefore a little less.

Table A5–13 treats, for the totality of motor vehicles, the other principal materials—lead, zinc, copper, and rubber. Lead is primarily a matter of original and replacement battery requirements and, given the future automobile population, may be projected with a relative degree of confidence. Zinc, on the other hand, has an even more uncertain future than do the ferrous metals and aluminum. Its rate of historical consumption has been determined from data on shipments of die castings (the form in which at present it finds nearly all of its automotive use), and the projections have been based on the trends in this rate as well as allowances for the possible substitution of plastics and aluminum on the one hand and for the introduction of new applications (undercoating, galvanized sheet) on the other. Copper has been projected on the basis of past shipments data of an even remoter character, in which it was necessary not only to rely upon a substantial degree of estimation as to gross shipments, but to make added allowance for return of industrial scrap. The copper projections reflect, among other things, uncertainty as to the continued degree of use of water-cooled engines. In the case of rubber, whose use other than for tires, tubes, recaps, etc., we have not attempted to project, the demand in the form of original-equipment tires is, by comparison with some of the other magnitudes with which we are dealing, fairly predictable (for a decade or so, at least). The replacement tire need, in view of substantial increases in average tire life on the one hand, and of an increased use of special purpose changeovers on the other hand, provides one more area of broad uncertainty.

Other than for motor vehicles, the only important consumption of raw materials for transportation occurs in the case of steel going into railway rolling stock and trackage (Tables A5–16 and 17). The two railway uses have been, in recent years, of somewhat comparable importance, but the prospects are that while improved track life and elimination of lines will cause the rail requirement to dwindle, rolling stock requirements will reverse recent trends and begin to increase. This conclusion is based on the projected increase in aggregate rail tonnage, sufficient to overbalance a concurrent increase in output of revenue tons per freight car. (The added output per car, moreover, is partly projected to be produced through added size and consequently added unit use of steel.) While a substitution of aluminum and other materials for steel is assumed to take place, a concurrent substitution of steel for wood is assumed to counterbalance it.

A particular point to note, in connection with Table A5–16, is the comparison at the table's end between consumption as measured on a bill-of-materials basis and consumption as measured on a net shipments basis. (Footnote 10 to the table explains the conceptual difference.) Similar considerations hold for steel and aluminum for automotive vehicles and other evaluations of materials consumption which are made wholly or partly on a bill-of-materials basis, but for which we do not have relevant historical series to compare. In the appendix to Chapter 16, the projections in each of these cases are adjusted to a net-shipments basis so that consistent historical/projected series on apparent total consumption for each of the metals concerned may eventually be obtained. Put in another way, the technical evaluation of end-product content serves to determine the course of future relative change, while a reconciliation of historical market distribution with historical apparent consumption (in appendix to Chapter 16) serves to establish the proper base magnitudes.

Fuels, the final item of projection in the transportation sector, are treated, in the case of motor vehicles, in Tables A5–14 and 15 and, in the case of railroads, in Table A5–18. For both categories, only liquid fuels are currently of any significance, and while gaseous fuels or atomic energy may come to play some role in the future, we have assumed that liquid fuels will continue as the overwhelming source of transportation energy. In the case of passenger cars, which account for about two-thirds of the automotive consumption, the projection has been based upon unchanging annual vehicle mileage and unchanging fuel efficiency, both assumptions being based upon the historical record and on judgments as to the kind of utilization of vehicles which is consistent with the projected stock. Annual mileage per truck has also been assumed to remain unchanged, in line with the historical indications, but in this case the historical trend of decreasing mileage per gallon has also been continued on the supposition that trucks will continue to get larger. Railroad fuel has been separately calculated for freight traffic, passenger traffic, and non-motive purposes, but it is only the first of these that promises to be of any real future importance. The projections, except for the High, assume modest rates of increase in fuel efficiency, presumably achievable through higher rates of utilization of hauled cars for revenue traffic and/or lower dead weight/capacity ratios.

Steel and aluminum requirements for transportation are summed up in Table A5–19 and fuel requirements in Table A5–20. Both make an over-all allowance for the sectors of transportation not specifically covered; the latter also makes a specific projection for the amounts of liquid fuel required for bunkering of vessels in foreign trade.

LIST OF TABLES

TABLE A5–1.   Automobile Stocks, Related to Adult Population, and Automobile Production and Purchases, 1921–60

	Auto stock, Jan. 1[1] (millions)	Population 20 yrs. & over[2] (millions)	Population 20 & over per auto	Auto production (factory sales)[3] (millions)	Exports[4] (millions)	Imports[5] (millions)	Apparent net domestic purchases (millions)	Net increase in stocks[6] (millions)	Apparent retirement (millions)
1921	8.1	64.3	7.94	1.47	.03	*	1.44	1.1	.3
1922	9.2	65.2	7.09	2.27	.07	*	2.20	1.5	.7
1923	10.7	66.5	6.21	3.62	.13	*	3.49	2.6	.9
1924	13.3	67.9	5.11	3.19	.15	*	3.04	2.1	.9
1925	15.4	69.1	4.49	3.74	.24	*	3.50	2.1	1.4
1926	17.5	70.3	4.02	3.69	.24	*	3.45	1.8	1.7
1927	19.3	71.6	3.71	2.94	.28	*	2.66	.9	1.8
1928	20.2	72.9	3.61	3.78	.37	*	3.41	1.2	2.2
1929	21.4	74.1	3.46	4.46	.34	*	4.12	1.7	2.4
1930	23.1	75.5	3.27	2.79	.15	*	2.64	−.1	2.7
1931	23.0	76.6	3.33	1.95	.08	*	1.87	−.6	2.5
1932	22.4	77.7	3.47	1.10	.04	*	1.06	−1.5	2.6
1933	20.9	78.8	3.77	1.56	.06	*	1.50	−.2	1.7
1934	20.7	79.9	3.86	2.16	.14	*	2.02	.8	1.2
1935	21.5	81.1	3.77	3.27	.17	*	3.10	1.1	2.0
1936	22.6	82.1	3.63	3.68	.18	*	3.50	1.6	1.9
1937	24.2	83.3	3.44	3.93	.23	*	3.70	1.3	2.4
1938	25.5	84.3	3.30	2.02	.16	*	1.86	−.2	2.1
1939	25.3	85.5	3.38	2.89	.14	*	2.75	.9	1.9
1940	26.2	86.8	3.31	3.72	.11	*	2.61	1.3	1.3
1941	27.5	88.2	3.21	3.78	.10	*	3.68	2.1	1.6
1942	29.6	89.6	3.05	.22	.01	*	.21	−1.6	1.8
1943	28.0	91.0	3.24	*	*	*	*	−2.0	2.0
1944	26.0	92.4	3.55	*	*	*	*	−.4	.4
1945	25.6	93.7	3.66	.07	*	*	.07	.2	[7]−.1
1946	25.8	94.9	3.68	2.15	.14	*	2.01	2.4	[7]−.4
1947	28.2	96.2	3.41	3.56	.26	*	3.30	2.6	.7
1948	30.8	97.6	3.17	3.91	.23	.03	3.71	2.6	1.1
1949	33.4	98.9	2.96	5.12	.16	.01	4.97	3.1	1.9
1950	36.5	100.3	2.75	6.67	.15	.02	6.54	3.8	2.7
1951	40.3	101.5	2.52	5.34	.25	.02	5.11	2.4	2.7
1952	42.7	102.6	2.40	4.32	.17	.03	4.18	1.1	3.1
1953	43.8	103.4	2.36	6.12	.19	.03	5.96	2.7	3.3
1954	46.5	104.3	2.24	5.56	.21	.04	5.39	2.0	3.4
1955	48.5	105.3	2.17	7.92	.25	.06	7.73	3.7	4.0
1956	52.2	106.3	2.04	5.82	.19	.11	5.74	2.0	3.7
1957	54.2	107.2	1.98	6.11	.16	.26	6.22	1.7	4.5
1958	55.9	108.2	1.94	4.26	.13	.44	4.58	1.0	3.6
1959	56.9	109.2	1.92	5.59	.12	.70	6.17	2.4	3.8
1960	59.3	110.3	1.86	6.67	.14	.47	7.00	[8]2.0	5.0

* Negligible.

1. Bureau of Public Roads data on total passenger-car registrations as of Dec. 31 of preceding year. Source: *Highway Statistics, Summary to 1955 and 1956, 1957, 1958, and 1959,* Table MV–1. The figures are probably an overstatement of actual stock; see Notes.

2. From U.S. Bureau of the Census, Current Population Reports, Series P–25, Nos. 98, 114, 146, 193, and 212.

3. Total sales, including exports and sales to the Federal Government. Source: Automobile Manufacturers Association, *Automobile Facts and Figures,* 1961, p. 3.

4. Data from 1921 to 1930 are for "passenger cars and chassis, except electric," 1931–39, for "new passenger cars and chassis," 1940–60, for "factory sales to foreign market from plants located in United States." Source: 1921–39 from U.S. Department of Commerce, *Foreign Commerce*

and Navigation; 1940–60 from *Automobile Facts and Figures,* 1961, p. 5. Data more or less include vehicle equivalent of parts exported for foreign assembly.

5. Includes new and used, including chassis. Data for 1940, 1946–60 from *Automobile Facts and Figures,* 1961, p. 5. Other years prior to 1946 assumed to be negligible.

6. From first column. Because of presumably increasing exaggeration in size of stock (see Notes), these figures tend to be overstated and retirements to be understated.

7. Represents vehicles taken out of temporary, wartime retirement.

8. Estimated on basis of rate of addition needed to reach estimated 1963 stock in Medium projection (see Table A5–3).

TABLE A5–2. Projected Stocks and Purchases of User-Operated Passenger Vehicles, and Reconciliation with Personal Consumption Expenditures[1]

	1950	1955	1960		1970	1980	1990	2000
Population 20+ per vehicle[2]				L	1.43	1.10	.84	.65
(millions)	2.75	2.17	1.86	M	1.53	1.26	1.04	.85
				H	1.57	1.32	1.11	.94
				L	127.1	150.1	168.4	187.4
Population 20+[3] (millions)	100.3	105.3	110.3	M	127.4	151.5	175.3	207.0
				H	130.1	158.0	192.6	241.9
				L	81.0	113.7	151.7	199.4
Total stock of vehicles[4] (millions)	36.5	48.5	59.3	M	83.3	120.2	168.6	243.5
				H	91.0	143.6	229.3	372.2
				L	8.7	11.1	13.7	16.9
Purchases of vehicles[5] (millions)	6.5	7.7	7.0	M	9.8	14.0	19.7	28.8
				H	12.6	21.6	38.9	73.7
Reconciliation:								
Purchases of vehicles for personal				L	7.1	9.1	11.2	13.9
consumption[6] (millions)	5.0	6.4	5.8	M	8.0	11.5	16.2	23.6
				H	10.3	17.7	31.9	60.4
Consumer expenditures on autos[7]				L	22.0	28.7	36.9	46.0
($ 1960 bil.)	12.8	17.3	15.8	M	23.1	33.1	47.2	66.0
				H	27.7	48.2	84.0	140.1
Implicit value per vehicle[8]				L	3.1	3.2	3.3	3.3
($ 1960 thous.)	2.6	2.7	2.8	M	2.9	2.9	2.9	2.8
				H	2.7	2.7	2.6	2.3
Consumer auto operating expendi-				L	28.7	38.4	50.8	65.3
tures[7] ($ 1960 bil.)	13.8	18.3	21.4	M	30.5	43.7	62.3	87.1
				H	34.6	55.7	89.7	141.9
Operating expenditures per				L	354	338	335	327
vehicle[9] ($ 1960)	378	377	361	M	366	364	370	358
				H	380	388	391	381

1. Projected data refer to all types of user-operated vehicles, including airborne. Historical data, following the National Income Division classification, are confined to automobiles; the NID classifies consumer operated aircraft under recreation expenditures.

2. Low ratio based on approximate average annual decrease 1942–60, or 2.6%; Medium ratio based on average annual decrease 1930–60, or 1.9%; High ratio based on average annual decrease of 1.7%—all applied to 1960 ratio of 1.86. Historical data from Table A5–1.

3. From Table A1–3.

4. Low—Low population ÷ High population per vehicle.
Medium—Medium population ÷ Medium population per vehicle.
High—High population ÷ Low population per vehicle.
Historical data from Table A5–1.

5. Historical data from Table A5–1. Projections are annual average of purchases shown in Table A5–3.

6. Purchases of vehicles multiplied by 82% (National Income Division estimate of consumer portion of total passenger vehicle sales). This is applied to number of units, assuming no significant difference between unit values of business and personal vehicles. For 1950, percentage used (also following NID) was 76.5%.

7. From Table A1–27.

8. Because "personal consumption expenditures" on automobiles include dealers' margins on used car turnover, these average values are overstated, probably by 5–10%. "Low" relates to low volume of automobile purchases, and "High" to high volume.

9. Auto operating expenditures related to total stock of vehicles. "Low" average relates to low stock and "High" to high stock.

TABLE A5–3. Projected Net Additions to Stock and Replacement Demand for User-Operated Passenger Vehicles

(Millions)

	Net additions to stock[1]			Replacement demand[2]			Total purchases[3]		
	L	M	H	L	M	H	L	M	H
1948–52[4]	—	13.0	—	—	11.5	—	—	24.5	—
1953–57[4]	—	12.1	—	—	18.9	—	—	31.0	—
1958–62	8.8	9.3	10.9	22.4	24.1	28.0	31.2	33.4	38.9
1963–67	10.9	12.1	16.5	25.5	28.1	33.3	36.4	40.2	49.8
1968–72	14.1	15.6	21.2	29.6	33.4	41.6	43.7	49.0	62.8
1973–77	16.9	18.9	26.6	32.8	40.1	57.3	49.7	59.0	83.9
1978–82	17.8	21.8	33.7	37.6	48.1	74.5	55.4	69.9	108.2
1983–87	19.1	24.1	43.6	42.0	57.7	103.9	61.1	81.8	147.5
1988–92	21.2	30.3	55.5	47.2	68.1	139.0	68.4	98.4	194.5
1993–97	24.2	38.1	73.4	51.6	81.3	206.1	75.8	119.4	279.5
1998–2002	27.1	46.3	94.9	57.6	97.7	273.6	84.7	144.0	368.5

1. Quinquennial average for decade in which period is centered (see Table A5–2). Last period (1998–2002) extrapolated. First period based on increase from 1958 stock needed to reach 1963 stock as interpolated from known 1960.
2. From Table A5–4.
3. Net additions plus replacements.
4. From Table A5–1.

TABLE A5–4. Retirements of User-Operated Passenger Vehicles, by Period of Purchase, 1948–2002[1]

(Millions)

Period in which retired[2]	Period in which purchased																				Ending stock
	Before 1958[3]		1958–62		1963–67		1968–72		1973–77		1978–82		1983–87		1988–92		1993–97		1998–2002		
	R	B	R	B	R	B	R	B	R	B	R	B	R	B	R	B	R	B	R	B	
Low purchase model:[4]																					
1953–57	18.9	55.9																			55.9
1958–62	22.4	33.5	–	31.2																	64.7
1963–67	13.4	20.1	12.1	19.1	–	36.4															75.6
1968–72	8.0	12.1	7.4	11.7	14.2	22.2	–	43.7													89.7
1973–77	4.8	7.3	4.6	7.1	8.6	13.6	14.8	28.9	–	49.7											106.6
1978–82	2.9	4.4	2.8	4.3	5.3	8.3	9.8	19.1	16.8	32.9	–	55.4									124.4
1983–87	1.8	2.6	1.7	2.6	3.2	5.1	6.5	12.6	11.1	21.8	17.7	37.7	–	61.1							143.5
1988–92	1.0	1.6	1.0	1.6	2.0	3.1	4.3	8.3	7.4	14.4	12.0	25.7	19.5	41.6	–	68.4					164.7
1993–97	.6	1.0	.6	1.0	1.2	1.9	2.8	5.5	4.9	9.5	8.2	17.5	13.3	28.3	20.0	48.4	–	75.8			188.9
1998–2002	.4	.6	.4	.6	.7	1.2	1.9	3.6	3.2	6.3	5.6	11.9	9.0	19.3	14.2	34.2	22.2	53.6	–	84.7	216.0
Medium purchase model:[5]																					
1948–52	11.5	43.8																			43.8
1953–57	18.9	55.9																			55.9
1958–62	24.1	31.8	–	33.4																	65.2
1963–67	13.7	18.1	14.4	19.0	–	40.2															77.3
1968–72	7.8	10.3	8.2	10.8	17.4	22.8	–	49.0													92.9
1973–77	4.4	5.9	4.7	6.1	9.8	13.0	21.2	27.8	–	59.0											111.8
1978–82	2.5	3.4	2.6	3.5	5.6	7.4	12.0	15.8	25.4	33.5	–	70.0									133.6
1983–87	1.5	1.9	1.5	2.0	3.2	4.2	6.8	9.0	14.5	19.0	30.2	39.8	–	81.8							157.7
1988–92	.8	1.1	.9	1.1	1.8	2.4	3.9	5.1	8.2	10.8	17.2	22.6	35.3	46.5	–	98.4					188.0
1993–97	.5	.6	.5	.6	1.0	1.4	2.2	2.9	4.7	6.1	9.8	12.8	20.1	26.4	42.5	55.9	–	119.4			226.1
1998–2002	.3	.3	.3	.3	.6	.8	1.3	1.6	2.6	3.5	5.5	7.3	11.4	15.0	24.1	31.8	51.6	67.8	–	144.0	272.4
High purchase model:[6]																					
1953–57	18.9	55.9																			55.9
1958–62	28.0	27.9	–	38.9																	66.8
1963–67	13.9	14.0	19.4	19.5	–	49.8															83.3
1968–72	7.0	7.0	9.7	9.8	24.9	24.9	–	62.8													104.5
1973–77	3.5	3.5	4.9	4.9	12.5	12.4	36.4	26.4	–	83.9											131.1
1978–82	1.8	1.7	2.5	2.4	6.2	6.2	15.3	11.1	48.7	35.2	–	108.2									164.8
1983–87	.8	.9	1.2	1.2	3.1	3.1	6.4	4.7	20.4	14.8	72.0	36.2	–	147.5							208.4
1988–92	.5	.4	.6	.6	1.5	1.6	2.7	2.0	8.6	6.2	24.1	12.1	101.0	46.5	–	194.5					263.9
1993–97	.2	.2	.3	.3	.8	.8	1.2	.8	3.6	2.6	8.0	4.1	31.9	14.6	160.1	34.4	–	279.5			337.3
1998–2002	.1	.1	.1	.2	.4	.4	.5	.3	1.5	1.1	2.7	1.4	10.0	4.6	28.3	6.1	230.0	49.5	–	368.5	432.2

Table A5–4 (cont'd)

R = retired.
B = balance in use.

1. Total purchases in each successive period based on stock change and total replacement demand, as summarized in Table A5–3.

2. Scrappage through 1957 from Table A5–1.

3. Based on apparent rate of attrition, 1953–57: 43.2% in 5 years, equivalent to median life of about 8½ years or average life of about 10¾ years, for "Medium purchase model"; 40% in 5 years, equivalent to median life of 9 or average of 12, for Low; and 50% in 5 years, equivalent to median life of 7½ and average of 9 1/3, for High.

4. Attrition rate declines from 38.9% in 5 years, or equivalent of median life of 9½ years (average of 12¼) for cars built in 1958–67, to 33.8%, or equivalent of 10½ years (average of 13¾), 1968–77; to 31.9%, or equivalent of 11½ years (average of 15),

1978–87; to 29.3%, or equivalent of 12½ years (average of 16), 1988–2003. Zero attrition rate assumed for period in which built; equivalent average lives include an allowance of 2½ years for this period.

5. Attrition rate continues at 1953–57 rate (see footnote 3).

6. Attrition rate rises from 50.0% in 5 years, or equivalent of median life of 7½ years (average of 9 1/3) for cars built in 1958–67, to 58.0% in 5 years, or equivalent of 6½ years (average of 7 4/5) for cars built in 1968–77; to 68.5% or equivalent of 5½ years (average of 6 1/3) for cars built in 1978–87; to 82.3% or equivalent of 4½ years (average of 5) for cars built in 1988–97. Zero attrition rate assumed for period in which built; equivalent average lives include an allowance of 2½ years for this period.

TABLE A5–5. Implicit Age Distribution of User-Operated Passenger Vehicles, 1963–2003[1]

	1963	1968	1973	1978	1983	1988	1993	1998	2003
Low projection:									
Vehicles in use, start of year (millions)	64.7	75.6	89.7	106.6	124.4	143.5	164.7	188.9	216.0
Per cent purchased:									
Prior to 1958	51.8	26.6	13.5	6.8	3.5	1.8	1.0	.5	.3
1958–62	48.2	25.3	13.0	6.7	3.5	1.8	1.0	.5	.3
1963–67	–	48.2	24.8	12.7	6.7	3.6	1.9	1.0	.6
1968–72	–	–	48.7	27.1	15.4	8.8	5.0	2.9	1.7
1973–77	–	–	–	46.6	26.4	15.2	8.7	5.0	2.9
1978–82	–	–	–	–	44.5	26.3	15.6	9.3	5.5
1983–87	–	–	–	–	–	42.6	25.3	15.0	8.9
1988–92	–	–	–	–	–	–	41.5	25.6	15.8
1993–97	–	–	–	–	–	–	–	40.1	24.8
1998–2002	–	–	–	–	–	–	–	–	39.2
Medium projection:									
Vehicles in use, start of year (millions)	65.2	77.3	92.9	111.8	133.6	157.7	188.0	226.1	272.4
Per cent purchased:									
Prior to 1958	48.8	23.4	11.1	5.3	2.5	1.2	.6	.3	.1
1958–62	51.2	24.6	11.6	5.5	2.6	1.3	.6	.3	.1
1963–67	–	52.0	24.5	11.6	5.5	2.7	1.3	.6	.3
1968–72	–	–	52.7	24.9	11.8	5.7	2.7	1.3	.6
1973–77	–	–	–	52.8	25.1	12.0	5.7	2.7	1.3
1978–82	–	–	–	–	52.4	25.2	12.0	5.7	2.7
1983–87	–	–	–	–	–	51.9	24.7	11.7	5.5
1988–92	–	–	–	–	–	–	52.3	24.7	11.7
1993–97	–	–	–	–	–	–	–	52.8	24.9
1998–2002	–	–	–	–	–	–	–	–	52.8
High projection:									
Vehicles in use, start of year (millions)	66.8	83.3	104.5	131.1	164.8	208.4	263.9	337.3	432.2
Per cent purchased:									
Prior to 1958	41.8	16.8	6.7	2.7	1.0	.4	.2	.1	.02
1958–62	58.2	23.4	9.4	3.7	1.5	.6	.2	.1	.05
1963–67	–	59.8	23.8	9.5	3.8	1.5	.6	.2	.09
1968–72	–	–	60.1	20.1	6.7	2.3	.8	.2	.07
1973–77	–	–	–	64.0	21.4	7.1	2.4	.8	.3
1978–82	–	–	–	–	65.7	17.4	4.6	1.2	.3
1983–87	–	–	–	–	–	70.8	17.6	4.3	1.1
1988–92	–	–	–	–	–	–	73.7	10.2	1.4
1993–97	–	–	–	–	–	–	–	82.9	11.4
1998–2002	–	–	–	–	–	–	–	–	85.3

1. Based on stock distributions shown in Table A5–4.

TABLE A5–6. Historical Data on Volume of Passenger Transportation on Public Carriers, by Mode of Travel

	1949	1950	1951	1952	1953	1954	1955	1956	1957	1958	1959	1960
Intercity common carrier:												
Surface:												
Revenue passenger-miles[1] (billions):												
Rail	30.5	27.5	30.4	30.0	27.5	24.7	23.9	23.8	21.4	18.8	17.9	17.2
Bus	27.9	26.4	27.4	28.7	28.4	25.6	25.5	25.2	21.5	20.8	20.4	20.4
Total	58.4	53.9	57.8	58.7	55.9	50.3	49.4	49.0	42.9	39.6	38.3	37.6
Population[2] (millions)	149	152	154	157	160	162	165	168	171	174	177	180
Revenue passenger-miles per capita:												
Rail	204.7	180.9	197.4	191.1	171.9	152.5	144.8	141.7	125.1	108.0	101.1	95.6
Bus	187.2	173.7	177.9	182.8	177.5	158.0	154.6	150.0	125.7	119.5	115.3	113.3
Total	391.9	354.6	375.3	373.9	349.4	310.5	299.4	291.7	250.8	227.5	216.4	208.9
Air:[3]												
Revenue passenger-miles[1] (billions)	8.6	10.1	12.9	15.0	17.4	19.6	22.7	25.5	28.1	28.5	32.4	34.6
Revenue passenger-miles per capita	57.7	66.4	83.8	95.5	108.8	121.0	137.6	151.8	164.3	163.8	183.1	192.2
Inland waterway:												
Revenue passenger-miles[1] (billions)	1.4	1.2	1.3	1.4	1.5	1.7	1.7	1.9	1.9	2.1	2.0	2.0
Revenue passenger-miles per capita	9.4	7.9	8.4	8.9	9.4	10.5	10.3	11.3	11.1	12.1	11.3	11.1
Total:												
Revenue passenger-miles (billions)	68.4	65.2	72.0	75.1	74.8	71.6	73.8	76.4	72.9	70.2	72.7	74.2
Revenue passenger-miles per capita	459	429	468	478	468	442	447	455	426	403	411	412
Local common carrier:												
Passenger volume[4] (billions)	19.3	17.5	16.4	15.4	14.2	12.6	11.8	11.2	10.6	10.0	9.8	9.5
Non-farm employment[5] (millions)	50.4	52.2	53.8	54.2	55.3	54.4	56.2	58.1	58.8	58.2	59.8	60.7
Ratio: Passenger volume to non-farm employment	383	335	305	284	257	232	210	193	180	172	163	157

School bus:

Enrollment in public and non-public elementary and secondary schools[6] (millions)	n.a.	28.6	n.a.	30.5	n.a.	33.3	n.a.	36.0	n.a.	39.3	n.a.	42.6
Per cent of enrolled public school pupils transported at public expense[7]	n.a.	27.7	28.0	28.6	30.0	30.4	31.6	31.7	33.2	33.9	35.3	35.0
Estimated total pupils transported by bus[8]	–	7.9	–	8.7	–	10.1	–	11.4	–	13.3	–	15

1. Excludes commutation traffic. From published and unpublished compilations of Bureau of Railway Economics, Association of American Railroads, and Interstate Commerce Commission.

2. From Table A1-1.

3. Includes revenue traffic of both scheduled and non-scheduled airlines, as well as a small proportion of passenger-miles in private business and pleasure flying. The carriage of Armed Forces personnel by commercial airlines is included, but not troop or other air movements by the Air Force, Military Air Transport Service, etc.

4. From American Transit Association, *Transit Fact Book*, 1953 and 1961 editions. Also includes railroad commutation traffic, from source cited in footnote 1.

5. From Table A1-1—civilian government plus private non-agricultural employment.

6. From U.S. Department of Health, Education, and Welfare, *Health, Education and Welfare Trends*, 1960, p. 56. Adjusted to omit enrollments in "subcollegiate" departments of institutions of higher learning.

7. From *Automobile Facts and Figures*, 1961 ed.

8. Product of preceding two lines. Percentage of private school pupils transported assumed to be the same as for public. Since only about 1/7 of all pupils attend private schools, any error would not be great. Likewise, while all types of transportation are included, all except a very small proportion of the children are transported by bus.

TABLE A5–7. Projected Volume of Passenger Transportation on Public Carriers, by Mode of Travel[1]

	1950	1955	1960		1970	1980	1990	2000
Intercity common carrier:								
Surface:								
Revenue passenger-miles per capita:[2]				L	140	105	85	77
Total	355	299	209	M	160	134	116	110
				H	175	158	150	150
				L	60	44	36	30
Rail	181	145	96	M	68	55	49	55
				H	80	73	71	70
				L	78	60	46	40
Bus	174	154	113	M	92	79	67	55
				H	100	90	85	85
				L	202	226	249	268
Population[3] (millions)	152	165	180	M	208	245	287	331
				H	223	279	349	433
Revenue passenger-miles[4] (billions):				L	28.3	23.7	21.2	20.6
Total	53.9	49.4	37.6	M	33.3	32.8	33.3	36.4
				H	39.0	44.1	52.4	65.0
				L	12.1	9.9	9.0	8.0
Rail	27.5	23.9	17.2	M	14.1	13.5	14.1	18.2
				H	17.8	20.4	24.8	30.3
				L	15.8	13.6	11.5	10.7
Bus	26.4	25.5	20.4	M	19.1	19.4	19.2	18.2
				H	22.3	25.1	29.7	36.8
Air:								
				L	300	400	500	600
Revenue passenger-miles per capita[5]	66.4	138	192	M	320	440	560	680
				H	340	480	620	760
				L	60.6	90.4	124.5	160.8
Revenue passenger-miles[4] (billions)	10.1	22.7	34.6	M	66.6	107.8	160.7	225.0
				H	75.8	133.9	216.4	329.1
Inland waterway:								
				L	2.2	2.5	2.7	2.9
Revenue passenger-miles[6] (billions)	1.2	1.7	2.0	M	2.3	2.7	3.2	3.6
				H	2.5	3.1	3.8	4.8
Total revenue passenger-miles				L	471	545	627	721
per capita[7]	429	447	412	M	491	585	687	801
				H	511	625	747	881
				L	95.1	123.2	156.1	193.2
Revenue passenger-miles[4] (billions)	65.2	73.8	74.2	M	102.1	143.3	197.2	265.1
				H	114.0	174.4	260.7	381.5
Check:								
Per capita personal consumption				L	1.8	2.4	3.3	4.3
expenditures on intercity com-	1.3	1.3	1.5	M	2.3	3.3	4.7	6.6
mon carriers ($ 1960)[8]				H	3.0	4.5	6.9	10.4
Implicit expenditures per revenue				L	1.9	1.9	2.1	2.2
passenger-mile (¢ 1960)[9]	2.0	1.8	2.0	M	2.3	2.3	2.4	2.5
				H	2.6	2.6	2.6	2.7

Table A5–7 (cont'd)

	1950	1955	1960		1970	1980	1990	2000
Local common carrier:								
Non-farm employment (millions)[10]	52.2	56.2	60.7	L	72	83	92	101
				M	76	91	107	129
				H	79	101	128	170
Ratio: Passenger volume to non-farm employment[11]	335	210	157	L	100	80	65	55
				M	125	115	105	90
				H	150	150	150	150
Passenger volume (billions of passengers)	17.5	11.8	9.5	L	7.2	6.7	6.0	5.6
				M	9.5	10.4	11.2	11.7
				H	11.9	15.1	19.2	25.5
School bus:								
Enrollment in public and non-public elementary and secondary schools[12] (millions of pupils)	28.6	[13]34.6	42.6	L	49.3	47.7	51.7	52.0
				M	51.1	56.9	69.9	77.6
				H	55.8	71.7	95.0	116.8
Per cent of pupils transported by bus[14]	28	32	35		41	45	48	50
Number of pupils transported by bus (millions)	8.0	11	15	L	20.2	21.5	24.8	26.0
				M	21.0	25.6	33.6	38.8
				H	22.9	32.3	45.6	58.4

1. Historical data from Table A5–6.
2. Total per capita use extrapolated graphically, with all three levels assuming a decline in the geometric rate of decline. Rail and bus shares projected so as to remain consistent with one another, with the basic assumption, in the Medium, that they will end up with roughly equal shares at the century's end. (This implies some recovery, in per capita terms, from the trough reached by rail around 1990.) Rail, on the assumption of greater sensitivity to air competition, has been projected to decline somewhat more than bus in the Low and to hold up relatively better than bus in the High.
3. From Table A1–2.
4. Per capita use is assumed to be independent of size of population. Hence Lows are multiplied by Lows and Highs by Highs.
5. The three levels represent alternate extrapolations of past trends.
6. Projected on assumption of 11 revenue passenger-miles per capita at all three levels. This is the 1949–60 average.
7. Compensation was assumed between air and surface. The Medium per capita surface was assumed also to represent the Low surface consistent with Low air and the High surface consistent with High air.

8. From Table A1–25.
9. Since consumer travel is only about half of all revenue traffic, the implicit average rates per passenger-mile are about double what is shown here. The higher costs in the High and the lower costs in the Low may be explained by the relative shares of surface and air.
10. From Table A1–2: civilian government employment plus private non-agricultural employment.
11. Low assumes continued decline in ratio, but at less rapid rate than in 1950–60. For the High, the ratio is kept constant roughly at the 1960 level. The Medium is approximately midway between the High and the Low. The 2000 Low implies about 1/9 of all workers making two trips per working day (assuming 240 working days a year); the High about 1/3 of the workers; the Medium about 1/5.
12. 85% of population levels projected for 5 to 19 age group in Table A1–3. This is approximate recent level.
13. Straight line interpolation between 1954 and 1956.
14. Extrapolation of long term historical trend. While historical data relate to public school students transported at public expense, it is assumed that the same percentage applies to non-public schools.

TABLE A5–8. Historical Data on Domestic Intercity Freight Transportation in Relation to Output of Goods and Construction

| | Volume of freight carried[1] (billion ton-miles) | | | | | | | | | | | Output of goods and construction[2] ($ 1960 bil.) | Ton-miles per $ 1960 of goods and construction | | | | | Production of crude petroleum[3] (mil. bbl.) | Oil pipeline ton-miles per bbl. of oil produced |
| | Rail | | Truck | | Inland waterway[4] | | Oil pipeline | | Air | | Total (= 100%) | | Rail | Truck | Water-ways[4] | Oil pipe-line | Total | | |
	Quan-tity	%	Quan-tity	%	Quan-tity	%	Quan-tity	%	Quan-tity	%									
1946	602.1	66.6	82.0	9.1	124.0	13.7	95.7	10.6	.09	.01	903.9	205.4	2.93	.40	.60	.47	4.40	1,734	55.2
1947	664.5	65.2	102.1	10.0	146.7	14.4	105.2	10.3	.20	.02	1,018.7	208.9	3.18	.49	.70	.50	4.88	1,857	56.7
1948	647.3	61.9	116.0	11.1	161.8	15.5	119.6	11.4	.22	.02	1,044.9	223.2	2.90	.52	.72	.54	4.68	2,020	59.2
1949	534.7	58.4	126.6	13.8	139.4	15.2	114.9	12.6	.24	.03	915.8	213.8	2.50	.59	.65	.54	4.28	1,842	62.4
1950	596.9	56.2	172.9	16.3	163.3	15.4	129.2	12.2	.32	.03	1,062.6	237.3	2.52	.73	.69	.54	4.48	1,974	65.5
1951	655.4	55.6	188.0	16.0	182.2	15.5	152.1	12.9	.38	.03	1,178.1	254.5	2.58	.74	.72	.60	4.63	2,248	67.7
1952	623.4	54.5	194.6	17.0	168.4	14.7	157.5	13.8	.42	.04	1,144.3	262.4	2.38	.74	.64	.60	4.36	2,290	68.8
1953	614.2	51.0	217.2	18.0	202.4	16.8	169.9	14.1	.41	.03	1,204.1	276.7	2.22	.78	.73	.61	4.35	2,357	72.1
1954	556.6	49.6	213.2	19.0	173.7	15.5	179.2	16.0	.40	.04	1,123.1	268.1	2.08	.80	.65	.67	4.19	2,315	77.4
1955	631.4	49.5	223.3	17.5	216.5	17.0	203.2	15.9	.48	.04	1,274.9	293.5	2.15	.76	.74	.69	4.34	2,484	81.8
1956	655.9	48.4	248.8	18.4	220.0	16.2	230.0	17.0	.56	.04	1,355.2	296.8	2.21	.84	.74	.77	4.57	2,617	87.9
1957	626.2	46.9	254.2	19.0	231.8	17.4	222.7	16.7	.57	.04	1,335.5	299.3	2.09	.85	.77	.74	4.46	2,616	85.1
1958	558.7	46.0	255.5	21.0	189.0	15.6	211.3	17.4	.58	.05	1,215.2	286.5	1.95	.89	.66	.74	4.24	2,449	86.3
1959	582.5	45.0	288.5	22.3	196.6	15.2	227.0	17.5	.65	.06	1,295.3	309.6	1.88	.93	.63	.73	4.18	2,575	88.2
1960	579.1	43.5	299.4	22.5	223.0	16.8	228.6	17.2	.69	.06	1,330.9	315.1	1.84	.95	.71	.73	4.22	2,575	88.8

1. From Interstate Commerce Commission, *Intercity Ton-Miles, 1939–1954*, and 71st–75th *Annual Report*, except air, 1959–60, which is estimated from data in American Automobile Association, *Motor Truck Facts*, 1961.

2. From Table A1-6.
3. From Bureau of Mines, *Mineral Facts and Problems* and *Minerals Yearbook*.
4. Including Great Lakes traffic.

TABLE A5–9. Projected Volume of Domestic Intercity Freight Transportation, by Type of Carrier[1]

	1950	1955	1960		1970	1980	1990	2000
Output of goods and construction[2]				L	395	501	634	812
($ 1960 bil.)	237	294	315	M	453	638	900	1,285
				H	525	829	1,311	2,128
Total ton-miles per dollar of goods				L	3.90	3.70	3.60	3.50
and construction[3]	4.48	4.34	4.22	M	4.18	4.14	4.10	4.10
				H	4.35	4.60	4.60	4.60
				L	1,540	1,854	2,282	2,842
Total ton-miles[4] (billions)	1,063	1,275	1,331	M	1,894	2,641	3,690	5,268
				H	2,284	3,813	6,031	9,789
Rail ton-miles per dollar of goods				L	1.50	1.22	1.03	.93
and construction[3]	2.52	2.15	1.84	M	1.63	1.43	1.31	1.24
				H	1.77	1.67	1.57	1.50
				L	592	611	653	755
Rail ton-miles[4] (billions)	597	631	579	M	738	912	1,179	1,593
				H	929	1,384	2,058	3,192
Truck ton-miles per dollar of goods				L	.95	1.05	1.15	1.20
and construction[3]	.73	.76	.95	M	1.08	1.18	1.25	1.30
				H	1.15	1.35	1.50	1.50
				L	375	526	729	974
Truck ton-miles[4] (billions)	173	223	299	M	489	753	1,125	1,671
				H	604	1,119	1,967	3,192
Inland-waterway ton-miles per dollar				L	.65	.61	.60	.60
of goods and construction[3]	.69	.74	.71	M	.70	.70	.70	.70
				H	.76	.80	.80	.80
				L	257	306	380	487
Inland waterway ton-miles[4] (billions)	163	216	223	M	317	447	630	900
				H	399	663	1,049	1,702
Oil pipeline ton-miles per dollar of				L	.69	.66	.65	.65
goods and construction[3]	.54	.69	.73	M	.78	.82	.84	.85
				H	.82	.90	.96	1.00
				L	273	331	412	528
Oil pipeline ton-miles[4] (billions)	129	203	229	M	353	523	756	1,092
				H	430	746	1,259	2,128
				L	1.25	1.70	2.10	2.30
Air ton-miles[5] (billions)	.33	.48	.69	M	1.45	2.70	4.60	6.30
				H	1.70	4.20	10.30	25.30
Type of carrier as per cent of total— medium projection:[6]								
Rail	56.2	49.5	43.5		39.0	34.5	32.0	30.2
Truck	16.3	17.5	22.5		25.8	28.5	30.5	31.7
Inland waterway	15.4	17.0	16.8		16.7	16.9	17.1	17.1
Oil pipeline	12.2	15.9	17.2		18.6	19.8	20.5	20.7
Check:								
				L	2.91	3.58	4.48	5.73
Crude oil production[7] (bil. bbl.)	1.97	2.48	2.57	M	3.30	4.29	5.79	7.81
				H	3.62	5.47	8.18	12.95
Implicit pipeline ton-miles/bbl.				L	94	92	92	92
of oil produced	66	82	89	M	107	122	131	140
				H	119	136	154	164

1. Historical data from Table A5–8.
2. From a preliminary version of Table A1–13. Subsequent changes were not sufficiently significant to warrant being carried forward to this calculation.
3. Projections are based on graphic extrapolation of historical relationships, adjusted to expected competitive conditions as described in Chapter 5, pp. 137–42. Because of compensation among the modes of transport, the total of the Low detail will be less than the Low total and that of the High detail greater than the High.

4. Volume of output and ton-miles per (constant) dollar are assumed to be not necessarily compensatory. Therefore, the Low factor has in each case been multiplied by Low goods and construction to obtain Low ton-miles, and similarly for the High.
5. Direct geometric extrapolation, on the assumption that rate of growth in air freight has only slight relation to rate of growth in the general economy.
6. Air accounts for less than 1% of the total.
7. Assumed domestic contribution to crude oil demand, as in Table A1–30.

TABLE A5–10.   Stock and Annual Demand for Trucks and Trailers, 1957–2000

	1957	1958	1959	1960		1970	1980	1990	2000
Stock of single-unit trucks:									
Output of goods and construction[1] ($ 1960 bil.)	299	286	310	315	L M H	395 453 525	501 638 829	634 900 1,311	812 1,285 2,128
Trucks in use per $ million of above[2]	33.7	36.1	33.9	34.7		34	34	34	34
Single-unit trucks in use[3] (millions)	10.08	10.33	10.52	10.94	L M H	13.4 15.4 17.8	17.0 21.7 28.2	21.6 30.6 44.6	27.6 43.7 72.4
Stock of combo's (tractor-trailers):									
Intercity truck ton-miles[4] (billions)	254	256	288	299	L M H	375 489 604	526 753 1,119	729 1,125 1,967	974 1,671 3,192
Per cent by combo's[5]	73	72	73	74		78	81	83	84
Intercity ton-miles by combo's (billions)	185	184	210	221	L M H	213 381 471	426 610 906	605 934 1,633	818 1,404 2,681
Ton-miles per combo[6] (millions)	.30	.29	.33	.32		.39	.47	.58	.70
Combo's in use[7] (millions)	.61	.63	.64	.68	L M H	.75 .98 1.21	.91 1.30 1.93	1.04 1.61 2.82	1.17 2.01 3.83
Total trucks in use[8] (millions)	10.69	10.96	11.16	11.62	L M H	14.2 16.4 19.0	17.9 23.0 30.1	22.6 32.2 47.4	28.8 45.7 76.2
Stock of trailers:									
Trailers per tractor[9]	1.61	1.63	1.66	1.65		1.75	1.85	1.95	2.05
Trailers in use (millions)	.98	1.03	1.06	1.12	L M H	1.31 1.72 2.12	1.68 2.40 3.57	2.03 3.14 5.50	2.40 4.12 7.85
Annual demand for trucks:									
Net additions to stock[10] (millions)	.27	.20	.46	.47	L M H	.33 .55 .86	.42 .77 1.40	.54 1.12 2.23	.72 1.65 3.64
Replacement demand[11] (millions)	.62	.50	.48	.50	L M H	.71 .82 .95	.90 1.15 1.50	1.13 1.61 2.37	1.44 2.28 3.81
Total domestic demand[12] (millions)	.89	.70	.94	.97	L M H	1.04 1.37 1.81	1.32 1.92 2.90	1.67 2.73 4.60	2.16 3.93 7.45
Total demand[13] (millions)	1.10	.87	1.13	1.19	L M H	1.20 1.58 2.08	1.52 2.21 3.34	1.92 3.14 5.29	2.48 4.52 8.57
Annual demand for trailers:									
Net additions to stock[10] (millions)	.05	.03	.06	.06	L M H	.03 .06 .11	.03 .07 .19	.04 .08 .19	.04 .10 .28
Replacement demand[11] (millions)	.01	.02	.01	–	L M H	.04 .05 .06	.05 .07 .11	.06 .09 .16	.07 .12 .24
Total demand[12] (millions)	.06	.05	.07	.06	L M H	.07 .11 .17	.08 .14 .30	.10 .17 .35	.11 .22 .52

Table A5–10 (cont'd)

1. From Table A1–6 and a preliminary version of Table A1–13. (See footnote 2, Table A5–9.)

2. Historical data calculated from number of trucks and output of goods and construction. Single level for future based on assumed relative increase in trucking, compensated by increased relative use of tractor-trailers.

3. Historical data calculated by subtracting tractor-trailer combinations, below, from total number of vehicles registered as of Jan. 1. Projections based on use per dollar of goods and services.

4. From Tables A5–8 and 9.

5. Projected on a judgment basis. Percentages for earlier years: 1956—76; 1955—75.

6. Historical data calculated from number of combo's and intercity ton-miles by combo. Projections assume increase in average size and speed of intercity freight carriers.

7. Historical data are tractor-trailer registrations reported in Bureau of Public Roads Table MV–9 (private and commercial trucks only), adjusted upward to benchmark (figure shown here for 1958) from "Third Progress Report," 1957 *Highway Cost Allocation Study* (86th Cong. 1st Sess., House Doc. No. 91, p. 7). Projections result from dividing ton-miles by ton-miles per combo.

8. Historical data from Bureau of Public Roads Table MV–1 or 9. Projections are sum of single unit trucks and combinations.

9. Includes a trailer for each tractor, as well as extras. Historical data based on trailers registered, from Bureau of Public Roads Table MV–11 (excluding light farm trailers, car trailers, house trailers, etc.). Projection is an extrapolation of apparent upward trend. (Increased piggybacking would help account for such a trend.) "Trailer," for the future, should be taken to include trailer-size separable containers, as well as bodies attached to chassis.

10. Annual average for 10 years, centered on the given year, except for 1957–59, which are the one-year differences, and 1960, which is interpolated.

11. Historical data deduced from net additions and total demand. Projections based on annual attrition rate of 5% of stock (equal to an average life of roughly 10 years) for trucks and 3% for trailers.

12. Historical data are sales for domestic market (from *Motor Truck Facts*, 1961). Projections are sum of net additions and replacement demand.

13. Historical data from source cited in preceding footnote. Projections assume exports at 15% of domestic production, which is a little under the post–World War II average.

TABLE A5–11. Projected Cast Iron, Steel, and Aluminum Content of User-Operated Passenger Vehicles[1]

	1960		1970	1980	1990	2000
Cast iron per vehicle[2] (lb.)	600	L	300	–	–	–
		M	450	300	180	100
		H	525	475	425	375
Cast aluminum per vehicle[3] (lb.)	45	L	70	85	105	120
		M	100	155	200	225
		H	165	285	285	285
Wrought aluminum per vehicle[4] (lb.)	15	L	35	63	71	79
		M	55	111	147	167
		H	115	255	271	280
Total aluminum per vehicle (lb.) (first approximation)	60	L	105	148	176	199
		M	155	266	347	392
		H	280	540	556	565
Steel displaced by wrought aluminum[4] (lb.)	–	L	50	120	140	160
		M	100	240	330	380
		H	250	600	640	660
Steel displaced by other materials[5] (lb.)	–	L	–	10	30	50
		M	10	25	65	200
		H	20	50	100	400
Steel per vehicle (lb.)	2,400	L	2,130	1,750	1,660	1,340
		M	2,290	2,135	2,005	1,820
		H	2,350	2,270	2,230	2,190
Weight saved per vehicle[6] (lb.)	–	L	80	165	215	275
		M	160	350	500	670
		H	340	750	805	995
Adjusted steel per vehicle[7] (lb.)	2,400	L	2,030	1,567	1,470	1,122
		M	2,240	2,031	1,864	1,639
		H	2,324	2,219	2,163	2,106
Adjusted wrought aluminum per vehicle[7] (lb.)	15	L	35	61	69	76
		M	54	105	137	150
		H	110	228	240	234
Adjusted total aluminum per vehicle (lb.)	60	L	105	146	174	196
		M	154	261	337	375
		H	275	513	525	519
Size of vehicle adjustment[8] (index, 1960 = 100)	100	L	80	70	60	50
		M	100	100	100	100
		H	120	130	140	150
Annual production of vehicles[9] (mil.)	6.7	L	8.3	10.5	13.0	16.1
		M	8.8	12.6	17.7	25.9
		H	10.7	18.4	33.1	62.6
Steel in automobiles[10] (mil. tons)	8.0	L	8.5	9.6	12.8	13.6
		M	9.9	12.8	16.5	21.2
		H	11.8	15.9	22.5	32.8
Aluminum in automobiles[11] (mil. tons)	.20	L	.52	1.00	1.58	2.37
		M	.68	1.64	2.98	4.86
		H	1.18	3.30	5.21	8.12
Cast iron in automobiles[12] (mil. tons)	2.0	L	1.25	–	–	–
		M	1.98	1.89	1.59	1.30
		H	2.67	3.41	4.43	5.85

Table A5–11 (cont'd)

1. The method of this table is to project, first, the Low, Medium, and High rates of substitution of cast aluminum for cast iron and of wrought aluminum for steel in the "automobile" (or other user-operated vehicle) of 1960 average size. This has a consequence in terms of total weight of car which permits further saving in steel (and wrought aluminum) structure. Superimposed upon the foregoing are changes in average size of car in connection with both the Low and the High rates of growth of automobile stock, in which increases in average size are assumed to accompany the Low rate of growth and vice versa.

The 1960 levels are estimated from spotty data on total weights of automobiles and on materials content, particularly:

"Metals in Automobiles," *Waste Trade Journal*, Oct. 5, 1957.

Consumer Reports, April 1960 and 1961 (tables listing weights of various model automobiles). These data were weighted by sales of various models, as reported by Automobile Manufacturers Association and Aluminum Company of America.

Press releases of Alcoa on aluminum content of various years' models.

Correspondence with automotive and metals industry sources.

2. In the Medium, half of the cast iron in automobiles is assumed to be replaced by aluminum by 1980 and two-thirds more by 2000. In the Low, replacement is assumed to be complete by 1980, and in the High, a fairly modest rate of replacement is assumed.

3. Of the 45 lb. shown for 1960, some 15–20 is in the form of small die castings and the remainder in applications otherwise fulfilled by cast iron. The great bulk of the growth in cast aluminum consumption is assumed to fall into the latter category, occurring at the rate of 1 lb. of aluminum for 3 lb. of cast iron replaced. (The Low cast aluminum projection is consistent with the High cast iron projection and vice versa.) While the specific gravities of the two metals are in the ratio of 2.67 to 1, the use of aluminum is assumed to have a derivative effect in permitting a decrease in size of engine, because of lower power requirements and/or the possibility of decreasing or eliminating the cooling jacket.

That part of cast aluminum which does not substitute for cast iron is presently used in trim and in die cast parts which substitute for zinc. The increase in this portion is assumed to be modest at best, being estimated at an additional 20% (in addition to the cast iron substitution) for the High, 10% for the Medium, and nil for the Low.

4. Projections are based on rates of replacement of steel (see below), starting with an estimated average steel content of 2,400 lb. In the High, about 25% of the steel is assumed to be replaced by 1980, in the Medium, 10%, and in the Low, 5%, followed by tapering off thereafter. While the specific gravities are in the ratio of 2.9 to 1, displacement is assumed at the ratio of 2½ lb. of steel for 1 lb. of aluminum, on the basis that equivalent structural characteristics will require somewhat greater volumes of aluminum.

The 1960 estimate is based partly on the following estimates by Alcoa of average aluminum use by model year: 1957, 41 lb.; 1958, 47 lb.; 1959, 51 lb.; 1960, 54 lb.; 1961, 63 lb. These include castings as well as wrought products.

5. In addition to the substitution by aluminum, it is assumed that there will also be some replacement of steel by plastics, glass, magnesium, and other materials. The amounts shown are arbitrary, the High being based on the assumption that some cars will dispense almost entirely with steel in body and structure but that this will not be true for all cars. The Low implies the continuation of essentially steel structure and body for most cars.

6. The cumulative difference between additional aluminum used and cast iron and steel replaced, plus an arbitrary 3/5 of steel displaced by other materials.

7. It was assumed that the weight saved would lead to a secondary weight saving in structural members equal to 1/3 of the primary saving. This was divided proportionately (on a steel equivalent basis) between the steel and the wrought aluminum.

8. The Medium assumes that the average size of car will remain at today's level. For the Low (associated with High use and production) a trend toward smaller cars is assumed to prevail. For the High, the trend toward larger vehicles is assumed to resume. (See implicit unit values in Table A5-2.)

9. Purchases of vehicles, from Table A5-2, less the following assumed levels of net imports: Low— 5%; Medium—10%; High—15%.

10. The Medium is the product of "adjusted steel per vehicle" times "size of vehicle adjustment" (= 100) times number of vehicles. The High is obtained by multiplying the High adjusted steel per vehicle by the High vehicle size by an annual production of vehicles which is derived by adjusting upward the Low production as originally calculated in proportion to the relationship between the High and the Low population of 20 years and over (Table A5-2); vice versa for the Low. This is because the higher levels of steel use depend more upon the retention of steel in relatively larger vehicles than upon an expansion in total vehicle use; however, the Low production as originally calculated relates to the Low population projections and has to be raised (even if roughly) to be consistent with the High.

11. The Medium is the product of "adjusted total aluminum per vehicle" times "size of vehicle adjustment" (= 100) times number of vehicles. The Low combines Low production and large size with Low unit use of aluminum, and the High vice versa. The underlying assumption is that relatively higher production levels are positively correlated with more rapid substitution and with decreasing average size of car, the latter being implied by the relatively higher level of second-car ownership needed to support the higher production levels.

12. Similar to calculation for steel.

TABLE A5–12. Projected Cast Iron, Steel, and Aluminum Content of Trucks and Trailers[1]

		1960		1970	1980	1990	2000
Cast iron:							
			L	1.20	1.52	1.92	2.48
Number of trucks built[2] (millions)		1.19	M	1.58	2.21	3.14	4.52
			H	2.08	3.34	5.29	8.57
			L	.20	–	–	–
Cast iron per truck[3] (tons)		.40	M	.30	.20	.12	.07
			H	.35	.32	.27	.23
			L	.24	–	–	–
Cast iron in trucks (mil. tons)		.48	M	.47	.44	.38	.32
			H	.73	1.07	1.43	1.97
Steel:							
Steel per truck or combo[4] (tons)		1.8		1.6	1.4	1.2	1.0
			L	1.92	2.13	2.30	2.48
Steel in trucks (mil. tons)		2.14	M	2.53	3.09	3.77	4.52
			H	3.33	4.68	6.35	8.57
Aluminum in trucks:							
Aluminum per truck[5] (excluding			L	27	38	45	51
trailers) (lb.)		15	M	38	65	84	94
			H	69	128	131	130
			L	.02	.03	.04	.06
Aluminum in trucks (mil. tons)		.01	M	.03	.07	.13	.21
			H	.07	.21	.35	.56
Aluminum in trailers:							
			L	.07	.08	.10	.11
Number of trailers built[2] (millions)		.06	M	.11	.14	.17	.22
			H	.17	.30	.35	.52
Per cent with aluminum bodies[6]		25		35	45	55	65
Aluminum per aluminum unit[7] (tons)		1.10		1.20	1.30	1.40	1.50
			L	.03	.05	.08	.11
Aluminum in trailers (mil. tons)		.02	M	.05	.08	.13	.21
			H	.07	.18	.27	.51
			L	.05	.08	.12	.17
Total aluminum (mil. tons)		.03	M	.08	.15	.26	.42
			H	.14	.39	.62	1.07

1. 1960 use of materials, as shown herein, is estimated from spotty historical data, including, in particular, those given in "Metals in Automobiles," *Waste Trade Journal,* Oct. 5, 1957.

2. From Table A5–10.

3. Assumed to average about 1/3 higher than average weight of cast iron in automobiles (see Table A5–11).

4. Assumed to decline moderately with lightening of structure through use of aluminum engines, etc. Average size of truck does not seem to be changing: although very heavy trucks are getting heavier, light trucks are expanding more rapidly in relative numbers. The estimated present level of 1.8 tons allows for trailer chassis as well as trucks and tractors.

5. Assumed to increase at same rate as aluminum in automobiles (see Table A5–11).

6. Present use is almost exclusively in van bodies, of which about half are now made of aluminum. It is assumed that this percentage will increase, as the result of (1) some increase in proportion of vans, (2) increasing use of aluminum for vans, and (3) increasing use of aluminum for tank trailers. "Van bodies" should be interpreted as including also separable van sized containers.

7. It is assumed that the average size of trailer will increase. 1960 figure is based on estimated weight of an all aluminum van body (2,000–2,500 lb.).

TABLE A5–13. Lead, Zinc, Copper, and Rubber Requirements for Motor Vehicles

	1955	1956	1957	1958	1959	1960		1970	1980	1990	2000
Lead:[1]											
Motor vehicle stock[2]	58.3	62.5	64.9	66.9	68.1	70.9	L	95.2	131.6	174.3	228.2
(millions)							M	99.7	143.2	200.8	289.2
							H	110.0	173.7	276.7	448.4
Replacement batteries (sold)[3]							L	22.8	19.7	17.4	13.7
(millions)	25.8	25.0	25.9	25.3	27.5	26.3	M	30.9	35.8	42.2	49.2
							H	37.4	52.1	77.5	116.6
Per cent of stock[4]							L	24	15	10	6
	44.2	40.0	39.9	37.8	40.4	37.1	M	31	25	21	17
							H	34	30	28	26
Motor vehicle output[5]							L	9.5	12.0	14.9	18.6
(millions)	9.2	6.9	7.2	5.1	6.7	7.9	M	10.4	14.8	20.8	30.4
							H	12.8	21.7	38.4	71.2
Tractor production[6] (millions)	.38	.27	.27	.26	.30	.18	L	.22	.21	.23	.25
							M	.32	.38	.45	.53
							H	.41	.56	.74	.94
Total automotive battery							L	32.5	31.9	32.5	32.5
production[7] (millions)	35.8	32.6	33.7	30.9	34.7	34.7	M	41.6	51.0	63.5	80.1
							H	50.6	74.4	116.6	188.7
Lead content of automotive							L	263	233	214	193
batteries[8] (thous. tons)	342	329	326	283	332	313	M	374	459	572	721
							H	481	744	1,224	2,076
Pounds per battery[9]							L	16.2	14.6	13.2	11.9
	19.1	20.2	19.3	18.3	19.1	18.0	M	18.0	18.0	18.0	18.0
							H	19.0	20.0	21.0	22.0
Zinc:[10]							L	238	300	372	465
Aggregate use (thous. tons)	260	220	224	132	175	190	M	260	370	520	760
							H	320	542	960	1,780
Pounds per motor vehicle	57	64	62	52	52	48		50	50	50	50
Copper:[11]							L	171	192	209	242
Aggregate use (thous. tons)	237	175	174	125	172	159	M	187	237	291	395
							H	230	347	538	926
Pounds per vehicle	52	51	48	49	51	40		36	32	28	26

(Cont'd on p. 658)

1. In addition to the lead for batteries which is shown here, lead is also used, importantly, in solder for motor vehicle radiators. The latter, however, is only about 1% of total lead consumption and is not likely to grow very much, if at all, in relative importance.

2. Automobile stock, from Tables A5–1 and 2, and truck stock, from Table A5–10, supplemented, for 1955–56, by data from *Automobile Facts and Figures*.

3. Historical data are from Association of American Battery Manufacturers, reported in *Automobile Facts and Figures*, 1961, and *Minerals Yearbook*, 1960. Projections based on relationship to stock, shown on following line.

4. All three projections assume a declining trend (lengthening average battery life), the Medium being at the approximate 1955–60 rate. The Low projection, while not out of line with recent trends, is presumed possible only if there is significant substitution of nickel-cadmium or other longer lasting types of storage batteries for the lead-acid type.

5. Automobile production, from Tables A5–1 and 11, and truck production, from Table A5–10, supplemented, for 1955–56, by data from *Motor Truck Facts*. Bus production omitted, but this is less than 1% of total vehicle production.

6. Historical data, which include exports and exclude garden tractors, are from U.S. Bureau of the Census, *Statistical Abstract*, 1959 and 1960, Tables 1118 and 1130, respectively, and from Bureau of the Census, Current Industrial Reports,

Series M35S. Projections are proportional to domestic investment in agricultural machinery and equipment, Table A6–4.

7. Sum of replacement batteries and of motor vehicle and tractor output (equals original equipment batteries), plus (for historical data only) a small number of exported batteries, as reported in source given in footnote 8. Does not, therefore, include miscellaneous industrial batteries or batteries used in battery driven equipment. For purposes of these projections, future automotive vehicles are assumed to continue to use storage batteries.

8. Historical figures are Bureau of Mines data on consumption of lead by the storage battery industry, less an estimated amount going into non-automotive batteries, as estimated by K. W. Green in *Daily Metal Reporter*, Jan. 15, 1960, Part II, p. 71, and Jan. 13, 1961, Part II, p. 106. Projections are calculated from coefficients, which follow, of lead use per battery. The historical, and hence projected, consumption data and coefficients are probably slightly understated.

9. Medium projection assumes that there will be a continuing trend toward higher voltage batteries, offset, so far as lead use is concerned, by more economical use of lead and by increased use of other battery materials. Low assumes a faster displacement of lead, and High, little or no displacement.

10. Data for 1955–60 represent tabulations by American

Table A5–13 (cont'd)

	1955	1956	1957	1958	1959	1960		1970	1980	1990	2000
Rubber for tires, etc.:[12]											
Automobile stocks[2] (millions)	48.5	52.2	54.2	55.9	56.9	59.3	L	81.0	113.7	151.7	199.4
							M	83.3	120.2	168.6	243.5
							H	91.0	143.6	229.3	372.2
Auto replacement tires shipped[13] (millions)	50.2	53.2	56.6	61.6	66.8	68.5	L	72.9	79.6	75.8	79.8
							M	91.6	120.2	151.7	194.8
							H	118.3	201.0	344.0	595.5
Tires per auto[14]	1.04	1.02	1.04	1.10	1.17	1.16	L	.90	.70	.50	.40
							M	1.10	1.00	.90	.80
							H	1.30	1.40	1.50	1.60
Stock of trucks[2] (millions)	9.8	10.3	10.7	11.0	11.2	11.6	L	14.2	17.9	22.6	28.8
							M	16.4	23.0	32.2	45.7
							H	19.0	30.1	47.4	76.2
Truck and bus replacement tires[13] (millions)	9.1	8.9	8.5	9.2	10.0	9.5	L	12.8	16.1	20.3	25.9
							M	14.8	20.7	29.0	41.1
							H	17.1	27.1	42.7	68.6
Tires per truck[15]	.93	.86	.79	.84	.89	.82		.9	.9	.9	.9
Automobile production[5] (millions)	7.9	5.8	6.1	4.3	5.6	6.7	L	8.3	10.5	13.0	16.1
							M	8.8	12.6	17.7	25.9
							H	10.7	18.4	33.1	62.6
Original equipment tires for autos[13] (millions)	42.6	30.9	32.7	23.4	29.8	36.0	L	40.7	49.4	58.5	69.2
							M	46.6	64.3	86.7	121.7
							H	58.8	101.2	182.0	344.3
Tires per auto[16]	5.4	5.3	5.4	5.4	5.3	5.3	L	4.9	4.7	4.5	4.3
							M	5.3	5.1	4.9	4.7
							H	5.5	5.5	5.5	5.5
Truck production[5] (millions)	1.2	1.1	1.1	.9	1.1	1.2	L	1.2	1.5	1.9	2.5
							M	1.6	2.2	3.1	4.5
							H	2.1	3.3	5.3	8.6
Original equipment tires for trucks and buses[13] (millions)	4.8	4.5	4.0	3.4	4.4	4.0	L	4.8	6.0	7.6	10.0
							M	6.4	8.8	12.4	18.0
							H	8.4	13.2	21.2	34.4
Tires per truck[15]	4.0	4.1	3.6	3.8	4.0	3.3		4.0	4.0	4.0	4.0
Total automotive tires[17] (millions)	108.5	99.3	103.6	98.9	112.5	119.7	L	133.3	153.5	164.8	187.9
							M	162.0	217.4	284.3	381.6
							H	205.8	348.0	599.3	1,059.5
Per cent for user-operated passenger vehicles	85.5	84.7	86.2	85.9	85.9	87.3	L	85.2	84.0	81.5	79.3
							M	85.3	84.9	83.9	82.9
							H	86.1	86.8	87.8	88.7
Rubber used in tires[18] (mil. long tons)	1.13	1.04	1.07	1.00	1.18	1.14	L	1.40	1.61	1.73	1.97
							M	1.70	2.28	2.99	4.01
							H	2.16	3.65	6.29	11.12
Tons per thousand tires[19]	10.4	10.5	10.3	10.1	10.5	9.5		10.5	10.5	10.5	10.5

Die Casting Institute of shipments of zinc castings by custom shops to the automotive industry, plus estimates, by the ADCI, of the proportion of "captive" die casting zinc use which is for the automotive industry. The estimates thus include a small amount of alloying material, but this may be counterbalanced by automotive use of zinc for purposes other than die casting. While the latter has been small or negligible in the past, the possible future use of zinc for automobile undercoatings may increase its importance.

The projection of unit use continues approximately the present level of utilization, on the assumption that decreased use of zinc for present die casting applications will probably be compensated by the appearance of new die casting applications, by the use of zinc for undercoating, and by the possible use of galvanized sheet for bodies. Since a more copious use of zinc is assumed to be associated with larger (and fewer) cars, and vice versa, the Medium projection is also taken as the Low consistent with Low automotive production and the high consistent with High.

11. Historical data are for shipments of copper mill products, adjusted to eliminate returned scrap (Table A16–39). The projection of unit use assumes a decline in copper use as the result of replacement by aluminum in radiators as well as of the complete elimination of radiators, partly compensated by increased use of copper in wiring, air conditioners, and such new applications as the plating of steel parts. As with zinc, the larger use is assumed to be associated with larger and fewer cars, and vice versa, so that the

Table A5–13 (cont'd)

one projection is also taken as the low consistent with Low automotive production and the high consistent with High.

12. The calculation is essentially in terms of casings, but allowance is made in the rubber-per-tire coefficient for average weight of tubes used (currently about 1/3 as many as tires) and for tire repair materials (camelback, etc., currently amounting to perhaps 1/10 the volume of rubber in tires). Rubber used elsewhere in the automobile has not been analyzed.

13. Historical data from Rubber Manufacturers Association, reported in *Automobile Facts and Figures*, 1961 ed. Projections calculated from coefficients which follow.

14. Apparent recent upward trend is assumed due to earlier replacement of tires owing to lower relative prices and to increased utilization of special purpose (snow) tires. This trend is assumed, in the Medium projection, to be nearing its peak and to be more than counterbalanced by (in the nearer future) longer tire life and (more distantly) some use of "tireless" vehicles. For the Low, the two latter factors are assumed to have even greater importance, and for the High, the trend toward higher replacement rates and use of special purpose changeovers is assumed to be the dominant one. Annual mileage per vehicle (see Table A5–15) is assumed to remain relatively unchanged.

15. The number of buses is small enough in relation to the number of trucks that no significant error is introduced by relating truck and bus tires to trucks alone. Replacement projection assumes that increased size of trucks (meaning more wheels) will be compensated by longer tire life. The low historical (and hence projected) ratio of original equipment tires to trucks is assumed due to the export of some trucks without tires and/or to the separate accounting for exported-truck tires so that they show up as exports rather than production for domestic use. (An export adjustment is made in the tire total; see footnote 17.)

16. Projections (except High) assume sooner (Low) or later (Medium) introduction of "tireless" vehicles, elimination of spares, and some diminution in the proportion of original equipment tires destined for vehicles for export.

17. Projections include an adjustment of +1.6% for net exports. Historical exports from source cited in footnote 13.

18. Historical data from U.S. Department of Commerce, Current Industrial Reports, *Rubber*, No. M30A (60)–11. Projections calculated from coefficients which follow.

19. Average size of tire (or tire-tube combination) assumed to remain unchanged, with larger truck and bus tires being compensated by smaller automobile tires and increasing percentage of tubeless tires.

TABLE A5–14. Historical Data on Vehicle Mileage and Fuel Requirements for Motor Vehicles

	Automobiles					Trucks					Buses		
	Total stock Jan. 1 [1] (millions)	Vehicle miles [2] (billions)	Miles per vehicle (thousands)	Fuel consumption [3] (bil. gal.)	Miles per gal.	Total stock Jan. 1 [4] (millions)	Vehicle miles [2] (billions)	Miles per vehicle (thousands)	Fuel consumption [3] (bil. gal.)	Miles per gal.	Vehicle miles [2]	Fuel consumption [3] (bil. gal.)	Miles per gal.
1936	22.6	209	9.25	13.65	15.3	3.9	41	10.5	4.00	10.2	2.4	.38	6.3
1937	24.2	223	9.21	14.62	15.3	4.3	44	10.2	4.36	10.1	2.5	.40	6.2
1938	25.5	224	8.78	14.66	15.3	4.5	44	9.8	4.46	9.9	2.5	.41	6.1
1939	25.3	236	9.33	15.41	15.3	4.5	47	10.4	4.81	9.8	2.6	.41	6.3
1940	26.2	250	9.54	16.32	15.3	4.7	50	10.6	5.16	9.7	2.7	.44	6.1
1941	27.5	276	10.04	18.03	15.3	4.9	55	11.2	5.75	9.6	2.8	.47	6.0
1942	29.6	219	7.40	14.43	15.2	5.2	46	8.8	4.89	9.4	3.1	.55	5.6
1943	28.0	163	5.82	10.82	15.1	4.9	42	8.6	4.53	9.3	3.4	.60	5.7
1944	26.0	167	6.42	11.11	15.0	4.7	42	8.9	4.58	9.2	3.8	.70	5.4
1945	25.6	200	7.81	13.32	15.0	4.8	46	9.6	5.06	9.1	3.8	.70	5.4
1946	25.8	281	10.89	18.76	15.0	5.1	56	11.0	6.07	9.2	4.1	.74	5.5
1947	28.2	300	10.64	20.09	14.9	6.0	66	11.0	7.24	9.1	4.3	.78	5.5
1948	30.8	320	10.39	21.37	15.0	6.8	74	10.9	8.19	9.0	4.3	.78	5.5
1949	33.4	341	10.21	n.a.	n.a.	7.5	79	10.5	n.a.	n.a.	4.3	n.a.	n.a.
1950	36.5	364	9.97	"	"	8.0	91	11.4	"	"	4.1	"	"
1951	40.3	392	9.73	"	"	8.6	95	11.0	"	"	4.1	"	"
1952	42.7	410	9.60	"	"	9.0	99	11.0	"	"	4.3	"	"
1953	43.8	435	9.93	"	"	9.2	105	11.4	"	"	4.4	"	"
1954	46.5	451	9.70	30.92	14.6	9.6	106	11.0	12.54	8.4	4.4	.76	5.8
1955	48.5	488	10.06	33.55	14.5	9.8	111	11.3	13.31	8.3	4.5	.77	5.8
1956	52.2	507	9.71	35.33	14.4	10.3	116	11.3	13.98	8.3	4.6	.80	5.8
1957	54.2	529	9.76	36.77	14.4	10.7	113	10.6	14.27	7.9	4.4	.82	5.4
1958	55.9	545	9.75	38.10	14.3	11.0	115	10.4	14.51	7.9	4.3	.81	5.3
1959	56.9	571	10.04	39.9	14.3	11.2	123	11.0	15.4	8.0	4.3	.82	5.2
1960	59.3	588	9.92	41.2	14.3	11.6	126	10.9	15.9	7.9	4.4	.83	5.3

1. From Table A5–1.

2. *Automobile Facts and Figures*, 1961 ed., p. 49, and for 1936–39, *Highway Statistics: Summary to 1955*, p. 40; 1959–60 directly from Bureau of Public Roads. (Data for 1957 and following years are not strictly comparable with those of previous years, owing to revision of estimated traffic distribution between trucks and other vehicles.)

3. *Highway Statistics: Summary to 1955*, p. 40; and for 1956–58, Table VM–1, published in *Highway Statistics: 1956* and *1958*; 1959–60 directly from Bureau of Public Roads.

4. *Highway Statistics: Summary to 1955*, p. 18; and for 1957–60, Table MV–9, *Highway Statistics* and separate releases.

TABLE A5–15. Projected Vehicle Mileage and Fuel Requirements for Motor Vehicles

	1940	1945	1950	1955	1960		1970	1980	1990	2000
Passenger cars:										
						L	8.10	113.7	151.7	199.4
Total stock (millions)[1]	26.2	25.6	36.5	48.5	59.3	M	83.3	120.2	168.6	243.5
						H	91.0	143.6	229.3	372.2
Miles per vehicle[2] (thousands)	9.5	7.8	10.0	10.1	9.9		9.8	9.8	9.8	9.8
						L	794	1,114	1,487	1,954
Passenger-car-miles (billions)	250	200	364	488	588	M	816	1,178	1,652	2,386
						H	892	1,407	2,247	3,648
Miles per gallon[3]	15.3	15.0	n.a.	14.5	14.3		14.5	14.5	14.5	14.5
Fuel consumption:										
						L	54.8	76.8	102.6	134.8
Gallons (billions)[4]	16.3	13.3	n.a.	33.5	41.2	M	56.3	81.2	113.9	164.6
						H	61.5	97.0	155.0	251.6
						L	1,305	1,829	2,443	3,210
Barrels (millions)	388	317	n.a.	798	981	M	1,340	1,933	2,712	3,919
						H	1,464	2,310	3,691	5,991
Trucks:										
						L	14.2	17.9	22.6	28.8
Total stock (millions)[5]	4.7	4.8	8.0	9.8	11.6	M	16.4	23.0	32.2	45.7
						H	19.0	30.1	47.4	76.2
						L	155	195	246	314
Truck-miles (billions)[6]	50	46	91	111	126	M	179	251	351	498
						H	207	328	517	831
Miles per gallon[3]	9.7	9.1	n.a.	8.3	7.9		7.3	6.9	6.5	6.5
Fuel consumption:										
						L	21.2	28.3	37.8	48.3
Gallons (billions)[4]	5.16	5.06	n.a.	13.3	15.9	M	24.5	36.4	54.0	76.6
						H	28.4	47.5	79.5	127.8
						L	505	674	900	1,150
Barrels (millions)	123	120	n.a.	317	379	M	583	867	1,286	1,824
						H	676	1,131	1,893	3,043
Buses:										
						L	91.0	87.6	86.7	85.6
Index of growth[7] (1960 = 100)	–	–	–	–	100	M	108.1	120.5	137.3	146.9
						H	127.4	162.2	210.6	272.2
						L	77.5	66.7	56.4	52.5
Interurban buses[8]	–	–	–	–	100	M	93.6	95.1	94.1	89.2
						H	109.3	123.0	145.6	180.4
						L	75.8	70.5	63.2	58.9
Local commercial buses[9]	–	–	–	–	100	M	100.0	109.5	117.9	123.2
						H	125.3	158.9	202.1	268.4
						L	134.7	143.3	165.3	173.3
School buses[10]	–	–	–	–	100	M	140.0	170.7	224.0	258.7
						H	152.7	215.2	304.0	389.3
						L	4.0	3.9	3.8	3.8
Bus-miles (billions)[11]	2.7	3.8	4.1	4.5	4.4	M	4.8	5.3	6.0	6.5
						H	5.6	7.1	9.3	12.0
Fuel consumption:										
						L	.76	.73	.72	.71
Gallons (billions)[12]	.44	.70	n.a.	.77	.83	M	.90	1.00	1.14	1.22
						H	1.06	1.35	1.75	2.26
						L	18.1	17.4	17.1	16.9
Barrels (millions)	10.5	16.7	n.a.	18.3	19.8	M	21.4	23.8	27.1	29.0
						H	25.2	32.1	41.7	53.8
Total fuel consumption:						L	1.83	2.52	3.36	4.38
(bil. bbl.)	.52	.45	n.a.	1.13	1.38	M	1.94	2.82	4.02	5.77
						H	2.16	3.47	5.63	9.09

Table A5–15 (cont'd)

1. From Tables A5–1 and A5–2.

2. Historical data from Table A5–14. Projected level assumes (for Medium) that the recent decline in miles per vehicle has about reached its limit. This level is also used as a "low" associated with the Low stock of automobiles and a "high" associated with the High stock, since there is compensation between the two factors.

3. Historical data from Table A5–14. For factors governing selection of assumed efficiency level, see Chapter 5, pp. 146–48. As with mileage, the figures shown represent not only the Medium, but High efficiency associated with Low mileage and Low efficiency associated with High mileage.

4. Historical data from Table A5–14. Projections calculated from preceding two lines.

5. From Table A5–10—total single units and combinations. Historical data from Table A5–14.

6. Stock multiplied by current level of 10,900 miles per truck. Historical data from Table A5–14.

7. The weights used in combining indexes are: interurban buses, 30; local commercial buses, 45; school buses, 25. These are based on approximate 1958 contribution to total fuel consumption.

8. Based on total passenger-miles by interurban bus, from Table A5–7.

9. Based on local transportation passenger volume, from Table A5–7.

10. Based on number of pupils transported, from Table A5–7.

11. Growth index multiplied by 4.4 billion miles (1960 level). Historical data from Table A5–14. (Mileage reached a peak in 1956 and then declined.)

12. Growth index multiplied by 830 million gallons, which is 1960 consumption. Future mileage per gallon assumed unchanged. Historical data from Table A5–14.

TABLE A5–16. Historical Data on Railway Rolling Stock and Use of Steel for Railroads

	1947	1948	1949	1950	1951	1952	1953	1954	1955	1956	1957	1958	1959	1960
Rail freight carried[1] (bil. ton-miles)	664	647	535	597	655	623	614	557	631	656	626	559	582	579
Rolling stock (thousands):														
Freight cars (domestic):														
Number in use, beginning of year[2]	2,055	2,050	2,076	2,070	2,033	2,071	2,082	2,099	2,059	2,018	2,031	2,075	2,052	2,000
Ton-miles per car (thousands)	323	316	258	288	322	301	295	265	306	325	308	269	284	290
Net additions to stock	-5	26	-6	-37	38	11	17	-40	-41	13	44	-23	-52	-15
New cars delivered[3]	69	113	93	44	96	78	81	36	38	67	100	43	38	57
Apparent retirements	74	87	99	81	58	67	64	76	79	54	55	66	90	72
Per cent of cars in use	3.60	4.24	4.77	3.91	2.85	3.24	3.07	3.62	3.84	2.68	2.71	3.18	4.38	3.60
Other rolling stock built:														
Passenger train cars[4]	1	1	1	1	*	*	*	*	1	*	1	*	*	*
Locomotives[5]	1	2	3	3	4	3	2	1	1	1	1	*	1	1
Freight cars exported[6]	28	2	3	*	*	2	3	3	4	*	1	2	1	*
Total	30	5	7	4	4	5	5	4	6	1	3	2	2	1
Per cent of new freight cars (domestic)	43.48	4.42	7.53	9.09	4.17	6.41	6.17	11.11	15.79	1.49	3.03	4.65	5.26	1.75
Total new cars:	99	118	100	48	100	83	86	40	44	68	102	45	40	58
Estimated steel content														
Per car[7] (tons)	21.2	20.3	21.0	22.0	21.7	22.0	24.1	23.1	24.5	21.7	24.8	24.5	25.7	26.0
Total (thous. tons)	2,099	2,395	2,100	1,056	2,170	1,826	2,073	924	1,078	1,476	2,530	1,102	1,028	1,508
Cf: Total steel shipments for car building[8]	2,713	3,173	1,775	2,029	3,477	2,240	2,471	1,055	1,901	2,605	2,703	867	1,572	1,763
Railroad trackage:														
Steel used (rail, etc., shipments)[8] (thous. tons)	2,099	1,997	1,829	2,222	2,257	1,711	2,278	1,379	1,580	1,590	1,406	584	763	723
Per million ton-miles of freight carried (tons)	3.16	3.09	3.42	3.72	3.45	2.75	3.71	2.48	2.50	2.42	2.25	1.04	1.31	1.25
Misc. maintenance and construction:														
Steel used[8] (thous. tons)	134	97	85	124	127	97	87	83	75	66	71	43	40	51
Total steel consumed[9] (thous. tons)	4,332	4,489	4,014	3,402	4,554	3,634	4,438	2,386	2,733	3,132	4,007	1,729	1,831	2,282
Cf: Net shipments for railroads[10] (mil. tons)	5.4	5.8	3.8	4.7	6.4	4.3	5.1	2.6	3.7	4.5	4.3	1.6	2.6	2.8
Ratio: Net shipments to consumption as calculated above[11]	1.25	1.29	.95	1.38	1.40	1.18	1.15	1.09	1.35	1.44	1.07	.92	1.42	1.23

Table A5–16 (cont'd)

* Negligible.

1. From Table A5–8.
2. From American Railway Car Institute, *Railroad Car Facts, 1960* (Oct. 1961), p. 1. Data are shown therein as of the preceding year, but apply to the year-end.
3. *Ibid.*, "cars built."
4. *Ibid.*, p. 55.
5. Data from Association of American Railroads, *Railroad Transportation—A Statistical Record, 1921–1957*, p. 11, and unpublished data.
6. American Railway Car Institute, *op. cit.*, p. 13.
7. Average total weight of newly installed freight cars on Class I railroads, less an arbitrary 10% to allow for wood and other materials. Data from source cited in footnote 2.
8. American Iron and Steel Institute, *Annual Statistical Report, 1960*, pp. 94–95. Does not include steel redistributed through warehouses.

9. An approximation based on estimated content of cars, the assumption that shipments are a good measure of trackage use (i.e., that there is little or no scrap loss), and that "warehouse" steel used by railroads is negligible. In addition to the amounts shown, very small quantities of steel shipped for local transit requirements are classified by the AISI as being for railroad use.

10. From Table A16-4. The differences between this and the preceding series should be comprised by differences in timing (equivalent to fluctuations in inventory in pipeline); irrecoverable losses of metal during transport, fabrication, and manufacture; statistical error in the estimation of scrap generation; and errors or differences in the assignment of shipments or consumption to end-uses.

11. 1947–60 average: 1.22.

TABLE A5–17. Projected Railway Rolling Stock and Use of Steel for Railroads[1]

	1950	1955	1960		1970	1980	1990	2000
Rail freight carried[2] (bil. ton-miles)	597	631	579	L	592	611	653	755
				M	738	912	1,179	1,593
				H	929	1,384	2,058	3,192
Rolling stock (thousands):								
Freight cars (domestic):								
Ton-miles per car[3]	288	306	290	L	300	300	300	300
				M	320	340	360	380
				H	340	380	420	460
Number in use[3]	2,070	2,059	2,000	L	1,973	2,037	2,177	2,517
				M	2,306	2,682	3,275	4,192
				H	2,732	3,642	4,900	6,939
Net additions to stock[4]	−37	−41	−15	L	8	8	24	46
				M	33	44	77	110
				H	75	106	168	233
Retirements[5]	81	79	72	L	59	61	65	76
				M	92	107	131	168
				H	137	182	245	347
New cars required	44	38	57	L	67	69	89	122
				M	125	151	208	278
				H	212	288	413	580
Total new rolling stock[6]	48	44	58	L	71	73	95	130
				M	133	160	221	295
				H	225	306	439	616
Steel per car[7] (tons)	22.0	24.5	26.0		30.3	34.7	39.1	43.5
Total steel for rolling stock (mil. tons)	1.06	1.08	1.51	L	2.15	2.53	3.71	5.37
				M	4.03	5.55	8.64	12.18
				H	6.82	10.62	17.16	25.44
Railroad trackage:								
Steel per million ton-miles[8] (tons)	3.72	2.50	1.25		.65	.55	.50	.48
Steel used (mil. tons)	2.22	1.58	.72	L	.38	.34	.33	.36
				M	.48	.50	.59	.76
				H	.60	.76	1.03	1.53
Steel for maintenance[9] (mil. tons)	.12	.08	.05	L	.07	.07	.08	.09
				M	.09	.11	.14	.19
				H	.11	.17	.25	.38
Total steel consumed (mil. tons)	3.4	2.7	2.3	L	2.6	2.9	4.1	5.8
				M	4.6	6.2	9.4	13.1
				H	7.5	11.6	18.4	27.4

1. Historical data are from Table A5–16.
2. From Table A5–9.
3. Except in Low, higher ton-mileage per car per year is assumed to accompany the increasing size of cars. Moreover, relatively higher freight traffic is assumed to be accompanied by relatively greater utilization of capacity. (Low ton-mileage per car associated with Low total carriage, High with High.)
4. Average of preceding and following five-year period (not here shown).
5. Projected at 3, 4, and 5% of stock for Low, Medium, and High, respectively, based on 1947–60 record.

6. 106.2% of domestic freight car requirements (1948–60 average).
7. Arithmetic extrapolation of 1947–60 trend. Use of other materials for freight cars (e.g., aluminum bodies) assumed to be counterbalanced by disappearance of wood and increased size of cars.
8. Judgment extrapolation, based on assumption that there is a limit to the ultimate possible economy which may be achieved.
9. Assumed to be .12 tons per million ton-miles (1947–60 average).

TABLE A5–18.   Fuel Requirements for Railroads

	1950	1952	1954	1956	1958	1960		1970	1980	1990	2000
Freight movement:											
							L	592	611	653	755
Intercity ton-miles[1] (billions)	597	623	557	656	559	579	M	738	912	1,179	1,593
							H	929	1,384	2,058	3,192
							L	2.87	2.85	2.92	3.23
Liquid fuel consumed[2] (bil. gal.)	3.08	3.13	2.69	2.93	2.74	2.92	M	3.65	4.42	5.61	7.42
							H	4.68	6.98	10.37	16.09
							L	4.85	4.66	4.47	4.28
Gallons per thousand ton-miles[3]	5.16	5.02	4.83	4.47	4.90	5.04	M	4.94	4.85	4.76	4.66
							H	5.04	5.04	5.04	5.04
Coal consumed[4] (mil. tons)	47.3	28.0	11.0	7.9	1.0	.03		–	–	–	–
Passenger movement: Intercity passenger-miles							L	12.1	9.9	9.0	8.0
(billions)[5]	27.5	30.0	24.7	23.8	18.8	17.2	M	14.1	13.5	14.1	18.2
							H	17.8	20.4	24.8	30.3
							L	.41	.34	.31	.27
Liquid fuel consumed[2] (bil. gal.)	1.04	1.02	.91	.84	.72	.66	M	.51	.49	.51	.66
							H	.68	.78	.94	1.15
Gallons per thousand							L	34	34	34	34
passenger-miles[6]	37.8	34.0	36.8	35.3	38.3	38.4	M	36	36	36	36
							H	38	38	38	38
Coal consumed[4] (mil. tons)	7.5	4.3	1.5	.6	.1	.005		–	–	–	–
Fuel for non-motive purposes:[7] Liquid fuel consumed[8]							L	.28	.22	.18	.14
(bil. gal.)	.44	.42	.35	.45	.34	.34	M	.40	.40	.40	.40
							H	.45	.45	.45	.45
Coal consumed[9] (mil. tons)	11.1	6.8	4.2	4.4	3.1	2.5		.6	.2	–	–
Total consumption: Liquid fuels:											
							L	3.56	3.41	3.41	3.64
Billion gallons	4.56	4.57	3.95	4.22	3.80	3.92	M	4.56	5.31	6.52	8.48
							H	5.81	8.21	11.76	17.69
							L	85	81	81	87
Million barrels	109	109	94	100	90	93	M	109	126	155	202
							H	138	195	280	421
Coal (mil. tons)	65.9	39.1	16.7	12.9	4.2	2.5		.6	.2	–	–

1. From Tables A5–8 and 9.
2. Mostly diesel, but also includes fuel oil and gasoline. Consumption for freight includes fuel used in yard switching, which is assumed to be preponderantly for freight service. Historical data from Interstate Commerce Commission Statement No. M–230 (OS–E). Projections calculated from coefficients which follow.
3. Historical data calculated. High projection assumes no change from recent level; Low assumes decline of 15% in 40 years; Medium is taken as midway between the two.
4. From ICC Statement M–230 (OS–E). Consumption tor freight includes coal used in yard switching. Future consumption assumed to be negligible, since coal burning locomotives have by now been completely eliminated from regular line service.

5. From Tables A5–6 and 7.
6. Historical data calculated. Projections assume no change from recent levels.
7. Historical data derived from ICC Statement M–230 (OS–E)—difference between "quantities of all fuel and power purchased and produced" and the quantities consumed by freight, passenger, and switching services. Projections as indicated below.
8. Medium and High both assume continuation of recent levels; Low, a decline flowing from decreased space heating requirements.
9. Judgment extrapolation of trend.

TABLE A5–19. Summary of Steel and Aluminum Requirements for Transportation

	1960		1970	1980	1990	2000
Steel (mil. tons):						
		L	8.5	9.6	12.8	13.6
In automobiles[1]	8.0	M	9.9	12.8	16.5	21.2
		H	11.8	15.9	22.5	32.8
		L	1.9	2.1	2.3	2.5
In trucks and trailers[2]	2.1	M	2.5	3.1	3.8	4.5
		H	3.3	4.7	6.4	8.6
		L	2.6	2.9	4.1	5.8
In railroads[3]	2.3	M	4.6	6.2	9.4	13.1
		H	7.5	11.6	18.4	27.4
		L	13.0	14.6	19.2	21.9
Total[4]	12.4	M	17.0	22.1	29.7	38.8
		H	22.6	32.2	47.3	68.8
		L	13.6	15.3	20.2	23.0
Adjusted total[5]	13.0	M	17.8	23.2	31.2	40.7
		H	23.7	33.8	49.7	72.2
Aluminum (mil. tons):						
		L	.52	1.00	1.58	2.37
In automobiles[1]	.20	M	.68	1.64	2.98	4.86
		H	1.18	3.30	5.21	8.12
		L	.05	.08	.12	.17
In trucks and trailers[2]	.03	M	.08	.15	.26	.42
		H	.14	.39	.62	1.07
		L	.57	1.08	1.70	2.54
Total	.23	M	.76	1.79	3.24	5.28
		H	1.32	3.69	5.83	9.19

1. From Table A5–11.
2. From Table A5–12.
3. From Table A5–17.
4. There is a slight understatement in the Lows and overstatement in the Highs, as the result of failure to take account of the compensation between railroad freight traffic and intercity trucking. The error, however, would be of very small significance in relation to total steel requirements.
5. Includes a 5% allowance for shipbuilding, aircraft, local transit, and miscellaneous transportation uses. This allowance is on the "low" side of recent averages.

TABLE A5–20. Summary of Liquid Fuel Requirements for Transportation

	1950	1955	1960		1970	1980	1990	2000
Motor vehicles[1] (bil. bbl.)	.85	1.13	1.38	L	1.83	2.52	3.36	4.38
				M	1.94	2.82	4.02	5.77
				H	2.16	3.47	5.63	9.09
Railroads[2] (bil. bbl.)	.11	.10	.09	L	.08	.08	.08	.09
				M	.11	.13	.16	.20
				H	.14	.20	.28	.42
Marine (foreign trade):								
Gross merchandise trade[3] ($ 1960 bil.)	21.7	26.3	34.0	L	46.6	63.7	86.6	119.7
				M	49.3	70.7	101.9	149.0
				H	55.6	90.4	148.7	253.4
Bunker fuel requirements[4] (bil. bbl.)	.06	.08	.08	L	.14	.19	.26	.36
				M	.15	.21	.30	.45
				H	.17	.27	.44	.76
Total liquid fuels (bil. bbl.):								
Uses specified above[5]	1.02	1.31	1.55	L	2.05	2.79	3.70	4.83
				M	2.20	3.16	4.48	6.42
				H	2.47	3.94	6.35	10.27
All transportation uses[6]	1.09	1.40	1.65	L	2.18	2.97	3.94	5.15
				M	2.34	3.37	4.77	6.84
				H	2.63	4.20	6.76	10.94

1. From Table A5–15. 1950 estimated.
2. From Table A5–18. 1955 estimated.
3. Imports plus exports, from Table A1–17.
4. Historical data as published by Foreign Trade Division, U.S. Bureau of the Census. Projections based on 1929–60 average of bunkerings per $1,000 of merchandise trade (2.99 bbl.). Includes fuel for both domestic and foreign vessels engaged in foreign trade and bunkering at U.S. ports.
5. There is a slight understatement in the lows and overstatement in the highs, as the result of failure to take account of the compensation between railroad freight traffic and intercity trucking. However, this involves only a very small part of total fuel consumption.
6. Total of specified uses raised by 6.54% (approximate present relationship) to allow for requirements for aviation, inland waterways, coastwise and intercoastal shipping, and oil pipelines. Requirements for the last three sectors (about half of the unaccounted-for balance) are closely related to total petroleum requirements (most water borne tonnage is petroleum). The specified transportation uses, in turn, are close to half of all petroleum consumption.

appendix
to
chapter
6

DURABLE GOODS

Notes

ALTHOUGH THIS section concerns itself to some extent with projections and relationships pertaining to durable goods as a whole, it would be more strictly labeled "Other Durables." Transportation durables and their materials implications have already been treated in the immediately preceding section; defense matériel, which is almost the equivalent of government durables, is treated in Chapter 9. Our interest here is in the volume of purchases and the materials content of producer and consumer purchases of hard goods other than for transportation.

Some of the details of even this restricted portion have been set in earlier parts of the study. Detailed projections of consumer durables purchases have already been made in the appendix to Chapter 1, as part of the process of distributing consumer purchases in general. And although the total of producer durables purchases is derived here, it has been reconciled with the total durables purchases of consumers and government in the tables in the appendix to Chapter 1 dealing with the gross national product. Since the considerations pertaining to the distribution of consumer purchases have been presented in Chapter 1 and its appendix, it is left for this appendix to supplement Chapter 6 only with regard to the producer durables projections (i.e., purchases in constant dollars) and to the materials evaluation of durables in general.

Because it provides the best means for integrating with the GNP projections, the basic measurement of producer durables purchases used herein has been the series developed by the National In-

come Division of the Department of Commerce on "Private Purchases of Producers' Durable Equipment." Unfortunately, since their publication in *U.S. Income and Output* (1958 supplement to *Survey of Current Business*), Tables V–5 and 6, for the years 1946–54, the series have not been brought up to date. The usefulness of this particular breakdown to the purposes of this study was such, however, that the extension of the series to 1960 was estimated, as indicated in footnote 1 to Table A6–2. The series were also aggregated into more summary categories, since the amounts involved in some of the detail were not great enough to warrant separate projection.

The full procedure utilized for obtaining the 1955–60 estimates is involved and has not been reproduced. It was carried out with the full *Income and Output* detail, aggregation being postponed until the end. Each of the categories was first estimated in current dollars, using the 1954 *Income and Output* value as a benchmark and extending the series as indicated in Table A6–2, footnote 1. The implicit price deflators, shown in *Income and Output*, Table VII–15, were extended on the basis of Bureau of Labor Statistics wholesale price indexes. The deflated series were totaled, then adjusted slightly so that the total would conform to the directly deflated producer durables series as given in Table A1–8.

It would have been perfectly possible, in projecting these series, to relate them directly to such parameters as GNP, goods output, etc. To have done so, however, would have obscured certain details of the interrelationship between equipment, plant, total investment, and output; it would also have deprived us of a means for the collateral projection of certain elements of construction. Hence, a prior analysis and projection was made (Tables A6–1 and 3) of industry-by-industry "investment" (plant and equipment expenditures) in relation to an output measure for each industry. Thus, for example, instead of electrical machinery purchases' being related directly to, say, output of public utilities, they were related to the investment projection for public utilities and communication combined, which was in turn a composite of the investment projection for public utilities, based on public utility activity (FRB index), and the investment projection for the communications industry, related to the GNP. Thus, in this case, two parameters were brought to bear instead of one. Similarly, purchases of industrial machinery could have been related directly to goods output. But by relating them first to manufacturing investment and then by building up the latter from components related separately to durable goods output and to non-durable goods output, we have exposed some of the underlying relationships in a way that better enabled us to apply judgment.

No attempt was made to utilize, except for general background, any of the copious research that has been done regarding the relationships between gross and net investment, investment and capital stock, capital stock and output, etc., on the assumption that such research has still not been definitive enough and specific enough to be applied to these kinds of projections. Such general findings as the recently declining relationships of plant to equipment were taken cognizance of, however, and the projections were fashioned on the basis of hypotheses as to why such trends should have taken place. It is recognized that there is no general agreement as to the continuation of such trends, and the ranges in the projected relationships reflect the uncertainty. We have proceeded on the general bias, however, that total investment in relation to output would, in the aggregate, tend to remain fairly stable and that the equipment portion of investment would tend, depending upon the industry, either to remain at its present proportion of the whole or to increase. One exception to the former hypothesis is in the area of durable goods output, which we feel may increase a little faster than the investment needed to produce it. The bias toward a possibly continuing increase in equipment/plant ratios is based on the increasing complexity of productive equipment in relation to the buildings in which such equipment is housed. Since for some industries "plant" and "equipment"

are virtually synonymous, but their installation is statistically classified mostly as "plant," this overall conclusion needs to be duly tempered.

The historical data and relationships on which the projections of plant and equipment expenditures are based are shown in Table A6–1, the projections themselves in Table A6–3. Table A6–5 shows the relationships which were used to derive projected durable goods purchases, which are in turn summarized in Table A6–4.

Tables A6–6 to 8 convert the non-transportation, non-government durables to raw materials, so far as these are quantitatively important and there is any statistical basis for derivation. This includes the metals for these durables in general and wood for furniture and fixtures. The statistical basis does not exist for determining the plastics content of durables output or for relating plastics to the other materials which they may displace; however, some relation between plastics and durables is drawn in Table A17–1.

Historical data on unit metal inputs are shown in Table A6–6. For none of these inputs is the derivation on a "technical coefficient" basis, as in the case, for example, of iron and steel and aluminum in automobiles (Table A5–11). The relationships have been derived, rather, on the "economic coefficient" basis of distributing the shipments of the various metals to end-uses and adjusting to eliminate the circulating industrial scrap generated in fabrication (appendix to Chapter 16). We also chose to confine the analysis to producer durables as a whole and consumer durables as a whole, despite the fact that this limited the possibilities for evaluation of substitution among the individual metals. The reason for this choice was a combination of the statistical difficulty in arriving at more specific input-output relationships for some of the metals and, more importantly, the fact that the non-transportation durables consumption as a proportion of the total consumption of any of the principal metals is not great enough to warrant further precision.

The basic method of projection was to examine the historical trend in input per unit value of output (Table A6–6) and to project this (Table A6–7) on a judgment basis. Only a single set of coefficients was used for each such relationship; this is to be interpreted as representing not only the judgment of what is most probable in each case but also of what is a reasonably probable Low unit input given the Low end-product projection and a reasonably probable High unit input given the High end-product projection. In general, the coefficients have been permitted to decline, in line with the considerations set forth in the text. As a crude measure of the inter-metal substitutions implicit in the coefficients, the various metals were converted into steel equivalents on a specific gravity basis and a calculation made of the resultant percentage distribution. The latter, as it worked out, appeared consistent with presumed technological trends toward the substitution of nonferrous for ferrous metals in consumer products. The absence of a similar trend in producer durables—in fact, a proportional increase in steel mill products—is more unexpected, but may plausibly be explained in terms of the increasing utilization of stainless and other alloy steels in the increasing number of applications where high temperature strength or strength combined with noncorrosiveness are important. It is also to be remembered that sheer mass is frequently a requirement in industrial and related equipment, and that in such cases iron and steel provide a specific gravity/strength/price combination which is superior to that of other materials.

In both the historical relationships and the projections, one element, of possibly substantial significance, must be subsumed among the "statistical errors." This is the matter of maintenance and repair parts, whose annual value may come to one-quarter or more of the value of expenditures on new producers' equipment. It is to be suspected that a good proportion of these do not get recorded as purchases of investment goods (producer durables) but are included among the other current business expenditures represented in the National Income Accounts by the value of other end-products. Our procedure of distributing all metal shipments by end-use insures that in one way or another all of the historical metal use gets accounted for. To the extent, however, that there are future shifts between the relative replacement parts content and the end-product content of our various producer durable categories, not already reflected in histori-

cal trends, the input-output ratios may be in error. They may also be in error by virtue of shifts in relative assignment of such parts (for National Accounts purposes) as between the analogous producer durables and the end-products, whatever they may be, of the corresponding purchasing industries.

Table A6–8, finally, converts furniture and fixture purchases, by consumers and producers combined, into equivalent lumber. It is assumed that the unit input of lumber cannot rise and that, more likely, the continued substitution of metal and plastics will prolong the historical decline. It is also assumed that the unit use of lumber will be all the higher the higher the total output of furniture and fixtures; but the wide range in possible utilization that results is more a consequence of the range in furniture and fixture projections than of the range in unit lumber inputs.

LIST OF TABLES

TABLE A6–1. Historical Data on New Plant and Equipment Expenditures, by Industry[1]

(Billion 1960 dollars)

	1939	1945	1946	1947	1948	1949	1950	1951	1952	1953	1954	1955	1956	1957	1958	1959	1960
Private expenditures on new plant and equipment[2]	17.0	21.3	31.8	39.0	41.4	37.6	40.5	42.9	42.6	44.5	42.8	46.5	50.0	50.0	41.6	43.9	47.1
Business (SEC/OBE basis)[3]	14.9	17.8	27.8	32.9	32.3	27.5	28.7	32.7	33.4	34.9	32.7	33.9	38.9	38.9	31.3	32.6	35.7
Agriculture[4]	1.9	2.1	3.4	5.1	6.0	6.3	6.1	6.1	5.8	5.5	4.9	4.8	4.2	4.1	4.4	4.5	4.1
Other[5]	.2	1.4	.6	1.0	3.1	3.8	5.7	4.1	3.4	4.1	5.2	7.8	6.9	7.0	5.9	6.8	7.3
Business plant and equipment expenditures:[3]																	
Manufacturing	5.26	8.17	12.69	13.90	13.39	10.18	10.43	13.86	14.65	14.66	13.44	13.52	16.61	16.80	11.74	12.11	14.48
Durables	2.06	3.26	5.82	5.44	5.11	3.69	4.37	6.60	7.07	6.96	6.20	6.43	8.47	8.44	5.62	5.79	7.18
Non-durables	3.22	4.91	6.87	8.46	8.29	6.49	6.07	7.26	7.58	7.71	7.24	7.10	8.14	8.36	6.12	6.31	7.30
Mining	.89	.78	.80	1.10	1.29	1.13	.98	1.19	1.24	1.21	1.19	1.13	1.38	1.31	.97	.99	.99
Transportation	1.73	2.30	2.81	3.49	3.82	3.19	3.24	3.79	3.65	3.54	2.88	2.98	3.27	3.34	2.31	2.95	2.97
Public utilities[6]	1.41	1.03	1.48	2.46	3.73	4.45	4.61	4.68	4.90	5.61	5.14	5.09	5.44	6.53	6.25	5.69	5.68
Communications[7]	5.64 }	5.54 }	1.53	2.23	2.55	1.88	1.54	1.68	1.94	2.08	2.09	2.34	2.98	3.19	2.69	2.68	3.13
Commercial and other[8]	{ 5.64	5.54 }	8.44	9.73	7.56	6.64	7.90	7.56	7.00	7.77	7.93	8.85	9.29	7.76	7.39	8.23	8.44
Ratios:[9]																	
Total exp./private GNP	8.8	7.3	11.3	13.4	13.7	12.5	12.3	12.3	11.8	11.7	11.5	11.5	12.1	11.8	10.0	9.9	10.3
Agriculture exp./farm product	11.2	12.1	19.3	31.5	32.4	35.8	33.0	35.3	32.2	29.4	25.1	23.4	20.9	20.7	22.0	22.6	19.7
Durables exp./durable goods output	7.2	3.7	9.6	8.6	8.1	6.2	5.9	7.7	8.1	7.4	7.5	6.8	8.7	8.6	6.8	6.1	7.4
Non-durables exp./non-durables output	3.9	4.1	5.7	7.3	6.8	5.4	5.0	5.7	5.8	5.6	5.3	4.9	5.5	5.6	4.1	4.0	4.5
Mining exp./total goods output	.79	.38	.44	.61	.70	.63	.50	.56	.57	.53	.54	.47	.56	.53	.42	.39	.38
Transportation exp./exp. on transportation equipment[10]	–	–	81.9	70.8	73.0	71.5	69.5	68.5	81.5	83.1	80.2	66.2	71.2	76.6	72.0	73.6	72.4
Public utilities exp./FRB public utilities index[11]	–	–	–	63.2	85.9	96.1	87.5	77.9	75.2	78.9	67.2	59.6	58.1	65.3	59.8	49.5	46.1
Communications exp./GNP		.475	.693	.763	.563	.425	.429	.477	.491	.501	.521	.649	.682	.585	.546	.620	
Commercial and other/private GNP	2.62[12]	1.50[12]	3.00	3.35	2.50	2.20	2.40	2.16	1.94	2.05	2.13	2.18	2.24	1.84	1.78	1.85	1.85
Private non-residential construction[13]	6.6	5.9	12.3	12.7	13.8	13.6	14.6	16.2	16.1	17.2	17.6	19.3	19.8	20.2	18.2	18.2	19.6
Per cent of plant & equipment exp.	38.8	27.7	38.7	32.6	33.3	36.2	36.1	37.8	37.8	38.7	41.1	41.5	39.6	40.4	43.8	41.5	41.6
Producers' durables[14]	10.3	15.5	19.6	26.4	27.7	24.1	25.8	26.7	26.5	27.4	25.3	27.4	30.3	29.9	23.6	25.9	27.5
Per cent of plant & equipment exp.	60.6	72.8	61.6	67.7	66.9	64.1	63.7	62.2	62.2	61.6	59.1	58.9	60.6	59.8	56.7	59.0	58.4
Deflators for plant & equipment (1960 = 100)[15]	36.9	48.7	53.5	62.6	68.2	70.2	71.8	78.3	79.4	81.2	82.1	84.6	90.0	95.0	97.4	99.7	100.0

1. Unless otherwise indicated, series are derived from data in current dollars from the sources cited in the footnotes that follow, and deflation is by the implicit deflator for total private plant and equipment expenditures, given below.

2. Sum of "private non-residential construction," (including farm residences) and "private purchases of producer durable equipment," in Table I-1, *U.S. Income & Output* (1958 supplement to *Survey of Current Business*) and July 1961 National Income Number of *Survey of Current Business*. This measure, which is the fixed non-residential investment portion of total private investment as shown in the National Income Accounts, differs from the SEC/OBE (Securities and Exchange Commission and Office of Business Economics, U.S. Department of Commerce) measure of total business expenditures for new plant and equipment by inclusion in the former of investment by farmers (including their homesteads), professional persons, and institutions, as well as of fixed investment charged to current account.

3. 1939–59 from *Economic Report of the President*, Jan. 1961, Table C-30, except for breakdown between "communications" and "commercial and other," which is from Table V-7, *U.S. Income and Output* and July 1961 National Income Number of *Survey of Current Business*. 1960 from July 1961 National Income Number.

4. *Economic Report*, 1961, Table C-8, except for 1960, which is from unpublished data of the Office of Business Economics. Includes all farm construction (residential and non-residential), plus farm machinery and equipment and farmers' purchases of tractors and motor vehicles.

5. Residual, which includes fixed investment by professional persons and non-profit institutions, as well as fixed investment charged to current account.

6. Gas, electricity, and water.

7. Telephone and telegraph, radio and television.

8. Trade, services, finance, and construction.

9. Per cent, unless otherwise specified. "Expenditures" (exp.) refers to the plant and equipment expenditure series above. Comparison is with the indicated output series in 1960 dollars. Latter from Table A1-6 unless otherwise indicated.

10. Transportation equipment from Table A6-2; data prior to 1946 not available. Plant and equipment expenditures for transportation are lower because the latter include the expenditures of the transportation industry alone, while the former include the expenditures of all industries for transportation (principally motor vehicle) equipment.

11. Million dollars per point of index. Federal Reserve Board index from Table A1-28. Data prior to 1947 not available.

12. Ratio based on private GNP.

13. Data in 1954 dollars (*U.S. Income and Output*, Table I-1), transposed to a 1960 base. (Includes farm dwellings.)

14. From Table A1-8.

15. Sum in current dollars (*U.S. Income and Output*, Table I-1), divided by sum in constant dollars (Table I-2), of new non-residential construction and purchases of producers' durables.

TABLE A6–2.   Historical Data on Producer Durables Purchases, by Type[1]

(Billion 1960 dollars)

	1946	1947	1948	1949	1950	1951	1952	1953	1954	1955	1956	1957	1958	1959	1960
Total	19.6	26.4	27.7	24.1	25.8	26.7	26.5	27.4	25.3	27.4	30.3	29.9	23.6	25.9	27.5
a. Passenger cars	1.56	2.69	2.82	3.54	3.98	3.18	2.59	2.99	2.79	3.58	2.96	3.06	2.40	3.13	3.27
b. Transportation equipment	3.43	4.93	5.23	4.46	4.66	5.53	4.48	4.26	3.59	4.50	4.59	4.36	3.21	4.01	4.10
c. Electrical machinery	1.99	3.10	2.74	2.33	2.52	2.51	2.84	2.88	2.77	3.02	3.58	3.36	2.77	3.18	3.45
d. Service industry machinery	.88	1.38	1.87	1.24	1.20	1.00	1.15	1.27	1.25	1.36	1.68	1.70	1.80	1.55	1.84
e. Furniture and fixtures	1.54	1.88	1.66	1.41	1.42	1.65	1.57	1.56	1.79	2.03	2.44	2.11	1.80	1.95	2.12
f. Industrial machinery	5.18	6.30	6.18	4.69	5.29	5.77	6.01	6.78	6.63	5.91	7.19	7.09	4.55	4.49	5.05
g. Other non-agricultural equipment	3.74	4.16	4.62	3.76	4.07	4.50	4.99	5.23	4.51	4.70	5.78	6.07	5.42	5.54	6.17
h. Agricultural machinery	1.27	2.07	2.71	2.70	2.61	2.78	2.83	2.44	2.01	2.34	1.95	2.08	2.10	2.06	1.48
Private purchases of—[2]															
"c," as per cent of investment in public util. and communications	66.1	66.1	43.6	36.8	41.0	39.5	41.5	37.5	38.3	40.6	42.5	34.6	31.0	38.0	39.2
"d," as per cent of commercial investment	10.4	14.2	24.7	18.7	15.2	13.2	16.4	16.3	15.8	15.4	18.1	21.9	18.8	18.8	21.8
"e," as per cent of private non-residential construction	12.5	14.8	12.0	10.4	9.7	10.2	9.8	9.1	10.2	10.5	12.3	10.4	9.9	10.7	10.8
"f," as per cent of investment in all manufacturing	40.8	45.3	46.2	46.1	50.7	41.6	41.0	46.2	49.3	43.7	43.3	42.2	38.8	37.1	34.9
"g," as per cent of total business investment	13.5	12.6	14.3	13.7	14.2	13.8	14.9	15.0	13.8	13.9	14.9	15.6	17.3	17.0	17.3
"h," as per cent of agricultural investment	37.4	40.6	45.2	43.0	42.8	45.6	48.8	44.4	41.0	48.8	46.4	50.7	47.7	45.8	36.1

1. These series, through 1954, are based on the more detailed series in *U.S. Income and Output*, Table V–6, aggregated as follows:

Passenger cars — Passenger cars

Transportation equipment — Trucks, buses, and trailers; aircraft; ships and boats; railroad equipment

Electrical machinery — Electrical machinery

Service industry machinery — Service industry and household machines

Furniture and fixtures — Furniture and fixtures; fabricated metal products (except cutlery and hand tools)

Industrial machinery — Engines and turbines; metal-working machinery; special-industry machinery, n.e.c.; general industrial machinery

Other non-agricultural equipment — Cutlery and hand tools; construction machinery; mining and oilfield machinery; office and store machines; instruments; miscellaneous equipment

Agricultural machinery — Tractors; agricultural machinery (except tractors)

Data beyond 1954 have not been published and it was necessary to estimate roughly the subsequent series and the deflators (including the 1954/1960 relationship for transposing the *Income and Output* series to 1960 dollars). Post-1954 extensions of the purchases series, in current dollars, were based on data in various Current Industrial Reports (Facts for Industry) of the U.S. Department of Commerce, with a few exceptions, in which the basis was either a Federal Reserve Board industrial production index or the *Income and Output* plant and equipment expenditures series or one of its components. Extensions of the deflators (*U.S. Income and Output*, Table VII–15) were on the basis of various of the Bureau of Labor Statistics wholesale price indexes. Finally, the individual series were adjusted to total to the producer durables series as given in Table A1–8.

2. Reference series are in Table A6–1. "Investment" refers to plant and equipment expenditures.

TABLE A6–3.   Projected New Plant and Equipment Expenditures, by Industry[1]

(Billion 1960 dollars)

	1939	1945	1950	1955	1960		1970	1980	1990	2000
Manufacturing[2]	5.3	8.2	10.4	13.5	14.5	L	16.4	18.7	22.4	26.8
						M	21.4	29.7	41.6	57.3
						H	27.2	43.7	69.3	110.6
Durables	2.06	3.26	4.37	6.43	7.18	L	8.42	9.82	12.2	14.9
						M	10.8	15.3	22.3	31.9
						H	14.1	24.2	40.5	68.8
Per cent of durable goods output	7.2	3.7	5.9	6.8	7.4	L	6.9	6.5	6.1	5.7
						M	7.0	6.7	6.5	6.2
						H	7.5	7.5	7.5	7.5
Non-durables	3.22	4.91	6.07	7.10	7.30	L	8.00	8.86	10.2	11.9
						M	10.6	14.4	19.3	25.4
						H	13.1	19.5	28.8	41.8
Per cent of non-durable goods output	3.9	4.1	5.0	4.9	4.5	L	4.0	3.6	3.4	3.4
						M	4.9	4.9	4.9	4.9
						H	5.5	5.5	5.5	5.5
Mining	.89	.78	.98	1.13	.99	L	.86	.84	.97	1.11
						M	.94	1.02	1.30	1.63
						H	1.04	1.25	1.74	2.40
Per cent of total goods output	.79	.38	.50	.47	.38		.26	.20	.18	.16
Transportation	1.73	2.30	3.24	2.98	2.97	L	3.39	4.17	5.26	6.52
						M	5.17	6.95	9.79	13.41
						H	7.91	12.66	20.24	31.53
Per cent of expenditures for transportation equipment[3]	n.a.	n.a.	69.5	66.2	72.4	L	64.0	61.0	58.0	55.0
						M	69.5	67.5	65.5	63.5
						H	75.0	75.0	75.0	75.0
Public utilities	1.41	10.3	4.61	5.09	5.68	L	6.0	5.9	5.4	5.9
						M	7.8	10.0	13.0	17.8
						H	10.8	16.8	25.9	40.5
Per point of FRB public utilities index[4] ($ mil.)	n.a.	n.a.	87.5	59.6	46.1	L	35	24	17	14
						M	39	32	29	28
						H	43	40	40	40
Communications	n.a.	n.a.	1.54	2.34	3.13	L	3.7	4.7	5.9	7.6
						M	4.5	6.4	9.1	13.2
						H	5.3	8.8	14.7	25.7
Per cent of GNP	—	—	.42	.52	.62	L	.52	.49	.47	.45
						M	.60	.60	.60	.60
						H	.66	.70	.74	.78
Commercial and other	n.a.	n.a.	7.90	8.85	8.44	L	9.0	10.6	14.0	18.8
						M	11.5	15.4	22.1	32.5
						H	14.4	22.7	36.2	60.1
Per cent of private GNP[5]	—	—	2.40	2.18	1.85	L	1.4	1.2	1.2	1.2
						M	1.7	1.6	1.6	1.6
						H	2.0	2.0	2.0	2.0
Total business expenditures on new plant and equipment[6]	14.9	17.8	28.7	33.9	35.7	L	39.4	44.9	53.9	66.7
						M	51.3	69.5	96.9	135.8
						H	66.6	105.9	168.1	270.8
Agricultural expenditures on new plant and equipment	1.9	2.1	6.1	4.8	4.1	L	4.0	3.7	4.0	4.3
						M	5.4	6.4	7.5	8.5
						H	6.4	8.7	11.5	14.7
Per cent of farm gross product[5]	11.2	12.1	33.0	23.4	19.7	L	18.0	15.0	15.0	15.0
						M	22.3	22.3	22.3	22.3
						H	23.9	25.9	27.1	27.5

Table A6–3 (cont'd)

(Billion 1960 dollars)

	1939	1945	1950	1955	1960		1970	1980	1990	2000
Total private expenditures on						L	62.0	76.1	90.9	109.6
new plant and equipment	17.0	21.3	40.5	46.5	47.1	M	74.4	106.2	152.2	223.4
						H	84.4	138.6	224.6	378.4
						L	9.6	8.6	7.8	7.0
Per cent of private GNP[5]	8.8	7.3	12.3	11.5	10.3	M	11.0	11.0	11.0	11.0
						H	11.7	12.2	12.4	12.6
"Other" and "nonallocable" plant						L	18.6	27.5	33.0	38.6
and equipment[7]	.2	1.4	5.7	7.8	7.3	M	17.7	30.3	47.8	79.1
						H	11.4	24.0	45.0	92.9
Private non-residential						L	21.8	24.7	28.2	32.9
construction[8]	6.6	5.9	14.6	19.3	19.6	M	28.3	39.3	54.8	78.2
						H	35.7	58.6	95.0	160.1
Per cent of new plant and						L	35.2	32.5	31.0	30.0
equipment expenditures	38.8	27.6	36.1	41.5	41.6	M	38.0	37.0	36.0	35.0
						H	42.3	42.3	42.3	42.3
Private purchases of producer						L	35.8	43.9	52.4	63.2
durables	10.3	15.5	25.8	27.4	27.5	M	46.1	66.9	97.4	145.2
						H	54.7	93.6	155.0	264.9
Per cent of new plant and						L	57.7	57.7	57.7	57.7
equipment expenditures	60.6	72.8	64.1	58.9	58.4	M	62.0	63.0	64.0	65.0
						H	64.8	67.5	69.0	70.0

1. Historical data from Table A6–1. Projections are derived by application of the coefficients shown in each case to the indicated reference series. Coefficients are projected on a judgment basis, taking into account factors discussed in Chapter 6, (pp. 151–53) and Notes, above. Unless otherwise indicated, reference series may be found in Tables A1–6, 8, and 13.
2. Sum of durables and non-durables.
3. Reference series in Table A6–5. For explanation of the fact that the whole appears to be smaller than the part, see footnote 10, Table A6–1.
4. Reference series in Table A1–29.
5. Reference series in Tables A1–6 and 18. Some slight discrepancies (less than one per cent) will be found in the calculations owing to the use of the reference series as it stood prior to final adjustment.
6. Total of the preceding detail.
7. Residual, after deduction of business and agricultural expenditures on new plant and equipment from the directly projected total. For content of "other," see footnote 5, Table A6–1. "Non-allocable" is the under- or over-allocation in the Low and the High, respectively, arising out of the fact that a reasonable range for the total is inconsistent with all the segments concurrently assuming either the Lows or the Highs which they might reasonably assume individually.
8. National Income Accounts definition: includes farm dwellings.

TABLE A6–4. Projected Private Purchases of Durable Goods, by Type

(Billion 1960 dollars)

	1950	1955	1960		1970	1980	1990	2000
Total purchases:[1]								
				L	26.6	34.6	44.5	55.5
Passenger cars	16.8	20.9	19.1	M	27.9	40.0	57.0	79.7
				H	33.4	58.2	101.4	169.1
				L	15.5	19.9	25.7	33.5
Electrical machinery and appliances	10.6	12.2	13.6	M	20.8	33.8	52.2	80.0
				H	27.2	51.0	92.7	164.6
				L	11.2	12.3	13.4	15.1
Furniture and fixtures	7.9	9.5	10.5	M	15.6	22.2	31.5	44.2
				H	18.7	30.3	49.4	79.8

Table A6–4 (cont'd)

(Billion 1960 dollars)

	1950	1955	1960		1970	1980	1990	2000
Consumer durables—total[2]	34.0	42.0	44.3	L	60.5	83.6	113.8	150.9
				M	65.1	98.6	148.2	217.8
				H	74.7	125.8	210.4	344.3
Passenger cars, parts, and accessories	15.4	20.0	18.6	L	25.6	33.3	41.8	52.4
				M	27.3	39.1	54.8	76.6
				H	33.6	58.7	100.1	164.3
Electrical appliances	6.9	7.8	8.3	L	9.9	13.4	18.0	23.5
				M	13.4	23.2	36.8	56.8
				H	17.3	33.9	63.2	112.4
Furniture and furnishings	6.5	7.5	8.4	L	9.0	9.8	10.6	11.8
				M	12.5	17.9	25.5	35.6
				H	14.4	23.3	38.0	60.6
Other	5.2	6.9	8.9	L	11.7	15.6	20.5	26.8
				M	13.3	20.5	31.2	46.2
				H	16.4	28.0	48.3	79.5
Non-allocable consumer durables	–	–	–	L	+4.3	+12.5	+22.9	+36.4
				M	—1.4	—2.1	—.1	+2.6
				H	—7.0	—18.1	—39.2	—72.5
Producer durables—total[3]	25.8	27.4	27.5	L	35.8	43.9	52.4	63.2
				M	46.1	66.9	97.4	145.2
				H	54.7	93.6	155.0	264.9
Transportation equipment including passenger cars	8.64	8.08	7.37	L	9.84	12.78	16.71	21.38
				M	12.22	17.15	24.70	34.78
				H	16.27	26.86	44.37	71.04
Electrical machinery	2.52	3.02	3.45	L	3.98	4.45	4.86	5.94
				M	5.17	7.22	10.17	14.88
				H	6.92	11.78	19.89	34.42
Service industry machinery	1.20	1.36	1.84	L	1.66	2.07	2.87	4.04
				M	2.24	3.31	5.19	8.29
				H	2.95	5.33	9.59	17.73
Furniture and fixtures	1.42	2.03	2.12	L	2.18	2.47	2.82	3.29
				M	3.11	4.32	6.03	8.60
				H	4.28	7.03	11.40	19.21
Industrial machinery, except electrical	5.29	5.91	5.05	L	5.77	6.26	7.28	8.44
				M	8.35	11.58	16.22	22.35
				H	11.15	18.79	31.18	51.98
Other non-agricultural equipment	4.07	4.70	6.17	L	7.18	8.62	10.97	14.28
				M	9.45	13.61	19.95	29.52
				H	12.43	21.08	35.81	62.01
Agricultural machinery including tractors	2.61	2.34	1.48	L	1.60	1.48	1.60	1.80
				M	2.27	2.69	3.15	3.57
				H	2.88	3.92	5.18	6.62
Non-allocable producer durables	–	–	–	L	+3.6	+5.8	+5.3	+4.0
				M	+3.3	+7.0	+12.0	+23.2
				H	—2.2	—1.2	—2.4	+1.9
Recap: Private purchases of producer durables excluding transportation equipment	17.2	19.3	20.1	L	26.0	31.1	35.7	41.8
				M	33.9	49.8	72.7	110.4
				H	38.4	66.7	110.6	193.9

1. Aggregated from the appropriate items in Table A1–27 and A6–5; for other than automobiles, also shown below. (Service industry machinery included with electrical.)

2. From Table A1–27. In some cases, the detail shown therein is aggregated into the categories listed here. "Non-allocable" represents statistical error plus the undistributed or overdistributed portion of the Low or High detail, respectively, compared with the corresponding directly projected durables aggregate.

3. Historical data from Table A6–2. Projections of the total from Table A6–3, projections of the detail aggregated from Table A6–5. For meaning of "non-allocable," see footnote 2.

TABLE A6–5. Derivation of Projected Producer Durables Purchases, by Type[1]

(Billion 1960 dollars)

	1950	1955	1960		1970	1980	1990	2000
Producer purchases of passenger cars[2]	3.98	3.58	3.27	L	4.55	5.94	7.64	9.52
				M	4.78	6.85	9.75	13.66
				H	5.73	9.98	17.39	29.00
Other producer purchases of transportation equipment	4.66	4.50	4.10	L	5.29	6.84	9.07	11.86
				M	7.44	10.30	14.95	21.12
				H	10.54	16.88	26.98	42.04
Purchases of selected types of transportation equipment (1960 = 100)[3]	n.a.	n.a.	100	L	123	152	193	242
				M	173	229	318	431
				H	245	375	574	858
All transportation equipment ($ mil. per point of index)	–	–	41.0		43	45	47	49
Purchases of electrical machinery	2.52	3.02	3.45	L	3.98	4.45	4.86	5.94
				M	5.17	7.22	10.17	14.88
				H	6.92	11.78	19.89	34.42
Investment in public utilities and communications[4]	6.15	7.43	8.81	L	9.7	10.6	11.3	13.5
				M	12.3	16.4	22.1	31.0
				H	16.1	25.6	40.6	66.2
Electrical machinery as per cent of do.	41.0	40.6	39.2	L	41.0	42.0	43.0	44.0
				M	42.0	44.0	46.0	48.0
				H	43.0	46.0	49.0	52.0
Purchases of service industry machinery	1.20	1.36	1.84	L	1.66	2.07	2.87	4.04
				M	2.24	3.31	5.19	8.29
				H	2.95	5.33	9.59	17.73
"Commercial and other" investment[4]	7.90	8.85	8.44	L	9.0	10.6	14.0	18.8
				M	11.5	15.4	22.1	32.5
				H	14.4	22.7	36.2	60.1
Service industry machinery as per cent of do.	15.2	15.4	21.8	L	18.5	19.5	20.5	21.5
				M	19.5	21.5	23.5	25.5
				H	20.5	23.5	26.5	29.5
Purchases of furniture and fixtures	1.42	2.03	2.12	L	2.18	2.47	2.82	3.29
				M	3.11	4.32	6.03	8.60
				H	4.28	7.03	11.40	19.21
Private non-residential construction[4]	14.6	19.3	19.6	L	21.8	24.7	28.2	32.9
				M	28.3	39.3	54.8	78.2
				H	35.7	58.6	95.0	160.1
Furniture and fixtures as per cent of do.	9.7	10.5	10.8	L	10.0	10.0	10.0	10.0
				M	11.0	11.0	11.0	11.0
				H	12.0	12.0	12.0	12.0
Purchases of industrial machinery	5.29	5.91	5.05	L	5.77	6.26	7.28	8.44
				M	8.35	11.58	16.22	22.35
				H	11.15	18.79	31.18	51.98
Total manufacturing investment[4]	10.43	13.52	14.48	L	16.4	18.7	22.4	26.8
				M	21.4	29.7	41.6	57.3
				H	27.2	43.7	69.3	110.6
Industrial machinery as per cent of do.	50.7	43.7	34.9	L	35.2	33.5	32.5	31.5
				M	39.0	39.0	39.0	39.0
				H	41.0	43.0	45.0	47.0

Table A6–5 (cont'd)

(Billion 1960 dollars)

	1950	1955	1960		1970	1980	1990	2000
Purchases of misc. non-agricultural equipment (tools, office equipment, etc.)	4.07	4.70	6.17	L	7.18	8.62	10.97	14.28
				M	9.45	13.61	19.95	29.52
				H	12.43	21.08	35.81	62.01
Total business expenditures on new plant and equipment[4]	28.7	33.9	35.7	L	39.4	44.9	53.9	66.7
				M	51.3	69.5	96.9	135.8
				H	66.6	105.9	168.1	270.8
Misc. non-agricultural equipment as per cent of do.	14.2	13.9	17.3	L	18.2	19.2	20.4	21.4
				M	18.4	19.6	20.6	21.7
				H	18.7	19.9	21.3	22.9
Purchases of agricultural machinery	2.61	2.34	1.48	L	1.60	1.48	1.60	1.80
				M	2.27	2.69	3.15	3.57
				H	2.88	3.92	5.18	6.62
Farm investment[4]	6.1	4.8	4.1	L	4.0	3.7	4.0	4.5
				M	5.4	6.4	7.5	8.5
				H	6.4	8.7	11.5	14.7
Agricultural machinery as per cent of do.	42.8	48.8	36.1	L	40	40	40	40
				M	42	42	42	42
				H	45	45	45	45

1. Historical data from Table A6–2, unless otherwise noted. Projections are made on the basis of the indicated coefficients, which are projected on a judgment basis, taking into account the 1946–60 trend.

2. Total sales of passenger cars are assumed to be distributed in accordance with the current allocation of the National Income Division, U.S. Department of Commerce: 82% to consumers, 17% to producers, and the remaining 1% to government. Consequently, producer purchases are projected as 20.7% (17/82) of consumer purchases, as projected in Table A1–27.

3. Based on projections in terms of units (motor trucks and trailers in Table A5–10 and railroad rolling stock in Table A5–17), weighted by approximate unit values, representing delivered cost to purchaser: trucks, $3,000; trailers, $7,000; and railroad rolling stock, $10,000.

4. From Table A6–3.

TABLE A6–6.   Historical Data on Durables' Use of Principal Metals[1]

	1950	1955	1956	1957	1958	1959	1960
Total consumption of metals, actual weight (mil. tons):							
Producer durables:							
Steel mill products[2]	9.2	10.8	11.4	9.9	8.3	10.2	9.6
Ferrous castings[3]	3.7	4.6	4.4	4.1	3.2	3.9	3.7
Total iron and steel	12.9	15.4	15.8	14.0	11.5	14.1	13.3
Aluminum[4]	.166	.201	.208	.197	.178	.219	.175
Copper[5]	.727	.767	.769	.681	.582	.705	.673
Zinc die castings[6]	.021	.036	.033	.035	.036	.048	.037
Lead[7]	.220	.205	.199	.189	.157	.188	.164
Consumer durables:							
Steel mill products[2]	3.7	3.8	3.8	2.8	2.8	3.3	3.2
Aluminum[4]	.244	.206	.207	.164	.158	.201	.187
Copper[5]	.193	.179	.174	.149	.144	.163	.133
Zinc die castings[6]	.044	.072	.063	.058	.068	.075	.053
Total consumption of metals, steel equivalent weight[8] (mil. tons):							
Producer durables:							
Steel mill products	9.2	10.8	11.4	9.9	8.3	10.2	9.6
Ferrous castings	4.0	5.0	4.8	4.4	3.5	4.2	4.0
Total iron and steel	13.2	15.8	16.2	14.3	11.8	14.4	13.6
Aluminum	.48	.58	.60	.57	.51	.63	.51
Copper	.64	.67	.68	.60	.51	.62	.59
Zinc die castings	.02	.04	.03	.04	.04	.05	.04
Lead	.15	.14	.14	.13	.11	.13	.11
Total use	14.5	17.2	17.6	15.6	13.0	15.8	14.9
Consumer durables:							
Steel mill products	3.7	3.8	3.8	2.8	2.8	3.3	3.2
Aluminum	.71	.60	.60	.47	.46	.58	.54
Copper	.17	.16	.15	.13	.13	.14	.12
Zinc die castings	.05	.07	.07	.06	.07	.08	.06
Total use	4.6	4.6	4.6	3.5	3.5	4.1	3.9
Consumption (actual weight) per $ 1960 mil. of private purchases:							
Producer durable purchases[9]							
($ 1960 bil.)	17.2	19.3	22.8	22.5	18.0	18.8	20.1
Tons per $ 1960 million:							
Steel mill products	535	560	500	440	461	543	478
Ferrous castings	215	238	193	182	178	207	184
Total iron and steel	750	798	693	622	639	750	662
Nonferrous metals:							
Aluminum	9.7	10.4	9.1	8.8	9.9	11.6	8.7
Copper	42.3	39.7	33.7	30.3	32.3	37.5	33.5
Lead	12.8	10.6	8.7	8.4	8.7	10.0	8.2
Zinc die castings	1.2	1.8	1.4	1.6	2.0	2.6	1.8
All major nonferrous	66.0	62.5	52.9	49.1	52.9	61.7	52.2
All major metals	816	860	746	671	692	812	714
Consumer durable purchases[10]							
($ 1960 bil.)	18.6	22.0	23.5	23.5	23.6	25.7	25.7
Tons per $ 1960 million:							
Steel mill products	199	173	162	119	119	128	125
Nonferrous metals:							
Aluminum	13.1	9.4	8.8	7.0	6.7	7.8	7.3
Copper	10.4	8.1	7.4	6.3	6.1	6.3	5.2
Zinc die castings	2.4	3.3	2.7	2.5	2.9	2.9	2.1
All major nonferrous	25.9	20.8	18.9	15.8	15.7	17.0	14.6
All major metals	225	194	181	135	135	145	140

Table A6–6 (cont'd)

	1950	1955	1956	1957	1958	1959	1960
Consumption (steel equivalent weight) per $ 1960 million of private purchases (tons):							
Producer durables:							
Steel mill products	535	560	500	440	461	543	478
Ferrous castings	233	259	211	196	195	223	199
Total iron and steel	768	819	711	636	656	766	677
Nonferrous metals:							
Aluminum	27.9	30.1	26.3	25.3	28.3	33.5	25.4
Copper	37.2	34.9	29.7	26.7	28.3	33.0	29.5
Lead	8.7	7.3	6.1	5.8	6.1	6.9	5.6
Zinc die castings	1.2	1.9	1.3	1.8	2.2	2.7	1.9
All major nonferrous	75.0	74.2	63.4	59.6	64.9	76.1	62.4
All major metals	843	893	774	696	721	842	739
Consumer durables:							
Steel mill products	199	173	162	119	119	128	125
Nonferrous metals:							
Aluminum	37.9	27.2	25.5	20.0	19.5	18.3	21.1
Copper	9.2	7.1	6.4	5.5	5.5	5.4	4.6
Zinc die castings	2.5	3.4	3.0	2.6	3.0	3.1	2.2
All major nonferrous	49.6	37.7	34.9	28.1	28.0	26.8	27.9
All major metals	249	211	197	147	147	155	153

1. Refers to all producer and consumer durables except transportation equipment, which is covered in Table A5–19. Data are net end-use consumption, i.e., net of amounts of metal returned as prompt industrial scrap.

2. From Table A16–4. Includes some additional adjustment in the allocation of steel shipments to producer and consumer durables, respectively, which in Table A16–4 was based upon a less detailed market classification.

3. Estimated on the basis of Census of Manufactures data on materials consumed and total shipments of ferrous castings, from U.S. Bureau of the Census, Current Industrial Reports, Series M33–A.

4. Weight of aluminum and aluminum alloy. From Table A16–31.

5. Copper content of copper and copper-base alloys. From Table A16–37.

6. Zinc content. From American Die Casting Institute press releases.

7. Lead content of lead and alloys containing lead. Computed from data in *Minerals Yearbook,* Lead chapters.

8. Converted on basis of the specific gravities listed herewith. While the actual ratio of substitution may differ considerably from this in some cases, the data are intended only to provide a rough guide to relative use.

	Specific gravities	Converted to steel equivalents; steel = 1.00
Steel	7.8	1.00
Iron	7.2	1.08
Aluminum	2.7	2.89
Copper	8.9	0.88
Zinc	7.5	1.04
Lead	11.4	0.685

9. From Table A6–2—total purchases, excluding passenger cars and transportation.

10. From Table A1–26—total durables, excluding passenger cars, parts, and accessories.

TABLE A6–7.　Projected Durables' Use of Principal Metals[1]

	1950	1955	1960		1970	1980	1990	2000
Private purchases of durables[2] ($ 1960 bil.):								
				L	26.0	31.1	35.7	41.8
Producer durables	17.2	19.3	20.1	M	33.9	49.8	72.7	110.4
				H	38.4	66.7	110.6	193.9
				L	34.9	50.3	72.0	98.5
Consumer durables	18.6	22.0	25.7	M	37.8	59.5	93.4	141.2
				H	41.1	67.1	110.3	180.0
Consumption of principal metals, actual weight[3] (mil. tons): For producer durables:								
				L	12.0	13.5	14.6	16.1
Steel mill products	9.2	10.8	9.6	M	15.6	21.6	29.7	42.4
				H	17.7	28.9	45.1	74.5
Tons per $ 1960 million	535	560	478		461	434	408	384
				L	4.3	4.6	4.6	4.8
Ferrous castings	3.7	4.6	3.7	M	5.7	7.3	9.5	12.6
				H	6.4	9.8	14.4	22.1
Tons per $ 1960 million	215	238	184		167	147	130	114
				L	.27	.34	.41	.50
Aluminum	.17	.20	.18	M	.36	.55	.84	1.32
				H	.40	.73	1.27	2.33
Tons per $ 1960 million	9.7	10.4	9.0		10.5	11.0	11.5	12.0
				L	.78	.84	.86	.92
Copper	.73	.77	.67	M	1.02	1.34	1.74	2.43
				H	1.15	1.80	2.65	4.27
Tons per $ 1960 million	42.3	39.7	33.4		30.0	27.0	24.0	22.0
				L	.18	.17	.16	.15
Lead	.22	.20	.16	M	.23	.27	.33	.39
				H	.26	.37	.50	.68
Tons per $ 1960 million	12.8	10.6	8.2		6.8	5.5	4.5	3.5
				L	.05	.06	.07	.08
Zinc die castings	.02	.04	.04	M	.07	.10	.15	.22
				H	.08	.13	.22	.39
Tons per $ 1960 million	1.2	1.8	1.8		2.0	2.0	2.0	2.0
For consumer durables:								
				L	3.5	4.0	4.7	5.4
Steel mill products	3.7	3.8	3.2	M	3.8	4.8	6.1	7.8
				H	4.1	5.4	7.2	9.9
Tons per $ 1960 million	199	173	125		100	80	65	55
				L	.28	.43	.65	.98
Aluminum	.24	.21	.19	M	.30	.51	.84	1.41
				H	.33	.57	.99	1.80
Tons per $ 1960 million	13.1	9.4	7.4		8.0	8.5	9.0	10.0
				L	.17	.23	.29	.34
Copper	.19	.18	.13	M	.19	.27	.37	.49
				H	.21	.30	.44	.63
Tons per $ 1960 million	10.4	8.1	5.2		5.0	4.5	4.0	3.5
				L	.09	.13	.18	.25
Zinc die castings	.04	.07	.05	M	.09	.15	.23	.35
				H	.10	.17	.28	.45
Tons per $ 1960 million	2.4	3.3	2.1		2.5	2.5	2.5	2.5

Table A6–7 (cont'd)

	1950	1955	1960		1970	1980	1990	2000
Consumption of principal metals, steel equivalent weight[4] (mil. tons):								
For producer durables:								
				L	12.0	13.5	14.6	16.1
Steel mill products	9.2	10.8	9.6	M	15.6	21.6	29.7	42.4
				H	17.7	28.9	45.1	74.5
Tons per $ 1960 million	535	560	478		461	434	408	384
				L	4.7	4.9	5.0	5.1
Ferrous castings	4.0	5.0	4.0	M	6.1	7.9	10.2	13.6
				H	6.9	10.6	15.5	23.8
Tons per $ 1960 million	233	259	199		180	159	140	123
Total iron and steel[5]	13.2	15.8	13.6		21.7	29.5	39.9	56.0
				L	.79	.99	1.19	1.45
Aluminum	.48	.58	.51	M	1.03	1.58	2.41	3.83
				H	1.16	2.12	3.67	6.73
Tons per $ 1960 million	27.9	30.1	25.4		30.3	31.8	33.2	34.7
				L	.69	.74	.75	.81
Copper	.64	.67	.59	M	.89	1.19	1.53	2.14
				H	1.01	1.59	2.33	3.76
Tons per $ 1960 million	37.2	34.9	29.4		26.4	23.8	21.1	19.4
				L	.12	.12	.11	.10
Lead	.15	.14	.11	M	.16	.19	.23	.26
				H	.18	.25	.34	.47
Tons per $ 1960 million	8.8	7.3	5.6		4.7	3.8	3.1	2.4
				L	.05	.07	.07	.09
Zinc die castings	.02	.04	.04	M	.07	.10	.15	.23
				H	.08	.14	.23	.41
Tons per $ 1960 million	1.2	1.9	1.9		2.1	2.1	2.1	2.1
All major nonferrous metals[5]	1.29	1.43	1.26		2.15	3.06	4.32	6.46
All principal metals[5]	14.5	17.2	14.9		23.8	32.6	44.2	62.5
Percentage distribution (Med.):								
Steel mill products	64	63	64		65	66	67	68
Ferrous castings	28	29	27		26	24	23	22
Aluminum	3	3	4		4	5	5	6
Copper	4	4	4		4	4	4	3
Lead and zinc	1	1	1		1	1	1	1
Total	100	100	100		100	100	100	100
All ferrous	92	92	91		91	90	90	90
All nonferrous	8	8	9		9	10	10	10
For consumer durables:								
				L	3.5	4.0	4.7	5.4
Steel mill products	3.7	3.8	3.2	M	3.8	4.8	6.1	7.8
				H	4.1	5.4	7.2	9.9
Tons per $ 1960 million	199	173	125		100	80	65	55
				L	.81	1.24	1.87	2.85
Aluminum	.71	.60	.54	M	.87	1.46	2.43	4.08
				H	.95	1.65	2.87	5.20
Tons per $ 1960 million	37.9	27.2	21.1		23.1	24.6	26.0	28.9

Table A6–7 (cont'd)

		1950	1955	1960		1970	1980	1990	2000
Copper		.17	.16	.12	L	.15	.20	.25	.31
					M	.17	.24	.33	.44
					H	.18	.27	.39	.56
Tons per $ 1960 million		9.2	7.1	4.6		4.4	4.0	3.5	3.1
Zinc die castings		.05	.07	.06	L	.09	.13	.19	.26
					M	.10	.15	.24	.37
					H	.11	.17	.29	.47
Tons per $ 1960 million		2.5	3.4	2.2		2.6	2.6	2.6	2.6
All major nonferrous metals[5]		.93	.83	.73		1.14	1.85	3.00	4.89
All principal metals[5]		4.6	4.6	3.9		4.9	6.6	9.1	12.7
Percentage distribution (Med.):									
Steel mill products		80	82	82		77	72	67	61
Aluminum		15	13	14		18	22	27	32
Copper		4	3	3		3	4	3	4
Zinc		1	2	1		2	2	3	3
Total		100	100	100		100	100	100	100
All nonferrous		20	18	18		23	28	33	39

1. Refers to all producer and consumer durables except transportation equipment, which is covered in Table A5–19. Data refer to net end-use consumption, i.e., net of amounts of metal returned as prompt industrial scrap.

2. From Table A6–4.

3. Projections are obtained, in each case, by application of the coefficients shown. Latter are extrapolations of the historical trends (see Table A6–6) adjusted on a judgment basis. For considerations involved, see Chapter 6, pp. 154–57, and Notes, above.

4. Converted on basis of specific gravities. See footnote 8, Table A6–6.

5. Lows and Highs omitted since, because of substitution among metals, they would be higher and lower, respectively, than the added totals. Composite Low and High models which are internally consistent are not needed for further derivations and have therefore not been calculated. The Medium model is additive and has been calculated in order to obtain the percentage distribution of metals as an implications check.

TABLE A6–8. Projected Consumption of Lumber for Furniture and Fixtures

	1948	1952	1953	1954	1958	1960		1970	1980	1990	2000
Total purchases of furniture and fixtures[1] ($ 1960 bil.)	7.7	8.0	8.3	8.2	9.7	10.5	L	11.2	12.3	13.4	15.1
							M	15.6	22.2	31.5	44.2
							H	18.7	30.3	49.4	79.8
Lumber used per $ billion of furniture and fixtures purchases[2] (bil. bd. ft.)	.25	.20	.19	.23	.23	.21	L	.18	.155	.13	.11
							M	.19	.17	.155	.14
							H	.21	.21	.21	.21
Total lumber used in furniture and fixtures[3] (bil. bd. ft.)	1.95	1.60	1.58	1.91	2.2	2.2	L	2.0	1.9	1.7	1.7
							M	3.0	3.8	4.9	6.2
							H	3.9	6.4	10.4	16.8

1. From Tables A1–26, A6–2, and A6–4.

2. Projected on a judgment basis, taking into account historical trend. For considerations, see Chapter 6, p. 155.

3. 1948 from U.S. Forest Service, *Timber Resources for America's Future* (Forest Resource Report No. 14,

Jan. 1958); 1952 and 1953 from U.S. Department of Commerce, *Facts for Industry,* No. M54A–03; 1954 and 1958 calculated from Census of Manufactures; 1960 estimated. Projections calculated by applying coefficients to aggregate purchases.

appendix
to
chapter
7

CONTAINERS AND PACKAGING

Notes

THE COMPARTMENTALIZATION of container production into what is essentially a group of quite separate industries is reflected in this appendix by separate successive treatment of the key materials used in containers—metal, wood, glass, paper, and plastics. One other traditional container material which heretofore has been of importance—textiles—has been omitted from the evaluation on two grounds: its resource significance is now, and is likely to be, negligible, and its present role and future importance compared to all container materials is a minor, and declining, one. Moreover, fiber consumption for containers is allowed for in the aggregates derived in the appendix to Chapter 3.

Essentially, two different methods have been employed to develop the projections. Future requirements for cans have been approached through projections of the principal items contained within cans, derived in turn from the food consumption projections in the appendix to Chapter 2. The range of items canned—principally certain kinds of fruits, vegetables, and beverages, plus shortening—is narrow enough so that it has been possible to relate future can requirements to these principal items alone. Moreover, we have comparatively good historical data on per capita consumption of canned foods as a result of the continuing series, *Consumption of Food in the United States,* published by the U.S. Department of Agriculture. For other kinds of metal containers, however, including metal foils and collapsible tubes, as well as pails, drums, barrels, cylinders, and other metal shapes, and for wood, glass, paper, and plastic containers the di-

versity of commodities packaged is so great, the percentage of the total which the principal items comprise is so small, and the historical data in general are so meager that it has been more practical to relate each major class of container to some appropriate aggregate series, not necessarily having to do directly with containers.

In general, each of the historical and projected series is evaluated in terms of its requirements for key materials, such as steel, aluminum, tin, and wood. There are two exceptions, however. Historical data on the actual consumption of glass for containers is not available, and we have therefore used Census data, plus the assumption of a declining coefficient, to estimate a few historical years as well as the projections. Also, we have not worked container and packaging requirements for paper back to the requirements for pulp, but have deferred this to Chapter 13, where all the paper requirements from various end-uses are brought together.

The Highs and Lows for each general class of container, such as cans, glass containers, and wooden containers, cannot be construed as being additive; for example, the High for wooden containers would imply less than the High for paper containers. Within each major class of container, however, no hard and fast rule applies. In the case of paper containers, the various subclasses are essentially non-competitive, and the Highs and Lows have thus been treated cumulatively to derive the High and Low for paper containers as a whole. For glass containers, the question does not arise, since we have not considered it necessary for purposes of our projections to break these down into types. Similarly, we have not divided wooden containers into separate categories. Among the plastic containers, molded and blown containers are non-competitive with the transparent films. Among the latter we have made a simple twofold division into the cellulosic and the petroleum based films, in which we have considered the Highs of one to be paired with the Lows of the other. Among cans, aluminum and steel are to be regarded as competitive with one another and have been so treated.

The spread between the Highs and Lows for the various kinds of container betokens a considerable range of uncertainty. This stems not so much from the possible variation in growth of containers as a whole as from the inherent possibilities of substitution among different types—and particularly between cans and plastics. Another reason for the wide spread is uncertainty as to how fast a decline there will be in inputs of materials per unit of output.

The problem of projecting requirements for steel, aluminum, and tin in can manufacture is typical of those obtaining for materials use in containers and packaging in general. We can be much more certain about future requirements for cans than about the quantities of particular metals which will be used in them. The approach which we have adopted here has been to relate historical inputs of "plate" to the leading uses of cans, for foods and malt beverages, which account for approximately 78 per cent of all plate consumed in can manufacture. The principal categories of canned foods are in turn derived from the total food consumption series in Tables A2–1 and 2, and per capita consumption of canned malt beverages is computed from data on total and canned consumption published by the U.S. Brewers Foundation.

As with total per capita consumption of particular foodstuffs, the consumption of the portion canned can be projected within relatively narrow ranges. In general, Table A7–2 indicates that future per capita consumption of the principal canned foods is likely to decline somewhat from current rates. On the other hand, per capita consumption of malt beverages has been remarkably stable for almost fifteen years, and we have therefore assumed future packaged consumption at present levels. The proportion canned has been rising steadily in recent years, however, and it is apparent that further shifts from glass to cans will occur before relative stability is reached. Because the exact equilibrium point is difficult to predict, we have projected three levels of further percentage displacement.

To the historical and projected consumption of

foods and malt beverages (Tables A7–1 and 2) is in turn related the consumption of metals for can manufacture (Table A7–3). The historical relationship between the weight of plate consumed for all cans and the weight of plate consumed for food and malt beverage cans has then been used to "blow up" future food and malt beverage can requirements to total plate requirements.

The term "plate," as used herein, encompasses mainly tin plate, but it includes also smaller amounts of terne plate and black plate. Common in the technical literature, it is used for want of a better word to cover all three products. Historically, steel has composed over 99 per cent of the total weight of plate reported as consumed in metal cans, but the precise percentage of steel and tin has varied—partly because of variations in the relative amounts of terne plate and black plate used in any one year but principally because of the historical shift from hot-dip to electrolytic tin plate, resulting in thinner films of tin over the steel base. The actual weights of steel and tin consumed in the manufacture of plate have been computed by the method detailed in Table A7–3, footnote 8. Data published by the Can Manufacturers Institute on the consumption of "steel" for cans actually include the weight of the tin coating, rather than the net weight of the steel alone.

In order to translate the projected consumption of cans into the projected consumption of steel for cans, four different kinds of factors which could affect the amount of steel required have been considered and built into the projections: (1) substitution of non-metals for metals, (2) substitution of aluminum for plate, (3) variations in the relative weights of steel and tin in plate, and (4) reductions in the weight of steel input stemming from the use of thinner gauge steel. It is of major importance in the evaluation of these projections to note that of these four factors, all except the second represent developments which were imminent in the year 1960 but for which there was no clear basis of judgment as to the timing, rate, or extent of possible impact on steel requirements. If and when non-metal substitution occurs for metals, the substituting material is likely to be one or more of the plastics, and the applications will be primarily in food packaging, but new food preservation techniques (probably irradiation) will have to be perfected first. No substitution had occurred by 1960. In the same year, the use of aluminum as an alternative to plate was significant enough for the first time to justify compilation of data. The shift to thinner gauge plate is still in the incipient commercial stage. Hence our uncertainties with respect to each of these three factors are sufficient to introduce a substantial range between the High and Low projected demand for steel in cans—a range which future analysis can narrow as the trends become clearer.

Starting with projections of conventional plate as a first approximation, the method of calculation was first to allow for non-metal can substitutions. In view of the unresolved technical problems which stand in the way of food irradiation, all three models are quite conjectural, the High and Low representing the limits of a reasonable spread of likely possibilities.

The second step was to consider the substitution of aluminum for plate. Although again we have no historical trends to help delimit the range, we can be certain that some substitution will occur in view both of the actual appearance of aluminum cans during the last several years and of the current plans for aluminum can production. Three different trends are postulated for the actual rate of replacement.

The third step involved the separation of the projected weight of plate into weights of steel and tin. In order to derive the steel, the historical trend of the ratio of steel to plate was projected to 2000 on the assumption that inputs of tin per unit of plate would continue their historical decline, partly because of residual displacement of hot-dipped by electrolytic tin plate, but more importantly because of the probable success of efforts to develop and use tinless cans.

The final step was to incorporate into the projections the likely effects of a shift to thinner gauge steels. Again we have assumed what appears to be a reasonable range between rapid adoption and slow adoption of thinner tin plate. Neither the High nor the Low assumption should be regarded as marking the extreme limits of possibilities.

The steel and aluminum figures thus arrived at represent gross consumption, rather than net metal content, since they fail to allow for scrap generated in the can manufacturing process. Adjustment for this scrap component is deferred to the end of Table A7–4, after use of steel in other forms of metal containers and consumption of aluminum in foil and collapsible tubes have been considered. At that point a final adjustment is made for scrap, as detailed in footnote 12.

About the only evidence we have as to the magnitude of steel consumption for containers other than cans is the shipments data compiled by the American Iron and Steel Institute. Ancillary estimates, discussed in Chapter 16 (see especially appendix Table A16–3), suggest that the amounts shown by the AISI as going directly to the manufacturers of containers other than cans are more or less equaled by amounts flowing indirectly to these manufacturers via steel warehouses and distributors. These adjusted data, even though they may include some steel utilized by container manufacturers for non-container products, are used as the output measure for this group of miscellaneous metal containers and are related to about the only available reference series that reflects the wide range of end-uses, namely, total national output of goods.

The final correction for that portion of steel consumption which ends up as industrial scrap rather than being incorporated into finished products—is made on the basis of a scrap generation ratio—12 per cent—derived as explained in Chapter 16.

The historical and the projected series on the use of lumber in containers have been related to the output of durable goods. Except for the continuing use of crating for the transport of certain kinds of fresh vegetables and fruits (particularly when transport is by refrigerated railway car), boxes and crating have been used principally for the transport of durable goods, particularly those entering the export trade. The declining trend in the consumption of lumber for boxes and crating per unit of goods output can be expected to persist, as substitution of paperboard for lumber continues. The recent appearance of paperboard containers even in the export trade confirms the likelihood of such a further decline.

The treatment of glass containers has been essentially similar to that of boxes and crating. Glass containers are used even more exclusively for non-durable goods, however, than boxes and crating are for durable goods. Their use is not confined to food and beverages, but spans a number of major non-durable groups; in fact, the diversity of commodities packaged in glass is probably greater than that in any other kind of container. The historical series indicates a gradual decline in the rate of increase in consumption of glass containers per dollar of non-durable goods output over the span of the last thirty years. It is because of this that in the Low projection an approximate leveling off at roughly the present level of consumption per unit of non-durable goods output is assumed. In the Medium and High projections there are continued increases, but at declining rates.

While a continuous historical series on the actual weight of glass consumed for containers is not available, approximate average weights of glass per gross in 1947, 1954, and 1958 could be computed from data in the 1954 and 1958 Censuses of Manufactures on the tonnages of glass sand used. To compute the weight of glass as such, it was assumed that 74.5 per cent of bottle glass is made up of SiO_2. Average weights per gross shown in Table A7–6 for 1950, 1955, and 1960 are interpolated or extrapolated.

It appears likely that the weight of bottle glass per gross will decline substantially in the years ahead—perhaps to less than half of what it is at present. Our Medium coefficient decreases, accordingly, from 70 pounds per gross in 1960 to 30 pounds in 2000.

The consumption of paper for containers and packaging is developed in Table A7–7, which shows the historical trends, and Table A7–8, which shows the projected series. In each case the relevant data have been set out in terms of the principal commercial classes or categories of paper, such as containerboard, special foodboard, and folding boxboard. In one case, several more or less related major types of paper have been grouped together: what we have called "set-up boxboards and special paperboards" include lined and unlined chipboard; tube, can, and drum stock; solid groundwood pulp board; bending board other than folding boxboard and other than special foodboard; and other miscellaneous special paperboards. The principal groups which we have used are those commonly recognized in the industry.

Most of the major commercial classes of paper and paperboard are used either exclusively or almost exclusively for containers and packaging or, alternatively, exclusively or almost exclusively for non-container and packaging uses. Three of the broad general groups, however, find wide uses both inside and outside the container and packaging industry. One is the "coarse and industrial papers" group, of which the coarse paper segment involves mostly wrapping, bag, shipping sack, and other packaging uses while the "special industrial" segment falls outside the container and packaging industries. Likewise, some of the predominantly non-packaging sanitary and tissue papers are used in packaging, and similarly for a good deal of what we have referred to as "set-up boxboards and special paperboards." We have allocated the consumption of these mixed categories on the basis of details on more specific types of paper within each group, as published by the U.S. Department of Commerce, Bureau of the Census, in *Pulp, Paper, and Board* (Current Industrial Reports, Series M26A). The particular percentages of each category estimated to be consumed for containers and packaging are detailed in the table footnotes.

The projections of the various individual classes

of paper and paperboard used for containers and packaging have been related in each case to one or a combination of three reference series: durable goods, non-durable goods, consumption of food and soft beverages. Containerboard has been related to goods output, since the containerboard carton has now become the standard container for the shipment of both durable and non-durable goods. Consumption of coarse and industrial paper by the container and packaging industries has also been related to goods output. Folding boxboards and set-up boxboards and special paperboards have been related to consumer purchases of non-durables, since these classes of paper and paperboard are used almost exclusively for non-durable goods. (Cigarette cartons and breakfast cereal boxes are good examples of the former, rigid shoe boxes a typical example of the latter.) Tissue paper in packaging has also been related to consumer purchases of non-durables. Finally, special foodboard, a bleached chemical pulpboard of which milk cartons are a good example, has been related to personal consumption expenditures on food and soft beverages.

Among the various materials used in containers and packaging, plastic resins have the least resource significance. All the synthetic resins for all purposes now utilize substantially less than 1 per cent of the total output of petroleum and gas in the United States, and the portion of plastic resins used for container products is well under one-tenth of all plastics consumption. Likewise, cellophane and other cellulosic plastics comprise only a very small, and a relatively declining, end-use for wood pulp. We have nevertheless included a brief tabular treatment of plastic containers, in order to provide a general view of all the materials likely to be of future significance for containers and packaging and to permit comparisons with other classes of containers in terms of possible future growth.

Statistical data relating to plastics are less satisfactory than those relating to any of the other major groups of container materials. (Cellophane, for which complete production data are available for every year since onset of production in 1924, is an exception.) At present there are about ten different types of plastic films—other than cellophane—on the market. Production and shipments data are not revealed directly, and it has been necessary to rely upon unofficial estimates of the Department of Commerce, based on knowledge of the industries involved and on the sizes of the companies operating, which are believed to provide a reasonably reliable indication of the historical trend. In the case of the rigid and semirigid plastic materials used in the container industry, the problem of securing adequate historical data is even more difficult. While the Tariff Commission publishes global statistics on molded and extruded plastics—the major types used for rigid and semirigid containers—there are no consistent and reliable figures on the portion so used. This reflects the fact that both production and sales data as reported by the synthetic plastics industries are either in terms of the kinds of plastics or in terms of the general forms of production, such as transparent films, moldings and extrusions, etc. End-use distribution is not collected in a systematic way, and since end-uses cut across both kinds of plastics and forms of production, we have at present only a very imperfect notion of the market allocation. The scattered data which do exist—for example, on the quantity of polyethylene consumed in the manufacture of plastic bottles—provide the rough basis for our estimate of all molded and extruded plastics ending up in containers.

The comparatively short period during which plastics have been used for containers and packaging, the current dynamic growth rates characteristic of this use, the likelihood of further discoveries and developments leading to the production of as yet unsynthesized plastics, and the further improvements to be expected in the properties of existing plastic materials all aggravate the difficulty of looking into the plastic container future with any degree of confidence. In general, our projections rest on the assumption that the growth curve for plastics used in containers and packaging will probably resemble that for many other new products, commencing with an early steep rate and eventually tapering off.

While at present plastic containers are used predominantly for foods, in years to come the propor-
tion so used can be expected to decline. Increased use will probably be made of custom molded plastic coverings for assembly line packing, and both films and rigid plastics will probably continue to add new packaging applications among items other than foods. However, food packaging is likely to remain the predominant use throughout the forty-year period, and our projections have therefore related total consumption of plastics for containers and packaging to personal consumption expenditures for food and tobacco.

LIST OF TABLES

690

APPENDIX TO CHAPTER 7

TABLE A7–1. Historical Data on Per Capita Consumption of Canned Food and Beverages[1]

(Pounds, retail weight)

	Principal items									
	Vegetables and soups		Fruits and fruit juices (except citrus)		Citrus fruit and juices (incl. frozen)		Condensed and evaporated milk		Shortening	
	Quantity[2]	Per cent of tomatoes and other vegetables, farm wt.[3]	Quantity[4]	Per cent of apples, other fruits, and melons, farm wt.[3]	Quantity[5]	Per cent of all citrus fruit, farm wt.[3]	Quantity	Per cent of all milk, whole milk equiv.[3]	Quantity	Per cent of fats and oils, retail wt.[3]
1937	30.2	10.8	14.3	7.8	2.2	4.3	16.7	2.1	12.3	18.9
1938	31.9	11.2	15.7	9.2	2.7	4.8	17.2	2.2	11.5	17.7
1939	33.3	11.6	16.7	9.5	3.6	5.0	17.8	2.2	10.7	15.7
1940	35.9	12.3	20.1	11.3	4.1	6.1	19.3	2.4	9.0	12.7
1941	38.3	13.3	18.5	10.5	5.8	8.0	18.5	2.3	10.4	14.9
1942	41.2	13.5	18.4	12.2	4.8	6.7	18.4	2.2	9.4	14.2
1943	37.5	11.9	13.5	10.3	4.0	5.6	18.8	2.5	9.6	14.3
1944	36.3	11.6	9.4	6.5	7.6	8.5	15.7	2.1	8.9	13.5
1945	35.6	10.6	15.0	9.3	7.8	8.8	18.3	2.3	9.1	14.9
1946	48.8	14.9	23.7	13.5	13.1	13.7	18.6	2.4	10.2	15.9
1947	42.7	14.1	19.2	11.7	11.8	12.5	20.4	2.7	9.4	14.5
1948	41.3	14.1	18.7	11.7	14.3	15.4	20.2	2.8	9.7	14.9
1949	42.3	15.1	20.2	12.8	12.4	15.0	19.7	2.7	9.7	14.9
1950	45.6	16.1	22.3	15.0	10.9	14.9	20.1	2.7	11.0	16.2
1951	46.4	16.5	20.2	13.4	13.0	15.7	18.3	2.6	9.0	13.8
1952	46.3	16.7	21.8	14.5	12.6	14.9	17.6	2.5	10.2	15.0
1953	47.8	17.4	22.4	14.7	12.7	14.8	17.4	2.5	10.2	15.7
1954	46.8	17.3	21.7	14.6	13.1	15.2	16.8	2.4	11.8	17.9
1955	48.6	17.9	23.2	15.8	14.2	15.5	16.2	2.3	11.5	16.9
1956	49.3	18.1	23.7	16.1	14.2	16.1	15.9	2.3	10.9	16.3
1957	49.6	18.4	24.1	16.7	14.9	16.7	15.4	2.3	10.4	16.0
1958	50.7	18.9	24.1	16.2	13.8	18.2	14.8	2.2	11.3	17.1
1959	51.4	19.3	23.7	16.1	13.6	16.4	14.3	2.2	12.6	18.3
1960	51.6	19.2	24.8	16.7	14.9	17.3	13.8	2.1	12.6	18.8

	Principal items (cont'd)			Total canned food		Malt beverages (packaged)			All canned food and beverages
	Coffee and cocoa						Canned		
	Quantity[6]	Per cent of coffee, tea, and cocoa, retail wt.[3]	Total	Quantity[7]	Ratio to principal items (%)	Total consumed[8]	Quantity[8]	Per cent of total	
1937	7.3	48.7	83.0	93.9	113.1	48.9	n.a.	–	n.a.
1938	7.6	47.5	86.6	98.0	113.2	47.1	n.a.	–	n.a.
1939	8.5	50.0	90.6	102.8	113.5	51.3	n.a.	–	n.a.
1940	8.7	51.2	97.1	109.4	112.7	52.3	5.2	9.9	114.6
1941	8.8	48.9	100.3	113.5	113.2	62.3	8.4	13.5	121.9
1942	7.4	49.3	99.6	107.8	108.2	72.5	1.3	1.8	109.1
1943	6.7	47.9	90.1	98.5	109.3	83.5	.4	.5	98.9
1944	7.5	46.9	85.4	94.8	111.0	92.4	2.4	2.6	97.2
1945	8.0	47.1	93.8	105.1	112.0	97.1	4.3	4.4	109.4
1946	9.8	46.7	124.2	139.5	112.3	96.7	.8	.8	140.3
1947	8.9	49.4	112.4	126.7	112.7	105.5	11.6	11.0	138.3
1948	8.9	46.8	113.1	128.4	113.5	103.3	15.4	14.9	143.8
1949	9.3	48.9	113.6	128.4	113.0	102.8	19.4	18.9	147.8
1950	8.8	48.9	118.7	134.8	113.6	101.2	26.1	25.8	160.9

Table A7–1 (cont'd)

(Pounds, retail weight)

| | Principal items (cont'd) | | | Total canned food | | Malt beverages (packaged) | | | |
| | Coffee and cocoa | | | | | | Canned | | |
	Quantity[6]	Per cent of coffee, tea, and cocoa, retail wt.[3]	Total	Quantity[7]	Ratio to principal items (%)	Total consumed[8]	Quantity[8]	Per cent of total	All canned food and beverages
1951	7.6	42.2	114.5	130.7	114.1	103.1	22.5	21.8	153.2
1952	7.7	42.8	116.2	133.1	114.5	104.1	25.2	24.2	158.3
1953	7.8	43.3	118.3	135.9	114.9	106.4	31.0	29.1	166.9
1954	7.0	43.8	117.2	134.4	114.7	101.6	32.0	31.5	166.4
1955	7.1	44.4	120.8	138.0	114.2	103.3	35.2	34.1	173.2
1956	7.4	43.5	121.4	139.6	115.0	102.9	36.7	35.7	176.3
1957	7.5	44.1	121.9	139.7	114.6	100.9	37.2	36.9	176.9
1958	7.2	42.4	121.9	139.6	114.5	99.5	37.9	38.1	177.5
1959	7.6	44.7	123.2	141.0	114.4	102.5	40.9	39.9	181.9
1960	7.4	43.5	125.1	143.0	114.3	103.0	42.4	41.2	185.4

1. Based on data in 1956 and 1960 supplements to *Consumption of Food in the United States* (USDA Agricultural Handbook No. 62).
2. Consists of vegetables listed in *Consumption of Food*, Table 18, and canned soup, Table 19, less asparagus, catsup and chili sauce, and pickles.
3. Reference series, which refer to total consumption, are in Table A2–1.
4. Consists of canned and chilled fruits listed in *Consumption of Food*, Table 12, less citrus segments, olives, and half the weight of cherries, plus berry juices, pineapple juice, and fruit sections, from Table 13.

5. Consists of the citrus items in *Consumption of Food*, Tables 12, 13, and 14.
6. One-third of total coffee, plus all cocoa, assumed to be in cans.
7. Includes, in addition to "principal items," canned meat, fish, peanuts, spices, and tree nuts. It has been assumed that half of total peanuts and spices and one-tenth of tree nuts are canned.
8. Computed from data in standard barrel equivalents in U.S. Brewers Foundation, *The Brewing Industry in the United States* (1960 ed.). Conversion factors employed: 31-gallon barrels and 258 pounds per 31-gallon barrel.

TABLE A7–2. Projected Per Capita Consumption of Canned Food and Beverages[1]

(Pounds, retail weight)

	1950	1955	1960		1970	1980	1990	2000
Principal items:								
Vegetables and soups[2]	45.6	48.6	51.6	L	39.2	36.8	36.8	36.8
				M	42.4	40.5	41.2	41.2
				H	46.1	44.7	46.5	46.5
Per capita consumption of tomatoes and other vegetables (farm wt.)	284	271	269	L	245	245	245	245
				M	265	270	275	275
				H	288	298	310	310
Per cent in cans (retail wt.)	16.1	17.9	19.2		16.0	15.0	15.0	15.0
Fruits and fruit juices (except citrus)[2]	22.3	23.2	24.8	L	22.2	21.2	21.0	21.0
				M	24.7	24.2	24.2	24.2
				H	26.4	26.2	26.2	26.2
Per capita consumption of apples, other fruit, and melons (farm wt.)	149	146	147	L	127	121	120	120
				M	141	138	138	138
				H	151	150	150	150
Per cent in cans (retail wt.)	15.0	15.8	16.7		17.5	17.5	17.5	17.5

Table A7–2 (cont'd)

(Pounds, retail weight)

	1950	1955	1960		1970	1980	1990	2000
Citrus fruit and juices				L	16.6	19.0	19.0	19.0
(incl. frozen)	10.9	14.2	14.9	M	19.4	21.8	21.8	21.8
				H	20.4	23.8	24.7	24.7
Per capita consumption of				L	90	100	100	100
citrus fruit (farm wt.)	73.3	91.4	86.3	M	105	115	115	115
				H	110	125	130	130
Per cent in cans (retail wt.)	14.9	15.5	17.3		18.5	19.0	19.0	19.0
				L	11.8	11.0	10.2	10.0
Condensed and evaporated milk	20.1	16.2	13.8	M	12.9	12.6	12.2	12.2
				H	13.5	13.6	13.6	13.6
Per capita consumption of all				L	590	550	510	500
milk (whole milk equiv.)	741	706	654	M	645	630	610	610
				H	675	680	680	680
Per cent in cans (retail wt.)	2.7	2.3	2.1		2.0	2.0	2.0	2.0
				L	9.6	8.7	8.4	8.4
Shortening	11.0	11.5	12.6	M	10.4	9.4	9.1	9.1
				H	11.2	10.2	9.8	9.8
Per capita consumption of fats				L	60	60	60	60
and oils (retail wt.)	68	68	67	M	65	65	65	65
				H	70	70	70	70
Per cent in cans	16.2	16.9	18.8		16.0	14.5	14.0	14.0
				L	6.6	6.6	6.6	6.6
Coffee and cocoa	8.8	7.1	7.4	M	7.5	7.5	7.5	7.5
				H	8.4	8.8	8.8	8.8
Per capita consumption of coffee,				L	15	15	15	15
tea, and cocoa (retail wt.)	18	16	17	M	17	17	17	17
				H	19	20	20	20
Per cent in cans	48.9	44.4	43.5		44.0	44.0	44.0	44.0
				L	106.0	103.3	102.0	101.8
Total, principal items	118.7	120.8	125.1	M	117.3	116.0	116.0	116.0
				H	126.0	127.3	129.6	129.6
Total canned food (except malt				L	121.9	118.8	117.3	117.1
beverages)[3]	134.8	138.0	143.0	M	134.9	133.4	133.4	133.4
				H	144.9	146.4	149.0	149.0
Ratio to principal items (%)	113.6	114.2	114.3		115	115	115	115
				L	55.6	62.4	64.7	64.7
Malt beverages[4]	26.1	35.2	42.4	M	56.6	64.9	68.7	70.1
				H	57.8	67.4	72.7	74.9
Per capita consumption of malt				L	101	99	97	95
beverages (packaged)	101	103	103	M	103	103	103	103
				H	105	107	109	110
Per cent in cans	25.8	34.1	41.2		55.0	63.0	66.7	68.1
				L	177.5	181.2	182.0	181.8
Total canned food and beverages	160.9	173.2	185.4	M	191.5	198.3	202.1	203.5
				H	202.7	213.8	221.7	223.9

1. Historical data from Tables A7–1 (canned food consumption) and A2–2 (reference series). Projections of each of the "principal items" are derived by applying the coefficients (percentages) shown to the accompanying reference series (from Table A2–2). The coefficients are projected on the basis of judgment and past trends.

2. For items included, see Table A7–1.
3. Includes, in addition to principal items, canned meat, fish, peanuts, spices, and tree nuts.
4. Calculated from the two series which follow, each of which is extrapolated on a judgment basis.

TABLE A7–3.   Historical Data on Use of Metals in Containers and Packaging

(Million tons, unless otherwise specified)

	1948	1949	1950	1951	1952	1953	1954	1955	1956	1957	1958	1959	1960
Cans:													
Consumption of canned foods and beverages[1]	10.5	11.0	12.2	11.8	12.4	13.3	13.5	14.3	14.8	15.1	15.5	16.1	16.7
Plate or equivalent consumed for canned food and beverages[2]	2.60	2.62	3.04	2.99	3.05	3.23	3.25	3.53	3.78	3.61	3.73	3.82	3.77
Pounds of plate per pound of content	.248	.238	.249	.253	.246	.243	.241	.247	.255	.239	.241	.237	.226
Plate or equivalent used for all cans[2]	3.25	3.28	3.89	3.80	3.84	4.08	4.14	4.48	4.79	4.59	4.76	4.95	4.82
Ratio to consumption for food and beverages (%)	125	125	128	127	126	126	127	127	127	127	128	130	128
Aluminum used in cans:													
Quantity[3]	–	–	–	–	–	–	–	–	–	–	–	.01	.02
Plate equivalent[4]												.02	.04
Steel plate used for all cans[5]	3.25	3.28	3.89	3.80	3.84	4.08	4.14	4.48	4.79	4.59	4.76	4.93	4.78
Tin used in cans[6] (thous. tons)	26	26	30	24	23	24	26	28	29	28	29	29	29
Ratio of tin to plate[7]	.81	.78	.77	.62	.60	.60	.63	.62	.61	.60	.60	.59	.60
Miscellaneous metal containers, closures, and packaging materials:													
Steel barrels, drums, pails, closures, etc.[8]	3.06	2.36	3.26	4.03	2.98	3.26	2.66	3.38	3.47	2.79	2.86	3.33	3.58
Output of goods[9] ($ 1960 bil.)	184.5	178.5	195.1	211.8	218.5	230.4	218.5	239.1	244.5	246.9	233.3	252.2	258.5
Tons per $ 1960 million	16.6	13.2	16.7	19.0	13.6	14.1	12.2	14.1	14.2	11.3	12.3	13.2	13.9
Aluminum in foil and collapsible tubes[10]	n.a.	n.a.	n.a.	n.a.	.032	.044	.055	.066	.078	.089	.092	.112	.127
Pounds per capita	–	–	–	–	.409	.550	.680	.792	.940	1.04	1.06	1.27	1.41
Gross consumption of steel in containers and packaging[11]	6.31	5.64	7.15	7.83	6.82	7.34	6.80	7.86	8.26	7.38	7.62	8.27	8.36
Net consumption of steel in containers and packaging[12]	5.55	4.96	6.29	6.89	6.00	6.46	5.98	6.92	7.27	6.70	6.71	7.28	7.36
Consumption of aluminum in containers and packaging	n.a.	n.a.	n.a.	n.a.	.03	.04	.06	.07	.08	.09	.09	.12	.15

1. Per capita consumption (Table A7–1), multiplied by population (Table A1–1).

2. Can Manufacturers Institute, *Annual Report of Steel and Tin Consumed in Metal Cans.* Includes tin plate, terne plate, and black plate. Data for 1959 and 1960 include also the plate equivalent of aluminum cans (see below in table).

3. For 1960, from Can Manufacturers Institute; 1959 estimated.

4. Based on assumed ratio of .45 tons of aluminum to 1 ton of steel (from study by Arthur D. Little, Inc., "Future Prospects for Aluminum Cans," 1959).

5. Actual tin plate or other steel plate; i.e., net of aluminum.

6. Derived by applying ratio which follows.

7. Derived as follows: ratios of tin to hot dipped and electrolytic tin plate, respectively (from U.S. Bureau of Mines, *Minerals Yearbook*), applied to tin and terne plate shipments to the canning industry, per American Iron and Steel Institute annual statement, "Shipments of Steel Products by Market Classifications" (AIS 16), to obtain tin used for canning; this quantity then applied to total shipments of

all types of plate (including black plate) to the canning industry. The error introduced by inclusion of terne plate in the first part of the calculation is negligible, since the ratio of terne plate to tin plate is very small (less than 1%).

8. Data are for direct shipments of steel for these uses, as reported by AISI, *op. cit.*, plus amounts needed to adjust from totals accounted for by AISI as going directly to the container industry as a whole and sum total of direct and indirect shipments to the container industry as a whole, as estimated in Table A16–3. For explanation, see Notes.

9. From Table A1–6.

10. Computed from Census data on conversion of aluminum foil by end-use and from data on collapsible tubes in U.S. Department of Commerce, Business and Defense Services Administration (BDSA), *Containers and Packaging* (quarterly).

11. Sum of steel in cans and steel in barrels, etc.

12. Gross consumption less an allowance for scrap generated in processing. The estimated ratio of 12% is from a study by Battelle Memorial Institute (see footnote 8, Table A16–4).

TABLE A7–4. Projected Use of Metals in Containers and Packaging[1]

(Million tons, unless otherwise specified)

	1950	1955	1960		1970	1980	1990	2000
Cans:								
Metal cans, in plate equivalent:								
Consumption for canned food				L	4.30	4.92	5.45	5.86
and beverages (unadjusted)	3.04	3.53	3.77	M	4.78	5.83	6.96	8.09
				H	5.42	7.15	9.29	11.64
Consumption of canned food				L	17.9	20.5	22.7	24.4
and beverages[2]	12.2	14.3	16.7	M	19.9	24.3	29.0	33.7
				H	22.6	29.8	38.7	48.5
Pounds of plate equivalent								
per pound of product[3]	.249	.247	.226		.240	.240	.240	.240
Consumption for all purposes				L	5.59	6.40	7.08	7.62
(unadjusted)	3.89	4.48	4.82	M	6.26	7.70	9.26	10.84
				H	7.15	9.58	12.63	16.06
Ratio to consumption for food				L	130	130	130	130
and beverages[4] (%)	128	127	128	M	131	132	133	134
				H	132	134	136	138
Per cent substitution of non-				L	–	8.4	16.8	25.0
metal containers[5]	–	–	–	M	–	2.0	6.0	10.0
				H	–	–	–	–
Consumption of metal, in plate				L	5.59	5.86	5.89	5.72
equivalent	3.89	4.48	4.82	M	6.26	7.55	8.70	9.76
				H	7.15	9.58	12.63	16.06
Aluminum consumption:								
Per cent of metal cans made				L	4	6	8	10
of aluminum[5]	–	–	.9	M	8	11	13	15
				H	10	14	18	20
Aluminum consumption in plate				L	.22	.35	.47	.57
equivalent	–	–	.04	M	.50	.83	1.13	1.46
				H	.72	1.34	2.27	3.21
				L	.10	.16	.21	.26
Aluminum consumption[6]	–	–	.02	M	.22	.37	.51	.66
				H	.32	.60	1.02	1.44
Steel consumption:								
Per cent of metal cans made of				L	90	86	82	80
conventional plate[7]	100.0	100.0	99.1	M	92	89	87	85
				H	96	94	92	90
Consumption of conventional				L	5.03	5.04	4.8	4.58
plate	3.89	4.48	4.78	M	5.76	6.72	7.57	8.30
				H	6.86	9.01	11.62	14.45
Adjusted steel in cans as a				L	82.3	68.1	55.3	49.8
percentage of steel in con-	100.0	100.0	100.0	M	95.8	88.1	80.6	73.2
ventional plate[8]				H	97.8	96.2	94.8	93.0
				L	4.14	3.43	2.68	2.28
Adjusted steel consumption	3.89	4.48	4.78	M	5.52	5.92	6.10	6.08
				H	6.71	8.67	11.01	13.44
Tin consumption:								
Ratio of tin to conventional				L	.38	.24	.15	.10
plate[9] (%)	.77	.62	.60	M	.48	.40	.32	.26
				H	.57	.55	.53	.51
				L	19	12	7	4
Thousands of tons	30	28	29	M	28	27	24	22
				H	39	50	62	74

Table A7–4 (cont'd)

(Million tons unless otherwise specified)

	1950	1955	1960		1970	1980	1990	2000
Miscellaneous metal containers, closures, and packaging materials:								
Steel barrels, drums, pails, closures, etc.				L	3.17	2.95	2.81	2.70
	3.26	3.38	3.58	M	3.88	4.51	5.20	6.01
				H	4.73	6.60	9.28	12.92
Output of goods[10] ($ 1960 bil.)				L	330	422	540	692
	195	239	258	M	363	512	722	1,019
				H	401	623	967	1,502
Tons/$ 1960 mil.[9]				L	9.6	7.0	5.2	3.9
	16.7	14.1	13.9	M	10.7	8.8	7.2	5.9
				H	11.8	10.6	9.6	8.6
Aluminum in foil and collapsible tubes				L	.21	.29	.35	.39
	n.a.	.07	.13	M	.25	.40	.55	.68
				H	.29	.50	.77	1.10
Pounds per capita[9]				L	2.1	2.6	2.8	2.9
	n.a.	.79	1.41	M	2.4	3.3	3.8	4.1
				H	2.6	3.6	4.4	5.1
Gross consumption of steel in containers and packaging				L	7.31	6.38	5.49	4.98
	7.15	7.86	8.36	M	9.40	10.43	11.30	12.09
				H	11.44	15.27	20.29	26.36
Net consumption of steel in containers and packaging[11]				L	6.43	5.61	4.83	4.38
	6.29	6.92	7.36	M	8.27	9.18	9.95	10.64
				H	10.07	13.44	17.86	23.20
Net consumption of aluminum in containers and packaging[12]				L	.29	.42	.52	.60
	.06	.06	.16	M	.43	.70	.97	1.22
				H	.55	.99	1.61	2.28

1. Historical data from Table A7–3, except as noted.

2. Per capita consumption, Table A7–2, multiplied by population, Table A1–2.

3. For purposes of a first approximation, the historical relationship (see Table A7–3) is assumed to remain unchanged. The effects of variation in types of container are developed below.

4. Historical ratios (Table A7–3), extrapolated on a judgment basis.

5. The Low refers to the amount of substitution consistent with Low metal consumption, the High with High metal consumption. Projections are on a judgment basis (see Chapter 7, p. 163, and Notes, above).

6. For conversion factor, see Table A7–3, footnote 4.

7. Complement of aluminum percentage. Low "conventional" is complement of High aluminum and vice versa.

8. Assumes a reduction in weight of steel as thinner gauge steels become common in the industry. The possible rates of reduction have been projected on the basis of estimates made by specialists in the field of metallurgy.

9. Projected on a judgment basis. See Chapter 7, p. 163, and Notes, above.

10. From Table A1–13.

11. 88% of gross; see footnote 12, Table A7–3.

12. Aluminum in foil and collapsible tubes, plus 82% of aluminum in cans. (Latter rate is from BDSA, *Industrial Scrap Generation,* 1957). Aluminum foil and collapsible tubes are already on a net, or content, basis. Historical data from Table A16–32.

TABLE A7–5.   Historical Data on Wood and Glass Containers

	Consumption of lumber in boxes and crating[1] (bil. bd. ft.)	Durable goods output[2] ($ 1960 bil.)	Consumption of lumber in boxes and crating/$ thous. durable goods output (bd. ft.)	Ship- ments of glass con- tainers[3] (mil. gross)	Non- durable goods output[2] ($ 1960 bil.)	Shipments of glass contain- ers/$ bil. non-dur- able goods (thous. gross)
1929	4.64	34.8	133	34	69.7	488
1930	4.04	23.4	173	32	68.2	469
1931	3.36	17.0	198	32	67.9	471
1932	2.42	8.8	275	27	61.4	440
1933	2.55	12.0	212	33	57.6	573
1934	2.66	17.6	151	35	61.3	571
1935	3.22	22.4	144	38	67.7	561
1936	3.66	29.7	123	46	73.5	626
1937	4.00	32.4	123	50	79.4	630
1938	3.84	22.3	172	44	80.2	549
1939	4.05	28.7	141	49	83.5	587
1940	4.29	37.4	115	52	88.7	586
1941	5.14	52.5	98	69	93.8	736
1942	9.14	59.8	153	80	103.8	771
1943	14.14	89.3	158	96	105.2	913
1944	15.24	100.5	152	95	113.5	837
1945	11.71	88.7	132	104	118.6	877
1946	5.72	60.7	94	114	119.9	951
1947	4.91	63.6	77	106	116.3	911
1948	3.99	63.4	63	94	121.1	776
1949	3.78	59.3	64	87	119.2	730
1950	4.29	73.9	58	105	121.2	866
1951	4.51	85.3	53	112	126.5	885
1952	4.69	87.2	54	111	131.3	845
1953	4.41	93.6	47	124	136.8	806
1954	4.09	82.7	49	122	135.8	898
1955	4.21	95.0	44	134	144.1	930
1956	4.54	97.2	47	138	147.5	936
1957	4.01	98.1	41	140	148.8	941
1958	4.23	82.5	51	140	150.8	928
1959	4.34	95.0	46	150	157.2	954
1960	4.09	96.7	42	156	161.8	964

1. National Lumber Manufacturers Association, *Lumber Facts.* Data represent mill shipments adjusted for changes in retail inventories.
2. From Table A1–6.
3. From U.S. Dept. of Commerce, *Containers and Packaging* (quarterly).

TABLE A7–6.   Projections of Wood and Glass Containers

	1950	1955	1960		1970	1980	1990	2000
Consumption of lumber in boxes and crating[1] (bil. bd. ft.)	4.3	4.2	4.1	L M H	3.0 5.7 7.9	2.1 6.6 10.9	1.6 7.2 14.0	1.3 6.7 16.5
Durable goods output[2] ($ 1960 bil.)	74	95	97	L M H	122 154 188	151 229 322	200 343 540	261 514 918
Consumption of lumber/$ thous. durable goods output[3] (bd. ft.)	58	44	42	L M H	25 37 42	14 29 34	8 21 26	5 13 18
Shipments of glass containers[1] (mil. gross)	105	134	156	L M H	194 220 253	239 311 400	290 424 622	339 570 950
Non-durable goods output[2] ($ 1960 bil.)	121	144	162	L M H	200 216 239	246 293 354	299 393 523	349 518 766
Glass containers shipped/$ bil. non-durable goods output[4] (mil. gross)	.867	.931	.964	L M H	.97 1.02 1.06	.97 1.06 1.13	.97 1.08 1.19	.97 1.10 1.25
Glass used in containers (bil. lb.)	7.6	9.4	10.9	L M H	11.2 13.2 16.4	10.8 15.6 24.0	9.4 17.0 34.2	6.8 17.1 47.5
Average weight per gross[5] (lb.)	72.8	70.0	70.0	L M H	57.5 60.0 65.0	45.0 50.0 60.0	32.5 40.0 55.0	20.0 30.0 50.0

1. Historical data from Table A7–5. Projections calculated from the factors which follow.
2. From Table A1–13.
3. Projections assume that coefficient will continue to decline, as it has historically, in spite of leveling off between 1955 and 1960.
4. Medium projection reflects historical trend in the coefficient, which has been increasing at a decreasing rate.
5. Assumes that technical progress toward thinner, lighter glass will occur throughout the 40–year period. Projections are based on estimates of weight reduction appearing in the technical literature.

TABLE A7-7.   Historical Data on Use of Paper in Containers and Packaging

	1929	1946	1947	1948	1949	1950	1951	1952	1953	1954	1955	1956	1957	1958	1959	1960
Goods output ($ 1960 bil.)[1]	104.5	180.6	179.9	184.5	178.5	195.1	211.8	218.5	230.4	218.5	239.1	244.5	246.9	233.3	252.2	258.5
Consumer purchases of non-durables ($ 1960 bil.)[2]	70.2	115.7	113.2	113.0	114.2	117.4	119.6	123.6	127.2	128.3	134.7	140.0	142.4	143.2	149.2	152.4
Personal consumption expenditures on food and soft beverages ($ 1960 bil.)[3]	–	55.2	54.3	54.4	54.7	55.4	56.8	58.0	59.9	60.9	63.5	66.2	67.2	67.1	69.0	70.2
Consumption of containerboard[4] (mil. tons)	2.21	4.28	4.89	5.02	4.63	5.77	6.19	5.69	6.54	6.34	7.35	7.62	7.39	7.41	8.09	8.16
Consumption per $ 1960 bil. goods output (thous. tons)	21.1	23.7	27.2	27.2	25.9	29.6	29.2	26.0	28.4	29.0	30.7	31.2	29.9	31.8	32.1	31.6
Consumption of folding boxboard[5] (mil. tons)	.99	2.27	2.30	2.23	2.09	2.46	2.46	2.66	2.56	2.54	2.74	2.84	2.83	2.87	2.93	2.92
Consumption per $ 1960 bil. consumer purchases of non-durables (thous. tons)	14.1	19.6	20.3	19.7	18.3	21.0	20.6	21.5	20.1	19.8	20.3	20.3	19.9	20.0	19.6	19.2
Consumption of special foodboard[4] (mil. tons)	–	.43	.46	.44	.52	.65	.77	.80	.97	1.00	1.16	1.26	1.28	1.33	1.46	1.49
Consumption per $ 1960 bil. personal consumption expenditures on food and soft beverages (thous. tons)	–	7.79	8.47	8.09	9.51	11.7	13.6	13.8	16.2	16.4	18.3	19.0	19.0	19.8	21.2	21.2
Consumption of set-up boxboards and special paperboards for containers[6] (mil. tons)	.60	.81	.87	.96	1.00	1.17	1.19	.91	1.24	1.23	1.40	1.34	1.29	1.29	1.46	1.42
Consumption per $ 1960 bil. consumer purchases of non-durables (thous. tons)	8.55	7.00	7.69	8.50	8.76	9.97	9.95	7.36	9.75	9.59	10.4	9.57	9.06	9.01	9.79	9.32
Consumption of coarse and industrial papers for packaging[7] (mil. tons)	1.35	2.43	2.63	2.75	2.46	2.99	3.28	2.94	3.15	3.14	3.40	3.69	3.42	3.44	3.80	3.80
Consumption per $ 1960 bil. goods output (thous. tons)	12.9	13.5	14.6	14.9	13.8	15.3	15.5	13.5	13.7	14.4	14.2	15.1	13.9	14.7	15.1	14.7
Consumption of tissue paper for packaging[8] (mil. tons)	.04	.10	.10	.11	.11	.13	.14	.13	.14	.15	.17	.18	.18	.19	.21	.20
Consumption per $ 1960 bil. consumer purchases of non-durables (thous. tons)	.569	.864	.883	.973	.963	1.107	1.171	1.052	1.101	1.169	1.262	1.286	1.264	1.327	1.408	1.312
Total consumption of paper in containers and packaging (mil. tons)	5.19	10.32	11.25	11.51	10.81	13.17	14.03	13.13	14.60	14.40	16.22	16.93	16.39	16.53	17.95	17.99

1. From Table A1-6.
2. From Table A1-8.
3. From Table A1-26.
4. House Committee on Interstate and Foreign Commerce, *Pulp, Paper, and Board—Supply-Demand* (H. Rept. No. 573, 85th Cong., First Sess.). Data for years 1957-60 are from U.S. Bureau of the Census, *Pulp, Paper, and Board* (Current Industrial Reports, Series M26A).
5. Reported as "bending board" in House Report No. 573.

6. Estimated as 54.0% of the total consumption of set-up boxboards and special paperboards (reported as "nonbending and other paperboards") in House Report No. 573. Consumption in 1957-60 for containers and packaging estimated from reported consumption by grades of paper in Bureau of the Census, *Pulp, Paper, and Board*.
7. Estimated as 80.3% of the total consumption of coarse and industrial paper. Sources as in footnote 6.
8. Estimated as 9.6% of the total consumption of sanitary and tissue paper. Sources as in footnote 6.

TABLE A7–8. Projected Use of Paper in Containers and Packaging[1]

	1950	1955	1960		1970	1980	1990	2000
Goods output ($ 1960 bil.) [2]	195.1	239.1	258.5	L	330	422	540	692
				M	363	512	722	1,019
				H	401	623	967	1,502
Consumer purchases of non-durables ($ 1960 bil.) [3]	117.4	134.7	152.4	L	191	237	287	335
				M	202	271	360	469
				H	221	323	473	680
Personal consumption expenditures on food and soft beverages ($ 1960 bil.) [3]	55.4	63.5	70.2	L	85.6	102.5	121.2	139.1
				M	90.6	117.8	154.8	198.0
				H	111.4	169.4	258.8	389.2
Consumption of containerboard (mil. tons)	5.77	7.35	8.16	L	11.55	15.87	21.28	28.03
				M	12.70	19.25	28.45	41.27
				H	14.04	23.42	38.10	60.83
Consumption per $ 1960 bil. goods output [4] (thous. tons)	29.6	30.7	31.6		35.0	37.6	39.4	40.5
Consumption of folding boxboard (mil. tons)	2.46	2.74	2.92	L	3.72	4.62	5.60	6.53
				M	3.94	5.28	7.02	9.15
				H	4.31	6.30	9.22	13.26
Consumption per $ 1960 bil. consumer purchases of non-durables [5] (thous. tons)	21.0	20.3	19.2		19.5	19.5	19.5	19.5
Consumption of special foodboard (mil. tons)	.65	1.16	1.49	L	2.25	2.77	3.27	3.76
				M	2.38	3.18	4.18	5.35
				H	2.93	4.57	6.99	10.51
Consumption per $ 1960 bil. personal consumption expenditures on food and soft beverages [6] (thous. tons)	11.7	18.3	21.2		26.3	27.0	27.0	27.0
Consumption of set-up boxboards and special paperboards for containers (mil. tons)	1.17	1.40	1.42	L	1.81	2.25	2.73	3.18
				M	1.92	2.57	3.42	4.46
				H	2.10	3.07	4.49	6.46
Consumption per $ 1960 bil. consumer purchases of non-durables [5] (thous. tons)	9.97	10.4	9.3		9.5	9.5	9.5	9.5
Consumption of coarse and industrial papers for packaging (mil. tons)	2.99	3.40	3.80	L	4.78	6.12	7.83	10.03
				M	5.26	7.42	10.47	14.78
				H	5.81	9.03	14.02	21.78
Consumption per $ 1960 bil. goods output [4] (thous. tons)	15.3	14.2	14.7		14.5	14.5	14.5	14.5
Consumption of tissue paper for packaging (mil. tons)	.13	.17	.20	L	.31	.40	.49	.57
				M	.33	.46	.61	.80
				H	.36	.55	.80	1.16
Consumption per $ 1960 bil. consumer purchases of non-durables [6] (thous. tons)	1.11	1.26	1.31		1.63	1.70	1.70	1.70
Total consumption of paper in containers and packaging (mil. tons)	13.2	16.2	18.0	L	24.42	32.03	41.20	52.10
				M	26.53	38.16	54.15	75.81
				H	29.55	46.94	73.62	114.00

1. Historical data from Table A7–7.
2. From Table A1–13.
3. From Table A1–27.
4. Projected on a judgment basis.

5. Projected coefficient is 1950–60 average.
6. Projected on a judgment basis at a declining rate of increase to 1980, and at a constant level thereafter.

TABLE A7–9.   Historical Data on Use of Plastics in Containers and Packaging

	1950	1951	1952	1953	1954	1955	1956	1957	1958	1959	1960
Personal consumption expenditures for food and tobacco[1] ($ 1960 bil.)	70.3	71.4	73.6	75.5	76.2	79.0	82.0	83.1	82.8	85.9	87.6
Total consumption of transparent plastic film for containers and packaging[2] (mil. lb.)	300	347	343	388	465	525	583	590	627	682	706
Consumption per $ 1960 thous. pers. cons. exp. for food and tobacco (lb.)	4.3	4.9	4.7	5.1	6.1	6.6	7.1	7.1	7.6	7.9	8.1
Percentage share:											
Cellophane	87.7	80.1	74.3	80.7	75.3	69.5	68.1	65.8	64.3	63.9	62.2
Petroleum-base films	12.3	19.9	25.7	19.3	24.7	30.5	31.9	34.2	35.7	36.1	37.8
Consumption of cellophane[3] (mil. lb.)	263	278	255	313	350	365	397	388	403	436	439
Consumption of petroleum-base films[4] (mil. lb.)	37	69	88	75	115	160	186	202	224	246	267
Consumption of molded and blown plastics for containers and packaging[5] (mil. lb.)	64	67	61	71	81	110	116	115	123	170	188
Consumption per $ 1960 thous. pers. cons. exp. for food and tobacco (lb.)	0.9	0.9	0.8	0.9	1.1	1.4	1.4	1.4	1.5	2.0	2.1
Total consumption of plastics in containers and packaging (mil. lb.)	364	414	404	459	546	635	699	705	750	852	894

1. From Table A1–26.
2. Sum of cellophane and petroleum-base plastic films.
3. U.S. Department of Commerce, BDSA, *Containers and Packaging*, Vol. XIII, No. 1 (Spring 1961).
4. Based on unpublished data compiled by BDSA, Containers and Packaging Division. Includes all transparent plastic films other than cellophane.
5. Estimates, based on assumption that 9.4% of all molded and extruded plastics are used in containers and packaging. Figure of 9.4% derived from various estimates and data in the technical literature. Data on total molded and extruded plastics are based on weight of resin production and sales for moldings and extrusions, as reported in U.S. Tariff Commission, *Synthetic Organic Chemicals*. In those cases where production data of specific resins used for moldings and extrusions are not disclosed, the ratio of resins sold for moldings and extrusions to total resins sold in each major class of resins has been used to arrive at an approximate production figure.

TABLE A7–10.   Projected Use of Plastics in Containers and Packaging[1]

	1950	1955	1960		1970	1980	1990	2000
Personal consumption expenditures for food and tobacco[2] ($ 1960 bil.)	70.3	79.0	87.6	L M H	107.5 112.7 136.1	130.5 147.0 207.1	156.4 190.7 316.2	181.9 240.2 475.8
Total consumption of transparent plastic films for containers and packaging[3] (bil. lb.)	.30	.52	.71	L M H	1.18 1.35 1.91	1.83 2.35 4.14	2.35 3.43 7.59	2.91 4.80 13.32
Consumption per $ 1960 thous. pers. cons. exp. for food and tobacco[4] (lb.)	4.3	6.6	8.1	L M H	11 12 14	14 16 20	15 18 24	16 20 28
Percentage share:								
Cellophane[5]	87.7	69.5	62.2	L M H	40 50 55	20 40 50	12.5 32.5 50	10 30 50
Petroleum-base plastics[5]	12.3	30.5	37.8	L M H	45 50 60	50 60 80	50 67.5 87.5	50 70 90
Consumption of cellophane (bil. lb.)	.26	.36	.44	L M H	.47 .67 1.05	.37 .94 2.07	.29 1.11 3.80	.29 1.44 6.66
Consumption of petroleum-base films (bil. lb.)	.04	.16	.27	L M H	.53 .68 1.15	.92 1.41 3.31	1.18 2.32 6.64	1.46 3.36 11.99
Consumption of molded and blown plastics for containers and packaging[3] (bil. lb.)	.06	.11	.19	L M H	.43 .68 1.63	.78 1.47 4.97	1.09 2.38 9.49	1.27 3.24 14.99
Consumption per $ 1960 thous. pers. cons. exp. for food and tobacco[4] (lb.)	0.9	1.4	2.1	L M H	4 6 12	6 10 24	7 12.5 30	7 13.5 31.5
Total consumption of plastics in containers and packaging (bil. lb.)	.364	.635	.894	L M H	1.61 2.03 3.54	2.61 3.82 9.11	3.44 5.81 17.08	4.18 8.04 28.31

1. Historical data from Table A7–9; projections as indicated below and Chapter 7, pp. 167–69.
2. From Table A1–27.
3. Highs and Lows are based on High and Low projections of personal income expenditures for food and tobacco paired with High and Low coefficients (below), respectively.

4. Projected on a judgment basis.
5. Continuation of the historical trend for polyethylene and other petroleum-base plastics to fill a larger share of the plastic resin market. Present and potential complementarity of cellophane to polyethylene and other petroleum-base plastics is such that complete disappearance of cellophane is not likely.

appendix
to
chapter
8

PAPER PRODUCTS

Notes

IN THIS APPENDIX historical data on and projections of paper consumption for all paper products are drawn together. Summary data on the consumption of the major categories of paper and paperboard in containers and packaging are carried forward from the appendix to Chapter 7, together with projections of building paper and board from the appendix to Chapter 4. Three classes of paper and board treated in the appendix to Chapter 7 in terms of their consumption for containers and packaging (coarse and industrial paper, sanitary and tissue paper, and set-up boxboards and other special paperboards) are treated in this appendix for their other uses. Several other important classes of paper are also treated here, namely, newsprint, printing papers, and fine papers. Finally, the wood pulp requirements for domestic paper and board production are projected by category of paper and board.

Historical data on consumption of sanitary and tissue paper, coarse and industrial paper, and set-up boxboards and other special paperboards for all uses other than for containers and packaging have been derived by subtracting consumption for containers and packaging, as derived in Table A7–7, from total apparent consumption, as given in the sources cited in Table A8–1, footnote 1. The resulting historical series have then been related, as appropriate, to personal consumption expenditures for paper products and other supplies, to goods production, and to consumer non-durables. Consumption of sanitary and tissue paper per $ 1960

billion of personal consumption expenditures for paper products and other supplies has been rising steeply in recent years, and the coefficient has been projected on a judgment basis to rise further, although at a decreasing rate. The coefficients for coarse and industrial paper and for set-up boxboards and other special paperboards have exhibited no pronounced trends in recent years, and the projections are based on extensions of the 1950–60 averages.

Projection of domestic newsprint production has necessitated first a projection of total domestic requirements and then an assumption regarding the future trend of newsprint imports, which may be expected to continue to be important in the supply picture. Newsprint requirements have been related directly to population with the assumption that the long-range trend toward higher per capita consumption will continue, but at a decreasing rate, particularly after 1980. Newspaper purchases are made almost entirely by individuals, at a cost which is relatively insignificant in relation to disposable personal income.

Discussed in Chapter 8 are the technological advances which should permit a growing proportion of U.S. newsprint requirements to be met from domestic production. The assumed decline in the percentage of domestic requirements imported, down to 45 per cent of the total in 2000, is shown in Table A8–2.

Both the printing papers and the fine papers have been related to disposable personal income. While the latter relationship has varied irregularly, with no clear trend either upward or downward, the former has shown a clear decline.

The 1954 ratios of wood pulp to paper, as detailed in the source cited in Table A8–3, footnote 1, have been assumed to remain constant to 2000 except in the cases of containerboard and building paper and board. Ratios of pulp to paperboard should continue to rise for containerboard as the use of secondary fibers—especially straw and waste paper—in manufacture continues to be displaced more completely by use of wood pulp, although at a decreasing rate. In the case of building paper and board, the projected change in ratio reflects an anticipated change in the "mix" of building paper and building board in this group as a whole. In 1955, building paper comprised 50 per cent of building paper and board as a group; by 2000 it is anticipated that this percentage will decline to 26. The pulp-paper ratios of building paper and building board were quite different in 1954: .321 and .795 respectively. Therefore the ratio of pulp required to building paper and board produced should continue to rise.

LIST OF TABLES

A8–

TABLE A8–1. Historical Data on Consumption and Production of Paper

(Million tons unless otherwise specified)

	1929	1946	1947	1948	1949	1950	1951	1952	1953	1954	1955	1956	1957	1958	1959	1960
Consumption of newsprint[1]	3.79	4.19	4.66	5.14	5.53	5.86	5.87	5.92	6.11	6.10	6.48	6.81	6.78	6.52	7.03	7.33
Population[2] (millions)	121.9	141.4	144.1	146.6	149.2	151.7	154.4	157.0	159.6	162.4	165.3	168.2	171.2	174.1	177.1	179.9
Consumption per million population (thous. tons)	31.1	29.6	32.3	35.1	37.1	38.6	38.0	37.7	38.3	37.6	39.2	40.5	39.6	37.4	39.7	40.7
Imports of newsprint[3]	2.42	3.49	3.96	4.40	4.64	4.86	4.96	5.03	5.00	4.99	5.16	5.57	5.22	4.88	5.26	5.42
Per cent of newsprint consumption	63.9	83.3	85.0	85.4	83.9	82.9	85.2	85.1	81.8	81.8	79.6	81.8	77.0	75.1	74.8	73.9
U.S. production of newsprint[3]	1.41	.77	.83	.88	.92	1.01	1.11	1.11	1.07	1.20	1.46	1.62	1.81	1.73	1.92	2.01
Consumption of printing paper[1]	1.84	2.75	3.05	3.19	2.97	3.31	3.51	3.36	3.59	3.58	3.91	4.31	4.04	4.02	4.19	4.71
Disposable personal income[4] ($ 1960 bil.)	148.7	230.7	221.2	232.8	235.3	253.9	260.9	268.2	280.8	282.9	300.6	315.7	323.3	326.7	342.8	351.8
Consumption per $ 1960 bil. disposable personal income (thous. tons)	12.4	11.9	13.8	13.7	12.6	13.0	13.5	12.5	12.8	12.7	13.0	13.7	12.5	12.3	12.2	13.4
Consumption of fine paper[1]	.73	1.07	1.11	1.10	.97	1.16	1.32	1.26	1.27	1.25	1.42	1.54	1.48	1.54	1.72	1.74
Consumption per $ 1960 bil. disposable personal income (thous. tons)	4.91	4.64	5.02	4.72	4.12	4.57	5.06	4.70	4.52	4.42	4.72	4.88	4.58	4.71	5.02	4.95
Consumption of sanitary and tissue paper: Consumption for other than packaging[5]	.34	.94	.98	1.07	1.08	1.23	1.33	1.22	1.37	1.46	1.59	1.60	1.73	1.76	1.92	2.02
Personal consumption expenditures for paper products and other supplies[6] ($ 1960 bil.)	n.a.	5.0	5.4	5.4	5.4	5.9	6.1	5.8	5.9	5.9	6.3	6.5	6.6	6.7	7.1	7.4
Consumption per $ 1960 bil. pers. cons. exp. for paper products and other supplies (thous. tons)	–	187.6	181.7	198.7	199.3	208.1	217.4	210.7	231.5	246.8	252.7	245.7	262.4	261.9	270.1	272.6
Consumption for packaging[7]	.04	.10	.10	.11	.11	.13	.14	.13	.14	.15	.17	.18	.18	.19	.21	.20
Total consumption	.38	1.04	1.08	1.18	1.19	1.36	1.47	1.35	1.51	1.61	1.76	1.78	1.91	1.95	2.13	2.22
Consumption of coarse and industrial paper: Consumption for other than packaging[5]	.33	.59	.64	.68	.60	.73	.81	.72	.77	.77	.83	.89	.89	.82	.95	.95
Goods output[8] ($ 1960 bil.)	104.5	180.6	179.9	184.5	178.5	195.1	211.8	218.5	230.4	218.5	239.1	244.5	246.9	233.3	252.2	258.5
Consumption per $ 1960 bil. goods output (thous. tons)	3.19	3.28	3.56	3.69	3.36	3.74	3.81	3.31	3.35	3.53	3.47	3.64	3.62	3.49	3.77	3.69
Consumption for packaging[7]	1.35	2.43	2.63	2.75	2.46	2.99	3.28	2.94	3.15	3.14	3.40	3.69	3.42	3.44	3.80	3.80
Total consumption	1.68	3.02	3.27	3.43	3.06	3.72	4.09	3.66	3.92	3.91	4.23	4.58	4.31	4.26	4.75	4.75

Consumption of boxboards and other special paperboards:

Consumption for other than containers and packaging [5]	.52	.69	.75	.80	.86	.99	1.01	.77	1.05	1.05	1.20	1.13	1.27	1.28	1.37	1.38
Consumer non-durables ($ 1960 bil.) [9]	70.2	115.7	113.2	113.0	114.2	117.4	119.6	123.6	127.2	128.3	134.7	140.0	142.4	143.2	149.2	152.4
Consumption per $ 1960 bil. of consumer non-durables (thous. tons)	7.44	5.97	6.64	7.12	7.51	8.41	8.43	6.22	8.23	8.16	8.91	8.08	8.90	8.92	9.20	9.08
Consumption for containers and packaging [7]	.60	.81	.87	.96	1.00	1.17	1.19	.91	1.24	1.23	1.40	1.34	1.29	1.29	1.46	1.42
Total consumption	1.12	1.50	1.62	1.76	1.86	2.16	2.20	1.68	2.29	2.28	2.60	2.47	2.56	2.57	2.83	2.80
Consumption of containerboard [7]	2.21	4.28	4.89	5.02	4.63	5.77	6.19	5.69	6.54	6.34	7.35	7.62	7.39	7.41	8.09	8.16
Consumption of folding boxboard [7]	.99	2.27	2.30	2.23	2.09	2.46	2.46	2.66	2.56	2.54	2.74	2.84	2.83	2.87	2.93	2.92
Consumption of special foodboard [7]	–	.43	.46	.44	.52	.65	.77	.80	.97	1.00	1.16	1.26	1.28	1.33	1.46	1.49
Consumption of building paper and board [1]	.65	1.99	2.34	2.57	1.98	2.65	2.66	2.60	2.69	2.89	3.19	3.12	2.93	3.03	3.48	3.21
Total consumption of paper and paperboard [1]	13.39	22.54	24.78	26.06	24.80	29.10	30.54	28.98	31.45	31.50	34.84	36.33	35.50	35.50	38.65	39.33
Total production of paper and paperboard [1]	11.14	19.26	21.11	21.90	20.32	24.38	26.05	24.42	26.53	26.72	30.14	31.34	30.70	30.82	34.05	34.46
Wood pulp consumed in paper production [1]	6.3	12.1	13.3	14.4	13.6	16.5	17.7	17.3	18.7	19.0	21.5	23.0	22.5	22.5	25.2	25.7

1. Data prior to 1956 from U.S. Congress, House Committee on Interstate and Foreign Commerce, *Pulp, Paper, and Board, Supply-Demand* (H. Rept. No. 573, 85th Cong., First Sess.). Data for 1956–60, which are in terms of reported production, from U.S. Bureau of the Census, *Pulp, Paper, and Board*, Series M 26A, except for newsprint, data for which are apparent consumption as reported in U.S. Department of Commerce, *Pulp, Paper, and Board Industry Report* (quarterly).

2. From Table A1–1.

3. Data prior to 1956 from House Committee on Interstate and Foreign Commerce, *op. cit.;* data for 1956–60 from U.S. Department of Commerce, *Pulp, Paper, and Board Industry Report* (quarterly).

4. From Table A1–26, except for 1929, which is the current-dollar figure (*U.S. Income and Output*, 1958 suppl. to *Survey of Current Business*), deflated by the index for personal consumption expenditures, Tables A1–7.

5. Total consumption, from sources in footnote 1, less consumption for packaging, Table A7–7.

6. From Table A1–26.

7. From Table A7–7.

8. From Table A1–6.

9. From Table A1–8.

TABLE A8–2. Projected Consumption and Production of Paper[1]

(Million tons unless otherwise specified)

	1950	1955	1960		1970	1980	1990	2000
Consumption of newsprint	5.86	6.48	7.33	L	8.8	10.4	11.8	12.9
				M	9.0	11.2	13.6	15.9
				H	9.7	12.8	16.6	20.8
Population[2] (millions)	151.7	165.3	179.9	L	202	226	249	268
				M	208	245	287	331
				H	223	279	349	433
Consumption per million population[3] (thous. tons)	38.6	39.2	40.7		43.4	45.9	47.5	48.0
Assumed percentage of newsprint consumption imported[4]	82.9	79.6	73.9		65	57	51	45
Imports of newsprint	4.86	5.16	5.42	L	5.7	5.9	6.0	5.8
				M	5.9	6.4	7.0	7.2
				H	6.3	7.3	8.5	9.4
Required U.S. production of newsprint[5]	1.01	1.46	2.01	L	3.1	4.5	5.8	7.1
				M	3.1	4.8	6.6	8.7
				H	3.4	5.5	8.1	11.4
Consumption of printing paper	3.31	3.91	4.71	L	5.8	7.4	9.4	11.6
				M	6.0	8.2	11.0	14.6
				H	6.5	9.6	14.1	20.4
Disposable personal income[6] ($ 1960 bil.)	253.9	300.6	351.8	L	479	647	868	1,134
				M	499	715	1,020	1,426
				H	542	840	1,305	1,998
Consumption per $ 1960 bil. disposable personal income[7] (thous. tons)	13.0	13.0	13.4		12.0	11.4	10.8	10.2
Consumption of fine paper	1.16	1.42	1.74	L	2.2	3.0	4.1	5.3
				M	2.4	3.4	4.8	6.7
				H	2.6	4.0	6.1	9.4
Consumption per $ 1960 bil. disposable personal income[8] (thous. tons)	4.57	4.72	4.95		4.7	4.7	4.7	4.7
Consumption of sanitary and tissue paper:								
Consumption for other than packaging	1.2	1.6	2.0	L	2.9	4.1	5.2	6.0
				M	3.2	4.9	7.1	9.0
				H	3.7	6.4	10.4	15.9
Personal consumption expenditures for paper products and other supplies[6] ($ 1960 bil.)	5.9	6.3	7.4	L	9.0	11.0	13.1	15.0
				M	9.7	13.2	17.9	22.4
				H	11.4	17.3	26.4	39.8
Consumption per $ 1960 bil. pers. cons. exp. for paper products and other supplies[9] (thous. tons)	208.1	252.7	272.6		325	370	395	400
Consumption for packaging[10]	.1	.2	.2	L	.3	.4	.5	.6
				M	.3	.5	.6	.8
				H	.4	.6	.8	1.2
Total consumption	1.4	1.8	2.2	L	3.2	4.5	5.7	6.6
				M	3.5	5.4	7.7	9.8
				H	4.1	7.0	11.2	17.1
Consumption of coarse and industrial paper:								
Consumption for other than packaging	.7	.8	1.0	L	1.2	1.5	1.9	2.5
				M	1.3	1.8	2.6	3.7
				H	1.4	2.2	3.5	5.4
Goods output[11] ($ 1960 bil.)	195.1	239.1	258.5	L	330	422	540	692
				M	363	512	722	1,019
				H	401	623	967	1,502
Consumption per $ 1960 bil. goods output[8] (thous. tons)	3.74	3.47	3.69		3.6	3.6	3.6	3.6

Table A8–2 (cont'd)

(Million tons unless otherwise specified)

	1950	1955	1960		1970	1980	1990	2000
Consumption for packaging [10]	3.0	3.4	3.8	L	4.8	6.1	7.8	10.0
				M	5.3	7.4	10.5	14.8
				H	5.8	9.0	14.0	21.8
Total consumption	3.7	4.2	4.8	L	6.0	7.6	9.7	12.5
				M	6.6	9.2	13.1	18.5
				H	7.2	11.2	17.5	27.2
Consumption of set-up boxboards and other special paperboards: Consumption for other than containers and packaging	1.0	1.2	1.4	L	1.7	2.1	2.6	3.0
				M	1.8	2.4	3.2	4.2
				H	2.0	2.9	4.3	6.1
Consumer non-durables [6] ($ 1960 bil.)	117.4	134.7	152.4	L	191	237	287	335
				M	202	271	360	469
				H	221	323	473	680
Consumption per $ 1960 bil. of consumer non-durables [8] (thous. tons)	8.41	8.91	9.08		9.0	9.0	9.0	9.0
Consumption for containers and packaging [10]	1.2	1.4	1.4	L	1.8	2.2	2.7	3.2
				M	1.9	2.6	3.4	4.5
				H	2.1	3.1	4.5	6.5
Total consumption	2.2	2.6	2.8	L	3.5	4.3	5.3	6.2
				M	3.7	5.0	6.6	8.7
				H	4.1	6.0	8.8	12.6
Consumption of containerboard [10]	5.8	7.4	8.2	L	11.6	15.9	21.3	28.0
				M	12.7	19.2	28.4	41.3
				H	14.0	23.4	38.1	60.8
Consumption of folding boxboard [10]	2.5	2.7	2.9	L	3.7	4.6	5.6	6.5
				M	3.9	5.3	7.0	9.2
				H	4.3	6.3	9.2	13.3
Consumption of special foodboard [10]	.6	1.2	1.5	L	2.2	2.8	3.3	3.8
				M	2.4	3.2	4.2	5.4
				H	2.9	4.6	7.0	10.5
Consumption of building paper and board [12]	2.6	3.2	3.2	L	3.6	4.1	4.5	5.3
				M	4.7	6.0	7.8	10.6
				H	6.0	8.8	12.9	21.0
Total consumption of paper and paperboard	29.1	34.8	39.3	L	50.6	64.6	80.7	98.7
				M	54.9	76.1	104.2	140.7
				H	61.4	93.7	141.5	213.1
Total production of paper and paperboard [5]	24.4	30.1	34.5	L	44.9	58.7	74.7	92.9
				M	49.0	69.7	97.2	133.5
				H	50.8	80.1	133.0	203.7

1. Historical data from Table A8–1. Projections as indicated in the footnotes which follow.
2. From Table A1–2.
3. Extrapolated on a judgment basis. See Chapter 8, p. 172, and Notes, above.
4. Extrapolation of historical trend.
5. Data for 1950, 1955, and 1960 show actual production. Projections relate entirely to required domestic consumption less imports; exports assumed negligible.

6. From Table A1–27.
7. Extrapolation of slow, irregular historical decline.
8. 1950–60 average.
9. Projected on a judgment basis.
10. From Table A7–8.
11. From Table A1–13.
12. From Table A4–7.

TABLE A8–3.   Projected Wood Pulp Requirements for Production of Paper[1]

(Million tons unless otherwise specified)

	1950	1955	1960		1970	1980	1990	2000
For newsprint[2]	1.1	1.6	2.2	L	3.3	4.8	6.2	7.6
				M	3.3	5.2	7.1	9.4
				H	3.7	5.9	8.7	12.3
For printing paper[3]	2.7	3.2	3.8	L	4.7	6.0	7.6	9.4
				M	4.9	6.7	8.9	11.9
				H	5.3	7.8	11.4	16.6
For fine paper[4]	1.1	1.3	1.5	L	2.0	2.7	3.7	4.8
				M	2.2	3.1	4.4	6.1
				H	2.4	3.6	5.6	8.6
For sanitary and tissue paper[5]	1.2	1.6	2.0	L	2.9	4.1	5.1	5.9
				M	3.2	4.9	6.9	8.8
				H	3.7	6.3	10.1	15.4
For coarse and industrial paper[6]	3.6	4.1	4.7	L	5.9	7.5	9.5	12.3
				M	6.5	9.1	12.9	18.2
				H	7.1	11.0	17.2	26.8
For set-up boxboards and other special paperboards[7]	.1	.2	.2	L	.2	.2	.3	.4
				M	.2	.3	.4	.5
				H	.2	.3	.5	.7
For containerboard[8]	4.3	6.1	7.5	L	10.9	15.3	20.6	27.2
				M	11.9	18.4	27.4	40.1
				H	13.1	22.5	36.8	59.0
Pulp requirements per ton of containerboard (tons)	.740	.820	.915		.938	.960	.965	.970
For folding boxboards[9]	.4	.5	.5	L	.7	.8	1.0	1.1
				M	.7	.9	1.2	1.6
				H	.8	1.1	1.6	2.3
For special foodboard[10]	.6	1.1	1.4	L	2.0	2.6	3.1	3.5
				M	2.2	3.0	3.9	5.0
				H	2.7	4.3	6.5	9.7
For building paper and board[8]	1.4	1.8	1.9	L	2.2	2.6	3.0	3.6
				M	2.8	3.8	5.2	7.1
				H	3.6	5.6	8.5	14.1
Pulp requirements per ton of building paper and board	.539	.558	.601		.605	.639	.662	.672
Total requirements	16.5	21.5	25.7	L	34.8	46.6	60.1	75.8
				M	37.9	55.4	78.3	108.7
				H	42.6	68.4	106.9	165.5

1. Historical data estimated on basis of 1954 ratios of wood pulp consumption to paper and board production given in House Committee on Interstate and Foreign Commerce, *Pulp, Paper, and Board, Supply-Demand* (H. Rept. No. 573, 85th Cong., First Sess.). Projected wood pulp requirements for paper assume continuation of 1954 ratios, as detailed below, except in the cases of containerboard and building paper and board.
   Paper consumption series in Table A8–2.

2. Ratio of 1.077 tons of pulp per ton of paper.
3. Ratio of .812.
4. Ratio of .910.
5. Ratio of .901.
6. Ratio of .984.
7. Ratio of .058.
8. For rationale of changing ratio, see Notes.
9. Ratio of .176.
10. Ratio of .927.

appendix
to
chapter
9

MILITARY GOODS

Notes

CHAPTER 9 outlines most of the basic rationale behind the projections both of defense expenditures and of materials requirements. It also points
out that for our ultimate goal of projecting total
requirements of the principal materials and fuels,
relatively crude, order-of-magnitude figures for the
defense portion are sufficient. These notes confine
themselves to some of the additional specifics behind each of the appendix tables, beyond what is
covered in the footnotes thereto.

The principal problem in arriving at a historical
breakdown of national defense expenditures (Table
A9–1) is that the available published data are on
a budget basis and only for fiscal years. While
there might have been some virtue in retaining the
fiscal year basis in order to allow for a reasonable
time lead of the expenditures by the material inputs which were to be related to them, the insignificance of this lead time so far as the projections
were concerned, plus the necessity for relating to
total national defense historical statistics and projections which were on a calendar year basis, decided in favor of conversion to calendar years. To
this end, the fiscal year data were averaged and the
tentative totals adjusted to the national defense
totals as derived from the National Income Accounts statistics. This process also disposed mechanically of some of the minor inconsistencies
between budget data and national income accounting practice. While these various adjustments could
have been made in more precise fashion, the differences would not have been significant for the

expenditure projections and input-output ratios
which it was desired to derive.

Another serious problem in dealing with defense
expenditures, as with government expenditures in
general, is the manner of national income deflation
of the pay of government employees. The assumption in the national income accounting is that all
changes in rates of pay of government personnel,
within broad categories, represent changes in the
price of the services they render, and not at all in
the real volume of output. It was concluded to be
most convenient, from the standpoint of insuring
consistency among the various projections in this
book, to retain essentially the national income approach. In fact, for practical reasons, the level of
deflation was limited to the two broad classes of
military and civilian personnel, respectively. If both
the gross national product and military product had
been adjusted, instead, to a concept of increasing
productivity per member of the Armed Forces (and
per civilian government employee as well), application of the basic defense expenditure assumptions
and some of the projection criteria used in this part
would have given significantly different results. It is
not believed, however, that any of the conclusions
as to materials usage would have been conspicuously different.

Table A9–2 projects defense expenditures, by
category, in two stages—first as if the level of
Armed Forces were to remain unchanged, and then
with adjustment to the globally projected national
defense expenditures (Table A1–12). The purpose

is to be able to give quantitative dimensions, in isolation, to presumed future changes in military technology. The subsequent adjustment to global expenditure levels is not proportionate, but takes account of the fact that differences in expenditure level will be reflected more in the amount expended upon objects rather than personnel than they will in the size of the Armed Forces. An arbitrary adjustment factor of eight-tenths was used to express this lesser impact upon personnel compensation.

Note should be taken of the fact that, so far as "end-product" expenditure is concerned, there is some duplication between this appendix and the appendix to Chapter 4, in that military construction is included in both places. So far as materials requirements are concerned, however, the effect of including military construction with construction is pretty much lost in the face of the other, larger categories which really determine construction material requirements. It figures only as part of the "public construction" whole and is left in only for convenience. Its retention in the defense totals is to give somewhat fuller perspective on total defense materials requirements, but again it does not account for appreciable portions of anything except carbon steel. The statistical error is eliminated, in the appendix to Chapter 16, at the stage of adapting the end-product "technical" evaluations to the total accounting for each metal in terms of market categories.

It should also be noted that the significance of "electronics" is a little different for the projected expenditures from what it is in the historical data. Historically, original electronics equipment in aircraft, missiles, etc., is included with the expenditures for these items and it is impracticable to separate it. For purposes of a more precise evaluation of future materials requirements, however, the projections of electronics are designed to include any increases over present levels in all electronics equipment procured, whether showing up as installed equipment or otherwise.

The rationale behind the rates of growth in the various expenditure categories is treated in Chapter 9.

Materials requirements. In principle, the raw material consumption generated by an order for some quantity of a procurement item is all of the material required directly or indirectly to support production lines for that order, including that not only for the prime contractor but for subcontractors, suppliers of subassemblies and parts to these contractors, and so on. As a practical matter, however, consumption by the prime contractor and one or two earlier stages of contractors covers

nearly all metals requirements, and these are the only large-volume materials for which defense production is an important end-use.

The principal present source of information on defense consumption of metals is the tabulations of requirements under the Defense Materials System (DMS), peacetime successor to the Controlled Materials Plan (CMP) of World War II and the Korean war. Under these plans, all defense procurement agencies (of which only the Department of Defense and the Atomic Energy Commission now remain), have been required to submit quarterly their own requirements for certain metals and the requirements for those metals by their contractors. Currently covered are various shapes and forms of carbon steel, alloy steel, nickel bearing stainless steel, several forms of copper and copper base alloy, and three nickel concentration classes of nickel alloys. The classification of the Defense Department DMS programs for which these metals are detailed is similar to that used for the classification of budget expenditures. AEC requirements under DMS are withheld on security grounds, but it is known that the amounts involved are small in relation to Department of Defense utilization.

DMS tabulations suffer from two major weaknesses: they omit magnesium, lead, zinc, and other important metals; and they cover only the direct requirements of prime contractors and their subcontractors in the production of the end-product. With a few exceptions, materials required to produce the general industrial components incorporated in these end-products are omitted. Some notion may be had as to these missing elements from World War II tabulations from "Form PD-25A," used in the Production Requirements Plan, CMP's predecessor.

Also used in arriving at the unit inputs given in Table A9–3 were Census data on ships and aircraft; Bureau of Mines tabulations on consumption of molybdenum, tungsten, and other metals; Dow Chemical Company estimates of magnesium consumption for aircraft and missiles; trade journals; congressional hearings; and personal interviews with personnel of the federal government, the Aircraft Industries Association (now Aerospace Industries Association), and the American Ordnance Association. Basically, however, a good deal of personal judgment was applied, in part because variations in the timing difference between material inputs as recorded in these various sources and Defense Department budget expenditures made exact input-output comparisons impossible. Additionally, the analysis was made before data for 1960 were available, and some amount of extrapolation, in order to arrive at these base year figures, was necessary.

Direct requirements for DMS materials in 1960 were estimated in two parts: (1) aggregate requirements by each expenditure category for steel, copper, and aluminum; (2) the breakdown of these aggregates and the relation of other metals to them. Indirect requirements were based on available information as to procurement of general industrial components (e.g., electric motors) by each category; the proportional share of each expenditure category in consumption of these components was assumed also to apply to their share in the materials inputs into such components. Finally, non-DMS materials—including the currently evolving family of high temperature alloys on which very

boosters, and for other applications made possible by improvements in aluminum alloys. For missiles, the aluminum loss, again from the 1960 base, was assumed to be 20 per cent by 1965, 20 per cent more by 1970, and a final 10 per cent by 1975, the 50 per cent loss reached to be no further affected thereafter.

The displaced aluminum was assumed to be replaced principally by stainless steel, in the case of aircraft, in the ratio of 1.4 pounds of steel per pound of aluminum, and in varying proportions first by magnesium, then by stainless steel, for missiles. These and other substitutions for the displaced aluminum in the two principal expenditure categories are summarized in the accompanying table.

Fuels. The general considerations behind the fuel

Per Cent Substitution for Displaced Aluminum

Metal	Aircraft			Missiles		
	1965	1970	1975	1965	1970	1975
Alloy steel (replacement ratio 1/1)	–	–	2	–	–	3
Nickel stainless (ratio 1.4/1)	75	75	75	30	55	55
Nickel alloy (ratio 2/1)	–	2	5	–	2	5
Magnesium (ratio 1/1)	5	3	2	60	30	24
Titanium (ratio 1/1)	20	20	16	10	13	13

few statistical data are available—were related, largely on the basis of World War II data, to the weights of the materials already accounted for.

In projection of the input-output ratios, first attention was given to judgments on the changing relation of aggregate metal consumption to aggregate expenditure in each category. Next, prospective substitutions among the metals were quantified, again on a judgment basis. The calculations were made in five-year intervals, given the rapidity of expected development, but the resulting figures for 1965 and 1975 were not further used in the projections. For manned aircraft, aluminum applications were assumed to decline from 22 per cent of total metals use in 1960 to 15 per cent in 1965, 8 per cent in 1970, and 5 per cent in 1975, to remain at that level to the end of the century. This means a relative loss from the 1960 base of 30 per cent for the first five-year period, another 30 per cent for the 1965–70 period, and an additional 15 per cent for 1970–75. The 25 per cent assumed to remain after 1975 might be needed for specialized ground equipment, for airframes of training and other slower aircraft, for parts of jettisonable rocket

projections are discussed in Chapter 9. Most important are the increasing relative importance of jet fuels and the decreasing importance of fuels in general in relation to aircraft procurement. Fuels for other purposes than aircraft use have so little significance in the total picture that they have been arbitrarily projected at a Medium level only, merely to round out the total.

LIST OF TABLES

TABLE A9–1.   Historical Data on National Defense Expenditures, by Category[1]

(Billion 1960 dollars)

	1953	1954	1955	1956	1957	1958	1959	1960
Department of Defense:								
Military personnel	15.0	14.1	13.0	12.7	12.3	11.5	11.5	11.0
Active forces	14.6	13.7	12.5	12.1	11.6	10.8	10.8	10.4
Reserve forces	.4	.4	.5	.6	.7	.7	.7	.6
Operation and maintenance	12.4	9.8	9.3	9.6	10.5	10.6	10.5	10.2
Procurement	21.5	16.3	14.3	13.8	15.2	15.1	14.8	13.9
Aircraft	11.2	10.1	9.4	8.8	9.5	8.7	7.3	6.0
Missiles and space craft	.4	.6	1.0	1.6	2.4	3.1	3.8	4.1
Ships	1.2	1.1	1.0	1.0	1.1	1.4	1.6	1.7
Ordnance, vehicles, etc.	5.2	2.6	1.4	1.0	.6	.4	.4	.4
Electronics and communications	1.0	.6	.6	.7	.8	.7	.9	1.0
Other	2.5	1.3	.9	.7	.8	.8	.8	.7
Research and development	2.8	2.5	2.4	2.4	2.7	2.8	3.3	3.6
Military construction	2.2	2.1	2.2	2.2	2.0	1.9	1.8	1.5
Department of Defense total	53.9	44.8	41.2	40.7	42.7	41.9	41.9	40.2
Atomic energy	2.4	2.1	2.0	1.9	2.3	2.5	2.6	2.5
Other	6.2	4.5	3.6	3.3	3.1	2.8	2.4	1.8
Total	62.5	51.4	46.8	45.9	48.1	47.2	46.9	44.5

1. Derived, except for military personnel expenditures, atomic energy, and missiles (in part), from fiscal year data in current dollars in Defense Department statement FAD–397, 28 March 1961. Fiscal year data averaged to approximate calendar year expenditures and deflated as follows:

   a. Construction—deflator shown in Table A4–2.
   b. Other items, except military personnel—deflator derived by dividing constant-dollar series in *Economic Report of the President*, Jan. 1961, Table C–2, by comparable current-dollar data in Table C–1.

For consistency with the National Income Accounts, expenditures on "space exploration and flight technology," which are now outside the Defense Department, have been added to the "missiles" expenditures, as shown in FAD–397.

Military personnel expenditures are the sum of the two components. Active forces expenditures are the product of the number of personnel in the Armed Forces and the average compensation for 1960 (estimated) in National Accounts terms. Payments to the reserve forces are based on FAD–397 and deflated by the implicit price deflator for active forces pay. Atomic energy expenditures are based on data in U.S. Bureau of the Budget, *The Budget in Brief*.

The components as calculated in the foregoing manner were finally adjusted (slightly) to add to national defense expenditures as given in the *Economic Report*, 1961. This differs slightly from the final figure of the National Income Division, Department of Commerce, shown in Table A1–8.

TABLE A9–2. Projected National Defense Expenditures, by Category

(Billion 1960 dollars)

	1955	1960		1970	1980	1990	2000
Base projections, on assumption of un-changed level of Armed Forces:[1]							
Military personnel	13.0	11.0		11.2	11.2	11.2	11.2
Armed Forces	12.5	10.4		10.5	10.5	10.5	10.5
Reserves	.5	.6		.7	.7	.7	.7
Operation and maintenance[2]	9.3	10.2		11.3	12.4	13.7	15.2
Procurement[3]	14.3	13.9		18.7	25.2	33.9	45.6
Aircraft[4]	9.4	6.0		7.4	8.3	8.5	11.2
Missiles and space craft[4]	1.0	4.1		6.6	10.7	17.0	22.5
Ships, etc.[5]	1.0	1.7		1.7	1.7	1.7	1.7
Ordnance, vehicles, etc.[5]	1.4	.4		.4	.4	.4	.4
Electronics, etc.[6]	.6	1.0		1.7	2.8	4.6	7.5
Other[3]	.9	.7		.9	1.3	1.7	2.3
Research and development[7]	2.4	3.6		6.4	11.5	15.2	18.6
Military construction[2]	2.2	1.5		1.7	1.9	2.1	2.3
Department of Defense total	41.2	40.2		49.3	62.2	76.1	92.9
Atomic energy and other[2]	5.6	4.3		4.7	5.1	5.7	6.3
Total	46.8	44.5		54.0	67.3	81.8	99.2
Adjusted projections:[1]							
Military personnel	13.0	11.0	L	9.7	6.1	6.4	6.8
			M	14.6	16.4	18.8	22.1
			H	19.7	26.3	34.6	46.9
Armed Forces	12.5	10.4	L	9.1	5.7	6.0	6.4
			M	13.7	15.4	17.6	20.7
			H	18.5	24.7	32.4	44.0
Reserves	.5	.6	L	.6	.4	.4	.4
			M	.9	1.0	1.2	1.4
			H	1.2	1.6	2.2	2.9
Operation and maintenance	9.3	10.2	L	9.3	5.0	6.1	7.5
			M	15.8	19.8	25.7	34.2
			H	22.5	34.2	50.5	77.2
Procurement	14.3	13.9	L	15.4	10.2	15.1	22.6
			M	26.2	40.3	63.5	102.5
			H	37.3	69.5	125.0	231.7
Aircraft	9.4	6.0	L	6.1	3.4	3.8	5.5
			M	10.4	13.3	15.9	25.2
			H	14.7	22.9	31.4	56.9
Missiles and space craft	1.0	4.1	L	5.4	4.3	7.6	11.1
			M	9.3	17.1	31.8	50.6
			H	13.2	29.5	62.7	114.3
Ships	1.0	1.7	L	1.4	.7	.8	.8
			M	2.4	2.7	3.2	3.8
			H	3.4	4.7	6.3	8.6
Ordnance, vehicles, etc.	1.4	.4	L	.3	.2	.2	.2
			M	.6	.6	.7	.9
			H	.8	1.1	1.5	2.0
Electronics and communications	.6	1.0	L	1.4	1.1	2.0	3.7
			M	2.4	4.5	8.6	16.9
			H	3.4	7.7	17.0	38.1
Other	.9	.7	L	.7	.5	.8	1.1
			M	1.3	2.1	3.2	5.2
			H	1.8	3.6	6.3	11.7

Table A9–2 (cont'd)

(Billion 1960 dollars)

	1955	1960		1970	1980	1990	2000
Adjusted projections (cont'd):							
			L	5.3	4.7	6.8	9.2
Research and development	2.4	3.6	M	9.0	18.4	28.5	41.8
			H	12.8	31.7	56.1	94.5
			L	1.4	.8	.9	1.1
Military construction	2.2	1.5	M	2.4	3.0	3.9	5.2
			H	3.4	5.2	7.7	11.7
			L	41.1	26.8	35.3	47.2
Department of Defense total	41.2	40.2	M	68.0	97.8	140.4	205.8
			H	95.7	166.9	273.9	462.0
			L	3.9	2.1	2.5	3.1
Atomic energy, etc.	5.6	4.3	M	6.6	8.1	10.7	14.2
			H	9.4	14.1	21.0	32.0
			L	45	29	38	50
Total	46.8	44.5	M	75	106	151	220
			H	105	181	295	494

1. The method of projection was first to estimate the effects of changing military technology upon an unchanged size of defense establishment, as measured by the number of persons in the Armed Forces, then to adjust to the levels of defense expenditure as independently projected (in effect, assumed) for each of the future years shown. (For rationale of the independent projections, see text, Chapters 1 and 9.) In making the latter adjustment, it was assumed that higher (or lower) expenditures than those arrived at as a base would be reflected less than proportionately in expenditures on personnel (80% of its proportionate base share) and more than proportionately in expenditures on materiel, operations, research and development, etc.

The particular assumptions as to base rates of increase are given in the footnotes that follow. They are all rough quantitative expressions of qualitative judgments as to the nature of future weapons systems, as discussed in Chapter 9, pp. 175–77, and Notes, above.

2. Assumed to rise at the rate of 1% a year.

3. Assumed to rise at the rate of 3% a year.

4. Aircraft and missiles projected in combination, as the residual between all other procurement categories and the procurement total. Within the combination, the missiles category (which, it should be remembered, includes space exploration expenditures) is assumed to increase at the rate of 5% a year until its annual total is twice that of aircraft (1990); thereafter the relationship is assumed to be stabilized.

5. Assumed to maintain an unchanged relationship to manpower.

6. Assumed to rise at the rate of 5% a year. This is meant to include the increasing amount of electronic equipment included in missiles, space vehicles, and aircraft. Although budget practice actually credits originally installed equipment to the procurement item in which it is installed, the reclassification of some of this as electronics is more useful as a guide to future materials requirements.

7. Assumed to rise at the rate of 6% a year until it becomes 20% of all "D.O.D." (Department of Defense) expenditures (1990).

TABLE A9–3.   Projected Defense Consumption of Metals per Million Dollars of Expenditure[1]

(Tons)

	1960	1970	1980	1990	2000
Aircraft	45	34	25	19	14
Carbon steel	17.1	12.3	9.02	6.69	4.98
Alloy steel	9.59	6.87	5.12	3.82	2.84
Nickel stainless steel	3.25	6.77	5.77	4.30	3.20
Copper and alloys	2.02	1.45	1.06	.79	.59
Aluminum	9.88	2.83	1.30	.96	.72
Nickel alloys	.74	.70	.77	.58	.43
Magnesium	.39	.40	.28	.21	.16
Titanium	.46	1.18	.86	.64	.48
Lead	.97	.69	.51	.38	.28
Cadmium	.02	.01	.01	.01	.01
Cobalt	.11	.11	.12	.09	.07
Chromium	.45	.42	.48	.35	.26
Missiles and space craft	24	23	17	13	10
Carbon steel	12.3	12.1	8.97	6.66	4.95
Alloy steel	2.85	2.79	2.13	1.58	1.18
Nickel stainless steel	1.47	3.05	2.50	1.87	1.38
Copper and alloys	.59	.58	.43	.32	.24
Aluminum	5.38	3.16	1.96	1.46	1.08
Nickel alloys	.16	.25	.24	.18	.14
Magnesium	.21	.29	.20	.15	.11
Titanium	.08	.35	.31	.23	.17
Lead	.43	.43	.32	.24	.18
Cadmium	.01	.01	.01	.01	.01
Cobalt	.02	.03	.03	.02	.02
Chromium	.09	.14	.14	.10	.08
Ships	194	194	194	194	194
Carbon steel	122	122	122	122	122
Alloy steel	49.5	49.5	49.5	49.5	49.5
Nickel stainless steel	2.57	2.57	2.57	2.57	2.57
Copper and alloys	8.53	8.53	8.53	8.53	8.53
Aluminum	5.43	5.43	5.43	5.43	5.43
Nickel alloys	.78	.78	.78	.78	.78
Lead	4.87	4.87	4.87	4.87	4.87
Cadmium	.03	.03	.03	.03	.03
Ordnance, vehicles, etc.	489	442	399	360	325
Carbon steel	327	295	267	240	217
Alloy steel	123	111	100	90	82
Nickel stainless steel	.98	.88	.80	.72	.65
Copper and alloys	24	22	20	18	16
Aluminum	13.2	11.9	10.8	9.7	8.8
Lead	.98	.88	.80	.72	.65
Cadmium	.49	.44	.40	.36	.32

Table A9–3 (cont'd)

(Tons)

	1960	1970	1980	1990	2000
Electronics	94	58	35	22	13
Carbon steel	53.3	32.7	20.1	12.3	7.58
Alloy steel	6.11	3.73	2.30	1.41	.86
Nickel stainless steel	1.83	1.13	.69	.42	.26
Copper and alloys	17.1	10.5	6.43	3.94	2.43
Aluminum	10.6	6.52	3.97	2.45	1.51
Nickel alloys	.50	.31	.19	.12	.07
Lead	4.00	2.46	1.51	.92	.57
Cadmium	.48	.29	.18	.11	.07
Other procurement	237	214	194	176	159
Carbon steel	219	198	180	163	147
Alloy steel	3.86	3.49	3.17	2.86	2.60
Nickel stainless steel	2.50	2.26	2.05	1.85	1.68
Copper and alloys	5.09	4.60	4.17	3.77	3.42
Aluminum	5.77	5.22	4.72	4.28	3.88
Nickel alloys	.32	.30	.27	.25	.22
Military construction	205	205	205	205	205
Carbon steel	198	198	198	198	198
Alloy steel	1.23	1.23	1.23	1.23	1.23
Nickel stainless steel	.68	.68	.68	.68	.68
Copper and alloys	4.54	4.54	4.54	4.54	4.54
Aluminum	.91	.91	.91	.91	.91
Nickel alloys	.02	.02	.02	.02	.02

1. 1960 base inputs are estimates based upon a number of sources—principally, unpublished Department of Defense data on DMS (Defense Materials System) requirements for the direct inputs of major metals, and World War II PD–25A tabulations for a notion of direct requirements for the minor metals and indirect requirements for all metals. These were supplemented by Census data (for ships and aircraft), Bureau of Mines consumption data for some metals, Dow Chemical Company estimates of magnesium consumption, Air Materiel Command bill-of-materials data, and information obtained from trade journals, congressional hearings, and personal interviews (particularly with the Aircraft Industries Association and the American Ordnance Association). In general, calendar year inputs, where available, were related to expenditures for the following fiscal year, to approximate the lag between materials procurement and payment for work on the relevant products. Indicated trends were extrapolated to 1960 in terms of total weight per dollar and the relative contributions of the different "bulk" materials (carbon steel, alloy steel, stainless steel, copper, and aluminum). Similarly the projections to 2000 were derived in terms of total unit inputs of metal and changes in the relative participation of each type. The total metal requirement per dollar was assumed to decrease at the rate of roughly 3% per annum for aircraft and missiles (the latter starting after 1970), 5% per annum for electronics, and 1% for ordnance, etc., and for "other procurement;" for other items it was assumed to remain unchanged. The basis for these judgments is discussed in Chapter 9, pp. 178–79.

TABLE A9–4. Projected Aggregate Consumption of Metals for Defense[1]

(Thousand tons)

			1960		1970	1980	1990	2000
Carbon steel:								
Aircraft		L			75	31	25	27
		M	103		128	120	106	125
		H			181	207	210	283
Missiles and space craft		L			65	39	51	55
		M	50		113	153	212	250
		H			160	265	418	566
Ships		L			171	85	98	98
		M	207		293	329	390	464
		H			415	573	769	1,049
Ordnance, vehicles, etc.		L			88	53	48	43
		M	131		177	160	168	195
		H			236	294	360	434
Electronics		L			46	22	25	28
		M	53		78	90	106	128
		H			111	155	209	289
Other procurement		L			139	90	130	162
		M	153		257	378	522	764
		H			356	648	1,027	1,720
Military construction		L			277	158	178	218
		M	297		475	594	772	1,030
		H			673	1,030	1,525	2,317
Total		L			861	478	555	631
		M	994		1,521	1,824	2,276	2,956
		H			2,132	3,172	4,518	6,658
Alloy steel:								
Aircraft		L			42	17	15	16
		M	58		71	68	61	72
		H			101	117	120	162
Missiles and space craft		L			15	9	12	13
		M	12		26	36	50	60
		H			37	63	99	135
Ships		L			69	35	40	40
		M	84		119	134	158	188
		H			168	233	312	426
Ordnance, vehicles, etc.		L			33	20	18	16
		M	49		67	60	63	73
		H			89	110	136	163
Electronics		L			5	3	3	3
		M	6		9	10	12	15
		H			13	18	24	33
Other procurement		L			2	2	2	3
		M	3		5	7	9	14
		H			6	11	18	30
Military construction		L			2	1	1	1
		M	2		3	4	5	6
		H			4	6	9	14
Total		L			168	87	91	92
		M	214		300	319	358	428
		H			418	558	718	963
Nickel stainless steel:								
Aircraft		L			41	20	16	18
		M	20		70	77	68	81
		H			100	132	135	182

APPENDIX TO CHAPTER 9

Table A9–4 (cont'd) (Thousand tons)

	1960		1970	1980	1990	2000
Nickel stainless steel (cont'd):						
		L	16	11	14	15
Missiles and space craft	6	M	28	43	59	70
		H	40	74	117	158
		L	3	2	2	2
Ships	4	M	6	7	8	10
		H	9	12	16	22
		L	–	–	–	–
Ordnance, vehicles, etc.	–	M	1	–	1	1
		H	1	1	1	1
		L	2	1	1	1
Electronics	2	M	3	3	4	4
		H	4	5	7	10
		L	2	1	1	2
Other procurement	2	M	3	4	6	9
		H	4	7	12	20
		L	1	1	1	1
Military construction	1	M	2	2	3	4
		H	2	4	5	8
		L	65	36	35	39
Total	35	M	113	136	149	179
		H	160	235	293	401
Copper and alloys:						
		L	9	4	3	3
Aircraft	12	M	15	14	13	15
		H	21	24	25	34
		L	3	2	2	3
Missiles and space craft	2	M	5	7	10	12
		H	8	13	20	27
		L	12	6	7	7
Ships	15	M	20	23	27	32
		H	29	40	54	73
		L	7	4	4	3
Ordnance, vehicles, etc.	10	M	13	12	13	15
		H	18	22	27	32
		L	15	7	8	9
Electronics	17	M	25	29	34	41
		H	36	50	67	93
		L	3	2	3	4
Other procurement	4	M	6	9	12	18
		H	8	15	24	40
		L	6	4	4	5
Military construction	7	M	11	14	18	24
		H	15	24	35	53
		L	55	29	31	34
Total	67	M	95	108	127	157
		H	135	188	252	352
Aluminum:						
		L	17	4	4	4
Aircraft	59	M	29	17	15	18
		H	42	30	30	41
		L	17	8	11	12
Missiles and space craft	22	M	29	34	46	55
		H	42	58	92	123
		L	8	4	4	4
Ships	9	M	13	15	17	21
		H	18	26	34	47

Table A9–4 (cont'd)   (Thousand tons)

		1960		1970	1980	1990	2000
Aluminum (cont'd):							
Ordnance, vehicles, etc.		5	L	4	2	2	2
			M	7	6	7	8
			H	10	12	15	18
Electronics		11	L	9	4	5	6
			M	16	18	21	26
			H	22	31	42	58
Other procurement		4	L	4	2	3	4
			M	7	10	14	20
			H	9	17	27	45
Military construction		1	L	1	1	1	1
			M	2	3	4	5
			H	3	5	7	11
Total		111	L	60	25	30	33
			M	103	103	124	153
			H	146	179	247	343
Nickel alloys:							
Aircraft		4.4	L	4.2	2.6	2.2	2.4
			M	7.3	10.2	9.2	10.8
			H	10.3	17.6	18.2	24.5
Missiles and space craft		.7	L	1.4	1.0	1.4	1.6
			M	2.3	4.1	5.7	7.1
			H	3.3	7.1	11.3	16.0
Ships		1.3	L	1.1	.5	.6	.6
			M	1.9	2.1	2.5	3.0
			H	2.7	3.7	4.9	6.7
Electronics		.5	L	.4	.2	.2	.3
			M	.7	.9	1.0	1.2
			H	1.1	1.5	2.0	2.7
Other procurement		.2	L	.2	.1	.2	.2
			M	.4	.6	.8	1.1
			H	.5	1.0	1.6	2.6
Military construction		–	L	–	–	–	–
			M	–	.1	.1	.1
			H	.1	.1	.1	.2
Total		7.1	L	7.3	4.4	4.6	5.1
			M	12.6	18.0	19.3	23.3
			H	18.0	31.0	38.1	52.1
Magnesium:							
Aircraft		2.3	L	2.4	1.0	.8	.9
			M	4.2	3.7	3.3	4.0
			H	5.9	6.4	6.6	9.1
Missiles and space craft		.9	L	1.6	.9	1.1	1.2
			M	2.7	3.4	4.8	5.6
			H	3.8	5.9	9.4	12.6
Total		3.2	L	4.0	1.9	1.9	2.1
			M	6.9	7.1	8.1	9.6
			H	9.7	12.3	16.0	21.7
Titanium:							
Aircraft		2.8	L	7.2	2.9	2.4	2.6
			M	12.3	11.4	10.2	12.1
			H	17.3	19.7	20.1	27.3
Missiles and space craft		.3	L	1.9	1.3	1.7	1.9
			M	3.3	5.3	7.3	8.6
			H	4.6	9.1	14.4	19.4
Total		3.1	L	9.1	4.2	4.1	4.5
			M	15.6	16.7	17.5	20.7
			H	21.9	28.8	34.5	46.7

Table A9–4 (cont'd)   (Thousand tons)

	1960		1970	1980	1990	2000
Lead:						
Aircraft	5.8	L M H	4.2 7.2 10.1	1.7 6.8 11.7	1.4 6.0 11.9	1.5 7.1 15.9
Missiles and space craft	1.8	L M H	2.3 4.0 5.7	1.4 5.5 9.4	1.8 7.6 15.0	2.0 9.1 20.6
Ships	8.3	L M H	6.8 11.7 16.6	3.4 13.1 22.9	3.9 15.6 30.7	3.9 18.5 41.9
Ordnance, vehicles, etc.	.4	L M H	.3 .5 .7	.2 .5 .9	.1 .5 1.1	.1 .6 1.3
Electronics	4.0	L M H	3.4 5.9 8.4	1.7 6.8 11.6	1.8 7.9 15.6	2.1 9.6 21.7
Total	20.3	L M H	17.0 29.3 41.5	8.4 32.7 56.5	9.0 37.6 74.3	9.6 44.9 101.4
Cadmium:						
Aircraft	.1	L M H	.1 .1 .1	– .1 .2	– .2 .3	.1 .3 .6
Missiles and space craft	–	L M H	– .1 .1	– .2 .3	.1 .3 .6	.1 .5 1.1
Ships	.1	L M H	– .1 .1	– .1 .1	– .1 .2	– .1 .3
Ordnance, vehicles, etc.	.1	L M H	.1 .3 .4	.1 .2 .4	.1 .2 .5	.1 .3 .6
Electronics	.5	L M H	.4 .7 1.0	.2 .8 1.4	.2 .9 1.9	.3 1.2 2.7
Total	.9	L M H	.6 1.3 1.7	.3 1.4 2.4	.4 1.7 3.5	.6 2.4 5.3
Cobalt:						
Aircraft	.7	L M H	.6 1.1 1.6	.4 1.6 2.7	.3 1.4 2.8	.4 1.8 4.0
Missiles and space craft	.1	L M H	.2 .3 .4	.1 .5 .9	.2 .6 1.3	.2 1.0 2.3
Total	.8	L M H	.8 1.4 2.0	.5 2.1 3.6	.5 2.0 4.1	.6 2.8 6.3
Chromium:						
Aircraft	2.7	L M H	2.6 4.4 6.2	1.6 6.4 11.0	1.3 5.6 11.0	1.4 6.6 14.8
Missiles and space craft	.4	L M H	.8 1.3 1.8	.6 2.4 4.1	.8 3.2 6.3	.9 4.0 9.1
Total	3.1	L M H	3.4 5.8 8.0	2.2 8.8 15.1	2.1 8.8 17.3	2.3 10.6 23.9

Table A9–4 (cont'd)

1. Evaluated herein are the principal metals-using categories, the unit requirements for which have been projected in Table A9–3. Additional requirements will be generated by research and development, operation and maintenance, and atomic energy activities. These are assumed to be relatively small, however, and are accounted for statistically when adjusting, in Appendix 16, to a total net shipments basis from the total of specifically accounted for end-uses.

The quantities shown for each expenditure category under each metal are obtained by multiplying the input factors in Table A9–3 by the respective dollar expenditures as projected in Table A9–2.

TABLE A9–5.   Projected Defense Consumption of Petroleum[1]

(Million barrels)

	Residual fuel oil[2]	Light distillates	Motor gasoline	Aviation fuel[3] Bbl./$ thous. of air- craft	Aviation fuel[3] Aggregate consumption	Total consumption (rounded)
Total consumption:						
1955[4]	28.4	10.9	10.6	10	93.5	143
1960[5]	59	21	14	28	168	[6]262
Domestic procurement:						
1960[7]	39	15	8	25	151	213
Per cent of total consumption	66	70	55	–	90	81
1970	31	15	8	21	L 128 M 218 H 309	180 270 360
1980	18	15	8	17	L 58 M 226 H 389	100 270 430
1990	10	15	8	14	L 53 M 223 H 440	86 260 470
2000	10	15	8	12	L 66 M 302 H 683	100 330 720

1. The minor items in this table are projected on an aggregate, judgment basis. The principal item—aviation fuel—is projected on the basis of its relation to aircraft procurement, which is taken as a rough measure of changes in military aviation activity. Only the domestically procured supply is comprehended in the projections.

2. The projection reflects a gradual shift to nuclear powered vessels.

3. Reference series on aircraft expenditures is in Table A9–2. (See also footnote 1, above.) The declining coefficient reflects an expectation (a) that large-bomber functions will be mostly taken over by missiles and that the remaining craft, of lesser average size, will cost increasingly more in relation to their fuel consumption and (b) that solid (rocket) fuel will gradually substitute for some of the jet fuel consumption.

4. From Schurr, Netschert, *et al.*, *Energy in the American Economy, 1850–1975* (Johns Hopkins Press, 1960), Appendix Table E–8.

5. Estimated.

6. According to the U.S. Bureau of Mines, delivery of petroleum products to the military agencies for the fiscal year ending June 30, 1961 was scheduled to be 697,000 barrels per day, or 255,000,000 barrels for the year.

7. Estimated on the basis of the percentages for each type of fuel; latter based primarily on *Energy in the American Economy*, Table E–7.

appendix
to
chapter
10

HEAT AND POWER

Notes

WITHOUT EXCEPTION the most reliable statistical data on energy demand are cast in terms either of aggregate disappearance—at the wholesale distribution rather than end-use level—or of broad classes of end-use. More methodical projections of future demand, on the other hand, can be derived from specific end-use data. Much of the statistical work, therefore, needs to be concerned with the derivation of a useful 1960 base and with the search for indications of change in that base. Fortunately, an analytical framework, suitable in many respects, is available in the comprehensive Resources for the Future study by Schurr, Netschert, *et al.* entitled *Energy in the American Economy, 1850–1975* (Baltimore: Johns Hopkins Press and Resources for the Future, 1960). Liberal use has been made of its methods and findings. Also of substantial help was a detailed analysis of energy consumption and production in the American economy in the year 1954, a draft of which was made available by the author prior to publication and which has since been published as a joint RFF–Bureau of Mines venture (Perry D. Teitelbaum, *Energy Production and Consumption in the United States: An Analytical Study Based on 1954 Data,* Bureau of Mines Report of Investigations 5821, 1961).

The steps in arriving at projections of energy demand in each of the consuming sectors are essentially the same: establishment of the 1960 base for all fuels combined, forward projection of that base, estimates of the future sharing of the aggregate by the different sources of energy, and, where necessary, conversion of the quantities into physical amounts (tons, barrels, cubic feet, etc.) through the use of efficiency factors and energy content measures. This approach has the advantage that it makes it difficult to overstate the possibilities of growth—or decline—of any given source of energy, since aggregate consumption, regardless of source, sets a ceiling within which all sources have to be accommodated. At the same time, it has the disadvantage that comparison with historical data is feasible only for large aggregates, since the specific end-use pattern is tailor-made for the base year.

Substantial reliance on data collected and disseminated by trade organizations or publications characterizes the energy estimates (e.g., American Gas Association, Edison Electric Institute, Gas Appliance Manufacturers Association, *Electrical World*). Wherever possible the outcome of aggregating estimated consumption based upon these data has been checked against government-compiled data on total apparent disappearance and the two sets have been reconciled by adjusting the 1960 aggregates to the latter. In this fashion historical continuity with published data is assured, and any errors due to faulty assumption concerning specific end-uses are offset. In no case were such discrepancies significant, so that projection of the series so adjusted presented no difficulty in either concept or technique. (This does not, of course, exclude the possibility that offsetting errors arising out of the use of trade association statistics can bring about a similarity with government data that is more apparent than real.)

The consumption segments which constitute the framework of the projection are the traditional ones: domestic (or residential), commercial, industrial, transportation, and miscellaneous, the last including governmental or public consumption at various levels, agriculture, defense, and the truly miscellaneous group of activities that go to round out demand and constitute the difference between the major identified uses and total apparent consumption. Cutting across this classification runs the division between use of electric energy and what is sometimes called the "direct" use of fuels, i.e., the burning of fuels and the use of the resulting heat or energy without conversion into electricity.

Domestic requirements can be conveniently split into space-heating, by far the most important field of consumption, and all other uses, some of which are dealt with individually. The first eleven appendix tables deal with the derivation of space-heating requirements.

The principal variables are the number of households, heat output per household, share of heat output supplied by different energy sources, and efficiency of heating devices. Statistically, these factors lead a shadow existence. In effect, for each year for which one wishes to obtain the heating pattern a special and rather cumbersome effort has to be made, and even then the results retain a significant element of speculation. For 1955 such an attempt was made in *Energy in the American Economy;* the results, to be found principally in Chapter 5, pp. 210–16, and Appendix Tables C–1 to C–5, have been useful in setting up a similar pattern for 1960 herein (Table A10–6). Projections, on the other hand, have been handled differently. For estimating the national average heat output per heated household, the data published by the American Gas Association relating to gas sales for residential use were adopted, despite some conceptual difficulties relating to both seasonal and regional factors. Table A10–1 presents these for the past decade and makes an adjustment for the seasonal problem.

For our purposes gas heating statistics suffer from two defects: (1) their geographic distribution is biased toward the Pacific and the West-South Central areas, and (2) they are recorded in terms of customers rather than households. Table A10–2 shows the regional distribution and its changes through the years. Both the unequal incidence of gas heating and a gradual extension toward the Northern states and the Atlantic Seaboard are in evidence. The extent of the bias thus introduced is suggested by Table A10–3, in which an attempt is made to calculate the average number of degree-days in the United States (i.e., the number of days during the heating season on which the average outside temperature fell below 65°, measured for every 24-hour period). Based on data collected by the U.S. Weather Bureau, regional estimates of degree-days were made and weighted by the population in each region. In a second calculation the weights were constituted by the gas-heating population only, and, as expected, the resulting weighted average is lower, roughly by 10 per cent. Thus application of gas use statistics would understate national heat requirements.

As for the second source of distortion, the transition from *customers* (in the statistics) to *households* (in these projections) calls for a downward adjustment, as each customer represents about 1.1 households. This relationship is implicit in calculations shown in *Energy in the American Economy,* especially Tables C–1 and C–13. The dual adjustment produces a figure that may be taken to represent as nearly as possible the average heat input per household for the country as a whole. At 75 per cent efficiency of the heating device, the resulting heat *output* per household would be more or less 70 million Btu.

The fact that the two principal adjustments work in opposite directions with just about identical force, and thus yield roughly the unadjusted figure as derived from published data, is purely accidental.

This calculation, which is basic to the projection, may be appraised in several ways. In the first place, the 1955 estimate for oil heating cited in *Energy in the American Economy* yields an average energy input of 150 million Btu per customer. At 60–65 per cent efficiency this would indicate effective heat output in the neighborhood of 90–95 million Btu, or 30–35 per cent above the 70 million just established. However, two factors are important for evaluating this estimate. First, as in the case of gas, there is more than one household per customer. Second, just as gas customers have been concentrated in the warmer parts of the country, so oil customers are more generally located in the country's colder areas, as shown in Table A10–3. New England and the Middle Atlantic states, especially New York, are among the heavy oil-heating areas; they are colder than the average location, with 20 per cent more degree-days than the national average.

An adjustment on both counts would have to be made from the raw per-customer figure, and it is a fair guess that we might land somewhere near 65–70 million Btu. Apart from statistical uncertainties in each of the factors, it is quite logical that, corrected for differences in location, Northern households should use somewhat less heat than others, since more often than not heat conserving practices, such as use of storm windows and the like, are a necessity and the same amount of heat therefore goes a longer way.

There is yet another way of looking at the matter. For estimating purposes, the American Gas Association uses, as a rule of thumb, an input of 22,500 Btu per degree-day deficiency per customer, which presumably is not derived from historical statistics. At 75 per cent efficiency this would correspond to heat output of 16,900 Btu per day. As shown in Table A10–3, the average degree-day deficiency in the country, i.e. number of degree-days in each state weighted by its population, is 4,590. At this rate the national average annual heating requirement would be 77 million Btu per customer, or some 70 million Btu per household, provided, as is reasonable to assume, that the American Gas Association rule of thumb applies indeed per customer—which is the unit of interest and record to the supplier—and not per household. In either event, the basic assumption of 70 million Btu that underlies the calculations shown in this appendix appears a reasonable estimate.

In *Energy in the American Economy,* we find that heat output from all sources, including what small amount of electricity was used in 1955, amounts to less than 60 million Btu per household. This undoubtedly reflects under-heating in the case of customers using fuels other than gas and oil or not using central heating, as well as the inclusion of households not heated at all and of dwelling units heated only part of the year (vacation homes, etc.). One may legitimately speculate that, as a general rule, coal heating is more frequently found in older, lower priced houses and that a great deal of heating in such dwellings is probably below the level found in the gas heated or oil heated home. Similarly, wood is probably to a large degree a supplementary rather than a primary source of heat, while a good deal of liquid petroleum gas is employed in temporary residences, vacation places, etc., which have a low annual occupancy rate and, consequently, a low rate of consumption. Altogether, the lower value, when use of all fuels and absence of heating are taken into account, does not appear unreasonable. In the absence of end-use statistics one can only guess at these magnitudes.

In projecting space-heating requirements we have taken into account the 1955 estimate and have postulated a gradual increase in the annual heat output per household, based upon improving heating standards that go hand in hand with the disappearance of outmoded methods of heating. Such changes are not likely to be violent or rapid since they are counteracted by increasingly effective insulation. Thus the projections made in Table A10–11 show only a moderate change in this particular variable.

More troublesome are the projections of heat source. Again, the pattern established for 1955 in *Energy in the American Economy* serves as a starting point (Table A10–6). Projections rest upon past trends in residential building practices with regard to space-heating installations. The tables reflecting these list changes in automatic heating equipment in use, by type of fuel (Table A10–4), and data relating to oil burner installations (Table A10–5); both kinds of data are reported regularly in *Fueloil and Oil Heat* (Heating Publishers, Inc., New York, N.Y.). In addition, data from *New Housing and its Materials, 1940–56* (Bureau of Labor Statistics Bulletin No. 1231) throw considerable light on changing building practices with regard to type of heating installation. Combined with projections of new residential construction, as presented in Chapter 4 (picked up in Table A10–7), these data have been used to estimate the future role of the different sources of heat.

Because in 1960 the electrical heating sector was still in its infancy and yet must be assumed to rise to substantial stature in the years to come, it has been given separate treatment and may need the most drastic revision in the future, as it now is least susceptible to analysis by growth rates. Table A10–7 contains the pertinent assumptions upon which calculation of the spread of electrical heating rests.

The heat sources other than electricity are developed in Tables A10–7 and 10. The share of gas is assumed to continue its dynamic growth, which, in terms of heat output, appears to have proceeded at a rate of over 1.5 percentage points per year between 1955 and 1960. Gas is by far the preferred choice in new dwellings, and, in addition, it has benefited from conversion from oil heating. In view of the fact that the recent share of gas heating has been some 70–75 per cent of all heating of new housing, and in view of the continuing strength of the conversion market (Table A10–5), the projections depict a further though gradually decreasing increase in gas heating. The decrease is based upon the belief that in certain areas oil or coal occupy positions of preference—if not in all then in a large share of the existing dwellings—from which it will be hard if not impossible to dislodge them, and that the conversion possibilities are bound to narrow and gradually disappear.

Only Medium projections were made for coal, liquid petroleum gas, and other fuels, partly because the trends seem less uncertain and partly because the significance of the residential heating market in the total consumption of these fuels is so small as to render establishment of ranges hardly worthwhile.

Lows and Highs for gas and oil on the other hand are called for, given the possibility that, through some technical innovation unmatched by its competitor, the trend away from oil may be halted and eventually reversed. Tables A10–6, 7, and 11 contain the statistical details of the rather complex assumptions and calculations.

The projection of efficiency of heating devices—depicted in Table A10–11—is not based upon the introduction of specific, predictable innovations, but rather on the assumption of a generally progressive improvement, larger in oil heaters than in gas heaters, on the basis that the oil heater is an older device than the gas furnace and thus has a better chance of catching up with modern, high-efficiency gas furnaces as replacement oil heating takes over. Because of the small range of possibilities no Low and High projections have been used.

There are, of course, a variety of sources that can be cited for a given set of rates, but in the last resort one must make a compromise between them. The most troublesome item is the electric heating efficiency, because of the wide disparity in efficiency of resistance heating and the heat pump. While, broadly speaking, the former operates at an efficiency of 100 per cent, i.e., one kilowatt-hour of energy input yields the equivalent in heat, or 3,412 Btu, the heat output of the pump is a multiple of the energy input. The efficiency, and in consequence the estimated heat *input,* therefore, may vary considerably, depending upon the share taken by each of these devices. At the moment, the heat pump is still very much in its infancy; or perhaps one should say that it is catching its second breath after a poor debut. In 1960, there were no more than 100,000 homes so heated in the entire country. And yet, this represents a tripling since 1959. While it seems sheer folly to base any projections on such a pinpoint, there are potent arguments—discussed in Chapter 10, pp. 190–91—in favor of an eventual significant place for the heat pump in the electrical heating field.

Table A10–9 represents an attempt to work out an "average efficiency" for all types of electric heating so that calculated heat output may be expressed in terms of the required electricity input.

The projections are simplified models in that they do not allow for conversion of existing dwellings from one source of heat to another. These have in the past run up to 10 per cent of new construction for any one type of fuel. In the future one may anticipate continuing conversion from coal to oil and gas and—less so—from oil and gas to electricity. It was felt that the gain in purity of concept was too small to outweigh the further complexities of calculation, especially given the basic uncertainties even in the base period. On balance, failure to allow for conversions probably leads to an overstatement of oil heated and understatement of gas and electric heated dwellings. As oil heating is in relative decline, and electric heating is projected to rise rapidly, this introduces a slightly dampening influence on the speed of both projected trends.

Tables A10–12 through A10–19 deal with residential uses for purposes other than space-heating. The use of a variety of electric appliances, and cooking and water-heating with gas, are the main items of analysis.

The procedure is fairly uniform and consists in establishing the number of customers in 1960, the consumption per unit, and the share of each of the fuels (where more than one is used). Past trends are used to project this picture into the future, but these trends are greatly modified over time. The details are spelled out in footnotes.

Unit consumption data are of course largely conjectural, and, as reported in *Energy in the American Economy* (Table C–32), experts vary widely in their opinion. The data here used purport to represent a middle estimate, partly on the basis of judgment of the possible bias in each of the existing estimates. As for the future, the uncertainties are augmented by the fact that changes in any one appliance may influence unit consumption of one or more other appliances or uses. There are probably instances of this in the past, such as reduction in room illumination during hours of TV watching, lower power consumption by refrigerators in air-conditioned homes, or higher heating consumption where fluorescent lamps are substituted for the heat-yielding incandescent bulb. These interrelationships are not taken into account, since the data are far too rough to make such refinement a reasonable venture. One must nonetheless be aware of them.

Another problem, not fully explored here, is the situation that arises when the saturation factor exceeds 100. The statistics compiled by the pertinent trade association are cast in terms not of numbers of appliances per household but rather of presence or absence of the given appliance. Obviously, this rate cannot exceed 100, but in terms of numbers it can do so (more than one refrigerator, TV set, etc., per household). Each appliance has been treated on its merits in the tables, but there is probably a good deal of work that can be done in further illuminating this area of consumption.

As a test of the reasonableness of the many assumptions that underlie the projections, there is totaled, in Tables A10–18 and 19, the energy consumption in the various segments of domestic use; these are compared with aggregate electricity and gas sales for residential purposes for 1960.

In the case of electricity, the aggregation of the end-use estimates accounts for roughly 90 per cent of consumption; this figure is reasonable since no account has been taken of innumerable uses of electricity in the home, in items ranging from the electric iron and toaster to the vacuum cleaner, radio, or shaver. An expanding category of "All other" is therefore in order and has been used as the vehicle for omissions as well as new future uses. The 1960 total thus equals the figure published by the Federal Power Commission as utility sales for residential purposes augmented by one-third of rural sales, deemed to represent the residential portion of those sales.

In the case of gas, coverage, which applies to space-heating, water heaters, ranges, and clothes dryers, exceeds 90 per cent. It would undoubtedly be higher if we could make a better guess at the portion of gas appliances burning liquid petroleum gas. Data for total residential and commercial LPG sales indicate that we may have over-allowed for LPG demand in individual uses and thus understated natural gas use. Most likely, many LPG appliances have only seasonal use; thus unit consumption per year is not as high as we have estimated. Secondly, some appliances using gas are not covered, such as gas refrigerators, incinerators, and more recently air-conditioners. We have therefore adjusted the 1960 aggregate end-uses to the 1960 residential gas sales, as reported by the American Gas Association. In the Medium projection we have let the resulting "All other" factor grow to provide for expanded new uses, but the rate of growth is far less than in the case of electricity. This appears reasonable in spite of the unrelenting efforts of the gas industry to extend gas applications in the home. While there is definitely such a thing as the "all-electric home," it is not so easy to conceive of an "all-gas home." Not only is there electric light, but gas appliances, including heating, require electric motors, thermostats, etc. Thus, the task of gas to extend its realm must be judged as more difficult than that of electricity. Neither the gas refrigerator nor gas air-conditioning has to date received broad-based acceptance. While this situa-

tion may change—and one must not underrate the resourcefulness or the resources of the gas industry, as exemplified in the idea of producing gas-based electricity in the individual home—there is not at this time enough of an aura of success in other applications of gas to justify a very dynamic approach to future new uses, especially those in which electricity has a firm footing.

A brief comment is in order regarding the projection of electric lighting (Table A10–14). The observation applies to the 1960 base, which in view of the historical series preceding it might be regarded as too low. However, as is true for all estimates of lighting consumption, the figures shown are derived *indirectly*, i.e., as a balancing item of total residential and estimated appliance consumption. In the light of the most recent *direct* survey of lighting consumption that has come to our attention, made by the Middle West Service Company, there can be little doubt that power consumption for lighting has been lower than estimated through the indirect approach. Indeed, in only one of the seven utility companies involved which undertook direct surveys did lighting account for as much as 700 kwh per year (or 23 per cent of all domestic uses), and this was in the largest metropolitan area included, Detroit. Other utility companies found lighting use as low as 332 kwh; the straight average of the seven was 474 kwh, or considerably below 20 per cent, as compared with the near-30 per cent generally assumed. It is legitimate, therefore, to infer that lighting use as estimated indirectly overstates consumption by the inclusion of many small appliances not separately accounted for. Under those circumstances, even the 825 kwh assumed for 1960 may be on the high side. (See also *Energy in the American Economy*, pp. 215–16, and Appendix Tables C–34 through C–36.)

Tables A10–20 through 26 are devoted to projections of energy demand in the commercial, public, and other non-industrial fields. These are based principally upon long-run direct or indirect relationships to residential trends. There is no certainty that these relationships will endure, but the historical evidence is very persuasive. Besides, there is practically complete absence of data that would permit independent estimates. In at least one instance, the so-called "other" gas sales, a big question mark attaches to the category and the projections we suggest. The reason is amply explained in the footnotes to Table A10–26.

With the exception of the last two tables (A10–46 and 47), which deal with the derivation of liquid fuel demand in agriculture, the balance of this appendix is devoted to projections of industrial use of energy. Tables A10–27 through 36 deal with electricity consumption, A10–37 through 45 with direct fuel consumption. Heavy reliance is placed upon Census of Manufactures data, though the data of the 1958 Census could, because of timing, be considered on only a very rough basis. Use has been made also of the Census Bureau's *Annual Survey of Manufactures,* though only in the case of electricity, since other sources of energy are carried in dollar terms only and it seemed too hazardous to add price deflators to the other uncertainties of projections.

Certain industries have been dealt with in more detail than others. The primary metals were singled out for the most thorough treatment, because of both their significance as energy consumers and the fortunate circumstance that ample data permit this approach, given the relative homogeneity of the industry's output (Tables A10–29–34 and 40–43). In direct fuel consumption, the petroleum refining industry was singled out for separate treatment for the same reasons (Tables A10–44 and 45).

All other manufacturing and mining has been dealt with in a more summary fashion by establishing a trend in the historical relationship between energy consumption and output (the latter represented by the Federal Reserve Board index of production) and projecting this relationship. Two tables in the case of electricity (A10–27 and 28) and three in the case of fuels (A10–37, 38, 39) contain the pertinent calculations.

The question arises whether the rather complex method, involving a good deal of adjusting and manipulating of basic sources and a good deal of judgment, is worth the effort, or whether it would not be simpler to project electric energy consumption on the basis of some reasonable rate of change in the aggregate power coefficient. There is no easy answer to such a query, except that one can have a little more confidence in the results arrived at by the more involved method and that such a method will in the future lend itself more easily to corrections and to better understanding of whatever deviations from the path here projected will actually occur. But this alone might still not justify the complexities introduced by the more detailed calculations.

There is, however, further merit in the industry-by-industry approach. Faced with increasing electric power consumption per unit of industrial output, many observers are led to look for one single cause and are tempted to interpret this phenomenon as the effect of an across-the-board "electrification"

of processes previously performed manually or by mechanical means not powered by electricity. They will then tend to equate electrification and automation and point to the rise in unit consumption of power as its visible evidence. The piecemeal approach here chosen erects some barrier against the simplification introduced by this concept; though a much finer industry or product breakdown would be desirable, the instances in which data would permit this with any degree of accuracy are the exception, not the rule.

In Table A10–28 the reader will note, perhaps with some puzzlement, that for each year a few of the industries show an index in the Low projection that is higher than the Medium and sometimes higher than the High. Similarly, some High index numbers are lower than the Medium and sometimes than the Low. This is because the weighted average of the Low industry indexes must equal the projection of the over-all Low manufacturing index, and the same must be true for the Highs. Not all of the industry indexes can be at their High (or Low) simultaneously, just as steel and aluminum—being partial substitutes—cannot be assumed to reach their Highs and Lows together. A deliberate distortion has been introduced, designed to yield the highest (or lowest) attainable power requirements that can be reconciled with the range of the production index. Some of the group Lows have been raised, some of the Highs lowered. In the method used here the least power-intensive industries (defined as those having the lowest number of kilowatt-hours per point of the FRB index) are made to bear the brunt of the upward adjustment in the Low projection and of the downward adjustment in the High projection. Thus, the industries that are most significant in power consumption are allowed to stay at their respective Lows and Highs, in order that the aggregate Lows and Highs in power consumption may be only minimally affected by these adjustments.

In the case of direct fuel use, it is necessary to allocate total fuel consumption to the different fuels (Table A10–39), whereas the demand for electricity is solely for one end-product: kilowatt-hours. The corresponding operation of determining the likely origin of required electricity is performed in the appendix to Chapter 15.

Projection of direct fuel consumption in less industry detail than electricity use is largely due to the nature of the data. For direct fuel use only Census year data are available, i.e. 1947, 1954, and most recently 1958. To establish trends on the basis of these three years is hazardous enough for manufacturing as a whole but, as is evident from a study of Teitelbaum's analysis for 1954 (*op. cit.*), much more so in terms of individual industries or groups. Thus projections in the latter instance were made for all manufacturing jointly, other than metals and petroleum refining. Even in the case of these two industries, where data are more fully available, simplifications have been applied. In the case of the iron and steel industry above all, we have bypassed some tricky points in the use of by-product fuels by relating ingot output to total coal equivalent (Tables A10–40 and 41) and considering the production and consumption of fuel within the industry as coming from the original fuel content of coal.

The least troublesome of these by-product fuels is blast furnace gas. Because of its low heat content —only some 90 Btu per cubic foot (compared with 1,000 to 1,050 Btu for natural gas)—its use is confined to the immediate physical vicinity of its origin, i.e., mainly the blast furnace; mill practice, however, provides also for its use in steam generation (for power production) or in various heating phases of steelmaking. In any event, we have treated blast furnace gas strictly as a by-product that is recycled in the same plant and thus constitutes merely one of the uses of the blast furnace reaction between coke and hot air. Any improvement in the exploitation of blast furnace gas would thus be considered an improvement in the efficiency of coal use.

Tar and pitch are conceptually somewhat more difficult to deal with in that they have a large variety of uses other than as fuel. Should improved technology facilitate the marketing of these by-products outside the industry at values higher than their fuel equivalent, our failure to consider them as an independent part of total fuel demand in the base-year would underestimate future fuel demand. Should outside use diminish, future requirements would be overstated. It is only because these two sources are quantitatively of little importance— they account for barely more than 1 per cent of all primary fuels used in the industry—that the problem can be bypassed.

Perhaps the most complex issue is raised by the production and use of coke oven gas, since this is a by-product fuel that finds immediate use outside the iron and steel industry. Strictly speaking, unless we consider it a separate independent source of fuel and try to estimate the degree of its future availability to the steel industry, any substantial change in the use pattern of coke oven gas would necessarily affect the fuel balance of the industry. Currently it is equivalent, in Btu terms, to some 10 per cent of all primary fuels used in the industry. However, with its gradual displacement by natural gas in the economy as a whole—especially in use by utilities—less than 5 per cent of all coke oven gas produced in the steel industry is now disposed of outside the industry. If we make the reasonably realistic assumption that there will be no resurgence in its use outside the steel industry, then the omission of the gas as an independent factor in fuel consumption does not significantly affect the validity of the projection. Indeed, one may study the fuel economy without worrying about the disposition of by-product fuels.

One further point needs comment. To the modest extent that a greater share of electric-furnace steel is projected, the ratio of pig iron to ingots declines at the same time. And smaller amounts of by-product fuels (from non-electric furnaces) will be available to the industry. To the extent that these are used in the production of ingots their loss would not be felt, since fewer ingots would be made in open hearth and other non-electric furnaces. In all subsequent processes, however, they would have to be replaced by purchased fuels, and these might not necessarily be coal. In the balance the main effect would be on the fuel pattern, since the steel industry's demand for coal for furnaces would decline as the demand of the other stages of the industry, deprived of by-product fuels, would increase. Considering the wide range of efficiency improvement merely through the replacement of old and addition of new units, and the possibilities afforded by maximum heat preservation in the flow of hot intermediate products, the further lack of precision produced by this particular deficiency is not considered to be of much consequence, bothersome as it might be conceptually.

A somewhat related problem arises in the case of petroleum refining (Tables A10–44, 45). To the extent that still gas originating in the course of refining is burned as fuel, it is sufficient to take into account the ratio of this and other by-product fuels per barrel of crude refined. To the extent that portions of still gas are increasingly shipped for their value as chemical feed stock, an additional, independent source of fuel demand arises. This may one day become a significant source of error in the direction of understating fuel requirements for refining. By not allowing for any improvement in efficiency in petroleum refining, we have—if not in motivation, at least in fact—allowed for maximum fuel demand through the operation of this particular factor.

Because liquid fuel consumption in agriculture is difficult to project, the method used (Table A10–

47) has been supplemented by a different approach based upon the past relationship between the displacement of horses and mules and the acquisition of tractors. The replacement ratios show a rather narrow range. The evident decline is to be expected as the work utilization of the horses retained on farms drops lower and lower so that each tractor acquired replaces fewer and fewer horses.

Years	Change in number of		Number of horses replaced per tractor
	Horses	Tractors	
	(thousands)		
1940–45	—2,528	+809	3.1
1945–50	—4,169	+1,045	4.0
1950–55	—3,472	+946	3.7
1955–60	—1,259	+430	3.0

Using a ratio of 3 animals to be replaced per tractor and assuming complete displacement of all work animals on farms would yield a figure of just over 1 million tractors yet to be acquired. Dropping the ratio to 2.5 would raise the tractor figure to 1.2 million. Raising it to 4.0 would lower the tractor figure to not quite 800,000. These rough calculations yield an order of magnitude very similar to that obtained by the previous approach, though their significance is impaired by the fact that the relationship between tractors acquired and workstock displaced is rendered increasingly tenuous by the special character and limited usefulness of the working animals left on farms.

In making the projection, a short cut was used in that estimated 1960 fuel consumption for all uses (other than those—such as use in trucks and automobiles—that are covered elsewhere) was related solely to the number of tractors rather than to the number of all farm machines and to any other fuel-burning activity (orchard-heating, weeding, etc.). The reasons for this procedure are of a purely practical nature: tractors are by far the most important factor in fuel consumption, since most other pieces of machinery are either tractor-drawn or otherwise tractor-powered through take-offs. It is, therefore, reasonable to have tractors represent all machinery—fortunately, since we can hazard a guess as to future number of tractors but would find it less rewarding to repeat the procedure for a variety of machines. We are left with the question of fuel burned in uses other than the driving of tractors and related vehicles. Here, both current statistics and bases for projection are unsatisfactory, and the grossly simplifying assumption has therefore been made that those uses of fuel will develop in step with tractor fuel consumption.

LIST OF TABLES

TABLE A10–1.   Estimated Sales of Gas for Residential Space
Heating, 1949–60[1]

	Gas utility sales to residential customers (tril. Btu)			Number of house heating customers (thous.)	Estimated annual heating sales per customer (mil. Btu)
	Total	Estimated non-heating[2]	Estimated heating[3]		
1949	1,183	572	611	7,443	82
1950	1,384	649	735	8,718	84
1951	1,620	697	923	10,046	92
1952	1,735	710	1,025	11,054	93
1953	1,803	748	1,055	12,297	86
1954	2,003	823	1,180	13,402	88
1955	2,239	894	1,345	14,711	91
1956	2,464	988	1,476	16,080	92
1957	2,598	994	1,604	17,188	93
1958	2,812	1,082	1,730	18,265	95
1959	2,974	1,082	1,892	19,446	97
1960[4]	3,188	1,168	2,020	20,739	97

1. Source of basic data: American Gas Association, *Gas Facts* (New York: various years).

2. Assumed to equal four times consumption in third calendar quarter, which is predominantly for non-heating uses, increased by 10% to balance likely underestimate of non-heating uses due to fact that third quarter includes vacation period and that non-heating uses in winter are likely to rise (hot water, including use in clothes washing; hot meals). There is no claim that this 10% adjustment is "right." Rather, it is a recognition of the likely underestimation of non-heating uses. It has been suggested that the sizable number of non-central-heating customers depress the heating data. However, it is remarkable that the rapid advance of central heating, as obvious from a comparison of the fourth column of this table with the number of automatic heaters calculable from Table A10–4, has not resulted in any substantial increase in per-customer use (fifth column) beyond what is reasonably explainable in terms of regional expansion.

3. Calculated as residual. Total (annual) sales include the liquid petroleum gas portion of sales that is sent through mains by utilities, but non-heating sales do not; heating sales are thus overstated. However, since LPG sales have amounted only to some 4 to 6 trillion Btu per year in the eleven years under consideration, no correction has been made for this inconsistency, which would amount to less than 0.5% in 1949 and probably less than 0.2% in 1959.

4. Includes negligible quantities and number of customers for Hawaii.

TABLE A10–2.   Regional Distribution of Gas House-Heating Customers, 1949–60

(Per cent)

	1949	1950	1951	1952	1953	1954	1955	1956	1957	1958	1959	1960
New England	.8	.8	.9	.8	.9	.9	1.0	1.2	1.4	1.6	1.7	1.9
Middle Atlantic	8.0	8.2	8.7	8.9	10.0	10.5	11.3	11.6	11.5	12.0	12.2	12.0
E. N. Central	13.0	15.1	16.3	17.1	17.2	17.5	18.3	18.8	19.3	19.8	20.3	21.0
W. N. Central	7.9	9.4	9.8	9.5	9.8	10.0	9.9	9.7	9.6	9.5	9.6	9.6
S. Atlantic	5.4	5.0	5.6	6.1	6.5	6.8	7.1	7.2	7.1	7.1	7.2	7.3
E. S. Central	4.6	4.8	5.1	5.2	5.3	5.3	5.3	5.5	5.7	5.7	5.7	5.7
W. S. Central	25.4	24.1	22.6	22.0	20.9	20.2	19.4	18.8	18.3	17.7	17.1	16.7
Mountain	5.1	4.9	5.0	5.1	5.3	5.3	5.1	5.1	5.2	5.2	5.2	5.3
Pacific	29.6	27.6	26.0	25.3	24.2	23.4	22.6	22.1	21.9	21.3	20.9	20.5
Total	100.0	100.0	100.0	100.0	100.0	100.0	100.0	100.0	100.0	100.0	100.0	100.0

Source: American Gas Association, *1954 Gas Facts*, p. 155; *1960 Gas Facts*, p. 144; *1961 Gas Facts*, p.147.

TABLE A10–3.   Average Number of Degree-Days for U.S. Population, Gas Heating Customers, and Oil Heating Households, 1957

	Estimated average degree-days[1] (thousands)	Resident population 1957 (millions)	Number of gas heating customers 1957[2] (thousands)	Number of central oil burners in use 1/2/58[3] (thousands)	Degree-days for—		
					Resident population (thousands)	Gas heating population (thousands)	Oil heating population (thousands)
New England	7.0	9.92	245	1,511	69.4	1.71	10.58
Middle Atlantic	6.0	32.75	1,971	3,096	196.5	11.83	18.58
E. N. Central	6.0	34.72	3,314	1,723	208.3	19.88	10.34
W. N. Central	5.5	15.14	1,656	785	83.3	9.11	4.32
S. Atlantic	2.5	24.62	1,226	999	61.6	3.06	2.50
E. S. Central	3.5	11.72	976	57	41.0	3.42	.20
W. S. Central	2.0	16.31	3,143	62	32.6	6.29	.12
Mountain	5.0	6.40	900	110	32.0	4.50	.55
Pacific	3.0	18.71	3,757	685	56.1	11.27	2.05
Total		170.29	17,188	9,028	780.8	71.07	49.24
U.S. average		–	–	–	[4]4.59	4.13	5.45

1. This regional simplification is derived from a state-by-state calculation. The U.S. average based upon these regional estimates comes within 1% of the average derived directly from the state-by-state data. (But see footnote 4.)

2. *1960 Gas Facts*, p. 144.

3. New York: Heating Publishers, Inc., *Fueloil and Oil Heat*, April 1958.

4. The Petroleum Economics Branch of the U.S. Bureau of Mines carries an "average degree-days" figure in its files which totals 4,775, i.e., about 4% above the one here estimated. The Bureau has a weighting system that emphasizes urban vs. rural areas.

TABLE A10–4. Automatic Heating Equipment in Use, 1941–60

At end of—	Total in use (thous.)	Gas burners	Oil burners (Per cent of total)	Stokers	Electric
1941	4,515	29.0	53.2	17.8	–
1942	4,616	29.3	51.7	19.0	–
1943	4,634	29.4	51.3	19.3	–
1944	4,700	29.4	50.9	19.7	–
1945	4,980	28.8	50.5	20.7	–
1946	6,009	33.7	47.0	19.3	–
1947	7,134	32.2	51.2	16.6	–
1948	7,152	32.7	51.3	16.0	–
1949	8,846	35.2	50.8	14.0	–
1950	10,435	39.1	49.6	11.3	–
1951	11,507	40.6	49.6	9.8	–
1952	12,758	41.8	49.7	8.5	–
1953	14,086	43.1	49.8	7.1	–
1954	15,423	45.0	49.2	5.8	–
1955	17,047	46.9	48.5	4.6	–
1956	18,452	48.7	47.3	4.0	–
1957	19,516	50.2	46.3	3.5	–
1958	20,742	52.1	45.0	2.9	–
1959	22,697	52.5	42.5	2.4	2.6
1960	23,968	54.0	41.0	2.0	3.0

Source: Fueloil and Oil Heat, Jan. 1961.

TABLE A10–5. Trends in Residential Oil Heating Installations, 1948–60[1]

(Thousands)

	Oil burner installations			Conversions to oil			Conversions from oil				Net additions
	Total	In new homes	Replacements of oil burners	Total	From coal	From gas	Total	To gas	To coal	To electricity	
1948	461	196	91	174	170	4	40.9	29.7	10.1	1.1	329
1949	570	172	58	340	335	5	38.2	30.3	2.9	5.1	474
1950	816	305	92	419	413	6	68.3	60.9	5.1	2.2	656
1951	692	262	94	336	327	9	50.8	44.9	1.9	3.9	547
1952	722	223	103	396	389	7	32.7	26.9	1.4	9.4	586
1953	794	312	101	381	374	7	47.1	43.2	.6	3.3	646
1954	767	330	123	314	299	15	55.6	47.8	.6	7.2	588
1955	835	361	132	342	330	12	75.1	68.5	2.1	5.5	628
1956	715	321	143	251	235	16	90.1	82.2	2.2	5.8	482
1957	609	224	151	234	222	12	133.4	122.2	2.0	9.2	325
1958	505	165	154	186	171	15	98.0	86.3	1.3	10.4	253
1959	637	213	205	219	208	11	109.3	96.0	1.6	11.7	323
1960	517	157	210	149	138	11	129.3	117.6	1.4	10.3	178

1. From *Fueloil and Oil Heat,* various issues. Installations are unrevised figures published each January following the year of reference. In most cases, these totals are later revised, but some of the breakdowns here shown are not conveniently available with the revised totals. The relationships observed are little affected by the revisions. Nonetheless, it is worth recording that the revised total for 1960 is 490,000, of which 149,000 is in new homes, 198,000 in replacements, and 141,000 in conversions.

TABLE A10–6.   Estimated Space Heating Pattern, by Source of Heat, 1955 and 1960

	Total	Gas	Oil	Coal	LPG	Electricity	Other, incl. unheated
1955:[1]							
Number of households (millions)	47.8	16.1	14.2	9.5	4.5	0.2	3.3
Per cent distribution	100.0	33.7	29.7	19.9	9.4	0.4	6.9
Energy input (tril. Btu)	4,424	1,423	1,874	891	128	[2]8	[3]100
Per cent distribution	100.0	32.2	42.4	20.1	2.9	0.2	2.3
Efficiency[4] (%)	(63.0)	75	60	50	75	100	40
Heat output (tril. Btu)	2,788	1,070	1,124	450	96	8	40
Per cent distribution	100.0	38.4	40.3	16.1	3.4	0.3	1.4
1960:							
Number of households[5] (millions)	52.6	21.7	16	6.5	5	0.9	2.5
Per cent distribution	100	[6]41.3	30.4	[7]12.4	9.5	1.7	4.8
Energy input (tril. Btu)	4,985	[8]2,120	[9]2,060	[10]550	[11]145	[12]30	[13]80
Per cent distribution	100.0	42.5	41.3	11.0	2.9	.6	1.6
Efficiency[4] (%)	(67.5)	76	62	51	76	[14]110	40
Heat output (tril. Btu)	3,347	1,611	1,280	280	110	33	32
Per cent distribution	100.0	48.1	38.2	8.4	3.3	1.0	1.0

1. Based on Schurr, Netschert, *et al.*, *Energy in the American Economy, 1850–1975* (Baltimore: Johns Hopkins Press and Resources for the Future, 1960), especially Tables C–6, C–7, C–11 (footnotes), with number of households adjusted from mid–1950 to mid–1955. 1955 household figure compares with 48.0 million in Table A1–1.

2. Estimated at 11,000 kwh per household (mostly resistance heating) and 3,412 Btu per kwh. In terms of fuel burned to generate this quantity of electricity, the entry would be 3 to 4 times as large, but still insignificant.

3. Does not figure in projections, and correctness of figure here assumed of relatively low order of importance.

4. Efficiency factors based on *op. cit.* footnote 1, p. 177. For further discussion of factors see Notes. Figure in parentheses is derived over-all average.

5. These estimates, except the one for electric heating, which comes from *Electrical World* (New York: McGraw-Hill) and represents a rounding of the mid-year point between their most recently revised estimates for the end of 1959 and for the end of 1960 (in *Proceedings of the Fifth Electrical Heating Conference,* Washington, Sept. 1961), and the one for gas, are patterned after the estimated changes in energy input below. (See footnotes 6 and 7.)

6. *1961 Gas Facts,* p. 144, shows 20.7 million gas heating customers. This figure was adjusted to pro-

vide for a reasonable amount of doubling-up of households per customer.

7. There is little to support any specific estimate, except that a lower figure would suggest a rate of decline that appears too rapid, given the pace of conversion to other fuels.

8. *1961 Gas Facts,* p. 98.

9. Based on evidence contained in continuing decrease in share of oil burners, which was used to adjust data on sales of heating oil. This is because sales of No. 2 oil show an unreasonable increase between 1955 and 1960, presumably because of a discontinuity in data collection method. Increase in input is assumed to be 10% from 1955 to 1960.

10. Based on 1960 retail sales of bituminous coal and consumption of anthracite, adjusted as suggested in Schurr, Netschert, *et al., op. cit.,* Table C–5, footnote 1.

11. Assumed to grow by 10% from 1955 and rounded (which is equivalent to preserving its 1955 market share). Because of its basically small share, this is not an important assumption but is grounded in the 54% rise of LPG sales for domestic and commercial use between 1955 and 1960.

12. Assumed to have increased in same proportion as number of electrically heated households.

13. Assumed to decline by 20%.

14. See Table A10–9.

TABLE A10–7.   Projected Number of Dwellings, by Source of Heat

		Pre–1960	1960–70	1970–80	1980–90	1990–2000	Total
Stock of dwellings [1] (millions):							
1960		58.5					58.5
	L	53.2	12.5				65.7
1970	M	47.9	20.9				68.8
	H	42.5	30.6				73.1
	L	47.1	12.1	18.0			77.2
1980	M	37.6	19.7	25.7			83.0
	H	29.0	27.9	35.2			92.1
	L	40.7	11.2	17.5	16.9		86.3
1990	M	28.3	16.9	24.1	27.6		96.9
	H	18.3	22.2	32.2	43.5		116.2
	L	35.0	9.8	16.2	16.4	18.2	95.6
2000	M	21.0	13.1	20.7	25.9	34.9	115.6
	H	10.9	14.8	25.6	39.7	60.2	151.2
Per cent electrically	L		10	15	20	25	
heated [2]	M	1.5	15	25	40	50	
	H		20	33	50	65	
Number electrically heated [3] (millions):							
1960		.9					.9
	L	.9	1.3				2.2
1970	M	.9	3.1				4.0
	H	.8	6.1				6.9
	L	.9	1.2	2.7			4.8
1980	M	.9	3.0	6.4			10.3
	H	.7	5.6	11.7			18.0
	L	.9	1.1	2.6	3.4		8.0
1990	M	.7	2.5	6.0	11.0		20.2
	H	.5	4.4	10.7	21.8		37.4
	L	.9	1.0	2.4	3.3	4.5	12.1
2000	M	.7	2.0	5.2	10.4	17.4	35.7
	H	.4	3.0	8.5	19.8	39.1	70.8
Per cent non-electri-	L		80	67	50	35	
cally heated [4]	M	98	85	75	60	50	
	H		90	85	80	75	
Number of dwellings non-electrically heated (millions):							
1960		57.6					57.6
	L	52.3	10.0				62.3
1970	M	47.0	17.8				64.8
	H	41.8	27.5				69.3
	L	46.2	9.7	12.1			68.0
1980	M	36.7	16.7	19.3			72.7
	H	28.3	25.1	29.9			83.3
	L	39.8	9.0	11.7	8.4		68.9
1990	M	27.5	14.4	18.1	16.6		76.6
	H	17.8	20.0	27.4	34.8		100.0
	L	34.1	7.8	10.8	8.2	6.4	67.3
2000	M	20.3	11.1	15.5	15.5	17.5	79.9
	H	10.5	13.3	21.8	31.8	45.2	122.6
Per cent of dwellings	L		65	54	39	25	
gas heated [5]	M	41	70	62	49	40	
	H		75	72	69	65	

Table A10–7 (cont'd)

		Period of construction						
		Pre–1960	1960–70	1970–80	1980–90	1990–2000	Total	
Number of dwellings gas heated (millions):								
1960		24.0					24.0	
1970	L	21.8	8.1				29.9	
	M	19.6	14.6				34.2	
	H	17.4	23.0				40.4	
1980	L	19.3	7.9	9.7			36.9	
	M	15.4	13.8	15.9			45.1	
	H	11.9	20.9	25.3			58.1	
1990	L	16.7	7.3	9.5	6.6		40.1	
	M	11.6	11.8	14.9	13.5		51.8	
	H	7.5	16.7	23.2	30.0		77.4	
2000	L	14.4	6.4	8.7	6.4	4.6	40.5	
	M	8.6	9.2	12.8	12.7	14.0	57.3	
	H	4.5	11.1	18.4	27.4	39.1	100.5	
Per cent of dwellings oil heated[5]		30	15	13	11	10		
Number of dwellings oil heated[6] (millions):							(Unadjusted)	(Adjusted)
1960		17.6					17.6	
1970	L	12.7	1.9				14.6	16.2
	M	14.4	3.1				17.5	17.5
	H	16.0	4.6				20.6	19.0
1980	L	8.7	1.8	2.3			12.8	15.3
	M	11.3	3.0	3.4			17.7	17.7
	H	14.1	4.2	4.5			22.8	20.3
1990	L	5.5	1.6	2.3	1.9		11.3	14.2
	M	8.5	2.6	3.1	3.0		17.2	17.2
	H	12.2	3.3	4.1	4.8		24.4	21.6
2000	L	3.3	1.5	2.1	1.8	1.8	10.5	13.3
	M	6.3	2.0	2.6	2.9	3.5	17.3	17.3
	H	10.5	2.3	3.3	4.4	6.0	26.5	23.8

1. From Table A4–6. In order to utilize the data in Table A4–6 without a time consuming conversion to households, the calculations are executed in terms of dwellings. Only in Tables A10–9 and A10–11 are the conversions made for the totals accumulated in this table. As a result, the 1960 data are not comparable with customer statistics as published by trade associations.

2. For basis of these ratios, see discussion in Chapter 10, pp. 188–91. They derive essentially from a 10% ratio in 1960 construction, and industry experience, plans, and expectations thereafter.

3. Because households already electrically heated in 1960 are the more recently built ones, a slower rate of attrition is assumed for this group than for the pre–1960 stock as a whole. For post–1960 dwellings, an increasing proportion (shown above) is assumed to be initially equipped with electrical heating. Conversions, which are currently about 25% of the electrical heating market, are not calculated separately, but the installation rates are kept high enough to allow for them.

4. Low non-electrical is the complement of High electrical, etc. Forms of heating equipment other than electricity, oil, or gas are assumed to be negligible in post–1960 construction. In pre–1960 stock, on the other hand, electric, oil, and gas heated dwellings add to only 73% of all dwellings (see Table A10–8).

5. The division of dwellings between oil and gas is based upon the assumption of a continuing decline from present pattern in oil heating equipment installed in new construction. The decline—starting from a level of 15% in 1960–70—is held to 2 percentage points per decade and half that rate in the final decade. In view of the low and declining share of oil heating equipment, no low and high shares are projected for oil, so that the oil heating variations are due solely to Lows and Highs in the totals. For basis of the 1960 distribution, see footnotes to Table A10–8.

6. The projected pattern of dwelling construction above is so set up as to yield Highs and Lows for construction activity. Since oil heating is assumed to decline in relative importance, its role at any time in the future will not be maximized by maximum construction, nor will it be at a low when construction is at a low. On the contrary, a high in oil heating equipment is likely to be associated with maximum carry-over of older houses. Consequently, the Highs and Lows are derived, in somewhat hybrid fashion, as explained in detail for Highs as follows:

The High projection assumes the lowest construction rate. It, therefore, takes as its point of origin the pre–1960 stock carried under the Low entry for stock of dwellings. To this is added the maximum new construction compatible with this stock; i.e., the sum of the pre–1960 stock plus new construction must not exceed the total high stock at the end of each decade.

Table A10–7 (cont'd)

To illustrate, the High projection for 1970 is composed of 53.2 million dwellings carried as the low pre–1960 stock plus the difference between the high stock in 1970, i.e., 73.1 million, and the pre–1960 stock as above, or 19.9 million dwellings. The ratio between this adjusted construction total and the unadjusted High of 30.6 million dwellings built in the 1960–70 period may be considered as an adjustment factor, in this instance amounting to 65%. Once these magnitudes are established the percentage figures for oil heated dwellings are applied to them. Low projections are set up in an analogous manner. The following table shows the adjustment factors that were applied to post–1960 construction projections in order to ensure compatibility as explained (the unadjusted and adjusted totals are also shown):

| | Dwellings added in period between 1960 and year shown (millions) | | | | | |
| | Adjustment factors | | Unadjusted | | Adjusted | |
Year	High	Low	High	Low	High	Low
1970	65	186	4.6	1.9	3.0	3.5
1980	71	160	8.7	4.1	6.2	6.6
1990	77	150	12.2	5.8	9.4	8.7
2000	83	140	16.0	7.2	13.3	10.0

TABLE A10–8. Projected Percentage Distribution of Dwellings, by Source of Heat

(Per cent)

		Gas[1]	Oil[1]	Electricity[1]	Coal[2]	LPG[2]	Other[3]
1955		34	30	0.4	20	9	7
1960		41	30	2	12	9	5
	L	46	25	3	5	8	–
1970	M	50	25	6	7	9	4
	H	55	26	10	10	10	–
	L	48	20	6	2	6	–
1980	M	54	21	12	3	7	3
	H	63	22	20	7	10	–
	L	46	16	9	–	5	–
1990	M	53	18	21	–	6	2
	H	67	19	32	4	10	–
	L	42	14	13	–	3	–
2000	M	50	15	31	–	5	–
	H	66	16	47	–	10	–

1. 1955–60 from Table A10–6; 1970–2000 derived from Table A10–7, column headed "Total."

2. 1955–60 from Table A10–6; 1970–2000 projected proportionately to changes in input shares as shown in Table A10–11.

3. Including unheated. Since figures in this column are not further used and since Lows and Highs can not be added across, no Low and High projections have been made.

TABLE A10–9.   Projected Electricity for Household Space Heating

	1960		1970	1980	1990	2000
Number of dwellings heated electrically[1]		L	2.2	4.8	8.0	12.1
(millions)	.90	M	4.0	10.3	20.2	35.7
		H	7.0	18.0	37.4	70.8
		L	.894	.890	.886	.880
Ratio of households to dwellings[2]		M	.890	.880	.870	.860
		H	.880	.860	.840	.820
Number of households heated electrically		L	2.0	5.2	7.1	10.6
(millions)	.90	M	3.6	9.1	17.6	30.7
		H	6.2	15.5	31.4	58.1
Electricity requirements per household[3] (thous. kwh), based on resistance heating	14		15	16	16	16
Efficiency factor adjustment:						
		L	15	20	25	30
Share of heat pumps[4] (%)	10	M	20	35	50	60
		H	25	40	60	75
Coefficient of performance[4] (including auxiliary resistance heating)	2		2.10	2.25	2.40	2.5
		L	85	80	75	70
Share of resistance heating[5] (%)	90	M	80	65	50	40
		H	75	60	40	25
		L	116	125	135	145
Combined average efficiency[6] (%)	110	M	122	134	170	190
		H	128	150	184	212
Adjusted requirement per household[7]		L	12.9	12.8	11.9	11.0
(thous. kwh)	13	M	12.3	11.9	9.4	8.4
		H	11.7	10.7	8.7	7.5
		L	25.8	66.6	84.5	117
Total electricity required[8] (bil. kwh)	11.7	M	44.3	108	165	258
		H	72.5	166	273	436

1. From Table A10–7.

2. Calculated from Table A4–5; "households" is equivalent to "occupied dwelling units" and "dwellings" to "total housing stock." For 1960, however, the vacancy rate of electrically heated dwellings is assumed to be negligible.

3. Based partly upon technical literature pertaining to resistance heating, and partly upon the average heat output factor of 70 million Btu developed in Chapter 10, pp. 187, 190–91. Assuming a heat loss reduction through proper insulation of one-third, this would yield a requirement of just below 14,000 kwh. One of the utilities deeply interested in and heavily promoting electric heating bases its projections on annual heating plus cooling load of 18,000 kwh (Harold Turner, American Electric Power Co., quoted in *Electrical World* of Nov. 16, 1959). Assuming some 3,500 Btu for cooling results in 14,500 for heating. Some studies appear to be based on lower, others on higher requirements; the 14,000 kwh level is chosen as a reasonable compromise. The effect of introduction of heat pumps is taken separate account of in the efficiency factor derived below. Increases in the unit requirement are expected to flow from increased sizes of dwelling units and the spread of electrical heating to colder parts of the country.

4. The projections both of the share of heat pumps and of their effective coefficient of performance are conjectures as to possible development, based upon a study of the technical literature and discussion with trade experts. While higher coefficients can be reached, the use of the pump in colder regions and the consequent need for auxiliary resistance heating would tend to limit this potential. In its 1960 Electric Heating Survey the editors of *Electrical World* project that by 1970 heat pumps will have taken 26% of the electrical heating market. This is slightly above our High projection.

5. The figures shown here for the Low are the shares that would accompany the low rate of introduction of heat pumps, since this leads to the lowest over-all efficiency factor; similarly for the High.

6. Efficiency of resistance heating is taken as 100%.

7. Low here denotes low efficiency; High denotes high efficiency.

8. The figures shown for the low are calculated by applying the unit requirements associated with low efficiency to the Low projection of electrically heated households, on the assumption that there will be a positive interdependence between the two factors; similarly for the High.

TABLE A10–10. Projected Gas and Oil Shares in Household Space Heating Output, Excluding Electricity (medium projections)

(Per cent)

	Share of gas	Share of oil	Total gas and oil
1960 shares in heat output[1]	48.6	38.6	87.2
Per cent change in share of dwellings 1960–70[2]	+24	—13	–
Preliminary 1970 shares in heat output[3]	60	34	94
Adjusted 1970 shares in heat output[4]	58	33	91
Per cent change in share of dwellings 1970–80[2]	+17	—10	–
Preliminary 1980 shares in heat output[3]	68	30	98
Adjusted 1980 shares in heat output[4]	64	28	92
Per cent change in share of dwellings 1980–90[2]	+9	—5	–
Preliminary 1990 shares in heat output[3]	70	27	97
Adjusted 1990 shares in heat output[4]	69	27	96
Per cent change in share of dwellings 1990–2000[2]	+6	—5	–
Preliminary 2000 shares in heat output[3]	73	26	99
Adjusted 2000 shares in heat output[4]	72	26	98

1. From Table A10–6, omitting electricity.

2. Percentage changes projected for number of dwellings heated by different sources are calculated from Table A10–8, excluding the share of electrically heated dwellings.

3. Percentage change in share of dwellings applied to percentage share in heat output of preceding period.

4. Adjusted to the projected joint gas-oil share in heat output, which is derived by deducting from 100 the shares of coal, LPG, and "other" as independently projected in Table A10–11. This method was selected because the possible range is quite small for these secondary fuels and may be projected with but little chance of gross miscalculation. The breakdown between gas and oil is then calculated by scaling down the preliminary shares to the projected gas-plus-oil level.

The need for this calculation arises out of the fact that gas and oil occupy a relatively larger share in heat output than in number of dwellings, owing to the fact that secondary fuel sources are either supplementary or found frequently in dwellings not as fully heated as those using oil and gas.

TABLE A10–11.　Projected Fuel Requirements for Non-Electrical Household Space Heating, by Source of Heat

	1955	1960		1970	1980	1990	2000
Dwellings excluding those heated			L	62.3	68.0	68.9	67.3
electrically[1] (millions)	52.8	57.6	M	64.8	72.7	76.6	79.9
			H	69.3	83.3	100.0	122.6
			L	.894	.890	.886	.880
Ratio of households to dwellings[2]	.901	.898	M	.890	.880	.870	.860
			H	.880	.860	.840	.820
Households not heated electrically[3]			L	55.7	60.5	61.0	59.2
(millions)	47.6	51.7	M	57.7	64.0	66.7	68.8
			H	61.0	71.6	84.0	100.5
Heat output per household[4] (mil. Btu)	58.6	65.7		68	70	65	60
			L	3,788	4,235	3,965	3,552
Total heat output required (tril. Btu)	2,788	3,400	M	3,924	4,480	4,335	4,128
			H	4,148	5,017	5,460	6,030
Fuel shares (%):[5]							
			L	48	55	58	62
Gas	38.5	48.6	M	58	64	69	72
			H	59	69	76	80
			L	25	20	16	15
Oil	40.4	38.6	M	33	28	27	26
			H	31	28	27	26
Coal	16.2	8.4		4.4	3.5	1.0	–
Liquid petroleum gas	3.4	3.4		4.0	4.0	3.0	2.0
Other	1.5	1.0		0.6	0.5	–	–
Fuel amounts:							
			L	1,818	2,329	2,300	2,202
Gas	1,070	1,650	M	2,276	2,867	2,991	2,972
			H	2,447	3,458	4,150	4,824
			L	947	847	634	533
Oil	1,124	1,310	M	1,295	1,254	1,170	1,073
			H	1,286	1,403	1,474	1,568
			L	167	148	40	–
Coal	450	280	M	173	157	43	–
			H	183	175	55	–
			L	152	169	119	71
LPG	96	110	M	157	179	130	83
			H	166	200	164	121
Fuel efficiency[6] (%):							
Gas, LPG	75	76		78	80	80	80
Oil	60	62		70	75	75	75
Coal	50	51		53	55	55	55

Table A10–11 (cont'd)

	1955	1960		1970	1980	1990	2000
Fuel input:							
Trillion Btu:							
			L	2,330	2,910	2,875	2,750
Gas	1,440	2,170	M	2,920	3,585	3,740	3,715
			H	3,135	4,320	5,185	6,030
			L	1,350	1,130	845	710
Oil	1,880	2,110	M	1,850	1,670	1,560	1,430
			H	1,840	1,870	1,965	2,090
			L	315	270	70	–
Coal	910	530	M	325	285	80	–
			H	345	320	100	–
			L	195	210	150	90
LPG	125	145	M	200	225	160	105
			H	210	250	205	150
Physical units:							
Gas (tril. cu. ft. at 1,035			L	2.251	2.812	2.778	2.657
Btu/cu. ft.)	1.390	2.096	M	2.821	3.464	3.614	3.589
			H	3.029	4.174	5.010	5.826
			L	237	198	148	125
Oil (mil. bbl. at 5.7 mil. Btu/bbl.)	330	[7]370	M	325	293	274	251
			H	323	328	345	367
			L	12.0	10.3	2.7	–
Coal (mil. tons at 26.2 mil. Btu/ton)	34.7	20.2	M	12.4	10.9	3.1	–
			H	13.2	12.2	3.8	–
			L	48.8	52.5	37.5	22.5
LPG (mil. bbl., at 4 mil. Btu/bbl.)	31.2	36.2	M	50.0	56.3	40.0	26.2
			H	52.5	62.5	51.3	37.5

1. From Table A10–7, except for 1955, which is approximated from the household distribution (third row, below) and the approximate vacancy rate. These, and the household data which follow, contain a small, and dwindling, percentage of unheated dwellings.

2. As in Table A10–9, except for 1955, which is estimated from the end-of-1955 ratio (complement of vacancy rate) in Table A4–5.

3. 1955 and 1960 from Table A10–6; projections calculated by applying occupancy ratios to dwelling units, above.

4. 1955 and 1960 calculated from Table A10–6. Projections based on attaining theoretically optimum heating by 1980, thereafter declining as the result of the spread of more complete insulation.

5. Medium projections for gas and oil from Table A10–10. Highs are calculated as the percentage that the high of the fuel in question is of the sum of that same High and the combined Lows of the other fuels (excluding electricity), all taken from Table A10–8. Lows are calculated by the corresponding reverse method. These percentage shares are based upon the distribution of dwellings rather than of heat input, but it was found that adjusting the projections to a fuel input basis would not sufficiently alter the results (less than 5%) to warrant further encrusting the procedure.

1955 and 1960 data for coal, LPG, and "other" are taken from Table A10–6, but adjusted so as to have fuel shares add up to 100. They are projected on the basis that LPG will conserve its share through 1980 and that coal will continuously decline (but retain a minimum market through 1990). Highs and Lows, which are retained in Table A10–8, are here dropped, because of the modest significance of these series.

6. Assumed to grow gradually for all four fuels, then to remain constant after reaching a high in 1980. Initial assumptions (1955, 1960) are based on whatever consensus can be distilled from written judgments of experts in various fields. See also Table A10–6.

7. It is difficult to apply any independent check upon the reasonableness of the quantity here computed. The 1955 figure checks closely with sales data for No. 1 and No. 2 heating oils and range oils, as adjusted in accordance with the judgment expressed in *Energy in the American Economy*, Appendix C, especially Tables C–2 and C–3. If the same method is applied to sales figures for 1959—the latest available—the resulting consumption estimate exceeds the one here arrived at for 1960 by some 10%. However, there is evidence that the sales data statistics suffered a break in continuity between 1957 and 1958, with the result that the post–1957 level is substantially higher. Thus the 10% excess in the heating oil total is not too disconcerting, and it is not thought useful to apply any kind of correction factors to the data here computed. Any error which may be involved is compensated for by the adjustment of identified end-use totals to total oil demand (apparent consumption) in Table A15–13.

TABLE A10–12.　Projected Energy Consumption for Household Cooking[1]

	1951	1952	1953	1954	1955	1956	1957	1958	1959	1960		1970	1980	1990	2000
Number of households[2] (millions)	44.8	45.7	46.5	47.1	48.0	49.0	49.8	50.7	51.6	52.6	L	58.7	68.7	76.5	84.3
											M	61.2	73.0	84.3	99.4
											H	64.3	79.2	97.6	124.1
Number of ranges in use, midyear estimate[3] (millions)	37.5	39.6	41.6	43.6	45.5	47.8	49.9	51.8	53.6	55.2	L	65.7	79.7	90.3	101.2
											M	68.5	84.7	99.5	119.3
											H	72.0	91.9	115.2	148.9
Per cent of households (saturation factor)	83.7	86.6	89.5	92.6	94.8	97.6	100.2	102.2	103.9	105.0		112	116	118	120
Electric ranges:															
Per cent of total[4]	23.5	24.7	25.7	26.8	27.5	28.7	29.8	30.9	31.5	32.3	L	37.5	42.0	46.0	49.0
											M	42.0	51.0	57.0	62.0
											H	47.5	61.0	70.0	77.0
Number (millions)	8.8	9.8	10.8	11.7	12.5	13.8	14.9	16.0	17.0	17.8	L	24.6	33.5	41.5	49.6
											M	28.8	43.2	56.7	74.0
											H	34.2	56.1	80.6	114.7
Gas ranges[5] (millions)	28.7	29.8	30.8	31.9	33.0	34.0	35.0	35.8	36.6	37.4	L	34.5	31.1	27.1	23.3
											M	39.7	41.5	42.8	45.3
											H	45.0	53.3	62.2	75.9
Annual consumption per range:[6]															
Electric (kwh)						n.a.				1,200		1,100	1,000	900	800
Gas (thous. Btu)										9,600		9,025	8,575	8,150	7,750
Annual energy consumption:															
Electricity (bil. kwh)						n.a.				21.4	L	27.1	33.5	37.4	39.7
											M	31.7	43.2	51.0	59.2
											H	37.6	56.1	72.5	91.8
Gas (tril. Btu)										359	L	311	267	221	181
											M	358	356	349	351
											H	406	457	507	588
LPG[7]										72	L	62	53	44	36
											M	72	71	70	70
											H	81	91	101	118
Natural gas										287	L	249	214	177	145
											M	286	285	279	281
											H	325	366	406	470

1. Historical data for number of ranges are from Gas Appliance Manufacturers Association (GAMA), *Statistical Highlights*, various issues.

2. From Tables A1–1 and 2.

3. Projections calculated from the saturation factors which follow. Latter have been extrapolated at a declining rate of increase, in line with recent past experience, owing to high degree of saturation.

4. Projected (Medium) at 1951–60 arithmetic rate of change through 1970, then at declining rate, to allow for gas stoves' retaining a core portion of the market.

5. Low is 100 minus the High electric percentage, applied to the Low total; High is 100 minus the Low electric percentage, applied to the High total.

6. The 1960 estimates are from *Energy in the American Economy*, Table C–32. Unit consumption is assumed to decline in the future, as the result principally of greater use of prepared foods. The more rapid decline in annual consumption by electric ranges is based on a more rapid increase in the volume of sales, which results in a more modern stock of equipment, presumably more efficient.

7. Assumed to be 20% of the total, based roughly upon the recent relationship of LPG ranges to total gas ranges.

TABLE A10–13. Projected Energy Consumption for Household Water Heating

	1950	1951	1952	1953	1954	1955	1956	1957	1958	1959	1960		1970	1980	1990	2000
Number of households[1] (millions)	43.8	44.8	45.7	46.5	47.1	48.0	49.0	49.8	50.7	51.6	52.6	L	58.7	68.7	76.5	84.3
												M	61.2	73.0	84.3	99.4
												H	64.3	79.2	97.6	124.1
Number of water heaters in use,[2] midyear estimate (millions)	18.5	19.9	21.2	22.5	23.7	25.1	26.6	27.9	29.3	30.7	32.0	L	44.6	58.4	71.9	84.3
												M	46.5	62.1	79.2	99.4
												H	48.9	67.3	91.7	124.1
Per cent of households[3] (saturation factor)	42.2	44.4	46.4	48.4	50.3	52.3	54.3	56.0	57.8	59.5	60.9		76	85	94	100
Electric water heaters:																
Per cent of total	22.2	24.6	25.9	27.1	27.8	28.7	29.3	29.4	29.7	30.0	30.0	L	32	34	37	41
												M	34.5	41	48	56
												H	37	45	54	64
Number (millions)	4.1	4.9	5.5	6.1	6.6	7.2	7.8	8.2	8.7	9.2	9.6	L	14.3	19.9	26.6	34.6
												M	16.0	25.5	38.0	55.7
												H	18.1	30.3	49.5	79.4
Gas heaters[4] (millions)	14.4	15.0	15.7	16.4	17.1	17.9	18.8	19.7	20.6	21.5	22.5	L	28.1	32.1	33.1	30.3
												M	30.5	36.6	41.2	43.7
												H	33.3	44.4	57.8	73.2
Annual energy consumption:																
Electricity[5] (bil. kwh)					n.a.						45.1	L	67.2	93.5	119.7	148.8
												M	75.2	119.9	171.0	239.5
												H	85.1	142.4	222.8	341.4
Gas[6] (tril. Btu)											585	L	731	835	828	727
												M	793	952	1,030	1,049
												H	866	1,154	1,445	1,757
LPG[7]											58	L	73	84	83	73
												M	79	95	103	105
												H	87	115	145	176
Natural gas											527	L	658	752	745	654
												M	714	857	927	944
												H	779	1,039	1,300	1,581

1. From Tables A1–1 and 2.
2. Data through 1960 from GAMA *Statistical Highlights*, 1960–2000 calculated from saturation factors.
3. Projected at declining arithmetic rate of increase, owing to increasing saturation.
4. Low is 100 minus the High electric percentage, applied to the Low total; high is 100 minus the Low electric percentage, applied to the High total.

5. Calculated at 4700 kwh per heater through 1980, declining by 200 kwh per decade thereafter, owing to assumed increases in efficiency.
6. Calculated at 26 million Btu per heater through 1980, declining by 1 million Btu per decade thereafter, owing to assumed increases in efficiency.
7. Assumed to be 10% of total gas, based upon recent trends in LPG vs. other gas water heater sales and use.

TABLE A10–14. Projected Electricity Consumption for Residential Lighting

	1940	1945	1950	1955	1960		1970	1980	1990	2000
Annual consumption per						L	975	1,125	1,275	1,425
customer[1] (kwh)	352	428	602	790	825	M	1,075	1,325	1,575	1,825
						H	2,100	2,500	2,900	3,300
Number of households[2]						L	58.7	68.7	76.5	84.3
(millions)	35.2	37.5	43.8	48.0	52.6	M	61.2	73.0	84.3	99.4
						H	64.3	79.2	97.6	124.1
Total consumption						L	57.2	77.3	97.5	120.1
(bil. kwh)	n.a.	n.a.	n.a.	n.a.	43.4	M	65.8	96.7	132.8	181.4
						H	135.0	198.0	283.0	409.5

1. 1940–55 from *Energy in the American Economy*, Table C–34, column 2 through 1950 and column 3, adjusted to level of column 2 in 1953, for 1955. For derivation of 1960 figure, see Notes. The rate of change in the Medium projection is similar to that in *Energy in the American Economy*.

The Medium projection is similar to that in *Energy in the American Economy;* the Low allows arbitrarily for a somewhat slower rate of gain. The High for 1970 is based upon the most optimistic industry fore-

casts (*op. cit.,* Table C–36), slightly modified by postponing to 1970 the industry estimate for 1965. Thereafter an increase of 400 kwh per decade is assumed. See Chapter 10, pp. 197–98, for further comment.

2. From Table A1–2. There is now so little difference between number of households and number of electricity customers that the distinction is not significant for purposes of the present projections.

TABLE A10–15.   Projected Number of Centrally Air-Conditioned Dwellings

		Period of construction					
		Pre–1960	1960–70	1970–80	1980–90	1990–2000	Total
Stock of dwellings[1] (millions):							
1960		58.5					58.5
1970	L	53.2	12.5				65.7
	M	47.9	20.9				68.8
	H	42.5	30.6				73.1
1980	L	47.1	12.1	18.0			77.2
	M	37.6	19.7	25.7			83.0
	H	29.0	27.9	35.2			92.1
1990	L	40.7	11.2	17.5	16.9		86.3
	M	28.3	16.9	24.1	27.6		96.9
	H	18.3	22.2	32.2	43.5		116.2
2000	L	35.0	9.8	16.2	16.4	18.2	95.6
	M	21.0	13.1	20.7	25.9	34.9	115.6
	H	10.9	14.8	25.6	39.7	60.2	151.2
Per cent having central air-conditioning:[2]							
When built	L		10	20	30	40	
	M		15	30	45	60	
	H		20	40	60	80	
10 years later	L		15	25	40		
	M	(³)	25	40	60		
	H		35	50	75		
20 and 30 years later	L		16	27			
	M		28	45			
	H		40	55			
Number of dwellings with central air-conditioning (millions):							
1960		.5					.50
1970	L		1.25				2.75
	M	1.5	3.14				4.64
	H		6.12				7.62
1980	L		1.82	3.60			7.22
	M	1.8	4.93	7.71			14.44
	H		9.77	14.08			25.65
1990	L		1.79	4.38	5.07		12.84
	M	1.6	4.73	9.64	12.42		28.39
	H		8.88	16.10	26.10		52.68
2000	L		1.57	4.37	6.56	7.28	21.18
	M	1.4	3.67	9.32	15.54	20.94	50.87
	H		5.92	14.08	29.78	48.16	99.34

1. From Table A4–6.

2. It is assumed that during the two decades following the decade of construction small additional amounts of air-conditioning will be installed, but none thereafter. It is further assumed that these additional rates of installation will decline as the houses get older. The initial—and crucial—rate of 15% in the 1960–70 decade to be constructed with air-conditioning in the Medium projection is based on the finding of a Bureau of Labor Statistics survey (*New Housing and its Materials,* Bull. 1231, Washington: 1958) that 6% of houses built in 1956 were centrally air-conditioned and that this rate rises to 15% in the class of houses priced $20,000 and over. It is likely that the average rate climbed to 10% by 1960 and will approach 20% by the end of the sixties. An average of 15% would thus appear reasonable, with substantial additional installations to follow in the seventies.

3. Installation of central air-conditioning in pre–1960 houses is assumed to occur on the following basis: None in houses built prior to 1940. Thereafter only in houses having air ducts for heating. Of these there were approximately 7 million in 1960, and 7% of these did have central air-conditioning. It is assumed that this ratio will rise to 20% during the sixties and 30% during the seventies; thereafter no further installations can be expected. Taking into account the attrition in pre–1960 houses, we obtain roughly the figures shown.

TABLE A10–16. Projected Energy Consumption for Residential Air-Conditioning

	1960		1970	1980	1990	2000
		L	58.7	68.7	76.5	84.3
Number of households[1] (millions)	52.6	M	61.2	73.0	84.3	99.4
		H	64.3	79.2	97.6	124.1
Saturation factor (%):						
		L	4.2	9.4	14.9	22.2
Central air-conditioning[2]	.9	M	6.7	17.4	29.3	44.0
		H	10.4	27.9	45.3	65.7
		L	21	28	33	38
Room air-conditioning[3]	14	M	29	40	50	35
		H	34	52	35	15
Number of households (millions) with:						
		L	2.47	6.46	11.4	18.7
Central air-conditioning	.5	M	4.10	12.7	24.7	43.7
		H	6.69	22.1	44.2	81.5
		L	12.3	19.2	25.2	32.0
Room air-conditioning	7.4	M	17.7	29.2	42.2	34.8
		H	21.9	41.2	34.2	18.6
Consumption/unit (kwh):						
Central[4]	3,500		3,400	3,200	2,900	2,500
Room[5]	800		750	700	650	600
Annual consumption (bil. kwh):						
		L	8.40	20.7	33.1	46.8
Central	1.75	M	13.9	40.6	71.6	109
		H	22.7	70.7	128	204
		L	9.23	13.4	16.4	19.2
Room	5.92	M	13.3	20.4	27.4	20.9
		H	16.4	28.8	22.2	11.2
		L	17.6	34.1	49.5	66.0
All air-conditioning	7.67	M	27.2	61.0	99.0	130
		H	39.1	99.5	150	215

1. Table A1–2.
2. Based on relationship of air-conditioned to total number of dwellings, shown in Table A10–15.
3. Based on extension of brief historic trend, as follows (midyear estimates):

	No. of households (millions)	No. of homes with air-conditioners (thousands)	Saturation factor
1948	40.9	93	.2
1949	42.5	128	.3
1950	43.8	186	.4
1951	44.8	286	.6
1952	45.7	460	1.0
1953	46.5	863	1.9
1954	47.1	1,475	3.1
1955	48.0	2,192	4.6
1956	49.0	3,092	6.3
1957	49.8	4,132	8.3
1958	50.6	5,208	10.3
1959	51.2	6,133	12.0
1960	52.6	7,150	13.6

Source: *Electrical Merchandising* (New York: McGraw-Hill), various issues.

In the Medium projection it is assumed that the saturation factor ("rate") will increase at an average 1.5 points per year through 1970, 1.1 points through 1980, and 1 point through

Table A10–16 (cont'd)

1990, and that it will sharply decline thereafter, owing to the substitution of central for room air-conditioning.

Since room and central air-conditioners are complementary, Highs in central air-conditioners, in the latter part of the series, are accompanied by Lows in room air-conditioners.

4. 1960 based on *Energy in the American Economy;* projected decline reflects the spread of insulation and other energy-saving devices, especially after 1980, accompanying increased electric heating installations; also reflecting extension to climatically cooler parts of country.

5. 1960 based on *Energy in the American Economy;* projected decline for reasons given in footnote 3 and also because part of growth will presumably consist of use of more than one unit per home, resulting in moderate decline in consumption per unit.

TABLE A10–17. Saturation Trends for Miscellaneous Appliances, 1946–60[1]

| | Number of house-holds[2] (millions) | Households owning— | | | | | | | |
| | | Refrigerators | | Television | | Home freezers | | Clothes dryers | |
		Number (millions)	Per cent of all households	Number (millions)	Per cent of all households	Number (millions)	Per cent of all households	Number (millions)	Per cent of all households
1946	38.4	20.6	53.6	*	*	*	*	*	*
1947	39.4	22.5	57.1	*	*	*	*	*	*
1948	40.9	25.2	61.6	*	*	*	*	*	*
1949	42.5	28.2	66.4	2.5	5.9	1.7	4.0	.2	.5
1950	43.8	31.6	72.1	7.2	16.4	2.4	5.5	.4	.9
1951	44.8	34.6	77.2	13.2	29.5	3.3	7.4	.7	1.6
1952	45.7	36.6	80.1	18.5	40.5	4.3	9.4	1.3	2.8
1953	46.5	38.6	83.0	24.4	52.5	5.3	11.4	1.9	4.1
1954	47.1	40.4	85.8	29.9	63.5	6.4	13.6	2.6	5.5
1955	48.0	42.2	87.9	33.5	69.8	7.2	15.0	3.6	7.5
1956	49.0	44.4	90.6	36.7	74.9	8.1	16.5	4.8	9.8
1957	49.8	46.4	93.2	40.2	80.7	8.9	17.9	6.1	12.2
1958	50.7	47.8	94.3	42.9	84.6	9.8	19.3	7.2	14.2
1959	51.6	48.9	94.8	44.7	86.6	10.8	20.9	8.4	16.3
1960	52.6	50.1	95.2	45.8	87.1	11.6	22.1	9.6	18.3

* Negligible.

1. Source: *Electrical Merchandising* and GAMA, *Statistical Highlights.* Since household numbers represent midyear estimates, year-end data for appliances in use were adjusted to midyear by straight-line interpolation between year-end points.

2. From Table A1–1.

TABLE A10–18.   Projected Energy Consumption for Miscellaneous Appliances

	1950	1955	1960		1970	1980	1990	2000
				L	58.7	68.7	76.5	84.3
Number of households[1] (millions)	43.8	48.0	52.6	M	61.2	73.0	84.3	99.4
				H	64.3	79.2	97.6	124.1
Saturation factors (%):[2]								
Refrigerators	72.1	88.3	95.2		100	100	100	100
Television	16.4	69.8	87.1		100	100	100	100
				L	34.0	44.0	53.0	60.0
Home freezers	5.5	15.0	22.1	M	38.0	53.0	62.5	70.0
				H	40.0	55.0	68.0	80.0
				L	33.0	44.0	53.0	60.0
Clothes dryers	0.9	7.5	18.3	M	42.0	60.0	68.0	75.0
				H	45.0	66.0	80.0	90.0
Number of appliances (millions):								
				L	117	137	153	169
Refrigerators and TV sets	38.8	75.9	95.9	M	122	146	169	199
				H	129	158	195	248
				L	20.0	30.2	40.5	50.6
Home freezers	2.4	7.2	11.6	M	23.3	38.7	52.7	69.6
				H	25.7	43.6	66.4	99.3
				L	19.4	30.2	40.5	50.6
Clothes dryers, total	0.4	3.6	9.6	M	25.7	43.8	57.3	74.6
				H	28.9	52.3	78.1	111.7
Per cent of clothes dryers electric[3]	90	80	70		60	50	50	50
				L	11.6	15.1	20.2	25.3
Electric clothes dryers	–	–	6.7	M	15.4	21.9	28.6	37.3
				H	17.3	26.2	39.0	55.9
				L	7.8	15.1	20.3	25.3
Gas clothes dryers	–	–	2.9	M	10.3	21.9	28.7	37.3
				H	11.6	26.1	39.1	55.8
Estimated energy consumption per unit:								
Average of refrigerator and TV set (kwh)[4]	n.a.	n.a.	300		300	300	300	300
Freezers (kwh)[5]	"	"	800		850	900	900	900
Clothes dryers, electric (kwh)[5]	"	"	1,300		1,200	1,100	1,000	1,000
Clothes dryers, gas (thous. Btu)[5]	"	"	4,500		4,250	4,000	3,750	3,500
All other electricity per household				L	450	550	650	750
(kwh)[6]	"	"	330	M	550	850	1,150	1,600
				H	650	1,000	1,450	2,000
Aggregate annual consumption:								
Electricity (bil. kwh):								
				L	35.1	41.1	45.9	50.7
Refrigerators and TV sets	"	"	28.5	M	36.6	43.8	50.7	59.7
				H	38.7	47.4	58.5	74.4
				L	17.0	27.2	36.4	45.5
Home freezers	"	"	9.3	M	19.8	34.8	47.4	62.6
				H	21.8	39.2	59.8	89.4
				L	13.9	16.6	20.2	25.3
Clothes dryers	"	"	8.7	M	18.5	24.1	28.6	37.3
				H	20.8	28.8	39.0	55.9
				L	26.4	37.8	49.7	63.2
All other electricity	"	"	17.2	M	33.7	62.1	96.9	159.0
				H	41.8	79.2	142.0	248.0
				L	92.4	123	152	185
Total	"	"	63.7	M	109	165	224	319
				H	123	195	299	468

Table A10–18 (cont'd)

	1950	1955	1960		1970	1980	1990	2000
Gas (tril. Btu):								
				L	33	60	76	89
Clothes dryers	n.a.	n.a.	13	M	44	88	108	131
				H	49	104	147	195
Oil (mil. bbl.):								
				L	59	50	37	31
Non-space heating uses[7]	"	78	92	M	81	73	68	63
				H	81	82	86	92

1. From Table A1–2.

2. Based on trends shown in Table A10–17. Refers to percentage of households owning, rather than sets per household. See footnote 3.

3. In absence of data on numbers in use based on sales data for 1950 through 1960 and the trend revealed by them (GAMA, *Statistical Highlights*). Decline in share of electric dryers assumed to terminate half-way through the period; as electric heating increases, this will presumably offset the trend to gas. By the end of the period, percentage will still exceed that of electrically heated dwellings.

4. Consumption of refrigerators assumed at 350 kwh and of television sets at 250 kwh per year. Historical decline in power consumption of refrigerators assumed to have moderated. Further declines assumed to be offset by emergence of more than one appliance per household, whereas projection of saturation factor above stops at 100%. Same reasoning applies to TV, where saturation, in terms of number of sets per household, may already exceed 100; therefore, declining use and power consumption per set for increasing number is replaced by holding saturation factor at 100 but keeping unit consumption steady.

5. Initial rates based on *Energy in the American Economy*, Table C–35. Growth in freezer unit consumption based on increasing importance of frozen food, more than offsetting better control of ambient temperature; also assumed that technical improvement will be relatively small as the freezer has benefited from the long history of the refrigerator. Decline in clothes dryer consumption based on increased role of fast drying clothing and higher efficiency.

6. This item reconciles consumption via uses identified in this study with total residential sales plus the estimated residential portion of rural sales. Annual use is projected to increase, at varying rates at the three levels, to reflect the entry of new uses of electricity as well as the spread of miscellaneous current uses now enjoying only a low degree of saturation.

The reconciliation for 1960 is as follows:

Estimated use, by categories (bil. kwh):

Water heaters	45.1
Domestic ranges	21.4
Lighting	43.4
Air-conditioning	7.7
Heating	11.7
Miscellaneous	46.5
Total	175.8
All other	17.2
Total	193.0

Estimated sales, as per Edison Electric Institute (bil. kwh):

Residential sales, 1960	189.0
Estimated residential portion of rural sales	4.0
Total residential sales	193.0

7. Estimated as 25% of oil used for space heating, as shown in Table A10–11. This appears to be roughly the relationship implied in the two types of use, as developed in *Energy in the American Economy*, Appendix Tables C–2 and C–3. However, the resulting estimate of total domestic consumption of oil for 1960 falls below what one would expect in view of the 1959 level. In fact, for 1959 a similar calculation, in which non-heating uses are estimated as the difference between total sales of domestic-type oils and heating use, shows the non-heating use to constitute more nearly one-third of heating use. The problem is connected with an apparent break in comparability in 1958 which has lifted the 1958 and 1959 data for distillates to a level substantially higher than prevailed previously. (See Table A10–11, footnote 7.)

If, as is possible, we have understated the 1960 use of oils in households for purposes other than space heating, this is compensated for in the summary table (A15–13), where the sum of the identified uses is boosted to the total consumption of all types of oil.

TABLE A10–19. Projected Total Residential Consumption of Natural Gas and Electricity

	1960		1970	1980	1990	2000
Gas (quadril. Btu):						
Space-heating[1]	2.17	L M H	2.33 2.92 3.13	2.91 3.58 4.32	2.88 3.74 5.18	2.75 3.72 6.03
Ranges[2]	.287	L M H	.249 .286 .325	.214 .285 .366	.177 .279 .406	.145 .281 .470
Water heaters[3]	.527	L M H	.658 .714 .779	.752 .857 1.039	.745 .927 1.300	.654 .944 1.581
Clothes dryers[4]	.013	L M H	.033 .044 .049	.060 .088 .104	.076 .108 .147	.089 .131 .195
Sub-total, identified fuel uses	3.00	L M H	3.27 3.96 4.28	3.94 4.81 5.83	3.88 5.05 7.03	3.64 5.08 8.28
Identified uses as per cent of all uses[5]	94	L M H	94 89 87	94 85 83	94 85 80	94 85 80
Total use	3.19	L M H	3.48 4.45 4.92	4.19 5.66 7.02	4.13 5.94 8.79	3.87 5.98 10.35
Total use, physical units (tril. cu. ft.)	3.08	L M H	3.36 4.30 4.75	4.05 5.47 6.78	3.99 5.74 8.49	3.74 5.78 10.00
Electricity (bil. kwh):						
Lighting[6]	43.4	L M H	57.2 65.8 135.1	77.3 96.7 198	98 133 283	120 181 409
Ranges[2]	21.4	L M H	27.1 31.7 37.6	33.5 43.2 56.1	37.4 51.0 72.5	39.7 59.2 91.8
Water heaters[3]	45.1	L M H	67.2 75.2 85.1	93.5 120 142	120 171 223	149 240 341
Air-conditioners[7]	7.7	L M H	17.6 27.2 39.1	34.1 61.0 99.5	49.5 99.0 150.0	66.0 131.0 215.0
Space-heating[8]	11.7	L M H	25.8 44.3 72.5	66.6 108.0 166.0	84 165 273	117 258 436
Miscellaneous[4]	63.7	L M H	92.4 109 123	123 165 195	152 224 299	185 319 468
Total	193	L M H	287 353 492	428 594 857	541 843 1,300	677 1,188 1,961
Average per household	3,669	L M H	4,889 5,768 7,652	6,230 8,137 10,820	7,072 10,000 13,320	8,031 11,952 15,802

Table A10–19 (cont'd)

1. From Table A10–11.
2. From Table A10–12.
3. From Table A10–13.
4. From Table A10–18.
5. The difference of 220 trillion Btu between uses identified and total residential sales in 1960 of 3.19 quadrillion Btu, as reported by the American Gas Association and shown below, is due to miscellaneous uses not here projected and probably also to an overestimate in our estimate of the extent of LPG use. (This is allowed for in the LPG summary table, A15–14.)

It has been assumed that identified uses will constitute a shrinking portion of total use, and coverage adjustment therefore increases in time, though only through 1980, except in the High projections, where increasing adjustments are made through 2000.

6. From Table A10–14.
7. From Table A10–16.
8. From Table A10–9.

TABLE A10–20. Relationship of Number of Commercial Electricity Consumers to Number of Households, 1930, 1940, 1947–60

	Households[1] (millions)	Commercial electricity customers[2] (thousands)		Commercial customers as per cent of households	
1930	30.0	3,610		12.0	
1940	35.2	4,240		12.0	
1947	39.4	4,830		12.3	
1948	40.9	5,050		12.3	
1949	42.5	5,210		12.3	
1950	43.8	5,380		12.3	
1951	44.8	5,500		12.3	
1952	45.7	5,580		12.2	
1953	46.5	5,750		12.4	
1954	47.1	5,930		12.6	
1955	48.0	6,020	(6,005)	12.5	(12.5)
1956	49.0	6,080	(6,060)	12.4	(12.4)
1957	49.8	6,160	(6,132)	12.4	(12.3)
1958	50.7	6,230	(6,210)	12.3	(12.2)
1959	51.6	6,320	(6,296)	12.2	(12.2)
1960	52.6	–	6,489	–	12.3

1. From Table A1–1.
2. Edison Electric Institute's data for "small light and power sales" customers are used as nearest available approximation. Data are interpolated as of midyear, for comparability with the households estimates. Source: Edison Electric Institute, *Electric Utility Industry Statistics in the United States for the year 1959*, p. 33, except for 1960, which appears in the 1960 edition. The figure for 1960 is not comparable with those for preceding years, as E.E.I. has reallocated the sales of a large utility between "small" and "large" light and power sales. The figures in parentheses are the revisions made by E.E.I. on that same basis. None are reported prior to 1955.

TABLE A10–21. Relationship of Commercial to Residential Electricity and Gas Consumption, 1930–60

	1930	1935	1940	1945	1950	1955	1960
Electricity:[1]							
Consumption per customer (kwh):							
Residential	547	677	952	1,229	1,830	2,751	3,825
Commercial	3,863	3,682	5,280	7,062	9,320	13,422	–
(Revised commercial data)	–	–	–	–	–	(12,722)	(17,105)
Ratio, commercial to residential	7.06	5.44	5.55	5.75	5.09	4.88	–
(Revised data)	–	–	–	–	–	(4.62)	(4.47)
Gas:[2]							
Aggregate consumption (tril. Btu):							
Residential	n.a.	444	582	775	1,384	2,239	3,188
Commercial	n.a.	121	160	250	410	603	920
Commercial as per cent of residential	n.a.	27.2	27.4	32.2	29.7	26.9	28.9

1. Except for 1955 and 1960, from Edison Electric Institute, *Statistical Yearbook of the Electric Utility Industry for 1960*, p. 50. Revisions made in the 1960 Yearbook for 1955 through 1960 render these years no longer comparable with preceding years. Consequently the series here shows the unrevised 1955 figure as it appeared in the 1959 Yearbook as well as the revised 1955 figure (in parentheses), so that trends may be compared through 1955 and from 1955 to 1960. One may reasonably assume that the ratio based upon unrevised data for 1960 would be of the order of 4.72. 1960 estimates from *Electrical World*, Feb. 27, 1961. Inasmuch as the commercial figure for 1960 is on a new basis, the ratio shown is based instead upon an estimated unrevised 1960 figure, in order to preserve comparability. The ratio computed from the revised figure would be 4.73.

2. Except for 1960, *Energy in the American Economy*, Table B–2; 1960 from *1961 Gas Facts*.

TABLE A10–22. Projected Commercial Consumption of Electricity

	1960		1970	1980	1990	2000
Number of households[1] (millions)	52.6	L	58.7	68.7	76.5	84.3
		M	61.2	73.0	84.3	99.4
		H	64.3	79.2	97.6	124.1
Number of commercial customers[2] (millions)	6.5	L	7.2	8.5	9.4	10.4
		M	7.5	9.0	10.4	12.2
		H	7.9	9.7	12.0	15.3
Average residential consumption per household[3] (kwh)	3,669	L	4,889	6,230	7,072	8,031
		M	5,768	8,137	10,000	11,952
		H	7,652	10,820	13,320	15,802
Commercial per customer as multiple of residential[4]	4.66		4.4	4.2	4.0	3.8
Average commercial consumption per customer[5] (kwh)	17,100	L	21,500	26,200	28,300	30,500
		M	25,400	34,200	40,000	45,400
		H	33,700	45,500	53,300	60,000
Total commercial consumption[6] (bil. kwh)	113	L	170	254	340	467
		M	190	308	416	554
		H	243	387	501	624

1. From Table A1–2.
2. Projected at 12.3% of number of households, based on Table A10–20.
3. From Table A10–19.
4. Based on Table A10–21. The 1960 ratio is that calculated from residential use per household (3,669) and commercial use per customer and thus differs slightly in concept from the comparison made in Table A10–21. The data in the latter table are helpful in showing the relative constancy of the ratio over time with just a suggestion of decline. Similarly, we have let the projected ratio decline moderately over the projection period (a reasonable course, as electrical heating is likely to raise residential consumption before it expands commercial use, while any new electricity uses by commercial customers are unlikely to be enough to offset this). No High and Low ratios are stipulated, as the trend seems rather clear and little can be gained from small variations introduced at this stage.
5. Product of preceding two series.
6. Low number of customers is combined with High per-customer consumption, on the basis that the more restricted the number, the more likely it is to exclude the smaller accounts. On analogous grounds the High number of customers times the Low per-customer consumption is used to obtain the Low projection.

TABLE A10–23.   Projected Commercial Consumption of Gas

		1960		1970	1980	1990	2000
Residential consumption[1]			L	3.48	4.19	4.13	3.87
(quadril. Btu)		3.19	M	4.45	5.66	5.94	5.98
			H	4.92	7.02	8.79	10.35
Commercial as per cent of			L	27.0	26.0	26.0	26.0
residential consumption[2]		28.9	M	28.0	28.0	28.0	28.0
			H	31.0	34.0	34.0	34.0
Commercial consumption[3]			L	1.08	1.42	1.40	1.32
(quadril. Btu)		.92	M	1.25	1.58	1.66	1.67
			H	1.33	1.83	2.29	2.69
Commercial consumption[4]			L	1.04	1.37	1.35	1.28
(tril. cu. ft.)		.89	M	1.21	1.53	1.60	1.61
			H	1.29	1.77	2.21	2.60

1. From Table A10–19.

2. From Table A10–21. Past relationships provide no firm clue as to future behavior of the ratio. Except for the war and immediate postwar years (shown in more detail in *Energy in the American Economy,* Table B–2), there has been notable stability around a level of 28%, and it is to this level that the ratio has recently been returning, after a dip of some years. The level of 28% has, therefore, been chosen for the Medium for the entire period. Short-range projections made by the American Gas Association foresee a relationship of 34% by 1970; we have taken this as a High for 1980, and assumed no further rise thereafter. For our Low we have assumed a percentage of 26, the lowest ever observed, to be reached by 1980, with no changes thereafter.

3. Lows are calculated by combining Low residential consumption with the High ratio; Highs are calculated by combining High residential consumption with the Low ratio.

4. Conversion factor—.967 trillion cubic feet per quadrillion Btu.

TABLE A10–24. Projected Commercial Consumption of Oil, Coal, and Liquid Petroleum Gas

	1955[1]	1960		1970	1980	1990	2000
Number of customers[2] (millions)	6.0	6.5	L	7.2	8.5	9.4	10.4
			M	7.5	9.0	10.4	12.2
			H	7.9	9.7	12.0	15.3
Energy consumption (tril. Btu):							
Total excl. electricity[3]	2,260	2,450	L	2,690	3,100	3,340	3,550
			M	2,830	3,390	3,880	4,540
			H	2,970	3,660	4,520	5,760
Gas[4]	603	920	L	1,080	1,420	1,400	1,320
			M	1,250	1,580	1,660	1,670
			H	1,330	1,830	2,290	2,690
All other[5]	1,660	1,520	L	1,480	1,550	1,650	1,890
			M	1,580	1,810	2,220	2,870
			H	1,780	1,990	2,630	3,620
Of which:							
Coal[6]	896	600	L	200	100	–	–
			M	300	225	200	200
			H	400	300	300	300
Oil, incl. LPG[7]	763	920	L	1,150	1,320	1,460	1,730
			M	1,280	1,590	2,020	2,670
			H	1,540	1,860	2,630	3,620
LPG only[8]	26	80		120	150	165	175
Oil only[9]	737	840	L	1,030	1,170	1,300	1,560
			M	1,160	1,440	1,860	2,500
			H	1,420	1,710	2,470	3,440
Physical quantities consumed:[10]							
Coal (mil. tons)	34	22	L	8	4	–	–
			M	11	9	8	8
			H	15	11	11	11
Oil (mil. bbl.)	121	138	L	166	189	210	252
			M	187	232	300	403
			H	229	276	398	555
LPG (mil. bbl.)	6	21		30	38	41	44

1. Unless otherwise specified, estimates are from *Energy in the American Economy*, Appendix Tables B–4, B–1.

2. From Table A10–22.

3. 1960 raised above 1955 in proportion to increase in number of customers. On the basis that (1) the bulk of consumption will be in space heating and will therefore roughly follow the trend in number of customers, but that (2) beginning in 1960 in the Low and 1980 in the Medium projection increases in electric heating will have a depressing effect upon non-electric heating, total energy use is projected as follows from 1960 to 2000 in relation to number of customers:

High—in exact proportion.

Medium—in exact proportion through 1980; thereafter at a rate representing approximately 95% of the growth rate in number of customers.

Low—at a rate equal to 90% of the growth rate in number of consumers between 1960 and 1970, this percentage declining by approximately 10 points every 10 years thereafter.

4. From Table A10–23, historical from Table A10–21.

5. Derived from preceding two items as follows:

Medium—arithmetic difference between two Medium projections.

High—difference between total High and gas Low, after the latter has been raised by the percentage difference between total High and Low.

Low—difference between total Low and gas High after the latter has been lowered by the percentage difference between total Low and High.

This procedure avoids exaggerated ranges by assuming that a High in total consumption will be associated with a Low in gas that is relatively higher than the Low gas associated with the Low in total consumption.

6. 1960 derived from preliminary data for retail deliveries of bituminous coal and for anthracite production, following procedures in *Energy in the American Economy*. Projection assumes a less sharp absolute decline in the future, given the very low level of current consumption.

7. Obtained as the difference between the two preceding items in a manner analogous to that described in footnote 5.

Table A10–24 (cont'd)

8. 1960 obtained from preliminary 1960 sales data, as the difference between total domestic and commercial sales on the one hand and (a) residential consumption, as estimated in Tables A10–11, 12, and 13, and (b) farm consumption of some 12 million barrels, as estimated in Table A10–47. It should be noted that this procedure allocates more LPG to commercial use than the procedure used in *Energy in the American Economy,* where it is assumed that 10% of combined residential and commercial sales represent commercial. The exact breakdown is significant only to the extent that the two portions—residential and commercial—are projected to grow at different rates.

Annual increases in domestic and commercial LPG sales have been on the order of 6%–7% from 1950 to 1958, and 20% and 10%, respectively, in the last two years. It is here assumed that residential sales are responsible for most of this spurt and that the increase in commercial LPG sales has been and will be moderate—this largely on the basis that commercial establishments are decreasingly likely to find themselves in such isolated locations as provide access neither to electricity nor to natural gas.

9. Obtained as difference. The figure for 1960 is slightly below that obtained by a summation of 1959 sales of those heating oils generally considered to be used in commercial establishments. However, dividing lines between different uses of each type of heating oil—as with coal—are not very firm and this result is therefore not considered significant. Moreover, the residual oil portion of commercial consumption, amounting currently to only about 9 million barrels, is picked up in the series dealing with industrial use.

10. 1 ton of coal = 26.2 million Btu.
1 barrel of oil = 6.2 million Btu (assumed to be principally heavy distillate and residual).
1 barrel of LPG = 4.0 million Btu.

TABLE A10–25.   Other Non-Industrial End-Uses of Electricity and Gas in Relation to Residential and Commercial, 1937–60

| | Electricity[1] (bil. kwh) | | | | | | Gas (tril. Btu) | | |
| | | Street and highway | | | Other public authorities | | | "Other" sales | |
	Residential (except rural)[2]	Total[2]	As per cent of residential	Commercial (small light and power)[2]	Total[2]	As per cent of commercial	Commercial sales[3]	Total[3]	As per cent of commercial
1937	17.7	1.86	10.5	18.1	2.40	13.3	138	36.4	26
1938	19.4	1.93	9.95	19.1	2.45	12.8	138	40.5	29
1939	21.1	2.00	9.48	20.7	2.52	12.2	147	40.0	27
1940	23.3	2.05	8.80	22.4	2.72	12.1	160	27.1	17
1941	25.1	2.11	8.41	24.6	3.09	12.6	165	29.2	18
1942	26.9	2.06	7.66	27.2	4.21	15.5	199	45.7	23
1943	28.6	2.08	7.27	28.2	9.14	32.4	208	74.8	36
1944	31.3	2.16	6.90	29.8	8.46	28.4	221	96.4	44
1945	34.2	2.18	6.37	30.4	7.59	25.0	250	110	44
1946	38.6	2.27	5.88	33.0	5.85	17.7	263	66.5	25
1947	44.2	2.36	5.34	38.4	5.92	15.4	311	89.7	29
1948	51.0	2.52	4.94	43.2	6.26	14.5	354	122	34
1949	58.1	2.72	4.68	46.3	6.58	14.2	372	126	34
1950	67.0	2.98	4.45	50.4	7.16	14.2	410	126	31
1951	77.0	3.28	4.26	57.3	7.99	13.9	456	194	43
1952	86.8	3.52	4.06	62.1	8.44	13.6	493	212	43
1953	97.1	3.78	3.89	69.2	9.01	13.0	498	269	54
1954	108.5	4.04	3.72	73.4	9.42	12.8	540	249	46
1955	120.5	4.37	3.63	80.8 (76.3)	10.2	12.6	603	282	47
1956	133.9	4.74	3.54	87.7 (82.9)	11.0	12.5	656	265	40
1957	147.1	5.09	3.46	95.1 (90.0)	11.8	12.4	699	358	51
1958	159.0	5.50	3.46	101.2 (96.0)	12.8	12.6	765	375	49
1959	173.4	5.87	3.40	112.4 (106.7)	14.2	12.6	827	427	52
1960	189.2	6.12	3.23	– 113.3	15.6	13.8	920	470	51

1. Agricultural electricity use should be included here, but historical data are not available.

2. Edison Electric Institute, *Electric Utility Industry Statistics,* various years. 1960 data not strictly comparable with data for earlier years. 1960 "commercial" revision for earlier years shown in parentheses. Based upon an estimated unrevised 1960 figure, the 1960 percentage that "other public authorities" is of "commercial sales" would be 13.0 rather than 13.8.

3. American Gas Association, *Gas Facts,* various years; data for "other" sales for 1952–57 are those revised in the 1957 edition.

TABLE A10–26.   Projections of Other Non-Industrial End-Uses of Electricity and Natural Gas

	1960		1970	1980	1990	2000
Electricity (bil. kwh):						
		L	8.6	12.0	14.1	16.2
Street and highway lighting[1]	6.1	M	10.6	16.5	21.9	28.5
		H	14.8	24.0	33.8	47.1
		L	287	428	541	677
Residential consumption[2]	193	M	353	594	843	1,188
		H	492	857	1,300	1,961
Street and highway lighting as per cent of residential consumption[3]	3.23		3.0	2.8	2.6	2.4
		L	21.2	31.8	42.5	58.4
Other public authorities[4]	15.6	M	23.8	38.5	52.0	69.3
		H	30.3	48.4	62.6	78.0
		L	170	254	340	467
Commercial consumption[5]	113	M	190	308	416	554
		H	243	387	501	624
Agriculture[6]	10		15	20	25	30
Total other non-industrial		L	44.8	63.8	81.6	104.6
end-uses	32	M	49.4	75.0	98.9	127.8
		H	60.1	92.4	121.4	155.1
Natural gas (tril. cu. ft.):						
"Other sales"[7]	.47		.67	.92	1.04	1.17
Commercial gas consumption[8]	.89		1.21	1.53	1.60	1.61
"Other sales" as per cent of commercial[9]	51		55	60	65	72.5

1. Derived from the two series which follow. It is worth noting that basing this projection upon commercial sales would result in a similar order of magnitude.

2. From Table A10–19.

3. Based on Table A10–25. In view of the slowdown in the decreasing trend of the ratio, a continuance of that slowdown has been assumed, on the basis that increasing attention to public lighting will tend to offset the fact that growing use by appliances is not a factor, as in residential use, exerting an upward force. In view of the relative insignificance of this category, it was not considered reasonable to establish ranges for the ratio.

4. Derived as 12.5% of commercial consumption. Table A10–25 shows a striking persistence of this ratio except during the disturbed 1940's.

5. From Table A10–22.

6. From U.S. Senate, Select Committee on National Water Resources, *Electric Power in Relation to the Nation's Water Resources* Committee Print No. 10 (86th Cong., 2nd Sess., 1960), p. 4.

7. Derived from the two series that follow. In view of the haphazard nature of the relationship among the three levels, as well as of the "accidental" character of the ratios (see footnote 9), High and Low projections have been deleted and only the Medium is further used, to represent Low and High as well, in aggregating to total gas consumption. In preliminary calculations the combination of Low commercial consumption and High ratio on the one hand, and High commercial consumption and Low ratio on the other, as would be logical to stipulate, results in "other" sales that are very close to the Medium projection.

8. From Table A10–23.

9. The relationship between commercial gas sales and "other sales" has been rather erratic, as shown in Table A10–25. Altogether, it trended upward until 1953, whereafter it has remained stable. Part of the difficulty stems from the catch-all nature of the "other" category, which makes it difficult to relate it meaningfully to any other end-use classes. The commercial category is the closest one but, as seen, far from satisfactory as a guide. Simply to extrapolate past trends would have been to depend overmuch on the year in which the projection was made. Consumption in a handful of states dominates the category, California accounting for one-third, the Southwestern oil and gas producing states, plus Kansas and Tennessee, for the balance. One of the large variables is the use of gas for power generation within the so-called "combination utilities." This use not only fluctuates from year

Table A10–26 (cont'd)

to year (depending upon the competitive position of residual oil) but also is subject to different statistical treatment depending upon accounting procedures: if the gas department sells it as it would sell a commodity, at a profit, it is considered an industrial sale; if sold at an approved rate, it enters the "other" category; and if its transfer results merely in a credit entry on the books of the gas department, it is not recorded in the sales data at all. Year-to-year changes of very large magnitude (for example "other" sales in California nearly doubled between 1956 and 1959 and grew sevenfold between 1955 and 1959 in Oklahoma) result from these various factors. In general, there has been an increase in the ratio of "other" to commercial sales, and the Medium projection continues that trend, although at a slower rate. Faster-than-national population growth in California and the Southwest should push in that direction, even though the California figures actually depend almost entirely on the degree to which thermal power generation supplements hydropower, since "other sales" in that state reflect almost exclusively the interdepartmental transfers of gas from gas to power departments of the combination utilities.

TABLE A10–27. Historical Data on Electricity Consumption in Manufacturing

	1947	1950	1951	1952	1953	1954	1955	1956	1957	1958
Electricity consumption[1] (bil. kwh):										
Food, beverages, and tobacco	10.4	12.9	13.2	13.5	12.7	14.3	15.4	16.5	15.9	18.2
Textiles, apparel, and leather	11.5	14.8	15.2	15.7	15.8	13.9	14.4	15.8	15.4	14.9
Paper and printing	16.7	20.9	22.8	23.5	24.7	25.2	27.6	29.6	30.4	32.3
Chemicals, petroleum, and rubber[2]	29.6	37.8	41.8	43.2	43.7	48.1	55.0	58.9	62.6	63.4
Clay, glass, and stone	7.9	9.9	11.0	11.0	10.5	11.6	13.0	13.9	14.1	14.4
Fabricated metal products	3.9	4.9	5.7	5.6	6.7	5.9	6.7	6.9	7.1	7.3
Non-electrical machinery	5.9	6.5	8.1	8.4	9.2	8.1	9.0	9.9	9.9	8.1
Electrical machinery	3.6	4.6	5.1	5.6	6.1	5.6	6.0	6.9	6.8	8.0
Transportation equipment	6.1	7.7	8.7	10.1	11.9	11.8	14.3	14.9	15.4	13.6
Primary metals[3]	40.6	50.1	54.5	54.5	61.7	66.8	76.0	78.7	77.8	70.5
All other, excl. AEC	4.8	7.4	8.7	9.7	10.2	9.9	10.8	11.0	10.9	9.4
Total, excl. AEC	141.0	177.5	194.8	200.8	213.2	221.2	248.2	263.0	266.3	260.1
Electricity consumption per point of index[4] (mil. kwh):										
Food, beverages, and tobacco	125	149	149	150	139	154	160	165	159	178
Textiles, apparel, and leather	138	161	169	170	169	155	146	156	154	150
Paper and printing	245	267	281	296	292	290	292	298	304	326
Chemicals, petroleum, and rubber[2]	585	584	582	580	545	607	599	612	626	642
Clay, glass, and stone	116	121	122	127	119	136	134	137	141	152
Fabricated metal products	52	58	63	64	68	66	69	71	71	80
Non-electrical machinery	80	92	90	86	91	94	97	96	99	98
Electrical machinery	71	68	75	72	68	69	65	68	68	90
Transportation equipment	151	146	147	147	138	150	149	163	154	162
All other, excl. primary metals and AEC	65	89	104	111	108	108	107	106	109	98

1. Data for 1953 through 1957 from U.S. Bureau of the Census, *Annual Survey of Manufactures;* for 1947, 1950, 1951, 1952 from special compilation published in *Electrical World* Jan. 23, 1956; for 1958 from Bureau of the Census, 1958 Census of Manufactures, MC58(1)–6.
Consumption includes electric energy purchased, and self-generation reduced by amount sold.
2. Excludes amount consumed by Atomic Energy Commission installations.
3. Here shown only for the sake of comprehensiveness.

Projections are derived independently (Tables A10–29 through A10–34).
4. Electric energy consumption divided by the appropriate group index of the Federal Reserve Board Industrial Production index (see Table A1–28). The index for the "all other" category includes lumber and products, furniture and miscellaneous, instruments and related products, and is derived from Table A1–28 as a weighted average of these indexes. The chemical index includes AEC operations, but their elimination, if feasible, would make no difference in the index as shown.

TABLE A10–28. Projected Electricity Consumption in Manufacturing, by Major Industrial Group[1]

Group	1960		1970	1980	1990	2000
1. Food, beverages, and tobacco (bil. kwh)	18.5	L	26.6	37.5	49.2	61.8
		M	28.0	42.3	60.0	81.8
		H	33.8	59.6	99.5	162.0
FRB index (1957=100)	109	L	133	163	197	229
		M	140	184	240	303
		H	169	259	398	600
Mil. kwh/index point	170		200	230	250	270
2. Textiles, apparel, and leather products (bil. kwh)	17.3	L	20.1	22.6	26.2	29.7
		M	21.8	28.0	36.2	46.4
		H	24.6	34.6	47.8	66.0
FRB index (1957=100)	115	L	134	151	175	198
		M	145	187	241	309
		H	164	231	319	440
Mil. kwh/index point	150		150	150	150	150
3. Paper and printing (bil. kwh)	35.8	L	55.9	81.6	111.3	147.0
		M	59.3	92.2	135.7	196.0
		H	62.7	105.4	178.0	279.0
FRB index (1957=100)	112	L	147	192	242	294
		M	156	217	295	392
		H	165	248	387	558
Mil. kwh/index point	320		380	425	460	500
4. Chemicals (incl. petroleum, rubber, and plastics, but excl. AEC) (bil. kwh)	76.7	L	112.4	161.6	231.3	298.8
		M	137.2	226.4	361.2	561.6
		H	178.9	364.0	707.8	1,330.2
FRB index (1957=100)	118	L	154	202	269	332
		M	188	283	420	624
		H	245	455	823	1,478
Mil. kwh/index point	650		730	800	860	900
5. Clay, glass, and stone products (bil. kwh)	16.5	L	23.4	33.4	45.4	62.7
		M	30.2	48.9	78.5	126.9
		H	29.2	50.0	81.1	139.6
FRB index (1957=100)	110	L	130	159	189	241
		M	168	233	327	488
		H	162	238	338	537
Mil. kwh/index point	150		180	210	240	260
6. Primary metals (bil. kwh)	76.3	L	86.4	103.7	125.4	162.0
		M	111.8	160.2	223.7	323.8
		H	152.7	260.9	398.1	654.1
7. Fabricated metal products (bil. kwh)	8.5	L	18.0	29.1	43.6	69.3
		M	18.0	30.6	49.3	81.4
		H	17.4	30.8	51.6	90.6
FRB index (1957=100)	106	L	164	224	301	433
		M	164	235	340	509
		H	158	237	356	566
Mil. kwh/index point	80		110	130	145	160
8. Machinery, non-electric (bil. kwh)	10.7	L	23.0	41.2	69.4	115.8
		M	21.3	39.4	68.6	117.2
		H	19.3	34.6	63.1	113.6
FRB index (1957=100)	102	L	200	317	496	772
		M	186	303	490	781
		H	168	266	451	757
Mil. kwh/index point	105		115	130	140	150

Table A10–28 (cont'd)

Group	1960		1970	1980	1990	2000
		L	13.3	21.3	32.6	48.6
9. Machinery, electric (bil. kwh)	7.8	M	12.4	20.7	32.3	49.9
		H	11.3	17.9	28.6	45.3
		L	190	304	465	694
FRB index (1957=100)	112	M	177	296	462	713
		H	162	256	409	647
Mil. kwh/index point	70		70	70	70	70
10. Transportation equipment		L	28.1	37.0	58.6	91.5
(bil. kwh)	16.8	M	37.6	71.2	131.6	243.0
		H	44.8	113.6	242.2	461.0
		L	148	176	255	366
FRB index (1957=100)	102	M	198	339	572	972
		H	236	541	1,053	1,844
Mil. kwh/index point	165		190	210	230	250
		L	18.1	35.0	52.7	75.5
11. Other manufactures (bil. kwh)	12.5	M	22.3	35.6	57.4	94.8
		H	20.0	31.2	51.5	84.0
		L	155	280	399	539
FRB index (1957=100)	115	M	191	285	435	677
		H	171	250	390	600
Mil. kwh/index point	110		117	125	132	140
		L	425.3	604.0	845.7	1,162.8
All manufacturing (bil. kwh)	297.4	M	499.9	795.5	1,234.5	1,922.8
		H	594.7	1,102.6	1,949.3	3,425.4
All manufacturing except primary		L	338.9	500.3	720.3	1,000.7
metals (bil. kwh)	221.1	M	388.1	635.3	1,010.8	1,599.0
		H	442.0	841.7	1,551.2	2,771.3

1. Projections for all but the primary metals group are the product of the production index and the indicated consumption per index point. The latter is projected with the aid of the historical data shown in Table A10–27, largely by the use of graphic extrapolation and interpretation of the trends emerging in each group between 1947 and 1958, including an examination of the behavior of the production index in the intervening years. In general, the 1950–57 rate of change was given greater weight, as compared with that of the earlier years. The primary metals are projected by reference to the actual trend in power consumption by each of its principal components (Table A10–34); total manufacturing is projected by summing the industry groups.

The projected index numbers are from Table A1–29, except that the Highs and Lows have been adjusted so that their weighted average coincides with the independently-arrived-at Highs and Lows of the manufacturing index, which make an allowance for the effects of substitution and are therefore less extreme. In making this adjustment, the principle was to adjust individual Lows upward and Highs downward starting with the least power-intensive industry (in terms of kwh per index point) and continuing in increasing order of power-intensiveness until the sum of the so adjusted indexes equalled the over-all index. This resulted in High and Low combinations of industry detail that implied High and Low total consumption, respectively, of electric power. These adjustments, being largely mechanical in nature, have the unfortunate by-product that for some groups the order of High, Low, and Medium projections is upset, in some or all years (e.g., non-electrical machinery). However, the special indexes have only one purpose, to lead to the reasonable maximization or minimization of total power consumption.

TABLE A10–29.   Output and Electricity Consumption in the Iron and Steel Industry, 1947–60

| | Power consumption (bil. kwh) | | | | Production of ingots and steel for castings[1] | | | Electric furnace as per cent of all steel | | Power consumption per ton of steel (kwh) | |
| | All steel | Electric furnaces[2] | | Other steel | All steel | Electric furnace | All other | Capacity | Production | Total steel industry consumption | Total, less electric furnace[3] |
		Steel	Ferro-alloys		(Mil. short tons)						
1947	21.0	2.6	4.9	13.5	84.9	3.8	81.1	5.6	4.5	247	159
1948	23.2	3.5	5.1	14.6	88.6	5.1	83.5	5.7	5.8	261	165
1949	19.7	2.6	5.1	12.0	78.0	3.8	74.2	6.4	4.9	253	154
1950	24.7	4.2	5.6	14.9	96.8	6.0	90.8	6.9	6.2	255	154
1951	27.6	4.9	7.1	15.6	105.2	7.1	98.1	7.2	6.7	262	148
1952	25.9	4.7	7.1	14.1	93.2	6.8	86.4	7.5	7.3	278	151
1953	31.1	5.0	8.1	18.0	111.6	7.3	104.3	8.7	6.5	279	161
1954	26.7	3.8	6.5	16.4	88.3	5.4	82.9	8.4	6.1	302	186
1955	34.6	5.6	8.6	20.4	117.0	8.0	109.0	8.6	6.8	297	174
1956	35.8	6.0	9.7	20.1	115.2	8.6	106.6	8.4	7.5	311	174
1957	35.7	5.6	8.8	21.3	112.7	8.0	104.7	8.6	7.1	317	189
1958	26.5	4.7	6.3	15.5	85.3	6.7	78.6	9.4	7.9	311	182
1959	27.1	6.0	8.1	13.0	93.4	8.5	84.9	9.2	9.1	290	139
1960	30.3	5.9	7.5	16.9	99.3	8.4	90.9	9.7	8.5	305	170

1. From *Annual Statistical Report* of the American Iron and Steel Institute (AISI). Comparison with Census of Manufactures data indicates 1954 coverage, in terms of power consumption, corresponding to 85% of Census coverage in Industry 331: Blast furnaces and steel mills (see footnote 4 to Table A10–30).

2. For 1947–57, from *Load* (Schenectady, N.Y.: General Electric Co.), Mar. 1958, adjusted for subsequent revisions in output of electric furnace steel and ferroalloys in 1955, 1956, and 1957. For 1958–60, calculated on the basis of *Load*'s consumption of 700 kwh per ingot ton of electric furnace steel and 6,000 kwh per ingot ton of ferroalloys.

3. This represents, essentially, the input-output ratio for the post-ingot-stage operations (principally rolling and drawing) of the steel industry. Because it is part of consumption and cannot be separated out, the very minor consumption by blast furnaces and non-electric steel furnaces (c. 10 kwh/ton) is also included. The input is related, on the other hand, to a steel figure which includes electric steel (inasmuch as this, too, participates in rolling and drawing operations), and the effect is therefore that the ratio shown slightly understates total unit consumption by the industry for other than electric furnace operations.

TABLE A10–30. Projected Electricity Consumption in the Iron and Steel Industry

	1960		1970	1980	1990	2000
Production of electric furnace		L	11	12	13	14
steel[1] (mil. tons)	8.4	M	15	21	29	41
		H	21	35	59	100
Production of all other		L	95	103	116	126
steel[1] (mil. tons)	90.9	M	126	155	196	253
		H	157	218	308	454
Ferroalloys produced in electric		L	1.7	1.8	2.0	2.1
furnaces[2] (mil. tons)	1.25	M	2.3	2.8	3.5	4.6
		H	2.9	4.1	5.8	8.8
Electric power required per ton of product (kwh):						
Electric furnaces (exc. ferro-alloys)[3]	700		650	600	550	500
Other steel operations[4]	200		230	265	300	350
Electric furnace ferroalloys[3]	6,000		5,500	5,000	4,500	4,250
Total power consumption (bil. kwh):						
Electric furnaces (exc.		L	7.2	7.2	7.2	7.0
ferroalloys)	5.9	M	9.7	12.6	16.0	20.5
		H	13.6	21.0	32.4	50.0
		L	22.3	27.2	34.8	44.1
All other steel operations	16.9	M	29.0	41.1	58.8	88.6
		H	36.1	57.8	92.4	158.9
		L	9.4	9.0	9.0	8.9
Electric furnace ferroalloys	7.5	M	12.6	14.0	15.8	19.6
		H	16.0	20.5	26.1	37.4
		L	38.9	43.4	51.0	60.0
Total[5]	30.3	M	51.3	67.7	90.6	128.7
		H	65.7	99.3	150.9	246.3

1. Steel ingot projection from Table A16–9. Electric furnace portion assumed to grow from 10% (roughly) in 1960 to 14% in 2000 in the Medium projection and to 18% in the High projection, and to remain stationary, at 10%, in the Low projection.

2. Projected as 60% of total ferroalloy requirements in Table A16–9, on basis of essentially constant ratio in past.

3. Based on *Load,* Mar. 1958. Represents power consumed not only in melting but also in such auxiliary operations as preheating, etc.

4. Based upon data in Table A10–29. The increase over time reflects various developments discussed in the text. The initial figure of 200 is somewhat above recent years for the same reason and also for the reasons stated in footnote 3 to Table A10–29. It compares with a calculated figure of 170 in 1960.

5. 1954 Census data suggest that this might represent less than the entire steel industry, the apparent shortfall being in the neighborhood of 15%. However, if we were to raise the steel totals by such a percentage, the difference between power consumption in primary metals, as annually reported by the Census Bureau, and that in the iron and steel industry as so adjusted would historically not be nearly large enough to account for power consumption in the nonferrous metals. We have therefore left both the past and projected totals unadjusted, in view of the fact that any balance of electric power consumption unaccounted for is dealt with as part of a lump sum adjustment in Table A15–1 and that the figure here calculated for 1960 does in any event exceed the power consumption reported in the AISI statistics by 10%.

TABLE A10–31. Electricity Consumption in Primary Aluminum Production, 1940–60

	Primary aluminum production[1] (thous. tons)	Kwh per ton[2]	Total power consumption[3] (mil. kwh)
1940	206	21,970	4,532
1941	309	21,888	6,765
1942	521	21,109	11,000
1943	920	20,506	18,869
1944	776	19,903	15,454
1945	495	19,300	9,555
1946	410	18,697	7,659
1947	572	18,092	10,344
1948	623	18,187	11,339
1949	603	18,282	11,032
1950	719	18,378	13,207
1951	837	18,282	15,300
1952	937	18,243	17,100
1953	1,252	18,290	22,900
1954	1,461	18,281	26,700
1955	1,566	18,266	28,600
1956	1,679	18,250	30,641
1957	1,648	18,215	30,100
1958	1,566	18,180	28,500
1959	1,953	18,140	35,400
1960	2,014	18,100	36,400

1. From Table A16–30.

2. Source: 1940–56—*Energy in the American Economy*, Table A–28; 1957–60—estimated on basis of moderately falling trend in kwh per ton. Assuming 10 kwh per pound of magnesium, the electricity consumption estimate published by *Electrical World* on Sept. 18, 1961, for aluminum and magnesium combined (1957:31.3, 1958:28.8, 1959:35.8, and 1960:37.0) is compatible with the estimates here made for aluminum only.

3. Source: 1940–56, see footnote 2 above; 1957–60, production multiplied by kwh per ton, and rounded.

TABLE A10–32.   Electricity Consumption in Selected Nonferrous Metals Production, 1947 and 1954[1]

		Primary production				
		Quantity (thous. tons)	Power consumption (mil. kwh)	Power consumption per ton (kwh)	Power consumed in processing[2] (mil. kwh)	Power consumed per ton, all phases (kwh)
1. Copper	1947	1,156	738	638	1,701	2,110
	1954	1,191	746	626	1,901	2,222
2. Zinc	1947	802	1,341	1,672	Included under "4," below	
	1954	802	1,686	2,102		
3. Lead	1947	441	141	320		
	1954	487	136	279		
4. Secondary and processing[3]	1947	–	583	–	–	–
	1954	–	995	–	–	–

1. Source: U.S. Bureau of the Census, Census of Manufactures, 1947, 1954.
2. Includes mill and foundry work and all wire drawing (even though some 20% or so is not copper wire—see 1954 Census, Vol. II, p. 33D–10, Table 5–B).
3. Includes secondary production of all nonferrous metals, rolling and drawing of all except aluminum and copper, and casting of all except aluminum. The inclusion of copper in two instances is unavoidable but the order of magnitude is small, compared to the portions of the copper industry isolated under "copper" above.

TABLE A10–33.   Projected Electricity Consumption in Nonferrous Metals Production

	1960		1970	1980	1990	2000
Aluminum:						
Primary production[1] (mil. tons)	2.01	L	2.05	2.75	3.52	4.50
		M	2.85	4.66	7.04	10.57
		H	4.26	8.50	13.43	23.68
Kwh/ton[2,3]	18,100		17,200	16,400	15,800	15,500
Power consumption (bil. kwh)	36.4	L	35.3	45.1	55.6	69.8
		M	49.0	76.4	111.2	163.8
		H	73.3	139.4	212.2	366.9
Adjusted power consumption (bil. kwh)[4]	38.2	L	37.1	47.4	58.4	73.3
		M	51.4	80.2	116.8	172.0
		H	77.0	146.4	222.8	385.2
Magnesium:						
Primary production[1] (thous. tons)	40	L	33	36	37	39
		M	46	62	75	92
		H	69	112	143	204
Kwh/ton[2,3]	19,000		17,400	16,200	15,600	15,000
Power consumption (bil. kwh)	.76	L	.57	.58	.58	.58
		M	.80	1.00	1.17	1.38
		H	1.20	1.81	2.23	3.06

Table A10–33 (cont'd)

	1960		1970	1980	1990	2000
Copper:						
		L	1.18	1.19	1.12	.96
Primary production[1] (mil. tons)	1.55	M	1.60	2.03	2.53	3.44
		H	1.97	2.96	4.45	7.61
Kwh/ton[3, 5]	2,100		2,200	2,300	2,400	2,500
		L	2.60	2.74	2.69	2.40
Power consumption (bil. kwh)	3.26	M	3.52	4.67	6.07	8.60
		H	4.33	6.81	10.68	19.02
Zinc:						
Primary (slab) production[1]		L	.77	.86	.96	1.10
(mil. tons)	.82	M	.99	1.26	1.63	2.20
		H	1.28	1.89	2.90	4.69
Kwh/ton[3, 5]	2,200		2,400	2,600	2,800	3,000
		L	1.85	2.24	2.69	3.30
Power consumption (bil. kwh)	1.80	M	2.38	3.28	4.56	6.60
		H	3.07	4.91	8.12	14.07
All other nonferrous metals power		L	2.02	2.37	2.75	3.24
consumption[6] (bil. kwh)	2.00	M	2.42	3.32	4.50	6.26
		H	3.12	5.23	7.68	12.78
		L	44.1	55.3	67.1	82.8
Total consumption[7] (bil. kwh)	46.0	M	60.5	92.5	133.1	194.8
		H	88.7	165.2	251.5	434.1

1. Based on projected FRB industrial production index, Table A1–29, with 1960, which is actual primary production, as base. 1960 data from *Yearbook* of the American Bureau of Metal Statistics.

2. Based on data shown in Table A10–31, and for magnesium on projections of similar data in *Energy in the American Economy*, Tables A–28 and A–29. Recently announced progress in electrode efficiency in aluminum production may make the Medium projection a conservative appraisal.

3. The single efficiency level projected is assumed to be as high as can be expected to prevail under conditions of high production and as low as can be expected to prevail under conditions of low production. While under high production conditions there will be relatively more up-to-date plant, it is also true that older plants will be kept in production and high demand will allow slack in efficiency. The opposite reasoning applies to low production. There is thus no clear-cut balance that would favor assuming a higher (or lower) efficiency for higher (or lower) production projections.

4. Raised 5% to allow for aluminum processing, other than the unidentifiable portion included in "All other nonferrous" below. Percentage based on Census data for recent years.

5. Based upon data shown in Table A10–32. Extrapolated on the basis that extension of electric processes will more than offset improving efficiency.

6. Includes all other nonferrous metals and such processing phases of aluminum, magnesium, and zinc as are not separately identifiable. Census data, shown in Table A10–32, indicate this category to consume power in the magnitude of 1 billion kwh. A somewhat increased requirement for titanium and other new metals may have raised this total to 2 billion kwh by 1960. One large element included here is aluminum casting, which must be expected to grow with at least the rapidity of primary aluminum production. Other elements are likely to exhibit a less rapid growth. As a compromise, the series is projected at a rate of growth one-half that of primary aluminum production.

7. The Highs and Lows are additions of the individual items. Ideally, they should both be modified for whatever degree of substitution can be assumed between the components. This is done for the nonferrous group as a whole versus steel in Table A10–34, but is neglected within the nonferrous group, because of the overwhelming significance of aluminum: the degree of future substitution between aluminum and copper and aluminum and zinc would, in the way these adjustments are made, affect power consumption in copper and zinc only, where it amounts to less than 10% of the nonferrous industry total. Finally, magnesium is closely linked to aluminum, of which it serves as an alloy, and thus adjustment would be most complex. Nonetheless, it should be borne in mind that the Highs and Lows here shown are exaggerated by a few percentage points.

TABLE A10–34. Projected Aggregate Electricity Consumption in the Primary Metals Industry

	1960		1970	1980	1990	2000
Industrial production indexes (1957=100):[1]						
Primary metals, total (weight in		L	102	112	131	154
index 7.73=100%)	90	M	129	168	222	303
		H	161	237	352	540
Iron and steel (weight in index		L	92	95	105	112
6.21=80.3%)	88	M	122	151	190	247
		H	156	220	316	474
Aluminum (weight in index		L	128	172	220	281
.24=3.1%)	126	M	178	292	439	661
		H	267	531	839	1,479
Other nonferrous (weight in index		L	109	128	168	215
1.28=16.6%)	95	M	139	197	286	433
		H	184	303	479	868
Low model:[2]						
Primary metals aggregate (index x weight)			10,200	11,200	13,100	15,400
Aluminum aggregate (index x weight)			397	533	682	871
Other nonferrous aggregate (index x weight)			1,809	2,125	2,789	3,659
Balance (=iron and steel)			7,994	8,542	9,629	11,870
Adjusted iron and steel index (aggregate divided by percentage weight)			100	106	120	148
High model:[2]						
Primary metals aggregate (index x weight)			16,100	23,700	35,200	54,000
Aluminum aggregate (index x weight)			828	1,646	2,601	4,585
Other nonferrous aggregate (index x weight)			3,054	5,030	7,951	14,409
Balance (=iron and steel)			12,218	17,024	24,648	35,006
Adjusted iron and steel index (aggregate divided by percentage weight)			152	212	307	436
Power consumption (bil. kwh):						
Steel:						
		L	38.9	43.4	51.0	60.0
Unadjusted[3]	30.3	M	51.3	67.7	90.6	128.7
		H	65.7	99.3	150.9	246.3
		L	42.3	48.4	58.3	79.3
Lows and Highs adjusted[4]	30.3	M	51.3	67.7	90.6	128.7
		H	64.0	95.7	146.6	220.0
		L	44.1	55.3	67.1	82.8
Nonferrous metals[5]	46.0	M	60.5	92.5	133.1	194.8
		H	88.7	165.2	251.5	434.1
		L	86.4	103.7	125.4	162.1
Primary metals, total	76.3	M	111.8	160.2	223.7	323.5
		H	152.7	260.9	398.1	654.1

1. From Table A1–29, "other nonferrous" equals "other nonferrous metals" plus "nonferrous shapes and castings."

2. Inasmuch as the weighted average of components in the High and Low primary metals index projections exceeds, or falls short of, the over-all primary metals index, the components have to be reduced to an additive model before they can be used to derive aggregate primary metals power consumption. To minimize the effect of this adjustment on power consumption, the adjustments are made entirely in the least power-intensive component, i.e., iron and steel.

3. From Table A10–30.

4. Unadjusted Low and High power consumption, multiplied by ratio of respective adjusted to unadjusted index.

5. From Table A10–33.

TABLE A10–35. Electricity Consumption in the Mineral Industries, 1935–56

	FRB production index[1] (1957=100)	Electricity consumption (mil. kwh)[2]	Electricity consumption per point of index (mil. kwh)
1935	42	6,559	156
1936	48	7,551	157
1937	54	8,543	158
1938	47	7,398	157
1939	52	8,085	155
1940	58	9,115	157
1941	62	9,894	160
1942	64	11,137	174
1943	66	11,676	177
1944	71	11,350	160
1945	70	11,306	162
1946	69	11,710	170
1947	76	12,950	170
1948	80	13,300	166
1949	71	12,750	180
1950	80	13,500	169
1951	87	14,200	163
1952	86	14,980	174
1953	89	15,780	177
1954	86	15,861	184
1955	95	15,942	168
1956	100	16,023	160

1. Revised index linked to old index in 1947.
2. U.S. Bureau of the Census, *Historical Statistics of the U.S.*, Series S 90. This series is the result of a one time effort by the Federal Power Commission, no longer pursued. It does not extend beyond 1956.

TABLE A10–36. Projected Electricity Consumption in the Mineral Industries

	1960		1970	1980	1990	2000
FRB index of mining[1] (1957=100)	97	L	109	130	152	188
		M	128	167	218	292
		H	149	222	325	514
Mil. kwh/index point[2]	170		185	200	210	210
Power consumption (bil. kwh)	16.5	L	20	26	32	39
		M	24	33	46	61
		H	28	44	68	108

1. From Table A1–29.
2. Derived on basis of past data shown in Table A10–35. It is assumed that initially there will be a somewhat faster growth than heretofore in this coefficient, owing to the growing importance of oil and gas and the greater importance within that category of electric pumping, followed by stability towards the end of the period. While it is possible to construct, for the years 1939–46 and for 1954, separate power consumption series for coal, metal, oil and gas, and all other minerals, the particular choice of years—i.e., the war years plus one Census year—and various difficulties of interpretation have made it advisable to operate here with the total mining industry. It is worth pointing out, however, that in 1954 the four branches enumerated above shared in power consumption in more or less equal parts.

TABLE A10–37. Consumption of Fuel in Manufacturing (excluding Primary Metals, Petroleum Refining, and AEC), for Purposes Other Than Electricity Generation, 1939, 1947, 1954, and 1958

	1939	1947		1954	1958
Fuels consumed (tril. Btu)	2,178[1]	3,375[1]	3,490[2]	4,263[2]	4,100[3]
Index of production:[4]					
1935–1939=100	108	194	–	–	–
1957=100	–	–	64.7	86.2	93.7
Btu per point of index (tril.)	20.2	17.4	53.9	49.5	43.8
Change in Btu/point of index (per cent between successive years)	–	—14	–	—8	—11

1. Based upon gross energy consumption cited in Perry D. Teitelbaum, *Energy Production and Consumption in the United States*, Bureau of Mines Report of Investigations 5821 (Washington: Bureau of Mines and Resources for the Future, 1961), p. 64, as comparable and adjusted for electricity and non-fossil fuel consumption in both years. The latter again is a rough adjustment, following the 1954 pattern.

2. Total energy consumption adjusted to exclude electricity (at central station heat rates), both purchased and generated, and such non-fossil fuels as wood and bagasse. 1954 is the only year for which all data are directly available in Teitelbaum, *op. cit.* The 1947 data shown next to the 1954 column are taken from the same source, but only aggregate energy is available. Electricity consumption was deducted on the basis of data given in Teitelbaum, *Nuclear Energy and the U.S. Fuel Economy 1955–1980* (Washington: National Planning Association, July 1958), and rough adjustments were made for non-fossil fuels. It is believed that the resultant figures are comparable to the 1954 data.

3. This is a very rough estimate, derived from the 1958 Census of Manufactures (Fuel and Electricity Consumed, MC58(1)-6) but in no way calculated with the care expended upon the data for earlier years, as the data became available at too late a stage in the completion of these estimates. Since the 1958 Census data show a sizable quantity of fuel not specified as to kind, this alone could throw off the magnitude. However, there can be little doubt that fuel consumption per unit of production declined between 1954 and 1958.

4. Federal Reserve Board index of manufacturing adjusted to exclude primary metals and petroleum refining. AEC production is not feasible to exclude but this inconsistency does not affect the index, since the weight of this component is exceedingly small.

TABLE A10–38. Projected Consumption of Fuel in Manufacturing (excluding Primary Metals, Petroleum Refining, and AEC), for Purposes Other Than Electricity Generation

	1960		1970	1980	1990	2000
Index of manufacturing, excl.		L	155	219	305	423
primary metals, petroleum	110	M	170	264	407	622
refining, and AEC[1]		H	187	320	543	908
Fuel coefficient[2] (tril. Btu/point of index)	45.0		38.7	33.3	29.3	26.4
		L	5,999	7,293	8,937	11,167
Fuel consumed (tril. Btu)	4,950	M	6,579	8,791	11,925	16,421
		H	7,237	10,656	15,910	23,971

1. Computed from Table A1–29.

2. Based upon historical data in Table A10–37. Reductions between years shown there vary from 1.2% to 3.3% per year, the latter being the rate based upon the less reliable 1954–58 comparison. Consequently an initial rate of 45 has been based on the 1954 figure, and reductions thereafter have been on the order of 1.5% per year during the first two decades, 1.25% during the third, and 1% during the last.

TABLE A10–39. Projection of Fuel Shares in Manufacturing (Other Than Primary Metals, Petroleum Refining, and AEC)

	1960		1970	1980	1990	2000
Total consumption (quadr. Btu) [1]	4.90	L	5.94	7.22	8.85	11.06
		M	6.51	8.70	11.81	16.26
		H	7.17	10.55	15.76	23.73
Fuel shares [2] (%):						
Coal	36		29	23	18	15
Natural gas	46		55	62	67	70
Oil	18		16	15	15	15
Consumption by type of fuel:						
Coal:						
Quadrillion Btu	1.76	L	1.72	1.66	1.59	1.66
		M	1.89	2.00	2.13	2.44
		H	2.08	2.43	2.84	3.56
Million tons (at 26.2 mil. Btu/ton)	67.0	L	66	63	61	63
		M	72	76	81	93
		H	79	93	108	136
Natural gas:						
Quadrillion Btu	2.25	L	3.27	4.48	5.93	7.74
		M	3.58	5.39	7.91	11.38
		H	3.94	6.54	10.56	16.61
Trillion cu. ft. (at 1,035 Btu/cu. ft.)	2.17	L	3.16	4.33	5.73	7.48
		M	3.46	5.21	7.64	10.99
		H	3.81	6.32	10.20	16.05
Oil:						
Quadrillion Btu	.88	L	0.95	1.08	1.33	1.66
		M	1.04	1.31	1.77	2.44
		H	1.15	1.58	2.36	3.56
Million bbl. (at 6.3 mil. Btu/bbl.)	140	L	151	171	211	263
		M	165	208	281	387
		H	183	251	375	565

1. From Table A10–38, but reduced by 1% to exclude use of natural gas liquids. If one-half of "Industry and miscellaneous" in Table A15–15 is industrial use, then in 1960 this use amounts roughly to 60 trillion Btu or a little over 1% of total 1960 consumption.

2. Based on findings for 1955 in *Energy in the American Economy,* projected to 1960 on basis of 1958 Census of Manufactures data and partial data on consumption in industry of coal and natural gas. For rationale of projections, see Chapter 10, pp. 215–17.

TABLE A10–40. Fuel Consumption in the Steel Industry, 1943–60[1]

	Natural gas		Fuel oil		Coal[2] (mil. tons)	Total coal equiv. consumption					Coal equiv. of power generated (mil. tons)[3]	Coal equiv. for non-electric uses (mil. tons)	Production of ingots[4] (mil. tons)	Coal equiv. per ingot (tons)	Tons of coke per ton of pig iron[1]
	Bil. cu. ft.	Mil. tons, coal equiv.	Bil. gal.	Mil. tons, coal equiv.		Mil. tons	Per cent								
							Natural gas	Fuel oil	Coal						
1943	155.3	6.5	2.1	12.7	90.9	110.1	5.9	11.5	82.6	4.7	105.4	84.2	1.251	.900
1944	144.7	6.1	2.1	12.4	94.2	112.7	5.4	11.0	83.6	5.6	107.0	85.4	1.253	.905
1945	148.1	6.2	2.0	12.1	84.9	103.2	6.0	11.7	82.3	5.9	97.3	76.2	1.276	.920
1946	144.4	6.1	1.8	10.7	74.4	91.2	6.7	11.7	81.6	5.2	86.0	64.0	1.343	.934
1947	148.9	6.3	2.2	13.0	94.3	113.5	5.5	11.5	83.0	6.0	107.5	81.1	1.325	.950
1948	167.2	7.0	2.2	13.2	97.7	117.9	5.9	11.2	82.9	6.3	111.5	83.6	1.334	.954
1949	163.0	6.8	1.8	11.0	82.9	100.7	6.8	10.9	82.3	5.0	95.7	74.2	1.290	.935
1950	203.9	8.5	2.3	13.8	92.5	114.9	7.4	12.0	80.6	5.3	109.5	90.8	1.206	.922
1951	206.8	8.7	2.5	15.1	100.2	124.0	7.0	12.2	80.8	5.2	118.8	98.1	1.211	.924
1952	209.0	8.8	2.2	13.4	87.3	109.5	8.0	12.3	79.7	4.8	104.7	86.4	1.212	.922
1953	224.0	9.4	2.4	14.4	101.3	125.1	7.5	11.5	81.0	6.1	119.0	104.3	1.140	.906
1954	213.7	11.8	1.8	10.8	81.8	104.3	11.3	10.3	78.4	5.7	98.6	82.9	1.190	.873
1955	273.1	11.2	2.3	13.7	100.3	125.2	9.0	10.9	80.1	4.9	120.3	108.7	1.107	.873
1956	283.7	11.3	2.3	13.6	97.7	122.6	9.2	11.1	79.7	5.0	117.6	106.1	1.109	.850
1957	281.1	11.8	2.0	11.8	102.2	125.8	9.4	9.4	81.2	6.0	119.8	104.1	1.151	.842
1958	278.7	11.7	1.6	9.6	74.7	96.1	12.2	10.0	77.8	4.7	91.3	77.3	1.182	.799
1959	317.0	13.3	1.7	10.4	75.8	99.6	13.4	10.5	76.1	4.5	95.1	84.9	1.120	.785
1960	360.9	14.3	1.7	10.4	78.7	103.5	13.8	10.0	76.2	5.1	98.4	90.9	1.082	.749

1. Basic data from various issues of American Iron and Steel Institute, *Annual Statistical Report*, and U.S. Steel Corp., *The Making, Shaping and Treating of Steel* (7th ed., 1957), p. 84.
2. Contains between 500,000 and 900,000 tons of anthracite.
3. Electricity generated converted to coal at heat rate of utility generation in year shown. This probably underestimates coal required slightly and thus overstates coal used for other uses.
4. Includes steel for castings. Excludes electric furnace steel, which is produced mostly from scrap (95% in 1960—see American Iron and Steel Institute, *Annual Statistical Report*, 1960, p. 17) and therefore does not participate in bulk of fuel consumption.

TABLE A10–41.   Projected Fuel Consumption in the Steel Industry

			1960		1970	1980	1990	2000
Ton of coal equiv. per ton of ingot, other than electric furnace[1]			1.082		.925	.800	.750	.700
Steel production, other than electric furnace[2] (mil. tons)		L			97	103	116	126
		M	90.9		126	155	196	253
		H			157	218	308	454
Total fuel consumption[3] (mil. tons of coal equiv.)		L			90	82	87	88
		M	103.5		116	124	146	177
		H			145	174	231	318
Fuel shares (%):[4]								
Coal			76		73.0	70.0	68.0	66.0
Fuel oil			10		11.0	12.0	13.0	14.0
Natural gas			14		16.0	18.0	19.0	20.0
Consumption by type of fuel (mil. tons coal equiv.):								
		L			65.7	57.4	59.2	58.1
Coal		M	78.7		84.7	86.8	99.3	116.8
		H			105.8	121.8	157.1	209.9
		L			9.9	9.8	11.3	12.3
Fuel oil		M	10.4		12.8	14.9	19.0	24.8
		H			16.0	20.9	30.0	44.5
		L			14.4	14.8	16.5	17.6
Natural gas		M	14.3		18.6	22.3	27.7	35.4
		H			23.2	31.3	43.9	63.6
Consumption in original units:								
Fuel oil (mil. bbl.—4.1 bbl./ton		L			40.6	40.2	46.3	50.4
of coal)		M	40.5		52.5	61.1	77.9	101.7
		H			65.6	85.7	123.0	182.5
Natural gas (bil. cu. ft., at 25.3 thous.		L			364.3	374.4	417.4	445.3
cu. ft./ton of coal)		M	361		470.6	564.2	700.8	895.6
		H			587.0	791.9	1,110.7	1,609.1

1. These coefficients are based partly on past events as reflected in Table A10–40 and partly on the expectation that improved ore preparation processes—such as are discussed in Chapter 10, pp. 212–14—and above all higher blast furnace and steel making efficiency, including greater continuity of product flow and thus less waste of heat, will lead to substantially lower unit requirements. The levels chosen are merely convenient guesses within the realm of what appears reasonable, given the fact that chemically the minimum is approximately 15 million Btu per ingot ton, or just below six-tenths of a pound of coal.

2. From Table A10–30.

3. 1960 from Table A10–40; projections based upon preceding two series.

4. The outstanding change in the fuel pattern has been the increase in the use of natural gas, at the expense of coal and, occasionally, of fuel oil. It may be expected that new techniques will accentuate this tendency, although coal—especially if a change can be made to powdered streams injected into furnaces—will remain the principal fuel. The projections provide for modest increases in the relative use of fuel oil and gas.

TABLE A10–42. Pattern of Fuel Consumption in Nonferrous Metals Production, 1954[1] and 1958[2]

	Primary production		Secondary production		Rolling and drawing[3]		Foundries		All phases			
									Original energy units		Btu equivalent (tril. Btu)	
	1954	1958	1954	1958	1954	1958	1954	1958	1954	1958	1954	1958
Coal (thous. tons)	1,134	1,379	122	20	748	849	169	26	2,173	2,274	56.9	59.6
Coke (thous. tons)	442	358	57	32	3	–	18	6	520	396	13.5	10.3
Fuel oil (thous. bbl.)	2,837	2,259	908	625	2,605	2,438	890	627	7,240	5,949	45.6	37.5
Natural gas (bil. cu. ft.)	152.6	148.6	7.3	6.5	23.2	40.6	11.8	12.5	194.9	208.2	201.7	215.5
Total (tril. Btu)[4]	n.c.	n.c.	n.c.	n.c.	n.c.	n.c.	n.c.	–	–	–	318	323
Electric energy generated (bil. kwh)	9.86	10.55	–	–	.29	.41	.05	–	10.20	10.96	n.c.	n.c.
Estimated thermal electric energy generated[5] (bil. kwh)	(estimated for total only)								7.5	8.3	[6]100	[6]105
Fuel use for purposes other than electricity generation (tril. Btu)	(estimated for total only)										[7]218	218

n.c. = Not calculated.
1. Source: 1954 Census of Manufactures.
2. Source: 1958 Census of Manufactures.
3. Includes a small amount of steel wire; the bulk is copper wire. In 1958 includes small amount of energy consumption for nonferrous forgings, not separately available in 1954.
4. No allowance is made for other fuels; the only known instance of the use of such is the Rockdale aluminum plant, which burns lignite.
5. Individual examination of generating installations of aluminum plants in 1954 indicates that about 75% of capacity is fuel-burning. Total power

generated in nonferrous metal production was about 10 billion kwh in 1954 and 11 billion in 1958.
6. Converted at heat rate of 13,000 Btu/net kwh in 1954 and 12,700 in 1958. Natural gas is the predominant fuel in aluminum plants; in succeeding calculations this quantity is, therefore, deducted entirely from gas input, an assumption of convenience not entirely in accordance with the facts. On that basis, coal, oil, and gas contributed 30%, 20%, and 50%, respectively, of non-electric fuel input in the industry.
7. If adjustment were made for failure to include forgings in 1954, consumption would be more nearly 222.

TABLE A10–43. Projected Fuel Consumption in Nonferrous Metals Production

	1960		1970	1980	1990	2000
Production index		L	117	145	185	235
(1957 = 100)[1]	100	M	157	237	351	532
		H	215	393	640	1,131
Fuel coefficient[2] (tril. Btu/ index point)	2.50		2.25	2.05	1.85	1.67
Fuel consumption, total[3]		L	263	297	342	392
(tril. Btu)	250	M	353	486	649	888
		H	484	806	1,184	1,889
Fuel consumption, by type of fuel:[4] Coal (incl. coke):						
		L	79	89	103	118
Trillion Btu	75	M	106	146	195	266
		H	145	242	355	567
Million tons (26.2		L	3	3	4	4
mil. Btu/tons)	3	M	4	6	7	10
		H	5	9	14	22
Natural gas:						
		L	132	148	171	196
Trillion Btu	125	M	176	243	324	444
		H	242	403	592	944
Billion cu. ft. (1,035		L	128	143	165	189
Btu/cu. ft.)	121	M	170	235	313	429
		H	234	389	572	912
Petroleum:						
		L	53	59	68	78
Trillion Btu	50	M	71	97	130	178
		H	97	161	237	378
Million bbl. (6.3 mil.		L	8	9	11	12
Btu./bbl.)	8	M	11	15	21	28
		H	15	26	38	60

1. From Table A1–29.
2. Based upon net fuel consumption developed in Table A10–42 for 1954 and 1958. The adjusted level of 222 trillion Btu at production index level of 86.8 (1957 =100) yields 2.56 trillion Btu per point of the index in 1954; and 218 trillion Btu at 1958 index level of 87.7 yields 2.48 trillion Btu. A moderate improvement in fuel efficiency has been assumed, equal to 1% per year, about the same as calculated between the two Census years. The 1960 starting figure is rounded to 2.50.
3. Entries in this category most likely overstate fuel consumption, since aluminum growth is the driving factor in the rise of the production index, but direct fuel consumption (i.e., other than via electricity) plays only a moderate part in aluminum production. No method for dealing with this source of error was found, given the undifferentiated nature of the underlying data.
4. Shares derived from distribution in Table A10–42 (footnote 6). Data are not sufficient to suggest changes in pattern for projection period. In any event, such changes, given the generally minor importance of this segment of industry, would have negligible effect upon the outcome.

TABLE A10–44.   Fuel Consumption in Petroleum Refining, 1954[1]

	Unit	Quantity	Equivalent Btu (trillions)
Coal	thous. tons	876	23.7
Coke	thous. tons	8	.2
Crude oil	thous. bbl.	633	3.6
Residual oil	mil. bbl.	49.9	313.8
Gasoline	thous. bbl.	237	1.2
Distillate oil	thous. bbl.	42	.2
Acid sludge	mil. bbl.	2.47	15.5
Petroleum coke	mil. bbl.	9.48	57.1
Still gas	bil. cu. ft.	480	597.3
Natural gas	bil. cu. ft.	563	583.0
Steam	–	–	8.7
Total			1,604.3
Used for generating electricity			47.2
Net of power generation			[2]1,557.1

1. Perry D. Teitelbaum, *Energy Production and Consumption in the United States,* Bureau of Mines Report of Investigations 5821 (Washington: Bureau of Mines and Resources for the Future, 1961), Table B–11, p. 102.
2. On basis of 2,540 million barrels run to stills in 1954, this is equivalent to 613,000 Btu per barrel run to stills.

TABLE A10–45.   Projected Fuel Consumption in Petroleum Refining

	1960		1970	1980	1990	2000
Petroleum demand, excluding refinery		L	3,552	4,339	5,396	6,813
fuel consumption, and prior to adjust-	3,129	M	4,035	5,222	6,953	9,509
ment for natural gas liquids[1] (mil. bbl.)		H	4,530	6,648	9,852	15,306
Petroleum required for refining purposes[2]		L	188	229	285	360
(mil. bbl.)	165	M	213	276	367	501
		H	239	351	520	810
Natural gas required for refining		L	.82	1.00	1.24	1.57
purposes[3] (tril. cu. ft.)	.72	M	.93	1.20	1.60	2.19
		H	1.02	1.53	2.26	3.54

1. From Table A15–13—sum of total identified and miscellaneous uses (which are those parts of demand that can be projected independently of total petroleum demand, including demand for refining operations). Although process fuel, which is excluded, itself generates a further requirement for process fuel (as only little of it takes the form of crude), these succeeding amounts may be integrated into a single coefficient (see footnote 2) which sums up the second, third, etc., order effects. Relating the fuel requirement to demand, rather than to production, also carries the implicit assumption of an unchanging proportion of demand to be met by refined-product imports. Although changes in the supply pattern are conceivable (see Chapter 20), this is as reasonable an assumption as any.
2. Based on a coefficient of 5.28% of demand. Adjusted for imports (see footnote 1), this is equivalent to about 5.9% of net production, or approximately 5.6% of total throughput, including amounts diverted for fuel use in refineries. This may be compared with the data given in Table A10–44, which suggest that fuel burned equals roughly 10% of the Btu value of crude input, and that of this amount some 60% is comprised of petroleum derivatives. This would point to fuel use of petroleum on the order of 6% of throughput, but the indications are that since 1954 there has been some shift in refinery fuel from petroleum to natural gas.
  The coefficient in relation to demand is actually calculated by applying the petroleum fuel throughput coefficient of 5.6% to 1960 runs to stills (2.96 bil. bbl.) and then expressing the resulting fuel demand as a ratio of total demand. This same coefficient is used for all future years, carrying the assumption that neither the future fuel mix nor the total unit fuel requirement will

Table A10–45 (cont'd)

change sufficiently to affect the order of magnitude. The latter factor, at least, has remained stable throughout the past three decades, and the shifts in fuel mix do not appear to have had a significant net effect.

3. Based on a coefficient of 3.84% of demand. This is derived in a manner paralleling that described in footnote 2, but with natural gas (as fuel) estimated to account for 4% of refinery throughput (40% of 10%). The resulting estimated fuel use is converted to its equivalent in cubic feet of natural gas on the basis of 6,000 cubic feet per barrel of oil—a convenient approximation of relative fuel values. It is possible that the apparent shift to relatively more natural gas fuel is a shift merely to a larger volume of lower unit heat value (owing to removal of high energy fractions for petro-chemical processing), rather than a real shift in Btu terms. However, this is only of minor consequence among many unresolved questions of the relative energy equivalents of different fuels in different uses which have to be begged herein.

TABLE A10–46.　Number of Principal Farm Machines on Farms, 1940–60[1]

(Thousands)

	Tractors (excl. steam and garden)		Grain combines		Corn pickers	
	Number on farms	Annual increase	Number on farms	Annual increase	Number on farms	Annual increase
1940[2]	1,567	–	190	–	110	–
1941	1,665	98	225	35	120	10
1942	1,860	195	275	50	130	10
1943	2,055	195	320	45	138	8
1944	2,160	105	345	25	146	8
1945	2,354	194	375	30	168	22
1946	2,480	126	420	45	203	35
1947	2,613	133	465	45	236	33
1948	2,821	208	535	70	299	63
1949	3,123	302	620	85	372	73
1950[2]	3,394	271	714	94	456	84
1951	3,678	279	810	96	522	66
1952	3,907	229	887	77	588	66
1953	4,100	193	930	43	630	42
1954	4,243	143	965	35	660	30
1955[3]	4,345	102	980	15	688	28
1956	4,515	170	1,000	20	705	17
1957	4,600	85	1,020	20	725	20
1958	4,685	85	1,040	20	745	25
1959	4,750	65	1,060	20	760	20
1960	4,770	20	1,065	5	780	20

1. *Changes in Farm Production and Efficiency* (USDA Statistical Bulletin No. 233, Revised July 1961). Data are as of Jan. 1, unless otherwise indicated.
2. As of Apr. 1.
3. As of Nov. 1, 1954.

TABLE A10–47. Projected Liquid Fuel Consumption in Agriculture

	1955	1960		1970	1980	1990	2000
Number of tractors[1]			L	5.25	5.50	–	–
(millions)	4.40	4.77	M	5.30	5.80	–	–
			H	5.45	6.10	–	–
Cropland acreage[2]			L	–	364	368	368
(mil. acres)	–	–	M	–	368	396	418
			H	–	368	409	456
Liquid fuel consumption[3]			L	148	156	158	159
(mil. bbl.)	125	135	M	150	164	176	186
			H	154	172	191	213
			L	16	19	21	24
LPG[4] (mil. bbl.)	11	12	M	16	20	24	28
			H	16	21	26	32
			L	132	137	137	135
Oil (mil. bbl.)	114	128	M	134	144	152	158
			H	138	151	165	181

1. Historical data from Table A10–46. For rationale of projections, see Chapter 10, pp. 218–20.
2. From Table A18–11.
3. Projections on basis of number of tractors through 1980, on basis of crop acreage 1980–2000. 1960 figure is for all productive uses; the bulk of it is, however, for tractor fuel, as shown in Table 10–8. Only gasoline for trucks and automobiles is excluded.
4. Estimated at 9% in 1960, based upon 1955 relationship shown in Table 10–8. Assumed to rise to 15% in 2000.

appendix
to
chapter
12

CROPS

Notes

IN ANALYZING non-agricultural statistics, if one wishes to distill trends from annual data it is necessary to contend primarily with the business cycle, whose beginnings and ends are fairly well defined and fairly well known. In agriculture, we must abstract not only from the fluctuations caused by more hazily defined agricultural economic cycles but from those resulting from the vagaries of weather and from the fluidity of a productive complex whose "plant" is readily adaptable to a variety of uses and whose very decentralized decision-making process is quickly and significantly influenced by almost random changes in market conditions and the detail of government control, but only slowly and uncertainly by the stream of technological development. The trends we have extracted, therefore, are necessarily of a lower order of dependability than those we have set forth for other areas of the economy, and thus, in general, the area of uncertainty as reflected in the breadth of our High-Low range is rather wide. Moreover, even our basic reference points for projections cannot be fixed with much precision. From all indications, 1960 agricultural output (or more precisely, 1959–60 crop year output) was in most sectors unusually high—particularly in respect to the important area of animal husbandry and animal feedstuffs—in comparison with the "trend" point which should, under the circumstances, be substituted as our "present" base. However, any precise fixing of 1960 trend points is almost impossible without several years of hindsight, which we do not yet have, and we have therefore allowed the estimated actual values to remain as, in some cases, rather poor reference

points for projections which on this basis sometimes exhibit, for the near future, rather anomalous drops.

The number and variability of interrelationships in agricultural production have also led to a certain amount of unevenness in the detail with which various items are analyzed. For example, the relationship between feed consumption of grains and the required output of the four principal feed grains has, despite its considerable significance in terms of acreage, been treated in a crude manner, as one over-all relationship, largely because our ignorance of what might determine the components (see footnote 4 to Table A12–10) suggested that we might more likely compound error than add precision by aggregating the details. On the other hand, we have gone into considerable detail (although still crudely, at many points) in evaluating the relationship between by-product feeds and grain requirements, despite the lesser significance of the outcome for acreage requirements, because it takes this much detail to sort out the answer to how much of a role the strictly by-product cottonseed leaves for the more dependently varying soybean, whose principal product, in turn, cannot *a priori* be designated as being oil or as being meal. (See Table A12–7.)

A further peculiarity of the agricultural projections is the fact that they are based on comparisons and combinations of series in which the annual data available historically are not consistent as to beginning and ending month. For example, the food consumption series utilized in the appendix to Chapter 2, upon which the agricultural projections are primarily based, are for calendar years. Live-stock production data are also on a calendar year basis, but feed and feeding statistics are generally on the basis of a "feeding year" beginning October 1. In this connection, work had already been done by Ralph D. Jennings (*Consumption of Feed by Livestock, 1909–56,* USDA Production Research Report No. 21, Washington, Nov. 1958) to relate feed inputs to outputs on a feeding year basis, but the basic data on some of the individual feed components, including the key "supply and distribution" tables, are frequently for other beginning and ending dates. For example, corn and sorghum grain statistics are generally for years beginning October 1, oat and barley statistics for years beginning July 1, hay statistics for years beginning May 1. Similarly, wheat statistics are on a July–June basis, soybeans on an October–September basis, and cotton on an August–July basis.

For the long-run future, these discrepancies are of no importance. One must necessarily assume away any year-to-year fluctuations and treat the decennial projections as magnitudes of central tendency for the 20 year period in which each is centered. The minor leads and lags, on this basis, would affect only the partial-year increases or decreases in average rate of commodity flow—negligible in relation to the general magnitudes of the estimates and their changes during the course of a decade. For the past, however, these discrepancies, because of the special year-to-year volatility that occurs in agriculture, create irrelevant variations in the various coefficients of relationship among series, which raise difficulties in determining their trend. Although it might have been possible in some instances, no attempt was made here to recast the readily available data onto a comparable-year basis. Rather, on the assumption that production generally "leads" consumption, consumption data on a calendar year basis were generally compared with production data for the crop year beginning during the preceding calendar year, and the year-to-year fluctuations were dealt with by regarding fairly long historical series and trying to extract therefrom either a trend (usually by "inspection") or a constant coefficient (by inspection or averaging). In doing so, we have generally labeled all the data with the calendar year of the consumption series to which they are related. Because of this, it should be noted, agricultural data, which are customarily labeled according to the year of the beginning month, will be found in this appendix, whenever they are not originally on a calendar year basis or in a table containing exclusively crop year statistics, designated as relating to the year following that for which they are designated in the usual statistical

sources. The specific usage is indicated in each table.

Another deviation herein from the usual agricultural statistical practice has been to define "use" of a crop as being net of seed requirements. This was for convenience in relating seed requirements to total utilization for end-uses. "Use" has been presented, in various places herein, either inclusive or exclusive of exports; which of the two is intended has either been specified in each instance or is clear from the context.

The principal part of this appendix is devoted to the determination of feed requirements—in general and in terms of kinds of feeds. Central to this calculation is the utilization of the common denominator, "feed unit." Based upon the work of Ralph D. Jennings, it appears to be the best common denominator available for dealing with the changing feed requirements of different animals and the possibilities of substitution of one feed for another. Data are also available for an alternative common denominator, "animal unit," and a related "production unit," but the published series do not as fully account for all feed and its composition or provide as ready a means for drawing feed-input/product-output relationships as the data worked out by Jennings.

From an acreage standpoint, the most important set of assumptions, by far, is that having to do with these particular input-output relationships, or "feed efficiencies," as projected in Table A12–1. Because of both the crudity of the measure and the uncertainties as to future livestock feeding practice, it has been necessary in the Low to High range to allow for a wide spread of possibilities, so that, in effect, the calculations that follow must essentially be regarded as only illustrative of our contingent liabilities for feed production (and ultimately land) in the light of our relative lack of knowledge. A background assumption—unrealistic in fact, but necessary to make the calculations manageable—is that the total amount of feed required for any unit of output will be the same (i.e., for any one product at any point in time) regardless of the particular feed mix employed. However, the final mixes, as worked out in succeeding tables, do not appear to deviate enough from present practice to imply any marked changes in the feeding values of the component feedstuffs. Another background assumption is that the approximate postwar average dressing yields will continue to prevail. Since even year-to-year fluctuations of several percentage points have been common in the past, it follows that the liveweight measures of product may, by reason of this assumption's being in error, be off by magnitudes of perhaps 10 or 20 per cent. Any such error, however, may be presumed to be more or less compensated by an error of opposite direction in the feed-input/product-output relationship. It should be noted, incidentally, that these dressing percentages are not consistent with those recorded for "federally inspected slaughter," but are the apparent percentages derived by comparing total liveweight and carcass weight production for each year.

The ancillary Table A12–2 establishes, in a relatively crude manner, the prospective product mix for poultry, calculation of which is desirable because of the by-product character of part of the production and the widely varying feed efficiencies. Since feed input for poultry meat accounts for only about 5 per cent of all feed units, a more refined derivation was not considered necessary. The results of the calculation are incorporated into Table A12–1.

Both in the case of eggs and in the case of milk, the feed required to produce the "current" product was calculated separately from the feed required to raise the animal. The coefficients were based on those given by Jennings for feed per 100 pounds of milk and feed per 100 eggs, as distinguished from the feed for raising cows and pullets. In the case of cows, the feed inputs ascribed to meat were assumed to be the same as for "cattle and calves." Historically, the results check closely with Jennings' figures of total feed going to beef and dairy cattle combined, but his separate data on feed fed to each of these two categories are different from ours.

The initial calculation of feed requirements and feed components, designed to establish the general concepts and relationships and the High to Low ranges, is carried forward from Table A12–1 through Tables A12–3, 7, and 10. The High is oriented toward a projection of High land requirements and thus develops the implications of a combination of High demand and Low efficiency. The Low, conversely, evaluates the implications of Low demand and High efficiency. Since the resultant Low, as may be learned from the subsequent calculations in Chapter 18, implies substantial land surpluses, and the High, substantial shortages, it becomes important also to know the approximate levels of land requirements which would follow from assumptions of Low demand with Low efficiency and High demand with High efficiency. These supplementary calculations are carried out, in an abbreviated manner, in Table A12–16, utilizing the coefficients of relationship set forth in the earlier tables just mentioned.

Table A12–3 seeks to establish the primary breakdown of feed requirements into concentrates and roughage. Since the distribution varies substantially from animal to animal (viewing even beef and dairy cattle as two different kinds of animals), this is done for each of the principal livestock products, and the requirements are then aggregated, with a percentage adjustment to account for animals not specifically evaluated, in order to arrive at total concentrates and roughage, respectively.

The historical background for distribution of the concentrates by subtypes is set forth in Table A12–4. Since the shape that this distribution takes is not merely a matter of independent trends in feeding custom, but also depends upon the exogenous factor of availability of by-product feeds, the latter has also had to be calculated; the relevant historical data are set forth in Tables A12–5 and 6, and the projections in Table A12–7. The "by-product" element in roughage feeding being quite small (essentially straw and stover, but also including such more esoteric items as bagasse and waste newsprint), its availability was not calculated, but instead the projections of roughage items were based on extrapolation of the percentage distribution.

Unlike the substitutability between roughage and concentrates, which is severely limited by the nature of the animal being fed, there is very substantial inter-product substitutability, regardless of animal, among the subcomponents within each of the categories. While this substitutability is not complete, it is extensive enough that consideration of these subcomponents on an animal-by-animal basis was not considered warranted.

Our final projections of individual feed components, which are not so different from today's consumption in their relative proportions as to suggest that the mix may be unrealistic, are set forth in Table A12–10. This table is carried through to the principal feeds on a crop, or "key material," basis: the four major feed grains, combined, in terms of feed units; hay, in both feed units and tons; and pasture, in feed units. Though it is "harvested" directly by the animals, pasture, for the purposes of this study, is no different from any other crop. Treatment as one crop of the principal feed grains (corn, barley, oats, and sorghum) was to avoid a hazardous allocation, which would have added nothing to the ultimate precision of the evaluation of land requirements. Yields of feed grains, which are set forth in Chapter 18, have, however, been calculated as weighted averages of the components, before being applied, in terms of feed units, to feed grain requirements.

Projections of the three other principal crops are set forth in Table A12–14, and the relevant historical background is given in Tables A12–11, 12, and 13. Since soybeans are valued essentially for their crushing products, oil and meal (soybeans grown not for the harvested beans but for forage, etc., are customarily considered as a separate crop), the oil and meal projections of Table A12–7 lead to domestic soybean demand, which has to be supplemented by an allowance for exports, direct feed use, and seed, in order to arrive at the crop projections. The domestic wheat projections flow directly from the requirements established in Chapter 2; the exports are separately established in Table A12–15. Cotton flows directly from the projections of Chapter 3; the cruder calculations on exports are included in Table A12–14.

LIST OF TABLES

TABLE A12–1.   Projected Feed Demand

	1940	1945	1950	1955	1960		1970	1980	1990	2000
Demand for animal products as produced: [1]										
Cattle and calves [2] (bil. lb. livewt.)	15.2	19.6	20.7	27.9	28.6	L M H	34.1 39.6 44.1	39.8 50.6 60.4	43.9 60.6 78.9	47.2 69.8 99.4
Hogs [3] (bil. lb. livewt.)	17.6	18.8	19.8	19.5	20.0	L M H	24.5 24.5 29.5	28.2 30.5 37.3	31.1 37.9 49.3	33.6 44.3 62.0
Milk [4] (bil. lb.)	109.1	120.1	116.7	122.2	122.5	L M H	119 134 151	124 154 190	127 175 237	134 202 294
Commercial broilers [5] (bil. lb. livewt.)	.31	1.11	1.94	3.35	6.02	L M H	8.2 7.1 6.7	9.9 9.2 8.6	11.0 10.8 10.8	11.8 12.4 13.6
Turkeys [5] (bil. lb. livewt.)	.50	.70	.82	1.09	1.51	L M H	2.1 2.0 2.0	2.5 2.5 2.5	2.7 2.9 3.0	3.0 3.3 3.8
Farm chickens raised [5] (bil. lb. livewt.)	3.30	3.83	2.79	2.14	1.58	L M H	1.5 1.7 1.9	1.5 1.7 2.2	1.5 1.9 2.8	1.7 2.4 3.3
Eggs [6] (billions)	39.5	56.3	58.7	59.6	62.0	L M H	67 75 87	75 88 112	82 103 140	88 119 173
Feed units per unit of output [7] **(lb.):**										
Cattle and calves	9.50	10.57	9.46	9.13	10.55	L M H	8.7 9.5 10.5	8.3 9.5 10.6	8.0 9.5 10.8	8.0 9.5 11.0
Hogs	5.06	5.58	5.34	5.15	5.73	L M H	4.7 5.2 5.7	4.4 5.1 5.7	4.2 5.0 5.7	4.0 4.8 5.7
Milk	1.07	1.20	1.11	1.07	1.09	L M H	.95 1.00 1.10	.87 .95 1.10	.81 .91 1.10	.75 .90 1.10
Commercial broilers	4.80	4.48	3.82	3.42	3.02	L M H	2.4 2.7 3.0	2.1 2.4 3.0	2.0 2.3 3.0	2.0 2.3 3.0
Turkeys	7.20	6.50	5.92	5.36	5.11	L M H	4.4 5.0 5.5	3.9 4.8 5.4	3.6 4.5 5.2	3.5 4.2 5.0
Farm chickens raised	5.22	5.82	6.21	5.38	5.84	L M H	4.9 5.5 6.0	4.6 5.3 6.0	4.2 5.2 6.0	4.0 5.0 6.0
Eggs	.59	.62	.64	.54	.56	L M H	.45 .52 .59	.38 .48 .55	.32 .43 .51	.31 .39 .47

Table A12–1 (cont'd)

	1940	1945	1950	1955	1960		1970	1980	1990	2000
Total feed units [8] (billions):										
Cattle and calves	144	207	196	255	302	L	297	330	351	378
						M	376	481	576	663
						H	463	640	852	1,093
Hogs	89	105	106	100	115	L	115	124	131	134
						M	127	156	190	213
						H	168	213	281	353
Milk	117	144	130	131	134	L	113	108	103	100
						M	134	146	159	182
						H	166	209	261	323
Commercial broilers	2	5	7	11	18	L	20	21	22	24
						M	19	22	25	28
						H	20	26	32	41
Turkeys	4	5	5	6	8	L	9	10	10	10
						M	10	12	13	14
						H	11	14	16	19
Farm chickens raised	17	22	17	12	9	L	7	7	6	7
						M	9	9	10	12
						H	11	13	17	20
Eggs	23	35	38	32	35	L	30	28	26	27
						M	39	42	44	46
						H	51	62	71	81

1. The Lows and Highs for cattle and calves, hogs, and poultry represent the quantities of each which would obtain in the combinations of these items which lead, respectively, to Low and High feed requirements (models V and I, respectively, in Table A2–6). Data for 1970–2000 are converted from product to liveweight on the basis of assumed dressing yields. Those for earlier years, unless otherwise indicated, are actual production, for feeding years beginning the preceding Oct. 1, as calculated by Ralph D. Jennings, in *Consumption of Feed by Livestock*, 1909–56 (USDA Production Research Report No. 21, Nov. 1958), Table 29, and unpublished USDA revisions thereof.

2. 1940–60 from source cited in footnote 1. 1970–2000 converted from data in Table A2–6 on basis of dressing yield of 54%. (1940–60 apparent average yield, 53.6%; 1948–60, 52.2%; 1953–60, 53.8%.)

3. 1940–60 from source cited in footnote 1. 1970–2000 converted from data in Table A2–6 on basis of dressing yield of 56%. (1940–60 average, 56.3%; 1948–60, 55.7%; 1953–60, 56.5%.)

4. 1940–60 from source cited in footnote 1. 1970–2000 from Table A2–4.

5. For division of poultry demand among farm chickens, commercial broilers, and turkeys see Table A12–2. Conversion from ready-to-cook weight to liveweight on the basis of yield of 72% for broilers and chickens, and 80% for turkeys (ratios in current use by USDA). Historical data from source cited in footnote 1, except for 1940, which is estimated.

6. From Table A12–2.

7. This is the inverse of so-called "feed efficiencies." A "feed unit" has the same feeding efficiency as one pound of corn. The factor varies from animal to animal. Historical data are for production year starting Oct. 1 of preceding calendar year (source cited in footnote 1, Table 76). For rationale of projections, see Chapter 12, pp. 236–39.

8. Product of two preceding sections, for historical data as well as projections. Because of differences in classification, historical data on dairy cattle and beef cattle, taken separately, will differ from quantities reported in Jennings, *op. cit.*, Table 65.

TABLE A12–2. Projected Poultry Demand

(All weights on ready-to-cook basis)

		Eggs[1] (bil-lions)	Farm chicken production		Total poultry consump-tion[4] (bil. lb.)	Commer-cial broilers and turkeys[5] (bil. lb.)	Turkeys[6] (bil. lb.)	Broilers[7] (bil. lb.)
			Pounds per 100 eggs[2]	Bil-lion pounds[3]				
1940			39.5	4.08	1.61	2.25	.64	.39	.25
1945			56.3	4.23	2.38	3.51	1.13	.55	.58
1950			58.7	3.13	1.84	3.75	1.91	.62	1.29
1955			59.6	2.11	1.26	4.36	3.10	.82	2.28
1960			62.0	1.45	.90	6.22	5.32	1.13	4.19
	L	66.7		1.1	8.7	7.6	1.7	5.9
1970	M	74.9	1.60	1.2	7.9	6.7	1.6	5.1
	H	87.0		1.4	7.8	6.4	1.6	4.8
	L	75		1.1	10.2	9.1	2.0	7.1
1980	M	88	1.40	1.2	9.8	8.6	2.0	6.6
	H	112		1.6	9.8	8.2	2.0	6.2
	L	82		1.1	11.2	10.1	2.2	7.9
1990	M	103	1.40	1.4	11.5	10.1	2.3	7.8
	H	140		2.0	12.2	10.2	2.4	7.8
	L	88		1.2	12.1	10.9	2.4	8.5
2000	M	119	1.40	1.7	13.2	11.5	2.6	8.9
	H	173		2.4	15.2	12.8	3.0	9.8

1. From Table A2–4. Data for 1940–60 are actual production, for production years beginning the preceding Oct. 1 as calculated by Jennings, *Consumption of Feed by Livestock,* Table 29, and unpublished USDA data.

2. Historical ratios derived from data on egg and farm chicken production. Projections take into account status of technical change in egg production and the fact that most of the effect of such change has already exhibited itself (see Notes).

3. 1940–45 from USDA, *Agricultural Statistics, 1957,* Table 601, converted from "dressed weight" at 75%. 1950–60, *ibid.,* Table 614, and unpublished

USDA data. 1970–2000 are product of first two columns.

4. 1940–60 from Table A2–4. Projections from Table A2–6. "Low" represents level of poultry consumption attendant upon Low red meat consumption and Low population; vice versa for High (cf. Table A2–4).

5. Total poultry consumption less farm chickens.

6. Historical data based on per capita data in 1960 supp. to USDA, *Consumption of Food in the United States.* Projections assume turkeys as 20% of total poultry consumption.

7. Broilers and turkeys, less turkeys.

TABLE A12–3. Projected Major Components of Feed Demand[1]

		1940	1945	1950	1955	1960		1970	1980	1990	2000
Concentrates:											
Concentrates as per cent of total feed units:[2]							L	18	20	20	20
Cattle and calves		15.8	14.1	17.4	17.0	19	M	21	23	25	27
							H	24	28	32	35
Hogs		94.4	94.3	94.3	96.0	94.8		95	95	95	95
							L	30	30	30	30
Milk cows		27.3	28.7	29.6	29.7	32	M	33	34	35	35
							H	34	36	38	40

Table A12–3 (cont'd)

	1940	1945	1950	1955	1960		1970	1980	1990	2000
Total concentrates[3] (bil. feed units):										
Cattle and calves	23	29	34	43	57	L	71	92	112	132
						M	78	110	144	179
						H	83	128	170	219
Hogs	84	99	100	96	109	L	109	118	125	127
						M	121	148	181	202
						H	160	202	267	335
Milk cows	32	41	38	39	43	L	38	39	39	40
						M	44	50	56	64
						H	50	63	78	97
Poultry (including eggs)[4]	46	67	67	64	70	L	66	66	64	68
						M	77	85	92	100
						H	93	115	136	161
Subtotal	185	236	239	242	279	L	284	315	340	367
						M	320	393	473	545
						H	386	508	651	812
Total[5]	207	264	257	254	317	L	312	346	374	404
						M	352	432	520	600
						H	425	559	716	893
Roughage[6] (bil. feed units):										
Cattle and calves	121	178	162	212	245	L	226	238	239	246
						M	297	370	432	484
						H	380	512	682	874
Hogs	5	5	5	5	5	L	6	6	7	7
						M	6	8	10	11
						H	8	11	14	18
Milk cows	85	103	92	92	91	L	75	69	64	60
						M	90	96	103	118
						H	116	146	183	226
Lambs and sheep[7]	37	36	22	22	19	L	11	12	12	12
						M	24	33	39	44
						H	38	51	68	87
Subtotal	248	322	281	331	360	L	318	325	322	325
						M	417	507	584	657
						H	542	720	947	1,205
Total[8]	301	367	315	351	377	L	334	341	338	341
						M	438	532	613	690
						H	569	756	994	1,265

1. This table is designed to derive the particular combinations of feed units that will illustrate the reasonably possible extremes in feed land requirements. The Low demand is coupled with that combination of feeding which exerts the lowest pressure on land and the High demand with the combination exerting highest pressure on land.

2. Extrapolations, by inspection, of historical trends. Historical data from, or based on, Ralph D. Jennings, *Consumption of Feed by Livestock,* Tables 70, 71, and 74. Relative consumption shown by Jennings for dairy cattle assumed to apply to milk production, and relative consumption for beef cattle assumed to apply to raising dairy cattle, with upward adjustments in the concentrate portion of each category to reconcile with Jennings' total concentrate consumption by cattle. (Adding dairy calves and heifers to "beef" and subtracting them from "dairy" would tend to raise the relative concentrate consumption of both categories.)

3. For total feed units for each type of animal, see Table A12–1. Since feeding of concentrates is gener-

ally more economical of land than feeding of roughage, the High percentage of concentrates is associated with Low demand and vice versa.

4. 100% concentrates.

5. For 1970–2000, preceding subtotal raised by 10% to account for other livestock (mostly horses, pets, etc.). 1940–60 from Table A12–4, for preceding year beginning Oct. 1.

6. The Low percentage of roughage (100%, less High percentage of concentrates) is associated with Low demand and vice versa. Historical data from Jennings, *op. cit.*

7. Derived roughly by taking following percentages of roughage consumption by cattle and calves: 1970, 5% for Low, 8% for Medium, and 10% for High; 1980–2000, 5% for Low, 9% for Medium and 10% for High. Historical data from Jennings, *op. cit.*, Table 72.

8. For 1970–2000, preceding subtotal raised by 5% to account for other livestock (horses, goats, etc.). 1940–60 from Table A12–8, for preceding crop year.

TABLE A12–4.   Historical Data on Feed Concentrate Pattern[1]

Year beginning Oct. 1	Feed consumption of concentrates, seeds, and milk (bil. feed units)					Percentage distribution				Per cent of total excluding high protein	
	Corn[2]	Other grains[3]	High protein feeds[4]	Other by-products,[5] seeds, and milk[6]	Total	Corn	Other grains	High protein feeds	Other by-products, seeds, and milk	Grains	Other
1926	126.6	41.4	14.7	25.8	208.5	60.7	19.9	7.0	12.4	86.7	13.3
1927	133.9	44.0	12.9	25.1	215.9	62.0	20.4	6.0	11.6	87.6	12.4
1928	124.6	50.0	14.6	25.1	214.3	58.2	23.3	6.8	11.7	87.4	12.6
1929	122.4	48.2	14.9	25.8	211.3	57.9	22.8	7.1	12.2	86.9	13.1
1930	97.7	55.2	13.6	25.7	192.2	50.8	28.7	7.1	13.4	85.6	14.4
1931	121.0	50.2	12.6	25.4	209.2	57.8	24.0	6.0	12.2	87.1	12.9
1932	139.0	46.3	12.8	25.0	223.1	62.3	20.8	5.7	11.2	88.1	11.9
1933	118.5	30.2	13.1	25.2	187.0	63.4	16.1	7.0	13.5	85.5	14.5
1934	80.9	27.6	13.2	23.9	145.6	55.6	19.0	9.0	16.4	82.0	18.0
1935	102.9	45.4	16.3	25.0	189.6	54.3	23.9	8.6	13.2	85.6	14.4
1936	77.4	34.3	17.6	24.7	154.0	50.3	22.3	11.4	16.0	81.9	18.1
1937	103.6	48.9	18.1	25.7	196.3	52.8	24.9	9.2	13.1	85.6	14.4
1938	109.1	47.1	18.7	25.4	200.3	54.5	23.5	9.3	12.7	86.0	14.0
1939	116.2	46.0	19.9	24.9	207.1	56.1	22.2	9.6	12.0	86.6	13.4
1940	119.7	52.5	23.5	26.1	221.8	53.9	23.7	10.6	11.8	86.8	13.2
1941	132.8	59.9	25.3	24.7	242.7	54.7	24.7	10.4	10.2	88.6	11.4
1942	155.7	80.8	30.8	25.8	293.1	53.1	27.6	10.5	8.8	90.2	9.8
1943	153.5	77.3	31.6	25.8	288.2	53.3	26.8	10.9	9.0	90.0	10.0
1944	144.1	63.7	30.8	25.8	264.4	54.5	24.1	11.6	9.8	89.0	11.0
1945	146.4	70.1	28.3	24.2	269.0	54.4	26.1	10.5	9.0	90.0	10.0
1946	140.7	52.2	29.7	25.6	248.2	56.7	21.0	12.0	10.3	88.3	11.7
1947	119.0	52.3	30.3	24.1	225.7	52.7	23.2	13.4	10.7	87.7	12.3
1948	133.0	52.0	34.7	23.2	242.9	54.7	21.4	14.3	9.6	88.9	11.1
1949	148.9	48.1	36.7	23.7	257.4	57.8	18.7	14.3	9.2	89.3	10.7
1950	146.2	55.2	40.9	23.1	265.4	55.1	20.8	15.4	8.7	89.7	10.3
1951	150.4	54.7	42.1	24.0	271.2	55.5	20.2	15.5	8.8	89.5	10.5
1952	135.5	48.8	41.1	23.6	249.0	54.4	19.6	16.5	9.5	88.6	11.4
1953	139.5	48.0	42.4	23.8	253.7	55.0	18.9	16.7	9.4	88.7	11.3
1954	131.9	54.6	42.2	24.8	253.5	52.0	21.5	16.6	9.8	88.3	11.7
1955	138.8	57.7	44.4	24.0	264.9	52.4	21.8	16.8	9.1	89.1	10.9
1956	139.8	52.4	46.5	24.3	263.0	53.2	19.9	17.7	9.2	88.8	11.2
1957	147.0	59.1	48.3	25.2	279.6	52.6	21.1	17.3	9.0	89.1	10.9
1958	160.7	64.4	53.1	25.1	303.3	53.0	21.2	17.5	8.3	90.0	10.0
1959	176.5	61.6	53.7	25.6	317.4	55.6	19.4	16.9	8.1	90.3	9.7

1. Including seeds and milk. Source: 1926–39 from Jennings, *Consumption of Feed by Livestock*, Table 64. Subsequent data from unpublished USDA material. (Although Jennings shows data to 1956, numerous revisions have since been made.)

2. Other than silage.

3. Includes principally oats, barley, and sorghum grain.

4. Includes oil meals, animal proteins, brewers' and distillers' grains, and gluten feed and meal.

5. Includes various millfeeds, other than gluten.

6. Seeds and milk are currently around 1½% of total concentrate feed units, having declined from over 2% prior to 1957.

TABLE A12–5.   Historical Data on Cottonseed and Soybean Oil and Meal

| | Cottonseed[1] | | | | | Soybeans[2] | | | | | | | | | |
| | Cotton ginned[3] (thous. bales) | Cottonseed oil produced[4] | | Cake & meal produced[4] | | Soybeans crushed (mil. bu.) | Soybean oil produced | | Cake and meal produced | | | Total soybean & cottonseed oil produced (mil. lb.) | Total food use of fats & oils following calendar year[5] (retail wt., mil. lb.) | Ratio of soybean & cottonseed oil production to total food use of fats & oils (%) |
		Million pounds	Oil per bale of cotton (lb.)	Million pounds	Cake & meal per pound of oil (lb.)		Million pounds	Oil per bushel of beans (lb.)	Million pounds	Cake & meal per pound of oil (lb.)	Cake & meal per bushel of beans crushed (lb.)			
1934	9,515	1,109	116.6	3,228	2.91	9.1	78	8.6	440	5.6	48.4	1,187	7,899	15.0
1935	10,403	1,164	111.9	3,478	2.99	25.2	209	8.3	1,226	5.9	48.7	1,373	8,333	16.5
1936	12,269	1,364	111.2	4,062	2.98	20.6	184	8.9	992	5.4	48.2	1,548	8,385	18.5
1937	18,284	1,961	107.3	5,660	2.89	30.3	279	9.2	1,448	5.2	47.8	2,240	8,450	26.5
1938	11,617	1,409	121.3	4,046	2.87	44.6	416	9.3	2,128	5.1	47.7	1,825	8,908	20.5
1939	11,420	1,325	116.0	3,764	2.84	56.7	533	9.4	2,698	5.1	47.6	1,858	9,379	19.8
1940	12,318	1,425	115.7	3,908	2.74	64.1	564	8.8	3,086	5.5	48.1	1,989	9,338	21.3
1941	10,552	1,250	118.5	3,506	2.80	77.1	707	9.2	3,690	5.2	47.9	1,957	8,903	22.0
1942	12,496	1,401	112.1	3,990	2.85	133.5	1,206	9.0	6,400	5.3	47.9	2,607	9,159	28.5
1943	11,083	1,236	111.5	3,668	2.97	142.3	1,219	8.6	6,892	5.7	48.4	2,455	9,134	26.9
1944	11,924	1,324	111.0	3,908	2.95	153.4	1,347	8.8	7,396	5.5	48.2	2,671	8,534	31.3
1945	8,852	1,018	115.0	2,868	2.82	159.5	1,415	8.9	6,674	4.7	41.8	2,433	9,050	26.9
1946	8,574	973	113.5	2,726	2.80	170.2	1,531	9.0	8,172	5.3	48.0	2,504	9,367	26.7
1947	11,648	1,276	109.6	3,796	2.97	161.4	1,534	9.5	7,666	5.0	47.5	2,810	9,529	29.5
1948	14,649	1,704	116.3	4,782	2.81	183.7	1,807	9.8	8,660	4.8	47.1	3,511	9,698	36.2
1949	15,921	1,847	116.0	5,110	2.77	195.3	1,937	9.9	9,172	4.7	47.0	3,784	10,316	36.7
1950	9,876	1,197	121.2	3,338	2.79	252.0	2,454	9.7	11,794	4.8	46.8	3,651	10,036	36.4
1951	15,069	1,751	116.2	5,096	2.91	244.4	2,444	10.0	11,408	4.7	46.7	4,195	10,676	39.3
1952	15,166	1,825	120.3	5,344	2.93	234.4	2,536	10.8	11,102	4.4	47.4	4,361	10,374	42.0
1953	16,402	2,074	126.4	5,922	2.86	213.2	2,350	11.0	10,102	4.3	47.4	4,424	10,718	41.3
1954	13,590	1,735	127.7	5,122	2.95	249.0	2,711	10.9	11,410	4.2	45.8	4,446	11,240	39.6
1955	14,680	1,894	129.0	5,262	2.78	283.1	3,143	11.1	13,092	4.2	46.2	5,037	11,269	44.7
1956	13,027	1,685	129.3	4,780	2.84	315.9	3,431	10.9	15,020	4.4	47.5	5,116	11,128	46.0
1957	10,920	1,438	131.7	3,916	2.72	353.8	3,800	10.7	16,568	4.4	46.8	5,238	11,491	45.6
1958	11,424	1,518	132.9	4,122	2.72	401.2	4,251	10.6	18,980	4.5	47.3	5,769	12,220	47.2
1959	14,555	1,861	127.9	5,094	2.74	393.4	4,338	11.0	18,305	4.2	46.5	6,199	12,053	51.4

1. Data are for seasons beginning Aug. 1 of year shown.
2. Data are for seasons beginning Oct. 1 of year shown. Source: 1934–47, *Agricultural Statistics, 1957*, Table 194; 1948–49, *Agricultural Statistics, 1958*, Table 192; 1950–59, USDA, *Fats and Oils Situation*, Nov. 1961, Tables 5, 6, and 7.
3. Includes city crop, 1946–60. Earlier years not available. Source: USDA, *The Cotton Situation*, Nov. 1961, Table 16.

4. Source: 1934–47, *Agricultural Statistics, 1957*, Table 162; 1948–59, *The Cotton Situation*, Nov. 1961, Table 45.
5. Per capita data for fats and oils (Table A2–1), multiplied by total population (Table A1–1).

APPENDIX TO CHAPTER 12

TABLE A12–6.   Historical Data on High Protein Feeds

Year beginning Oct. 1	Cottonseed cake & meal consumed for feed[1] (mil. lb.)	Soybean cake & meal consumed for feed[1] (mil. lb.)	Feed unit equivalents[2] (bil. feed units)			Total high protein feeds[3] (bil. feed units)	Cottonseed & soybean as per cent of total high protein feeds
			Cottonseed meal	Soybean meal	Total		
1934	3,048	534	4.1	0.9	5.0	13.2	37.9
1935	3,436	1,228	4.6	2.0	6.6	16.3	40.5
1936	4,198	1,064	5.7	1.8	7.5	17.6	42.6
1937	4,664	1,438	6.3	2.4	8.7	18.1	48.1
1938	4,026	2,040	5.4	3.4	8.8	18.7	47.1
1939	3,524	2,552	4.8	4.2	9.0	19.9	45.2
1940	3,724	2,982	5.0	4.9	9.9	23.5	42.1
1941	3,642	3,570	4.9	5.9	10.8	25.3	42.7
1942	4,156	6,148	5.6	10.1	15.7	30.8	51.0
1943	3,580	6,646	4.8	11.0	15.8	31.6	50.0
1944	3,964	7,254	5.4	12.0	17.4	30.8	56.5
1945	2,866	7,310	3.9	12.1	16.0	28.3	56.5
1946	2,868	7,490	3.9	12.4	16.3	29.7	54.9
1947	3,906	6,766	5.3	11.2	16.5	30.3	54.5
1948	4,542	8,278	6.1	13.7	19.8	34.7	57.1
1949	4,764	9,034	6.4	14.9	21.3	36.7	58.0
1950	3,706	11,436	5.0	18.9	23.9	40.9	58.4
1951	5,300	11,280	7.2	18.6	25.8	42.1	61.3
1952	5,242	11,020	7.1	18.2	25.3	41.1	61.6
1953	5,852	9,930	7.9	16.4	24.3	42.4	57.3
1954	4,810	10,852	6.5	17.9	24.4	42.2	57.8
1955	5,022	12,084	6.8	19.9	26.7	44.4	60.1
1956	4,440	14,186	6.0	23.4	29.4	46.5	63.2
1957	4,196	15,924	5.7	26.3	32.0	48.3	66.3
1958	4,396	17,876	5.9	29.5	35.4	53.1	66.7
1959	4,660	16,840	6.3	27.8	34.1	53.7	63.5

1. Source: *Agricultural Statistics, 1957,* Table 75 (1934–46); *1958,* Table 74 (1947–55); *1960,* Table 80 (1956–59).

2. Converted at average feeding efficiency given in Jennings, *Consumption of Feed by Livestock,* Table 26: cottonseed meal, 135% of corn; soybean meal, 165%.

3. From Table A12–4.

TABLE A12–7.   Projected High Protein Feed Concentrates

	1940	1945	1950	1955	1960		1970	1980	1990	2000
Domestic food use of fats and oils[1]						L	12.1	13.6	14.9	16.1
(retail wt., bil. lb.)	9.4	8.5	10.3	11.2	12.1	M	13.5	15.9	18.7	21.5
						H	15.6	19.5	24.4	30.3
Production of soybean and cottonseed						L	58	60	60	60
oil in relation to food use of	19.8	31.3	36.7	39.6	51.4	M	70	80	86	90
fats and oils[2] (%)						H	75	90	97	100
Production of soybean and cottonseed						L	9.1	12.2	14.5	16.1
oil[3] (bil. lb.)	1.86	2.67	3.78	4.45	6.2	M	9.4	12.7	16.1	19.4
						H	9.0	11.7	14.6	18.2
Cotton production (ginnings)[4]						L	13.3	13.3	13.5	13.5
(mil. bales)	11.4	11.9	15.9	13.6	14.6	M	17.9	21.9	26.7	33.1
						H	20.8	28.5	40.0	57.7
Oil per bale of cotton[5] (lb.)						L	125	125	125	125
	116.0	111.0	116.0	127.7	127.9	M	131	133	135	135
						H	142	146	148	150
Cottonseed oil produced[6] (bil. lb.)						L	1.9	1.9	2.0	2.0
	1.33	1.32	1.85	1.74	1.86	M	2.3	2.9	3.6	4.5
						H	2.6	3.6	5.0	7.2
Soybean oil produced[7] (bil. lb.)						L	7.2	10.3	12.5	14.1
	.53	1.35	1.94	2.71	4.34	M	7.1	9.8	12.5	14.9
						H	6.4	8.1	9.6	11.0
Cottonseed cake and meal per						L	2.7	2.7	2.7	2.7
pound of oil[5] (lb.)	2.84	2.95	2.77	2.95	2.74	M	2.8	2.8	2.8	2.8
						H	3.0	3.0	3.0	3.0
Soybean cake and meal per						L	4.1	3.9	3.7	3.5
pound of oil[5] (lb.)	5.1	5.5	4.7	4.2	4.2	M	4.3	4.2	4.1	4.0
						H	4.5	4.5	4.5	4.5
Cake and meal produced[8] (bil. lb.):										
Cottonseed						L	5.7	5.7	6.0	6.0
	3.8	3.9	5.1	5.1	5.1	M	6.4	8.1	10.1	12.6
						H	7.0	9.7	13.5	19.4
Soybean						L	32.4	46.4	56.2	63.4
	2.7	7.4	9.2	11.4	18.3	M	30.5	41.2	51.2	59.6
						H	26.2	31.6	35.5	38.5
Cake and meal consumed[9] (bil. lb.):										
Cottonseed						L	5.5	5.5	5.8	5.8
	3.5	4.0	4.8	4.8	4.7	M	6.2	7.9	9.8	12.2
						H	6.8	9.4	13.1	18.8
Soybean						L	30.8	44.1	53.4	60.2
	2.6	7.3	9.0	10.9	16.8	M	29.0	39.1	48.6	56.6
						H	24.9	30.0	33.7	36.6
Cake and meal consumed (bil. feed units):[10]										
Cottonseed						L	7.4	7.4	7.8	7.8
	4.8	5.4	6.4	6.5	6.3	M	8.4	10.7	13.2	16.5
						H	9.2	12.7	17.7	25.4
Soybean						L	50.8	72.8	88.1	99.3
	4.2	12.0	14.9	17.9	27.8	M	47.8	64.5	80.2	93.4
						H	41.1	49.5	55.6	60.4
Combined						L	58.2	80.2	95.9	107.1
	9.0	17.4	21.3	24.4	34.1	M	56.2	75.2	93.4	109.9
						H	50.3	62.2	73.3	85.8

Table A12–7 (cont'd)

	1940	1945	1950	1955	1960		1970	1980	1990	2000
Cottonseed and soybean meal as per cent of total high protein feeds in feed units [11]	45.2	56.5	58.0	57.8	63.5	L M H	69 74 78	71 76 82	73 78 86	75 80 90
High protein feeds—Projection I [12] (bil. feed units)	19.9	30.8	36.7	42.2	53.7	L M H	84 76 64	113 99 76	131 120 85	143 137 95
High protein feeds as per cent of total concentrate feeds [13]	9.6	11.6	14.3	16.6	16.9	L M H	16.9 17.2 18.0	17.1 17.6 19.0	17.3 18.0 20.0	17.5 18.4 21.0
High protein feeds—Projection II [14] (bil. feed units)	19.9	30.8	36.7	42.2	53.7	L M H	56 61 72	66 77 96	75 94 124	85 110 156
High protein feeds—Final Projection [15] (bil. feed units)	19.9	30.8	36.7	42.2	53.7	L M H	84 76 72	113 99 96	131 120 124	143 137 156
Adjusted "high": Soybean/cottonseed meal consumed [16] (bil. feed units)						H	56.2	78.7	106.6	140.4
Soybean meal consumed [17] (bil. feed units)						H	47.0	66.0	88.9	115.0
Soybean meal consumed (bil. lb.) [18]						H	28.5	40.0	53.9	69.7
Soybean meal produced (bil. lb.) [19]						H	30.0	42.1	56.7	73.4

1. From Table A2–4. It is assumed that consumption of fats and oils is not compensatory with consumption of meat, and that a High (or Low) in the one could accompany a High (or Low) in the other.

2. Extrapolations by inspection, based on data in Table A12–5. Implicitly includes oil produced for export (which accounts for the otherwise implausible level shown in the High). Historical data from same source, for preceding crop year.

3. The High percentages of soybean/cottonseed oil are assumed to accompany Low fats and oils demand and the Low percentages, High demand. This may be justified on the assumption that export demand (for lard and butter, as well as for vegetable oil) becomes a proportionately larger factor under the Low assumption than under the High (see footnote 2). In addition, because of the proportionately greater differences in meat consumption than in fats and oils consumption at the different projection levels, there is a relatively greater availability of animal fats for the Low fats and oils consumption than for the High. Historical data from Table A12–5, for preceding crop year.

4. From Table A12–14. Refers to preceding crop year.

5. Extrapolations by inspection, based on data in Table A12–5. Historical data from same source, for preceding crop year.

6. Since cottonseed oil is purely by-product and there is therefore a net land saving despite the lower yield in meal than for soybeans, the High assumption on cottonseed oil per bale is combined with Low cotton ginnings, in order to minimize the soybean oil and meal; vice versa for the High. Historical data from Table A12–5.

7. Low cottonseed subtracted from Low total, etc. Historical data from Table A12–5.

8. In the projections, the High yield in meal is associated with the Low oil, to give the Low meal produced, and vice versa. Historical data from Table A12–5, for preceding crop year.

9. Deduction of 3% made for cottonseed meal exports, 5% for soybean meal exports (recent averages). Historical data from Table A12–6, for preceding crop year.

10. Converted at 135 feed units per 100 pounds cottonseed meal, 165 units per 100 pounds soybean meal. Historical data from Table A12–6. Conversion factor from Jennings, *Consumption of Feed for Livestock,* Table 26.

11. Extrapolations based on historical data in Table A12–6.

12. Based on immediately preceding relationship, using Low ÷ Low, etc. Historical data from Table A12–6.

13. Extrapolations based on historical data in Table A12–4.

14. Low total concentrates multiplied by High percentage, and vice versa, on assumption that there is compensation between the two factors. Total concentrates from Table A12–3.

15. On assumption that consumption will be determined by by-product availability (Projection I) or trend in high protein demand (Projection II), if latter is higher and assumption is one of Low efficiency. (Soybean meal involves a lower feed unit yield per acre than do feed grains.)

16. Applying High percentage of soybean plus cottonseed meal to high protein feeds, final projection.

17. Soybean/cottonseed, less High cottonseed.

18. Converted at 165 units per hundred pounds.

19. Using consumption/production relationship given in footnote 9.

TABLE A12–8. Historical Data on Roughage Feeding Pattern[1]

Year beginning Oct. 1	Consumption in billion feed units				Percentage distribution			
	Hay	Silage[2]	Pasture	Total[3]	Hay	Silage	Pasture	Other
1919	73.7	9.1	241.0	364.3	20.2	2.5	66.2	11.1
1920	67.7	9.6	227.8	347.7	19.5	2.8	65.5	12.2
1921	73.3	9.2	222.9	343.2	21.4	2.7	64.9	11.0
1922	74.8	9.4	222.3	341.2	21.9	2.8	65.2	10.1
1923	72.1	10.2	211.1	327.8	22.0	3.1	64.4	10.5
1924	71.5	8.8	182.9	306.4	23.3	2.9	59.7	14.1
1925	65.9	10.0	194.1	303.9	21.7	3.3	63.9	11.1
1926	62.2	10.3	202.8	305.7	20.3	3.4	66.3	10.0
1927	74.9	10.2	190.6	295.9	25.3	3.4	64.4	6.9
1928	72.4	10.2	192.1	296.2	24.4	3.4	64.9	7.3
1929	70.2	10.0	171.3	274.5	25.6	3.6	62.4	8.4
1930	61.8	10.3	179.3	280.2	22.1	3.6	64.0	10.3
1931	60.2	11.3	191.7	293.9	20.5	3.8	65.2	10.5
1932	66.1	11.3	182.0	288.8	22.9	3.9	63.0	10.2
1933	62.6	11.7	156.6	264.9	23.6	4.4	59.1	12.9
1934	51.1	12.5	198.7	298.5	17.1	4.2	66.6	12.1
1935	66.1	13.7	161.4	266.1	24.8	5.1	60.7	9.4
1936	63.2	12.3	182.0	284.6	22.2	4.3	63.9	9.6
1937	61.9	13.6	197.9	297.0	20.8	4.6	66.6	8.0
1938	71.3	13.5	176.3	283.6	25.1	4.8	62.2	7.9
1939	73.8	12.7	193.8	300.9	24.5	4.2	64.4	6.9
1940	75.8	13.8	211.7	321.3	23.6	4.3	65.9	6.2
1941	78.7	14.0	235.0	350.1	22.5	4.0	67.1	6.4
1942	85.5	13.3	230.7	350.6	24.4	3.8	65.8	6.0
1943	85.8	12.7	234.4	355.5	24.1	3.6	65.9	6.4
1944	82.0	13.4	247.3	367.4	22.3	3.6	67.3	6.8
1945	83.8	13.1	227.4	343.2	24.4	3.8	66.3	5.5
1946	84.8	13.6	222.3	337.0	25.2	4.0	66.0	4.8
1947	82.8	13.3	206.2	316.7	26.1	4.2	65.1	4.6
1948	78.9	14.9	205.6	313.8	25.1	4.7	65.5	4.7
1949	79.0	15.6	205.3	315.3	25.0	4.9	65.1	5.0
1950	84.2	17.1	214.6	330.2	25.5	5.2	65.0	4.3
1951	89.5	17.8	214.8	335.0	26.7	5.3	64.1	3.9
1952	87.0	18.7	216.3	341.1	25.5	5.5	63.4	5.6
1953	87.9	21.0	215.1	341.9	25.7	6.1	62.9	5.3
1954	88.5	23.0	223.2	351.4	25.2	6.5	63.5	4.8
1955	91.1	23.8	209.3	340.9	26.7	7.0	61.4	4.9
1956	87.3	24.2	233.3	360.4	24.2	6.7	64.7	4.4
1957	91.0	26.5	240.7	373.2	24.4	7.1	64.5	4.0
1958	98.7	25.8	229.3	365.6	27.0	7.1	62.7	3.2
1959	99.6	26.7	240.6	376.7	26.4	7.1	63.9	2.6

1. Source: 1919–40 from Jennings, *Consumption of Feed by Livestock*, Table 64. Subsequent data from unpublished USDA material.

2. Tabulated by Jennings as "silage and beet pulp," but beet pulp component is insignificant.

3. Included in total, in addition to items shown, are stover and straw. These are assumed to arise as by-products on acreage otherwise accounted for.

TABLE A12–9. Historical Data on Feed Grains

Crop year	Total disappearance, including non-feed use, seed, and exports									Feed consumption of all grains[3] (mil. feed units)	Ratio: disappearance of 4 grains to total feed consumption
	Million bushels[1]				Billion feed units (lb.)[2]						
	Corn[4]	Oats[5]	Barley[5]	Sorghum grain[4]	Corn[4]	Oats[5]	Barley[5]	Sorghum grain[4]	Total		
1934	1,759	611	149	19	98.5	17.6	6.4	1.0	123.5	108.5	1.14
1935	2,209	1,009	250	58	123.7	29.1	10.8	3.1	166.7	148.3	1.12
1936	1,720	983	219	30	96.3	28.3	9.5	1.6	135.7	111.7	1.21
1937	2,349	1,059	216	70	131.5	30.5	9.3	3.7	175.0	152.5	1.15
1938	2,327	1,103	242	67	130.3	31.8	10.5	3.6	176.2	156.2	1.13
1939	2,478	1,016	282	53	138.8	29.3	12.2	2.8	183.1	162.2	1.13
1940	2,501	1,182	303	86	140.1	34.0	13.1	4.6	191.8	172.2	1.11
1941	2,806	1,213	355	114	157.1	34.9	15.3	6.1	213.4	192.7	1.11
1942	3,197	1,355	437	110	179.0	39.0	18.9	5.9	242.8	236.5	1.03
1943	3,123	1,272	409	110	174.9	36.6	17.7	5.9	235.1	230.8	1.02
1944	3,010	1,192	295	185	168.6	34.3	12.7	9.8	225.4	207.8	1.08
1945	3,013	1,492	309	96	168.7	43.0	13.3	5.1	230.1	216.5	1.06
1946	3,106	1,495	272	106	173.9	43.1	11.8	5.6	234.4	192.9	1.22
1947	2,515	1,270	286	94	140.8	36.6	12.4	5.0	194.8	171.3	1.14
1948	2,916	1,361	279	119	163.3	39.2	12.1	6.3	220.9	185.0	1.19
1949	3,207	1,323	276	107	179.6	38.1	11.9	5.7	235.3	197.0	1.19
1950	3,181	1,321	304	255	178.1	38.0	13.1	13.6	242.8	201.4	1.21
1951	3,179	1,349	290	191	178.0	38.9	12.5	10.2	239.6	205.1	1.17
1952	3,011	1,314	275	93	168.6	37.8	11.9	4.9	223.2	184.3	1.21
1953	3,060	1,255	265	101	171.4	36.1	11.4	5.4	224.3	187.5	1.20
1954	2,944	1,354	344	183	164.9	39.0	14.9	9.7	228.5	186.5	1.23
1955	3,100	1,462	443	236	173.6	42.1	19.1	12.6	247.4	196.5	1.26
1956	3,202	1,286	393	208	179.3	37.0	17.0	11.1	244.4	192.2	1.27
1957	3,373	1,241	421	334	188.9	35.7	18.2	17.8	260.6	206.1	1.26
1958	3,742	1,376	463	410	209.6	39.6	20.0	21.8	291.0	225.1	1.29
1959	4,024	1,168	467	514	225.3	33.6	20.2	27.3	306.4	238.1	1.29

1. Source: USDA, *Grain and Feed Statistics Through 1956* (Statistical Bulletin No. 159, May 1957) and 1960 supplement (March 1961).

2. Converted at 56 lb./bu. for corn, 32 lb. for oats, 48 lb. for barley, and 56 lb. for sorghum, combined with following feed values relative to corn as 100: oats and barley, 90; sorghum, 95. Source of feed values: Jennings, *Consumption of Feed by Livestock,* Table 26.

3. From Table A12–4. Excludes corn in silage and includes feed consumption of wheat and rye.

4. Years beginning Oct. 1.

5. Years beginning July 1.

TABLE A12–10. Projected Individual Feed Components

	1940	1945	1950	1955	1960		1970	1980	1990	2000
Concentrates:										
Total concentrates[1] (bil. feed units)	207.1	264.4	257.4	253.5	317.4	L M H	312 352 425	346 432 559	374 520 716	404 600 893
High protein feeds[2] (bil. feed units)	19.9	30.8	36.7	42.2	53.7	L M H	84 76 72	113 99 96	131 120 124	143 137 156
Total grains and miscellaneous concentrates (bil. feed units)	187.2	233.6	220.7	211.3	263.7	L M H	228 276 353	233 333 463	243 400 592	261 463 737
Per cent grains[3]	86.6	89.0	89.3	88.3	90.3		90	90	90	90
Grains (bil. feed units)	162	208	197	186	238	L M H	205 248 318	210 300 417	219 360 533	235 417 663
Total disappearance of 4 principal feed grains[4] (bil. feed units)	183	225	235	229	306	L M H	256 310 398	262 375 521	274 450 666	294 521 829
Roughage:										
Total roughage[1] (bil. feed units)	301	367	315	351	377	L M H	334 438 569	341 532 756	338 613 994	341 690 1,265
Percentage distribution in—										
Low land model:[5]										
Hay	24.5	22.3	25.0	25.2	26.4		34	40	45	50
Pasture	64.4	67.3	65.1	63.5	63.9		54	47	41	35
Other	11.1	10.4	9.9	11.3	9.7		12	13	14	15
Medium land model:[5]										
Hay	24.5	22.3	25.0	25.2	26.4		31	35	39	43
Pasture	64.4	67.3	65.1	63.5	63.9		58	54	50	46
Other	11.1	10.4	9.9	11.3	9.7		11	11	11	11
High land model:[5]										
Hay	24.5	22.3	25.0	25.2	26.4		27.5	28.5	29.5	30.5
Pasture	64.4	67.3	65.1	63.5	63.9		63	63	63	63
Other	11.1	10.4	9.9	11.3	9.7		9.5	8.5	7.5	6.5
Billion feed units:[6]										
Hay	74	82	79	88	100	L M H	114 136 156	136 186 215	152 239 293	170 297 386
Pasture	194	247	205	223	241	L M H	180 254 358	160 287 476	139 306 626	119 317 797
Other[7]	33	38	31	40	36	L M H	40 48 54	44 58 64	47 67 75	51 76 82
Hay feed units per ton[8]	812	813	814	818	835		824	828	832	836
Consumption in million tons[9]	91	101	97	108	119	L M H	138 165 189	164 225 260	183 287 352	203 355 462

1. From Table A12–3. Historical data from Table A12–4.

2. From Table A12–7.

3. Based on historical data in Table A12–4, for preceding feeding year. Projections based on percentage which follows, which is kept constant because of relative historical stability.

4. Corn (including silage), oats, barley, and grain sorghums. Feed consumption of grain as calculated herein

raised by 25% (see historical ratios, Table A12–9) to account for export and non-feed uses, seed, and quantities used for silage, less feed consumption of wheat (accounted for under wheat, Table A12–14) and rye (included, in Chapter V, in acreage not specifically accounted for). Historical data from Table A12–9, for preceding crop year.

5. Based on historical trends shown in Table A12–8. Distribution in High and Low models based on relative

Table A12–10 (cont'd)

productivity of each type of roughage in terms of yield in feed units per acre. (Heaviest demand on land occurs from following order of emphasis: (1) pasture, (2) hay, (3) silage, (4) other.)

6. Low, Medium, and High refer to respective land models. Historical data from Table A12–8, for preceding feeding year.

7. Includes silage, which becomes a progressively larger proportion of this category.

8. Historical values are those implicit in Jennings,

Consumption of Feed by Livestock, Tables 44 and 64, and unpublished USDA data (years beginning preceding Oct. 1). Because of trend toward alfalfa and latitude for increasing efficiency in use of hay (see footnote 1, Table 26 in Jennings), there is a clear prospect for increasing feed unit values. Extrapolation continues Jennings' implicit arithmetic trend.

9. Historical data from Jennings, Table 44, except for 1960, which is from unpublished USDA data.

TABLE A12–11.   Historical Data on Wheat Consumption[1]

(Million bushels, unless otherwise indicated)

Year beginning July 1	Processed for food[2]	Total domestic use[3]			Exports and shipments to territories[4]	Total use	Retained for seed		Food consumption following calendar year	
		Quantity	As per cent of quantity processed for food				Quantity	Per cent of total use	Quantity[5]	Ratio to "processed for food" preceding crop year (%)
1934	473.8	570.9	120		13.6	584.5	82.7	14.1	477.7	100.8
1935	490.1	573.5	117		7.5	581.0	87.5	15.1	502.2	102.5
1936	493.3	594.5	121		12.7	607.2	95.9	15.8	490.2	99.4
1937	489.4	604.3	123		107.3	711.5	93.1	13.1	496.2	101.4
1938	496.2	638.0	129		111.1	749.1	74.2	9.9	491.3	99.0
1939	488.8	589.9	121		48.9	638.8	73.0	11.4	484.3	99.1
1940	489.4	601.2	123		36.6	637.8	74.4	11.7	491.3	100.4
1941	472.9	605.0	128		32.2	637.2	62.5	9.8	501.3	106.0
1942	495.0	880.4	178		36.5	916.9	65.5	7.1	521.7	105.4
1943	477.3	1,159.4	243		45.8	1,205.2	77.4	6.4	486.7	102.0
1944	472.7	1,006.0	213		53.4	1,059.4	80.5	7.6	536.3	113.5
1945	473.7	882.5	186		324.3	1,206.8	82.0	6.8	504.3	106.5
1946	479.4	749.4	156		332.2	1,081.6	86.8	8.0	470.7	98.2
1947	484.1	811.7	168		344.2	1,155.9	91.1	7.9	474.0	97.9
1948	471.5	758.6	161		331.5	1,090.1	95.0	8.7	480.0	101.8
1949	484.2	719.2	149		183.2	902.4	80.9	9.0	485.5	100.3
1950	479.6	629.8	131		338.4	968.2	87.9	9.1	489.0	102.0
1951	481.1	601.1	125		474.3	1,075.4	88.2	8.2	492	102.3
1952	473.6	569.9	120		319.5	889.4	89.1	10.0	484.2	102.2
1953	472.7	561.5	119		219.7	781.2	69.5	8.9	481.8	101.9
1954	473.0	543.2	115		277.4	820.6	64.8	7.9	479.3	101.3
1955	469.5	531.9	113		350.2	882.1	67.7	7.7	476.5	101.5
1956	469.8	526.5	112		553.6	1,080.1	57.7	5.3	476.5	101.4
1957	474.6	524.5	111		406.8	931.3	63.2	6.8	490.3	103.3
1958	485.8	538.8	111		447.2	986.0	65.1	6.6	493.0	101.5
1959	487.4	534.0	110		512.4	1,046.4	63.7	6.1	494.7	101.5

1. Unless otherwise noted, from *Agricultural Statistics, 1957*, Table 12, and *Wheat Situation*, Aug. 1961.

2. Does not include military procurement, which, however, is included in total domestic use.

3. Includes feed and other uses, except seed, in continental United States, plus military procurement, which, in the war and early postwar years, has been largely for civilian feeding abroad.

4. Includes shipments to Alaska, Hawaii, and Puerto Rico, among other places.

5. Per capita consumption from Table A2–1, multiplied by population from Table A1–1. This, rather than total disappearance, is used in order to eliminate the effect of abnormal military purchases. (The per capita data are on a civilian consumption basis and expressed in pounds. Converted to bushels at 60 pounds per bushel.)

TABLE A12–12. Historical Data on Cotton Consumption and Production

	Domestic consumption in finished goods[1] (bil. lb.)	Exports of semi-finished goods[2] (bil. lb.)	Total end-use consumption (bil. lb.)	Total end-use consumption—equivalent bales[3] (millions)	Exports of raw cotton[4] (mil. bales)	Approximate total use of crop[5] (mil. bales)	Ginnings[4] (mil. bales)	Ratio: ginnings to calculated use (%)
1949	3.40	.37	3.77	7.85	4.75	12.60	14.65	116.3
1950	3.80	.25	4.05	8.44	5.77	14.21	15.92	112.0
1951	3.74	.43	4.17	8.69	4.11	12.80	9.88	77.2
1952	3.69	.34	4.03	8.40	5.51	13.91	15.07	108.3
1953	3.78	.31	4.09	8.52	3.05	11.57	15.17	131.1
1954	3.70	.28	3.98	8.29	3.76	12.05	16.40	136.1
1955	3.95	.24	4.19	8.73	3.45	12.18	13.59	111.6
1956	3.95	.25	4.20	8.75	2.21	10.96	14.68	133.9
1957	3.82	.29	4.11	8.56	7.60	16.16	13.03	80.6
1958	3.74	.27	4.01	8.35	5.72	14.07	10.92	77.6
1959	4.06	.25	4.31	8.98	2.79	11.77	11.42	97.0
1960	3.96	.24	4.20	8.75	7.18	15.93	14.56	91.4
1949–1960 totals						158.21	165.29	104.5

1. From Table A3–1. Includes finished goods exported. Allocable processing waste is included (see Table A3–1 and *Textile Organon*, Nov. 1961).

2. Includes yarn and spinnable waste, broad woven and knit fabric. Source: Textile Economics Bureau, *Textile Organon*, Nov. 1961.

3. Converted at 480 lb./bale.

4. Crop year beginning Aug. 1 of preceding calendar year. Source: *Agricultural Statistics, 1958*, Table 81, and *1960*, Table 89; and *The Cotton Situation*, Nov. 1961, Table 16.

5. Includes the very small quantities of imported cotton used.

TABLE A12–13. Historical Data on Soybean Consumption[1]

(Million bushels, unless otherwise indicated)

Year beginning Oct. 1	Crushed	Exports and direct feed use[2]	Total use	Retained for seed Quantity	Retained for seed Per cent of total use
1942	133.5	26.6	160.1	21.0	13.1
1943	142.3	26.5	168.8	19.8	11.7
1944	153.4	26.2	179.6	18.9	10.5
1945	159.5	20.3	179.8	16.7	9.3
1946	170.2	14.7	184.9	17.5	9.5
1947	161.4	11.8	173.2	16.1	9.3
1948	183.7	27.0	210.7	15.9	7.5
1949	195.3	20.3	215.6	18.9	8.8
1950	252.0	27.0	279.0	19.0	6.8
1951	244.4	20.2	264.6	19.8	7.5
1952	234.4	37.2	271.6	20.7	7.6
1953	213.2	41.9	255.1	22.9	9.0
1954	249.0	60.0	309.0	23.4	7.6
1955	283.1	70.5	353.6	26.1	7.4
1956	315.9	101.1	417.0	26.2	6.3
1957	353.8	89.4	443.2	29.4	6.6
1958	401.2	110.8	512.0	27.2	5.3
1959	393.4	149.3	542.7	29.1	5.4

1. Source: 1942–52, *Agricultural Statistics, 1957* and *1958*, Table 191, *1960*, Table 202; 1953–59, *Fats and Oils Situation*, Nov. 1961, Table 3.

2. Includes statistical error. Direct feed use has been very small or negligible.

TABLE A12–14.   Projected Wheat, Cotton, and Soybeans[1]

	1940	1945	1950	1955	1960		1970	1980	1990	2000
Wheat:										
Domestic food consumption[2]						L	31.3	32.8	34.9	37.5
(bil. lb.)	29.1	32.2	29.1	28.8	29.7	M	30.1	33.0	35.9	39.7
						H	30.1	33.5	38.4	43.3
Domestic food consumption[3]						L	522	547	582	625
(mil. bu.)	484	536	485	479	495	M	502	550	598	662
						H	502	558	640	722
Adjustment to total domestic										
use[4] (per cent)	122	188	148	113	108		110	109	108	107
						L	574	596	629	669
Total domestic use[5] (mil. bu.)	590	1,006	719	543	534	M	552	600	646	708
						H	552	608	691	773
Shipments outside continental						L	359	372	420	474
U.S.[6] (mil. bu.)	49	53	183	277	512	M	372	405	493	610
						H	375	416	523	685
						L	933	968	1,049	1,143
Total use (mil. bu.)	639	1,059	902	821	1,046	M	924	1,005	1,139	1,318
						H	927	1,024	1,214	1,458
Seed as per cent of total use[4]	11.4	7.6	9.0	7.9	6.1		6.5	5.8	5.4	5.0
						L	994	1,024	1,106	1,200
Use, including seed (mil. bu.)	712	1,140	983	886	1,110	M	984	1,063	1,200	1,384
						H	987	1,083	1,280	1,531
Cotton:										
Domestic end-use consump-						L	3.86	3.98	4.33	4.70
tion[7] (bil. lb.)	n.a.	n.a.	3.80	3.95	3.96	M	4.53	5.52	6.72	8.35
						H	5.40	7.40	10.49	15.19
						L	2.27	2.15	1.91	1.53
Exports[8] (bil. lb.)	–	–	3.02	1.90	3.69	M	3.65	4.46	5.48	6.77
						H	4.11	5.62	7.81	11.11
Free World population[9]						L	2,065	2,385	2,722	3,069
(millions)	–	–	1,513	1,615	1,794	M	2,146	2,622	3,222	3,980
						H	2,162	2,674	3,397	4,443
						L	1.1	.9	.7	.5
Per capita exports[10] (lb.)	–	–	1.98	1.18	2.11	M	1.7	1.7	1.7	1.7
						H	1.9	2.1	2.3	2.5
						L	6.1	6.1	6.2	6.2
Total consumption (bil. lb.)	–	–	6.82	5.85	7.65	M	8.2	10.0	12.2	15.1
						H	9.5	13.0	18.3	26.3
						L	6.4	6.4	6.5	6.5
Total ginnings[11] (bil. lb.)	5.5	5.7	7.6	6.5	7.0	M	8.6	10.5	12.8	15.9
						H	10.0	13.7	19.2	27.6
						L	13.3	13.3	13.5	13.5
Total ginnings (mil. bales)[12]	11.4	11.9	15.9	13.6	14.6	M	17.9	21.9	26.7	33.1
						H	20.8	28.5	40.0	57.5

Table A12–14 (cont'd)

	1940	1945	1950	1955	1960		1970	1980	1990	2000
Soybeans:										
Soybean meal produced[13]						L	32.4	46.4	56.2	63.4
(bil. lb.)	2.7	7.4	9.2	11.4	18.3	M	30.5	41.2	51.2	59.6
						H	30.0	42.1	56.7	73.4
Meal per bushel of beans						L	46.5	46.5	46.5	46.5
crushed[14] (lb.)	47.6	48.2	47.0	45.8	46.5	M	47.5	47.5	47.5	47.5
						H	48.5	48.5	48.5	48.5
						L	670	960	1,160	1,310
Soybeans crushed[15] (mil. bu.)	56.7	153.4	195.3	249.0	393.4	M	640	870	1,080	1,250
						H	620	870	1,170	1,510
Exports and direct feed use[16]						L	100	100	100	100
(mil. bu.)	n.a.	26.2	20.3	60.0	149.3	M	140	160	180	200
						H	210	260	320	400
						L	770	1,060	1,260	1,410
Total use (mil. bu.)	n.a.	179.6	215.6	309.0	542.7	M	780	1,030	1,260	1,450
						H	830	1,130	1,490	1,910
Seed as per cent of total use[17]	n.a.	10.5	8.8	7.6	5.4		6	6	6	6
						L	820	1,120	1,340	1,490
Use including seed (mil. bu.)	n.a.	198.5	234.6	332.5	571.8	M	830	1,090	1,340	1,540
						H	880	1,200	1,580	2,020

1. The historical data on crop use which are given herein refer to the immediately preceding crop year. End-use data are on a calendar year basis.

2. The Low and High projections here differ from those in Table A2–4, since the Low per capita consumption of meat used here to obtain the Low land model implies a High consumption of wheat, and vice versa. Consequently the Low here is obtained by applying the High per capita projections in Table A2–2 to the Low population (Table A1–2), etc. Historical data from Table A2–4.

3. Converted to bushels at 60 lb/bu.

4. Extrapolation of recent ratios (see Table A12–11). Historical data are actual relationships of series shown.

5. Historical data from Table A12–11.

6. From Table A12–15. Historical data from Table A12–11.

7. From Table A3–3.

8. Historical data from Table A12–12—semifinished, plus raw cotton converted at 480 lb/bale. Projections are product of population projections and per capita exports which follow.

9. From Table A12–15, with the addition of U.N. projections for Canada.

10. Extrapolated by inspection.

11. Total consumption, plus an allowance of 5%, which is approximate 1949–60 experience on ratio of total use (calculated in this manner) to total ginnings. This allows for a gradual stock increase. Historical data from Table A12–12 and from *Agricultural Statistics, 1957* and *1958,* Table 81, converted at 480 lb/bale.

12. Converted at 480 lb/bale.

13. From Table A12–7, using adjusted projection for High.

14. Extrapolation of historical ratios in Table A12–5, consistently with oil ratios in Table A12–7. Meal plus oil should almost equal beans crushed.

15. Calculated from preceding two items, except for historical data, which are from Table A12–13. The High unit yield is associated with both the Low and High meal projections and the Medium unit yield is associated with the Medium meal projection.

16. Extrapolations of historical data in Table A12–13. Apparent inconsistency between 1960 and the projection is due to the assumption that the 1960 figure is well above the trend. Direct feed use in future considered to be negligible, so that "exports and direct feed use" essentially equals exports.

17. 6% assumed to be approximate lower limit, based on trends shown in Table A12–13.

TABLE A12–15.   Projected Wheat Exports

	1950	1955	1960		1970	1980	1990	2000
Population[1] (millions):								
				L	254	312	377	445
Latin America[2]	163	182	206	M	265	348	455	592
				H	265	349	471	651
				L	343	360	370	376
Western Europe[3]	300	309	328	M	351	379	408	436
				H	351	380	414	454
				L	1,164	1,360	1,569	1,784
Asia and Oceania[4]	837	892	998	M	1,220	1,524	1,904	2,381
				H	1,220	1,531	1,971	2,614
				L	284	330	380	436
Africa	199	216	244	M	289	346	426	537
				H	305	389	511	688
U.S. exports per								
capita[5] (bu.):								
Latin America	.18	.21	.44		.3	.3	.3	.3
Western Europe	.42	.47	.33		.25	.21	.2	.2
Asia and Oceania	.03	.09	.26		.12	.1	.1	.1
Africa	.01	.04	.23		.2	.2	.2	.2
Aggregate exports[6]								
(mil. bu.):								
				L	76	.94	113	134
Latin America	30	39	90	M	80	104	136	178
				H	80	105	141	195
				L	86	76	74	75
Western Europe	126	146	107	M	88	80	82	87
				H	88	80	83	91
				L	140	136	157	178
Asia and Oceania	25	83	260	M	146	152	190	238
				H	146	153	197	261
				L	57	66	76	87
Africa	2	9	55	M	58	69	85	107
				H	61	78	102	138
				L	359	372	420	474
Total	183	277	512	M	372	405	493	610
				H	375	416	523	685

1. From United Nations, *Future Growth of World Population* (1958), Appendix C, with projections proportionally adjusted to actual 1960 levels as reported in U.N., *Population and Vital Statistics Report* (Stat. Papers, Series A, Vol. XIII, No. 4), 1961.

2. Including Central America and Caribbean.

3. Including Yugoslavia and Greece.

4. Excluding Communist countries.

5. Based on the gradual disappearance of "non-commercial" exports between now and 1980. This would affect mostly per capita exports to Europe and Asia. Commercial exports to Europe are also expected to decline, in the face of rapidly increasing European output.

6. Historical data, from Table A12–11 for totals, are for crop year beginning July 1 of preceding calendar year and include shipments to U.S. territories but not military shipments for civilian feeding abroad. In estimated geographical distribution, territories included under Latin America. 1955 estimate from *Agricultural Statistics, 1957,* Table 14; 1960 based on 1959–60 distribution, *Wheat Situation,* Aug. 1961, Table 8. 1950 estimated from data including military exports in *Agricultural Statistics, 1952;* military exports of 119,000 bushels (1958 supp. to *Grain and Feed Statistics,* Table 45) assumed all to have gone to Germany and Japan. Apparent inconsistency between 1960 and the projections is due to the assumption that the 1960 figure is well above the trend.

TABLE A12–16. Alternate Projections of Feed Grains, Soybeans, Hay, and Pasture[1]

	1940	1945	1950	1955	1960		1970	1980	1990	2000
Total feed units required[2] (billions):										
						LL	297	330	351	378
						HL	358	422	474	519
Cattle and calves	144	207	196	255	302	M	376	481	576	663
						LH	384	501	631	795
						HH	463	640	852	1,093
						LL	115	124	131	134
						HL	140	161	177	192
Hogs	89	105	106	100	115	M	127	156	190	213
						LH	139	164	207	248
						HH	168	213	281	353
						LL	113	108	103	100
						HL	131	136	140	147
Milk cows	117	144	130	131	134	M	134	146	159	182
						LH	143	165	192	220
						HH	166	209	261	323
						LL	20	21	22	24
						HL	25	30	33	35
Commercial broilers	2	5	7	11	18	M	19	22	25	28
						LH	16	18	22	27
						HH	20	26	32	41
						LL	9	10	10	10
						HL	12	14	14	15
Turkeys	4	5	5	6	8	M	10	12	13	14
						LH	9	10	11	13
						HH	11	14	16	19
						LL	7	7	6	7
						HL	9	9	9	10
Farm chickens raised	17	22	17	12	9	M	9	9	10	12
						LH	9	10	12	13
						HH	11	13	17	20
						LL	30	28	26	27
						HL	40	41	42	41
Eggs	23	35	38	32	35	M	39	42	44	46
						LH	39	43	45	54
						HH	51	62	71	81
Total concentrates[3] (bil. feed units):										
						LL	71	92	112	132
						HL	64	84	95	104
Cattle and calves	23	29	34	43	57	M	78	110	144	179
						LH	92	140	202	278
						HH	83	128	170	219
						LL	109	118	125	127
						HL	133	153	168	182
Hogs	84	99	100	96	109	M	121	148	181	202
						LH	132	156	197	236
						HH	160	202	267	335
						LL	38	39	39	40
						HL	39	41	42	44
Milk cows	32	41	38	39	43	M	44	50	56	64
						LH	49	59	73	88
						HH	50	63	78	97
						LL	66	66	64	68
						HL	86	94	98	101
Poultry (including eggs)	46	67	67	64	70	M	77	85	92	100
						LH	73	81	90	107
						HH	93	115	136	161

Table A12–16 (cont'd)

	1940	1945	1950	1955	1960		1970	1980	1990	2000
Total concentrates (cont'd)										
						LL	284	315	340	367
						HL	322	372	403	431
Subtotal	185	236	239	242	279	M	320	393	473	545
						LH	346	436	562	709
						HH	386	508	651	812
						LL	312	346	374	404
						HL	354	409	443	474
Total	207	264	257	254	317	M	352	432	520	600
						LH	381	480	618	780
						HH	425	559	716	893
Roughage [4] (bil. feed units):						LL	226	238	239	246
						HL	294	338	379	415
Cattle and calves	121	178	162	212	245	M	297	370	432	484
						LH	292	361	429	517
						HH	380	512	682	874
						LL	6	6	7	7
						HL	7	8	9	10
Hogs	5	5	5	5	5	M	6	8	10	11
						LH	7	8	10	12
						HH	8	11	14	18
						LL	75	69	64	60
						HL	92	95	98	103
Milk cows	85	103	92	92	91	M	90	96	103	118
						LH	94	106	119	132
						HH	116	146	183	226
						LL	11	12	12	12
						HL	15	17	19	21
Lambs and sheep	37	36	22	22	19	M	24	33	39	44
						LH	29	36	43	52
						HH	38	51	68	87
						LL	318	325	322	325
						HL	408	458	505	549
Subtotal	248	322	281	331	360	M	417	507	584	657
						LH	422	511	601	713
						HH	542	720	947	1,205
						LL	334	341	338	341
						HL	428	481	530	576
Total	301	367	315	351	377	M	438	532	613	690
						LH	443	537	631	749
						HH	569	756	994	1,265
						LL	1.9	1.9	2.0	2.0
						HL	1.7	1.7	1.7	1.7
Cottonseed oil produced [5] (bil. lb.)	1.33	1.32	1.85	1.74	1.86	M	2.3	2.9	3.6	4.5
						LH	3.0	4.2	5.9	8.7
						HH	2.6	3.6	5.0	7.2
						LL	7.2	10.3	12.5	14.1
						HL	7.4	10.5	12.8	14.4
Soybean oil produced [4] (bil. lb.)	.53	1.35	1.94	2.71	4.34	M	7.1	9.8	12.5	14.9
						LH	6.0	7.5	8.7	9.5
						HH	6.4	8.1	9.6	11.0

Table A12–16 (cont'd)

	1940	1945	1950	1955	1960		1970	1980	1990	2000
Cake and meal produced[6] (bil. lb.):						LL	5.7	5.7	6.0	6.0
						HL	4.6	4.6	4.6	4.6
Cottonseed	3.8	3.9	5.1	5.1	5.1	M	6.4	8.1	10.1	12.6
						LH	9.0	12.6	17.7	26.1
						HH	7.0	9.7	13.5	19.4
						LL	32.4	46.4	56.2	63.4
						HL	30.3	41.0	47.4	50.4
Soybean	2.7	7.4	9.2	11.4	18.3	M	30.5	41.2	51.2	59.6
						LH	27.0	33.8	39.2	42.8
						HH	26.2	31.6	35.5	38.5
Cake and meal consumed[7] (bil. lb.):						LL	5.5	5.5	5.8	5.8
						HL	4.5	4.5	4.5	4.5
Cottonseed	3.5	4.0	4.8	4.8	4.7	M	6.2	7.9	9.8	12.2
						LH	8.7	12.2	17.2	25.3
						HH	6.8	9.4	13.1	18.8
						LL	30.8	44.1	53.4	60.2
						HL	28.8	39.0	45.0	47.9
Soybean	2.6	7.3	9.0	10.9	16.8	M	29.0	39.1	48.6	56.6
						LH	25.7	32.1	37.2	40.7
						HH	24.9	30.0	33.7	36.6
Cake and meal consumed[8] (bil. feed units):						LL	7.4	7.4	7.8	7.8
						HL	6.1	6.1	6.1	6.1
Cottonseed	4.8	5.4	6.4	6.5	6.3	M	8.4	10.7	13.2	16.5
						LH	11.7	16.5	23.2	34.2
						HH	9.2	12.7	17.7	25.4
						LL	50.8	72.8	88.1	99.3
						HL	47.5	64.4	74.2	79.0
Soybean	4.2	12.0	14.9	17.9	27.8	M	47.8	64.5	80.2	93.4
						LH	42.4	53.0	61.4	67.2
						HH	41.1	49.5	55.6	60.4
						LL	58.2	80.2	95.9	107.1
						HL	53.6	70.5	80.3	85.1
Combined	9.0	17.4	21.3	24.4	34.1	M	56.2	75.2	93.4	109.9
						LH	54.1	69.5	84.6	101.4
						HH	50.3	62.2	73.3	85.8
						LL	84	113	131	143
High protein feeds—projection						HL	69	86	93	95
I[9] (bil. feed units)	19.9	30.8	36.7	42.2	53.7	M	76	99	120	137
						LH	78	98	116	135
						HH	64	76	85	95
						LL	56	66	75	85
High protein feeds—projection						HL	64	78	89	100
II[10] (bil. feed units)	19.9	30.8	36.7	42.2	53.7	M	61	77	94	110
						LH	64	82	107	136
						HH	72	96	124	156
						LL	84	113	131	143
High protein feeds—final projec-						HL	69	86	93	100
tion[11] (bil. feed units)	19.9	30.8	36.7	42.2	53.7	M	76	99	120	137
						LH	78	98	116	135
						HH	72	96	124	156

Table A12–16 (cont'd)

	1940	1945	1950	1955	1960		1970	1980	1990	2000
Feed grains:						LL	228	233	243	261
Total grains and miscella-						HL	285	323	350	374
neous concentrates[12]	187	234	221	211	264	M	276	333	400	463
(bil. feed units)						LH	303	382	502	645
						HH	353	463	592	737
						LL	205	210	219	235
Feed grains (domestic feed						HL	256	291	315	337
use)[13] (bil. feed units)	162	208	197	186	238	M	248	300	360	417
						LH	273	344	452	580
						HH	318	417	533	663
						LL	256	262	274	294
Total disappearance of 4						HL	320	364	394	421
principal feed grains[14]	183	225	235	229	306	M	310	375	450	521
(bil. feed units)						LH	341	430	565	725
						HH	398	521	666	829
Adjusted cake and meal:						LL	58.2	80.2	95.9	107.1
Soybean/cottonseed meal						HL	53.6	70.5	80.3	90.0
consumed[15] (bil. feed units)	9.0	17.4	21.3	24.4	34.1	M	56.2	75.2	93.4	109.9
						LH	54.1	69.5	84.6	101.4
						HH	56.2	78.7	106.6	140.4
						LL	50.8	72.8	88.1	99.3
Soybean meal consumed[16]						HL	47.5	64.4	74.2	83.9
(bil. feed units)	4.2	12.0	14.9	17.9	27.8	M	47.8	64.5	80.2	93.4
						LH	42.4	53.0	61.4	67.2
						HH	47.0	66.0	88.9	115.0
						LL	30.8	44.1	53.4	60.2
Soybean meal consumed						HL	28.8	39.0	45.0	50.8
(bil. lb.)[17]	2.6	7.3	9.0	10.9	16.8	M	29.0	39.1	48.6	56.6
						LH	25.7	32.1	37.2	40.7
						HH	28.5	40.0	53.9	69.7
						LL	32.4	46.4	56.2	63.4
Soybean meal produced[18]						HL	30.3	41.0	47.4	53.5
(bil. lb.)	27.7	7.4	9.2	11.4	18.3	M	30.5	41.2	51.2	59.6
						LH	27.0	33.8	39.2	42.8
						HH	30.0	42.1	56.7	73.4
Soybeans:						LL	670	960	1,160	1,310
						HL	650	880	1,020	1,150
Soybeans crushed[19] (mil. bu.)	56.7	153.4	195.3	249.0	393	M	640	870	1,080	1,250
						LH	560	700	810	880
						HH	620	870	1,170	1,510
						LL	100	100	100	100
Exports and direct feed						HL	100	100	100	100
use[20] (mil. bu.)	n.a.	26.2	20.3	60.0	149.3	M	140	160	180	200
						LH	210	260	320	400
						HH	210	260	320	400
						LL	770	1,060	1,260	1,410
						HL	750	980	1,120	1,250
Total use (mil. bu.)	n.a.	179.6	215.6	309.0	542.7	M	780	1,030	1,260	1,450
						LH	770	960	1,130	1,280
						HH	830	1,130	1,490	1,910
						LL	820	1,120	1,340	1,490
						HL	800	1,040	1,190	1,320
Use, including seed[21] (mil. bu.)	n.a.	198.5	234.6	332.5	571.8	M	830	1,090	1,340	1,540
						LH	820	1,020	1,200	1,360
						HH	880	1,200	1,580	2,020

Table A12–16 (cont'd)

	1940	1945	1950	1955	1960		1970	1980	1990	2000
Hay and pasture [22] (bil. feed units):						LL	114	136	152	170
						HL	118	137	156	176
Hay	74	82	79	88	100	M	136	186	239	297
						LH	151	215	284	374
						HH	156	215	293	386
						LL	180	160	139	119
						HL	270	303	334	363
Pasture	194	247	205	223	241	M	254	287	306	317
						LH	239	252	259	262
						HH	358	476	626	797
						LL	138	164	183	203
						HL	143	165	187	210
Tons of hay (millions) [23]	91	101	97	108	119	M	165	225	287	355
						LH	183	260	341	447
						HH	189	260	352	462

LL = "Low-Low" projections based on Low (in terms of land) food and fiber demand, and High efficiency in meeting it.
HL = "High-Low": Low demand, Low efficiency.
LH = "Low-High": High demand, High efficiency.
HH = "High-High": High demand, Low efficiency.

1. Based on originally projected demand levels for meat and for fats and oils, as in Tables A12–1 and 7. Following footnotes refer only to derivation of projections. For historical data, see Tables A12–1, 3, 7, 10, and 14.
2. LL = Low demand and High feeding efficiency.
  HL = Low demand and Low feeding efficiency.
  LH = High demand and High feeding efficiency.
  HH = High demand and Low feeding efficiency.
  Basic data from Table A12–1.
3. LL = LL total feed units and High proportion of concentrates.
  HL = HL total feed units and Low proportion of concentrates.
  LH = LH total feed units and High proportion of concentrates.
  HH = HH total feed units and Low proportion of concentrates.
  Basic data from Table A12–3. Subtotals for 1970 to 2000 raised by 10% to account for other livestock.
4. Residuals. For combined cottonseed/soybean oil production, see Table A12–7.
5. LL = Low cotton, High oil/bale.
  HL = Low cotton, Low oil/bale.
  LH = High cotton, High oil/bale.
  HH = High cotton, Low oil/bale.
  Basic data in Table A12–7.
6. LL = LL oil, High meal/oil ratio.
  HL = HL oil, Low meal/oil ratio.
  LH = LH oil, High meal/oil ratio.
  HH = HH oil, Low meal/oil ratio.
  Basic data in Table A12–7.
7. Deduction of 3% for cottonseed meal exports, 5% for soybean meal exports.
8. Converted at 135 feed units per 100 lb. for cottonseed meal, and 165 for soybean.
9. LL = LL cottonseed/soybean, Low % of total high protein.
  HL = HL cottonseed/soybean, High % of total high protein.
  LH = LH cottonseed/soybean, Low % of total high protein.

HH = HH cottonseed/soybean, High % of total high protein.
  Basic data in Table A12–7.
10. LL = LL concentrates, High % of high protein.
  HL = HL concentrates, High % of high protein.
  LH = LH concentrates, Low % of high protein.
  HH = HH concentrates, Low % of high protein.
  On assumption that there is compensation between the two factors. Basic data in Table A12–7.
11. Projection I, in every case where higher. Projection II, where it is higher *and* assumption is one of Low efficiency (HL or HH). (Soybean meal involves a lower feed unit yield per acre than do feed grains.)
12. Total concentrates, less high protein concentrates, for each level.
13. 90% of grains and miscellaneous (1970–2000). Historical data from Table A12–10.
14. Feed use of feed grains, increased by 25%. See footnote 4, Table A12–10.
15. Applying percentages cited in footnote 9. (Originally calculated values used where Projection I controls.)
16. Soybean/cottonseed, less cottonseed.
17. Converted at 165 units per 100 lb.
18. Making same percentage allowance for exports as indicated in footnote 7.
19. LL = LL soybean meal (above), High ratio to beans (48.5).
  HL = HL soybean meal, Low ratio to beans (46.5).
  LH = LH soybean meal, High ratio to beans.
  HH = HH soybean meal, High ratio to beans (because of assumed emphasis on meal as the principal product).
20. Low of Table A12–14 used for LL and HL, high for LH and HH.
21. Seed assumed as 6% of use exclusive of seed at all levels.
22. LL = LL roughage (above), percentages as in "Low land model," Table A12–10.
  HL = HL roughage, percentages as in "High land model."
  LH = LH roughage, percentages as in "Low land model."
  HH = HH roughage, percentages as in "High land model."
23. Conversion factor from Table A12–10.

appendix

to

chapter

13

LUMBER AND WOODPULP

Notes

THE FIRST FOUR tables in this appendix are designed to show some of the quantitative relationships which have prevailed since 1929 between the consumption of wood products, the output of principal wood products such as lumber and pulp, and the attendant drain on the forest resource base of the United States. The effects of imports, and to a lesser extent of exports, on new supply of wood products are also detailed.

In Tables A13–5 and 6, the input-output trends of the past four decades are used in conjunction with projections of timber products consumption, by principal end-use categories, drawn from the appendixes to Part I, to establish the general dimensions of the likely future requirements for forest resources. In these projections, it has seemed best to look at aggregate demand for key timber products —lumber, veneer, pulp, etc.—and to defer to Chapter 18 any consideration of the portions of such demand that might reasonably be met through imports. A partial exception is paper, the imports of which in the form of newsprint are treated, in Chapter 8, as a factor reducing U.S. demand for the key material, pulp.

The information which is presented in the historical tables necessarily reflects the general kinds of forest product statistics collected in the United States. Thus, the data in Table A13–1 on timber products output are not the same as data on annual cut from growing stock; the latter exist for only a few selected years when special studies were made, such as 1952. Instead, timber products output, as

shown in the table, includes wood derived from dead trees and culls, wood from non-commercial forest land, and some wood from trees and parts of trees below growing stock diameter. Thus, an important fraction of the output shown is derived from supplies not classified as part of our "forest inventory," which is measured exclusively in terms of commercial growing stock. At the same time it excludes "logging residues"—growing stock, cut or otherwise killed but not removed from the forest.

Wood products are commonly reported both in official data and in data from the separate wood product industries in a number of different units, such as "board-feet International ¼-inch log rule," "board-feet lumber tally," cords, and square feet. Both the data on new supply of principal wood products and the data on consumption by end-use categories, when available, have been expressed herein in terms of such conventional units. Since we are ultimately concerned, however, with comparisons between demand for and supply of forest products as a whole, we have, in Tables A13–2 and 6, rendered the historical data on new supply and the data on projected demand for wood products into the only practical common denominator, namely, the cubic volume of roundwood from which the products are derived. In spite of the advantages of so doing, this statistical exercise can be misleading if not interpreted in terms of three important qualifications:

(1) The conversions are based upon historical experience with logs designated for removal from

the forest for particular purposes. The figures do not express the total cubic footage of all logs cut, much less the volume of merchantable timber in the trees from which the logs were cut; moreover, as already noted, the trees from which the measured log volumes are cut are not synonymous with "growing stock"—living trees of merchantable quality with minimum diameters of five inches at breast height. The U.S. Forest Service has estimated that in 1952 approximately 1.4 billion cubic feet, or 13 per cent of the growing stock actually cut became logging residues which never left the forest. We may also note that in this year, according to the U.S. Forest Service, domestic output of timber products—estimated as total demand minus net imports—was 11.1 billion cubic feet, of which 1.7 billion was derived not from growing stock but from dead and cull trees. The roundwood output from growing stock was therefore 9.4 billion cubic feet, but the actual cut from growing stock on commercial forest lands (including lands in coastal Alaska) in the same year was 10.8 billion. It is assumed herein that the net of these compensations permits projected total demand for timber, in roundwood equivalent, to be used as a good approximation of what actually is to be cut from commercial growing stock.

(2) While a summation of gross roundwood requirements is attempted, in order to compare the total availability of wood supply with demand, the cubic volume equivalents of the several timber products categories will have to be met in large part from separate and generally mutually exclusive categories of roundwood. For example, the projected requirements for lumber and for veneer and plywood will have to be drawn almost entirely from logs derived from trees at least 9 inches in diameter at breast height. For important uses, one general variety of wood will not substitute for another. In Table A13–6 the aggregate cubic volume requirements for sawlogs for lumber, and for veneer logs separated into softwood and hardwood components, are detailed.

(3) The projected roundwood volumes for the several principal categories of wood products have been derived on the basis of the approximate relationships between the various roundwood inputs and product outputs which have prevailed since 1945. Changes in future input-output relationships could therefore result in errors in the projected roundwood requirements at any particular demand level.

The demand for wood in its raw material form (lumber and pulp), as distinguished from its resource form (logs), is covered in Tables A13–3, 4, and 5. Adequate historical series (Tables A13–3 and 4) are limited to lumber and to pulp; in the case of plywood—especially hardwood plywood and veneer—the coverage is incomplete. Thus, the few historical figures for plywood given in Table A13–5 are estimated on the same basis as the projections. It may be seen from Table A13–6, however, that the estimates thus made, when converted to roundwood equivalent, add to the directly compiled series on veneer log consumption (Table A13–2). The relative proportions of softwood and hardwood also check out with the proportions in data on veneer log production available in similarly broken down form (U.S. Department of Agriculture, *The Demand and Price Situation for Forest Products,* Nov. 1961, Table 12).

In addition to the relationships between the projected demands for principal types of wood products and the volumes of wood needed, we must also consider the degree to which mill and fabricating plant residues may substitute for roundwood. Fairly sizable residues are inevitable at sawmills, although there has been much progress in recent years toward fuller utilization of sawlogs, so that actual "waste" of wood compared to output of wood products has declined markedly. The most important use for mill residues is for fuel, but pulp mills have now also become important consumers of slabs, edgings, and other mill scrap. In Table A13–2 we have considered the use of residues for pulp, since for our purposes residues are of interest wherever they substitute for logs. Apart from those that go into the making of pulp, most mill residues do not so substitute. An exception is the use of mill residues in manufacture of particle board; its substitution for other roundwood products may become significant, but reliable historical data are not available.

Projections of the pulpwood requirements for pulp are developed in Table A13–6, first in terms of the total wood requirement, expressed in cubic feet of roundwood equivalent. Then, in order to derive the net requirements for roundwood, this is projected as a percentage of total requirements. Historically, the proportion of the total consumption of pulpwood derived from residues has increased rapidly in recent years (Table A13–2), reaching 18 per cent in 1960. The Low, Medium, and High projections all assume that this proportion will reach 25 per cent by 1980. The models also assume that the full proportional displacement of roundwood by residues will have reached its probably practical limits by 1980.

TABLE A13–1.   Historical Data on Timber Products Output, by Type

(Million cubic feet)

Year	Total utilized cut[1]	Distribution of cut — Industrial wood[1]											Fuel wood[2]
		Total	Sawlogs for lumber			Veneer logs			Pulpwood			Other products[3]	
			Total	Soft-wood[4]	Hard-wood[4]	Total	Soft-wood[5]	Hard-wood[5]	Total	Soft-wood[6]	Hard-wood[6]		
1929	11,220	8,050	6,020	n.a.	n.a.	200	64	136	455	n.a.	n.a.	1,380	3,170
1930	10,135	6,345	4,560	3,634	926	155	n.a.	n.a.	430	374	56	1,195	3,790
1931	9,015	4,625	3,105	n.a.	n.a.	125	37	88	420	n.a.	n.a.	970	4,390
1932	8,375	3,395	2,100	"	"	120	n.a.	n.a.	345	"	"	830	4,980
1933	9,050	4,045	2,665	"	"	125	45	80	425	"	"	835	5,005
1934	9,180	4,355	2,925	"	"	130	n.a.	n.a.	445	"	"	855	4,825
1935	9,605	5,095	3,565	2,857	708	145	54	91	485	419	66	895	4,510
1936	10,255	5,990	4,295	n.a.	n.a.	165	n.a.	n.a.	555	n.a.	n.a.	975	4,265
1937	10,445	6,370	4,505	"	"	195	73	122	645	"	"	1,020	4,075
1938	9,895	5,570	3,860	"	"	195	n.a.	n.a.	595	"	"	920	4,325
1939	10,565	6,375	4,470	"	"	210	87	123	730	"	"	965	4,190
1940	10,865	6,975	4,845	4,012	833	235	n.a.	n.a.	935	"	"	965	3,890
1941	11,645	8,050	5,680	4,680	1,000	265	"	"	1,075	938	137	1,030	3,595
1942	10,950	8,085	5,645	4,617	1,028	305	128	177	1,135	990	145	1,000	2,865
1943	10,345	7,560	5,325	4,200	1,125	280	105	175	1,030	894	136	920	2,785
1944	10,370	7,455	5,115	3,928	1,187	270	103	167	1,165	1,014	151	905	2,915
1945	9,580	6,605	4,365	3,313	1,052	250	88	162	1,140	976	164	845	2,975
1946	10,380	7,705	5,295	4,045	1,250	255	n.a.	n.a.	1,260	1,067	193	890	2,675
1947	10,775	8,090	5,500	4,370	1,130	275	121	154	1,375	1,189	186	940	2,685
1948	11,030	8,365	5,750	4,623	1,127	290	n.a.	n.a.	1,475	1,291	184	850	2,665
1949	10,160	7,340	5,000	4,131	869	320	"	"	1,275	1,108	167	745	2,820
1950	10,795	8,525	5,905	4,781	1,124	345	"	"	1,500	1,275	225	770	2,270
1951	10,960	8,730	5,780	4,602	1,178	395	199	196	1,830	1,537	293	730	2,230
1952	10,775	8,750	5,820	4,717	1,103	420	248	172	1,810	1,520	290	700	2,025
1953	10,810	8,740	5,710	4,607	1,103	475	296	179	1,895	1,573	322	660	2,070
1954	10,675	8,670	5,650	4,565	1,085	490	317	173	1,930	1,563	367	600	2,005
1955	11,045	9,205	5,785	4,637	1,148	575	388	187	2,155	1,767	388	690	1,840
1956	11,510	9,680	5,920	4,711	1,209	580	400	180	2,420	1,960	460	760	1,830
1957	10,430	8,690	5,100	4,224	876	555	394	161	2,305	1,844	461	730	1,740
1958	10,280	8,575	5,160	4,258	902	620	460	160	2,115	1,692	423	680	1,705
1959	11,135	9,480	5,730	4,752	978	755	556	199	2,285	1,737	548	710	1,655
1960	10,770	9,270	5,410	4,477	933	730	560	170	2,450	1,838	612	680	1,500

Table A13–1 (cont'd)

1. Source: U.S. Department of Agriculture, Forest Service and Agricultural Stabilization and Conservation Service, *The Demand and Price Situation for Forest Products,* Nov. 1961, Table 2.

2. Includes small quantities of imported fuel wood.

3. Includes timber used for poles and piling, round mine timbers, hewn ties, fence posts, cooperage, excelsior, and other miscellaneous items.

4. Derived from USDA, *op. cit.,* Table 7, using regional softwood and hardwood conversion factors specified in U.S. Forest Service, *Timber Resources for America's Future* (Forest Resource Report No. 14, Jan. 1958),

p. 642.

5. Based on conversion of board-foot data for softwoods and hardwoods in USDA, *op. cit.,* Table 12. Conversion factors employed:
   softwoods: 160 cubic feet per thousand board feet.
   hardwoods: 188 cubic feet per thousand board feet.
   Components adjusted to agree with data in "Total" column.

6. Distribution assumed to be identical with distribution indicated in *ibid.,* Table 9.

TABLE A13–2.   Historical Data on Total Consumption of Wood, by Type

(Million cubic feet)

	Total new supply[1]	Sawlogs[2]			Veneer logs[2]			Pulpwood[2]				Total consumption	Per cent from residues	Other products—new supply[2]	Fuel wood—new supply[2]
		Domestic production	Net imports	New supply	Domestic production	Net imports	New supply	Domestic production	Net imports[3]	New supply	Residues[4]				
1929	11,280	6,020	—255	5,765	200	—5	195	455	314	769	43	812	5.30	1,380	3,170
1930	10,250	4,560	—175	4,385	155	—5	150	430	298	728	46	774	5.94	1,195	3,790
1931	9,095	3,105	—150	2,960	125	—5	120	420	242	662	43	705	6.10	970	4,390
1932	8,470	2,100	—120	1,980	120	*	115	345	229	574	34	608	5.59	830	4,980
1933	9,175	2,665	—145	2,520	125	—5	120	425	271	696	37	733	5.05	835	5,005
1934	9,270	2,925	—165	2,760	130	—5	125	445	262	707	18	725	2.48	855	4,825
1935	9,950	3,565	—135	3,630	145	—5	140	485	291	776	23	799	2.88	895	4,510
1936	10,290	4,295	—95	3,995	165	—5	160	555	342	897	25	922	2.71	975	4,265
1937	10,320	4,505	—115	4,015	195	*	195	645	364	1,009	44	1,053	4.18	1,020	4,075
1938	9,995	3,860	—70	3,680	195	*	195	595	284	879	18	897	2.01	920	4,325
1939	10,815	4,470	—60	4,410	210	*	210	730	310	1,040	25	1,065	2.35	965	4,190
1940	11,555	4,845	—35	5,340	235	—5	230	935	195	1,130	21	1,151	1.82	965	3,890
1941	11,860	5,680	105	5,630	265	—5	260	1,075	269	1,344	17	1,361	1.25	1,030	3,595
1942	12,400	5,645	170	6,830	305	—5	300	1,135	269	1,404	15	1,419	1.06	1,000	2,865
1943	11,275	5,325	85	6,020	280	—15	265	1,030	250	1,280	15	1,295	1.16	920	2,785
1944	10,865	5,115	100	5,385	270	—10	260	1,165	228	1,393	22	1,415	1.55	905	2,915
1945	10,280	4,365	100	4,745	250	—10	240	1,140	324	1,464	35	1,499	2.33	845	2,975
1946	10,650	5,295	90	5,200	255	—5	250	1,260	361	1,621	46	1,667	2.76	890	2,675
1947	10,955	5,500	—5	5,260	275	5	265	1,375	417	1,792	58	1,850	3.14	940	2,685
1948	11,370	5,750	190	5,645	290	*	295	1,475	424	1,899	71	1,970	3.60	850	2,665
1949	10,840	5,000	140	5,345	320	*	320	1,275	323	1,598	83	1,681	4.94	745	2,820
1950	11,640	5,905	455	6,330	345	10	350	1,500	414	1,914	96	2,010	4.78	770	2,270
1951	11,565	5,780	235	5,895	395	15	410	1,830	462	2,292	108	2,400	4.50	730	2,225
1952	11,500	5,820	275	6,140	420	15	435	1,810	384	2,194	121	2,315	5.23	700	2,025
1953	11,405	5,710	330	5,915	475	25	500	1,895	358	2,253	133	2,386	5.57	660	2,070
1954	10,855	5,650	365	6,070	490	45	530	1,930	315	2,245	146	2,391	6.11	600	2,005
1955	11,895	5,785	430	6,230	575	60	640	2,155	333	2,488	206	2,694	7.65	690	1,840
1956	12,230	5,920	420	6,205	580	65	645	2,420	361	2,781	270	3,051	8.85	760	1,830
1957	11,400	5,100	335	5,680	555	75	625	2,305	306	2,611	329	2,940	11.19	730	1,740
1958	11,100	5,160	415	5,600	620	80	700	2,115	296	2,411	417	2,828	14.74	680	1,705
1959	11,995	5,730	515	6,165	755	115	870	2,285	300	2,585	511	3,096	16.50	710	1,655
1960	11,475	5,410	480	5,780	730	95	820	2,450	239	2,689	604	3,293	18.34	680	1,500

* Negligible.
1. Sum of components excluding pulpwood residues.
2. *The Demand and Price Situation for Forest Products*, Nov. 1961, Table 2, except as indicated in footnotes 3 and 4.
3. U.S. Bureau of the Census, *Historical Statistics of the United States, Colonial Times to 1957*, 1960, Series L 62 multiplied by 77 (conversion factor for cords of pulpwood), plus L 65 multiplied by 120 (conversion factor for the pulpwood equivalent of pulp). Data for 1958–60 from U.S. Bureau of the Census, *Pulp, Paper and Board* (Current Industrial Reports, Series M26A), 1958, 1959, and 1960. Imports of paper and paperboard are treated in the section on paper (App. A8).
4. *The Demand and Price Situation for Forest Products*, Table 9, converted to cubic feet at the rate of 77 cubic feet per cord.

TABLE A13–3.   Historical Data on Supply and Consumption of Lumber, by End-Use

(Billion board feet)

	Domestic production[1]	Exports[1]	Imports[1]	New supply	Per cent softwoods[2]	End-use consumption[3]				Ratio, new supply to end-use consumption
						Total	Construction[4]	Containers[5]	Other manufactures[6]	
1929	38.7	3.2	1.5	37.1	79.8	32.6	23.8	4.6	4.2	1.14
1930	29.4	2.4	1.2	28.2	79.8	24.2	16.9	4.0	3.3	1.17
1931	20.0	1.7	.7	19.0	80.0	17.4	11.7	3.4	2.3	1.09
1932	13.5	1.2	.4	12.7	80.3	12.0	8.1	2.4	1.4	1.06
1933	17.2	1.3	.4	16.2	80.9	13.9	9.7	2.6	1.6	1.17
1934	18.8	1.3	.3	17.8	77.5	14.1	9.8	2.7	1.7	1.26
1935	22.9	1.3	.4	22.1	79.6	18.0	12.6	3.2	2.2	1.23
1936	27.6	1.3	.7	27.0	80.0	22.3	16.2	3.7	2.5	1.21
1937	29.0	1.4	.7	28.2	80.5	23.7	16.9	4.0	2.8	1.19
1938	24.8	1.0	.5	24.4	80.7	21.5	15.1	3.8	2.5	1.13
1939	28.8	1.1	.7	28.4	81.3	25.3	18.5	4.1	2.8	1.12
1940	31.2	1.0	.7	30.9	82.5	29.6	22.3	4.3	3.0	1.04
1941	36.5	.7	1.4	37.2	82.0	34.2	25.3	5.1	3.8	1.09
1942	36.3	.5	1.5	37.4	81.8	42.0	28.2	9.1	4.7	.89
1943	34.3	.3	.9	34.8	78.7	37.0	17.9	14.1	5.0	.94
1944	32.9	.4	1.0	33.6	76.5	34.0	14.1	15.2	4.7	.99
1945	28.1	.4	1.1	28.7	75.6	31.1	15.6	11.7	3.8	.92
1946	34.1	.6	1.2	34.7	76.1	32.9	22.7	5.7	4.5	1.05
1947	35.4	1.4	1.3	35.4	79.4	33.3	23.7	4.9	4.7	1.06
1948	37.0	.6	1.9	38.2	80.6	35.9	27.5	4.0	4.4	1.06
1949	32.2	.7	1.6	33.1	82.8	33.7	25.8	3.8	4.1	.98
1950	38.0	.5	3.4	40.9	81.7	41.6	32.5	4.3	4.8	.98
1951	37.2	1.0	2.5	38.7	79.8	37.6	28.4	4.5	4.7	1.03
1952	37.5	.7	2.5	39.2	81.4	39.4	30.0	4.7	4.8	.99
1953	36.7	.6	2.8	38.9	81.2	38.1	28.7	4.4	4.9	1.02
1954	36.4	.7	3.1	38.8	81.7	38.5	29.9	4.1	4.5	1.01
1955	37.4	.8	3.6	40.2	80.8	41.1	32.3	4.2	4.6	1.02
1956	38.2	.8	3.4	40.8	81.4	40.5	31.0	4.5	4.9	1.01
1957	32.9	.8	3.0	35.1	83.2	35.5	27.2	4.0	4.3	.99
1958	33.4	.7	3.4	36.1	83.1	36.4	27.6	4.2	4.6	.99
1959	37.1	.8	4.1	40.4	83.7	39.9	30.8	4.3	4.7	1.01
1960	35.0	.9	3.9	38.0	83.5	36.8	28.3	4.1	4.4	1.03

1. 1929–54 from *Timber Resources for America's Future,* Tables 265 and 266. 1955–60 from *The Demand and Price Situation for Forest Products,* Nov. 1961, Table 6.

2. Derived from: 1929–54, *Timber Resources for America's Future,* Table 265; 1955–59, Lumber Manufacturers Association, *Lumber Industry Facts,* 1960–61, Tables 25 and 50; 1960, production plus imports minus exports, in *The Demand and Price Situation for Forest Products,* Table 6, and U.S. Department of Commerce, *U.S. Lumber Exports 1960* (June 1961) and *U.S. Lumber Imports 1960* (Oct. 1961).

3. Mill shipments, less exports, compiled by National Lumber Manufacturers Association. Source: *Lumber Industry Facts,* 1960–61.

4. Includes lumber consumed in railroad box car construction, railroad ties (except hewn), and other railroad uses.

5. Includes only boxes and crating.

6. Includes furniture, fixtures, caskets, vehicle bodies, wooden-ware and novelties, handles, and other miscellaneous wooden items, as well as shipping pallets.

TABLE A13–4. Historical Data on Supply and Consumption of Woodpulp

(Million short tons)

	Domestic production[1]	Net imports[1]	New supply[1]	Per cent softwoods[2]	End-use consumption[3]			Ratio, new supply to end-use consumption
					Total	Paper	Other uses[4]	
1929	4.9	1.8	6.7	n.a.	6.7	6.3	.4	1.00
1930	4.6	1.8	6.4	86.9	n.a.	n.a.	n.a.	–
1931	4.4	1.5	5.9	n.a.	"	"	"	–
1932	3.8	1.4	5.2	"	"	"	"	–
1933	4.3	1.9	6.2	"	"	"	"	–
1934	4.4	1.7	6.1	"	"	"	"	–
1935	4.9	1.8	6.7	86.4	6.6	6.4	.2	1.02
1936	5.7	2.1	7.8	n.a.	n.a.	n.a.	n.a.	–
1937	6.6	2.1	8.7	"	"	"	"	–
1938	5.9	1.6	7.5	"	"	"	"	–
1939	7.0	1.9	8.9	"	8.9	8.7	.2	1.00
1940	9.0	.7	9.7	"	10.1	9.8	.3	.96
1941	10.4	.8	11.2	86.6	11.7	11.4	.3	.96
1942	10.8	.9	11.6	87.2	11.5	11.0	.5	1.01
1943	9.7	1.0	10.7	86.8	11.1	10.6	.5	.96
1944	10.1	.8	11.0	87.6	11.1	10.5	.6	.99
1945	10.2	1.6	11.8	85.6	11.3	10.8	.5	1.04
1946	10.6	1.8	12.4	84.7	12.6	12.1	.5	.98
1947	11.9	2.2	14.1	86.5	13.9	13.3	.6	1.01
1948	12.9	2.1	15.0	87.5	15.0	14.4	.6	1.00
1949	12.2	1.6	13.8	86.9	14.1	13.6	.5	.98
1950	14.8	2.3	17.1	86.0	17.2	16.5	.6	.99
1951	16.5	2.2	18.7	84.9	18.5	17.7	.8	1.01
1952	16.5	1.7	18.2	85.3	18.0	17.3	.8	1.01
1953	17.5	2.0	19.5	84.0	19.5	18.7	.8	1.00
1954	18.3	1.6	19.9	82.2	19.7	19.0	.8	1.01
1955	20.7	1.6	22.3	82.8	22.3	21.5	.8	1.00
1956	22.1	1.8	23.9	82.7	23.8	23.0	.8	1.00
1957	21.8	1.5	23.3	82.0	23.3	22.5	.9	1.00
1958	21.8	1.6	23.4	82.2	23.3	22.5	.8	1.00
1959	24.4	1.8	26.2	79.3	26.1	25.2	.9	1.00
1960	25.3	1.2	26.5	78.8	26.6	25.7	.9	1.00

1. 1929–56 from U.S. Bureau of the Census, *Historical Statistics of the United States,* Series L 64–66. 1957–60 from U.S. Bureau of the Census, *Pulp, Paper and Board* (Current Industrial Reports, Series M26A), 1958, 1959, and 1960.

2. Distribution assumed to be the same as distribution for pulpwood in USDA, *The Demand and Price Situation for Forest Products,* Nov. 1961, Table 9.

3. 1929 and 1935 from U.S. Bureau of the Census (in cooperation with U.S. Forest Service), *Forest Products,* 1929, 1935. 1939–56 from U.S. Congress, House Committee on Interstate and Foreign Commerce, *Pulp, Paper, and Board, Supply-Demand* (H. Rept. No. 573, 85th Cong., 1st Sess.), Table 86. 1957–60 from U.S. Bureau of the Census, *Pulp, Paper and Board,* 1958, 1959, and 1960.

4. Includes rayon and acetate yarn, cellophane, and other cellulosics.

TABLE A13–5.   Projected End-Use Consumption of Principal Wood Products

	1950	1955	1960		1970	1980	1990	2000
Lumber[1] (bil. bd. ft.):								
Use in construction[2]	32.5	32.3	28.3	L	26.5	26.2	24.9	26.2
				M	38.8	46.4	57.4	76.3
				H	50.3	67.6	97.5	157.5
Use in manufacture of containers[3]	4.3	4.2	4.1	L	3.0	2.1	1.6	1.3
				M	5.7	6.6	7.2	6.7
				H	7.9	10.9	14.0	16.5
Use in all manufactures other than containers[4]	4.8	4.6	4.4	L	4.7	4.5	4.0	4.0
				M	7.1	8.9	11.5	14.6
				H	9.2	15.0	24.4	39.5
Use in furniture and fixtures[5]	1.8	2.0	2.2	L	2.0	1.9	1.7	1.7
				M	3.0	3.8	4.9	6.2
				H	3.9	6.4	10.4	16.8
Total consumption	41.6	41.1	36.8	L	34.2	32.8	30.5	31.5
				M	51.6	61.9	76.1	97.6
				H	67.4	93.5	135.9	213.5
Softwoods[6]	34.0	33.2	30.7	L	28.4	27.2	25.3	26.1
				M	42.8	51.4	63.2	81.0
				H	55.9	77.6	112.8	177.2
Hardwoods[6]	7.6	7.9	6.1	L	5.8	5.6	5.2	5.4
				M	8.8	10.5	12.9	16.6
				H	11.5	15.9	23.1	36.3
Plywood and veneer (bil. sq. ft.):								
Softwood[7]	2.7	5.3	7.7	L	11.1	15.9	20.2	25.8
				M	16.8	26.6	42.0	62.7
				H	22.9	43.5	77.5	137.4
Adjusted softwood[8]				L	11.6	17.0	22.3	29.1
				H	21.8	39.3	66.7	118.2
Hardwood[9]	10.6	13.6	14.2	L	16.8	20.0	23.4	29.8
				M	23.3	32.5	46.2	70.2
				H	30.9	49.9	81.4	147.4
Pulp[10] (mil. short tons)	17.2	22.3	26.6	L	35.4	47.1	60.7	76.4
				M	38.8	56.4	79.5	110.1
				H	43.9	70.3	109.6	169.6
Consumption for paper[11]	16.5	21.5	25.7	L	34.8	46.6	60.1	75.8
				M	37.9	55.4	78.3	108.7
				H	42.6	68.4	106.9	165.5
Ratio, total consumption to consumption for paper[12]	104.2	103.7	103.5	L	101.7	101.1	101.0	100.8
				M	102.4	101.8	101.5	101.3
				H	103.1	102.8	102.5	102.5

Table A13–5 (cont'd)

1. Historical data from Table A13–3.
2. From Table A4–7.
3. From Table A7–6.
4. Projections calculated at 2.35 times lumber used in furniture and fixtures. This is the average for 1948, 1952, 1953, and 1954, years for which data on consumption of lumber in furniture and consumption of lumber in all manufactures other than boxes and crating are available. It is assumed that the relationship will continue.
5. From Table A6–8. 1950 and 1955 derived by straight-line interpolation between selected years there shown.
6. Based on recent experience (Table A13–3), softwoods assumed to constitute 83% of total consumption. Hardwoods are the residual.
7. Arithmetically the same as total plywood for construction, projected in Table A4–7. The roughly one-fourth of construction plywood which is hardwood has been approximately balanced by the proportion of softwood plywood which is not for construction, and it is assumed that this relationship will continue.
8. The Low and the High shown here are those consistent with the corresponding levels of lumber consumption, using the adjusted plywood projections given at the end of Table A4–7. Compensation in non-construction uses is assumed to be negligible.
9. Of which perhaps half may be veneer. Projected at 2.5 square feet per $ 1960 billion of new construction (Table A4–3). While only a minor portion of hardwood plywood and veneer goes directly into construction, many of its other uses (e.g., furniture) tend to vary roughly with construction activity. The same coefficient, based on relationship in 1952, 1953, and 1955, was also used to estimate the historical data.
10. Historical data from Table A13–4. Projections on basis of series that follow.
11. From Table A8–3.
12. Projected on the basis of trial calculations as to relative requirements of pulp for fibers and plastics.

TABLE A13–6. Projected End-Use Consumption of Wood, in Roundwood Equivalent

(Billion cubic feet)

	1950	1955	1960		1970	1980	1990	2000
Sawlogs for lumber[1]	6.3	6.2	5.8	L	5.3	5.1	4.7	4.9
				M	8.0	9.6	11.9	15.1
				H	10.5	14.5	21.1	33.2
Softwood	5.2	4.9	4.9	L	4.4	4.2	3.9	4.1
				M	6.7	8.0	9.9	12.6
				H	8.7	12.1	17.6	27.6
Hardwood	1.1	1.3	.9	L	.9	.9	.8	.8
				M	1.3	1.6	2.0	2.5
				H	1.8	2.4	3.5	5.6
Veneer logs[2]	.4	.6	.8	L	1.2	1.6	2.0	2.6
				M	1.6	2.5	3.9	5.8
				H	2.1	3.7	6.3	11.2
Softwood	.2	.4	.6	L	.8	1.2	1.5	1.9
				M	1.2	2.0	3.1	4.6
				H	1.7	3.2	5.7	10.1
Adjusted softwood	–	–	–	L	.9	1.3	1.6	2.1
				H	1.6	2.9	4.9	8.7
Hardwood	.2	.2	.2	L	.3	.3	.4	.5
				M	.4	.5	.8	1.2
				H	.5	.8	1.4	2.5
Pulpwood:								
Total requirements for wood[3]	2.0	2.7	3.3	L	4.2	5.7	7.3	9.2
				M	4.7	6.8	9.5	13.2
				H	5.3	8.4	13.2	20.4
Per cent from roundwood[4]	95.22	92.35	81.66		78.3	75.0	75.0	75.0
Net requirements for roundwood	1.9	2.5	2.7	L	3.3	4.3	5.5	6.9
				M	3.7	5.1	7.1	9.9
				H	4.1	6.3	9.9	15.3
Per cent softwoods[5]	86.0	82.8	78.8		76.6	74.4	72.2	70.0
Softwood	1.6	2.1	2.1	L	2.5	3.2	4.0	4.8
				M	2.8	3.8	5.1	6.9
				H	3.1	4.7	7.1	10.7
Hardwood	.3	.4	.6	L	.8	1.1	1.5	2.1
				M	.9	1.3	2.0	3.0
				H	1.0	1.6	2.8	4.6
Total, principal types	8.5	9.3	9.2	L	9.8	11.0	12.2	14.4
				M	13.3	17.2	22.9	30.8
				H	16.7	24.5	37.3	59.7
Softwood	7.0	7.4	7.5	L	7.8	8.7	9.5	11.0
				M	10.7	13.8	18.1	24.1
				H	13.4	19.7	29.6	47.0
Hardwood	1.5	1.9	1.7	L	2.0	2.3	2.7	3.4
				M	2.6	3.4	4.8	6.7
				H	3.3	4.8	7.7	12.7
Miscellaneous timber:								
Minor structural wood products[6]	.37	.38	.36	L	.31	.26	.24	.22
				M	.41	.42	.48	.54
				H	.52	.63	.84	1.11
Total miscellaneous timber[7]	.77	.69	.68	L	.50	.42	.38	.35
				M	.66	.67	.77	.86
				H	.83	1.01	1.34	1.78

Table A13–6 (cont'd)

(Billion cubic feet)

	1950	1955	1960		1970	1980	1990	2000
Softwood	.36	.32	.32	L	.24	.20	.18	.16
				M	.31	.31	.36	.40
				H	.39	.47	.63	.84
Hardwood	.41	.37	.36	L	.26	.22	.20	.19
				M	.35	.36	.41	.46
				H	.44	.54	.71	.94
Fuel wood (from forest and woodland cuttings)[8]	2.3	1.8	1.4	L	.98	.65	.43	.30
				M	1.08	.81	.66	.60
				H	1.16	1.00	.92	.90
Softwood	.55	.43	.34	L	.24	.16	.10	.07
				M	.26	.19	.16	.14
				H	.28	.24	.22	.22
Hardwood	1.75	1.37	1.06	L	.74	.49	.33	.23
				M	.82	.62	.50	.46
				H	.88	.76	.70	.68
Total timber consumption	11.6	11.9	11.5	L	11.3	12.1	13.0	15.0
				M	15.1	18.7	24.3	32.3
				H	18.7	26.5	39.6	62.4
Softwood	7.9	8.2	8.3	L	8.3	9.1	9.8	11.2
				M	11.3	14.3	18.6	24.7
				H	14.1	20.4	30.5	48.1
Hardwood	3.7	3.7	3.2	L	3.0	3.0	3.2	3.8
				M	3.8	4.4	5.7	7.6
				H	4.6	6.1	9.1	14.3

1. Historical data based on "new supply," Table A13–2, and percentage softwood, Table A13–3. Projected figures for total lumber are sums of components, which are conversions of board-foot data in Table A13–5. Conversion factors:
        Softwood—156 cubic feet per thousand board feet
        Hardwood—153 cubic feet per thousand board feet

2. Historical data based on "new supply," Table A13–2, and hardwood-softwood proportions of veneer-log production, *The Demand and Price Situation for Forest Products*, Nov. 1961, Table 12. Projected figures for total plywood are sums of plywood components, using adjusted "Low" and "High" consumption of softwood to allow for compensation between lumber and plywood (Table A13–5). Conversion factors derived as follows:
        Softwood—(.46 M bd. ft. per M sq. ft.) $\times$ (160 cu. ft. per M bd. ft.) = 73.6 cu. ft. per M sq. ft. Bd. ft. per sq. ft. derived as average of 1951–60 ratios between board feet in *The Demand and Price Situation for Forest Products*, Table 12, and square feet in U.S. Bureau of the Census, *Softwood Plywood and Veneer*, 1960 (Current Industrial Reports, No. M24 H(60)–1, Table 2.
        Hardwood—(.09 M bd. ft. per M sq. ft.) $\times$ (188 cu. ft. per M bd. ft.) = 16.9 cu. ft. per M sq. ft. Bd. ft. per sq. ft. derived as average of 1952–53 ratios between bd. ft. in *The Demand and Price Situation*, Table 12, and square feet in *Timber Resources for America's Future*, pp. 445 and 447.

3. Historical data from Table A13–2. Projections converted from Table A13–5 using 120 cubic feet per ton of pulp.

4. Historical data represent residual of "total consumption of wood for pulp" minus "per cent from residues," Table A13–2. The single extrapolated percentage series is taken to represent not only the Medium, but the Low percentage consistent with Low consumption and the High percentage consistent with High consumption.

5. Historical percentage assumed to be same as for wood pulp production (Table A13–4). Projected on a judgment basis, taking into account recent technological developments (see Chapter 13, p. 255).

6. From Table A4–7. Includes posts, poles, piling, and mine timbers.

7. Historical data (for total) from Table A13–2. Assumed to stabilize, in the future, at 1.6 times the consumption of timber for minor structural products. Some 47% of miscellaneous timber was derived from softwoods in 1952. Continuation of this percentage assumed.

8. Totals extrapolated on a judgment basis. Twenty-four per cent of fuelwood was softwood in 1952; continuation of this percentage is assumed.

appendix
to
chapter
14

WATER

Notes

IN CHAPTER 14, fresh water uses were divided into three categories: *withdrawal* uses; *flow* uses; and *on site* uses. The total demand which these uses make upon fresh water supplies was defined as the depletion (evapotranspiration plus discharges of effluent into saline water) attributable to *withdrawal* and *on site* uses and the demand for stream-flow as such. Where quantitative projections of *flow* and *on site* demands were used in the text they were straightforwardly adopted from the reports to the Senate Select Committee on National Water Resources (86th Cong., 2nd Sess.). Demand (water depletion) stemming from *withdrawal* uses was independently projected for the three geographical regions shown in Figure 14–1. These projections were based on the framework projections of economic and demographic growth which underlie all sections of this volume. Other general economic and technical assumptions basic to the projections are stated in Chapter 14. Specific calculation procedures are outlined in the footnotes to the appendix tables. The purpose of the present note is to explain certain matters of methodology and concept in more detail than was used in the text.

The major withdrawal uses of fresh water are for municipal, thermal-electric power, manufacturing, and irrigation purposes. A brief section is devoted to each of these.

Municipal Supplies

The depletion of water in municipal systems (including municipally supplied minor industrial use)

was taken to be the sum of evapotranspiration losses (largely occurring in yard watering and air cooling) and water withdrawals of municipal systems which discharge effluent into the ocean or saline bays and estuaries. The increase in these losses is the co-ordinate result of changes in their per capita amounts and changes in population served by municipal systems. High, Low, and Medium projections of urban population were taken to represent the latter variable. The projection of regional distribution of urban population used was that provided by Resources for the Future to the Senate Select Committee on Water Resources (U.S. Senate, Select Committee on National Water Resources, *Water Resource Activities in the United States,* Committee Print No. 5, *Population Projections and Economic Assumptions,* Washington, Mar. 1960). In all calculations of municipal water use and depletion, large industrial users connected to municipal supplies were excluded. They are included in the estimates of manufacturing depletion.

For reasons explained in Chapter 14 (pp. 262–63), per capita withdrawals and per capita evapotranspiration were assumed to be constant at their 1954 level over the projection period. Consequently gross withdrawals for a given region in a given year were obtained by multiplying the urban population projected for that year by 1954 per capita withdrawals of 106 gallons per day in the East, 129 in the West, and 141 in the Pacific Northwest.

The procedure adopted for the estimation of depletion losses required that the proportion of regional withdrawals made by cities which discharge effluent into saline receiving water be estimated. The withdrawals of cities where this was judged to be the case were tabulated from the U.S. Public Health Service publication, *Municipal Water Facilities, Communities of 25,000 Population and Over, 1960,* and compared with estimated regional municipal withdrawals. The percentages of withdrawals destined for saline discharge were computed to be 38 in the East, 50 in the West, and 59 in the Pacific Northwest. These percentages were assumed to hold for all three levels of projections and to be unchanged over the projection period. The calculated portion of withdrawals destined for saline discharge was counted a loss or depletion in each region.

Losses due to evapotranspiration were calculated for the remainder of projected municipal gross withdrawals. This was done on the assumption that these losses would be 10 per cent of withdrawals in the East and Pacific Northwest and 20 per cent of withdrawals in the balance of the West. The percentages (with the exception of the one for the Pacific Northwest) are estimates which were used by the Senate Select Committee. There are no direct estimates of municipal evapotranspiration available.

Projected levels of evapotranspiration and withdrawals of systems discharging into saline supplies were summed to yield the estimates of total depletion due to municipal use. It is interesting to note that the latter source of municipal losses is a multiple of the former in each region.

Because of the relative importance of calculated losses due to effluent discharge into saline water, it must be noted that the appropriate handling of these discharges in water demand estimates presents a somewhat complex problem. Simply treating them as losses represents the judgment that this will come closer to indicating their importance than any other simple assumption. However, some brief discussion of the conceptual problem they present is in order. This discussion may usefully proceed by exploring three possible types of situations:

1. *No flow requirement.* If evapotranspiration is taken to be the only factor bearing upon reuse possibilities for water (i.e., there is no streamflow requirement), an increase in withdrawal by a coastal user (short for a municipality or other user withdrawing fresh water and discharging into saline water) will reduce the potential depletion at other points on the stream by a roughly equivalent amount. This is independent of whether the coastal user operates the "last" intake or makes his withdrawals upstream, since an increase in withdrawals at a downstream point will require an increase in

flow commitment to that point. There may be some amount of saving in evapotranspiration if the coastal user taps his supply far upstream. In the absence of evapotranspiration from the stream, the point of diversion by coastal users would make no difference to the impact on physical supply. This view of the matter is consistent with some recent analyses of the water supply outlook which have simply compared evapotranspiration and an estimate of flow. The implication is that flow can be "used up." This view, however, neglects the fact that some amount of flow will ordinarily be required for navigation and/or waste dilution.

2. *Flow requirement—coastal user withdrawals at last feasible point of use.* If a streamflow requirement for either of the above purposes is imposed, some amount of flow into saline water is associated with the requirement. In this case upstream potential use (depletion plus flow use) will not be reduced *until some minimum amount is withdrawn at the coastal location* (i.e., one of the consequences of a streamflow requirement is that not all of the flow may be depleted at locations upstream from the coastal user). Once the coastal user's withdrawal reaches the required flow, presuming the stream's capacity is fully utilized, any increase will require a cutback upstream sufficient to yield the additional flow. Since the minimum flow standard was previously met, this will mean an increase in flow which serves no useful purpose upstream. It follows that the largest permissible withdrawal and depletion is achieved when upstream withdrawals are just high enough to permit the minimum flow requirement to be met and the coastal user withdraws the exact amount of flow reaching his intake. If the coastal user withdraws less than this, he could withdraw more without displacing upstream use. If he withdraws more, the upstream users must release an equivalent amount of flow.

Where required dilution (or navigation) flows are heavy in relation to depletion, projected withdrawals at coastal locations may have *no* effect on upstream potential, i.e., these withdrawals and attendant evapotranspiration should simply be neglected in assessing the adequacy of supplies. In areas where dilution flows are low in relation to depletion (or more accurately, where the residual flow destined for the ocean in any case is small in relation to projected withdrawal at coastal sites), projected levels will cut back upstream potential depletion. The diminution will be by the full amount by which coastal withdrawals exceed waste dilution flow. In other words, when coastal withdrawal exceeds the dilution flow, dilution requirements become irrelevant and upstream depletion plus coastal withdrawal cannot exceed streamflow. Thus the situation reverts to that described in paragraph 1 above.

One other matter deserves mention. If a certain fresh water flow is needed to maintain a barrier against saline water intrusion in estuaries, the discharge of a coastal user may or may not help to meet the requirement. If the coastal user discharges into the upper reaches of an estuary (but where the water is already too saline for subsequent use), the discharge will help to maintain the barrier. But if wastes are discharged at sea, say to avoid pollution of estuaries or bays, the withdrawal of the coastal user will not help maintain the barrier. If the flow requirement for maintaining the barrier dominates other flow requirements, the first case requires that evapotranspiration attributable to the coastal user be counted as depletion. The second case requires that the entire withdrawal of the coastal user be considered a loss.

3. *Flow requirement—upstream withdrawal.* Where a coastal user withdraws his water far upstream, appropriate handling of his withdrawals is more straightforward. Presuming, for simplicity, that he withdraws it at the headwaters of the stream, the amount available for dilution and depletion by users at locations intermediate between his intake and the ocean is reduced by a quantity equivalent to his withdrawal, i.e., his withdrawal can be straightforwardly added to the depletions and flow requirements of other users in order to arrive at total requirements. The effect of his withdrawal is exactly the same as that of a reduction in streamflow. This third case seems to fit roughly the situation with respect to a number of large coastal cities. In general this is the case to which municipal coastal users (with their high quality requirements for intake water) are assumed to conform in the set of projections made for this section.

To handle discharges into saline water in a really precise fashion would require detailed examination of individual cases, an undertaking beyond the scope of the present study. The procedure adopted somewhat overstates the losses attributable to municipal discharges into saline water. Investigation of individual cases would undoubtedly identify some which make withdrawals at coastal points not going beyond the flow required for purposes not adversely affected by such withdrawals.

Thermal-electric Power Generation

Virtually all the water loss in thermal-electric power production results from evaporation of water which has been used for cooling. There are no data available which show the magnitude of this loss.

The reason is that published information on water withdrawals and discharge by thermal-electric plants reveals only water lost in the plant. An additional amount of induced evaporation occurs when the warmed cooling water is discharged into a body of receiving water. Consequently a method of computing losses is necessary which permits estimation of total depletion (depletion in the plant and in the stream) attributable to thermal-electric power generation.

In the thermal-electric power industry (and other industries where water is used for condenser cooling or other cooling during which the water is confined) there is no loss in the actual cooling process itself. However, when cooling water is recirculated it must be recooled after emerging from the condenser, and this step does involve evaporation. A cooling tower cools by causing a small part of the total water passing through it to evaporate. The amount of water so lost can be accurately forecast since it is a straightforward function of the amount of water being cooled and the temperature loss entailed. In general, about one per cent of the water going through the tower will be evaporated for each 10°F temperature drop.

The difference between water intake and discharge shown by Federal Power Commission statistics is a direct function of the amount of recirculation. Some plants recirculate water many times and cause virtually all of the water they take in to evaporate; others do not recirculate at all and no loss is recorded for them. In regional and national figures, these plants are averaged together. The figures on losses show marked regional variation since there is a tendency to recirculate where water is in stringent supply.

If losses occurred only in the plant itself, existing information would supply a satisfactory indication of water physically removed from regional supply by thermal-electric power plants. Such information, in the form of an "input-output" coefficient adjusted for changing efficiency, might then be utilized in conjunction with kilowatt-hour output projections, to estimate water depletion. However, if water is discharged into a stream or pond at a higher temperature than when it was withdrawn from the source, some additional evaporation is induced in the receiving water. In other words, once-through cooling water may not sustain *any* evaporation loss in the plant but some subsequent loss will occur from the stream surface after discharge. This loss occurs because stream temperature is raised to some degree. How large a loss it will be is somewhat problematical.

Three physical processes are involved in water temperature change—evaporation, convection, and radiation. George O. G. Löf, a consulting engineer and consultant to Resources for the Future, gives the opinion that the latter two are of modest net significance in the cooling of warm water effluents. The projected values for water losses in thermal-electric power generation, therefore, assume that a reasonably predictable amount of evaporation is induced by the recooling of water after it has been warmed by a pass through a condenser, and that the amount of this loss is about the same whether it occurs in a stream or in a cooling tower. There is little or no relevant empirical evidence on heat losses from streams. The technique used to calculate such losses in this study yields an estimate of the maximum loss, given the amount of heat to be dissipated.

In other words, at a given rate of generating efficiency (Btu equivalent of fuel input compared to Btu equivalent electric energy produced), a certain amount of heat must be dissipated by the cooling water and the amount of evaporation induced is directly related to the temperature rise whether the water is subsequently recirculated or not. Using this rule of thumb, a simple factor (adjusted for changing efficiency over time) can be applied to projected kwh generation to obtain losses which include those resulting from the discharge of a warm effluent into a water course.

At present efficiency about 6,230 Btu's of heat must be dissipated by cooling water per kwh generated. This is the result of a Btu equivalent fuel consumption of about 10,700, of which some 10 per cent goes up the stack or is lost in a number of individually minor ways (estimate by Mr. Löf), about 3,400 is converted into electrical energy, and the remainder (about 6,230) is transferred to the cooling water.

The evaporation of about a pound of water is required for the dissipation of 1,000 Btu's. A 10°F temperature drop in a pound of water requires the removal of about 10 Btu's. Thus in order to cool 100 pounds of water 10°, 1,000 Btu's must be removed; this can be done by evaporating 1 pound or 1 per cent of the water.

The portion of heat transferred to the cooling water in the generation of one kwh of electricity is sufficient to raise approximately 75 gallons of water 10°F. Since about 1 per cent of the water must be evaporated to cool 10°, this means that about three-fourths of a gallon of water must be evaporated for each kwh generated.

Improvement in the conversion of fuel energy to electrical energy has been reducing cooling requirements for many years. In 1954, approximately 12,180 Btu's on the average were needed to generate one kwh. By 1980, this may well decline to about 9,050 Btu's, a figure comparable to the performance of the most advanced plants at the present time. The rate of further advance after 1980 will depend in part on the relative cost of fuels. However, in the course of time a situation will be approached in which the marginal costs of further improvements in plant efficiency cease to be justified by savings in fuel expenditure. Consequently, it appears that there will be a gradual slowing down in the rate of increase in generating efficiency in the latter part of the century. On the basis of this reasoning, it is assumed that the heat requirement will have fallen to about 7,600 Btu's per kwh by the year 2000. (See Chapter 15, under "Efficiency: The Heat Rate" for discussion of the reasoning underlying the assumed heat rate and Table A15–10 for the basic data from which this estimate was constructed). The attendant reductions in evaporation per kwh result from less Btu *use* per kwh in relation to the constant (3,413) number of Btu's actually *converted* to electricity. Only the residual heat needs to be dissipated.

On the basis of projected fuel use per kwh generated, the water evaporated per kwh is projected as follows:

Year	Gallons
1954	.92
1960	.76
1970	.67
1980	.58
1990	.50
2000	.42

These amounts were multiplied by the regional High, Medium, and Low projections of kwh generation to obtain projected total cooling water depletion for each region. The regional projections of kwh generation were made on the assumption that the present distribution of generating activity (as estimated in Edward A. Ackerman and George O. G. Löf, *Technology in American Water Development,* Baltimore: Johns Hopkins Press and Resources for the Future, 1959) would change in proportion to projected population shifts. Regional population distributions used in making this calculation were the same as those provided by Resources for the Future to the Senate Select Committee on National Water Resources (*op. cit.*). Fresh water depletion was estimated on the assumption that the present relationship (as estimated from Federal Power Commission statistics) between brackish and fresh water use would persist in each of the regions.

The projections of fresh water depletion are independent of the degree to which recirculation is adopted in the future. Since the focus of the study is upon water depletion rather than withdrawals, no attempt was made to project future rates of recirculation. It was not considered necessary to take special account of the effects of fresh water withdrawals and discharge of effluent into saline water bodies as was done in the case of municipal supplies. Most plants with coastal locations either use ocean water for cooling already or could do so should a situation of water stringency develop.

Manufacturing

About two-thirds of all water used by industry is for cooling, and the remainder serves a great variety of other purposes in industrial processing. The cooling function accounts for by far the largest proportion of industrial water losses. As in the case of thermal power plants, available statistics do not reveal losses which occur subsequent to discharges of hot effluents into water courses. The procedure by which these losses were calculated is described below.

As in the case of thermal-electric plants, no effort was made to project recirculation rates or water withdrawals. Also it was assumed that the 1954 relationship (as shown by the U.S. Census of Manufactures) between fresh and saline water use would persist over the projection period, and that non-water-using types of cooling would not substantially affect industrial water use beyond the degree they now do. In contrast, however, to the assumption made in projecting water depletion by thermal-electric power plants, it was assumed that there would be no reflection of an over-all gain in energy use efficiency in future cooling water use per unit of manufacturing output.

Petroleum refining is discussed first, not because it is the most important source of industrial water depletion, but because most of the water used in the industry (over 80 per cent) is for cooling and the technique used to estimate losses is most nearly like that used for thermal-electric power.

In principle, the best way to determine cooling water evaporation is to calculate the amount of heat transferred to water as a function of the output of the industry and directly deduce the implied evaporation, as was done in the case of thermal-electric generation. However, information necessary to do this for industry is lacking. There are no figures on the amount of heat directly dissipated to the air, for example, and accurate data on the Btu value of fuel input are not available. However, a rough estimate of total (in-plant and post-discharge) evaporation due to petroleum refining can be obtained from Census data by computing evaporation of the recirculated portion of the water used and attribut-

ing the same evaporation rate to that portion not recirculated. This rests on the assumption, explained in the section on thermal power, above, that a given temperature rise in cooling water induces about the same amount of evaporation whether the water is recooled in a tower or in a stream receiving the warmed effluent. It may be noted that, since recirculation rates are much higher in refining than in thermal power (reflecting the different location pattern of the industry), the in-plant losses recorded by the Census are a much larger proportion of total losses.

The 1954 Census of Manufactures shows the following pertinent information for the petroleum refining industry:

		Billion gallons per year (bgy)
A	Water intake—total	1,220
	A_1 Water intake—fresh	655
	A_2 Water intake—brackish	565
B	Water discharge	1,111
C	Water use	4,083*

* The total amount of water serving cooling or other purposes in the plant. It is the sum of water intake and water recirculation net of losses in cooling towers.

From this it may be computed that water evaporation in the plants of the industry was (D) 109 bgy $= (A - B)$ and that the total water use provided by recirculated water in the industry was (E) 2,863 bgy $= (C - A)$. It seems reasonable to assume that the losses in the industry resulted from recooling of water to be recirculated, so the entire loss was attributed to the recirculated portion of water use. About 3.7 per cent of the total amount of water put through the recooling processes was lost, $\dfrac{D}{E+D}$. This would imply a heat gain of about 37°F in the cooling process—an apparently reasonable figure.[1]

Fresh water depletion for 1954 was computed by

1. An alternative formulation of the idea explained above follows:

Fresh water intake in petroleum refining in 1954 was 665 bgy, consequently the average rate of fresh water recirculation =
$$\frac{(E + D)}{655 \text{ bgy}} = \frac{2,972 \text{ bgy}}{655 \text{ bgy}} = 4.5.$$
Since only fresh water is recirculated, fresh water losses as a proportion of intake =
$$\frac{109 \text{ bgy}}{655 \text{ bgy}} = .166.$$
Since fresh water intake is sent through the cooling towers on an average of 4.5 times, the proportion lost in each pass =
$$\frac{.166}{4.5} = .037.$$

applying .04 (rounded from .037 in the actual calculations because of the imprecision of the basic data) to fresh water use in 1954.[2] This calculation yielded an estimate of total *fresh* water losses (in-plant and post-discharge). Projected water losses were computed on the assumption that water depletion per unit of output will remain constant over the projection period. Consequently the projected percentage increase in production was applied di-rectly to computed 1954 water losses. The same procedure was used for all three levels of the projection, i.e., the projections vary only because projected production varies.

If we visualize the data provided by the Census as applying to a single large plant, we can sketch the considerations discussed above as follows (figures in billion gallons per year):

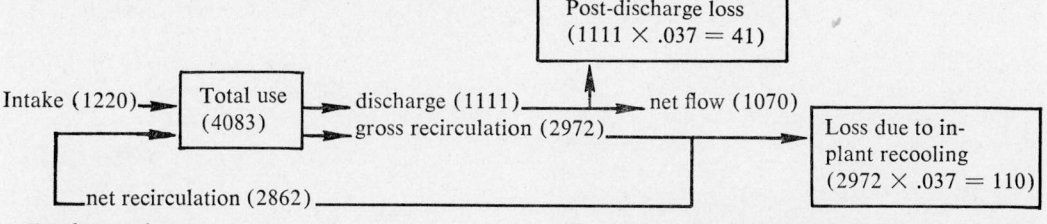

Total water loss
110 loss in plant
 41 post-discharge loss
151 total loss = .037 × total use

Fresh water loss = .037 × fresh water use, i.e., .037 × 3518 = 130.
Alternatively, fresh water loss = 110 (loss in plant) + .037 times fresh water discharge, i.e., 110 + .037 (655 − 110) = 130.

The chemicals industry presents a more complex problem. The relevant figures are provided directly by the Census or calculated from the data provided there.

		Billion gallons per year
A	Water intake	2,810
B	Water discharge	2,554
C	Water use—total	5,004
D	Water loss in plant	256
E	Water net recirculation	2,194
F	Water intake—brackish	513

Calculation of loss as a per cent of water beginning the recirculation process (in the same manner as for the petroleum industry) yields roughly 10 per cent—a figure too high to be accounted for by losses in cooling towers since it implies a tem-perature rise of about 100°F. Other factors, such as embodiment of water in product, evaporation losses in process uses, and open air cooling, are apparently significantly large. Consequently the following procedure was adopted to derive a factor for application to water use to obtain a loss figure which comprehends post-effluent discharge as well as in-plant losses.

First, it was assumed, on the basis of engineering advice, that the average discharge temperature of chemical plants is about 20° higher than intake temperature. This implies that about 2 per cent of the effluent would be lost by evaporation after discharge. Again visualizing the data provided by the Census as applying to a single, large plant, the relevant variables can be outlined as follows (figures in billion gallons per year):

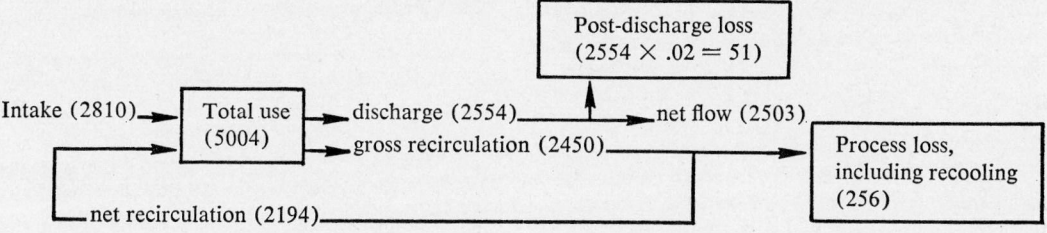

Total water loss
256 loss in plant
 51 post-discharge loss
307 total loss = .06 × total use

It was assumed that the relationship between the various kinds of cooling water and process losses remains constant, and that the temperature of water going to cooling towers and that going into the stream is about the same. This permits 6 per cent to be applied to use in order to obtain total losses regardless of the degree of recirculation adopted in the industry. Consequently, *fresh water* loss for 1954 (in-plant and post-discharge) was calculated by applying .06 to *fresh water use*. Fresh water use = total use minus brackish water intake (which is not recirculated) or 5,004 bgy − 513 bgy = 4491 bgy. Total fresh water loss in 1954 is thus estimated as about 270 bgy. This was projected in the same manner as described for petroleum refining. It may be noted that changing the assumption concerning discharge temperature by a relatively large amount affects the over-all result comparatively little. For example, if it is assumed that the discharge temperature is 30°F rather than 20°F higher than intake, the over-all percentage of loss changes by only about .6 per cent.

Calculations similar to that for chemicals were made for iron and steel, food, coke, and nonferrous metals production. In each case the discharge temperature was, on the basis of engineering judgment, assumed to be 20° to 30° higher than intake (specifically, iron and steel 30°, coke 30°, food 20°, nonferrous metals 20°), and losses as a percentage of *use* tended to be in the 4–6 per cent range.

For pulp and paper manufacturing, another major water using industry, no post-discharge losses were computed, primarily because the industry uses comparatively little cooling water—only about 20 per cent of total intake. Process water losses on the other hand are comparatively large. It was assumed that in-plant losses would continue to hold their present relationship to output in this industry.

A large factor in the computation of municipal losses was, as explained earlier, the discharge of municipal effluents into saline water. In principle, the same considerations apply to industries which withdraw fresh water supplies and discharge effluent into saline water. No separate calculations of the withdrawals of such industrial users were made, however. One reason is that among the heavy water using industries, coastal locations are comparatively uncommon in the pulp and paper, food, and coke industries. Chemical plants and petroleum refining plants, which frequently do have coastal locations, are heavy users of cooling water. With respect to them the same assumption was made as for thermal-electric plants, i.e., that they either use saline water for cooling already or could do so should a situation of stringency develop.

Irrigation

The basic projections of irrigation water use and depletion were not linked directly to projected growth of population and output as were projections of other withdrawal uses. Rather, the various levels of projected irrigated acreage (to which the water use and depletion projections are in turn linked) rest upon extrapolations of trend, existing irrigation and irrigation plans, and judgments as to maximum irrigation potential. The specific steps in the computations are explained in the footnotes to Table A14–4. This note is directed to the elaboration of certain assumptions underlying the rates of water application and depletion per acre which were used.

Water use and water depletion in Western irrigation. Water depletion in irrigation is composed of two elements: (1) The sustenance and growth of a plant involve transpiration of water through its leaves. The amount of transpiration for a given type of plant depends primarily upon the moisture available in the root zone and the atmospheric temperature and humidity. (2) Some amount of water is lost (evaporated) during the process of delivering water to the plants. If sprinkler irrigation (typical of the East) is used, the amount so dissipated is comparatively small. In Western irrigation, however, water is ordinarily led by gravity flow along a series of main and lateral ditches and then carried along furrows to the plants. For some crops, the fields are flooded. Consequently the process of getting water to the plants offers ample opportunity for water to be lost by ditch seepage (some of this becomes return flow to a usable fresh water source and some is evapotranspired), evaporation from irrigation canal surfaces, and transpiration through deep rooted plants which tap canal water. This means that, on the average, perhaps two and one half times as much water must be diverted from the source as the plants actually use.

The diversion figures in the irrigation table (A14–4) refer to the amount of water actually taken from a fresh water source. They are based upon the assumption that four acre-feet of water per year per acre are diverted. According to the Bureau of Reclamation, in Senate Select Committee on National Water Resources, *op. cit.,* Print No. 14, *Future Needs for Reclamation in the Western States* (Washington, Apr. 1960), this is the present average diversion requirement in the Western states. The amount of diversion is not varied for any of the three levels of projection and is assumed to remain constant over time.

This constancy over time is assumed to result

from the counteracting effects of two currently foreseeable tendencies. The first is that water applied per acre will increase in the future. Present rates of application are generally far below optimum levels, and a number of recent Bureau of Reclamation projects have had as their primary objective the provision of supplementary water to undersupplied acreages. The second foreseeable trend is a substantial increase in delivery efficiency. Measures such as ditch lining, ditch covering, and eradication of phreatophytic plants (water loving weed trees and plants) along ditches can substantially reduce the difference between the amount of water diverted from a source and the amount reaching the plant. The projections assume that the increasing application of these measures will leave the level of diversion unchanged even though more moisture effectively reaches the plant and higher yields per acre are produced. This procedure differs considerably from that used in the Department of Agriculture report to the Senate Select Committee on National Water Resources (*op. cit.,* Print No. 12, *Land and Water Potential and Future Requirements for Irrigation,* Washington, Dec. 1959). That report assumes that crops will receive as much water as they can use; this would have required the withdrawal of 6.9 feet of water in 1954, the amount gradually declining as efficiency increases. Our study assumes that, in the future as in the past, irrigated cropland will not get as much water as it can utilize fully.

It is assumed, on the basis of Department of Agriculture estimates (Senate Select Committee, *op. cit.*), that 60 per cent of the water diverted in 1954 was evapotranspired and 40 per cent was return flow. Of the 60 per cent lost it is estimated that a little more than half is actually transpired by the plant and the rest is evapotranspiration loss in transit. As the efficiency of irrigation rises, the amount of water which must be diverted per acre (only part of which is lost) falls in relation to the amount which is transpired by the crop plant (all of which is lost). This means that the over-all percentage of diversion which is lost increases. The projections assume that this percentage gradually increases from 58 per cent in 1954 to 65 per cent in 2000. Other things being equal, a more rapid gain in efficiency than was assumed would result in

a reduction of diversion per acre but even greater increases in the proportion evapotranspired.

Water use and water losses in Eastern irrigation. In the projections of water diversion and water losses in Eastern irrigation, rates of diversion and losses were straightforwardly adopted from Department of Agriculture estimates in Senate Select Committee, *op. cit.,* Print No. 12. These estimates are based on the assumption that optimal moisture will be provided in the root zone. There is no reason to suppose that application rates in the East, in contrast to the West, will be limited by water shortage. On this basis the diversion rate in 1954 would have been 2.7 acre-feet per acre. Since optimal moisture provision was assumed to prevail throughout the period projected, efficiency gain would cause the rate of diversion to fall gradually to 1.9 acre-feet per acre in 2000. This differs from the situation in the West, where higher rates of application were assumed to cancel the effects of efficiency gain. As in the West, the same rates of application were assumed for all three levels of projection.

Since almost all Eastern irrigation is applied by means of sprinklers, there is a far smaller relative difference between the amount of water diverted per acre and the amount actually transpired by the crop plants. This means that there is less opportunity for return flow and that a higher percentage of water diverted is depleted. It was estimated that in 1954, 88 per cent of the irrigation water diverted in the East was lost. This loss was assumed to rise to 91 per cent by the year 2000.

LIST OF TABLES

A14–

TABLE A14–1.   Projected Regional Fresh Water Losses from Municipal Use

(Million gallons per day)

	1954	1960		1970	1980	1990	2000
Municipal water losses in East:							
Urban population in East[1] (millions)	81.8	93.1	L M H	104.6 112.3 124.4	116.0 136.3 163.7	126.0 162.4 212.5	132.8 189.9 269.4
Total withdrawals for municipal uses[2]	8,705	9,869	L M H	11,088 11,904 13,186	12,296 14,448 17,352	13,356 17,214 22,525	14,077 20,129 28,556
Municipal withdrawals destined for discharge into saline water[3]	3,308	3,750	L M H	4,213 4,524 5,011	4,672 5,490 6,594	5,075 6,541 8,560	5,349 7,649 10,851
Municipal withdrawals destined for discharge into fresh water[4]	5,397	6,119	L M H	6,875 7,380 8,175	7,624 8,958 10,758	8,281 10,673 13,965	8,728 12,480 17,705
Depletion of withdrawals destined for discharge into fresh water[5]	540	612	L M H	688 738 818	762 896 1,076	828 1,067 1,396	873 1,248 1,770
Total municipal losses in East[6]	3,848	4,362	L M H	4,901 5,262 5,829	5,434 6,386 7,670	5,903 7,608 9,956	6,222 8,897 12,621
Municipal water losses in Pacific Northwest:							
Urban population in Pacific Northwest[1] (millions)	3.1	3.8	L M H	4.5 4.8 5.3	5.2 6.2 7.4	6.1 7.9 10.3	7.0 10.1 14.3
Total withdrawals for municipal uses[7]	436	536	L M H	634 677 747	733 874 1,043	860 1,114 1,452	987 1,424 2,016
Municipal withdrawals destined for discharge into saline water[8]	257	316	L M H	374 399 441	432 516 615	507 657 857	582 840 1,189
Municipal withdrawals destined for discharge into fresh water[4]	179	220	L M H	260 278 306	301 358 428	353 457 595	405 584 827
Depletion of withdrawals destined for discharge into fresh water[5]	18	22	L M H	26 28 31	30 36 43	35 46 60	40 58 83
Total municipal losses in Pacific Northwest[6]	275	338	L M H	400 427 472	462 552 658	542 703 917	622 898 1,272
Total municipal water losses in high runoff regions (East plus Pacific Northwest)[6]	4,123	4,700	L M H	5,301 5,689 6,301	5,896 6,938 8,328	6,445 8,311 10,873	6,844 9,795 13,893
Total municipal water losses in West (except Pacific Northwest):							
Urban population in West[1] (millions)	23.0	28.7	L M H	36.3 37.8 41.0	44.9 50.4 58.7	53.5 64.4 80.4	61.6 79.2 106.5
Total withdrawals for municipal uses[9]	2,967	3,702	L M H	4,683 4,876 5,289	5,792 6,502 7,572	6,902 8,308 10,372	7,946 10,217 13,738
Municipal withdrawals destined for discharge into saline water[10]	1,484	1,851	L M H	2,342 2,438 2,645	2,896 3,251 3,786	3,451 4,154 5,186	3,973 5,109 6,869

Table A14–1 (cont'd)

(Million gallons per day)

	1954	1960		1970	1980	1990	2000
Municipal withdrawals destined for discharge into fresh water[4]	1,483	1,851	L M H	2,341 2,438 2,644	2,896 3,251 3,786	3,451 4,154 5,186	3,973 5,108 6,869
Depletion of withdrawals destined for discharge into fresh water[11]	297	370	L M H	468 488 529	579 650 757	690 831 1,037	795 1,022 1,374
Total municipal losses in West[6]	1,781	2,221	L M H	2,810 2,926 3,174	3,475 3,901 4,543	4,141 4,985 6,223	4,768 6,131 8,243

1. U.S. Public Health Service, *Future Water Requirements for Municipal Use* (U.S. Senate Select Committee on National Water Resources, Committee Print No. 7, Jan. 1960), Table 2.
2. Per capita water use for municipal purposes in 1954 calculated to be 106 gallons per day. Calculations based on water use data in *ibid.*, Table 4, from which industrial withdrawals from municipal systems, as detailed in U.S. Bureau of the Census, 1954 Census of Manufactures, "Industrial Water Use," Table 5, have been subtracted.
3. Ratio of withdrawals of municipal systems discharging into saline water to total municipal withdrawals assumed to be 38%. Ratio derived on a judgment basis from data on municipal plant output in U.S. Public Health Service, *Municipal Water Facilities, Communities of 25,000 Population and Over* (Dec. 1955). Discharge from all coastal communities assumed to be into saline water. Ratio assumed

constant to 2000.
4. Balance of withdrawals.
5. Assumed to be 10% (see Notes).
6. Withdrawals of coastal communities plus depletion from municipal systems discharging into fresh water.
7. Per capita water use for municipal purposes in 1954 calculated (basis as in footnote 2) to be 141 gallons per day.
8. Withdrawals of municipal systems discharging into saline water to total municipal withdrawals assumed to be 59%. Derived as in footnote 3.
9. Per capita water use for municipal purposes in 1954 calculated (basis as in footnote 2) to be 129 gallons per day.
10. Withdrawals of municipal systems discharging into saline water to total municipal withdrawals assumed to be 50%. Derived as in footnote 3.
11. Assumed to be 20% (see Notes).

TABLE A14–2.　Projected Regional Fresh Water Losses from Thermal-Electric Power Generation

(Million gallons per day)

	1954	1960		1970	1980	1990	2000
Thermal-electric utility output[1] (bil. kwh)	365	608	L M H	854 1,039 1,389	1,318 1,801 2,577	1,814 2,722 4,190	2,490 4,104 6,808
Heat rates assumed, Btu per kwh[2]	12,180	10,700		9,880	9,050	8,320	7,630
Water evaporated per kwh generated[3] (gal.)	.92	.76		.67	.58	.50	.42
Total water evaporated by thermal-electric plants in U.S.	336	462	L M H	572 696 931	764 1,045 1,495	907 1,361 2,095	1,046 1,724 2,859
Fresh water losses from thermal-electric plants in East:							
Regional share of national population[4] (%)	76.92	75.84		74.48	73.11	71.80	70.49
Regional percentage departure from 1954 share of U.S. population		—1.41		—3.17	—4.95	—6.66	—8.36
Regional share of national thermal-electric water use[5] (%)	83.49	82.64		81.49	80.31	79.27	78.21

Table A14–2 (cont'd)

(Million gallons per day)

	1954	1960		1970	1980	1990	2000
Fresh water losses from thermal-electric water use (cont'd)							
Total water evaporated by thermal-electric plants in East[6]	281	382	L	466	614	719	818
			M	567	839	1,079	1,348
			H	759	1,201	1,661	2,236
Total fresh water evaporated[7]	230	313	L	382	503	590	671
			M	465	688	885	1,105
			H	622	985	1,362	1,834
Fresh water losses from thermal-electric plants in Pacific Northwest:							
Regional share of national population[4] (%)	3.14	3.28		3.34	3.40	3.58	3.77
Regional percentage departure from 1954 share of U.S. population		+4.46		+6.37	+8.28	+14.01	+20.06
Regional share of national thermal-electric water use[5]	0.02	0.02		0.02	0.02	0.02	0.02
Total water evaporated by thermal-electric plants in Pacific Northwest[6]	–	–	L	–	–	–	–
			M	–	–	–	–
			H	–	–	–	1
Total fresh water evaporated[8]	–	–	L	–	–	–	–
			M	–	–	–	–
			H	–	–	–	1
Total fresh water evaporated by thermal-electric plants in high runoff regions (East plus Pacific Northwest)	230	313	L	382	503	590	671
			M	465	688	885	1,105
			H	622	985	1,362	1,835
Fresh water losses from thermal-electric plants in West (except Pacific Northwest):							
Regional share of national population[4] (%)	19.94	20.88		22.18	23.49	24.62	25.74
Regional percentage departure from 1954 share of U.S. population		+4.71		+11.23	+17.80	+23.47	+29.09
Regional share of national thermal-electric water use[5]	16.49	17.34		18.49	19.66	20.71	21.77
Total water evaporated by thermal-electric plants in West[6]	55	80	L	106	150	188	228
			M	129	205	282	375
			H	172	294	434	622
Total fresh water evaporated[9]	36	52	L	69	98	122	148
			M	84	133	183	244
			H	112	191	282	404

1. 1954 from Edison Electric Institute, *Statistical Yearbook*, 1960. All other data derived from Tables A15–1 and 10. Generation from nuclear power included; self-supplied industrial power excluded. Water losses associated with self-supplied industrial generation are included in Table A14–4.

2. From Table A15–17, adjusted to reflect utility generation only (see Table A15–10, footnote 6). 1954 from Table A15–8.

3. Based on the assumption that 10% of Btu input is dissipated in the stack and through other miscellaneous heat transfers (other than that accomplished by the cooling water), and that one pound of water will be evaporated for each 980 Btu dissipated.

4. From Nathaniel Wollman, *A Preliminary Report on the Supply of and Demand for Water in the United States as Estimated for 1980 and 2000* (Senate Select Committee on National Water Resources, Committee Print No. 32, Aug. 1960), Table 8, medium projection. Regional percentages of national population for 1954, 1970, and 1990 derived by straight-line interpolation.

5. Regional share in 1954 from Edward A. Ackerman and George O. G. Löf, *Technology in American Water Development* (Baltimore: Johns Hopkins Press and Resources for the Future, 1959), Table 32; regional shares in subsequent years projected on the assumption of a percentage departure from the 1954 regional share equal to the projected percentage departures from the 1954 regional share of national population, adjusted to 100%.

6. Percentage in line above applied to total water evaporated by thermal-electric plants in the United States.

7. Ratio of fresh to total water use was 82% in the East in 1954. Unchanging ratio to 2000 assumed.

8. All water used by thermal-electric plants in the Pacific Northwest in 1954 was fresh. Continuing non-use of brackish water assumed in projections.

9. Ratio of fresh to total water use was 65% in the West in 1954. Unchanging ratio to 2000 assumed.

TABLE A14–3. Projected Regional Fresh Water Losses from Manufacturing

(Million gallons per day)

	1954	1960		1970	1980	1990	2000
FRB indexes of industrial production (1954 = 100): [1]							
			L	115	118	131	140
Iron and steel	100	110	M	153	189	237	309
			H	195	275	396	593
			L	206	272	355	453
Chemicals and products	100	158	M	253	383	567	836
			H	335	619	1,114	1,974
			L	141	172	210	260
Petroleum refining (petroleum products)	100	122	M	158	208	279	385
			H	179	267	402	622
			L	144	176	212	247
Food, beverages, and tobacco	100	118	M	151	198	259	326
			H	182	279	429	646
			L	135	167	213	271
Nonferrous metals	100	116	M	182	274	406	614
			H	248	454	739	1,306
			L	172	227	290	363
Pulp and paper	100	130	M	188	269	378	522
			H	195	309	517	796
			L	175	242	334	460
Total manufacturing	100	126	M	193	296	451	684
			H	214	362	608	1,014
			L	80	70	72	71
Index of coke production [2]	100	96	M	104	106	121	143
			H	129	149	192	256
National water use and depletion by industry group:							
Iron and steel:							
			L	11,344	11,640	12,922	13,810
Total water use [3]	9,864	10,850	M	15,092	18,643	23,378	30,480
			H	19,235	27,126	39,061	58,494
			L	10,958	11,244	12,483	13,340
Total fresh water use [4]	9,532	10,481	M	14,579	18,009	22,583	29,444
			H	18,581	26,204	37,733	56,505
			L	548	562	624	667
Total fresh water depletion [5]	477	524	M	729	900	1,129	1,472
			H	929	1,310	1,887	2,825
Chemicals and products:							
			L	28,245	37,294	48,674	62,111
Total water use [3]	13,711	21,663	M	34,689	52,513	77,741	114,624
			H	45,932	84,871	152,741	270,655
			L	25,336	33,453	43,661	55,714
Total fresh water use [4]	12,305	19,432	M	31,116	47,104	69,734	102,818
			H	41,201	76,129	137,009	242,778
			L	1,520	2,007	2,620	3,343
Total fresh water depletion [5]	738	1,166	M	1,867	2,826	4,184	6,169
			H	2,472	4,568	8,221	14,567

Table A14–3 (cont'd)

(Million gallons per day)

	1954	1960		1970	1980	1990	2000
Petroleum refining:							
			L	15,774	19,242	23,493	29,086
Total water use [3]	11,187	13,648	M	17,675	23,269	31,212	43,070
			H	20,025	29,869	44,972	69,583
			L	13,597	16,587	20,251	25,072
Total fresh water use [4]	9,639	11,765	M	15,236	20,058	26,905	37,126
			H	17,262	25,747	38,766	59,981
			L	544	663	810	1,003
Total fresh water depletion [5]	386	471	M	609	802	1,076	1,485
			H	690	1,030	1,551	2,399
Food products:							
			L	4,925	6,019	7,250	8,447
Total water use [3]	3,420	4,036	M	5,164	6,772	8,858	11,149
			H	6,224	9,542	14,672	22,093
			L	4,689	5,730	6,902	8,042
Total fresh water use [4]	3,255	3,842	M	4,916	6,447	8,433	10,614
			H	5,925	9,084	13,968	21,033
			L	281	344	414	483
Total fresh water depletion [5]	195	231	M	295	387	506	637
			H	356	545	838	1,262
Nonferrous metals:							
			L	2,326	2,877	3,670	4,669
Total water use [3]	1,723	1,999	M	3,136	4,721	6,995	10,579
			H	4,273	7,822	12,733	22,502
			L	1,970	2,437	3,108	3,955
Total fresh water use [4]	1,460	1,693	M	2,656	3,999	5,925	8,960
			H	3,619	6,625	10,785	19,059
			L	118	146	186	237
Total fresh water depletion [5]	88	102	M	159	240	356	538
			H	217	398	647	1,144
Pulp and paper:							
			L	19,458	25,681	32,808	41,066
Total water use [3]	11,313	14,707	M	21,268	30,432	42,763	59,054
			H	22,060	34,957	58,488	90,051
			L	18,816	24,834	31,725	39,711
Total fresh water use [4]	10,944	14,222	M	20,566	29,428	41,352	57,105
			H	21,332	33,803	56,558	87,079
			L	753	993	1,269	1,588
Total fresh water depletion [5]	438	569	M	823	1,177	1,654	2,284
			H	853	1,352	2,262	3,483
Coke:							
			L	789	690	710	700
Total water use [3]	986	947	M	1,025	1,045	1,193	1,410
			H	1,272	1,469	1,893	2,824
			L	712	623	641	632
Total fresh water use [4]	890	855	M	926	944	1,077	1,273
			H	1,149	1,327	1,709	2,550
			L	50	44	45	44
Total fresh water depletion [5]	62	60	M	65	66	75	89
			H	80	93	120	179

Table A14–3 (cont'd)

(Million gallons per day)

	1954	1960		1970	1980	1990	2000
Miscellaneous industries:							
			L	13,682	18,920	26,112	35,963
Total water use [3]	7,818	9,851	M	15,089	23,141	35,259	53,475
			H	16,731	28,301	47,533	79,275
			L	13,217	18,277	25,224	34,740
Total fresh water use [4]	7,553	9,516	M	14,576	22,354	34,060	51,657
			H	16,162	27,339	45,917	76,580
			L	1,057	1,462	2,018	2,779
Total fresh water depletion [5]	604	761	M	1,166	1,788	2,725	4,133
			H	1,293	2,187	3,673	6,126
Regional shares of national industrial output by industrial category [6] (%):							
East:							
Iron and steel	92.77	92.55		92.12	91.68	91.22	90.76
Chemicals and products	93.99	93.16		92.82	92.46	92.09	91.72
Petroleum refining	39.62	39.77		40.02	40.26	40.26	40.25
Food products	77.83	76.20		74.94	73.68	72.57	71.47
Nonferrous metals	48.71	56.01		55.69	55.36	55.18	54.99
Pulp and paper	86.54	83.49		75.71	67.93	64.01	60.08
Coke	92.77	92.55		92.12	91.68	91.22	90.76
Miscellaneous industries	81.75	80.07		77.27	74.46	71.98	69.50
Pacific Northwest:							
Iron and steel	0.46	0.37		0.37	0.38	0.39	0.40
Chemicals and products	0.67	0.75		0.76	0.77	0.78	0.80
Petroleum refining	–	0.04		0.10	0.16	0.16	0.16
Food products	3.14	3.30		3.35	3.39	3.50	3.60
Nonferrous metals	21.79	19.19		22.03	24.88	25.45	26.02
Pulp and paper	9.52	12.51		20.23	27.95	26.93	25.91
Coke	0.40	0.37		0.37	0.38	0.39	0.40
Miscellaneous industries	3.62	4.70		6.51	8.32	8.38	8.43
West, except Pacific Northwest:							
Iron and steel	6.77	7.08		7.51	7.94	8.39	8.84
Chemicals and products	5.34	6.09		6.43	6.77	7.12	7.48
Petroleum refining	60.38	60.19		59.88	59.58	59.58	59.59
Food products	19.03	20.50		21.71	22.93	23.93	24.93
Nonferrous metals	29.50	24.80		22.28	19.76	19.37	18.99
Pulp and paper	3.94	4.00		4.06	4.12	9.06	14.01
Coke	6.77	7.08		7.51	7.94	8.39	8.84
Miscellaneous industries	14.63	15.23		16.22	17.22	19.64	22.07
Fresh water depletion in East: [7]							
			L	505	515	569	605
Iron and steel	443	485	M	672	825	1,030	1,336
			H	856	1,201	1,721	2,564
			L	1,411	1,856	2,413	3,066
Chemicals and products	694	1,086	M	1,733	2,613	3,853	5,658
			H	2,295	4,224	7,571	13,361
			L	218	267	326	404
Petroleum refining	153	187	M	244	323	433	598
			H	276	415	624	966
			L	211	253	300	345
Food products	152	176	M	221	285	367	455
			H	267	402	608	902
			L	66	81	103	130
Nonferrous metals	43	57	M	89	133	196	296
			H	121	220	357	629

Table A14–3 (cont'd)

(Million gallons per day)

	1954	1960		1970	1980	1990	2000
Pulp and paper	379	475	L	570	675	812	954
			M	623	800	1,059	1,372
			H	646	918	1,448	2,093
Coke	58	56	L	46	40	41	40
			M	60	61	68	81
			H	74	85	109	162
Miscellaneous industries	494	609	L	817	1,089	1,453	1,931
			M	901	1,331	1,961	2,872
			H	999	1,628	2,644	4,258
Total	2,416	3,131	L	3,844	4,776	6,017	7,475
			M	4,543	6,371	8,967	12,668
			H	5,534	9,093	15,082	24,935
Fresh water depletion in Pacific Northwest: [7]							
Iron and steel	2	2	L	2	2	2	3
			M	3	3	4	6
			H	3	5	7	11
Chemicals and products	5	9	L	12	15	20	27
			M	14	22	33	49
			H	19	35	64	117
Petroleum refining	–	–	L	1	1	1	2
			M	1	1	2	2
			H	1	2	2	4
Food products	6	8	L	9	12	14	17
			M	10	13	18	23
			H	12	18	29	45
Nonferrous metals	19	20	L	26	36	47	62
			M	35	60	91	140
			H	48	99	165	298
Pulp and paper	42	71	L	152	278	342	411
			M	166	329	445	592
			H	173	378	609	902
Coke	–	–	L	–	–	–	–
			M	–	–	–	–
			H	–	–	–	1
Miscellaneous industries	22	36	L	69	122	169	234
			M	76	149	228	348
			H	84	182	308	516
Total	96	146	L	271	466	595	756
			M	305	577	821	1,160
			H	340	719	1,184	1,895
Total fresh water depletion in high runoff regions (East plus Pacific Northwest)	2,512	3,277	L	4,115	5,242	6,612	8,231
			M	4,848	6,948	9,788	13,828
			H	5,874	9,812	16,266	26,830
Fresh water depletion in West (except Pacific Northwest): [7]							
Iron and steel	32	37	L	41	45	52	59
			M	55	71	95	130
			H	70	104	158	250
Chemicals and products	39	71	L	98	136	187	250
			M	120	191	298	461
			H	159	309	585	1,090

Table A14–3 (cont'd)

(Million gallons per day)

	1954	1960		1970	1980	1990	2000
Petroleum refining	233	283	L	326	395	483	598
			M	365	478	641	885
			H	413	614	924	1,430
Food products	37	47	L	61	79	99	120
			M	64	89	121	159
			H	77	125	201	315
Nonferrous metals	26	25	L	26	29	36	45
			M	35	47	69	102
			H	48	79	125	217
Pulp and paper	17	23	L	31	41	115	222
			M	33	48	150	320
			H	35	56	205	488
Coke	4	4	L	4	3	4	4
			M	5	5	6	8
			H	6	7	10	16
Miscellaneous industries	88	116	L	171	252	396	613
			M	189	308	535	912
			H	210	377	721	1,352
Total	476	606	L	758	980	1,372	1,911
			M	866	1,237	1,915	2,977
			H	1,018	1,671	2,929	5,158

1. From Tables A1–28 and A1–29; transposed from 1957 to 1954 base.

2. Derived from projected coal consumption in the iron and steel industry (Table A10–41).

3. Total water use in 1954 from U.S. Bureau of the Census, 1954 Census of Manufactures; water use in 1960 and later years projected on basis of corresponding Federal Reserve Board index. Ratio of water use to product output assumed to remain constant to 2000.

4. The following percentages of fresh water use to total water use prevailed in 1954, as calculated from data in 1954 Census of Manufactures:

Iron and steel	96.6
Chemicals and products	89.7
Petroleum refining	86.2
Food products	95.2
Nonferrous metals	84.7
Pulp and paper	96.7
Coke	90.3
Miscellaneous industries	96.6

Percentages assumed to remain constant to 2000.

5. The following percentages of fresh water depletion to fresh water use, including post-discharge evaporation in all cases except pulp and paper and the group of miscellaneous industries, are assumed to apply:

Iron and steel	5
Chemicals and products	6
Petroleum refining	4
Food	6
Nonferrous metals	6
Pulp and paper	4
Coke	7
Miscellaneous	8

Miscellaneous fresh water use derived by subtracting from U.S. total fresh water use the total fresh water use of the industries listed separately above.

6. Regional shares of each category except miscellaneous industries calculated from data in U.S. Department of Commerce and U.S. Bureau of Mines, *Future Water Requirements of Principal Water-Using Industries* (U.S. Senate Select Committee on National Water Resources, Committee Print No. 8, Apr. 1960), Part I, Appendixes C, D, E, F, G, and H, and Part II, "Water Use in the Mineral Industry," Table 6. Regional estimates of water use for iron and steel, chemicals and products, food products, nonferrous metals, and pulp and paper related to regional production data supplied by Resources for the Future. Production estimates for the water use regions comprising the East, the Pacific Northwest, and the balance of the West compared to national totals to derive the percentage estimates for these three major regions for 1954, 1959, 1980, and 2000. Percentages for 1960, 1970, and 1990 interpolated on a straight-line basis. Regional shares of coke production assumed to be the same as the share for iron and steel. Regional shares of petroleum refining estimated from water use data in Part II, Table 6. Regional shares of miscellaneous industries estimated from data in Wollman, Tables 12, 13, and 14 (see Table A14–2, footnote 4).

7. Total fresh water depletion multiplied by the estimated regional percentages of national production.

TABLE A14–4.   Projected Regional Fresh Water Losses from Irrigation

	1954	1960		1970	1980	1990	2000
East:							
			L	3,808	4,910	6,012	7,113
Irrigated acreage[1] (thous. acres)	2,002	2,877	M	4,549	6,220	7,891	9,562
			H	4,500	6,123	17,653	31,200
Requirements for diversion of irrigation water:							
			L	9,139	10,802	12,024	13,515
Thousands of acre-feet per year[2]	5,405	7,480	M	10,918	13,684	15,782	18,168
			H	10,800	13,471	35,306	59,280
Assumed diversion rate per irrigated acre[3] (acre-feet)	2.7	2.6		2.4	2.2	2.0	1.9
Mil. gallons per day (at 325,851			L	8,159	9,642	10,733	12,067
gal./acre-foot)	4,826	6,678	M	9,746	12,219	14,093	16,224
			H	9,642	12,029	31,521	52,926
Depletion of water[4] (mil. gallons			L	7,180	8,581	9,660	10,981
per day)	4,247	5,877	M	8,576	10,875	12,684	14,764
			H	8,485	10,706	28,369	48,163
Depletion as percentage of diversion[5]	88	88		88	89	90	91
Pacific Northwest:							
			L	5,057	5,057	5,057	5,057
Irrigated acreage[6] (thous. acres)	4,353	5,057	M	5,057	5,592	6,768	7,730
			H	5,057	5,427	6,563	7,900
Requirements for diversion of irrigation water:							
			L	20,228	20,228	20,228	20,228
Thousands of acre-feet per year[2]	17,412	20,228	M	20,228	22,368	27,072	30,920
			H	20,228	21,708	26,252	31,600
Assumed diversion rate per irrigated acre[7] (acre-feet)	4	4		4	4	4	4
Mil. gallons per day (at 325,851			L	18,055	18,055	18,055	18,055
gal./acre-foot)	15,543	18,055	M	18,055	19,972	24,170	27,603
			H	18,055	19,383	23,438	28,212
Depletion of water[4] (mil. gallons			L	10,833	11,194	11,555	11,736
per day)	9,015	10,652	M	10,833	12,383	15,469	17,942
			H	10,833	12,017	15,000	18,337
Depletion as percentage of diversion[5]	58	59		60	62	64	65
Total depletion from high runoff			L	18,013	19,775	21,215	22,717
regions (East plus Pacific	13,262	16,529	M	19,409	23,258	28,153	32,706
Northwest)			H	19,318	22,723	43,369	66,500

Table A14–4 (cont'd)

	1954	1960		1970	1980	1990	2000
West (except Pacific Northwest):							
Irrigated acreage[8] (thous. acres)	23,197	26,947	L	26,947	26,947	26,947	26,947
			M	26,947	28,655	32,413	35,488
			H	26,947	28,969	35,190	42,500
Requirements for diversion of irrigation water							
			L	107,788	107,788	107,788	107,788
Thousands of acre-feet per year[2]	92,788	107,788	M	107,788	114,620	129,652	141,952
			H	107,788	115,876	140,760	170,000
Assumed diversion rate per irrigated acre[7] (acre-feet)	4	4		4	4	4	4
Mil. gallons per day (at 325,851 gal./acre-foot)			L	96,228	96,228	96,228	96,228
	82,837	96,228	M	96,228	102,336	115,757	126,727
			H	96,228	103,457	125,676	151,766
Depletion of water[4] (mil. gallons per day)			L	57,737	59,661	61,586	62,548
	48,045	56,775	M	57,737	63,448	74,084	82,373
			H	57,737	64,143	80,433	98,648
Depletion as percentage of diversion[5]	58	59		60	62	64	65

1. Low acreage projection is an arithmetic extrapolation of 1939–57 rate of increase in irrigated acreage in the East; Medium projection is an arithmetic extrapolation of the 1949–57 rate of increase. Irrigated acreages in 1939, 1949, and 1957 from U.S. Department of Agriculture, *Land and Water Potentials and Future Requirements for Irrigation* (Senate Select Committee on National Water Resources, Committee Print No. 12, Dec. 1959), Table 11. In the High projection, the acreage figure for 2000 is the maximum potential irrigable area of the East (land where soils are suitable and water is available) as estimated by the U.S. Department of Agriculture, *op. cit.*, Table 20. High projections for 1980 and 1990 are derived by allocating to 1957–80 and 1957–90, respectively, the same proportions of the 1957–2000 irrigated area increase as correspond with the 1960–80 and 1960–90 proportions of the 1960–2000 increase in total cropland to be harvested, from Table A18–11 (10 and 55%). The 1970 figure is a straight-line interpolation.

2. Projected irrigated acreage multiplied by the assumed diversion rate per irrigated acre below.

3. Rates for 1954, 1980, and 2000 calculated from data in Department of Agriculture, *op. cit.*, Tables 43 and 45; rates for 1960, 1970, and 1990 interpolated on a straight-line basis.

4. Requirements for diversion multiplied by assumed depletion percentages detailed below.

5. 1954, 1980, and 2000 calculated from data in Department of Agriculture, *op. cit.*, Tables 39, 40, and 41; depletion percentages in 1960, 1970, and 1990 interpolated on a straight-line basis. Depletion is assumed to equal all losses not recovered plus all water

transpired by plants.

6. Low acreage projection is the irrigated acreage in 1957 (*ibid.*, Table 11). Medium acreage projection for the year 2000 is the acreage potentially irrigable under Potential II assumptions in *ibid.*, Table 11, i.e., the 1957 irrigated acreage plus U.S. Bureau of Reclamation "proposed project acreages and all foreseeable future projects for which data are available as listed in the 1958 report of the Commissioner of the Bureau of Reclamation." Medium projected irrigated acreages in 1960, 1970, 1980, and 1990 have been related to the Medium projections of acreage required to be harvested (Table A18–11) in a manner identical to that detailed in footnote 1. These percentages are: 1960, 0; 1970, 0; 1980, 20; 1990, 64. High acreage projection for 2000 is the maximum potential irrigable area in the Pacific Northwest (land where soils are suitable and water is available) as estimated by the U.S. Department of Agriculture, *op. cit.*, Table 20. Irrigated acreages in 1970, 1980, and 1990 interpolated on the basis of the High projection of cropland requirements (Table A18–11) in the same manner that the Medium irrigated acreages were derived. These percentages are: 1970, 4; 1980, 34; 1990, 61.

7. Assumed to remain constant throughout the projection period.

8. Computed in the same manner and from the same sources as the irrigated acreage projections for the Pacific Northwest (see footnote 6). Includes all Western water resource regions listed in Department of Agriculture, *op. cit.*, Tables 11 and 20, except Pacific Northwest.

appendix
to
chapter
15

MINERAL FUELS

Notes

THE MAIN burden of the tables in this part is to bring together, in terms of physical quantities, the demand for individual fuels and other primary sources of energy. A major part of this effort consists of determining the origin of electric energy, which is treated as an object of primary demand in Part I but must be disaggregated into demand for specific fuels, as well as for water power and nuclear power, if meaningful tests of adequacy are to be applied.

Tables A15–1 through 10 are devoted to this effort. The important requirements are to estimate the quantities that have to be generated in order to supply the quantities that are projected to be consumed; to isolate the amounts that can be expected to be generated through hydro and nuclear installations; to project the future efficiency of power generation; and lastly, to determine the share that each of the mineral fuels will capture of the power market. A minor, but troublesome, sub-requirement is to allow for the lower efficiency of that part of power generation that lies outside the utilities.

Given the ample footnoting of the individual tables, little need be said in the way of introduction. The separation of non-utility generation is made necessary by two factors: the absence, for all practical purposes, of transmission losses, and the lower efficiency. As the importance of non-utility generation diminishes further, so does the significance of the corrections made for the two factors, but at this time they have sufficient effect to call for adjustment. The assumption of "no loss" outside utilities is sufficiently realistic to raise no issue of docu-

mentation. Loss experience in utility generation, on the other hand, can be supported by statistical data, albeit with some qualifications.

"Losses" as used herein consist of losses in fact sustained in transmission and distribution, and energy used by producers for purposes not connected with generation (i.e., other than auxiliary services that constitute the difference between gross and net generation). Thus a better term is "losses and unaccounted for." Conceptually the two categories here shown together should be treated separately. This treatment is not, however, feasible, as the "energy used by producers," when projections are called for, is merely a statistical device arising out of the fact that these amounts are not "sold" and are therefore eliminated from utility statistics before sales to different customer classes are developed. The Federal Power Commission attempts to allocate these amounts to the proper categories, and the "losses and unaccounted for" category is therefore smaller, but still exists. Most of these amounts are, in fact, consumed by industry and public authorities since they originate in industrial plants that are for one reason or another classified as utilities, or in municipal and other publicly owned utilities which do not consider transfers to other departments of the same authority as sales. This matter is a major cause, incidentally, for existing small discrepancies between consumption statistics as compiled by the FPC and by the industry, category by category. In its release of 1960 data the Edison Electric Institute, and following it *Electrical World,* has largely corrected this situation, but at the same time badly damaged historical comparability (cf. Table A15–1, footnote 11). For the purposes of this study, it suffices for the reader to keep in mind that, of the actual amounts shown under "losses and unaccounted for," some 25 per cent does not represent actual physical loss.

On the question of efficiency, the adjustment is arbitrary; there is little to go on in the literature. As on other occasions, it has seemed preferable to make an adjustment, however little supported, in the direction that we know to be correct rather than let the matter drop by the wayside.

A somewhat picayune adjustment will be found in Table A15–4, where hydro non-utility generation is allowed for in the projection. This is a matter usually conspicuous for the disregard it receives. Quantitatively it makes little difference, but a signpost has nevertheless been erected to call attention to a statistical weakness. Otherwise, the projection sticks closely to the judgment of the Federal Power Commission.

In projecting the entry and development of nuclear energy we have drawn heavily on detailed work done by others in the belief that the work was of such caliber that little benefit would result from doing it over, given the early stage at which nuclear power generation finds itself at this time. In general, these earlier estimates have been somewhat dampened, as the pace of commercial development has been slow, compared with earlier expectations only. From one point of view the Medium projection might be considered conservative, in that it makes no provision for replacement of obsolete conventional plant by nuclear installations. There will undoubtedly be some such movement. However, relatively few of the very large generating units—and they are the primary candidates for nuclear generation—are of such age as to be candidates for early retirement. Indeed, it will probably not be until the last 10 or 15 years of the 40-year period that the time will arise for replacement of any of the large conventional units in existence now and to be installed in the sixties and thereafter. Any understatement will therefore arise only during the last years of the century. Failure to allow for this contingency does not, in view of the energy pattern as it emerges, significantly affect the conclusions regarding adequacy.

The fuel price comparison, which is shown in Table A15–7, throws only relative light upon the competitive position of coal and gas. Much remains to be done in terms of regional and state prices, and perhaps even in terms of prices paid by individual systems and installations. The data are fully available, but time and space do not permit

this analysis to exceed the dimensions that it is here allotted. However, mention of the subject cannot be made without reference to the abundance of statistical material for further work.

The crucial items in Table A15–10 are the heat rate and the fuel shares. The first is projected by 2000 to approach for the industry as a whole a level —7,500 Btu per Kwh—that is coming into sight for the latest installations. Indeed, if one considers that the rate for the utility industry has declined from 15,700 British thermal units per net kilowatt-hour in 1946 to 10,700 in 1960, the further drop to 7,500 by the year 2000—given the best current performance in the neighborhood of 8,900—seems almost too moderate, but it must be recalled that the road from now on is a far more difficult one than it has been in the past. As the physical limits of heat-to-electricity conversion are approached, the gradient will tend to flatten out, and the projected decline of 30 per cent over the next 40 years has substantially different connotations from the drop of roughly the same magnitude over the past 14 years. More difficult to judge is the future sharing of the utility market by the different fuels. Regional considerations above all, plus the seemingly inevitable closing of the gap between gas and coal prices, are the principal determinants. However, it must be readily admitted that the fuel pattern could develop quite differently. On the one hand, even the High projection of the gas share might turn out to have been conservative; on the other, the High projection of coal might look less extreme a decade or two from now.

Tables A15–11 and 12 fill a gap in the treatment of that part of natural gas demand that arises out of the role of gas as a raw material rather than a fuel, and above all out of the various incidental uses that accompany its production and distribution and thus are necessary concomitants of end-use demand as projected in Chapter 10. Only the introduction here of amounts wasted and vented is in need of comment. While these amounts are projected as a declining fraction, there will presumably always be a certain amount of gas that will be so lost, and if we want to compare total consumption with availability we must take into account not merely identifiable end-uses but also the losses that occur in the course of production. Thus our definition of consumption must include the volume that is flared or otherwise lost, not ordinarily so considered.

Tables A15–13 through 16 are the heart of this appendix. In them are brought together the projections for each of the identified uses, and adjustments are made to bring each total into line with official statistics for 1960. Actually, the need for adjustment is quite small. In other words, the cumulated end-uses estimated by us for 1960 come close to equaling the apparent consumption as calculated from statistics of production, foreign trade, and inventory changes. In the case of coal and petroleum the two sets check almost to the barrel; and for natural gas the comparable data are within 1.5 per cent of one another. Only in the instance of natural gas liquids does the gap approach 10 per cent. But then, the natural gas liquids industry altogether presents an unusual array of statistical difficulties which, one may hope, may be cleared up gradually as the increasing importance of this sector calls forth better analysis. As is pointed out in Table A15–15, the mere fact that the demand for the products of the natural gas liquids industry is joint, but that one cannot complete the analysis for either the gas or the petroleum industry without attributing to each a part of the NGL demand, leads to a good deal of conjecture. So does the growing importance, and the confused state of statistics, of the natural gas liquids as raw material supplies for the chemical industry. The arbitrary allocations made carry with them hope that increasingly better informed projections may be made.

This portion of the appendix closes with three tables (A15–17 through 19) that present, in ten-year intervals up to the year 2000, the projected demand for each source of energy and each major category of use. Since neither hydro nor nuclear energy can be reduced to conventional fuel equivalents, they are shown in these tables in terms of kilowatt-hours, that are in turn converted to British thermal units, for across-the-board comparisons, on the basis of the heat rates in conventional generation then projected to prevail. Conventional thermal electricity is shown both in kwh and in terms of coal, oil, and gas. Perhaps in the future this procedure will have to be abandoned and nuclear energy converted at least to the corresponding quantities of uranium and the energy content of those quantities. For the time being, we have followed the conventional approach, given the extreme range in future efficiency of this conversion process. The implications for uranium are explored in the text of Chapter 20.

LIST OF TABLES

A15–

TABLE A15–1.   Projected End-Use Consumption and Generation of Electricity

(Billion kilowatt-hours)

	1960		1970	1980	1990	2000
1. Residential[1]	193	L M H	287 353 492	428 594 857	541 843 1,300	677 1,188 1,961
2. Commercial[2]	113	L M H	170 190 243	254 308 387	340 416 501	467 554 624
3. Other non-industrial uses[3]	32	L M H	45 49 60	64 75 92	82 99 121	105 128 155
4. Iron and steel industry[4]	30	L M H	42 51 64	48 68 96	58 91 147	79 129 220
5. Nonferrous metals industry[4]	46	L M H	44 60 89	55 92 165	67 133 251	83 195 434
6. Atomic Energy Commission installations[5]	60	L M H	60 60 68	60 60 75	60 60 83	60 60 90
7. All other manufacturing[6]	221	L M H	339 388 442	500 635 842	720 1,011 1,551	1,001 1,599 2,771
8. Mining[7]	16	L M H	20 24 28	26 33 44	32 46 68	39 61 108
9. All identified end-uses	711	L M H	1,007 1,175 1,486	1,435 1,865 2,558	1,900 2,700 4,022	2,511 3,914 6,363
10. All other end-uses[8]	42	L M H	70 82 104	115 149 205	171 243 362	251 391 636
11. All end-uses	753	L M H	1,077 1,257 1,590	1,550 2,014 2,763	2,071 2,943 4,384	2,762 4,305 6,999
12. Recapitulation: Total industry use[9]	415	L M H	575 665 795	804 1,037 1,427	1,108 1,584 2,462	1,513 2,435 4,259
13. Self-generation as per cent of industry use[10]	21.3	L M H	16.5 17.0 18.0	13.0 14.0 16.0	10.5 12.1 15.0	8.0 10.0 14.0
14. Amount self-generated	88	L M H	95 113 143	105 145 228	116 192 369	121 244 596
15. Recapitulation: Utility sales[11]	665	L M H	982 1,144 1,447	1,445 1,869 2,535	1,955 2,751 4,015	2,641 4,061 6,403
16. Losses, etc., as per cent of utility sales[12]	14.0	L M H	12.2 12.5 13.1	10.8 11.5 12.8	9.4 10.7 12.4	8.0 10.0 12.0
17. Amount of losses, etc.	92	L M H	120 143 190	156 215 325	184 294 498	212 406 768
18. Generation required[13]	845	L M H	1,197 1,400 1,780	1,706 2,229 3,088	2,255 3,237 4,882	2,974 4,711 7,767

Table A15–1 (cont'd)

1. From Table A10–19.
2. From Table A10–22.
3. From Table A10–26.
4. From Table A10–34.
5. Low and Medium assumed to remain at current levels; High assumed to rise 50% by 2000.
6. From Table A10–28.
7. From Table A10–36.
8. Derived in 1960 as difference between all identified uses and total end-uses (sales to ultimate consumers plus non-utility generation) as reported by *Electrical World,* Feb. 27, 1961, on basis of Federal Power Commission data. This category includes use of electricity in construction and railroads, and industrial and commercial uses not covered by the specific categories here listed, and serves as a balancing item generally. It includes 5 billion kwh of imports. Projected to rise from 6% of identified uses in 1960 to 10% in 2000.
9. Sum of items 4 through 8 plus 10. Defined to include Atomic Energy Commission for purposes of comparison with non-utility generation.
10. Based on trends shown in Table A15–2. 1960 derived from relationship of amount self-generated and identified industrial consumption above.
11. Total end-use consumption (item 11) minus amount self-generated. A recent revision by the Edison Electric Institute, incorporated in *Electrical World* estimates (Feb. 26, 1962), has raised this figure to 684 and lowered the "losses and unaccounted for" item correspondingly, leaving the generation estimate shown below unaffected. Last-minute adaptation of this revision in our estimates would have badly interfered with historical comparability and, because changes are offsetting (higher utility and identified end-use figures vs. lower "losses and unaccounted for"), brought little if any change in the generation estimates which are the figures that are carried forward in subsequent tables.
12. Based on trends shown in Table A15–3.
13. Item 11 plus item 17. Includes imports in 1960 of 5 billion kwh, or 0.5% of total.

TABLE A15–2.   Non-utility Generation of Electricity, 1940 and 1945–60

	Estimated electricity consumption in industry[1] (bil. kwh)	Non-utility plant			Non-utility generation as per cent of industrial consumption
		Installed capacity (in mil. kw at end of year shown)[2]	Generation (bil. kwh)[2]	Utilization (kwh per kw installed at year-end)[3]	
1940	92.4	11.0	38.1	3,450	41.2
1945	143.2	12.8	48.8	3,823	34.1
1946	133.8	12.7	46.4	3,644	34.7
1947	153.9	12.8	51.7	4,027	33.6
1948	169.2	13.1	54.1	4,145	32.0
1949	165.7	13.5	54.0	4,006	32.6
1950	191.0	13.9	59.5	4,274	31.2
1951	215.3	14.4	62.7	4,368	29.1
1952	224.3	15.1	63.8	4,231	27.8
1953	254.7	15.9	71.5	4,511	28.4
1954	266.2	16.3	73.0	4,480	27.4
1955	323.7	16.4	82.0	4,991	25.3
1956	358.0	16.6	84.1	5,055	23.8
1957	368.0	17.1	84.8	4,959	23.4
1958	355.0	18.1	79.7	4,403	22.5
1959	388.0	17.5	85.2	4,868	22.0
1960	405.0	17.8	87.6	4,921	21.6

1. 1940 and 1945–55 from *Energy in the American Economy, 1850–1975* (Baltimore: Johns Hopkins Press, for Resources for the Future, 1960), Pt. II, Appendix Table B–8. Figures for 1956–59 estimated from "large light and power sales" and "other generation," as shown in Edison Electric Institute, *Electric Utility Industry Statistics* (New York: 1959), for 1960 from *Electrical World,* Feb. 7, 1961. The 1960 figure compares with an estimated 415 billion kilowatt-hours for industry and "all other uses," as combined in Table A15–1, item 12.
2. Edison Electric Institute, *Electric Utility Industry Statistics,* various years.
3. Calculated from data prior to rounding.

TABLE A15–3.   Losses in Utility Generation, 1942–60[1]

	Generation plus imports (bil. kwh)	Losses and unaccounted for (bil. kwh)	Losses only (bil. kwh)	Sales (bil. kwh)	Losses and unaccounted for as per cent of sales	Losses only as per cent of generation plus imports
1942	187.4	28.0	21.4	159.4	17.5	11.4
1943	219.3	33.4	24.7	185.9	18.0	11.3
1944	229.8	31.6	25.1	198.2	15.9	10.9
1945	224.3	30.7	27.3	193.6	15.9	12.2
1946	224.8	34.0	29.5	190.8	17.8	13.1
1947	257.0	39.4	33.2	217.6	18.1	12.9
1948	283.8	43.1	36.7	240.7	17.9	12.9
1949	292.1	43.6	37.7	248.5	17.5	12.9
1950	330.4	49.9	41.4	280.5	17.8	12.5
1951	372.4	54.2	44.9	318.2	17.0	12.1
1952	401.0	58.5	47.7	342.5	17.1	11.9
1953	444.0	59.8	50.4	384.2	15.6	11.4
1954	473.4	62.5	51.6	410.9	15.2	10.9
1955	550.3	69.4	55.5	480.9	14.4	10.1
1956	605.2	75.1	58.5	530.1	14.2	9.7
1957	635.2	77.4	59.0	557.8	13.9	9.3
1958	648.4	78.9	61.2	569.2	13.9	9.1
1959	713.6	86.9	64.8	626.7	13.9	9.1
1960	757.4	92.5	67.2	664.9	14.0	8.9

1. Basic data from *Electrical World*, Feb. 23, 1959, p. 88, and Feb. 27, 1961, p. 80. See also Table A15–1, footnote 11, for latest revision and problems raised thereby.

TABLE A15–4.   Historical and Projected Hydro Generation (Medium Projection)

	Genera-tion by utility[1] (mil. kwh)	Utility end-year capacity[1] (thous. kw)	Utility utilization (kwh per estimated kw installed at midyear)[2]	Generation by industrial establishments[3] (mil. kwh)	Generation by utilities and non-utilities[4] (bil. kwh)
1950	95,938	17,675	5,589	4,946	102
1951	99,750	18,868	5,459	4,626	104
1952	105,103	20,419	5,350	4,606	110
1953	105,233	22,045	4,956	4,384	110
1954	107,069	23,211	4,732	4,571	112
1955	112,975	25,005	4,686	3,261	116
1956	122,029	25,654	4,818	3,208	125
1957	130,232	27,036	4,943	3,125	133
1958	140,262	29,359	4,975	3,353	144
1959	137,782	31,074	4,560	3,373	141
1960	145,513	32,373	4,587	3,550	149
1965	203,000	45,000[5]	4,500	[7]	206
1970	245,000	55,000	4,450	[7]	248
1975	265,000	60,000	4,000	[7]	268
1980	280,000	65,000[6]	4,300	[7]	283
1985	300,000	71,000	4,200	[7]	303
1990	320,000	78,000	4,100	[7]	323
1995	336,000	84,000	4,000	[7]	339
2000	360,000	90,000	4,000	[7]	363

1. Data for 1950–60 from Edison Electric Institute, *Electric Utility Industry Statistics*, 1959, and *Electrical World*, Feb. 27, 1961. Estimates for 1980 and 2000 from FPC projection in release dated Dec. 17, 1959, adjusted for the year 2000 so as to allow for somewhat higher capacity and lower utilization. Other years estimated by interpolation. Quinquennial estimates, useful here as benchmarks, not used in further projections.
2. Midyear capacity estimated as halfway point between end-year figures shown.
3. From *Historical Statistics of the United States, Colonial Times to 1957*, and *Statistical Abstract*, both Bureau of the Census.
4. FPC estimates a future constant installed capacity of 700,000 kw of non-utility hydropower, the level reached in 1955, after five hydro installations of the Carolina Aluminum Co. had been absorbed into the utility system. It is unlikely that significant additional non-utility hydro capacity will be installed in the future or that annual utilization will vary much from the 4,000–5,000 hours per year at which the plants had been operating in the past. Consequently a constant 3 billion kwh is added to utility generation after 1960.
5. Late in 1961 nearly 11 million kw of new capacity were identifiable by location as due for commercial operation by 1965. Further additions will be small, but may be expected.
6. In a most recent revision (FPC press release No. 11,829, dated Jan. 30, 1962) this figure has been revised upward to 71,000,000 kw. Owing to the advanced stage of completion of these calculations and those derived from them no account could be taken of this revision, nor does it seem to have affected the subsequent two decades. The revision includes Alaska and Hawaii.
7. Included in utility and non-utility generation (last column).

TABLE A15–5. Projected Nuclear Power Generation
(Medium Projection)

	Total electricity demand (=generation)[1] (bil. kwh)	Nuclear generation		
		As per cent of total generation[2]	In billion kwh[3]	
			As calculated	Adjusted and rounded[4]
1960	845	–	–	–
1965	1,114	0.8	9	8
1970	1,400	3.5	49	35
1975	1,800	11.2	202	160
1980	2,229	21.0	468	400
1985	2,706	31.4	850	770
1990	3,237	39.4	1,275	1,200
1995	3,899	44.7	1,742	1,750
2000	4,711	50.6	2,384	2,400

1. From Table A15–1, except for years ending in 5, for which projections were derived for this table only.

2. For 1965–1980, from Perry D. Teitelbaum, *Nuclear Energy and the U.S. Fuel Economy, 1955–1980* (Washington: National Planning Association, July 1958), App. 8, Table 12. While the percentages derive from a more conservative total growth projection, the NPA approach of applying cost criteria to projected growth data permits the use of the percentage figures despite the difference in total growth. This involves the reasonable assumption that the cost structure of the larger projection does not differ from that assumed in the NPA calculation.

3. 1960–80: the result of applying the percentages in the second column to the first column; thereafter: 80% of increase in total generation in each period added to level of nuclear generation in 1980. For derivation of the 80% assumption see Table A15–6; the overall percentage of 84% there established is here rounded to 80%.

4. Adjusted in view of plans known in mid–1961. 1970 estimated on basis of installation of 3 bil. kw capacity in period 1966–70, equal to 70% of calculated amount. 1975 estimated at 80% of calculated amount, 1980 at 85%, 1990 at 95%, and no adjustments thereafter. This implies installation of 7 million kw nuclear generating capacity per year in the latter part of the seventies, or a fully mature industry twelve to fifteen years from now. Some put this date in the late sixties, but current trends do not suggest a speedup of that magnitude.

TABLE A15–6. Assumptions Underlying Projected Share of Nuclear Power Generation, 1980–2000

FPC region	Regional share in utility electricity requirements (%)			Estimated electricity requirements[4] (bil. kwh)		Increase in electricity requirements 1980–2000 (bil. kwh)	Nuclear energy generation as per cent of increase in total electricity requirements[5]		Increases in electricity requirements 1980–2000 met by nuclear generation (bil. kwh)
	Actual 1955–59 average[1]	Estimated 1980[2]	Estimated 2000[3]	1980	2000		1975–80	1980–2000	
I	19.7	17.9	16.3	399	768	369	[6]111.9	100	369
II	19.6	18.6	17.5	415	824	409	88.1	95	389
III	19.6	18.7	17.8	417	839	422	54.0	75	316
IV	11.9	12.4	12.9	276	608	332	96.9	100	332
V	9.7	10.5	11.3	234	532	298	45.4	60	179
VI	1.9	2.3	2.7	51	127	76	49.0	60	46
VII	8.3	9.1	9.6	203	452	249	34.5	50	125
VIII	9.2	10.5	11.9	234	561	327	96.4	100	327
U.S.	100.0	100.0	100.0	2,229	4,711	2,482	76.1	[7]84	2,085

1. From Federal Power Commission, *Estimated Future Power Requirements of the United States* (Washington: various years).
2. FPC, in *Water Resources Activities in the United States* (Senate Select Committee, 86th Cong., 2nd Sess., Committee Print No. 10), p. 6.
3. Estimated as extension of trend between 1955–59 average and 1980, and adjusted to add to 100%.
4. U.S. totals, Medium projection, from Table A15–1, allocated to FPC regions by use of percentage shares in preceding columns.

5. Share of nuclear power extended to 2000 on basis of trends shown by Karl M. Mayer, in *Nuclear Energy and the U.S. Fuel Economy* (Washington: National Planning Association, 1958), Appendix 8, Table 13, of which 1975–80 change reported here for comparison.
6. Percentage above 100 implies replacement of some existing conventional steam capacity.
7. This figure is not an assumed share but emerges as the result of relating increases met by nuclear generation to U.S. electricity requirements.

TABLE A15–7. Fuel Prices Paid by Electric Utilities, 1948–60[1]

	Coal			Oil			Natural gas		
	Dollars per ton	Btu per lb.	Cents per mil. Btu	Dollars per bbl.	Btu per bbl. (thous.)	Cents per mil. Btu	Cents per thous. cu. ft.	Btu per cu. ft.	Cents per mil. Btu
1948	6.69	11,980	27.9	2.81	6,201	45.3	11.0	1,053	10.4
1949	6.50	12,011	27.1	2.15	6,293	34.2	12.3	1,046	11.8
1950	6.38	11,839	26.9	2.00	6,287	31.8	11.8	960	12.3
1951	6.42	11,968	26.8	2.11	6,306	33.5	13.6	972	14.0
1952	6.54	12,059	27.1	2.14	6,318	33.9	14.7	965	15.2
1953	6.52	12,011	27.1	2.05	6,325	32.4	16.7	1,000	16.7
1954	6.25	12,087	25.9	2.11	6,319	33.4	18.3	1,019	18.0
1955	6.01	12,048	24.9	2.12	6,322	33.5	18.8	1,006	18.7
1956	6.29	12,030	26.1	2.42	6,314	38.3	18.9	1,001	18.9
1957	6.62	12,029	27.5	2.79	6,309	44.2	20.1	994	20.2
1958	6.55	12,025	27.2	2.47	6,294	39.2	21.9	1,016	21.6
1959	6.29	12,032	26.1	2.22	6,334	35.0	23.6	1,017	23.2
1960	6.26	12,041	26.0	2.17	6,322	34.3	25.2	1,034	24.4

1. Edison Electric Institute, *Electric Utility Industry Statistics,* various years.

TABLE A15–8.   Thermal Efficiency in Utility Generation, 1948–60[1]

| | Coal per net kwh | | Gas per net kwh | | Oil per net kwh | | All fuels per net kwh, Btu[4] |
	Lb.[2]	Btu[3]	Cu. ft.[2]	Btu[3]	Bbl.[2]	Btu[3]	
1948	1.30	15,574	15,884	16,726	2.54	15,752	15,738
1949	1.24	14,894	14,868	15,552	2.33	14,664	15,033
1950	1.19	14,088	14,101	13,537	2.24	14,084	14,030
1951	1.14	13,644	13,497	13,119	2.23	14,062	13,641
1952	1.10	13,265	13,286	12,821	2.26	14,279	13,361
1953	1.06	12,732	12,960	12,960	2.14	13,535	12,889
1954	0.99	11,966	12,438	12,674	2.12	13,397	12,180
1955	0.95	11,446	12,101	12,174	2.03	12,834	11,699
1956	0.94	11,308	11,916	11,928	2.02	12,754	11,456
1957	0.93	11,206	11,700	11,758	1.97	12,444	11,365
1958	0.91	10,966	11,469	11,526	1.92	12,128	11,090
1959	0.89	10,708	11,109	11,298	1.89	11,971	10,879
1960	0.88	10,596	10,911	11,282	1.85	11,696	10,701

1. Power is measured net of auxiliary services in generating stations.
2. *Electrical World,* Feb. 27, 1961.
3. Converted on basis of Btu values per physical unit from Edison Electric Institute, *Electric Utility Industry Statistics,* various issues.
4. *Ibid.,* 1960, Table 41. If all-fuel heat rates for 1948–60 are reconstructed from fuel consumption data and Btu content per unit of each fuel, they work out slightly (not quite 2%) above the figures estimated by EEI and shown in this column. This difference is most likely due to inclusion, in the individual fuel Btu equivalents on which the three Btu/kwh rates are based, of small amounts of fuels other than the three listed (wood, lignite, tar, waste gas, etc.).

TABLE A15–9.   Sources of Energy for Utility Generation, Selected Years, 1940–60[1]

(Per cent)

| | Shares in total generation | | Coal as per cent of | | Natural gas as per cent of | | Oil as per cent of | |
	Hydro	Thermal	Total generation	Thermal generation	Total generation	Thermal generation	Total generation	Thermal generation
1940	33.4	66.6	54.6	81.8	7.7	11.6	4.4	6.6
1945	35.9	64.1	51.7	80.6	8.9	13.9	3.5	5.5
1950	29.1	70.9	47.1	66.4	13.5	19.2	10.2	14.4
1955	20.6	79.4	55.1	69.5	17.4	21.9	6.8	8.6
1956	20.3	79.7	56.4	70.8	17.3	21.7	6.0	7.5
1957	20.6	79.4	54.9	69.1	18.1	22.8	6.4	8.1
1958	21.7	78.3	53.4	68.2	18.6	23.8	6.3	8.0
1959	19.4	80.6	53.4	66.3	20.7	25.7	6.6	8.2
1960	19.3	80.7	53.6	66.4	21.0	26.0	6.1	7.6

1. Federal Power Commission, *Annual Reports.*

TABLE A15–10.   Projected Electricity Generation, by Source of Energy

	1960		1970	1980	1990	2000
Total generation[1] (bil. kwh)	845	L	1,197	1,706	2,255	2,974
		M	1,400	2,229	3,237	4,711
		H	1,780	3,088	4,882	7,767
Nuclear[2] (bil. kwh)	–	L	20	220	620	1,230
		M	35	400	1,200	2,400
		H	50	580	1,680	3,480
Hydro[3] (bil. kwh)	149		248	283	323	363
Thermal conventional (bil. kwh)	696	L	929	1,203	1,312	1,381
		M	1,117	1,546	1,714	1,948
		H	1,482	2,225	2,879	3,924
Natural gas:						
Share in thermal generation[4] (%)	26		30	26	24	22
Gas-based generation (bil. kwh)	181	L	279	313	315	304
		M	335	402	411	429
		H	445	578	691	863
Fuel rate (cu. ft/net kwh)[5]	10,910		10,100	9,300	8,600	7,875
Amount used, unadjusted (bil. cu. ft.)	1,975	L	2,818	2,911	2,709	2,394
		M	3,384	3,739	3,535	3,378
		H	4,494	5,375	5,943	6,796
Amount used, adjusted for non-utility generation[6] (bil. cu. ft.)	2,034	L	2,903	2,998	2,790	2,466
		M	3,486	3,851	3,641	3,479
		H	4,629	5,536	6,121	7,000
Oil:						
Share in thermal generation[4] (%)	7.6		6.3	5.0	5.0	5.0
Oil based generation (bil. kwh)	53	L	59	60	66	69
		M	70	77	86	97
		H	93	111	144	196
Fuel rate (bbl/Th. kwh)[7]	1.85		1.70	1.58	1.46	1.36
Amount used, unadjusted (mil. bbl.)	98	L	100	95	96	94
		M	119	122	126	132
		H	158	175	210	267
Amount used, adjusted for non-utility generation[6] (mil. bbl.)	101	L	103	98	99	97
		M	123	126	129	136
		H	163	180	216	275
Coal:						
Share in thermal generation[4] (%)	66.4	L				
		M	63.7	69.0	71.0	73.0
		H				
Coal based generation (bil. kwh)	461	L	592	830	932	1,008
		M	712	1,067	1,217	1,422
		H	944	1,535	2,044	2,865
Fuel rate[8] (lb/net kwh)	0.88		0.805	0.740	0.680	0.625
Amount used, unadjusted (mil. tons)	202	L	238	307	317	315
		M	287	395	414	444
		H	380	568	695	895
Amount used, adjusted for non-utility generation[6] (mil. tons)	208	L	245	316	327	324
		M	296	407	426	457
		H	391	585	716	922

Table A15–10 (cont'd)

1. From Table A15–1. Includes some 4 billion imported kwh for which no adjustment is made.

2. Medium projection: Table A15–5. Low projection: half the additions of nuclear generation per decade. High projection: 50% larger additions than in medium.

3. From Table A15–4.

4. 1960: Table A15–9. Projection based upon considerations discussed fully in text.

5. 1960: Table A15–8. Projection based upon coal heat rate projection, but raised 5% throughout the period (and rounded) to reflect the fact that heat rate of gas fired plants has in the past exceeded that of coal fired plants by that percentage (see Table A15–8). Despite the projected rise in the relative importance of this sector it is not anticipated that the relative change in the fuel pattern will be enough to change the picture significantly.

Conversion from coal to gas based upon 12,000 Btu per pound of coal (see note 8 below) and 1,000 Btu per cubic foot of gas. The latter is slightly below the average prevailing in recent years and reflects the increasing tendency to remove the more valuable (and heat-intensive) hydrocarbon fractions from the pipeline gas prior to transmission and combustion.

6. Adjusted for the fact that calculated fuel rates are valid only for utility generation, while generation in this table comprises also non-utility power plants. The error is likely to be a diminishing one, given the declining role of non-utility generation, and the adjustment is minor to begin with. It has been approached as follows: in 1960, when the error can be presumed to have been at its peak for the 40-year period, roughly 10% of the total electricity supply of 845 billion kwh is estimated to have been generated in non-utility plants. If we assumed that the fuel rate in this segment exceeded that of the utilities by 40%, the resulting increase in energy input requirements would be about 4%, or, put differently, there would be an understatement of some 4% if we were to neglect making an adjustment for the higher non-utility fuel rate. By 2000 a 40% excess in the non-utility fuel rate would result in a mere 2% rise in energy input requirements. As a rough measure of differences, we have increased the calculated quantities of fuel by 3% throughout, thus being generous in the allowance for higher fuel rates in non-utility generation.

No adjustment has been found feasible for possible differences in fuel pattern between utility and non-utility generation. For utilities only, 1960 gas consumption amounted to 1,724 billion cubic feet, oil consumption to 85.3 million barrels, and coal consumption to 176.5 million tons.

7. 1960: Table A15–8; projection based upon coal heat rate, but raised, in rounded form, from 11% in 1960 (see Table A15–8) to 14% in 2000, with intermediate years interpolated, to reflect increasing excess of oil heat rate over that of coal; the further rise to the year 2000 is based upon an anticipated declining share of oil fired plants and a continuation of a past trend widening the spread between the two heat rates. Conversion from coal to oil based upon 12,000 Btu per pound of coal (see note 8 below) and 6.3 million Btu per barrel of oil, the rate for residual oil.

8. Assumed to reach 7,500 Btu per net kwh by 2000, equal, at 12,000 Btu per pound of coal (which is the characteristic energy content of utility-type coal), to 0.625 pounds of coal. Figures for other years derived by semilog graphic interpolation.

TABLE A15–11. Projected Chemical Industry Demand for Natural Gas Liquids as Raw Material

	1960		1970	1980	1990	2000
Selected organic crudes and		L	13.9	18.5	23.8	30.1
intermediates[1] (bil. lb.)	9.3	M	18.7	30.7	47.9	73.8
		H	26.8	56.5	111.2	215.0
Above group as per cent of oil		L	31	25	20	15
and gas derived material[2]	36	M	33	30	25	20
		H	38	40	40	40
Oil and gas derived[3]		L	44.8	74.0	119	201
material (bil. lb.)	26.1	M	56.7	102.0	192	369
		H	70.5	141.0	278	536
Same in equivalent		L	148	247	397	670
volume[4] (mil. bbl.)	87	M	189	340	640	1,230
		H	240	470	930	1,790

1. From Table A17–10.

2. 1960 percentage derived from data immediately above and below. It is assumed that, in the Medium projection, this percentage can be expected to shrink as new products not now foreseen begin to enlarge the total. In the Low model it is assumed that this shrinkage will be even more pronounced, thus the smaller percentage figures; whereas in the High projection it is assumed that the high absolute growth in the underlying series will at the same time constitute a large percentage, taken here as a constant percentage, of the total.

3. 1960: U.S. Tariff Commission, *Synthetic Organic Chemicals, United States Production and Sales, 1960* (Washington: 1961), Table 5A, p. 4. Projections derived from data above.

4. The conversion of this highly mixed and changing bag of products poses a nearly insurmountable problem. Some of the products have very high, others very low, specific weight. A compromise figure of 7 pounds per gallon has here been chosen, corresponding to roughly 300 pounds per barrel. This might be on the high side, especially as ethylene, a material of very low specific weight, is a significant and growing item. On the other hand, materials such as styrene or formaldehyde have a very high mass/volume factor. The compromise coefficient can no doubt be greatly improved upon, but in the context of the very rough assumptions that have gone into building these aggregate projections, and the uncertainties concerning even the precise nature of many of the base year data, there seems little call here for anything more refined.

TABLE A15–12. Historical Data on Disposition of Natural Gas[1]

	Net withdrawal[2] (bil. cu. ft.)	Net marketed production[3] (bil. cu. ft.)	Field use, including NGL extraction		NGL extraction		Field use, excluding NGL extraction		Wasted and vented		Transmission losses		Pipeline fuel		Net increase in underground storage (bil. cu. ft.)
			Bil. cu. ft.	Per cent of net marketed production	Mil. bbl.	Bil. cu. ft.[4]	Bil. cu. ft.	Per cent of net marketed production[5]	Bil. cu. ft.	Per cent of net marketed production	Bil. cu. ft.	Per cent of net marketed production	Bil. cu. ft.	Per cent of net marketed production	
1935	2,408	1,336	580	43	41	55	525	39.3	–	–	41	3.1	n.a.	n.a.	n.a.
1936	2,571	1,549	618	40	45	60	558	36.0	393	25	47	3.0	n.a.	n.a.	n.a.
1937	2,854	1,756	651	37	51	68	583	33.2	526	30	52	3.0	n.a.	n.a.	14
1938	2,960	1,636	659	40	53	71	588	35.9	649	40	48	2.9	n.a.	n.a.	15
1939	3,162	1,796	681	38	54	73	608	33.9	677	38	54	3.0	n.a.	n.a.	8
1940	3,331	1,948	712	37	58	78	634	32.5	656	34	59	3.0	n.a.	n.a.	15
1941	3,459	2,127	686	32	84	113	575	27.0	630	30	65	3.1	n.a.	n.a.	16
1942	3,701	2,332	721	31	87	117	604	25.9	627	27	71	3.0	n.a.	n.a.	18
1943	4,336	2,634	781	30	91	122	659	25.0	684	26	82	3.1	n.a.	n.a.	19
1944	4,731	2,856	855	30	104	140	715	25.0	1,010	35	94	3.3	n.a.	n.a.	10
1945	4,840	3,002	917	31	117	157	760	25.3	896	30	98	3.3	n.a.	n.a.	25
1946	5,152	3,133	898	29	121	163	735	23.5	1,102	35	103	3.3	n.a.	n.a.	19
1947	5,650	3,511	934	27	132	177	757	21.6	1,068	30	128	3.6	n.a.	n.a.	10
1948	5,958	3,942	1,022	26	147	197	825	20.9	810	21	127	3.2	n.a.	n.a.	57
1949	6,274	4,156	1,059	25	157	211	848	20.4	854	21	139	3.3	n.a.	n.a.	66
1950	7,084	4,865	1,187	24	182	244	943	19.4	801	16	175	3.6	126	2.6	54
1951	8,251	5,685	1,442	25	205	275	1,167	20.5	793	14	192	3.4	192	3.4	135
1952	8,862	6,149	1,484	24	224	300	1,184	19.3	849	14	204	3.3	207	3.4	178
1953	9,207	6,257	1,471	24	239	321	1,150	17.6	810	13	240	3.8	230	3.7	158
1954	9,466	6,968	1,457	21	252	338	1,119	16.0	724	10	216	3.1	231	3.3	102
1955	10,179	7,583	1,508	20	281	377	1,131	14.9	774	10	247	3.3	245	3.2	68
1956	10,946	8,312	1,421	17	293	393	1,028	12.4	864	10	213	2.6	296	3.6	136
1957	11,489	8,804	1,480	17	295	396	1,084	12.3	809	9	205	2.3	299	3.4	191
1958	11,664	9,059	1,604	18	295	396	1,208	13.3	633	7	284	3.1	312	3.4	123
1959	12,617	9,967	1,737	17	321	431	1,306	13.1	571	6	223	2.2	349	3.5	119
1960	13,334	10,585	1,780	17	339	455	1,325	12.5	563	5	274	2.6	347	3.3	132

1. All data except 1960 from U.S. Bureau of Mines, *Minerals Yearbook*. 1960 natural gas liquids extraction from special release of Bureau of Mines; 1960 data, unless otherwise specified, from Bureau of Mines, *Mineral Market Report* (MMS No. 3298, Sept. 5, 1961), and American Gas Association, *1961 Gas Facts*.

2. Gross production from oil and gas wells, minus amounts used for repressuring; equal to net marketed production plus field use, wasted and vented and transmission losses, plus net storage changes.

3. Net withdrawals minus amounts wasted and vented, field use, net storage changes, and transmission losses. Marketed production, in Bureau of Mines usage, is net withdrawal minus amounts wasted and vented. The concept used in this table is dictated by the fact that the sum of the end-use estimates as projected equals net marketed production which in turn forms the basis for estimating the remaining quantities.

4. Converted from barrels on the basis of 1,343 cubic feet per barrel (see Table A15–14, footnote 12).

5. With the greater emphasis that was placed on natural gasoline in the past this ratio is undoubtedly too high for the earlier years, as heavier fractions are equivalent to lower volume. Thus the percentage relationship depicted in this column exaggerates the decline in the portion that is devoted to field use other than extraction loss. However, the declining tendency is beyond dispute.

APPENDIX TO CHAPTER 15

TABLE A15–13. Projected Petroleum Demand in All Uses

(Million barrels)

	1960		1970	1980	1990	2000
Residential—Space heating[1]	370	L	237	198	148	125
		M	325	293	274	251
		H	323	328	345	367
Residential—All other[2]	92	L	59	50	37	31
		M	81	73	68	63
		H	81	82	86	92
Commercial[3]	138	L	166	192	210	252
		M	187	232	300	403
		H	229	276	398	555
General manufacturing[4]	140	L	151	171	211	263
		M	165	208	281	387
		H	183	251	375	565
Iron and steel industry[5]	40	L	41	40	46	50
		M	52	61	78	102
		H	66	86	123	183
Nonferrous metals[6]	8	L	8	9	11	12
		M	11	15	21	28
		H	15	26	38	60
Defense[7]	213	L	182	99	86	99
		M	272	267	256	335
		H	363	430	473	716
Electricity generation[8]	101	L	103	98	99	97
		M	123	126	129	136
		H	163	180	216	275
Agriculture[9]	128	L	132	137	137	135
		M	134	144	152	158
		H	138	151	165	181
Asphalt and road oil[10]	111	L	146	197	257	334
		M	157	224	313	448
		H	176	277	440	710
Transportation[11]	1,639	L	2,160	2,940	3,900	5,090
		M	2,320	3,340	4,730	6,780
		H	2,610	4,170	6,720	10,880
All uses identified above	2,980	L	3,385	4,128	5,142	6,488
		M	3,827	4,983	6,602	9,091
		H	4,347	6,257	9,379	14,584
Miscellaneous uses[12]	149	L	169	206	257	324
		M	191	249	330	455
		H	217	313	469	729

Table A15–13 (cont'd)

(Million barrels)

		1960		1970	1980	1990	2000
Liquid refinery gas[13]		78	L	100	141	190	277
			M	116	175	273	462
			H	134	222	377	658
Petroleum refinery fuel[14]		165	L	188	229	285	360
			M	213	276	367	501
			H	239	351	520	810
Less: Natural gasoline originating in gas processing[13]		185	L	230	280	310	340
			M	270	340	400	480
			H	310	420	580	780
Total consumption[15] (bil. bbl.)		3.19	L	3.61	4.42	5.56	7.11
			M	4.08	5.34	7.17	10.03
			H	4.63	6.72	10.16	16.00

1. From Table A10–11.
2. From Table A10–18.
3. From Table A10–24.
4. From Table A10–39.
5. From Table A10–41.
6. From Table A10–43.
7. From Table A9–5.
8. From Table A15–10.
9. From Table A10–47.
10. From Table A4–10.
11. Liquid fuel consumption for all transportation uses as shown in Table A5–20, adjusted for small content of liquid petroleum gas used as motor fuel, especially in trucks and other heavy equipment. These amounts that are deducted are shown in Table A15–15, under "Motor fuel." While the correction is almost insignificant in quantitative terms and the LPG figures themselves suffer from a good deal of ambiguity as to end-use, the correction is made, nonetheless, as a reminder of the existence of this problem.
12. Represents 5% of identified uses. For rationale see the section in Chapter 15, "Other Fuel Requirements."
13. From Table A15–15. Liquid refinery gas is not included in preceding end-uses.
14. From Table A10–45.
15. For 1960, this total compares with the preliminary estimate of the Bureau of Mines, adjusted to a basis, in figures comparable to ours, of 3.2 billion barrels. No further adjustment was therefore deemed necessary. The Bureau of Mines figure was derived as follows:

Crude production	2.575 bil. bbl.
Crude net imports	.369 " "
Product net imports	.223 " "
Stock change, crude	.017 " " (decline)
Stock change, products	.017 " " (decline)
Apparent consumption	3,201 bil. bbl.

The figures shown include Alaska and Hawaii. Comparability is affected only in exports of refined products, which are no longer included. Thus the comparable export figure is more likely to be 235 than 223, and the apparent consumption 3.21 billion. This does not invalidate the conclusion reached above.

TABLE A15–14.   Projected Natural Gas Demand in All Uses

(Trillion cubic feet)

	1960		1970	1980	1990	2000
Residential[1]	3.08	L M H	3.36 4.30 4.75	4.05 5.47 6.78	3.99 5.74 8.49	3.74 5.78 10.00
Commercial[2]	.89	L M H	1.04 1.21 1.29	1.37 1.53 1.77	1.35 1.60 2.21	1.28 1.61 2.60
Public[3]	.47		.67	.92	1.04	1.17
General manufacturing[4]	2.17	L M H	3.16 3.46 3.81	4.33 5.21 6.32	5.73 7.64 10.20	7.48 10.99 16.05
Iron and steel industry[5]	.36	L M H	.36 .47 .59	.37 .56 .79	.42 .70 1.11	.45 .90 1.61
Nonferrous metals[6]	.12	L M H	.13 .18 .24	.15 .24 .40	.17 .32 .59	.20 .44 .94
Petroleum refining[7]	.72	L M H	.82 .93 1.02	1.00 1.20 1.53	1.24 1.60 2.26	1.57 2.19 3.54
Carbon black manufacture[8]	.20		.16	.12	.10	.10
Electricity generation[9]	2.03	L M H	2.90 3.49 4.63	3.00 3.85 5.54	2.79 3.64 6.12	2.47 3.48 7.00
Total identified uses	10.04	L M H	12.60 14.87 17.16	15.31 19.10 24.17	16.83 22.38 32.12	18.46 26.66 43.01
Total identified uses plus pipeline fuel (net marketed)[10]	10.40	L M H	13.06 15.41 17.78	15.86 19.79 25.05	17.44 23.19 33.28	19.13 27.63 44.57
Transmission losses[11]	.26	L M H	.33 .39 .44	.40 .49 .63	.44 .58 .83	.48 .69 1.14
Field use, excluding NGL extraction loss[12]	1.32	L M H	1.44 1.70 1.96	1.59 1.98 2.50	1.74 2.32 3.33	1.91 2.76 4.46
End-use consumption, excluding NGL extraction loss	11.98	L M H	14.83 17.50 20.18	17.85 22.26 28.18	19.62 26.09 37.44	21.52 31.08 50.17
Same adjusted to level shown for comparable coverage by Bureau of Mines data[13]	12.31	L M H	15.25 17.99 20.75	18.35 22.88 28.97	20.17 26.82 38.49	22.12 31.95 51.57
Wasted and vented as per cent of net marketed[14]	5.4		4.0	3.0	3.0	3.0
Amount wasted and vented	.56	L M H	.52 .62 .71	.48 .59 .75	.52 .70 1.00	.57 .83 1.34

Table A15–14 (cont'd)

(Trillion cubic feet)

		1960		1970	1980	1990	2000
Total disappearance including			L	15.77	18.83	20.69	22.69
amounts wasted and vented		12.87	M	18.61	23.47	27.52	32.78
			H	21.46	29.72	39.49	52.91
NGL originating in natural			L	.62	.82	1.01	1.32
gas processing [15]		.46	M	.73	1.00	1.39	2.09
			H	.84	1.26	1.96	3.11
Net withdrawals [16]			L	16.4	19.6	21.7	24.0
		13.33	M	19.3	24.5	28.9	34.9
			H	22.3	31.0	41.4	56.0

1. From Table A10–19.
2. From Table A10–23.
3. From Table A10–26.
4. From Table A10–39.
5. From Table A10–41.
6. From Table A10–43.
7. From Table A10–45.
8. 1960 based upon Bureau of Mines data. Projected as a declining amount (following past trend), but reaching stable level after 1980.
9. From Table A15–10.
10. Preceding totals assumed to represent 96.5% of total including pipeline fuel. The percentage of pipeline fuel to total gas consumption has remained very stable during the past decade (Table A15–12) and is not assumed to undergo any change. Any large-scale switch to the transportation of gas by ship might, however, depress the percentage and correspondingly raise petroleum consumption. Such changes might occur in the second half of the period under review in this country, though undoubtedly much sooner in other parts of the world. The total falls short of the total calculated in Table A15–12 by 0.18 trillion cubic feet. Adjustment for this and allowance for storage changes is made in subsequent line (cf. footnote 13).
11. Based upon Table A15–12; percentage assumed to remain at 2.5 of net marketable amounts as here defined.
12. Field use, as reported by the Bureau of Mines, includes quantities stripped from natural gas in processing plants. We have approximated these amounts by assuming the equivalence of 1,343 cubic feet of gas to one barrel of liquids produced (see Schurr, *et al.*, *Energy in the American Economy, 1850–1975*, Johns Hopkins Press, for Resources for the Future, 1960, p. 434). While this factor cannot be a constant but must vary with the composition of the liquids extracted, and probably other factors as well, the simplification here introduced is not considered of importance in the context. Natural gas liquids originating in the natural gas industry, reported in barrels, can thus be excluded, and all other field use (pumping, drilling, etc.) be obtained as the balance. So defined and calculated, field use has been declining from 20% of marketed production in 1950 to 13% in recent years and 12.7% in 1960 (Table A15–12). Given the rising value of gas in the market place, it is assumed that it will decline further but more slowly, as shown in the calculation, and will stabilize at 10%, beginning in 1980.
13. The figure shown for 1960 represents the Bureau of Mines estimate of marketed production (other than NGL extraction), which includes storage and pipeline fill changes, not identified in the calculation up to this point. Storage changes in 1960 amount to 132 million cubic feet, so that the residual difference amounts to 190 million cubic feet, consisting of changes in pipeline fill and a residual error, due to underestimates of individual end-uses above. This residual error amounts to about 2.5% of consumption, and therefore the adjustment to the Bureau of Mines level is made without hesitation to provide historical comparability.
14. 1960 ratio based upon historical record as shown in Table A15–12; this ratio is assumed to decline further, as shown.
15. From Table A15–15: last row converted to natural gas equivalent volume on the basis of factor described in footnote 12, above.
16. Equals amounts withdrawn from wells minus quantities used for repressuring.

TABLE A15–15.   Projected Natural Gas Liquids Demand in All Uses

(Million barrels)

		1960		1970	1980	1990	2000
Residential space heating[1]		36	L M H	49 50 52	52 56 62	38 40 51	22 26 38
Cooking[2]		18	L M H	15 18 20	13 18 23	11 17 25	9 17 29
Water heating[3]		14	L M H	18 20 22	21 24 29	21 26 36	18 26 44
Commercial[4]		21		30	38	41	44
Chemical industry feed stock[5]		87	L M H	150 190 240	250 340 470	400 640 930	670 1,230 1,790
Agriculture[6]		12	L M H	16 16 16	19 20 21	21 24 26	24 28 32
Motor fuel[7]		12		18	29	44	63
Industry (excluding chemical feed stock) and miscellaneous[8]		32	L M H	39 43 47	47 57 69	58 77 103	72 106 155
Total NGL use (other than natural gasoline)		232	L M H	335 385 445	469 582 741	634 909 1,256	922 1,540 2,195
Originating in petroleum refining[9]		78	L M H	100 116 134	141 175 222	190 273 377	277 462 658
Originating in natural gas processing[9]		154	L M H	234 270 312	328 407 519	444 636 879	645 1,078 1,536
Natural gasoline including LPG blended into gasoline[10]		185	L M H	230 270 310	280 340 420	310 400 580	330 480 780
Total originating in natural gas processing[11]		339	L M H	464 540 622	608 747 939	754 1,036 1,459	985 1,558 2,316

Table A15–15 (cont'd)

1. From Table A10–11.
2. From Table A10–12; converted at 4,011,000 Btu per barrel.
3. From Table A10–13; converted at 4,011,000 Btu per barrel.
4. From Table A10–24; converted at 4,011,000 Btu per barrel.
5. From Table A15–11, rounded.
6. From Table A10–47.
7. 1960 represents reported sales of liquid petroleum gas for motor fuel of 21 million barrels (Bureau of Mines, *Mineral Market Report,* MMS No. 3297, Aug. 3, 1961), minus amount so used in agriculture, which is estimated at 75% of quantity shown in line above. Projected at annual increments rising slowly from those recently experienced (about 1 million barrels per year for *all* uses of motor fuel in 1955–60 period).
8. For 1960, represents difference between total demand below, as reported by U.S. Bureau of Mines, and uses identified above. Includes principally industrial use of LPG other than as feed stock for chemicals (including synthetic rubber). The projection is based upon that of total fuel use in manufacturing (excluding primary metals and petroleum refining) as in Table A10–38. This category also includes LPG used in secondary oil recovery, which has recently been rising steeply. In a sense, this is not consumption but temporary disappearance. No attempt has been made to estimate future use for this purpose, which might in time greatly exceed other LPG uses, but which has not to date been sufficiently analyzed for separate consideration.
9. There is no demand as such for LPG originating in the processing of natural gas or in petroleum refining, but only for LPG regardless of origin. For measuring total petroleum or total natural gas demand, the joint demand has to be allocated by industrial origin. For 1960, this can be done on the basis of Bureau of Mines data most recently available in an undated release entitled "Production, Stocks, and Demand of Natural Gas Liquids and Liquefied Refinery Gases in the United States." Unfortunately, only production and not consumption is shown by origin. In addition, it is not clear whether the data include figures for refinery gases consumed in the plants where they originate. Our guess would be that they do not, for while the amount is small, the quantities that one concludes from the statistics are going to gasoline blending are far too small in that they appear to be zero. The figures are thus more likely to represent sales or shipments. There is, however, no better way of dealing with the matter. It has therefore been assumed that all liquefied refinery gases are consumed in uses other than gasoline. On that basis the portions originating in refining and gas processing respectively can be determined. By the same token, all natural gasoline and all LPG used for blending must be assumed to originate in gas processing. Fortunately, the amounts involved, in terms of either total oil or total gas, are not significant.

While there will undoubtedly be shifts in the ratio in which total natural gas liquid supplies are obtained from the two sources, there is little basis for determining future sources of supply. For the purposes of this study we have assumed a continuation of the current relationship, which, in turn, has been simplified to 30% from petroleum refining and 70% from gas processing. There is some indication that the balance might shift towards petroleum, since the resulting portion that would have to be stripped from natural gas in future years is substantially beyond current practice and touches what experts at present consider the feasible limits. Related to gross withdrawals of gas, excluding only the gas wasted and vented, the amount stripped would have to rise from the current approximate 1 gallon per thousand cubic feet (comparable to 1.47 per thousand cubic feet of the 70% or so that is currently treated) to 1.4 in 1980 and 1.8 in 2000. Part of this increase could come about by treatment of a larger percentage of all gas withdrawn, but part would also have to come from more intensive stripping. Certainly, achieving the indicated level of liquid gas production would be predicated upon a much more intensive exploitation of the potential, including the proper installation of equipment which becomes more and more expensive as more of the lighter fractions are stripped.
10. 1960 from Bureau of Mines release cited in footnote 9 above. Projected in rough proportion to increase in end-use demand for natural gas. The assumption that consumption is at a constant ratio between gas and natural gasoline production is probably the most realistic that can be made at a time when the accent is not on the heavier hydrocarbon fractions. It is also likely that, for technical reasons, all natural strippable gasoline fractions are now being extracted, leaving little room for growth.
11. Sum of preceding two items. For significance, see footnote 9.

TABLE A15–16. Projected Bituminous Coal and Anthracite Demand in All Uses

(Million short tons)

	1960		1970	1980	1990	2000
Residential[1]	20	L	12	10	3	–
		M	12	11	3	–
		H	13	12	4	–
Commercial[2]	22	L	8	4	–	–
		M	11	9	8	8
		H	15	11	11	11
Iron and steel industry[3]	79	L	66	57	59	58
		M	85	87	99	117
		H	106	122	157	210
Nonferrous metals[4]	3	L	3	3	4	4
		M	4	6	7	10
		H	5	9	14	22
General manufacturing[5]	67	L	66	63	61	63
		M	72	76	81	93
		H	79	93	108	136
Railroads[6]	3		1	–	–	–
Electricity generation[7]	208	L	245	316	327	324
		M	296	407	426	457
		H	391	585	716	922
Total identified uses	402	L	401	453	454	449
		M	481	596	624	685
		H	610	832	1,010	1,301
Total domestic consumption[8]	398	L	397	448	449	445
		M	476	590	618	678
		H	604	824	1,000	1,288
Total consumption, incl. exports[9]	436	L	437	488	489	485
		M	516	630	658	718
		H	644	864	1,040	1,328

1. From Table A10–11.
2. From Table A10–24.
3. From Table A10–41.
4. From Table A10–43.
5. From Table A10–39.
6. From Table A5–18.
7. From Table A15–10.
8. 1960 adjusted to the level of consumption reported by the Bureau of Mines, and projections adjusted proportionately.
9. Projected by raising domestic consumption by 40 million tons throughout the period and at all three levels (compared with 38 million tons actually exported in 1960). This adjustment is based upon the prospect of gradually increasing shipments to Canada, declining shipments to Western Europe, and possibly growing exports to developing countries. However, the balancing of these factors is quite uncertain and could be done only on the basis of long-range studies of potential export markets, not now available. The adjustment is, therefore, only a reminder of the existence of this segment of demand.

TABLE A15–17. Allocation of Electricity Consumption, including Losses, to Economic Sectors, by Type of Generation (Medium Projection)

	Consumption [1]		Losses and unaccounted for [1] (bil. kwh)	Consumption plus losses (bil. kwh)	Heat rate [2] (Btu/kwh)	Btu consumed in generation (quadrillion)	Energy shares (quadrillion Btu) [3]				
	Bil. kwh	Per cent of total					Coal	Oil	Natural gas	Hydro	Nuclear
1960:											
Total	753	100	92	845 ⎤		9.30	4.99	.64	2.03	1.64	–
Residential	193	26	24	217 ⎥		2.39	1.28	.16	.52	.42	–
Commercial	113	15	14	127 ⎬ 11,010		1.40	.75	.10	.30	.25	–
Industrial	355	47	43	398 ⎥		4.38	2.35	.30	.95	.77	–
All other	92	12	11	103 ⎦		1.13	.61	.08	.25	.20	–
1970:											
Total	1,257	100	143	1,400 ⎤		14.24	7.10	.78	3.49	2.52	.36
Residential	353	28	40	393 ⎥		4.00	2.00	.22	.98	.71	.10
Commercial	190	15	21	211 ⎬ 10,175		2.15	1.07	.12	.53	.38	.05
Industrial	605	48	69	674 ⎥		6.86	3.42	.38	1.68	1.21	.17
All other	109	9	13	122 ⎦		1.24	.62	.07	.30	.22	.03
1980:											
Total	2,014	100	215	2,229 ⎤		20.77	9.77	.79	3.85	2.64	3.72
Residential	594	29	62	656 ⎥		6.11	2.87	.23	1.13	.78	1.10
Commercial	308	15	32	340 ⎬ 9,320		3.17	1.49	.12	.59	.40	.57
Industrial	977	49	105	1,082 ⎥		10.08	4.74	.38	1.87	.28	1.81
All other	135	7	15	150 ⎦		1.40	.66	.05	.26	.18	.25
1990:											
Total	2,943	100	294	3,237 ⎤		27.72	10.22	.81	3.64	2.77	10.28
Residential	843	29	85	928 ⎥		7.95	2.93	.23	1.04	.80	2.95
Commercial	416	14	41	457 ⎬ 8,565		3.91	1.44	.11	.51	.39	1.45
Industrial	1,524	52	153	1,678 ⎥		14.36	5.30	.42	1.88	1.43	5.33
All other	159	5	15	174 ⎦		1.49	.55	.04	.20	.15	.55
2000:											
Total	4,305	100	406	4,711 ⎤		37.01	10.95	.86	3.48	2.82	18.90
Residential	1,188	28	114	1,302 ⎥		10.23	3.03	.23	.96	.78	5.23
Commercial	554	13	53	607 ⎬ 7,860		4.77	1.41	.11	.45	.36	2.44
Industrial	2,375	55	223	2,598 ⎥		20.42	6.04	.47	1.92	1.55	10.43
All other	188	4	16	204 ⎦		1.60	.47	.04	.15	.12	.82

Items do not always add up to total because of rounding.

1. From Table A15–1. Procedure makes simplified assumption that losses are proportional to consumption.
2. Computed from Table A15–10; adjusted fuel consumption converted to Btu and related to generation.

Average rates so calculated applied to hydro and nuclear generation.
3. From Table A15–10; fuel amounts converted to Btu and averages applied to hydro and nuclear shares. Procedure involves simplified assumption that over-all pattern of different generating modes applies equally to all sectors.

TABLE A15–18. Projected Consumption of Energy, by Economic Sectors and Sources[1] (Medium Projection)

(Quadrillion Btu)

	Coal			Petroleum (excl. liquid refinery gas)			Natural gas (excl. NGL)			NGL (incl. liquid refinery gas and natural gasoline)	Hydro power	Nuclear power	Consumption via electricity only	All sources of energy
	Direct	Via electricity generation (incl. losses)	Total	Direct	Via electricity generation (incl. losses)	Total	Direct	Via electricity generation (incl. losses)	Total					
Residential[3]														
1960	.53	1.28	1.81	2.63	.16	2.79	3.19	.52	3.71	.28	.42	–	2.38	9.01
1970	.33	2.00	2.33	2.31	.22	2.53	4.45	.98	5.43	.35	.71	.10	4.00	11.45
1980	.29	2.87	3.16	2.09	.23	2.32	5.66	1.13	6.79	.39	.78	1.10	6.11	14.54
1990	.08	2.93	3.01	1.95	.23	2.18	5.94	1.04	6.98	.33	.80	2.95	7.95	16.25
2000	–	3.03	3.03	1.79	.23	2.02	5.98	.96	6.94	.28	.78	5.23	10.23	18.28
Commercial[4]														
1960	.60	.75	1.35	.84	.10	.94	.92	.30	1.22	.08	.25	–	1.40	3.84
1970	.30	1.07	1.37	1.16	.12	1.28	1.25	.53	1.78	.12	.38	.05	2.15	4.98
1980	.23	1.49	1.72	1.44	.12	1.56	1.58	.59	2.17	.15	.40	.57	3.17	6.57
1990	.20	1.44	1.64	1.86	.11	1.97	1.66	.51	2.17	.17	.39	1.45	3.91	7.79
2000	.20	1.41	1.61	2.50	.11	2.61	1.67	.45	2.12	.18	.36	2.44	4.77	9.32
Transportation[5]														
1960	.08	–	.08	7.71	–	7.71	.37	–	.37	1.03	–	–	–	9.19
1970	.03	–	.03	10.87	–	10.87	.56	–	.56	1.50	–	–	–	12.96
1980	–	–	–	15.90	–	15.90	.71	–	.71	1.92	–	–	–	18.53
1990	–	–	–	22.95	–	22.95	.84	–	.84	2.30	–	–	–	26.09
2000	–	–	–	33.39	–	33.39	1.00	–	1.00	2.80	–	–	–	37.19
Industrial[6]														
1960	3.90	2.35	6.25	2.13	.30	2.43	5.07	.95	6.03	.48	.77	–	4.37	15.95
1970	4.22	3.42	7.64	2.66	.38	3.04	7.14	1.68	8.82	.93	1.21	.17	6.86	21.81
1980	4.43	4.74	9.17	3.36	.38	3.74	9.64	1.87	11.51	1.59	1.28	1.81	10.08	29.10
1990	4.90	5.30	10.20	4.48	.42	4.90	13.12	1.88	15.00	2.87	1.43	5.33	14.36	39.73
2000	5.76	6.04	11.80	6.12	.47	6.59	18.00	1.92	19.92	5.33	1.55	10.43	20.42	55.62
All other[7]														
1960	1.00	.61	1.61	3.48	.08	3.56	1.68	.25	1.93	.05	.20	–	1.13	7.35
1970	1.05	.62	1.67	4.39	.07	4.46	2.25	.30	2.55	.06	.22	.03	1.24	8.99
1980	1.05	.66	1.71	5.20	.05	5.25	2.71	.26	2.97	.08	.18	.25	1.40	10.44
1990	1.05	.55	1.60	6.23	.04	6.27	3.16	.20	3.36	.10	.15	.55	1.49	12.03
2000	1.05	.47	1.52	8.31	.04	8.35	3.68	.15	3.83	.11	.12	.82	1.60	14.75

All sectors													
1960	6.11	4.99	11.10	16.79	.64	17.43	11.23	2.03	13.26	1.92	1.64	—	9.30	45.35
1970	5.93	7.10	13.03	21.39	.78	22.18	15.65	3.49	19.14	2.96	2.52	.36	14.24	60.19
1980	6.00	9.77	15.77	27.99	.79	28.78	20.30	3.85	24.15	4.13	2.64	3.72	20.77	79.19
1990	6.23	10.22	16.45	37.47	.81	38.28	24.72	3.64	28.36	5.77	2.77	10.28	27.72	101.91
2000	7.01	10.95	17.96	52.11	.86	52.97	30.33	3.48	33.81	8.70	2.82	18.90	37.01	135.16

Sum of individual items does not always equal total because of rounding.

1. Where Btu values are not stated in the tables from which data in this table have been collected, they have been calculated by applying the most appropriate conversion factor, depending upon the type or mixture of types of fuel in each use. This is of significance principally in oil, where there is a range from 5.2 million Btu per barrel for gasoline to 6.4 million Btu for residual fuel oil.

2. From Table A15–17.

3. Direct uses from Tables A10–11, 12, 13, 18, 19.

4. Direct uses from Table A10–24.

5. Includes pipeline fuel (Table A15–14). Other uses from Tables A15–

13 and 15, with petroleum and natural gasoline converted at 5.3 mil. Btu/ bbl. and natural gas liquids at 4.0 mil. Btu/bbl. Small amounts of electricity used by transportation media are ignored.

6. Direct uses include use for iron and steel, nonferrous metals, petroleum refining, general manufacturing; field use of natural gas (which is principal component of fuel use in mineral production); use for carbon black; use of NGL as chemical feed stock; and industry and miscellaneous use of NGL, in the following tables: A10–39, 41, 43, 45, A15–14, 15, 16.

7. Direct uses include use for defense, agriculture, asphalt and road oil; public use of natural gas; gas transmission losses; miscellaneous petroleum uses; gas wasted and vented and coal exports, in Tables A15–13, 14, and 16 and underlying tables.

TABLE A15–19.   Historical and Projected Consumption of Energy in Physical Quantities and Percentages of Total (Medium projection)

	1940[1]	1950[1]	1960	1970	1980	1990	2000
In physical quantities:[2]							
Coal, bituminous & anthracite (mil. tons)	499	523	436	516	630	658	718
Oil, incl. liquid refinery gas (bil. bbl.)	1.41	2.29	3.19	4.08	5.34	7.17	10.03
Natural gas, excluding NGL (tril. cu. ft.)	3.29	6.79	12.87	18.61	23.47	27.52	32.78
Natural gas liquids, incl. nat. gasoline (mil. bbl.)	60	179	339	540	747	1,036	1,558
Electricity, all modes (bil. kwh)	182	390	845	1,400	2,229	3,237	4,711
Electricity, thermal (bil. kwh)	130	289	696	1,117	1,546	1,714	1,948
Electricity, hydro (bil. kwh)	52	101	149	248	283	323	363
Electricity, nuclear (bil. kwh)	–	–	–	35	400	1,200	2,400
In quadrillion Btu:[3]							
Coal	13.00	13.70	11.10	13.03	15.77	16.45	17.96
Oil	8.20	13.30	17.74	22.64	29.48	39.37	54.82
Natural gas	3.41	7.03	13.26	19.14	24.15	28.36	33.81
Natural gas liquids	.24	.72	1.61	2.50	3.43	4.68	6.85
Hydro power	.92	1.60	1.64	2.52	2.64	2.77	2.82
Nuclear power	–	–	–	.36	3.72	10.28	18.90
(All electricity	2.98	5.47	9.30	14.24	20.77	27.72	37.01)
Total	25.77	36.35	45.35	60.19	79.19	101.91	135.16
Percentage shares:							
Coal	50.4	37.7	24.5	21.6	19.9	16.2	13.3
Oil	31.8	36.6	39.1	37.6	37.2	38.6	40.5
Natural gas	13.3	19.3	29.2	31.8	30.5	27.8	25.0
Natural gas liquids	0.9	2.0	3.6	4.2	4.3	4.6	5.1
Hydro power	3.6	4.4	3.6	4.2	3.4	2.7	2.1
Nuclear power	–	–	–	0.6	4.7	10.1	14.0
(All electricity	11.6	15.1	20.5	23.7	26.2	27.2	27.4)
Total	100.0	100.0	100.0	100.0	100.0	100.0	100.0

1. From *Energy in the American Economy 1850–1975*, Tables VI and VII and Table 39 (natural gas, including transmission losses, and gas wasted and vented), adjusted to include coal and oil exports; total electricity from *Electric Utility Industry Statistics*, 1960, Table 8, converted to Btu on basis of heat rates, Table 40.

2. Except as indicated, data are from Tables A15–10, 13, 14, 15, 16. Fuels include amounts burned in generating electricity.

3. Except as indicated, data are from Table A15–18, in which different uses have been converted at different caloric rates. Actually, direct conversion of physical data, given above, at standard rates would not materially alter the results. Fuels include amounts burned in generating electricity. NGL derived from liquid refinery gas included in NGL in Table A15–18, here transferred to Oil line.

appendix
to
chapter
16

METALS

Notes

AMONG THE many users of metals, four sectors of the economy stand out as major consumers: the construction industry, the manufacture of transportation equipment, producer and consumer durables manufacture, and—less prominent, but by no means unimportant—container manufacture. The requirements of these four groups for the most widely used metals have been evolved in various sections of Part I. The main tasks of the tables in this appendix are:

a) to supplement the projections of demand for major metals in the four above-mentioned sectors with those for the numerous quantitatively less important uses, including uses in which a metal loses its identity, in order to arrive at estimates of total requirements for specific metals;

b) to analyze the demand for certain "minor" metals—specifically, those primarily used as additives in the making of steel;

c) to translate the net quantities of metals consumed in end uses into requirements for primary metal; i.e., to net out the recovery from obsolete scrap. These primary requirements, in turn, are in Chapter 21 compared with mineral resources, both within the borders of this country and abroad.

In relation to these tasks, two characteristics of metals, more fully discussed in Chapter 16, are of particular importance:

1) One, which they share with many other materials, is the fact that they can substitute for one another and can also be substituted for by other materials, such as wood or plastics. This implies that there are no absolute requirements for any specific metal. Our projections refer essentially to the relative usages that will prevail given existing long-term price trends and visible technological change. Even with these criteria there is room for wide variations in judgment. In the Medium projections we have made our best judgment for each metal, and (leaving aside problems of common denominators) the various metals are therefore additive. In the Lows and the Highs we have made more extreme judgments for each metal, most of which would not be consistent with one another, since each in turn assumes that the metal in question is either the least favored (Low) or the most favored (High) in the competitive race; the Lows and Highs, as a consequence, are not additive.

2) Another characteristic, in respect of which the metals are almost unique, is the fact that metal used in an end-product is not ordinarily lost to further consumption, since it can later be recovered and can be used over and over again. Large quantities of metal also become waste or scrap before reaching the end of the processing line; much of this is immediately reusable. We thus are faced with a considerable conceptual problem in defining when it is that a metal should be considered consumed.

Statistically, the definition of "when" can be in terms of form or time. For our purposes, we have used both references, in a seemingly contradictory way. The "point of measurement" at which we have aimed, in determining *time* of consumption, is the point at which semi-fabricated metal products are shipped from mill and foundry; this happens to provide, generally, the optimum combination of reasonably adequate historical statistics and closeness to the point of consumption as the latter term is used in the National Accounts. The *form* of consumption in which we are interested is similarly defined by National Accounting custom: we have sought to measure only that amount of metal which actually is incorporated into items of "final demand"—or, more precisely, is either incorporated into end-items or irretrievably lost along the way. This amount of metal happens to coincide (in quantity, not in time of consumption) with what is known as "apparent consumption of new supply"— the sum of metal newly recovered from natural resources and metal re-recovered from quantities consumed in past years. What is lost in the calculation is the metal recovered during the industrial production process from scrap and other reusable waste which never reaches the *form* of end-use consumption; this is a circular flow and makes no demand upon new supply. The basic equivalences may be summarized, roughly, as follows.[1]

Recoverable metal content of mine production + recovery of metal from obsolete scrap + net imports of metal in any form (except obsolete scrap) up to the mill and foundry product stage =

New supply, or apparent consumption =

Gross shipments from mills and foundries + previous irrecoverable losses − recoverable metal content of scrap generated in subsequent manufacturing processes =

Metal content of products finally consumed + all irrecoverable processing losses.

Obsolete scrap is excluded from gross imports because of its being already accounted for in the item "recovery from obsolete scrap." It is excluded from gross exports because of our particular approach in accounting for the contribution of obsolete scrap as a "credit" against demand for new metal at the time the obsolete scrap is actually used; on this basis, exports of old scrap are neutral so far as new metal demand is concerned. There has been no attempt to account for metals-in-use as a reserve and hence for exports of old scrap as

a diminution of that reserve, in the same way that ore which is either consumed domestically or shipped for export is compared (in Chapter 21) with our natural resource reserve.

The basic procedure of our metals analysis has been (1) to establish the historical comparison between the first and the third of these four equivalents; (2) to project the third by category of consumption, based primarily on the analysis in Part I; and (3) to adjust, if necessary, to the levels of the first equivalent on the basis of the historical "statistical error" revealed in step (1). A subsequent projection of the quantities recovered in future years from obsolete scrap yields as a final residual the implied demand upon natural resources, domestic or foreign, measured in recoverable metal content of ore.

The specific implementation of this basic procedure has differed somewhat from metal to metal. In particular, the nature of the available statistics and the traditional interest in steel ingot production and the inputs thereto have dictated a somewhat different approach to iron and steel from that used for the nonferrous metals. These details are discussed below.

Iron and Steel

The principal statistical sources used were the *Annual Statistical Reports* of the American Iron and Steel Institute; *Iron Age,* published by Chilton Company, Philadelphia; and *A Survey and Analysis of the Supply and Availability of Obsolete Iron and Steel Scrap,* prepared for the U.S. Department of Commerce by the Battelle Memorial Institute, Columbus, Ohio (1957).

The first step was to derive historical data on total annual net end-use consumption of iron and steel and to reconcile this total with the end-uses by the main consuming sectors of the economy, set forth in Part I. Detailed annual data are available only for shipments of steel to the various steel consuming industries (or in AISI terminology, to the various "market classifications"). Even these detailed statements do not give a complete industrial breakdown. Some 20 per cent of shipments volume is not allocated; most of this percentage is listed as shipments to the "warehouses and distributors" through which much of the steel consumed finds its way to fabricators of finished products. Other "basket" categories are: (1) steel for converting and processing; (2) forgings; (3) bolts, nuts, rivets, screws; and (4) non-classified. In order to arrive at an estimated end-use breakdown for all steel mill shipments, these last four comparatively small

1. A more precise statement would also allow for consumption in the form of *permanent* additions to industrial in-process stocks. Year-to-year stock increases (or decreases, considered as negative increases) have to be *deducted* in order to obtain apparent consumption, as a practical statistical matter. Although they include an element of permanent increase which actually constitutes consumption, for the most part these short-term fluctuations reflect only differences in timing (year of accounting) of quantities passing through successive processing stages.

groups were distributed among the 15 specific AISI major-end-use categories proportionately to the percentage shares of shipments going directly to the major categories. The large warehouse and distributor group, which in 1960 accounted for 18 per cent of all domestic steel shipments, was allocated on the basis of a report on the disposition of steel by U.S. Steel Corporation warehouses (see U.S. Congress, Temporary National Economic Committee, *Papers,* Vol. I, 1940), and a detailed analysis of warehouse shipments, by product, to individual steel-consuming industries for the years 1946, 1955, and 1957. For example, contractors are more likely to obtain their steel through warehouses than are railroads.

The major AISI categories, and the average percentage of warehouse shipments going to each, during the period 1940–60, follow:

Construction (including oil and gas well drilling and excluding railroad transportation)	40%
Contractors' products	10%
Automotive	15%
Agriculture	10%
Machinery and tools	8%
Electrical machinery	7%
Appliances, etc.	3%
Other domestic and commercial equipment	3%
Containers	4%
Total	100%

Amounts shipped from warehouses to other end-use categories (e.g., railroads, shipbuilding, etc.) were assumed to be negligible.

For 1929–39, *Iron Age* statistics on the distribution of steel mill products by market categories were expanded for 100 per cent coverage and reclassified to correspond to the AISI market classifications on the basis of a comparison and reconciliation of the two sets of statistics for the period 1940–49.

The adjusted historical data on steel shipments are shown in Table A16–3.

The next step consisted in estimating that amount of iron and steel which in the process of fabricating finished products is "lost" as borings, clippings, etc., or faulty intermediate or finished products. This so-called "prompt industrial scrap" is usually within a short period resold to mills and foundries for resmelting or remelting and thus is not really lost to the economy. In the individual steel and iron consuming industries the proportion of prompt industrial scrap automatically generated in the manufacture of finished goods varies from 3 per cent (as in construction) to more than 30 per cent (as in the aircraft industry). The generation factors

employed in this study for the various industries are set forth in footnote 8 of Table A16–4; that table also shows the actual quantities of all prompt industrial scrap generated each year and the over-all generation factor, which varies from year to year according to the changing product mix. If these amounts of prompt industrial scrap are subtracted from the adjusted steel shipments, industry by industry, one arrives at a measure of net end-use consumption by each of the various market classifications, which, for the historical period, is shown in the main part of Table A16–4.

Since even for these historical data some 20 per cent of all steel shipments had to be allocated on a judgment basis, and since the prompt industrial scrap generation factors are at best an approximation, it is obvious that the net end-use consumption estimates cannot claim a high degree of precision. They must be considered as approximations, which, it is hoped, come closer to measuring net consumption than do the published statistical series.

This reservation applies also, and to a much higher degree, to the projected net end-use consumption data for the various market classifications, shown in Tables A16–10 and A16–12. The building of these tables started from the projections of net iron and steel consumption by major use groups, set forth in the appendices to Part I. These were supplemented by projections for a number of other uses, not dealt with in Part I, such as water and air transportation. Furthermore, some of the data given in Part I were adjusted to include additional quantities of steel and iron consumed by major use groups. (For example, Table A5–19 shows only the net steel consumption by automobiles and trucks, while Table A16–10 includes also the projected consumption in buses, school buses, motorcycles, and automotive repair and replacement parts.)

Tables A16–10 and 12 furnish the principal basis for the other series of projections included in the iron and steel section. If these tables show three or four significant digits, it should be kept in mind that this does not at all indicate the order of precision; rather, the figures were retained as a convenient device for subsequent computations and to enable the reader to follow our procedure step by step from net end-use consumption to requirements for pig iron.

If we raise these estimates of future iron and steel end-use consumption by the amounts of prompt industrial scrap generated in the process of fabrication (see Table A16–14), we arrive at projections of gross shipments. Next come projections of steel ingot production required to support the gross shipments, as well as sum total projections of gross output of steel mills and foundries (i.e., gross shipments plus net loss) and, finally, projected requirements for ferrous metallics. These are summarized in Table A16–9.

Since a substantial portion of the requirements for ferrous metallics is met by ferrous scrap, it is necessary to subtract scrap from the projected requirements for ferrous metallics in order to arrive at requirements for primary metal. This is comparatively simple for two types of scrap: home scrap and prompt industrial. For the former there exists historical information which can serve as the basis for projections; the latter is a function of the level of projected production of finished goods and of the product mix and can easily, though only approximately, be computed (as has been done in Table A16–14). An attempt to estimate the quantities of obsolete ferrous scrap potentially available and the amounts likely to be withdrawn for consumption, however, raises intricate problems. Historical information is lacking, except for one pilot study, the above-cited Battelle Survey. In the concepts of that Survey, which we have by and large followed, the quantity of obsolete scrap becoming potentially available each year (the annual crop) is a function of the iron and steel content of fabricated goods which were produced a number of years earlier. The number of years is related to the average useful life of the iron and/or steel containing goods (the life cycle). Obviously, not the total amount of metal which went into finished goods can be recovered, partly for technical reasons (corrosion, etc.), partly for economic reasons (exports of finished goods, inaccessible location, too-small size of certain goods, etc.), although in times of emergency the recoverability factor can be pushed far beyond what normally would appear to be economically feasible. Also, the useful life of finished goods can vary considerably according to availability and cost of replacements. Thus, the "potential recovery factors" and the "life cycles" shown in Table A16–15 must be considered rough approximations, even for the historical period. To project them as constant for some forty years into the future, even if broken down by market categories, is admittedly unsatisfactory. But data which would indicate an upward or downward trend in the average life cycles or recovery percentages of the various market categories were not available and could not be developed quickly.

Additional error may have been introduced by the fact that for categories with a long life cycle, e.g., certain types of construction, data on end-use consumption of specific metals several decades ago are lacking and had to be estimated. This is less of a problem in the case of iron and steel, for which we computed these data by market categories back to 1929, than for nonferrous metals. In the latter case we had to rely on a crude "backward extrapolation" in numerous cases.

It is obviously not realistic to assume that all items of one category, say all automobiles produced in one year, are retired in the same year one life cycle later. Any year's output in any one market category has a distribution of useful lives extending over a number of years, some individual items becoming obsolete earlier, some later. In order to allow for this, the Battelle Survey developed a method which we have adopted and employed for our calculations of the potential annual supply of obsolete scrap. "The mechanics of computation for this method," to quote Battelle (App. G–8), "result in obsoleting $1/(L)$ of the production in the first year and the balance, $\frac{(L-1)}{(L)}$, after (L) years, where (L) equals the life cycle period. . . . This can be interpreted as assuming that the bulk of the obsolescence occurs at the end of one life cycle plus some fraction of input from succeeding years. The $1/(L)$ is assumed to be the summation of these fractions." This method was tested by the Battelle Memorial Institute for the automotive industry, and it predicted within one per cent the number of automobiles actually removed from registration between 1951 and 1953. Although this is a rather brief test run and applies to only one of the major iron and steel consuming industries, its results seem far superior to those of a simpler method which would assume that all of each year's output in any particular category became obsolete after one average life cycle. For more realistic and more complex calculations—based on the distribution pattern of the average life cycles of each class of products within each of the major market classifications—empirical data were lacking. For this reason we applied the above described method to all market classifications. The results are set forth in Table A16–15.

There is, of course, a great difference between the amounts of obsolete scrap which under "normal" conditions can be expected to become available and the quantities actually withdrawn from the scrap reservoir (or out of the annual crop) and consumed or exported. By subtracting home scrap and prompt industrial scrap from the total scrap consumed by steel furnaces, by iron furnaces, and in other uses (given in U.S. Bureau of Mines, *Minerals Yearbook,* chapters on "Iron and Steel Scrap"), and by making adjustments for foreign trade and stock changes, one may arrive at estimates of total withdrawals and domestic consumption of obsolete scrap for the historical period. Total withdrawals are shown in Table A16–6.

Domestic consumption of obsolete scrap in iron and steel production in the 1950–60 period and projected consumption for different levels of output are shown in Table A16–16. In these projections the *total* domestic consumption of ferrous scrap by steel mills and foundries has been estimated as a percentage of the total input of ferrous metallics— the percentage being determined on the basis of long-term historical trends. Of this total, the share of home scrap was calculated as a function of the gross output of steel mills and foundries. The share of prompt industrial scrap was calculated as a function of the projected level of production of finished goods and changing product mix (see Table A16–14). By subtracting these two types of scrap from the estimated total ferrous scrap consumption, we arrive at a residual demand for scrap which is assumed to be met by withdrawals of obsolete scrap for consumption by domestic steel mills and foundries. Finally, by deducting all types of scrap from the total input of ferrous metallics required for the projected gross output of the iron and steel industry, we arrive at estimates of the domestic demand for primary (pig) iron, obtained from domestic or imported iron ore (see Tables A16–9 and A16–17).

The last three tables in the iron and steel section show the annual rates of growth of end-use consumption by major market categories for the 1940–60 period and projected to the year 2000; the changing relative importance of the main iron and steel consuming industries, beginning with 1929 and projected to 2000; and the relationship of steel ingot production, gross domestic shipments, and net end-use consumption to the gross national product, the production of durable goods and construction, and the growing population. In the last table it is noteworthy that the relationship to two variables—GNP and population—shows a wide spread between the Low, Medium, and High projections, while the input for durable goods and construction is almost the same for all projection levels. This results from the underlying projections of GNP, which between the Low and the High vary by less than 1:2 for the 1960–2000 period, and of the population, with a variation still less than this ratio. Durable goods and construction, on the other hand, account for only little more than one-fifth of GNP in the Low but almost one-half in the High projection.

Steel Additives

Of the fairly numerous additive and alloying elements used in steelmaking, seven (manganese, nickel, chromium, molybdenum, tungsten, vanadium, and cobalt) are treated statistically herein. Save for manganese, whose use is essential to all steelmaking, the quantities demanded of these various additives are closely related to the production of alloy steel, a category which as we have used it herein includes not only the varieties generally designated as alloy steel by the American Iron and Steel Institute but also those which the Institute refers to as stainless and as heat-resisting, since these differ in the amounts more than in the kinds of additives used.

Table A16–18 lays the groundwork for the additive (except manganese) projections by establishing the quantities of alloy steels. The projections of alloy steel quantities have been made essentially by extrapolation of the historical ratios of alloy to total steel in each of the principal use categories, tempered by judgments as to the effects of expected shifts in technology.

Except, once more, in the case of manganese, the ferroalloy tables (A16–22 to 29) do not attempt to arrive at apparent consumption, but stop with reported, or surveyed, consumption, both historically and in the projections. The reason is that the substantial scale of stockpiling operations in these commodities renders relatively meaningless any historical apparent consumption series which is not corrected for stockpiling, and the data are not obtainable which would permit a systematic correction for stockpile changes. This deficiency also holds for manganese, but it was assumed that the difference between surveyed and apparent consumption in 1960 was small enough to represent essentially the undercoverage of reporting rather than significant stockpile accretions.

It should be noted, in the case of manganese (Table A16–22), that the indicated 18 pounds per ingot ton is somewhat larger than the roughly 13 pounds which has been used in steelmaking in recent years (as ferromanganese or otherwise). The difference is the implicit loss in the making of ferromanganese, since it is the manganese content of inputs into ferromanganese (plus directly used ore) that Table A16–22 seeks to measure. Additional amounts of manganese enter the steel furnace via pig iron and via scrap, but these are not relevant to manganese ore requirements.

In general, the additive elements were related to alloy steel by means of a coefficient based on the historical relationship between the production of alloy steel and consumption of the additive either for steelmaking or for metallurgical uses in general. In the case of nickel, the historical analysis (shown in Table A16–23) was somewhat more elaborate than for the other additives, involving a separate calculation of the nickel content of stainless and of other alloy steels as produced, the combination of the two to get a combined percentage of nickel content, and the application of this percentage to the net end-use consumption of alloy (including stainless) steel. The nickel content, year by year, of stainless and of other alloy steel respectively was derived by applying to the production of each subtype within each of these two categories the midrange percentage of nickel content shown for each such subtype in U.S. Steel Corporation's *The Making, Shaping and Treating of Steel* (7th Ed., 1957).

Each of the additive elements finds only part of its use in alloy steel. The projection tables derive the other principal uses, in addition to the alloy use, in order to arrive at total consumption.

Nonferrous Metals

In general, the approach to all the nonferrous metals follows closely that outlined at the start of these notes—the establishment of historical series on net end-use of the metal, based on mill shipments less the generation of fabricating scrap, and the confrontation of these quantities with apparent consumption derived from production, net imports, and reported stock changes. Except in the case of copper, where the correspondence is relatively close, the difference between the accounted-for uses (in some cases including one or two "direct consumption" categories) and apparent consumption has been termed "other disappearance" and the historical relationship of this series to the accounted-for total has been used as a basis for adjusting the specifically projected consumption to apparent consumption levels. The chief element in this "other disappearance," aside from statistical error and undercoverage in the reported end-use consumption, is usually the accretions to government stockpile, data on which are not ordinarily available. Since stockpiling is in general not assumed to continue at past levels, the amount of adjustment carried into the projections is somewhat less than would be indicated by the historical experience.

Following the basic historical table (A16–30, 38, 50, 59, and 69), the following sequence of tables appears for each of the principal nonferrous metals (aluminum, copper, lead, zinc, and tin):

A historical table establishing the market breakdown of net end-use consumption, and in some cases relating this to gross mill and foundry shipments (A16–31, 39, 51, 60, and 70)

A similar table projecting net end-use consumption (A16–32, 44, 52, 61, and 71)

A table (except for tin) deriving, on the basis of

past end-use consumption, the projected generation of obsolete scrap (A16–33, 45, 54, and 64)

A table (except for tin) deriving the projected recovery of individual metals from each of the various kinds of nonferrous scrap (A16–34, 46, 55, and 65)

A projected apparent consumption table, ending with requirements for primary metal (A16–35, 47, 56, 66, and 72)

A table summarizing the rates of growth in end-use consumption, by market category (A16–36, 48, 57, 67, and 73)

A table summarizing the changing percentage participation of the various market categories (A16–37, 49, 58, 68, and 74).

In addition, there are some special subsidiary tables pertinent to particular metals and there are tables (A16–46, 55, and 75) cumulating the availabilities of each metal from all its obsolete scrap sources.

The omission of the standard scrap tables for tin is due to the virtually negligible recovery of tin or any other nonferrous metal from obsolete tin scrap. There is recovery of tin from obsolete copper and lead scrap, however, and these amounts are picked up in Tables A16–46, 55, and 75 and deducted to obtain primary tin requirements in Table A16–72. Table A16–55 actually treats lead- and tin-base scrap jointly and thus implicitly also picks up the small amount of lead recovered from the latter.

The special tables on copper (A16–40 to 43) have to do with the breakdowns in consumption among brass mill (now known as copper mill) products, wire mill products, and foundry products. We have included these partly because the data are reported in this form, but also to establish the distribution of copper-base products among copper as such, brass, and bronze, which is in turn necessary to establish average copper content (as well as content of major alloying metals). A special table for lead (A16–53) establishes the consumption of solder as a composite of its declining use in automobile radiators and its increasing use elsewhere. A special table for zinc (A16–63) establishes its consumption in die castings and in oxides—intermediate products which it was inappropriate to explore adequately in the appendices to Part I.

LIST OF TABLES

A16–
Iron and Steel

TABLE A16–1.   Historical Data on Production and Consumption of Iron and Steel

(Million tons)

	Shipments			Prompt indus-trial scrap gener-ation[4]	Net ex-ports of steel mill products and ferrous castings[5]	Net do-mestic iron and steel con-sump-tion[6]	Steel ingot pro-duc-tion[7]	Ingot produc-tion as per cent of steel shipments	Produc-tion of steel for castings[8]
	Steel mill prod-ucts[1]	Fer-rous cast-ings[2]	Iron and steel products total[3]						
1926	40.7						52.9	130	.3
1927	37.7						49.3	131	.2
1928	43.2	°17.0	°57.5	°6.7	°1.7	°49.1	56.4	131	.3
1929	47.1						61.4	130	.3
1930	33.8						44.4	131	.2
1931	22.0						28.5	130	.1
1932	12.0						15.1	126	.0
1933	17.6	°7.4	°26.8	°3.5	°.6	°22.7	25.6	146	.1
1934	20.0						29.1	146	.1
1935	25.3						38.0	150	.2
1936	35.7						53.2	149	.3
1937	39.2						56.4	144	.3
1938	21.8	°11.2	°47.1	°6.0	°3.2	°37.9	31.6	145	.2
1939	35.8						52.5	147	.3
1940	47.0						66.6	142	.3
1941	65.6	10.5	76.1	10.2	6.5	59.4	82.4	126	.4
1942	63.4	10.5	73.9	10.0	7.1	56.8	85.6	135	.5
1943	65.1	12.6	77.7	11.4	7.2	59.2	88.4	136	.5
1944	64.8	13.2	78.0	11.2	6.0	60.9	82.2	127	.4
1945	57.6	12.5	70.1	9.3	5.0	55.8	79.4	138	.3
1946	49.0	12.7	61.7	7.8	4.9	49.0	66.3	135	.3
1947	63.4	15.3	78.7	10.1	6.8	61.8	84.6	133	.3
1948	66.3	15.9	82.2	11.1	4.3	66.9	88.4	133	.3
1949	58.5	13.0	71.5	9.8	4.5	57.2	77.7	133	.2
1950	73.0	16.2	89.1	13.0	1.9	74.2	96.5	132	.3
1951	80.1	18.1	98.2	14.1	1.1	83.1	104.8	131	.3
1952	69.0	15.7	84.7	11.8	3.0	69.9	92.8	134	.3
1953	80.2	16.5	96.7	14.4	1.4	80.8	111.3	139	.3
1954	63.2	13.5	76.7	11.1	2.0	63.6	88.1	139	.2
1955	84.7	17.5	102.2	15.5	3.1	83.6	116.8	138	.2
1956	83.2	16.7	100.0	14.3	3.0	82.7	114.9	138	.3
1957	79.9	15.3	95.2	13.1	4.4	77.7	112.4	141	.3
1958	59.9	12.2	72.1	10.5	1.2	60.4	85.1	142	.2
1959	69.4	14.6	84.0	13.3	—2.9	73.6	93.3	134	.2
1960	71.1	13.8	84.9	13.3	—0.7	72.3	99.1	139	.2

1. From Table A16–3 or from American Iron and Steel Institute (AISI), *Annual Statistical Report*. Represents net shipments after deducting shipments to reporting steel companies for conversion or resale. Includes all grades of steel: carbon, stainless and heat resisting, and alloy other than stainless.

2. 1959–60: from Bureau of the Census, Current Industrial Reports, Series M33–1–09. 1943–58: from Facts for Industry, Series M–21–C. 1929–42: based on computations by Battelle Memorial Institute in *A Survey and Analysis of the Supply and Availability of Obsolete Iron and Steel Scrap*, prepared for the Business and Defense Services Administration, Department of Commerce (Columbus, Ohio: Jan. 15, 1957), Appendix A, Table A–1. Represents shipments of foundry products for sale or own use by foundries. Includes gray iron, malleable iron, and steel castings.

3. Steel mill products plus ferrous castings.

4. From Table A16–6.

5. Aggregated from Table A16–5.

6. Total shipments of iron and steel products less prompt industrial scrap generated and less net exports.

7. AISI, *Annual Statistical Report*, "Ingots and Steel for Castings" section.

8. AISI, *ibid*. Represents only steel castings produced in foundries operated by companies producing steel ingots. An undeterminable portion of these steel castings may be included in shipments of steel mill products as well as shipments of ferrous castings. Hence, total shipments of iron and steel mill products may be slightly overstated, by some 0.2 to 0.3% in the decade 1951–60.

9. Annual averages of the periods 1926–30, 1931–35, and 1936–40.

TABLE A16–2.   Historical Data on Consumption of Ferrous Metallics and Gross Output of Steel Mills and Foundries

(Million tons)

	Consumption of ferrous metallics				Gross output[5]	Input/output ratio[6] (%)
	Total	Pig iron[1]	Ferrous scrap[2]	Iron ore[3]	Ferro-alloys[4]		
1929	89	46.7	39.3	1.7	1.0		
1930	64	33.6	27.8	1.3	.8		
1931	41	20.0	19.3	.8	.5	37	102.7
1932	21	9.7	10.6	.4	.3		
1933	36	16.2	18.6	.7	.5		
1934	39	17.6	20.1	.8	.5		
1935	53	23.1	27.8	1.3	.7		
1936	75	33.7	38.4	1.9	1.0		
1937	81	38.1	39.9	2.0	1.0		
1938	45	20.7	22.7	1.1	.5	68	107.4
1939	72	35.2	34.4	1.8	1.0		
1940	92	46.2	42.4	2.3	1.3		
1941	117	56.2	56.3	2.9	1.7	111	105.4
1942	120	59.0	56.1	3.0	1.9	109	110.1
1943	122	60.3	56.8	3.1	2.0	114	107.0
1944	122	61.0	56.4	3.2	1.9	115	106.1
1945	109	53.2	51.6	2.6	1.7	102	106.9
1946	95	45.1	46.0	2.2	1.6	89	106.7
1947	120	58.3	56.6	2.9	1.9	112	107.1
1948	125	60.0	60.4	3.0	2.0	116	107.8
1949	108	53.4	50.1	2.7	1.5	102	105.9
1950	133	64.9	63.0	3.3	2.1	126	105.6
1951	149	71.4	70.8	4.1	2.3	139	107.2
1952	131	61.6	63.6	3.8	2.1	122	107.4
1953	153	74.7	70.9	4.8	2.4	140	109.3
1954	121	58.7	56.6	3.9	1.8	112	108.0
1955	160	77.2	75.3	5.1	2.6	148	108.1
1956	157	75.0	74.6	5.1	2.7	144	109.0
1957	153	76.4	68.2	5.6	2.7	139	110.1
1958	116	57.3	52.6	4.5	1.8	106	109.4
1959	130	61.8	61.8	4.4	2.1	121	107.4
1960	136	66.6	62.1	4.6	2.1	125	108.8

1. From Table A16–7.
2. From Table A16–6.
3. 1943–60: from Table A16–7. 1935–1942: estimated at 2.5% of the total consumption of ferrous metallics. 1929–1934: estimated at 2% of total consumption. Data represent iron content of iron ore and sinter consumed by steel furnaces.
4. *Minerals Yearbook,* chapter on Ferroalloys. Data represent apparent consumption, i.e., shipments minus exports plus imports.
5. Shipments of iron and steel, from Table A16–1, plus home scrap generated, from Table A16–6. Prior to 1941, annual averages for the periods 1931–35 and 1936–40; 1926–30 average: 75.
6. Ratio of total consumption of ferrous metallics to gross output of steel mills and foundries. Prior to 1941, annual averages for the periods 1931–35 and 1936–40; 1929–30 average: 102.7.

TABLE A16–3.   Historical Data on Adjusted Shipments of Steel Mill Products, by Market Category[1]

(Million tons)

	Total ship-ments	Ex-ports[2]	Im-ports[2]	Adjusted gross domes-tic ship-ments[3]	Construc-tion in-cluding mainte-nance, excluding railroads	Con-trac-tors' prod-ucts	Auto-mo-tive	Rail trans-porta-tion	Ship-build-ing	Air-craft
1929	47.1	2.4	.4	45.0	15.3	[4]	8.8	9.8	.4	[5]
1930	33.8	1.5	.3	32.6	12.5	[4]	5.8	6.2	.4	[5]
1931	22.0	.8	.3	21.4	7.4	[4]	4.1	3.6	.3	[5]
1932	12.0	.4	.2	11.8	4.0	[4]	2.5	1.4	.1	[5]
1933	17.6	.6	.1	17.1	4.8	[4]	4.6	1.7	.1	[5]
1934	20.0	1.0	.1	19.1	5.4	[4]	5.0	2.8	.2	[5]
1935	25.3	1.1	.2	24.5	6.7	[4]	7.6	2.2	.2	[5]
1936	35.7	1.3	.3	34.7	10.7	[4]	8.8	4.8	.3	[5]
1937	39.2	2.8	.3	36.7	10.6	[4]	9.1	5.5	.5	[5]
1938	21.8	1.8	.2	20.2	7.0	[4]	4.6	1.6	.4	[5]
1939	35.8	2.4	.2	33.5	10.5	[4]	7.8	4.3	.7	[5]
1940	47.0	7.8	*	39.2	11.3	[4]	9.8	4.7	1.1	.1
1941	65.6	6.3	*	59.2	17.4	[4]	12.1	6.8	3.2	.2
1942	63.4	7.0	*	56.5	15.2	[4]	4.5	5.2	11.2	.6
1943	65.1	6.9	*	58.2	11.1	[4]	4.9	5.6	13.9	1.1
1944	64.8	5.8	.1	59.1	12.0	[4]	5.1	6.7	12.5	.6
1945	57.6	4.8	.1	52.9	13.6	[4]	6.3	6.3	3.3	.4
1946	49.0	4.6	*	44.4	9.5	2.8	9.0	4.5	.3	*
1947	63.4	6.5	*	56.9	11.9	3.7	12.3	5.8	.4	*
1948	66.3	4.3	.2	62.2	13.0	4.1	13.6	6.2	.8	*
1949	58.5	4.6	.3	54.1	12.1	3.3	13.6	4.1	.7	*
1950	73.0	2.9	1.1	71.2	15.1	4.9	18.6	5.1	.4	.1
1951	80.1	3.3	2.3	79.1	17.0	5.1	17.4	6.9	1.0	.2
1952	69.0	4.2	1.2	66.1	14.2	4.3	14.4	4.6	1.2	.2
1953	80.2	3.1	1.7	78.8	16.9	5.2	18.7	5.5	1.0	.2
1954	63.2	2.8	.9	61.2	13.8	4.4	14.6	2.8	.6	.1
1955	84.7	4.1	1.1	81.7	16.7	5.9	23.0	4.0	.7	.1
1956	83.2	4.4	1.5	80.4	18.1	6.2	18.2	4.8	.8	.2
1957	79.9	5.6	1.3	75.6	19.0	5.1	17.6	4.6	1.4	.1
1958	59.9	3.0	1.8	58.8	14.2	5.0	13.0	1.7	.9	.1
1959	69.4	1.7	4.6	72.3	15.4	5.6	18.9	2.8	.8	.1
1960	71.1	2.9	3.6	71.8	16.3	5.5	19.3	3.0	.8	.1

Table A16–3 (cont'd)

(Million tons)

	Oil and gas drilling	Mining, quarrying, and lumbering	Agricultural equipment	Machinery, industrial equipment, and tools	Electrical machinery and equipment	Appliances, utensils, and cutlery	Other domestic and commercial equipment	Containers	Ordnance and other military
1929	[4]	[4]	3.7	2.4		2.4		2.3	[5]
1930	[4]	[4]	2.0	1.6		1.9		2.2	[5]
1931	[4]	[4]	1.6	.9		1.7		1.9	[5]
1932	[4]	[4]	.7	.5		1.2		1.4	[5]
1933	[4]	[4]	1.3	.9		1.3		2.3	[5]
1934	[4]	[4]	1.4	.9		1.4		1.9	[5]
1935	[4]	[4]	2.2	1.2		1.8		2.6	[5]
1936	[4]	[4]	2.6	2.0		2.3		3.2	[5]
1937	[4]	[4]	2.7	2.1		2.4		3.8	[5]
1938	[4]	[4]	1.2	.9		2.0		2.4	[5]
1939	[4]	[4]	1.9	1.9		2.4		3.9	[5]
1940	[4]	.2	1.8	1.9	1.4	1.4	1.7	3.8	[5]
1941	[4]	.3	2.3	2.6	2.1	2.3	2.6	5.6	1.7
1942	[4]	.3	1.4	2.5	1.6	.7	1.6	4.6	7.2
1943	[4]	.2	1.6	2.7	1.5	.6	1.4	4.6	9.0
1944	[4]	.3	2.2	2.8	1.6	.7	1.8	4.8	8.0
1945	[4]	.3	2.5	2.8	1.8	1.2	2.1	5.7	6.7
1946	1.4	.2	2.2	3.6	2.0	1.7	1.9	5.3	*
1947	2.2	.3	2.5	4.4	2.6	2.1	2.3	6.3	.1
1948	2.5	.4	2.8	4.6	2.7	2.6	2.3	6.6	.1
1949	2.2	.3	2.6	3.8	2.0	1.8	1.8	5.6	.1
1950	2.6	.3	3.1	5.1	3.0	2.8	2.5	7.3	.2
1951	3.0	.4	3.4	6.2	3.4	2.6	2.8	8.2	1.4
1952	2.5	.4	2.9	5.4	2.8	2.0	2.2	6.8	2.4
1953	2.8	.4	2.9	6.0	3.4	2.7	2.8	7.4	3.0
1954	2.9	.2	2.4	4.7	2.7	1.9	2.2	6.9	1.1
1955	3.3	.3	3.0	6.4	3.6	2.9	2.9	8.0	1.0
1956	3.4	.4	2.8	6.9	3.9	2.9	3.0	8.3	.6
1957	3.3	.4	2.5	6.0	3.2	2.1	2.4	7.4	.4
1958	1.5	.2	2.4	4.5	2.8	2.1	2.3	7.8	.3
1959	2.9	.3	2.8	6.0	3.4	2.6	2.6	8.0	.2
1960	1.6	.4	2.4	5.7	3.3	2.5	2.7	8.2	.2

* Negligible.

1. Derived from available shipments data by reallocating to end-uses, as necessary, the steel shipped to warehouses and other intermediate distributors. For details of the adjustment, see introductory Notes. Sources of basic data:

1940–60: AISI, *Annual Statistical Report*, section on "Shipments of Steel Products." For 1953–60 the AISI statistics cover 100% of the shipments; for 1940–52 the coverage varies from 95.3% to 99.5%. For these years the data were expanded to include all shipments (see Battelle Memorial Institute, *A Survey and Analysis of the Supply and Availability of Obsolete Iron and Steel Scrap*, Appendix B, Table B–1).

1929–39: from *Iron Age*, Anniversary Issue of 1955. Data have been inflated by a factor of 1.023, which represents the 1940 ratio of AISI to *Iron Age* series on shipments.

2. From Table A16–5.

3. "Gross domestic shipments" means consumption before deduction of prompt industrial scrap generated. Equals total shipments minus exports plus imports; or the sum of the following 15 market classifications. Detail may not add up to total because of rounding.

4. Included in "Construction."

5. Insignificant or included in "Appliances."

TABLE A16–4. Historical Data on Net Consumption of Steel Mill Products and Ferrous Castings, by Market Category, and Prompt Industrial Scrap Generated

(Million tons)

	Steel mill products												Ferrous castings	
	Construction[1]	Automotive	Rail transportation	Water and air transport[2]	Agricultural machinery	Other producer durables[3]	Consumer durables[4]	Containers	Ordnance[5]	Total net domestic consumption[6]	Prompt industrial scrap generated[7]	Generation factor[8] (%)	Total consumption[9]	Prompt industrial scrap generated[10]
1929	14.6	6.1	9.1	.3	3.0	1.8	2.0	2.0	–	38.8	6.2	14		
1930	11.9	4.0	5.7	.3	1.6	1.2	1.6	1.9	–	28.3	4.3	13		
1931	7.1	2.9	3.3	.2	1.3	.7	1.4	1.6	–	18.5	3.0	14		
1932	3.8	1.7	1.3	.1	.6	.4	1.0	1.2	–	10.1	1.7	14		
1933	4.6	3.2	1.6	.1	1.0	.7	1.1	2.0	–	14.3	2.8	16	[11]6.8	.6
1934	5.2	3.5	2.6	.2	1.1	.7	1.2	1.7	–	16.2	3.0	16		
1935	6.4	5.2	2.1	.2	1.8	.9	1.5	2.3	–	20.4	4.2	17		
1936	10.2	6.1	4.4	.3	2.1	1.5	1.9	2.8	–	29.3	5.3	15		
1937	10.1	6.3	5.1	.4	2.2	1.6	2.0	3.3	–	31.0	5.7	16	[11]10.3	.9
1938	6.7	3.2	1.5	.3	1.0	.7	1.7	2.1	–	17.2	3.0	15		
1939	10.0	5.4	4.0	.5	1.5	1.4	2.0	3.5	–	28.3	5.1	15		
1940	11.0	6.8	4.4	.9	1.5	2.5	2.5	3.4	–	33.0	6.0	16		
1941	16.9	8.4	6.3	2.6	1.9	3.5	4.2	5.0	1.3	50.1	9.3	16	9.7	.8
1942	14.7	3.1	4.8	9.0	1.1	3.0	2.0	4.1	5.5	47.3	9.2	16	9.7	.8
1943	10.8	3.4	5.2	11.4	1.3	3.1	1.7	4.1	6.9	47.9	10.4	18	11.6	1.0
1944	11.7	3.5	6.2	10.0	1.8	3.2	2.1	4.3	6.1	48.9	10.1	17	12.1	1.1
1945	13.2	4.4	5.9	2.8	2.0	3.4	2.7	5.0	5.1	44.5	8.3	16	11.5	1.0
1946	13.3	6.2	4.2	.3	1.8	4.1	3.0	4.7	–	37.6	6.9	16	11.7	1.0
1947	17.3	8.5	5.4	.4	2.0	4.2	3.7	5.5	–	47.0	8.9	16	14.1	1.2
1948	19.0	9.4	5.8	.6	2.3	5.4	4.2	5.8	.1	52.5	9.8	16	14.6	1.3
1949	17.2	9.4	3.8	.6	2.1	4.3	3.0	4.9	.1	45.4	8.7	16	12.0	1.3
1950	21.9	12.9	4.7	.3	2.5	6.0	4.4	6.4	.2	59.3	11.8	17	14.9	1.3
1951	24.4	12.0	6.4	.9	2.8	7.1	4.6	7.2	1.1	66.5	12.6	16	16.7	1.4
1952	20.6	9.9	4.3	1.0	2.3	6.1	3.5	6.0	1.8	55.5	10.6	16	14.4	1.3
1953	24.2	12.9	5.1	.9	2.3	7.0	4.6	6.5	2.3	65.8	13.1	17	15.2	1.3
1954	20.3	10.1	2.6	.5	1.9	5.5	3.5	6.1	.8	51.3	10.0	16	12.4	1.1
1955	25.0	15.9	3.7	.6	2.4	7.4	4.8	7.1	.7	67.6	14.1	17	16.1	1.4
1956	26.7	12.6	4.5	.8	2.3	8.0	4.9	7.3	.4	67.5	13.0	16	15.4	1.3
1957	26.6	12.3	4.3	1.2	2.1	6.8	3.8	6.5	.3	63.9	11.9	16	14.1	1.2
1958	19.9	9.0	1.6	.7	2.0	5.4	3.7	6.9	.2	49.4	9.5	16	11.2	1.0
1959	23.0	13.0	2.6	.7	2.3	6.9	4.3	7.1	.1	60.0	12.1	17	13.4	1.2
1960	22.5	13.3	2.8	.6	1.9	6.6	4.3	7.2	.2	59.4	12.2	17	12.7	1.1

Table A16–4 (cont'd)

1. Except railroad construction. Includes maintenance; oil and gas drilling; mining, quarrying, and lumbering; and contractors' products.

2. Includes military equipment.

3. Includes electrical machinery and equipment.

4. Other than passenger cars. Includes appliances, utensils, and cutlery; and other domestic and commercial equipment.

5. Includes other military. 1929–40 and 1946–48 insignificant or included in consumer durables.

6. Represents sum of the preceding end-use categories; as well as gross domestic shipments (see Table A16–3) minus prompt industrial scrap generated. Detail may not add to totals because of rounding.

7. Represents scrap produced during the fabrication of finished steel products that is usually sold within a short time after being generated, such as: cutoffs, trimmings, turnings, and borings. Calculated for each of the 15 AISI end-use categories (as listed in Table A16–3) by applying the respective scrap generation factors to gross domestic consumption.

8. Represents prompt industrial scrap generation as a percentage of gross domestic consumption. Based on generation factors developed by the Battelle Memorial Institute (*A Survey and Analysis of the Supply and Availability of Obsolete Iron and Steel Scrap,* Appendix D, Table D–1). The Battelle generation factors, which in turn are based largely on a survey conducted by the Industry Division, Bureau of the Census, covering actual iron and steel consumption and scrap shipments for the year 1954, are as follows:

	1954 (Battelle) (%)	1960 (RFF estimate; based on 1954 ratios, modified for 1960 product mix) (%)
Oil and gas drilling	3.0	
Mining, quarrying, and lumbering	3.0	
Automotive	31.0	31.0
Railroad transportation	7.0	7.0
Water and air transport	–	24.0
Shipbuilding	23.0	–
Aircraft	31.0	
Agricultural machinery	19.0	19.0
Producer durables		19.0 ⎱
Machinery and tools	26.0	26.0 ⎰ 25.0
Machinery, excluding electrical	26.0	
Electrical machinery	26.0	
Consumer durables	–	16.0
Appliances, etc.	17.1	
Other domestic and commercial equipment	15.0	
Containers	12.0	12.0
Ordnance	24.0	24.0
All construction, excluding railroads	–	5.0
Construction, including maintenance	3.0	–
Contractors' products	10.3	–

Where two or more end-use categories were aggregated, an average scrap generation factor was calculated, using gross domestic consumption during the earliest year of detailed breakdown as weight. Thus, for the earlier period the following factors were applied to gross domestic consumption: All construction, excluding railroads, 1929–45: 4.5%. Machinery and equipment, including electrical machinery, 1929–39: 26.0%. Appliances and other domestic and commercial equipment, 1929–39: 16.3%.

9. Equals shipments (from Table A16–1) minus prompt industrial scrap generated. Exports and imports of ferrous castings are negligible and have been disregarded in computing prompt industrial scrap.

10. As a result of the final tabulations based on the survey of the Industry Division, Bureau of the Census (see footnote 8), the prompt industrial scrap generation factor has been raised from 4% (as given in Battelle study, Appendix D, Table D–1) to 8% of shipments of ferrous castings.

11. Annual averages for 1931–35 and 1936–40; 1926–30 averages: 15.6 consumption and 1.4 scrap.

TABLE A16–5.   Historical Data on Foreign Trade in Iron and Steel

(Million tons)

	Exports					Imports				
	Steel mill products[1]	Ferrous castings[2]	Pig iron[3]	Ferrous scrap[4]	Ferroalloys[5]	Steel mill products[6]	Ferrous castings[7]	Pig iron[3]	Ferrous scrap[4]	Ferroalloys[5]
1929	2.43	.14	.05	.62	*	.36	.07	.17	.10	.08
1930	1.54	.10	.02	.40	*	.29	.02	.15	.03	.05
1931	.81	.05	.01	.15	*	.29	.01	.09	.02	.04
1932	.36	.02	*	.26	*	.21	*	.15	.01	.03
1933	.62	.03	*	.87	*	.14	*	.18	.06	.07
1934	1.00	.05	*	2.06	*	.12	*	.13	.05	.05
1935	1.06	.05	*	2.36	*	.22	*	.15	.07	.07
1936	1.27	.06	.01	2.17	*	.27	*	.14	.16	.10
1937	2.84	.12	.88	4.59	*	.30	.01	.13	.09	.06
1938	1.78	.09	.48	3.36	*	.17	.01	.03	.03	.05
1939	2.44	.12	.18	4.01	.01	.18	*	.04	.03	.10
1940	7.85	.18	.55	3.16	.04	.02	*	.01	*	.04
1941	6.34	.20	.58	.90	.02	.02	*	*	.07	.03
1942	6.96	.20	.11	.14	.02	.02	*	*	.08	.03
1943	6.90	.27	.14	.06	.05	.02	*	*	.15	.02
1944	5.77	.26	.16	.10	.01	.06	*	.01	.11	.03
1945	4.79	.30	.09	.10	.01	.07	*	.02	.05	.07
1946	4.62	.28	.10	.15	.02	.02	*	.01	.03	.04
1947	6.47	.31	.04	.19	.03	.03	*	.03	.04	.11
1948	4.28	.19	.01	.24	.08	.15	*	.22	.42	.11
1949	4.65	.18	.08	.30	.02	.30	*	.10	1.09	.08
1950	2.86	.10	.01	.22	.05	1.08	.01	.80	.79	.16
1951	3.27	.12	.01	.25	.06	2.28	.01	1.07	.42	.18
1952	4.15	.14	.01	.35	.06	1.23	.01	.38	.15	.10
1953	3.07	.11	.02	.32	.03	1.74	*	.59	.17	.18
1954	2.80	.08	.01	1.70	.03	.88	.01	.29	.24	.09
1955	4.08	.09	.03	5.17	.06	1.08	.01	.28	.23	.12
1956	4.38	.11	.27	6.45	.09	1.48	.02	.33	.26	.23
1957	5.58	.12	.88	6.77	.07	1.30	.02	.23	.24	.41
1958	2.96	.09	.10	2.93	.05	1.83	.02	.21	.33	.17
1959	1.69	.08	.01	4.94	.07	4.63	.04	.70	.31	.21
1960	2.88	.08	.11	7.19	.07	3.58	.04	.33	.18	.19

* Negligible.

1. 1947–60: from AISI, *Annual Statistical Report,* section on Export Statistics. Includes all products enumerated under exports of "Total Steel Mill Products" plus the following semi-manufactures, listed in AISI export statistics under "Other Iron and Steel Products": plates, fabricated; structural shapes, fabricated; rails, relaying; railroad bolts, nuts, and washers; bolts, nuts, rivets, and washers, except railroad; welding rods, electric; wire rope and strand; other wire and manufactures; tacks; other nails, including staples; forgings.
1940–46: same source as above. Includes products enumerated under "Exports of Iron and Steel—semi-finished and finished products" except: iron bars; boiler plate; iron sheets, black; welded boiler tubes; frames and sashes; car wheels, tires, and axles.
1929–39: from Department of Commerce, Bureau of Foreign and Domestic Commerce, annual reports, *Foreign Commerce and Navigation of the United States,* cited in Bureau of the Census, *Statistical Abstract of the United States.* The products included are the same as for later years. (For enumeration of products see *Statistical Abstract,* 1942, p. 855.)
2. 1929–60: same sources as in footnote 1. Includes: iron

bars; cast iron pressure pipe; cast iron soil pipe; cast and malleable iron pipe fittings; iron castings and ingot molds; steel castings.
3. From *Minerals Yearbook,* chapter on Iron and Steel.
4. From *Minerals Yearbook,* chapter on Iron and Steel Scrap.
5. From *Minerals Yearbook,* chapter on Ferroalloys.
6. 1947–60: from AISI, *Annual Statistical Report,* section on Import Statistics. Includes all products enumerated under imports of "Total Steel Mill Products" plus the following semi-manufactures, listed in AISI import statistics under "Other Iron and Steel Products": castings and forgings; structural shapes, fabricated; wire rope and strand; nails and staples; bolts, nuts, and rivets; bale ties; cotton ties and other ties.
1940–46: same source as above. Includes products enumerated under "Imports of Iron and Steel—semi-finished and finished products" except: iron bars and slabs; die blocks and blanks.
1929–39: same as for exports 1929–39. (For enumeration of products see *Statistical Abstract,* 1942, pp. 658–59.)
7. 1929–60: same sources as in footnote 6. Includes: iron bars, slabs, blooms; die blocks and blanks; cast iron pipe and fittings; malleable iron pipe fittings.

TABLE A16–6.   Historical Data on Supply of and Requirements for Ferrous Scrap

(Million tons)

Year	Home scrap[1] Generated	Home scrap[1] As per cent of iron and steel shipments	Prompt industrial scrap generated[2]	Obsolete scrap Potential new supply[3]	Obsolete scrap Withdrawals[4]	Obsolete scrap Withdrawals as per cent of new supply	Total new supply of ferrous scrap[5]	Requirements Net exports[6]	Requirements Stock changes[7]	Requirements Blast furnaces[7]	Requirements Ferroalloy production[9]	Requirements Miscellaneous uses[10]	Ferrous scrap available for consumption by steel furnaces and iron foundries[11]
1929	18.8		7.8	n.a.	16.0	—	42.6	.5	n.a.	2.8	n.a.	n.a.	39.3
1930	13.4		5.4	"	11.4	—	30.2	.4	"	2.0	"	"	27.8
1931	8.5		3.6	"	8.5	—	20.6	.1		1.2	"	"	19.3
1932	4.7		2.0	"	4.8	—	11.5	1.3		.6	"	"	10.6
1933	10.5	[12]37.5	3.4	"	6.9	—	20.8	.8		.9	"	"	19.1
1934	10.9		3.6	"	8.6	—	23.1	2.0		1.0	"	"	20.1
1935	15.7		5.0	"	11.2	—	31.9	2.3		1.7	"	"	27.8
1936	22.2		6.2	"	14.3	—	42.7	2.0		2.3	"	"	38.4
1937	23.3		6.7	"	17.0	—	47.0	4.5		2.7	"	"	39.9
1938	13.3	[12]44.8	3.5	"	10.4	—	27.2	3.3		1.2	"	"	22.7
1939	20.5		6.0	"	13.8	—	40.3	4.0		1.9	"	"	34.4
1940	26.1		7.4	"	14.4	—	47.9	3.2	.2	2.1	"	"	42.4
1941	35.0	46.0	10.2	"	13.1	—	58.3	.8	−1.7	2.9	"	"	56.3
1942	35.1	47.5	10.0	"	17.8	—	62.9	.1	2.6	2.9	.3	.9	56.1
1943	36.8	47.4	11.4	"	12.9	—	61.1	−.1	−.4	3.6	.4	.9	56.8
1944	36.9	47.3	11.2	"	11.8	—	59.9	*	−1.4	3.6	.3	1.0	56.4
1945	32.2	46.0	9.3	"	14.2	—	55.7	*	−.5	3.3	.3	1.0	51.6
1946	27.3	44.3	7.8	"	13.9	—	49.0	.1	−.6	2.3	.3	1.0	46.0
1947	33.3	42.3	10.1	"	18.8	—	62.2	.1	1.1	2.7	.3	1.2	56.6
1948	34.1	41.5	11.1	"	21.6	—	66.8	−.2	2.0	2.9	.4	1.2	60.4
1949	30.5	42.6	9.8	"	12.4	—	52.7	−.8	−.8	3.0	.3	1.0	50.1
1950	37.0	41.5	13.0	39.5	18.1	46	68.1	−.6	−.2	4.4	.4	1.1	63.0
1951	40.8	40.7	14.1	39.8	21.3	54	76.2	−.2	−1.0	4.5	.4	1.0	71.5
1952	36.9	43.0	11.8	39.6	23.5	59	72.2	.2	2.5	4.3	.3	.8	64.1
1953	43.8	45.5	14.4	39.6	19.2	48	77.4	.1	.2	5.0	.4	.9	70.7
1954	35.7	46.5	11.1	39.7	16.1	41	62.9	1.4	.2	3.6	.3	.8	56.6
1955	45.5	44.5	15.5	38.6	25.1	65	86.1	4.9	−.1	4.7	.3	.8	75.3
1956	43.7	43.7	14.3	38.9	28.6	74	86.6	6.2	.2	4.4	.4	1.0	74.6
1957	44.0	46.2	13.1	38.6	24.4	63	81.5	6.5	1.4	4.2	.4	.8	68.2
1958	33.7	46.7	10.5	39.0	15.5	40	59.7	2.6	.7	2.9	.3	.7	52.6
1959	37.4	44.5	13.3	39.2	20.3	52	71.0	4.6	.4	3.2	.2	.8	61.8
1960	39.6	46.6	13.3	42.4	19.9	51	72.8	7.0	−.7	3.5	.3	.6	62.1

* Negligible.

1. 1929–52: from *Minerals Yearbook*, chapter on Iron and Steel Scrap. Represents home scrap consumption, plus (or minus) stock changes, adjusted by adding home scrap included in purchased scrap and subtracting obsolete scrap consumed by the steel industry as home scrap. These adjustments were based on estimates prepared by Battelle Memorial Institute (*A Survey and Analysis of the Supply and Availability of Obsolete Iron and Steel Scrap*, Appendix H, Table H–1). Prior to 1940 statistics on scrap inventories are not available; data for 1929–39 represent home scrap consumption, similarly adjusted.

1953–60: home scrap production from *Survey of Current Business*. Monthly data aggregated.

2. The method of computing prompt industrial scrap generation is described in Table A16–4, footnote 8.

3. See note on the method of computing the potential new supply of obsolete scrap in Table A16–15.

4. 1929–52: computed by subtracting prompt industrial scrap generation from the new supply data on consumption of purchased scrap (from *Minerals Yearbook*, chapter on Iron and Steel Scrap), adding net exports of ferrous scrap (from Table A16–5) to consumption, and then subtracting home scrap included in purchased scrap and adding obsolete scrap consumed as home scrap (see footnote 1).

1953–60: new supply of ferrous scrap minus home scrap generation and prompt industrial scrap generation.

5. 1929–52: the sum of home scrap generated, prompt industrial scrap generated, and obsolete scrap withdrawn.

1953–60: ferrous scrap available for consumption by iron and steel furnaces plus requirements for net exports, stocks, blast furnaces, ferroalloy production, and miscellaneous uses.

6. From Table A16–5.

7. 1929–39: not available. 1940–60: from *Minerals Yearbook*, chapter on Iron and Steel Scrap. Represents stocks at scrap consumers' plants only.

8. 1935–60: consumption of ferrous scrap by blast furnaces from *Minerals Yearbook*, chapter on Iron and Steel Scrap.

1929–34: estimated at 5.9% of pig iron production.

9. 1929–41: not available. 1942–60: from *Minerals Yearbook*, chapters on Iron and Steel Scrap and on Ferroalloys.

10. 1929–41: not available. 1942–60: from *Minerals Yearbook*, chapter on Iron and Steel Scrap. Represents use of scrap in rerolling, in nonferrous metallurgy, and as a chemical agent.

11. Equals total new supply of ferrous scrap minus net exports, stock increases, and consumption by blast furnaces, in ferroalloy production, and for miscellaneous uses. Data for 1929–41 are overstated by the small amounts consumed in ferroalloy production and miscellaneous uses.

12. Annual averages for the periods 1931–35 and 1936–40; 1926–30 average: 28.5% (17.0).

TABLE A16–7. Historical Data on Consumption and Production of Pig Iron and Iron Ore

(Million tons)

	Pig iron				Blast furnace consumption of ore and scrap[5]	Consumption of metallics as per cent of pig iron produced[6]	Iron ore consumption[7] (iron content)				Stock changes[8]
	Consumption[1]	Net exports[2]	Stock changes[3]	Production[4]			Blast furnaces	Steel furnaces	Miscellaneous uses	Total	
1929	46.7	—.1	.2	46.8	44.5	95.1	41.7	n.a.	n.a.	43.4	—1.2
1930	33.6	—.1	1.2	34.7	32.6	93.9	30.6	"	"	32.0	2.0
1931	20.0	—.1	.2	20.1	18.1	90.0	16.9	"	"	16.5	1.7
1932	9.7	—.1	*	9.6	7.9	82.3	7.3	"	"	3.3	2.6
1933	16.2	—.2	—1.5	14.6	12.9	88.4	12.0	"	"	14.2	—4.0
1934	17.6	—.1	*	17.6	15.7	89.2	14.7	"	"	14.9	—.4
1935	23.1	—.2	.3	23.3	21.4	91.8	19.7	"	"	19.2	—1.4
1936	33.7	—.2	.3	33.8	31.0	91.7	28.7	"	"	29.7	—1.0
1937	38.1	.8	1.6	40.5	37.4	92.1	34.7	"	"	41.2	.5
1938	20.7	.4	—.4	20.8	19.2	92.3	18.0	"	"	15.7	1.3
1939	35.2	.1	—.6	34.8	31.5	90.5	29.6	"	"	31.5	—1.4
1940	46.2	.5	—.7	46.1	42.6	92.4	40.5	"	"	43.6	—.9
1941	56.2	.6	—1.7	55.1	50.5	91.6	47.6	"	"	59.8	—.2
1942	59.0	.1	*	59.1	55.4	93.7	52.5	"	"	66.8	—.1
1943	60.3	.1	.4	60.8	58.9	96.9	55.3	3.1	.4	58.8	—2.2
1944	61.0	.2	—.1	61.0	58.7	96.2	55.1	3.2	.4	58.7	—5.7
1945	53.2	.1	*	53.2	51.2	96.2	47.9	2.6	.3	50.8	—.3
1946	45.1	.1	—.4	44.8	43.6	97.3	41.3	2.2	.3	43.8	—2.8
1947	58.3	*	*	58.3	56.4	96.7	53.7	2.9	.3	56.9	—2.8
1948	60.0	—.2	.2	60.1	57.9	96.3	55.0	3.0	.4	58.4	*
1949	53.4	*	*	53.4	52.6	98.5	49.6	2.7	.3	52.6	—1.6
1950	64.9	—.8	.4	64.6	63.2	97.8	58.8	3.3	.4	62.5	—3.8
1951	71.4	—1.1	.9	70.3	70.9	100.8	66.4	4.1	.6	71.1	—.6
1952	61.6	—.4	.1	61.3	60.6	98.9	56.3	3.8	.5	60.6	—2.6
1953	74.7	—.6	.8	74.9	73.1	97.6	68.1	4.8	.4	73.3	—2.6
1954	58.7	—.3	—.4	58.0	57.3	98.8	53.7	3.9	1.2	58.8	—5.7
1955	77.2	—.2	—.1	76.9	76.3	99.2	71.6	5.1	.4	77.1	—5.5
1956	75.0	—.1	.1	75.1	73.1	97.3	68.7	5.1	.5	74.3	—1.7
1957	76.4	.6	1.4	78.4	77.4	98.7	73.2	5.6	.4	79.2	.7
1958	57.3	—.1	*	57.2	56.2	98.3	53.3	4.5	.6	58.4	—2.1
1959	61.8	—.7	—.9	60.2	58.8	97.7	55.6	4.4	.7	60.7	—3.0
1960	66.6	—.2	.1	66.5	64.9	97.6	61.3	4.6	.6	66.5	6.9

* Negligible.

1. From *Minerals Yearbook*, chapter on Iron and Steel, series on "consumption of pig iron in the U.S. by type of furnace." Prior to 1935: apparent consumption (i.e., shipments minus net exports) from same source. That is, prior to 1935 changes in stocks at consumers of pig iron are not taken into account.

2. From Table A16–5.

3. Equals production minus consumption and minus net exports (or plus net imports).

4. From AISI, *Annual Statistical Report*.

5. Represents the iron content of iron ore, agglomerates, ferruginous manganese ore and manganiferous ore (see footnote 7) plus ferrous scrap consumed by blast furnaces from Table A16–6.

6. Consumption of metallics is smaller than production of pig iron because mill cinder, scale, and open-hearth slag are excluded from the consumption data.

7. Computed by deflating the gross weight of iron ore,

agglomerates, and manganiferous ores consumed by the percentage iron content of ore consumed in the United States (from Table A16–8). The term "iron ore" refers to all iron containing ores which do not have a manganese content of more than 5%. The term "manganiferous ores" refers to manganiferous iron ores, which contain 5% to 10% manganese, and to ferruginous manganese ores, which contain 10% to 35% manganese. Iron bearing ores having a manganese content of more than 35% —commonly called "manganese ores"—are excluded.

1943–60: from *Minerals Yearbook*, chapters on Iron Ore and on Manganese. Miscellaneous includes consumption of iron ore in ferroalloy, cement, and paint production and other primary manufactures.

1929–42: from *Minerals Yearbook*, chapters on Iron Ore and on Iron and Steel. Total consumption computed from shipments by subtracting net exports or adding net imports. Consumption by blast furnaces from series on "iron ore consumption for the production of pig iron,"

Table A16–7 (cont'd)

which includes manganiferous ores. The difference between total consumption and blast furnace consumption represents not only consumption by steel furnaces and for miscellaneous uses, but also changes in stocks held by consumers of iron ore.

8. Calculated as production-plus-imports minus consumption-plus-exports. Data for 1943–60 represent stock changes at mines, docks, sintering and agglomerating plants, and final consumers. Data for 1929–42 represent stock changes at mines only, not in the hands of iron ore consumers such as blast furnaces, etc.

TABLE A16–8.   Historical Data on Requirements and Supply of Iron Ore

(Million tons)

	Gross domestic requirements		Iron content of ore (% of gross weight)		Domestic production		Exports, gross wt.[7]	Imports, gross wt.[7]	Net imports, iron content[8]	Net imports as per cent of gross domestic requirements, iron content[9]
	Iron content[1]	Gross wt.[2]	Consumed in U.S.[3]	Produced in U.S.[4]	Iron content[5]	Gross wt.[6]				
1929	42.2	83.9	50	50	41.0	81.8	1.46	3.52	1.13	2.7
1930	34.0	67.7	50	50	32.7	65.4	.84	3.11	1.25	3.7
1931	18.2	36.0	50	50	17.5	34.9	.49	1.64	.63	3.5
1932	5.9	11.6	50	50	5.5	11.0	.01	.65	.35	5.9
1933	10.2	20.4	50	50	9.8	19.7	.17	.96	.43	4.2
1934	14.5	28.5	50	50	13.9	27.5	.68	1.60	.51	3.5
1935	17.8	35.1	50	50	17.2	34.2	.74	1.67	.53	3.0
1936	28.7	56.4	50	50	27.7	54.6	.72	2.50	1.03	3.6
1937	41.7	82.1	50	50	40.8	80.7	1.42	2.74	.78	1.9
1938	17.0	33.6	50	50	15.8	31.9	.66	2.38	1.05	6.2
1939	30.1	59.5	50	50	29.1	57.9	1.18	2.70	.93	3.1
1940	42.7	83.8	51	51	41.8	82.5	1.50	2.78	.78	1.8
1941	59.6	116.4	51	51	59.1	115.9	2.14	2.63	.29	.5
1942	66.7	130.4	51	51	67.6	132.4	2.82	.82	—1.02	—1.5
1943	56.6	110.8	51	51	57.9	113.4	3.05	.45	—1.33	—2.3
1944	53.0	103.2	51	51	54.1	105.4	2.71	.52	—1.11	—2.1
1945	50.5	98.0	51	51	50.9	99.0	2.31	1.33	—.50	—1.0
1946	41.0	80.4	51	51	40.2	79.3	1.69	3.15	.84	2.0
1947	54.1	106.1	51	50	52.5	104.2	2.81	5.48	1.55	2.9
1948	58.4	116.8	50	50	56.2	113.1	3.08	6.82	2.21	3.8
1949	51.0	100.0	51	50	47.7	95.1	2.72	8.28	3.28	6.4
1950	58.7	117.4	50	50	54.9	109.8	2.86	9.20	3.80	6.5
1951	70.5	135.6	52	51	66.6	130.5	4.85	11.36	3.91	5.5
1952	58.0	113.7	51	50	54.9	109.7	5.74	10.93	3.11	5.4
1953	70.7	138.6	51	50	66.1	132.1	4.76	12.42	4.60	6.5
1954	53.1	100.2	53	51	44.6	87.5	3.48	17.68	8.52	16.0
1955	71.6	135.1	53	51	58.9	115.4	5.04	26.26	12.73	17.8
1956	72.6	137.0	53	51	55.9	109.6	6.15	34.00	16.71	23.0
1957	79.9	148.0	54	51	60.6	118.9	5.59	37.77	19.31	24.2
1958	56.3	102.4	55	53	40.2	75.8	4.00	30.85	16.11	28.6
1959	57.7	103.1	56	53	35.8	67.5	3.32	39.89	21.94	38.0
1960	73.4	131.1	56	54	53.7	99.4	5.86	38.77	19.75	26.9

1. From Table A16–7. Represents total domestic consumption plus increase, or less decrease, in stocks.

2. Iron content of gross domestic requirements divided by average iron content of ore consumed in the United States multiplied by 100.

3. From *Minerals Yearbook,* chapter on Iron Ore. Calculated as weighted average of the iron content of ore produced in the United States and of iron ore imported for consumption.

4. Same source as footnote 3. There is no information available on the iron content of the small amounts of manganiferous iron ores and ferruginous manganese ores consumed in blast furnaces. It is assumed to be the same as that of iron ore produced in the United States.

5. Gross weight (see footnote 6) deflated by iron content of ore produced in the United States.

6. From *Minerals Yearbook,* chapter on Iron Ore. Represents usable iron ore mined, including direct shipping ore, agglomerates produced at mines, concentrates, and by-product ore. Cinder and sinter obtained by treating pyrites are not included.

7. From *Minerals Yearbook,* chapter on Iron Ore.

8. Same source as footnote 7. Represents weighted average of iron content of iron ore imported for consumption.

9. Iron content of net imports divided by the iron content of gross domestic requirements for iron ore.

TABLE A16–9. Projected Requirements for Ferrous Metallics[1]

(Million tons)

	1950	1955	1960		1970	1980	1990	2000
Net domestic iron and steel				L	73	76	82	89
consumption[2]	74	84	72	M	99	121	151	194
				H	126	176	252	378
				L	14	16	18	20
Prompt industrial scrap generation[3]	13	16	13	M	18	23	30	39
				H	22	32	46	69
Net exports of steel mill products				L	.7	.8	.9	1.0
and ferrous castings[4]	1.9	3.1	—.7	M	1.0	1.3	1.6	2.1
				H	2.2	3.3	4.1	5.9
Shipments of:								
				L	76	82	92	100
Steel mill products[5]	73	85	71	M	101	126	161	210
				H	127	181	262	396
				L	12	10	9	9
Ferrous castings[6]	16	18	14	M	17	19	21	25
				H	22	30	40	57
				L	88	92	101	109
Iron and steel[7]	89	102	85	M	118	145	182	235
				H	149	211	302	453
				L	106	115	129	140
Steel ingot production[8]	96	117	99	M	141	176	225	294
				H	178	253	367	554
Per cent of steel mill shipments[9]	132	138	139		140	140	140	140
Gross output of steel mills and				L	128	133	146	158
foundries[10]	126	148	125	M	171	210	264	341
				H	216	306	438	657
Requirements for ferrous metallics as per cent of gross output of iron and steel[11]	106	108	109		110	110	110	110
				L	141	146	161	174
Requirements for ferrous metallics[12]	133	160	136	M	188	231	290	375
				H	238	337	482	723
				L	2.8	2.9	3.2	3.5
Ferroalloys[13]	2.1	2.6	2.1	M	3.8	4.6	5.8	7.5
				H	4.8	6.7	9.6	14.5
				L	5.8	6.7	8.0	9.4
Direct ore[14]	3.3	5.1	4.6	M	7.7	10.6	14.5	20.2
				H	9.8	15.5	24.1	39.0
Per cent of total metallics	2.5	3.2	3.4	M	4.1	4.6	5.0	5.4
				L	66	69	76	82
Consumption of ferrous scrap[15]	63	75	62	M	88	109	136	176
				H	112	158	227	340
				L	66	67	74	79
Consumption of pig iron[16]	65	77	67	M	88	107	134	171
				H	111	157	221	330

1. Historical data from Tables A16–1 and 2; projections as indicated below.
2. From Tables A16–10 and 12.
3. From Table A16–14.
4. From Table A16–13.
5. From Table A16–11.
6. From Table A16–12.
7. The sum of shipments of steel mill products and ferrous castings.
8. Projections by application of percentage which follows.
9. Based on historical record.
10. Shipments of iron and steel, plus home scrap from Table A16–16.

Table A16–9 (cont'd)

11. Include an allowance for accumulation of stocks as well as for permanent loss in processing. Estimated on the basis of historical trends.

12. Based on two preceding lines.

13. Estimated at 2.0% of total metallics requirements.

14. Represents the iron content of ore and sinter used by steel furnaces. Calculated by applying the percentages shown in the following line to total metallics requirements. These percentages are estimated on the basis of historical trends.

15. From Table A16–16.

16. Represents the residual after subtraction of ferroalloys, direct ore, and ferrous scrap from total metallics requirements.

TABLE A16–10. Projected Net Consumption of Steel Mill Products, by Market Category[1]

(Million tons)

	1950	1955	1960		1970	1980	1990	2000
Construction[2]	21.9	25.0	22.5	L M H	22.1 32.4 44.2	23.3 38.0 59.8	23.1 45.2 83.9	24.1 57.6 128.7
Automotive[3]	12.9	15.9	13.3	L M H	13.5 16.1 19.6	15.2 20.7 26.8	19.6 26.4 37.6	20.9 33.4 53.8
Rail transportation[4]	4.7	3.7	2.8	L M H	2.9 5.2 8.6	3.3 7.0 13.1	4.7 10.7 21.0	6.6 15.0 31.2
Water and air transportation[5]	.3	.6	.6	L M H	1.1 1.2 1.3	1.6 1.7 2.0	2.0 2.4 3.2	2.7 3.5 5.3
Other producer durables[6]	9.2	10.8	9.6	L M H	12.0 15.6 17.7	13.5 21.6 28.9	14.6 29.7 45.1	16.1 42.4 74.5
Consumer durables[6]	3.7	3.8	3.2	L M H	3.5 3.8 4.1	4.0 4.8 5.4	4.7 6.1 7.2	5.4 7.8 9.9
Containers[7]	6.4	7.1	7.2	L M H	6.4 8.3 10.1	5.6 9.2 13.4	4.8 10.0 17.9	4.4 10.6 23.2
Ordnance[8]	.2	.7	.2	L M H	.1 .3 .4	.1 .2 .4	.1 .3 .5	.1 .3 .6
Total net domestic end-use consumption	59.3	67.6	59.4	L M H	61.6 82.9 106.0	66.6 103.2 149.8	73.6 130.8 216.4	80.3 170.6 327.2

1. Historical data from Table A16–4, except as indicated in footnote 6.

2. From Table A4–9.

3. From Table A5–19: steel consumed in production of passenger cars and trucks, increased by 30% to account for buses, school buses, motorcycles, and repair and replacement parts. Based on a historical comparison of adjusted gross shipments to and net consumption by the automotive industry.

4. From Table A5–17: steel consumed in production of rolling stock, increased by 15%, based upon a comparison of the historical steel content (shown in Table A5–16) with the apparent net consumption of steel for rolling stock, computed from adjusted gross shipments less estimated prompt industrial scrap generated.

5. Based on 1.6 tons of steel per million dollars of GNP; present consumption is predominantly for defense requirements (which use relatively less steel per dollar because of the heavy air component), but the defense proportion of expenditures is expected to decrease.

6. From Table A6–7. The 1950–60 consumption differs from the figures shown in Table A16–4 because part of the consumption by "Other domestic and commercial equipment" (mainly office and professional equipment) has here been shifted to "Producer durables."

7. From Table A7–4.

8. From Table A9–4—"Ordnance, vehicles, etc."

TABLE A16–11. Projected Gross Shipments of Steel Mill Products, by Market Category[1]

(Million tons)

	1960		1970	1980	1990	2000
Construction	23.8	L	23.3	24.5	24.3	25.4
		M	34.1	40.0	47.6	60.7
		H	46.5	63.0	88.3	135.5
Automotive	19.3	L	19.6	22.0	28.4	30.3
		M	23.3	30.0	38.3	48.4
		H	28.4	38.9	54.5	78.0
Rail transportation	3.0	L	3.1	3.5	5.0	7.1
		M	5.6	7.5	11.5	16.1
		H	9.2	14.1	22.6	33.5
Water and air transportation	.9	L	1.4	2.1	2.6	3.6
		M	1.6	2.2	3.2	4.6
		H	1.7	2.6	4.2	7.0
Other producer durables	12.8	L	16.0	18.0	19.5	21.5
		M	20.8	28.8	39.6	56.5
		H	23.6	38.5	60.1	99.3
Consumer durables	3.8	L	4.2	4.8	5.6	6.4
		M	4.5	5.7	7.3	9.3
		H	4.9	6.4	8.6	11.8
Containers	8.2	L	7.3	6.4	5.5	5.0
		M	9.4	10.5	11.4	12.0
		H	11.5	15.2	20.3	26.4
Ordnance	.2	L	.1	.1	.1	.1
		M	.4	.3	.4	.4
		H	.5	.5	.7	.8
Total domestic shipments	72	L	75	81	91	99
		M	100	125	159	208
		H	126	179	259	392
Net exports	—.7	L	.8	.8	.9	1.0
		M	1.0	1.3	1.6	2.1
		H	1.2	1.8	2.6	3.9
Total shipments	71	L	76	82	92	100
		M	101	126	161	210
		H	127	181	262	396
Prompt industrial scrap generated[2]	12.2	L	13.4	14.8	17.5	19.1
		M	16.8	21.8	28.5	37.3
		H	20.3	29.4	42.9	65.1
Scrap generation factor (prompt industrial scrap as per cent of domestic shipments)	17.4	L	17.9	18.3	19.2	19.3
		M	16.8	17.4	17.9	17.9
		H	16.1	16.4	16.6	16.6

1. Historical data from A16–3. Projections calculated by dividing net shipments, Table A16–10, by the complements of scrap generation factors shown in Table A16–4, footnote 8.
2. From Table A16–14.

TABLE A16–12. Projected Net Consumption and Gross Shipments of Ferrous Castings, by Market Category

(Million tons)

	1960		1970	1980	1990	2000
Construction[1]	3.8	L	3.1	3.0	2.8	2.4
		M	4.5	4.9	5.4	5.8
		H	6.2	7.8	10.1	12.9
Transportation[2]	3.2	L	1.9	–	–	–
		M	3.2	3.0	2.6	2.1
		H	4.4	5.8	7.6	10.2
Other producer durables[3]	3.7	L	4.3	4.6	4.6	4.8
		M	5.7	7.3	9.5	12.6
		H	6.4	9.8	14.4	22.1
Steel industry[4]	2.0	L	1.6	1.4	1.3	1.4
		M	2.1	2.1	2.3	2.9
		H	2.7	3.0	3.7	5.5
Total net domestic end-use consumption	12.7	L	10.9	9.0	8.7	8.6
		M	15.5	17.3	19.8	23.4
		H	19.7	26.4	35.8	50.7
Prompt industrial scrap generated[5]	1.1	L	.9	.7	.7	.7
		M	1.2	1.4	1.6	1.9
		H	1.6	2.1	2.9	4.1
Gross domestic shipments[6]	13.8	L	11.8	9.7	9.4	9.3
		M	16.7	18.7	21.4	25.3
		H	21.3	28.5	38.7	54.8
Net exports[7]	.04	L	*	*	*	*
		M	*	*	*	*
		H	1.0	1.5	1.5	2.0
Total shipments[8]	13.8	L	11.8	9.7	9.4	9.3
		M	16.7	18.7	21.4	25.3
		H	22.3	30.0	40.2	56.8

* Negligible.

1. Estimate based on steel consumption in construction (excluding railroads) shown in Table A4–9:

        1960: 17%   1990: 12%
        1970: 14%   2000: 10%
        1980: 13%

2. From Tables A5–11 and 12—ferrous castings consumption by automobiles and trucks, raised by 30% to include consumption by other transportation equipment. (See footnote 3, Table A16–10.)

3. From Table A6–7.

4. Based on the following amounts consumed per 100 tons of steel ingots produced:

        1960: 2.0 tons   1990: 1.0 tons
              1980: 1.2 tons
        1970: 1.5 tons   2000: 1.0 tons

Steel ingot production shown in Table A16–9.

5. Estimated at 8% of domestic shipments.

6. The sum of net end-use consumption and prompt industrial scrap generated.

7. Estimated on a judgment basis taking into account historical trends.

8. The sum of domestic shipments and net exports.

TABLE A16–13.   Projected Foreign Trade in Steel Mill Products and Ferrous Castings

(Million tons unless otherwise specified)

	1950	1955	1960		1970	1980	1990	2000
Steel mill products:								
				L	75	81	91	99
Domestic shipments[1]	71	82	72	M	100	125	159	208
				H	126	179	259	392
				L	2.6	2.8	3.2	3.5
Exports[2]	2.9	4.1	2.9	M	3.5	4.4	5.6	7.3
				H	4.4	6.3	9.1	13.7
Per cent of domestic shipments[3]	4.1	5.0	4.0		3.5	3.5	3.5	3.5
				L	1.9	2.0	2.3	2.5
Imports[2]	1.1	1.1	3.6	M	2.5	3.1	4.0	5.2
				H	3.2	4.5	6.5	9.8
Per cent of domestic shipments[3]	1.5	1.3	5.0		2.5	2.5	2.5	2.5
				L	.7	.8	.9	1.0
Net exports	1.8	3.0	—.7	M	1.0	1.3	1.6	2.1
				H	1.2	1.8	2.6	3.9
Ferrous castings:								
				L	*	*	*	*
Net exports[4]	.09	.07	.04	M	*	*	*	*
				H	1.0	1.5	1.5	2.0
Net exports of steel mill products and ferrous castings				L	.7	.8	.9	1.0
	1.9	3.1	—.7	M	1.0	1.3	1.6	2.1
				H	2.2	3.3	4.1	5.9

1. Historical data from Table A16–3; projections from Table A16–11.
2. Historical data aggregated from Table A16–5; projections calculated by applying percentage figures that follow.
3. Historical data calculated from Table A16–5; projection on a judgment basis.
4. Historical data from Table A16–5; projections from Table A16–12.

TABLE A16–14. Projected Prompt Industrial Scrap Generated by Steel Product Manufacturers[1]

(Million tons)

	1960		1970	1980	1990	2000
Construction	1.2	L	1.2	1.2	1.2	1.3
		M	1.7	2.0	2.4	3.0
		H	2.3	3.2	4.4	6.8
Automotive	6.0	L	6.1	6.8	8.8	9.4
		M	7.2	9.3	11.9	15.0
		H	8.8	12.1	16.9	24.2
Rail transportation	.2	L	.2	.2	.4	.5
		M	.4	.5	.8	1.1
		H	.6	1.0	1.6	2.3
Water and air transportation	.2	L	.3	.5	.6	.9
		M	.4	.5	.8	1.1
		H	.4	.6	1.0	1.7
Other producer durables	2.8	L	4.0	4.5	4.9	5.4
		M	5.2	7.2	9.9	14.1
		H	5.9	9.6	15.0	24.8
Consumer durables	.8	L	.7	.8	.9	1.0
		M	.7	.9	1.2	1.5
		H	.8	1.0	1.4	1.9
Containers	1.0	L	.9	.8	.7	.6
		M	1.1	1.3	1.4	1.4
		H	1.4	1.8	2.4	3.2
Ordnance	*	L	*	*	*	*
		M	.1	.1	.1	.1
		H	.1	.1	.2	.2
All prompt industrial scrap generated by steel mills	12.2	L	13.4	14.8	17.5	19.1
		M	16.8	21.8	28.5	37.3
		H	20.3	29.4	42.9	65.1
All prompt industrial scrap generated by foundries[2]	1.1	L	.9	.7	.7	.7
		M	1.2	1.4	1.6	1.9
		H	1.6	2.1	2.9	4.1
Total prompt industrial scrap generated by iron and steel industry	13.3	L	14.3	15.5	18.2	19.8
		M	18.0	23.2	30.1	39.2
		H	21.9	31.5	45.8	69.2

* Negligible.

1. Data represent the difference between gross shipments, Table A16–11, and net shipments, Table A16–10.
2. From Table A16–12.

TABLE A16–15.   Potential Supply of Obsolete Ferrous Scrap[1]

(Million tons unless otherwise specified)

	Metal content potentially recoverable[2] (%)	Average life cycle[3] (years)	1950	1955	1960		1970	1980	1990	2000
All construction	88	50 40 30	7.5	8.1	8.8	L M H	8.7 9.7 11.3	9.4 10.9 20.4	10.4 19.8 21.6	19.3 20.8 41.3
Automotive	95	10	7.0	8.2	12.3	L M H	12.7 12.9 13.2	13.0 15.7 19.3	14.9 20.2 26.5	18.7 25.7 37.3
Rail transportation	86	25	7.1	4.3	2.7	L M H	4.4 4.5 4.6	3.2 3.3 3.5	2.1 4.2 6.7	2.7 5.5 9.8
Water and air transportation	95	30	.3	.3	.3	L M H	.3 .3 .3	.3 .3 .3	.6 .6 .7	1.1 1.2 1.4
Other producer durables	90	20	2.4	3.2	4.2	L M H	8.4 8.6 8.7	8.8 9.2 9.5	10.9 14.7 17.2	12.3 20.4 28.1
Consumer durables	65	10	1.8	1.9	2.4	L M H	2.1 2.1 2.1	2.3 2.5 2.7	2.7 3.2 3.6	3.1 4.1 4.9
Containers	13	15	.3	.4	.6	L M H	.8 .9 1.2	.9 1.0 1.3	.8 1.1 1.5	.7 1.2 2.0
Ordnance	36	20	.1	.2	.1		.1	.1	.1	.1
Ferrous castings	100	25	13.0	12.0	11.0	L M H	11.5 11.7 11.8	15.8 16.2 16.6	11.7 15.0 18.0	10.8 17.8 25.5
Total potential supply	–	–	39.5	38.6	42.4	L M H	49.0 50.8 53.3	53.8 59.2 73.7	54.2 78.9 95.9	68.8 96.8 150.4
Domestic consumption of obsolete scrap as per cent of total potential supply[4]	–	–	32.9	37.0	21.7	L M H	25.3 34.1 43.0	21.7 34.1 43.3	18.9 30.8 46.7	18.9 32.2 44.4

1. Refers to the estimated recoverable metal content of scrap becoming available in the year indicated upon abandonment or other disposal of articles as the result, ordinarily, of completion of their useful lives (not including mere retirement to "standby" use, use in the form of cannibalized parts, and other uses not involving availability for scrap). The method used is patterned after one suggested by Battelle Memorial Institute in its report to the U.S. Department of Commerce (*A Survey and Analysis of the Supply and Availability of Obsolete Iron and Steel Scrap,* Jan. 15, 1957). To allow for the fact that articles become available for scrapping over a period of time and not exactly one lifetime after their consumption, an estimate of total scrap of any one category becoming available in a particular year has to approximate the sum of the portions of various age-cohorts (amounts of the article consumed in successive past periods) which become available in the given year. Since there is some continuity in production trends, this sum may be approximated by summation of the following two fractions:

$$(1)\quad \frac{1}{L} \quad \text{of the current year's consumption of the article}$$

$$(2)\quad \frac{L-1}{L} \quad \text{of the consumption one life cycle earlier}$$

where L = the average life cycle.

The foregoing formula, which was applied to get the historical estimates as well as the projections, gives only the scrap potential and not what is actually processed for recovery, which is shown as the last item in the table. To apply the formula, it was necessary, in some cases, to make an estimate of actual consumption in the earlier years of the century. This was done crudely, usually by extrapolation.

For further details on the concept and methods, see Notes to this appendix.

2. Based on data in Battelle study cited in footnote 1. Allows for loss due to abrasion, corrosion, inaccessibility, exports of used material, etc.

3. Based on data in Battelle study cited in footnote 1.

4. From Table A16–16.

TABLE A16–16. Projected Consumption of Ferrous Scrap by Steel Mills and Foundries

(Million tons unless otherwise specified)

	1950	1955	1960		1970	1980	1990	2000
Gross output of steel mills and foundries[1]				L	128	133	146	158
	126	148	125	M	171	210	264	341
				H	216	306	438	657
Total input of ferrous metallics[1]				L	141	146	161	174
	133	160	136	M	188	231	290	375
				H	238	337	482	723
Per cent of output[1]	106	108	109		110	110	110	110
Total consumption of ferrous scrap[2]				L	66.3	68.6	75.7	81.8
	63.0	75.3	62.1	M	88.4	108.6	136.3	176.2
				H	111.9	158.4	226.5	339.8
Per cent of total input[3]	47.4	47.1	45.6		47	47	47	47
Prompt industrial scrap[4]				L	14.3	15.5	18.2	19.8
	13.0	15.5	13.3	M	18.0	23.2	30.1	39.2
				H	21.9	31.5	45.8	69.2
Home scrap[5]				L	39.6	41.4	45.4	49.0
	37.0	45.5	39.6	M	53.1	65.2	81.9	105.8
				H	67.1	95.0	135.9	203.8
Obsolete scrap[6]				L	12.4	11.7	12.1	13.0
	13.0	14.3	9.2	M	17.3	20.2	24.3	31.2
				H	22.9	31.9	44.8	66.8

1. From Table A16–9.

2. Historical data from Table A16–2; projections are the products of total input of ferrous metallics, above, and per cent of total input, below.

3. Historical data based on second and fourth items; projections based on long-term historical record.

4. From Table A16–14. Prompt industrial scrap generation is assumed to equal consumption.

5. Historical data from Table A16–6; projections computed as 45% (1951–60 average) of total iron and steel shipments from Table A16–9.

6. This series is a residual, representing the difference between the sum of prompt industrial scrap plus home scrap consumption and total consumption of ferrous scrap. Historical data differ from those on withdrawals of obsolete scrap, shown in Table A16–6, because they do not include exports and scrap consumed by blast furnaces, in the production of ferroalloys, and in miscellaneous uses. They represent consumption by steel mills and steel and iron foundries only.

TABLE A16–17.   Projected Pig Iron Production and Iron Ore Requirements[1]

(Million tons unless otherwise specified)

	1950	1955	1960		1970	1980	1990	2000
Pig iron consumption[2]	64.9	77.2	66.6	L	66	67	74	79
				M	88	107	134	171
				H	111	157	221	330
Net exports[3]	—.8	—.2	—.2		*	*	*	*
Production[3]	64.6	76.9	66.5	L	66	67	74	79
				M	88	107	134	171
				H	111	157	221	330
Blast furnace consumption of ferrous metallics[4]	63.2	76.3	64.9	L	65	66	73	77
				M	86	105	131	168
				H	109	154	217	323
Per cent of pig iron production[5]	97.8	97.2	97.6		98	98	98	98
Ferrous scrap consumption by blast furnaces[6]	4.4	4.7	3.6	L	3.6	3.8	4.2	4.5
				M	4.9	6.0	7.5	9.7
				H	6.1	8.7	12.5	18.7
Requirements for iron ore:								
Blast furnaces (iron content)[7]	58.8	71.6	61.3	L	61.4	62.2	68.8	72.5
				M	81.1	99.0	123.5	158.3
				H	102.9	145.3	204.5	304.3
Steel furnaces (iron content)[8]	3.3	5.1	4.6	L	5.8	6.7	8.0	9.4
				M	7.7	10.6	14.5	20.2
				H	9.8	15.5	24.1	39.0
Miscellaneous (iron content)[9]	.4	.4	.6	L	.7	.7	.7	.8
				M	1.1	1.3	1.6	2.1
				H	1.6	2.3	3.3	4.8
Total domestic requirements for iron ore (iron content)[10]	62.5	77.1	66.5	L	67.9	69.6	77.5	82.7
				M	89.9	110.9	139.6	180.6
				H	114.3	163.1	231.9	348.1
Total domestic requirements for iron ore (gross weight)[11]	117.4	135.1	131.1	L	128.1	131.3	146.2	156.0
				M	169.6	209.2	263.4	340.7
				H	215.6	307.7	437.5	656.8

* Negligible.

1. Historical data from Table A16–7.
2. Projections from Table A16–9.
3. In the projections, production is equated with consumption because of the historical insignificance of foreign trade in pig iron. This trend is expected to continue.
4. Projections are the products of the preceding and the following line.
5. Projected ratio based on historical record. Ratio is less than 100 per cent because of omission of the input of recycled steel mill slag; this does not affect the final calculation.
6. Projections assume that 5.5% of the total domestic consumption of ferrous scrap, shown in Table A16–16, is used by blast furnaces.

7. Represents the difference between "Blast furnace consumption of ferrous metallics" and "Ferrous scrap consumption by blast furnaces," above.
8. From Table A16–9.
9. Projections assume that 1.0%, 1.25%, and 1.5% of "Blast furnace consumption of ferrous metallics" would be consumed in miscellaneous uses in the Low, Medium, and High projection, respectively.
10. Sum of the preceding three lines.
11. Projections based on an iron content of 53%, the weighted average of domestically produced and imported iron ore.

TABLE A16–18.   Net Consumption of Alloy (including Stainless) Steel, by Market Category

	1950	1955	1956	1957	1958	1959	1960		1970	1980	1990	2000
Net-end-use consumption of alloy (including stainless) steel as per cent of total steel consumption:[1]												
Construction	2.4	3.2	3.1	2.9	2.2	2.9	3.0		3.2	3.4	3.6	3.8
Automotive	12.8	11.8	11.6	10.6	9.4	10.2	8.8		9.2	9.6	10.0	11.0
Rail transportation	3.8	4.8	5.4	5.8	6.7	7.5	9.2		8.0	8.5	9.5	10.0
Water and air transportation	29.8	32.1	36.7	21.0	26.5	33.3	32.9		34.0	36.0	38.0	40.0
Other producer durables	12.5	12.4	13.2	11.7	11.1	12.7	11.9		13.0	14.0	15.0	16.0
Consumer durables	3.6	4.4	3.5	3.3	3.0	3.2	3.2		3.4	3.6	3.8	4.0
Ordnance	22.7	11.9	17.8	24.1	32.6	16.7	35.0		35.0	35.0	35.0	35.0
Containers and other	.5	.8	1.2	.8	.6	.7	.6		.7	.9	1.0	1.0
Net end-use consumption (million tons):[2]												
Construction	.53	.80	.83	.76	.44	.67	.67	L	.71	.79	.83	.92
								M	1.04	1.29	1.63	2.19
								H	1.41	2.03	3.02	4.89
Automotive	1.64	1.88	1.46	1.28	.94	1.33	1.17	L	1.24	1.46	1.96	2.30
								M	1.48	1.99	2.64	3.67
								H	1.80	2.57	3.76	5.92
Rail transportation	.19	.18	.24	.25	.11	.20	.26	L	.23	.28	.45	.66
								M	.42	.60	1.02	1.50
								H	.69	1.11	2.00	3.12
Water and air transportation	.10	.19	.28	.24	.19	.21	.20	L	.37	.58	.76	1.08
								M	.41	.61	.91	1.40
								H	.44	.72	1.22	2.12
Other producer durables	1.15	1.34	1.51	1.16	.92	1.29	1.15	L	1.56	1.89	2.19	2.58
								M	2.03	3.02	4.46	6.78
								H	2.30	4.05	6.76	11.92
Consumer durables	.13	.13	.13	.10	.08	.11	.11	L	.12	.14	.18	.22
								M	.13	.17	.23	.31
								H	.14	.19	.27	.40
Ordnance	.04	.09	.08	.07	.07	.02	.07	L	.04	.04	.04	.04
								M	.10	.07	.10	.10
								H	.14	.14	.18	.21
Containers and other	.03	.06	.09	.05	.04	.05	.04	L	.04	.05	.05	.04
								M	.06	.08	.10	.11
								H	.07	.12	.18	.23
Total	3.81	4.66	4.62	3.91	2.79	3.88	3.67	L	4.31	5.23	6.46	7.84
								M	5.67	7.83	11.09	16.06
								H	6.99	10.93	17.39	28.81

1. Source: American Iron and Steel Institute, Form AIS–16, AIS–C, AIS–A, and AIS–S. The historical percentage figures have been derived by calculating adjusted gross shipments and net end-use consumption of alloy (including stainless) steel by the same method as used for total steel shipments and total steel consumption. See footnotes to Tables A16–3 and 4. The projected percentage figures have been extrapolated on a judgment basis, taking into account historical trends, expected future changes of the product-mix within the various market classifications, and expected technological changes (such as increasing use of stainless steel in aircraft production).

2. The net end-use consumption has been calculated by applying the above percentage figures to the historical and projected data on total steel consumption shown in Tables A16–4 and 10.

TABLE A16–19.   Relative Changes in Net End-Use Consumption of Steel Mill Products and Ferrous Castings, by Market Category[1]

(Per cent per annum)

		Steel mill products								Ferrous castings	Total
		Construction	Automotive	Rail trans-portation	Water and air transportation	Other producer durables	Consumer durables	Containers	Ordnance		
1940–60		3.6	3.4	—2.2	—2.0	5.0	2.8	3.8	–	–	2.3
1960–80	L	0.2	0.7	0.8	5.0	1.7	1.1	—1.2	—3.4	—1.7	0.3
	M	2.7	2.2	4.7	5.3	4.1	2.0	1.2	–	1.6	2.7
	H	5.0	3.6	8.0	6.2	5.7	2.7	3.2	3.5	3.7	4.6
1980–2000	L	0.2	1.6	3.5	2.7	0.9	1.5	—1.2	–	—0.2	0.8
	M	2.1	2.4	3.9	3.7	3.4	2.5	0.7	2.0	1.5	2.4
	H	3.9	3.5	4.4	5.0	4.9	3.1	2.8	2.0	3.3	3.9
1960–2000	L	0.2	1.1	2.2	3.8	1.3	1.3	—1.2	—1.7	—1.0	0.5
	M	2.4	2.3	4.3	4.5	3.8	2.2	1.0	1.0	1.5	2.5
	H	4.5	3.5	6.4	5.6	5.3	2.9	3.0	1.7	3.5	4.2

1. From Tables A16–4, 10, and 12.

TABLE A16–20. Percentage Distribution of Net End-Use Consumption of Steel Mill Products and Ferrous Castings, by Market Category[1]

		Steel mill products								Ferrous castings	Total
		Construction	Automotive	Rail transportation	Water and air transportation	Other producer durables	Consumer durables	Containers	Ordnance		
1929		26.8	11.2	16.7	.5	8.8	3.7	3.7	*	28.6	100.0
1930		27.2	9.1	13.0	.7	6.4	3.7	4.3	*	35.6	100.0
1931		28.1	11.5	13.0	.8	7.9	5.5	6.3	*	26.9	100.0
1932		22.5	10.1	7.7	.6	5.9	5.9	7.1	*	40.2	100.0
1933		21.8	15.2	7.6	.5	8.0	5.2	9.5	*	32.2	100.0
1934		22.6	15.2	11.3	.9	7.8	5.2	7.4	*	29.6	100.0
1935		23.5	19.1	7.7	.8	9.9	5.5	8.5	*	25.0	100.0
1936		25.7	15.4	11.1	.8	9.1	4.8	7.1	*	26.0	100.0
1937		24.5	15.3	12.3	1.0	9.2	4.8	8.0	*	24.9	100.0
1938		24.4	11.6	5.5	1.1	6.2	6.2	7.6	*	37.4	100.0
1939		25.9	14.0	10.3	1.3	7.5	5.2	9.1	*	26.7	100.0
1940		25.4	15.7	10.2	2.1	9.2	5.8	7.8	*	23.8	100.0
1941		28.3	14.1	10.5	4.3	9.0	7.0	8.4	2.2	16.2	100.0
1942		25.8	5.4	8.4	15.8	7.2	3.5	7.2	9.7	17.0	100.0
1943		18.1	5.7	8.7	19.2	7.4	2.9	6.9	11.6	19.5	100.0
1944		19.2	5.7	10.2	16.4	8.2	3.4	7.1	10.0	19.8	100.0
1945		23.6	7.9	10.5	5.0	9.7	4.8	8.9	9.1	20.5	100.0
1946		27.0	12.6	8.5	.6	12.0	6.1	9.5	*	23.7	100.0
1947		28.3	13.9	8.8	.7	10.1	6.1	9.0	*	23.1	100.0
1948		28.3	14.0	8.6	.9	11.5	6.3	8.6	*	21.8	100.0
1949		30.0	16.4	6.6	1.0	11.2	5.2	8.5	.2	20.9	100.0
1950		29.5	17.4	6.3	.4	11.5	5.9	8.6	.3	20.1	100.0
1951		29.3	14.4	7.7	1.1	11.9	5.5	8.7	1.3	20.1	100.0
1952		29.5	14.2	6.1	1.4	12.0	5.0	8.6	2.6	20.6	100.0
1953		29.9	15.9	6.3	1.1	11.5	5.7	8.0	2.8	18.8	100.0
1954		31.9	15.8	4.1	.8	11.6	5.5	9.6	1.3	19.4	100.0
1955		29.9	19.0	4.4	.7	11.7	5.7	8.5	.8	19.2	100.0
1956		32.2	15.2	5.4	1.0	12.4	5.9	8.8	.5	18.6	100.0
1957		34.1	15.8	5.5	1.5	11.4	4.9	8.3	.4	18.1	100.0
1958		32.8	14.9	2.6	1.2	12.2	6.1	11.4	.3	18.5	100.0
1959		31.3	17.7	3.5	1.0	12.5	5.9	9.7	.1	18.3	100.0
1960		31.2	18.4	3.9	.8	11.8	6.0	10.0	.3	17.6	100.0
	L	30.5	18.6	4.0	1.5	16.6	4.8	8.8	.1	15.1	100.0
1970	M	32.9	16.4	5.3	1.2	15.8	3.9	8.4	.3	15.8	100.0
	H	35.2	15.6	6.8	1.0	14.1	3.3	8.0	.3	15.7	100.0
	L	30.8	20.1	4.4	2.1	17.9	5.3	7.4	.1	11.9	100.0
1980	M	31.5	17.2	5.8	1.4	17.9	4.0	7.6	.2	14.4	100.0
	H	34.0	15.2	7.4	1.1	16.4	3.1	7.6	.2	15.0	100.0
	L	28.1	23.8	5.7	2.4	17.7	5.7	5.9	.1	10.6	100.0
1990	M	30.0	17.5	7.1	1.6	19.7	4.1	6.6	.2	13.2	100.0
	H	33.3	14.9	8.3	1.3	17.9	2.8	7.1	.2	14.2	100.0
	L	27.1	23.5	7.4	3.0	18.1	6.1	5.0	.1	9.7	100.0
2000	M	29.7	17.2	7.7	1.8	21.9	4.0	5.5	.1	12.1	100.0
	H	34.1	14.2	8.3	1.4	19.7	2.6	6.1	.2	13.4	100.0

* Negligible.

1. From Tables A16-4, 10, and 12.

TABLE A16–21.   Production and Consumption of Iron and Steel in Relation to GNP and Durable Goods and Per Capita[1]

		Production of steel ingots			Gross iron and steel shipments			Net domestic consumption		
		Per $ 1960 bil. of GNP (mil. tons)	Per $ 1960 bil. of durable goods and construction (mil. tons)	Per capita (tons)	Per $ 1960 bil. of GNP (mil. tons)	Per $ 1960 bil. of durable goods and construction (mil. tons)	Per capita (tons)	Per $ 1960 bil. of GNP (mil. tons)	Per $ 1960 bil. of durable goods and construction (mil. tons)	Per capita (tons)
1929		.30	.93	.50	.32	1.02	.55	.27	.85	.46
1930		.24	.90	.36	.26	.97	.39	.22	.84	.34
1931		.16	.75	.23	.17	.80	.24	.15	.70	.21
1932		.10	.66	.12	.11	.73	.13	.10	.63	.12
1933		.18	1.16	.20	.17	1.10	.19	.14	.93	.16
1934		.18	1.02	.23	.17	.97	.22	.15	.81	.18
1935		.22	1.08	.30	.20	.99	.27	.17	.82	.23
1936		.27	1.12	.41	.24	.98	.37	.20	.84	.31
1937		.27	1.09	.44	.25	.99	.40	.20	.82	.33
1938		.16	.78	.24	.14	.71	.22	.12	.58	.18
1939		.24	1.02	.40	.22	.92	.36	.18	.76	.30
1940		.29	1.09	.50	.26	1.01	.47	.19	.74	.34
1941		.30	.98	.62	.28	.91	.57	.22	.71	.44
1942		.28	.92	.63	.24	.80	.55	.18	.62	.42
1943		.25	.82	.65	.22	.72	.57	.17	.55	.43
1944		.22	.73	.59	.21	.69	.56	.16	.54	.44
1945		.22	.78	.57	.19	.69	.50	.15	.55	.40
1946		.21	.78	.47	.19	.72	.44	.15	.57	.35
1947		.26	.91	.59	.24	.85	.55	.19	.67	.43
1948		.26	.91	.60	.25	.85	.56	.20	.69	.46
1949		.23	.82	.52	.21	.76	.48	.17	.61	.38
1950		.27	.83	.64	.25	.77	.59	.20	.64	.49
1951		.27	.82	.68	.25	.77	.64	.21	.65	.54
1952		.23	.71	.59	.21	.65	.54	.17	.53	.45
1953		.26	.80	.70	.23	.69	.61	.19	.58	.51
1954		.21	.67	.54	.18	.58	.47	.15	.48	.39
1955		.26	.78	.71	.23	.68	.62	.19	.56	.51
1956		.25	.77	.68	.22	.67	.59	.18	.55	.49
1957		.24	.75	.66	.20	.63	.56	.17	.52	.46
1958		.18	.63	.49	.16	.53	.41	.13	.45	.35
1959		.19	.61	.53	.17	.55	.47	.15	.48	.41
1960		.20	.65	.55	.17	.55	.47	.14	.47	.40
1970	L	.15	.56	.53	.12	.47	.44	.10	.39	.36
	M	.19	.57	.68	.16	.48	.57	.13	.40	.48
	H	.22	.57	.80	.19	.48	.67	.16	.40	.56
1980	L	.12	.50	.51	.10	.40	.41	.08	.33	.34
	M	.17	.49	.72	.14	.40	.60	.11	.34	.49
	H	.20	.48	.91	.17	.40	.76	.14	.34	.63
1990	L	.10	.44	.52	.08	.34	.41	.07	.28	.33
	M	.15	.43	.78	.12	.34	.63	.10	.29	.53
	H	.18	.42	1.05	.15	.35	.87	.13	.29	.72
2000	L	.08	.37	.52	.06	.29	.41	.05	.23	.33
	M	.10	.37	.90	.11	.30	.71	.09	.24	.59
	H	.19	.37	1.44	.14	.30	1.05	.11	.25	.87

1. Calculated from data in Tables A16–1 and 9 (steel production and consumption), A1–6 and 13 (GNP, durable goods and construction), and A1–1 and 2 (population).

TABLE A16–22. Projected Consumption of Manganese

(Million tons manganese content unless otherwise specified)

	1950	1955	1960		1970	1980	1990	2000
Consumption of ferromanganese and				L	.86	.93	1.04	1.13
direct ore in steel ingot production[1]	.72	.85	.84	M	1.13	1.40	1.76	2.28
				H	1.41	1.96	2.77	4.09
Production of steel ingots, excluding				L	95	103	116	126
electric furnace steel[2] (mil. tons)	91	109	91	M	126	155	196	253
				H	157	218	308	454
Manganese per ton[3] (lb.)	15.8	15.7	18.4		18	18	18	18
Consumption of ferromanganese in				L	.07	.07	.08	.09
iron and steel castings[4]	.06	.07	.07	M	.09	.11	.14	.18
				H	.11	.16	.22	.33
Consumption by dry cell and				L	.05	.07	.09	.11
chemical industries[5]	.04	.03	.04	M	.06	.08	.12	.17
				H	.06	.10	.16	.26
				L	.98	1.07	1.21	1.33
Total domestic consumption	.82	.95	.95	M	1.28	1.59	2.02	2.63
				H	1.58	2.22	3.15	4.68
Apparent consumption as per cent								
of surveyed consumption[6]	126	121	111		110	110	110	110
				L	1.08	1.18	1.33	1.46
Apparent domestic consumption[7]	1.03	1.15	1.05	M	1.41	1.75	2.22	2.89
				H	1.74	2.44	3.46	5.15

1. Historical data from *Minerals Yearbook,* chapter on Manganese. Manganese content of ore and ferromanganese, etc., consumed is calculated on the basis of weighted average content of domestic and imported ferroalloying materials and implicitly includes ferroalloy blast furnace losses. Does not include manganese content of iron ores used or of iron and steel scrap. Projections are the product of the following two lines.

2. From Tables A10–29 and 30.

3. Historical data computed from lines 1 and 2. The single projection is assumed to be as low an input ratio as may accompany Low steel output and as high a ratio as may accompany High steel production.

4. Estimated at 8% of consumption in steel ingot production—the same ratio as in recent years.

5. Historical data from *Minerals Yearbook.* Projected on a judgment basis.

6. Historical data computed from preceding and following lines. Differences presumably stem from government stockpiling and from undercoverage of surveyed consumption. The 1960 relationship is assumed to represent the latter only and is therefore rounded and used as the correction factor for the future.

7. Historical data calculated on the basis of manganese content of domestic production, imports, and stock changes of ore and ferromanganese, as reported in, or estimated from, *Minerals Yearbook.*

TABLE A16–23. Historical Data on Consumption of Nickel[1]

(Thousand tons unless otherwise specified)

	1950	1951	1952	1953	1954	1955	1956	1957	1958	1959	1960
Nickel in stainless steel produced:											
Stainless steel ingots produced[2]	832.3	933.7	930.2	1,049.1	848.2	1,218.2	1,248.3	1,043.7	893.0	1,128.5	1,000.7
Average per cent nickel[3]	5.63	4.44	5.22	4.33	5.60	5.30	5.96	6.32	5.94	6.03	6.28
Nickel content	46.9	41.4	48.5	45.4	47.5	64.6	74.4	66.0	53.0	68.0	62.8
Nickel in other alloy steel produced:											
Other alloy steel ingots produced[2]	7,614	9,062	8,087	9,208	6,296	9,374	9,012	7,794	5,725	7,729	7,355
Average per cent nickel[3]	0.874	0.816	0.728	0.701	0.722	0.688	0.706	0.685	0.742	0.738	0.717
Nickel content	66.6	74.0	58.9	64.6	45.5	64.5	63.6	53.4	42.5	57.1	52.8
Nickel in all alloy (including stainless) steel produced:											
Total alloy (including stainless) steel ingots produced	8,446	9,996	9,017	10,257	7,144	10,592	10,260	8,838	6,618	8,857	8,356
Average per cent nickel[4]	1.34	1.15	1.19	1.07	1.30	1.22	1.34	1.35	1.44	1.41	1.38
Nickel content	113.5	115.4	107.4	110.0	93.0	129.1	138.0	119.4	95.5	125.1	115.6
Net domestic end-use consumption of alloy (including stainless) steel[5] (mil. tons)	3.81	n.a.	n.a.	n.a.	n.a.	4.66	4.62	3.91	2.79	3.88	3.67
Nickel content of alloy (including stainless) steel consumed[6] (thous. tons)	51.1	–	–	–	–	56.9	61.9	52.8	40.2	54.7	50.6

1. The purpose of this table is to calculate the average nickel content of total net end-use consumption of stainless and other alloy steels. The method employed is described somewhat further in the Notes to this appendix.

2. From American Iron and Steel Institute, *Annual Statistical Report,* 1960.

3. Based on the output of about 30 categories of stainless and other alloy steel and the range of nickel content for each. (Source:

U.S. Steel Corp., *The Making, Shaping, and Treating of Steel,* 1957 ed.) The midpoint of each range was used, along with the quantities, to obtain a weighted average content.

4. The percentage, in this case, was computed from total alloy (including stainless) output, above, and total nickel content, below.

5. From Table A16–18.

6. Total nickel content of ingot multiplied by the ratio of end-use consumption to ingot production.

TABLE A16–24.   Projected Consumption of Nickel

(Thousand tons unless otherwise specified)

	1950	1955	1960		1970	1980	1990	2000
Consumption in alloy (including				L	60.3	78.4	103.4	133.3
stainless) steel[1]	51.1	56.9	50.6	M	79.4	117.4	177.4	273.0
				H	97.9	164.0	278.2	489.8
Net end-use consumption of alloy (in-				L	4.31	5.23	6.46	7.84
cluding stainless) steel[2] (mil. tons)	3.81	4.66	3.67	M	5.67	7.83	11.09	16.06
				H	6.99	10.93	17.39	28.81
Per cent nickel content[3]	1.34	1.22	1.38		1.40	1.50	1.60	1.70
				L	4.4	4.0	4.2	4.5
Consumption in ferrous castings[4]	4.9	5.4	4.6	M	6.2	7.6	9.5	12.2
				H	7.9	11.6	17.2	26.4
Net end-use consumption of ferrous				L	10.9	9.0	8.7	8.6
castings[5] (mil. tons)	14.8	16.0	12.7	M	15.5	17.3	19.8	23.4
				H	19.7	26.4	35.8	50.7
Per cent nickel content[6]	.033	.034	.036		.040	.044	.048	.052
Total net end-use consumption by				L	64.7	82.4	107.6	137.8
iron and steel industry	56.0	62.3	55.2	M	85.6	125.0	186.9	285.2
				H	105.8	175.6	295.4	516.2
Net end-use consumption by non-				L	48.3	54.4	61.0	72.0
ferrous metals industry[7]	40.7	45.5	41.4	M	69.2	100.4	146.1	217.8
				H	92.6	172.2	302.2	535.1
Purchases of producer durable				L	35.8	43.9	52.4	63.2
goods[8] ($ 1960 bil.)	25.8	27.4	27.5	M	46.1	66.9	97.4	145.2
				H	54.8	93.6	155.0	264.9
				L	1.35	1.24	1.17	1.14
Tons of nickel/$ 1960 mil.[9]	1.58	1.66	1.51	M	1.50	1.50	1.50	1.50
				H	1.69	1.84	1.95	2.02
				L	20.6	25.1	29.6	33.2
Consumption in electro-plating[7]	17.4	16.0	16.8	M	22.1	29.6	38.5	48.0
				H	25.4	37.7	54.6	75.7
Purchases of consumer durables[8]				L	60.5	83.6	114.0	151.0
($ 1960 bil.)	34.0	42.0	44.3	M	65.1	98.6	148.0	218.0
				H	74.7	125.8	210.0	344.0
Tons of nickel/$ 1960 mil.[9]	.51	.38	.38		.34	.30	.26	.22
				L	5.5	6.6	7.9	9.5
Minor uses[10]	3.2	5.2	4.7	M	6.0	7.5	9.5	12.0
				H	6.2	8.3	11.2	15.0
				L	139.1	168.5	206.1	252.5
Total net end-use consumption[11]	117.3	129.0	118.1	M	182.9	262.5	381.0	563.0
				H	230.0	393.8	663.4	1,142.0

1. Historical data from Table A16–23. Projections are the product of the following two lines.
2. From Table A16–18.
3. Historical data from Table A16–23. Projected on a judgment basis, taking account of historical trends and expected faster growth of stainless, compared with other alloy, steel.
4. Historical data from *Minerals Yearbook*, chapter on Nickel. These refer to primary nickel only; the utilization of old scrap in ferrous castings appears to be negligible. Projections are product of following two lines.
5. From Table A16–12.
6. Historical data calculated from two preceding lines. Projected on a judgment basis.
7. Historical data on consumption of primary nickel, shown in *Minerals Yearbook*, chapter on Nickel, has

been raised by the estimated amounts of nickel recovered from scrap. This gross consumption has then been reduced by excluding estimated prompt industrial scrap. Projections computed from the following two lines.
8. From Table A1–14.
9. Historical data computed from the two preceding lines. Projected on a judgment basis.
10. Historical data aggregated from *Minerals Yearbook*. Projected on a judgment basis.
11. Historical estimates compare with the following data, from *Minerals Yearbook*, on reported primary consumption plus recovery from old scrap: 1950—103.7 thousand tons; 1955—117.5; 1960—112.8. Owing to the sporadic (and largely unpublished) record of acquisitions for and sales from government stockpiles, a usable apparent consumption series is not calculable.

TABLE A16–25. Projected Consumption of Chromium[1]

(Million tons Cr_2O_3 equivalent unless otherwise specified)

	1950	1955	1960		1970	1980	1990	2000
Consumption in metallurgical uses[2]	.23	.47	.31	L	.38	.46	.57	.69
				M	.50	.69	.98	1.41
				H	.62	.96	1.53	2.54
Per cent of alloy (including stainless) steel consumption	6.0	10.1	8.4		8.8	8.8	8.8	8.8
Refractory uses[3]	.12	.15	.14	L	.14	.14	.15	.16
				M	.18	.22	.27	.35
				H	.23	.32	.45	.68
Tons/thousand tons of pig iron	1.85	1.95	2.09		2.05	2.05	2.05	2.05
Chemical uses[4]	.06	.07	.07		.09	.10	.12	.13
Total domestic consumption[5]	.41	.69	.52	L	.61	.70	.84	.98
				M	.77	1.01	1.37	1.89
				H	.94	1.38	2.10	3.35

1. Historical data based on *Minerals Yearbook,* chapter on Chromium. Chromic oxide content calculated as follows:

Cr_2O_3 content as per cent of gross consumption of chromite, by primary use groups (1960):

Metallurgical	Refractory	Chemical	Total
46.4	34.9	45.3	42.6

2. Represents the chromic oxide content of chromite consumed in the production of chromium ferroalloys and chromium metal. Since some 9/10 of all chromium ferroalloys consumed are used in stainless and other alloy steels, the projections of chromium consumption in metallurgical uses have been tied to the projected use of alloy steels, shown in Table A16–18. The percentages represent this abstract relationship and not the average chromium content of alloy steels.

3. This item represents chrome brick, chrome mortar, chrome-magnesite brick, plastic chrome, etc. used by ferrous and nonferrous metal smelters. As shown, projections have been related to the major refractory use, namely, pig iron production. Latter from Table A16–9.

4. Include consumption in the manufacture of pigments, in leather tanning, in chrome-plating, etc. The chemical industry proper consumes only a small fraction of all chromium used by this category. For this reason the projections assume only a slow rise in consumption.

5. Owing to the sporadic (and largely unpublished) record of acquisitions for and sales from government stockpiles, a usable apparent consumption series is not calculable.

TABLE A16–26. Projected Consumption of Molybdenum[1]

(Thousand tons molybdenum content unless otherwise specified)

	1960		1970	1980	1990	2000
Molybdenum consumption in alloy (including stainless) steel[2]	11.7	L	17.2	26.2	38.8	54.9
		M	22.7	39.2	66.5	112.4
		H	28.0	54.6	104.3	201.7
Per cent of alloy (including stainless) steel consumption[3]	.32		.40	.50	.60	.70
Molybdenum consumption in ferrous castings[4]	1.4	L	1.6	1.6	1.7	2.0
		M	2.2	3.0	4.0	5.5
		H	2.9	4.8	7.6	12.5
Per cent of ferrous castings shipments[5]	.10		.13	.16	.19	.22
Molybdenum consumption by chemical industry[6]	.5	L	.6	.8	1.1	1.4
		M	.8	1.2	1.7	2.6
		H	1.0	1.9	3.4	6.1
Molybdenum metal and alloys[7]	2.3	L	3	2	4	7
		M	5	9	17	31
		H	7	16	33	70
Tons/$ 1960 bil. of defense procurement[8]	165		199	233	267	300
Total domestic consumption[9]	15.9	L	22.4	30.6	45.6	65.3
		M	30.7	52.4	89.2	151.5
		H	38.9	77.3	148.3	290.3

1. 1960 figures, except consumption in Defense, based on data in *Minerals Yearbook*, chapter on Molybdenum.

2. Projected by applying percentages in following line to alloy steel consumption shown in Table A16–18.

3. Projections assume increase in molybdenum content by 0.01% per year; the resulting percentage is rounded to .40 in the initial projection year, 1970.

4. For shipments of ferrous castings see Table A16–9.

5. Projected on a judgment basis, assuming rate of increase similar to that of alloy steel.

6. Projected as 4 tons per point of FRB index for chemicals and allied products, shown in Table A1–29.

7. Based on coefficients shown in following line.

8. Military expenditures from Table A9–2.

9. Owing to the sporadic (and largely unpublished) record of acquisitions for and sales from government stockpiles, a usable apparent consumption series is not calculable.

TABLE A16–27.   Projected Consumption of Tungsten[1]

(Thousand tons tungsten content unless otherwise specified)

		1960		1970	1980	1990	2000
Consumption by alloy (including			L	1.5	1.8	2.3	2.7
stainless) steels[2]		1.2	M	2.0	2.7	3.9	5.6
			H	2.4	3.8	6.1	10.1
Per cent of alloy (including							
stainless) steel consumption[3]		.033		.035	.035	.035	.035
Consumption by nonferrous alloys,			L	1.8	2.0	2.2	2.7
tungsten metal, and chemicals[4]		1.5	M	2.3	3.2	4.6	6.7
			H	3.1	5.3	9.0	15.5
Tons/$ 1960 bil. of electrical machinery[5]		435		450	450	450	450
			L	2.3	2.5	2.9	3.4
Consumption by carbides[6]		1.9	M	3.3	4.6	6.5	8.9
			H	4.5	7.5	12.5	20.8
Tons/$ 1960 bil. of industrial machinery[7]		376		400	400	400	400
			L	6	6	7	9
Total domestic consumption[8]		4.6	M	8	10	15	21
			H	10	17	28	46

1. Source for 1960 distribution: *Minerals Yearbook*, chapter on Tungsten.
2. Projected by applying percentages in line below to figures in Table A16–18.
3. Projected on a judgment basis.
4. Based on coefficient shown in following line applied to purchases of electrical equipment shown in Table A6–4.
5. Projected on a judgment basis.
6. Based on coefficient shown in following line applied to purchases of industrial machinery shown in Table A6–4.
7. Projected on a judgment basis.
8. Owing to the sporadic (and largely unpublished) record of acquisitions for and sales from government stockpiles, a usable apparent consumption series is not calculable.

TABLE A16–28.   Projected Consumption of Vanadium[1]

(Thousand tons unless otherwise specified)

	1955	1960		1970	1980	1990	2000
Consumption in alloy (including			L	1.7	2.1	2.6	3.1
stainless) steels[2]	1.4	1.5	M	2.3	3.1	4.4	6.4
			H	2.8	4.4	7.0	11.5
Per cent of alloy (including stain-							
less) steel consumption[3]	.03	.04		.04	.04	.04	.04
			L	.6	.7	.9	1.0
Other uses[4]	.5	.5	M	.8	1.0	1.5	2.1
			H	.9	1.5	2.3	3.8
			L	2.3	2.8	3.5	4.1
Total domestic consumption[5]	1.9	2.0	M	3.1	4.1	5.9	8.5
			H	3.7	5.9	9.3	15.3

1. Consumption mainly in the form of ferrovanadium.
2. Historical data from AISI *Annual Report;* projected by applying percentages in line below to figures in Table A16–18.
3. Historical data computed from line 1 and Table A16–18; projected on a judgment basis.
4. Historical data aggregated from *Minerals Yearbook*, chapter on Vanadium. Include consumption in cast iron, nonferrous alloys, chemicals, ceramics, glass, etc. Projected as 25% of total consumption, or, in other words, 1/3 of consumption in alloy steel, based on trend in recent years.
5. Owing to the sporadic (and largely unpublished) record of acquisitions for and sales from government stockpiles, a usable apparent consumption series is not calculable.

TABLE A16–29.   Projected Consumption of Cobalt[1]

(Thousand tons unless otherwise specified)

	1955	1960		1970	1980	1990	2000
Consumption in permanent			L	1.4	1.8	2.3	3.0
magnet alloys[2]	1.4	1.2	M	1.9	3.0	4.7	7.2
			H	2.4	4.6	8.3	14.8
Tons/$ 1960 bil. of purchases of electrical machinery and appliances[3]	115	88		90	90	90	90
Consumption in high temperature,			L	1.2	1.4	1.7	2.0
high strength alloys[4]	1.6	1.0	M	1.8	2.9	3.5	4.2
			H	2.5	4.5	5.1	7.9
			L	1.4	1.6	1.9	2.2
Other metallic uses[5]	.9	1.2	M	2.0	2.9	4.1	5.8
			H	2.7	4.7	8.0	13.5
Tons/$ 1960 bil. of purchases of industrial machinery[6]	170	240		245	250	255	260
Non-metallic uses[7]	1.0	1.1		1.4	1.6	1.8	2.0
			L	5.4	6.4	7.7	9.2
Total domestic consumption[8]	4.7	4.5	M	7.1	10.4	14.1	19.2
			H	9.0	15.4	23.2	38.2

1. Historical data aggregated from *Minerals Yearbook,* chapter on Cobalt.
2. Projections based on coefficients in following line. In the absence of any clear upward or downward trend in recent years these coefficients have been held constant close to the 1960 level.
3. Based on purchases of electrical machinery and appliances, shown in Table A6–4.
4. Primarily used in aircraft, missiles, and spacecraft. For 1960, Defense consumption of cobalt has been estimated at 800 tons. Assuming that most of this was in high temperature, high strength alloys, Defense use would have accounted for about 4/5 of the total consumption of this type of cobalt-bearing alloy. The High projections for 1970 to 2000 and the Medium projection for 1970 are based on consumption for Defense (shown in Table A9–4) raised by a factor of 1.25 to include civilian uses. The Low projections for 1970 to 2000 and the Medium projections for 1980 to 2000 have been estimated independently.
5. Include alloy steels (other than high temperature, high strength alloys), cutting and wear-resisting materials, alloy hard-facing rods, nonferrous alloys, cemented carbides, and "other." Projections based on coefficients in following line. Since the larger portion of cobalt in these uses is consumed in special steels for industrial equipment, the projections have been tied to the increasing percentage share of alloy steels in producer durables (shown in Table A16–18), but a somewhat slower rate of increase has been assumed for cobalt, about 20% per billion dollars of purchases of industrial machinery during the 1960 to 2000 period.
6. Based on purchases of industrial machinery, shown in Table A6–4.
7. Include consumption in ground-coat frit, pigments, salts, and driers. Projected on a judgment basis, assuming a slower absolute increase in consumption of cobalt in these uses than in metallic uses.
8. Owing to the sporadic (and largely unpublished) record of acquisitions for and sales from government stockpiles, a usable apparent consumption series is not calculable.

TABLE A16–30.   Historical Data on Production and Consumption of Aluminum

(Thousand tons)

	Domestic production		Stock changes[3]	Net imports[4]	Apparent domestic consumption[5]	Net end-use consumption[6]	Direct uses[7]	Other disappearance[8]	Gross exports[9]	Apparent total requirements[10]	Requirements for primary metal[11]
	Primary[1]	Recovery from obsolete scrap[2]									
1929	114	32	15	15	146	120	26		10	156	124
1930	115	28	48	3	98	80	18		10	108	80
1931	89	21	35	4	79	65	14		3	82	61
1932	52	18	20	1	51	40	11		3	54	36
1933	43	25	−4	4	76	60	16		3	79	54
1934	37	35	−26	5	103	85	18		4	107	72
1935	60	36	−28	8	132	110	22		2	134	98
1936	112	33	−13	11	169	140	29		1	170	137
1937	146	40	−2	19	207	170	37		3	210	170
1938	143	26	56	2	115	94	21		7	122	96
1939	164	38	−31	−24	209	170	39		38	247	209
1940	206	46	−30	−11	271	220	51		29	300	254
1941	309	43	12	6	346	280	66		8	354	311
1942	521	42	6	70	627	447	58	122	42	669	627
1943	920	33	61	14	906	616	55	235	122	1,028	995
1944	776	23	−55	−91	763	685	63	15	194	957	934
1945	495	27	29	332	825	560	69	196	7	832	805
1946	410	91	−26	37	563	547	52	−36	18	582	491
1947	572	164	1	−35	700	687	50	−37	65	765	601
1948	623	96	−2	101	822	820	58	−56	53	875	779
1949	603	44	16	84	716	585	40	91	39	755	710
1950	719	76	−5	212	1,012	914	67	31	22	1,034	958
1951	837	77	−12	142	1,068	897	74	97	15	1,083	1,006
1952	937	71	8	138	1,138	949	68	121	10	1,148	1,077
1953	1,252	79	34	330	1,627	1,186	82	359	21	1,648	1,569
1954	1,461	60	−20	204	1,745	1,075	73	597	36	1,781	1,721
1955	1,566	76	−6	193	1,841	1,429	96	316	35	1,876	1,800
1956	1,679	72	94	190	1,847	1,466	95	286	66	1,913	1,841
1957	1,648	72	67	190	1,843	1,368	98	377	64	1,907	1,835
1958	1,566	64	−25	211	1,866	1,322	85	459	81	1,947	1,883
1959	1,953	78	−30	142	2,203	1,707	94	402	160	2,363	2,285
1960	2,014	63	149	−166	1,762	1,557	101	104	366	2,128	2,065

Table A16–30 (cont'd)

1. From *Minerals Yearbook,* chapter on "Aluminum" or "Bauxite and Aluminum."
2. Same source as for footnote 1. 1929–38 estimated from data on recovery of aluminum from old and new scrap combined. Data for 1929–53 represent recovered aluminum alloy content, data for 1954–60 recovered aluminum content.
3. Same source as for footnote 1. Data represent stocks of pig and ingot at primary and secondary producers. Information on stocks of mill shapes and castings, stocks at consumers' plants, and government stockpiling is not available. Consequently, these items are included in "Apparent domestic consumption."
4. 1929–48 from U.S. Department of Commerce, *Foreign Commerce and Navigation of the United States,* annual reports. 1949–60 from U.S. Bureau of the Census, cited in *Minerals Yearbook.* Includes crude metal (pig, ingot, slab), new scrap converted into ingot equivalent (.9 times the weight of scrap), and wrought and cast products (plates, sheets, bars, rods, extruded shapes, and other semifabricated products).
5. Equals total domestic production plus (or minus) stock changes, plus net imports.
6. Represents the sum of the net end-use consumption by all market categories, i.e., shipments minus prompt industrial scrap generated. For method of calculating prompt industrial scrap, see Table A16–4, footnote 8.

7. Represents uses in which aluminum loses its identity and cannot be recovered as scrap. The bulk of these uses is accounted for by steel production (deoxidizing and alloying), by production of ferroalloys, and by production of zinc-base die casting alloys. (See U.S. Department of Commerce, Business and Defense Services Administration, *Shipments of Aluminum for Detailed End-Product Uses, 1952,* Apr. 1955.) Data for 1942–55 are from BDSA, *Materials Survey: Aluminum* (Nov. 1956). Data for 1956–60 have been estimated on the basis of detailed end-use data for 1952 and the ratio of aluminum use in the production of steel, ferroalloys, and zinc-base die casting alloys. For 1929–41 "direct uses" and "other disappearance" were combined and computed as the difference between "Apparent domestic consumption" and "Net end-use consumption."
8. Represents the difference between "Apparent domestic consumption" and the sum of "Net end-use consumption" and "direct uses." Includes increases in government stockpiles, stock increases of rollers, drawers, fabricators, and warehouses, and permanent processing losses.
9. Same sources as cited in footnote 4.
10. Represents the sum of "Apparent domestic consumption" and "Gross exports."
11. Equals "Apparent total requirements" minus "Recovery from obsolete scrap."

TABLE A16–31.　Historical Data on Gross Shipments, Prompt Industrial Scrap Generation, and Net Consumption of Aluminum Mill and Foundry Products, by Market Category

(Thousand tons)

	1950	1952	1954	1955	1956	1957	1958	1959	1960
Gross shipments:[1]									
Building construction	247	197	361	462	463	477	503	633	627
Electric power construction	72	92	74	78	94	91	87	98	94
Consumer durables	289	131	177	241	242	192	185	232	217
Producer durables	202	192	155	242	250	237	212	260	208
Containers and packaging	71	44	66	77	89	109	114	168	188
Transportation	183	124	318	466	462	429	357	452	388
Military and other	47	452	187	219	228	155	145	226	150
Exports	27	6	12	18	13	21	14	20	29
Total shipments	1,138	1,238	1,350	1,803	1,841	1,711	1,617	2,089	1,901
Imports	[2]	[2]	15	23	24	21	31	55	41
Domestic shipments, adjusted for inclusion of imports:[3]									
Building construction	247	197	365	468	469	483	513	650	641
Electric power construction	72	92	75	79	95	92	89	101	96
Consumer durables	289	131	179	244	245	194	188	238	222
Producer durables	202	192	157	245	253	240	216	267	213
Containers and packaging	71	44	67	78	90	110	116	172	192
Transportation	183	124	322	472	468	434	364	464	396
Military and other	47	452	189	222	231	157	148	232	153
Total	1,111	1,232	1,354	1,808	1,851	1,710	1,634	2,124	1,913
Prompt industrial scrap generated:[4]									
Building construction	22	17	32	41	41	43	45	57	56
Electric power construction	2	3	2	2	3	3	3	3	3
Consumer durables	45	20	28	38	38	30	30	37	35
Producer durables	36	34	28	44	45	43	38	48	38
Containers and packaging	13	8	12	14	16	20	21	31	35
Transportation	63	43	111	162	161	149	126	160	136
Military and other	16	158	66	78	81	55	521	81	54
Total	197	283	279	379	385	343	315	417	357
Reconciliation:[5]									
Domestic consumption of new scrap	181	265	272	321	337	360	284	364	351
Exports of new scrap	1	1	30	14	15	14	15	25	60
Stock changes	—2	6	—4	2	5	*	2	5	—3
Total	180	272	298	337	357	374	301	394	408
Per cent of estimated prompt industrial scrap generation	91.4	96.1	106.8	88.7	92.7	109.0	95.3	94.5	114.3
Net end-use consumption:[6]									
Building construction	225	180	333	427	428	441	468	593	585
Electric power construction	70	89	73	77	92	89	86	98	93
Consumer durables	244	111	151	206	207	164	158	201	187
Producer durables	166	158	129	201	208	197	178	219	175
Containers and packaging	58	36	55	64	74	90	95	141	157
Transportation	120	81	211	310	307	285	238	304	260
Military and other	31	294	123	144	150	102	96	151	100
Total	914	949	1,075	1,429	1,466	1,368	1,319	1,707	1,557

* Negligible.

1. This table brings together shipments of aluminum mill, wrought, and foundry products (including die castings) by market category, adjusted to *Minerals Yearbook* totals. Data for 1950 and 1952 are derived from U.S. Department of Commerce, Facts for Industry, No. BDSAF–122–03 (May 1954). Data for 1954–60 are computed from percentage distributions reported by the Aluminum Association and from reports of the American Die Casting Institute.

2. Imports are included with gross shipments.

3. Imports distributed proportionately.

4. The prompt industrial scrap generation factors are based on estimates published in Business and Defense Services Administration, *Industrial Scrap Generation,* 1957.

5. Data from *Minerals Yearbook;* exports estimated. This exercise is intended to check on the reasonableness of the prompt industrial scrap generation factors.

6. Domestic shipments adjusted for imports, minus prompt industrial scrap.

TABLE A16–32.   Projected Net End-Use Consumption of Aluminum, by Market Category[1]

(Million tons)

	1950	1955	1960		1970	1980	1990	2000
Building construction[2]	.22	.43	.58	L	.74	.95	1.16	1.59
				M	1.08	1.60	2.49	4.25
				H	1.60	3.00	5.66	12.61
Electric power construction[2]	.07	.08	.09	L	.06	.04	.02	.01
				M	.12	.16	.22	.32
				H	.24	.44	.72	1.17
Consumer durables[3] (excluding passenger cars)	.24	.21	.19	L	.28	.43	.65	.98
				M	.30	.51	.84	1.41
				H	.33	.57	.99	1.80
Producer durables[3] (excluding transportation equip.)	.17	.20	.18	L	.27	.34	.41	.50
				M	.36	.55	.84	1.32
				H	.40	.73	1.27	2.33
Containers and packaging[4]	.06	.06	.16	L	.29	.42	.52	.60
				M	.43	.70	.97	1.22
				H	.55	.99	1.61	2.28
Transportation equipment[5]	.12	.31	.26	L	.65	1.23	1.95	2.92
				M	.86	2.04	3.71	6.07
				H	1.50	4.21	6.68	10.57
Defense and miscellaneous[6]	.03	.14	.10	L	.05	.02	.03	.03
				M	.09	.09	.11	.13
				H	.13	.15	.22	.30
Net end-use consumption by all market categories	.91	1.43	1.56	L	2.34	3.43	4.74	6.63
				M	3.24	5.65	9.18	14.72
				H	4.75	10.09	17.15	31.06

1. Historical data from Table A16–31. Data do not include direct uses or "other disappearance," for which see Table A16–35.
2. From Table A4–12.
3. From Table A6–7.
4. From Table A7–4.
5. From Table A5–19. Figures shown in Table A5–19 increased as follows to include aluminum consumed in transportation equipment other than automobiles and trucks (compared with an actual difference of 13.0% in 1960):

1970—13.5%	1990—14.5%
1980—14.0%	2000—15.0%

6. From Table A9–4, excluding military construction (which is included in construction) and excluding electronics (which is included in durables), less prompt industrial scrap, estimated as follows: aircraft, missiles, and spacecraft—40% of shipments; ships, ordnance, and vehicles—20% of shipments; other procurement—15% of shipments. The resulting data were raised by 60% (the 1960 ratio between Defense and miscellaneous) to account for miscellaneous.

TABLE A16–33. Projected Supply and Consumption of Obsolete Aluminum Scrap, by Market Category[1]

(Thousand tons metal weight unless otherwise specified)

	Metal content potentially recoverable[2] (%)	Average life cycle[3] (years)	1950	1955	1960		1970	1980	1990	2000
Potential supply:[4]										
Building construction	85	30	10	16	20	L M H	30 40 53	185 200 235	460 490 570	580 890 1,470
Electric power construction	80	50	1	2	2	L M H	2 3 5	3 5 10	10 15 25	55 60 75
Consumer durables	45	10	23	50	100	L M H	90 90 92	130 145 160	200 245 275	310 405 480
Producer durables	60	20	15	14	23	L M H	105 108 110	112 120 125	165 230 265	210 350 485
Containers	10	15	–	–	2	L M H	8 9 9	22 32 40	38 59 83	48 88 136
Transportation	75	10	73	87	100	L M H	224 240 290	530 734 1,328	975 1,655 3,340	1,535 2,960 5,295
Defense	75	10	32	40	28	L M H	71 74 77	35 68 99	16 69 118	22 84 171
Total (mil. tons)	–	–	.15	.21	.28	L M H	.53 .56 .64	1.02 1.30 2.00	1.86 2.76 4.68	2.76 4.84 8.11
Domestic consumption[5]	–	–	.09	.11	.09	L M H	.25 .27 .31	.59 .75 1.16	1.23 1.82 3.09	1.99 3.48 5.84
Ratio of domestic consumption to potential supply[6]	–	–	60.0	52.3	32.1		48	58	66	72

1. This table—and subsequent tables with similar headings for other major nonferrous metals—is similar to Table A16–15 in concept and statistical treatment (described in the notes to that table); Table A16–15 estimates the potentially recoverable amounts of metal contained in fabricated metal goods. However, there is one important distinction: The percentages of metal potentially recoverable from fabricated metal products and the average life cycles of those finished products, as shown in Table A16–15, are the result of a careful pioneer study by the Battelle Memorial Institute. For nonferrous metals no such study was available at the time of this writing. Consequently, the recovery ratios and average life cycles for nonferrous metals contained in fabricated metal goods had to be roughly estimated with some guidance from the Battelle ferrous metals data.

2. The recovery ratios here listed have been estimated by taking account of probable losses due to size and usage of the products included in the various market categories. Other losses, due to abrasion, corrosion, geographic location, deficient scrap collecting organization, and shipments of used equipment during its life cycle to other countries (including military aid), are roughly estimated.

3. The life cycles listed are estimated, weighted averages for aluminum-consuming goods produced in recent years. The projections thus assume not only that the current average life cycles will not change but also that they will not be materially affected by changes in the product mix within each of the various market categories.

4. Potential scrap that might be withdrawn from annual "crop" of obsolete scrap if aggregate demand is high and losses are held to a minimum. In order to take account of the wide distribution of retirement periods of

Table A16–33 (cont'd)

finished products, the formula used to obtain the potential scrap crop in each year is $\frac{1}{L}$% of present consumption, plus $\frac{L-1}{L}$% of the consumption one average life cycle earlier; L representing the average life cycle in years. This method, which is recommended by Battelle, also tends to mitigate the effect of imperfect data for the early part of this century, for the better part of which crude, conjectural estimates of consumption by market category had to be used. (See also Notes to this appendix.) Historical data are computed on the same basis as the projections.

5. Historical data represent actual domestic consumption, plus or minus stock changes and exports of obsolete scrap, from *Minerals Yearbook;* projections are based on the coefficient which follows.

6. Historical data represent the ratio of actual withdrawals to computed potential supply. Projections on a judgment basis, assuming increasing relative demand and improving collection as amounts in use become larger.

TABLE A16–34. Projected Metallics Recovery from Obsolete Aluminum-Base Scrap[1]

(Thousand tons metal weight unless otherwise specified)

	1950	1955	1960		1970	1980	1990	2000
Domestic consumption of obsolete scrap[2]	92	106	90	L	250	590	1,230	1,990
				M	270	750	1,820	3,480
				H	310	1,160	3,090	5,840
Total metallics recovery[3]	79	81	67	L	210	507	1,082	1,791
				M	227	645	1,602	3,132
				H	260	998	2,719	5,256
Per cent of domestic consumption[4]	86	76	74		84	86	88	90
Metals recovered: Per cent:[5]								
Aluminum	95.6	93.7	92.8		93.0	93.0	93.0	93.0
Copper	2.9	3.1	3.8		4.0	4.0	4.0	4.0
Zinc	.3	2.3	2.1		2.0	2.0	2.0	2.0
Quantities:								
Aluminum	76	75	62	L	195	472	1,006	1,666
				M	211	600	1,490	2,913
				H	242	928	2,529	4,888
Copper	2	3	3	L	8	20	43	72
				M	9	26	64	125
				H	10	40	109	210
Zinc	1	2	1	L	4	10	22	36
				M	5	13	32	63
				H	5	20	54	105

1. The purpose of this table is to approximate the quantities of secondary aluminum (and other nonferrous metals) recovered from domestically consumed aluminum-base scrap. Since obsolete scrap contains a certain portion of impurities, the quantities of metals recovered are smaller than the quantities of scrap consumed, varying between 75% and 90%. Also, aluminum-base scrap includes small recoverable amounts of other nonferrous metals, reducing the quantity of secondary aluminum proper to about 93% of the total metals obtained.

2. From Table A16–33; historical data from source cited in footnote 5 hereto.

3. Historical data from *Minerals Yearbook;* projections are the product of the preceding and the following lines.

4. Historical data computed from *Minerals Yearbook;* projections have been extrapolated on a judgment basis, assuming increasing quality of scrap owing to changes in relative uses.

5. Historical data computed from *Minerals Yearbook;* projections on a judgment basis. The percentages do not quite add to 100, because small amounts of other metals, such as nickel, are disregarded.

TABLE A16–35.   Projected Consumption and Requirements for Primary Aluminum

(Million tons)

	1950	1955	1960		1970	1980	1990	2000
Net end-use consumption by all market categories[1]				L	2.34	3.43	4.74	6.63
	.91	1.43	1.56	M	3.24	5.65	9.18	14.72
				H	4.75	10.09	17.15	31.06
Direct uses[2]				L	.10	.11	.13	.14
	.07	.10	.10	M	.13	.16	.22	.29
				H	.16	.23	.37	.55
Other disappearance[3]				L	.12	.17	.24	.33
	.03	.32	.10	M	.16	.28	.46	.74
				H	.24	.53	.86	1.55
Apparent domestic consumption				L	2.56	3.71	5.11	7.10
	1.01	1.85	1.76	M	3.53	6.09	9.86	15.75
				H	5.15	10.85	18.38	33.16
Gross exports[4]				L	.08	.11	.15	.21
	.02	.04	.37	M	.10	.18	.30	.47
				H	.16	.33	.57	.99
Apparent total requirements				L	2.64	3.82	5.26	7.31
	1.03	1.88	2.13	M	3.63	6.27	10.16	16.22
				H	5.31	11.18	18.95	34.15
Secondary recovery from obsolete scrap[5]				L	.20	.48	1.02	1.68
	.08	.08	.06	M	.21	.61	1.50	2.94
				H	.24	.94	2.55	4.94
Requirements for primary aluminum				L	2.44	3.34	4.24	5.65
	.95	1.80	2.06	M	3.42	5.66	8.66	13.28
				H	5.07	10.24	16.40	29.21

1. From Table A16–32.
2. Related to steel ingot production (Table A16–9) as follows: 1970 and 1980—550 tons of aluminum per million tons of steel ingot; 1990 and 2000—600 tons. The resulting figure assumed to be 60% of all direct uses in which aluminum loses its identity. See footnote 7, Table A16–30, for explanation of "direct uses."
3. Assumed to be 5% of total end-use consumption.
4. Estimated at 3% of apparent domestic consumption.
5. From Table A16–75, which adjusts the recovery shown in Table A16–34 by a factor of 1.01 to include aluminum recovered from other than aluminum-base scrap.

TABLE A16–36. Relative Changes in Net End-Use Consumption of Aluminum, by Market Category[1]

(Rates of increase in per cent per annum)

		Building construction	Electric power construction	Consumer durables	Producer durables	Containers	Transportation	Defense & miscellaneous	Direct uses	Other disappearance	Total
1950–60		10.2	2.5	—2.3	0.6	10.3	8.0	12.8	3.6	12.8	5.7
1960–80	L	2.5	—4.0	4.2	3.2	4.9	8.1	—7.7	0.5	2.7	3.8
	M	5.2	2.9	5.1	5.7	7.7	10.9	—0.5	2.4	5.3	6.3
	H	8.6	8.3	5.6	7.3	9.5	14.9	2.1	4.3	8.7	9.5
1980–2000	L	2.6	—6.6	4.2	2.0	1.8	4.4	2.1	1.2	3.4	3.3
	M	5.0	3.5	5.2	4.5	2.8	5.6	1.9	3.0	5.0	4.9
	H	7.4	5.0	5.9	6.0	4.3	4.7	3.5	4.5	5.5	5.8
1960–2000	L	2.6	—5.3	4.2	2.6	3.4	6.2	—3.0	0.8	3.0	3.6
	M	5.1	3.2	5.1	5.1	5.2	8.2	0.7	2.7	5.1	5.6
	H	8.0	6.6	5.8	6.6	6.9	9.7	2.8	4.4	7.1	7.6

1. Calculated from Tables A16–32 and 35. Totals are equivalent to "apparent domestic consumption."

TABLE A16–37. Percentage Distribution of Net End-Use Consumption of Aluminum, by Market Category[1]

		Building construction	Electric power construction	Consumer durables	Producer durables	Containers	Transportation	Defense and miscellaneous	Direct uses	Other disappearance
1950		21.8	6.9	23.8	16.8	5.9	11.9	3.0	6.9	3.0
1955		23.2	4.3	11.4	10.8	3.2	16.8	7.6	5.4	17.3
1960		32.9	5.1	10.8	10.2	9.1	14.8	5.7	5.7	5.7
1970	L	28.9	2.3	10.9	10.6	11.3	25.4	2.0	3.9	4.7
	M	30.6	3.4	8.5	10.2	12.2	24.4	2.5	3.7	4.5
	H	31.0	4.8	6.4	7.8	10.7	29.1	2.5	3.1	4.6
1980	L	25.6	1.1	11.6	9.2	11.3	33.1	.5	3.0	4.6
	M	26.3	2.6	8.4	9.0	11.5	33.5	1.5	2.6	4.6
	H	27.6	4.1	5.3	6.7	9.1	38.8	1.4	2.1	4.9
1990	L	22.7	.4	12.7	8.0	10.2	38.2	.6	2.5	4.7
	M	25.3	2.2	8.5	8.5	9.9	37.6	1.1	2.2	4.7
	H	30.8	3.9	5.4	6.9	8.8	36.3	1.2	2.0	4.7
2000	L	22.4	.1	13.8	7.0	8.5	41.1	.4	2.0	4.7
	M	27.0	2.0	9.0	8.4	7.7	38.5	.8	1.9	4.7
	H	38.0	3.5	5.4	7.0	6.9	31.9	.9	1.7	4.7

1. Computed from Tables A16–32 and 35. Totals (100%) are equivalent to "apparent domestic consumption."

TABLE A16–38. Historical Data on Production and Consumption of Copper

(Thousand tons copper content)

	Domestic production			Stock changes[2]	Net imports[3]	Apparent domestic consumption[4]	Net domestic end-use consumption[5]	Gross exports[6]	Apparent total requirements[7]	Requirements for primary metal[8]
	Primary[1]	Recovery from obsolete scrap[1]	Total							
1929	1,370	404	1,774	96	—402	1,276	n.a.	499	1,775	1,371
1930	1,079	342	1,421	155	—310	956	"	377	1,333	991
1931	751	261	1,012	154	—151	707	"	279	986	725
1932	340	181	521	40	—43	438	"	164	602	421
1933	371	260	631	—96	—133	594	"	175	769	509
1934	445	311	756	—122	—279	599	"	313	912	601
1935	589	362	951	—109	—273	787	"	303	1,090	728
1936	822	383	1,205	—65	—235	1,035	"	262	1,297	914
1937	1,067	409	1,476	69	—317	1,090	"	350	1,440	1,031
1938	792	267	1,059	2	—391	666	"	422	1,088	821
1939	1,010	287	1,297	—85	—390	992	"	428	1,420	1,133
1940	1,314	334	1,648	—4	—410	1,242	"	428	1,670	1,336
1941	1,395	413	1,808	59	170	1,919	"	159	2,078	1,665
1942	1,415	427	1,842	128	150	1,864	"	214	2,078	1,651
1943	1,379	428	1,807	—77	64	1,948	"	396	2,344	1,916
1944	1,221	457	1,678	—7	198	1,883	"	238	2,121	1,664
1945	1,109	497	1,606	91	387	1,902	"	133	2,035	1,538
1946	879	406	1,285	1	54	1,338	"	97	1,435	938
1947	1,160	503	1,663	—24	—50	1,637	"	197	1,834	1,331
1948	1,107	505	1,611	—37	53	1,702	"	209	1,911	1,406
1949	928	384	1,312	—30	106	1,448	"	196	1,644	1,260
1950	1,240	485	1,725	—100	161	1,986	1,827	193	2,179	1,694
1951	1,207	458	1,665	—1	94	1,760	n.a.	166	1,926	1,468
1952	1,178	415	1,593	42	169	1,720	1,745	213	1,933	1,518
1953	1,293	429	1,722	73	154	1,803	1,781	172	1,975	1,546
1954	1,212	407	1,619	—45	1	1,665	n.a.	315	1,980	1,573
1955	1,342	514	1,856	39	10	1,827	1,876	273	2,100	1,586
1956	1,443	468	1,911	91	—13	1,807	1,814	294	2,101	1,633
1957	1,454	444	1,898	24	—168	1,706	1,647	446	2,152	1,708
1958	1,352	411	1,763	—45	—212	1,596	1,540	442	2,038	1,627
1959	1,098	471	1,569	—62	112	1,743	1,847	203	1,946	1,475
1960	1,519	429	1,948	121	—240	1,587	1,647	529	2,116	1,687

1. From *Minerals Yearbook*, Copper chapter.
2. Refers to stocks in the hands of primary producers and fabricators only. From *Minerals Yearbook*, Copper chapter. Data for 1929–40 include producers' stocks only.
3. Consists of imports less exports of refined copper and copper-base mill and foundry products. Refined imports are "general," i.e., they include copper imported for immediate consumption plus bonded material. Exports include re-exports of foreign refined copper, which are negligible. They also include copper refined under toll arrangements from foreign ores. Imports and exports of mill shapes and castings include both unalloyed and alloyed products. Copper-base alloys are estimated at 75% pure copper content. This is lower than the copper content of domestic shipments, because of the preponderance of brass mill products in foreign trade. Exports include gross weight of insulated wire and cable, even though these items are made of various other metals; inadequacy of data makes it impossible to exclude these other metals.
Data for 1929–45 comprise refined copper only. Im-

ports of copper-base and foundry products from U.S. Department of Commerce, Business and Defense Services Administration, *Copper Industry Report,* plus unpublished data.
4. Includes primary refined copper, secondary recovery from obsolete scrap, and net imports, less net increase in stocks.
5. Total shipments of copper at mill and foundry level, adjusted to exclude prompt industrial scrap. From Table A16–39.
6. Includes concentrates, unrefined and refined copper-base mill and foundry products, new and old scrap. Excludes exports of alloyed mill shapes, castings, and scrap in order to maintain comparability with long-term Bureau of Mines series. Conceptually, all mill and foundry products should be included, and old scrap excluded; because of the compensating nature of the deviations from this concept, the net error is assumed to be small.
7. Apparent domestic consumption, plus gross exports.
8. Apparent total requirements, less secondary recovery from obsolete scrap.

TABLE A16–39. Historical Data on Gross Shipments, Prompt Industrial Scrap Generation, and Net Consumption of Copper-Base Mill and Foundry Products, by Market Category

(Thousand tons)

	1950	1952	1953	1955	1956	1957	1958	1959	1960
Gross shipments of brass, copper wire, bronze, and powder-mill products: [1]									
Motor vehicles	326	178	210	284	208	206	147	200	186
Consumer durables	235	104	131	215	208	178	170	192	156
Producer durables	908	932	912	949	946	834	706	851	812
Building construction	436	294	318	481	439	430	440	506	468
Communications construction	72	64	64	70	90	96	80	80	88
Electric power construction	85	84	77	57	50	49	46	37	32
Railroad equipment	84	125	134	112	114	114	112	111	103
Defense	76	434	380	84	58	52	40	36	39
Maintenance, repair, and operation	136	142	150	148	147	146	147	163	154
Miscellaneous	128	80	124	141	146	80	118	204	91
Exports	33	28	26	25	28	30	21	25	22
Total shipments	2,519	2,465	2,526	2,566	2,434	2,215	2,022	2,405	2,151
Imports	20	32	24	42	54	58	78	102	89
Shipments, excluding exports, including imports	2,506	2,469	2,524	2,583	2,460	2,243	2,079	2,482	2,218
Domestic shipments, adjusted for inclusion of imports: [2]									
Motor vehicles	329	180	212	289	213	212	153	209	194
Consumer durables	237	105	132	219	213	183	177	200	163
Producer durables	915	944	921	965	967	856	733	887	846
Building construction, fabricated	250	131	164	259	247	251	265	312	292
Building construction, on-site	189	167	157	230	202	190	192	216	195
Communications construction	72	65	65	71	92	99	83	83	92
Electric power construction	86	85	78	58	51	50	48	39	33
Railroad equipment	85	127	135	114	117	117	116	116	107
Defense	77	440	384	85	59	53	42	37	41
Maintenance, repair, and operation	137	144	151	150	150	150	147	170	160
Miscellaneous	129	81	125	143	149	82	123	212	95
Total shipments	2,506	2,469	2,524	2,583	2,460	2,243	2,079	2,481	2,218
Prompt industrial scrap generated: [3]									
Motor vehicles	59	32	38	52	38	38	27	37	35
Consumer durables	44	19	24	40	39	34	33	37	30
Producer durables	188	194	189	198	198	175	150	182	173
Building construction, fabricated	68	36	45	71	67	69	72	85	80
Building construction, on-site	6	5	5	7	6	6	6	6	6
Communications construction	2	2	2	2	3	3	3	1	3
Electric power construction	3	3	2	2	2	2	2	1	1
Railroad equipment	29	43	45	38	39	39	39	39	36
Defense	17	95	83	18	13	11	9	8	9
Maintenance, repair, and operation	28	30	31	31	31	31	30	35	33
Total scrap	444	459	464	459	436	408	371	431	406

Table A16–39 (cont'd)

(Thousand tons)

	1950	1952	1953	1955	1956	1957	1958	1959	1960
Net end-use consumption (metal weight):									
Motor vehicles	270	148	174	237	175	174	125	172	159
Consumer durables	193	86	108	179	174	149	144	163	133
Producer durables	727	750	732	767	769	681	582	705	673
Building construction	365	257	271	411	376	366	380	437	401
Communications construction	70	62	63	69	89	96	81	82	89
Electric power construction	83	82	76	56	49	48	46	38	32
Railroad equipment	56	84	90	76	78	78	78	77	71
Defense	60	346	301	67	46	42	32	29	32
Maintenance, repair, and operation	109	114	120	119	119	119	117	135	127
Miscellaneous	129	81	125	143	149	82	123	212	95
Total domestic consumption	2,062	2,010	2,060	2,124	2,024	1,835	1,708	2,050	1,812
Exports	33	28	26	25	28	30	21	25	22
Total consumption	2,095	2,038	2,086	2,149	2,052	1,865	1,729	2,075	1,834
Net end-use consumption (copper content):[4]									
Motor vehicles	231	125	145	204	152	152	108	151	142
Consumer durables	162	72	89	150	148	128	123	140	116
Producer durables	635	646	626	669	681	606	518	626	608
Building construction	324	226	239	360	335	328	340	390	360
Communications construction	70	62	62	70	89	95	81	82	89
Electric power construction	84	82	75	56	49	48	46	38	32
Railroad equipment	51	74	80	67	70	68	72	70	66
Defense	52	288	248	57	42	38	28	26	29
Maintenance, repair, and operation	101	103	110	110	110	112	110	126	119
Miscellaneous	117	67	107	133	138	72	114	198	86
Total domestic consumption	1,827	1,745	1,781	1,876	1,814	1,647	1,540	1,847	1,647
Exports	30	26	26	24	27	29	21	23	19
Total consumption	1,857	1,771	1,807	1,900	1,841	1,676	1,561	1,870	1,666

1. Aggregated from Table A16–40.

2. Imports distributed proportionally among market categories.

3. For method of calculating prompt industrial scrap see Table A16–4, footnote 8. The scrap generation factors, applied to the domestic shipments plus imports, are as follows:

Motor vehicles	17.9%	Communications	
Consumer durables	18.4%	construction	3.0%
Producer durables	20.5%	Electric power	
		construction	3.0%
Railroad equipment	33.6%	Maintenance, repair,	
Defense	21.6%	and operation	20.5%
		Miscellaneous	Nil

For building construction, scrap generation was estimated as 3.0% for on-site construction and 27.3% for fabricated construction (i.e., for the metal entering into building materials). The breakdown between these direct and indirect construction uses has been estimated by extrapolating the data for 1950–53 (see footnote 1, Table A16–40).

The foregoing percentages were estimated by applying the detailed scrap generation factors given in Business and Defense Services Administration, *Industrial Scrap Generation* (1957) to the composition of shipments to end-use categories in 1952, from BDSA, *Uses of Copper* (in three parts, Feb. and Apr. 1955). For comparative classifications, see footnote 1 to Table A16–40.

4. Aggregated from Tables A16–42 and 43.

TABLE A16–40. Historical Data on Gross Shipments of Brass Mill (Copper Mill), Wire Mill, Bronze, and Powder Mill Products, by Market Category[1]

(Thousand tons)

	1950	1952	1953	1955	1956	1957	1958	1959	1960
Brass mill shipments (metal weight):									
Motor vehicles	230	128	150	200	143	138	98	136	112
Consumer durables	196	82	104	183	175	144	140	158	120
Producer durables	492	482	482	488	455	367	339	440	362
Building construction	199	137	146	258	222	215	224	266	242
Railroad equipment	9	14	14	7	10	10	8	8	10
Defense	46	328	295	54	34	30	18	14	20
Maintenance, repair, and operation	40	46	48	42	40	36	34	48	40
Miscellaneous	47	48	64	26	22	22	24	28	21
Exports	18	12	11	10	10	11	11	12	12
Total brass mill shipments	1,277	1,277	1,314	1,268	1,111	973	896	1,110	939
Imports	20	31	243	37	45	55	77	100	82
Shipments, excluding exports, including imports	1,279	1,296	1,546	1,295	1,146	1,017	962	1,198	1,009
Wire mill shipments (copper content):									
Motor vehicles	74	43	51	74	58	60	43	57	66
Consumer durables	28	18	23	28	28	27	26	30	32
Producer durables	170	197	193	206	232	235	190	221	255
Building construction	117	102	110	146	142	140	141	158	150
Communications construction	72	64	64	70	90	96	80	80	88
Electric power construction	86	84	77	57	50	49	46	37	32
Railroad equipment	10	12	12	12	13	12	11	12	12
Defense	20	76	52	13	14	14	13	13	14
Maintenance, repair, and operation	66	69	79	83	84	86	84	90	90
Miscellaneous	59	5	22	74	86	38	62	84	14
Exports	14	15	16	15	18	20	11	12	8
Total wire mill shipments	716	685	699	778	815	777	707	794	761
Imports	*	2	*	5	10	4	1	2	6
Total, excluding exports, including imports	702	672	683	768	807	761	697	784	759
Bronze shipments (gross weight):									
Motor vehicles	22	8	8	10	8	8	6	8	8
Consumer durables	11	4	4	4	4	4	4	5	5
Producer durables	248	253	236	254	259	232	176	190	194
Building construction	120	55	62	78	75	74	74	82	75
Railroad equipment	66	98	108	92	91	92	94	92	82
Defense	10	28	30	16	10	8	8	10	6
Maintenance, repair, and operation	31	28	23	22	23	24	23	24	23
Miscellaneous	22	15	24	20	19	1	17	70	38
Exports	1	1	1	1	1	1	*	*	1
Total bronze shipments	531	490	496	497	490	444	402	481	432
Powder mill shipments (gross weight):									
Defense	n.a.	3	2	*	*	*	*	*	*
Miscellaneous	n.a.	12	15	21	18	18	16	22	19
Exports	n.a.	*	*	*	*	*	1	1	1
Total powder mill shipments	n.a.	15	17	21	18	18	17	23	20
Imports of powder	*	*	*	*	1	1	1	1	1
Total, excluding exports, including imports	n.a.	15	17	21	19	19	17	23	20

Table A16–40 (cont'd)

* Negligible.

1. The purpose of this table is to estimate the gross shipments (metal content) for each market category. The estimates are based primarily upon Korean War Controlled Materials Plan data published in U.S. Department of Commerce, Facts for Industry, Nos. BDSAF 84–1–3 (Feb. 16, 1954) and BDSAF 84.1–2–3 (July 26, 1954) and a Business and Defense Services Administration report on *Uses of Copper* (in three parts, Feb. and Apr. 1955). The market categories used herein are assumed to correspond with BDSA categories as follows:

This table	BDSA
Motor vehicles	Motor vehicles
Consumer durables	Consumer durables
	30 per cent of "Other deliveries" (less exports)
Producer durables	Communications equipment
	Electrical equipment
	Electronics
	Engines and turbines
	General components
	General industrial equipment
	Metalworking equipment
	Scientific and technical equipment
	"Other industries"
	30 per cent of "Other deliveries" (less exports)
Building construction	Construction ("Other construction," in the case of wire mills)
Building materials	Building materials
Communications construction	Communications construction
Electric power construction	Electric power construction
Railroad equipment (including maintenance, repair, and operation)	Railroad equipment, plus: 3.2% of brass mills "MRO" 8.0% of wire mills "MRO" 51.4% of foundry "MRO"
MRO (Maintenance, repair, and operating supplies)	MRO, other than above
Military	Military
Other domestic	40 per cent of "Other deliveries" (less exports)

The breakdown of "other deliveries" (after deduction of exports) is conjectural, but it is based on indications in *Uses of Copper*. Unless otherwise indicated, exports and imports are from BDSA's *Copper Industry Report* and from Census series FT 110 and 410 (Foreign Trade Statistics Division). Military, 1952 ff., is from *Copper Industry Report;* where this differs from the amounts indicated by the market distribution in the other sources, proportional adjustment is made in remaining categories.

Data for 1950–53 were estimated as indicated above. 1955–60 data are from the percentage market distribution compiled by the Copper and Brass Research Association (CABRA) and published in the American Bureau of Metal Statistics *Yearbook,* as applied to total shipments reported by BDSA (*Copper Industry Report,* Annual No. 4, 1961). The CABRA classifications were adapted to the market categories in this table as follows:

This table	CABRA
Motor vehicles	Automotive (excluding ignition and other electrical), divided by .95 to allow for the excluded items (based on 1952 relationship)
Consumer durables	Appliances, utensils, and cutlery (including electrical)
	Other domestic, commercial, and professional equipment
	10% of Jobbers, dealers, and distributors
Producer durables	Redrawers and rerollers
	Metal working
	Fastenings—industrial and commercial
	Machinery and machinery parts (excluding electrical)
	Electrical machinery and equipment, less the adjustment added to motor vehicles
	20% of Jobbers, dealers, and distributors (see Building construction below)
	20% of Transportation (other than automotive) (see Railroad equipment below)
	Less the amounts estimated below as applicable to MRO
Building construction	Heavy construction
	Contractors' products
	60 per cent of Jobbers, dealers, and distributors
Railroad equipment (including MRO)	80 per cent of Transportation (other than automotive) (based on 1952 relationship)
Maintenance, repair, and operation	Estimated at 8% of Producer durables (including MRO) for 1955 and 1956, 9% for 1957 and 1958, 10% for 1959 and 1960
Other	10% of Jobbers, dealers, and distributors

TABLE A16–41. Historical Data on Percentage Distribution of Copper-Base Mill and Foundry Products among Copper, Brass, and Bronze[1]

		1950	1952	1953	1955	1956	1957	1958	1959	1960
Motor vehicles	Copper	22.7	24.2	24.3	26.2	27.6	29.1	29.2	28.4	35.5
	Brass	70.6	71.6	71.6	70.2	68.6	66.8	66.7	67.8	60.2
	Bronze	6.7	4.2	4.1	3.5	3.8	4.1	4.1	3.7	4.3
Consumer durables	Copper	11.7	17.4	17.6	12.8	13.5	15.2	15.3	15.4	20.1
	Brass	83.6	79.2	79.4	85.1	84.3	82.3	82.1	82.0	76.7
	Bronze	4.7	3.4	3.0	2.1	2.2	2.5	2.6	2.6	3.2
Producer durables	Copper	18.7	21.1	21.2	21.7	24.6	28.2	27.0	26.0	31.4
	Brass	54.1	51.7	52.9	51.5	48.1	44.0	48.1	51.7	44.7
	Bronze	27.2	27.2	25.9	26.8	27.4	27.9	24.9	22.3	23.9
Building construction	Copper	26.9	34.7	34.5	30.2	32.3	32.7	32.1	31.1	32.2
	Brass	45.7	46.6	46.0	53.5	50.6	50.0	50.9	52.6	51.8
	Bronze	27.4	18.7	19.5	16.2	17.1	17.3	17.0	16.3	16.0
Communications and electric power construction	Copper	100.0	100.0	100.0	100.0	100.0	100.0	100.0	100.0	100.0
Railroads	Copper	11.3	10.0	8.9	11.2	11.4	11.0	9.8	10.3	11.2
	Brass	10.7	11.2	10.8	6.2	9.2	8.4	7.1	6.7	9.2
	Bronze	78.0	78.8	80.3	82.6	79.5	80.6	83.1	83.0	79.6
Maintenance, repair, and operation	Copper	48.4	48.6	52.5	56.3	57.5	59.0	59.7	55.2	58.9
	Brass	28.9	32.0	32.2	28.5	26.9	24.9	24.0	29.8	26.1
	Bronze	22.7	19.4	15.3	15.2	15.6	16.1	16.3	15.0	15.0
Defense	Copper	26.5	18.2	14.4	15.6	24.3	27.6	32.9	36.1	34.6
	Brass	60.9	75.5	77.7	64.7	59.1	56.2	46.8	37.5	50.0
	Bronze	12.6	6.3	7.9	19.8	16.5	16.2	20.3	26.4	15.4
Miscellaneous	Copper	46.1	6.2	17.6	52.1	58.9	48.7	52.1	41.2	15.4
	Brass	36.7	60.0	51.2	18.3	15.1	28.2	20.2	13.7	23.1
	Bronze	17.2	33.8	31.2	29.6	26.0	23.1	27.7	45.1	61.5

1. These percentage distributions are based on shipments by end-use categories in gross metal content (Table A16–40). Brass mill shipments are here regarded as brass; brass and bronze foundry shipments as bronze; and wire mill shipments as copper. Powder mill shipments are included with bronze mill products.

TABLE A16–42.   Historical Data on Net End-Use Consumption of Copper, Brass, and Bronze, by Market Category[1]

(Thousand tons)

	1950	1952	1953	1955	1956	1957	1958	1959	1960
Copper:									
Motor vehicles	60	36	42	62	48	51	36	49	56
Consumer durables	22	15	19	23	24	23	22	25	27
Producer durables	136	158	155	166	190	192	157	183	211
Building construction	98	89	94	124	122	120	122	136	129
Communications construction	70	62	62	70	89	95	81	82	89
Electric power construction	84	82	75	56	49	48	46	38	32
Railroad equipment	6	8	8	8	9	8	8	8	8
Defense	16	63	44	10	12	12	11	10	11
Maintenance, repair, and operation	53	56	64	67	68	70	70	75	75
Miscellaneous	59	5	22	74	86	38	63	87	15
Exports	14	15	16	15	18	20	11	12	8
Total	618	589	601	675	715	677	627	705	661
Brass:									
Motor vehicles	190	106	124	168	120	116	83	117	96
Consumer durables	162	68	86	152	146	123	118	134	102
Producer durables	394	388	387	395	370	300	280	364	301
Building construction	167	120	125	220	190	184	193	230	208
Railroad equipment	6	10	10	4	7	6	6	5	7
Defense	36	261	234	43	28	24	15	11	16
Maintenance, repair, and operation	32	36	39	34	32	30	28	40	33
Miscellaneous	47	48	64	26	22	22	24	29	22
Exports	18	12	11	10	10	10	11	12	12
Total	1,052	1,049	1,080	1,052	925	815	758	942	797
Bronze:									
Motor vehicles	18	6	7	8	6	7	5	6	7
Consumer durables	9	3	3	4	4	4	4	4	4
Producer durables	198	204	190	206	210	190	145	157	161
Building construction	100	48	53	66	64	64	65	71	64
Railroad equipment	44	66	72	62	62	62	65	64	57
Defense	8	22	24	13	8	7	6	8	5
Maintenance, repair, and operation	25	22	18	18	18	19	19	20	19
Miscellaneous	22	27	39	42	38	18	34	96	58
Exports	1	1	1	1	1	1	1	1	1
Total	425	399	407	420	411	372	344	427	376

1. Computed by applying the percentage distribution of copper, brass, and bronze in Table A16–41 to Table A16–39, section on "Net end-use consumption (metal weight)." Exports from Table A16–40.

TABLE A16–43. Historical Data on Net End-Use Consumption of Brass and Bronze Products, by Component Metal Content[1]

(Thousand tons)

	1950	1952	1953	1955	1956	1957	1958	1959	1960
Brass components:									
Copper:									
Motor vehicles	155	84	97	135	99	95	68	97	80
Consumer durables	132	54	67	123	120	101	97	111	85
Producer durables	321	307	302	318	305	245	230	301	251
Building construction	136	95	98	177	156	151	159	190	173
Railroad equipment	5	8	8	3	6	5	5	4	6
Defense	29	206	183	35	23	20	12	9	13
Maintenance, repair, and operation	26	28	30	27	26	25	23	33	27
Miscellaneous	38	38	50	21	18	18	20	24	18
Exports	15	9	9	8	8	8	9	10	10
Total	857	829	843	848	761	667	623	780	664
Zinc:									
All market categories	182	214	230	196	158	142	130	156	127
Nickel and aluminum:									
All market categories	13	6	7	8	6	6	5	6	6
Bronze components:									
Copper:									
Motor vehicles	16	5	6	7	5	6	4	5	6
Consumer durables	8	3	3	4	4	4	4	4	4
Producer durables	178	181	169	185	186	169	131	142	146
Building construction	90	42	47	59	57	57	59	64	58
Railroad equipment	40	58	64	56	55	55	59	58	52
Defense	7	19	21	12	7	6	5	7	5
Maintenance, repair, and operation	22	19	16	16	16	17	17	18	17
Miscellaneous	20	24	35	38	34	16	31	87	53
Exports	1	1	1	1	1	1	1	1	1
Total	382	353	362	377	365	331	311	386	341
Lead:									
All market categories	24	26	26	24	27	24	20	24	21
Tin:[2]									
All market categories	19	20	19	19	19	17	14	17	15

1. Brass mill products are estimated as comprising (per cent):

	1950	1952	1953	1955	1956	1957	1958	1959	1960
Copper	81.5	79.0	78.1	80.6	82.3	81.8	82.2	82.8	83.3
Zinc	17.3	20.4	21.3	18.6	17.1	17.5	17.1	16.6	15.9
Nickel and aluminum	1.2	.6	.6	.8	.6	.7	.7	.6	.8

Bronze mill and foundry products:

	1950	1952	1953	1955	1956	1957	1958	1959	1960
Copper	89.9	88.5	88.9	89.8	88.8	89.0	90.1	90.4	90.7
Lead	5.6	6.5	6.4	5.7	6.6	6.5	5.8	5.6	5.3
Tin	4.5	5.0	4.7	4.5	4.6	4.5	4.1	4.0	4.0

The percentages are arrived at from data in *Minerals Yearbook* giving consumption of the principal alloying elements in brass and bronze and obtaining copper content as a residual; consumption is adjusted to eliminate quantities obtained from new scrap.

Percentages applied to quantities given in Table A16–42.

2. Includes minor quantities of other metals. Cf. tin consumption for brass and bronze, Table A16–70.

TABLE A16–44. Projected Net Consumption of Copper and Copper Alloys, by Market Category[1]

(Thousand tons unless otherwise specified)

	1950	1955	1960		1970	1980	1990	2000
Motor vehicles[2]	270	237	159	L	171	192	209	242
				M	187	237	291	395
				H	230	347	538	926
Consumer durables[3]	193	179	133	L	174	226	288	345
				M	189	268	374	494
				H	206	302	441	630
Producer durables[3]	727	767	673	L	780	840	857	920
				M	1,017	1,345	1,745	2,429
				H	1,152	1,801	2,654	4,266
New building construction[4]	365	411	401	L	431	515	584	745
				M	663	889	1,254	1,947
				H	932	1,490	2,448	4,685
Communications construction[4]	70	69	89	L	78	101	109	121
				M	121	186	288	437
				H	134	231	483	983
Electric power construction[4]	83	56	32	L	8	2	*	*
				M	24	19	17	12
				H	58	86	112	139
Railroad equipment[5]	56	76	71	L	69	67	67	76
				M	86	101	123	157
				H	112	160	230	347
Rolling stock in use (number)	2,070	2,059	2,000	L	1,973	2,037	2,177	2,517
				M	2,306	2,682	3,275	4,192
				H	2,732	3,642	4,900	6,939
Pounds of copper and copper alloys per car	54	74	72	L	70	66	62	60
				M	75	75	75	75
				H	82	88	94	100
Defense[6]	60	67	32	L	24	13	13	14
				M	41	46	52	64
				H	59	80	105	151
Maintenance, repair, and operation[7]	109	119	127	L	130	147	160	184
				M	175	232	311	445
				H	216	338	526	910
Miscellaneous[7]	129	143	95	L	130	147	160	184
				M	175	232	311	445
				H	216	338	526	910
Net end-use consumption by all categories (mil. tons)	2.06	2.12	1.81	L	2.00	2.25	2.45	2.83
				M	2.68	3.55	4.77	6.83
				H	3.32	5.17	8.06	13.95

* Negligible.

1. Historical data from Table A16–39, section on "Domestic net end-use consumption (metal weight)."
2. From Table A5–13.
3. From unrounded data underlying Table A6–7.
4. From Table A4–12.
5. Copper consumption related to stock, rather than production, because of its principal use in journal bearings, which are regularly replaced. Number of rolling stock in use from Table A5–17. Copper and copper alloy content computed from Table A16–39 and extrapolated on a judgment basis. The outlook for future preferences in bearings is very uncertain and could involve either less copper or more.
6. From Table A9–4, less military construction, which is included in building construction; less electronics, which is included in producer durables; and less prompt industrial scrap generation, estimated at 30% of gross copper consumption for defense.
7. Estimate based on the historical ratio of these two items to total net consumption of copper and copper alloys by all specified market categories. That is, 15% of the latter was divided equally between "Maintenance, repair, and operation" and "Miscellaneous."

TABLE A16–45. Projected Potential Supply of Obsolete Copper-Base Scrap, by Market Category[1]

(Thousand tons metal weight unless otherwise specified)

	Metal content potentially recoverable (%)	Average life cycle (years)	1950	1955	1960		1970	1980	1990	2000
Motor vehicles	50	10	140	110	130	L	80	86	97	106
						M	81	96	121	151
						H	83	121	183	288
Consumer durables	45	10	52	58	83	L	62	81	104	132
						M	62	89	125	174
						H	63	97	142	207
Producer durables	65	20	95	158	364	L	474	443	510	549
						M	482	459	684	909
						H	487	474	798	1,250
New building construction	70	40	75	88	106	L	135	145	260	290
						M	140	150	270	310
						H	145	165	290	355
Communications and electric power construction	100	50	101	125	150	L	247	370	149	152
						M	248	373	153	160
						H	249	375	160	176
Railroad equipment	90	15	20	25	40	L	68	62	61	61
						M	69	74	86	101
						H	71	87	125	180
Maintenance, repair, and operation	70	15	35	53	75	L	84	83	99	107
						M	86	108	146	195
						H	88	129	204	322
Defense	75	15	15	23	32	L	48	21	13	9
						M	49	29	33	38
						H	50	36	55	71
Potential scrap supply	–	–	530	640	980	L	1,200	1,290	1,290	1,410
						M	1,220	1,380	1,620	2,040
						H	1,240	1,480	1,960	2,850
Domestic consumption of obsolete scrap	–	–	735	702	600	L	720	774	903	1,128
						M	915	1,104	1,458	2,040
						H	1,116	1,554	2,254	3,562
Ratio of domestic consumption to potential supply	–	–	139	110	61	L	60	60	70	80
						M	75	80	90	100
						H	90	105	115	125

1. For sources and method of calculating potential obsolete scrap and ratio of domestic consumption to potential supply see footnotes to Table A16–33 and introductory Notes to this appendix.

TABLE A16–46.   Projected Metallics Recovery from Obsolete Copper-Base Scrap[1]

(Thousand tons metal weight unless otherwise specified)

	1950	1955	1960		1970	1980	1990	2000
Domestic consumption of				L	720	774	903	1,128
obsolete scrap[2]	735	702	600	M	915	1,104	1,458	2,040
				H	1,116	1,554	2,254	3,562
				L	605	666	795	1,015
Total metallics recovery[3]	556	596	483	M	769	949	1,283	1,836
				H	937	1,336	1,984	3,206
Per cent of domestic								
consumption[4]	74	85	80		84	86	88	90
Metals recovered:								
Per cent of total metallics								
recovery:[5]								
Copper	86.5	85.7	88.2		89.3	90.2	90.3	90.4
Lead	3.9	4.2	3.7		3.3	3.0	3.0	3.0
Tin	2.2	2.0	1.9		1.8	1.7	1.6	1.5
Zinc	7.2	8.1	6.0		5.5	5.0	5.0	5.0
Nickel	.2	*	.2		.1	.1	.1	.1
Quantities:[6]								
				L	540	601	718	918
Copper	481	511	426	M	687	856	1,159	1,660
				H	837	1,205	1,792	2,898
				L	20	20	24	30
Lead	22	25	18	M	25	28	38	55
				H	31	40	60	96
				L	33	33	40	51
Zinc	40	48	29	M	42	47	64	92
				H	52	67	64	160
				L	11	11	13	15
Tin	12	12	9	M	14	16	21	28
				H	17	23	32	48
				L	1	1	1	1
Nickel	1	*	1	M	1	1	1	2
				H	1	1	2	3

* Negligible.

1. See footnote 1 to Table A16–34.
2. From Table A16–45.
3. Historical data from *Minerals Yearbook*. Projections by application of the percentages which follow.
4. Average recovery computed from *Minerals Yearbook* data and projected on a judgment basis.
5. Historical breakdown from absolute data which follow. Projections on a judgment basis, assuming an increasing emphasis on consumption of copper (e.g., in wire-mill products) compared with brass and bronze.
6. Historical data from *Minerals Yearbook*. Projections are product of total metallics recovery and percentages shown above.

TABLE A16–47. Projected Copper Consumption and Requirements for Primary Metal

(Million tons copper content)

		1950	1955	1960		1970	1980	1990	2000
Net end-use consumption by all market categories[1]					L	1.80	2.02	2.20	2.55
		1.83	1.88	1.65	M	2.41	3.20	4.29	6.15
					H	2.99	4.65	7.25	12.56
Gross exports[2]					L	.20	.10	–	–
		.19	.27	.53	M	.26	.22	.18	.14
					H	.30	.30	.30	.30
Apparent total consumption[3]					L	2.00	2.12	2.20	2.55
		2.18	2.10	2.12	M	2.67	3.42	4.47	6.29
					H	3.29	4.95	7.55	12.86
Secondary recovery from obsolete scrap[4]					L	.55	.63	.77	1.00
		.48	.52	.43	M	.70	.89	1.23	1.80
					H	.85	1.26	1.92	3.13
Requirements for primary copper					L	1.45	1.49	1.43	1.55
		1.69	1.59	1.69	M	1.97	2.53	3.24	4.49
					H	2.44	3.69	5.63	9.73
Equivalent recoverable copper content of ore[5]					L	1.49	1.53	1.47	1.60
		1.74	1.63	1.74	M	2.03	2.61	3.34	4.62
					H	2.51	3.80	5.80	10.02

1. Historical data from Table A16–39. Projections from Table A16–44 reduced to 90% to include copper content only (approximate historical relationship—see Table A16–39).
2. Historical data from Table A16–38. Projections on a judgment basis.
3. Historical data from Table A16–38. Projections are sum of preceding two items.
4. From Table A16–75.
5. Requirements multiplied by 1.03 to compensate for smelting losses.

TABLE A16–48. Relative Changes in Net End-Use Consumption of Copper and Copper Alloys, by Market Category[1]

(Rates of increase in per cent per annum)

		Motor vehicles	Consumer durables	Producer durables	Building construction	Communications construction	Electric power construction	Railroad equipment	Defense	Maintenance, repair, and operation	Miscellaneous	Total
1950–60		—5.2	—3.7	—0.8	0.9	2.4	—9.3	2.4	—6.1	1.5	—3.0	—1.3
	L	0.9	2.7	1.1	1.3	0.6	—13.0	0.3	—4.4	0.7	2.2	1.1
1960–80	M	2.0	3.6	3.5	4.1	3.7	—2.6	1.8	1.8	3.1	4.6	3.4
	H	4.0	4.2	5.0	6.8	4.9	5.1	4.1	4.7	5.0	6.6	5.4
	L	1.2	2.1	0.5	1.9	0.9	–	0.6	0.4	1.1	1.1	1.2
1980–2000	M	2.6	3.1	3.0	4.0	4.4	—2.3	2.2	1.7	3.3	3.3	3.3
	H	5.0	3.8	4.4	5.9	7.5	2.4	3.9	3.2	5.1	5.1	5.1
	L	1.1	2.4	0.8	1.6	0.8	–	0.2	—2.0	0.9	1.7	1.1
1960–2000	M	2.3	3.3	3.3	4.0	4.1	—2.4	2.0	1.7	3.2	3.9	3.4
	H	4.5	4.0	4.7	6.3	6.2	3.7	4.0	3.9	5.0	5.8	5.2

1. Calculated from Table A16–44.

TABLE A16–49. Percentage Distribution of Net End-Use Consumption of Copper and Copper Alloys, by Market Category[1]

		Motor vehicles	Consumer durables	Producer durables	Building construction	Communications construction	Electric power construction	Railroad equipment	Defense	Maintenance, repair, and operation	Miscellaneous
1950		13.1	9.4	35.3	17.7	3.4	4.0	2.7	2.9	5.3	6.2
1955		11.2	8.4	36.1	19.4	3.2	2.6	3.6	3.2	5.6	6.7
1960		8.8	7.3	37.1	22.1	4.9	1.8	3.9	1.8	7.0	5.3
	L	8.6	8.7	39.1	21.6	3.9	.4	3.5	1.2	6.5	6.5
1970	M	7.0	7.1	38.0	24.7	4.5	.9	3.2	1.6	6.5	6.5
	H	6.9	6.2	34.7	28.1	4.0	1.7	3.4	1.8	6.5	6.5
	L	8.5	10.0	37.3	22.9	4.5	.1	3.0	.6	6.5	6.5
1980	M	6.7	7.5	37.9	25.0	5.2	.5	2.8	1.3	6.5	6.5
	H	6.7	5.8	34.8	28.8	4.5	1.7	3.1	1.5	6.5	6.5
	L	8.5	11.8	35.0	23.8	4.4	*	2.7	.5	6.5	6.5
1990	M	6.1	7.8	36.6	26.3	6.0	.4	2.6	1.1	6.5	6.5
	H	6.7	5.5	32.9	30.4	6.0	1.4	2.8	1.3	6.5	6.5
	L	8.5	12.2	32.5	26.3	4.3	*	2.7	.5	6.5	6.5
2000	M	5.8	7.2	35.6	28.5	6.4	.2	2.3	.9	6.5	6.5
	H	6.6	4.5	30.6	33.6	7.0	1.0	2.5	1.1	6.5	6.5

* Negligible.
1. Calculated from Table A16–44.

TABLE A16–50.   Historical Data on Production and Consumption of Lead

(Thousand tons)

	Production of primary refined lead[1]			Secondary recovery from obsolete scrap[2]	Stock changes[3]	Net imports[4]	Production of leaded zinc oxide[5]	Apparent domestic consumption[6]	Net domestic end-use consumption[7]	Other disappearance[8]	Gross exports[9]	Apparent total requirements[10]	Requirements for primary metal[11]
	Soft lead	Lead in antimonial lead	Total										
1940	533	10	543	260	−18	125	17	963	782	181	29	992	732
1941	571	23	594	390	−21	250	24	1,279	1,050	229	26	1,305	915
1942	567	37	604	317	15	360	17	1,283	1,043	240	7	1,290	973
1943	470	27	497	333	−2	238	16	1,086	1,113	−27	10	1,096	763
1944	465	18	483	323	−14	206	20	1,046	1,119	−73	24	1,070	747
1945	444	10	454	355	26	241	19	1,043	1,051	−8	11	1,054	699
1946	338	13	351	385	2	112	19	865	956	−91	6	871	486
1947	441	25	466	505	−26	157	21	1,175	1,172	3	5	1,180	675
1948	407	45	452	492	44	257	18	1,175	1,134	41	4	1,179	686
1949	477	5	482	407	9	277	9	1,166	958	208	5	1,171	763
1950	508	15	523	474	*	450	15	1,462	1,238	224	7	1,469	996
1951	418	27	445	510	−40	198	13	1,206	1,185	21	5	1,211	702
1952	473	19	492	463	34	517	10	1,448	1,131	317	6	1,454	991
1953	468	21	489	479	27	387	10	1,338	1,202	136	5	1,343	867
1954	487	13	500	475	23	278	8	1,237	1,095	142	4	1,241	870
1955	479	15	494	495	−66	278	6	1,339	1,213	126	5	1,344	852
1956	542	14	556	501	27	277	6	1,313	1,210	103	11	1,324	825
1957	534	20	554	484	50	335	5	1,328	1,138	190	10	1,338	855
1958	470	16	486	397	96	379	3	1,169	986	183	7	1,176	780
1959	341	12	353	445	−65	280	4	1,147	1,091	56	7	1,154	710
1960	382	2	384	465	11	230	3	1,071	1,021	50	6	1,077	615

* Negligible.

1. From *Minerals Yearbook*, chapter on Lead.

2. Prior to 1957, from *Minerals Yearbook*, Secondary Metals—Nonferrous chapter, old scrap plus new scrap except copper-base. Later years, Lead chapter, same items. The reason for including "new," lead- and tin-base scrap is that this consists nearly entirely of "drosses and residues," which are, in turn, mostly a by-product of the process of recovery from old scrap.

3. From *Minerals Yearbook*, chapter on Lead. Computed as change in stocks of refined pig, lead in antimonial lead at primary smelters and refineries, and all consumers' stocks, except scrap.

4. From American Bureau of Metal Statistics *Yearbook* and from *Minerals Yearbook*, chapter on Lead. Includes pigs and bars, sheets, pipe and shot; lead content of miscellaneous products; and lead content of lead pigments and salts (assumed to be 85%).

5. From *Minerals Yearbook*, chapter on Lead. Represents the lead

content of leaded zinc oxide produced from domestic and foreign ore.

6. The sum of "Production of primary refined lead," "Secondary recovery from obsolete scrap," "Net imports," and "Production of leaded zinc oxide," minus "Stock changes."

7. 1940–58 from U.S. Bureau of Mines, *Mineral Facts and Problems*, Lead chapter, Table 8 of 1956 edition and Table 7 of 1960 edition. 1959–60 from *Minerals Yearbook*, Lead chapter.

8. Difference between "Apparent domestic consumption" and "Net domestic end-use consumption."

9. Includes ore, matte, and base bullion, in addition to exports of items listed in footnote 4.

10. Sum of "Apparent domestic consumption" and "Gross exports."

11. Difference between "Apparent total requirements" and "Secondary recovery from obsolete scrap."

TABLE A16–51.   Historical Data on Net End-Use Consumption of Lead, by Market Category[1]

(Thousand tons lead content)

	1950	1955	1956	1957	1958	1959	1960
Metal products:							
Storage batteries[2]	398	380	371	361	313	381	353
Automotive	366	342	329	326	283	332	313
Industrial	32	38	42	35	30	49	40
Solder	95	89	75	71	60	69	60
Cable covering	132	121	134	108	75	62	60
Caulking lead	53	59	65	66	71	80	67
Brass and bronze	24	24	27	24	20	24	21
Other metal products	212	202	187	180	157	173	162
Total in metal products	914	875	859	810	696	789	723
Dissipative uses:							
Tetraethyl and tetramethyl fluid	114	165	192	177	159	160	164
Other	210	172	157	151	131	143	134
Total net domestic end-use consumption	1,238	1,213	1,210	1,138	986	1,091	1,021

1. From *Minerals Yearbook,* chapter on Lead.
2. Breakdown of storage batteries into the above components from Table A5–13, which shows lead content of automotive batteries.

TABLE A16–52. Projected Net End-Use Consumption of Lead, by Market Category[1]

(Thousand tons lead content)

	1950	1955	1960		1970	1980	1990	2000
Storage batteries[2]	398	380	353	L M H	305 421 533	278 514 811	262 637 1,311	244 798 2,188
Automotive batteries[3]	366	342	313	L M H	263 374 481	233 459 744	214 572 1,224	193 721 2,076
Industrial batteries[4]	32	38	40	L M H	42 47 52	45 55 67	48 65 87	51 77 112
Solder[5]	95	89	60	L M H	62 83 107	66 105 160	73 137 239	85 183 372
Cable covering[6]	132	121	60	L M H	70 82 103	82 106 143	86 121 176	87 133 211
Caulking lead[7]	53	59	67	L M H	74 90 119	74 111 163	73 132 218	70 154 276
Brass and bronze[8]	24	24	21	L M H	23 31 38	26 41 60	28 55 94	33 79 163
Other metal products (mainly producer durables)[9]	212	202	162	L M H	151 191 233	139 211 296	134 230 362	128 252 450
Total lead in metal products	914	875	723	L M H	685 898 1,133	665 1,088 1,633	656 1,312 2,400	647 1,599 3,660
Tetraethyl and tetramethyl fluid[10]	114	165	164	L M H	210 223 248	265 296 364	343 410 574	420 554 873
Other dissipative uses[11]	210	172	134	L M H	97 113 145	75 107 169	71 121 242	81 150 370
Total net domestic end-use consumption	1,238	1,213	1,021	L M H	992 1,234 1,526	1,005 1,491 2,166	1,070 1,843 3,216	1,148 2,303 4,903

1. Historical data from Table A16–51, except as otherwise noted.

2. Projections are sum of automotive and industrial batteries.

3. From Table A5–13.

4. For historical years, difference between lead content of all and that of automotive batteries. Projections related to FRB manufacturing index (Table A1–29) by a coefficient which declines from .37 ton per index point in 1960 to .13 ton in 2000.

5. Projections from Table A16–53.

6. Related to FRB index of electric power production (Table A1–29) by a coefficient which declines from .49 ton in 1960 to .18 ton in 2000.

7. Related to expenditures on "water and sewerage construction" (Table A4–4) by a coefficient which declines from 45 tons per $ 1960 mil. in 1960 to 29 tons in 2000.

8. Practically all lead consumed in copper alloys is a component of brass and bronze foundry products. Projected on basis of implicit relationship of lead in brass and bronze (Table A16–43) to net end-use consumption of copper and copper alloys (Table A16–44).

9. Projections related to output of durable goods (Table A1–13) by a coefficient which declines from 1.6 tons per $ 1960 bil. in 1960 to .5 ton in 2000.

10. Based on the following quantities of lead in tons per million barrels of motor fuel: 1960—120; 1970—115; 1980—105; 1990—102; 2000—96. Motor fuel consumption from Table A5–15.

11. Represents almost exclusively consumption of lead in paints, varnishes, and lacquers. Projections based on the following quantities of lead in tons per million gallons of paints, varnishes, and lacquers: 1960—202; 1970—180; 1980—163; 1990—150; 2000—140. Projected consumption of paints, varnishes, and lacquers from Table A17–12.

TABLE A16–53.   Projected Net Consumption of Lead in Solder

(Thousand tons unless otherwise specified)

	1950	1955	1960		1970	1980	1990	2000
Motor vehicle production (millions)[1]	8.0	9.2	7.9	L	9.5	12.0	14.9	18.6
				M	10.4	14.8	20.8	30.4
				H	12.8	21.7	38.4	71.2
Use of solder in radiators, etc.[2]				L	1.4	.6	.3	.1
(pounds/motor vehicle)	7.5	5.2	3.3	M	2.1	1.4	.9	.6
				H	2.7	2.2	1.8	1.4
Expenditures for durable goods and				L	189	231	293	380
construction[3] ($ 1960 bil.)	116	149	154	M	247	359	528	795
				H	312	522	866	1,508
Tons of solder/$ 1960 bil. expenditures[4] (excluding use in radiators)	828	624	422		384	347	314	283
Solder requirements:								
Radiators[5]	30	24	13	L	7	4	2	1
				M	11	10	9	9
				H	17	24	35	50
Other[6]	96	93	65	L	73	80	92	108
				M	95	125	166	225
				H	120	181	272	427
Total	126	117	78	L	80	84	94	109
				M	106	135	175	234
				H	137	205	307	477
Lead content (%)[7]	75.4	78.1	78		78	78	78	78
Tin content (%)	24.6	21.9	22		22	22	22	22
Lead content	95	89	60	L	62	66	73	85
				M	83	105	137	183
				H	107	160	239	372
Tin content	31	25	20	L	18	18	21	24
				M	23	30	38	51
				H	30	45	68	105

1. From Table A5–13 and (1950) *Automobile Facts and Figures.*
2. Line 5 divided by line 1. Projected on a judgment basis.
3. From Table A1–13.
4. Line 6 divided by line 3. Projected on a judgment basis.
5. From American Bureau of Metal Statistics, *Metal Statistics,* 1960. Adjusted for lead and tin content on the basis of Bureau of Mines information. Solder used in radiators may include some other automotive use. Projections computed from first two lines.
6. Includes wiring, electronics, plumbing, canning, etc. Projections computed from lines 3 and 4.
7. Lead and tin comprised roughly 99% of solder produced during 1948–60. Breakdown is adjusted to 100%; the error introduced is negligible.

TABLE A16–54. Projected Potential Supply of Obsolete Lead-Base Scrap, by Market Category[1]

(Thousand tons metal weight unless otherwise specified)

	Metal content potentially recoverable (%)	Average life cycle (years)	1950	1955	1960		1970	1980	1990	2000
Batteries scrapped[2] (millions)	–	–	28.6	31.0	31.7	L	29.4	28.1	27.9	26.6
						M	38.4	46.6	57.4	71.0
						H	46.7	68.5	107.7	175.1
Lead/battery, 2 years earlier[3] (lb.)	–	–	20.6	20.7	18.3	L	16.6	14.9	13.5	12.1
						M	18.0	18.0	18.0	18.0
						H	18.8	19.8	20.8	21.8
Lead from automotive batteries[4]	–	–	295	320	290	L	245	210	190	160
						M	345	420	520	640
						H	440	680	1,120	1,910
Lead from all batteries[5]	–	–	320	360	330	L	285	255	240	210
						M	390	475	585	715
						H	490	745	1,205	2,020
Cable coverings	100	50	30	60	70		100	140	130	120
Other lead scrap, including radiators	65	25	120	90	105	L	180	135	100	95
						M	190	140	130	140
						H	200	145	160	200
Antimony in lead scrap[6]	100	2	30	30	30	L	25	20	20	20
						M	35	45	50	65
						H	45	70	110	180
Potential scrap supply	–	–	500	540	535	L	590	550	490	445
						M	715	800	895	1,040
						H	835	1,100	1,605	2,520
Domestic consumption of obsolete lead- and tin-base scrap[7]	–	–	615	658	614	L	650	605	540	490
						M	785	880	985	1,145
						H	920	1,210	1,765	2,770
Percentage of potential supply[8]	–	–	123	122	115		110	110	110	110

1. See introductory Notes and footnotes to Tables A16–15 and 33 for general method of calculating obsolete scrap supply.

2. Sum of batteries for replacement and annual scrappage of motor vehicles, from Tables A5–1, 3, 10, and 13. (Historical data partially estimated.)

3. From or interpolated from Table A5–13. (Some of the historical data similarly estimated.)

4. A 2–year average life is assumed, and complete recovery.

5. Automotive battery lead plus lead from industrial batteries (assumed to be mostly for replacement).

6. 9% of battery scrap.

7. Historical data from *Minerals Yearbook*. Projections by application of percentage that follows.

8. Sources of lead-base scrap other than those enumerated have been declining in importance. The projected percentage represents a judgment, based on future uses of lead, as to the point at which the relationship will stabilize.

TABLE A16–55.   Projected Metallics Recovery from Obsolete Lead- and Tin-Base Scrap

(Thousand tons metal weight unless otherwise specified)

	1950	1955	1960		1970	1980	1990	2000
Domestic consumption of				L	650	605	540	490
obsolete lead- and	615	658	614	M	785	880	985	1,145
tin-base scrap[1]				H	920	1,210	1,765	2,770
				L	520	484	432	392
Total metallics recovery[2]	489	507	476	M	628	704	788	916
				H	736	968	1,412	2,216
Per cent of consumption	80	77	78		80	80	80	80
Quantities:[3]								
				L	478	445	397	361
Lead	452	470	446	M	578	648	725	843
				H	677	891	1,299	2,039
				L	26	24	22	20
Antimony	22	24	20	M	31	35	39	46
				H	37	48	71	111
				L	16	15	13	11
Tin	16	13	10	M	19	21	24	27
				H	22	29	42	66

1. From Table A16–54.
2. Historical data calculated from *Minerals Yearbook;* projections by application of percentage which follows.
3. Lead projected as 92% of total metallics recovery; antimony as 5%; and tin as residual.

TABLE A16–56.   Projected Consumption of Lead and Requirements for Primary Metal

(Million tons lead content)

	1950	1955	1960		1970	1980	1990	2000
Net domestic end-use				L	.99	1.00	1.07	1.15
consumption[1]	1.24	1.21	1.02	M	1.23	1.49	1.84	2.30
				H	1.53	2.17	3.22	4.90
				L	—.02	—.02	—.02	—.02
Other disappearance[2]	.22	.13	.05	M	.05	.06	.08	.10
				H	.16	.22	.34	.53
				L	.97	.98	1.05	1.13
Apparent total requirements[3]	1.47	1.34	1.08	M	1.28	1.55	1.92	2.40
				H	1.69	2.39	3.56	5.43
				L	.50	.46	.42	.39
Recovery from obsolete scrap[4]	.47	.50	.46	M	.60	.68	.76	.90
				H	.71	.93	1.36	2.14
				L	.47	.52	.63	.74
Requirements for primary metal	1.00	.85	.62	M	.68	.87	1.16	1.50
				H	.98	1.46	2.20	3.29
Gross requirements for				L	.48	.54	.65	.76
primary metal[5]	1.03	.88	.64	M	.70	.90	1.19	1.54
				H	1.01	1.50	2.27	3.39

1. Historical data from Table A16–51. Projections from Table A16–52.
2. Historical data from Table A16–50; projections on a judgment basis.
3. Equals apparent domestic consumption, after 1960.
4. From Table A16–75.
5. Preceding line multiplied by a factor of 1.03 to allow for long-term stock increases and permanent losses at the refining stage.

TABLE A16–57. Relative Changes in Net End-Use Consumption of Lead, by Market Category[1]

(Rates of increase in per cent per annum)

		Storage batteries	Solder	Cable covering	Caulking lead	Brass and bronze	Other metal products	Tetraethyl & tetramethyl fluid	Other dissipative uses	Total
1950–60		—1.2	—4.5	—7.7	2.4	—1.3	—2.7	3.7	—4.4	—1.9
1960–80	L	—1.2	0.5	—1.6	0.5	1.1	—0.7	2.4	—2.9	—0.1
	M	1.9	2.8	2.9	2.6	3.4	1.3	3.0	0.9	1.9
	H	4.2	5.0	4.4	4.5	5.4	3.1	4.1	1.2	3.9
1980–2000	L	—0.6	1.3	0.4	—0.3	1.2	—0.4	2.3	0.4	0.7
	M	2.2	2.8	1.1	1.6	3.4	0.9	3.2	1.7	2.2
	H	5.1	4.3	2.0	2.7	5.1	2.1	4.5	4.0	4.2
1960–2000	L	—1.1	0.9	0.9	0.1	1.1	—0.5	2.4	—1.2	0.3
	M	2.1	2.8	2.0	2.1	3.4	1.1	3.1	0.3	2.1
	H	4.7	4.7	3.2	3.6	5.3	2.6	4.3	2.6	4.0

1. Calculated from Table A16–52.

TABLE A16–58. Percentage Distribution of Net End-Use Consumption of Lead, by Market Category[1]

		Storage batteries	Solder	Cable covering	Caulking lead	Brass and bronze	Other metal products	Tetraethyl & tetramethyl fluid	Other dissipative uses	Total
1950		32.1	7.6	10.7	4.3	1.9	17.1	9.2	17.0	100.0
1955		31.3	7.3	10.0	4.9	2.0	16.6	13.6	14.2	100.0
1960		34.6	5.9	5.9	6.6	2.1	15.9	16.1	13.1	100.0
1970	L	30.7	6.2	7.1	7.5	2.3	15.2	21.2	9.8	100.0
	M	34.1	6.7	6.6	7.3	2.5	15.5	18.1	9.2	100.0
	H	34.9	7.0	6.7	7.8	2.5	15.3	16.3	9.5	100.0
1980	L	27.7	6.6	8.2	7.4	2.6	13.8	26.4	7.5	100.0
	M	34.5	7.0	7.1	7.4	2.7	14.2	19.9	7.2	100.0
	H	37.4	7.4	6.6	7.5	2.8	13.7	16.8	7.8	100.0
1990	L	24.5	6.8	8.0	6.8	2.6	12.5	32.1	6.6	100.0
	M	34.6	7.4	6.6	7.2	3.0	12.5	22.2	6.6	100.0
	H	40.8	7.4	5.5	6.8	2.9	11.3	17.8	7.5	100.0
2000	L	21.3	7.4	7.6	6.1	2.9	11.1	36.6	7.1	100.0
	M	34.6	7.9	5.8	6.7	3.4	10.9	24.1	6.5	100.0
	H	44.6	7.6	4.3	5.6	3.3	9.2	17.8	7.5	100.0

1. Calculated from Table A16–52.

TABLE A16–59. Historical Data on Production and Consumption of Zinc

(Thousand tons)

	Primary slab zinc production[1]	Secondary recovery from obsolete scrap[2]	Stock changes[3]	Direct use of ore (zinc content)[4]	Net imports[5]	Apparent domestic consumption	Net end-use consumption[6]	Government stockpiling[7]	Other disappearance[8]	Gross exports[5]	Apparent total requirements[9]	Requirements for primary metal[10]
1940	675	64	—2	96	—62	775				79	854	790
1941	822	81	—11	135	—54	995				89	1,084	1,003
1942	892	73	68	115	—94	918				134	1,052	979
1943	942	84	97	115	—36	1,008				97	1,105	1,021
1944	869	113	42	142	48	1,130				22	1,152	1,039
1945	765	91	32	131	94	1,049		53		8	1,057	966
1946	728	77	—63	134	60	1,062		62		47	1,109	1,032
1947	802	75	—129	146	—30	1,122		140		107	1,229	1,154
1948	788	74	30	133	36	1,001		58		66	1,067	993
1949	815	52	58	88	71	968		92		59	1,027	975
1950	844	74	—101	134	138	1,291	963	128	200	19	1,310	1,236
1951	882	68	*	134	53	1,137	1,021	40	76	41	1,178	1,110
1952	904	75	98	109	60	1,050	922	37	91	59	1,109	1,034
1953	916	64	86	118	219	1,231	1,062	42	127	19	1,250	1,186
1954	802	73	—35	99	115	1,124	872	109	143	42	1,166	1,093
1955	964	84	—57	118	156	1,379	1,188	97	93	40	1,419	1,335
1956	984	74	2	113	222	1,391	1,052	237	102	24	1,415	1,341
1957	986	77	69	110	253	1,357	1,002	373	—18	16	1,373	1,296
1958	781	70	32	95	189	1,104	934	75	94	7	1,111	1,041
1959	799	74	—17	108	135	1,133	1,023	31	79	23	1,156	1,082
1960	804	68	—6	88	35	1,001	945	5	51	87	1,088	1,020

* Negligible.

1. From *Minerals Yearbook*, chapters on Zinc and on Lead and Zinc Oxides. Includes production from domestic and imported ore; excludes redistilled secondary slab zinc.

2. From *Minerals Yearbook*, chapters on Zinc or on Secondary Metals—Nonferrous.

3. Includes slab zinc stocks at metallurgical works, in transit to consumers, and at consumers, i.e., at galvanizers, brass mills, etc. Excludes government stocks, secondary zinc stocks, and zinc scrap. From *Minerals Yearbook*, chapter on Zinc.

4. From *Minerals Yearbook*, chapter on Zinc.

5. Includes zinc slab, pigs, and blocks, and new scrap. Exports include some ore and old scrap. In the case of zinc there are no comprehensive data on imports and exports of what corresponds to "metal shapes," i.e., galvanized steel, brass and bronze, die castings, etc. Net exports of zinc in these products are therefore included—not quite properly—in both apparent domestic consumption and end-use consumption; in effect these intermediate materials are treated as fabricated products.

6. From Table A16–60.

7. Since 1956, includes foreign zinc acquired under the Government Barter Program as well as additions to the Strategic Stockpile.

8. Equals "Apparent domestic consumption" minus "Net end-use consumption" and minus "Government stockpiling."

9. Equals "Apparent domestic consumption" plus "Gross exports."

10. Equals "Apparent total requirements" minus "Secondary recovery from obsolete scrap."

TABLE A16–60. Historical Data on Net End-Use Consumption of Zinc, by Market Category[1]

(Thousand tons)

	1950	1951	1952	1953	1954	1955	1956	1957	1958	1959	1960
Galvanizing	320	320	301	336	316	376	358	309	322	302	312
Sheet and strip	136	115	116	136	142	167	166	141	164	147	165
Other steel	184	205	185	200	174	209	192	168	158	155	147
Brass products	182	203	214	230	152	196	158	142	130	156	127
Light metal alloys	2	3	4	8	5	6	8	7	5	5	5
Die castings	206	226	180	245	187	348	285	306	261	320	278
Rolled zinc[2]	70	66	54	56	49	53	48	40	39	41	37
Other zinc-base alloys[3]	12	16	14	13	16	24	21	23	21	20	18
Zinc oxides	116	122	103	119	99	128	116	116	101	114	100
Other metallurgical and chemical uses[4]	55	65	52	55	48	57	58	59	55	65	68
Total	963	1,021	922	1,062	872	1,188	1,052	1,002	934	1,023	945

1. Shipments by end-use aggregated from *Minerals Yearbook,* chapter on Zinc, data on distribution of slab zinc, secondary zinc, and direct ore consumption. End-use consumption calculated by: (1) subtracting recoverable zinc content of new copper- and light-metal-base scrap from shipments to "brass products" and "light metal alloys" and (2) subtracting secondary zinc recovered from new zinc-base scrap from remaining categories allocated in proportion to shipments.

2. Represents production, a part of which is currently exported.

3. Includes alloy dies and rods, slush and sand castings, and all zinc-base alloys produced from secondary sources.

4. Such as use in wet batteries, desilvering lead, zinc dust, zinc sulfate, and other chemicals.

TABLE A16–61.   Projected Net End-Use Consumption of Zinc, by Market Category[1]

(Thousand tons unless otherwise specified)

	1950	1955	1960		1970	1980	1990	2000
Galvanizing	320	376	312	L	344	364	400	444
				M	475	586	762	1,029
				H	633	918	1,393	2,247
Sheet and strip	136	167	165	L	196	222	258	298
				M	283	378	517	733
				H	389	616	986	1,663
Galvanized sheet shipments[2] (mil. tons)	2.26	2.86	3.06	L	4.01	4.94	6.01	7.26
				M	5.54	7.71	10.78	15.59
				H	7.20	11.40	18.26	30.80
Tons of zinc/ton of sheet	.060	.058	.054	L	.049	.045	.043	.041
				M	.051	.049	.048	.047
				H	.054	.054	.054	.054
Other steel	184	209	147	L	148	142	142	146
				M	192	208	245	296
				H	244	302	407	584
Expenditures on all construction[3] ($ 1960 bil.)	58.6	72.8	76.2	L	92.7	113.5	134.9	172.2
				M	120.3	166.3	233.6	348.4
				H	152.4	241.4	387.6	687.0
Tons consumed/$ 1960 mil.	3.14	2.87	1.93		1.60	1.25	1.05	.85
Brass products[4]	182	196	127	L	160	180	196	226
				M	241	320	429	615
				H	332	517	806	1,395
Die castings[5]	206	348	278	L	377	490	626	802
				M	429	631	921	1,377
				H	513	865	1,488	2,681
Rolled zinc[6]	70	53	37	L	7	3	–	–
				M	15	15	15	15
				H	30	40	50	55
Other zinc-base alloys[7]	14	30	23	L	30	39	50	64
				M	34	50	74	110
				H	41	69	119	214
Other zinc-base alloys as per cent of die castings	5.8	6.9	8.3		8.0	8.0	8.0	8.0
Zinc oxides[5]	116	128	100	L	98	92	93	95
				M	116	131	157	193
				H	145	203	312	489
Other metallurgical and chemical uses[8]	55	57	68	L	58	58	58	58
				M	75	83	91	101
				H	83	102	125	152
Total net domestic end-use consumption by all market categories	963	1,188	945	L	1,074	1,226	1,423	1,689
				M	1,385	1,816	2,449	3,440
				H	1,777	2,714	4,293	7,233

1. Historical data from Table A16–60.
2. From Table A16–62.
3. From Table A4–3.
4. Projected as 8%, 9%, and 10% of the net domestic end-use consumption of copper and alloys (Table A16–44), for the Low, Medium, and High level, respectively.
5. Projections from Table A16–63.
6. Represents production, a part of which is exported. Projected on a judgment basis.
7. Projected as a percentage of die castings, shown in the following line. Includes "light metal alloys."
8. Projected by extrapolation: Low level same as 1950–60 average; Medium, 1% per annum growth; High, 2% per annum.

TABLE A16–62. Projected Consumption and Shipments of Galvanized Steel Sheet

(Million tons unless otherwise specified)

	1950	1955	1960		1970	1980	1990	2000
Net end-use consumption of galvanized steel as per cent of total steel net consumption:[1]								
Construction	5.3	6.1	7.4		9.0	10.0	11.0	12.0
Producer durables	3.5	3.2	3.6		4.2	4.6	5.0	5.4
Consumer durables	4.9	5.3	7.8		9.0	10.0	11.0	12.0
Automotive and railroads	1.0	1.1	1.8		3.0	4.0	5.0	6.0
Other	1.3	1.1	1.0		1.5	1.5	1.5	1.5
Net end-use consumption:[2]								
				L	1.99	2.33	2.54	2.89
Construction	1.16	1.52	1.67	M	2.92	3.80	4.97	6.91
				H	3.98	5.98	9.23	15.44
				L	.50	.62	.73	.87
Producer durables	.32	.35	.35	M	.66	.99	1.48	2.29
				H	.74	1.33	2.26	4.02
				L	.32	.40	.52	.65
Consumer durables	.18	.20	.25	M	.34	.48	.67	.94
				H	.37	.54	.79	1.19
				L	.49	.74	1.22	1.65
Automotive and railroads	.17	.22	.29	M	.64	1.11	1.86	2.90
				H	.85	1.60	2.93	5.10
				L	.11	.11	.10	.11
Other	.09	.09	.08	M	.15	.17	.19	.22
				H	.18	.24	.32	.44
				L	3.41	4.20	5.11	6.17
Total	1.92	2.38	2.64	M	4.71	6.55	9.17	13.26
				H	6.12	9.69	15.53	26.19
				L	4.01	4.94	6.01	7.26
Gross shipments[3]	2.26	2.86	3.06	M	5.54	7.71	10.78	15.59
				H	7.20	11.40	18.26	30.80

1. Source: American Iron and Steel Institute, Form AIS–16. The historical percentage figures have been derived by calculating adjusted gross shipments and net end-use consumption of galvanized steel by the same method as used for total steel shipments and total steel net end–use consumption. See footnotes to Tables A16–3 and 4. The projected percentage figures have been extrapolated on a judgment basis, taking into account historical trends and expected future changes of the product-mix within the various market classifications and expected technological changes (such as increasing use of galvanized steel in construction).

2. The net end-use consumption has been calculated by applying the above percentage figures to the historical and projected data on total steel net end-use consumption, shown in Table A16–10.

3. Represents net end-use consumption plus estimated net exports and prompt industrial scrap generated. The scrap generation factor has been estimated at 15% of projected gross shipments.

TABLE A16–63.　Projected Net Consumption of Zinc in Die Castings and Zinc Oxides

(Thousand tons unless otherwise specified)

	1950	1955	1960		1970	1980	1990	2000
Die castings (zinc content):								
				L	52	62	71	84
Producer durables[1]	21	36	37	M	68	100	145	221
				H	77	133	221	388
				L	214	270	335	418
Transportation[2]	130	225	171	M	234	333	468	684
				H	288	488	864	1,602
				L	87	126	180	246
Consumer durables[1]	44	72	53	M	94	149	234	353
				H	103	168	276	450
				L	24	32	40	54
Contractors' products[3]	11	15	17	M	33	49	74	119
				H	45	76	127	241
New building construc-				L	43.5	53.1	61.5	80.1
tion[4] ($ 1960 bil.)	27.3	34.5	36.0	M	60.3	80.8	114.0	177.0
				H	81.0	124.2	195.8	360.4
Die castings/$ mil. (tons)	.40	.43	.47		.55	.61	.65	.67
				L	377	490	626	802
Total[5]	206	348	278	M	429	631	921	1,377
				H	513	865	1,488	2,681
Zinc oxides:[6]								
				L	53	52	53	56
Rubber	47	59	49	M	64	74	91	114
				H	81	119	192	317
Rubber consumption in				L	1.40	1.61	1.73	1.97
tires[7] (mil. long tons)	.96	1.13	1.14	M	1.70	2.28	2.99	4.01
				H	2.16	3.65	6.29	11.12
Zinc oxides/100 long tons of rubber (tons)	4.89	5.22	4.30		3.75	3.25	3.05	2.85
				L	21	16	16	15
Paints	47	37	27	M	23	22	24	28
				H	29	32	43	58
Production of paints, var-				L	555	494	535	608
nishes, and lacquers[8]	641	719	663	M	629	670	829	1,105
(mil. gal.)				H	771	974	1,467	2,322
Zinc oxides/mil. gal. (tons)	73.3	51.5	40.7		37	33	29	25
				L	24	24	24	24
Other uses[9]	22	32	24	M	29	35	42	51
				H	35	52	77	114
				L	98	92	93	95
Total	116	128	100	M	116	131	157	193
				H	145	203	312	489

1. From Table A6–7, prior to rounding.
2. Ninety per cent of zinc in motor vehicles, Table A5–13, assuming increased use of zinc for under-coatings.
3. Historical data from American Die Casting Institute press releases. Projections are product of following two lines.
4. From Table A4–12.
5. Includes die castings for National Defense, projected as negligible.
6. Historical data from *Minerals Yearbook,* Lead and Zinc Pigments chapter, table on shipments of zinc oxide by uses, adjusted for zinc content and new scrap generated. Zinc content of all leaded zinc oxide shipments included with paint consumption. Other uses include use in ceramics, coated fabrics (rayon), floor coverings, cosmetics, pharmaceuticals, and other miscellaneous chemicals.
7. From Table A5–13.
8. From Table A17–12.
9. Assumed to increase at zero, 2, and 4 per cent per year, respectively, in the Low, Medium, and High.

TABLE A16–64. Projected Potential Supply of Obsolete Zinc-Base Scrap, by Market Category[1]

(Thousand tons metal weight unless otherwise specified)

	Metal content potentially recoverable[2] (%)	Average life cycle[3] (years)	1950	1955	1960		1970	1980	1990	2000
Potential supply:[4]						L	144	194	252	322
Die castings	50	10	40	50	107	M	147	225	330	483
						H	151	274	464	804
						L	7	1	1	–
Rolled zinc	20	10	13	20	13	M	7	3	3	3
						H	7	6	8	10
						L	12	19	24	31
Other zinc-base alloys	60	10	10	7	9	M	14	21	31	47
						H	15	26	44	77
						L	163	214	277	353
Total	–	–	63	77	129	M	168	249	364	533
						H	173	306	516	891
						L	65	86	111	141
Domestic consumption[5]	–	–	42	41	47	M	81	144	240	384
						H	102	226	428	793
Ratio of domestic						L	.40	.40	.40	.40
consumption to	–	–	.67	.53	.36	M	.48	.58	.66	.72
potential supply[6]						H	.59	.74	.83	.89

1. See Notes to this appendix and footnotes to Tables A16–15 and 33.
2. See footnote 2 to Table A16–33.
3. Estimated; see footnote 3, Table A16–15.
4. See footnote 4 to Table A16–33.
5. See footnote 5 to Table A16–33.
6. See footnote 6 to Table A16–33.

TABLE A16–65.   Projected Metallics Recovery from Obsolete Zinc-Base Scrap

(Thousand tons metal weight unless otherwise specified)

	1950	1955	1960		1970	1980	1990	2000
Domestic consumption of				L	65	86	111	141
obsolete zinc scrap[1]	42	41	47	M	81	144	240	384
				H	102	226	428	793
				L	53	71	91	116
Total metallics recovery[2]	35	34	39	M	66	118	197	315
				H	84	185	351	650
Per cent of domestic								
consumption[3]	83	83	83		82	82	82	82
Zinc as per cent of total								
metallics recovery[3]	98.8	98.7	98.4		98.0	98.0	98.0	98.0
				L	52	70	89	114
Secondary recovery of zinc	34	34	38	M	65	116	193	309
				H	82	181	344	637

1. Historical data from *Minerals Yearbook;* projections from Table A16–64.
2. Historical data from *Minerals Yearbook;* projections are the product of the preceding and following lines.
3. Historical data computed from *Minerals Yearbook;* projection on a judgment basis.

TABLE A16–66. Projected Zinc Consumption and Requirements for Primary Metal[1]

(Million tons)

	1950	1955	1960		1970	1980	1990	2000
Net end-use consumption[2]	.96	1.19	.95	L	1.07	1.23	1.42	1.69
				M	1.38	1.82	2.45	3.44
				H	1.78	2.71	4.29	7.23
Other disappearance[3]	.20	.09	.05	L	.05	.06	.07	.08
				M	.07	.09	.12	.17
				H	.09	.14	.21	.36
Apparent domestic consumption[4]	1.29	1.38	1.00	L	1.12	1.29	1.49	1.77
				M	1.45	1.91	2.57	3.61
				H	1.87	2.85	4.50	7.60
Gross exports	.02	.04	.09		*	*	*	*
Apparent total consumption	1.31	1.42	1.09	L	1.12	1.29	1.49	1.77
				M	1.45	1.91	2.57	3.61
				H	1.87	2.85	4.50	7.60
Secondary recovery from obsolete scrap[5]	.07	.08	.07	L	.09	.11	.15	.20
				M	.11	.18	.29	.46
				H	.14	.27	.46	.92
Requirements for primary metal	1.24	1.34	1.02	L	1.03	1.18	1.34	1.57
				M	1.34	1.73	2.28	3.15
				H	1.73	2.58	4.04	6.68
Gross requirements for ore[6] (recoverable zinc content)	1.28	1.38	1.05	L	1.06	1.22	1.38	1.62
				M	1.38	1.78	2.35	3.24
				H	1.78	2.66	4.16	6.88

* Negligible.

1. Historical data from Table A16–59; projections as indicated below.
2. From Table A16–61.
3. Projected, on a judgment basis, as 5% of end-use consumption.
4. Historical data include government stockpiling.
5. From Table A16–75.
6. Preceding line multiplied by a factor of 1.03 to allow for expansion of stocks.

TABLE A16–67.   Relative Changes in Net End-Use Consumption of Zinc, by Market Category[1]

(Rates of increase in per cent per annum)

		Gal-vaniz-ing	Brass prod-ucts	Die cast-ings	Rolled zinc	Other zinc-base alloys	Zinc oxide	Other metal-lurgical and chem-ical uses	Total
1950–60		—0.2	—3.5	3.0	—6.2	5.1	—1.5	2.1	—0.2
	L	0.8	1.8	2.9	—12.2	2.7	—0.4	—.08	1.3
1960–80	M	3.2	4.7	4.2	—4.4	4.0	1.4	1.0	3.3
	H	5.5	7.3	5.8	0.4	5.6	3.6	2.0	5.4
	L	1.0	1.1	2.5	–	2.5	0.2	–	1.6
1980–2000	M	2.9	3.3	4.0	–	4.0	2.0	1.0	3.2
	H	4.6	5.1	5.8	1.6	4.0	4.5	2.0	5.0
	L	0.9	1.5	2.7	–	2.6	—0.1	—0.4	1.5
1960–2000	M	3.0	4.0	4.1	—2.2	4.0	1.7	1.0	3.3
	H	5.1	6.2	5.8	1.0	5.7	4.0	2.0	5.2

1. Computed from Table A16–61.

TABLE A16–68.   Percentage Distribution of Net End-Use Consumption of Zinc, by Market Category[1]

		Gal-vaniz-ing	Brass prod-ucts	Die cast-ings	Rolled zinc	Other zinc-base alloys	Zinc oxide	Other metal-lurgi-cal and chem-ical uses	Total
1950		33.2	18.9	21.4	7.3	1.5	12.0	5.7	100.0
1955		31.6	16.5	29.3	4.5	2.5	10.8	4.8	100.0
1960		33.0	13.4	29.5	3.9	2.4	10.5	7.2	100.0
	L	32.0	14.9	35.1	0.7	2.8	9.1	5.4	100.0
1970	M	34.3	17.4	31.0	1.0	2.4	8.4	5.4	100.0
	H	35.6	18.7	28.9	1.7	2.3	8.1	4.7	100.0
	L	29.7	14.7	40.0	0.2	3.2	7.5	4.7	100.0
1980	M	32.3	17.6	34.7	0.8	2.8	7.2	4.6	100.0
	H	33.8	19.0	31.9	1.5	2.5	7.5	3.8	100.0
	L	28.1	13.8	44.0	–	3.5	6.5	4.1	100.0
1990	M	31.1	17.5	37.6	0.6	3.1	6.4	3.7	100.0
	H	32.4	18.8	34.6	1.2	2.8	7.3	2.9	100.0
	L	26.3	13.4	47.5	–	3.8	5.6	3.4	100.0
2000	M	29.9	17.9	40.0	0.5	3.2	5.6	2.9	100.0
	H	31.1	19.3	37.1	0.7	2.9	6.8	2.1	100.0

1. Computed from Table A16–61.

TABLE A16–69. Historical Data on Production and Consumption of Tin[1]

(Thousand tons)

	Primary smelter production[2]	Secondary recovery from obsolete scrap[3]	Stock changes[4]	Net imports[5]	Apparent domestic consumption[6]	Net domestic end-use consumption[7]	Other disappearance[8]	Gross exports[9]	Apparent total consumption[10]	Requirements for primary metal[11]
1942	18.1	28.6								
1943	24.1	29.1								
1944	34.3	24.1								
1945	45.5	27.1								
1946	48.7	21.4								
1947	37.3	23.5								
1948	41.1	23.3								
1949	40.4	19.3								
1950	36.0	27.6	4.1	89.4	148.9	104.8	44.1	5.4	154.3	126.7
1951	34.6	27.1	—16.1	25.4	103.2	87.4	15.8	6.3	109.5	82.4
1952	25.3	26.9	7.6	91.2	135.8	77.7	58.1	4.8	140.6	113.7
1953	42.1	24.9	—1.9	83.7	152.6	85.3	67.3	3.8	156.4	131.5
1954	30.7	22.7	3.7	71.0	120.7	82.7	38.0	6.2	126.9	104.2
1955	25.0	25.1	4.8	70.6	115.9	90.3	25.6	7.1	123.0	97.9
1956	19.7	26.2	1.1	66.3	111.1	90.1	21.0	6.2	117.3	91.1
1957	1.8	21.1	—.7	60.1	83.7	82.2	1.5	6.3	90.0	68.9
1958	5.9	19.6	—1.2	44.8	71.5	72.4	—.9	3.9	75.4	55.8
1959	12.0	19.9	7.4	48.8	73.3	77.4	—4.1	3.4	76.7	56.8
1960	15.1	18.7	—1.3	43.3	78.4	80.5	—2.1	4.4	82.8	64.1

1. From *Minerals Yearbook,* chapter on Tin unless stated otherwise.
2. From ABMS *Yearbook.*
3. Includes secondary recovery from tin cans, and tin-base, lead-base, and copper-base scrap, plus new tin-base and lead-base scrap, considered as old scrap for these purposes. (See footnote 2, Table A16–50.)
4. Total for industry, including tin-plate makers, other fabricators, importers, tin in transit. Excludes stocks of tin-bearing scrap and government stocks.
5. Includes pig, grain, and granulated tin, tin in tin plate, cans and tin-plate scrap, bars, blocks, and the tin content of tin-base alloys. Prior to 1952 data on tin-base alloy imports are not available, but they amounted to less than 1,000 tons per year.
6. Represents the sum of columns 1, 2, and 4 minus column 3.
7. From Table A16–70.
8. Difference between "Apparent domestic consumption" and "Net domestic end-use consumption." Represents mainly additions to and diminutions of government stocks, including the National Strategic Stockpile.
9. Includes, pig, bars, tin in tin plate, tin-plate scrap, and tin cans. Exports of ore and tin compounds are negligible.
10. The sum of "Apparent domestic consumption" and "Gross exports." Does not include additions to stocks.
11. Equals "Apparent total consumption" less "Secondary recovery from obsolete scrap."

TABLE A16–70. Historical Data on Net End-Use Consumption of Tin, by Market Category[1]

(Thousand tons)

	Tin and terne plate[2]	Solder[3]	Brass and bronze[4]	Miscellaneous tin products[5]	Net domestic end-use consumption by all market categories
1950	35.8	30.8	18.0	20.2	104.8
1951	30.8	22.2	19.0	15.4	87.4
1952	27.5	20.1	17.8	12.3	77.7
1953	31.5	22.6	17.1	14.1	85.3
1954	32.9	21.7	14.5	13.6	82.7
1955	33.4	24.9	17.2	14.8	90.3
1956	34.6	23.1	17.0	15.4	90.1
1957	31.9	21.2	15.0	14.1	82.2
1958	29.1	18.3	12.4	12.6	72.4
1959	25.2	22.4	15.0	14.8	77.4
1960	33.3	20.5	13.4	13.3	80.5

1. Historical data from *Minerals Yearbook*, Tin chapter, corrected for new scrap generation as indicated in footnotes below.
2. Reduced by 12% (scrap generation factor).
3. No scrap generation.
4. Reduced by 22% (scrap generation factor).
5. This category includes all items not previously enumerated, reduced by 10% (scrap generation factor).

TABLE A16–71.   Projected Net End-Use Consumption of Tin, by Market Category[1]

(Thousand tons unless otherwise specified)

	1950	1955	1960		1970	1980	1990	2000
				L	20	13	7	4
Tin and terne plate[2]	35.8	33.4	33.3	M	29	28	25	23
				H	41	52	65	78
				L	18	18	21	24
Solder[3]	30.8	24.9	20.5	M	23	30	38	51
				H	30	45	68	105
				L	14	16	17	20
Brass and bronze[4]	18.0	17.2	13.4	M	21	28	38	55
				H	30	47	73	126
				L	10	8	8	10
Miscellaneous tin products[5]	20.2	14.8	13.3	M	15	18	24	36
				H	24	35	54	92
Output of durable goods[6]				L	122	151	200	261
($ 1960 bil.)	74	95	97	M	154	229	343	514
				H	188	322	540	918
				L	.08	.05	.04	.04
Tons/$ 1960 mil.[7]	.27	.16	.14	M	.10	.08	.07	.07
				H	.13	.11	.10	.10
Net domestic end-use consumption				L	62	55	53	58
by all market categories	105	90	81	M	88	104	125	165
				H	125	179	260	401

1. Historical data from Table A16–70, unless indicated otherwise.
2. Projected by raising series on tin consumption by container industry, Table A7–4, by 5%, to cover other uses.
3. From Table A16–53.
4. Assumed tin content of end-use consumption of copper-base mill products, Table A16–44: .7% in the Low; .8% in the Medium; and .9% in the High. These assumptions are based on historical relationship implicit in Tables A16–39 and 43.
5. Projections are the product of the two succeeding lines.
6. From Table A1–13.
7. Historical relationship between lines 5 and 6 projected on a judgment basis.

TABLE A16–72.   Projected Tin Consumption and Requirements for Primary Metal

(Thousand tons)

	1950	1955	1960		1970	1980	1990	2000
Net end-use consumption by				L	62	55	53	58
all market categories[1]	105	90	81	M	88	104	125	165
				H	125	179	260	401
				L	2	2	2	2
Other disappearance[2]	44	26	—2	M	2	3	3	4
				H	4	5	7	10
Apparent domestic				L	64	57	55	60
consumption	149	116	79	M	90	107	128	169
				H	129	184	267	411
Gross exports[3]	5	7	4		*	*	*	*
				L	64	57	55	60
Apparent total requirements	154	123	83	M	90	107	128	169
				H	129	184	267	411
Secondary recovery from				L	27	26	26	26
obsolete scrap[4]	28	25	19	M	35	37	45	55
				H	39	52	74	114
				L	37	31	29	34
Requirements for primary tin	127	98	64	M	55	70	83	114
				H	90	132	193	297
Gross requirements for ore				L	38	32	30	35
(recoverable tin content)[5]	130	101	66	M	57	72	85	117
				H	93	136	199	306

* Negligible.

1. From Table A16–71.
2. Historical data from Table A16–69. Projected as 3% of end-use consumption at all three levels.
3. Historical data from Table A16–69. Future exports should be negligible.
4. From Table A16–75.
5. Previous line multiplied by 1.03, to allow for stock accumulations of pig tin or other tin bearing raw material.

TABLE A16–73.   Relative Changes in Net End-Use Consumption of Tin, by Market Category[1]

(Rates of increase in per cent per annum)

		Tin and terne plate	Solder	Brass and bronze	Miscellaneous tin products	Total
1950–60		—0.7	—4.0	—2.9	—4.1	—2.6
	L	—4.6	—0.6	0.9	—2.5	—1.9
1960–80	M	—0.8	1.9	3.8	1.5	1.3
	H	2.3	4.0	6.5	5.0	4.0
	L	—5.7	1.4	1.1	1.1	0.3
1980–2000	M	—1.0	2.7	3.4	3.5	2.3
	H	2.0	4.3	5.1	5.0	4.1
	L	—5.2	0.4	1.0	—0.7	—1.1
1960–2000	M	—0.9	2.3	3.6	2.5	1.8
	H	2.2	4.2	5.8	5.0	4.1

1. Computed from Table A16–71.

TABLE A16–74. Percentage Distribution of Net End-Use Consumption of Tin, by Market Category[1]

		Tin and terne plate	Solder	Brass and bronze	Miscellaneous tin products	Total
1950		34.1	29.3	17.1	19.2	100.0
1955		37.0	27.6	19.0	16.4	100.0
1960		41.4	25.5	16.6	16.5	100.0
	L	32.3	29.0	22.6	16.1	100.0
1970	M	33.0	26.1	23.9	17.0	100.0
	H	32.8	24.0	24.0	19.2	100.0
	L	23.6	32.7	29.1	14.6	100.0
1980	M	26.9	28.9	26.9	17.3	100.0
	H	29.0	25.1	26.3	19.6	100.0
	L	13.2	39.6	32.1	15.1	100.0
1990	M	20.0	30.4	30.4	19.2	100.0
	H	25.0	26.1	28.1	20.8	100.0
	L	6.9	41.4	34.5	17.2	100.0
2000	M	14.0	30.9	33.3	21.8	100.0
	H	19.5	26.2	31.4	22.9	100.0

1. Computed from Table A16–71.

TABLE A16–75. Secondary Recovery of Major Nonferrous Metals from Obsolete Scrap

(Thousand tons)

	1950	1955	1960		1970	1980	1990	2000
Aluminum[1]	76	76	63	L	197	477	1,016	1,683
				M	213	606	1,505	2,942
				H	244	937	2,554	4,937
Copper[2]	485	515	429	L	552	626	767	998
				M	702	889	1,233	1,799
				H	854	1,255	1,916	3,134
Lead[3]	474	495	465	L	498	465	421	391
				M	603	676	763	898
				H	708	931	1,359	2,135
Zinc[4]	75	84	68	L	89	113	151	201
				M	112	176	289	464
				H	139	268	458	920
Tin[3]	28	25	19	L	27	26	26	26
				M	35	37	45	55
				H	39	52	74	114

1. Secondary aluminum recovered, from Table A16–34, multiplied by the factor 1.01 to include aluminum recovered from other obsolete nonferrous scrap.
2. From Tables A16–34 and 46, multiplied by 1.008 to account for copper recovered from nickel-base, tin-base, and zinc-base scrap.
3. From Tables A16–46 and 55.
4. From Tables A16–34, 46, and 65.

appendix
to
chapter
17

CHEMICALS

Notes

OF THE following twelve tables, the first ten, simple in concept but complex in execution, form the statistical skeleton of the projections made for the synthetics branch of the chemical industry; the other two, for specific end-products, are almost self-explanatory. Because of this feature the last two—A17–11 and 12—are considered first. They represent an effort to project the use of two leading classes of chemical products—soaps and paints. Neither seems destined to share in the rapidly rising trend of many other branches of the industry; they are interesting mainly because they have undergone, and to some extent are still undergoing, a thorough reorientation in their resource base: from natural fats and oils, vegetable and animal, to synthetic materials, especially those derived from oil and gas and, decreasingly, from coal. The production of paints, as projected, forms part of the calculations carried on in the first ten tables of this appendix. The materials on which the detergents are based are not further analyzed. The series as offered may be used by experts in the field to serve as starting points for such calculations in terms of raw materials as they might wish to pursue.

It is the first ten tables that require extended comment, since to the best of our knowledge no similar broad-based, long-term projection has been made in this field in the past. A good many considerations apply to more than one table and are discussed in this introductory statement, but most are intimately connected with the construction of each individual series and are therefore presented with the particular table and series to which they apply, even though

this involves providing footnotes of unusual length and substance for most of the tables. It is, however, unlikely that readers who do not possess a fair degree of familiarity with the structure and operations of this particular industry will in any event undertake the arduous voyage through this portion of the statistical appendix. Their purpose is best served by reading the text of Chapter 17. On the other hand, the technical reader will most likely prefer to find out our reasons for doing one thing rather than another not in a general preface but while looking at the figures that have resulted from our reasoning. Thus these notes are limited to a few general remarks—specifically (1) the scheme of the subsequent statistical material and (2) the most significant among the general problems and weaknesses encountered.

The field covered here comprises three closely related branches: the man-made fibers (other than rayon), the man-made rubbers (or elastomers), and, most difficult of all to define properly, the man-made resins. The last are the ingredients for what is popularly conceived as the "plastics" or "synthetics" industry. As the terminology is inconsistent and often vague, a few comments may help to orient the reader. The Business and Defense Services Administration of the U.S. Department of Commerce defines plastics as materials "composed wholly or partly of various combinations of carbon, oxygen, hydrogen, chlorine, fluorine, and/or nitrogen, together with certain inorganic or organic substances, which though solid in the finished state [are] at some stage during [their] manufacture sufficiently fluid to be formed into various shapes, usually through the application of heat or pressure, or both."

We are not here concerned with finished *products,* but with plastic *materials* that are also used in products other than plastic ones as commonly understood, such as paint (going here under the name of protective coating), adhesives, fabric-treating materials, etc. Strictly speaking, plastic materials is a more inclusive category than synthetic materials since it includes also natural substances, of animal or vegetable origin, such as rosin, shellac, casein, cellulose, etc. However, the natural materials are by now quantitatively so insignificant that the calculations here undertaken have been limited to the synthetic portion of the plastics, except where consideration of a natural material is essential in figuring out the raw material pattern of a particular line of products (e.g., cellulosic moldings).

In their final, marketed form, plastic materials contain various secondary materials, such as fillers, extenders, plasticizers, coloring matter, and lubricants, all designed either to make the product cheaper, to impart desirable qualities, or to facilitate processing. In the tables only the bonding agents themselves are considered, except where inclusion of additives is dictated by the data (as is frequently the case).

The plastic materials thus defined, comprising fibers, resins, and rubbers, differ more in terms of external characteristics of the final product and method of manufacture than in terms of basic ingredients. For example, polystyrene is used as both monofilament (man-made fiber), and synthetic resin (molding powder, film, etc.); the best known synthetic rubber is a copolymer of styrene and butadiene; butadiene in turn is one of the raw materials for some nylons and for several synthetic resins, including a fast growing one in which it is polymerized with styrene and acrylonitrile. Thus, the underlying material is, so to speak, "neutral" until processed.

While everyone understands what synthetic fiber or rubber is, the term "synthetic resin" causes more difficulty. Properly defined, synthetic resins are amorphous solid or semisolid complex organic compounds with no definite melting point or tendency to crystallize, produced by chemical means and used as the major component of plastic materials (powders, granules, liquids containing additives), which in turn either are cast, extruded, calendered, etc. into such things as blocks, tubes, or film or have some other application (e.g., as a film-forming ingredient in paint).

Though the same definition would seem to fit the materials from which fibers and rubber are manufactured, the term "resin" is used here in the more common, restricted sense, mainly because the figures for resinous materials going into fibers or rubber are not included with the synthetic resin statistics, though there are exceptions to this generalization as well. Data on synthetic resinous materials treated in any way other than extrusion into monofilaments, spinning into yarn, blowing into staple, or processing like natural rubber or used for any purpose other than those just named are thus the substance of those tables that deal with resins.

The key materials that are synthesized into resins, fiber, or rubber may be called organic intermediates (e.g., styrene, phenol, phthalic anhydride, etc.) and organic crudes (e.g., ethylene, benzene, etc.). The ideal procedure would be to derive first the requirements for intermediates, then for crudes, and then relate the latter to the primary resource, typically a fossil fuel. However, in this study we have stopped short of the final step, i.e., the reduction of the intermediates to the crudes (the industry, incidentally, does not generally use this last term except in the coal-derived materials, where crudes have their origin in both fact and name). The principal reason is that there is characteristically more than one way in which the intermediate may be obtained. For example, vinyl chloride, a common resin material, may be obtained from acetylene and hydrogen chloride, or from ethylene dichloride. Acetylene itself may be produced from calcium carbide or from certain hydrocarbon fractions obtainable from natural gas or oil. Indeed, one may almost legitimately generalize that increasingly the opportunity to derive the intermediates directly from natural gas or petroleum fractions opens up a sufficient number of alternative ways of obtaining the intermediates that the calculations are becoming too difficult to set up meaningfully. The fact that since 1950 methane has been one of the starting materials for production of acetylene, which in turn can be a starting point for a wide variety of resins, greatly widens the range of such alternatives. In this study, therefore, no effort has been made to go beyond developing the intermediate stage.

Another general preface must be directed toward the treatment of the historical statistics. Because the industry is young and therefore constantly—and rapidly—changing in composition, the statistics not only have but a brief history but sometimes lack year to year comparability. They also tend to behave erratically, as processes, end-uses, and other factors change. Finally, end-use information is scarce; available, if at all, only sporadically, in an article in one trade journal or another, for this year or that; and of questionable authenticity. All these data, aided by systematic exposition in two or three basic books, have been carefully studied and used to arrive at the best possible reconstruction of the industry pattern. More than in most other industries, knowledge of processes, even to the extent of being familiar with those employed by a specific company, is often a prerequisite for interpretation and manipulation of published statistics.

By no means all this information is shown in the tables. For the past, even though data on intermediate years have provided useful guidance, information for only 1950 and 1955 is shown (where available) and not all the adjustments (frequently, informed guesses) that had to be made to achieve a modicum of comparability have been spelled out in the footnotes. This would have led to a superabundance of notes quite out of keeping with the eventual use made of the series. For it must be remembered that (1) the final projections of this particular group of products are further expanded by rather crude methods to arrive at totals that are assumed to represent the aggregate demand for oil and gas emanating from the chemical industry; (2) the total demand from this particular direction represents only a small portion of demand for oil and gas altogether; and (3) the sum total of the demand for raw materials thus derived is compared, without differentiation between the various forms in which they enter the manufacturing process, with the gross production of oil and gas. Thus the precise type and magnitude of each of the various materials, while of interest, is not in this study used at its full value, that is, for determining the cost implications for each of the different materials, based upon ease of availability. This is further discussed in Chapter 17 (see pp. 320–25).

When it comes to projecting the use of each of the materials, the uncertainty as to past performance is compounded by the well known fluidity of the industry, the ready substitutability of one material for another, the radical price changes that characterize the industry and play a large part in relative growth rates, and, above all, the paucity of reliable end-use information, i.e., data relating to end *products* as opposed to end *markets*.

For these reasons many of the data are presented, without much background documentation, as our best guesses crystalized from a thorough study of the raw data available mainly from the U.S. Tariff Commission, the Census Bureau, and the trade press.

The organization of the statistical tables is as follows: Table A17–1 shows the principal markets (in terms of broad end-use classes) of plastics and resin materials in the past and develops the projection of each, based upon the most applicable available reference series. Table A17–2 illustrates the procedure in some detail in the case of moldings and extrusions. Table A17–3 shows the share of each of the major chemical groups of materials in each of the markets and projects these shares. Table A17–4 combines the projections made in Tables A17–1 and 3 and thus arrives at projections of aggregate demand for each resin material, first in the eight major markets that have been specifically projected and then, by consideration of likely growth in unspecified, minor markets, in all markets. In Table A17–5 the demand for each of the resin materials is reduced to the demand for the major ingredients used in their production. The information used in this particular phase is gleaned from a large variety of sources but presented in terms of those single coefficients into which it has been feasible to compress it. Undoubtedly, since we are here dealing with averages and a large assortment of materials and processes, the expert will have much to criticize in this phase, but he should be aware of the statistical limitations, as to both availability of data and the need for ruthless averaging. In a highly competitive industry, it is not the custom of the participants to shout details of their bills for materials and processes from the roof tops, and all is thus approximate.

Tables A17–6 and 7 deal with the role and projection of synthetic rubber in the manufacture of both tires and other products. The second of the two tables reduces the requirements for synthetic rubber to the requirements for the basic raw materials; this step yields a reasonably close approximation in the case of standard (S-type) rubber, made from styrene and butadiene, but proves less satisfactory in the case of the rapidly developing other types, which appear to be moving into prominence both in tires and in the non-automotive field. Here the procedure is rather primitive, being based solely on the relationship between production of one of the several non-S-type rubbers (viz. N-type) and that of the two principal ingredients known, in approximate quantities, to compose it. There is little doubt that future developments will substantially alter these projections, and that polyisoprene and polybutadiene will before long deserve separate recognition.

Table A17–8 contains projections for the third member of the synthetics family, i.e., man-made fibers, and reduces demand for them into demand for key materials. Unfortunately, this group cannot be fully covered, as the necessary data are not available for the growing variety of synthetic fibers. Only for nylon and the acrylic fibers is there anywhere nearly enough information available to make reasonable accuracy possible. So a substantial percentage of man-made fiber production is omitted; in the aggregate, however, the man-made fibers are not produced in significant quantities compared to either the rubbers or the plastics, so that the omissions are not too disturbing.

Table A17–9 is devoted to two types of material that are manufactured in significant amounts by at least two substantially different routes and which therefore cannot be reduced to key materials in the same kind of shortcut method that is used in Table A17–5. The two materials are acrylonitrile, an ingredient of both fibers and plastics, and vinyl chloride, one of the older and more versatile resin intermediates.

Table A17–10 is a summary in which uses in all three synthetic fields are brought together and reduced to uses of organic crudes and intermediates, through bills for materials that are based upon as thorough a review of the technical literature as is feasible in a basically non-technical study. It should be noted that the final materials to which demand is here reduced are neither a comprehensive list of all synthetics (as explained throughout the tables, there are omissions all along the line) nor do they represent the "ultimate ingredients" of the synthetics. For example, we have already mentioned that synthetic rubbers are in the main a mixture of butadiene and styrene, where the latter is made from ethylene and benzene. Other instances of this sort will be obvious to the expert. The reason we have refrained from taking the next—and last—step, i.e., reducing the materials given to their ultimate ingredients, is that most of the elements here listed can be, and are being, produced in more than one way and that it proved too difficult to disentangle the production processes and their relative importance. Therefore, Table A17–10, for the purposes of this study, is the end of the road.

One final note in regard to looking forward to future research in this field: The principal difficulty, other than that of mastering the technical intricacies, lies on one hand, in the vast and growing applicability of synthetic materials and, on the other, in failure to consider them jointly with other basic materials, such as metals, wood, non-metallic construction materials, etc., in larger, more universal aggregates, in an effort to determine their current and prospective share of such larger aggregates. Such consideration would call for elaboration of equivalents in use, for close price comparisons, and for intelligent evaluation of changes in consumer acceptability. Ultimately, as the synthetic materials become a major segment of the economy, this must be the approach. Considering the synthetics industry in isolation, as a branch of the chemical industry, will become increasingly fruitless and futile, as growth rates are determined not by demand for the material as such but by its demand as shares of larger aggregates. In that direction we hope to have made a beginning.

LIST OF TABLES

TABLE A17–1.   Projected Synthetic Resin Materials, by Major Markets[1]

(Billion pounds, unless otherwise stated)

	1950	1955	1960		1970	1980	1990	2000
Moldings and extrusions[2]	.677	1.166	1.809	L	3.42	5.25	7.86	10.88
				M	4.59	8.78	15.34	25.60
				H	6.54	15.52	32.28	64.19
Output of durable goods[3] ($ 1960 bil.)	73.9	95.0	96.7	L	120	150	199	259
				M	153	228	341	512
				H	187	320	538	917
Pounds/$ 1960 thous.	90	122	187	L	285	350	395	420
				M	300	385	450	500
				H	350	485	600	700
Bondings and adhesives[4]	.257	.415	.566	L	.742	.972	1.20	1.56
				M	1.30	1.840	2.90	4.63
				H	1.740	3.710	7.53	16.08
New and maintenance construction[5] ($ 1960 bil.)	58.6	72.8	76.2	L	92.7	113	135	172
				M	120.3	166	234	348
				H	152.4	241	388	687
Pounds/$ 1960 thous.	4.4	5.7	7.4	L	8.0	8.6	8.9	9.1
				M	9.4	11.1	12.4	13.3
				H	11.4	15.4	19.4	23.4
Film for packaging[6]	.30	.52	.71	L	1.18	1.83	2.35	2.91
				M	1.35	2.35	3.43	4.80
				H	1.91	4.14	7.59	13.32
Sheeting and film, excluding packaging[7]	.170	.189	.419	L	.611	.844	1.05	1.32
				M	.851	1.380	1.90	2.60
				H	1.155	2.221	3.62	5.66
Domestic consumption of man-made fibers[8]	1.20	1.53	1.78	L	1.91	2.22	2.56	2.96
				M	2.66	3.63	4.56	5.85
				H	3.61	5.84	8.73	12.73
Sheeting and film as per cent of man-made fibers	14	12.3	23.5		32.0	38.0	41.5	44.5

Table A17–1 (cont'd)

(Billion pounds, unless otherwise stated)

	1950	1955	1960		1970	1980	1990	2000
Reinforced plastics[9]	n.a.	.064	.186	L	.508	1.00	1.69	2.54
				M	.586	1.38	2.81	5.23
				H	.896	2.52	5.88	12.38
Purchases of consumer durable goods[10] ($ 1960 bil.)	34.0	42.0	44.3	L	60.5	83.6	114	151
				M	65.1	98.6	148	218
				H	74.7	126	210	344
Pounds/$ 1960 thous.	n.a.	1.5	4.2	L	8.4	12.0	14.8	16.8
				M	9.0	14.0	19.0	24.0
				H	12.0	20.0	28.0	36.0
Flooring[11]	.150	.352	.431	L	.700	.995	1.14	1.51
				M	1.013	1.527	2.26	3.58
				H	1.418	2.517	4.41	8.10
Residential and large building construction[5] ($ 1960 bil.)	27.3	34.5	36.0	L	43.5	53.2	61.5	80.2
				M	60.4	80.8	114	177
				H	80.9	124	196	360
Pounds/$ 1960 thous.	5.4	10.1	12.0	L	16.1	17.8	18.6	18.8
				M	16.8	18.9	19.8	20.2
				H	17.5	20.3	22.5	22.5
Protective coatings[12]	.639	.918	1.010	L	.938	.892	1.015	1.178
				M	1.063	1.211	1.573	2.140
				H	1.303	1.760	2.784	4.498
Textile treating and coating[13]	.82	.116	.115	L	.164	.208	.260	.321
				M	.185	.264	.359	.493
				H	.210	.332	.524	.823
Total fiber use[14]	5.94	6.60	7.08	L	8.21	9.47	10.82	12.36
				M	9.25	12.01	14.94	18.97
				H	10.49	15.10	21.85	31.64
Pounds of resin/hundred pounds of fiber	1.4	1.8	1.6		2.0	2.2	2.4	2.6
Total (Medium only)	–	–	5.240		–	18.73	–	49.07
Synthetic resin use in all markets (from Table A17–4) (Medium only)	–	–	6.142		–	24.16	–	66.00
Major markets as per cent of total use	–	–	84.8		–	77.5	–	74.3

Table A17–1 (cont'd)

1. Source of historical data is the annual reports of the U.S. Tariff Commission, *Synthetic Organic Chemicals, United States Production and Sales*. Production is measured on a "dry basis," i.e., total weight of the material including resin, plasticizers, fillers, etc., but excluding liquids; production of vinyl resins is measured in resin content. Historical data on market totals are aggregated from breakdowns of individual resin materials "by classes and uses," hence exclude resins for which statistics in a given market are not available. Allowance is made in the projections for the resulting understatements, which are small in all cases.

2. Excludes alkyd, urea, and melamine moldings and extrusions among others. The projection is based, in the final analysis, on trends in the growth of plastic moldings and extrusions in several more detailed end-uses, and in the relationship of the aggregate of these to the output of durable goods. This analysis yields a year–2000 output per dollar of durable goods production that is roughly 2½ times the 1960 ratio. Since, at the same time, durables output is projected to increase nearly fivefold, the consequent growth in plastic moldings and extrusions over the four decades is approximately thirteen times. A similar calculation for 1980 was adjusted to yield a smoother line between 1950, 1960, and 2000, and all the remaining benchmark years are results of interpolation, with the rate of growth in the plastics durable coefficient assumed to decline gradually. Some of the underlying detail is shown in Table A17–2, to illustrate the methods used.

3. From Table A1–14.

4. Includes only phenolics, urea and melamines, and polyvinyl acetate. The projection is based upon the growth in construction, on the grounds that the major use of this type of plastic material is in the production of plywood and of other construction materials, for laminating, impregnating, or other treatment (e.g., thermal insulation). The mechanics of the projection consist in taking the increase in the rate of plywood use per dollar of construction (Table A4–9) as a reference series for the projection of bondings and adhesives, at least in the Low and Medium projections, in the sense that the Low projection equals that growth rate and the Medium slightly exceeds it. In the High projection it is assumed that other applications will show a substantially greater growth than those in construction, and the ratio is therefore assumed to rise by four percentage points per decade.

5. From Table A4–3.

6. From Table A7–10. Excludes small amounts of styrene copolymers. Includes cellophane, which is not further considered in these tables.

7. Polyethylene and polyvinyl chloride only. Roughly three-fourths of sheeting and film use (other than for packaging) is in applications that compete directly with those of synthetic fibers. The projection is, therefore, cast in terms of the relationship to that group. The increase in the ratio is not as drastic as it would have been on a straight extension of the experience during the last five years. On the other hand, even though many uses can now be considered to have entered a phase of "maturity," i.e., slower growth, there are others which have hardly scratched the surface, in both household furnishings and apparel. This is the consideration underlying the projected near-doubling in the relationship between 1960 and 2000.

8. Sum of rayon and acetate and other man-made fiber consumption (actual weight), from Table A3–3.

9. Sales of all reinforced plastics. Reinforced plastics have most diversified use: in transportation (automotive, water), appliances, electrical and other consumer products, construction (panels), aircraft and missiles, and pipes, tanks, ducts, and similar items. At the moment, consumer durables appear to dominate the use pattern and have therefore been utilized as the reference series. Motor vehicles and construction are by all odds the most promising future fields of application, because of features of weight saving and ease of maintenance, tooling, repair, etc. Price is the major drawback; building codes and tradition are a different type of obstacle in construction. Given the diversity of uses, the relationship to the reference series has been allowed to increase significantly throughout the period, as it has done during the fifties. In the Medium projection, no radical breakthrough in construction is assumed, with the slow decline in rate of growth in such uses as boat-building to be offset by greater use in other fields (motor vehicles above all).

10. From Table A1–14.

11. Excludes certain plastic tiles (polystyrene), but includes some coumarone-indene and petroleum resins in applications other than asphalt tile. Resulting errors believed to be offsetting.

The projection is tied, as one would expect, to construction activity and is based upon further growth in the share taken by this material, which in 1960 was estimated to account for nearly 40% of all flooring. It is assumed that asphalt felt base and linoleum flooring above all will lose out to plastic flooring during the balance of the century, so that the share of the former will be reduced to negligible proportions. The three projection levels assume different competitive strengths for the other materials (such as rubber tile, wooden floors, etc.), but all of them project continuing gains for plastics.

12. From Table A17–12.

13. Excludes polystyrene (over 50% of total shown in 1960), phenolics, and other thermosetting resins, because no historical data are available. Includes small amounts of polyvinyl chloride used in treatment and coating of paper. Figure for 1950 actually 1951.

Chemical treatment of fibers is projected to continue at increasing rates compared to total fiber use, which is the reference series applied. Flame-proofing, rot- and mildew-proofing, shrink-proofing, increasing water repellancy and crease and wrinkle resistance should all gain in acceptance, although the rather slow increases during the fifties (possibly the result of poor statistics) commend caution. As total use is quite small, errors of judgment here are not especially significant.

14. From Table A3–2; measured in cotton equivalents.

TABLE A17–2. Major End-Uses of Synthetic Moldings and Extrusions, 1958 and 2000[1]

(Million pounds)

End-use category	Phenolic		Polystyrene		Polyethylene		Polyvinyl		Cellulosic		Other		Total		Percentage share	
	1958	2000	1958	2000	1958	2000	1958	2000	1958	2000	1958	2000	1958	2000	1958	2000
Housewares, toys, etc.	27	160	93	1,500	112	2,270	9	450	n.a.	–	45	800	286	5,180	27	27
Radio, TV, appliances, etc.	37	450	89	1,620	n.a.	2,270	35	360	n.a.	–	n.a.	n.e.	161	4,700	15	24
Automotive	10	70	n.a.	n.a.	n.a.	140	n.a.	–	50	250	n.a.	n.e.	60	460	6	2
Bottles, closures, etc.	12	60	67	1,000	26	3,000	n.a.	440	n.a.	–	18	850	123	4,910	12	25
Electronics	75	660	n.a.	n.e.	87	900	90	580	n.a.	–	n.a.	n.e.	252	2,000	24	10
Moldings and profiles	n.a.	n.e.	n.a.	n.e.	n.a.	n.e.	80	580	n.a.	–	n.a.	n.e.	80	580	7	4
Pipe and tile	n.a.	n.e.	33	250	52	400	6	880	n.a.	–	n.a.	n.e.	91	1,530	9	8
Total of above	161	1,400	282	4,370	280	8,980	220	2,710	50	250	63	1,650	1,053	19,370	100	100
Grand total[2]	167	1,500	476	6,500	280	10,000	234	2,900	94	450	63	2,680	1,314	24,030	–	–
Percentage shares	13	6	36	27	21	42	18	12	7	2	5	11	100	100	–	–

N.a.—not available; n.e.—not estimated.

1. This table illustrates, to a limited degree, the kinds of considerations and statistical speculation that went into the projections of the several pieces going to make up the projections of the synthetics. Only the end results are shown here. The 1958 data are derived principally from figures published for that year in the *Oil, Paint and Drug Reporter's* "Chemical Forecast for 1964," supplemented by guesses based upon other scraps of information and related to the data published by the U.S. Tariff Commission. The projections are derived from the growth trends in the reference series, on the one hand, and assumptions as to the role of plastics in each of them. Such reference series are, for example, personal consumption expenditures on tableware and utensils and books, toys, etc., for projecting plastics use in the first category; personal consumption expenditures on household appli-

ances for projecting plastics use for radio, TV, etc. By evaluating the possible spread of plastics in each of these fields and compounding this with the growth shown by the reference series, we evolved certain orders of magnitude. This procedure accounts for the seeming precision, which is not, of course, commensurate with the precision of the concepts but is only a mechanical product of the calculations. In Table A17-1, the aggregates here derived are related to an aggregate reference series, and it is the relationship between the two in the years 1960 and 2000 that sets the tone for the entire projection.

2. Adjusted to include uses not shown separately and resins not covered. These adjustments are made partly on the basis of current data and partly to compensate for future developments (reflected also in the major boost in the 2000 figure for "other" resins materials).

TABLE A17–3.   Projected Shares of Selected Resin Materials in Major Markets[1]

(Per cent)

Market	1950	1955	1960	1970	1980	1990	2000
Moldings and extrusions[2]	100.0	100.0	100.0	100.0	100.0	100.0	100.0
Cellulosics	12.1	7.9	5.0	3.2	1.8	1.2	1.0
Phenolics	32.8	18.9	11.4	7.4	5.7	4.5	4.3
Polystyrene	38.4	36.3	40.5	35.0	31.4	30.6	29.5
Polyolefins[3]	–	15.9	20.0	29.0	34.5	38.0	39.5
Vinyls	16.7	16.6	17.6	15.0	14.0	13.0	13.0
Miscellaneous[4]	–	4.4	5.5	10.4	12.6	12.7	12.7
Bondings and adhesives[5]	100.0	100.0	100.0	100.0	100.0	100.0	100.0
Phenolics	60.7	60.0	58.7	52.5	50.0	50.0	50.0
Urea and melamine	33.5	30.8	28.1	27.0	24.5	21.0	19.5
Polyvinyl acetate	5.8	9.2	13.2	20.5	25.5	29.0	30.5
Film for packaging[6]	100.0	100.0	100.0	100.0	100.0	100.0	100.0
Cellophane	87.7	69.5	62	50	40	32.5	30
Polyolefins	12.3	30.5	38	50	60	67.5	70
Sheeting and film, excluding packaging[7]	100.0	100.0	100.0	100.0	100.0	100.0	100.0
Polyolefins[8]	–	24.9	41.5	55	67	75	75
Polyvinyl chloride	100	75.1	58.5	45	33	25	25
Reinforced plastics[8]	–	100.0	100.0	100.0	100.0	100.0	100.0
Polyesters	–	77	82	75	67	59	51
Other[9]	–	23	18	25	33	41	49
Flooring[10]	100.0	100.0	100.0	100.0	100.0	100.0	100.0
Coumarone-indene and petroleum resins	95	83	62	42	33	33	33
Polyvinyl chloride	5	17	38	58	67	67	67
Protective coatings[11]	100.0	100.0	100.0	100.0	100.0	100.0	100.0
Alkyds	64	59	54.0	45.0	38.5	35.5	35
Polystyrenes	4	11	7.9	5.8	4.8	4.4	4
Urea and melamines	4	4	4.4	4.0	4.0	4.0	4
Other[12]	28	26	33.7	45.2	52.7	56.1	57
Of which miscellaneous only	(6)	(10)	(16)	(32)	(40)	(47)	(50)
Textile treating and coating[13]	100.0	100.0	100.0	100.0	100.0	100.0	100.0
Urea and melamines	42	41	39	40	40	40	40
Polyvinyl chloride	58	59	61	60	60	60	60

Table A17–3 (cont'd)

1. Historical data based on U.S. Tariff Commission, *Synthetic Organic Chemicals, United States Production and Sales*. For make-up of individual series, see footnotes to Table A17–1. While percentages add up to 100, the totals themselves (to which they add) are not all-inclusive, i.e., in most instances resins not listed also have a (small) share of the particular end-use market. The mechanics (as opposed to the rationale) of setting rates of change may be easily inferred from the sequence of the figures in each series, except for the figures for polystyrene in moldings, which are obtained as a residual.

2. General comparison may be made with the results of Table A17–2. The data shown here are smoothed to yield a more manageable group of series, but the orders of magnitude shown in Table A17–2 are maintained.

3. Includes, besides polyethylene, the newer polymers of propylene, formaldehyde, etc. Data for 1950 not available, but data for 1951 suggest that polyolefin use was negligible.

4. Estimated moldings use of "miscellaneous" group, which contains mainly acrylic, polyamide, toluenesulfonamide, and other newer resins.

5. Phenolics, though recently losing ground to polyvinyl acetate in miscellaneous minor applications, are not assumed to drop below 50%, owing to their place in plywood manufacture, insulation, and foundry use (shell casting). Urea and melamine assumed to lose ground to polyvinyl acetate.

6. From Table A7–10. Petroleum based assumed to be all polyolefins.

7. Polystyrene not considered, since no data available. Polyvinyl chloride has been under growing competitive pressure from polyethylene, as price of the latter has been reduced to approach that of polyvinyl chloride (which currently is still lower). Growing invasion into traditional uses of polyvinyl chloride plus development of new fields, especially in agriculture and construction, seems to argue for rapid and substantial relative gains by polyethylene.

8. Polyesters practically monopolize the field today, owing to low price and easy workability. Most polyesters, however, are inflammable and suffer from poor water and weather resistance. New uses, therefore, might well favor increased reliance on other resins.

9. Mainly epoxies and methamylates.

10. Expansion in use of asphalt tile, based principally upon coumarone-indene, appears to have been stopped by the newer resins (polyvinyl chloride and rubber tile). This trend, which seems to have more than doubled the share of the vinyls between 1955 and 1960, is projected to moderate, with a stable relationship assumed to exist from 1980 to 2000, largely because of the price advantages of the asphalt type. Data shown for 1950 refer to 1951.

11. The gradual decline in the alkyd-based paints is projected to continue, but at a less rapid rate, in favor of other new types that have shown more dynamic growth in the past decade and are aggregated under "miscellaneous" (consisting principally of phenolics and vinyl). There is little doubt that the "miscellaneous" group base figure in 1960 is only a very rough approximation and that its rapid relative growth here projected is equally highly conjectural.

12. Includes acetates, phenolics, vinyl chloride, and others.

13. No change is anticipated in the historic pattern in which the market is shared. Data in 1950 column refer to 1951.

TABLE A17–4.   Projected Synthetic Resin Materials, by Major Groups of Resins[1]

(Billion pounds)

	1950	1955	1960		1970	1980	1990	2000
Phenolic and other tar acid resins:								
				L	.253	.299	.354	.468
Moldings	.222	.220	.207	M	.340	.500	.691	1.100
				H	.484	.885	1.450	2.760
				L	.389	.486	.605	.780
Bondings and adhesives	.156	.249	.334	M	.593	.920	1.450	2.320
				H	.914	1.850	3.860	8.040
				L	.642	.785	.959	1.25
All major markets	.378	.469	.541	M	.933	1.420	2.141	3.42
				H	1.40	2.735	5.310	10.80
				L	.770	.942	1.15	1.50
Total[2]	.451	.563	.651	M	1.120	1.700	2.57	4.10
				H	1.680	3.280	6.37	12.96
Alkyd resins:								
				L	.422	.343	.360	.412
Protective coatings	n.a.	.537	.526	M	.478	.466	.558	.749
				H	.586	.678	.988	1.57
				L	.460	.388	.421	.499
Total[3]	.402	.543	.552	M	.521	.527	.653	.906
				H	.639	.766	1.156	1.900
Styrene resins:								
				L	1.20	1.65	2.40	3.21
Moldings	.260	.423	.731	M	1.61	2.76	4.70	7.55
				H	2.29	4.87	9.88	18.94
				L	.054	.043	.047	.047
Protective coatings	.026	.103	.077	M	.062	.058	.069	.086
				H	.076	.084	.122	.180
				L	1.25	1.69	2.45	3.26
All major markets	.286	.526	.808	M	1.67	2.82	4.77	7.64
				H	2.37	4.95	10.00	19.12
				L	1.68	2.28	3.31	4.40
Total[4]	.355	.619	1.062	M	2.25	3.81	6.44	10.31
				H	3.20	6.68	13.50	25.81
Polyester resins:								
				L	.381	.672	.995	1.29
Reinforced plastics	n.a.	.049	.153	M	.440	.925	1.66	2.67
				H	.672	1.69	3.47	6.32
				L	.572	1.01	1.49	1.94
Total[5]	n.a.	.062	.190	M	.660	1.39	2.49	4.00
				H	1.01	2.53	5.20	9.47
Polyethylene, other olefins:								
				L	.53	.92	1.18	1.46
Film for packaging[6]	.04	.160	.270	M	.68	1.41	2.32	3.36
				H	1.15	3.31	6.64	11.99
				L	.336	.565	.788	.990
Film for other uses[7]	n.a.	.047	.174	M	.468	.925	1.430	1.950
				H	.635	1.490	2.710	4.200
				L	.992	1.81	2.99	4.30
Moldings and extrusions	n.a.	.185	.361	M	1.33	3.03	5.83	10.11
				H	1.90	5.35	12.27	25.59
				L	1.86	3.20	4.95	6.71
All major markets	n.a.	.392	.805	M	2.48	5.34	9.57	15.39
				H	4.28	10.15	21.66	41.81
				L	2.66	4.27	6.43	8.75
Total[8]	.055	.402	1.337	M	3.55	6.96	12.44	20.04
				H	5.26	13.20	28.12	54.33

Table A17–4 (cont'd)

(Billion pounds)

	1950	1955	1960		1970	1980	1990	2000
Urea and melamine resins:								
Bondings and adhesives	.079	.128	.159	L	.200	.238	.252	.304
				M	.305	.451	.609	.903
				H	.470	.909	1.581	3.136
Textile treatment and coatings	.034	.048	.045	L	.066	.083	.104	.128
				M	.074	.106	.144	.197
				H	.087	.133	.210	.329
Protective coatings	.025	.039	.043	L	.037	.036	.040	.047
				M	.042	.048	.063	.086
				H	.052	.070	.111	.180
All major markets	.138	.214	.245	L	.303	.357	.396	.479
				M	.421	.605	.816	1.186
				H	.609	1.112	1.902	3.645
Total[9]	.237	.328	.399	L	.530	.660	.772	.982
				M	.737	1.119	1.591	2.431
				H	1.066	2.057	3.709	7.472
Vinyl and vinyl copolymer resins:								
Moldings and extrusions	.113	.194	.319	L	.513	.735	1.020	1.410
				M	.688	1.230	1.990	3.330
				H	.982	2.170	4.200	8.340
Bondings and adhesives	.015	.038	.075	L	.152	.248	.348	.476
				M	.232	.469	.841	1.412
				H	.357	.946	2.180	4.900
Film and sheeting (not for packaging)	.182	.142	.245	L	.275	.278	.262	.330
				M	.383	.455	.475	.650
				H	.520	.733	.905	1.400
Textile and paper treatment and coating	.046	.068	.070	L	.098	.125	.156	.193
				M	.111	.158	.215	.296
				H	.126	.199	..314	.494
Floor tile	.025	.059	.166	L	.406	.667	.764	1.010
				M	.588	1.020	1.510	2.400
				H	.822	1.690	2.950	5.430
All major markets	n.a.	.504	.875	L	1.44	2.05	2.55	3.42
				M	2.00	3.33	5.03	8.09
				H	2.81	5.74	10.55	20.56
Total[10]	n.a.	.703	1.203	L	2.02	2.87	3.57	4.79
				M	2.80	4.66	7.04	11.33
				H	3.93	8.04	14.77	28.78
Coumarone-indene and petroleum polymer resins, total (flooring)	.143	.293	.265	L	.294	.328	.376	.498
				M	.425	.504	.746	1.18
				H	.596	.830	1.450	2.670
Other resins:[11]								
Molding materials	n.a.	.052	.100	L	.356	.662	.998	1.38
				M	.477	1.110	1.950	3.25
				H	.681	1.960	4.100	8.15
Protective coatings	n.a.	.085	.156	L	.300	.357	.477	.589
				M	.340	.484	.739	1.07
				H	.417	.704	1.310	2.25
Reinforced plastics	n.a.	.015	.033	L	.127	.331	.692	1.24
				M	.146	.455	1.150	2.56
				H	.224	.832	2.410	6.07
All major markets	n.a.	.152	.289	L	.783	1.35	2.17	3.22
				M	.963	2.05	3.84	6.88
				H	1.322	3.50	7.82	16.47

Table A17–4 (cont'd)

(Billion pounds)

	1950	1955	1960		1970	1980	1990	2000
Total [12]	.139	.225	.479	L	1.33	2.30	3.69	5.47
				M	1.64	3.49	6.53	11.70
				H	2.25	5.95	13.29	28.00
Grand total [13]	2.151	3.739	6.142	L	10.32	15.05	21.21	28.83
				M	13.70	24.16	40.50	66.00
				H	19.63	43.33	87.56	171.39

1. Based upon Tables A17–1 and A17–3. Projected uses in major markets allocated to specific groups of resins on basis of projected market shares. Major market totals raised to assumed total use, as specified under individual items. Each of the groups includes a number of mixtures of different resins.

Because of rounding at various stages, items may not add exactly to totals shown.

2. 20% above use in major markets, based upon past experience. Other uses include protective coatings, reinforced plastics, textile treating, and coatings.

3. 5% above use in major markets in 1960, 9% in 1970, and so on to 21% in 2000, to reflect expected increases in other uses (e.g., moldings and extrusions) relative to protective coatings, the dominant current market.

4. 35% above use in major markets throughout the projection period, in line with past experience. No disproportionate growth in minor uses is anticipated, as exports are likely to decline and new uses (especially foam in construction) to grow in a balancing development.

5. 50% above use in reinforced plastics. The reinforced plastics figure for 1955 is a rough estimate; the relationship between total and reinforced plastics use has fluctuated considerably in the past few years. Miscellaneous use as foam and molding powder should grow no less rapidly than reinforced plastics use.

6. From Table A7–10.

7. Division between end-uses of film in historical data is based upon types of film produced, to extent known, and is somewhat arbitrary. In securing distribution of physical production by end-uses, the available data on value of shipments were utilized. No reasonably reliable data are available for any sequence of years.

8. Polyethylene has had a major export market that needs to be considered in the projection. This market is expected to decline sharply in the future, as production, especially in Europe, increases. However, other—currently minor—applications, such as in protective coatings, should soften the impact and after 1980 in fact balance the loss of export markets.

It has been assumed, therefore, that other markets will gradually decline in importance through 1980 and that total use, which has been between 50 and 60% above use in major markets in the past few years, will decline in 1970 to 43% and in 1980 and thereafter to 30% above major market use.

9. Major markets account for barely one-half of the total end-use consumption of this resin group and are well established, i.e., not fast expanding, a condition that is likely to become even more pronounced in the future. Consequently, minor uses are expected to grow disproportionately fast, and major market totals have been raised by 10 percentage points every ten years, beginning with a rounded 1.65 ratio in 1960, to reflect this expectation.

10. Foam, water based paints, metal coatings are some of the minor uses. None is expected to affect the use pattern now existing in this well established material. Total use is thus projected to exceed major market totals by a constant percentage throughout the period, namely, 40%, as observed in the recent past.

11. Includes polymethane and other polyethers, acrylates, epoxies, polyamide (nylon), silicones, acetal resin, fluorocarbons, etc. The data for 1960 given in the subgroupings are the result of distributing unallocated totals on the basis of distributed data for earlier years and spotty indications of uses in 1960. The figure for protective coatings includes modified resins.

12. Projected to exceed major market totals by 70% throughout the period, in accordance with experience in recent years and absence of indications to the contrary.

13. 1950 and 1955 totals are not the sum of the individual items above but the aggregate production figure as published by the U.S. Tariff Commission. The sum of the items in both years is smaller (by some 25% in 1950 but by only 2% in 1955) owing to the fact that for the earlier years the Tariff Commission totals contain a larger number of resins that for those years are not as yet individually listed by type and are therefore not covered in the itemized lines of this tabulation. ("Other resins" refers only to resins itemized in footnote 11.)

TABLE A17–5. Projected Monomers and Other Organic Intermediates Used in Synthetic Resin Manufacture[1]

(Billion pounds)

	1950	1955	1960		1970	1980	1990	2000
Phenolic and other tar acid resins: [2]								
Use of:								
				L	.801	1.09	1.33	1.74
Formaldehyde (37% solution) [2]	.289	.445	.597	M	1.165	1.97	2.98	4.76
				H	1.747	3.80	7.39	15.03
Per pound of resin (lb.)	.70	.75	.92		1.04	1.16	1.16	1.16
				L	.439	.537	.656	.855
Phenol [2]	.257	.321	.370	M	.638	.969	1.465	2.337
				H	.958	1.870	3.631	7.387
Phthalic alkyd resins:								
				L	.384	.323	.352	.417
Output [3]	.333	.456	.464	M	.435	.440	.545	.756
				H	.534	.640	.965	1.586
Use of:								
				L	.134	.113	.123	.146
Phthalic anhydride [4]	.117	.160	.162	M	.152	.154	.191	.265
				H	.187	.224	.338	.555
				L	.054	.045	.049	.058
Pentaerythritol [5]	.036	.061	.065	M	.061	.062	.076	.106
				H	.075	.090	.135	.222
Styrene resins: [6]								
				L	1.36	1.75	2.48	3.22
Styrene (monomer)	.308	.530	.903	M	1.82	2.93	4.83	7.52
				H	2.59	5.14	10.12	18.84
Per pound of resin (lb.)	.87	.86	.85		.81	.77	.75	.73
Polyester resins: [7]								
Use of:								
				L	.086	.131	.194	.252
Phthalic anhydride	.001	.012	.032	M	.099	.180	.323	.520
				H	.151	.329	.677	1.23
Per pound of resin (lb.)	.30	.20	.17		.15	.13	.13	.13
				L	.200	.353	.522	.679
Styrene (monomer)	.002	.022	.066	M	.231	.486	.871	1.400
				H	.353	.866	1.820	3.320
Polyolefins: [8]								
Share of (%):								
Polypropylene	–	–	1.7		21.2	30.7	38.2	43.5
Polyethylene	100	100	98.3		78.8	69.3	61.8	56.5
Use of: [9]								
				L	.563	1.31	2.46	3.81
Propylene (99+ %)	–	–	.023	M	.752	2.14	4.75	8.72
				H	1.12	4.05	10.74	23.63
				L	2.09	2.95	3.97	4.94
Ethylene (99+ %)	.055	.402	1.314	M	2.79	4.82	7.69	11.32
				H	4.14	9.15	17.38	30.70
Urea and melamine resins: [10]								
Use of:								
				L	.784	1.02	1.24	1.63
Formaldehyde (37% solution)	.228	.407	.567	M	1.091	1.72	2.55	4.04
				H	1.578	3.17	5.93	12.40
Per pound of resin (lb.)	1.04	1.24	1.42		1.48	1.54	1.60	1.66

Table A17–5 (cont'd)

(Billion pounds)

	1950	1955	1960		1970	1980	1990	2000
Vinyl resins: [11]								
Use of:								
Vinyl chloride (monomer)	.250	.529	.930	L	1.52	2.11	2.58	3.42
				M	2.11	3.43	5.08	8.08
				H	2.96	5.91	10.66	20.52
Per cent of all vinyls	65.6	75.2	77.3		75.2	73.5	72.2	71.3
Vinyl acetate	n.a.	.134	.247	L	.444	.663	.850	1.15
				M	.616	1.076	1.676	2.73
				H	.865	1.857	3.515	6.94
Per cent of all vinyls	n.a.	19.1	20.5		22.0	23.1	23.8	24.1
Phthalic anhydride (via phthalic ester plasticizers)	.070	.104	.153	L	.190	.210	.225	.287
				M	.263	.340	.444	.680
				H	.369	.587	.931	1.727
Per cent of all vinyls	18.4	14.8	12.7		9.4	7.3	6.3	6.0
Other resins:								
Use of propylene in epoxies, polyurethanes, and other [12]	–	–	.129	L	.359	.621	.996	1.48
				M	.443	.942	1.763	3.16
				H	.608	1.606	3.588	7.56

1. Data in this table calculated by multiplying estimated key material requirements per pound of resin by production of pertinent resin classes as projected in Table A17-4. It should be noted at the outset that the synthetic resins projected "by type" in Table A17-4 are really groups of resins generally using the same class of raw materials, but in differing combinations (straight polymers, copolymers, condensation products, etc.). Since raw material requirements can be determined precisely only for individual synthetic materials, each with its own chemical composition, and since the number of such individual synthetics is virtually infinite (one is tempted to say: a different compound for each use!), the raw materials figures derived on the basis of group outputs are rough approximations only. They also tend to understate true requirements by virtue of the omission of particular resins from consideration.

2. Coefficients of .57 pounds of phenol and .92 pounds (1960) to 1.16 pounds (1980) of formaldehyde per pound of resin based on following considerations:

Bakelite, resinox, crystallin, fiberlon, durex, haveg, catalin, formica, indur are only a fraction of the variety of phenolic and other tar acid resins, each with its own composition. Even materials of the same trade name may vary in chemical composition. But establishment of the general order of magnitude of materials requirements is possible from scattered sources of information.

The groups of resins included under "phenolics" are copolymers of a "phenolic body" and an "aldehyde." The most frequently used raw materials are phenol and formaldehyde. Although other combinations are also included in the group (e.g., phenol-furfural, phenol-glycerol, cresylic acid-formaldehyde, and resorcinol-formaldehyde), phenol or formaldehyde is almost always one of the constituents, and in over 85% of the total poundage involved, both materials are present in the combination. The exact amount of the two materials required per pound of resin cannot be established because of the large variety of resins included and because of lack of continuous data on end-use distribution of either of the two materials. On the other hand, a rough approxi-

mation of the relative needs of phenol and formaldehyde can be obtained from coefficients implied by aggregate phenolic resin production and the estimated share of the two materials in that application in 1958 (Cf. *Oil, Paint and Drug Reporter,* "Chemical Forecast for 1964," pp. 48 and 56). On this basis, .8 pounds of formaldehyde (37% basis) and .57 pounds of phenol appear required to make one pound of phenolic resins on the average. This is consistent with Shreve's figures for "a typical phenolic molding powder" (R. Norris Shreve, *Chemical Process Industries,* p. 779 [McGraw-Hill, 1956]), which are .73 pounds of formaldehyde and .42 pounds of phenol. Since moldings use larger quantities of fillers and plasticizers in addition to the basic constituents than do bonding resins, average requirements for all phenolic resins should be above the requirements that prevail for molding compounds. Excluding the wood flour input, for example, one pound of resin would require 1.27 pounds of formaldehyde and .73 pounds of phenol. Because of the continued decrease of the share of moldings assumed through 1980, formaldehyde requirements per pound of resin are projected to rise from .92 to 1.16 by 1980. This also takes into account the hexamethylene tetramine requirement, most of which is used in phenol (see W. L. Faith, Donald B. Keyes, Ronald L. Clark, *Industrial Chemicals, 2nd Ed.* p. 419 [New York: John Wiley & Sons, 1957]). Phenol requirements are not expected to be affected by the change, mainly because phenol coefficients have shown remarkable stability in the past despite changes in production mix.

3. This series represents only 83.5% of all alkyd resins, as all non-phthalic alkyds are excluded. The past relationship between all and phthalic alkyd resins is remarkably steady (varying between a high of 84.5% and a low of 82.7% between 1950 and 1960) and has therefore been assumed for the projections. Basic components from which alkyd resins are condensed (excluding such natural oils as rosin) are a dicarboxylic acid (most important: phthalic and maleic anhydride) and a polyhydric alcohol (ethylene glycol, glycerol, pentaerythritol or sorbitol). Although synthetic resins are all-important consumers of these materials, maleic anhydride and

Table A17–5 (cont'd)

glycerol are not considered here because of their negligible importance for the resources they in turn use (maleic anhydride uses 3%–4% of annual benzene output; synthetic glycerine uses 3%–4% of propylene output). In the case of glycols, in turn, other applications, such as antifreeze, overshadow the use in synthetics. That leaves only phthalic anhydride and pentaerythritol to consider.

4. By volume, phthalic anhydride (hereafter referred to as "p.a.") is the most important raw material of alkyd resins. On the basis of various sources (e.g., *Industrial Chemicals*, p. 613; Stanford Research Institute *Chemical Economics Newsletter*, March 1960; and *Chemical Week*, Dec. 10, 1960) an average of .35 pounds of p.a. is needed to produce one pound of phthalic alkyd resin. Historical data indicate no change in the p.a. consumption ratio by alkyds over the period 1950–60. Nor do its two potential competitors, terephthalic and isophthalic acid (made from xylene) represent a significant threat, because of their much higher price. Consequently p.a. consumption in alkyd resins is projected as 35% of phthalic alkyd output throughout the period.

5. Pentaerythritol (hereafter referred to as "p.e.") is used in alkyd and polyester resins, in plasticizers, and in the upgrading of drying oils, in competition with glycerol, glycols, sorbitol, etc. Since the bulk of p.e. output is consumed in the manufacture of phthalic alkyd resins, it is here related to the production of phthalic alkyds. Despite the relatively higher rates of increase of other applications (e.g., polyesters, plasticizers), p.e. use per pound of phthalic alkyd resin shows no sign of rise since 1953 (fluctuating between .13 and .15 pounds). The process of substitution of p.e. for glycerol, which is responsible for the rapid rise of p.e. following World War II, seems to have come to an end, either as a result of the price stability of synthetic glycerine (compared to by-product glycerin) or as a result of countervailing losses of p.e. to other competitors, e.g. sorbitol. It is projected as 14%—the 1953–59 average—of phthalic alkyd resin output.

6. Although many organic chemicals are used in the manufacture of styrene resins (e.g., butadiene, acrylonitrile, phthalic anhydride, glycerol, etc.), only the monomer styrene is of quantitative significance. Because of the inclusion of several copolymers along with polystyrene in the styrene resin group, the establishment of styrene requirements runs into considerable difficulty. Reasoning from technical discussions in *Industrial Chemicals* and in George S. Brady, *Materials Handbook*, Eighth Ed. (McGraw-Hill, 1956) and from the 1960 distribution of styrene (monomer) by end-uses, one can derive average styrene requirements for polystyrene and two major copolymer groups, which when applied to the production of these groups (Manufacturing Chemists' Association, *Chemical Statistics Handbook*, 5th edition, p. 229) can be reconciled with total monomer output during the years 1950 through 1959. The coefficients used are:

1.00 for polystyrene (5% loss, offset by additives)
.70 for styrene-butadiene
.35 for other styrene resins

.85 average for current product mix

The styrene-butadiene (latex, foam) copolymer is expected to increase at a high rate relative to straight polystyrene. Consequently, average styrene needs per pound of resin are projected to decrease by .04 pounds every ten years from the starting point of .85 pounds in 1960 through 1980, and half as fast thereafter.

7. Though currently not significant consumers of any synthetic intermediates, polyester resins through

their high rate of projected growth (see Table A17–3) are expected to exert a growing influence on demand for phthalic anhydride and styrene. Consequently, the implications of polyester projections for these two intermediates are presented. The coefficient of .35 pounds of styrene per pound of polyester is derived together with the coefficients for styrene resins described above. The use of phthalic anhydride appears to have continuously declined, from .30 pounds per pound of resin to .17 pounds in 1960. It is therefore projected to decline further, but far more slowly to .13 by 1980, remaining constant thereafter. (See especially *Chemical Economics Newsletter*, March 1960.)

The precarious nature of these assumptions and averages must be clearly understood. Polyesters embrace a large variety of combinations, mostly but not always containing a phthalate and styrene. For example, dacron, a polyester fiber, is the condensation product of dimethyl terephthalate (made from terephthalic acid rather than phthalic anhydride) and ethylene glycol. Furthermore, there are many substitutes (e.g. maleic anhydride) which might be favored in the future as raw materials for polyester plastics. The degree of replacement is unpredictable; hence one must rely on more or less arbitrary assumptions.

8. The raw materials problem connected with polyolefins arises from difficulties not of estimating input coefficients (one pound of high purity, 99+ % monomer is required to produce one pound of each polymer) but of predicting the share of polypropylene—and possibly even newer polyolefins—versus polyethylene in the total. As late as 1958, polypropylene was not produced commercially; its output in 1960 was 41 million pounds, with expectations of sharp increases over the years to come. The material offers possibilities in all applications in which polyethylene is now used, including fibers.

In these projections it is assumed that the share of polypropylene will increase at the same rate within polyolefin groups as the share of polyethylene increased within molding and extrusion plastics during the fifties. Since polyolefins themselves are a fast-growing resin group, such assumption results in a steep projection for polypropylene. The share of polyethylene among polyolefins includes polyfluoroethylene and other modified forms (e.g., copolymers of ethylene and other monomers), as well as straight polyethylene. Because most of these newer materials will require ethylene, even if in smaller amounts, and in view of the large margin for error, a separate projection of "other polyolefins" is not warranted.

9. Percentage shares applied to polyolefin totals in Table A17–4.

10. Urea and melamine plastics refer to two groups of copolymers: urea-formaldehyde and melamine-formaldehyde. Resin applications are only a small part of the use of both urea (from ammonia) and melamine (trimer of a cyanamide). Urea and melamine resins, however, are the largest end-users of formaldehyde. According to Shreve (*op cit.*), a typical urea molding compound requires 1.13 pounds of formaldehyde (37% basis). This implies, on the basis of recent end-use distribution, a residual requirement of approximately 2 pounds of formaldehyde per pound of melamine resins. Since molding applications —which are heavy users of melamines—are projected to increase at a higher rate than other uses, formaldehyde requirements per pound of urea and melamine resins are projected to increase.

11. The most important raw materials used in the manufacture of vinyl resins are vinyl chloride, vinyl acetate, and a group of plasticizers (mostly phthalic esters, though they are not exclusively used for this purpose). Since phthalic esters represent currently the

Table A17–5 (cont'd)

major end-use of phthalic anhydride, they are projected separately.

Because of the predominance of copolymers in the vinyl resin family, it is impossible to establish historically the relative shares of polyvinyl chloride and resins made from vinyl acetate (e.g., polyvinyl acetate, polyvinyl alcohol, formal, butyral, etc.—often called acetals). In a large proportion of its applications, vinyl acetate is copolymerized with vinyl or vinylidene chloride; the latter is copolymerized with other materials. But there are annual statistics on vinyl chloride (monomer) production, which can be projected as a percentage of all vinyls. This percentage, varying between 76 and 70, with one or two exceptions, shows no trend during the last ten years. Since vinyl projections assume a faster rise in adhesives and water-paints (major end-uses of acetates) than in other applications (cf. Table A17–3), vinyl chloride requirements are projected as a moderately declining share of the total, roughly parallel to the increase of the adhesives share in the above table.

The share of vinyl acetate increases less than proportionately to the decrease in vinyl chloride, because of the expected rise in the utilization of other monomers, not here treated.

The use of phthalic esters relative to vinyl output has been declining over the past decade. Since it is not clear what has caused this decline, phthalic anhydride use is projected on the basis of the historical trend established by converting esters to anhydride on the basis of .49 pounds of anhydride per pound of ester and relating the resulting figures to total vinyl and vinyl copolymer output.

12. Calculated as .27 pounds per pound of "other resins." Includes also polyethylene used in polymethane rubbers. Data available for 1959 only (*Chemical Economics Newsletter,* Nov. 1960).

TABLE A17–6.   Projected Rubber Consumption, by Type[1]

(Million long tons, unless otherwise stated)

	1950	1955	1960		1970	1980	1990	2000
Consumption in tires and tire products[2]	.961	1.13	1.14	L	1.40	1.61	1.73	1.97
				M	1.70	2.28	2.99	4.01
				H	2.16	3.65	6.29	11.12
Consumption in non-tire products[3]	.601	.715	.689	L	.858	1.056	1.279	1.520
				M	1.009	1.469	2.119	3.046
				H	1.383	2.684	5.212	9.865
FRB index of industrial production (1957 = 100)[4]	74.5	96.0	108	L	148	203	278	380
				M	164	249	375	564
				H	182	305	506	836
Rubber consumption per point of of index (thous. long tons)	8.01	7.45	6.38	L	5.80	5.20	4.60	4.00
				M	6.15	5.90	5.65	5.40
				H	7.60	8.80	10.30	11.80
Total consumption	1.562	1.842	1.833	L	2.258	2.666	3.008	3.490
				M	2.709	3.749	5.116	7.056
				H	3.543	6.334	11.502	20.986
Percentage shares of different types:[5]								
Tires and tire products:[6]								
Natural	49.7	36.3	28.3		21.2	15.7	12.2	12.0
S-type	28.6	44.3	54.2	L	59.6	61.4	59.2	53.0
				M	61.6	65.4	65.2	61.0
				H	63.6	69.4	71.2	69.0
Other synthetic	6.9	4.4	4.5	L	2.7	2.8	4.9	7.7
				M	4.7	6.8	10.9	15.7
				H	6.7	10.8	16.9	23.7
Reclaim	14.9	14.4	13.1		12.5	12.1	11.7	11.3
Other products:[7]								
Natural	40.4	31.5	22.6		13.1	8.1	7.0	7.0
S-type	23.5	33.9	40.6	L	44.8	44.4	40.0	31.6
				M	46.8	48.4	46.0	39.6
				H	48.8	52.4	52.0	47.6
Other synthetic	9.5	14.0	18.0	L	25.2	31.0	35.3	40.9
				M	27.2	35.0	41.3	48.9
				H	29.2	39.0	47.3	56.9
Reclaim	26.8	20.3	18.9		12.9	8.5	5.7	4.5
Consumption of natural rubber:[8]								
Tires	.478	.410	.324	L	.297	.253	.167	.236
				M	.360	.358	.365	.481
				H	.458	.573	.767	1.336
Non-tire products	.243	.225	.156	L	.112	.086	.090	.106
				M	.132	.119	.149	.213
				H	.181	.217	.365	.691
Total	.720	.635	.480	L	.409	.339	.257	.342
				M	.492	.477	.514	.694
				H	.639	.790	1.132	2.027
Consumption of S-type rubber:[8, 9]								
Tires	.275	.500	.621	L	.834	.989	1.024	1.044
				M	1.047	1.491	1.949	2.446
				H	1.374	2.533	4.478	7.680
Non-tire products	.141	.242	.280	L	.384	.469	.511	.480
				M	.472	.711	.978	1.206
				H	.675	1.406	2.710	4.696
Total	.416	.742	.901	L	1.218	1.458	1.535	1.524
				M	1.519	2.202	2.927	3.652
				H	2.049	3.939	7.188	12.376

Table A17–6 (cont'd)

(Million long tons, unless otherwise stated)

	1950	1955	1960		1970	1980	1990	2000
Consumption of other synthetic rubbers: [8, 10]								
Tires	.066	.050	.051	L	.038	.045	.085	.152
				M	.080	.155	.326	.629
				H	.145	.286	1.063	2.638
Non-tire products	.057	.100	.124	L	.216	.327	.451	.622
				M	.274	.514	.878	1.490
				H	.404	1.047	1.465	5.613
Total	.122	.153	.175	L	.254	.372	.536	.774
				M	.354	.669	1.204	2.119
				H	.549	1.333	3.528	8.251

1. Historical data on rubber consumption, unless otherwise stated, are from U.S. Bureau of the Census, *Rubber* (Current Industrial Reports, Series M30A).

2. From Table A5–13. Includes rubber consumed in tires, tubes, and camelback and other repair materials.

3. Includes rubber consumed in footwear, latex foam, belting, hose, cement, flooring, sporting wear, and a large number of other products.

Projections are based upon the index of industrial production (below in table), in view of the wide variety of uses of rubber outside the field of tires and tubes. No single, relatively homogeneous use accounts for as much as even 5% of non-tire use of rubber. Rubber is employed in durable as well as non-durable consumer goods, in capital equipment, and in construction material. In order to test the appropriateness of this projection procedure, a test was run in which rubber uses in the principal subseries (latex foam; footwear; wire and cable; textiles; balloons, toys, sporting goods, etc.; mechanical goods) were each related to an appropriate reference series (such as major consumer durables, footwear, producer durables, etc.) and projected in accordance with these reference series. The result checks closely with the more convenient aggregate projection using the FRB index of industrial production.

Although historically there has been a substantial decline in the ratio between non-tire rubber use and the production index (see below), the Medium projection rests upon a more stable though still declining ratio, in the belief that the principal reason for the past decline has been the heavy impact of non-rubber synthetics and that this particular phase is on the decline. In the Low projection, however, the strongly declining trend is continued, whereas the assumption of an upward trend in the high projection (an increase of 2% per year in rubber use per index point) reflects the possible emergence of radically new rubber uses in the economy, such as rubber roads or inflatable aircraft.

4. From Table A1–29.

5. Projection of reclaim: lowered by 0.4% every ten years, in continuation of 1950–60 trend. Projection of natural: assumes slowdown in rate of decline, with 12% as lower limit; latter suggested by 1951 experience during natural rubber shortage. Synthetic rubber as a whole is assumed to continue its rise vis-a-vis natural and reclaimed, but to be especially dynamic for the types other than the traditional S-type (the styrene-butadiene mixture). The "other" types have a relatively short history, especially those not yet included in the statistics (such as "stereospecific" rubbers—polybutadiene and polyisoprene). Their current use is quite insignificant in quantitative terms, but this is not at all likely to be the case in the future. There has been trade talk of capacity for 200,000 long tons for the "new rubbers" by the end of 1961. Abrasion resistance and strength generally are among their desirable attributes. In the opposite direction we must consider high price and the inclusion in this group of some of the older rubbers (e.g., butyl), whose growth is not likely to be rapid and which may even lose their markets.

6. Within the general framework given in footnote 5 and in view of the lack of good data on the subject, the growth assumptions have been rather mechanical: The declining growth trend for S-type rubber has been extended at all three levels. In the Medium projection a rate of 7.4% for the first decade was assumed, diminishing as shown and turning into a decline. Highs and Lows are set above and below. In the calculations five-year intervals not here shown were used. The Medium projection for other synthetic rubber is the balance between the total and the sum of the other three categories. The Low projection is calculated as the difference between total synthetic share (100 minus natural and reclaimed) and the High S-type share; the High projection is calculated as the difference between the total synthetic share and the Low S-type share.

7. Follows general reasoning of footnote 6, except that growth in S-type use is assumed to be much slower than in tires, and role of new-type rubbers far more dynamic, overtaking S-type late in the century and filling nearly half of all demand by 2000. Mechanically, the high projection for S-type rubber represents the continuation of the historical trend, diminished by two percentage points every ten years. The Medium projection is set two and the Low projection four points lower in 1970, with differences increasing thereafter. Projections for "other types" are derived in a manner analogous to that described in footnote 6.

8. Percentages projected above, applied to rubber consumption in tires and non-tire products respectively. All groups include gross weight of latex as well as dry rubber.

9. GR-S, or general purpose synthetic rubber of the butadiene-styrene type, including oil content.

10. Includes neoprene, butyl, and N-type rubbers as well as new types of synthetic rubbers being produced or to be produced in the future (e.g., polymethane, silicone, and polybutadiene types).

TABLE A17-7. Projected Key Materials in Rubber Manufacturing[1]

	1950	1955	1960		1970	1980	1990	2000
Natural rubber, imported[2]				L	.409	.339	.257	.342
(mil. long tons)	.720	.635	.480	M	.492	.477	.514	.694
				H	.639	.790	1.132	2.027
Synthetic rubber:								
				L	2.25	2.89	3.29	3.69
Total production[3] (mil. long tons)	.483	.988	1.469	M	2.72	4.07	5.62	7.48
				H	3.59	6.86	12.56	22.21
S-type only:								
Production[4] (mil. long tons,				L	1.61	1.81	1.81	1.71
gross weight)	.358	.791	1.166	M	2.01	2.73	3.45	4.09
				H	2.70	4.88	8.48	13.86
Per cent of domestic consumption[5]	86	107	128		132	124	118	112
Elastomer content[6] (%)	100	92.5	87.4		82	84	86	88
Elastomer consumption[7]				L	1.32	1.52	1.56	1.50
(mil. long tons)	.358	.732	1.019	M	1.65	2.29	2.97	3.60
				H	2.21	4.10	7.29	12.20
Requirements for:								
				L	2.30	2.64	2.71	2.61
Butadiene[8] (bil. lb.)	.618	1.274	1.773	M	2.87	3.98	5.17	6.26
				H	3.84	7.13	12.68	21.23
				L	.660	.760	.780	.750
Styrene[8] (bil. lb.)	.184	.366	.510	M	.825	1.145	1.485	1.800
				H	1.105	2.050	3.645	6.100
Other types:								
				L	.508	.744	.965	1.238
Production (mil. long tons)[9]	.125	.197	.303	M	.708	1.338	2.167	3.390
				H	1.098	2.666	6.350	13.202
Per cent of domestic consumption[10]	102	129	172		200	200	180	160
Requirements for:								
				L	.132	.193	.251	.322
Butadiene[11] (bil. lb.)	.019	.051	.059	M	.184	.348	.563	.881
				H	.286	.693	1.651	3.432
Pounds of butadiene/ton of rubber[11]	151	259	196		260	260	260	260
				L	.437	.551	.598	.619
Chloroprene[12] (bil. lb.)	.112	.205	.301	M	.609	.990	1.344	1.695
				H	.944	1.973	3.937	6.601
Pounds of chloroprene/ton of rubber[12]	896	1,041	993		860	740	620	500

1. For source of historical rubber production statistics, see footnote 1 to Table A17–6. Historical data on key materials are from annual reports of the U.S. Tariff Commission, *Synthetic Organic Chemicals*. Consumption by type of rubber, from which projections of total use are here derived, is projected in Table A17–6. Calculations performed prior to rounding. Reclaim rubber not considered in this tabulation.

2. Equals projected consumption as shown in Table A17-6.

3. Sum of projections of S-type and other synthetic rubber as developed below. Highs and Lows here adjusted to range of total rubber consumption, in Table A17-6, by computing Lows and Highs as percentages

of Medium for each year shown and applying those percentages to the Medium projection.

4. Represents total domestic production of synthetic rubber, including the content of oil added to the basic ingredients in the course of master-batching. This procedure, which is an economizing move, as the oil added is substantially cheaper than the special hydrocarbon ingredients, necessitates certain extra steps in the calculations and close attention to the make-up of the particular series under review. In general, the data emanating from the Tariff Commission are cast in terms of elastomer content only, whereas the Census Bureau data include oil content. This holds true for S-type rubber only, since master-batching is not practiced elsewhere. Projected as de-

Table A17–7 (cont'd)

clining multiple of consumption by use of percentages shown in subsequent line.

5. Difference between consumption (Table A17–6) and production is principally foreign trade, as stocks tend to be small in relation to consumption and their variations have therefore had little impact. Whereas natural rubber stockpiling can be considered a thing of the past and consumption can thus be assumed to equal imports in the future, the foreign trade picture in synthetic rubber requires more care in order to make the projection realistic. Following a period of imports, mainly from Canadian facilities built during World War II with U.S. Government cooperation, exports began a rapid rise in the mid-fifties. By 1960 exports accounted for nearly one-fourth of S-type rubber output. Since European capacity is slated to expand at an accelerating pace, the export share is bound to decline after 1965. Arbitrarily we have assumed an export peak for 1965, at which time production will exceed domestic demand by 36%. From then on the ratio is projected to decline by 4 percentage points every five years through 1980 and by 3 points thereafter. Only the ten year intervals are shown here, but without the preceding explanation their derivation would not be intelligible. It should be noted, in connection with the historical comparison, that the low ratio for 1950 arises partly because consumption did not then include oil content, but the situation was not widespread, and the ratio is low primarily because the United States was on a net import basis.

6. The historical decline in this ratio reflects the spread of master-batching. In 1950, statistics indicate its absence. In 1952, elastomer content was 98% of gross weight. It is assumed that the practice will reach its limit within the next few years. As it is little used in rubber for non-tire products, and as these products will gradually increase in relation to tire production until they account for nearly one-half, it is unlikely that master-batching will ever affect more than one-half of all S-type rubber. Since even now 45% is so prepared, it is difficult to see a substantial further spread of the practice. On the contrary, it is likely that there will be a slow reversal. The projections reflect these considerations.

7. Gross weight multiplied by percentage of elastomer content.

8. Calculated on the basis of a technical coefficient of 500 pounds of styrene and 1,740 pounds of butadiene per long ton of S-type rubber. This represents a change from the original formula of 30%

styrene and 70% butadiene. No assumptions as to future change are made.

9. Includes neoprene, N-type, butyl, and the "new elastomers" such as polymethane. The material requirements for the latter are, however, submerged in those for the other synthetics.

10. It is assumed that the leading position of U.S. producers and the consequent demand for exports will further increase and remain high for a long time to come, i.e., for the next twenty years, declining only gradually thereafter. Patent protection of neoprene, the largest export material, is a key factor in this picture. It is assumed that Europe will continue to lag in the development of new rubbers, as it has in the past, and that in the "non-conventional" types exports will therefore have a brighter future.

11. The materials picture is complex, given the variety of rubbers included in this category. Unfortunately, there are no historical data on any but butadiene and chloroprene, and it is not feasible to project each of the new types of rubber separately. Consequently, projection here must proceed on the basis of selection, dictated by data availability.

Butadiene is an important constituent of both nitrile rubber and polybutadiene (to be blended with natural rubber or isoprene to increase toughness, abrasion resistance). Assuming a 70% butadiene content in N-type rubber, the relationship between butadiene use and total "other" synthetic rubber output has fluctuated between 200 and 300 pounds per ton in the recent past. As the share of N-type rubber is likely to decline, but that of butadiene polymer and copolymer rubber equally likely to rise, it has been assumed that butadiene content per ton of "other" synthetic rubbers will remain stable. Obviously, these are very rough assumptions and calculations.

12. Use of chloroprene (which can for all practical purposes be considered the equivalent of neoprene production) per ton of "other" synthetic rubbers has been steadily rising, reflecting the progress of neoprene as a constituent of that group. However, 1960 saw the first drop in that ratio. It is expected that neoprene will gradually decline in relative importance, owing to the discovery of new oil- and chemical-resistant elastomers, and consequently the ratio is allowed to decline by 120 pounds per ton of "other" synthetics every ten years, a decline equivalent in the beginning of the period to 1% per year and toward the end of the period to 2% per year.

TABLE A17–8. Projected Non-cellulosic Fiber Production and Key Materials

(Billion pounds, unless otherwise stated)

	1950	1955	1960		1970	1980	1990	2000
Production of non-cellulosic and				L	1.35	1.90	2.48	3.01
textile glass fibers[1]	.146	.455	.854	M	1.88	3.08	4.28	5.81
				H	2.50	4.62	7.60	11.77
				L	.43	.68	.98	1.27
Textile glass fiber production[2]	.024	.076	.177	M	.49	.94	1.63	2.61
				H	.75	1.71	3.41	6.19
Per pound of reinforced								
plastics (lb.)	n.a.	1.19	1.95		.84	.68	.58	.50
Production of non-cellulosic fibers,				L	.92	1.22	1.50	1.74
other than glass fiber	.122	.379	.677	M	1.39	2.14	2.65	3.20
				H	1.75	2.91	4.19	5.58
Percentage shares:[3]								
Nylon	75.6	65.1	62		56	52	50	50
Acrylics	.8	15.4	19		20	20	20	20
Other	23.6	19.5	19		24	28	30	30
Production:								
				L	.52	.63	.75	.87
Nylon	.092	.247	.42	M	.78	1.11	1.32	1.60
				H	.98	1.51	2.10	2.79
				L	.18	.24	.30	.35
Acrylics[4]	.001	.058	.14	M	.28	.43	.53	.64
				H	.35	.58	.84	1.12
				L	.22	.34	.45	.52
Other	.029	.074	.13	M	.33	.60	.80	.96
				H	.42	.81	1.26	1.67
Key material requirements:[5]								
				L	.31	.38	.45	.52
Adipic acid[6]	.055	.148	.25	M	.47	.67	.79	.96
				H	.59	.91	1.26	1.67

1. Historical data from Textile Economics Bureau, *Textile Organon.* Projection: 1.10 (Low), 1.135 (Medium), and 1.175 (High) times end-use consumption as projected in Table A3–3. Different ratios reflect principally different levels of export assumptions.

2. Related to sales of reinforced plastics—projected in Table A17–1—by declining coefficients below; these coefficients are based upon statistics for 1954 and 1957–60, showing textile glass fibers rising much less rapidly than reinforced plastics. This trend has been extended at a rate by which pounds of glass fiber per pound of reinforced plastics decline by 16 pounds every 10 years from a rounded 1.00 in 1960 through 1980 and more slowly thereafter.

3. Acrylics include acrilan, orlon, dynel, creslan, etc. "Other" includes the polyesters (dacron), the polyvinyls (saran, vinyon), the polyolefins (teflon, polypropylene fibers), polymethane (spandex), and many other lesser known, and in many cases just developed, synthetic fibers. Historical data from *Textile Organon,* based upon shipments (609 mil. lb. in 1960).

Projection of shares is based upon postwar trends. Acrylics presumed to remain at 1960 share, after fast postwar growth, on the basis that the lower growth rate of its market—clothing and apparel—will be offset by future application in the industrial market (not now existing). Share of "others" assumed to increase, since it not only comprises the multitude of new fibers but must also accommodate fibers yet to be developed. This development is most likely to occur at the expense of nylon—the oldest and largest of non-cellulosic fibers. The resulting relationships are worked out to physical production projections in the subsequent lines. The increase in nylon production rests largely on the assumed replacement of rayon by nylon cord in automobile tires. Introduction of metal-cord tires would, of course, seriously upset this picture.

4. Acrylonitrile assumed to be required at 1:1 ratio. Therefore the figures here shown represent equally the acrylonitrile requirements.

5. The mixture of fibers included under "other" (polyesters, polyolefins, polyvinyl chloride, etc.) and the difficulty of obtaining adequate processing data make it impossible to reduce these totals to key material requirements. The material requirements shown here are therefore confined to those for nylon. For acrylic fibers see footnote 4.

6. Adipic acid requirements assumed to equal nylon production. All other materials are omitted, since their use in nylon manufacture is either only a small part of their total consumption (for instance butane, one of the possible sources of hexamethylenediamine, the second most important nylon ingredi-

Table A17–8 (cont'd)

ent) or can be traced to materials that are in large prospective supply (e.g., caustic soda in the manufacture of sodium cyanide, another nylon-manufacturing intermediate).

To illustrate the difficulty of reducing a well-established synthetic material such as Nylon 66 to its ingredients it is perhaps well to point out that there are a variety of ways of arriving at nylon. It results from reaction of adipic acid with hexamethylenediamine. Adipic acid in turn is derived from benzene via phenol, or through hydrogenation via cyclohexane. The latter may also be obtained from the heavier petroleum fractions, and in still other ways. Hexamethylenediamine may equally be derived from adipic acid (via adiponitrile), or it may be produced from furfural (a plant life product that can alternatively be produced synthetically from acetylene and formaldehyde) or from butadiene. In each instance different catalysts and reagents are involved. The ratio here chosen is that of Nylon 66. If one were to take into account other processes, it is possible that the conversion ratio would be more nearly 1:1. Our source material did not, however, allow us to make these adjustments.

This multiplicity of producing processes is more nearly typical than unique in the synthetics field.

TABLE A17–9. Projected Key Materials for Acrylonitrile and Vinyl Chloride[1]

(Billion pounds, unless otherwise stated)

	1950	1955	1960		1970	1980	1990	2000
Acrylonitrile:								
Use in:								
Synthetic fibers[2]				L	.18	.24	.30	.35
	.001	.058	.140	M	.28	.43	.53	.64
				H	.35	.58	.84	1.12
Synthetic resins and				L	.226	.299	.406	.492
miscellaneous[3]	.014	.060	.101	M	.312	.593	1.110	1.989
				H	.518	1.488	3.854	9.240
Per pound of "other resin"				L	.17	.13	.11	.09
output (lb.)	.10	.27	.210	M	.19	.17	.17	.17
				H	.23	.25	.29	.33
				L	.406	.539	.706	.842
Total use	.015	.118	.241	M	.592	1.023	1.640	2.629
				H	.868	2.068	4.694	10.360
Derived from:[4]								
Ethylene cyanohydrin	.015	.037	.043		.050	.010	–	–
				L	.277	.363	.452	.520
Acetylene-hydrogen cyanide	–	.081	.198	M	.370	.605	.919	1.413
				H	.508	1.128	2.446	5.279
				L	.079	.165	.254	.322
Propylene-ammonia	–	–	–	M	.172	.407	.721	1.215
				H	.310	.930	2.248	5.081
Key material requirements:								
				L	.166	.218	.271	.312
Acetylene[5]	–	.049	.119	M	.222	.363	.551	.848
				H	.305	.677	1.468	3.167
				L	.203	.224	.271	.312
Hydrogen cyanide	.012	.078	.152	M	.260	.369	.551	.848
				H	.346	.683	1.468	3.167
Per pound of acrylonitrile manufactured from acetylene and ethylene[6]	.79	.66	.63		.62	.60	.60	.60

Table A17–9 (cont'd)

(Billion pounds, unless otherwise stated)

	1950	1955	1960		1970	1980	1990	2000
Vinyl chloride:								
				L	1.52	2.11	2.58	3.42
Total use[7]	.250	.529	.930	M	2.11	3.43	5.08	8.08
				H	2.96	5.91	10.66	20.47
Key material requirements:[8]								
				L	.334	.464	.568	.752
Acetylene	n.a.	1.48	.205	M	.464	.755	1.118	1.778
				H	.651	1.300	2.345	4.503
				L	.456	.633	.774	1.026
Hydrogen chloride	n.a.	n.a.	.280	M	.633	1.029	1.524	2.424
				H	.888	1.773	3.198	6.141
				L	1.25	1.74	2.13	2.82
Ethylene dichloride	n.a.	.320	.767	M	1.74	2.83	4.19	6.67
				H	2.44	4.88	8.79	16.89

1. Historical data are from Manufacturing Chemists Association, *Chemical Statistics Handbook;* U.S. Tariff Commission, *Synthetic Organic Chemicals;* and U.S. Department of Commerce, *Chemical and Rubber Industry Reports.*

2. From Table A17–8.

3. Includes acrylonitrile consumed in acrylates and metacrylates, as well as nitrile rubbers and miscellaneous chemical uses. "Other resins" projected in Table A17–4. Ratio has recently been declining and is so continued (reflecting the diminishing importance of the rubber outlet) in the Medium projection, with variations in the High and Low projections.

The Low coefficient assumes that usage of acrylics will continue to be restricted owing to high price. A drastic—nearly 40%—price cut made in July 1961 may make this Low projection, made prior to the cut, unrealistically Low. (The event illustrates strikingly the ephemeral nature of long-range projections in the chemical field.) The High coefficient is based upon favorable expectations in the dynamic field of reinforced plastics, which should receive a strong stimulus from the price reduction.

4. Acrylics may be manufactured in at least three different ways. Originally, they were made by dehydrating ethylene cyanohydrin, which in turn is the product of the reaction of ethylene oxide with hydrogen cyanide. After 1952 the acetylene-hydrogen cyanide process was introduced and appears to have surpassed the older process in importance as early as 1955. In 1959 only one plant, representing about one-fourth of total capacity, was operating via ethylene, and no new plants of that type are expected to be built. Consequently, the projection is cast in terms of abandonment of that route before the end of the projection period; it is allowed to decline beginning in 1970.

Future requirements for both acetylene and hydrogen cyanide depend upon the success of a new and allegedly more economical process employing propylene and ammonia. Since at the time of writing no plant had as yet entered commercial production via this new route, it has been assumed in the projection that any demand above the 1960 level other than by the ethylene cyanohydrin route will be evenly divided between the acetylene and the propylene route, with the acetylene route retaining in addition its 1960 share. Only requirements for acetylene and hydrogen cyanide are projected, as the production of acrylics is a negligible outlet for the other ingredients.

5. Technical writings suggest that it takes 0.6 pounds of acetylene to make 1 pound of acrylonitrile via the acetylene route.

6. Based upon data in *Industrial Chemicals* (see Table A17–5, footnote 2), and in U.S. Bureau of the Census, *Inorganic Chemicals* (Current Industrial Reports, Series M28A).

7. From Table A17–5.

8. The question of material requirements boils down to the question of how future vinyl chloride production will be distributed between two competing processes: one using acetylene and hydrochloric acid (approximately 880 and 1,200 pounds respectively per ton of vinyl chloride), the other using ethylene dichloride (approximately 3,300 pounds per ton), which in turn is made from ethylene and chlorine. There is even conflicting evidence as to the past share of the market, according to whether one looks at what data there are or listens to observers of the scene in the literature. On balance it appears that the acetylene route was the favored one in the mid-fifties but has been losing ground. Most recently, more than half the production seems to have been via the ethylene route. Changes in relative prices may be the most important factor in deciding the future allocation of the market.

Given the uncertainties described, we have based the projections upon a 50:50 sharing of production, mainly for the following reasons: (1) there is nothing that indicates a significant change in the price relationship between ethylene and acetylene; (2) there exists the possibility of increasing adoption of a "combination process" using both acetylene and ethylene, which would be more economical than either of the other two because of the utilization of by-products previously wasted. No estimates are submitted for past consumption of materials, but assuming equal amounts of vinyl chloride produced from acetylene and ethylene in 1960 and in the future, material requirements per pound of vinyl chloride appear to be: acetylene, .22 pounds; hydrogen chloride, .30 pounds; ethylene dichloride, .825 pounds.

TABLE A17–10. Summary Projections of Organic Crudes and Intermediates Used in Synthetics Manufacture[1]

(Billion pounds)

	1950	1955	1960		1970	1980	1990	2000
Acetylene:								
Acrylonitrile[2]	–	.049	.119	L	.166	.218	.271	.312
				M	.222	.363	.551	.848
				H	.305	.677	1.468	3.167
Chloroprene[3]	.091	.167	.246	L	.357	.450	.488	.505
				M	.497	.808	1.097	1.383
				H	.770	1.610	3.210	5.386
Vinyl chloride[2]	n.a.	.148	.205	L	.334	.464	.568	.752
				M	.464	.755	1.118	1.778
				H	.651	1.300	2.345	4.503
Major chemical uses	n.a.	.364	.570	L	.857	1.131	1.327	1.569
				M	1.183	1.926	2.766	4.009
				H	1.726	3.587	7.023	13.056
Total chemical uses[4]	n.a.	.398	.638	L	.977	1.31	1.56	1.88
				M	1.350	2.23	3.26	4.81
				H	1.970	4.16	8.29	15.66
Adipic acid:								
Nylon[5]	.055	.148	.250	L	.31	.38	.45	.52
				M	.47	.67	.79	.96
				H	.59	.91	1.26	1.67
Total use[6]	n.a.	[7].125	.285	L	.36	.44	.52	.60
				M	.57	.82	1.07	1.38
				H	.76	1.31	2.04	3.02
Per cent of nylon use	n.a.	[7]106	114	L	115	115	115	115
				M	121	128	136	144
				H	128	144	162	181
Butadiene (rubber grade):								
Synthetic rubber[8]	.637	1.325	1.832	L	2.43	2.83	2.96	2.93
				M	3.05	4.33	5.73	7.14
				H	4.13	7.82	14.33	24.66
Total use[9]	n.a.	1.411	1.920	L	2.55	2.97	3.11	3.08
				M	3.20	4.55	6.02	7.50
				H	4.34	8.21	15.05	25.89
Ethylene (99+ %)[10]	.055	.402	1.314	L	2.09	2.95	3.97	4.94
				M	2.79	4.82	7.69	11.32
				H	4.14	9.15	17.38	30.70
Ethylene dichloride[11]	n.a.	.320	.767	L	1.25	1.74	2.13	2.82
				M	1.74	2.83	4.19	6.67
				H	2.44	4.88	8.79	16.89
Formaldehyde (37% basis):								
Phenolic resins[12, 13]	.289	.445	.597	L	.801	1.09	1.33	1.74
				M	1.165	1.97	2.98	4.76
				H	1.747	3.80	7.39	15.03
Urea and melamine resins[13]	.228	.407	.567	L	.784	1.02	1.24	1.63
				M	1.091	1.72	2.55	4.04
				H	1.578	3.17	5.93	12.40
Pentaerythritol[14]	.114	.193	.206	L	.171	.143	.156	.184
				M	.194	.197	.241	.337
				H	.238	.286	.429	.705
All major uses	.631	1.045	1.370	L	1.76	2.25	2.73	3.55
				M	2.45	3.89	5.77	9.14
				H	3.56	7.26	13.75	28.14
Total use[15]	.835	1.259	1.750	L	2.32	3.02	3.71	4.90
				M	3.38	5.68	8.89	14.81
				H	5.06	11.18	22.82	50.09

Table A17–10 (cont'd)

(Billion pounds)

	1950	1955	1960		1970	1980	1990	2000
Formaldehyde (37% basis) (cont'd)								
				L	132	134	136	138
Per cent of major uses	132	121	128	M	138	146	154	162
				H	142	154	166	178
Phenol:								
				L	.439	.537	.656	.855
Phenolic resins [13]	.257	.321	.370	M	.638	.969	1.465	2.337
				H	.958	1.870	3.631	7.387
Phthalic anhydride:								
				L	.134	.113	.123	.146
Alkyd resins [13]	.117	.160	.162	M	.152	.154	.191	.265
				H	.187	.224	.338	.555
				L	.086	.131	.194	.252
Polyester resins [13]	.001	.012	.032	M	.099	.180	.323	.520
				H	.151	.329	.677	1.230
				L	.190	.210	.225	.287
Plasticizers [13]	.070	.104	.153	M	.263	.340	.444	.680
				H	.369	.587	.931	1.727
				L	.410	.454	.542	.685
All major uses	.189	.276	.347	M	.514	.674	.958	1.465
				H	.707	1.140	1.946	3.512
				L	.455	.504	.602	.760
Total use [16]	.216	.331	.385	M	.571	.748	1.063	1.626
				H	.785	1.265	2.160	3.898
Propylene (99+ %): [17]								
				L	.563	1.31	2.46	3.81
Propylene	–	–	.023	M	.752	2.14	4.75	8.72
				H	1.12	4.05	10.74	23.63
Epoxies, polymethanes, and				L	.359	.621	.996	1.48
other resins	–	–	.129	M	.443	.942	1.763	3.16
				H	.608	1.606	3.588	7.56
Total use (identified				L	.922	1.931	3.456	5.29
synthetic uses)	–		.152	M	1.195	3.082	6.513	11.88
				H	1.908	5.656	14.328	31.19
Styrene:								
				L	1.36	1.75	2.48	3.22
Styrene resins [13,18]	.308	.530	.903	M	1.82	2.93	4.83	7.52
				H	2.59	5.14	10.12	18.84
				L	.200	.353	.522	.679
Polyesters [13]	.002	.022	.066	M	.231	.486	.871	1.400
				H	.353	.886	1.820	3.320
				L	.660	.760	.780	.750
Synthetic rubber [19]	.184	.366	.510	M	.825	1.145	1.485	1.800
				H	1.105	2.050	3.645	6.100
				L	2.22	2.86	3.78	4.65
All major uses	.494	.918	1.479	M	2.88	4.56	7.19	10.72
				H	4.05	8.08	15.58	28.26
				L	2.51	3.12	4.04	4.98
Total use [20]	.539	1.014	1.730	M	3.25	4.97	7.69	11.47
				H	4.58	8.81	16.67	30.24
Per cent of major uses	109	110	117		113	109	107	107
				L	13.9	18.5	23.8	30.1
Total, identified uses [21]	–	–	9.31	M	18.7	30.7	47.9	73.8
				H	26.8	56.5	111.2	215.0

Table A17–10 (cont'd)

1. Sources of historical data for production statistics: U.S. Department of Commerce, Current Industrial Reports, and U.S. Tariff Commission, annual reports on *Synthetic Organic Chemicals.* A convenient alternate source for the latter is the *Chemical Statistics Handbook,* issued by the Manufacturing Chemists Association, Inc. End-use series are computed on the basis of output data derived in preceding tables and technical input coefficients derived principally from *Industrial Chemicals, Chemical Process Industries,* and *Materials Handbook,* cited in Table A17–5, footnotes 2 and 6.

2. From Table A17–9.

3. 81.6% of chloroprene requirements, projected in Table A17–7. Under the assumption of 72% yield, 1,632 pounds of acetylene is required to produce one ton of chloroprene.

4. Major chemical uses raised increasingly: 12% in 1960 up to 20% in 2000, to account for all chemical uses. Some recent, but discontinuous, data suggest that these may be understated, but no correction is feasible. The basic source is a complete statistical breakdown of acetylene use in *Industrial Chemicals,* p. 38. "Other" chemical uses include the manufacture of vinyl acetate, acetaldehyde, acetic acid, tri- and per-chloroethylenes, etc.

5. From Table A17–8.

6. Historical data estimated as the sum of use in nylon (0.6 pounds per pound of nylon production) and adipic acid sales from *Industrial Chemicals.* Ratio of total to nylon use assumed to increase by 6% every ten years in the Medium and by 12% in the High projection, based upon faster growth of non-nylon uses. Although demand for nylon alone is sufficient to insure substantial growth in adipic acid output, its other uses give it a further potential growth factor. For example, adipic acid esters are becoming established as a major plasticizer. Polyesters based on adipic acid are reacted with diisocyanates to yield polyester rubber and foam (polymethane). If adipic acid were the only raw material suitable to produce polymethane, its future growth could be expected to exceed that of "other synthetic rubbers," projected in Table A17–6; its position, however, is already threatened by polyether glycols, which are much cheaper than the polyester varieties and serve almost as well in most uses. To be conservative, adipic acid demand in uses other than nylon is projected to remain proportional to nylon in the Low and to rise at roughly the same rate as "other synthetic rubbers" in the Medium and High projections.

7. 1954.

8. Sum of butadiene requirements in S-type and other synthetic rubbers, projected in Table A17–7.

9. Use in synthetic rubber raised 5% (1955–60 average) in projection. Other applications include manufacture of nylon and synthetic resins.

10. From Table A17–5. Accounts for ethylene used in polyethylene manufacture only. Ethylene also enters synthetic materials via ethylene dichloride, ethyl alcohol, ethylene glycol, and styrene.

11. Used in vinyl chloride, projected in Table A17–9.

12. Including formaldehyde used in hexamethylenetetramine, a small portion of which is consumed in uses other than phenolics manufacture.

13. Figures shown in Table A17–5.

14. Figures shown in Table A17–5 multiplied by 3.175, which, according to *Industrial Chemicals,* is unit requirement.

15. Other uses include paraformaldehyde, trioxane, and other formaldehyde polymers. Also included are formaldehyde applications not directly connected with synthetics manufacture, e.g., dyestuffs, sequesterants, ethylene glycol, explosives, tanning agents, drugs, and many more. Production in the fifties has shown no real trend in the share of the minor uses but the outlook is bright for some of them (formaldehyde polymers).

Consequently, starting with an average excess of total over major uses of 30% as a base, the Low projection is assumed to rise by only 2 percentage points every ten years, the Medium projection by 8 points, and the High projection by 12 points.

16. Assumed at 11% above all major uses. Other uses include use in dyes, chlorinated products, pharmaceuticals, insecticides, etc. Although the share of minor phthalic anhydride uses (other than alkyds, polyester resins and plasticizers) increased slightly between 1954 and 1960, production as a per cent of major uses showed a declining tendency, because of constant export levels, high imports, and declining inventories. In view of these contrary tendencies, total use is projected as a constant proportion of major uses based on the 1950–60 average.

17. From Table A17–5. Propylene used in polypropylene, epoxies, and polymethanes only. Propylene also enters synthetic materials via acrylonitrile, propylene, glycol, cumene (benzene), isopropyl alcohol, etc., and as the key material of polypropylene fibers.

18. Includes styrene consumed in polystyrene, styrene-butadiene copolymer, styrene-alkyd polyesters, styrene-divinylbenzene copolymer, and others.

19. From Table A17–7.

20. The increase of the share of "other" disappearance over the fifties, especially since 1956, reflects the sudden expansion of export outlets (principal foreign consumers: synthetic rubber makers). Without exports, "other uses" grew in proportion to the major outlets. Foreign demand for the monomer is assumed to drop, resulting in a decreasing ratio between total styrene use and major applications. Beginning in 1990, the relative fall in exports is assumed to be counterbalanced by the development of new domestic uses for the material.

21. 1950 and 1955 not totaled because of lack of comparability; totals for remaining years computed prior to rounding of subtotals; thus subtotals may not add to totals shown here.

TABLE A17–11.   Projected Soap and Detergent Production

	1940	1945	1950	1955	1960		1970	1980	1990	2000
Per capita production[1] (lb.):										
Soap	24.8	27.8	19.5	9.8	7.0		4.0	3.0	3.0	3.0
Synthetic detergents	.23	1.07	9.51	16.36	22.0		26.0	28.0	28.0	28.0
Total	25.03	28.87	29.01	26.16	29.0		30.0	31.0	31.0	31.0
Aggregate production[2] (mil. lb.):										
Soap	3,273	3,888	2,958	1,625	1,250	L	808	678	747	804
						M	832	735	861	993
						H	890	837	1,050	1,300
Synthetic detergents	30	150	1,443	2,704	3,970	L	5,250	6,330	6,970	7,500
						M	5,410	6,860	8,040	9,270
						H	5,800	7,810	9,770	12,100
Total	3,303	4,038	4,401	4,329	5,220	L	6,060	7,010	7,720	8,300
						M	6,240	7,600	8,900	10,300
						H	6,690	8,650	10,800	13,400

1. Historical data from U.S. Department of Agriculture, *Fats and Oils Situation*, Mar. 1959, p. 24; 1960 based upon census of producers compiled by Association of American Soap and Glycerine Producers, Inc., and adjusted to historical series to allow for incomplete coverage. The adjustment is based upon the relationship in the late fifties but does not yet take into account the results of the 1958 Census of Manufactures. Figures for soap represent factory shipments adjusted to represent production, but detergent data represent sales.

The projection rests upon the assumption of a very modest rise in the per capita use of soap and detergents jointly, given the great stability of this factor in the past. What small rise there has been is assumed to continue; it is likely to stem from the greater availability of washable—as opposed to dry cleaned—fabrics. Use of natural soap is projected to decline further, but much more slowly than in the past, and to reach by 1980, and maintain thereafter, the level that has prevailed for per capita use of toilet soap in the past. This implies that all other uses of soap will be taken over by detergents. The latter are derived as the difference between total and soap consumption.

2. Per capita use multiplied by population projections taken from Table A1–2.

TABLE A17–12.   Projected Paint, Varnish, and Lacquer Production

	1946	1950	1955	1960		1970	1980	1990	2000
Production of paints, varnishes, and lacquers[1] (mil. gal.)	586	641	719	663	L	555	494	535	608
					M	629	670	829	1,105
					H	771	974	1,467	2,322
Production of trade sales products[2] (mil. gal.)	311	344	375	347	L	332	327	307	306
					M	356	373	394	452
					H	390	471	625	945
Maintenance and repair construction[3] ($ 1960 bil.)	15.0	16.4	18.4	19.6	L	25.7	33.4	41.5	52.8
					M	27.0	36.2	48.7	67.5
					H	28.7	41.7	61.9	97.4
Gallons/$ 1960 thous.[4]	20.7	21.0	20.4	17.7	L	12.9	9.8	7.4	5.8
					M	13.2	10.3	8.1	6.7
					H	13.6	11.3	10.1	9.7
Production of industrial products finishes[5] (mil. gal.)	275	297	344	316	L	223	167	228	302
					M	273	296	445	653
					H	381	503	842	1,377
Purchases of consumer durables ($ 1960 bil.)[6]	18.5	34.0	42.0	44.3	L	60.5	83.6	113.8	150.9
					M	65.1	98.6	148.2	217.8
					H	74.7	125.8	210.4	344.3
Gallons/$ 1960 thous.[7]	14.9	8.4	8.1	7.4	L	3.7	2.0	2.0	2.0
					M	4.2	3.0	3.0	3.0
					H	5.1	4.0	4.0	4.0
Requirements for film-forming materials (resins and drying oils)[8] (bil. lb.)	1.081	1.519	1.760	1.724	L	1.443	1.284	1.391	1.581
					M	1.635	1.742	2.155	2.873
					H	2.005	2.532	3.814	6.037
Share of synthetic resins[9] (%)	30.4	42.3	52.1	58.5	L				
					M	65.0	69.5	73.0	74.5
					H				
Requirements for synthetic resins[10] (bil. lb.)	.298	.639	.918	1.010	L	.938	.892	1.015	1.178
					M	1.063	1.211	1.573	2.140
					H	1.303	1.760	2.784	4.498

1. Historical data from U.S. Department of Agriculture, *Fats and Oils Situation,* May 1961, p. 21. Projections are the sum of "trade sales products"—stock-type commodities distributed through wholesale-retail channels, and most overwhelmingly in maintenance construction; and "industrial product finishes"—manufactured to industrial specifications and used as coatings for automobiles, furniture, appliances, and other durable goods.

2. Historical data derived from line above by using share of trade in total products as shown in U.S. Bureau of Census, *Paint, Varnish, and Lacquer* (Current Industrial Reports, Series M28F).

3. From Tables A4–1 and 3.

4. Projected as declining percentage extending trend observed in 1946–60 period when use per $1,000 dropped from 20.7 to 17.7 gallons. Newer paints have increased durability and hiding power and have captured a larger share of the market because of greater attractiveness (ease of application and clean-up, lack of odor). Also, there has been increased use of materials requiring less or no paint to maintain (synthetic tile, reinforced plastic, aluminum, etc.).

5. Obtained as difference between total and trade sales products for 1950, 1955, 1960, and as sum of trade sale and projections from two succeeding series thereafter.

6. From Tables A1–26 and 27.

7. Projected to decrease in extension of past trend, which has witnessed decline from 14.9 to 7.4 gallons per $1,000 between 1946 and 1960. Factors analogous to those in footnote 4, and above all more effective methods and new materials, are likely to be responsible for this trend.

8. Historical data from *Fats and Oils Situation,* May 1961, with 1960 and projections calculated by applying factor of 2.6 lb/gal. to total production (line 1), based on historical data.

9. Projected as increasing more slowly in the future. 1959 ratio, latest available from *Fats and Oils Situation,* was 55.5.

10. Historical data from *Fats and Oils Situation,* May 1961, p. 21; 1960 represents difference between total film-forming requirements and fats and oils used, as given in *op. cit.*

appendix
to
chapter
18

LAND

Notes

THE PRINCIPAL variable item in converting into land requirements the projected food and fiber needs evolved in Chapter 12 and detailed in Tables A12–1 to 16 is that of yield of product per acre. Historical yield data are available for most major crops for a long look back, but since the significant upward march of yields is of relatively recent origin, the projections are based as much on judging what may be accomplished in the future as on what has been accomplished in the past. The length of the time period over which yields have been rising, combined with regional and even farm-to-farm differences and reinforced by scientific experimentation, put these improvements in yields into the category of long-run trends rather than short-term flukes occasioned by favorable weather or other fortuitous factors. This does not place the actual projections here adopted beyond the reach of controversy. It merely justifies an extension into the future of the upward movement of recent years. The degree of that movement has been assumed to differ between different crops, for reasons detailed in the textual material.

The situation here is essentially different from that prevailing in industry. It is not a matter of what can technically be achieved, for we have practical proof that the yields postulated for the end of the century are if anything conservative in terms of what has been achieved under proper production controls even today. In other words, the potential is all there. What is lacking is the application. In industry, on the other hand, we must speculate not on the rapid application of what is potentially pos-

sible but upon the extension of the potential, through expansion of technology. Thus, the type of conjecture involved in the projection of crop yields is more dependent upon the economic and social variables, less on the technical elements. For this reason the Low estimate takes on special significance. A glance at Tables A18–1 and 2 shows that the Low assumption for the end of the period puts yields at levels that exceed current experience only by modest margins. This surely is a very conservative assumption, and consequently the calculations based on the Low yields set a most generous goal of inefficiency and, it follows, of land requirements.

A word of explanation is due regarding the choice of the acreage assumed to be cropland. This figure—470 million acres—is a rounded halfway choice between the recorded cropland acreages in the two Census years 1950 (478) and 1954 (465). It has no physical connotation, such as suitability for growing crops, but merely an economic one, i.e., it is the area in fact cultivated by farmers for the raising of crops, including pasture. Thus an excess of requirements over this base figure indicates that, at the assumed level of efficiency and yield, additional land will have to be cultivated if the demand for farm products is to be met. Conversely, an excess of the base figure over projected acreage requirements indicates that farmers can supply projected farm products without cultivating the acreage they did in fact cultivate in the early fifties.

The paradox that the High projection results in a surplus of land, the Low projection in a deficit (Table A18–11), finds its explanation in the fact that the High projection maximizes the use of concentrates and hay and minimizes the use of pasture, while it is at the same time assumed that grazing efficiency rises. Consequently, there is a minimum need for cropland pasture and a resulting excess of cropland acreage. The reverse holds true for the Low model. What is more likely to develop in fact, of course, is the use of cropland for pasture and the consequent release of grazing land for uses other than feeding, as discussed in the conclusion to Chapter 18.

Some of the difficulties in discussing land use arise from the nature of the statistics. They have their origin principally in differing concepts of land use. The Department of Agriculture figures have distinguished parcels of land basically by their vegetative cover: i.e., tree-bearing land is called wooded or forest land, even though it may be used principally for grazing, and land in natural grass is called grazing land, even though it may not be so used or may form part of a recreation area. Marion Clawson and his co-authors, in *Land for the Future* (Baltimore: Johns Hopkins Press and Resources for the Future, 1960), have attempted to establish a use classification: only wooded land commercially exploited or exploitable for lumber is considered forest land—following U.S. Forest Service data—and only land primarily grazed by livestock is included under the category of grazing; any forest or other stretches of land used primarily for recreation, wildlife, etc., are so designated.

Clawson's approach, while introducing an element of personal judgment, has the advantage of permitting allocation by principal use and preventing the danger of overlaps and double-counting. In official statistics, on the other hand, forest land shades into grazing land and both into "miscellaneous" land—the kind whose only use, it has been said, is "to hold the world together." To illustrate, the 1950 statistics show 631 million acres of open (non-wooded) grazing land and 287 million acres of forest land without grazing potential. Some 319 million additional acres form the bridge between the two uses: they carry trees and are being grazed. One may, therefore, speak of 950 (631 + 319) million grazing acres, and of 606 (287 + 319) million forest acres. One may not, however, speak of 1,556 acres of grazing and forest land. The principal result of Clawson's approach is to reduce the area of grazing. Within this general framework text Table 18–15 requires some comment to explain how the forest and grazing areas are arrived at.

Grazing land is the rounded sum of the 631 million acres of open grazing land mentioned above and about half of the 138 million acres of non-commercial forest land (exclusive of park and other special uses) that Clawson estimates can be properly considered as falling into the grazing category. The remaining half is distributed over other uses, including the catch-all "other land." It follows, incidentally, that some 250 million acres—or over half—of commercial forest land is presumably grazed. Only in this fashion can one arrive at total woodland grazing of 300 to 320 million acres, as estimated by the Department of Agriculture.

Tables A18–1, 2, and 3 concern past and projected yields of principal crops. Table A18–4 serves as background material for estimating the cropland required for crops other than those specifically dealt with. Application of a constant percentage implicitly assumes that yields in crops not individually covered will follow the trend projected for the major crops. In Table A18–5 there are brought together some historical data bearing on cropland acreage that is not harvested, for one reason or another. The logic of projecting this category is exposed in Chapter 18, pp. 347–48. Tables A18–6 and 7 contain projections for yields that can be expected from different types of grazing land.

Tables A18–8 through 13 bring together the separate projections of acreage requirements for crops and pasture and compare total cropland requirements with cropland availability, at various levels of yield and efficiency. For the purpose of these calculations available cropland (including pasture) is set at 470 million acres, which seems to have been the area for most of the fifties.

The by now classical treatise on future requirements for forest products and the outlook for growth was published in 1958 by the Forest Service of the U.S. Department of Agriculture under the title *Timber Resources for America's Future*. It is suggested that the reader who desires to have a more than casual acquaintance with both method and substance in the field of forest economics, statistics, and especially projections, study the relevant portions of that report. The few calculations that are here presented relating to likely supply have drawn heavily upon the Forest Service's data for 1952 and the methodology. Results differ principally because of differences in demand projections and the far more summary treatment here provided.

Tables A18–14 and 15 present, for softwood and hardwood species separately, and for Western softwood distinguished from Eastern softwood forests, the size of the growing stock as it would change from decade to decade under the stated consumptions of demand, mortality, and annual rate of growth. The underlying calculations are complex and are not here shown. They were patterned after the formula suggested by the Forest Service, as noted in the footnotes to the two tables. Difficulties arise mostly from the fact that not a whole year's growth is harvested. Mortality takes its toll and so does cutting. Furthermore, growth rates must be assumed to change, as the volume of growing stock rises or falls, quite apart from improvements in forest management and protection against insect, disease, fire, and windstorm damage. In contrast to most other fields dealt with in this book, data on growth of forests become available only as the result of special surveys, such as the one that underlies the above-mentioned Forest Service report. In other years, the total cut is estimated, but not the growth. Consequently, projections of future supply are quite speculative, especially when note is taken of the great potential, put by the Forest Service at twice present rates of growth (realizable growth) or even four times present rates of growth as the ultimate capacity under ideal conditions.

The two tables are the rock-bottom minimum in two respects: they do not distinguish between different species other than softwood and hardwood, nor between sawtimber (roughly speaking, commercial species trees measuring at least between 9 and 11 inches diameter at breast height, depending upon type and region) and poletimber (same, but 5 to 9 or 11 inches in diameter). Because of the nature of the results, which suggest that even if such important distinctions are disregarded there is no chance of meeting the projected demand and maintaining adequate forest cover, no effort was made to provide breakdowns. The likely consequences are, however, discussed in Chapter 18, pp. 365–67.

Table A18–16 summarizes the data and shows the results of certain variations in the basic assumption. Only the Medium projections are here worked out, as the Medium level appears to be the crucial one; the Low projection suggests no supply problem, and the High projection is merely an intensified version of the critical Medium projection.

The variations are worked out by use of the same formula. They are merely illustrative of the impact that any one variation or a combination might have upon the future supply situation. The implications are discussed in Chapter 18.

No data are shown regarding acreage required to meet the gap between net growth and demand in 2000 as suggested by the projections. A rough measure of such acreage may be found in Chapter 18, p. 364.

LIST OF TABLES

TABLE A18–1.　Yields per Harvested Acre of Four Major Crops, Actual 1878–82 to 1960,[1] and Projections[2]

		Wheat (bu/acre)		Corn (bu/acre)		Cotton (lb/acre)		Hay (tons/acre)	
		Actual and projected	1940–44 = 100	Actual and projected	1940–44 = 100	Actual and projected	1940–44 = 100	Actual and projected	1940–44 = 100
1878–82		13.2	77	25.6	80	179	68	[3]1.14	84
1920–24		13.9	81	27.2	85	154	59	1.21	90
1925–29		14.1	82	26.4	83	171	65	1.20	89
1930–34		13.3	78	23.8	75	185	71	1.08	80
1935–39		13.2	77	22.5	71	226	86	1.24	92
1940–44		17.1	100	31.9	100	262	100	1.35	100
1945–49		17.0	99	35.6	112	270	103	1.35	100
1950–54		17.3	101	38.5	121	297	113	1.43	106
1955–59		22.1	129	47.3	148	429	164	1.58	117
1960		26.2	153	53	166	446	170	1.76	130
	L	26	152	65	204	530	202	1.7	126
1970	M	28	164	70	219	560	214	2.0	148
	H	30	175	75	239	595	227	2.2	163
	L	28	164	73	229	590	225	1.8	133
1980	M	31	181	80	251	640	244	2.3	170
	H	33	193	87	273	700	267	2.7	200
	L	29	170	81	254	650	248	2.0	148
1990	M	33	193	90	282	720	275	2.6	193
	H	35	205	99	310	810	309	3.2	237
	L	30	175	89	279	710	271	2.2	163
2000	M	35	205	100	313	800	305	3.0	222
	H	37	216	110	345	930	355	3.7	274

1. U.S. Department of Agriculture, *Agricultural Statistics* and *Crop Production, Annual Summary*.
2. Judgment basis, discussed in Chapter 18, pp. 336–46.
3. Estimated from data on tame hay alone.

TABLE A18–2.   Yields per Harvested Acre for Oats, Barley, Grain Sorghum, and Soybeans, 1948–57, 1958, 1959, 1960, and Projections[1]

(Bushels)

	1948–57	1958	1959	1960		1970	1980	1990	2000
Oats	34.9	44.8	37.9	43.4	L	46	49	52	55
					M	49	54	58	61
					H	53	62	71	80
Barley	27.5	32.3	28.3	30.9	L	32	34	36	38
					M	35	38	41	45
					H	37	40	44	48
Grain sorghum	20.8	35.2	36.0	39.8	L	50	54	55	56
					M	52	55	57	59
					H	53	59	63	65
Soybeans	21.0	24.2	23.5	23.5	L	26	27	28	29
					M	27.5	30	32.5	35
					H	29	32	35	38

1. Historical data from USDA, *Crop Production, Annual Summary,* various years. Projections on judgment basis and discussed in text.

TABLE A18–3.   Projected Feed Grain Yields

(Feed units per acre)

		Corn[1]	Oats[1]	Barley[1]	Grain sorghum[1]	Weighted average[2]
1960		2,968	1,259	1,329	2,109	2,352
1970	L	3,640	1,334	1,376	2,650	2,821
	M	3,920	1,421	1,505	2,756	3,022
	H	4,200	1,537	1,591	2,809	3,229
1980	L	4,088	1,421	1,462	2,862	3,126
	M	4,480	1,566	1,634	2,915	3,416
	H	4,872	1,798	1,720	3,127	3,728
1990	L	4,536	1,508	1,548	2,915	3,427
	M	5,040	1,682	1,763	3,021	3,799
	H	5,544	2,059	1,892	3,339	4,223
2000	L	4,984	1,595	1,634	2,968	3,728
	M	5,600	1,769	1,935	3,127	4,179
	H	6,160	2,320	2,064	3,445	4,677

1. Derived by converting yields in bushels (Tables A18–1 and 2) to yields in feed units as follows:
   Feed units per bushel:
       Corn, 56
       Oats, 29
       Barley, 43
       Grain sorghum, 53
2. Composition of feed grain ratios assumed to remain constant as follows:
       Corn, 60%
       Oats, 23%
       Barley, 10%
       Sorghum grains, 7%

TABLE A18–4. Relationship of Crops for Which Projections Are Made to Total Crop Acreage, 1939–60

(Million acres except for ratios)

	Feed grains	Wheat	Cotton	Soybeans	Hay	Total selected for projections	59 crops harvested	Bearing acreage, fruits & nuts	59 crops plus bearing acreage, fruits & nuts	Acreage not covered by selected crops	Acreage not covered as % of selected crop acreage
									(9= 7+8)	(10= 9—6)	(11= 10÷6)
	(1)	(2)	(3)	(4)	(5)	(6)	(7)	(8)			
1939	139.2	52.7	23.8	4.3	69.2	289.2	322.1	3.9	326.0	36.8	12.7
1940	141.8	53.3	23.9	4.8	73.1	296.9	331.7	3.9	335.6	38.7	13.0
1941	143.8	55.9	22.2	5.9	73.1	300.9	335.5	3.9	339.4	38.5	12.8
1942	148.5	49.8	22.6	9.9	74.8	305.6	339.5	3.9	343.4	37.8	12.3
1943	152.8	51.4	21.6	10.4	77.0	313.2	348.0	3.9	351.9	38.7	12.4
1944	155.4	59.7	19.6	10.2	77.6	322.5	352.9	3.9	356.8	34.3	10.6
1945	146.1	65.2	17.0	10.7	76.7	315.7	345.6	3.8	349.4	33.7	10.7
1946	147.4	67.1	17.6	9.9	73.7	315.7	343.0	3.7	346.8	31.1	9.8
1947	137.2	74.5	21.3	11.4	74.7	319.1	346.4	3.7	350.1	31.0	9.7
1948	143.3	72.4	22.9	10.7	71.8	321.1	348.0	3.6	351.6	30.5	9.5
1949	139.9	75.9	27.4	10.5	72.8	326.5	352.3	3.4	355.7	29.2	8.9
1950	142.6	61.6	17.8	13.8	75.2	311.0	336.4	3.3	339.7	28.7	9.2
1951	133.9	61.9	26.9	13.6	75.0	311.3	336.1	3.2	339.3	28.0	9.0
1952	131.5	71.1	25.9	14.4	75.1	318.0	341.3	3.1	344.4	26.4	8.3
1953	133.0	67.8	24.3	14.8	75.0	314.9	340.7	3.0	343.7	28.8	9.1
1954	145.8	54.4	19.3	17.0	73.7	310.2	338.2	3.0	341.2	31.0	10.0
1955	145.8	47.3	16.9	18.6	75.0	303.6	331.9	3.0	334.9	31.3	10.3
1956	130.6	49.8	15.6	20.6	72.3	288.9	316.2	2.9	319.1	30.2	10.5
1957	140.5	43.8	13.6	20.9	71.9	290.7	315.6	2.8	318.4	27.7	9.5
1958	134.8	53.0	11.8	24.0	70.5	294.1	315.7	2.8	318.5	24.4	8.3
1959	140.0	51.8	15.1	22.6	66.3	295.8	316.5	2.9	319.4	23.6	8.0
1960	137.1	51.9	15.3	23.7	67.2	295.2	316.2	2.9	319.1	23.9	8.1

Source: USDA, *Crop Production, Annual Summary;* latest volume used is that for 1961, issued Dec. 15, 1961.

TABLE A18–5.   Acreage Neither Cropped nor Pastured

(Million acres)

Census Data[1]

	Total	Cultivated summer-fallow, 17 Western states	Other not harvested, 17 Western states (mostly failure)	Idle in 31 Eastern states	Planted but not harvested, 31 Eastern states
1924	46.9				
1929	54.0				
1934	119.7				
1939	77.5				
1944	50.3				
1949	64.1	25.6			
1954	60.7	28.6	13.7	13.5	4.9

U.S. Department of Agriculture, Bureau of Agricultural Economics Estimates[2]

	Crop failure	Fallow	Idle or soil-improvement	Total
1910–19	11.1	5.0	29.0	45.1
1920–29	13.2	7.3	30.0	50.5
1930–39	25.8	15.8	33.0	74.6
1940–49	10.5	18.4	29.9	58.8
1950–53	12.7	23.6	30.8	67.1
1950–59	18.0	–	–	–

1954 Regional Data (Census) [1]

Western states	Summer fallow	Failure & idle	Total	Eastern states	Idle
Montana	5.0	0.4	5.4	Georgia	1.2
Kansas	4.5	2.3	6.8	Alabama	0.9
North Dakota	4.4	1.3	5.7	Michigan	0.9
Colorado	3.1	1.8	4.9	Kentucky	0.8
Washington	2.5	0.3	2.8	Tennessee	0.8
Nebraska	2.1	0.7	2.8	Minnesota	0.7
Texas	1.2	3.2	4.4	Pennsylvania	0.7
California	1.2	0.7	1.9	New York	0.7
Idaho	1.0	0.2	1.2	Arkansas	0.6
Oregon	1.0	0.2	1.2	Mississippi	0.6
Oklahoma	0.8	1.1	1.9	North Carolina	0.6
Other	1.8	1.5	3.3	Ohio	0.6
Total	28.6	13.7	42.3	South Carolina	0.5
				Florida	0.5
				Other	3.4
				Total	13.5

1. From U.S. Bureau of the Census, U.S. Census of Agriculture, 1954, Vol. II, General Report, Chap. I, "Farms and Land in Farms," Tables 17 and 18.

2. From USDA, *Agricultural Land Resources;* Agricultural Information Bulletin No. 140, June 1955; also *Crop Production, Annual Summary.*

TABLE A18–6.   Yields of Different Types of Pasture, 1950 and Projections

(Feed units per acre)

	Hay	Crop-land		Perma-nent open (farm)	Wood-land (farm)	Graz-ing (off-farm)
1950	1,150	985		195	95	56
1960	1,440	1,230		220	100	60
1970	1,640	1,410	L	200	100	60
			M	240	107	64
			H	280	115	68
1980	1,890	1,622	L	200	100	60
			M	260	112	67
			H	320	125	74
1990	2,130	1,834	L	200	100	60
			M	290	117	70
			H	360	135	80
2000	2,460	2,116	L	200	100	60
			M	310	125	74
			H	420	150	88

Basic Assumptions:
  Hay: Tonnage figures (Table A18–1) converted to feed units on basis of 820 feed units per ton.
  Cropland: 1950 based on USDA Statistical Bulletin No. 153, p. 53; projections at same rate as hay.
  Permanent open farm: 1950—19.8% of cropland (USDA Information Bulletin No. 162).
  Woodland farm: 1950—9.6% of cropland (USDA Information Bulletin No. 162).
  Grazing off farm: 1950—5.7% of cropland (USDA Information Bulletin No. 162).
Projections (other than hay and cropland):
  Low: 1950 level throughout (rounded).
  High: For open farm—same rate of growth as that of cropland pasture. For woodland and off-farm grazing—half rate of growth of cropland pasture.
  Medium: Halfway between High and Low.
Note: All computations carried on with rounded figures.

TABLE A18–7. Feed Availability from Grazing Land other than Cropland Pasture

| Unit | Open permanent pasture (on farms) | Woodland pasture (on farms) | Grazing land not on farms | Total feed units from— | | |
				Grazing other than cropland	Aftermath	Grazing and aftermath
1950, Million acres	416	135	400	–	–	–
1960, Feed units/acre	220	100	60	–	–	–
Billion feed units	92	13	24	129	15	144
1970, Feed units/acre						
L	200	100	60	–	–	–
M	240	107	64	–	–	–
H	280	115	68	–	–	–
Billion feed units						
L	83	13	24	120	15	135
M	100	14	26	140	15	155
H	116	16	27	159	15	174
1980, Feed units/acre						
L	200	100	60	–	–	–
M	260	112	67	–	–	–
H	320	125	74	–	–	–
Billion feed units						
L	83	13	24	120	16	136
M	108	15	27	150	15	165
H	133	17	30	180	16	196
1990, Feed units/acre						
L	200	100	60	–	–	–
M	290	117	70	–	–	–
H	360	135	80	–	–	–
Billion feed units						
L	83	13	24	120	16	136
M	121	16	28	165	16	181
H	150	18	32	200	17	217
2000, Feed units/acre						
L	200	100	60	–	–	–
M	310	125	74	–	–	–
H	420	150	88	–	–	–
Billion feed units						
L	83	13	24	120	16	136
M	129	17	30	176	17	193
H	175	20	36	231	18	249

Sources:
Acreage from *U.S. Census of Agriculture,* 1950.
Feed units per acre from Table A18–6.
Feed units from aftermath:
16.7 billion feed units in 1950 on 280 million acres of feed and feed grain and hay land (USDA Statistical Bulletin No. 153), i.e., 60 feed units per acre. This yield applied to projected acreage of four feed grains, wheat, and hay in 1960, 1980, and 2000. Other years interpolated.

TABLE A18–8.   Distribution of Cropland Acreage, 1950–59, 1960, 1980, and 2000 (Medium projection)

| | 1950–59[1] | | 1960[2] | | | 1980[3] | | 2000[3] | |
| | Million acres | % of total | Million acres | | % of total | Million acres | % of total | Million acres | % of total |
			Calculated	Actual					
Feed grains	139	29.6	134	(139)	28.4	110	23.6	125	26.3
Wheat	56	11.9	46	(52)	9.8	34	7.2	40	8.4
Cotton	19	4.0	16	(15)	3.4	16	3.4	20	4.2
Soybeans	18	3.8	24	(23)	5.1	36	7.7	44	9.2
Hay	74	15.7	68	(67)	14.8	98	20.9	118	24.8
All other crops (incl. fruits and nuts)	28	6.0	26	(24)	5.1	27	5.8	31	6.5
Total crops harvested	334	71.0	313	(319)	66.6	323	68.6	378	79.4
Cropland pasture	70	14.9	79		16.8	75	16.0	58	12.2
Total crops and pasture	404	85.9	392	398	83.4	398	84.6	436	91.6
Fallow, idle, failure	60	12.8	55		11.7	45	9.6	40	8.4
Excess cropland acreage[4]	6	1.3	23	17	4.9	27	5.8	–6	–
Total cropland (1950–54 level)	470	100.0	470		100.0	470	100.0	470	100.0

1. Historical data for crops based upon USDA, *Crop Production, Annual Summary,* 1960, 1961. Pasture, Fallow, etc., and total cropland are estimates based upon Census of Agriculture, 1950, 1954.

2. Calculated are estimated from acreage requirements, Table A18–9; actual are rounded recorded 1959–1960 averages; they include acreage for crops grown beyond requirements. Cropland pasture estimate from Table A18–11.

3. Table A18–9.

4. Obtained as residual.

Note: Totals may not equal sum of items because of rounding.

TABLE A18–9.   Projected Acreage Required for Crops under Different Demand and Yield Assumptions[1]

	1960		1970	1980	1990	2000
Feed grains:						
		LL	256	262	274	294
		HL	320	364	394	421
Demand[2] (bil. feed units)	306	M	310	375	450	521
		LH	341	430	565	725
		HH	398	521	666	829
		LL	3,230	3,730	4,220	4,680
		HL	2,820	3,130	3,430	3,730
Yield[3] (feed units/acre)	2,290	M	3,020	3,420	3,800	4,180
		LH	3,230	3,730	4,220	4,680
		HH	2,820	3,130	3,430	3,730
		LL	79.3	70.2	64.9	62.8
		HL	113.5	116.3	114.9	112.9
Land required (mil. acres)	133.6	M	102.6	109.6	118.4	124.6
		LH	105.6	115.3	133.9	154.9
		HH	141.1	166.5	194.2	222.2
Wheat:						
		LL	} 994	1,024	1,106	1,200
		HL				
Demand[2] (mil. bu.)	1,110	M	984	1,063	1,200	1,384
		LH	} 987	1,083	1,280	1,531
		HH				
		LL	30.0	33.0	35.0	37.0
		HL	26.0	28.0	29.0	30.0
Yield[3] (bu/acre)	24.0	M	28.0	31.0	33.0	35.0
		LH	30.0	33.0	35.0	37.0
		HH	26.0	28.0	29.0	30.0
		LL	33.1	31.0	31.6	32.4
		HL	38.2	36.6	38.1	40.0
Land required (mil. acres)	45.8	M	35.1	34.3	36.4	39.5
		LH	32.9	32.8	36.6	41.4
		HH	38.0	38.7	44.1	51.0
Cotton:						
		LL	} 6.4	6.4	6.5	6.5
		HL				
Demand[2] (bil. lb.)	7.0	M	8.6	10.5	12.8	15.9
		LH	} 10.0	13.7	19.2	27.6
		HH				
		LL	595	700	810	930
		HL	530	590	650	710
Yield[3] (lb/acre)	446	M	560	640	720	800
		LH	595	700	810	930
		HH	530	590	650	710
		LL	9.3	9.1	8.0	7.0
		HL	12.1	10.8	10.0	9.2
Land required (mil. acres)	15.7	M	15.4	16.4	17.8	19.9
		LH	16.8	19.6	23.7	29.7
		HH	18.9	23.2	29.5	38.9

Table A18–9 (cont'd)

		1960		1970	1980	1990	2000
Soybeans:							
	LL			820	1,120	1,340	1,490
	HL			800	1,040	1,190	1,320
Demand[2] (mil. bu.)	M	572		830	1,090	1,340	1,540
	LH			820	1,020	1,200	1,360
	HH			880	1,200	1,580	2,020
	LL			29.0	32.0	35.0	38.0
	HL			26.0	27.0	28.0	29.0
Yield[3] (bu/acre)	M	23.5		27.5	30.0	32.5	35.0
	LH			29.0	32.0	35.0	38.0
	HH			26.0	27.0	28.0	29.0
	LL			28.3	35.0	38.3	39.2
	HL			30.8	38.5	42.5	45.5
Land required (mil. acres)	M	24.3		30.2	36.3	41.2	44.0
	LH			28.3	31.9	34.3	35.8
	HH			33.8	44.4	56.4	69.7
Hay:							
	LL			138	164	183	203
	HL			143	165	187	210
Demand[2] (mil. tons)	M	119		165	225	287	355
	LH			183	260	341	447
	HH			189	260	352	462
	LL			2.20	2.70	3.20	3.70
	HL			1.70	1.80	2.00	2.20
Yield[3] (tons/acre)	M	1.76		2.00	2.30	2.60	3.00
	LH			2.20	2.70	3.20	3.70
	HH			1.70	1.80	2.00	2.20
	LL			62.7	60.7	57.2	54.9
	HL			84.1	91.7	93.5	95.5
Land required (mil. acres)	M	67.6		82.5	97.8	110.4	118.3
	LH			83.2	96.3	106.6	120.8
	HH			111.2	144.4	176.0	210.0
	LL			212	206	200	196
Total land required for above	HL			278	294	294	303
crops (mil. acres)	M	287		266	296	324	346
	LH			264	296	335	383
	HH			343	417	500	592
	LL			231	225	218	214
Total crop land required to be	HL			303	319	325	328
harvested[4] (mil. acres)	M	313		290	323	353	378
	LH			288	323	366	416
	HH			374	445	545	645

1. The Low-Low model minimizes acreage requirements by combining Low demand, High feed efficiency, High use of concentrates with High crop yields. The conditions are relaxed in the High-Low model, which stipulates Low feed efficiency, Low use of concentrates, and Low yields. The Medium projection is based on Medium assumptions for both demand and yields. The High-High model maximizes acreage requirements by combining High demand, Low feed efficiency, and Low use of concentrates with Low crop yields. In the Low-High model those conditions are relaxed by assuming High feed efficiency, High use of concentrates, and High crop yields.

2. From Tables A12–14 and A12–16. Notes to the tables cited contain full explanation of the meaning of the different models.

3. From Tables A18–1, 2, and 3. 1960 yields are averages for 1959/60 and 1960/61 to match the calendar year basis upon which demand estimates are built and to broaden yield base.

4. Equivalent to 109% of 5-crop total, based upon historical record, Table A18–4.

TABLE A18–10.   Acreage Requirements for Crops of Extreme Demand Models at Yields Mitigating Extreme Acreage Demand, 1980 and 2000

(Acreage in millions)

Demand model Yield assumption	1980				2000			
	LL M	LL L	HH H	HH M	LL M	LL L	HH H	HH M
Feed grains:								
Demand (bil. feed units)	262	262	521	521	294	294	829	829
Yield (feed units/acre)	3,420	3,130	3,730	3,420	4,180	3,730	4,680	4,180
Acreage	76.6	83.7	139.7	152.3	70.3	78.8	177.1	198.3
Wheat:								
Demand (mil. bu.)	1,024	1,024	1,083	1,083	1,200	1,200	1,531	1,531
Yield (bu./acre)	31	28	33	31	35	30	37	35
Acreage	33.0	36.6	32.8	34.9	34.3	40.0	41.4	43.7
Cotton:								
Demand (bil. lb.)	6.4	6.4	13.7	13.7	6.5	6.5	27.6	27.6
Yield (lb./acre)	640	590	700	640	800	710	930	800
Acreage	10.0	10.8	19.6	21.4	8.1	9.2	29.8	34.6
Soybeans:								
Demand (mil. bu.)	1,120	1,120	1,200	1,200	1,490	1,490	2,020	2,020
Yield (bu./acre)	30	27	32	30	35	29	38	35
Acreage	37.3	41.5	37.5	40.0	42.6	51.4	53.2	57.7
Hay:								
Demand (mil. tons)	164	164	260	260	203	203	462	462
Yield (tons/acre)	2.3	1.8	2.7	2.3	3.0	2.2	3.7	3.0
Acreage	71.3	91.1	96.7	113.5	67.7	92.3	124.9	154.0
Total acreage, major crops	228	264	326	362	223	272	426	488
All crops (109% of major crop acreage)	249	288	355	395	243	296	464	532

Source: Table A18–9.

TABLE A18–11.   Projected Cropland Acreage Required for Crops and Grazing

	1960		1970	1980	1990	2000
Acreage required to be harvested		HL	303	319	325	328
(mil. acres) [1]	313	M	290	323	353	378
		LH	288	323	366	416
Crop failure, idleness, summer						
fallow (mil. acres) [2]	55		50	45	43	40
Total cropland required other		HL	353	364	368	368
than pasture (mil. acres)	368	M	340	368	396	418
		LH	338	368	409	456
Acreage in excess of requirement given		HL	117	106	102	102
a base of 470 million acres of	102	M	130	102	74	52
cropland (mil. acres)		LH	132	102	61	14
Roughage required from pasture		HL	270	303	334	363
(bil. feed units) [3]	241	M	254	287	306	317
		LH	239	252	259	262
Roughage available from pasture		HL	135	136	136	136
other than cropland	144	M	155	165	181	193
(bil. feed units) [4]		LH	174	196	217	249
Roughage required from cropland		HL	135	167	198	227
pasture (bil. feed units)	97	M	99	122	125	124
		LH	65	56	42	13
Cropland pasture yield						
(feed units/acre) [5]	1,230		1,410	1,620	1,830	2,120
		HL	96	103	108	107
Cropland pasture required (mil. acres)	79	M	70	75	68	58
		LH	46	35	23	6
Cropland in excess or short of		HL	+21	+3	—6	—5
combined crop and pasture	+23	M	+60	+27	+6	—6
requirements (mil. acres) [6]		LH	+86	+67	+38	+8

1. From Table A18–9.
2. Based upon Table A18–5, and assumed to decline slowly.
3. From Table A12–16.
4. From Table A18–7.
5. From Table A18–6, rounded.
6. 470 million acres minus "total cropland required other than pasture" and "cropland pasture required."

TABLE A18–12. Cropland Requirements to Meet High and Low Demand at Different Crop Yield Levels, 1980 and 2000

	Cropland			Roughage				
	Harvested[1]	Idle, fallow, etc.[2]	Total required (excl. pasture)	Required from grazing[3]	Available from non-cropland grazing[2]	Needed from cropland pasture	Cropland equiv. of feed units required from pasture[4]	Total cropland required[5]
	(million acres)			(billion feed units)			(million acres)	
	(1)	(2)	(3)=(1)+(2)	(4)	(5)	(6)=(4)—(5)	(7)	(8)=(3)+(7)
High demand, 1980:								
at Low crop yields	445		490		136	340	210	700
at Medium crop yields	395	45	440	476	165	311	192	632
at High crop yields	355		400		196	280	173	573
High demand, 2000:								
at Low crop yields	645		685		136	661	312	997
at Medium crop yields	532	40	572	797	193	604	285	857
at High crop yields	464		504		249	548	258	762
Low demand, 1980:								
at High crop yields	225		270		196	(36)	(22)	270
at Medium crop yields	249	45	294	160	165	(5)	(3)	294
at Low crop yields	288		333		136	24	15	348
Low demand, 2000:								
at High crop yields	214		254		249	(130)	(61)	254
at Medium crop yields	243	40	283	119	193	(74)	(35)	283
at Low crop yields	296		336		136	(17)	(8)	336

1. From Tables A18–9 and 10.
2. From Table A18–11.
3. From Table A12–16; highest and lowest demand respectively.
4. Preceding column converted into acres on basis of per acre yields in Table A18–11.
5. Sum of cropland required for crops and cropland for grazing. Where latter is smaller than zero, the figure entered here is the same as that for cropland required for crops.

TABLE A18–13.   Acreage Requirements, Medium Demand, with High and Low Yields, 1980 and 2000[1]

(Acreage in millions)

	1980, medium demand		2000, medium demand	
	Low yield	High yield	Low yield	High yield
Feed grains:				
Demand (bil. feed units)	375		521	
Yield (feed units/acre)	3,130	3,730	3,730	4,680
Acreage	120	101	140	111
Wheat:				
Demand (mil. bu.)	1,063		1,384	
Yield (bu./acre)	28	33	30	37
Acreage	38	32	46	37
Cotton:				
Demand (bil. lb.)	10.5		15.9	
Yield (lb./acre)	590	700	710	930
Acreage	18	15	22	17
Soybeans:				
Demand (mil. bu.)	1,090		1,540	
Yield (bu./acre)	27	32	29	38
Acreage	40	34	53	41
Hay:				
Demand (mil. tons)	225		355	
Yield (tons/acre)	1.8	2.7	2.2	3.7
Acreage	125	83	161	96
Total acreage, 5 crops	340	265	422	302
Total acreage, all crops (109% of above)	371	289	460	329

1. All data from Table A18–9.

TABLE A18–14. Implications for Growth and Growing Stock of Softwood Species of Projected Forest Products Demand

(Physical amounts in bil. cu. ft. roundwood or roundwood equivalent)

	1952[1]	1960		1970	1980	1990	2000
			L	8.3	9.1	9.8	11.2
Demand for softwood[2]	8.2	8.3	M	11.3	14.3	18.6	24.7
			H	14.1	20.4	30.5	48.1
Net imports of softwood and prod-			L	1.2	1.6	2.0	2.4
ucts, in roundwood equivalent[3]	0.7	0.8	M	1.4	2.0	2.6	3.0
			H	1.6	2.4	3.2	4.0
Demand for domestic softwood			L	7.1	7.5	7.8	8.8
(cut from U.S. growing stock)	7.5	7.5	M	9.9	12.3	16.0	21.7
			H	12.5	18.0	27.3	44.1
Annual cut from East, equal to			L	3.6	3.8	3.9	4.4
annual cut from West[4]	3.75	3.75	M	5.0	6.1	8.0	10.8
			H	6.2	9.0	13.6	22.0
Mortality rate, East[5]		.0063		.0056	.0048	.0046	.0046
Mortality rate, West[5]		.0063		.0058	.0054	.0052	.0052
			L	.056	.054	.052	.050
Net growth rate, East[6]	.059	.060	M	.060	.060	.060	.060
			H	.065	.070	.072	.072
			L	.013	.015	.015	.015
Net growth rate, West[6]	.94	.010	M	.014	.017	.019	.021
			H	.015	.019	.023	.027
			L	4.9	5.5	6.2	7.2
Net growth, East[7]	4.4	4.6	M	4.8	4.1	1.7	–
			H	4.8	1.8	–	–
			L	3.2	3.6	3.5	3.5
Net growth, West[7]	2.6	2.5	M	3.2	3.6	3.4	2.4
			H	3.4	3.6	2.3	–
			L	89.7	103.9	123.1	148.0
Growing stock, East[7]	74.2	79.2	M	82.6	72.0	32.8	–
			H	76.5	35.7	–	–
			L	246	244	241	234
Growing stock, West[7]	262	253	M	238	219	185	121
			H	234	193	112	–

1. From Forest Service, USDA, *Timber Resources for America's Future,* Forest Resources Report No. 14, 1958, especially Appendix Tables 8 and 57 and p. 486.

2. From Table A13–6.

3. Exclusive of equivalent of paper imports, which are allowed for in projection of paper demand; cf. Table A8–2.

4. Cut assumed to continue 1952 experience of originating one-half each in Eastern and Western forest areas. This assumption is changed in Table A18–16.

5. From Forest Service, *op. cit.,* especially p. 486.

6. Growth rate assumed to rise with decrease in growing stock, and vice versa, except that some increase is allowed for even if there is no change in size of growing stock and no increase or only a small one in Medium and High growth rate in East in second half of period, since rates are already very high.

7. 1952 data from *ibid.;* 1960 and projections calculated on basis of projected cut, mortality, and growth rates by formulas suggested in *ibid.,* p. 667:

$$\text{Net growth} = (GS - \frac{C}{2} - M)\, .0s - M$$

$$\text{Addition to growing stock} = [(GS - \frac{C}{2} - M)\, .0s - (C + M)]\, \frac{1.0x^n - 1}{.0x} \text{ where}$$

GS = growing stock at beginning of period (or year)

C = average annual cut during period (or year)

M = mortality in first year of period (or during year)

$.0s$ = average annual gross growth rate during period (or year)

$.0x$ = gross growth rate minus mortality rate (= net growth rate)

TABLE A18–15. Implications for Growth and Growing Stock of Hardwood Species of Projected Forest Products Demand

(Physical amounts in bil. cu. ft. roundwood or roundwood equivalent)

	1952[1]	1960		1970	1980	1990	2000
Demand for hardwood[2]	3.3	3.2	L	3.0	3.0	3.2	3.8
			M	3.8	4.4	5.7	7.6
			H	4.6	6.1	9.1	14.3
Net imports of hardwood and products in roundwood equivalent[3]	.04	.08		.11	.14	.17	.20
Demand for domestic hardwood (cut from U.S. growing stock)	3.3	3.12	L	2.89	2.86	3.03	3.60
			M	3.69	4.26	5.53	7.40
			H	4.49	5.96	8.93	14.10
Mortality rate[4]	.0060	.0060		.0050	.0048	.0045	.0045
Net growth rate[5]	.0046	.042	L	.037	.031	.024	.016
			M	.038	.034	.030	.026
			H	.040	.036	.032	.032
Net growth[6]	7.23	8.0	L	8.9	9.8	8.8	4.9
			M	9.2	10.0	10.4	10.0
			H	9.6	10.2	9.7	9.0
Growing stock[6]	162	192	L	244	308	372	416
			M	244	299	352	389
			H	242	287	311	290

1. From Forest Service, *Timber Resources for America's Future,* especially Appendix Tables 8 and 56 and p. 486.
2. From Table A13–6.
3. See Chapter 18, pp. 367–69, for discussion.
4. From Forest Service, *op. cit.,* p. 486.
5. Growth rate assumed to decline with increase in growing stock and vice versa, at different speeds.
6. See Table A18–14, footnote 7.

TABLE A18–16.   Effects upon Growing Stock of Variations in Ways of Meeting Projected Forest Products Demand (medium projection only)

(Billion cubic feet of roundwood or roundwood equivalent)

	1960	1970	1980	1990	2000
Demand for forest products[1]	11.5	15.1	18.7	24.3	32.3
Net imports[1]	.9	1.5	2.1	2.8	3.2
Demand for domestic forest products[1]	10.6	13.6	16.6	21.5	29.1
Net growth, softwood and hardwood[1]	15.1	17.1	17.6	15.4	12.4
Growing stock, softwood, West[2]	253	238	219	185	121
Growing stock, softwood, East[2]	79	83	72	33	–
Growing stock, hardwood[3]	192	244	299	352	389
Growing stock when percentage of cut met by hardwood reaches 40% in 2000:[4]					
Softwood, West	253	240	227	218	182
Softwood, East	79	86	86	72	24
Hardwood	192	240	280	300	282
Growing stock when cut shifted to West:[5] Softwood, West, at growth rate of					
Table A18–14	253	237	212	166	79
Same, but net growth rate reaching					
3% by 1990–2000[6]	253	249	236	210	151
Softwood, East	79	84	82	63	25
Combined effect of regional and species shifts and more rapid growth:[7]					
Growing stock, Western softwood	253	242	228	205	158
Growing stock, Eastern softwood	79	87	94	95	84
Growing stock, hardwood	192	240	280	300	282

1. From Tables A18–14 and 15, computed from unrounded figures.
2. From Table A18–14.
3. From Table A18–15.
4. At present hardwood supplies not quite 29% of demand for all domestic forest products. Excluding fuelwood, the percentage is not quite 20. Assuming the percentage to reach 40 by the end of the century implies the average doubling of the share of hardwood in saw logs, veneer logs, and pulpwood.
5. Present 50/50 division of cut between East and West assumed to shift gradually until West supplies 60% of demand by 2000.
6. Net growth rate of Western forests assumed to rise from present 1.0% not to 2.0% in last decade of century but to 3.0%.
7. Assuming change to 40% of hardwood and 60% of total softwood from West by end of century, as above, aided by a rise in Western softwood net growth rate from 1.0% not to 3.0% as above but only to 2.5%.

Index

Index